SHAKESPEARE
for Students
BOOK II

SHAKESPEARE
for Students
B O O K II

Critical Interpretations of:

Henry IV, Part One
Henry V
King Lear
Much Ado About Nothing
Richard III
The Taming of the Shrew
The Tempest
Twelfth Night

Catherine C. Dominic, editor

Advisors:

Cynthia Burnstein
Plymouth-Salem School District, Michigan

Gladys V. Veidemanis
Oshkosh Area Public Schools, Wisconsin

Copyright 1997

GALE

DETROIT • NEW YORK • TORONTO • LONDON

STAFF

Catherine C. Dominic, *Editor*
Dana Ramel Barnes, Jelena O. Krstović, Marie Lazzari,
Mary Onorato, James E. Person, Jr., *Contributing Editors*
Susan Trosky, *Managing Editor*

Cynthia Burnstein, Gladys Veidemanis, *Advisors*
Nancy Brown, *Contributing Advisor*

Marlene Hurst, *Permissions Manager*
Margaret A. Chamberlain, Maria Franklin, Kimberly F. Smilay, *Permissions Specialists*
Diane Cooper, Edna Hedblad, Michele Lonoconus, Maureen Puhl,
Susan Salas, Shalice Shah, Barbara A. Wallace, *Permissions Associates*
Sarah Chesney, Margaret Weyhing, *Permissions Assistants*

Victoria B. Cariappa, *Research Manager*
Barbara McNeil, *Research Specialist*
Alicia Noel Biggers, Julia C. Daniel, Tamara C. Nott,
Michele P. Pica, Tracie A. Richardson, Cheryl Warnock, *Research Associates*

Mary Beth Trimper, *Production Director*; Shanna P. Heilveil, *Production Assistant*

Barbara J. Yarrow, *Graphic Services Manager*
Randy Bassett, *Image Database Supervisor*
Pamela A. Hayes, *Photography Coordinator*

Cynthia Baldwin, *Product Design Manager*; Pamela A. E. Galbreath, *Art Director*

Library of Congress Cataloging-in-Publication Data

Shakespeare for students, Book II: critical interpretations of Henry IV, part one, Henry V, King Lear, Much ado about nothing, Richard III, The taming of the shrew, The tempest, and Twelfth night / Catherine C. Dominic, editor ; advisors, Cynthia Burnstein, Gladys V. Veidemanis.

    p.   cm.

    Includes bibliographic references and index.
    ISBN 0-7876-0157-8 (alk. paper)
    1. Shakespeare, William, 1564-1616--Criticism and interpretation.
I. Dominic, Catherine C., 1970-
PR2987.S468   1996
822.3'3--dc20
                                        96-24206
                                        CIP

∞™ This book is printed on acid-free paper that meets the minimum requirements of American National Standard for information Sciences—Permanence Paper for Printed Library Materials, ANSI Z39.48.1984.

Printed in the United States of America

Gale Research

10 9 8 7 6 5 4 3 2 1

Contents

How to Get the Most out of *Shakespeare for Students, Book II*

Purpose of the Book

Like *Shakespeare for Students, Shakespeare for Students, Book II* is intended to present the beginning student of Shakespeare and other interested readers with information on Shakespeare's most popular and frequently taught plays. A further purpose of the *Shakespeare for Students* books is to acquaint the reader with the use and function of literary criticism itself. Selected from the immense and often bewildering body of Shakespearean commentary, the essays and excerpts in these volumes offer insights into Shakespeare's plays from a wide range of commentators representing many different critical viewpoints. Readers do not need a wide background in literary studies to use these books. Students can benefit from using the *Shakespeare for Students* books as a basis for class discussion and written assignments, new perspectives on the plays, and noteworthy analyses of Shakespeare's artistry.

Less than twenty-five percent of the essays and excerpts reprinted in the *Shakespeare for Students* books can be found in Gale's companion literary series, *Shakespearean Criticism,* a multi-volume set which provides a comprehensive collection of published criticism, spanning four centuries, on all of Shakespeare's plays and poems. Like all of the essays selected for inclusion in the *Shakespeare for Students* books, material chosen from *Shakespearean Criticism* was carefully reviewed and excerpted in an effort to provide information that is interesting and accessible to students.

How an Entry is Organized

Each play entry consists of the following elements: an introduction to the play, essays and excerpts of critical commentary on the play prefaced by explanatory annotations, and an annotated bibliography of sources for further study.

- The **Introduction** provides basic information about the play, discussing when the play was written, commenting on the sources from which Shakespeare drew, and identifying the major conflicts and themes within each play. The remainder of the introduction is divided into the following sections: **Principal Characters,** a descriptive list of the play's characters; **Plot Synopsis,** an act-by-act summary of the main events in the play; **Principal Topics,** a discussion of the principal thematic issues in the play; **Character Studies,** a discussion of the actions and possible motivations of each of the major characters in the play; and a brief **Conclusion.** In *Shakespeare for Students, Book II,* the **Principal Topics** and **Character Studies** sections are subdivided by topic and character.

- The **literary criticism** is arranged by important topics and themes that have emerged in published commentary. In *Shakespeare for Students, Book II,* each section of criticism is prefaced by a brief discussion of the major critical issues relevant to the topic or character being covered in that section. The names of critics whose essays are featured in that entry appear in boldface. The works of other critics mentioned in these critical introductions are cited in the **Sources for Further Study** portion of the entry.

- A complete **bibliographic citation** precedes each piece of criticism. This enables the interested reader to locate the original book or article from which the reprint is taken.

- **Explanatory annotations** preface each critical essay and excerpt as an additional aid to students. These notes provide helpful information regarding the criticism that follows, providing an overview of the essay and some insight into the critic's stance regarding the topic or character being discussed.

- The **Sources for Further Study** list at the end of each entry includes suggested sources for further study of the play and informs the reader of radio, motion picture, and television adaptations of the play (many available on videocassette).

Other Features

- Throughout the book, various **illustrations**—including artist's renditions of certain scenes and performance photographs—add a visual dimension, enhancing the reader's understanding of the critical discussion of each play.

- A **Chronology of Shakespeare's Life and Major Works** helps students place the writing of various plays within the context of major events in Shakespeare's life. For *Book II*, this chronology has been expanded and includes composition information (the date Shakespeare probably wrote the play or poem) for all of Shakespeare's works.

- *Shakespeare for Students, Book II* offers a **Glossary** of terms students are likely to encounter in the study of Shakespeare's work.

- An **Index to Major Themes and Characters** at the end of each volume identifies the principal topics and characters from each play. The index covers themes and characters of plays treated in *Shakespeare for Students* and *Shakespeare for Students, Book II*.

A Note to the Reader

When writing papers, students who quote from *Shakespeare for Students, Book II* may use the following general formats to cite reprinted criticism. The first example pertains to material from periodicals, the second to material reprinted from books.

[1]Anne Marie McNamara, "Henry IV: The King as Protagonist," *Shakespeare Quarterly* X, No. 3 (Summer, 1959): 423-31; excerpted and reprinted in *Shakespeare for Students, Book II*, ed. Catherine C. Dominic (Detroit: Gale Research, 1996), 28-33.

[2] Moody E. Prior, "Ideas of History: *Richard II, 1* and *2 Henry IV, Henry V*" in *The Drama of Power: Studies in Shakespeare's History Plays* (Northwestern University Press, 1973), 199-218; excerpted and reprinted in *Shakespeare for Students, Book II*, ed. Catherine C. Dominic (Detroit: Gale Research, 1996), 14-16.

Acknowledgments

The editors wish to thank the copyright holders of the excerpted criticism included in this volume and the permissions managers of many book and magazine publishing companies for assisting us in securing reprint rights. We are also grateful to the staffs of the Detroit Public Library, the Library of Congress, the University of Detroit Mercy Library, Wayne State University Purdy/Kresge Library Complex, and the University of Michigan Libraries for making their resources available to us. Following is a list of the copyright holders who have granted us permission to reproduce material in *Shakespeare for Students, Book II*. Every effort has been made to trace copyright, but if omissions have been made, please let us know.

COPYRIGHTED EXCERPTS IN *SHAKESPEARE FOR STUDENTS, BOOK II*, WERE REPRODUCED FROM THE FOLLOWING PERIODICALS:

Arizona Quarterly, v. 20, Winter, 1964 for "A Shakespeare All too Modern?" by Herbert Weisinger. Copyright © 1964, renewed 1992 by Arizona Quarterly. Reproduced by permission of the publisher and the author.—*Cahiers Elisabethains*, n. 17, April, 1980. Reproduced by permission of the publisher.—*College English*, v. 32, November, 1970 for "Act One, Scene One, of 'Lear'" by Simon O. Lesser. Copyright © 1970 by the National Council of Teachers of English. Reproduced by permission of the publisher and the author.—*Critical Quarterly*, v. 16, Spring, 1974. © Manchester University Press 1974. Reproduced by permission of Basil Blackwell Limited.—*Criticism*, v. XIV, Summer, 1972 for "How Do We Judge King Lear?" by Judd Arnold. Copyright, 1972, Wayne State University Press. Reproduced by permission of the publisher and the author.—*Educational Theatre Journal*, v. XIX, October, 1967. © 1967 University College Theatre Association of the American Theatre Association. Reproduced by permission of the publisher.—*ELH*, v. 40, Winter, 1973. Copyright © 1973 by The Johns Hopkins University Press. All rights reserved. Reproduced by permission of the publisher.—*English,* v. 41, Summer, 1992. © The English Association 1992. Reproduced by permission of the publisher.—*English Language Notes*, v. IV, March, 1967. Reproduced by permission of the publisher.—*English Studies*, (Netherlands), v. 45, April, 1964. © 1964 by Swets & Zeitlinger B.V. Reproduced by permission of the publisher.—*English Studies in Canada*, v. XIII, March, 1987 for "Shakespeare's Female Twins in *Twelfth Night*: In Defense of Olivia" by Douglas H. Parker. © Association of Canadian University Teachers of English 1987. Reproduced by permission of the publisher and the author.—*Essays in Criticism*, v. XXIII, April, 1973 for "Much Ado About Nothing: The Individual in Society" by Michael Taylor. Reproduced by permission of the Editors of *Essays in Criticism* and the author.—*Essays in Literature*, v. 1, Fall, 1974; v. 13, Fall 1986. Copyright 1974, 1986 by Western Illinois University. Both reproduced by permission of the publisher.—*Wascana Review*, v. 10, Spring 1977. Copyright © 1977, The University of Regina, Canada. Reproduced by permission of the publisher.—*Hebrew University Studies in Literature*, v. 4, Spring, 1976. © 1976 by HSLA. All rights reserved. Reproduced by permission of the publisher.—*Interpretation: A Journal of Political Philosophy*, v. 20, Spring, 1993 for "Shakespeare's Richard III and the Soul of the Tyrant" by Morton J. Frisch. Reproduced by permission of the publisher and the author.—*Iowa State Journal of Research*, v. 56, August, 1981. Reproduced by permission of the publisher.—*JEGP: Journal of English and Germanic Philology*, v. XII, 1963 for "The Tempest: An Interpretation" by Frank Davidson. Renewed 1991 by the Board of Trustees of the University of Illinois. Reproduced by permission of the publisher and the author.—*Modern Language Quarterly*, v. 33, September, 1972. © 1972 University of Washington. Reproduced by permission of Duke University Press.—*Modern Language Studies*, v. V, Spring, 1975 for "*The Taming of the Shrew*: Shakespeare's Mirror of Marriage" by Coppélia Kahn. Copyright, Northeast Modern Language Association, 1975. Reproduced by permission of the publisher and the author.—*Papers on Language and Literature*, v. VII, Spring, 1971. Copyright © 1971 by the Board of Trustees, Southern Illinois University at Edwardsville. Reproduced by permission of the publisher.—*Shakespeare Jahrbuch*, v. 114, 1978. Reproduced by permission of the publisher.—*Shakespeare Quarterly*, v. 2, January 1951; v. 13, Autumn, 1962; v. 14, Summer 1962; v. 23, Spring, 1972; v. 27, Spring, 1976; v. 29, Winter 1978; v. 30, Winter, 1979; v. 35, Spring, 1984. © The Folger Shakespeare Library 1951, 1962, 1963, 1972, 1976, 1978, 1979, 1984. All reproduced by permission of the publisher.—*Shakespeare Survey: An Annual Survey of Shakespearean Study and Production*, v. 13, 1960 for "Madness in 'King Lear'" by Kenneth Muir; v. 20, 1967 for "Shakespeare's Thematic Modes of Speech: Richard II to Henry V" by Robert Hapgood; v. 21, 1968 for "Imagery and Irony in Henry V" by C. H. Hobday; v. 30, 1977 for "Whatever Happened to Prince Hal? An Essay on Henry V" by William Babula; v. 31, 1978 for

Chronology of Shakespeare's Life and Works

1564   William Shakespeare is born in Stratford-upon-Avon. His notice of baptism is entered in the parish register at Holy Trinity Church on April 26th. While the actual date of his birth is not known, it is traditionally celebrated on April 23rd.

1571   Shakespeare probably enters grammar school, seven years being the usual age for admission.

1575   Queen Elizabeth visits Kenilworth Castle, near Stratford. Popular legend holds that the eleven-year-old William Shakespeare witnessed the pageantry attendant on the royal progress and later recreated it in his dramatic works.

1582   Shakespeare marries Anne Hathaway of Shottery. The eighteen-year-old Shakespeare and twenty-six-year-old Hathaway are married on November 27th at Temple Grafton, a village about five miles from Stratford.

1583   Susanna, the first child of William and Anne Shakespeare, is born. Susanna's birth occurs five months after Shakespeare and Hathaway

wed. Susanna dies in 1649.

1585(?)   Shakespeare leaves Stratford sometime between 1585 and 1592, and joins a company of actors as a performer and playwright.

1585   Twins Hamnet and Judith Shakespeare born. Hamnet dies in 1596. Judith dies in 1662.

1589-90   Shakespeare probably writes *Henry VI, Part One*. The dates given for the composition of Shakespeare's plays, though based in scholarship, are somewhat conjectural.

1590-91   Shakespeare probably writes *Henry VI, Part Two* and *Henry VI, Part Three*.

1592   Shakespeare was known in London as an actor and playwright by this time as evidenced by his being mentioned in Robert Greene's pamphlet *A Groats-worth of Wit*. In this pamphlet (published this year), Greene chides Shakespeare as an "upstart crow" on the theater scene. Greene charges that Shakespeare is an unschooled player and writer who "borrows" material from his well-educated betters for his own productions.

London theaters are closed due to plague.

1592-93   Shakespeare probably writes *Venus and Adonis*, *Richard III*, and *The Two Gentlemen of Verona*.

1592-94   Shakespeare probably writes *The Comedy of Errors*.

1593   Shakespeare probably begins composing his sonnets. He will eventually write 154 sonnets.

Shakespeare's narrative poem *Venus and Adonis* is published.

1593-94   Shakespeare probably writes *The Rape of Lucrece*, *Titus Andronicus*, and *The Taming of the Shrew*.

1594   Shakespeare performs with the theater troupe the Lord Chamberlain's Men. The group includes leading actor Richard Burbage and noted comic performer Will Kempe.

1594-95   Shakespeare probably writes *Love's Labour's Lost*.

1594-96   Shakespeare probably writes *King John*.

1595   Shakespeare probably writes *Richard II*. The play is first performed the same year.

Shakespeare probably writes *A Midsummer Night's Dream*. The play is probably composed for performance at a wedding.

Shakespeare probably writes *Romeo and Juliet*.

1596   Henry Carey, Lord Hunsdon, Lord Chamberlain, and patron of the Lord Chamberlain's Men, dies.

Shakespeare's company comes under the patronage of George Carey, second Lord Hunsdon.

Shakespeare probably writes *The Merry Wives of Windsor*. The play was performed before the Queen during the Christmas revels.

1596-97   Shakespeare probably writes *The Merchant of Venice*, and *Henry IV, Part One*.

1597   Shakespeare purchases New Place and the grounds surrounding the spacious Stratford home.

1598   Shakespeare appears in a performance of Ben Jonson's *Every Man in His Humour*, and is listed as a principal actor in the London performance.

Shakespeare probably writes *Henry IV, Part Two*.

1598-99   Shakespeare probably writes *Much Ado About Nothing*.

1599   Shakespeare probably writes *Julius Caesar*, *Henry V*, and *As You Like It*.

The Lord Chamberlain's Men lease land for the Globe Theatre. Nicholas Brend leases the land to leading shareholders in the Lord Chamberlain's Men, including Shakespeare. Later this year, the Globe Theatre opens.

Earliest known performance of *Julius Caesar*. Thomas Platter, a German traveler, mentions the production at the Globe Theatre on

September 21st in his diary.

John Weever publishes the poem "Ad Guglielmum Shakespeare," in which he praises Shakespeare's *Venus and Adonis*, *The Rape of Lucrece*, *Romeo and Juliet*, and other works.

1600-01   Shakespeare probably writes *Hamlet*.

1601   Shakespeare probably writes the narrative poem *The Phoenix and Turtle*.

1601-02   Shakespeare probably writes *Twelfth Night; or, What You Will* and *Troilus and Cressida*.

Shakespeare probably writes *All's Well That Ends Well*.

1603   *A Midsummer Night's Dream* is performed before the Queen at Hampton Court.

Queen Elizabeth dies. The new king, James I (James VI of Scotland), arrives in London a month later, and proves to be a generous patron of the theater and of acting troupes.

King James grants a patent, or license, to Shakespeare's acting troupe, the Lord Chamberlain's Men. The patent is required for the troupe to perform. They take the name the King's Men to honor the new king.

The King's Men enact a play, probably *As You Like It*, before King James at Wilton.

Shakespeare appears in a performance of Ben Jonson's *Sejanus*. This is the last recorded occasion of Shakespeare appearing in a theatrical production.

An epidemic of the Black Death kills at least 33,000 in London. This is the worst outbreak of disease in London until the plague recurs in 1608.

1604   Shakespeare probably writes *Measure for Measure*. The play is staged at court before King James.

Shakespeare probably writes *Othello*. The play is first performed at Whitehall on November 1st.

1605   Shakespeare probably writes *King Lear*.

The Merchant of Venice is performed at court. The play is performed twice and is commended by the king.

Shakespeare probably writes *Macbeth*. This play's Scottish background was almost certainly intended to celebrate the new king's ancestry.

1606   Shakespeare probably writes *Antony and Cleopatra*.

1607   *Hamlet* and *Richard III* are performed. The plays are acted aboard the British ship *Dragon* at Sierra Leone.

1607-08   Shakespeare probably writes *Coriolanus*, *Timon of Athens*, and *Pericles*.

1608   The King's Men lease the Blackfriars Theatre. The Blackfriars was the first permanent enclosed theater in London. Shakespeare, Richard Burbage, Cuthbert Burbage, Thomas Evans, John Hemminges, Henry Condell, and William Sly lease the theatre for a period of twenty-one years. Stage directions indicate that Shakespeare wrote *The Tempest* with specific features of the new playhouse in mind.

London theaters are closed due to plague. This is one of the longest periods of theater closure due to plague: the playhouses are shut from spring 1608 throughout 1609.

1609 Shakespeare's sonnets are published. This publication of Shakespeare's sonnets is unauthorized.

1609-10 Shakespeare probably writes *Cymbeline*.

1610 The King's Men perform *Othello* at Oxford College during the summer touring season. An Oxford don records his impressions of the play in Latin, finding the spectacle of Desdemona's death, in particular, deeply moving.

1610-11 Shakespeare probably writes *The Winter's Tale*.

1611 Shakespeare probably writes *The Tempest*.

1612-13 Frederick V, the elector platine and future king of Bohemia, arrives in England to marry Elizabeth, King James's daughter. The King's Men perform several plays, including *Othello* and *Julius Caesar*.

Shakespeare probably writes *Henry VIII*, most likely collaborating with John Fletcher, another highly reputed dramatist, on this history play.

Shakespeare probably writes *Cardenio*, the only play of Shakespeare's that has been completely lost.

1613 Shakespeare probably writes *The*

Two Noble Kinsmen. An entry in the Stationer's Register for 1634 indicates that this play was jointly written by Shakespeare and John Fletcher.

The Globe Theatre burns down.

1614 The Globe Theatre reopens on the opposite bank of the Thames.

1616 Shakespeare dies on April 23rd. His burial is recorded in the register of Stratford's Holy Trinity Church on April 25th.

1619 *Hamlet* and several other of Shakespeare's plays are performed at court as part of the Christmas festivities.

1623 Anne Hathaway Shakespeare dies.

Shakespeare's fellow actors, John Hemminges and Henry Condell, compile and publish thirty-six of the dramatist's works. This collection is known as the First Folio.

To the Student: An Introduction to *Shakespeare for Students, Book II*

by Cynthia Burnstein, Plymouth-Salem High School, Canton, Michigan

This may be a scene from your experience: You have been assigned to read a play by William Shakespeare in your literature class. The students look a little skeptical as the books are distributed. That evening at home you do your best to understand as you read the play alone, fiercely studying the footnotes and employing a dictionary, but you still have serious doubts that you are correctly grasping the plot. Although the next day's class discussion helps enormously, you are now positive that you will never get all the characters' names straight. Then one day in class a couple of students disagree about the motivation of the main character and press each other to back up their interpretations with evidence from the text. The rest of the class sits forward in their seats. The debate is intense. For some reason, your teacher is smiling. Hours later you find yourself thinking about the play. Finally, you watch a film version of the play, or, if you are really lucky, you see it performed live. Now everyone in the class has a question as well as an opinion, and the discussions that ensue take a tone of authority that is new and exhilarating.

Someone has said that books are like having the smartest, wittiest, most profound and poetic friends in the world, friends who are there to speak to you anytime you wish. Literary criticism, which is what the book you are holding in your hands is primarily concerned with, is valuable for just the same reason. It is a way of having a thought-provoking conversation about a piece of literature with an intelligent friend. As sometimes happens between friends, you may not always agree with or fully grasp his or her point. Other times, a particular interpretation may seem so preposterous that you stomp off, sputtering. But then there are times you listen and say, "I never thought of it *that* way . . ." or better yet, "Wow!"

The purpose of this book, then, is to enable you to continue those discussions. The heart of *Shakespeare for Students, Book II* is a collection of essays by Shakespeare scholars which have been carefully selected to be of interest to students at the high school or undergraduate college level. Some essays appear as excerpts for your convenience. For efficiency's sake, you may want to read the general introductions to the essays on certain characters or topics to determine whether that subject is what you're interested in. If it is, you can then turn to the specific introduction for each separate essay. This will help you determine which essays are the most promising. If you are still hungry for more discussion, you will find the Sources for Further Study section to be very helpful. This section lists not only more titles of essays about the plays, but can also aid you in locating other valuable resources such as Shakespeare on video.

Shakespeare for Students, Book II contains a number of other features that will help you as you study Shakespeare's plays. For each of the eight plays, there is:

1. an **introduction**, which provides basic background information about the play
2. a **character list**, which briefly describes the role and personality of each character in the play
3. a **plot synopsis**, which summarizes the action by act
4. an overview of the **principal topics**, which are the most commonly discussed issues the play explores
5. **character studies**, which provide a closer look at the play's major characters, and
6. a **conclusion**, which is a summary of what some of the critics have had to say about the play through the years.

Here is a scene I am imagining about your future: Scholars from the past and students from the present are speaking to each other intensely. They are discussing the plays of William Shakespeare. Ideas are everywhere—in the air, careening off of walls, bouncing through space. As I look around the room at the faces that glow with energy, I see one that looks very familiar. It is yours.

SHAKESPEARE
for Students
BOOK II

HENRY IV, PART ONE

INTRODUCTION

Henry IV, Part One continues the story Shakespeare began telling in *Richard II*. To understand the events of *Henry IV, Part One*, readers must know that in *Richard II*, Henry IV, who was then known as Bolingbroke, returns from exile, has King Richard imprisoned, and declares himself King. In *Henry IV, Part One*, Henry's former supporters, those who helped put him in power, join forces against him. Henry and his son, Hal, fight together against the rebels. The story continues in *Henry IV, Part Two* with civil war still threatening the nation. Henry dies and Hal becomes King Henry V. Finally, in *Henry V*, the last of the group of plays known as the Lancastrian tetralogy (Lancaster refers to the family, or house, from which Henry was descended), Henry V conquers France, establishes peace, and marries Katherine, the French princess.

Scholars estimate that *Henry IV, Part One* was written and performed in late 1596 or early 1597. The play was published in 1598. For the historical plot of the play, Shakespeare drew from several sources of English history which were written during Elizabethan times. His primary source was Raphael Holinshed's *Chronicles of England, Scotland, and Ireland* (2nd edition, 1586-87). Shakespeare also consulted Samuel Daniel's narrative poem entitled *The Civile Wars between the two houses of Lancaster and York* (1595) and Edward Hall's *Chronicle of the Union of the Two Noble and Illustre Famelies of Lancastre and Yorke* (1540). Finally, Shakespeare seems to have drawn heavily from an anonymous play, *The Famous Victories of Henry V* (1594?), for the Hal-Falstaff plot.

Although little was written about the play until the mid-seventeenth century, when Samuel Pepys commented that the performance "did not please" him (*Diary and Correspondence*, 1660), it is known that Shakespeare was persuaded to change Falstaff's name, which was Jockey Oldcastle when the play was originally performed. When the play was first printed, the name had been changed. Scholars suggest that perhaps an Elizabethan descendent of the historical Oldcastle was offended by Shakespeare's representation of the family name.

The major conflicts in the play include Hal's strained relationship with his father. Henry IV is concerned that Hal is tarnishing his princely reputation with his association with the corrupt Falstaff. Falstaff is often associated with the idea of disorder, as his friendship with Hal appears to threaten the Prince's ability to mature into a responsible ruler. Critics argue whether Hal, who, after a confrontation with his father suddenly transforms himself into the prince his father wants him to be, was actually only using Falstaff to heighten the impact of his transformation. Others attempt to demonstrate Hal's sincerity.

Critics are also concerned with the rebellion against the crown and one of its chief instigators, Hotspur. The rebellion, led in part by Hotspur, threatens the stability and order of the nation. Hotspur's valor is admired by many in the play, especially by Henry, who suggests to Hal that Hotspur is perhaps a more deserving heir to the throne. Henry's comparison of the two often leads critics to do the same. Many commentators focus their comparison on the two distinct views of honor expressed by Hal and Hotspur.

PRINCIPAL CHARACTERS

(in order of appearance)

King Henry IV: Formerly known as Bolingbroke, Henry, who won the crown through rebellion, faces the same threat that he once posed. He is fearful that his son, Prince Hal, will lose the crown to the rebellious Hotspur. (See **Henry** *in the* **CHARACTER STUDIES** *section.*)

John of Lancaster: The younger brother of Prince Hal, John fights valiantly in battle but seems to lack many of his brother's skills and virtues.

Earl of Westmoreland: A nobleman who, with Sir Walter Blunt, leads King Henry IV's army.

Sir Walter Blunt: A nobleman who, with the Earl of Westmoreland, leads King Henry IV's army.

Henry, Prince of Wales: Known as Prince Hal and son of King Henry IV. Hal is a courteous, noble, high-spirited youth who provokes his father's anger and disapproval by associating with the common people, especially with Falstaff. Hal regains his father's favor when he vows to change his ways and best Hotspur in battle. (See **Hal** *in the* **CHARACTER STUDIES** *section.*)

Sir John Falstaff: An irresponsible, merry, and often

drunk companion of Prince Hal. Falstaff tempts Hal into a variety of mischievous deeds, but eventually loses his influence over the Prince as Hal accepts his responsibilities as heir to the throne. (*See* **Falstaff** *in the* **CHARACTER STUDIES** *section.*)

Ned Poins: A companion of Hal at the Boar's Head Tavern.

Henry Percy, Earl of Northumberland: Hotspur's father. Northumberland was one of the original supporters of Henry IV, then Bolingbroke. He now turns on the King who he believes turned his back on those who helped him gain power.

Thomas Percy, Earl of Worcester: Hotspur's uncle. Like his brother, Northumberland, Worcester questions King Henry IV's treatment of his former supporters.

Henry Percy: Nicknamed Hotspur. Hotspur is a passionate, hot-headed youth who prices honor, chivalry, and bravery in battle above all else. With his father and uncle, Hotspur plots a rebellion against King Henry IV. (*See* **Hotspur** *in the* **CHARACTER STUDIES** *section.*)

Gadshill: Falstaff's unruly Boar's Head Tavern companion.

Peto: Another of Falstaff's rambunctious Boar's Head Tavern companions.

Lady Percy: Hotspur's witty and affectionate wife.

Mistress Quickly: Hostess of the Boar's Head Tavern.

Bardolph: Another of Falstaff's rowdy Boar's Head Tavern companions.

Edmund Mortimer, Earl of March: Lady Percy's brother, and rightful heir of the deceased Richard II. Mortimer joins forces with the rebels.

Owen Glendower: A Welsh soldier and ally of the Percys, he is reputed to have magical powers.

Lady Mortimer: Glendower's daughter and Mortimer's wife, she speaks and understands only Welsh, while her husband speak or comprehends only English.

Archibald, Earl of Douglas: Leader of the Scottish army, Douglas forms an alliance with the Percys, his former enemies, to rally against King Henry IV.

Sir Richard Vernon: A nobleman and rebel.

Richard Scroop, Archbishop of York: Supporter of the Percy rebellion against King Henry IV.

Sir Michael: A follower of the Archbishop.

PLOT SYNOPSIS

Act I: Henry postpones his planned trip to the Holy Land, which he had hoped to offer as penance for the death of Richard II. Hotspur refuses to surrender to Henry the Scottish prisoners he has captured unless Henry agrees to pay the ransom for Edmund Mortimer. Mortimer, Hotspur's brother-in-law and Richard II's rightful heir, was captured by Owen Glendower when English forces attacked Wales. Henry refuses to ransom Mortimer and demands Hotspur to release the Scottish prisoners. Hotspur again refuses and returns to his home in Northern England with his father (Northumberland) and his uncle (Worcester). The three plan to raise a rebellion against the King by joining their forces with those of the Archbishop of York, Owen Glendower, Edmund Mortimer, and Douglas. In the meantime, Prince Hal is plotting with Falstaff and other companions to rob a group of travelers passing through Gadshill, near London.

Act II: After Falstaff's group has robbed the travelers, they are attacked by Prince Hal and Ned Poins, who are masked and disguised in buckram (a certain, stiff type of fabric). Back in the tavern, Falstaff exclaims that he fought valiantly against eleven men in buckram. Hal explains the practical joke, much to the amusements of the other patrons in the tavern. Later, Hal and Falstaff, act out a scene between Hal and his father, in which the two discuss Hal's unprincely activities and his friendship with Falstaff. Initially, Hal plays himself and Falstaff plays Henry, but the two switch roles. Falstaff, playing the role of Hal, finds himself defending himself to Hal, who is playing Henry. The group's story-telling, jesting, and play-acting is interrupted by a nobleman who has come to summon Prince Hal to court due to the impending rebellion.

Act III: The rebels agree on a plan to attack the King's forces and discuss how they will divide the country after they have won. In the meantime, Henry confronts Hal about the Prince's wild ways. The King suggests that Hotspur would make a better king than Hal, a comment which leads Hal to vow that he will redeem his reputation "on Percy's head." Henry, much pleased with his son's promise to change his behavior, forgives Hal and puts him in charge of a division of the royal army. Henry even allows Falstaff to command a company of foot soldiers.

Act IV: Near Shrewsbury, in the rebel camp, Hotspur and Douglas discover that they have been deserted by Northumberland and Glendower. Hotspur and Douglas plan to lead their forces into battle despite these losses. Westmoreland, Prince John of Lancaster, and Hal are leading the royal forces. The Archbishop of York foresees the failure of the rebellion and makes plans to meet with the King sometime after the battle is over.

Act V: Henry meets with Worcester and Sir Richard Vernon to offer a complete pardon to all of the rebels if they will disband. Worcester, however, is suspicious of the King's motives and does not tell the rebel forces of the King's offer. Rather, he claims that the King has challenged them to immediate battle. During the fighting, Hal saves his father from an attack by Douglas. Hal then finds himself engaged in battle with Hotspur, whom he kills. Hal praises Hotspur's valor and then sees Falstaff lying on the ground. Falstaff, attacked by Douglas, fell down and pretended to be dead. He continues his sham as Prince Hal briefly laments his death and exits. Falstaff then rises up and stabs the body of Hotspur. When Hal returns with this brother, John, Falstaff claims that he, not Hal, has slain Hotspur. Hal allows the lie to stand. By battle's end, the rebel forces have been defeated and have all run off. Worcester and Vernon are taken prisoner and executed. Douglas is also taken prisoner but Hal releases him. The play ends with Prince John in pursuit of Northumberland and the Archbishop, Henry, and Hal departing to find and attack Glendower and Mortimer.

PRINCIPAL TOPICS

Language

The study of the language of *Henry IV, Part One* has focussed primarily on the use of prose and verse. Critics have examined how the use of prose and verse helps differentiate between the two worlds of the play. In the world of the tavern, Falstaff's world, prose is spoken, and in the world of the court, also identified as the historical world, verse is spoken. Hal, at ease in both worlds, uses the appropriate language when in the tavern or at court. Falstaff, in complete opposition to the courtly world, speaks only in prose. It has been noted that Hotspur speaks the best verse in the play. His speeches, like Hotspur himself, are straightforward and hard.

The use of oaths, or promises, has also been examined, as has the frequent manipulation of language in the play. Oaths, which are contradicted repeatedly by many characters including Falstaff, can be used to evaluate character as they indicate the possible moral superiority of characters who remain true to their word. Hal learns how to manipulate language and some critics have pointed out that his skill is a significant part of Hal's education. He learns how to speak like Hotspur when necessary, to speak like a commoner, to speak like a king, and to speak like himself.

Honor

In *Henry IV, Part One* Hal and Hotspur represent two distinct versions of honor. Hotspur's honor is achieved through warfare, and is marked by chivalrous action. It has been argued that Hotspur's aggressive pursuit of honor shows his disregard for human life. Some critics have maintained that this view of honor, prevalent throughout the play and not just in Hotspur's character, runs deeper than warfare and chivalry; that in fact, it emphasizes family loyalty as well as patriotism.

Many commentators have noted that Hotspur's conception of honor is an outdated one and the Hal's view is more in line with what Elizabethans would have been familiar with and approving of. Scholars cite two Elizabethan sources (*The Courtier* and *The Governour*) as containing references to the type of honor represented by Hal, which is sometimes labeled "courtesy." Hal's honor is demonstrated, some critics maintain, by his loyalty to his father, to his country, and to his fellowman. Some commentators have noted that Hal's sense of honor is more humane than Hotspur's in that Hal does not seek warfare, but fights when necessary against rebellion in order to preserve the nation's unity.

In examinations of the theme of honor in *Henry IV, Part One*, some interest has been paid to Falstaff. Scholars studying the subject have maintained that Falstaff serves as a commentator on the futility of honor, and that this is especially true during the battle scene in the last act of the play. Falstaff seems to recognize the human cost of honor, at least of honor as Hotspur views it. Other critics argue that Falstaff represents a complete rejection of honor.

Fathers and Sons

The father/son relationship is played out in three different ways in *Henry IV, Part One*. It can be seen in the relationship between Henry and Hal, between Henry and Hotspur, and between Falstaff and Hal. Falstaff serves as a father-figure to Hal in that he teaches Hal about the world of commoners, the people Hal will one day rule; Falstaff also teaches Hal some of the useful "skills" he has learned in this world, including drinking and high-way robbery. Critics have argued that Hal rejects Falstaff's teachings, just as he rejects those of his own father. Others maintain that Henry's instruction of Hal is crucial to the Prince's success as a ruler. One of the most significant lessons that Henry teaches Hal, some commentators have pointed out, is that kingship is not inherited; it must be earned.

In the process of instructing Hal in his responsibilities as heir, Henry expresses his impression that Hotspur would be a more deserving heir than Hal. At one point, Henry even states his wish that Hotspur were his son instead of Hal. Henry feels as though he has more in common with Hotspur than Hal in that he sees himself and Hotspur as clear-thinking, passionate leaders. Henry also aligns himself with Hotspur because he also led a rebellion against the King.

It should also be noted that Hal's journey through Falstaff's world and back to the world of is father has been compared to that of the Biblical Prodigal Son, who returns home and wins his father's favor after a period of wanton living.

Time

There are numerous references to time in *Henry IV, Part One*. The one most frequently studied appears at the end of the second scene in Act I when Hal says that he will "redeem time." Many editors of the text of the play have noted that by this Hal means he will attempt to make up for the time he has spent unwisely or carelessly. Other critics argue that Hal means that he plans to begin spending his time well, that he will waste no more of it. References in Elizabethan religious literature seem to support the belief during that period that misspent time can not be made up for.

In addition to analyzing references to time made by the main characters, critics have discussed the views on the nature of time held by these characters. These critics demonstrate Henry's fear of and frequent misreading of time. They point out that Hal seems to have a firm understanding of the importance of good timing, that Hotspur is driven to action and uses up time, and that Falstaff, to whom it seems that time is completely irrelevant, fails to use time well, first by avoiding having to deal with its consequences, then by trying to make up lost time.

CHARACTER STUDIES

King Henry IV

Henry appears in the first scene of the play discussing his decision not to visit the Holy Land due to the civil unrest in his kingdom. (He had made the decision to go on the journey at the end of *Richard II* when he vowed to atone for the guilt he felt when Richard was murdered by Sir Pierce of Exton. Sir Pierce, an associate of Henry, then Bolingbroke, acted

upon Henry's comment that the death of Richard would ease his fears.) Henry refuses to give in to Hotspur's demand that Edmund Mortimer be ransomed. Rather, he presents his own demand that Hotspur's Scottish prisoners be turned over to him. Hotspur refuses.

Henry then begins to prepare for war with the Percys, who have shown themselves to be rebels against the crown. This preparation includes Henry's successful attempt to reclaim his son, Hal, from the negative influence of Sir John Falstaff. After Hal promises his father that he will redeem his reputation through battle with Hotspur, Henry awards him command of a division of the royal army. During the battle of Shrewsbury, Hal saves his father's life. After the battle, father and son depart in search of Glendower and Mortimer.

Few critics acknowledge that Henry has more than a supporting role in the play, with many critics claiming that Hal is the protagonist, despite the play's title. Others have argued for Henry's prominence, showing how he influences all of the major events within the play.

Most critics also agree that Henry's character is somewhat mysterious, that he leaves much unsaid or only hinted at. Some say that Shakespeare's indirect characterization of Henry allows the reader to understand the King through what others say about him, and through what Henry leaves unsaid. Also, most critics seem to agree that despite this indirect characterization, it is plain to see that Henry is a Machiavel, that he uses any means to achieve his political goals.

Hal

Hal appears in the first act of the play, plotting with Falstaff and company to rob a group of travelers. Hal decides to play a practical joke on Falstaff, and with Ned Poins, robs Falstaff of the loot stolen from the travelers. Back at the Boar's Head Tavern, he reveals the practical joke to Falstaff. He is soon called away to court where he is confronted by his father. Henry chastises his son for his crude behavior. Hal asks for forgiveness, but the king continues with his lecture, in which he praises Hotspur's ambition and valor. At this, Hal promises to change his ways, to put down Hotspur, and, in making such vows, wins his father's favor. Hal proceeds to lead his troops in the battle of Shrewsbury, where he saves his father's life and kills Hotspur.

Hal's motivation to behave the way he does—first irresponsibly participating in illegal activities and tarnishing his reputation as a nobleman and prince and later making a radical transformation, so impressive that Henry allows him to command troops in warfare—is a subject of much debate. Many critics argue that Hal's motives are Machiavellian, that his political ambitions are such that he can coldly use Falstaff to make his transformation from careless youth to responsible prince seem dramatic, deeply impressive, and well-timed. Other critics take a similar approach but argue that Hal's manipulation of Falstaff is for the purpose of gaining knowledge about the people he will one day rule. Still other critics believe that Hal actually learns a great deal from Falstaff and that the Prince's transformation is not staged but quite sincere. Finally, some believe that Hal has to deal with two conflicting natures within himself—the carefree youth and the ambitious prince. His ambition is strong and he understands his responsibilities as heir, and so suppresses his easy-going, laid back nature in order to assume those responsibilities.

Falstaff

Falstaff, often called a tempter or a corrupting force, is first seen living up to these accusations. In the first act of the play, he cajoles Hal into joining him in a robbery. But Falstaff is duped by Hal and Ned Poins, who attack Falstaff after he has robbed the travelers. Back at the tavern, Falstaff tells everyone that he was attacked by a group of men (in the course of his story-telling, Falstaff changes the number of men in this group repeatedly, finally agreeing that there were eleven men involved), and that he fought them all. Hal finally lets Falstaff in on the joke. Later, Falstaff and Hal jokingly portray Hal and his father discussing Hal's association with Falstaff, with Hal playing the part of Henry and Falstaff playing the part of Hal. In this exchange, Hal admits that he would banish Falstaff from his company. Although Hal is acting the part of his father, Falstaff seems to understand that there is some truth in Hal's words, that Hal indeed would leave his company.

When the action moves to the battle of Shrewsbury, where Falstaff is in command of a troop of foot soldiers, Falstaff attempts to joke with the Prince. Hal asks Falstaff to lend him his sword. Falstaff tells the Prince that he has a pistol in his holster that Hal is welcome to use, but when Hal reaches for the pistol, he finds a bottle of sack (a type of wine) in the holster instead. The Prince, caught up in the seriousness of the battle, takes the bottle and throws it at Falstaff. Later, Douglas appears and attacks Falstaff, who falls down and pretends to be dead. He lies there while Hal, nearby, kills Hotspur. After Hal leaves the scene, Falstaff stabs the dead Hotspur. Hal returns with his brother and is surprised to see Falstaff alive. Falstaff then takes credit for killing Hotspur, while Hal protests little to the lie. Falstaff exits the scene carrying Hotspur's body and looking forward to the award he expects to receive.

Falstaff's primary motivation throughout the play, some would argue, is his cowardice. These critics cite Falstaff's hiding when the Sheriff is looking for him, his running away from his attackers after the Gadshill robbery and then lying about what really happened, his playing dead at the battle, and his stabbing of the dead Hotspur then claiming that he had killed him, as examples of Falstaff's cowardice. Other critics claim that Falstaff only appears to be a coward. They argue that he is actually a courageous figure.

Falstaff is also analyzed in terms of his relationship with Hal and his commentary on Hotspur's character, especially Hotspur's honor. Some critics have observed that Falstaff's influence over Hal diminishes gradually throughout the play and that by the play's end, even Falstaff's role as a comic figure has been severely diminished.

Hotspur

Hotspur first appears in the play as a hot-headed soldier, boldly demanding that the King ransom Edmund Mortimer in exchange for Hotspur's release of the Scottish prisoners to the crown. When Henry refuses, Hotspur returns home with his uncle and father and begins to plot a rebellion against the "vile politician" (Henry). Despite the tension among the rebel forces, especially between Hotspur and Glendower, they agree on a plan of attack and begin to plan the division of the kingdom. Later, the rebels listen to Lady Mortimer sing. During this performance, Hotspur and his wife playfully engage in a verbal sparring match. Shortly before the battle, Hotspur learns that his father and Glendower have claimed to be ill and are unable to join the rebels, but Hotspur decides to fight the royal army anyway. During the battle, Hotspur is killed by the Prince.

Many critics admire Hotspur's sense of honor, and some argue that his obsession with it is foolish and deadly. Hotspur is also charged with being childishly unable to control his passions, with being a central force in the disorder in the world of *Henry IV, Part One*, and with failing to mature or change during the course of the play. Despite these criticisms, Hotspur's passionate nature, his impulsiveness, and his youthful need for action are the qualities that attract audiences and critics alike to him.

CONCLUSION

Increasingly, criticism on *Henry IV, Part One* has shifted from an emphasis on character studies and the historical sources from which Shakespeare drew to define his characters and plot to an emphasis on the language and structure of the play. The debate over the exact relationship between the two parts of *Henry IV* has intensified during the twentieth century as well, although an understanding of the conjectures on this topic is not necessary to understand and enjoy either play. *Henry IV, Part One* is considered to be one of the more controversial and popular of Shakespeare's histories, partly due to the political and moral implications as well as to the fascinating nature of the characters struggling for power in the play. It is enjoyed by many due to the comic relief provided by Falstaff. Additionally, many audiences and readers can relate to the situation Hal and his father find themselves in, in which an exasperated parent disapproves of a child's behavior and friends and the child struggles to find a balance between winning parental approval and finding his or her own identity.

(See also *Shakespearean Criticism*, Vols. 1 and 14)

OVERVIEWS

Maynard Mack

SOURCE: In an introduction to *The History of Henry IV, Part One*, by William Shakespeare, edited by Maynard Mack, New American Library, 1965, pp. xxiii-xxxvi.

[*Mack provides basic information about the play, discussing the dates it was written, performed, and published. In identifying the historical sources Shakespeare used to write* Henry IV, Part One, *Mack points out some of the historical facts that Shakespeare alters. The critic explains why topics covered in the play, such as the succession of English monarchs, were of interest to Elizabethan audiences.*]

The *First Part of Henry IV* was published in 1598; it was probably written and acted in 1596-97. There are some topical allusions in the play to these years, notably the Second Carrier's reference to the high cost of oats that killed Robin Ostler (II.i.12). Topical in a more important sense, during the whole of the 1590's, was the play's general subject matter. Though contemporary concern about succession to the throne need not (though it may) have influenced Shakespeare's choice of materials for his English histories, it inevitably gave them an extra dimension. Elizabeth was now in her sixties, and there was no assured heir, only a multiplicity of candidates, including her sometimes favorite, the Earl of Essex. Many recalled anxiously the chaos in times past when the center of power in the monarchical system had ceased to be sharply defined and clearly visible. This had occurred

to an extent after Henry VIII's death, and earlier after Henry V's, and still earlier after the murder of Richard II.

If Shakespeare was at all influenced by these anxieties, his rendering of them is on the whole buoyant and optimistic in his second English tetralogy and especially so in *1 Henry IV*. True, the England seen in this play and its immediate successor is far from reassuring. It has even been described as

> . . . an England, on the one side, of bawdy house and thieves'-kitchen, of waylaid merchants, badgered and bewildered Justices, and a peasantry wretched, betrayed, and recruited for the wars; an England, on the other side, of the chivalrous wolf pack of Hotspur and Douglas, and of state-sponsored treachery in the person of Prince John—the whole presided over by a sick King, hagridden by conscience, dreaming of a Crusade to the Holy Land as M. Remorse [i.e., Falstaff] thinks of slimming and repentance [Danby, J.F., *Shakespeare's Doctrine of Nature: A Study of King Lear*, 1949].

But this is only half the picture. Beside it, for the first Henry IV play, we must place the warmth, wit, and high spirits of the tavern scenes, the impetuous charm of Hotspur, the amusing domesticities of Kate and Glendower's daughter, the touching loyalty of Francis, the affections that (along with sponging) bind Falstaff to Hal, and Hal's own magnanimity and self-command. For both the first and second plays, we must weigh heavily into the account the character of the story told. This, the greatest of monarchical success stories in English popular history, traces the evolution of an engaging scapegrace [rascal] into one of the most admired of English kings. Chicanery [trickery] and appetite in the first play, apathy and corruption in the second, form an effective theatrical background against which the oncoming sunbright majesty of the future Henry V may shine more brightly—as we are assured precisely that it will do on our first meeting with him (I.ii).

When Shakespeare turned to this subject in 1596-97, he found in his historical sources, mainly Holinshed's *Chronicles*, two dominant motifs. One was the moral and theological interpretation of the troubles attending Henry IV's reign in consequence of his usurpation. . . .

The other was the legend of the madcap youth of Henry's son and heir—a legend already exploited in an anonymous play of which we have today only a debased and possibly abbreviated text: *The Famous Victories of Henry the Fifth*. The *Famous Victories* contributes to *1 Henry IV* the germ of the robbery incident (though the Prince's involvement in a thieving episode is found in the chronicles as well); the germ of the tavern high jinks and parodying of authority;

the germ of the expectation of Hal's reign as a golden age of rascals; and the germ of the reconciliation scene between the Prince and his father. The extent to which these hints are fleshed out and transfigured by Shakespeare's imagination may be seen in the character of Mistress Quickly. Her entire original in the *Famous Victories* is a sentence spoken by the Prince, favoring a rendezvous at "the old tavern in Eastcheap" because "there is a pretty wench that can talk well."

From the *Famous Victories* come also the names Gad's Hill (for the arranger of the robbery), Ned (our Ned Poins), and Jockey Oldcastle. The last was Shakespeare's name for Falstaff when the play was first performed, as references throughout the early seventeenth century show; Hal's addressing him as "my old lad of the castle" in the play as we have it (I.ii.43-44) is a survival from this. By the time the play was printed, the name had been altered to Falstaff for reasons that can now only be guessed at. Possibly there had been a protest by Oldcastle's descendants, one of whom was Lord Chamberlain during part of 1596-97. How the historical Oldcastle (d.1417), a man of character who was made High Sheriff of Herefordshire and eventually Lord Cobham, came to be metamorphosed into the roisterer of the *Famous Victories* is also an unsolved mystery, though no more mysterious than the dramatic imagination that exalted this dull stage roisterer, lacking eloquence, wit, mendacity, thirst, and fat, into the Falstaff we know.

On Holinshed and minor sources like Samuel Daniel's epic *The First Four Books of the Civil Wars between the Two Houses of Lancaster and York* [1595], Shakespeare based his treatment of the Percy rebellion, recasting the materials to give them an inner coherence. The Hotspur of history, for example, was twenty-three years older than Hal and two years older than the King himself, who at the date of the battle of Shrewsbury was only thirty-seven, his eldest son being then sixteen, and Prince John thirteen. Shakespeare followed the lead of Daniel and made Hotspur a youth, in order to establish dramatic rivalry between him and Hal. He then aged Henry rapidly so that by the time of the battle the King can speak of crushing his "old limbs in ungentle steel" and be the more appropriately rescued (this episode is also derived from Daniel) by his vigorous heir. For the same dramatic purpose, he assigned to Hal the triumph over Hotspur—though the inspiration for this may have come from misreading an ambiguous sentence in Holinshed. The reconciliation of Prince and King, touched on in the chronicles and dramatized briefly in the *Famous Victories* as occurring in Henry's latter years, he moved forward to a position before Shrewsbury, in order to enhance the human drama of father and son and further sharpen our anticipation of Hal's meeting with Hotspur. Hotspur's blunt uncourtly humor, the conception of Glendower as scholar and poet fired by a Celtic imagination, the entertaining clash of temperament and mood that this makes possible at Glendower's house, not only between Welshman and Englishman, but between romantic lovers and seasoned man and wife—all this again is Shakespeare's invention. His transformation of Holinshed, like his transformation of the *Famous Victories*, may best be indicated by a specific example. All of Hotspur's deliciously impetuous speech about the popinjay lord who came to Holmedon to demand his prisoners, not to mention the wonderfully ebullient scene in which it occurs, has behind it in Holinshed only seventeen words: "the King demanded of the Earl and his son such Scottish prisoners as were taken at Homeldon. . . ."

Hal's triumphant journey from tippling in taverns to glory on the field of battle derives from one other "source," more influential than any yet mentioned here. This is the *psychomachia* of the morality plays—that is, the struggle of virtues and vices for possession of a man's soul, a theme acted again and again in the plays of the early sixteenth century, which the drama of Marlowe and Shakespeare superseded. In these plays, youthful virtue is beset by temptations and misleaders but customarily sees the true light at last and is saved. In the same general manner, Prince Hal "has to choose, Morality-fashion, between Sloth or Vanity, to which he is drawn by his bad companions, and Chivalry, to which he is drawn by his father and brothers. And he chooses Chivalry" [Tillyard, E. M. W. *Shakespeare's History Plays*, 1944].

Norrie Epstein

SOURCE: "The Histories," in *The Friendly Shakespeare: A Thoroughly Painless Guide to the Best of the Bard*, Viking, 1993, pp. 156-235.

[*Epstein offers a definition of the history play, comments on the themes typically covered in history plays, and offers, in historical order, an account of the events that take place in Shakespeare's histories.*]

**The History Play
Defined**

The terms "history" and "chronicle" plays refer to the two tetralogies, or the eight plays covering the reigns of English monarchs from that of Richard II to that of Richard III, roughly from the late 1390s through the establishment of the Tudor dynasty in 1485. The cycle begins with the abdication of Richard II and ends with the death of Richard III. Shakespeare also wrote two other history plays that don't fall within this time span, *King John* and *Henry VIII*, but they won't immediately concern us, since *John* isn't all that interesting and *Henry VIII* was written with a collaborator. Shakespeare probably invented

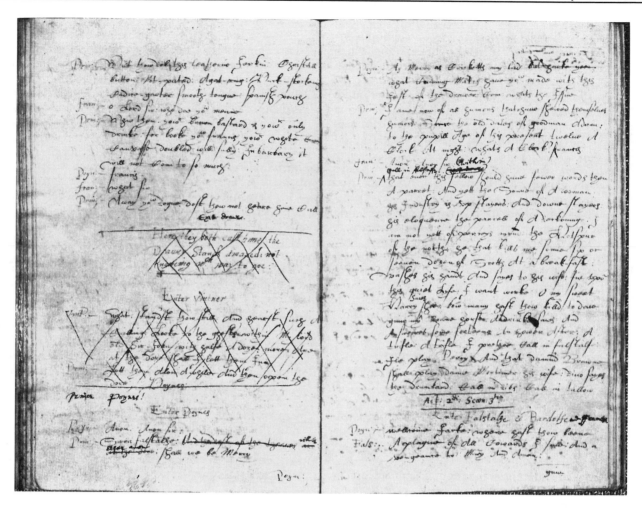

A manuscript of Henry IV, *prepared about the year 1611, known as the Dering Manuscript.*

this genre, and there is nothing like it today, although the old historical movie epics come close. The plays are a wonderful mix of battlefield heroics, familial relationships, feisty characters, power politics, and covert scheming.

Shakespeare's histories have been compared with "Dallas" and "Dynasty," but they also are a Tudor version of "Lifestyles of the Rich and Famous." Like these television shows, the history plays are about royalty and other moneyed people in high places, and their struggle for power. The Wars of the Roses, between the Houses of Lancaster and York, are nothing more than an elaborate family feud over the crown. By substituting a major corporation for England, the plot of, say, *Richard III* could easily be a miniseries about two warring scions fighting for corporate control. Thematically, however, the history plays perhaps most closely resemble the movie *The Godfather*; both are concerned with the father-son relationship, family honor, and the acquisition of power. More important, they both examine the question

of dynastic succession—a particularly weighty issue for the Elizabethans, who had an aging virgin queen on the throne and no heir in sight.

Although the history plays can be—and often are—enjoyed as separate dramas, they are more fully understood when seen as a whole, since each play forms part of an ongoing saga. In each tetralogy, characters appear, rise to power, and are killed, only to be replaced by their descendants, who in turn emerge, rise to power, and are killed.

Outline of Events

Here is a chronology of the history plays—not in the order Shakespeare wrote them, but according to the events they describe:

Richard II: Richard II renounces his throne and is later murdered, an act that divides the succession into two dynastic strains, Lancaster and York, primary contenders for the crown in the Wars of the Roses. Henry IV, formerly called Bolingbroke, is crowned.

Henry IV, Part 1: Henry's old supporters, the Percys, raise forces against him. Relations between Henry and his heir, Hal, are strained; Hal comes of age when he valiantly fights in his father's cause.

Henry IV, Part 2: Civil disruptions continue as Henry struggles to maintain his throne; he dies and is succeeded by his son, Hal, who becomes Henry V.

Henry V: Henry V conquers France and woos the French princess Katherine. The first tetralogy concludes with civil peace, triumph, and a royal marriage.

Henry VI, Part 1: Henry V dies while Henry VI is still an infant; uncles vie for power; civil war is imminent; France is lost.

Henry VI, Part 2: Henry VI grows up to become a weak and ineffectual ruler; the Wars of the Roses begin. (Henry is a Lancastrian.)

Henry VI, Part 3: Henry is defeated; the House of York triumphs. Edward III, brother of Richard of Gloucester (soon Richard III), is crowned.

Richard III: Edward III dies; Richard, fourth in line for the throne, removes all obstacles and is crowned. At the Battle of Bosworth, he is slain by Henry Richmond, later Henry VII, the first Tudor king and Elizabeth's grandfather.

There is supposedly a moment in a grade B historical epic when a character yells, "Come on, men! Let's go fight the Hundred Years' War!" This ironic, retrospective view of history must have been similar to what the Elizabethans felt as they watched their own past being enacted on stage. The Wars of the Roses were still vivid in the minds of Shakespeare's audience; they knew the outcome of the plot and the fates of all the major characters. Lancaster and York were household names, with all the familiarity and appeal of the name Kennedy today. The members of the audience could smile at the irony of Richard III's boast of power, since they knew that in Act V he would be defeated at the hands of Henry Richmond. This double perspective allowed them to observe the past while knowing its outcome—both in history and on stage. Thus the characters' words were given an extra level of meaning that is lost to us today.

The Elizabethans loved watching their past come alive, and the histories were among Shakespeare's most popular plays. The *Henry VI* trilogy was a box-office smash that turned an unremarkable actor named William Shakespeare into the most successful playwright of the day.

LANGUAGE

The study of the language of *Henry IV, Part One* has included an examination of the puns used in the play as well as analyses of unfamiliar words and phrases. Criticism has largely focused on the use of prose and verse within the play. **Milton Crane**, Brian Vickers, and others have studied this issue. Crane shows how the use of prose and verse by the main characters in the play differentiates between the worlds of the court and the tavern and helps flesh out each character's role within the play. Vickers maintains that Falstaff's "very existence depends on prose" but that Hal easily uses prose and verse. Other critics, including **Ronald R. MacDonald** have examined the frequency of the use of oaths in the play and how the use of oaths can be used to evaluate character. MacDonald also offers an analysis of the means by which language is manipulated by various characters and how the exploitation of language is an integral part of Hal's education.

Milton Crane

SOURCE: "Shakespeare: The Comedies," in *Shakespeare's Prose*, The University of Chicago Press, 1951, pp. 66-127.

[*Crane examines the use of prose and verse in the play and shows how the two modes of speech differentiate between the two worlds of the play—the world of the court and Falstaff's world. Crane demonstrates how Falstaff mimics the play's serious action through his use of prose. Falstaff's world, argues Crane, is in complete opposition to the world of the court; therefore it is appropriate that he never speaks in verse, the language of the court. Crane also shows how Hal moves easily from one world to the other, speaking prose in the tavern and verse in court. Crane analyzes Hotspur's speech as well, arguing that he speaks the best verse in the play.*]

Nowhere in Shakespeare are the boundaries of two worlds so clearly delimited by the use of prose and verse as in the *Henry IV* plays (1597, 1598). The scenes relating to the historical matter are in verse, the scenes of Falstaff and his followers in prose. There are trifling exceptions: the conventional usages, as in Hotspur's letter (II, iii); Hotspur's short comic dialogue with his lady (III, i), with its startling shifts between prose and verse; and the mock verse of Pistol. [All references to Shakespeare's text are to George Lyman Kittredge's *The Complete Works of Shakespeare*, 1936.] One can hardly say of plays which fall so neatly into two actions and two spheres of influence that the form of either action is basic and the form of the other is the exception. Between the two worlds lies a huge and fundamental opposition, but each is autonomous within itself; Pistol's verse in the Boar's Head tavern is burlesque, not a sadly distorted recollection that the "serious business" of the play is going on elsewhere in verse.

Falstaff is Shakespeare's most brilliant speaker of comic prose, as Hamlet is his most gifted speaker of a prose which defies categories. But why does Falstaff speak prose? This may seem an idle question: Falstaff is a clown, although a nobleman, and must therefore speak prose; he must, furthermore, represent "the whole world" that Hal has to banish before he can become England's Harry, and Falstaff must therefore be opposed in every conceivable way to the world of high action and noble verse in which Hal is destined to move. But beyond all this, Falstaff speaks prose because it is inconceivable that he should speak anything else. . . .

Burlesque [a form of comedy, typically mockery or ridiculous exaggeration] lies near the heart of Shakespearean comedy, from *The Comedy of Errors* to *As You Like It*. In the two *Henry IV* plays, the Falstaff-plot offers the broadest conceivable burlesque on the serious action. Falstaff derides the chivalric ideal, the forms of noble behavior, the law itself; he robs the travelers, suffers himself to be robbed in turn without fighting, and at last lies grossly and complacently about the whole affair and is totally unabashed at being found out. He is an unrepentant sinner, and, notwithstanding, is handsomely rewarded for his evil life until the moment of his banishment. He is a particularly noisome stench in the nostrils of the godly. His burlesque of their world is conducted on every plane: he robs them, flouts their ideals, and corrupts their prince. And, because he is in such constant opposition to their world, it is only fitting that he should never really speak its language. The powerful contrast is expressed on the level of speech as on every other, and thus Falstaff speaks prose because of what he represents as well as what he is.

Most of the characters can be assigned easily enough to one group or the other—Hal's position remaining always ambiguous—but Hotspur's case is somewhat odd. He accepts the code completely; he is honor's fool, and is killed for it. But he is a very downright man, whose hard and realistic common sense makes him impatient with both poetry and milk-and-water oaths; language must speak clearly, directly, and forcefully, or he will have none of it. It is therefore inevitable that he should speak the very best of language, and that especially in verse. His verse is so hard, colloquial, and simple that he really has no need for prose. George Rylands [in *Words and Poetry*, 1928] says that Hotspur's speech marks an important stage in the development of Shakespeare's verse style, a stage at which Shakespeare incorporated into his verse many of the qualities of his prose. And yet one feels that Shakespeare must have known what he was about

when he made Hotspur speak much more verse than prose. Hotspur belongs, after all, to the world of the knights, and he must speak their idiom even if only to mock them in it. Occasionally he uses prose, and very well, as in the prose letter in II, iii—a furious stream of prose: letter, comment, and vituperation, all well jumbled together. But as soon as Lady Percy enters, we have verse dialogue. The prose of this first long monologue should perhaps be put down to a combination of conventional epistolary prose and the dramatic necessity for continuing the letter scene in prose, even after the reading of the letter is finished.

In III, i, where Hotspur taunts and enrages the fiery Glendower, he begins in broken verse:

> Lord Mortimer, and cousin Glendower,
> Will you sit down?
> And uncle Worcester. A plague upon it!
> I have forgot the map.

> (III, i, 3-5)

Glendower's reply has been rearranged as most irregular verse by Pope from the prose of the Quartos. Hotspur's next speech is in prose, whereas Glendower at once breaks into the pompous, inflated verse so characteristic of him. Hotspur then varies between prose and verse; the length of the individual speech appears to be the only determinant. Thus he says at first:

> Why, so it would have done at the same
>   season, if your mother's cat
> had but kitten'd, though yourself had never
>   been born.

> (18-20).

But, a moment later, he goes on:

> And I say the earth was not of my mind,
> If you suppose as fearing you it shook.

> . . . . .

> O, then the earth shook to see the heavens
>   on fire,
> And not in fear of your nativity.
> Diseased nature oftentimes breaks forth
> In strange eruptions; oft the teeming earth
> Is with a kind of colic pinch'd and vex'd
> By the imprisoning of unruly wind
> Within her womb, which, for enlargement
>   striving,
> Shakes the old beldame earth and topples
>   down
> Steeples and mossgrown towers. At your birth
> Our grandam earth, having this
>   distemp'rature,
> In passion shook.

> (22-23, 25-34)

After Glendower's reply, Hotspur returns to prose for a two-line retort, and, a little later, speaks verse again. Hotspur's prose in this scene appears to be restricted to short gibes, whereas he speaks verse when he becomes aroused.

He uses prose again, briefly, toward the end of the scene, when he jokes with his wife and reproaches her for her genteel swearing. It is difficult to assign any specific reason for this prose, largely because of the general uncertainty of media in this passage (227-265). Hotspur speaks prose, then verse, then prose again; after the Welsh lady's song, Hotspur's protest against his lady's "in good sooth" begins in prose and drops suddenly into verse. His last speech is again in prose. . . .

The Prince, in general, takes his cue from his company, speaking prose in the tavern and verse in the court with equal facility. His one violation of this division is, consequently, all the more striking. He enters in V, iii, to find Falstaff moralizing over the corpse of Sir Walter Blunt. Hal is now no longer the boon companion, but the valiant knight, and reproves Falstaff in straightforward verse. Falstaff replies with a jest in prose, and the rest of the scene—a matter of a half-dozen speeches—is wound up in prose. But Falstaff himself has brought his prose into a verse scene, one of noble words and deeds, and he has used Sir Walter's "grinning honour" as a telling proof of his conclusions in his own catechism of honor. The scene thus contains a double contrast between prose and verse, and the old use of prose and verse characters within a single scene is here given a new and effective turn.

In V, i, Falstaff is for the first time brought into the world of the court, and at once sets about his favorite task of deriding it. Worcester pleads his innocence, and to the King's ironic question about the rebellion, "You have not sought it! How comes it then?" (V, i, 27), Falstaff interjects a reply: "Rebellion lay in his way, and he found it." Only Hal's injunction to remain quiet keeps Falstaff from making further comments on the action of the scene. He must needs hold his peace until the nobles have left, but immediately thereafter rediscovers his vein. Hal is short with him, for he is keenly aware of the seriousness of the situation. And so Falstaff must wait for even Hal to leave before he can make his most devastating comment on the ideals of a world he so ambiguously serves.

Shakespeare was too keen a dramatist not to have understood that the most powerful impression a scene creates in the mind of an audience is the final one. The first scene of Act V begins with King Henry, Worcester and the rest; but it ends with Falstaff. The *dramatic* point of the scene is well made and the main action is appreciably advanced. But at the side, and attempting always to intrude, is Falstaff, and when the rest have left, he has the stage entirely to himself. The net effect is produced not by the heroics of the nobles, but by the cynical realism of Falstaff. This is not to say that Falstaff dominates the play as he dominates this scene; as Professor Van Doren has well expressed it [in *Shakespeare*, 1939]: "History is enlarged here to make room for taverns and trollops and potations of sack, and the heroic drama is modified by gigantic mockery, by the roared voice of truth; but the result is more rather than less reality, just as a cathedral, instead of being demolished by merriment among its aisles, stands more august."

Hal must, as he says, "imitate the sun," and Falstaff's charm must be made so great as to convince the spectator that Hal's enjoyment of low life is not caused by a natural preference for the stew or the alehouse. But so charming (to use the word strictly) is Falstaff that Hal's necessary renunciation of him cannot be anything but priggish. . . .

Ronald R. MacDonald

SOURCE: "Uneasy Lies: Language and History in Shakespeare's Lancastrian Tetralogy," in *Shakespeare Quarterly*, Vol. 35, No. 1, Spring, 1984, pp. 22-39.

[*MacDonald explores the use and manipulation of language in* Henry IV, Part One. *He shows how oaths are made and contradicted and how the use of oaths indicates the moral superiority of characters in the play. MacDonald goes on to show how the exploitation of language has become a necessity in the new world, that is, the world created when Henry usurped Richard II. MacDonald argues that much of Hal's education is devoted to his learning how to manipulate language.*]

. . . Here is a sampling of oaths, selected not quite at random from the literally hundreds that stuff the language of *1 Henry IV*:

1. By the Lord, and I do not, I am a villain.
   (I.ii.96)

2. I'll make one, an' I do not, call me villain and baffle me.
   (I.ii.100-101)

3. By God, he shall not have a Scot of them,
   No, if a Scot would save his soul, he shall not!
   (I.iii.214-15)

4. An' it be not four by the day, I'll be hang'd.
   (II.i.1-2)

I choose these because they represent a situation, not

at all uncommon in the play, where an oath is given and then immediately contravened [contradicted]. The first two, and the clearest examples, are Falstaff's. With the first he swears to reform his wicked ways; with the second, a mere five lines later, he swears to join Hal in stealing a purse. Falstaff makes the outrageous contradiction highly visible by invoking the same penalty (being reduced to the rank of villain) on two incompatible performances. We should be exceedingly wary of believing (as Hal seems to do here) that Falstaff has been caught out, that the contradiction is inadvertent. He *displays* the contradiction, invites our attention to it, precisely in the way he will later underscore a patent fabrication by multiplying men in buckram suits (II.iv.191 ff.). In that later instance Hal will accuse him with some heat of lying about his exploits. The accusation imprudently overlooks the fact that Falstaff's exaggerations are clearly designed to be seen through. He isn't lying, he claims implicitly, but spinning a yarn, and to accuse a yarn-spinner of lying, is to make yourself look something of a sore-headed spoilsport. One of the weakest kinds of triumph is to think you have caught a man in a lie, and then have him show that he was only trying to entertain you. The stakes are perhaps somewhat lower in the matter of Falstaff's contradictory oaths, but the principles are similar: catch him out, and you become a killjoy; let the contradiction pass unremarked, and you seem to connive in degrading the whole institution of promising. This real dilemma, conjured up with a couple of apparently casual oaths, suggests that Falstaff's verbal skill is of a very high order.

Not so with the next oath in our sample, which belongs to Hotspur. He is denying his Scottish prisoners to King Henry, and doing this with some force; but fifty lines later, when Worcester has broached the conspiracy against the King, he agrees without demur to deliver them up unransomed. He is by no means aware of the contradiction; he has simply forgotten, in his characteristically hare-brained way, that he has promised anything at all.

The shrewd man may very well break a promise: this is the case with our last oath, which belongs to the unnamed carrier in II.i. He swears that it is four o'clock in the morning (if it is not, he will be hanged); he even offers supporting astronomical evidence: "Charles' wain is over the new chimney" (1. 1-2). Yet when the thief Gadshill, about whom the carrier has every reason to be suspicious, asks him the time, he says "I think it be two a' clock" (1. 33). He is very wisely denying a potential highjacker information about a time when he may expect to find portable property on the road. This is clearly more important in the circumstances than the very remote possibility that anyone will actually offer to hang him for contravening his initial oath. Perhaps the worst that can happen is that Gadshill will glance at Charles's wain over the new chimney and conclude that the carrier is lying. But that risk is certainly worth taking: if it succeeds, the advantage gained is real; if it fails, the consequences are trivial.

But no such careful calculation informs the promises that Hotspur makes and breaks. It may be argued that genuinely to forget a promise is not the same as to break it, and that the forgetful man enjoys a certain moral superiority over the consciously duplicitous one. But there is, for all that, a very high price to be paid for this moral superiority, for you deliver yourself over, body and soul, to those with a deeper understanding of the institution of promising, to those who are more than willing to suffer your old-fashioned talk about honor and justice and right, and then let you pay, for an hour or so of chivalric masquerading at Shrewsbury, with your life. The day belongs, even as it did in Richard's time, to the man who thinks in and through the language he speaks, and not to the man who allows that language to think in him.

The day belongs, in short, at least in the world of *1 Henry IV,* to Falstaff. He has fully mastered one of the lessons that Richard has to teach, that weakness, properly managed, may result in real power. Another characteristic locutionary [location refers to a particular way of expressing oneself] act in the play, one closely related to the oath, is the boast, an assertion of personal power peculiarly vulnerable to deflation:

> *Gadshill*   We steal as in a castle, cock-sure; we have the receipt of fern-seed, we walk invisible.
>
> *Chamberlain*   Nay, by my faith, I think you are more beholding to the night than to fern-seed for your walking invisible.
>
>   (II.i.85-90)

> *Glendower*   I can call spirits from the vasty deep.
>
> *Hotspur*   Why, so can I, or so can any man,
> But will they come when you do call for them?
>
>   (III.i.52-54)

> *Falstaff*   But, as the devil would have it, three misbegotten knaves in Kendal green came at my back and let drive at me, for it was so dark, Hal, that thou couldest not see thy hand.
>
> *Prince*   These lies are like their father that begets them, gross as a mountain, open, palpable.
>
>   (II.iv.221-26)

The difference between Falstaff's boast and those of

Gadshill and Glendower is simply that Falstaff offers his in full awareness of the way in which it renders him vulnerable. Indeed, his vulnerability is so obvious that the prudent man will be wary of it, and suspect that it conceals a trap. . . .

To speak effectively in the new world created by the usurpation [Bolingbroke's (Henry IV) stealing the Crown from Richard II] requires the exploitation of all the figurative resources of language, of irony, of understatement, of wary hyperbole [wild exaggeration] and deft paronomasia [puns; a pun is a play on words]. The days are gone when simple grandiloquence of the "This land of such dear souls, this dear dear land" kind will do. When in the deposition scene of *Richard II* Bullingbrook asks Richard if he is contented to resign the crown, Richard's riddling reply, "Ay, no, no ay" (IV.i.201), is something more than idle play with the homophones [words that sound alike but have different meanings or spellings] "ay" and "I." Richard has come to realize that a language that can only speak of either/or, that can generate no discourse governing the in-between, is inadequate to cover the complex of feelings he is now experiencing. His equivocation is the true expression of his inability to answer Bullingbrook's bald question with anything like the clarity Bullingbrook seems to require.

The changes of history demand changes of language, and to survive in the world of the two parts of *Henry IV* is to learn to speak in ways that are adequate to the occasion. Much of Hal's "education" in the course of the plays, if that is what it is, may be described as his attempt to master new languages, to be able to "drink with any tinker in his own language" (II.iv.19); to be able to speak like Hotspur ("'Give my roan horse a drench,' says he, and answers, 'Some fourteen,' an hour after; 'a trifle, a trifle,'" II.iv.106-8); to speak like a king; or to speak like himself:

> I know you all, and will a while uphold
> The unyok'd humor of your idleness,
> Yet herein will I imitate the sun.
> (*1 Henry IV*, I.ii.195-97)

The homophonic play (which at this early stage, when Hal tends to sound a bit smug, may not be fully conscious) suggests "imitate the son." The real task, in the shifting and ambiguous world created by the usurpation, is to be yourself. This is not a matter of the "naturalness" of manner tirelessly recommended in books of etiquette and treatises on how to succeed. It is a rigorous process of learning the languages of others and inventing a language of your own. When in the first reconciliation scene, Hal replies to his father's long sermon on the proper behavior exemplified by his aristocratic ancestors, his reply is anything but casual: "I shall hereafter, my thrice-gracious lord, / *Be more myself*" (III.ii.92-93). And we will not

be surprised to find him at the very end of *Henry V* learning yet another language, this time the French of his affianced Kate.

It is those who do not grow in language, who do not submit themselves to its shifting substance and stubborn materiality, who are defeated by history in the world of the Henry IV plays. Hotspur is first in this group, because, for all his eloquence, he has a thoroughly naive relation to the language he speaks. There is so much in him to remind us of the new order that it is easy to underestimate the extent to which he abandons himself to the aristocratic myths of the old order. Yet his gaze is basically retrospective, and it is in his casualness with language, and particularly in his unreflective relation to the institution of promising, that we can discover his allegiances most clearly. Here is Hotspur in soliloquy, congratulating himself warmly on the excellence of the anti-Lancastrian conspiracy:

> By the Lord, our plot is a good plot as ever was laid, our friends true and constant; a good plot, good friends, and full of expectation; an excellent plot, very good friends. . . . Is there not my father, my uncle, and myself? Lord Edmund Mortimer, my Lord of York, and Owen Glendower? is there not besides the Douglas? have I not all their letters to meet me in arms by ninth of the next month?
> (*1 Henry IV*, II.iii.15-19, 23-28)

We should be suspicious of Hotspur's way of upping the verbal ante here ("a good plot, good friends. . . . an excellent plot, very good friends"), for, as the example of Richard made clear, you can't make a thing so by saying it, nor a friend true by heaping him with honorific adjectives. Wishes are not horses, they are words, and that is why beggars have to walk. Hotspur's touching faith in the written promises of his fellow conspirators, in the letters he has in hand, is rather cruelly rewarded when, of the good friends he mentions here, all but two fail to show up and do battle.

HONOR

The theme of honor in *Henry IV, Part One* is most often examined by critics as it relates to Hal, Hotspur, and Falstaff. Critics such as **Moody E. Prior** argue that Falstaff represents a rejection of honor. Gordon Zeeveld maintains that Falstaff does not cynically respond to honor, he simply and realistically recognizes that warfare (pursued by Hotspur in the name of honor) is inhumane. Similarly, Carmen Rogers points out that Falstaff observes and comments on "false honor" as represented by Hotspur. Most critics, including Paul Siegel, **G. M. Pinciss**, and Prior, generally agree that the honor so enthusiastically pursued by Hotspur is related primarily to chivalry and warfare. Zeeveld comments that this pursuit demonstrates Hotspur's blatant disregard for human life. Siegel and Pinciss also demonstrate how this sense of honor is, in the world of *Henry IV, Part One,* an outdated one. Hal is most often associated with what critics like Rogers refer to as "true honor." Zeeveld shows how this sense of honor is entirely humane, unlike Hotspur's view of honor. Siegel discusses Hal's honor as a striving for "Christian humanism" which is demonstrated by Hal's virtuous and loyal service to his countrymen. Pinciss states that Hal is actually a representative of a more modern (in Elizabethan terms) version of honor: courtesy. While many critics speculate on how Shakespeare's portrayal of these different views on honor may indicate what the playwright's own feelings on the subject were, Patrick Cruttwell asserts that Shakespeare does not favor any of these views; he simply presents all the options.

Moody E. Prior

SOURCE: "Ideas of History: *Richard II, 1* and *2 Henry IV, Henry V,*" in *The Drama of Power: Studies in Shakespeare's History Plays,* Northwestern University Press, 1973, pp. 199-218.

[*Prior examines the place of honor in the disorderly world of* Henry IV, Part One. *On the surface, argues Prior, honor appears to serve only in the context of chivalry and warfare. Prior shows how a closer examination reveals that Hotspur, Hal, and Henry have a deeper understanding of the concept of honor. Prior also illuminates the limitations of honor. He first focusses on how little attention is paid in the play to the broken promises and rebellion related to Henry's road to kingship. Next, Prior notes that Falstaff denies "the reality of honor" by seeing honor only as an intangible, valueless result of bravery in battle. Prior contrasts Hotspur's extravagant desire for honor with Falstaff's rejection of honor, commenting that Falstaff overlooks those aspects of honor which are unrelated to warfare and which could therefore be useful to him. Finally, Prior discusses Hal's conception of honor, showing it to be demonstrated by Hal's loyalty to the King and to the nation.*]

The word "honor" occurs frequently in Part 1, and its presence has raised some troublesome questions. What place can honor have in a world in which subjects rebel against a usurper whom they placed in office, the prince plays at robbery with a dissolute knight, and the contending parties in government seem guided by "policy" rather than principle? Superficially, the answer appears to be that honor has little to do with the conduct of most of the characters, and where it is invoked the concept often seems narrow. At first glance honor seems to mean no more than a reputa-

tion for prowess and skill in arms gained in battle by noblemen and knights. That is the implication when the word first appears in the opening scene, in which the king contrasts the victorious Hotspur, "the theme of honor's tongue," with his son, who was not at the battle and whose brow is stained with "riot and dishonor" (1.1.80, 84), and also when, later in the play, the king upbraids the prince, comparing his son's dissoluteness and negligence with the boldness of young Hotspur leading his rebellious followers "to bloody battles and to bruising arms" and to the "never-dying honor" which he gained against Douglas (3.2.105-6). It is also the prince's meaning when he promises to redeem his bad reputation against the "child of honor and renown" and exchange his own shames "for every honor sitting on his helm" (3.2.139, 142). Hotspur glorifies the honor to be gained in battle against worthy foes, and the more hazardous the enterprise the greater the chance of gaining honor. The extravagance of his speech about plucking "bright honor from the pale-faced moon" and "drowned honor by the locks" (1.3.199 ff.) is inspired by Worcester's warning that the matter he is about to reveal is "deep and dangerous" (1.3.188).

Even in this narrow military context, however, honor demands from these warriors something more than bravery and success in battle. This is a society in which the nobility constitutes an elite expected to bear arms, and honor stands for the special virtues which distinguish this class in the exercise of its vocation—gallantry in combat with a worthy foe, adherence to the accepted code of arms, and individual loyalty to friends, family, and comrades in arms. These qualities are taken seriously and have currency in *I Henry IV,* even though men accuse each other of breaking their solemn word, rebellions are plotted, and warriors fight for something less than the highest moral principles and national glory. It says something for the world of *I Henry IV* that such distinctions can be made. . . . The battle of Shrewsbury is a deadly serious affair, yet the prince can call Hotspur "a valiant rebel of that name" before engaging him in fair fight to the death.

There are further shades of meaning which extend the idea of honor in *I Henry IV* beyond the demands of chivalry and war. Even for Hotspur honor can mean something more than meeting dangers and triumphing over great warriors in battle. His first use of the word is, in fact, not in connection with warfare at all. He upbraids his father and uncle for having dishonored themselves by putting down Richard, setting the crown on Bolingbroke, and having to endure the humiliation of being discarded by him now that he is Henry IV. From these shames, he urges,

time serves wherein you may redeem
Your banished honors and restore yourselves

Into the good thoughts of the world again.

(1.3.178-80)

The dishonor that the king attributes to his son is not simply that he failed to distinguish himself in battle, but that by indulging in riot and bad company at a time when the king's interest was in danger he failed in a principal obligation of a prince. The king rejoices when his son joins him, not only because Hal has promised to use Hotspur's glory to redeem his own, but because he has returned to his proper princely role. "A hundred thousand rebels die in this," Henry exclaims (3.2.160). Honor, then, goes beyond chivalry and military fame.

Nevertheless, at its broadest it is a concept with serious limitations. Henry's perjury is a case in point. It is charged against him by his former supporters that in taking the crown from Richard II he had broken an oath which he made to them on returning from exile, that he had come only to claim his inheritance; but, in spite of the gravity of this charge, little enough is made of it, because the oath was taken for expedient reasons and broken with the connivance of his then allies, now his enemies. And yet for most of the characters, including the king, honor is a serious matter. Judgment of conduct is referred to it, and it is invoked to bind men to a cause and to inspire the exercise of such private virtues as are demanded by one's public obligations. Its prominence is thus a mark of the secular atmosphere of *I Henry IV*, in which the characters do not normally look beyond the immediate present to a cosmic scheme of justice or expect the wrath of God for neglecting a solemn obligation. In a world of politics and civil war it functions as a substitute for moral principle. It is not a static or a univocal concept, however; in the changing patterns of the play its merits are revealed, its limitations exposed, and in due course even the reality of honor is questioned.

The most direct, and indeed the only, denial of the reality of honor comes from Falstaff. His soliloquy on honor is a virtuoso performance of clever negation. It comes just after the king has ended his interview with the rebel leaders and the royal party awaits the almost certain sign for battle. Falstaff, the realist, says apprehensively, "I would 'twere bedtime, Hal, and all well." The prince's casual reply, "Why, thou owest God a death," provides the cue to the opening line of Falstaff's reflections, "'Tis not due yet, I would be loath to pay him before his day" (5.1.125-28). Restricting honor to its limited sense of the intangible rewards for valor in battle, Falstaff rejects it as empty and valueless, incapable of repairing wounds or surviving detraction after death. The sight of Sir Walter Blunt dead on the field of battle confirms him in his views—"There's honor for you" (5.3.32-33)— and it leads him to his final word on the subject: "I

like not such grinning honor as Sir Walter hath. Give me life, which if I can save, so; if not, honor comes unlooked for, and there's an end" (5.3.58-61). "'Tis not due yet," "Give me life"—these phrases sum up Falstaff's determination to hold on to life as the final good, even if it is only a precarious hold defiantly maintained against the decay of youth and the coming of age, the loss of moral virtue and of the world's esteem. The direct opposite of this is summed up in Hotspur's remarks shortly before the battle. A messenger comes with letters and Hotspur dismisses them— "I cannot read them now"; and as though this incident has suddenly brought home to him the realization that nothing matters now until the dangerous business is over, he continues,

O gentlemen, the time of life is short!
To spend that shortness basely were too long
If life did ride upon a dial's point,
Still ending at the arrival of an hour.

(5.2.81-84)

There are things which are more important to Hotspur than life. Though addressing his men, Hotspur seems in these lines almost to be speaking to himself, surprised by the circumstances into a moment of self-revelation which suggests something of the depth of feeling that underlies his earlier extravagant sentiments about honor or the apparent flippancy of his comment when he learns of the big odds against them in the battle, "Doomsday is near; die all, die merrily" (4.1.134).

Shakespeare has made both of these spokesmen for opposing attitudes attractive, each in his own extraordinary way. They have, moreover, some basic traits in common. Both conduct their lives and make their choices in accordance with a settled principle. Both have a distaste for the reserve and calculation of official public life. Their loyalties are narrow. Falstaff's loyalty is to himself and his cronies when they are useful, and Hotspur's is personal and clannish. Both reveal a lively extravagance at times when they feel challenged or aroused, and both display a trace of desperation in seeking to extract the full measure of gratification out of life. Both men have a zest for life, though Falstaff's inclinations carry him to dissoluteness and even degeneracy, and Hotspur's valor and sense of personal integrity sometimes express themselves in discourtesy, eccentricity, and foolhardiness. It is in the aberration of qualities which can enhance life that the danger lies in these two men Hotspur's sense of honor which makes him despise Henry as a "vile politician" and a "king of smiles" also makes him the victim of politicians who need his virtues to glamorize a rebellion, and his wholly personal coveting of honor "without corrival" inspires him to seek out occasions to exercise his youth and virtues in the destructive enterprise of war. Falstaff's ridicule of honor is a corollary of his guiding principle, "give me life," as he understands it; honor at Shrewsbury involves the danger of self-sacrifice, and so he will not seek it. If we see his position as a reply to the extravagances of Hotspur, we may be inclined to agree with him that honor is an empty illusion—Falstaff would not have ordered the charge of the Light Brigade. But by strictly limiting the scope of the term, Falstaff excludes its usefulness in defining a secular idea of loyalty and of dedication to the best demands of a serious calling, and thus as a means of maintaining one's self-esteem. Oddly enough, Falstaff has not completely lost the need for some modicum of that last quality. When they decide to do a play extempore and the prince proposes, "the argument shall be thy running away," Falstaff replies, "Ah, no more of that, Hal, and thou lovest me" (2.4.277-78). But Falstaff's chief use for the respectable world is to exploit it for his own purposes. He welcomes the rebellion as an opportunity to replenish his purse: "Well, God be thanked for these rebels, they offend none but the virtuous; I laud them, I praise them" (3.3.189-91). Lacking a sense of honor, he is capable of leading his wretched recruits to the thick of the battle where most of them will be killed so that he can keep their pay for himself. . . .

The prince, early in the play, shows a distaste for the questing after military victory that is the bad side of Hotspur's love of honor:

> I am not yet of Percy's mind, the Hotspur of the North, he that kills me some six or seven dozen of Scots at a breakfast, washes his hands, and says to his wife, "Fie upon this quiet life, I want work." "O my sweet Harry," says she, "how many hast thou killed today?" "Give my roan horse a drench," says he, and answers, "Some fourteen," an hour after, "a trifle, a trifle." (2.4.99-106)

Just before this he had described a drinking bout with a group of tapsters at the inn, and tells Poins, "I tell thee, Ned, thou hast lost much honor that thou wert not with me in this action" (2.4.19-21). This fleering use of "honor" may represent an indirect attempt to justify his present truancy, but the use of the military term "this action" to describe the heavy drinking and the "honor" gained by staying with it may also express some impatience with the cant of the warrior class. In comparison with Hotspur, Hal's attitude toward honor may be likened to Starbuck's attitude toward courage in *Moby Dick*—"one of the great staple outfits of the ship in their hazardous work of whaling, thought Starbuck, and, like her beer and bread, not to be wasted." The prince accepts the idea of honor as a mark of the warrior when he promises to exchange his shames for Hotspur's honors, but it is not an exact exchange. There are certain features of Hotspur's code which Hal does not take on. He does not have an excessive craving for military exploits or

gloat publicly over his success—he is willing, for the sake of a joke, to allow Falstaff to claim credit for killing Hotspur; and his sense of loyalty is not as clannish as Hotspur's nor as provincial ("this Northern youth" [3.2.145], he calls him)—it is to his father as king and therefore to the nation. It is an idea of honor more befitting a London courtier than a northern earl, and more useful to a national king than to a feudal lord. Hal appreciates Hotspur's gallantry—he honors the dead Hotspur by placing his "favors" on the body of his adversary; and in this connection Falstaff shows up to disadvantage, for we see him dishonoring Hotspur's corpse with a coarse comic bravado that is as unpleasant as it is funny.

This view of the significance of the scheme of multiple comparisons is in keeping with the way the conflicts are resolved at the end. The victory of the king's party seems the only acceptable conclusion—not merely the one imposed by history—and even the most unsympathetic critics do not express offense at the defeat of the rebels at Shrewsbury as they do, for instance, at the sophistry of Prince John at Gaultree or the rejection of Falstaff in Part 2. Nevertheless, it is questionable whether Shakespeare ever fully redresses the balance in favor of Henry and his son in *I Henry IV*, for the rebels are not pictured in a wholly reprehensible light. Once the rebellion gets under way, Hotspur's leadership lends it an air of gallantry and glamor. Aside from Worcester, who seems incapable of controlling the enterprise of which he was the political engineer, the others all have an almost amateurish quality which contributes to their undoing. This comes out in the one scene in which they all assemble to map out their strategy (3.1); they quarrel and show themselves more eager to divide the spoils of a hoped-for victory than to resolve the divisions within the kingdom, and hence appear as a worse choice politically than the king. Nevertheless, the conclusion which Shakespeare contrives for this episode comes as a surprising close to a scene of rebellious plotting. Glendower ushers in their wives, and there follows an engaging exchange of sentiments between Mortimer and his Welsh wife, with Glendower acting as interpreter, the contrasting affectionate sparring of Hotspur and his Kate, and finally the ethereal music invoked by Glendower which accompanies the Welsh song sung by Mortimer's wife. And these are the men who are threatening the center of order in the kingdom! There is nothing in the whole play that associates the king or the prince with as much charm and genial humanity. . . .

G. M. Pinciss

SOURCE: "The Old Honor and the New Courtesy: *1 Henry IV*," in *Shakespeare Survey: An Annual Survey of Shakespearian Study and Production*, Vol. 31, 1978, pp. 85-91.

[*Pinciss argues that while Hotspur is primarily concerned with honor throughout the play, Hal represents a comparable virtue: courtesy. Prior bases his examination of honor and courtesy on two books that were commonly read at the time Shakespeare wrote* Henry IV, Part One. The Courtier, *written by Castiglione and translated from Italian in 1561, and* The Governour, *written by Sir Thomas Elyot in 1531, were guides to the proper manners and behavior for upper class gentleman, or nobleman. Pinciss shows that Hotspur fails as a nobleman when measured against these standards. His code of honor is that of a soldier, and it is obsolete compared to Hal's courtesy. Hal's manners are approved of by these sources. Pinciss points out that without knowing that in Shakespeare's time the virtues represented by Hal were more highly valued than those represented by Hotspur, readers might be likely to misunderstand the two characters and what happens to them in the play.*]

Central to any reading of *1 Henry IV* is the dramatic opposition of the Prince of Wales with his arch-rival Henry Percy: the seriousness, energy, and courage of Hotspur are held up against the frivolous, bored, and irresponsible behavior of Hal. In large measure, the two young men, whom Shakespeare has intentionally portrayed as comparable in age, behave differently because they value differing codes of conduct. For Hotspur honor is of over-riding concern; by contrast, Hal acts as chief spokesman of another virtue, one especially appropriate for a Renaissance prince: courtesy. By analyzing the actions of both men according to the two most influential Elizabethan handbooks on courtly manners, we may arrive at a more precise evaluation of these two virtues and of those qualities that, it seems, ultimately mark Hal superior to Hotspur.

The two most prominent Elizabethan guides to courtly behavior were Castiglione's *The Courtier*, especially as translated by Sir Thomas Hoby in 1561, and the English version of Italian manner books, Sir Thomas Elyot's *The Governour* (1531). Something of a national character shaped the priorities of each writer: Castiglione and his countrymen, for example, stress personal perfection and aesthetic matters; Elyot and his readers place greater weight on civil usefulness and moral considerations. Nevertheless, the two works have more in common between them than either shares with a medieval manual on knightly conduct and they agree on the manners that characterize a Renaissance gentleman.

Hotspur's behavior and ethics are intimately associated with the striving for honor. He is the 'king of honour'; according to the envious Bolingbroke, he is the 'son who is the theme of honour's tongue'. For him public acclaim and reputation are to be earned chiefly by performance as a soldier—if not for, then against the crown. He is first mentioned at the very opening of the play in connection with a major victory over the Scots at Holmedon and the impressive list of his prisoners is described to the king as an 'honourable spoil'. At his first appearance in scene iii Hotspur displays something of his warrior nature, for he is plain-dealing, quick-tempered, and fearless, all those traits common to the best Elizabethan soldierstereotype: something of his nature can be found in men like Kent, or Enobarbus, or Othello. As Hal satirizes him, the young Percy 'kills me some six or seven dozen Scots at a breakfast, washes his hands, and says to his wife, "Fie upon this quiet life, I want work."' There is more than a grain of truth in this exaggeration of Hotspur's aggressive determination.

Hotspur is also concerned with the king's treatment of his family since this, too, reflects on his honor. Bolingbroke's refusal to ransom Hotspur's brother-in-law Mortimer, to consult with his father and uncle on matters of state, and to acknowledge the assistance of the Percys in taking the throne from Richard II are cited as particular reasons for rebelling. But all of these causes should be subsumed under one heading: his desire to 'pluck bright honour from the pale faced moon'. . . . Exasperated by Bolingbroke's tactics and encouraged to rebellion by his uncle, Hotspur in act II no longer supports the crown against the Scots but joins them and the Welsh in an effort to unseat the king. He calls this 'so honourable an action', an action by which his father and uncle 'may redeem your banished honours'.

Hotspur is not interested in material profit. And Shakespeare takes great pains to make this clear. In response to Sir Walter Blunt's hope that he will negotiate a peaceful settlement and accept an offer full of 'grace and love' from Bolingbroke, Hotspur answers, 'And maybe so we shall'. Indeed, Hotspur's motivation is so pure and his reply to Sir Walter so honest, that Worcester, Hotspur's uncle, never tells him of 'the liberal and kind offer of the king'. Worcester persuades his companion, Sir Richard Vernon, perhaps wisely, that his nephew must never learn what Bolingbroke promised. Unlike the open and rather naive and gullible Hotspur, it is Worcester who truly understands that the politic Bolingbroke knows 'at what time to promise, when to pay'. But actually, Hotspur's honesty and directness, although laudable and appealing to us, are not entirely praiseworthy traits for a Renaissance courtier. To attain the kind of reputation Hotspur is seeking, both craftiness and calculation are occasionally excusable practices.

As a Renaissance courtier Hotspur is inept. Shakespeare systematically displays his failures in the many skills, talents, and graces that every sixteenth-century nobleman should exhibit. And the deficiencies in Hotspur's nature are repeatedly displayed to the audience not only by his own actions but also by pointed comment from others. In his very first speech he confesses to the court that he answered the king's messenger 'neglectingly, I know not what . . . for he made me mad'. Although his conduct might be excusable in special circumstances, it is hardly correct or controlled behavior. Hotspur then proceeds to contradict Bolingbroke flatly, using neither the Retort Courteous nor the Quip Modest, but the Countercheck Quarrelsome and the Lie Direct. Men of good sense like Touchstone or his equally argumentative opponent stop short of such an offensive reply—from which there is no retreating without an 'if'. Bolingbroke in fury orders the Percys away. Finally, unable still to control his anger, Hotspur cannot allow his uncle to hold the floor without behaving like a 'wasp-stung and impatient fool . . . Tying thine ear to no tongue but thine own!' All this in his opening scene. Surely we are watching a young man lacking patience, moderation, and prudence, those virtues Elyot thought so essential in one who looked for a place at court.

Like Elyot, Castiglione, too, would have observed several deficiencies in Hotspur's behavior. His impetuous nature and quick tongue are obviously liabilities at the council table, but in the pleasures of civilized life he is equally undeveloped and uninterested. Glendower, the Welsh chieftain, boasts that he has composed English lyrics, 'a virtue that was never seen' in Hotspur. But the younger man has no shame at his deafness to the beauties of language:

> I had rather be a kitten and cry 'mew'
> Than one of these same metre ballad-
>   mongers.
> I had rather hear a brazen canstick turn'd
> Or a dry wheel grate on the axle-tree,
> And that would set my teeth nothing on
>   edge,
> Nothing so much as mincing poetry.
>   (III, i, 123-8) [References are to the Arden
>   Edition, ed. A. R. Humphreys, (1960)]

Obstinate in his ways, he takes delight neither in verse nor music. A lady's song is a subject for teasing his wife, and a lullaby in Welsh is less pleasing to him than the howling of his Irish wolf-hound; presumably neither the music nor the language held appeal. Had he followed the advice of Castiglione, Hotspur would have known how untutored (and French!) was his insistence on knowing 'onely the nobleness of armes'. A true courtier should

> exercise him selfe in Poets, and no lesse in Oratours and Historiogaphers, and also in writing both rime and prose, and especially in this our vulgar tongue. For beside the contentation that hee shall receive thereby him selfe, hee shall by this means never want pleasant intertainements with women which ordinarily love such matters.

And like the great warrior Achilles, taught to play the harp by Chiron, a soldier is no less heroic for his talent with music. Castiglione insists that such skill is not effeminate: 'musicke is not an ornament, but also necessarie for a Courtier'.

Hotspur's weaknesses are more than implied. His peccadilloes and his faults are named by his uncle lest we overlook them. Shakespeare must have suspected that Hotspur with his candor and spirit would draw our applause so whole-heartedly, especially when we discover him surrounded by intriguers, that we would tend to ignore his serious defects. Although Worcester may not appear the ideal teacher, his experience at dealing with men is unquestionably greater than his nephew's and his admonition is worth the heeding:

> In faith, my lord, you are too wilful-blame,
>
> . . . . .
>
> You must needs learn, lord, to amend this
>   fault.
> Though sometimes it show greatness,
>   courage,
>   blood—
> And that's the dearest grace it renders you—
> Yet oftentimes it doth present harsh rage,
> Defect of manners, want of government,
> Pride, haughtiness, opinion, and disdain,
> The least of which haunting a nobleman
> Loseth men's hearts, and leaves behind a
>   stain
> Upon the beauty of all parts besides,
> Beguiling them of commendation.
>   (III, i, 171, 174-83)

The charges Worcester recites sum up a rather complete bill of particulars against Hotspur. But there still remains at least one fact about the young man's attitude that shows to what an extent it is uncharacteristic of his time. When he learns that his father is unable to bring his support to the confrontation with Bolingbroke, Hotspur argues that 'It lends a larger dare to our great enterprise'. When he learns that Glendower, too, will be unable to join them, Hotspur still insists on rushing into battle. His courage and enthusiasm are admirable; his eagerness to encounter an enemy who vastly outnumbers him—'Die all, die merrily'—reveals the extent of his idealism. But rushing into battle, rejoicing to display bravery, enduring suffering and loss or even meeting death gladly as a reward for valor are the actions of a medieval knight demonstrating the code of chivalry. Such deeds, however, are not those of a Renaissance gentleman; the ideal performance of a crusader in a romance is not the same as that of a courtier in a sixteenth-century manners book and the behavior of a hero in a tale by Malory hardly agrees with Castiglione's recommendation:

it is behovefull both for himselfe and for his friendes, that he have a foresight in the quarrels and controversies that may happen, and let hime beware of the vantages, declaring alwaies in everie point both courage and wisedom. Neither let him runne rashly to these combats. . . . for beside the great daunger that is in the doubtful lot, he that goeth headlong to these thinges deserveth great blame.

On this subject it is interesting to review the career of the Douglas, Hotspur's Scots ally. Before the battle of Shrewsbury, Hotspur praises him as the best of soldiers, 'a braver place / In my heart's love hath no man than yourself'. And, indeed, the Douglas urges a speedy confrontation with Bolingbroke, actively seeks him in battle, and systematically attempts to kill each of those dressed like the king. His fight with the real king, however, is interrupted by Prince Hal who comes to aid his failing father. Rather than meet death at Hal's hand, the Douglas flees. All of this, of course, serves to enhance Hal's reputation in his father's and his audience's eyes. None of it is unexpected until Hal's very last speech in the play. In this, he instructs his brother John to free the imprisoned Douglas without ransom, for

> His valours shown upon our crests today
> Have taught us how to cherish such high
>   deeds
> Even in the bosom of our adversaries.
>
>   (v, v, 29-31)

That Hal would commit a public act reflecting what Prince John calls 'high courtesy' is not unlikely, but that Hal would praise for his courage an enemy who ran away when he saw defeat and death approaching is a little startling if one considers what Hotspur might have said had he seen it all! By and large it seems that Hotspur's values are not the same as those of his enemies or his friends, for unlike him both Hal and the Douglas approve of that advice that teaches one to flee when one is outnumbered or outclassed.

Hotspur's chief virtue—and he is called the 'king of honour' by the Douglas—is defined by a code of manners that is obsolete; he represents an age that is past or passing. Prince Hal on the other hand embodies the new virtues: even before he inherits the kingdom from his father he is dubbed the 'king of courtesy'.

Courtesy, Hal's most distinctive attribute, is considered by both English and Italian authorities a necessary quality for a nobleman's temperament; one so central to the concept that Spenser devoted a whole book of *The Faeie Queene* to it. Courtesy is exercised by knowing what is fitting for oneself and others, and for enacting this with graciousness. One's conduct, then, is affected in part by awareness of class and the lines between classes and in part by the desire

to draw praise and admiration for the grace of one's behavior, especially from one's equals and betters. Such a person in Elyot's terms possesses 'a gentil and familiare visage' able to procure men's love, and 'a beautie or comelynesse in his countenance, langage, and gesture apt to his dignitie, and accomodate to time, place, and company'. When a leash of drawers name him the 'king of courtesy' and promise he 'shall command all the good lads of Eastcheap', the Prince of Wales has proven something of his real worth. He is both truthful and slyly ironic when he says to Poins, 'thou hast lost much honour that thou wert not with me in this action'. Drinking-deep and sounding the very bass string of humility are evidence of his princeliness, for Hal has followed Castiglione's injunction:

> in companie with men and women of al degrees, in sporting, in laughing, and in jesting, he hath in him certaine sweetnes, and so comely demeanours, that who so speaketh with him, or yet beholdeth him, must needs beare him an affection for ever.

In fact, Hal satisfies most of Castiglione's criteria for courtesy: he is noble by birth, witty by nature, comely in person and countenance, and attractive with 'a certaine grace, and (as they say) a hewe, that shall make him at the first sight acceptable and loving unto who so beholdeth him'. These aspects of courtesy are perhaps more gifts of nature than manners consciously learned and artificially cultivated, but such gifts, as one might expect, are part of the legacy of a royal offspring.

Recognizing Hal's natural courtesy and his supremacy in this virtue allows us to reinterpret the claims of others. For example, Hotspur's threat that Hal will 'shrink under my courtesy' seems a hollow boast when one realizes Hal's true value, and his father's criticism of Hal's conduct should also be regarded with some skepticism. Bolingbroke has 'majesty', the quality that impresses his public; but this is only half of what Elyot finds necessary for courtesy. The king never gains his public's affection, lacking what Elyot would have called 'affability', the other component of courtesy. In fact, Bolingbroke is a fraud; like Macbeth in borrowed robes, he 'dressed' himself in humility to pluck allegiance from men's hearts, and 'stole all courtesy from heaven'. His rebuke to his son, a parallel to Worcester's reprimanding Hotspur, reflects Bolingbroke's own obtuseness. Even Sir Richard Vernon, who could scarcely be expected to think favorably of Bolingbroke's heir, appreciates Hal's innate graciousness of manner and speech. He describes to Hotspur how the Prince delivered his offer of single combat:

> I never in my life
> Did hear a challenge urg'd more modestly,

Unless a brother should a brother dare
To gentle exercise and proof of arms.
He gave you all the duties of a man;
Trimm'd up your praises with a princely
   tongue,
Spoke your deservings like a chronicle,
Making you ever better than his praise
By still dispraising praise valu'd with you,
And, which became him like a prince indeed,
He made a blushing cital of himself,
And chid his truant youth with such a grace
As if he mast'red there a double spirit
Of teaching and of learning instantly.

                 (V, ii, 51-64)

From Vernon's account it is clear that Hal can act with modesty, ease, and charm. . . .

Indeed, Hal's princely challenge to fight Hotspur alone, made before the leaders of the opposing parties, is in accordance with Castiglione's precepts for winning 'most estimation' in time of war; Hal's proposal is effective in 'separating him selfe from the multitude' and in offering to 'undertake notable and bolde feates'.

   The Prince of Wales doth join with all the
      world
   In praise of Henry Percy: by my hopes,
   This present enterprise set off his head,
   I do not think a braver gentleman,
   More active-valiant or more valiant-young,
   More daring or more bold, is now alive
   To grace this latter age with noble deeds.
   For my part, I may speak it to my shame,
   I have a truant been to chivalry,
   And so I hear he doth account me too.
   Yet this before my father's majesty—
   I am content that he shall take the odds
   Of his great name and estimation,
   And will, to save the blood on either side,
   Try fortune with him in a single fight.

                 (V, i, 86-100)

In addition, his language reveals what Castiglione calls

   a simplicitie of such meekenesse of minde, that a
   man would weene nature her selfe spake to make
   them tender and (as it were) dronken with
   sweetnes; and with such conveyance of easinesse,
   that who so heareth him, may conceive a good
   opinion of him selfe and thinke that he also . . .
   mighte attaine to that perfection.

That he is 'facile or easie to be spoken unto' by all except poor Francis, the puny drawer, who can barely speak at all, is half of Hal's attraction; the other half is his talent for speaking 'courtaisely, with a swere speche or countenance, wherewith the herers (as it

were with a delicate odour) be refressed, and alured to loue hym in whom is this most delectable qualitie'.

Even what appears Hal's failing must be reconsidered by the criteria for behavior that Castiglione and Elyot describe: one should not expect that all Hal's vices will metamorphose into virtues, but at least the mold of form will be defined by the expectancy of Shakespeare's times. Bolingbroke and Hotspur both criticize Hal for his friends: he has acted like a 'sword and buckler Prince of Wales' and has 'mingled his royalty with capering fools'. But both of Hal's critics are unsympathetic to the importance of public affection, and, as we have noted, both are out of touch with the advice published in the best Renaissance guides. Castiglione, for example, believes if 'the Courtier in jesting and speaking merry conceites have a respect to the time, to the persons, to his degree, and not use it too often . . . hee may be called pleasant and' a man of humor. That Hal knows something of this is clear when in the last act he scolds Falstaff for his impertinent answer to Bolingbroke's question about the reasons for the rebellion, or again when Hal on the field of battle asks his fat friend rhetorically, 'What, is it a time to jest and dally now?' Perhaps Hal is excessively given to the frivolous, but even his taste for practical jokes merits some approval: according to *The Courtier* 'a merrie prancke is nothing els, but a friendly deceite in matters that offend not at al or very little'.

Indeed, Hal's worst faults can be used to display the basic goodness of his nature. Elyot illustrates the importance of 'placability' by relating the story of Hal, the madcap prince, and the chief justice who put him in prison. By obeying the court, Hal

   a prince and sonne and heire of the kynge, in the
   middes of his furye, more considered his iuell
   example, and the iuges constance in iustice, than
   his owne astate or wylfull appetite. . . . Wherefore
   I conclude that nothing is more honorable, or to be
   desired in a prince or noble man, than placabilitie.

Finally, Hal's horsemanship symbolizes his prowess as a Renaissance prince, for it offers the most hyperbolic image of the wastrel turned courtly hero in the play. On horseback he emerges completely cleansed from the stains of riot and dishonor, appearing as Bellerophon, glittering in a golden coat:

   I saw young Harry with his beaver on,
   His cushes on his thighs, gallantly arm'd,
   Rise from the ground like feather'd Mercury,
   And vaulted with such ease into his seat
   As if an angel dropp'd down from the clouds
   To turn and wind a fiery Pegasus,
   And witch the world with noble horsemanship.

                 (IV, i, 104-10)

Such skills as Hal exhibits he might have practised at the recommendation of either Elyot or Castiglione. Elyot endorses the ability 'to ryde surely and clene on a great horse and a roughe' as 'the most honorable exercise, in myne opinion, and that besemeth the astate of euery noble persone'. *The Governour* also commends as 'a ryght good exercise which is also expendient to lerne, whiche is named the vauntynge of a horse: that is to lepe on him at euery side without stirroppe or other helpe, specially whiles the horse is goynge'. For his part, Castiglione would have a Courtier 'a perfect horseman for everie saddle. And beside the skill in horses . . . let him set all his delight and diligence to wade in everie thing a little farther than other men' while accompanying 'all his motion with a certaine good judgment and grace'.

To sum up this argument, we discover that judged by the standards of conduct recommended in *The Courtier* and *The Governour*, the two most influential manners books in sixteenth-century England, Hal is not truly a wastrel [a wild, extravagent person] nor Hotspur a paragon [a model of excellent behavior]. In fact, the behavior of the Prince at Shrewsbury and even his subsequent career as king are simply the further development of those character and personality traits which Castiglione and Elyot had considered essential for success. Indeed, it is not surprising that Hal, as one of England's greatest rulers, should embody the talents and skills Elizabethans looked for in the best representatives of nobility. What is surprising is that judged by these standards Hal proves a young man of more promise and Hotspur of less than we today might appreciate without such guides to courtly behavior, for without these handbooks for reference we might well overvalue Hotspur's virtues and underrate Hal's.

FATHERS AND SONS

The conflict between father and son, an issue examined by many critics, is outlined by **Ernst Kris**. Kris points to the relationships analyzed in most discussions of this issue: the relationships between Henry and Hal; Henry and Hotspur; and Falstaff and Hal. Falstaff, many critics agree, is a father-figure to Hal in the sense that he teaches the Prince the ways of the world, or at least the ways of *his* (Falstaff's) world. Kris argues that Hal rejects this guidance, just as Hal rejects his own father as a paternal image. Critics such as Barabara Baines, however, attempt to show that Hal takes his father's advice at significant moments in the play and that Henry's teachings contribute substantially to Hal's success. Other critics, including M. M. Reese, highlight Henry's failure to relate to his son. George Ian Duthie and John Lawlor continue the analysis of the father/son conflict with an examination of Hotspur's role as a surrogate son

to Henry. Duthie argues that Henry wishes Hotspur were his son, seeing him as a more worthy heir than Hal, and as a person very much like himself. Critics such as **Robert B. Pierce** view the relationship between Henry and Hal as central to an understanding of the play. Pierce arues that familial order, as demonstrated by Henry and Hal, is presented as a means of grasping the the political structure and issues conveyed in the play.

Ernst Kris

SOURCE: "Prince Hal's Conflict," in *The Psychoanalytic Quarterly*, Vol. XVII, No. 4, 1948, pp. 487-506.

[*Kris observes that the conflict between fathers and sons appears in three different versions in* Henry IV, Part One: *in the conflict between 1) Henry and Hal; 2) Henry and Hotspur; and 3) Falstaff and Hal. Kris discusses how these relationships are brought to the attention of the reader and how in order to present the conflict in this manner, Shakespeare deviated from his historical sources. Kris demonstrates Hal's rejection of both Falstaff and Henry as "unsatisfactory" father-figures.*]

The conflict between father and son appears in Part I of Henry IV in three versions, each time enacted by one central and two related characters. The theme is manifestly stated by the King in the introductory scene of the trilogy, when he compares Henry of Monmouth [Prince Hal] to Henry Percy [Hotspur].

> Yea, there thou makest me sad and makest
>   me sin
> In envy that my Lord Northumberland
> Should be the father to so blest a son,
> A son who is the theme of honour's tongue;
> Amongst a grove, the very straightest plant;
> Who is sweet fortune's minion and her
>   pride:
> Whilst I, by looking on the praise of him,
> See riot and dishonour stain the brow
> Of my young Harry. O! that it could be
>   prov'd
> That some night-tripping fairy had exchang'd
> In cradle-clothes our children where they lay,
> And called mine Percy, his Plantagene!
> Then would I have his Harry, and he mine.
>   [*King Henry IV, Part I*, Act 1, Sc. 1.]

The position of the Prince between Falstaff and the King is almost as explicitly stated; he has two fathers, as the King has two sons. When he enacts with Falstaff his forthcoming interview with his father, the theme is brought into the open. It is not limited to court and tavern, the centers of the 'double plot', as W. Empson calls it, but extends to the rebel camp. Henry Percy stands between a weak father, Northumberland, who is prevented by illness from participating in the decisive battle, and a scheming uncle, Worcester, who plans the rebellion, conceals from Percy that the King offers reconciliation and drives him thus to battle and to death.

The three versions of the father-son conflict compelled Shakespeare to deviate from his sources and thereby to enrich the stage: he sharpened the report of the chronicles on the rebellion of the Percies in order to create the contrast of Worcester and Northumberland; he reduced Henry Percy's age from a slightly older contemporary of Henry IV to a somewhat older contemporary of the Prince—and he invented Falstaff.

The triangular relationships are not only similar to each other, since they all contain variations of the theme of good and bad fathers and sons, but within each triangle the parallel figures are closely interconnected; thus the two Harrys, whom Henry IV compares, form a unit; Hotspur's rebellion represents also Prince Hal's unconscious parricidal impulses. Hotspur is the Prince's double. Impulses pertaining to one situation have thus been divided between two personages; but though in the triangles the characters are paired and contrasted, each of the play's personages transcends the bondage to his function in this thematic configuration. They have all out-grown the symmetry which they serve, into the fullness of life.

To appraise Falstaff as a depreciated father figure is to grasp the superficial aspect of a character who, more than any other of Shakespeare, has enchanted readers and audiences since his creation. Franz finds two principal psychoanalytic explanations for this universal enchantment: Falstaff's hedonism, he says, represents the uninhibited gratification of an infantile and narcissistic quest for pleasure, a craving alive to some extent in everyone of us; this hedonism, moreover, is made acceptable by contrast: one turns with relief from the court or the rebel camp to the tavern. In accordance with the last is the traditional antithesis of 'tragic King and comic people' (Empson) used by Shakespeare to emphasize a moral antithesis. From Prince Hal's point of view, Falstaff is a contrast to the King, who represents another version of the unsatisfactory paternal image. Henry IV succeeded his cousin Richard II by rebellion and regicide.

Robert B. Pierce

SOURCE: "The Henry IV Plays," in *Shakespeare's History Plays: The Family and the State*, Ohio State University Press, 1971, pp. 171-224.

[*Pierce maintains that in* Henry IV, Part One, *personal, familial order is presented as a way of understanding the larger, political structure in the play. He shows how the basic conflicts in the play—the struggle of Henry, and the nation, to create harmony from civil war, the struggle of Prince Hal to mature from a careless youth into an independent king—illuminate the larger conflict—the struggle to create order from disorder—being examined. Pierce shows how the play is essentially divided between the public story of rebellion and the private story of Hal's adventures with Falstaff and how the additional plot of Hal's estrangement from Henry links the play's public and private worlds.*]

Shakespeare's Henry IV plays explore the theme of political order with a new depth and subtlety. Not only does the state pass through civil war to harmony, but Prince Hal develops into a king fit to lead his newly united state in war against France. Although political order is central to the plays, Shakespeare uses a more personal order, that of the family, to illuminate his theme. In the early history plays harmony and strife in family relationships become symbols of order and disorder in the kingdom. This device expresses political ideas by analogy with another realm of experience. But in the two Henry IV plays the symbol merges with its referent; Shakespeare displays the quest for political order as fundamentally like the quest for personal order within the family. The values are the same, the problems the same; only the scale is different.

In Hal and his father the historical given of Shakespeare's plot combines the two levels: prince and king, son and father. While Henry IV struggles to keep his throne and the rebels to replace him, England is hungry for renewed order. Though he is in many ways a good ruler, he cannot be the hero-king who compels loyalty as well as submission. Prince Hal is to be such a king, but before he can assume his destined role, he must attain personal maturity. He must find a viable order for his own life, one centered on his duty to become England's king. Only thus will he be saved from self-destruction or personal insignificance, and only thus will England be saved (for a time) from civil war.

Finding in his sources the legend of Hal the wild prince, Shakespeare turns it into an expression of this theme. Like any young man reaching maturity, Hal must emulate his father's role, but at the same time he must escape his father in order to establish his autonomy. Even in the ideal family this task is difficult. In *1 Henry VI* young Talbot must defy his father's command to flee the battlefield so that he may be like his father and hence show a family loyalty deeper than explicit obedience. But Hal's father is a guilty man, one whose piety is tainted by Richard II's blood on his hands. In his personal inheritance from his father, Hal faces the same problem as the realm, how to generate an ordered future out of a disordered present. He must transcend his inheritance without denying it. It is part of the extraordinary scope of the Henry IV plays to study this spiritual process. An abstractly conceived Providence can bring peace to the England of *Richard III* because the process is external to Richard, but only a newly personal and psychological drama can show Hal's development into the king who will lead England to unity and glory.

The portrayal of Hal's growth follows a popular motif in Elizabethan drama, the Prodigal Son story. Hal leaves his responsibilities and his father for a life of tavern brawls, behavior typical of the prodigal, though Hal avoids contamination with the worst evils around him, reckless gambling, wenching, and such. Falstaff, "that villainous abominable misleader of youth" (II.iv.456), parallels a Vice-figure [a stock character in the morality play who, as a tempter, has both evil and comic qualities]. . . . Henry IV has much in common with the typical father, noble and sententious but somewhat ineffectual toward his son. . . . Appropriately enough, the parable of the Prodigal Son occurs among Falstaff's frequent allusions to scripture. This theme extends through both plays, since Hal is not completely reconciled to his father until the end of *2 Henry IV*.

In one sense Shakespeare is burlesquing an old dramatic form. . . . After all, it is the prodigal who mischievously denounces his tempter as "that reverend vice, that grey iniquity, that father ruffian, that vanity in years" (*1 Henry IV*, II.iv.447-49). And Falstaff himself delights in acting the prodigal, corrupted by his evil companions: "Before I knew thee, Hal, I knew nothing, and now am I, if a man should speak truly, little better than one of the wicked" (*1 Henry IV*, I.ii.90-92). This lightheartedness suggests even more clearly than Hal's soliloquy at the end of I.ii that he will not be significantly corrupted. Yet at the same time Falstaff is a serious threat to Hal's maturity, and the reconciliation with his father is a necessary step in his growth.

. . . For all Shakespeare's modifications to burlesque the pattern and to make it psychologically plausible, he uses the religious theme embodied in it. In the parable the Prodigal Son restored to his father is man restored to God, and in the Elizabethan system of correspondences the king is to his kingdom as God is to the universe. Hal's reconciliation with his father symbolizes a larger commitment to all that is good and orderly in the world.

The first of the two plays has an obvious division into two levels, the public story of the rebellion of the Percies and the private story of Hal's dissipations [self. indulgent activities] with Falstaff. Part of what raises this play above the typical Elizabethan two-plot drama is the ingenuity with which the two are interwoven, so that the Falstaff scenes parody many of the episodes and characters of the serious scenes. However, there is a third plot, less extended than the other two, that helps to mediate between them. It is the story of Hal's estrangement from his father and their reconciliation. Only in this plot is Hal clearly the central figure, though all three contribute to the most important theme of this and the next play, Hal's preparation for kingship over a united England. The rebellion of the Percies provides the battlefield on which he can prove his chivalric merit; and Hotspur, the dominant figure of the Percy camp, gives a dramatic contrast that illuminates Hal's growth. The scenes with Falstaff show Hal avoiding his duty, but they also help to educate him in the whole order (and disorder) of his future kingdom. Although Shakespeare allows us to glimpse the domestic life of the Percies, they live primarily in a public world, a world of treaties and defiances and battles, of blank verse. Although Falstaff appears, ludicrously out of place, at Shrewsbury, his is essentially a private world without clocks, a world of sack and tavern jests and highway robbery, of prose.

What gives the relationship of Henry IV and Hal special complexity is that in it the public and private worlds merge. As king and prince they embody all the political ideas implied in that relationship throughout the history plays. Hal must inherit the heroic and regal virtues of his father so that he may be a king worthy of his Lancastrian forebears. To teach Hal this lesson, Henry points to the ominous example of Richard II, who betrayed the heritage of the Black Prince with a frivolity that Henry sees in Hal too. Also the public theme of inherited guilt is an important one. Henry fears that his crime in deposing Richard will infect the kingdom even after his death (and Hal in *Henry V* shares that fear). As a public figure Henry IV has a double significance. He is the king, the center of order and virtue in the realm and hence the prime object of Hal's duty. But at the same time he is guilty; all the conscious piety of his life cannot entirely justify him, even to himself.

If Henry were simply a public figure, an emblem like John of Gaunt in *Richard II*, this ambiguity of meaning would destroy him as a dramatic character. What saves him is that he is given a private identity, an individual nature that expresses itself apart from his public stance. A public symbol cannot be ambiguous, but a man can be so various as to evoke two different symbolisms. In the same way Hal can both laugh at and be the Prodigal Son because he has a private identity that transcends both burlesque and symbolism. Henry IV and Hal are not only king and prince; they are also a very concrete father and son, going through all the painful misunderstanding that fathers and sons have always faced.

Henry appears first of all as king. As John Dover

Prince Hal, Falstaff, and Ned Poins at the Boar's Head Tavern.

Wilson points out [in *The First Part of the History of Henry IV*, 1946, in a note at I. i. 1], he speaks for himself and the kingdom in his opening words:

> So shaken as we are, so wan with care,
> Find we a time for frighted peace to pant,
> And breathe short-winded accents of new
>   broils
> To be commenc'd in stronds afar remote:
> No more the thirsty entrance of this soil
> Shall daub her lips with her own children's
>   blood.
>
> (I.i.1-6)

The sense of powers declining under strain, the desperate longing for peace, and the vague hope for glory in foreign wars—all these Henry shares with his land. It is a sign of his worthiness as a king that he expresses so accurately the spirit of his realm. The stark family image of lines 5-6, with its biblical echo, is typical of the severe formality of the speech. Henry's language shows the tightly linked world of Elizabethan correspondences, in which the state is a family and civil war opposes those "of one substance bred," so that they war "Against acquaintance, kindred, and allies" (11, 16).

Since most of the audience must have known that this was to be a play about civil war, they would notice the self-deception in Henry's prediction of peace; and it soon emerges that he is willfully deceiving himself, because he knows that England is still wracked with strife and even that the Percies show ominous signs of disloyalty. Henry represents a generation of Englishmen who have fought each other and will go on fighting until they can hardly remember the purpose of the battles and can only say:

> We are all diseas'd,
> And with our surfeiting, and wanton hours,
> Have brought ourselves into a burning fever,
> And we must bleed for it.
>
> (*2 Henry IV*, IV.i.54-57)

After his description of civil war in terms of violence within the family, there is irony in Henry's turning to speak with pain of his son's degeneracy. At the moment he seems unconscious of any connection between public and familial disorder. It may seem like a heartless repudiation of family bonds when he wishes:

> O that it could be prov'd
> That some night-tripping fairy had exchang'd
> In cradle-clothes our children where they lay,
> And call'd mine Percy, his Plantagenet!
>
> (85-88)

But the suffering is clear enough behind the petulant rejection. It is "my young Harry" (85) whose dishonor he feels; the repeated "mine" of the passage shows the grief of an estranged father, not unfeeling repudiation. If the audience perceived the irony of his wish to go to the Holy Land, they must also have seen the happier irony of his despair at the character of the future hero-king, the legendary example of wildness reformed. This speech establishes a contrast between the two young men that runs through the play and reaches its climax in their confrontation at Shrewsbury.

If in the first scene Henry IV seems like an old man, tired and sick from the strains of rule, it soon becomes apparent that he has not lost the strength of will and imposing presence that won him the crown. He sends for the Percies to explain their holding back the Scottish prisoners, and when Worcester shows signs of more pride than is fitting in a subject, Henry abruptly banishes him from the court. Questionable though his accession is, he is a royal king, and Hal can learn only from him the dignity that a king must have. The curious episode of the men in Henry's coats whom Douglas slays at Shrewsbury raises the issue of who is really king when Douglas challenges Henry:

> What art thou
> That counterfeit'st the person of a king?
>
> (V.iv.26-27)

But Douglas himself gives a worthy answer:

> I fear thou art another counterfeit,
> And yet, in faith, thou bearest thee like a
>   king.
>
> (34-35)

By a great act of will Henry is able to bear himself like a king. If the effort gradually saps his strength, there is little external evidence of his decline until his sickness in *2 Henry IV*. Only in one scene of this play does he fully reveal the private man behind the king, when he is alone with his son in III.ii. The sense of tension, of a will kept forcibly taut in his public appearances, suggests the terrible penalty of being king.

In contrast with his father in the opening scene, Hal in the second appears young, full of vitality, and gaily irresponsible. While his father wrestles with the problems of state, Falstaff and Hal can jest about how he will behave as king. "I prithee sweet wag, when thou art king, as God save thy Grace—Majesty I should say, for grace thou wilt have none" (I.ii.16-18). The fact that the major theme of Hal's development toward the ideal king can be suggested in a pun shows the characteristic tone of the scene. When he comes to this world where time is irrelevant and chivalry no more than the code of the highwayman, he is escaping from the court, from his father, and from his own place as heir apparent.

One can take too solemnly his assertion of virtue in the much-discussed soliloquy that closes the scene. The speech may seem priggish, as though Hal were condescending to sport with Falstaff even while maintaining a severe inner virtue. He says, "I know you all" (I.ii.190), implying that Falstaff's sinfulness is no threat to his self-confident virtue. However, direct exposition of one's moral state is characteristic of Elizabethan soliloquies. It is dangerous to read too much self-consciousness into Hal's proclamation of his own worth. Many critics note that this soliloquy is primarily a device to assure the audience of Hal's final reformation, an assurance especially needed just after he has agreed to join in a highway robbery. And his treatment of Falstaff is not really condescending; he too obviously rejoices in the battle of wits that keeps them on equal terms.

On the other hand, the fact that the soliloquy is a conventional device need not compel one to take it as absolutely true. Only someone determined to believe in Hal's spotless virtue (or his priggishness) could accept at face value the argument that a king gains his people's loyalty from having been a youthful sinner. No doubt Hal plans to reform, but he has not undertaken his sins in order to abandon them with a spectacular public gesture. There is an undertone to his argument that suggests his main reason for avoiding the court:

> If all the year were playing holidays,
> To sport would be as tedious as to work;
> But when they seldom come, they wish'd-for
>   come,
> And nothing pleaseth but rare accidents.
>
> (199-202)

Explicitly he is arguing that the contrast between a dissolute youth and a reformed king heightens the latter, just as the contrast with working days makes holidays pleasant. Yet at the same time he half-admits to snatching a few last bits of pleasure before assuming the heavy duties of kingship. . . .

Hal's sport with Falstaff is not only a young man's escape from responsibility, however. The public world of the play is one of disorder and treachery. Hotspur is caught in the political schemes of his father and uncle and manipulated by them. Henry IV is a nobler man than his former allies (except for Hotspur), but even he is trapped by his dubious past into suspicion and cold scheming. His projected crusade to the Holy Land is never more than a dream of expiation. Thus Hal escapes a tainted atmosphere by leaving the court. The evils of the tavern to which he turns are "like their father that begets them, gross as a mountain, open, palpable" (II.iv.220-21). Even though Falstaff's company sometimes parodies the public world, it is not corrupted by the pervasive disorder of the kingdom. "A plague upon it when thieves cannot be true one to another!" (II.ii.27-28). Falstaff's complaint foreshadows the disintegration among the rebels, but in fact the disloyalty in his band of "thieves" is harmless and even illusory.

In general the vices of Falstaff's group are timeless; the characters themselves are an anachronism brought into the play from Elizabethan life. This habit is not unusual among low-comedy scenes in Tudor drama, but here it is significant in that it provides an escape from the political disorder of the public scenes. In the three parts of *Henry VI* disorder spreads out from the court to infect the whole kingdom, but in *1 Henry IV* the life of England goes on in spite of treachery and rebellion among the governors. Hostlers worry about the price of oats, and Falstaff about the purity of sack. Leaving the court, Hal finds England with all its vices and jests, but also its abiding strength. What Faulconbridge brings to the court of King John, Hal reaches by going out into London.

Yet if Hal can gain strength from contact with English life, there is also the threat of forgetting his special role as England's future king. Just as he must escape from the court and his father to grow beyond them, so he must escape the unreasonable claims on him of his London companions. "O for a fine thief of the age of two and twenty or thereabouts: I am heinously unprovided," says Falstaff (III.iii.187-89). He is unprovided because Hal has kept himself a king's son on a lark. His characteristic defense against Falstaff is his irony, an amused detachment from whatever he is doing. Curiously enough, it is the same quality that allows him to show no concern for the deed when he proves his chivalric merit by killing Hotspur, the key symbolic act of the play. His nature is not "subdued / To what it works in" (Sonnet 111), whether he rubs elbows with Falstaff or fights against Hotspur.

Critics find this ironic detachment offensive in Hal

. . . when it rebuffs Falstaff's claims to intimacy. There is unconscious humor in the fugitive and cloistered vice of literary scholars who condemn Hal for repudiating the free life of a tavern roisterer and highway robber; one explanation of such a view is the absence in our day of much feeling for the importance of calling. Hal is called to be the next king of England, and so he cannot be an ordinary man. He is not denying his humanity in accepting his duty to prepare for royalty, because a man's vocation is the center of his manhood. In this play his calling is defined by his rivalry with Hotspur. He must demonstrate to his father and all the land that he is the true prince, not only in title but in worth. Thus he can turn from the boyish jest of giving Falstaff a company of foot soldiers to a vigorous assertion of his family's destiny:

> The land is burning, Percy stands on high,
> And either we or they must lower lie.
>
> (III.iii.202-3)

Henry IV and his son come together for the first time at III.ii. Ironically, Shakespeare has just shown the charming domesticity of the rebel camp when he turns to the estrangement of the king and crown prince. Henry's speeches to his son are curiously poised between his typical stiff formality and a father's anxious sincerity. His opening words are full of the traditional doctrines of the family. Thus for the first time he acknowledges that Hal's wildness may be punishment for "my mistreadings" (11). He measures Hal against the ideal of aristocratic inheritance, asking how he can reconcile "the greatness of thy blood" (16) with such low pursuits. He misunderstands his son, since he assumes that Hal is "match'd withal, and grafted to" these pleasures (15), the imagery suggesting that their corruption has entered the fibers of his being. But this speech is so formal that it suggests only abstract parenthood, and Hal's reply is in the same vein. They have expressed their abstract relationship, but little of the personal feeling in it.

Up to this point Henry has hidden the intensity of his emotions behind a mask of formality, but in his next speech his grief precariously warps the formality. After an affectionate "Harry" in line 29, he quickly pulls back into the commonplaces of aristocratic inheritance. He again charges Hal with betraying the tradition of his ancestors and losing the affection of his kinsmen. The king's hurt ego swings around to brood on his own past successes as he compares Hal with Richard II. He asserts that Hal has repudiated the moral heritage of the Lancastrians for Richard's corrupted "line" (85). (Primarily the word means "category" here, but it suggests the whole idea of a station in life established by birth.) His emotion gradually rises during the speech until he suddenly finds himself weeping as he complains of his son's neglect in what is no longer a king's reproof but the complaint of a lonely father.

Hal's reply to this display of emotion is embarrassed and terse, though it may reveal a deeper contrition than did his first speech. But the tide of Henry's grief cannot stop, and so he returns to comparing Hal with Richard. Now he raises the most irritating comparison, that with Hotspur. He contrasts Hal's dynastic inheritance with Hotspur's supposed moral superiority:

Now by my sceptre, and my soul to boot,
He hath more worthy interest to the state
Than thou the shadow of succession.

(97-99)

This pragmatic king has learned that even a title as unstained as Richard II's is only a shadow without *virtù*, the quality that he thinks he sees in Hotspur. The way that he associates Hotspur with himself hints that he wishes Hotspur were his heir. But that wish is no more than a desperate evasion of his parental grief, as the petulance of his next few lines indicates. He even charges that Hal will fight under Percy against his own family.

This final turn allows Hal to feel a cleansing anger. His characteristic irony overcome by hurt love and pride, he makes his most complete and open declaration of aims. The abrupt, almost non-metrical beginning suggests his anger: "Do not think so, you shall not find it so" (129). And the next few lines illuminate its cause; if Hotspur is the barrier between Hal and Henry's love, then Hotspur must die. By Henry's own standard the warrior ideal is the measure of moral worth, and Hal means to establish himself before his father and the kingdom. Already the duel of Act V is foreshadowed and weighted with public and private meaning. Conquering Hotspur will cleanse Hal's name and make him a hero worthy of royalty, but at the same time it will complete the reconciliation of this father and son. Hence the angry reproach of Hal's contrast between "This gallant Hotspur, this all-praised knight, / And your unthought-of Harry" (140-41).

Like most fathers Henry is only too eager to be reconciled. Delighted by his son's heroic zeal and by the affection implied in Hal's hurt feelings, he regains his kingly dignity and his confidence together:

A hundred thousand rebels die in this—
Thou shalt have charge and sovereign trust
herein.

(160-61)

Now that he knows the cleavage in his own house to be healed, he can face the challenge of the Percy rebellion with poise. When Blunt reports the gathering of the enemy, Henry gives orders with brisk efficiency and assigns Hal an important place in the plans. This father and son standing together are a symbol of unity in the realm, just as in *1 Henry VI* Talbot and his son fighting together stand for the unity that will die with them. But because Shakespeare has shown their reconciliation in an intensely personal scene, Henry and Hal are more than just symbols of order. Above all, the scene is a step in Hal's growth toward full readiness for kingship, but it also reveals Henry's human struggle to endure the weight of kingly office. The symbol of unity is there, but it is surrounded by a richness of meanings such as the early Shakespeare never achieved.

The king and Hal appear together again at Shrewsbury, now in perfect harmony. Henry is so full of confidence that he can laugh at the ill omen of a gloomy morning. Throughout the day Hal is the picture of a true prince, extorting praise even from his enemies. With becoming humility in his words, he challenges Hotspur to single combat. Henry forbids that, perhaps because of still-continuing doubts in his son, but mainly because it would be foolish to give up the advantage of superior numbers. In the battle Hal shows brotherly pride at Prince John's valor, and afterward he allows his brother the honor of giving Douglas his freedom. When Hal saves his father's life from Douglas, the king recalls the charges that Hal has sought his death. The sincerity of Hal's indignation is supported by his deeds, and in fact only the king's remark makes him point out the significance of his act. Finally Hotspur, Hal's rival, dies under his sword, and the last picture of the prince is with his family on the battlefield won by their united valor. If the expression of this newly firm tie between the king and his son is almost entirely public and formal at Shrewsbury, those qualities make the last scenes complementary to the personal reconciliation of III.ii. Shrewsbury establishes the forces of order as dominant in the kingdom, and its final moment is this public symbol of unity, a king and his crown prince, reconciled and victorious.

The path of Hal's growth is a great arc. He must move away from his father and the court so that he may find his personal autonomy. He must revitalize the Lancastrian line by renewed contact with the source of all political power, the commonwealth itself. Yet there is peril in this journey. If he plunges too deeply into the world of Falstaff and his companions, he will lose contact with his own heritage, with the birth that calls him to prepare himself for England's throne. And so the arc turns back. Hal must return to his father and prove his worthiness to be the Lancastrian heir. Now he must act for himself, yet to defend the primacy of the House of Lancaster. Only half-understanding what has happened to his son, Henry IV senses the ardor and enthusiasm that Hal has brought with him. The returned prodigal is the new hope of the forces of order, and especially of the king his father. "For this my son was dead, and is alive again: he was lost and is found." Hal, and with him the Lancastrian line, are renewed.

KING HENRY IV

Henry IV is perhaps the play's most mysterious character. A few critics, including **Ann Marie McNamara**, maintain that Henry is the protagonist and a hero. Most other critics view the King's claim to being the central character as weak, with most critics seeing Hal as the protagonist, and some arguing in favor of Falstaff or Hotspur. **Robert J. Fehrenbach** sides with the scholars who believe Henry is a secondary character in the play. He argues that Shakespeare's indirect characterization of Henry offers some insight into the King's thinking and motivation, but also inhibits the reader's gaining a real understanding of Henry. Most critics agree that Henry is a Machiavel, that is, that Henry uses whatever means necessary, including deceit and manipulation, to achieve his political goals. Critics such as John Dover Wilson and A. R. Humphrey's agree with this assessment to a degree, but also believe that Henry is not truly a villain. For further analysis of Henry's character, see the essays by **Ernst Kris** and **Robert B. Pierce** in the FATHERS AND SONS section.

Anne Marie McNamara

SOURCE: "*Henry IV*: The King as Protagonist," in *Shakespeare Quarterly*, Vol. X, No. 3, Summer, 1959, pp. 423-31.

[*McNamara examines* Henry IV, Part One *as a history play and argues that if the work is seen as such, there can be no debate over who the protagonist is; it must be Henry IV. McNamara outlines the differences between history plays and tragedies, and reasons that other critics overlook Henry as the main character because they are viewing the play as a tragedy. McNamara goes on to discount the legitimacy of claims that Hal, Falstaff, or Hotspur are the protagonists of the drama. Finally, she demonstrates Henry's prominence throughout the play.*]

In discussions of the problems of unity and of structural relationship between the two Parts of Shakespeare's *Henry IV*, the dominance of the titular character has been unaccountably neglected. Yet, according to the avowed nature, function, and theme of the history play, he is the only possible protagonist.

The Tudor history play, like all kinds of historical writing in the English Renaissance, was primarily didactic. Functioning specifically to teach lessons of patriotism to Englishmen, it had its own special method, the method of drama. . . . Specifically, it taught through historical examples the political lessons that the Tudors thought necessary and proper for all Englishmen to learn, lessons of the duties of ruler and subject in a divinely organized hierarchy of degree, the preservation of which was the only guard against the reversion of man's world to chaos. In particular, these lessons were, for the ruler, precepts of responsibility to God and to His people, and for the subject, those of obedience to the ruler as God's deputy. Through this scale or chain of rule and submission the maintenance of order in God's earthly kingdom would be assured. The Tudor state was built on such a theocratic conception of society. God was King of all. The reigning king of the realm was God's regent on earth, manifesting His providence and justice. The King's magistrates participated in God's direction of His world by substituting for His chief representative in less important offices. Subjects were bound to obey God and His deputies on earth. All human beings were bound to perform duties conducive to the maintenance of harmony and peace.

The famous *Mirrour for Magistrates*, which ran through seven editions in the reign of Queen Elizabeth I, exemplifies the didactic quality and use of historical writing in which the history play participated. It is crucial for our purpose to notice that in each of its accounts of the downfall of rulers and the destruction of subjects the cause of the ruin is *political* sin, that is, sin of commission or omission against the good of the nation, and that the emphasis is placed on the inevitability of the strict vengeance of God on those who fail to fulfill their prescribed roles in God's plan for men and nations. Although the *Mirrour* presents a group of individuals chosen from history to illustrate the destruction attendant upon the willful disruption of this plan, its focus is the state, not the individual. It is always concerned with public, never with private, sin. Its voices are those of rulers who failed to execute God's justice against rebellious subjects and those of subjects who opposed God's representatives, the king or the king's magistrates. Its laments are always for sins against the public weal. The history play, sharing this general function of Renaissance historical writing, aimed to teach nations, rulers, and subjects how to avoid unhappiness, destruction, and infamous report in the future by moving obediently in their appointed orbits in the universe.

The concept of the nature and function of the Tudor history play, here very briefly recalled, prescribes the theme of the genre: "questions of good government and national patriotism" (so says Brooke) [*The Tudor Drama*, 1911], or "the welfare of a nation as a nation (so says Charlton) [*Shakespeare, Politics, and Politicians*, 1929]. It is the fortunes of a *nation* that form the theme of the history plays. It is, therefore, the fortunes of England in a particular time and under a particular ruler that constitute the theme of any one of Shakespeare's history plays.

Just as the nature and function of such plays should not be confused with those of tragedy, so the theme of the plays, with its public and political concern, should not be construed as that of tragedy, the concern of which is private and ethical. Indeed, the dramatic representation of a succession of public events involving a group of individuals in a political context is not at all the same thing as the dramatic representation of a private individual working out a personal problem in an ethical context. In a word, history is not tragedy. *Henry IV* is not *King Lear*.

This distinction should lie at the very heart of the problem in any discussion of Shakespeare's history plays. It seems to me to demand an approach on grounds relevant to the nature, function, and theme of the genre, to forbid an approach on any other terms, and to reject the validity of any conclusion about the structure of the history plays that is arrived at in ignorance, defiance, or neglect of the genre. Surely, one would shrink from discussing tragedy in terms of comedy as instinctively as he would from trying to determine the structure of a lyric poem by applying to it criteria which are relevant only to an epic. Yet some commentators do examine the Shakespearian history play in the patently irrelevant terms of tragedy or of a strange hybrid genre that can only be designated as "history-comedy". Moreover, analyses of the history plays are too often analyses of the *characters* in the history plays. They are concerned with the rise and fall of individuals rather than with the change in fortune of a nation. We are asked to study the Elizabethan history play by examining it as if it were something other than it is.

That such misapprehension of the genre is disastrous to criticism of the history plays is evident in the naming of the protagonist in the play we are about to consider, *Henry IV*. By some commentators the role is assigned to Prince Hal, by others to Hotspur, by still others to Falstaff. One critic names two protagonists, Hal and Hotspur. Another speaks of Hotspur and Falstaff as "two other chief characters" in addition to Hal. As far as I know, no one names the most obvious candidate—to my mind the only possible choice—the titular character, the one whose reign is the matter and the theme of the play, the King, King Henry IV.

I propose that Prince Hal is not the protagonist and that the theme of the play is not "the education of the Prince". I disagree with the assertion that "it must be remembered that the entire plot turns on Hal and Hotspur". I suggest that it is not accurate to speak of

I Henry IV as an "induction to the treatment of the hero's [Prince Hal's] triumphant reign" and as a play "devoted to the prince's preparation for sovereignty. . . ." I suggest that it is incorrect to say that "*Henry IV* is no more than a label. They [the two Parts] are *Falstaff, Parts I and II*."—a flat statement that Falstaff is the hero. Naturally, I do not deny that Prince Hal is an important figure in the play or that his "preparation" for kingship goes on, but I cannot consider his "preparation" the central theme. I do not deny that Hotspur is an important figure in the play, but I think that his importance is controlled by that of the character with whom he is in conflict, the King. I do not deny that Falstaff is an important figure in the play, but I think that he is important because he is a formidable obstacle in the path of the King in his efforts to fulfill the prescribed duties of royalty. Yet I am prohibited from accepting Hal, Hotspur, or Falstaff as protagonist in this play by my awareness of the nature and function of its genre. My contention is that the sole protagonist of *Henry IV, Part I*, and of *Henry IV, Part II,* is the titular character, the King, and that the theme of each of the two Parts is his successful effort to maintain the well-being of England. I believe that the King must be the hero, for in the history-play the center of interest is the fate of a nation, and to an Elizabethan "the welfare of England was in the hands of its sovereign."

It is against the background that I have very briefly presented that I wish to attempt a structural analysis of Henry IV, Part I, "the best of the histories", "perhaps the fullest and richest of all the histories", one of the "perfect specimens . . . of a dramatic type which, even in an age of creative dramatists, only Shakespeare's genius could invent",—as a history-play. "Perhaps no one but Shakespeare wrote the History Play proper", says Charlton. "Others made plays on historical themes [but] almost all serious plays on historical subjects are tragedies, not history plays . . ." (p.7).

The uniqueness of the genre suggests a reason for the lack of some "standard" pattern for an analysis of its plot. A. C. Bradley has provided the classical conception of the structure of tragedy. For comedy there are less dependable guides. But for the history-play, as Professor Cain has reminded us, there seems to be no pattern for plot analysis at all. My approach is through the postulate that the King is the central figure and that his actions control the plot. We must follow the King, then, from his initiation of the action of the play through the complication of forces brought about by opposition to him, through crisis, through climax, to denouement.

The King figures in each of the five acts and in eighteen of the nineteen scenes into which *Henry IV, Part I,* is separated [All references to the text of *Henry*

IV, Part I are to the edition of George Lyman Kittredge: *The Complete Works of Shakespeare*, 1936]. In six of the eighteen scenes he is present and active (I.i; I.iii; III.ii; V.i; V.iv; V.v). In twelve, he is mentioned and acted against, either directly or indirectly, but more frequently directly (in ten scenes) than indirectly (in two scenes). In only one scene is there no reference of any kind to him, the Rochester innyard scene (II.i), in which Gadshill and the chamberlain set up the robbery for the Poins-Falstaff-Hal group. In five of the six scenes in which the King is present and active, he is the dominant and directive force (I.i; I.iii; III.ii; V.i; V.v). In the one exception (V.iv) he may seem to be weak, but his appearance of weakness should not be misconstrued: the King is figuring in an action (the Douglas-King-Hal episode) by which the necessity of his leadership and the sacredness of his person as King are emphasized. It is my task now to illustrate these statistics and to elucidate their significance by a reading of the text.

The play opens with the King's order for a report of his Council on his projected expedition to the Holy Land. Informed by Westmoreland that the Council's consideration of it had been interrupted by news from Wales that Mortimer had been captured by Glendower and by news from the North that Harry Percy had fought with the Scots to an uncertain issue, the King is not disturbed. He has a report from an eye-witness that Harry Percy [Hotspur] has successfully overcome the Scots and has taken several honorable prisoners. His pleasure in Hotspur's success is impaired, however, by Westmoreland's use of the term "prince" in his concurrence in the praise of Hotspur: "In faith / It is a conquest for a prince to boast of" (76-77). The word impels the King to a regretful contrast between Hotspur's "honour" (81) and Prince Hal's "riot and dishonour" (85). But he dismisses the contrast from his mind to call into question the refusal of Hotspur to send to London all but one of his noble prisoners (92-96). The King has already acted upon Hotspur's "pride" (92) by sending for him to explain his recalcitrance (100), which Westmoreland attributes to the unfriendliness towards the Crown of Hotspur's uncle, Worcester. The King therefore defers all plans for his pilgrimage to the Holy Land and calls a Council for the following Wednesday to hear and settle Hotspur's apparent disobedience. Thus, the King initiates the action of the play.

The King opens the investigation by interrogating Hotspur (I.iii), charging that the Percies have strained his patience and asserting that he will henceforth show them his authority and power as their ruler (1-9). Reminded by Worcester that the Percies were instrumental in his gaining that power and authority and therefore do not deserve harsh treatment, the King orders him from his presence as a threat of "danger and disobedience" (16) to "majesty" (18). Explanations

by Northumberland and spirited denials by Hotspur (both attempting mitigation on the plea of misunderstanding) and mediatory efforts by Blunt to conclude the meeting amicably prove unavailing. The King sharply rejects them, putting his finger on the price of Hotspur's obedience, the ransom of Mortimer, his brother-in-law, by the Crown. This the King flatly refuses on the grounds that Mortimer is a traitor (86). He declares unequivocally that he will not ransom him and insists that anyone who asks this favor brands himself as unfriendly. To Hotspur's heated defence of Mortimer's loyalty, the King gives the lie (113-118), forbids any further mention of Mortimer, and, ordering Hotspur to deliver his prisoners immediately under threat of punishment (120-122), he dismisses the Percies. Repeating his threatening demand for Hotspur's obedience, he leaves the meeting-room. At his departure, the Percies hatch a plot against him, justifying their revolt in a rehearsal of the King's ingratitude for their past assistance and of his fear of their present power to unsettle his right to the throne (130-300). Thus, the King sets himself in potential conflict with opponents of his authority.

In III.ii, the King is in action to protect the throne against an active and dangerous rebellion. The preparation and progress of the Percy plot have been made known to him. He moves against his enemies by making his ally one whom up to this time he has had sufficient cause to nominate (as he later says) his "nearest and dearest enemy" (123). It is the heir apparent to the throne, Harry Monmouth, Prince Hal. To win him, the King moves with expert shrewdness. He has summoned the Prince to the Palace from the young man's undesirable haunt in Eastcheap among companions ill-suited to one of royal blood. He dismisses his councillors that he may confront his son in private. He appraises Hal's irresponsible conduct as a probable judgment of God against him (the King) "to punish my misreadings" (11).

In answer to the Prince's immediate suggestion of malice in the reports of many of his irregularities and his expression of regret for his real offences, the King makes his second move. Taking advantage of the Prince's rueful attitude, the King paints a full portrait of the Prince as he appears to the Court and the public. He asserts that Prince Hal seems temperamentally disinclined from the interests of all his forebears, that is, from political interests (29-31). He presents the evidence: the Prince has lost his Council seat to his younger brother, Prince John (32-33); he has lost the goodwill of his relatives and the confidence of the Court (34-35); he has caused direful prophecies about his future "fall" (38). In a word, he has become a very unpromising heir-apparent. His irresponsibility for affairs of state augurs his failure when he succeeds to the throne. The King is acutely aware of these disturbing facts and prophecies. The strong possibility of the fall of his line from power urges him to move on to repair its strength by retrieving and invigorating this weak heir. The immediate exigency of the brewing rebellion of the Percies presents a cause through which he may strike for a double *coup*, the quelling of the northern rebels against his kingly power and the quelling of the youthful revolt of his son against his princely responsibilities.

The King now shows himself an excellent strategist. He enters upon a telling contrast between himself as a youthful aspirant to the throne and his son at this moment (39-84). He emphasizes the Prince's deviation from political propriety by recalling his own early attitude as Bolingbroke (39-45): he was sparing in his public appearance (46); he was therefore sought after on his occasional appearances (47-49); he acted with utmost regard for rank, position, hierarchy ("courtesy") (50); he thus won approbation and allegiance from men even in the presence of King Richard II (50-54). In contrast to this restraint, Richard was constantly in public, indulged in frivolity with worthless companions, adulterated his kingliness by promiscuous and indiscriminate association, and devoted himself to popularity (60-69). As a result, men surfeited with Richard; men loathed him; men finally disregarded him. They lost their respect for him, "being with his presence glutted, gorg'd, and full" (84).

Bluntly, the King presses the point of application on the pride of Prince Hal.

> And in that very line, Harry, standest thou;
> For thou hast lost thy princely privilege
> With vile participation. Not an eye
> But is aweary of thy common sight. . . .
>
> (85-88)

Shrewdly, he turns it to the young man's sentiment:

> Not an eye
> But is aweary of thy common sight,
> *Save mine,* which hath desir'd to see thee
> more. . . .
>
> [critic's emphasis]

Wisely, he weeps. Then, he continues:

> Save mine, which hath desired to see thee
> more;
> Which now doth that I would not have it do—
> Make blind itself with foolish tenderness.
>
> (88-91)

The King wins ground. For the Prince answers,

> I shall hereafter my thrice-gracious lord
> Be more myself.
>
> (92-93)

He will act hereafter like a prince and heir to the throne of England.

But the King is not satisfied. He is fighting for a full victory. He must have more than conventional contrition. He does not comment on the Prince's reply. He has achieved a promise of his son's future attention to the dignity of his position as a prince and heir-apparent. But there is an immediate need: the promise of Hal's active and enthusiastic support of the throne in the forthcoming struggle with the rebellious Percies. His strategy in the first stage of his attempt was the contrasting of a successful aspirant (himself as Bolingbroke) and an unsuccessful incumbent (Richard II) in order to emphasize the probability of Hal's failure as a king. His strategy in the second stage of his plan is equally clever. Beside the unimpressive figure of Richard, he places Hal:

> For all the world,
> As thou art to this hour, was Richard then
> When I from France set foot at
> Ravenspurgh. . . .
>
> (93-95)

Quickly, he draws into the pattern the one person calculated to stir the young Prince's pride, Harry Percy, Hotspur. With this fiery young Northerner, the King identifies his own youthful spirit: "And even as I was then is Percy now." He goads Hal with praise of Hotspur's reputation, his "worthy interest to the state" (98), his leadership, his honor in battle against the renowned warrior, Douglas (107). He hurls at Hal this undeniable proof of Hotspur's valor: at this very moment, Hotspur, with his father, Northumberland, Douglas, Mortimer, and the Archbishop of York, is in arms against the throne. The peace and safety of the realm are in jeopardy (117-120). Then, artfully, he sorrowfully questions the use of revealing all his troubles to this son, who, he implies, has no interest in the welfare of his kingdom. Suddenly, he names his son his "nearest and . . . dearest enemy" (123) and assails him with a bitter accusation of likely defection to Percy through fear, low inclinations, latent anger, and craven spite against his father (124-128). "Do not think so. You shall not find it so," cries Hal. He capitulates.

The King thus wins a critical encounter. He hears the Prince, stung by his taunts, pour out promises of the redemption of his name and valor. He hears him swear to God the sincerity of his reunion with his father against the Percy rebellion (132-159). He acknowledges Hal's protestations and his own victory by an approving shout: "A hundred thousand rebels die in this!" (160). This is the result for which he has planned and fought. In it he sees the death of the Percy rebellion and of Hal's inner revolt. Immediately, he places his complete confidence in his newly-won ally. He promises him a military command. His plans against the rebels are already made. With Hal's assumption of his proper role, the unification of the Crown's forces is accomplished. Henry IV—the King of England—is ready to fulfill his duty as monarch of the realm: to maintain on the field of battle, if necessary, the authority of the King against rebellion.

In V.i, the King significantly displays his sense of the authority and dignity of his position. He refuses the offer of Prince Hal to settle the differences between the rebels and the Crown by a single combat with Hotspur. His reason is clear: it is the King's duty to put down rebellion:

> Rebuke and dread correction wait on us,
> And they shall do their office.
>
> (111-112)

This uprising cannot be settled by a private contest on the field of chivalry. It is a public thing. A public demonstration of revolt has been made and it must be publicly rebuked. It is a threat against the Crown—and the King, not the Prince, wears the Crown. He orders all to their posts. He declares the justice of the cause of the Crown.

On the battlefield of Shrewsbury (V.iii) the primacy of the King as leader and symbol is clear. It is the *King* who is sought by Douglas. The death of the *King* is the desire of the rebels. The preservation of the life of the *King* is the concern of the loyal lords. "The King hath many marching in his coats" (25) for a very good reason: *his* person will be the center of attack. When Douglas mistakenly thinks that he has killed the King, he shouts that the battle is over: "All's done, all's won. Here breathless lies the King" (16). In V.iv, the King's concern for Prince Hal's wounds causes him to withdraw temporarily from the battle. But the Prince urges him to go back, lest the men become confused without his (the King's) leadership.

> I do beseech your Majesty make up,
> Lest your retirement do amaze your friends.
>
> (5-6)

The King is the leader of the national defence and the symbol of unity in the battle. When his identity is finally discovered by Douglas—"Thou bearest thee like a king" (36)—he fights with him and is in danger at the hands of this renowned warrior (III.ii.108-111). The strongest of the rebels has sought out the King and is determined to destroy him. Prince Hal intervenes, engages Douglas, and drives him off. The King's person, symbol of the Crown and of the realm, has been saved.

In V.v, as the battle of Shrewsbury is won by the royal armies, the King brings to a successful conclusion the action which he initiated at the beginning of the play when he saw "disobedience and danger" in the unfriendly eyes of the Percies. He sentences the chief rebels to death. "Thus ever did rebellion find rebuke" (1). Action to preserve order and peace in the kingdom has been his one concern. His words to Worcester in the camp at Shrewsbury on the eve of battle had that burden:

> . . . . Will you again unknit
> This churlish knot of all-abhorred war,
> And move in that obedient orb again
> Where you did give a fair and natural light,
> And be no more an exhal'd meteor,
> A prodigy of fear, and a portent
> Of broached mischief to the unborn times?
>
> (V.i.15-21)

His last words at Shrewsbury at the favorable conclusion of the battle are a sober emphasis of the purpose which has impelled him from the beginning:

> Rebellion in this land shall lose his sway
> Meeting the check of such another day. . . .
>
> (V.v.41-42)

This is a statement not only of the successful accomplishment of determined action incumbent on a King but also of sober realization that such action must be repeated if that duty is to be completely fulfilled. For there is more mischief afoot. Scroop and Northumberland are up in arms. They must now be put down. The Percy rebellion has been crushed. The rebellion in the north must be similarly crushed. England—embodied in the King—will not brook rebellion.

The problems of structural unity and of relationship between Part I and Part II seem to me less vexing when they are approached with the assumption that the King is the protagonist. It seems clear, for example, that Part I is a complete and separate play—a dramatic entity: " . . . this business so fair is done . . ." (V.v.45). This action is at an end. The drama initiated by the King when he moved against the Percies' threat to the throne (Act I) has been completed by his victory over them (Act V). It seems clear, too, that Part II is a complete and separate play—a dramatic entity in itself:

> Rebellion in this land shall lose his sway,
> Meeting the check of such another day

another action, another victory, another enemy, on another day.

This centering of our study on the King as protagonist and on his action as the plot of the history play need not preclude our awareness of all the other elements present and operative in it. The "honour" theme, the "preparation" theme, the "reparation" theme, the "vengeance" theme may all be present, but they are present in a larger reference and as adumbrations of future plays rather than as primary forces in this one. No one of them can possibly be the central theme here. Similarly, the characters other than King Henry IV, whose specific actions we have followed, are indeed important. It is true that Hotspur, Falstaff, and Prince Hal play indispensable parts. But they are indispensable because they are all antagonists of the King. Hotspur, the fiery rebel, is his antagonist in the formation of the major conflict. Falstaff, the old opportunist, is his antagonist in the conflict for Hal's allegiance. The Prince, the young escapist, is his antagonist in "the long grown wounds of . . . intemperance", but his is an antagonism of youth—more seeming than real—and he transforms it to fealty as he joins the King and assists him at Shrewsbury. That the Prince is an embryonic hero cannot be denied, but he is a prospective hero of a prospective play, one which will bear *his* name and concern the affairs of *his* reign. Here he is the ally and support of his father the King against the Percies, just as his brother, Prince John, is the ally and support of his father the King in another play about another group of rebels, *Henry IV, Part II*. No one of these characters, it seems to me, can possibly claim the major role in this play. No one of them holds the position which the hero of the English history-play must hold to fulfill the requirements of its genre, the position of embodiment of England and of guardian and director of the fortunes of England. . . .

Robert J. Fehrenbach

SOURCE: "The Characterization of the King in *1 Henry IV*," in *Shakespeare Quarterly*, Vol. 30, No. 1, Winter, 1979, pp. 42-50.

[*Fehrenbach argues that Henry is not the protagonist of the play. He states that, unlike Hal, Hotspur, and Falstaff, the King is characterized by indirect means. Fehrenbach shows that Shakespeare teaches the reader about Henry not through Henry's words and actions, but through the words and actions of other characters. Pointing to the criticisms made of Henry by Hotspur and Worcester and to the scene in which Hal and Falstaff take turns play-acting as Henry, Fehrenbach analyzes what these scenes say about how the reader should interpret Henry's character. Fehrenbach, urging the reader not to take anything Henry says at face value, maintains that there is much to learn about Henry by examining what he doesn't say. The critic gives special attention to the fact that throughout the play, Henry avoids discussing how he became King.*]

Despite the play's title, critics generally regard the central figure of *1 Henry IV* as just about anybody except Henry IV. The usual candidates, of course, are

Hal and Falstaff, but one also finds an occasional scholar asserting that Hotspur all but runs away with the play as the appealingly passionate quasi-tragic figure. Now and again someone will argue for the elevation of Henry to his rightful place as chief protagonist of his play as against those usurpers Hal, Hotspur, and Falstaff; but these departures from the critical tradition are rare and usually are not as revolutionary as they might first seem.

Relegation of the King to the status of a secondary character is understandable: when compared to Hal, Hotspur, and Falstaff, he has fewer speeches and fewer lines; he is generally less active in the play and arouses less interest in the audience. As Bolingbroke in *Richard II*, a significant and immensely interesting antagonist, he has been the subject of considerable study. But as King in *1 Henry IV*, Henry has received little attention, and virtually nothing has been written on the method employed by Shakespeare to make his character. This inattention is unfortunate, for Shakespeare's method of creating Henry is instructive. It illustrates how a master playwright marries characterization with character.

In a successfully constructed drama—and *1 Henry IV* has always been considered one of Shakespeare's best plays—one expects to find methods of characterization appropriate to the characters depicted. This expectation is not disappointed in *1 Henry IV*. The excessively passionate and open Hotspur is primarily revealed by honest and direct, if immature and unguarded, speeches, by active movement, and only incidentally by the more indirect method of description, which generally supports the characterization already created by what the young nobleman says and does. Falstaff, too, is an open book. His actions and statements on their face reveal a vain, irresponsible, and indulgent, if nonetheless likable, personality—a characterization supported by the less direct method of characterization: statements by others. Thanks to his famous soliloquy at the end of Act I, scene ii, Hal is also an open book. To be sure, he appears to be the profligate—and to a considerable degree he is a lover of good times—but owing to his soliloquy we know him to be a responsible and serious, even calculating prince. The several unfavorable comments about his character are made by men who lack the perspective of the audience; none of these comments coincides with Hal's true personality. Primarily by his actions and by his statements—which occasionally contain an irony clearly apparent to the audience because of the soliloquy in I. ii—and only to a small degree by the descriptions of others, do we understand the person of the Prince of Wales.

King Henry is a different kind of person, and his characterization is formed differently. He is by no means an open book; he is secretive and distant, more guessed at than known. He is a man we know but do not know, a man we watch but are not sure of. For reasons as selfless and politically necessary as they are self-serving and ambitious, Henry is a private man and a Machiavellian king, alone with his own thoughts of political responsibility and personal guilt. While Hal, Hotspur, and Falstaff are primarily created by direct means—appropriate to their open characters— Henry is formed primarily by indirect means—appropriate to his close character. For example, in contrast to the ways in which the speeches and actions of Hal, Hotspur, and Falstaff inform the audience about them, Henry's speeches and actions say more about him through indirection, through irony, and through a peculiar emphasis on what is left unsaid. Also, in a play abounding in character foils, Henry's person is especially dependent upon other characters, juxtaposed and compared to him, for his characterization. At the same time, descriptions of the King play a much larger role in creating the person Shakespeare intends us to know than do descriptions of the other three major figures. In short, to portray King Henry IV, Shakespeare employs methods of characterization that appropriately deny us intimacy with this necessarily private man, this troubled ruler who in his dual struggle against past sins and present threats must always be the masker. However advantageous masking is to Henry the King ruling a beleaguered state, it does not make Henry the man a warm and sympathetic figure.

Occasionally, Henry's speeches and actions can be trusted to be literal and accurate presentations of his character. For example, his expression of concern about his son's apparent profligacy in I. i. 78-90 and his agonizing, nearly confessional conference with Hal in III. ii convey his sincere fears for England and for the throne. [All Shakespeare quotations are from *The Complete Works of Shakespeare*, eds. Hardin Craig and David Bevington, rev. ed., 1973.] His comment before the battle of Shrewsbury that "nothing can seem foul to those that win" (V. i. 8), along with his orders preparing for war in III. ii. 170-80 and those speeches and actions throughout Act V with which he directs his forces and swiftly metes out justice after Shrewsbury, reveal the King to be an adroit, efficient ruler and a no-nonsense military leader.

Usually, however, the King says or does little that can be taken at face value, little that does not ironically reveal an otherwise hidden part of his character. But the kind of irony associated with Henry IV is not the same as the dramatic irony surrounding Hal's words and deeds. Because of the Prince's soliloquy in I. ii, the audience enjoys a peculiar and intimate relationship with him, a relationship that allows us generally to know how to respond to him at particular moments. The irony surrounding Henry's words causes us to suspect and to guess, not really to know. There remains a distance between us and the

King, and because we never get close to him we can never feel sure of him.

In his opening statement to the court in Act I, scene i, Henry would have us believe that now, tired of war but pleased with the end of civil strife, he would give thanks to God by traveling to Jerusalem on a crusade. Consider this pious vow in terms of the rest of that scene, especially Henry's subsequent speeches. The long-delayed crusade, if he sincerely wishes to organize one, is an act of penance for a sin Henry scrupulously and characteristically avoids mentioning (his responsibility for the murder of Richard II), but by the end of the scene we must question his guilt-born intention. It is likely that Henry has known all through his speech that the wars are not really over—in which case his call for a crusade becomes only a show of kingly piety. His haste in vowing to go to the Holy Land is matched only by his haste to "Brake off" (I. i. 48) the intended crusade, which he "must neglect" (I. i. 101) until the matter of Hotspur's refusal to send him the prisoners captured at the battle of Holmedon is settled. Certainly the King had known of the battles in the North and of Hotspur's refusal when he made his public call for a crusade, for Henry himself relates to the court the details of young Percy's acts from news brought to him by Sir Walter Blunt. Before Henry made his vow to go on the crusade, he had already sent for Hotspur to provide an explanation for his decision to keep the prisoners (I. i. 100-102). Henry's penitential speech is, therefore, difficult to take at face value, and consequently we soon find ourselves suspecting the King's public expression of Christian commitment.

Henry's statement to Westmoreland which closes this first scene—

> But come yourself with speed to us again;
> For more is to be said and to be done
> Than out of anger can be uttered
>
> (I. i. 105-7)

—clearly tells the audience that the King does not consider a public, open discussion of Hotspur's rebuff (*utter* carries the Elizabethan meaning, "to make public") to be the most effective way of preparing for his confrontation with the Percy family. In secret, therefore, he and Westmoreland will prepare a strategy to counter the Percies.

When Henry next appears (I. iii), his plan has been determined and put into action. He now plays the role of a long-suffering ruler whose patience has been mistaken for weakness by his subjects. But a perceptive audience will probably laugh silently at such a picture of Henry. His characterization of himself as "smooth as oil, soft as young down" (I. iii. 7), and "Unapt" to have his "cold and temperate" blood stirred

(I. iii. 1-2), only serves to disclose to the audience, through irony, an imperious nature and a real anger. If Henry has lost the "title of respect" as he says (I. iii. 8), the loss has hardly occurred because he has been too humble and malleable. Though Henry's words may deceive the Percies, Shakespeare reveals to the audience by ironic indirection that the King is angered, yet controlled, and, above all, that Henry is a subtle defender when crossed or threatened.

The royal dismissal of Worcester continues the indirect characterization of Henry. The King would have it understood that he dismisses Worcester because of the Earl's impertinence to "majesty," but what must equally offend him is Worcester's implicit reference to Henry's usurpation by reminding the King that the Percies aided him in gaining the throne:

> Our house, my sovereign liege, little deserves
> The scourge of greatness to be us'd on it;
> And that same greatness too which our own
>   hands
> Have holp to make so portly.
>
>   (I. iii. 10-13)

Henry's testy reaction and his dismissal of Worcester with a self-serving statement about his majesty call our attention to his extreme sensitivity to the history of his climb to the throne—a subject he scrupulously avoids speaking about candidly throughout the entire play. Though Worcester's statement is uncomfortably pointed, his charge that the Percy house is being oppressed is substantiated by the facts. In requiring Hotspur to turn over all his prisoners to the crown, the King is demanding more than military custom allows. However accurately Henry judges Worcester to be a danger, therefore, the temper of the King's reaction, his defensive imperiousness, reveals that the Earl has touched a sensitive nerve and that one subtle plotter has recognized the threat of another almost intuitively.

The rest of this important scene finds Henry insisting that Edmund Mortimer, the Earl of March and brother-in-law to Hotspur, traitorously surrendered to Glendower during the recent civil wars. This charge is not accepted by the Percies, nor is it accepted unequivocally by Shakespeare's sources: Holinshed's *Chronicles* and Samuel Daniel's *Civil Wars*. Holinshed, Daniel, and Shakespeare all agree (historically inaccurate though we know them to have been) that Mortimer was Richard II's designated successor, a fact known by Worcester and Northumberland and, one must assume, by Henry—though in keeping with his close nature the King never openly refers to that line of succession. More important, the Percies and Shakespeare's sources agree that when Henry charges Mortimer with treason, making him a traitor not deserving ransom, his objective is to avoid enlarging a rival to the throne. Although the audience is not likely to know Holinshed or Daniel, the force of the Percies' argument—the dramatic expression of the authority of the playwright's sources—causes us to suspect the King's motives to be politically self-serving (see I. iii. 145-59). Henry's speeches in these two early scenes arouse our skepticism not so much by what they say as by what they leave unsaid. The King's real motives, his true feelings, are kept at a remove from the audience, but they are not as well hidden as he would wish.

Appearing next in Act III, scene ii, Henry once again ironically and indirectly reveals what he, but not the dramatist, would hide. A. R. Humphreys has noted that Henry IV's expression of sadness at Hal's behavior indicates a "covert sense of guilt," guilt about his usurpation to which he will not openly admit and on which he attempts to put a good face for Hal. Moreover, as he compares himself to Hotspur in praising the young man's leadership and prowess in battle, Henry ironically and unintentionally identifies himself with a plotter against the throne:

> For all the world
> As thou art to this hour was Richard then
> When I from France set foot at Ravenspurgh,
> And even as I was then is Percy now.
>
>   (III. ii. 93-96)

Later in this scene, Henry says that Hal is morally capable of joining the rebels, allying with the Percies to fight against his own father. Such an unfair attack reveals by indirection the King's own values and his own covert guilt. This is the "politician" talking, the man who views ambition for the throne as paramount and as a motive annihilating all other considerations. However profligate Hal may appear to the King, there is nothing in the son's actions to warrant the charge of treason and perfidy which the father lays against him.

After an absence of several scenes, Henry next enters in Act V, scene i. There he engages in an interesting exchange with the man who has become his archenemy: Worcester. The hostility between these men can be explained as much by their similar personalities as by their different goals. Worcester, who seeks Henry's dethronement as earnestly as the King seeks to retain his position, is as subtle and shrewd as the King himself. He is therefore more dangerous to Henry than the passionate, open, and frequently foolish Hotspur. The King attempts to disarm Worcester with statements. When they do not work, he treats Worcester with disdain, making an offer he must know Worcester will reject for the very reason the Earl has hinted at earlier: distrust of Henry.

Henry's self-serving description of Worcester's disruption of the King's peace and his call for his cousin's obedience, to say nothing of his attempt to elicit sympathy as an aging man reluctantly but dutifully suffering the discomforts of war (V. i. 9-21), contrasts sharply with Worcester's detailed, substantive charge that Henry is responsible for the civil strife because he broke faith with his early supporters:

> Whereby we stand opposed by such means
> As you yourself have forg'd against yourself
> By unkind usage, dangerous countenance,
> And violation of all faith and troth
> Sworn to us in your younger enterprise.
> (V. i. 67-71)

Worcester's accusation cannot be entirely dismissed as an *argumentum ex nihilo* [argument from nothing] after what we have seen of Henry's relationship with the Percies earlier in the play and heard in Henry's private conversation with Hal. As usual, Henry will not actually deny the accusation; rather, from the position of majesty, he disdainfully and sarcastically charges that Worcester has merely found a deceptively plausible justification for rebellion (V. i. 72-82). To be sure. Henry does not want war, but the peace must be on his terms. His offer of pardon, capped with the contemptuous and peremptory "So, be gone; / We will not now be troubled with reply: / We offer fair; take it advisedly" (V. i. 112-14), must be taken in context with his refusal to deal with the substance of Worcester's argument, no small part of which is the Earl's belief that the King cannot be trusted to keep his word. For the second time in the play Henry curtly dismisses Worcester. None of this is to suggest that Worcester's view of the King is the entire story or that his rebellious attitude is wholly without fault. But again, Shakespeare, through indirection, causes us to see more of the person of Henry than the close King would allow. What Henry leaves unsaid suggests more than what he says informs.

In the end, Henry is understandably indignant with Worcester in his public chastisement of the Earl for not conveying the royal offer of pardon (V. v. 1-10), and Worcester admits to an attempt to save his own skin by his deceitful actions. But there was never any question about Worcester's concern for his safety. The important question, whether Henry could have been trusted to keep his promise to pardon all rebels, is not answered. The seeds of doubt, having been planted so plausibly by Worcester's statements and by Henry's reaction, grow so that Henry's character is affected as much by what we do not know as by what we do.

As our understanding of Henry comes less from what he says than from what he does not say, our acquaintance with other characters in association with Henry often tells us more about the King than do his own actions. In a play virtually structured around character-foils, Henry's character is notable for its subtly rich contrasts and comparisons with other actors in the drama. Thus the almost natural hostility revealed in the exchanges of Worcester and Henry—appropriate antagonists—is in great part explained by their similarity in cunning, shrewdness, and self-concern. As Henry makes his own comparison with Hotspur (III. ii. 96), we note his ironic self-identification with rebellion. Their argument over Hotspur's prisoners and Mortimer's behavior in battle, however, causes us to be aware of the two men's contrasting temperaments and, further, forces us to doubt Henry's sense of honor when his highly questionable motives are compared with his honor-driven young cousin's impulses. And, of course, Hal, who asserts that he is the "king of courtesy" (II. iv. 10) and who promises when he is King of England to command the "good lads of Eastcheap" (II. iv. 14), contrasts markedly with the present King of England, who demonstrates no particular friendship with the commons and is anything but a "king of courtesy." Because each of the other characters is more open, even more visible in these comparisons with Henry, the foil-relationships are more indirectly informing about Henry than they are about Worcester, Hotspur, and Hal.

The incident, however, that serves most vividly to characterize Henry through other characters is the famous mock-king scene (II. iv. 413-528) in which both Falstaff and Hal play the King. When Falstaff first stands for Henry IV, he chooses props at hand to represent the accoutrements of office, Hal's humorous comments on these objects carry ironic implications about his father's realm: "Thy state is taken for a joined-stool, thy golden sceptre for a leaden dagger, and thy precious rich crown for a pitiful bald crown!" (II. iv. 418-20). The King's regality as parodied by Falstaff and Hal is considerably less than grand, appropriate for a throne that is as unmajestic and troubled as Henry's.

Hal's rotund drinking companion then adopts the broad rhetorical style of Preston's Cambises, saying: "Give me a cup of sack to make my eyes look red, that it may be thought I have wept; for I must speak in passion, and I will do it in King Cambyses' vein" (II. iv. 423-26). Falstaff's role as a weeping king is appropriate to the character of the suffering Henry IV, who, guilt-ridden, grieves over his son's apparent irresponsibility and sees it as divine retribution for Richard's murder. At least three instances of the King crying are found in the play—weeping which derives from fear of his son's profligacy, from guilt (III. ii. 90-91), and, as Hotspur would have it, from deceit (see IV. iii. 63, 81-84).

King Falstaff's jocular comment that Hal is unlike his father parodies the King's earlier speech about Hal's lineage (I. i. 78-90) and prepares us for the King's later chastisement of Hal in Act III, scene ii. Falstaff's charge that Hal would depose King Falstaff-Henry (II. iv. 479) parodies the threat of the rebels and introduces the King's fear, as yet unexpressed in the play by the King himself, that Hal will turn against him. Only after Act III, scene ii (the private conversation between the King and the Prince at court) do the serious implications of these otherwise comic exchanges become clear. When Henry appears in that scene with his son, his actions and speeches are reminiscent of the earlier tavern scene, and their full meaning is underscored by what Falstaff-Henry has already shown us. In short, if we have been perceptive, we already know a significant part of Henry's personality—especially regarding his attitude toward Hal—through another: Falstaff.

Hal also presents a side of Henry not introduced by the worried, less than majestic King Falstaff-Henry. It is the severe, intolerant, no-nonsense Henry IV that King Hal-Henry portrays in his rhetorical attack upon the "villainous abominable misleader of youth, Falstaff, that old white-bearded Satan" (II. iv. 508-9). As Hal reveals to those who would hear how he as Henry V will react to Falstaff and the world old Jack represents ("I will," he says to Sir John's plea not to banish Falstaff), he also conveys Henry IV's reaction to the corpulent old man: "I do," he says to the same plea as the Prince-King (II. iv. 528).

Whether or not Hal and Falstaff are consciously portraying these facets of the character of the King—I suspect that Hal, with his perception, knows precisely how accurate his portrayal of the King is and is suggesting, however indirectly, that he is Henry's son and will be so proven in the future—it is clear that one of Shakespeare's purposes in this delightful scene is to disclose as much, if not more, of the character of the King by this indirect method as we already know by Henry's actual speeches and actions.

The third major indirect method utilized by Shakespeare to create the character of Henry from a distance is description. References to Henry are often neutral, such as when he is called "king" or "father." Occasionally, however, they are totally unfair, such as when Hotspur says, "I think his father loves him not / And would be glad he met with some mischance" (I. iii. 231-32). But most of the descriptive comments provide both a credible and an unsympathetic picture of Henry. The major sources of the portrayal of the King by this method are hardly objective persons. But the contribution these descriptions make to our attitude to this guilt-ridden politician—through their cumulation and by their often powerful rhetoric, whatever their source—cannot be denied.

One of the first descriptions not only provides an unfavorable view of Henry, but utilizes as well the earlier device of character-comparison. Hotspur chastises his father and uncle for having "put down Richard, that sweet lovely rose, / And plant[ed] this thorn, this canker, Bolingbroke" (I. iii. 175-76). The several uncomplimentary references to Henry by his patronymic and his dukedom—he is called Bolingbroke six times (I. iii. 137, 176, 229, 241, 246; III. i. 64) and Lancaster once (III. i. 8)—have the effect of portraying the King as a usurper and an impoverished claimant to majesty. The King's Machiavellian side is kept before us as Hotspur in his several speeches in I. iii describes Henry as "subtle," a "proud king, who studies," a "vile politician," the "king of smiles," a "fawning greyhound." To the youthful Percy, the King is an "ingrate," "unthankful" and "forgetful" of what others have done for him, a man who once offered the young supporter of his rebellion against Richard a "candy deal of courtesy" only later to prove himself a "cozener."

Henry's dismissal of the Percies with threats in I. i (an incident manufactured by Shakespeare) is cited by Worcester as an indication of the King's dangerous disloyalty to his earlier supporters. According to Worcester, this danger makes it necessary for them to defend themselves by taking arms (I. iii. 283-90). As self-serving as the Earl's speech is, its argument is sufficiently credible to make one wonder about the King. Henry the politician cannot be trusted. In a later attack upon the King that is more substantive than any of the charges brought by the firebrand Hotspur, Worcester details Henry's history of broken oaths (V. i. 30-71). Despite his dishonesty, even his treachery, Worcester offers a plausible justification for his refusal to convey the King's offer of pardon to the rebels (V. ii. 3-23), a justification also manufactured by Shakespeare. One must wonder why Shakespeare chose to relate the history of the usurpation and of Henry's ingratitude to his supporters twice in less than a hundred lines (IV. iii. 52-105 and V. i. 30-71) if not to impress us with the plausibility, perhaps even veracity, of the Percies' perspective on Henry. Never does the King openly deny the charges: he merely ignores or dismisses them with disdain.

Hotspur's sarcastic statement to Blunt, Henry's conveyor of pardon, that

> The king is kind; and well we know the king
> Knows at what time to promise, when to pay
>
> (IV. iii. 52-53)

is a fitting introduction to that passionate young man's unattractive description of Henry's earlier actions. According to Hotspur, when Henry arrived in England seeking his Lancastrian lands, he was "Sick in the world's regard," "wretched," "low," an "outlaw sneaking home." He appeared "to weep / Over his country's wrongs," and with this "face" captured the loyalty of all those he "did angle for." More recently, Hotspur says, the King unfairly "Disgraced" him in the midst of his victories and sought to "entrap" him with spies. Now Henry refuses to enlarge the Earl of March, captured by Glendower while fighting for the King's cause (see IV. iii. 52-105). Percy's rhetorically powerful denunciation of the King effectively overwhelms Sir Walter Blunt's earlier favorable, but by comparison formal and pedestrian, description (IV. iii. 38-51), neutralizing Blunt's representation of Henry as a merciful king offering pardon.

As a threatened, conscience-ridden, yet ambitious and coldly effective politician, Shakespeare's Henry IV must perforce mask both his personal self and his political self. Appropriately, the playwright forms this masking character not by means of intimate contact and not directly and openly, but as from a distance and indirectly. These indirect methods of characterizing Henry, methods that inhibit a familiarity with the man, create an almost unfailingly private man and an always political prince, who—to alter the meaning of Henry's description of himself—is "Ne'er seen but wond'red at" (III. ii. 57).

PRINCE HAL

The primary debate regarding the character of Hal concerns his reformation, or transformation, as it has been called by various critics. Some critics, including **Gareth Lloyd Evans** and **Herbert Weisinger** maintain that Hal's reformation is an act. The "act" involves Hal's friendship with Falstaff, his immersion in the world of England's commoners, his seeming irresponsibility and the carelessness he seems to demonstrate where his reputation as Prince is concerned. Evans argues that Hal's purpose is to gather information about the common people, the people he will one day rule. Weisinger contends that the purpose of the act is the dramatic and political impact resulting when Hal gives up this life in Falstaff's world. Weisinger also argues that Hal is an ideal hero, and other critics, including G. I. Duthie, agree with this assessment. Some critics take a harsher view of Hal, accusing him of manipulating Falstaff, of insincerity, of being cold and calculating. He has, like his father, been labeled a Machiavel, a politician who will do whatever it takes to achieve his political goals.

Other critics, including **Charles Mitchell** believe that Hal learns a great deal through his journey in Falstaff's world, and that his transformation from an irresponsible youth into a responsible prince is legitimate and

sincere. Elisa Sjoberg argues that Hal struggles to evolve and in succeeding, secures his right to be king. Similarly, Hugh Dickinson shows that Hal's actions prove that he has undergone a real transformation. Harold C. Goddard attempts to reconcile the question of Hal's motives by concluding that Hal possesses two distinct natures: a free and unique young man, and the ambitious Prince who must give up his freedom in favor of power. For further analysis of Hal's character, see the essays by **Ernst Kris** and **Robert B. Pierce** in the FATHERS AND SONS section; and the essays by **G. M. Pinciss** and **Moody E. Prior** in the HONOR section.

Gareth Lloyd Evans

SOURCE: "The Comical-Tragical-Historical Method—*Henry IV*," in *Early Shakespeare*, Edward Arnold (Publishers) Ltd., 1961, pp. 144-63.

[*Evans asserts that Hal's reformation is a carefully planned event. Evans discusses the two worlds of the play: that of kingship and ceremony, and the natural world, and argues that Hal is the connection between these worlds. Evans shows that Hal voluntarily isolates himself from the world of his father so that he may study the world of Falstaff. In order to demonstrate that Hal is never truly a part of Falstaff's world, Evans describes in detail several aspects of Hal's association with Falstaff. Evans also maintains that while Hal assures his father that he will change and accept his role as the future king, Hal is also his own person who's kingship will reject rebellion, represented by Henry and Hotspur, and political and moral anarchy, represented by Falstaff.*]

. . . The two parts of *Henry IV* encompass two worlds—the world of Kingship and ceremony, and the natural world. The connecting link is Prince Hal; he has commerce with both, and it is what the one world teaches him that enables him finally to take up his habitation in the other. In each world he is confronted with living example of kingship—his own father, and his 'adopted' father, Falstaff, emperor of the natural. Both 'kings' have a kingdom to bequeath—the one the realm of England, the other, a realm of knowledge and experience. Both kings perish so that Hal may come into his kingdoms—the one by the natural order of death, the other by rejection.

In *1 Henry IV* Hal begins his 'education'. No other prince of England in Shakespeare's histories is shown making himself deliberately a semi-fugitive from the world of royalty so that he may more certainly and dramatically enter into his heritage with the aura of man and royalty re-born. The process is self-imposed, and in some measure, self-denying, and one ironic result of it is to set up a poignant personal tension between himself and his father. The conscious purpose of Hal is emphasized time and again. For the present his creed reads 'wisdom cries out in the streets, and no man regards it', but there is more than a touch of conceit, a sort of satisfied self-seeing in his private ruminations through the stews of London. There is much in Hal that loves flourish and drama. He looks forward to the great re-birth with youthful relish.

> If all the year were playing holidays,
> To sport would be as tedious as to work;
> But when they seldom come, they wish'd for
>   come,
> And nothing pleaseth but rare accidents.
> So, when this loose behaviour I throw off,
> And pay the debt I never promised,
> By how much better than my word I am,
> By so much shall I falsify men's hopes;
> And like bright metal on a sullen ground,
> My reformation, glittering o'er my fault,
> Shall show more goodly and attract more
>   eyes,
> Than that which hath no foil to set it off.
>   (I. ii. 227)

Boyish conceit perhaps, but there is a calculated reasoning about it and a sense of high purpose. Here is a man assuming a false face, putting on a madcap disposition to ensure a desired result. The 'reformation' is a calculated effect—its inevitability is a species of faith for Hal—and this self-conscious responsibility is the keynote of his relationship with Falstaff. Hal has never actually sinned—the early remarks about wenching have the flavour of verbal artifice and nothing else.

When the Gadshill plans are made, the whole tone is that of persuasion. There is a strong impression that this is the first time that Hal has ever considered the possibility of an actual indulgence in the nefarious escapades of Falstaff.

> HAL: Well then, once in my days I'll be a madcap.
> FALSTAFF: Why, that's well said.
> HAL: Well, come what will, I'll tarry at home.
> FALSTAFF: By the Lord, I'll be a traitor then, when thou art king.
> HAL: I care not.
> POINS: Sir John, I prithee, leave the prince and me alone: I will lay him down such reasons for this adventure that he shall go.
> FALSTAFF: Well, God give thee the spirit of persuasion and him the ears of profiting, that what thou speakest may move and what he hears may be believed, that the true prince may, for recreation's sake, prove a false thief.
>
>   (I. ii. 160)

The emphasis here is plan. It is not merely that the prince is having to be persuaded to join in the affair; more pertinently it is the sense that his participation is a kind of formality 'for recreation's sake'. There was never a less villainous planning than this for Gadshill. It is no more nor less than tomfoolery. Its 'chief virtue' is the unmasking of Falstaff's braggadocio [a braggart's] cowardice. The action and the results of Gadshill remain carefully within the atmosphere with which the robbery is planned. In no sense is the prince involved in the actual robbery; in every sense he has a care to be disguised—his first words to Poins before the travellers arrive, are 'Ned, where are our disguises?' This prince remains unstained—his committal to the world of Falstaff is academic; he observes and learns. Any doors that might lead us to question the actual propriety of Hal are carefully closed by Shakespeare. Hal lays no hands upon the travellers. Their money is returned, the 'jest' is all.

Even so Hal's preoccupation with this world, academic though it may be, when contrasted with the idealized Hotspur, and in the light of the anguish of the King who sees nothing but 'riot and dishonour' stain the brow of his son, is sufficient not only to sketch the outlines of the personal tensions which are to well up later between father and son, but also to give an ironic depth to the widening theme of rebellion and the need for strong succession.

Yet, because of his self-conscious responsibility Hal has about him something too good to be true. He dips only his fingertips in mud, and Shakespeare is careful to wipe them clean. He has about him the self-conscious pride of the man whose indulgence is very circumspect.

The first appearance of Hal after Gadshill has, however, a different complexion. He and Poins meet together at the Boar's Head to await Falstaff, and there occurs the puzzling action with Francis the drawer. As Dover, Wilson says, in *The Fortunes of Falstaff,* 'Critics have solemnly entered it up in their black book of Hal's iniquities and accused him on the strength of it of "heartlessly endangering the poor drawer's means of subsistence".' Yet it is difficult to find Dover Wilson's cheery explanation that 'the main purpose of this trifling episode, apart from giving Falstaff's voice a rest after the roaring and in preparation for the strain of the scene ahead, is to keep the audience waiting agog for him', any more convincing. The actor playing Falstaff has already had a scene—that between Hotspur and Kate—in which to rest his voice. As to keeping the audience 'agog' for the fat wonder, surely the Hotspur scene fulfils that purpose, especially since in location and tone it takes our minds sufficiently far away from the fooleries of Gadshill to make a return to that atmosphere seem overdue. And if it were necessary for us to be introduced to the Boar's Head and the Prince in order to set the atmosphere for the arrival of Falstaff, why continue the scene-setting so long with this 'trifling episode'? Perhaps the explanation of the scene may lie within the boundaries of the knowledge of the Prince which has so far been vouchsafed to us. He is the pure Prince, the conscious wearer of a mask of very harmless anarchy. Indeed all he has done is to wear a mask—he has not indulged in a dance of anarchy. In this scene, however, it may be suggested that Shakespeare, in order to give some depth of credibility to Hal's sojourn in the kingdom of Falstaff, and to the tension between Henry IV's conception of his wild son and the reality, here shows something more than the academic observer of Falstaff's dominion. Here for a short time the Prince is committed to that dominion in a positive, though still relatively harmless, way. For a short time he relaxes his hold on the conscious curriculum of his 'education', and engages with that he had decided to observe. In short, he is drunk.

When Poins asks him where he has been, Hal replies

> With three or four loggerheads amongst three or four score hogsheads. I have sounded the very base-string of humility. Sirrah, I am sworn brother to a leash of drawers. (II. iv. 4)

In the interim, since Gadshill, Hal has been pursuing his 'education' and, like a naughty boy who steals the dregs at a wedding feast, is as much intoxicated by his sense of sin as by what he has drunk. Hal relishes the 'dyeing scarlet' of drinking, and that he can 'drink with any tinker in his own language'. His language has the flush of drinking on its face, and the repetitive sibilants of alcohol, and he has entered into the lovely world of hail-fellow-well-met:

> I am no proud Jack, like Falstaff, but a Corinthian, a lad of mettle, a good boy, by the Lord, so they call me, and when I am king of England, I shall command all the good lads in Eastcheap.

He has the tipsy man's giggly desire for a game, and Francis is the victim. When he asks Poins to call Francis, and Poins does so, Hal, with that pointless verbal backslapping which is the temporary gift of alcohol, murmurs—'Thou art perfect'. And the jest with Francis is pointless, it *is* a 'trifling episode' in the manner in which much pub gaming is pointless and trifling, and by its pointlessness mitigates the discomfiture of the victim. Even Poins, who has not been with Hal amongst 'three or four score hogsheads' cannot fathom the game. 'Come, what's the issue?' The truth is that there is no 'issue' that Hal could possibly explain to Poins. But Hal is not so tipsy that he does not dimly remember the issue himself. His answer is:

> I am now of all humours that have showed themselves humours since the old days of goodman Adam to the pupil age of this present twelve o'clock at midnight.

Now, in his own mind, he can confirm what he had earlier promised.

> I know you all, and will awhile uphold
> The unyok'd humour of your idleness.
>   (I. ii. 218)

Drink has taken Hal deeper into the world of Falstaff than he has ever been or ever will be again. In his fuddled state he thinks of Hotspur, but he talks of Hotspur in the language of Falstaff.

> I am not yet of Percy's mind, the Hotspur of the north; he that kills me some six or seven dozen of Scots at a breakfast, washes his hands, and says to his wife 'Fie upon this quiet life! I want work'. 'O my sweet Harry,' says she, 'how many hast thou killed today?' 'Give my roan horse a drench', says he; and answers 'Some fourteen', an hour after; 'a trifle, a trifle'. I prithee, call in Falstaff: I'll play Percy, and that damned brawn shall play Dame Mortimer his wife. (II. iv. 212)

This is the same comic-cynical vision that sees honour in terms of 'he that died a Wednesday'; in a few moments when Falstaff arrives we are to hear just such another 'parcel of reckoning' in Falstaff's monstrous fantasies of the men he fought at Gadshill. The possibilities of Hal disengaging himself from this definite descent into the world of Falstaff are, to say the least, tenuous. Falstaff at bay is Falstaff at his most dangerous. Hal, in the flush of wanting to rub home the discomfiture of Falstaff, faces an adversary adept, not only in the art of verbal escapology [escapism], but one, when cornered, capable of taunting, corrupting, verbal sword-play. The great scene in which Falstaff relates his version of Gadshill moves impeccably on two lines which intertwine and separate and intertwine, enfolding in their pattern a rich and total image of the education of Hal, his relationship with Falstaff, and through both a vision of kingship which, when it is seen in relation to the royal world Hal returns to, creates the most moving and mature comment in the history plays. The developments of I. iv, after the entry of Falstaff, are firstly the comic surface where Falstaff and Hal, indeed the rest of the crew of the Boar's Head, exist, as it were, man to man—it is the comedy which unites them; secondly the relationship between Hal and Falstaff which exists below the surface of their comic union and is constantly tending to disunite Hal from the kingdom of Falstaff. Ironically, it is the very advantage which Falstaff attempts to seize through his comic largesse of wit that gradually pushes Hal further away from his world, and actually helps to redeem Hal from slipping further into a state he had vowed merely to observe. Falstaff's great comic flaw is his inability to know when to stop—or rather it is both his strength and his weakness. It gives him his monumental self-glowing status and takes away from him his ability to 'hold' his most illustrious subject, Prince Henry.

When he enters, Falstaff is hot, dishevelled and angry. He rouses Hal to a pitch of anger by equating 'coward' with 'Prince'. Hal is caught on the raw, confronted with a direct image of himself coined in the realm of Falstaff. But the heat of anger passes, and Falstaff's imagination gathers strength. Out of his dangerous rage, the monstrous comedy of his account of Gadshill grows. Under the Prince's swift questioning and frustration Falstaff ascends to the highest peak of his comic dominion. The corner into which he has been pushed, cannot hold him, and there comes what Dover Wilson calls his 'consummate retort',

> By the Lord, I knew ye as well as he that
>   made ye.

There is no doubt that the brilliance of Falstaff's verbal gymnastics during this scene endears him to that part of us which revels in the bright machinations of roguery. Never again was Shakespeare to create such a sustained example of the magnificence of the solitary comic spirit. It rests at the opposite pole of the tragic hero's awareness of self. Where his is self-immolating, self-examining, inward turning, Falstaff's is self-expanding, outward turning, feeding on its own audacity, and gloriously aware of the incredible but magnetic effect it creates. But what is equally plain throughout this scene is that Falstaff is meticulously and unconsciously digging his own grave: his future grows less as he builds himself great. Falstaff's account of Gadshill is a superb essay in the art of cowardice. By the very deviousness of his description he proves the falsity and enormity of his naming Hal a coward. The coward is anatomized here—first his rage at apparent exposure, then his outrageous exaggeration, as if cloud-capped towers of falsehood will hide the earthy truth, and finally the hollow, audacious, magnificent trump-card—the attempt to put himself on the side of the angels.

Hal does not let the meaning of the essay go unmarked, 'the argument shall be thy running away'.

The relish with which Hal accepts Falstaff's invitation to 'stand for' his father the King, and to examine the particulars of his life, is an appetite based less on love of the 'game' than on the assurance of his own inviolable, secret purposes.

The mock trial scene is of very great significance since it is the last time that Falstaff is seen 'in state' with his chief subject, Hal. His reign over Hal is much shorter than is often admitted, and this scene represents a final audience before a long-drawn-out abdication. Shakespeare allows Falstaff to retain the high comic status he has achieved in his description of Gadshill. Falstaff sits on the throne first. But this over-indulgence of his comic craft once again causes a gap to widen between himself and Hal. He takes up his symbols and effects of office: 'this chair shall be my state, this dagger my sceptre, and this cushion my crown' (II. iv. 415). And the Prince's repetition: 'Thy state is taken for a joined stool, thy golden sceptre for a leaden dagger, and thy precious rich crown for a pitiful bald crown', with its emphasis on 'thy', sharply distinguishes comic licence and hard reality. Falstaff plays the game of King-father to Hal, but turns the occasion once more to his favourite theme, himself. The previous swelling fantasies of Gadshill are forgotten, and the new theme is a mocking catalogue of virtues. Yet there creeps into this feast of fooling a shadow of uncertainty, 'If then the tree may be known by the fruit, as the fruit by the tree, then peremptorily I speak it, there is virtue in that Falstaff; him keep with, the rest banish' (469).

There is a cold silence implied between this and the Prince's next words. Hal does not reply to the challenge—his mind has leapt to another world of consideration; 'Dost thou speak like a king? Do thou stand for me, and I'll play my father'.

Hal forces him on to the defensive—once more the shadow falls, and banishment is uttered. It is as if Falstaff is fatally fascinated by the need for an answer. He dare not question, but uses an appealing imperative:

> No, my good lord; banish Peto, banish Bardolph, banish Poins: but for sweet Jack Falstaff, kind Jack Falstaff, true Jack Falstaff, valiant Jack Falstaff, and therefore more valiant, being as he is, old Jack Falstaff, banish not him thy Harry's company, banish not him thy Harry's company; banish plump Jack, and banish all the world.

But he gets an unequivocal answer: 'I do, I will'.

There are no more dramatic interruptions than that which suddenly cuts across the stage at this point. Bardolph runs in shouting that the sheriff is at the door. Falstaff has been left in an agony of apprehension by Hal's words—he hardly takes in the fact that the law stands outside his door. He says to Bardolph, 'Out, ye rogue! Play out the play; I have much to say in the behalf of that Falstaff.'

Indeed he has much to say, but nothing ever again that can gainsay what Hal has said. Dover Wilson, observing that following Hal's words the Cambridge and other modern editions supply a stage direction, *'A knocking heard, exeunt Hostess, Francis and Bardolph'*, notes that neither quartos nor Folio supply previous exits for these three, and complains that firstly, this would leave the stage silent for several moments ('which is absurd'), and secondly the direction is unnecessary since Bardolph and the Hostess could exit at any time during the scene unnoticed by the audience. But it may be said that the instinct of the editors is correct. Nothing could be less absurd than a silence at this point, with Falstaff and Hal left alone momentarily until Bardolph runs back with his dread news. Falstaff hardly hears Bardolph, nor the Hostess when she repeats that the sheriff is at the door. He is still alone with Hal. His tone is still pleadingly imperative: 'Dost thou hear, Hal? never call a true piece of gold a counterfeit; thou art essentially made without seeming so'. Falstaff asks Hal not to mistake his (Falstaff's) counterfeiting (i.e. cowardice) for his real character (a true piece of gold). Hal is one thing while seeming to be another—so, the inference is, why should not he, Falstaff, counterfeit too? This is an interpretation of Falstaff's activities which Hal in the next line completely rejects: 'And thou a natural coward, without instinct'.

With the intervention of the sheriff, Falstaff leaves and Hal does an office of friendship. He puts the sheriff off the scent. There is, however, an attitude of strong decision about him now. He seems to be slipping away from this world of riot. It is as if he is putting his effects in order before setting out on a journey from which he will not return the same person. He engages his word to the sheriff that Falstaff will answer to the charges; he promises that Falstaff will be answerable if found guilty; he says that all must go to the wars; that the money will be paid back with advantage. As for himself: 'I'll go to the court in the morning.'

The themes and issues of this great scene irradiate both parts of the play. The magnificence of its comedy, and the meanings which emerge from Hal's verbal encounters with Falstaff make it a scene central to both parts of the play. On the battlefield of Shrewsbury its memory strikes home with a sharp nostalgia, 'I fear the shot here; here's no scoring but upon the pate' (V. iii. 31). And when Hal meets Falstaff:

> FALSTAFF: Nay, before God, Hal, if Percy be alive, thou get'st not my sword; but take my pistol, if thou wilt.
>
> HAL: Give it me: what, is it in the case?
> FALSTAFF: Ay, Hal; 'tis hot, 'tis hot; there's that will sack a city.

And Hal finds it to be a bottle of sack. Again in Falstaff's scenes with Shallow and Silence, there is

constant backward looking at haunts now deserted. And even in *Henry V* the long aroma of the Boar's Head stretches into the field of Agincourt, 'Would I were in an alehouse in London! I would give all my fame for a pot of ale and safety' (III. ii. 12).

But the suffusion of the atmosphere of the tavern throughout the plays is secondary to the depth of effect the action between Hal and Falstaff, within its walls, imposes upon the flow of the historical action. The comic anatomization [analysis] of kingship and cowardice in their interplay—the interplay between a world of royalty feigning and a counterfeit world which has the greatness of influence thrust upon it by the shrewd audacity of comic genius, the knowledge we receive of Hal and his purposes—all this colours our acceptance of the historical narrative.

The two scenes following, for example, take on a deep irony. The rebellious leaders Hotspur and Glendower, whom we meet immediately afterwards, have no glow of greatness about them. Shakespeare does not make the mistake of creating too great a contrast with the Hotspur whom Hal has pictured in the exaggerated comedy of his intoxication. This Hotspur is a long way in stature from the man we met in the early scenes arguing with the king about prisoners. There he was coldly determined, arrogant, a champion of rights, now he is petulantly mulish, irritating. Hal has seen below the chivalric generalizations of his own father's picture of Hotspur as:

> A son who is the theme of honour's tongue;
> Amongst a grove, the very straightest plant;
> Who is sweet Fortune's minion and her pride
>
> (I. i. 81)

And the proof of Hotspur's other self is revealed in this cavilling taunting youth who rows with Glendower about magic and pieces of land. But, to the king, Hotspur remains the perfect son some 'night-tripping fairy' exchanged for his own. When Hal goes to him from the tavern, he is treated to a long regretful diatribe on his own iniquities—his 'low desires', 'mean attempts', 'barren pleasures', words which curiously fit the Hotspur we have just seen. Hal, who keeps his intentions always to himself, does not break his silence. Henry ruminates bitterly on the similarity of Hal's and Richard II's behaviour, and draws a picture of himself in isolated regal splendour—a kind of altar at which all genuflect in awe:

> Thus did I keep my person fresh and new;
> My presence, like a robe pontifical,
> Ne'er seen but wondered at; and so my state,
> Seldom but sumptuous, showed like a feast
> And won by rareness such solemnity.
>
> (III. ii. 55)

Hal's reply is tight-lipped:

> I shall hereafter, my thrice gracious lord,
> Be more myself.

It is only when the king brings up the name of Hotspur that Hal speaks at length. He does not explain away his 'iniquity', but formally avows his determination to startle the king and the world, and Hotspur:

> for the time will come,
> That I shall make this northern youth exchange
> His glorious deeds for my indignities.

The tensions which inhabit this interview arise directly out of the commenting, revealing power of the Boar's Head scene. The King remains within the dim shadows of formal royalty. His picture of himself as Prince and King seems utterly and pathetically remote from the sharp realities of the kind of Prince that Hal is showing himself to be, and the kind of king he may become. Henry cannot see beyond the abstractions that surround royalty, and his stricken gaze falls upon the possibility that his usurping reign can only be succeeded by his stained son. Stuck as he is within ideas of kingship, he could never understand the practicalities of Hal's reasons for temporarily forsaking his world, in order to gouge out of experience a wisdom about men and about himself. Henry's tragedy, unlike that of his predecessor Richard, is seen to be less the result of an insufficiency to fit the royal condition, than complete isolation from the new world which is being born in the person of his son. To a king who can only see himself in terms of a cypher, a symbol, fixed and ceremonial, and all this ironically meaningless in the echo-chamber of usurpation, no other world can offer any meaning. And so Hal relieves the King of some of his grief in the only way in which Henry can understand—in a formal promise to change, and to wreak vengeance on Hotspur.

Hal has already set his face clearly in the direction of a return to a royal world—but on his own terms and of his own building. Throughout the rest of the history of the reign of Henry IV, the character of Hal constantly gains in integration, while the world of Henry and Hotspur—the political world of usurpation and rebellion—and the world of Falstaff, the anarchic comic, constantly gain a momentum towards disintegration. As the history advances towards the Kingship of Hal, he is seen more and more as a rock of unity, a Prince of total experience, around which the rest disintegrates.

Herbert Weisinger

SOURCE: "A Shakespeare All too Modern?" in *Arizona Quarterly*, Vol. 20, No. 4, Winter, 1964, pp. 293-316.

[*Weisinger argues that Hal is "the ideal hero" and that his reformation is calculated. Weisinger states that Hal takes on the role of the Prodigal Son in order to increase the political impact of his transformation from an irresponsible boy into a good, responsible, legitimate future king. Weisinger also comments on how Hal uses Falstaff to accomplish this dramatic reformation.*]

. . . In the character of Prince Hal, Shakespeare created the ideal hero. Confronted with the necessity of ridding the nation of a legitimate but bad king, a man morally corrupt, incapable of decisive action, and without the slightest sense of his regal obligations, Bolingbroke [Hal's father, Henry] seizes the throne at the cost of his own troubled conscience; he becomes King Henry IV, the good but illegitimate king. To his son he bequeaths the task of becoming both a legitimate and good king, a problem which Hal solves in his own way, a way misunderstood, ironically enough, by his father who had ascended to the throne by paths not unlike those followed by his son. Hal puts on the mask of irresponsibility so that when he chooses to drop the disguise his seeming reformation will appear all the more surprising and therefore all the more politically effective; he deliberately chooses to play the role of the Prodigal Son. He uses Falstaff as the screen behind which he conceals his intentions, and the tragedy of Falstaff is that, clever as he is, he is yet not clever enough to realize that he is nothing but a simple pawn in Hal's game. For Falstaff is to the son what Richard was to the father: the symbol of irresponsibility whose final defeat is the signal for a new order of law and justice. Falstaff is therefore never rejected for the simple reason that he has never been accepted, and his destruction is foretold him in the mock court scene of *I Henry IV*: Falstaff: "No, my good lord; banish Peto, banish Bardolf, banish Poins; but for sweet Jack Falstaff, kind Jack Falstaff, true Jack Falstaff, valiant Jack Falstaff, and therefore more valiant, being, as he is, old Jack Falstaff, banish not him thy Harry's company, banish not him thy Harry's company. Banish plump Jack, and banish all the world." Prince: "I do, I will." And he does, in *II Henry IV*, when Falstaff calls out to him in the coronation procession: "My king! My Jove! I speak to thee, my heart!" King: "I know thee not, old man; fall to thy prayers. . . . I have long dreamt of such a kind of man, / . . . But, being awak'd, I do despise my dream." Yet before Hal can conquer the symbol of moral irresponsibility, the threat from within, he has to overcome the symbol of political irresponsibility, the threat from without, in the person of Hotspur. Brilliant, egotistical, undisciplined, Hotspur possesses qualities which Hal does not have: warmth, love, wit, color, gaiety. But his virtues are defects in a man who has no control over himself. By defeating Hotspur, Hal acquires at little cost the reputation for bravery and daring Hotspur has spent a lifetime in the fields acquiring; it is a triumph of cold intellect over hot passion:

> For the time will come
> That I shall make this northern youth exchange
> His glorious deeds for my indignities.
> Percy is but my factor, good my lord,
> To engross up glorious deeds on my behalf; . . .

Thus, as by a dialectical transformation, Hal is changed from the Prodigal Son into the good and legitimate King Henry V. . . .

Charles Mitchell

SOURCE: "The Education of the True Prince," in *Tennessee Studies in Literature,* Vol. XII, 1967, pp. 13-21.

[*Mitchell offers a detailed account of Hal's education, drawing attention to the characters Hal learns from. In discussing Hal's relationship with Falstaff, Mitchell argues that Hal explores aspects of human weakness. Mitchell also examines how Hal's conception of honor changes through the course of the play due to the King's lecture on the subject and to Hal's association with Falstaff. Hal's view of Hotspur's conception of honor also aids the Prince in confirming his own understanding of honor, observes Mitchell. The critic also notes that the battle between Hal and Hotspur is representative of the "confrontation of true and false honor."*]

. . . By definition, a king must be superior to other men; on the other hand, if he feels only the superiority of his rank, as does Henry IV, he is not qualified to rule; indeed, moral superiority, upon which rank is ideally founded, recognizes no significant difference between the socially noble and the ignoble man. . . . Hal learns that the concept of hierarchy depends upon equality: that hierarchy mirrors the degree of awareness of one's equality to others. Falstaff never rises above his baseness as a man, and Henry IV does not rise to, by descending from, his political rank, because neither is guided by the awareness of moral truth. Falstaff and Henry IV represent Hal's two fathers, the one standing for Hal's condition as a man and the other for his status as a prince; the two extremes of man and prince—baseness and superiority—are synthesized in Hal by his moral sense of true honor.

The two-part setting of the play helps to distinguish the two stages of its action. In the first half, Hal as a man enjoys the life of ease and inactivity; in the second half, Hal as prince performs the active duties required by his rank. That Hal's character is to be reviewed under the dual aspects of man and prince is indicated by the distinction which Falstaff makes repeatedly: "Why, Hal, thou know'st, as thou art but man I dare; but as thou art Prince I fear thee" (III, iii, 165-66). [All references to Shakespeare's text are from *The Complete Plays and Poems of William Shakespeare,* 1942.] It would be unwise to assume that the two aspects of Hal's character are unrelated and that his conversion from man to prince is sudden. Hal's ability to span the poles of baseness and nobility demonstrates the paradox of honor—that he who is highest is also lowest, since he who is highest on the ethical scale is lowest on the social scale (as "servant" to the state). When he is pal to Falstaff, Hal is looked upon as the basest of men; when, however, Hal leaves Eastcheap to assume his role as Prince, he is described as "an angel dropped down from the clouds" (IV, ii, 108). The lowness and the highness exist simultaneously in a true prince; neither unprincipled baseness, obviously, (as in Falstaff) nor unprincipled nobility (as in Hotspur) establishes one's inner nobility.

With Falstaff's help, Hal discovers both his common weakness as a man and his special strength as a man, which together enable him to be the true Prince. The weaknesses which Hal permits himself are associated with Falstaff's physical appetites; the weakness which Hal does not allow himself is associated with Falstaff's comic wit, which is related to Falstaff's flouting of moral consciousness. Although Hal admittedly permits himself the release of physical appetites which express his nature as a man—an admission which proud kings tend not to make—he does not permit himself to surrender moral principles, as does Falstaff. As for the former weaknesses, Hal readily acknowledges them: "I am now of all humours that have showed themselves humours since the old days of goodman Adam to the pupil age of this twelve o'clock at midnight" (II, iv, 104-08). This kind of surrender to baseness is necessary for Hal's achievement of virtue; Hal says at one point, "I have sounded the very basestring of humility. Sirrah, I am sworn brother to a leash of drawers" (II, iv, 5-7). That Hal's "humility" has a moral cast is indicated by the remark that he is "no proud Jack, like Falstaff." At the same time that he is base, Hal is said to be "the king of courtesy," a phrase which competes favorably with Hotspur's "king of honor."

That Hal's lessons in humility prepare him for his role as king becomes clear when he assumes that position in the future; but now his consciousness of his future role helps him to combat the other temptation which Falstaff presents to Hal—laughter at wit. Laughter is, of course, related to the temptation of appetite as part of the appeal of worldly folly. Moreover, whereas Hotspur flouts morality with the power of valorous action, Falstaff flouts it with the sheer force of his wit. Falstaff delights in finding himself in a moral pickle, for the moral accusation offers him the occasion to prove the power of his imagination. His method is to explode accusatory fact with such brilliantly outlandish fictions that his accuser laughs away his own moral accusation. The essence of Falstaff's wit is not that it dodges moral issues but that it meets them head on, producing enormously funny clashes between wit and morality, with the intention not of evading but of marching straight through moral opposition. For a moral man like Hal, the danger of Falstaff's wit is that it may produce moral anarchy, its purpose being to laugh Hal out of moral consciousness. That Hal withstands the great temptation of laughter is indicated by his restrained response to each witty reply Falstaff makes.

In the first half of the play, Hal explores his weaknesses as a man, but these weaknesses are kept in check by the superior moral consciousness which makes him worthy of his superior rank. In the second half of the play, he is confronted with opportunities not to revel in baseness, but, on the contrary, to plume his honor in the public eye; he is protected from that temptation, however, by the sense of humility which he gained in the recent past. Two definitions of honor are operative in the second half of the play, one based on external, and the other on internal value. Henry IV and the rebels conceive of honor in terms of mere rank and mere valorous action unrelated to the virtue of true motive. Since Hal's concept of honor is internal and hence contrary to that of the King and the rebels, it is not surprising that Henry is at odds with his son but admires his enemy, Hotspur.

When Hal returns to the court, the King delivers a biting disquisition on the theme of honor. The King defines honor as a value synonymous with seriousness, although with seriousness of a ceremonial, external kind which contrasts with Richard II's levity:

> and so my state,
> Seldom but sumptuous, show'd like a feast
> And won by rareness such *solemnity*.
> The skipping King, he ambled up and down
> With shallow jesters and rash bavin wits
>   (III, ii, 57-61).

The King accuses Hal of having, like Richard, lost honor through levity and base association:

> For thou hast lost thy princely privilege
> With vile participation.

The King argues that royalty should not be seen too much because its power over the people is "blunted with community." While the King berates Hal for

his dishonor, the King unwittingly subverts his own concept of honor. The implication of Henry's discourse is that he depends so heavily on the outer appearance of royalty, which he describes as "My presence, like a robe pontifical, Ne'er seen but wond'red at," because he lacks the inner royalty founded on true purpose, which was defined earlier in Gadshill's remark that "they pray continually to their saint, the commonwealth; or rather, not pray to her, but pray on her" (II, i, 87-90). Henry contends that the outward royalty of mere rank cannot stand the test of repeated appearance and mingling with commoners:

> Had I so lavish of my presence been,
> So common-hackney'd in the eyes of men,
> So stale and cheap to vulgar company,
> Opinion, that did help me to the crown,
> Had still kept loyal to possession
> And left me in reputeless banishment,
> A fellow of no mark nor likelihood.

But true honor does not rub off when a king rubs shoulders with commoners—a fact which is evident from Hal's demeanor as true Prince and as Henry V. However, Henry IV, who defines honor in terms of outward appearance, cannot perceive Hal's inner truth; he sees only that Hal is "degenerate," but praises Hotspur's "neverdying honour" in spite of the fact that Hotspur is inwardly degenerate, rebelling against Henry's government for selfish interest. It is ironic that Henry should identify Hal with the true King, Richard II, and himself with the degenerate Hotspur:

> For all the world
> As thou art to this hour was Richard then
> When I from France set foot at Ravenspurgh,
> And even as I was then is Percy now.

Although the King feels that base association and greatness of rank are irremediably opposed:

> Tell me else,
> Could such inordinate and low desires,
> Such poor, such bare, such lewd, such mean
>   attempts,
> Such barren pleasures, rude society,
> As thou art match'd withal and grafted to,
> Accompany the greatness of thy blood
> And hold their level with thy princely heart?

Hal realizes that he has not lost honor by base association, but, rather, gained it; his association with Falstaff has taught him a kind of true humility (in contrast to the King's false humility), founded on the admission of human weaknesses, and has made him realize that royalty symbolizes the kind of superior moral consciousness he exercised when he reproved Falstaff and withstood the temptation to laugh away the reproof.

Hal's education in the presence of Falstaff may be interpreted as a progression away from the position expressed by the King in his lecture to the Prince. At the beginning of the play, however, Hal's attitude toward honor seems, in part at least, to resemble his father's. In his first soliloquy, Hal defines honor primarily as the external fact of rank; moreover, the principle whereby he intends to assume the honor which shall engender wonder in his viewers is rather similar to the King's. Just as by exercising the device of contrasting behavior, the King becomes "like a comet . . . wond'red at" (III, ii, 47), so likewise, Hal says,

> Yet herein will I imitate the sun,
> Who doth permit the base contagious clouds
> To smother up his beauty from the world,
> That when he please again to be himself
> Being wanted, he may be more *wond'red at*
> By breaking through the foul and ugly mists
> Of vapours that did seem to strangle him. . . .
> So, when this loose behaviour I throw off
> And pay the debt I never promised,
> By how much better than my word I am,
> By so much shall I falsify men's hopes
>   (I, i, 22-34).

Hal does not "pocket up his wrong" here, but pretends that his loose behavior is merely a "skill" or device whereby to enhance a glittering honor. He attributes the baseness not to himself but to others, pretending that he "doth permit" their presence, which he will "throw off" by some kind of mechanical reformation, suddenly, when he sees fit, not when he is morally prepared to.

In his speech to Falstaff after the Gadshill robbery, when Hal assumes the role of the King and addresses Falstaff as though he were the Prince, Hal acts out, though in a conscious fiction, the acceptance of baseness in himself: "Swearest thou ungracious boy? Henceforth ne'er look on me. Thou art violently carried away from grace" (II, iv, 490-92). When Falstaff, acting as King, spoke irresponsibly, saying, "there is virtue in that Falstaff; him keep with; the rest banish," Hal replied, "Dost thou speak like a king? Do thou stand for me, and I'll play my father." And when Falstaff, as Prince, pleads, "banish not him thy Harry's company," Hal replies, "I do, I will." Here, though in a play within a play, superiority of rank would seem to go hand in hand with superiority of moral consciousness. Hal loves both his fathers, but perceives the moral limits of the one through the character of the other.

When he is at last chastised by his father in fact instead of in fiction, Hal expresses a shrewd understanding of honor. His final reply to the King's rebuke of his past behavior is a comprehensive one. Hal indicates that he will not merely "throw off"

dishonor as he had earlier intended, but will "scour [his] shame" with the blood of action. Furthermore, says Hal,

> that shall be the day, whene'er it lights,
> That this same child of honour and renown,
> This gallant Hotspur, this all-praised knight,
> And your unthought-of Harry chance to meet.
> For every honour sitting on his helm,
> Would they were multitudes, and on my head
> My shames redoubled! For the time will come
> That I shall make this northern youth exchange
> His glorious deeds for my indignities.
> Percy is but my factor, good my lord,
> To engross up glorious deeds on my behalf;
> And I will call him to so strict account
> That he shall render every glory up,
> Yea, even the slightest worship of his time,
> Or I will tear the reckoning from his heart.
> This, in the name of God, I promise here;
> The which if He be pleas'd I shall perform.

As the concluding lines indicate, this speech is informed by a dignified moral seriousness. Hal's prophecy does not so much express a witty boast about exchanging honors with Hotspur as it indicates Hal's moral discrimination between his character and Hotspur's. True honor belongs not to the rebellious Hotspur, who is merely his factor. Hal is now prepared to call Hotspur to a reckoning, just as he is prepared to do with Falstaff, in both cases setting the inverted moral perspective aright. Hal is aware that he has still to earn his honor because so far he has displayed only "loose behaviour." Contrariwise, Hal feels that Hotspur has worked a little too industriously for honor: "I am not yet of Percy's mind, the Hotspur of the north; he that kills me some six or seven Scots at a breakfast, washes his hands, and says to his wife, 'Fie upon this quiet life! I want work'" (II, iv, 113-17).

The humility which Hal has earned through his past association with Falstaff guides him to his present understanding of the concept of honor. Hal is, in short, superior to Falstaff on the one hand and to Hotspur on the other, for Falstaff does not check his baseness, nor on the contrary, does Hotspur limit his sense of superiority. The two extremes share a common moral irresponsibility, for the coward and the foolhardy act upon the principle of unlicenced self-regard.

Hal demonstrates his moral consciousness by evincing a valorous selflessness grounded in a sense of humility. When he challenges Hotspur to personal combat, his avowed aim is not to gain personal honor, but to risk his life to save the lives of his countrymen, both partisan and foe. Even Vernon, one of the enemy chiefs, calls attention to Hal's modesty:

> I never in my life
> Did hear a challenge urg'd more modestly. . . .
> He made a blushing cital of himself,
> And chid his truant youth with such a
>   grace. . . .

Hal also exercises moral discrimination when he observes that Hotspur's valor has deserved honor, but only until the present enterprise:

> By my hopes,
> This present enterprise set off his head,
> I do not think a braver gentleman,
> More active-valiant or more valiant-young,
> More daring or more bold, is now alive
> To grace this latter age with noble deeds
>   (V, i, 87-92).

Hal's martial encounter with Hotspur is emblematic of the confronation of true and false honor. Hence Hal lets honor as reward (which is associated with rank, V, iv, 146) go to Falstaff, who will "follow, as they say, for reward." Hal remains satisfied with virtue performed. Falstaff's allegation that he has slain Hotspur is perhaps the most blatant of all his witty exaggerations: that essential cowardice has slain essential valor. But Falstaff means to be taken seriously (see V, v, 148-56) and in fact has taken himself seriously in rationalizing his sword-thrust into Hotspur's dead body. For the first time in the play, Hal does not confound Falstaff's ludicrous contention:

> For my part, if a lie may do thee grace,
> I'll gild it with the happiest terms I have.

But also for the first time the issue is not a moral one: that external honor which initially Hal had hoped to gain he now freely relinquishes to the kind of man who seeks it. Hotspur's counterfeit honor suits the counterfeit man, not the true Prince.

FALSTAFF

Falstaff has inspired an abundance of criticism, to say the least. Critics tend to agree that Shakespeare's characterization of Falstaff is one of the playwright's greatest achievements. Probably the most debated aspect of Falstaff's character is his cowardice. Eighteenth-century commentary, beginning with Maurice Morgann's study of Falstaff, focussed heavily on this subject. Morgan argued that the "real" Falstaff was a courageous figure, not the drunken coward he appeared to be. **A. C. Bradley** continued this line of argument in the nineteenth century. Bradley maintains that while Falstaff may act in a cowardly manner at times, he is actually not a coward. Other critics, including **Robert Willson**, conclude that in naming Falstaff, Shakespeare intended to indicate that cowardice, as well as gluttony, are aspects of Falstaff's character.

Taking a wider approach to the analysis of Falstaff are critics such as **Axel Clark**, who examines Falstaff's role and power as a comic figure throughout the play. Clark concludes that, by the end of the play, Falstaff's influence over other characters is diminished, as is his comic view of life. Other commentators, including Lois Bueler have analyzed the responses of critics and audiences to the character of Falstaff. Bueler points out that the majority of criticism on Falstaff has been written from the point of view of middle-aged or elderly males. She argues that women and younger readers may respond less favorably to Falstaff than the older male critics who view the "fat knight" as a figure of wish fulfillment. For further analysis of Falstaff's character, see the essay by **Robert B. Pierce** in the FATHERS AND SONS section, and the essays by **Gareth Lloyd Evans** and **Charles Mitchell** in the section on PRINCE HAL.

A. C. Bradley

SOURCE: "The Rejection of Falstaff," in *Shakespeare: Henry IV Parts I and II*, edited by G. K. Hunter, Macmillan and Co. Ltd., 1970, pp. 56-78.

[In an excerpt from a lecture first published in 1909, Bradley maintains that Falstaff is not a coward, even though his behavior sometimes appears cowardly. Bradley offers a definition of a coward, and, after a brief commentary on the history of the stock comic figure Falstaff represents, shows how Falstaff does not fit his definition. Bradely cites a number of examples to support his argument and includes an explanation of why Falstaff ran away during the Gadshill incident and why he pretended to be dead at Shrewsbury.]

. . . That Falstaff sometimes behaves in what we should generally call a cowardly way is certain; but that does not show that he was a coward; and if the word means a person who feels painful fear in the presence of danger, and yields to that fear in spite of his better feelings and convictions, then assuredly Falstaff was no coward. The stock bully and boaster of comedy is one, but not Falstaff. It is perfectly clear in the first place that, though he had unfortunately a reputation for stabbing and caring not what mischief he did if his weapon were out, he had not a reputation for cowardice. Shallow remembered him five-and-fifty years ago breaking Scogan's head at the court-gate when he was a crack not thus high; and Shallow knew him later a good back-swordsman.

Then we lose sight of him till about twenty years after, when his association with Bardolph began; and that association implies that by the time he was thirty-five or forty he had sunk into the mode of life we witness in the plays. Yet, even as we see him there, he remains a person of consideration in the army. Twelve captains hurry about London searching for him. He is present at the Council of War in the King's tent at Shrewsbury, where the only other persons are the King, the two princes, a nobleman and Sir Walter Blunt. The messenger who brings the false report of the battle to Northumberland mentions, as one of the important incidents, the death of Sir John Falstaff. Colvile, expressly described as a famous rebel, surrenders to him as soon as he hears his name. And if his own wish that his name were not so terrible to the enemy, and his own boast of his European reputation, are not evidence of the first rank, they must not be entirely ignored in presence of these other facts. What do these facts mean? Does Shakespeare put them all in with no purpose at all, or in defiance of his own intentions? It is not credible.

And when, in the second place, we look at Falstaff's actions, what do we find? He boldly confronted Colvile, he was quite ready to fight with him, however pleased that Colvile, like a kind fellow, gave himself away. When he saw Henry and Hotspur fighting, Falstaff, instead of making off in a panic, stayed to take his chance if Hotspur should be the victor. He *led* his hundred and fifty ragamuffins where they were peppered, he did not *send* them. To draw upon Pistol and force him downstairs and wound him in the shoulder was no great feat, perhaps, but the stock coward would have shrunk from it. When the Sheriff came to the inn to arrest him for an offence whose penalty was death, Falstaff, who was hidden behind the arras, did not stand there quaking for fear, he immediately fell asleep and snored. When he stood in the battle reflecting on what would happen if the weight of his paunch should be increased by that of a bullet, he cannot have been in a tremor of craven fear. He *never* shows such fear; and surely the man who, in danger of his life, and with no one by to hear him, meditates thus: 'I like not such grinning honour as Sir Walter hath. Give me life: which if I can save, so; if not, honour comes unlooked-for, and there's an end,' is not what we commonly call a coward.

'Well,' it will be answered, 'but he ran away on Gadshill; and when Douglas attacked him he fell down and shammed dead.' Yes, I am thankful to say, he did. For of course he did not want to be dead. He wanted to live and be merry. And as he had reduced the idea of honour *ad absurdum* [to absurdity], had scarcely any self-respect, and only a respect for reputation as a means to life, naturally he avoided death when he could do so without a ruinous loss of reputation, and (observe) with the satisfaction of playing a colossal practical joke. For *that* after all was his first object. If his one thought had been to avoid death he would not have faced Douglas at all, but would have run away as fast as his legs could carry him; and unless Douglas had been one of those exceptional Scotchmen who have no sense of humour, he would never have thought of pursuing so ridiculous an object as Falstaff running. So that, as Mr Swinburne remarks, Poins is right when he thus distinguishes Falstaff from his companions in robbery: 'For two of them, I know them to be as true-bred cowards as ever turned back; and for the third, if he fight longer than he sees reason, I'll forswear arms.' And the event justifies this distinction. For it is exactly thus that, according to the original stage-direction, Falstaff behaves when Henry and Poins attack him and the others. The rest run away at once; Falstaff, here as afterwards with Douglas, fights for a blow or two, but, finding himself deserted and outmatched, runs away also. Of course. He saw no reason to stay. *Any* man who had risen superior to all serious motives would have run away. But it does not follow that he would run from mere fear, or be, in the ordinary sense, a coward.

Axel Clark

SOURCE: "The Battle of Shrewsbury," in *The Critical Review*, Melbourne, No. 15, 1972, pp. 29-45.

[*Clark examines Falstaff's comic role in the play and comments on the limitations of that role. Clark traces Falstaff's movement in the play from his stature as the principal character in what appears to be a comedy to his role as a subordinate character wielding little power by the end of the play. Throughout the play, Clark argues, Falstaff's jests point to truths that other characters fail to recognize. By the end of the play, Falstaff has come to understand the limitations of his comic view of life, in that he realizes that preserving his own life is a serious matter.*]

The Battle of Shrewsbury is the consummation of this mixed historical and comic drama which constitutes *Henry IV* Part One, but it is also a transitional stage in the development towards the puzzlingly different drama of Part Two. On the one hand, the conflict between the comic and serious views of events, which has continued throughout the drama, reaches its climax. For the first time all the main characters of Part One are brought together on the stage. So Falstaff's witty comments are more obviously relevant to the serious political issues of the play than ever before, and the criticisms of the great men and events he sees are often devastating. But on the other hand, the scope of the comedy is at times more limited than ever before, as Falstaff is partly detached

James Henry Hackett plays Falstaff in Henry IV, Part One *in 1828.*

from the battle, though physically close to it; his words and actions, in the context of a battle crucial to men's lives and the nation's future, are no longer infallibly amusing, and sometimes shallow or repellent.

The move from the Boar's Head to Shrewsbury shows Falstaff in a different light (as it does Hal). The evil effects of his determination to preserve his freedom—the suffering it causes others, the corruption it produces in himself—are realized more deeply, and with increasing horror and disgust, in each successive scene in which he appears. When, on the road to Shrewsbury, he defends his misuse of the king's press—"good enough to toss; food for powder, food for powder; they'll fill a pit as well as better: tush, man, mortal men, mortal men" (IV, ii, 63-5)—he may seem to be criticizing the war mentality, but he is also reflecting this mentality, condoning this attitude, even endorsing and using it for his own profit.

Falstaff's ability to exploit every situation is evident right to the end of Part One, but at Shrewsbury he often appears more limited than ever before. He is unable (or refuses) to comprehend the full moral significance of his actions, and he has little influence over the events in which he participates. Though he is the master and exploiter of his soldiers, and though unlike them he understands and utilizes his situation, he is at one with them in being a participant in events shaped by the decisions of the great politicians. His actions are still comic, and he is the greatest example of the savagery and falsity that characterize the whole battle, but his finest speeches are now soliloquies, commentaries; he sees and conveys the comedy of a piece of history in which he is only partly involved. Whereas Falstaff was once the creator of and principal actor in the comedy, he is by the time of the battle a subordinate actor, though a central figure. His significance is great—he may be seen as symbolizing the forces which triumph at Shrewsbury—but his influence over the battle (and more personally over the behaviour of Hal) is slight. His most important comic and historical role is that of commentator. He sometimes seems like Thersites in the battle-scenes of *Troilus and Cressida*, watching, understanding, mocking and fearing the conflict—apparently the very opposite of the royal and rebel leaders, who are completely absorbed in the action.

This impression, that Falstaff is different from the other leading characters at Shrewsbury, is strong in the first two scenes of Act V, but as the battle develops, the similarities between them become increasingly important. In the first scene of Act V, though Falstaff enters with royal leaders, and listens to the parley with Worcester and Vernon, he appears to be quite alien to these politicians. He is almost completely silent till the king and Worcester have finished their argument and left. He speaks only one line in this time, which is a deadly comment on Worcester:

> *Worcester* . . . I protest
>   I have not sought the day of this dislike.
> *King Henry* You have not sought it! How
>   comes it then?
> *Falstaff* Rebellion lay in his way, and he
>   found it.
> *Prince* Peace, chewet, peace!
>
>   (V, i, 25-9)

The prince's remark shows how much of an embarrassment Falstaff is, how out of place he is in a military parley. To act the clown in this situation indicates a complete want of tact, a complete failure to recognize and respect the gravity of the situation. But Falstaff's remark is true, as Worcester shows when he excuses the rebellion with a mixture of misrepresentations, anger and vanity. Some kinds of truth are out of place in this company, and Falstaff holds his tongue until the king and Worcester finish their fruitless parley and leave the stage.

Left alone with Hal, Falstaff (unlike anyone else in this scene) unashamedly acknowledges that his principles in the battle will really be self-help and self-preservation. He can be seen in several ways here: as the honest man, who will openly acknowledge the supposedly base motives that the king and Worcester seek to conceal behind their proud posturing; as the irresponsible coward, decrying honour because he does not have it, while the Douglas, Hotspur and Hal are obviously brave, and honourable in that sense at least; or as the simple (but shrewd) human amongst wolves, the only man to feel and express spontaneously the fear of death, and a complete cynicism about all honours won by defying or suffering death. Perhaps the last view of Falstaff comes out most strongly at this point, because of the sheer nakedness of his emotions, and the consequent power of his expression. When he confides to the Prince, "I would 'twere bedtime, Hal, and all well" (V, i, 125), he is more than merely a base coward: his remark stands out as one of the most candid, deeply felt and universal utterances in the whole play. Falstaff's words thus provide an especially sharp contrast with what has been said before (by the king for instance, whose prayer, "God befriend us, as our cause is just!" (V, i, 120), is a mere gesture, a cliché used to gloss over an essentially confused situation).

This strain of genuine personal feeling and candour runs right through the famous soliloquy on honour (V, i, 127-40), and makes it a very moving as well as a witty and intelligent comment: "Can honour set to a leg? No. Or an arm? No. Or take away the grief of a wound? No. Honour hath no skill in surgery, then? No." When Falstaff speaks of "the grief of a wound", he invokes something undeniably real, which the politicians in their arguments about the rights and wrongs of the battle conveniently forget. Though his final assertion that "honour is a mere scutcheon" reveals the limitations of his own attitudes, it also points to the inadequancies of the concept of honour in a battle like Shrewsbury.

Hotspur's speech to his troops at the end of the following scene shows how inadequate and suicidal honourable ambitions may be. He is single-mindedly brave, to the exclusion of any considerations of his own welfare, or the wisdom of his own behaviour. His imagination is generous, and his words have a fine ring, but they constantly reveal his carelessness, his thoughtlessness and his vanity. Twice he protests that he cannot speak well, and does not enjoy speaking, yet in this scene as always he shows himself a most voluble character and exciting speaker:

> O gentlemen, the time of life is short!
> To spend that shortness basely were too
>   long,
> If life did ride upon a dial's point,
> Still ending at the arrival of an hour.
> An if we live, we live to tread on kings;
> If die, brave death, when princes die with us!
> Now, for our consciences, the arms are fair,
> When the intent of bearing them is just.
>
> (V, ii, 82-9)

Hotspur's excitement is increasing at the expense of his understanding: the consolation offered by the thought that, if he dies, princes are dying with him, he finds completely satisfying. There is no identifiable aim or desire behind his rush into battle, beyond the simple ideal of bravery or "honour". There is a glorious abandon in his determination not to live basely, but behind that lies a simple refusal to consider the merits of any situation, as the pathetic tautology of the last two lines demonstrates. The magnificance of Hotspur's martial vision is born of his intellectual, moral and political shallowness, and bears a close (though half-hidden) relationship to despair:

> Sound all the lofty instruments of war,
> And by that music let us all embrace;
> For, heaven to earth, some of us never shall
> A second time do such a courtesy.
>
> (V, ii, 98-101)

The suggestions of emptiness, desperation and futility in Hotspur's speeches here (they have the same frenzied excitement as his cry, "Doomsday is near; die all, die merrily." (IV, i, 134), on the eve of the battle) are more obvious and significant because they come so soon after Falstaff's soliloquy on honour. If Falstaff seemed out of place in the parley between the king and Worcester, it was partly because his jest contained the awkward truth; now the awkward truths of his soliloquy make Hotspur seem out of place, a hopelessly dated romantic in a new sort of battle, with a new and complicated political background. Falstaff does not dictate the rules of the battle, but he understands and follows them unerringly, while Hotspur, for all that he has an impressiveness, is simply out of his depth.

On the other hand, Hotspur's bravery (and Hal's, and Douglas's, and even the king's—when he actually faces danger himself) gives the battle a dimension which Falstaff simply does not recognize, and this means that Falstaff's cynical attitude has at least one fundamental limitation. Though he illuminates all the corruptness and selfishness of the principal participants in the battle, and all the futility of gaining honour by dying, he cannot conceive that a selfless act may be both intelligent and worthwhile, because he is the most selfish and corrupt participant in the battle himself. He can see that the death of Sir Walter Blunt in the disguise of the king is in a way absurd, but he cannot see that Blunt's bravery and disguise, while bringing death to himself, may have assisted a larger cause, the commonwealth, by keeping the king alive. Falstaff is completely unable to comprehend the notion of the common weal, and is therefore the most thorough anarchist.

This is why he makes a joke of everything, indiscriminately. When he reappears after the slaying of Blunt he jests continually, but the seriousness of the situation reveals the shortcomings of his clowning, more than he is able to expose the absurdity of the battle. He jests beautifully at his own expense, but he also treats the grimmest effects of his own irresponsibility as a joke: "I have led my ragamuffins where they are pepper'd; there's not three of my hundred and fifty left alive, and they are for the town's end, to beg during life." Falstaff's wish to turn everything to laughter becomes more embarrassing when Hal enters:

> *Prince* What, stand'st thou idle here? Lend
>   me thy sword.
> Many a nobleman lies stark and stiff
> Under the hoofs of vaunting enemies,
>   Whose deaths are yet unreveng'd. I prithee
>   lend me thy sword.
> *Falstaff* . . . I have paid Percy, I have made
>   him sure.
> *Prince* He is, indeed, and living to kill thee. I
>   prithee lend me thy sword.
> *Falstaff* Nay, before God, Hal, if Percy be
>   alive, thou get'st not my sword; but take
>   my pistol, if thou wilt.
> *Prince* Give it me. What, is it in the case?
> *Falstaff* Ay, Hal, 'tis hot, 'tis hot; there's that
>   will sack a city.
> (*The prince draws it out, and finds it to be a*

> *bottle of sack*).
> *Prince* What, is it a time to jest and dally
> now?
> (*He throws the bottle at him, Exit.*)
> (V, iii, 39-43, 46-54.)

It is quite common for this incident to raise a laugh at a performance, but this happens when the actors yield to the same temptation as Falstaff: they wish to excite laughter, and give little weight to Hal's words. His final angry question, and his action in throwing the bottle at Falstaff, make any attempt at comical effect seem cheap. Many times earlier in the drama, and often enough here at Shrewsbury, comedy completely deflates a serious judgement, or radically alters it; here the tables are turned, and clownish behaviour loses its power to amuse because it comes at such a desperately urgent time. Falstaff's determination to treat all places on earth as variants of the tavern always has something pathetic and unfunny about it, even when his attempts are successful; in this episode the pathos and hollowness of the comedian are exposed in quite a painful way, because his natural and typical attempt to make a joke fails.

Thus this incident is part of the constant interaction and conflict between seriousness and comedy which pervade *Henry IV* Part One, but it also points away from universal comedy to the markedly different drama of Part Two. The limitations of comedy are beginning to be felt as Part One nears its end, and Falstaff's indiscriminate attempts to make a joke of everything give rise to embarrassment and exasperation. Indeed, Hal's momentary angry rejection of him seems entirely just. Yet the comedy is still a universal presence, a universal influence: even in this incident, a comic view is being asserted. At this point, it is still possible to say that everything in the drama has been subjected to a comic interpretation, as well as a serious one.

Furthermore, this incident is by no means a final comment on Falstaff. As William Empson says, "the main fact about Falstaff. . . . is that it is hard to get one's mind all around him." ("Falstaff and Mr Dover Wilson", *Kenyon Review*, Spring 1953, p. 221) Any judgement of him based on one incident is liable to be modified or fundamentally changed by what he does next. When Hal leaves the stage after throwing the bottle at him, Falstaff immediately shows himself in a much more impressive light:

> Well, if Percy be alive, I'll pierce him. If he do come in my way, so; if he do not, if I come in his willingly, let him make a carbonado of me. I like not such grinning honour as Sir Walter hath. Give me life, which if I can save, so; if not, honour comes unlook'd for, and there's an end. (V, iii, 55-end)

Being unashamedly self-centred, Falstaff is able to speak with a kind of humorous dignity and sanity. He reveals a powerful apprehension of the grim realities of the battle, and an equally powerful grasp of what is valuable. His great instinct for survival, and his great vitality, are concentrated in the cry, "give me life", which might be his credo. His eye for the main chance often seems to be a simple and profound ability to see what is important; his tenacious clinging to life seems sensible as well as shameless, in a battle where all others, except, significantly, the king himself, seem quite prepared for death. Falstaff might fall much lower in the audience's estimation were it not for his unremitting efforts to ensure his survival. He acquires a kind of quintessence lacking in any other character in the play. He endures, because unlike the others he has not invested his pride or his person in the conflict.

Falstaff's behaviour during and after the duel between Hotspur and Hal reflects quite fully the changed attitude to him which has been slowly evolving in the last three acts of Part One, ever since the tavern play. The encounter between Hal and Hotspur has been frequently foreseen since the opening of Part One, and it now seems to be of crucial importance in determining the political future of the nation. Falstaff walks in at the end of the verbal exchange between them, and as they fight, he says gaily: "Well said, Hal! to it, Hal! Nay, you shall find no boy's play here, I can tell you." (V, iv, 76-7) Falstaff, as he presents himself, is simply the jocular partisan spectator at a sporting event. He is the barracker, shouting encouragement to one of the participants; and then he turns around and speaks to the audience on equal terms with them, rejoicing in the manly contest where, it is implied, he is just as much a spectator as they are. But after this he becomes momentarily involved in the action. Douglas enters and fights with him; he falls down as if he were dead, and Douglas leaves. His behaviour contrasts radically with both Hal's and Hotspur's. Hal and Falstaff are involved in comparable contests, because Hotspur and Douglas are almost identical in both attitude and military prowess. But Hal fights bravely against Hotspur, and kills him, thus (as the drama presents the case) assuring victory for the royal party; while Falstaff, to whom both bravery and a cause larger than himself have no appeal, fights cannily and counterfeits death. Hotspur dies for his name; Hal accepts the risk of death for his name, and for the cause of his family, perhaps even for the cause of order in the nation; Falstaff lives, for himself.

Unlike Falstaff, Hotspur has no flexibility, no resilience, and, though he is very quick to see the deceptions and falsities in the images which others present of themselves, he shows no realism in his attitude to himself. His ideals are a delusion, and his ambitions are futile, as he shows signs of recognizing for the first time in the few lines he speaks before he dies:

> I better brook the loss of brittle life
> Than those proud titles thou hast won of
>   me:
> They wound my thoughts worse than thy
>   sword my flesh;
> But thoughts, the slaves of life, and life,
>   time's fool,
> And time, that takes survey of all the world,
> Must have a stop.
>
> (V, iv, 78-83)

Hotspur begins typically by claiming that injury causes him less pain than the loss of honour through defeat. But then he realizes that honour only has value for him while he is alive to enjoy it, that thoughts are the slaves of life, and that life is itself therefore more valuable to him than the "proud titles" which he has made the consuming interest of his life. These beginnings of a new kind of self-knowledge make Hotspur at his death more than a noble but shallow cavalier; they give his end a touch of tragedy, which is deepened when his self-knowledge leads him to a sudden, universal comprehension that life is time's fool. Thus the man who thought he feared death least, comes to feel its absoluteness most, and this is one reason why his death is singularly poignant.

But this is not the reason why Hal is moved after he has killed Hotspur. In his speech over the body (V, iv, 87-101), the emphasis falls entirely on the bravery and noble spirit which Hotspur has always shown. The old medieval chivalrous qualities—"brave", "great heart", "spirit", "stout gentleman", "courtesy"—are dwelt on, while the odium attaching to Hotspur for being a rebel is deliberately forgotten. Hal evidently does not understand that chivalrous qualities have hardly any relevance in this battle, where victory is to the subtle rather than to the great-hearted: bravery is admirable, perhaps, but not necessarily useful by itself, and Hotspur, who has never learned to temper his old-fashioned valour with any modern discretion, has been simply out of his depth. Hal is so absorbed in his role of Hotspur's rival for honour that he is oblivious of these considerations, and as the victor he shows Hotspur the reverence due to an honourable adversary. Then, seeing Falstaff lying on the ground, he makes another speech, mostly in couplets and containing an idle pun, a kind of afterthought following the drama of Hotspur's death, a slight piece of praise for the embarrassing clown whose last meeting with the prince ended in the bottle-throwing incident.

Hal's increasing coolness towards Falstaff is understandable after their last encounter, but the tone of casual acceptance in his lines over Falstaff's body suggests he feels Falstaff's death has come at a convenient

time in his own royal career. Falstaff can now be finally tucked away in Hal's memory as an "old acquaintance", and in this way Hal can speak more fondly of Hotspur, with whom he is now identifying himself in speech and manners.

> Death hath not struck so fat a deer today,
> Though many dearer, in this bloody fray.
> Embowell'd will I see thee by and by;
> Till then in blood by noble Percy lie.
>
> (V, iv, 107-10)

To Hal, the dead Falstaff is a faintly pathetic, faintly ludicrous figure, a fat deer; and the prince, with a rather casual pun, asserts that there are many others dead in the battle who are dearer both in his affection and his estimation. The casual and distant attitude suggested by the use of this kind of pun on such an occasion (when John of Gaunt used wordplay at his death (*Richard II*, II, i, 73-83)) it was a completely serious means of expressing more fully his bodily condition and his state of mind) is confirmed by the final couplet, in which Hal implies that he is being very generous to Falstaff's memory even to think of comparing him to such a noble man as Percy. A simple hierarchy is being established: Falstaff is a mere acquaintance from the past, whose passing is sad but timely; Hotspur is a great and noble adversary; Hal, the conqueror of Hotspur, is greater and nobler.

But Falstaff does not accept, as Hal does, that the traditions of honour are relevant or important in the present battle. Falstaff is not, as one old-guard Marxist critic maintains, a dependent on the old feudal order (T. A. Jackson, "Marx and Shakespeare", *Labour Monthly*, London, April 1964, p. 170); he is the most thoroughgoing exponent of the opportunist philosophy which suplanted the feudal order when Bolingbroke usurped Richard's throne. After Hal's epitaph, Falstaff rises, and proves once again that he is not easily subjected to the kind of neat categorizing and fond farewelling with which the prince imagines he has finally succeeded in dismissing him. He then proceeds to prove quite brutally that Hotspur's ideal of honour is utterly outdated and defeated in this battle fought by the essentially feudal Percy against the successful new type of dissembling politician.

When Falstaff rises, the first thing he does is to crack a couple of jokes, so that for a moment he appears to be primarily a comic figure, following the traditional formula of comic relief after a serious scene, where the lesser mortal comically escapes after the greater has suffered death. Falstaff's feigned death may seem to make him the clown, compared with the great figure of Hotspur, who suffers real death. . . . [The] reasons Falstaff gives for feigning death cast him and Hotspur in an entirely different light:

'Sblood, 'twas time to counterfeit, or that hot termagant Scot had paid me scot and lot too. Counterfeit? I lie, I am no counterfeit: to die is to be a counterfeit; for he is but the counterfeit of a man who hath not the life of a man; but to counterfeit dying, when a man thereby liveth, is to be no counterfeit, but the true and perfect image of life indeed. (V, iv, 114-22)

Falstaff's action has been at least as serious as Hotspur's; in fact, by feigning death, Falstaff has shown that he takes himself and his life much more seriously than Hotspur, and that his intelligence is much greater. He applies the word "counterfeit", in one sense or another, to both himself and Hotspur, but his constant play on the word finally attaches a much greater falsity to Hotspur than to himself. His own counterfeiting is successful deception of others, whereas Hotspur's is the idealistic self-deception which leads to failure and death. In calling his counterfeiting of death "the true and perfect image of life indeed", Falstaff is exaggerating, but his exaggeration, as so often elsewhere, brings out the fundamental value of his action: he is a great survivor, and a great believer in life.

Because both Hotspur and Falstaff are called counterfeits, a comparison is invited between them and the king, to whom Douglas has twice applied the word a short while before in challenging him (V, iv, 28, 35). Though Hotspur and the king are superficially more similar to each other than either is to Falstaff—they are ostensibly the serious characters, the politicians, while he is apparently the odd man out—at a deeper level the connection between the king and Falstaff is the strongest. Hotspur's counterfeiting is self-deception, but Henry and Falstaff both counterfeit cunningly to preserve their lives. Henry's methods in the battle are essentially the same as Falstaff's (except that he uses his followers to counterfeit his death, whereas Falstaff is obliged to do all his counterfeiting on his own behalf), and their motives are also the same: to preserve their own lives, and to advance their own interests. Falstaff is the most thoroughgoing exponent and unashamed representative of the king's military principles at Shrewsbury.

This is only natural, in a play which sees Falstaff as the product of Henry's usurpation of the throne, and the questioning and disruption of national order which accompanied it. Where power proceeds from strength rather than from ordained right, as it does in the case of Henry, it may be challenged by anybody with pretensions to greater strength or a better right, as Hotspur and Mortimer have challenged it. . . . [The] victory at Shrewsbury does not go to the noble, careless bravery of Hotspur, but to those whose valour is tempered by discretion. Even Hal, with all his bravery, is very calculating, and his greater discretion is the main reason why his killing of Hotspur seems a just

comment on their relative status, in the conditions of English political life since Richard's death. While Hal triumphs over Hotspur in personal combat, his father successfully leads the army which defeats Hotspur's rebellion, and that success is only achieved with the aid of the various royal counterfeits who die to preserve Henry's life. It remains to Falstaff, the most unashamedly self-interested character in the play, to set the seal on Hotspur's fall by giving his body a gratuitous and indecent new wound in the thigh. The decision to inflict this wound is inspired by a repellent amalgam of perversion, desire for gain, and barely-mastered terror, and a moment later Falstaff barefacedly claims to Hal that he killed Hotspur himself. The idea of the cowardly, mendacious, parasitical Falstaff killing such a military champion as Hotspur would seem ludicrous even if the drama had not just shown Hal killing him. But astonishingly, this assertion of Falstaff's, like many of his other great lies, contains an essential truth. Though Hal killed Hotspur's body, Falstaff, through the success of his self-interested policy at Shrewsbury, has signalled the end of the outworn conception of honour for which Hotspur stood; the thigh wound both epitomises and clinches the triumph of vandalism over chivalry.

So Falstaff is an essentially serious figure in English political life. This seriousness was implied in the king's speech which began the drama, and throughout Part One his anarchical energy and appetite have been seen as representative of the national condition. These qualities lie at the heart of the comedy whose influence is felt everywhere in Part One, but in the last three acts, as the political crisis has drawn to a climax, the doubts about Falstaff's irresponsibility have deepened to revulsion, and the understanding of his serious political significance has constantly developed. When he rises and wounds Hotspur, the feelings of revulsion at his viciousness and the understanding of his political importance both reach their deepest level in the drama: this is the typically repellent behaviour of the age, amongst those who have won power, and are continuing to hold it.

As the full implications of Falstaff's role as survivor are revealed, the drama suggests limitations in his comic role. His clowning, which has already failed to amuse on one occasion, is only a partial success here. Though the spectacle of Falstaff rising when he has appeared to be dead is amusing, there is at least a partial failure to raise the intended laugh, a renewed sense of embarrassment, mixed in with the delight at his cunning and his great wit. Falstaff suffers from a basic lack of tact: he knows what is good in life, but he does not know how much is enough. He is like an actor who is so pleased with the success of his death that he decides to act his part over again; we feel that he may have been wiser to stay dead, even to rest content with Hal's epitaph of faint praise. It seems likely that his continued existence will only make him less dear, more tiresome and more unpleasant, and the likelihood is quickly confirmed when he stabs Hotspur and then claims to have killed him. The cunning that enables him to survive, and the sovereign with that gives him a quicker and wider understanding of the battle than anyone else, seem more and more directed to sordid and miserable ends.

Other limitations in Falstaff's comic role also emerge at this time. By rising after he had seemed dead, he is announcing the end of the "full" comedy, which up to this moment in Part One has seemed to take the whole world as its subject. Because he is utterly serious about preserving his own life, he is in fact accepting that there are some things which simply cannot be laughed out of serious consideration, and thus he accepts limits on the range of his comic vision. All Falstaff's history in Part Two may be seen as the consequence of his resurrection: he has taken on a new lease of life, on different terms from the old. Though the resurrection and the new life are comical, Falstaff rises primarily as a survivor, for whom life is all-important, and the comment this makes on the battle, and on himself, is intrinsically more serious than comical. The implications of his survival are in some ways enlarging for Falstaff himself, but they are unequivocally limiting for comedy.

Thus the pattern of Falstaff's role in Part Two is in substance set at his last appearance in Part One. He is now obviously one who preys on mankind, as he shows when he leaves the stage, hot on the heels of the two princes, with the avowed intention of "following for reward", like a hound after the hunt being rewarded with part of the kill. But his hopes that he may "grow great", and then "grow less . . . purge, and leave sack, and live cleanly, as a nobleman should do" (V, iv, 163-end) are pathetic rather than sordid. Chinks are appearing in his armour, which once appeared impenetrable. Falstaff's life is changing and disintegrating, with a speed that increases in Part Two; he is still the great seeker after life, but the manner of the search and the life itself are becoming more sordid and pathetic.

But though the scope of Falstaff's comedy is seen as a finite thing for the first time at Shrewsbury, his comic vision colours and determines the audience's view of historical events more directly here than ever before in Part One. He treats everything he sees in the battle as a comedy. All the characters and events seem serious in themselves, until Falstaff demonstrates or discovers some inherent comedy in them. Hotspur, Hal, the king, Douglas and Blunt are all made part of the comic vision of the drama through Falstaff's emulation of or witty commentary on their actions. By not taking anything seriously except his own survival, by laughing at honour, bravery and policy,

he undermines the serious view which everyone else takes of the battle. And by continuing his role as a comedian, while pursuing a highly successful course in the battle, he goes a long way (but not the whole way, as Hal suggests by throwing the bottle at him) towards proving that a man may treat all places on earth as variants of the tavern, and that comic behaviour is always possible and a comic vision of life is universally tenable.

Hal ends Part One having apparently grown up and come of age, but the appearance is more than a little deceptive. He obviously feels that he has judged Falstaff satisfactorily, and can now pass him by. Even though Hal's epitaph over the body of his "old acquaintance" proves to be premature, he shows essentially the same attitude to Falstaff at their meeting soon after. When Falstaff claims Hotspur as his victim, Hal plays along with him, too tired to assert the truth any more, and not interested in doing so. Both this and his previous encounter with Falstaff on the battle-field, which ended with the bottle-throwing incident, can give the impression that Falstaff the dallier, coward and liar is being simply judged and found wanting in comparison with a noble prince.

But such a comparison, quite apart from presenting a grossly simplified and one-sided picture of Falstaff, rests on a superficial view of Hal's part in the battle. There can be little dispute about the impressiveness of his actions. Hal shows that he is capable of mastering a military crisis with wonderful ease. What causes misgivings about him is the increasingly hollow ring of his utterances, as his actions make him theoretically more admirable. He shows bravery spontaneously and without effort, but in other ways he is only acting the part he thinks he ought to play. Ever since the meeting with his father (III, ii), he has been trying to live the part of the young prince going off to war. Sometimes he tries to follow the courtly ideal of *sprezzatura,* of modesty and careless ease; sometimes he forgets his affectation of modesty, and adopts the more self-assertive manners and values of Hotspur. In his speech over Hotspur's body Hal is so caught up with his own chivalrous display that he idealizes himself, and makes a simple, final judgment on Falstaff—a judgment which is immediately shown to be hopelessly inadequate. Hal overestimates the importance of honour, nobility, chivalry, even of bravery, in this battle, and in doing so he underestimates the importance of the cunning, the calculation and the self-centredness which are really as marked in his character as in anyone else's. At Shrewsbury, as always, he satisfies himself by the same arguments and displays that he uses to satisfy others: the private world of his conscience is a kind of mirror world, in which he preens himself, so that he sees no true reflection of his character and actions, but that image with which he wishes to impress others, and by which he is himself convinced and satisfied:

> But let my favours hide thy mangled face,
> And, even in thy behalf, I'll thank myself
> For doing these fair rites of tenderness.
>
> (V, iv, 96-8)

Hal is so pleased with the role he plays as the princely slayer-mourner of Hotspur that he forgets his genuine emotion over Hotspur's death, and allots every part in the scene to himself. His pleasure at the noble part he is playing is no less when he makes a show of modesty and generosity: the insipidity, the lack of spontaneity that showed through his vows after the king rebuked him at court (III, ii, 129-59) are observable again in his earnest appreciation of his brother's soldiery, and in his final act of generosity to the Douglas. His praise of Lancaster is seemly and uninteresting:

> I did not think thee lord of such a spirit;
> Before, I lov'd thee as a brother, John,
> But now I do respect thee as my soul.
>
> (V, iv, 18-20)

His praise of the Douglas is in the same style:

> His valours shown upon our crests to-day
> Have taught us how to cherish such high
> 　　deeds
> Even in the bosom of our adversaries.
>
> (V, v, 29-31)

Valour, one might say, knows no national bounds. The whole speech comes at second hand, and the emotion is gushing rather than deeply felt.

So Hal at the end of Part One is not a simple figure at all. He is pleased to be a hero in the battle, distastefully glad to behave and speak as he believes a Prince of Wales should. But his delight and belief in military action are in many ways quite genuine, as the beauty and energy of Vernon's description of him riding to Shrewsbury (IV, i, 97-110), and the spontaneous anger he shows when Falstaff tries to make a tavern jest in the battle, both demonstrate. Like the duel with Hotspur, the bottle-throwing incident contributes to the impression that Hal's role of heroic prince is partly natural, as well as being a stage in the young man's unedifying search for an acceptable identity. Hal *is* a man of action and responsibility, however much he is not yet able to be that man except under physical stress, as well as one who composes speeches to suit his idea of the part. In making a step forward to fitness for kingship—albeit a temporary step—he has become more impressive, as well as more distasteful. By throwing the bottle at Falstaff, and later on tiredly but gently accepting his lies, Hal has suggested that the tavern moralist is superfluous in matters of national policy. The suggestion has not

even been made explicit, and the drama's endorsement of it is only partial. The view of the relations between Hal and Falstaff, and between Falstaff and the grim national events in which he takes part, is not clear-cut, but it is not a spineless balancing of ambiguities.

Nor is Part One as a whole: it does without "irritable reaching after fact and reason", and is a coherent work. For all the conflicts of interests, families, morals, attitudes to and visions of life it presents, it achieves a unity that does not require conflicts to be resolved decisively. Its ending is more appropriate, a more balanced "answer to its problems", than the spectacular pronouncements rounding off Part Two. It offers imperfect characters and imperfect views on all sides, and gives a flexible, relative value to each of them. All the history it dramatizes is subjected to a comic interpretation and a serious one, and these conflicting interpretations frequently interact and merge. The tavern and the court, the revels and the national crisis, may appear at times to be mighty opposites, but in England after Richard's death the mighty opposites share fundamental affinities: there is no natural order, there are no unquestioned absolutes, everything is contingent, relative. And there is no ladder of standards, no progression to an ending with the appearance of moral and dramatic finality. The end of the Battle of Shrewsbury is just one situation, suggesting some views. There have been other suggestions previously, not necessarily less important, and there is a whole new drama to come, rising out of this one. Part One is a balanced work, finishing with a sense of incompleteness entirely appropriate to its conception and form, and the sense of incompleteness demands another drama to follow this one.

But it is impossible to be sanguine about the course Part Two will take. At the end of the battle of Shrewsbury, the king's hopes of establishing order in the kingdom, and of leading a great English crusade (hopes largely inspired by the fear of rebellion), are indefinitely postponed because of the need to quell many more rebellions. Rebellion is in fact more endemic in England than before the battle, although Hotspur, the most attractive rebel, is dead. Falstaff remains alive, more embarrassing and predatory. Hal's success in action is coupled with a depressingly unconvincing assumption of what he believes to be royal behaviour. Part Two sinks into a great slough of despond as the mixed drama undergoes an inevitable decline. This decline is foreshadowed in Part One at the Battle of Shrewsbury, principally by the change in Falstaff's role. But the dramatization of the battle is markedly different from what we see in Part Two. In the Shrewsbury scenes we see neither the confused depression that vitiates Part Two at various points, nor the allied potentially tragic interest in exploring "the revolutions of the times"—the diseases, illusions, disappointments and humiliations to which all but

Bolingbroke's sons are subject. The idea that all things in life, including the most serious political issues, are subject matter for comedy, an idea which is embodied by the figure of Falstaff in Part One, achieves its fullest expression at Shrewsbury, where its limitations are revealed and a more depressing future is foreseen.

Robert F. Willson

SOURCE: "Falstaff in *1 Henry IV*: What's in a Name?" in *Shakespeare Quarterly*, Vol. 27, No. 2, Spring, 1976, pp. 199-200.

[*Willson argues that when Shakespeare changed the character of Falstaff's name from Oldcastle to Falstaff (the Elizabethan ancestor of Oldcastle was offended by the use of his family name in this context) he rendered the spelling as he did for specific reasons. Willson goes on to show how Falstaff's name is symbolic of the character's cowardice and gluttony.*]

It has been a custom of editors and critics of *1 Henry IV* to account for Shakespeare's change of Oldcastle's name to Falstaff by referring to the objection of one of that family's members to the shoddy treatment of his ancestor on the stage. These editors and critics argue that Shakespeare looked back in history to unearth the title of the cowardly knight, Sir John Fastolfe, which he used as a convenient means of silencing the bitter and threatening complaints of the humorless Lord Cobham. This explanation may indeed illustrate the playwright's problems of production, but in the rush to uncover a source for the naming of Falstaff it fails to take into account, or at least to weight heavily enough, the noticeable change in the spelling of the supposed source name: in Q1 we do not have "Fastolfe" but "Falstalffe." Surely Shakespeare did not alter *this* name to protect himself from charges of libel by the Fastolfe family! On the contrary, I believe the name as we now have it was carefully fashioned to suggest Falstaff's symbolic role in the play. My conclusion is supported by the instructive nature of the comedy/history, and by Shakespeare's recognized habit of stylizing his comic heroes in such a way as to illustrate their burlesque relationship to a given play's main themes and characters. In Falstaff's case, his name, like his personality, is rich in connotation.

In the first connotative sense, the name suggests an image of "fallen staffs," with staff here representing "a pole used as a weapon" [*Oxford English Dictionary* (*OED*)] Shakespeare has thus handily underscored Sir John's cowardice ("false staff" is another possible reading). Whether at Gadshill or Shrewsbury, we regularly expect to hear of Falstaff dropping his weapon and departing in an act of discretion. In addition, this interpretation invites us to conclude that Falstaff was dubbed as carefully as Hotspur, who stands as a contrasting symbolic figure: when spurs glow with the heat of blind courage the staffs of cowardice are sure to fall.

In a second sense of "staff"—staple or the "staff of life" (*OED*)—the name could be intended to highlight another side of Falstaff's character—his gluttony. Falling staffs evoke the image of harvest, a time of year in which the glutton may be expected to enjoy the fruits of plenty while others do the reaping. Of course the irony in this reading consists in Falstaff's use of the grain; instead of consuming it as bread ("Item . . . ob."), he assumes the role of Bacchus and downs his beloved sack in great amounts. Without doubt the notion of harvest and its uncontrolled alcoholic pleasures is attached to the fallen knight's name.

Finally, the comic name points to a favorite Elizabethan sexual pun—the wilted phallus—that illustrates both Falstaff's cowardice and the effects of excessive drinking on desire. . . . Combined with the other two connotations, the sexual pun provides a fittingly ironic and instructive finish to Shakespeare's portrait of a man devoted to fleshly pursuits that are never totally satisfying.

Even if Shakespeare intended none of these connotations, a conclusion that is strongly challenged by the bawdy action and dialogue (see especially the exchanges between Hal and Falstaff in *1 Henry IV*, II. iv. 375 ff.), we cannot ignore the picture of Falstaff, drawn frequently in the play, as lying in a horizontal position. Whether being flattened in the Gadshill doublecross, or sleeping in the Boar's Head Tavern, or counterfeiting death at Shrewsbury, Sir John is a literal depiction of fallen man, weighed down by his cowardice and gluttony. Since these are two vices Hal and the audience must see in their most extreme forms if they are to understand the education of the prince, it is fitting that Shakespeare should name his comic hero in such a symbolic way.

In any case, the literal and historical explanation of the name "Falstaff," which is concerned solely with the Oldcastle family objections, does not recognize Shakespeare's more central structural reasons, devoted to matters of characterization and theme, for giving the fat knight his memorable name.

HOTSPUR

Hotspur has been described by critics as passionate, hot-tempered, and self-centered, among other things. But his sense of honor is the trait that has fueled much of the commentary on his character. While many critics, including **Colin Gardner**, respect Hotspur's commitment to honor, others believe that he is foolishly obsessed with it. For example, **E. M. W. Tillyard** argues that from the beginning of the play, Hotspur is almost "ridiculous" because he is unable to control his passions, including his passion for honor. Many critics such as Raymond H. Reno and Derek Cohen are quick to point out Hotspur's flaws. Reno observes that Hotspur's obsession with chivalry is instrumental in causing disorder. Cohen, while pointing out the tragic nature of Hotspur's character, asserts that Hotspur never shows any signs of growth or change throughout the play and that his death is necessary if healing is to occur. Overall, it is to Hotspur's extremely obsessive nature that many critics object. Yet the passion—characteristic of this trait—and the object of the obsession—honor—are aspects of Hotspur's character that appeal to other critics and to many readers as well. For further analysis of Hotspur's character, see the essay by **Robert B. Pierce** in the FATHERS AND SONS section; and the essays by **G. M. Pinciss** and **Moody E. Prior** in the HONOR section.

E. M. W. Tillyard

SOURCE: "The Second Tetralogy," in *Shakespeare's History Plays*, Barnes & Noble, Inc., 1964, pp. 264-304.

[*Tillyard argues that while some may consider Hotspur to be the hero of* Henry IV, Part One, *he is definitely not. Tillyard comments on the reasons why people might confuse Hotspur as the play's protagonist, focussing especially on the fact that Shakespeare gave Hotspur's character the play's best poetry to speak. The reason Shakespeare developed Hotspur's character in this manner, Tillyard maintains, was to allow Hotspur to represent the positive characteristics, such as straightforwardness and kindness, of Elizabethan Englishmen.*]

. . . I fancy there are still many people who regard Hotspur as the hero of the first part of the play. They are wrong, and their error may spring from two causes. First they may inherit a romantic approval for mere vehemence of passion, and secondly they may assume that Shakespeare must somehow be on the side of any character in whose mouth he puts his finest poetry. For proof of the first error take the frequent habit of reading Hotspur's lines on honour,

> By heaven, methinks it were an easy leap
> To pluck bright honour from the pale-fac'd
>   moon,
> Or dive into the bottom of the deep,
> Where fathom-line could never touch the
>   ground,
> And pluck up drowned honour by the locks,

as the kind of great poetry to which we surrender

without reserve. The lines are of course partly satirical at Hotspur's expense. Hotspur, however captivating his vitality, verges on the ridiculous from the very beginning, through his childish inability to control his passions. At his first appearance he follows his gloriously vivid and humorous account of the "certain lord, neat and trimly dress'd" demanding the prisoners on the field of battle, an account where he has his passions under control and all his native wit has scope, with his violent description, grotesquely heightened by excessive passion, of the duel between Glendower and Mortimer. From this second description (whose inflation gets overwhelming confirmation immediately after and throughout the rest of the first part) it should be plain that Shakespeare held up Hotspur's excesses to ridicule and never for a moment intended him for his hero. That Hotspur speaks some of the best poetry in the play is undoubted. There is nothing finer, for instance, than Hotspur's account to Blunt before the Battle of Shrewsbury of Henry's past career from the time he was

> A poor unminded outlaw sneaking home

till his present quarrel with the Percies. But to interpret the poetry as a sign of Shakespeare's sympathy with Hotspur's excesses is as wrong as to imagine that Shakespeare approved of Cleopatra's influence on Antony's character because he puts such poetry into her mouth. What the poetry proves is that Shakespeare was much interested in these characters and that he had something important to say through them.

Why then did Shakespeare develop Hotspur's character so highly and put such poetry into his mouth, when a less elaborate figure would have done to symbolise, as was necessary for the play's structure, the principle of honour carried to an absurd excess? It is that he uses him as one of his principal means of creating his picture of England. . . .

For though, as said above, Hotspur is satirised as the northern provincial in contrast to that finished Renaissance gentleman, the Prince, he does express positive English qualities and in so doing has his part in the great composite picture Shakespeare was constructing. . . . His fits of English passion are utterly opposed to the Welsh dream-world inhabited by Glendower, while Glendower's solemn profession of being given to the arts of poetry and music sting him into an attack on them that is not necessarily in keeping with his nature at all:

> I had rather be a kitten and cry mew
> Than one of these same metre ballad
>   mongers;
> I had rather hear a brazen canstick turn'd,
> Or a dry wheel grate on the axle-tree:
> And that would set my teeth nothing on

edge,
Nothing so much as mincing poetry.

kittens, ballad mongers, candlesticks and cartwheels, though by no means exclusively English, were very much a part of English life; and Hotspur had noted them and a great deal else with an eye sharp with the zest of the man who adores the solid and reassuring traffic of the everyday world. The forthright Englishman had long been a stock figure in the drama, often contrasted with the effeminate French. . . . Shakespeare does not spare "all the faults" of this Englishman yet he makes us "love him still." Similarly though Hotspur teases his wife outrageously, bringing her to the verge of tears with his rebuffs, maddening her with his offhandedness, he yet reassures us of the Englishman's rough kindliness somewhere underneath. There is no real cruelty in his roughness. And when he rates her for "swearing like a comfit-maker's wife," he does in his own (and not indelicate) way make love to her as well as show with what wide-open eyes he passed through the England of which in this play he is so important an expression.

> *Hot.* Come, Kate, I'll have your song too.
> *Lady P.* Not mine, in good sooth.
> *Hot.* Not yours, in good sooth! Heart! You
> 　swear like a comfit- maker's wife. 'Not
> 　you, in good sooth,' and 'as true as I live,'
> 　and 'as God shall mend me,' and 'as sure
> 　as day.'
>
> 　And givest such sarcenet surety for thy
> oaths,
> 　As if thou never walk'st further than
> Finsbury.
> 　Swear me, Kate, like a lady as thou art,
> 　A good mouth-filling oath and leave 'in
> sooth'
> 　And such protest of pepper-gingerbread
> 　To velvet-guards and Sunday-citizens.
> 　Come, sing.

Colin Gardner

SOURCE: "Hotspur," in *Southern Review*, Australia, Vol. III, No. 1, 1968, pp. 34-51.

[*Gardner attempts to show how critics have misunderstood Hotspur. Recognizing Hotspur's flaws and commenting that the young rebel is "almost ludicrous" Gardner also argues that Hotspur possesses extremely attractive and heroic qualities. Gardner discusses in detail several scenes which highlight Hotspur's virtues.*]

. . . My concern in this essay is with Hotspur, but not because I believe Hotspur to be intrinsically more important than Hal or Falstaff. It seems to me . . . that Hotspur has often, and especially in recent years,

been given less than his due. This certainly cannot be said of Falstaff, whose importance and whose values have seldom been unappreciated—though some critics have had difficulty in explaining their affection for him to their own consciences. Moreover Falstaff, in his astonishing fleshly self-awareness, is clearly a phenomenon to which every modern "bosom returns an echo". Indeed a characteristic fault of some modern criticism is a tendency to put too complete an emphasis upon Falstaff, to make him . . . the centre of the play. . . .

I am not going to attempt a complete account of Hotspur's character. It is less rich and intricate than Falstaff's, but rich and intricate it undoubtedly is; a full and just picture would require a considerable amount of space. Like Falstaff, Hotspur is to Hal both guide and temper. I do not propose to emphasize and elaborate upon Hotspur's many faults . . . — not because I wish to gloss over them, but simply because no intelligent person is likely to miss them. Hotspur is often intemperate, fantastic, self-centred, irresponsible; at his worst moments he is boyish and almost ludicrous. And throughout the play, especially at the end, we see him partly trapped and "placed" by webs of comment and dramatic irony.

It is what is valuable in Hotspur that I wish to talk of; and Hotspur's value I see (again, as in the case of Falstaff) as coexisting at almost every moment with his flaws, his excesses.

Most modern critics, even the most unsympathetic, respond fairly approvingly to Hotspur's speech about the "lord, neat and trimly dress'd", and to his deflation of the pretensions of the magniloquent Glendower. But they are apt to be less happy about his treatment of his wife, and even less so about his obviously impetuous and reckless conduct of the war. As for this famous speech on honour in Act I scene iii, it is almost always dealt with, and condemned, in exclusively and narrowly moral terms. The remarks of Richard J. Beck, who is in other respects unusually just to Hotspur, are representative:

> Honour can mean either a man's self-respect, or the esteem in which he is held by others; to Hotspur, the second and more selfish interpretation is the one that matters. Hotspur may have won more decorations and greater popular acclaim than the Prince; but he is outdone in magnanimity. His sort of honour brooks no rival, and the contrast between his sneering condemnation of "the nimble-footed madcap Prince of Wales" (IV. i. 95) and the Prince's generous tribute to him is both striking and significant.

This selfish pursuit of personal glory won on the field of battle is a limited virtue, the virtue of an Achilles or a Turnus. It is a virtue to be surpassed and superseded . . . Admirable though Hotspur is, therefore, his pursuit of honour is made to appear out of date when set beside the more sophisticated and complex ideal of leadership personified by the Prince, who rightly overcomes Hotspur at the end of part I of the play (*Shakespeare: Henry IV*, Studies in English Literature, No. 24, London, 1961, p. 39).

It should be obvious from what I have said earlier that I approve of the drift of Beck's comments. What I object to is their incompleteness. Hotspur's desire for honour is certainly an imperfection, and somewhat improper; yet there is within it a vital and colourful energy, a manly courage and imaginativeness, and a warmth, which are—if the reader or audience will but *listen* to the words—most powerful and attractive. The word "selfish" which Beck uses is not wrong, but it is inadequate.

> By heaven, methinks it were an easy leap
> To pluck bright Honour from the pale-fac'd
> moon,
> Or dive into the bottom of the deep,
> Where fathom-line could never touch the
> ground,
> And pluck up drowned Honour by the
> locks,
> So he that doth redeem her thence might
> wear
> Without corrival all her dignities:
> But out upon this half-fac'd fellowship!
>
>   (I. iii. 201-8)

Life, for Hotspur, is bold fiery activity: the proud "dignity" of "bright honour" is defined by the contrast with the passive universe ("the pale-fac'd moon") and with human mediocrity ("this half-fac'd fellowship"). It seems to me that, despite all the reservations that one must make, it is impossible not to react sympathetically to this speech. . . .

[Hotspur's] passion, his vigour, his humour, his bravery (in all senses of the word), even his bravado, have more than a touch of the heroic about them. And it seems to me that it is *this*, this tang of the heroic, which makes up the core of Hotspur's character, the central flame in the light of which everything else in him is to be seen.

In that famous first speech of his, for example, it is the fact that Hotspur so obviously is wholly superior to the person he describes that makes us respond so willingly, so joyfully:

> My liege, I did deny no prisoners;
> But I remember, when the fight was done,
> When I was dry with rage and extreme toil,
> Breathless and faint, leaning upon my sword,
> Came there a certain lord, neat, and trimly
> dress'd,

> Fresh as a bridegroom; and his chin new
> reap'd
> Show'd like a stubble-land at harvest-home.
> He was perfumed like a milliner,
> And 'twixt his finger and his thumb he held
> A pouncet-box, which ever and anon
> He gave his nose, and took't away again—
> Who therewith angry, when it next came
> there,
> Took it in snuff—and still he smil'd and
> talk'd;
> And as the soldiers bore dead bodies by,
> He call'd them untaught knaves,
> unmannerly,
> To bring a slovenly unhandsome corpse
> Betwixt the wind and his nobility.
> With many holiday and lady terms
> He question'd me; amongst the rest,
> demanded
> My prisoners in your majesty's behalf.
> I then, all smarting with my wounds being
> cold,
> To be so pester'd with a popinjay,
> Out of my grief and my impatience
> Answer'd neglectingly, I know not what,
> He should, or he should not; . . .
>
>   (I. iii. 29-53)

The imaginative life of the speech—its verbal delight, its rhythmical firmness, its unmalicious mockery—convinces us of the life and the validity of the feelings (circumscribed though they are) which nourish Hotspur's warrior heroism. Shakespeare allows us to feel the very pulse of a passionate nobility. Hotspur's complete lack of the effeminate fastidiousness which he yet so sharply observes is a sign of his manly fullness; his controlled anger is a sign of emotional largeness. And of his sincerity and honesty there can be no doubt. Hotspur is altogether more admirable, and lovable, than the cool Worcester or the cowardly Northumberland, or than the ruthless King Henry.

Similarly, in his blunt humorous defiance of Glendower's magic, it is the passional value, the grandeur even, of his soldier's sense of reality that impresses us:

> Glendower: I cannot blame him: at my
> nativity
> The front of heaven was full of fiery shapes,
> Of burning cressets; and at my birth
> The frame and huge foundation of the earth
> Shak'd like a coward.
>
> Hotspur: Why, so it would have done at the same season, if your mother's cat had but kittened, though yourself had never been born.
>
> Glendower: I say the earth did shake when I was born.

Hotspur: And I say the earth was not of my
  mind,
If you suppose as fearing you it shook.

(III. i. 13-23)

And in the first of the senses with Kate, his good-humoured aloofness, his determination not to be sentimental at any cost, is superb.

Hotspur: Away,
Away, you trifler! Love! I love thee not,
I care not for thee, Kate; this is no world
To play with mammets, and to tilt with lips:
We must have bloody noses and crack'd
  crowns,
And pass them current too. God's me, my
  horse!
What say'st thou, Kate? What wouldst thou
  have with me?

Lady Percy: Do you not love me? Do you
  not indeed!
Well, do not then, for since you love me not,

I will not love myself. Do you not love me?
Nay, tell me if you speak in jest or no.

Hotspur: Come, wilt thou see me ride?
And when I am o' horseback, I will swear
I love thee infinitely.

(II. iii. 94-107)

And of course she loves him for it. Hotspur behaves naturally and Spontaneously, yet we can feel that he is, quite properly, by no means unaware of his wife's response to him. The sudden gentleness of his closing words is not always noticed:

But, hark you, Kate;
Whither I go, thither shall you go too;
Today will I set forth, tomorrow you.
Will this content you, Kate?

Lady Percy: It must, of force.
(II. iii. 119-123)

In fact, then, his considerateness cannot really be faulted; and this warmth is an expression of the animation with which the whole exchange has vibrated. But now she in her turn refuses to be docilely sentimental. It is a healthy and beautiful relationship.

I have perhaps been looking at some of Hotspur's more acceptable moments. Is there very much to be said for him when he is at his most unreasonable? Let us consider an obvious passage, that which immediately follows his statement about honour:

. . . But out upon this half-fac'd fellowship!

Worcester: He apprehends a world of figures
  here,
But not the form of what he should attend:
Good cousin, give me audience for a while.
Hotspur: I cry your mercy.

Worcester: Those same noble Scots
That are your prisoners,—

Hotspur: I'll keep them all;
By God he shall not have a Scot of them:
No, if a Scot would save his soul he shall not.
I'll keep them, by this hand.

Worcester: You start away,
And lend no ear unto my purposes:
The prisoners you shall keep—

Hotspur: Nay, I will; that's flat:
He said he would not ransom Mortimer;
Forbade my tongue to speak of Mortimer;
But I will find him when he lies asleep,
And in his ear I'll holla "Mortimer?"

*Hotspur, Worcester, Mortimer, and Glendower in Wales, plotting
their rebellion.*

Nay, I'll have a starling shall be taught to
    speak
Nothing but "Mortimer", and give it him,
To keep his anger still in motion.

Worcester: Hear you, cousin; a word.

Hotspur: All studies here I solemnly defy,
Save how to gall and pinch this Bolingbroke:
And that same sword-and-buckler Prince of Wales,
But that I think his father loves him not,
And would be glad he met with some
    mischance,
I would have him poison'd with a pot of ale.

Worcester: Farewell, kinsman: I'll talk to you
When you are better temper'd to attend.

Northumberland: Why, what a wasp-stung
    and impatient fool
Art thou to break into this woman's mood,
Tying thine ear to no tongue but thine own!

Hotspur: Why, look you, I am whipp'd and
    scourg'd with rods,
Nettled, and stung with pismires, when I hear
Of this vile politician Bolingbroke.
                     (I. iii. 208-241)

Certainly *this* Hotspur deserves a good deal of the
moral censure that critics have lavished upon him.
He is on the brink of absurdity. And yet his passionate indignation is full-blooded and sincere, and as a
reaction to the prickly and evasive high-handedness
of Henry it is not absolutely unjustified. Worcester
and Northumberland are cold men: for them, self-
control is no great achievement. . . .

There are many other moments of Hotspur, many
other facets—his fiery allegiance to his friends, his
political insight, his yearning for the "sport" of battle, his contempt for those he considers ungrateful or
cowardly, his brave and rash optimism, his dislike of
"mincing poetry", his combination of wide generosity and cavilling, in the way of bargaining, on the
ninth part of a hair, his laughing bawdy talk to Kate,
his warm-heartedness on the battle-field and vigorous
irritation at hearing his enemy and rival praised, his
impatience for the decisive encounter—

    Come, let me taste my horse,
Who is to bear me like a thunderbolt
Against the bosom of the Prince of Wales:
Harry to Harry shall, hot horse to horse,
Meet and ne'er part till one drop down a corse—
                     (IV. i. 119-123)

his gay and solemn heroism as he approaches the
battle itself, the courage and the despair of his last

moments. In all this he is flawed; but in all, or almost
all, he is—in spite of Falstaff's penetrating and valid
comments on some aspects of the matter—genuinely
and movingly *honourable* too. . . .

SOURCES FOR FURTHER STUDY

Literary Commentary

Baines, Barbara J. "Kingship of the Silent King: A Study
of Shakespeare's Bolingbroke. *English Studies* 61, No. 1
(February 1980): 24-36.

    Baines analyzes the lessons that Henry teaches his
    son, giving special attention to Henry's instruction
    that kingship is not simply inherited; it must be
    earned.

Bennett, Robert B. "Hal's Crisis of Timing." *Cahiers
Elisabethains*, No. 13 (April 1978): 15-23.

    Argues that critics underestimate the tension and
    the crisis of the tavern scene. Shows how Hal's
    "political readiness" is weakened by this incident.

Bueler, Lois. "Falstaff in the Eye of the Beholder." *Essays
in Literature* 1, No. 1 (January 1973): 1-12.

    Examines the array of critical opinions on Falstaff,
    arguing that age and gender affect the reader's view
    of Falstaff. Explains that older, male critics view
    Falstaff as a figure of wish-fulfillment.

Callahan, E. F. "Lyric Origins of the Unity of *1 Henry
IV*." *Costerus* 3 (1972): 9-22.

    Analyzes how Shakespeare's use of the lyric form
    in his other works influenced the formal structure
    of *Henry IV, Part One*. Callahan also examines other
    forces that help unify the play, including the interplay
    between words and actions.

Cohen, Derek. "The Rite of Violence in *1 Henry IV*."
Shakespeare Survey 38 (1985): 77-84.

    Examines Shakespeare's portrayal of Hotspur in
    Henry IV, Part One as ranging from comic to heroic
    to tragic. Concludes that Hotspur is essentially a
    tragic character and that his death is necessary for
    any healing in the world of *Henry IV* to occur.

Cox, Gerard H. "'Like a Prince Indeed': Hal's Triumph
of Honor in *1 Henry IV*." *Pageantry in the Shakespearean
Theater*, pp. 130-49. Edited by David M. Bergeron. Athens:
University of Georgia Press, 1985.

    Argues that Hal's character is easily misread if one
    overlooks the significance of the pageantry and
    chivalry of the Renaissance. Maintains that in his
    battle with Hotspur, Hal does not receive any public
    recognition, as he lets Falstaff take credit for the
    kill, and that the absence of this public triumph

makes Hal's deed that much more honorable.

Cruttwell, Patrick. *The Shakespearean Moment and its Place in the Poetry of the Seventeenth Century*, pp. 27-28. London: Chatto & Windus, 1954.

Brief discussion of Shakespeare's views on honor as presented by Hotspur, Hal, and Falstaff. Cruttwell argues that Shakespeare does not indicate a preference for any particular view.

Dickinson, Hugh. "The Reformation of Prince Hal." *Shakespeare Quarterly* XII, No. 1 (Winter 1961): 33-46.

Takes a theatrical approach to the reading of the play and argues that based on this reading, Hal, as the protagonist and hero, demonstrates that "the supreme attribute of kingship" is self-sacrifice, not honor.

Duthie, George Ian. "History." *Shakespeare*, pp. 115-56. New York: Hutchinson's University Library, 1951.

Duthie argues that Henry wishes that Hotspur were his son instead of Hal. Demonstrating Henry's fears that Hal would be a poor king, Duthie shows how this fear feeds into the King's anxiety that, once king, Hal would be usurped by Hotspur.

Goddard, Harold C. *"Henry IV." The Meaning of Shakespeare*. Chicago: University of Chicago Press, 1951, pp. 161-214.

Offers an overview of *Henry IV*, arguing that the two parts are actually "a single drama in ten acts." Goddard maintains that the play's complexity is illustrated by the fact that Henry, Hal, Falstaff, and even Hotspur have some claim to being the play's hero.

Gross, Alan Gerald. "The Justification of Prince Hal." *Texas Studies in Literature and Language* X, No. 1 (Spring 1978): 27-35.

Argues that by drawing on the work of Raphael Holinshed, Shakespeare was able to provide moral and political justification of Hal's behavior.

Humphreys, A. R. "Shakespeare's Political Justice in *Richard II* and *Henry IV*." *Stratford Papers on Shakespeare, 1964*. Edited by B. W. Jackson. Toronto: Gage, 1965, pp. 30-50.

Examines the political and philosophical instruction provided by these two plays. Argues that while King Henry IV's rule was unarguably Machiavellian, Henry was not villainous and actually remained a man of considerable worth throughout his reign.

Jorgensen, Paul A. "'Redeeming Time' in Shakespeare's *Henry IV*." *Tennessee Studies in Literature* V (1960): 101-09.

Jorgensen discusses the theme of the "redemption of time", a concept which Hal refers to in a soliloquy. Jorgensen argues that in the past, other critics have failed to understand what Hal meant by redeeming

time and that if they had paid attention to Elizabethan religious literature they would have realized that redeeming time does not refer to making up lost time.

Lawlor, John. "Appearance and Reality." *Tragic Sense in Shakespeare*. London: Chatto & Windus, 1960, pp. 17-44.

Explores the symmetrical nature and the patterns of reversal in the parent/child relationships in the two parts of *Henry IV*. Argues that these relationships highlight the discrepancies between appearance and reality within the plays.

Maclean, Hugh. "Time and Horsemanship in Shakespeare's Histories." *University of Toronto Quarterly* XXXV (October-July 1965-66): 229-45.

Maclean assesses the views of time held by the primary characters in the play. Maclean also shows how a character's horsemanship supports his (Maclean's) assessment of the character's view of time. For example, Hotspur is, in a sense, "overmaster[ed]" by the horse that carries him a way. Similarly, time is "using him up."

Morgann, Maurice. "An Essay on the Dramatic Character of Sir John Falstaff." London: T. Davies, 1777. Reprinted in *Shakespearian Criticism*. Edited by Daniel A. Fineman. Oxford: Clarendon Press, 1972, 444 p.

Offers one of the earliest defenses of Falstaff's character. Argues that Falstaff was not a coward.

Reese, M. M. "Shakespeare's England: *Henry IV*." *The Cease of Majesty: A Study of Shakespeare's History Plays*, pp. 286-317. London: Edward Arnold (Publishers) Ltd., 1961.

Reese focusses on Henry's failure as a king and as a father. The critic shows how Henry is unable to be the peaceful king he wants to be and how he fails to control the rebels who helped him claim the throne. Reese goes on to argue that Henry judges others by their appearance which results in his misunderstanding and underestimation of Hal, Hotspur, and Falstaff.

Reno, Raymond. "Hotspur: The Integration of Character and Theme." *Renaissance Papers* (April 1962): 17-26.

Argues that Hotspur represents disorder and reflects the disorder of the kingdom.

Rogers, Carmen. "The Renaissance Code of Honor in Shakespeare's *Henry IV, Part I*." *The Shakespeare Newsletter* IV, No. 1 (February 1954): 8.

In this summary of a paper delivered at the 1953 South Atlantic Modern Language Association Meeting, Rogers argues that Hal and Hotspur represent contrasting views of honor, with Hal representing "true" honor, and Hotspur representing "false" honor. Rogers also states that Falstaff offers commentary on false honor.

Rowse, A. L. "The First Part of *King Henry IV.*" In *Prefaces to Shakespeare's Plays*, pp. 49-53. London: Orbis, 1984.

> Offers an overview of the play, providing background information as well as a discussion of the play's plot and major characters.

Siegel, Paul N. "Shakespeare and the Neo-Chivalric Cult of Honor." *Centennial Review* 8 (1964): 39-70.

> Argues that Hotspur is devoted to a sense of honor based on chivalry, and seeks honor through revenge, whereas Hal strives toward "Christian humanism" in which honor is based on virtue and patriotism.

Sjoberg, Elisa. "From Madcap Prince to King: The Evolution of Prince Hal." *Shakespeare Quarterly* XX, No. 1 (Winter 1969): 11-16.

> Maintains that Hal is never fully "madcap," that is, he never joins in Falstaff's exploits wholeheartedly; rather, he is secretly preparing to be king all along.

Stribrny, Zdenek. "The Idea and Image of Time in Shakespeare's Second Historical Tetralogy." *Shakespeare Jahrbuch* III (1975): 51-66.

> Stribrny examines the references to time within the play and attempts to show the significance of these references. He also comments on the use of time by the principal characters.

Vickers, Brian. *The Artistry of Shakespeare's Prose*. London: Methuen, 1968, pp. 1-51, 89-141.

> Compares the use of prose and verse by the characters in *Henry IV*.

Wilson, John Dover. "The Political Background of Shakespeare's Richard II and Henry IV." *Shakespeare Jahrbuch* 75 (1939): 36-51.

> Discusses the influence of Elizabethan attitudes and opinions on Shakespeare's historical and political views and argues that Henry is more of a "tragic figure" than a villain.

———. *The Fortunes of Falstaff*. Cambridge: Cambridge University Press, 1964, 143 p.

> Offers a thorough examination of the character of Falstaff and his influence over and relationship with Prince Hal.

Zeeveld, Gordon. "'Food for Powder'—'Food for Worms?'" *Shakespeare Quarterly* 3 (1952): 249-53.

> Argues that honor is the theme of *Henry IV, Part One*, and demonstrates the views of honor held by Falstaff, Hal, and Hotspur.

Media Adaptations

Henry IV, Part I. University of Michigan, 1961.

> Depicts England as a society split by civil war and the Prince of Wales as a young man preparing to become the next king. Distributed by Film Video Library. 29 minutes.

Henry IV, Part I. Cedric Messina, Dr. Jonathan Miller, BBC, 1980.

> Prince Hal, heir to the throne, appears to be wasting his youth in the company of the drunkard, Falstaff. Price Hal redeems himself at the battle of Shrewsbury, where the tension between King Henry IV and the rebels has come to a head. Part of the "Shakespeare Plays" series. Distributed by Ambrose Video Publishing, Inc. 147 minutes.

Henry IV, Part I: Act II, Scene IV; Act V, Scene IV. Seabourne Enterprises Ltd., 1971.

> Portrayal of these scenes enables students to focus on the atmosphere and theme of the play. Distributed by Phoenix/BFA Films. 17 minutes.

HENRY V

INTRODUCTION

It is widely agreed that *Henry V* was written in 1599. This date is based on what is generally perceived as a topical allusion in the play; Gerard Langbaine, writing in 1691, was the first to suggest that the reference to "the general of our gracious Empress" in the Chorus preceding Act V is an allusion to the Earl of Essex, who led an English expedition to put down an Irish rebellion in March of 1599. Essex and his men returned to London in disgrace on September 28 of that same year, for the Irish campaign was a humiliating failure. Most modern scholars endorse the thesis that the description of a triumphant general "from Ireland coming/Bringing rebellion broached on his sword" (Chorus, V, 31-2)—if indeed it is a reference to Essex—would have been terribly inappropriate after the Earl's actual return; thus, they conclude that Shakespeare must have composed *Henry V* sometime between March and early September 1599. There is no record of a performance of *Henry V* before January 7, 1605, when it was presented at Court by the King's Majesty's Players.

Most modern critics maintain that there is strong evidence that Shakespeare consulted both Raphael Holinshed's *Chronicles of England, Scotlande, and Irelande* (1577; 1587) and Edward Hall's *The Union of the Two Noble and Illustre Famelies of Lancastre and York* (2d ed., 1548) as sources for *Henry V*. Commentators note that such passages as Canterbury's Salic law speech in Act I, Scene ii is a paraphrase in verse of Holinshed's narrative of this episode, with only minimal variations from the original. On the other hand, Shakespeare made no reference to many events that appear in Holinshed's and Hall's accounts of the reign of Henry V; in addition, the dramatist implied only a short passage of time between Agincourt and the achievement of a treaty with France, when in fact the two were separated by a period of nearly four years. A lost and anonymous play from the 1580s, *The Famous Victories of Henry the Fifth*, survives only in a corrupt edition of 1598, so that it has proved difficult to determine the degree of Shakespeare's familiarity with this work. However, several critics have noticed parallels between Shakespeare's *Henry V* and *The Famous Victories*, including similarities in structure, the prominence in each of the Dauphin's gift of tennis balls to Henry, and the inclusion in both of a wooing scene between Henry and Katherine.

Henry V has been praised by many scholars as a vigorous portrayal of one of England's most popular national heroes. While the central issue for critics has been the character of the king and whether he represents Shakespeare's ideal ruler, modern commentary has increasingly explored both Henry's positive and negative attributes. Although the personality of the king has attracted significant criticism, commentators have also shown renewed interest in Shakespeare's attitude toward patriotism and war, his use of language and imagery, the absence of Falstaff, and the play's epic elements, particularly Shakespeare's use of the Chorus.

PRINCIPAL CHARACTERS

(in order of appearance)

Chorus: The presenter of the dramatic action. The Chorus begins the play by apologizing to the audience for the inadequacies of the stage. (See **Epic Elements** *in the* **PRINCIPAL TOPICS** *section.*)

The Archbishop of Canterbury and the Bishop of Ely: In order to keep their land, they counsel Henry to wage war on France.

King Henry V: Known as Prince Hal in *Henry IV Parts 1 and 2*, Henry has recently acquired the title of king. He is concerned about gaining his subjects' loyalty, and decides to wage war on France in order to "busy giddy minds with foreign quarrels" and quiet rebellion at home. (See **Henry** *in the* **CHARACTER STUDIES** *section.*)

The Duke of Clarence, the Duke of Gloucester, and the Duke of Bedford: Henry's brothers.

The Duke of Exeter: Henry's uncle. He was the half-brother of Henry IV.

The Earl of Huntingdon, the Earl of Salisbury, the Earl of Warwick, and the Earl of Westmorland: Leaders of the English forces in France.

Pistol, Nym, and Bardolph: The three are part of the old Boar's Head Tavern group from *Henry IV, Part One* and *Part Two*. In *Henry V*, they have become camp-followers, cheaters, and thieves in the English army in France.

Hostess: Formerly Nell Quickly, she is now the wife of Pistol. She tells Pistol, Nym, and Bardolph of Falstaff's death.

A Boy: Falstaff's page; attends Pistol, Nym and Bardolph in France.

Richard, Earl of Cambridge; Henry, Lord Scroop of Masham; and Sir Thomas Grey: English traitors who conspire with the French against the life of Henry V. Soon after he discovers the conspiracy, Henry sentences them to death.

Charles VI: King of France.

Lewis, the Dauphin: Eldest son of King Charles and Queen Isabel. The Dauphin continuously overestimates himself and underestimates Henry V and the English army, with disastrous consequences for the French.

The Constable of France, the Duke of Berry, the Duke of Britain, the Duke of Orleans, and the Duke of Bourbon: Leaders of the French army at the Battle of Agincourt.

Fluellen: A Welsh captain in the English army. Fluellen helps overtake the French city of Harfleur.

Sir Thomas Erpingham and Captain Gower: English officers in Henry's army.

Jamy: A Scots captain in the English army. Jamy, along with Fluellen and Macmorris, captures the city of Harfleur.

Macmorris: An Irish captain in the English army. Macmorris bravely contributes to the victory at Harfleur.

The Governor of Harfleur: After failing to receive help from the Dauphin, the Governor yields his city to the English, who occupy it and defend it against the French.

Katherine: Daughter of King Charles and Queen Isabel. She eventually marries Henry to restore peace to France and unite the two countries.

Alice: Waiting-lady attending Katherine. Because she has been to England and has some familiarity with the language, she serves as Katherine's instructor and interpreter.

Montjoy: A French herald. He brings messages to Henry from Charles first demanding Henry's surrender, then later acknowledging Henry's victory.

Lord Rambures and the Earl of Grandpré: Noblemen in the French army.

John Bates, Alexander Court, and Michael Williams: Common soldiers in the English army. They talk with Henry the night before Agincourt as he wanders throughout the camp disguised, and Williams argues with Henry over the king's responsibility for his men.

The Duke of York: Henry's cousin.

Isabel: Queen of France.

The Duke of Burgundy: Acts as peacemaker between France and England.

PLOT SYNOPSIS

Act I: The Archbishop of Canterbury, in light of a bill that would confiscate half of the church's wealth, explains to the Bishop of Ely that he has made an offer to the king "upon our spiritual conviction" to make a substantial donation should the king decide to go to war with France. Canterbury and Ely then meet with Henry and several of his advisors to discuss Henry's legal claim to the French throne. Canterbury advises Henry to wage war on France and take back the crown which (according to Canterbury) legally belongs to Henry, and the king makes plans to attack France. His cause is strengthened when messengers sent by the Dauphin arrive. The French ambassador asserts that Henry has no claim over France and presents him with an insulting gift of tennis balls. Henry becomes angry and tells the ambassador that the war between France and England is now the Dauphin's responsibility.

Act II: In Southampton, Henry consults with three of his officers— Scroop, Cambridge, and Grey—who have conspired with the French to assassinate him. Henry instructs Scroop to release a soldier that was arrested earlier for treason, but Scroop advises Henry to punish the soldier as an example to others. Henry then confronts the traitors with their own crime and sentences them to death. Meanwhile, the Hostess relates Falstaff's final moments to Nym, Bardolph, and Pistol before the three leave for France. In scene v, Exeter visits the French court with a message from Henry to surrender the throne. The Dauphin, confident that Henry is "a vain, giddy, shallow, humorous youth," insists that they will not surrender.

Act III: Henry, rejecting an offer made by King Charles of his daughter Katherine and "some petty and unprofitable dukedoms," continues his assault against France. The Governor of Harfleur surrenders his city to the English army, and Henry instructs Exeter to occupy the city but to show mercy to the residents. The French King, Dauphin, Duke of Britain, and Constable of France meet to discuss Henry's invasion, confidently concluding that he will be no match for their full army. A French herald approaches Henry with a message from Charles urging his surrender, but Henry, while admitting his army is weak and small, vows to continue on and prepares for the next morning's battle at Agincourt.

Act IV: On the eve of Agincourt, Henry, disguised in a cloak, wanders through the English camp and talks to several of the soldiers. Henry argues with Williams after he expresses doubt in the king's cause and his concern for his soldiers; after Williams leaves, Henry offers a prayer for the courage and safety of his men. The next morning, the French commanders confidently discuss their coming victory, while the English leaders simultaneously lament their impending doom. Henry then gives his famous "Crispin Day" speech, in which he talks of the glory that each warrior will receive if they win the battle. Off stage, the English army surprisingly takes over the French warriors, and King Charles sends a message to Henry asking for mercy and declaring him the victor.

Act V: Henry and his officers join Charles, Isabel, Katherine, and the Duke of Burgundy to finalize the peace treaty. He meets separately with Katherine and tries to "woo" her, and she finally agrees to marry him in order to restore peace to France. King Charles then crowns Henry King of France.

PRINCIPAL TOPICS

Kingship

Henry establishes his right to kingship by fulfilling the qualities required of a true king in several different ways. He focuses on both securing his right to the English crown and capturing the French throne. He follows the advice given to him by his father at the end of *Henry IV, Part Two,* to "busy giddy minds with foreign quarrels." He accomplishes this task by waging war on France and asserting his claim to the French throne, which was denied his great-great-grandmother because of the Salic law which made succession through the female line illegal. The war against France establishes both Henry's legal and moral right to the throne; by discrediting the Salic law and defeating the French army Henry captures the crown, and by accepting responsibility and showing concern for his subjects he earns the ethical right to kingship as well.

Henry's moral growth and acceptance of his role as king is seen throughout the play. Some of the characteristics of kingship include the king's relationship to his counselors, his divinity, his valid succession, and the burden of kingship. As king, Henry serves as the link between personal order and political unity and is required to show complete dedication to his office. He cannot allow selfishness or weakness to interfere with his duties as king. Most critics agree that although Henry struggles to achieve a balance between the demands of the crown and his own personal desires, by the end of the play he accepts his role and learns to integrate his humanity.

Language and Imagery

While analysis of the language in *Henry V* has yielded a variety of critical interpretations, most scholars concur that the kind of rhetoric used makes a significant contribution to the play's theme, tone, and meaning. Some critics point to the strenuous effort that the language requires of its speaker and requests of its audience and how this effort relates to the atmosphere of activity found in the play. Still others focus on the disputative tone of the language and its parallel to the dominant theme of war. This mode of speech can be traced throughout the play, as it begins with a tone of agreement (the choric appeal to English nationalism, the request for cooperation between the performer and the audience, and the first scenes showing the church and state working together), moves to dispute and war, and then concludes with a return to peace. Criticism of the imagery in *Henry V* also concentrates on the transition to war, particularly through Shakespeare's use of death imagery.

Critics have often debated whether the language of *Henry V* equals that found in the first three plays of the tetralogy. A number of scholars contend that the language is flatter and less powerful than that of the previous plays. However, others maintain that because the prose is so natural and deceptively close to common speech, the depth and artistry of the language is more subtle and no less artful than in the more prominent speeches.

Epic Elements

Shakespeare's use of epic elements in *Henry V* has elicited much critical attention. By far the most panoramic of his plays, *Henry V* dramatizes an epic theme and celebrates a legendary hero. According to several scholars, the play therefore fulfills most of the formal requirements of classical epic: its hero is of national significance; it emphasizes destiny and the will of God; its action is impressive in scale and centers upon war; and it includes a narrator, an invocation to the Muse, a large number of warriors, battle taunts and challenges, and other traditional epic devices. Most commentators agree that Shakespeare's use of epic elements contributes significantly to the success of the play, stating that an epic drama was the only fitting way to celebrate the noble deeds of Henry V.

Scholars repeatedly focus on the role of the Chorus in exposing the limitations of the Elizabethan stage. Many critics remark that the function of the Chorus is to apologise for the unsuitability of the stage in depicting the grandeur of an epic. However, other commentators contend that Shakespeare's audience would never have expected the kind of cinematic "realism" that the Chorus makes apology for lacking. Though the Chorus fulfills several functions as narrator—creating atmosphere, explaining lapses of time and shifts in locale, apologizing for the limitations of the theater—its most important function is to evoke an epic mood. The Chorus also creates structural unity in the play itself by building narrative bridges between the five acts. The play's choric prologues have similarly received critical praise for their eloquence and contribution to the epic tone of the play.

Patriotism and War

Many twentieth-century critics have explored the pervasive concern with war and patriotism in *Henry V*. Some commentators contend that the play is primarily concerned with the price of patriotism, arguing that Henry finally becomes controlled by the role he has assumed. The interaction between structure and theme can be seen in Shakespeare's development throughout the three central movements of the plot: the preparation for war, the combat itself, and the concluding of peace. In addition, scholars have praised Shakespeare's accurate portrayal of Renaissance warfare through his use of specific details such as the slaughter of the prisoners and threats of plundering, sacking, and burning.

CHARACTER STUDIES

Henry V

A majority of modern critics have concentrated on the character of Henry V and have been divided over whether Shakespeare intended to portray Henry as an ideal monarch and military hero or as a ruthless plotter. Many critics condemn Henry for his self-interestedness, brutality, and lack of emotion, and note Henry's tendency to manipulate his environment for his benefit. For example, in Act I, Henry places the responsibility of the war with France on both the church ("For God doth know how many

now in health/Shall drop their blood in approbation/Of what your reverence shall incite us to") and the Dauphin ("his soul/Shall stand sore charged for the wasteful vengeance/That shall fly"), completely evading his own role in the decision. However, some modern commentators praise him for his piety, heroism, and statesmanship, as he matures and learns to care for his subjects.

One of the most significant issues debated by commentators remains whether Henry embodies Shakespeare's ideal king. Some critics cite the use of irony and death imagery in the play as indicative of Shakespeare's lack of compassion for the central character; however, other scholars maintain that Shakespeare sought to present Henry as the ideal hero, one who reflects the Elizabethan notion of a perfect monarch.

Falstaff

Although Falstaff plays a significant role in the Henry IV plays, he never appears in *Henry V*. The last act of *Henry IV, Part Two* contains what is often referred to as "the rejection scene." The scene takes place during a royal procession in which Hal (as Henry V was formerly known), who has recently been crowned king, is approached by Falstaff. When Falstaff calls out to his friend, Hal replies, "I know thee not, old man." Although critics debate the implications of this scene, many feel that Hal's rejection of Falstaff is motivated by his understanding of his responsibilities as king, and the knowledge that in order to fulfill his duties, he must leave behind the friends and activities of his youth. The epilogue of *Henry IV, Part Two* tells the audience that Falstaff will return in *Henry V*, but he never does.

Falstaff's only presence in *Henry V* is Mistress Quickly's report of his death. She tells Nym, Pistol, and Bardolph that "The King hath killed his heart," and it appears that that is exactly what has happened. While most critics agree that Falstaff had to be removed from the play in order for Henry to mature into his position as king, they also concur that his absence from the play is disappointing.

CONCLUSION

Critics continue to focus their attention on the character of Henry V. While many commentators view him as a self-centered, ruthless leader, several have praised his heroism and his maturation throughout the play. Although Henry has attracted the majority of critical study, modern scholars have also concentrated on the epic elements, the absence of Falstaff, and the language and imagery of *Henry V*, as well as how each contributes to the tone of the play.

(See also *Shakespearean Criticism*, Vols. 5, 14, and 30)

OVERVIEWS

E. F. C. Ludowyk

SOURCE: "*Henry V*," in *Understanding Shakespeare*, Cambridge at the University Press, 1962, pp. 144-71.

[*In the excerpt below, Ludowyk praises* Henry V *as a celebration of an honoured and national hero of England. He contends that the play is a combination of fact and myth, and that it must be considered in relation to the Elizabethan audience. Ludowyk also reviews the structure of the play, the theme of war, and the character of Henry.*]

The national hero

Henry V is Shakespeare's celebration of one of England's national heroes—the warrior prince, Henry of Monmouth, who defeated the French at Agincourt, a battle remembered and honoured nearly 180 years later. In 3. 7. 31-2 the Dauphin speaks of 'varying' (inventing variations on the theme of) the deserved praises of his palfrey. In this play Shakespeare, in dramatic terms, is 'varying' the deserved praise of Henry V. His story was known to Elizabethans, as 5 Prologue states. Henry is Shakespeare's theme, the legendary subject of his panegyric [formal praise].

We have to consider the play against the background of the meaning of the legend of Henry V to Elizabethans, and not in connection with any promises made in the epilogue to *2 Henry IV*. It is related to that play, and even to *Richard II*, but it exists in its own right independently of them, and we should look at it in the light of its own intentions and achievement.

His legend. The legend of Henry of Monmouth was the familiar story of the young man who appears to be a wastrel and a ne'er-do-well, but who makes a glorious reformation, and becomes a heroic figure. It is like those stories of the ugly duckling who grows into a beautiful swan. For his play Shakespeare used the sober historical material of his time—the chronicles of Hall and Holinshed. In them, and also in contemporary plays, there were popular stories of the hero. The subject would therefore be a combination of fact, and, what is more important, belief in the myth which years of tradition had sanctioned.

Something more comes into Shakespeare's play, and this is his own memory of England at his time. Behind all the histories is a strong nationalist and patriotic feeling, given a new consciousness of itself after the defeat of the Spanish Armada. The England Shakespeare writes of in this play is the England of his time, though the events described are nearly two centuries old. So into this play comes an explicit reference to contemporary events, when Shakespeare, asking his audience to picture the welcome given to Henry after Agincourt, thinks of Essex, as 'happily he might', returning successful from Ireland. But more important than this reference is the complex of feelings which must have been the attitude of many men, when they thought of England in 1599, when the play was written.

This complex of feelings must have been made up of satisfaction and pride in the past, and confidence in the future if, as Falconbridge said in *King John*, 'England to itself remained but true'. But there would also be apprehension and uncertainty about both present and future. The Queen was as glorious a figure as any past hero. But she was old. She had reigned for just over forty years, and the end of her reign was in sight. Yet no successor to the kingdom had been formally named, and, as Tudor political wisdom had pointed out, and Shakespeare's own chronicle histories had maintained, the dangers of a disputed succession were plain for all to see.

So if *Henry V* is the celebration of England's national hero at a momentous period in the country's history, it should not be forgotten that there are other tones, suggesting the limitations of any heroic figure, and doubts of the future.

The play is a paean [song] of praise for Henry V. But other things come into it too—the crime of Henry's father who had usurped the throne; disloyal nobles; the boon companions of the king's youth; and the savagery of war. It could be supposed that Shakespeare, intending the play as tribute to the national hero, found that the presentation of a man so variously celebrated had its natural disadvantages. Inherent in the theme are the difficulties present in any artistic medium attempting to present the complete hero. The picture of the good man is usually dull and unattractive. So the hero 'full-fraught and best induced' (the all-round man endowed with all the graces) would seem wooden and unlifelike, or at any rate less plausible and human than the less 'complete' man.

We might remember, too, that our attitudes to persons, even those we admire and revere, are rarely without contradictory impulses of criticism and even of hostility. There is a human tendency to derive satisfaction from feelings of aggression to persons whom we honour and love. If, therefore, as it has so often been held of this play, into this vehicle for

Act II, scene ii. Exeter, Bedford, and Westmoreland watch as Henry V condemns Scroop, Cambridge, and Grey to death for treason.

Henry's glory comes in material tending to his hero's dispraise, it could be put down to Shakespeare's common humanity. The play must then be regarded as Shakespeare's 'varying' of the theme of the heroic and ideal stature of Henry V, together with whatever of a contrary significance naturally attached to such exercises.

Structure

The play is made up of five prologues or choruses, which enunciate some part of the theme which the following scenes illustrate. All of them contribute to the general suggestion made in 1 Prologue that the great theme is that of the warrior-king. This Prologue states the general theme: Henry of Monmouth as the hero who, if the medium used by the dramatist was equal to the task, would 'assume the port of Mars', that is, formally take on himself as was his right the bearing of Mars, the god of war. As 1 Prologue is general introduction, we should take 1.1 as being a further specific prologue to the scenes illustrating it. The epilogue reiterates the main theme, and apologizes, as do all the Prologues, for the unworthy treatment of a subject too great for the dramatist's powers.

We should see the structure of the play as dramatic illustration of the theme enunciated in the several prologues. The latter provide the statement, the acts and scenes which follow are their amplification. There is an additional feature in the content of these illustrative scenes. Quite often there will be found in them material of another kind, seemingly opposed in its effect to the general intention of the prologues. The scenes which follow the prologues should therefore be looked at as both extending the statement of the prologue, and also contributing something antithetical. . . .

The prologues

Before we examine this structure in greater detail, it is necessary to ask one question: why did Shakespeare use these prologues? Of course they were not unusual on the Elizabethan stage, and in earlier drama there was a 'presenter' whose function was to state to the audience the content of the play, and to draw their attention to any special points made by the dramatist.

The Prologues in this play will be seen to fall into three parts. They are, like all prologues, informative, and announce what has happened in the interim between the scenes just played on the stage and the appearance of the chorus. Secondly, they apologize for the inadequate means employed by the dramatist in putting his material on the stage, and acknowledge his 'abuse' of such things as 'time', 'place', and 'numbers'. As 1 Prologue puts it the dramatist has had to 'jump' over 'times'. This 'abuse' of time, according to Renaissance notions of playwriting, was the inclusion in the plot of events covering a greater period of time than that conventionally allowed.

In 2 Prologue the chorus undertakes to make the audience 'digest' another abuse—that of 'distance', or the fact that in the play we are at one time in one place and the next moment in another. Thus, again, by Renaissance 'rules' was inadmissible.

And both in 1 Prologue and elsewhere the dramatist, unable with the few actors in a stock company to put as many people as would be required on the stage, apologizes for the 'abuse' of 'numbers'.

Finally, the chorus urges the audience to compensate for the stage's deficiencies by using their 'imaginary forces', that is their imaginations are to work, and so 'piece out' or patch up what is wanting in the stage's treatment of its subject.

Why should Shakespeare have felt, in the first place, that he was infringing the 'rules' and, in the second, that his stage was unable to present scenes of battle and a war between two mighty countries? In every single one of his plays up to this time, he had not troubled himself with any 'rules' of time and place, and he was always working with the same slender resources of a stock company. Further, he had never felt, or stated his feelings, that his stage was incapable of giving his audiences scenes of war, or of famous battles. In *Henry VI* the most popular scenes with the London audiences had been those of Talbot in battle. In *Richard III* he had made such a success of the battle of Bosworth that Burbage's cry in his play seemed to be the most memorable thing in it. And in the plays yet to come he was to put on the stage momentous conflicts like those between Augustus Caesar and the conspirators, Actium, and the campaigns of Coriolanus.

The most favoured explanation is that Shakespeare taking up the story of England's national hero has a subject on his hands better suited to epic poetry than to drama. Such a subject was hedged about with literary conventions so powerful at that time, that anyone hardy enough to undertake it would neglect the 'rules' only at grave risk to his reputation. Shakespeare's subject, as he seems to see it in 1 Prologue, required epic narration and epic description. There had been plays on these subjects of England's wars and England's heroic figures before, but the dramatist, feeling that his form could scarcely do justice to his material, continually aspires (in his images of fire and air, and in the urgency of his tones with the repeated admonitions to the audience to 'think', to 'look', to 'work with their thoughts') to the height of epic grandeur and excellence.

There is something more. Shakespeare's difficulty, if this account of it is accepted, was not only one of the literary form he chose, but of his medium of presentation. In this play he excuses himself not only for offences against literary canons, but also for the ineptitudes of his stage. This avowal need not be taken too seriously, for he continued to do just what he apologizes for here. What is more, in 3 Prologue, he adds a dramatic touch at the very moment of his admission that dramatic modes are inadequate for his 'task'. His passionate 'work, work your thoughts and therein see a siege' (3 Prol. 25) is followed by the firing of a cannon off stage. The stage direction at 1.33 'alarum, and chambers go off', proves that imagination, for all its resolution, did not disdain stage effects.

This may seem the unconscious revenge of the theatre on the dramatist a little too prone to slight its resources. The combination in this prologue of the acknowledgement that the medium is inadequate with its efficient use seems typical of other contraries in the play, its material being the celebration of Henry together with a glance at what is unattractive in his character.

Focus on Henry

This is Henry's play. He is the one person on whom attention is continually focused. All the others in the play are there to pay their tribute to him as the ideal king. Numerous persons fill out this long play, but however interesting in their own right—the Dauphin, the typical vaunting knight, or the pedantic and honourable Welshman—their real function is to lend dramatic contrast and illustration to the main character.

Henry—'full of grace'. Two prelates open the play with a scene of exposition which should be taken as the specific prologue to Act 1. They see that the church's best defence is the king's character itself, rather than diverting him, with the offer of a large subsidy, to a war against France. Protestant historians linked the church's offer to the king with its support of Henry's claims to France, but it is clear, in the answer to Ely's question in 1. 1. 21, that the king will not countenance the bill against church properties because he has become the king he is. It is important that in the legend of Henry as the young man addicted to 'courses vain' ('open haunts and popularity' of 1. 1. 59), a less strongly stressed detail should not be overlooked. The king has undergone spiritual conversion.

We should note too how strongly Canterbury opens in 1. 22 with 'the king is full of grace and fair regard'. 'Grace' is a condition which the Christian continually strives after. It is a stronger word than mercy, and should be interpreted as being in a state of reconciliation with God and given power by God to persevere in right action.

The images. The intention of Canterbury's speeches is clear: to present the king as the epitome of kingly excellence. The verse is oratorically full and easy, the images employed—from the service of baptism, from the Bible, and the classical fable of Hercules cleansing the Augean stables—lending their weight to the figure being projected. Is there a feeling, however, that we are being given not a human being, but an unnatural prodigy? The threefold repetition of 'never' in lines 32-5, and the parenthetical 'all at once' in line 36 indicate the determination of the speaker to force into life an unbelievable figure of a man.

When Canterbury goes on in line 38 he indulges in a hyperbolic extension of this superhuman king. Again with a biblical reference—to the wind that bloweth where it listeth—he claims that the air, a 'libertine' because it does exactly what it wishes, is so charmed by the king's excellence of discourse that, dumbfounded and wondering, it hangs about men's ears, just to catch his beautifully expressed maxims. These 'sweet and honeyed sentences' seem to have two tones; of statement which may be sincere and also of crude flattery. Is there anything more in this hyperbole than straightforward praise, or does it, in trying to attain its object, overreach itself, and leave an impression of a kind of person too good to be true, or a speaker too flattering to be sincere?

In this passage and elsewhere in the play it is possible to see that the image, as Shakespeare uses it now, is so embedded in its dramatic context that it is not, as might have been the case in earlier plays, a device of the poetry as distinct from the drama. The image illuminates mental attitudes; it helps us to sense the dramatist's feelings towards the material he is shaping, to its persons and its situations; it reveals the relations of the persons of the play to each other.

Ely notes (1. 1. 60-6), as Canterbury had done, the wonder of the king's character, and, using an illustration from gardening, he points out how the king's

study of life had developed and matured under the cover of scapegrace behaviour in his youth. This image is like that of the Constable of France in 2. 4. 39-40, describing the contrast between the wildness of his youth and the nobility of his present character. Ely goes on to remark that the king's powers grew, like summer grass at night, unobserved, because they had the innate ability to do just this. Canterbury agrees. It is no miracle; the king's present perfection must be due to the natural cause ('means') of his inborn goodness of character. . . .

Henry—defender of the commonweal

On this follows an outburst of patriotism and national pride from churchmen and nobles who cite the glorious precedents of the past—the victories of Edward III and the Black Prince in France. They are all off in their rousing speeches to defeat the French again, but it is the king, with his care for the commonweal, who debates in his mind what will happen in England should the main force of the country be divided with the best part away in France. He has to calculate how his forces should be deployed and how the 'ill neighbourhood'—the hostile feelings of their neighbours the Scots—has to be feared. Could the king be away and the main strength of the country be safely divided?

Nobles and churchmen now reassure the king about the health and sound condition of the kingdom. The substance of what they say is: Do not fear to divide up your forces, setting out with the main body to France, for out of the division of parts comes the full harmony of the whole. Exeter's image in 1. 2. 180-4 was frequently used by Shakespeare to illustrate the concord made up of the voices singing the notes of their various parts. . . .

Henry—the Christian king

So the spiritual counsellor calms the king's apprehensions through an argument from parallels. Satisfied that the country will be in no danger, the king asks for the embassy from France. He indicates to the ambassador at once that he is

> a Christian king,
> Unto whose grace our passion is as subject
> As is our wretches fettered in our prisons

—a statement of one of his great virtues. Time and time again—with Montjoy, with his soldiers, with the French—the king shows perfect control of himself and of the impulse to give way to passion. Only once in the play does he say that he has been 'angered' (4. 7. 54).

His reply, therefore, to the insulting message of the

Dauphin is a neat and witty rejoinder. Punning on references to tennis as played at that time, he tells the Dauphin that the opponent ('wrangler') he has taken on will undo France and himself. The king speaks as king; of himself he uses the language conventionally used of kings. Like a lion he will 'rouse himself' in his throne of France. Like the sun he will dazzle the eyes of the French.

Twice in his speech which closes the scene, God's help is invoked. The sentiments may be conventional, but the formal occasion demands formal speech. But is there besides the dignity of the speech a sinister touch of grim seriousness in lines 282-99? The destruction of war, its slaughter and devastation are taken by the verse in its stride, but it leaves an impression of hardness and ruthlessness. The 'merry message' has an undertone of grimness.

The second Prologue is off with its description of the preparations for the war. But as soon as the chorus has announced the promise held out to the king and his chivalrous knights, it goes on to state that all is not well with the country. The French, through their spies, have corrupted three important nobles. . . .

Henry—as lawgiver

The king shows Christian mercy in pardoning the man who had abused him when drunk. The conspirators' objection to this, with their distinction between mercy and justice—always a fruitful theme with Shakespeare—is ironically turned aside by the king in 2. 2. 52-60. In seeming to give them their letters of appointment he hands them writs impeaching them for high treason.

The long speech (2. 2. 79-144) places this sudden turn of events in the setting the dramatist intends for it. Dramatic effectiveness and surprise probably account for the king's having played cat and mouse with them. The attitude he takes up shows that their crime makes the conspirators extraordinary creatures, to be pointed at and looked at as queer freaks were at fairs. They are English monsters, just as Caliban could have been thought of as an 'Indian' (or American) monster. For their crime is against 'proportion', the harmony of the well-ordered state. It is more than the disloyalty of a 'bedfellow' to his friend, bad as that might be.

Everything in lines 109 to the end of the speech depends on the enormity of the sin. It is so 'preposterous' (it turns the natural order upside down) that the king rises to a height of eloquence in underlining its illogicality, its combination of treason, murder and inexplicability. Scroop's crime has poisoned the sweet water of trust ('with jealousy infected the sweetness of affiance'). It seems nothing less than a 'second fall of man', as Bolingbroke's crime was to the

queen in *Richard II*. Yet when the king says in line 140 'I will weep for thee', are the words sincere, or are they an oratorical device? And the references to God's mercy in lines 166, and 177-81—are they the king's fervent wish, or do they imply that even God would find it hard to forgive such wrongs?

The king's behaviour is obviously in keeping with the traditions of political wisdom. He must tender the safety of the kingdom more than any threat to his person. But does this scene in showing him as wise in his handling of such emergencies leave a trace of dissatisfaction at the sternness of 'this grace of kings'? . . .

Henry—as man of war

The theme of the third Prologue is war. Henry goes to France in pursuance of a claim supported by his spiritual counsellors and by the whole country.

3. 1 opens with the army on the stage with their 'scaling ladders' before the gate of Harfleur. The whole of the scene is a warrior's call to arms. As usual on the Elizabethan stage war is conveyed most effectively through the speeches of the combatants.

Henry's lines in 3. 1 are the exaltation of the man of war. The human being is turned into an abstraction which combines the animal and the machine. The movement of the tiger, the eye threatening like the cannon as it points at the enemy through its embrasure, the brow in anger hanging like a worn crag over the raging sea greedily devouring its base—these images in the speech are unnatural portents.

It is true that this is the disguise which the warrior must put on. But there is in the organization of the lines such force and strain that we feel doubtful here of the panegyric lavished on Henry as 'this grace of kings'. . . .

Henry—the man

Of all the Prologues the fourth is the most interesting, because it creates a scene free from the extravagance and the hyperboles of the earlier prologues, and places squarely in it neither a 'grace of kings', nor a god of war, but the man Harry. If the earlier prologues are busy with a hero soon to 'assume the port of Mars', or a statesman unravelling the Gordian knot of policy, here the 'touch of Harry in the night' makes us conscious that Shakespeare's hero was a human being too.

In this Prologue the poet's sensitiveness to the great event of which he is writing enables him to provide a strong impression of expectancy, movement, and life. The references to darkness which strains the eyes, to the fires which are springing up all over the field, to darkened faces caught up in their dull light, have dramatic reality.

In this setting he gives us the French army 'secure' (an intensification of the Latin sense of *'securus'*, free from care) and the English as victims destined for the sacrifice on the morrow. The hero of his play is treated not as king, but as the captain of a band of soldiers. To him now his men are not the horrid engines he had urged them to become at the gates of Harfleur, but 'brothers, friends and countrymen'. The 'touch of Harry in the night' is a 'little touch' only because the dramatist is conventionally doubtful of his ability to put the man on the stage. 'As may unworthiness define' shows us this. But we may be grateful for this little 'touch', or account of the king, for it does much to humanize the idealized figure the play has been putting before us.

The great difference is that for the first time we have a king who speaks in natural tones. In the bluff humour of the scenes in Act 4 which follow we are made aware of a man, and not a hero. The king is capable now of seeing the reality of his situation. In both his prose and verse in 4. 1 we note tones of liveliness and criticism which have not entered his speech till now. His remark in 4. 1 4-7 on the 'soul of goodness in things evil' is not a solemn moral tag, it is the rueful joke of a man who in the worst position of all resolves that the best thing to do is to turn off most things with a laugh. To dwell on the uncomfortable reality would be to discountenance his men, so he continues with a good jest on 'dressing fairly for our end', and drops the light-hearted remark that even the devil himself, if need be, could be put to good moralistic use.

In the same strain are his remarks to Erpingham that if an analogy (an 'example') helps a man to endure distress, why should it not be used, for if the mind is revived, then the physical frame is once more active, like the snake which has sloughed off its skin. The dramatist is exhibiting here another facet of the character of the ideal monarch—his ability to keep up the spirits of his men. . . .

Henry—as peacemaker

The fifth Prologue, having established Henry as national hero and Christian prince, goes on to complete the study of Henry as the ideal king. He is first in peace as he was first in war. His character, both as statesman and the architect of peace, will be filled in. So 5. 2 will show how the warrior sets about making peace and restoring order to both countries, in the only way in which peace was then secured—by a dynastic marriage. Henry will be exhibited to us, not as lover, but as statesman. . . .

Henry as statesman

5. 2 for the first time brings the two mighty monarchs, France and England, on the stage together for the purpose of discussing the terms of peace. The English king is not the engine of war of the earlier acts, nor is he yet a romantic squire who will look 'greenly' or love-sick. Henry in this scene is the statesman who keeps the affairs of the commonwealth very clearly in front of him. He has certain justified claims on France, and he does not abate a jot of them. The marriage proposal is item no. 1 in his list, as he says in 5. 2. 96-8. The peace he is interested in has to be 'bought' from him, as he has won it through his victory over the French. We should not read this scene therefore only as an amusing sketch of the warrior unskilful in love wooing his princess. It is a demonstration of one of the qualities of the ideal king. Here Henry unlooses the Gordian knot of policy. How skilful he is in the role of suitor, though with conventional modesty he depreciates his abilities, the scene will show.

That peace is necessary to the French is shown in Burgundy's speech in 5. 2. 31-67. His is a picture of the waste of civil war, the fair garden ruined and turning to wildness because war has upset the natural order. The image of the country as a garden which it is the duty of the king to tend, and which cannot flourish unless order prevails, is already familiar through *Richard II*. What Burgundy says of France would come home to the imaginations of the English, to whom the threat of civil war was always a fearful possibility. The comparison of France to a garden, the symbol of the state, sets the level at which the scene of courtship should be taken. It is no real love-scene. Wise forethought which must benefit both states is its main impulse.

Henry as 'lover'

In the scene with Katharine, Henry is the blunt soldier who though, he says, he lacks skill in words, yet has a good sense of the occasion and an impressive readiness of speech. Two details in the make-up of an ideal king are stressed in it: his devotion to his country and his honesty of purpose as man. As lover he is, like the best of Shakespeare's lovers, not romantic but full of good sense: 'To say to thee that I shall die is true; but for thy love, by the Lord, no: yet I love thee too.' Comedy enters into it too, both in its breezy references to the physical and in the contrast between the soldier and the man.

So the match is made; Henry gets all he specified, even to the details of his royal titles; and the French king hails a union which will plant 'neighbourhood' and Christian-like accord between two kingdoms.

A grand procession crowns the play, and the chorus enters for the last time as epilogue. The actor apologizes, as usual, for the shortcomings of the dramatic medium. He is also careful to point out that none of the fine hopes raised by the last scene was ever fulfilled. Though no reason is given for this, there is in the words 'whose state so many had the managing', an eloquent hint, that England was divided and there was lack of unity in the country. So France was lost and England bled. Shakespeare has dramatically 'varied' the praises of England's ideal king at a time when the wonderful reign of a monarch her people idealized was drawing to its close. The connection between England at the beginning of the fifteenth century and at the end of the sixteenth was clear. This play, like the other histories, was a 'mirror' for England.

Robert B. Pierce

SOURCE: *"Henry V,"* in *Shakespeare's History Plays: The Family and the State,* Ohio State University Press, 1971, pp. 225-40.

[*In the following essay, Pierce analyzes the symbol of the family as an echo of political themes in* Henry V. *He contends that the traditional themes associated with family—inheritance of virtue, threat of political disorder to its unity, and need for companionship—are significant to the development of Henry's moral and political character.*]

Among the history plays, *Henry V* is something of a paradox. It is good without being great, and that is not at all what one would predict following the Henry IV plays. One might expect to see the triumph of Shakespeare's historical vision, the capstone of his second tetralogy, with the ideal king appearing in action against France, England's traditional enemy. Or one would not have been surprised by a daring failure, a play that starts off in a new direction with only partial success, like *Measure for Measure.* Some critics, including Derek Traversi [in *Shakespeare from Richard II to Henry V;* 1957], have seen just such experimentation in *Henry V;* but the foreshadowings of a new Shakespeare are of the faintest even in his account. Besides, *Henry V* is preeminently a successful play; significantly, it has produced one of the best of the Shakespearian films, Sir Laurence Oliver's spectacle.

Clearly *Henry V* is the last of Shakespeare's series of history plays in the 1590s. One can with some confidence date it in the spring or summer of 1599, though it is possible that there was an earlier form or even that it was later revised. In this last of the series, Shakespeare turns to epic drama in order to glorify his ideal king, Henry V, a national hero of legendary proportions and the product of Hal's education in the Henry IV plays. Since Renaissance epic

is not characteristically strong in dramatic power, there is peril in such handling. Both the idealized type-characters and the high decorum of language could cripple the stageworthiness of the play. In particular, overemphasis on Shakespeare's lofty manner could have brought back much of the stiffness of the first tetralogy as he tried to duplicate in dramatic verse the stateliness and pictorial richness of *The Faerie Queene* and Chapman's Homer. Such a play might have been all too like *Richard III* without the villain.

However, Shakespeare is too professional a dramatist to leave his hero merely a stiff epic figure. Once again he explores the man behind the public role, the kind of study that yields such rich results in the Henry IV plays. What is difficult to explain is why this approach is less rewarding in *Henry V* than in the two previous plays. Somehow the two sides of this king, public and private, exist parallel to each other but without much interaction. We see a Henry V who relaxes as a man among men, but when he takes on his regal authority, it is as though in gathering his robes about him he becomes a different person. Only in IV.i, perhaps the finest scene in the play, does Henry seem to be trying to define himself, to find some reconciliation of these two sides, as Henry IV and Prince Hal are constantly doing. As a result Henry V does not really seem like Hal grown older. The pressure of Hal's questing intellect is for the most part absent in this confident monarch, and so his intelligence is not so dramatically convincing. Hal is equal to Falstaff's wit—in a sense more than equal, for he can spar with the knight while holding part of himself in reserve. He is not subdued to the quality of his environment, whether in the tavern or on the battlefield at Shrewsbury.

Henry never faces an antagonist of Falstaff's brilliance, and he shows Hal's intellectual detachment only occasionally. Thus he is harder to see apart from the moral ambiguities of his environment. In I.ii he listens to his counselor's advice and makes his decision to invade France, but Shakespeare does little to suggest the thought processes by which he does so. Hence one is left wondering about his motives. Is he a noble patriot being duped by the clergy with their interested motive in supporting a French war? Is he unconcerned with the moral issue of his title as long as it is plausible, since what he wants is a war to unify the English after their long civil strife? Or does he allow for the clergy's bias even while being genuinely concerned with the validity of his title? Though Shakespeare may well have intended the last of these possibilities, one wishes that he had dramatized it more clearly. Perhaps he was overwhelmed by a sense of pervasive evil and corruption in even the noblest undertaking when he wrote *Henry V.* Hence he could not afford to make his king quite so aware of unpleasant reality as Hal is and still have him a patriotic man of action. If so, there is only a short step from this epic-comic history to the tragedy of Brutus, who can be moral only at the cost of willful blindness. (Shakespeare probably wrote *Julius Caesar* at about this time.)

Through most of the play we perceive King Henry V much more clearly than Harry LeRoy. This unresolved public-private duality spreads out from him to affect the whole play, including the use of the family. Throughout, the family is prominent as a public symbol. Although rhetorical allusions to the family are characteristic of all the history plays, *Henry V* relies more on this device than any other play since the first tetralogy. Woven into the public speeches of the English and French leaders are the traditional themes: the inheritance of virtue, the family as a symbol of unity, and political disorder as a threat to the family. Henry's reliance on his brothers' counsel and support is appropriate to his position as the leader of a unified and vigorous nation. The ideal king depends on his family, not on favorites, and Henry follows his father's advice in doing this (*2 Henry IV*, IV.iv.20-48).

Likewise *Henry V* progresses toward a marriage that both effects and symbolizes union (a momentary one) between the two ancient rivals, France and England. Queen Isabel makes this symbolism explicit at the end of the play:

> God, the best maker of all marriages,
> Combine your hearts in one, your realms in
>   one!
> As man and wife, being two, are one in love,
> So be there 'twixt your kingdoms such a
>   spousal
> That never may ill office, or fell jealousy,
> Which troubles oft the bed of blessed
>   marriage,
> Thrust in between the paction of these
>   kingdoms,
> To make divorce of their incorporate league.
>
>   (V.ii.377-84)

This is a formal speech in the old vein, based on the system of correspondences. But this speech has the effect of gratuitous embroidery after the lively comedy of the wooing scene and the cynical realism of the negotiations. Whereas *Richard III* points with solemn inevitability toward the marriage that unites the two warring houses, *Henry V* modulates from a military victory to a playful courtship that suddenly turns out to have symbolic significance.

Similarly, the few episodes of family life in the comic plot lack any thematic connection with the serious plot, unlike the Henry IV plays. Even if one reads *Henry V* as a satire on militarism and hence emphasizes

the parodic side of the comic plot, it remains all too directionless and only partly relevant. Pistol arrives onstage in II.i as a bridegroom and promptly engages in a thrasonical [boastful] quarrel with Nym, a rejected suitor. Their squabbles begin a burlesque of soldierly heroism that runs through the comic episodes, but Shakespeare makes no attempt to parody Henry V's marriage in advance as he had parodied the interview between Hal and his father in *1 Henry IV*.

Perhaps the lack of organic connection comes from the absence of a character like Prince Hal to mediate between the comic and serious plots. A Henry V who can comment without emotion or even wit on Bardolph's execution has lost touch with Falstaff's world, whether or not he finds some community with the tidier low life of Williams and the other common soldiers. Still, though the role of the family may be simpler and less developed than in the Henry IV plays, it is of genuine significance both in general and specifically in developing Henry's character.

One of the Renaissance doctrines on which Shakespeare relies in *Henry V* is moral inheritance. The English and the French agree that breeding should reveal itself in courage and military skill, but the French are puzzled to explain the tenacity of these "Norman bastards" (III.v.10). The Dauphin puts their attitude with vigorous contempt:

> O Dieu vivant! shall a few sprays of us,
> The emptying of our fathers' luxury,
> Our scions, put in wild and savage stock,
> Spirt up so suddenly into the clouds,
> And overlook their grafters?
>
>   (III.v.5-9)

In this commonplace imagery even his association of birth with growing plants is traditional. Both son and father have to admit the inbred strength and courage of the English. Weightier because less flippant than this speech is the French king's fearful awareness that Henry descends from Edward III, the victor of Crècy. The grandiloquent mouthings of the French nobles express their decadence and their unwilling admiration for English valor and tenacity. In spite of themselves they praise the breeding of these "mastiffs in robustious and rough coming on" (III.vii.148).

Meanwhile the English proclaim their duty to uphold a noble heritage. The point at issue is whether Henry has a better title to the French crown than its present holder. For all Shakespeare's consciousness of the mixed motives that lead men to war, there seems to be no doubt in the play that the English title to France is valid. The French themselves never question it, and the extraordinary triumph at Agincourt is a sign of God's support for the righteous claims of a united England. However, Shakespeare does raise the question of Henry's title to his own crown, vaguely at first in the conspiracy scene and then explicitly in the king's prayer the night before Agincourt. Even though the English heritage is superior in law and virtue to the French, it has within it a flaw that will lead to the collapse of order and civil war, "Which oft our stage hath shown" (Closing Chorus, 13). The warrior son that Henry and Katherine are to breed is the weakling Henry VI. Nonetheless, the primary contrast is between degenerate chivalry in the French and hereditary valor in the English under their warrior king.

In its rhetoric *Henry V* derives England's glory from its mighty heritage. All of Henry's counselors incite him by means of this heritage when he nears the decision to invade France. In words that foreshadow the French king's reference to Edward III, the Archbishop of Canterbury caps an appeal to Henry's forebears with a picture of that king smiling while his son defeats the French with only half the English forces. The Bishop of Ely and the Duke of Exeter are quick to second this appeal to the warrior blood in Henry's veins. The doctrines of inheritance are woven into Henry's own speech as well. In his grief at the betrayal by Lord Scroop, he includes with Scroop's apparent virtues the noble birth that should have guaranteed them.

As a warrior rallying his troops Henry places special emphasis on the doctrine of inherited virtue. At Harfleur the climax of his speech is a reminder of his men's heroic ancestry, first to the nobles and then to the common soldiers:

> On, on, you noblest English!
> Whose blood is fet from fathers of war-
>   proof;
> Fathers that, like so many Alexanders,
> Have in these parts from morn till even
>   fought,
> And sheath'd their swords for lack of
>   argument.
> Dishonour not your mothers; now attest
> That those whom you call'd fathers did beget
>   you.
> Be copy now to men of grosser blood,
> And teach them how to war. And you, good
>   yeomen,
> Whose limbs were made in England, show us
>   here
> The mettle of your pasture; let us swear
> That you are worth your breeding; which I
>   doubt not;
> For there is none of you so mean and base
> That hath not noble lustre in your eyes.
>   (III.i.17-30)

If Traversi is right in finding unconscious irony suggested by the language just before this, a powerful

suggestion that war is unnatural to man, this passage is a curious reversal. Here the warrior is a natural product of his birth. Surely this effect is where the primary emphasis of the speech, and the play, lies. If the appeal to inheritance in Henry's oration has a leanness and vigor beyond Shakespeare's early style, still it is traditional in content and in its abstractness of phrasing.

Related to the doctrine of inheritance is the conception of patriotic unity, symbolized by the bonds of family, as a precondition of political and military success. When Henry makes a decision, he gives due consideration to the counsels of his brothers and uncle, while in the French court the king engages in unseemly and fruitless squabbles with his son. The movement toward temporary harmony at the end is decorated by the two kings' constant references to each other as "brother France" and "brother England." This rhetoric of diplomacy is entirely hollow, as is clear from the fact that Charles invokes the bonds of kinship while agreeing to disinherit his son so that he may keep the throne during his lifetime, just as Henry VI does. Henry V never pretends to take this diplomatic rhetoric seriously. All through Act V he shows a playfulness that reminds one of Faulconbridge laughing at the false language of diplomacy. Even the French king catches this spirit long enough to exchange hard-headed appraisals of the bargaining under the veil of a joke about virginity.

Such formal language need not be a cloak for the realities of power politics, however. After the moving revelation in IV.i of his personal affection for his men, Henry's celebrated lines at Agincourt ring true:

> We few, we happy few, we band of brothers;
> For he to-day that sheds his blood with me
> Shall be my brother; be he ne'er so vile
> This day shall gentle his condition.
>   (IV.iii.60-63)

Shedding blood together becomes a figurative union of bloods. Under such a king the terrible chain of hereditary enmity that has bound England is for the moment broken.

Facing the task of a righteous war, England draws together like one family. There are both truth and irony in the traitor Grey's words:

> Those that were your father's
>   enemies
> Have steep'd their galls in honey, and do
>   serve you
> With hearts create of duty and of zeal.
>   (II.ii.29-31)

The treachery by Grey and his companions is not

enough to prevent the triumph at Agincourt, though it foreshadows developments that will eventually lose the fruits of victory. The chorus uses the language of correspondences to describe this imperfect unity:

> O England! model to thy inward greatness,
> Like little body with a mighty heart,
> What might'st thou do, that honour would
> 　　thee do,
> Were all thy children kind and natural!
> 　　　　　　　　　(Chorus to Act II, 16-19)

In the happy ending of victory in battle and a marriage that combines love and political union, we have only a vague consciousness that there will be unnatural, "kindless" disorder in the family of England, that this precarious unity will collapse.

Nearly as prominent as these two themes is a darker use of the family to express the horrors of war. In the first tetralogy civil war destroys not only love and family loyalty but also wives and children, innocent victims of the conflict. If *Henry V* glorifies the victory at Agincourt, it does so without concealing any of the violence and corruption that taint the English triumph. In contrast with the jesting Dauphin, Henry is determined to assure the justice of his cause before pursuing it into battle because he knows the evils that he will unleash, even on the innocent. At the French court Exeter proclaims Henry's guiltlessness in the war:

> 　　　　　　　　　on your head
> Turning the widow's tears, the orphans'
> 　　cries,
> The dead men's blood, the prived maidens'
> 　　groans.
> For husbands, fathers, and betrothed lovers,
> That shall be swallow'd in this controversy.
> 　　　　　　　　　(II.iv.105-109)

Though Shakespeare may well be paraphrasing Hall, the sentiments are an Elizabethan commonplace. He gives a striking visual quality to another such passage when Henry warns the citizens of Harfleur that continued resistance will expose them and their families to violence. Although this theme does not go beyond the language to permeate the dramatic structure as the other two do and as it did in the plays of civil war, it is still an important part of the imagery of *Henry V*.

Insofar as the family theme goes beyond this essentially public and traditional handling, it does so through Henry himself. Because he is in part an epic figure, the ideal king and warrior, the public language of the family with all its severe dignity is appropriate to him. After all, he represents in the state the moral values that the family stands for in private life. But

if Henry is an epic hero, he has more in common with Odysseus than with Achilles. He is the balanced hero, the prudent man, and his story moves toward reconciliation and marriage rather than toward tragedy. Such a hero can be more at his ease than his sterner counterpart, and he is seen in a broader environment, one that includes his personal relationships. Tamburlaine, the Achilles of the English stage, cannot stoop to prose comedy or to wandering among his men in disguise; he is too unitary a character for either. At least in flashes Henry shows a broader, more Odyssean nature.

What is most effectively human about Henry is his desire for companionship. He refuses to accept the isolation involved in royalty. When he does for a moment break through the forms of his office, in the comradeship of battle or in wooing Katherine, he shows a gaiety reminiscent of Prince Hal escaped from the court. When something makes him newly conscious of his isolation, his spirits fall. This side of him is hidden during the formal ceremonies of Act I, but even in his public reproof of the treacherous Scroop something of his personal feeling comes through. He voices the grief of betrayed friendship, a powerful theme in many of the plays and sonnets. As Henry goes to France, he seems entirely alone, there being no hint that he is personally close to any of his brothers.

In the communal effort that leads to Agincourt, he finds the contact with other men that he desires. His spirits rise as the battle nears, especially during the previous night. Although the companionship that he finds is mostly that of brothers in arms rather than actual kin, the family does play some part in the language of IV.i, and in the first few lines he appears among his blood brothers. Now they talk without the solemn formality of the scene in the English court. Henry's moralizing is playful as he shuffles off his kingly distance, first with them and then with the men while he wanders around the camp. Episodes involving the king in disguise are a favorite device of Elizabethan drama, in part because they emphasize his humanity and community with the people. Thus Henry whimsically identifies himself to Pistol as a kinsman to Fluellen, that embodiment of the commonplace virtues.

Henry's debate with the common soldiers implicitly defines the king's similarities and differences from other men. They talk of the king as a man with fears and hopes like theirs, and the disguised Henry is one of them both in physical presence and in manner. The point at issue is how far he is differentiated by his office, especially by responsibility for the individual fates of his soldiers. Both Williams and he think of the family in their dispute. Williams recalls with graphic literalness the effects of war on widows and children, and Henry argues by analogy to a father

Pistol (Bernard Horsfall) bids farewell to Mistress Quickly (Patricia Routledge) in the 1984 Royal Shakespeare Theatre production of Henry V.

and son: "So, if a son that is by his father sent about merchandise do sinfully miscarry upon the sea, the imputation of his wickedness, by your rule, should be imposed upon his father that sent him" (IV.i.150-53). Here the fatherhood of the king, a traditional figure of speech, implies what Henry himself illustrates, the combination of authority and personal affection in an ideal king. One thinks of the autocratic Elizabeth and her love for her countrymen. During a scene in which Henry escapes from his formal role, Shakespeare gives these stock references to the family a new immediacy. Henry and Williams argue in the same terms because they are men with the same concerns and values, yet this sameness can emerge only because the king is disguised.

In his soliloquy on ceremony and his prayer, Henry's isolation becomes all the more poignant because for a moment he has been just a man among men. He is left to himself with the responsibilities of kingship and his father's guilt. As king and father to all England, he has to be inhumanly strong and wise; alone before the God whose magistrate he is, he must bear the responsibility that ordinary men escape.

Henry's gaiety and sense of community return with the rising sun. The experience of the past night colors his words to his companions. The high rhetoric of Harfleur mixes with the plain manliness of phrases like "Good God! why should they mock poor fellows thus?" (IV.iii.92). In this way a bridge is made between the formal king of I.ii and the lusty wooer, the plain-speaking man, of V.ii. Henry V is both man and king; his royalty is personal virtue expanded to the larger sphere of public affairs. If this bridge between the private and public man is not so strong as in the Henry IV plays, if it is fully apparent in only one scene, still it is there as an indication of the relationship between man and office.

In the courtship itself we see the man Henry clearly enough, but Shakespeare makes little effort to show the epic king. Johnson remarks discontentedly, "I know not why Shakespeare now gives the king nearly such a character as he made him formerly ridicule in Percy." That is not quite fair, since presumably Henry is playing a part out of sheer exuberance. In one way like Richard III, he exults in the strength that lets him win a lady's love under the most adverse circumstances. Still Johnson's discontent is justified. Ingratiating though the scene may be, it is not really a part of the epic story. Henry plays the farmer seeking a wife, and the game sheds little light on the nature of kingship and on the precarious union between France and England. Hence the ending with its use of the coming marriage as a symbol seems perfunctory, neither triumphant nor effectively ironic.

The excellence of *Henry V* has little to do with the

family, partly because Henry's isolation, unlike that of the two Richards, has no moral significance. Despite its traditional role in the language, the family has no broader dramatic role. *Henry V* carries out the pattern of making the family an echo of political themes, but it does not deepen this function.

Moody E. Prior

SOURCE: "Of Diplomacy, War, and Peace: *Henry V*," in *The Drama of Power: Studies in Shakespeare's History Plays*, Northwestern University Press, 1973, pp. 263-82.

[*In the following excerpt, Prior discusses* Henry V's *emphasis on war. He traces the structure of the play, from the preparations for war to the negotiations for peace, noting that no other of Shakespeare's histories focus on war so exclusively as subject or setting.*]

Henry V is constructed on bold, simple lines. It is dominated by the figure of the warrior king, and it moves in a sequence of well-defined acts without the complex interrelations of an intrigue plot and subplots, and with strongly contrasting scenes. There are, however, several clearly established links between *Henry V* and the preceding plays. The prince's youthful wildness and later reformation, so large a feature of *1* and *2 Henry IV*, is the topic of conversation between the two bishops in the opening scene. In *2 Henry IV* Henry warns his son that his title, though got by direct succession, is but newly won, and advises him to busy giddy minds in foreign wars in order to unify his country; and the last speech of that play, spoken by Prince John, predicts the easing of civil tensions by means of a war with France:

> I will lay odds that, ere this year expire,
> We bear our civil swords and native fire
> As far as France. I heard a bird so sing,
> Whose music, to my thinking, pleased the
>   king.
>
>   (5.5.105-8)

War with France is the main issue in the first act of *Henry V*. Henry IV confesses to his son in *2 Henry IV* that his own title was dubiously got, and in his prayer before Agincourt Henry V alludes to his father's guilt in compassing the crown. All of Hal's tavern companions are back except Falstaff. The connections are numerous and provocative and it is natural to suppose that, as in the case of the interrelationships among the other plays in the series, the links indicate significant lines of development which may be followed through with some consistency in any serious study of *Henry V*. One consequence of approaching *Henry V* in this way is that the directness and straightforward simplicity of *Henry V* begin to disappear in complexities, and it becomes necessary to ask how far the method can really be applied in this case. The epilogue to *2 Henry IV* promises more of Falstaff, but Falstaff does not appear again; thus anyone unfamiliar with that remarkable figure from the two previous plays would not know what to make of the talk of his death in the early scenes of *Henry V*, and might be puzzled by Fluellen's praise of the king for casting him off. An individual play that is destined for performance must, simply as a condition of its intelligibility in the theatre, be able to stand pretty much alone. To the extent that this consideration determines the primary impression which the play can make, it must be respected in criticism. . . .

Politically and geographically, *Henry V* represents a distinct change from the previous plays. The scene enlarges to include the Continent, and most of the action takes place across the sea in France. The kinds of political issues which are at the center of the other plays—the struggles for power, the legal questions of legitimacy, the relations of power to sovereign authority, the evils of civil strife, and the crises of ambition and conscience which trouble a nation and distress or destroy its leaders—these cause no major concern here. The internal politics at the outset has to do with the interplay of special interests which influence the decision to go to war, with the internal dangers that must be met, and with the wedding out of a few traitors. These all, however, are ultimately related to the negotiations between the rival nations. The politics of *Henry V* is, in the broadest sense, international politics, or, more specifically, war politics, for the entire play is about war. To this central emphasis the construction is a clue. The effect of the play is not that of a tightly knit series of events, but of a sequence of five large episodes, almost pageant-like in quality, separated by the choruses into the five acts designated by modern editions, each dealing with one stage in the course of events that unfolds when two great nations become involved in war.

The first act is the prelude to war—the debate which justifies the going to war and establishes its aims, and the formal diplomatic confrontation the failure of which leads to hostilities. It is puzzling that Shakespeare introduced *Henry V* with the two bishops worrying over a proposed bill to expropriate temporal lands willed to the church. This topic does lead directly to the laudatory descriptions, amounting to near reverence, of the reformed king, who will shortly appear on the scene, but the connection has its purpose: the bishops see in this "true lover of the holy Church" a possible ally, and their offer of great sums in support of a possible campaign against France is calculated to influence the king in their favor. This heroic play thus opens in an atmosphere of devious politics in undisguised form, and it does not improve our impression of the archbishop when we learn that

the church wealth which Parliament proposes to confiscate would be used to

> maintain, to the King's
>   honor,
> Full fifteen earls and fifteen hundred knights.
> Six thousand and two hundred good esquires,
> And to relief of lazars, and weak age,
> Of indigent faint souls past corporal toil,
> A hundred almshouses right well supplied;
> And to the coffers of the King beside,
> A thousand pounds by the year.
>
> (1.1.12-19)

A modest and apparently laudable social revolution. What is further disturbing is that the man to whom the king appeals to expound whether he can "with right and conscience make this claim" (1.2.96) to the French lands is none other than "my gracious Lord of Canterbury," "my dear and faithful lord" (1.2.1, 13), who had made the offer of church funds to support a possible war with France. Thus, before the play is scarcely under way, we find ourselves among people who seem to have been brought up on *The Prince* and Bacon's "Of Negotiating," and it is not surprising that many critics find this conniving distasteful and so turn against Henry. As one of his modern biographers puts it [Harold Hutchinson, in *Henry V: A Biography*, 1967], "If Shakespeare is to be believed, the renewal of what we now call 'The Hundred Years War' was entirely due to the cynical advice of English Churchmen." Shakespeare, it is true, gives a more favorable picture of the churchmen and their efforts to influence the king than do his sources, but even in his modified form the calculated, conniving conduct of the churchmen serves well enough. Aided by recollections of "that vile politician Bolingbroke," the business at Gaultree Forest, and Henry IV's dying advice, our impulse at the outset is to involve the king in this sad business and mark him down for a sharp and conniving operator.

This is probably a mistake, and subsequent developments might make one think so. Shakespeare does not spare the churchmen, but it is they who are busy being politicians, and not Henry. The odd thing about *Henry V* is that as we look at the king's conduct at home and abroad, he turns out in all his dealings to be the most straightforward, candid political man of the whole lot. Even when he is courting Kate with tedious gallantry, he is blunt about his purpose: "No, it is not possible you should love the enemy of France, Kate; but in loving me you should love the friend of France, for I love France so well that I will not part with a village of it; I will have it all mine" (5.2.176-80). It should be noted, moreover, that negotiations between the countries had been in progress before the offer of the bishops. As the play opens, the French envoys are waiting to present their reply to an embassy sent by the king, before the play begins, to state his claims to France. As Shakespeare arranges the order of events, the offer of money is not the primary incentive to undertaking the war, and so in solemnly warning Canterbury to state the case of his French claims honestly and without sophistry Henry need not be pretending piety or indulging in irony. On the score of learning and logic—too much for us as audience—Canterbury's speech shows that Henry has asked the right man. Today the long harangue on the Salic law is a bore, and whether, as has been alleged, it was more interesting to an age that had to listen to long sermons can be no more than a hopeful guess. But Shakespeare introduces it as though he wished it to be taken as reasonable, and it is doubtful that he put it in for laughs—which is the only way Olivier saw of getting by with it in the film version of the play. By itself the play does not readily support the charge that Henry trumped up an unjust war—a charge, incidentally, which, as the Arden editor [J. H. Walter] points out, would not have been supported by the eminent sixteenth-century jurist, Gentili.

Shakespeare's dramatic strategy has induced numerous unfavorable responses, but it can be accounted for. Henry is presented as a model king, but he rules over an ordinarily imperfect nation—it is one way of bringing a sense of reality into the affairs of this near-perfect epic hero. The play moves on to high moments of patriotism and heroism, but in the course of events there are unsentimental glances now and then at the realities which accompany such great actions of state. The canny and self-serving politicking of the churchmen is to the deliberations that precede the hostilities with France what the discreditable conduct of a few of the king's soldiers is to the heroism of Agincourt. They impinge on Henry, they are part of the nation he must lead to glory, but he is not tarnished by them. There are politicians among the clergy, traitors among the nobles, and shabby characters among the soldiers, but the king employs or disposes of these as he must, moving about them without losing his independence and national regard. There are, moreover, two nations involved in these negotiations. The answer which the French embassy brings in act 1 is not from the king of France but from the dauphin, and it is an insult, which therefore renders further diplomatic negotiations impossible. National honor is a concept which our times have made to seem shabby, but it is nevertheless still true that in diplomacy a public insult from a weak nation is easier to disregard than from an equal. In the setting of the play, the uncompromising reply and the dauphin's contemptuous gift of tennis balls allows a choice only between humiliation and war. Act 1 is thus a dramatization of the cross-currents of debate, negotiation, and diplomacy which precede and in their mixed and sometimes irrelevant way combine to bring nations to war.

The second act encompasses the events between the breakdown of diplomatic missions and the actual fighting, in a loose sequence of events. The chorus tells of the contagious excitement that makes youth eager to take part in the national adventure:

> Now all the youth of England are on fire,
> And silken dalliance in the wardrobe lies;
> Now thrive the armorers, and honor's thought
> Reigns solely in the breast of every man.
> They sell the pasture now to buy the horse,
> Following the mirror of all Christian kings
> With winged heels, as English Mercuries.
>
> (1-7)

The play, however, shows us none of this. The odd assortment of characters from the tavern at Eastcheap are all we actually see responding to the war fever, and they are about to join Henry's forces for sordid reasons. In Pistol's inelegant but vivid language, "Let us to France, like horse-leeches, my boys, / To suck, to suck, the very blood to suck" (2.3.56-57). They threaten the lofty tone, like the practical politics of the bishops. We do not see the Gowers and Fluellens, the Williamses and the Courts being moved by the spirit of the moment to join the troops, though they are there at Harfleur and at Agincourt to carry the honor of their country while the Pistols and Bardolphs come to a bad end. The second major episode of act 2, clearly anticipated with appropriate comment by the chorus, is the discovery of the traitors. The final scene is in the French court, and while the picture suggested by the chorus, of the French quaking with fear and pale policy, is not borne out by the dramatization of the episode, the king of France warns the arrogant dauphin not to underestimate the English, and even the dauphin agrees to prudent preparations. The scene ends with the arrival of Exeter bringing an English ultimatum which is dismissed by the French with defiance. In the midst of these miscellaneous scenes, only Henry's confident words after he has dismissed the traitors match the high promise of the opening lines of the chorus:

> We doubt not now
> But every rub is smoothed on our way.
> Then forth, dear countrymen. Let us deliver
> Our puissance into the hand of God,
> Putting it straight in expedition.
> Cheerly to sea; the signs of war advance:
> No king of England, if not king of France!
>
> (2.2.187-93)

The next two acts depict the war itself. Act 3 presents two phases of it. The act opens with the siege of Harfleur, the kind of early victory, deceptively easy, which falls to an eager army against a foe not yet prepared to take the invasion seriously. The talk of

Henry before Harfleur is in this spirit: "Once more unto the breach, dear friends, once more; / Or close the wall up with our English dead!" (3.1.1-2). It is easy enough to talk about closing the wall up with English dead when casualties are still few and the army still fresh. Even the cowardly buffoonery of Pistol, Nym, and Bardolph is not enough to sully the occasion, since it is balanced by the solid character of the professionals, Gower, Jamie, Macmorris, and Fluellen. The comedy of the latter group, arising as it does out of their shop talk and their temperamental and national differences, does not diminish them as capable trained officers. The concluding portion of the third act brings us, with considerable foreshortening of time, to a later and more sober stage in the war, when sickness, lack of supplies, and war-weariness have taken their toll and the once spirited forces before Harfleur, now badly reduced, face an aroused and prepared enemy. At this stage there is no patience with the comic parody of soldiering provided by the Eastcheap gang, and the darkening of the situation is marked by Pistol's inability to get a reprieve for Bardolph, who must hang for not observing the king's stern orders against theft.

The fourth act carries the war portion to its climax at Agincourt. It opens with a series of episodes which show the king meeting with various parts of his army to assess their spirit, a device that provides a view of all the diverse groups that combined to make up his expeditionary force. These opening episodes prepare the mood for the battle, and for Henry's speech to the camp—a very different oration from the one before Harfleur. There is no talk of imitating the action of the tiger, no battle cries of "Harry, England, and St. George." The confidence expressed in this instance comes from the knowledge that this small, beleaguered army is united in waiting to face a common danger with courage. "We band of brothers," Henry calls them, "For he today that sheds his blood with me / Shall be my brother" (4.3.60-62).

The decisive victory at Agincourt is followed in the next act by the negotiations that conclude the peace. Burgundy is the go-between:

> I have labored
> With all my wits, my pains, and strong
> endeavors
> To bring your most imperial majesties
> Unto this bar and royal interview.
>   (5.2.24-27)

And he prefaces the negotiations with an eloquent plea for peace, the "dear nurse of arts, plenties, and joyful births" (5.2.35). Henry, with all the advantages on his side, proves a firm negotiator—"You must buy that peace / With full accord to all our just demands" (5.2.70-71). His victory is total: his demands

are met, he wins the princess Katherine for his wife, and the two erstwhile enemies seal the bargain with hopes for future amity. There is some justice in the common criticism that the last act is dramatically a letdown, but it is certainly a fitting completion of the design called for by the general idea which governs the play.

The structure of the play is straightforward and simple, and it makes clear the controlling idea. We begin with the debates and diplomatic mission that lead to war, and end with the negotiations that lead to peace. These two acts frame the portions of the action which involve the preparations preliminary to the war, and which deal with the war itself, from its buoyant beginning to the dark moment of danger, and then to its splendid victory. Everything in *Henry V* is accommodated to this design. Battles and fighting occur in all the other history plays, but in none of the others is war so exclusively the setting and the subject. . . .

Mark Van Doren

SOURCE: "*Henry V*," in *Shakespeare*, Henry Holt and Company, 1939, pp. 170-79.

[*In the following excerpt, Van Doren criticizes the lack of unity in* Henry V, *stating that the spectacle of the play does not compensate for the inadequate dramatic matter. He condemns Shakespeare's use of the chorus, the inflated style, the sentimental appeal to patriotism, and the weak humor in the play. Van Doren also asserts that Shakespeare fails to establish a relation between Henry's actions and his experiences.*]

Shakespeare in *Henry IV* had still been able to pour all of his thought and feeling into the heroic drama without demolishing its form. His respect for English history as a subject, his tendency to conceive kings in tragic terms, his interest in exalted dialogue as a medium through which important actions could be advanced—these, corrected by comedy which flooded the whole with the wisdom of a warm and proper light, may have reached their natural limit, but that limit was not transgressed. *Henry IV*, in other words, both was and is a successful play; it answers the questions it raises, it satisfies every instinct of the spectator, it is remembered as fabulously rich and at the same time simply ordered. *Henry V* is no such play. It has its splendors and its secondary attractions, but the forces in it are not unified. The reason probably is that for Shakespeare they had ceased to be genuine forces. He marshals for his task a host of substitute powers, but the effect is often hollow. The style strains itself to bursting, the hero is stretched until he struts on tiptoe and is still strutting at the last insignificant exit, and war is emptied of its tragic content. The form of the historical drama had been the tragic form; its dress is borrowed here, but only borrowed. The heroic idea splinters into a thousand starry fragments, fine as fragments but lighted from no single source.

Everywhere efforts are made to be striking, and they succeed. But the success is local. *Henry V* does not succeed as a whole because its author lacks adequate dramatic matter; or because, veering so suddenly away from tragedy, he is unable to free himself from the accidents of its form; or because, with *Julius Caesar* and *Hamlet* on his horizon, he finds himself less interested than before in heroes who are men of action and yet is not at the moment provided with a dramatic language for saying so. Whatever the cause, we discover that we are being entertained from the top of his mind. There is much there to glitter and please us, but what pleases us has less body than what once did so and soon will do so with still greater abundance again.

The prologues are the first sign of Shakespeare's imperfect dramatic faith. Their verse is wonderful but it has to be, for it is doing the work which the play ought to be doing, it is a substitute for scene and action. "O for a Muse of fire," the poet's apology begins. The prologues are everywhere apologetic; they are saying that no stage, this one or any other, is big enough or wealthy enough to present the "huge and proper life" of Henry's wars; this cockpit cannot hold the vasty fields of France, there will be no veritable horses in any scene, the ship-boys on the masts and the camp-fires at Agincourt will simply have to be imagined. Which it is the business of the play to make them be, as Shakespeare has known and will know again. The author of *Romeo and Juliet* had not been sorry because his stage was a piece of London rather than the whole of Verona, and the storm in *King Lear* will begin without benefit of description. The description here is always very fine, as for example at the opening of the fourth act:

> Now entertain conjecture of a time
> When creeping murmur and the poring dark
> Fills the wide vessel of the universe.
> From camp to camp through the foul womb
>   of night
> The hum of either army stilly sounds,
> That the fix'd sentinels almost receive
> The secret whispers of each other's watch;
> Fire answers fire, and through their paly
>   flames
> Each battle sees the other's umber'd face;
> Steed threatens steed, in high and boastful
>   neighs
> Piercing the night's dull ear; and from the
>   tents
> The armourers, accomplishing the knights,
> With busy hammers closing rivets up,

> Give dreadful note of preparation.

But it is still description, and it is being asked to do what description can never do—turn spectacle into plot, tableau into tragedy.

The second sign of genius at loose ends is a radical and indeed an astounding inflation in the style. Passages of boasting and exhortation are in place, but even the best of them, whether from the French or from the English side, have a forced, shrill, windy sound, as if their author were pumping his muse for dear life in the hope that mere speed and plangency might take the place of matter. For a few lines like

> Familiar in his mouth as household words
>   (IV, iii, 52)

> The singing masons building roofs of gold
>   (I, ii, 198)

> I see you stand like greyhounds in the slips,
> Straining upon the start
>   (III, i, 31-2)

there are hundreds like

> The native mightiness and fate of him
>   (II, iv, 64)

> With ample and brim fullness of his force
>   (I, ii, 150)

> That caves and womby vaultages of France
> Shall chide your trespass and return your
>   mock.
>   (II, iv, 124-5)

Mightiness and fate, ample and brim, caves and vaultages, trespass and mock—such couplings attest the poet's desperation, the rhetorician's extremity. They spring up everywhere, like birds from undergrowth: sweet and honey'd, open haunts and popularity, thrive and ripen, crown and seat, right and title, right and conscience, kings and monarchs, means and might, aim and butt, large and ample, taken and impounded, frank and uncurbed, success and conquest, desert and merit, weight and worthiness, duty and zeal, savage and inhuman, botch and bungle, garnish'd and deck'd, assembled and collected, sinister and awkward, culled and choice-drawn, o'erhang and jutty, waste and desolation, cool and temperate, flexure and low bending, signal and ostent, vainness and self-glorious pride. Shakespeare has perpetrated them before, as when in *Henry VI* he coupled ominous and fearful, trouble and disturb, substance and authority, and absurd and reasonless. But never has he perpetrated them with such thoughtless frequency. Nor has he at this point developed the compound epithet into that interesting mannerism—the only mannerism he ever submitted to—which is to be so noticeable in his next half-dozen plays, including *Hamlet*. The device he is to use will involve more than the pairing of adjectives or nouns; one part of speech will assume the duties of another, and a certain very sudden concentration of meaning will result. There is, to be sure, one approximation to the device in *Henry V*—"the quick forge and working-house of thought" (Prologue, v, 23). . . .

The third sign is a direct and puerile [juvenile] appeal to the patriotism of the audience, a dependence upon sentiments outside the play that can be counted on, once they are tapped, to pour in and repair the deficiencies of the action. Unable to achieve a dramatic unity out of the materials before him, Shakespeare must grow lyrical about the unity of England; politics must substitute for poetry. He cannot take England for granted as the scene of conflicts whose greatness will imply its greatness. It must be great itself, and the play says so—unconvincingly. There are no conflicts. The traitors Scroop, Cambridge, and Grey are

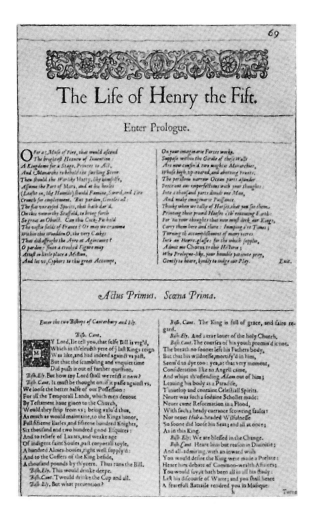

Title page of Henry V *taken from the First Folio (1623).*

happy to lose their heads for England (II, ii), and the battles in France, even though the enemy's host is huge and starvation takes its toll, are bound to be won by such fine English fellows as we have here. If the French have boasted beforehand, the irony of their doing so was obvious from the start. But it was patriotism, shared as a secret between the author and his audience, that made it obvious. It was not drama.

And a fourth sign is the note of gaiety that takes the place here of high passion. The treasure sent to Henry by the Dauphin is discovered at the end of the first act to be tennis-balls: an insult which the young king returns in a speech about matching rackets and playing sets—his idiom for bloody war. When the treachery of Scroop, Cambridge, and Grey is detected on the eve of his departure for France he stages their discomfiture somewhat as games are undertaken, and with a certain sporting relish watches their faces as they read their dooms. The conversation of the French leaders as they wait for the sun to rise on Agincourt is nervous as thoroughbreds are nervous, or champion athletes impatient for a tournament to commerce; their camp is a locker room, littered with attitudes no less than uniforms (III, vii). The deaths of York and Suffolk the next day are images of how young knights should die. They kiss each other's gashes, wearing their red blood like roses in the field, and spending their last breath in terms so fine that Exeter, reporting to the King, is overcome by "the pretty and sweet manner of it" (IV, vi, 28). And of course there are the scenes where Katharine makes fritters of English, waiting to be wooed (III, iv) and wooed at last (V, ii) by Henry Plantagenet, "king of good fellows." "The truth is," said Dr. Johnson, "that the poet's matter failed him in the fifth act, and he was glad to fill it up with whatever he could get; and not even Shakespeare can write well without a proper subject. It is a vain endeavour for the most skilful hand to cultivate barrenness, or to paint upon vacuity." That is harsh, but its essence cannot be ignored. The high spirits in which the scenes are written have their attraction, but they are no substitute for intensity.

Nor do they give us the king we thought we had. "I speak to thee plain soldier," boasts Henry in homespun vein. "I am glad thou canst speak no better English; for, if thou couldst, thou wouldst find me such a plain king that thou wouldst think I had sold my farm to buy my crown. I know no ways to mince it in love, but directly to say, 'I love you.' . . . These fellows of infinite tongue, that can rhyme themselves into ladies' favours, they do always reason themselves out again. . . . By mine honour, in true English, I love thee, Kate" (V, ii). . . .

Shakespeare has forgotten the glittering young god whom Vernon described in *Henry IV*—plumed like an estridge or like an eagle lately bathed, shining like an image in his golden coat, as full of spirit as the month of May, wanton as a youthful goat, a feathered Mercury, an angel dropped down from the clouds. The figure whom he has groomed to be the ideal English king, all plumes and smiles and decorated courage, collapses here into a mere good fellow, a hearty undergraduate with enormous initials on his chest. The reason must be that Shakespeare has little interest in the ideal English king. He has done what rhetoric could do to give us a young heart whole in honor, but his imagination has already sped forward to Brutus and Hamlet: to a kind of hero who is no less honorable than Henry but who will tread on thorns as he takes the path of duty—itself unclear, and crossed by other paths of no man's making. Henry is Shakespeare's last attempt at the great man who is also simple. Henceforth he will show greatness as either perplexing or perplexed; and Hamlet will be both.

Meanwhile his imagination undermines the very eminence on which Henry struts. For the King and his nobles the war may be a handsome game, but an undercurrent of realism reminds us of the "poor souls" for whom it is no such thing. We hear of widows' tears and orphans' cries, of dead men's blood and pining maidens' groans (II, iv, 104-7). Such horrors had been touched on in earlier Histories; now they are given a scene to themselves (IV, i). While the French leaders chaff one another through the night before Agincourt the English common soldiers have their hour. Men with names as plain as John Bates and Michael Williams walk up and down the dark field thinking of legs and arms and heads chopped off in battle, of faint cries for surgeons, of men in misery because of their children who will be rawly left. Henry, moving among them in the disguise of clothes like theirs, asks them to remember that the King's cause is just and his quarrel honorable. "That's more than we know," comes back the disturbing cool voice of Michael Williams. Henry answers with much fair prose, and the episode ends with a wager—sportsmanship again—which in turn leads to an amusing recognition scene (IV, viii). But the honest voice of Williams still has the edge on Henry's patronizing tone:

Williams. Your Majesty came not like yourself. You appear'd to me but as a common man; witness the night, your garments, your lowliness; and what your Highness suffer'd under that shape, I beseech you take it for your own fault and not mine. . . .

King Henry. Here, uncle Exeter, fill this
glove with crowns,
And give it to this fellow. Keep it, fellow;
And wear it for an honour in thy cap
    Till I do challenge it.
                                    (IV, viii, 53-64)

Henry has not learned that Williams knows. He is

still the plumed king, prancing on oratory and waving wagers as he goes. That he finally has no place to go is the result of Shakespeare's failure to establish any relation between a hero and his experience. Henry has not absorbed the vision either of Williams or of Shakespeare. This shrinks him in his armor, and it leaves the vision hanging.

The humor of the play, rich as it sometimes is, suffers likewise from a lack of vital function. The celebrated scene (II, iii) in which the Hostess describes Falstaff's death shuts the door forever on *Henry IV* and its gigantic comedy. Pistol and Bardolph continue in their respective styles, and continue cleverly; the first scene of the second act, which finds them still in London, may be indeed the best one ever written for them—and for Nym in his pompous brevity.

I cannot tell. Things must be as they may. Men may sleep, and they may have their throats about them at that time; and some say knives have edges. It must be as it may.

Pistol was never excited to funnier effect.

O hound of Crete, think'st thou my spouse
    to get?
No! to the spital go,
And from the powdering-tub of infamy
Fetch forth the lazar kite of Cressid's kind,
Doll Tearsheet she by name, and her
    espouse.
I have, and I will hold, the quondam
    Quickly
For the only she; and—*pauca,* there's enough.
Go to.

Yet this leads on to little in France beyond a series of rather mechanically arranged encounters in which the high talk of heroes is echoed by the rough cries of rascals. "To the breach, to the breach!" yells Bardolph after Henry, and that is parody. But Henry has already parodied himself; the device is not needed, any more than the rascals are. Shakespeare seems to admit as much when he permits lectures to be delivered against their moral characters, first by the boy who serves them (III, ii 28-57) and next by the sober Gower (III, vi, 70-85), and when he arranges bad ends for them as thieves, cutpurses, and bawds.

There is a clearer function for Fluellen, the fussy Welsh pedant who is for fighting wars out of books. Always fretting and out of breath, he mourns "the disciplines of the wars," the pristine wars of the Romans, now in these latter days lost with all other learning. There was not this tiddle taddle and pibble pabble in Pompey's camp. The law of arms was once well known, and men—strong, silent men such as he fancies himself to be—observed it without prawls and prabbles. He has no shrewdness; he mistakes Pistol for a brave man because he talks bravely, and there is his classic comparison of Henry with Alexander because one lived in Monmouth and the other in Macedon and each city had a river and there were salmons in both. He has only his schoolmaster's eloquence; it breaks out on him like a rash, and is the one style here that surpasses the King's in fullness.

> *Fluellen.* It is not well done, mark you now, to take the tales out of my mouth, ere it is made and finished. I speak but in the figures and comparisons of it. As Alexander kill'd his friend Cleitus, being in his ales and his cups; so also Harry Monmouth, being in his right wits and his good judgements, turn'd away the fat knight with the great belly doublet. He was full of jests, and gipes, and knaveries, and mocks; I have forgot his name.
>
> *Gower.* Sir John Falstaff.
>
> *Fluellen.* That is he.
>
> (IV, vii, 43-55)

Fluellen reminds us of Falstaff. That is a function, but he has another. It is to let the war theme finally down. Agincourt is won not only by a tennis-player but by a school-teacher. Saint Crispin's day is to be remembered as much in the pibble pabble of a pedant as in the golden throatings of a hollow god. Fluellen is one of Shakespeare's most humorous men, and one of his best used.

KINGSHIP

Scholars have discussed a number of characteristics of Henry V's kingship, including the validity of his succession and the burden of the role of king. Critics such as **Charles Mitchell** and **Harold C. Goddard** have assessed Henry's right to both the English and French thrones. Mitchell contends that while Henry is proving his right to the French throne, he is also securing his right to the English crown. Other critics, including **D. A. Traversi** and Peter G. Phialas, focus on the burden of the position of king and Henry's inner conflict between self-control and passion. Phialas asserts that while Henry struggles to achieve a balance between the demands of the crown and his right as a human being to express personal feelings, he does not fully accomplish this reconciliation until the close of the play. Alice Shalvi, however, contends that Henry is an ideal king precisely because of his human qualities. She states that Henry's courage and leadership, combined with his knowledge of and love for his people, serve as the basis of his success as king. Herbert R. Coursen, Jr. examines Henry's inability to act like a mere man now that he is king, and also notes that limited vision and the ability to

make morality subservient to politics are essential to the successful ruler. Karl E. Snyder reviews Henry's fulfillment of several aspects of kingship, including his relationship with his counselors and his divinity.

Harold C. Goddard

SOURCE: "*Henry V*," in *The Meaning of Shakespeare*, The University of Chicago Press, 1951, pp. 215-68.

[*In the excerpt below, Goddard discusses Henry's claim to the French throne and his discrediting of the Salic law. This law made it illegal for a woman to take the throne, thus denying Henry's great-great-grandmother from rightfully succeeding her father. Goddard notes that Henry uses this argument as a basis for waging war on France.*]

Henry V opens with war on France as good as decided on. Henry would have resented it if someone had told him that. Who doesn't resent being told that his mind is made up when he thinks it is still open? The resentment is a confession that it is closed.

The previous play ended with these words from John of Lancaster:

> I will lay odds, that, ere this year expire,
> We bear our civil swords and native fire
> As far as France. I heard a bird so sing,
> Whose music, to my thinking, pleas'd the king.
> Come, will you hence?

The present play, after a Chorus that forecasts the coming conflict, opens with a conversation between the Archbishop of Canterbury and the Bishop of Ely that takes war for granted, though Canterbury does not refer to it in so blunt a term but, more tactfully, as "causes now in hand . . . as touching France." What the King's brother, a little bird, a Chorus, and two Bishops agree in foreseeing is certainly coming. Henry has obviously made up his mind to follow his father's advice to busy giddy minds with foreign quarrels.

War being deemed desirable, the next thing is to find a reason for it. The opening of the play is dedicated to a search for sound moral ground for the attack on France. Fortunately for Henry, the Archbishop of Canterbury not only has such a sanction at hand but has a motive for bringing it forward. By a happy chance, he has discovered that what is good for the church coincides with what the King has decided is good for his kingdom. In Henry IV's reign a bill had been introduced to confiscate the better half of the church's wealth. Because of the troubled times it had never come to passage. But now it has been revived:

CANT.:   Thus runs the bill.
ELY: This would drink deep.
CANT.:   'Twould drink the cup and all.
ELY: But what prevention?
CANT.: The king is full of grace and fair
    regard.
ELY: And a true lover of the holy church.
CANT.: The courses of his youth promis'd it
    not . . .

and the two men digress from the subject in hand to comment on the miraculous change that has come over Henry. "But, my good lord," says Ely, returning to the main point,

How now for mitigation of this bill
Urg'd by the commons? Doth his majesty
    Incline to it, or no?
CANT.:   He seems indifferent,
Or rather swaying more upon our part
Than cherishing the exhibiters against us;
For I have made an offer to his majesty. . . .

This offer, he goes on to explain, is that the clergy shall make the greatest contribution ever recorded to the war chest of the sovereign. It will obviously be better for the church to make a large gift and so forestall confiscation than to give little or nothing and have its wealth expropriated.

ELY: How did this offer seem receiv'd, my
    lord?

(There is another word, also of five letters, that would define the nature of the proposed transaction more precisely than "offer." But it would be too much to expect either of these churchmen to employ it.)

With good acceptance of his majesty,

says Canterbury, answering Ely's question,

Save that there was not time enough to
    hear,—
As I perceiv'd his Grace would fain have
    done. . . .

and the Archbishop proceeds to tell of another trump card he had up his sleeve which an interruption prevented him from putting on the table before the King:

The severals and unhidden passages
Of his true titles to some certain dukedoms,
And generally to the crown and seat of
    France
Deriv'd from Edward, his great-grandfather.

In a word, the Church will supply not only treasure for the war chest but a justification for making the

war. What more could Henry ask? This is far more than his spiritual and political "father," the Lord Chief Justice of the previous play, would have had to offer in the circumstances. That may seem a cynical way of putting it, and Henry's words, when he resumes the interrupted conversation in the next scene, seem to make it utterly unwarranted. The King begins by warning the Archbishop not to incite him to war on specious grounds. Think of the blood that will be spilt, he reminds him, every drop of which will be a just complaint against whoever begins an unrighteous conflict.

We charge you in the name of God, take
    heed. . . .
Under this conjuration speak, my lord,
And we will hear, note, and believe in
    heart,
That what you speak is in your conscience
    wash'd
As pure as sin with baptism.

Nothing could sound more moral and humane (though a suspicious mind might find a Chaucerian ambiguity in that last phrase). But we must judge Henry by his acts, not by his words.

The King must have an irreproachable reason for making war. The one thing that his claim to the French throne must be is *clear*. But when the Archbishop goes on to expound that claim, clear is the one thing it does not seem to be. The sixty-odd lines Canterbury devotes to it make one of the most complicated passages of pure exposition in Shakespeare and one of the most difficult to assimilate without an opportunity to study it minutely. No one could possibly take it in in the theater. Any stage director would be certain to cut it drastically. Yet attention to it in detail is indispensable to an understanding of the scene.

The gist of Henry's claim rests on the fact that his great-great-grandmother was the daughter of Philip IV of France, the only bar to its legitimacy being the Salic law under which succession through the female line is illegal. Even if the title had been a technically good one, time had had the same effect on it as a statute of limitations. But its very age seems to recommend it all the more to the learned Archbishop. His speech consists of an elaborate discrediting of the Salic law. Under analysis it turns out to be (as it is even in Holinshed whom Shakespeare follows closely here) a colossal piece of ecclesiastical casuistry [resolving of duty or conduct through ethical principles or religious doctrine] with a highly ironical application to the situation in which Henry finds himself.

That situation itself, without any historical assistance, is ironical enough. Henry's father had seized the English throne—with disillusioning consequences. His son now proposes to seize the French throne in the hope—shall we say, of wiping out his father's sin? The Archbishop's speech rubs in the irony, for all the genealogical details he cites fit with damning neatness the situation in which Henry finds himself, and tend to undermine the very claim they are brought forward to substantiate. How far the learned Archbishop is intentionally obscuring the issue, and how far it is obscuring him, is difficult at times to make out. But if the style is the man we are entitled to believe the worst.

To prove that Henry will not be a usurper if he seizes the crown of France in defiance of the Salic law he cites the cases of three French kings who themselves inherited through the female. The first one deposed another king (*as Henry IV did Richard II*). The second "usurped the crown" by pressing his title

> with some shows of truth,
> Though in pure truth it was corrupt and
>   naught,

(*just as the Archbishop is urging Henry to press a similar title at the moment*). The third, who was sole heir to this usurper (*as Henry V was to Henry IV*), was so uneasy in his mind about his title (*as the first Henry was*) that he could not keep quiet in his conscience (*as the second Henry is now, by his present enterprise, proving that he cannot*). The allusiveness of all this to the pending question makes cynical in the extreme the citation of titles "corrupt and naught" as precedents in support of a claim supposed to be pure and substantial. It is like pointing to a dog's mongrel ancestors to prove it a thoroughbred. But the effrontery of the Archbishop's reasoning exceeds even this. The kings of France unto this day, he says to Henry in conclusion, want to bar your title to their throne because you inherit it through the female line, when, all the while, their own titles are crooked and were usurped from you and your progenitors because they were inherited in precisely the same way. The very thing that proves the title of a French king crooked—namely, inheritance through the female—serves, by some twist of ecclesiastical logic, to prove the title of an English king good. Heads you lose, tails I win.

Canterbury's long argument and its conclusion, which he pronounces "as clear as is the summer's sun," bewilder Henry as much as they do the reader. Or perhaps he prefers not to understand, that the responsibility may rest on the Archbishop. At any rate, quite as if he had not taken in a word of Canterbury's magnificent effort, he merely reiterates his original question:

> May I with right and conscience make this
>   claim?

To which the Archbishop replies:

> The sin upon my head, dread sovereign!
> For in the book of Numbers is it writ,
> When the son dies, let the inheritance
> Descend unto the daughter.

The Book of Numbers! The Archbishop has been holding back his ace. All those tedious genealogical details, then, were only a foil against which the crowning precedent should shine forth. (Quite in Henry's own style.) It was a considerable step back to the King's great-great-grandmother. But Moses, or whoever wrote the Pentateuch, is an even more venerable authority. When, in the next act, Exeter, in Henry's name, demands that the French King resign the crown and adds, as he presents his sovereign's pedigree:

> That you may know
> 'Tis no sinister nor no awkward claim,
> Pick'd from the worm-holes of long-vanish'd
>   days,
> Nor from the dust of old oblivion rak'd,
> He sends you this most memorable line,
> In every branch truly demonstrative,

we remember the learned Archbishop's researches and the Book of Numbers, and perceive that Exeter's vehement denial that there is anything shady or far-fetched in Henry's claim is the poet's oblique way of telling us that shady and far-fetched is exactly what it is.

And there is irony in this scene at a still deeper level. Henry bases his title on inheritance through the female line. But by this very rule under which he claims the French, he must surrender the English throne, for, allow inheritance through the female, and Edmund Mortimer, who is descended from the third son of Edward III through his grandmother, has a prior claim over Henry, who is descended from the fourth son. Shakespeare leaves it to anyone who will to remember this little fact. With it, the play is one thing; without it, quite another.

> Cheerly to sea! the signs of war advance,

cries Henry when the decision to cross the Channel is announced,

> No king of England, if not king of France.

"I am not worthy to be your king," he means, "if we cannot beat these Frenchmen." But attending to truth rather than to meter, the line ought to read:

> No king of England, if king of France.

Between war and law, Henry is bound to lose. If he wins the war, he confirms inheritance through the female and is "no king of England." If he loses it, he is no king of France.

We interrupted the Archbishop at the Book of Numbers. Let us return to his speech. "Gracious lord," he exclaims, passing from learning to exhortation,

> Gracious lord,
> Stand for your own! Unwind your bloody
> 　flag!
> Look back into your mighty ancestors!
> Go, my dread lord, to your great-grandsire's
> 　tomb,
> From whom you claim.

It is indeed a tombstone claim.

> For in his tomb lie my affections,

Henry, we may recall, said of his father. Now they go still deeper into the family burial chambers. Could anything make clearer the atavistic character of the change that is coming over Henry than these references to blood and ancestry and graves? His nobler self is regressing not merely into his father but into "the fathers."

In what follows one might imagine that that nobler self makes a final attempt to assert itself, for Henry says nothing for forty lines, while Canterbury, Ely, Exeter, and Westmoreland vie with one another in urging him to rouse himself like "the former lions" of his blood to "forage in the blood of French nobility" as did that "lion's whelp," the Black Prince, in his great-grandfather's day. Their verbal violence suggests both a suppressed thirst for blood on their own parts and a fear that Henry is hesitating to give the final word. Your subjects' hearts have already left their bodies and lie pavilioned on the fields of France, says Westmoreland.

> O, let their bodies follow, my dear liege,

cries the Archbishop,

> With blood and sword and fire to win your
> 　right;
> In aid whereof we of the spiritualty
> Will raise your highness such a mighty sum
> As never did the clergy at one time
> Bring in to any of your ancestors.

Fire, blood, lucre, and spiritualty! The witches' brew in *Macbeth* scarcely exceeds that.

It is evidently at just this moment that Henry overcomes any lingering scruples. With the tension removed, all these men, including the King, let themselves go a bit and their metaphors grow correspondingly revealing. The Scots, who are likely to attack England when her back is turned, are called petty thieves, snatchers, and weasels who suck princely eggs.

England is an eagle in prey—and a cat. But the Archbishop's comparison is a worse giveaway than any of these. He likens human polity in a well-ordered state to that of the bees. The bees, it turns out, have nearly everything in their community that men have except archbishops and armies. No high churchmen of the hive are mentioned. And as for fighters, this is the way the Archbishop tries to squeeze them in:

> Others, like soldiers, armed in their stings,
> Make boot upon the summer's velvet buds,
> Which pillage they with merry march bring
> 　home
> To the tent-royal of their emperor.

As if bees hovering above flowers, or the fruitful communion of the two, could be compared to the clash of enemies on the battlefield, or honey to the spoils of war! The Archbishop is as deficient in his science as in his symbolism. His childhood was plainly not spent in the meadows of Stratford. And his logic, that theological and ecclesiastical specialty, is no better. The bees are united and harmonious in a perfect division of labor, he says; "therefore" Henry should "divide" his forces into four parts, attack France with one, and leave the other three for home defense. What these two kinds of division have to do with each other only a mind more concerned with words than realities could figure out. What fun Shakespeare must have had making such a fool of his Archbishop, knowing all the while that his audience would swallow his utterances as grave political wisdom.

The King evidently accepts them as such, for as the Archbishop concludes, he gives the order:

> Call in the messengers sent from the
> 　Dauphin.
> Now are we well resolv'd.

The French ambassadors enter and ask whether they shall speak their sovereign's intent plainly or veil it in diplomatic language.

Henry tells them to speak out:

> We are no tyrant, but a Christian king;
> Unto whose grace our passion is as subject
> As are our wretches fetter'd in our prisons:
> Therefore with frank and with uncurbed
> 　plainness
> Tell us the Dauphin's mind.

The metaphor is worth nothing, for it is presently going to escape, as prisoners sometimes do, and stab its user in the back. "Whatever praises itself but in the deed," Shakespeare was to write a year or two later, "devours the deed in the praise." He knew it already.

Accepting Henry's invitation not to mince their words, the ambassadors declare that the Dauphin thinks Henry's claims (to certain lands in France—they have not yet heard his claim to the throne) "savour too much of your youth," a plain allusion to the part Hal had taken in *robberies;* that he cannot *dance* and *revel* himself into French dukedoms. Therefore he sends. Henry, in satisfaction of his claims and as more appropriate to his spirit, a tun of treasure. The treasure turns out to be—tennis balls!

This allusion to his gay youth touches Henry where he is sorest. On the instant his passions, which a moment before he had boasted were his subjects and prisoners, break their chains in such a threat of violence that it sounds more like the barbarous license of some Goth or Norseman in the days of Beowulf than the utterance of a supposedly responsible monarch. Go tell the Dauphin that

> many a thousand widows
> Shall this his mock mock out of their dear
>   husbands;
> Mock mothers from their sons, mock castles
>   down;
> And some are yet ungotten and unborn
> That shall have cause to curse the Dauphin's
>   scorn.

Diplomatic insults have often precipitated wars, and it isn't easy even for the Mirror of all Christian Kings to be twitted in the presence of his court on the subject of his misspent youth. Yet somehow all those widows and mothers and unborn babes seem more than an equivalent for a few tennis balls.

Intoxicated by his own strong speech, the King becomes so consumed with this idea of dominating France that England begins to seem like a mere side issue, a vacation spot where he has given himself up to gaiety while absent from his "home," the throne of France:

> We never valu'd this poor seat of England;
> And therefore, living hence, did give ourself
> To barbarous license; as 'tis ever common
> That men are merriest when they are from
>   home.

(What would Faulconbridge and John of Gaunt have said to that?) But when I come back to that home, Henry declares,

> I will rise there with so full a glory
> That I will dazzle all the eyes of France,
> Yea, strike the Dauphin blind to look on us.

That same old metaphor of the sun is still troubling him! Possessing him rather, we should say, for the sun is now turning from a glorious thing into a deadly one.

Evidently the "barbarous license" that the rejection of Falstaff supposedly ended forever did not include the barbarous license of speech in which Henry indulges in this interview with the ambassadors. But something within his unconsciousness (where the rejected Hal, it should be remembered, now resides) is evidently uneasy and attempts to strike a balance by making Henry introduce references to God, three in a score of lines, immediately following his bragging outbreak. This is one of the King's most interesting psychological symptoms. Those tennis balls shall turn to cannon balls, he boasts in one breath, and the Dauphin's soul at the Judgment Day shall be charged for the vengeance they bring.

> But this lies all within the will of God,

he adds in the next breath, as if catching himself up, "in whose name . . . I am coming on," he concludes in a third breath, "to venge me." He cannot leave himself out after all. *Vengeance is mine, saith the Lord*—and Henry V of England is my instrument. So reads Henry's revised version.

And thus the first act ends. One wonders whether any who find it lacking in drama may possibly have missed some of its irony. . . .

D. A. Traversi

SOURCE: *"Henry IV—Parts I and II, and Henry V,"* in *An Approach to Shakespeare*, third edition, Doubleday & Company, Inc., 1969, pp. 191-258.

[*In the following excerpt from an essay first published in 1956, Traversi observes Henry's moral and political conflict between self-control and passion. He contends that as king, Henry must possess a complete devotion to his position and cannot allow selfishness to affect his decisions. Traversi argues that Henry V provides the link between political unity and personal order in England. He also traces Henry's struggle throughout the play with personal control and order.*]

The political success aimed at by Henry IV is finally achieved, in the last play of the series, by his son. The general theme of *Henry V* is the establishment in England of an order based on consecrated authority and crowned by action against France. The conditions of this order are, again in accordance with the main conception, moral as well as political. The crime of regicide which had stood between Bolingbroke and the attainment of peace no longer hangs over Henry V—unless as a disturbing memory—and the crusading purpose which had run as an unfulfilled aspiration through the father's life is replaced by the reality, at once brilliant and ruthless, of the son's victorious campaign.

This, as critics have not always realized, is less a conclusion than a point of departure for the understanding of *Henry V*. It was the conditions of kingship, at least as much as its results, that interested Shakespeare in these plays: and these conditions are viewed, by the time the last of them came to be conceived, in a light definitely akin to the tragic. The problem of political unity and that of personal order have been brought in the course of these historical studies into the closest relationship. The former has been achieved, in the preceding plays, by the development of a political capacity that recalls, in various of its aspects, the Machiavellian conception of the Prince; but success of this kind increasingly poses for Shakespeare, whose thought was at once more traditional and less limited to the political than that of the great Florentine, wider problems more definitely moral, even religious, in kind. Just as the state, already in *Henry IV*-Part II, is regarded in its divisions as a diseased body ravaged by a consuming fever, so is the individual seen increasingly as torn between the violence of his passions and the direction of reason; and just as the remedy to political anarchy lies in unquestioned allegiance to an authority divinely constituted, so does personal coherence depend upon the submission to reason of our uncontrolled desires. The link between the two states, political and personal, is provided in these plays by concentration upon the figure of the king. The problem of the state becomes that of the individual at its head. The king, who properly demands unquestioning allegiance from his subjects, is first called upon to show, through the perfection of his dedication, a complete and selfless devotion to his office. The personal implications, as well as the patriotic triumphs, which that devotion brings with it are considered in *Henry V*.

It demands, in the first place, an absolute measure of self-domination. Called upon to exercise justice and shape policies for the common good, the king can allow no trace of selfishness or frailty to affect his decisions. He must continually examine his motives, confirm them in the light of reason; and this means that he is engaged in a continual struggle against his share of human weakness. As the play proceeds, we become increasingly aware that there is in Henry an uneasy balance between violent passion, in certain of its forms, and firm self-control. The control is, indeed, an essential part of his political capacity and of his personal stature. Without it, Henry would not be a true king at all; but, precisely because he is a man and not a crowned puppet, there are times when an unmistakable sense of constraint makes itself felt, as for instance in his greeting to the French ambassador:

> We are no tyrant, but a Christian king;
> Unto whose grace our passion is as subject
> As are our wretches fettered in our prisons.
>
> (I. ii)

The harshness of the comparison is, to say the least, remarkable. Such control, though admirable, and doubly so in a king, is necessarily precarious. The passions, "fettered," treated with a disdain similar to that which, as Prince Hal, he has already displayed to the considerations of normal feeling when the fulfillment of his vocation imposed the renunciation of his past, may be expected to break out in forms not immediately attractive.

Almost at once, in fact, they do so. The French envoys, in fulfilling their mission by presenting him with the Dauphin's tennis balls, touch upon a raw spot in Henry's sensibility; they expose him to ridicule and, worst of all, they refer—by the observation that "You cannot revel into dukedoms here"—to the abjured but not forgotten past. Henry's reaction, in spite of the opening affirmation of self-control, takes the form of one of those outbursts which are habitual with him whenever his will is crossed. As when France was to be "bent" or "broken," his rhetoric, measured and even cold on the surface, is full of accumulated passion:

> When we have match'd our rackets to these
>   balls,
> We will, in France, by God's grace, play a
>   set
> Shall strike his father's crown into the
>   hazard.
>
> (I. ii)

The reference to "God's grace," rarely omitted from Henry's official utterances, clearly befits a Christian king, and we need not deny its propriety; but from the personal point of view, which the play is also concerned to stress, the note of resentment which rises through the speech is equally significant. It rankles at this point until the real motive, or an important part of it, becomes at last explicit:

> we understand him well,
> How he comes o'er us with our wilder days,
> Not measuring what use we made of them.
>
> (I. ii)

The personal offense once mentioned, the considerations of conscience are swept aside, at least for so long as the new emotion is in command. The horrors of war, the slaughter and misery attendant upon it, are once again mentioned, but only that he may disclaim responsibility for them. The tone of his words, following the swell of emotion, rises to one of ruthless and triumphant egoism:

But *I* will rise there with so full a glory
That *I* will dazzle all the eyes of France,
Yea, strike the Dauphin blind to look on us.
And tell the pleasant prince this mock of his
Hath turn'd his balls to gun-stones; and his
   soul
Shall stand sore charged for the wasteful
   vengeance
That shall fly with them: for many a
   thousand widows
Shall this his mock mock out of their dear
   husbands;
Mock mothers from their sons, mock castles
   down;
And some are yet ungotten and unborn
That shall have cause to curse the Dauphin's
   scorn.

                                        (I. ii)

"*I* will rise there"; "*I* will dazzle all the eyes of France."
The Dauphin's gibe has set free Henry's "fettered"
passions and these express themselves in a cumulative
vision of destruction. The tone of the utterance—the
impact of "strike," the harsh reference to the balls
which have been turned to "gun-*stones*," the sense of
irresistible, ruinous force behind "mock castles down"—
reflects the new feeling and anticipates the later, more
masterly picture of Coriolanus in action. This is not
to say that we are to regard Henry as a monster at
this point, or to deny that a proper sense of royal
responsibility underlies his words. He is uttering a
warning, condemning the real irresponsibility of others; but the speech has, beyond this, an intimate
content which is also part of the complete effect. The
sense of power, inhuman and destructive beneath the
surface of righteous anger, has been unleashed in the
king. The responsibility for coming events, already
assumed by the Archbishop of Canterbury earlier in
the same scene, has now been further fastened upon
the Dauphin, and Henry is in a position to announce
his coming descent upon France with a phrase that
incorporates into his new vehemence the convenient
certainty of righteousness:

But all this lies within the will of God,
To whom I do appeal.

No doubt the conviction is sincere; but the fact remains that the will of God and the will of Henry, now
fused in the passion released by the Dauphin's jest,
have become identical.

It is not until the opening of the French campaign
that Henry's utterances are translated into action. The
poetry of war in this play deserves careful attention.
Much of it, corresponding to the spirit of the patriotic chronicle, is full of life and vigor; such is the
elaborate description in the Prologue to this same act
of the "fleet majestical" which bears the English forces

Act III, scene iii. Henry V takes over the city of Harfleur.

to Harfleur. The king "embarks his royalty" on a
"brave fleet," adorned and lighted by the dawn:

behold the threaden sails,
Borne with the invisible and creeping wind,
Draw the huge bottoms through the
   furrow'd sea,
Breasting the lofty surge: O, do but think
You stand upon the rivage and behold
A city on the inconstant billows dancing;
For so appears this fleet majestical.
                                        (III. Prologue)

Such imagery, splendidly and consciously laden for
its effect, is a contribution to the spirit of the play.
It may be that some of its deeper notes are not included in it, but the effect of a pageant, of the confident
display of might in beauty, is undoubtedly part of
Shakespeare's debt to his theme which, whilst balancing it against other elements, it was no part of his
intention to forgo. If, in much of this play, he qualifies the note of majesty with more somber and reflective tones, the effect of these tones is in part

gained by the contrast with the appeal of majesty itself.

Yet when, immediately after, Henry himself appears, much of his first utterance, as he incites his followers to battle, has about it a strong flavor of artificiality and strain:

> Then imitate the action of the tiger;
> Stiffen the sinews, summon up the blood,
> Disguise fair nature with hard-favour'd rage;
> Then lend the eye a terrible aspect;
> Let it pry through the portage of the head
> Like the brass cannon; let the brow
>   o'erwhelm it
> As fearfully as doth a galled rock
> O'erhang and jutty his confounded base,
> Swill'd with the wild and wasteful ocean.
> Now set the teeth and stretch the nostril
>   wide,
> Hold hard the breath and bend up every
>   spirit
> To his full height.
>
> (III. i)

There is about this incitation something forced, incongruous, even (if we may risk taking the point a little too far) slightly absurd. The action of the warrior is an imitation, and an imitation of a wild beast at that, carried out by a deliberate exclusion of "fair nature." The blood is to be summoned up, the sinews stiffened to the necessary degree of artificial savagery, while the involved rhetorical comparisons which follow the references to the "brass cannon" and the "galled rock" strengthen the impression of something very like unreality. In stressing this note of inhumanity, the speech does not intend to deny the poetry of war, which, as we have just seen, Shakespeare expresses most fully in certain passages from the various prologues of this play; but, as later in *Coriolanus*, he balances the conception of the warrior in his triumphant energy as "a greyhound straining at the leash" against that, not less forcible, of a ruthless and inhuman engine of destruction. Both ruthlessness and splendor are inseparable aspects of the complete picture.

Henry's treatment of the governor and citizens of Harfleur relates this conception of the warrior to tensions already apparent in his own character. Not for the first time, two scenes are placed together to point a contrast. The way in which he presents his ultimatum is full of that sense of conflict between control and passion that was so prominent in his early utterances. The grotesque inhumanity implicit in his words is balanced by a suggestion of tragic destiny. Beneath his callousness is a sense that the horrors of war, once unleashed, freed from the sternest control, are irresistible. His soldiers, he warns the

governor, are still held uneasily in check. "The cool and temperate wind of grace," whose control over passion is the mark of a Christian soldier, still exercises its authority; but "licentious wickedness" and "the filthy and contagious clouds" of *heady* murder" threaten to break out at any moment. In his catalogue of the horrors of war stress is laid upon rape and the crimes of "blood." The "fresh-fair" virgins of Harfleur will become the victims of the soldiery, whose destructive atrocities are significantly referred to in terms of "liberty":

> What rein can hold licentious wickedness
> When down the hill he holds his fierce
>   career?
>
> (III. iii)

The process of evil, once unleashed, follows courses fatally determined; but Henry, having described them in words which emphasize his awareness of their horror, ends by disclaiming all responsibility for them, just as he had once disclaimed all responsibility for the outbreak of the war. The whole matter, thus taken out of his hands, becomes indifferent to him:

> What is't to me, *when you yourselves are
>   cause,*
> If your pure maidens fall into the hand
> Of hot and forcing violation?
>
> (III. iii)

Yet this very assertion of indifference carries with it, at bottom, a sense of the tragedy of the royal position. Only this denial of responsibility, it would seem, only the exclusion of humanity and the acceptance of a complete dualism between controlling "grace" and the promptings of irresponsible passion, make possible that success in war which is, for the purposes of this play, the crown of kingship.

For it would certainly be wrong to suppose that Shakespeare, in portraying Henry, intends to stress a note of hypocrisy. Rather, his purpose is to bring out the burden of royalty, to point to certain contradictions, human and moral, which seem to be inherent in the notion of a successful king. As the play proceeds, Henry seems at times to be, at least in a moral sense, almost the victim of his position. The treasonable activities of Cambridge, Grey, and Scroop are indications of the duplicity with which monarchs are fated by their position to deal. Somewhere at the heart of this court there is a fundamental flaw which must constantly be allowed for by a successful ruler. It appears to Henry, in his dealings with the conspirators, as something deep-rooted enough to be associated with the original fall of man:

> seem they religious?
> Why, so didst thou: or are they spare in

diet,
Free from gross passion or of mirth or anger,
Constant in spirit, not swerving with the
    blood,
Garnish'd and deck'd in modest complement,
Not working with the eye without the ear,
And but in purged judgement trusting
    neither?
Such and so finely bolted didst thou seem:
And thus thy fall hath left a kind of blot,
To mark the full-fraught man and best
    indued
With some suspicion. I will weep for thee;
For this revolt of thine, methinks, is like
Another fall of man.

                              (II. ii)

It is remarkable that Henry, in meditating upon this betrayal, should return once more to that theme of control, of freedom from passion, which is so prominent in his own nature. By concentrating on the functioning of the body, and on the sense of mutual divergence between eye, ear, and judgment in the difficult balance of the personality, the speech sets spiritual control in contrast with a sense of anarchy that proceeds, most typically, from the contemplation of physical processes. "*Gross* passion"—the adjective is significant—is associated with the irrational "swerving of the blood," and the judgment which controls it needs to be "purged" by fasting ("spare in diet") before it can attain a scarcely human freedom from "mirth or anger." By thus emphasizing the difficult and even unnatural nature of such control, the speech casts a shadow, at least by implication, over that of Henry himself; but it is also seen to be necessary, inseparable from his office. The administration of justice, upon which depends order within the kingdom and success in its foreign wars, demands in the monarch a detachment which borders on the inhuman. The state must be purged of "treason lurking in its way" before it can be led, with that single-mindedness of purpose which is both Henry's strength and, perhaps, in the long run, his limitation, to the victorious enterprise in France.

It is clear, indeed, that *Henry V* represents, however tentatively, a step in the realization of themes fully developed in the tragedies. Inheriting from his sources the conception of a victorious king, perfectly aware of his responsibilities and religiously devoted to the idea of duty, Shakespeare seems, in the most individual scenes of his play, to emphasize the difficulties of the conception, the obstacles, both personal and political, which lie between it and fulfillment. These difficulties, however, never amount to a questioning of the royal judgment. Even in the disguised Henry's debate with Williams and Bates on the morning of Agincourt (IV. i), where the implications of his power are most searchingly discussed, the king's right to

command obedience is never in question. For Bates the duty of a subject lies in loyal execution of the royal will, and the responsibility for wrong action rests beyond the simple soldier with the king: "we know enough, if we know we are the king's subjects." Nor does Williams, though more skeptical in his attitude, question the postulate that the subject is bound to obey; for to disobey, as he puts it, "were against all property of subjection," and the emphasis is still upon the "proportion" to be observed between king and subject, directing head and executing body, and upon the proper submission which the successful prosecution of the military effort requires.

Henry, of course, accepts this view of his position; but although the questionings of his followers do not—and cannot—lead him to doubt his own authority, they do force him to reflect deeply upon the weaknesses which even kings cannot overcome. "The king is but a man as I am; the violet smells to him as it doth to me; . . . all his senses have but human conditions; his ceremonies laid by, in his nakedness he appears but a man; and though his affections are higher mounted than ours, yet when they stoop they stoop with the like wing." There is about the argument a universality which transcends the royal situation. Men, differentiated by vain "ceremony," are united in their common "nakedness," and the most notable feature of human behavior seems to the speaker to be its domination by impulse, its helplessness before the stooping of the affections. In this respect the king is one with his men; and just because he is so like them, because his senses too "have but human conditions" and are constantly liable to break through the guard of rigid self-control imposed upon him by his vocation, there is something precarious, potentially disproportionate in his absolute claim upon the allegiance of his followers.

The royal isolation is further underlined by Williams when he points out the spiritual consequences of a conflict for which the king has accepted full responsibility: "For how can they [Henry's soldiers] charitably dispose of anything when blood is their argument? Now, if these men do not die well, it will be a black matter for the king that led them to it" (IV. i). These words repeat once more, but with a greater urgency, a preoccupation with the horrors of war which Henry has already expressed, even if he succeeded in shaking off responsibility for them, to the French envoys and the governor of Harfleur. They imply, beyond the sense of responsibility which derives from the traditional conception of monarchy, a contrast—already familiar—between the Christian law of "charity" and the impulse to destruction that threatens it in the necessary acts of war with the consequences of unlimited brutality. The connection between this conflict of flesh and spirit and the tendency of human societies, states and families alike, to dissolve by the questioning of "degree" into anarchy is not established in this play as it is in the tragedies which followed. But Hamlet himself might have reflected like Henry on the precarious basis of human pretensions, and Angelo defined in similar terms the catastrophic realization of it brought about by his encounter with Isabella. Had Henry once followed his line of speculation far enough to doubt the validity of his motives for action, or—on the other hand—had he given free play to the sinister impulses dimly recognized in himself, he would of course have been the protagonist of another and quite different play; but the possibilities are there as a premonition, a first indication of issues brought fully to light in later actions.

For the moment, Henry counters the implications of this argument by pointing out that soldiers "purpose not their death, when they purpose their services." Williams' somber reflections, however, impose themselves upon him, attach themselves to his own meditations, and are profoundly echoed in his own words. Connecting war with sin, he repeats the tone of earlier statements: "Besides, there is no king, be his cause never so spotless, if it come to the arbitrament of swords, can try it out with all unspotted soldiers: some peradventure have on them the guilt of premeditated and contrived murder; some, of beguiling virgins with the broken seal of perjury" (IV. i). The result is, in part, a fresh emphasis on meticulous self-examination as a means of conserving spiritual health—"Therefore should every soldier in the wars do as every sick man in his bed, wash every mote out of his conscience"—and, in the verse soliloquy which closes the scene, one of those outbursts of nostalgic craving for release which have appeared already, in his father's mouth, in *Henry IV*—Part II, and which will be reflected with a new, more *physical* apprehension of existence in Hamlet's soliloquies and in the Duke's incitations to Claudio in *Measure for Measure:*

> what infinite heart's ease
> Must kings neglect, that private men enjoy!
>
> (IV. i)

The craving for "heart's ease" in this long speech is still, generally speaking, what it is in *Henry IV:* a desire to be freed from the burden of an office in which human purposes seem fatally divorced from human achievement. The development of the verse is still painstaking, leisurely in the expansion of its long periods, and a little rhetorical; but there are moments which foreshadow the association in *Hamlet* of this nostalgia with a desire to be free from the encumbrances, the "fardels," the "things rank and gross in nature" by which the flesh persistently seems to obstruct the workings of the spirit. "Greatness" is a "fiery fever" which consumes its royal victim like a bodily disease, and the contrasted peace of the humble

subject is described with a curious ambiguity of tone:

> Not all these, laid in bed majestical,
> Can sleep so soundly as the wretched slave,
> Who with a body fill'd and vacant mind
> Gets him to rest, cramm'd with distressful
>   bread.
>
> (IV. i)

In the association of peace with bodily fullness and vacancy of mind, in the impression, harshly and directly physical, behind "fill'd" and "cramm'd," there is a distinct suggestion of certain descriptions of satiated, idle contentment in plays as far apart as *Troilus and Cressida* and *Coriolanus*. Here already such imagery represents a kind of residue, intractable and irreducible, in direct contrast to the king's increasing emphasis on the need for spiritual discipline. It is no more than a suggestion, unabsorbed as yet into the main imaginative design of a play conceived on different, simpler lines; but, tentative as it is, it stands in a certain relationship to the clash of flesh and spirit—"passion" and "grace"—which exacts continual vigilance from Henry and which is slowly moving through these developments of imagery to more open realization.

A similar potential cleavage can be detected in the treatment of the two sides drawn up for battle at Agincourt. Shakespeare differentiates between the French and English forces in a way which sometimes seems to foreshadow the balance held in *Troilus and Cressida* between Greeks and Trojans, though it is true that the unfavorable estimate of the English, which is scarcely compatible with the spirit of the play, is expressed only in the words of their enemies. The English are morally worthy of their victory, but the French account does go a little way to anticipate the possibility of criticism. The French, combining a touch of the unsubstantial chivalry of Troilus with a more than Trojan emptiness, are, like the Trojans, and more justly, defeated; the English, whom they represent as gross and dull-witted, are as undeniably successful as the Greeks. Shakespeare's handling of the battle carries on this conception. The French, trusting in a thin and rhetorical belief in their own aristocracy, rush hastily and incompetently to their deaths; the English, deriving their spirit from their king, win the day by their perseverance and self-control. Self-control, however, which is—as in Henry himself—not without some suggestion of harshness and inhumanity. Henry's righteousness does not prevent him from inflicting merciless reprisals on his prisoners, and, though these matters need to be looked at in the spirit of the times, and the play is careful to emphasize the base act of treachery which rouses Henry to righteous anger, there is something finally sardonic about Gower's comment that "the king, *most worthily,* hath caused every soldier to cut his prisoner's throat. O, 'tis *a gallant king*"

(IV. vii). By such excellence, Shakespeare would seem to say, must even the most just and patriotic of wars be won. . . .

Charles Mitchell

SOURCE: "Henry V: The Essential King," in *Shakespearean Essays*, No.2, 1964, pp. 97-103.

[*In this essay, Mitchell examines Henry's attempts to establish his legal and moral right to kingship. He notes that by proving his right to the French throne, Henry simultaneously secures his claim to the English crown. Mitchell also discusses the concept of honor in* Henry V *and ways Henry achieves these ideals.*]

The war in Shakespeare's *Henry V* is significant because it provides the occasion for Henry's proving his right to kingship. Henry's need to establish his legal right to the throne of France serves the more pressing need to ensure his right to the English throne: [according to John Palmer in his *Political Characters of Shakespeare*, 1952] he "has invaded France in order that he may acquire a second crown which is to secure him yet more firmly in possession of a crown already in his grasp." The traitorous Scroop, Cambridge, and Grey challenge Henry's English rights, but by publicly laying claim to the French throne on the basis of his lineage, he simultaneously proves his right to the English crown. Henry's pedigree allegedly proves his right to the French crown, and the possession of that French crown would in turn prove the pedigree, which entitles him to rule England. At the same time that he establishes his legal right, Henry must also demonstrate his moral right to the English throne. Because Henry IV usurped the throne from Richard II, Henry feels that his legal right is dubious; others may be satisfied that his right can be supported by policy and power, but for Henry the legal dubiety is underlined by his doubt that he has an ethical right to kingship. In trying to satisfy his conscience that he deserves to be king, he discovers the qualities and attitudes which a truly virtuous ruler should possess. He gradually develops the proper ethical responses to concepts of conscience and commonwealth, honor and degree. At the end of the play Henry has become an embodiment of the ideals of political honor.

In spite of the fact that Henry is eulogized for being able to "reason in divinity," "debate on commonwealth affairs," and "turn him to any cause of policy," the events of Act I suggest that he possesses a strong self-interest which hinders the accurate translation of the "theoric" into the "practic part of life" (I.i.37-52). Ely and Exeter tempt Henry with attractions similar to those Cassius presents Brutus—degree and noble ancestry, which Henry must affirm and extend for himself:

> Awake remembrance of these valiant dead,
> And with your puissant arm renew their feats.
> You are their heir; you sit upon their throne;
> The blood and courage that renowned them
> Runs in your veins; and my thrice-puissant liege
> Is in the very May-morn of his youth,
> Ripe for exploits and mighty enterprises
> (I.ii.115-24).

Canterbury enriches Ely's temptation with a speech leading up to the "chronicle . . . rich with praise" (I.ii.162). That Henry is attracted by this reward of the war against France is indicated in his reply to Ely, Exeter, and Canterbury:

> Either our history shall with full mouth
> Speak freely of our acts, or else our grave,
> Like Turkish mute, shall have a tongueless mouth,
> Not worshipp'd with a waxen epitaph
> (I.ii.230-33).

Great fame will accrue to Henry should he do what none of his ancestors could: make good the English claim to the French throne. Henry's sense of the power of personal accomplishment is expressed in his conclusion:

> Now are we well resolv'd; and by God's help
> And yours, the noble sinews of our power
> France being ours, we'll bend it to our awe,
> Or break it all to pieces
> (I.ii.222-25).

Although more than lip service is being paid to divine providence, Henry's emphasis is on his own power and sense of high position. The insult from the Dauphin is certainly a circumstance which partially excuses Henry's pride; nevertheless, it does cause Henry to reveal his self-interest in the impending war. Henry's sense of his glory chronicled in the future is linked with his present vanity about his royal importance:

> But tell the Dauphin I will keep my estate,
> Be like a king, and show my sail of greatness
> When I do rouse me in my throne of France. . . .
> But I will rise there with so full a glory
> That I will dazzle all the eyes of France,
> Yea, strike the Dauphin blind to look on us
> (I.ii.273-80).

At the beginning of the play divine providence is

more like a means to an end, Henry's personal victory; at the close, Henry views his personal victory as a means of implementing a higher end, God's providence.

As an instrument of policy, the war is a necessity and seems to Henry a positive good. But viewed as an experience rather than an instrument of policy, the war is a gruesome reality which startles him out of his self-interest and into an enlarged sense of responsibility. His initial attitude toward war, supported by the Dauphin's insult, enlivens Henry's self-interest, but the second attitude modifies that self-interest and transmutes it into concern for his subjects. By that transformation Henry earns the ethical right to kingship. War as policy makes Henry legally a king; but war as horrible experience makes him ethically a king.

In his essay on *Henry V* [*An Approach to Shakespeare*, 1956] Derek Traversi remarks that "Called upon to . . . shape policies for the common good, the king can allow no trace of selfishness or frailty to affect his decisions. He must continually examine his motives." If Henry's motives for entering the war are not stirred by conscience, they are at least checked and examined by it. Though he frequently tries to evade his conscience by placing his responsibilities on others, he finds himself increasingly unable to act without its sanction. At the outset, he tries to satisfy his conscience that the war is legally justified, by requiring Canterbury to supply the legal justification:

> For we will hear, note, and believe in heart
> That what you speak is in your conscience
> wash'd
> As pure as sin with baptism
>
> (I.ii.30-32).

And after Canterbury's long justification Henry asks again, "May I with right and conscience make this claim?" (I.ii.96). Henry's repetition of the question would seem to indicate that he doubts Canterbury's somewhat tangled argument; perhaps he realizes that his motive is not itself pure but is being purified by the character of the ecclesiastical authority who adduces the argument and whose own conscience has perhaps been bought, intentionally or not, by Henry's recent political favors. At any rate, the exchange between Henry and Canterbury suggests that Henry both meets and evades his conscience by placing responsibility on the Archbishop. The fact that Henry allows the three traitors to judge themselves may express both his objectivity and his unwillingness to assume full responsibility:

> The mercy that was quick in us but late
> By your own counsel is suppress'd and
> kill'd
>
> (II.ii.79-80).

Simultaneously Henry justifies and evades responsibility for a harsh judgment. Again, at Harfleur, Henry places the blame for impending martial destruction on his enemy; they will be "guilty in defence" (III.iii.43), whereas his own soldiers,

> In liberty of bloody hand shall range
> With conscience wide as hell, mowing like
> grass
> Your fresh fair virgins and your flow'ring
> infants.

The grotesqueness of the imminent carnage and the linking of conscience with hell have robbed conscience of meaning, turning it into a mere word which supplants the principle.

[Palmer notes that two] common soldiers, Bates and Williams, accuse Henry: "out of the mouth of John Bates, he finds himself charged with precisely the burden he has always sought to avoid. . . . Driven to the wall, Henry is prompt in defence. Despite his lifelong evasions he has been brought to a point where the imminent death of twenty thousand men is laid to his account." It is not difficult to shift responsibility for an unfought war, and for the penalty imposed on traitors, and for the contemplated destruction of the enemy; but it is more difficult for Henry to justify the impending slaughter of his own countrymen. Henry seeks to evade the blame for the death of his men: "every subject's soul is his own. Therefore should every soldier in the wars do as every sick man in his bed, wash every mote out of his conscience" (IV.i.188-89). He has given only a partial solution to a difficult problem, and hence when the soldiers leave him with their accusation, Henry reluctantly accepts in private his moral responsibilities:

> Upon the King! let us our lives, our souls,
> Our debts, our careful wives,
> Our children, and our sins lay on the King!
>
> (IV.i.247-49).

Unlike Coriolanus, Henry permits himself to be upbraided by a plebeian: in so far as the master becomes servant to his servant, the servant may on occasion discipline his master, perhaps serving as an outward conscience questioning the master's motives.

Henry questions his motives in private and is less able than Brutus to evade the probing eye of conscience. Pressed hard by his conscience, Henry ferrets out one of the motives he has screened from himself, and in the process of that self-analysis, he reaches some remarkable conclusions about kingship and degree. In the process of trying to define the role of king, which includes the need to clarify the distinction between king and subject, Henry admits that his motives include the desire for ceremony and degree

(IV.i. 247-301). He is, of course, unlike Coriolanus and Brutus in his admission to himself that such a desire is a part of his motive. Unlike them again, Henry admits his common humanity and identifies himself, the highest figure in the social hierarchy, with his men, the lowest figures in it. He admits that as a man there is no essential difference between himself and his subjects; the only difference is the unessential one of ceremony and rank:

> but for ceremony, such a wretch,
> Winding up days with toil and nights with
>   sleep
> Had the fore-hand and vantage of a king.

Ceremony and degree, which before Henry had esteemed when defending himself against the Dauphin's mock, he now mocks:

> O Ceremony, show me but thy worth!
> What is thy soul of adoration?
> Art thou aught else but place, degree, and
>   form,
> Creating awe and fear in other men?

Divorced from ethical function, ceremonial degree becomes valueless, a "proud dream." More important and basic than the concept of degree is the concept of equality, demonstrated by Henry's mixing with everyone both "mean and gentle" (IV. prol. 45) and by the basic political assumption of the play. That assumption is that political harmony is achieved by equal contributions from all members of society directed at the target of common interest:

> I this infer,
> That many things, having full reference
> To one consent, may work contrariously.
> As many arrows, loosed several ways,
> Come to one mark; as many ways meet in
>   one town;
> As many fresh streams meet in one salt sea;
> As many lines close in the dial's centre;
> So may a thousand actions, once afoot,
> End in one purpose
>
> (I.ii.204-12).

Yet fused with the concept of ordered equality is a hierarchical arrangement expressed in Canterbury's progression from king downward to drone (I.ii.190-204). The two concepts of hierarchy and equality compose the single paradoxical principle of political rule: that the king is both master and servant to his people. In *The Education of a Christian Prince*, [1936, Desiderius] Erasmus says that the king serves as both the mind and heart to his people: "the rule of a prince over his people is no different from the mind over the body. The mind dominates the body because it knows more than the physical body. . . . What the heart is

in the body of a living creature, that the prince is in the state." As the embodiment of mind the king dominates his subjects, but as the embodiment of heart, he is lowered to their level: "The heart is situated in the middle of the body. Just so should a prince always be found among his people." Henry is the living embodiment of the paradox. When he rids himself of the sterile concept of ceremonial degree, Henry admits the essential equality between himself and his subjects. That admission leads back to the principle of hierarchy: Henry realizes that since ceremonial degree does not differentiate a king from other men, a king must be superior to others ethically in that he deserves to rule because he is most willing and able to serve. Henry thus concludes his soliloquy with a reference to the "watch the King keeps to maintain peace." It is a bitter truth, realized on the eve of battle. When he next addresses his men, he states that social hierarchy should be a reflection of ethical hierarchy, the degree of inner goodness revealed by selfless valor:

> For he today that sheds his blood with me
> Shall be my brother; be he ne'er so vile,
> This day shall *gentle* his condition;
> And gentlemen in England now a-bed
> Shall think themselves accurs'd they were
>   not here.

At the same time Henry expresses a willingness to share that glory which before he had sought for himself.

Having denied hierarchy in the name of equality, Henry has, in effect, reaffirmed hierarchy in the name of equality: he affirms that a man is superior only in so far as he recognizes his equality with others by serving them. Henry's progress toward moral superiority is marked by a kind of symbolic social progress: in rising above most men in his willingness to accept responsibility and to serve others, he casts off the garb which disguised him as a common man and assumes the rights of kingship. These rights require that he now assert the concept of hierarchy in order to maintain harmony. Whereas before he had neglected degree, he has newly discovered its meaning and therefore can newly affirm it: thus he cannot accept Williams' challenge: "It may be his enemy is a gentleman of great sort, quite from the answer of degree" (IV.viii.141-43). At the end Henry may with perfect moral rectitude both covet glorious honor and be "free from vainness and self-glorious pride" (V. prol. 20). The honor Henry seeks is not external, false honor:

> It yearns me not if men my garments wear;
> Such outward things dwell not in my
>   desires;
> But if it be a sin to covet honour
> I am the most offending soul alive
>
> (IV.iii.26-29).

It is morally a sin to covet honor if it is the mere outer garment of social degree, but if that honor is true—one's moral goodness as it is confirmed by the judgment of good men—it becomes a sin, as it does in *Coriolanus*, not to seek it, since the minds of good men serve as the collective conscience which corrects, and rewards, individual conscience. At the close, therefore, Henry can both covet honor and efface his own power:

> O God, thy arm was here;
> And not to me, but to thy arm alone
> Ascribe we all!
>
> (IV.viii.111-13).

The opposing terms in the paradoxical concept of honor are resolved in Henry: he deserves because he makes no claim to desert, he merits rank because he affirms equality, and he merits praise because he does not seek it but seeks the inner spirit of praise—honor as "a certeine testimonie of vertue shining of yt self, given of some man by the judgement of good men."

LANGUAGE AND IMAGERY

Analysis of the language and imagery in *Henry V* has yielded a variety of critical interpretations. Michael Goldman studies the use of language to exhort and to motivate listeners to action. He asserts that the speeches in the play are passionate and require great physical effort by the speaker. **Robert Hapgood** concentrates on the disputative tone of the language in the play, maintaining that the speech contributes to the constant arguments and the movement from peace to war. **C. H. Hobday** also notes the transition to war by assessing the references to death imagery in *Henry V*. For further analysis of the language and imagery of *Henry V*, see the essay by **Landon C. Burns, Jr.** in the EPIC ELEMENTS section.

Robert Hapgood

SOURCE: "Shakespeare's Thematic Modes of Speech: *Richard II* to *Henry V*," in *Shakespeare Survey: An Annual Survey of Shakespearian Study and Production*, Vol. 20, 1967, pp. 41-9.

[*In the excerpt below, Hapgood contends that the argumentative language of* Henry V *contributes to the tone and meaning of the play. He observes that disputes take place within the two camps more frequently than between the two enemies. Hapgood also notes that Henry's most characteristic mode of speech is that of agreement, which results in the nobility's loyalty to the king.*]

The central mode of speech in *Henry V* is that of dispute. Unlike the other three Lancastrian plays, each of which announces its central mode at the outset, *Henry V* begins with its main anti-mode, concert and agreement: the Prologue invokes a Muse of fire, appeals to English national feeling, and apologetically seeks the cooperation of spectator with performer; and the first scenes show the church and the crown working out the terms of their mutual assistance. Not until the end of the second scene, when the Ambassadors of France arrive with their tennis balls, is the dominant mode sounded. Disputes between the two enemies were of course to be expected in this play, and we are not disappointed; shamelessly weighted to favour the English, they continue until the agreements of the finale. What might not have been expected is the extent to which the two sides quarrel among themselves. Such disputes are even more frequent than those between the two sides.

The French mode of dispute is that of mocking insult. This is emphatically the manner of the Dauphin's gift of tennis balls and of the Constable's advice that the English repent before they die (IV, iii, 83-7). Among themselves, it marks the Constable's barbed raillery with the Dauphin and Orleans (III, vii) and seems even to be the mode of French women; the Dauphin protests:

> Our madams mock at us, and plainly say
> Our mettle is bred out and they will give
> Their bodies to the lust of English youth . . .
>
> (III, v, 28-30)

The French are much given, also, to bragging, both to the English and among themselves. As King Henry jokes to Montjoy:

> forgive me, God,
> That I do brag thus! This your air of France
> Hath blown that vice in me; I must repent.
>
> (III, vi, 159-61)

Yet they are quickly reduced to unconditional surrender, most abjectly in Monsieur le Fer's cries: 'O, je vous supplie, pour l'amour de Dieu, me pardonner!' (IV, iv, 42).

Like the top levels of the French court, the lower orders of the English army are constantly in dispute; yet unlike the French, whose disagreements are often left hanging in the air, theirs are always resolved, as in the quarrel (II, i) between Nym and Pistol over Nell Quickly. Captain Fluellen, the very embodiment of disputatiousness, is at the centre of these disputes. His 'prawls, and prabbles, and quarrels, and dissensions' are what he lives for, and he is too prone to equate love of dispute with valour in battle. He grossly

Katherine's English lesson.

underestimates Captain Macmorris, who is all fight and no talk; while he at first grossly overestimates Pistol, who—as the Boy puts it—'hath a killing tongue and a quiet sword'. Fluellen is so disputatious that he can even provoke a slight tiff with the otherwise ever-agreeable Gower (IV, i, 76), but his main disputes are of course with Pistol. Their contention echoes the international dispute, as the braggart's mocking insults give way to easy and total submission: 'Must I bite?' King Henry's magnanimity to a conquered foe is reflected in the groat Fluellen gives Pistol to 'heal your pate'.

Apart from his international exchanges, King Henry's chief disputes come when he is in disguise—first, as Harry le Roi, with Pistol (IV, i, 35-63); then, later in the scene, with Williams. The latter is easily the most searching of the play's disputes, the disguised king and his men debating the highest issues of duty and rule before descending to embroilments about the king's 'foolish saying' and Williams's 'something too round' reproof.

The king's most characteristic mode of speech, however, is the play's chief anti-mode: concert and agreement. Among the English nobility, especially in contrast to the French, there is notable amity among themselves and loyalty to the king. If the three traitors pervert this solidarity in their false expressions of fidelity (II, ii, 18-51), the king is not deceived; and their exception is more than counter-balanced by Exeter's account of the deaths of Suffolk and York (IV, vi, 7-32), which is the most extreme expression of amity in the play, perhaps in Shakespeare. Henry knows how to knit his band of brothers. Of course there are those who do not respond to his appeals. Among the stragglers, Bardolph can only parody the king's battle-cry: 'On, on, on, on, on! to the breach, to the breach!' (III, ii). The king is prepared to sacrifice their friendship. In their place, he welcomes Fluellen, who does respond to his cry and echoes it, if very much in his own idiom: 'Up to the breach, you dogs! avaunt, you cullions!'

With France, Henry's is again the voice of unity: not

as a mediator—he is not a Bardolph or a Bates or, at the international level, a Burgundy—but as a magnanimous conqueror. Typically, his victory with Kate is on his own terms—she goes much further than he in an attempt to 'talk the same language'—yet he has the magnanimity to attempt a little French.

C. H. Hobday

SOURCE: "Imagery and Irony in *Henry V*," in *Shakespeare Survey: An Annual Survey of Shakespearian Study and Production*, Vol. 21, 1968, pp. 107-14.

[*In the following essay, Hobday explores the use of death imagery in* Henry V *and the emotional significance that the imagery had for Shakespeare. He notes that Shakespeare constantly places the language of honor and religion amidst the realities of greed and cruelty.*]

During the last century and a half many of the most distinguished Shakespearian critics, from Hazlitt to J. Dover Wilson, have disputed over the character of Shakespeare's Henry V. When such a debate has continued so long, without showing any sign of reaching a conclusion, it seems reasonable to assume that the division of opinion among critics may reflect a division in Shakespeare's own mind, and that his emotions may have rebelled against his conscious intentions in writing the play. One criterion by which we can attempt to ascertain the feelings with which he wrote is through his image-clusters, which afford a clue to the emotional associations which certain words possessed for him. In *Henry V* one image-cluster plays an especially significant part, that associated with death.

Some two dozen images were linked in Shakespeare's mind with the idea of death, and can be roughly divided into seven groups: bones, leanness, pallor, rottenness, and ghost; hollowness, grave, vault or cave, earth, and womb; mouth or teeth, and eating; eyes and weeping; war, cannon, blood, and fire; sea, rocks, and wind or storm; and lion or tiger and roaring. The train of thought linking many of these ideas is obvious enough. Shakespeare saw death personified as a meagre, white-faced, ghostly figure, a rotting corpse, a skeleton, or a monster feeding on men—hence the association with the mouth and eating. Death, weeping, and hence eyes is a natural sequence of ideas, but the connexion between them is strengthened by the fact, which Caroline Spurgeon noted [in *Shakespeare's Imagery*, 1935], that when Shakespeare thought of a skull it was often the empty eye-sockets which first came into his mind. The grave, vaults, and earth are obviously connected with death, but they are also linked with one another, with the womb and caves, with cannon, and with the skull and its eye-sockets, by the common idea of hollowness. The association between the last three groups of images

may have arisen from the fact that Petruchio refers to roaring lions, the sea, winds, cannon, thunder, battle, and fire when enumerating louder noises than that of a woman's tongue (*The Taming of the Shrew*, I, ii, 201-10); the speech has nothing to do with death, but *tongue* may have suggested *mouth*, and hence Death the devourer. Again, the story of Pyramus and Thisbe may have contributed to bring together in Shakespeare's mind *tomb, hole* (hollowness), *lion, roar, mouth, blood* and *death*: in *Titus Andronicus* Pyramus is mentioned in a passage containing a long sequence of death-images (II, iii, 227-49). Finally, lions and tigers are linked with the sea by the application of 'roaring' to both (*Romeo and Juliet*, V, iii, 39; *Hamlet*, I, iv, 77-83).

This complex of images seems to have possessed an intense emotional significance for Shakespeare. It is found in passages relating, not merely to death, but to the murder of the innocent—the murder of Gloucester (*2 Henry VI*, III, ii, 141-76), the appearance of the ghost to Hamlet (I, iv, 47-50, 77-90), Lear's entry with the dead Cordelia (V, iii, 258-61), the discovery of Duncan's murder (*Macbeth,* II, iii, 69-103), and the appearance of Banquo's ghost (III, iv, 71-101). It occurs, too, at moments which mark a turning-point in the action of a play, such as the death of Gloucester, the final parting of Romeo and Juliet (III, V, 17-20, 56-9), or Northumberland's announcement of Bolingbroke's return (*Richard II*, II, i, 263-70). In *Henry V* such a turning point comes at the end of Act II and the beginning of Act III with the outbreak of war, and it is here that Shakespeare's death-imagery is concentrated.

Death-imagery dominates Exeter's warning to the French king:

> Therefore in fierce *tempest* is he coming,
> In thunder and in earthquake, like a Jove,
> That if requiring fail, he will compel;
> And bids you, in the bowels of the Lord,
> Deliver up the crown, and to take mercy
> On the poor souls for whom this hungry
>   *war*
> Opens his vasty *jaws:* and on your heads
> Turns he the widows' *tears,* the orphans'
>   cries,
> The *dead* men's *blood*, the pining maidens'
>   groans,
> For husbands, fathers, and betrothed lovers
> That shall be *swallowed* in this controversy.
>   (II, iv, 99-109)

More death-images follow in Exeter's defiance to the Dauphin:

> He'll call you to so hot an answer of it
> That *caves* and *womby vaultages* of France

Shall chide your trespass, and return your
    mock
In second accent of his *ordinance.*

                        (123-6)

The theme of Exeter's first speech, it will be noticed, is the death of innocent. He, of course, blames the French king, but it would be a poor diplomat who could not prove the other side responsible for any war. The question remains, whom did Shakespeare himself hold responsible?

Death-imagery (wind, sea, dead, ordnance, mouths, cannon) continues throughout the following chorus, with which we move from peace to war, and the first fifteen lines of Henry's speech before Harfleur (dead, blast, tiger, blood, eye, cannon, rock, ocean, teeth). If it is not heresy to say so, this passage is surely very badly written. Rhetoric has been defined as the will doing the work of the imagination, and by this criterion the speech is not poetry but rhetoric. Shakespeare's imagination is not engaged, and he forces the note. The result, when Henry issues detailed orders on the exact expression to be worn in battle, is unintentionally comic.

The implications of the death-images in this speech are disturbing. Henry's picture of the breach in the wall packed tight with corpses looks forward to Octavia's horrifying image:

       Wars 'twixt you twain would be
As if the world should cleave, and that slain
    men
Should solder up the rift.
      (*Antony and Cleopatra,* III, iv, 30-2)

Again, why should Henry order his men to 'imitate the action of the tiger'? Why not the lion? To Shakespeare the lion was a noble beast with a 'royal disposition' and 'a vice of mercy', but the tiger was above all cruel and merciless. Heroic figures such as Richard I, the Black Prince, Julius Caesar, and Antony are compared to lions in his plays, but the six characters who are compared to tigers—Aaron, Tamora, Queen Margaret, Richard III, Goneril, and Regan—are all notorious for cruelty. The details of the expression which Henry's soldiers are to assume are full of significant echoes. 'Hard-favoured rage' suggests 'hard-favoured death' (*1 Henry VI,* IV, vii, 23) and 'that devil's butcher, hard-favoured Richard' (*3 Henry VI,* V, V, 77-8). 'Let the brow o'erwhelm it' recalls the 'overwhelming brows' of the apothecary in *Romeo and Juliet* (V, i, 39), whom Shakespeare seems to envisage as an incarnation of death; note the death-images running through the scene (vault, pale, meagre, bones, earthen, thinly, death, fired, cannon's womb, eyes, food, grave). 'Now set the teeth' is echoed in Antony's lines in another passage full of death-imagery:

         Men did ransom lives
Of me for jests: but now I'll set my teeth
And send to darkness all that stop me.
    (*Antony and Cleopatra,* III, xiii, 180-2)

Setting the teeth for Shakespeare was evidently associated with refusal of mercy in battle. 'Stretch the nostril wide' echoes Warwick's description of the murdered Gloucester, 'his nostrils stretched with struggling' (*2 Henry VI,* III, ii, 171). Thus these fifteen lines contain a whole succession of images associated not only with death but with cruelty and murder.

That such images recur almost continuously through a passage of about a hundred lines, and are placed in the mouths of Henry himself and his spokesman, can hardly be accidental. They would seem to suggest that, whatever Shakespeare may say about Henry, in his heart he regarded him as a murderer. Faced with the demand to depict such a man as a hero, he took refuge in the irony which permeates the whole play, and constantly juxtaposed the fine talk of honour and religion with the realities of human greed and cruelty.

Such a contrast occurs at the very beginning of the play, when immediately after praying for a muse of fire Shakespeare introduces two bishops who discuss how they can prevent Church property from being confiscated for public and charitable purposes, and decide to encourage the King to invade France. An audience in Protestant and anti-clerical London would automatically have assumed that the two Popish prelates were up to no good, and would have thought the confiscation of Church property an excellent idea. Shakespeare probably sympathized with their views. His Catholic bishops and cardinals—Beaufort, Pandulph, Wolsey, Gardiner—are an unsavoury bunch, in contrast with the Protestant Cranmer; the Bishop of Carlisle in *Richard II* might be cited as an exception, but even he takes part in a murder plot. The terms in which Shakespeare refers to the use to which the Church's wealth might be put—

      to relief of lazars and weak age,
Of indigent faint souls past corporal toil
                   (I, i, 15-16)

—have an emotional note, unlike Holinshed's dry 'for reliefe onelie of the poore, impotent, and needie persons,' which suggests that he would have favoured its use for such purposes. That the bishop's testimonial to Henry's Christian virtues is interpolated in the middle of their plot to frustrate the relief of the poor would seem to throw some doubt upon its value.

In defence of the bishops, Dover Wilson points out that they do not initiate the idea of the war. Shakespeare's own views on its origin can be found in *2 Henry IV,* where Henry IV advises his son 'to busy giddy minds with foreign quarrels' (IV, V, 214-15) in order to divert attention from the weakness of his claim to the throne, and at the end of the same play it is suggested that Henry is planning to

> bear our civil swords and native fire
> As far as France.
>
> (V, V, 112-13)

This fact lessens the Archbishop's guilt, but it only increases Henry's.

Dover Wilson goes on to argue that 'the sole connection between the subject of the Archbishop's speech (on the Salic Law) and the question of Church lands is that both are spoken of in the conversation of the two bishops which constitutes the opening scene'; that in the 'perfectly legitimate desire' of removing any temptation for the King to finance his war by expropriating Church property the Archbishop offers him a large subsidy towards its cost; and that there is 'not a hint of a bribe on the Archbishop's part, still less of his provoking the King to war in order to protect Church property'. This argument ignores Shakespeare's text. If there is no connexion between the Church property question and the Archbishop's support for the war, why should the play open with a completely irrelevant discussion? There is not a word anywhere about Henry's being tempted to finance the war at the Church's expense. On the King's attitude towards the Church property bill, the Archbishop says that he seems

> rather swaying more upon our part
> Than cherishing th'exhibiters against us;
> For I have made an offer to his majesty,
> Upon our spiritual convocation,
> And in regard of causes now in hand,
> Which I have opened to his grace at large,
> As touching France, to give a greater sum
> Than ever at one time the clergy yet
> Did to his predecessors part withal.
>
> (I, i, 73-81)

That word *for* is decisive; Henry does not support the bill, because the Archbishop has offered him a large subsidy. If this is not a bribe, what is it? When later the Archbishop urges the King to war he again reminds him of his offer:

> O let their bodies follow, my dear liege,
> With blood and sword and fire to win your
>   right;
> In aid whereof we of the spiritualty
> Will raise your highness such a mighty
>   sum
> As never did the clergy at one time
> Bring in to any of your ancestors.
>
> (I, ii, 130-5)

The virtual repetition of lines from the Archbishop's earlier speech is clearly intended to emphasize that the motive for his support of the war is his fears for the Church's lands. When the spokesman of the 'spiritualty' advocates a policy of 'blood and sword and fire' for fear that Church property will be used to relieve 'indigent faint souls', Shakespeare's irony becomes Swiftian. . . .

The Archbishop's argument in support of Henry's claim to the French throne—that a claimant descended in the female line from the senior branch of a royal house takes precedence in the succession over one descended in the male line from a junior branch—in reality proves, not that Henry is the rightful King of France, but that he is not the rightful King of England. As Shakespeare himself had twice demonstrated at length in earlier plays, the house of Mortimer was descended in the female line from the third son of Edward III, through whom Henry claimed the

Frontispiece to a 1773 edition of Henry V, *depicting Pistol, a French soldier, and a boy.*

French throne, whereas the house of Lancaster was descended in the male line from the fourth son (*1 Henry VI*, II, V, 71-8; *2 Henry VI*, II, ii). To assume that Shakespeare regarded Henry's claim to the French throne as justified is therefore to assume that he was incapable of reasoning. As he saw the matter, Henry put forward a legally unjustifiable claim to the French throne because he had no legal right to the English throne either. The suffering which the resultant war was bound to cause the innocent is repeatedly stressed in the play—in Exeter's speech already quoted, in Henry's threats to the citizens of Harfleur (III, iii, 1-43), in Williams's reflections on the King's responsibility (IV, i, 140-53), and in Burgundy's description of desolated France (V, ii, 38-62). Hence when Shakespeare reached the actual outbreak of war, his feelings found expression in his imagery.

There is an implied comment on the nature of the war in the fate of Bardolph. Holinshed states that Henry had a soldier hanged for stealing a pyx (a box for consecrated wafers); Bardolph is hanged for stealing a pax (a tablet depicting the crucifixion, which was kissed by the communicants at mass). The Quarto text, which reads 'packs', shows that 'pax' in the Folio is not a misprint. J. H. Walter comments that 'Shakespeare, who surely must have known the difference, may have substituted "pax" for some reason not now clear'. The reason seems clear enough; Shakespeare equates Bardolph morally with Henry, who has stolen the peace of England and France.

> Through tattered clothes great vices do
>   appear:
> Robes and furred gowns hide all. Plate sin
>   with gold,
> And the strong lance of justice hurtless
>   breaks:
> Arm it in rags, a pigmy's straw does pierce
>   it.
>
>   (*King Lear*, IV, vi, 168-71)

Even if Shakespeare wrote 'pax' by mistake for 'pyx', the slip was surely a Freudian one; his unconscious mind insisted on giving vent to his real feelings about the war.

His divided mind is most apparent in the Agincourt scenes. There is much in them that is eloquent and deeply felt—the preliminary chorus, the Crispin's day speech, the description of the deaths of Suffolk and York. But the most moving passage of all is Williams's indictment of Henry: 'But if the cause be not good, the king himself hath a heavy reckoning to make, when all those legs and arms and heads, chopped off in a battle, shall join together at the latter day, and cry all, "We died at such a place"; some swearing, some crying for a surgeon, some upon their wives left poor behind them, some upon the debts

they owe, some upon their children rawly left' (IV, i, 140-6). In his laboured reply Henry answers Williams's suggestion that he is responsible for the fate of his subjects' souls, but completely evades the issue of his responsibility for the death of their bodies and the sufferings of their dependants. Left alone, he whines in an orgy of self-pity that his subjects do not appreciate 'what watch the king keeps to maintain the peace' (IV, i, 300). Shakespeare's irony here is palpable enough.

After the heroics of the Crispin's day speech, the first we see of the actual battle is Pistol extorting a ransom from his prisoner. This is indeed to reduce Agincourt to a 'brawl ridiculous'! As for Henry's contribution to the victory, it is apparently confined to an order for the massacre of the prisoners. Walter defends this order on the ground that 'he is moved to rage by the treacherous attack on the boys and lackeys in his tents', but in fact when he gives it all Henry knows is that 'the French have reinforced their scattered men' (IV, vi, 36)—another example of how his defenders are forced to ignore Shakespeare's text. Shakespeare's own ironic comment, which he puts into Gower's mouth—'the king most worthily hath caused every soldier to cut his prisoner's throat. O,'tis a gallant king!' (IV, vii, 8-10)—is typical of the method of the play in its juxtaposition of the patriotic illusion ('most worthily', 'gallant') with the stark reality ('cut his prisoner's throat'). In the Quarto text, which may preserve Shakespeare's original intention, immediately after Henry gives his order Pistol utters his catch-phrase 'Coupe le gorge!' In the very next line we learn that the French have massacred the boys in the English camp. Thus Henry, Pistol, and the chivalry of France are shown within a few lines to move on the same moral level.

Then there is what Sherlock Holmes would have called the curious incident of Henry's fight with Alençon. In earlier battle scenes Shakespeare had introduced completely unhistorical hand-to-hand combats between leading figures on the two sides—Richard III and Richmond, Henry himself and Hotspur. When his sources for this play of all others afforded him an opportunity to show a historical combat between his hero and a French nobleman, one would have expected him to seize on it eagerly, yet all we hear of the incident is a passing reference after the battle (IV, vii, 161-8). Walter seeks to explain the omission by suggesting that 'physical prowess in Henry was not at this point the most important quality. It is Henry's spiritual strength, his faith and moral courage which inspire and uphold his whole army'—the spiritual strength and moral courage, presumably, being shown in the order for the massacre of the prisoners. The real explanation surely is that by this time Shakespeare could not bring himself to show Henry as a heroic figure. There is something Brechtian in his depiction of Agincourt, not as a heroic feat of arms, but as a brutal and sordid affair of plunder and massacre.

It may be objected that this conclusion attributes to Shakespeare a pacifism alien to the Elizabethan age. Such an argument ignores historical facts. By 1599 the Spanish war had been in progress for over ten years, and the country was weary of it. The popular mood is often reflected in the drama of the last years of the century. The pressing of unwilling workmen, recruiting scandals, the neglect of the disabled soldier, and the stealing of their soldiers' pay by corrupt officers are frequent themes for protest or satire. The author of *I Jeronimo*, for example, wrote:

> O dear Andrea, pray, let's have no wars.
> First let them pay the soldiers that were
>   maimed
> In the last battle ere more wretches fall.
>
> (I, ii, 31-3)

Shakespeare's implicit condemnation of the Archbishop in *Henry V* is paralleled in the priest's speech in Fulke Greville's *Mustapha*:

>   we are untrue
> And spiritual forges under tyrants' might;
> God only doth command what's good for
>   you,
> Where we do preach your bodies to the
>   war . . .
>
> (IV, iv, 45-8)

The hero of *The Shoemaker's Holiday*, when commissioned to serve under Henry V in France, prefers to stay at home and carry on a love affair. Dekker apparently finds nothing dishonourable in such conduct; the moral of the play might in fact be 'Make love, not war'. It would be surprising if Shakespeare had not been affected by the widespread anti-war feeling.

If he found Henry V so unsympathetic, why did he write about him at all? Presumably he had no choice. He had committed himself to write such a play in the epilogue to *2 Henry IV*, and was under an obligation to his company—perhaps under pressure from them—to supply it. There may also have been a demand for a patriotic play that would arouse public enthusiasm for Essex's Irish campaign. If there was, Shakespeare failed to supply it; his incidental compliment to Essex, the leader of the war party, in the chorus to Act V could hardly be more tepid. Once engaged on the play he did his best to supply what was expected of him, but his own feelings would insist on asserting themselves. This may explain why he did not keep his promise that the play would have 'Sir John in it.' The case put forward by Dover Wilson and Walter

for believing that Falstaff appeared in the first draft is a strong one, but their suggested reasons for his subsequent omission are unconvincing; neither Will Kempe's absence nor Lord Cobham's hypothetical objections prevented the Chamberlain's Men from continuing to act the Falstaff plays. It seems more probable that Falstaff acted as Shakespeare's mouthpiece, and that he rewrote the play without him because he realized that his patriotic play was turning into a satire on war. Two such stars as Henry and Falstaff could not keep their motion in one sphere, and with Sir John in it *Henry V* might have done for the Hundred Years' War what *Troilus and Cressida* did for the Trojan War, with Falstaff playing a similar role to Thersites. Bernard Shaw was probably not far from the truth when he suggested that 'it was to expose and avenge his mistake and failure in writing *Henry V* that he wrote *Troilus and Cressida*'.

This does not mean that Shakespeare was necessarily insincere when he wrote, say, the Crispin's day speech. He was repelled by the callous cynicism of Henry V's aggression against France, but his imagination and his sympathies were stirred by the Dunkirk situation of a small English army with its back to the wall. That is why the Harfleur speech is so bad and the Crispin's day speech so good. Like most of us, Shakespeare had something of the patriot and something of the pacifist in his make-up. He was no more inconsistent than the arch-pacifist Tolstoy, who wrote the great epic of Russian patriotism and, long after he had reached the conclusion that war is always wrong, wept with shame at the news of the surrender of Port Arthur. Much of the interest in *Henry V* arises from the tensions in Shakespeare's mind between conflicting emotions, and between his own feelings and the external pressures to which he was subjected. We may apply to him what a contemporary has written of poets in general: 'The poet is always a double man, an internal émigré, a hostage in enemy country. His task is to try and reconcile the short-term public demand and the long-term private vision and to express the tension which this task necessarily brings with it' [Lacieu Rey, *New Left Review*, no. 38].

EPIC ELEMENTS

Shakespeare's use of the Chorus and other epic elements has attracted significant critical attention. Many commentators, including Anthony S. Brennan, Lawrence Danson, and Paul Dean, have speculated on the role of the Chorus. Brennan disputes the assumption that Shakespeare used the Chorus to express his own feelings, contending instead that the Chorus adds significantly to the patriotic theme. Danson asserts that the Chorus exists to provide a sense of perspective, praising its contribution to the tone of the play. Dean analyzes the relationship between the Chorus and Henry, stating that the Chorus praises Henry's achievements but also cautions against blindly accepting his success. Other critics have explored Shakespeare's representation of Henry V as an ideal epic hero; **Landon C. Burns, Jr.** examines this magnification of the king through the nationalistic theme in the play, in which Shakespeare glorifies all things English. **Helen J. Schwartz** analyzes the idealization of Henry by studying the comic scenes and contending that these episodes prove Henry's ability as king. J. H. Walter praises Shakespeare's ability to incorporate an epic tone in the play, contending that he did not merely extract material from an epic story, but gave the illusion of an epic whole. For further analysis of the epic elements in *Henry V*, see the essay by **E. F. C. Ludowyk** in the OVERVIEWS section, and the essay by **William Babula** in the HENRY section.

Landon C. Burns, Jr.

SOURCE: "Three Views of *King Henry V*," in *Drama Survey*, Vol. 1, No. 3, February, 1962, pp. 278-300.

[*In this excerpt, Burns examines* Henry V *as a patriotic play which glorifies England and its hero-king. Burns contends that Shakespeare uses this nationalistic theme to praise all things English and eliminate anything that could spoil this image. He also argues that although Henry seems to represent the ideal king, Shakespeare does not present him as a flawless ruler. Burns concludes by comparing the comic scenes and language in* Henry V *with that found in* Henry IV.]

Shakespeare's *Henry V* is a very different kind of play from his other histories, for, as has often been pointed out, it is an epic pageant rather than a character study. Whereas in *Henry IV* and the Richard plays we are intensely interested in the kings as men, here the interest is in the king as political hero. Henry V was a symbol of the great hero-king; popular opinion remembered his reign as the one really bright and glorious interlude in the whole long, wretched period of the civil wars. He was a symbol, too, of the unity of the people, of England's most impressive military and territorial strength before the Tudors. Thus, conventional opinion may, in part, have determined the direction which the play took. Various conjectures have also been made about Shakespeare's motives: the play may have been a not-very-subtle compliment to Elizabeth, for in some ways both the times and the monarchs were similar; or, having written, in *Richard III*, the history of the lowest point to which the kingship ever sank, Shakespeare felt compelled to balance it by writing the history of one of the highest points; to round off the tetralogy (*Richard II, 1 & 2 Henry IV*) he needed a hero of great stature who

would fulfill the promise at the end of *2 Henry IV*.

Whatever the causes, the play remains Shakespeare's glowing tribute to England, to the King, and to the people. And while it is splendid in this respect and exciting in its pageantry, it is not really one of Shakespeare's best plays. National heroes do not make very good dramatic ones unless they are treated as men rather than as paragons of virtue and symbols of majesty (and if they are treated as men, they tend to lose their viability as patriotic symbols). For one thing, the national hero must be a composite man; indeed, Henry becomes almost a universal hero, excelling all others in whatever business is at hand. Henry, as Shakespeare portrays him, is the ideal king, just, cautious, brave, tactful, conscientious, considerate, a successful general and lover. Real men are not like this. Hal of *Henry IV* was not, and even allowing for reform and growth, could never have become so. But Hal was a character in whom Shakespeare was interested *qua* character; Henry V is not. Here the interest (albeit a sporadic one) is in Henry the symbol and hero. The loss in dramatic power and effectiveness is enormous, but the patriotic symbol so created is superb.

Henry V, then, is a patriotic play, glorifying England and things English. Everything which could possibly detract from this central focus is eliminated. Thus, Falstaff must go. The rarefied and exalted sentiment of *Henry V* could never support his weight, for Falstaff's charm and vitality, the very essence of his character, come from his parody of noble sentiments. Falstaff was representative of the warm, human, fallible side of Hal, and he was symbolically rejected at the end of *2 Henry IV*, but now he must go entirely. And significantly he dies from the cold, the coldheartedness of the practical Lancastrian character which even Falstaff could not withstand. In the same manner, the riotous, disorderly Eastcheap world has become domesticated. Mistress Quickly has married; Pistol and Nym leave off their quarrel to fight for the King. In short, anything which could serve either as a reminder of the old Hal or detract from the new one as the center of interest and exemplar of virtue and valor has been excised. Again the dramatic loss is regrettable, though the practical necessity is obvious.

In another way Shakespeare uses some rather mechanical devices to show Henry as the man who can unite antagonistic elements for his great cause. Fluellen, Jamy, and Macmorris, representing the Welsh, Scottish, and Irish, fight shoulder to shoulder with their English brothers. The symbolic meaning here is evident. Just as Henry could draw Pistol and Nym from their quarrelling, so too he unites all the British national elements in a way that could only be brought about by his dynamic and universal character. But there is something a little too obvious about these

The Battle of Agincourt.

characters. Fluellen achieves a certain amount of individual importance; the others remain rather wooden and dramatically ineffective. Thematically, of course, they are important because they illustrate Henry's ability to wed inharmonious elements in allegiance, but they are certainly not among Shakespeare's memorable characters.

Henry is able not only to bring together antagonistic groups, but also to command the loyalty of men holding two entirely different kinds of values. Old Sir Thomas Erpingham is in the play for a specific purpose; he represents the good side of the old chivalric world that had been repudiated with Hotspur's defeat. His devotion to the King is sacramental, for, though he is old, and perhaps fearful about the outcome of the battle, he knows his place is beside the King. And significantly, Henry borrows Sir Thomas' cloak, for Henry needs what it symbolizes just as much as he needs the cool, practical, determined mind he has inherited from his father. He inherited his father's concern about this problem, and now, taking Sir Thomas' cloak, he takes in so far as possible, the sacramental principle unto himself. But most of all Henry needs the English long-bowman, the common man. It is upon these common men that the victory depends, and it is to them that Henry pays his allegiance. The days of chivalry, of knights in armor and codes of honor are past, and Henry knows it. He sees

(as Richard II never did or could) that his responsibility is to the people, not to a chivalric code or a concept of divine right:

> Canst thou, when thou command'st the
>   beggar's knee,
> Command the health of it? No, thou proud
>   dream,
> That play'st so subtly with a king's repose;
> I am a king that find thee; and I know
> 'Tis not the balm, the sceptre and the ball,
> The sword, the mace, the crown imperial,
> The intertissued robe of gold and pearl,
> The farced title running 'fore the king,
> The throne he sits on, nor the tide of pomp
> That beats upon the high shore of this
>   world,
> No, not all these, thrice-gorgeous ceremony,
> Not all these, laid in bed majestical,
> Can sleep so soundly as the wretched slave,
> Who, with a body fill'd and vacant mind
> Gets him to rest, cramm'd with distressful
>   bread;
>
> . . . . .
>
>   but in gross brain little wots
> What watch the king keeps to maintain the
>   peace,

Whose hours the peasant best advantages.
(IV.i.262-290)

The King must protect his people, lead and inspire them; in fact, he is their servant. This is a far cry from the concept of kingship as Richard saw it.

It is a concept which has as its corollary the implied fact that it is not the ceremony, pomp, and regal trappings which make the King, but rather the man. Of course, this is a very convenient philosophy for the Lancastrians since their usurpation (and neither Henry nor his father was ever quite able to rationalize that away) depended on opportunistic employment of power rather than sacramental consecration. But it is more than an expedient position for Henry here; it is the realization that the King who is to lead these long-bowmen needs more than "the sceptre and the ball,/The sword, the mace, the crown imperial." These things were enough to lead the old chivalric knights who paid allegiance to a sacramental, inviolable kingship. But Henry IV changed all that, and Henry V knows it when he speaks incognito to Bates:

> I think the king is but a man, as I am: the violet smells to him as it doth to me; the element shows to him as it doth to me; all his senses have but human conditions: his ceremonies laid by, in his nakedness he appears but a man; and though his affections are higher mounted than ours, yet when they stoop, they stoop with the like wing. Therefore when he sees reason of fears, as we do, his fears, out of doubt, be of the same relish as ours are: yet, in reason, no man should possess him with any appearance of fear, lest he, by showing it, should dishearten his army. (IV.i.101-113)

The French, however, have not changed. They are still playing the old game and not playing it very well. The nobles in the French camp give the appearance of acting by the rules of the old chivalric code, but they are deluded, frivolous, concerned with armor, horses, and mistresses rather than with policy and the business at hand. Their overconfidence is chronic, and nothing could illustrate their weakness better than the list of casualties in Act IV. Of the French losses, over eighty per cent were noblemen of some kind; on the eve of the battle five hundred new knights had been created as if to terrorize the English by the very number of their titles, as if to imply that superiority and valor inhered in a name. There was a day when such strategy might have had some effect, but not any more. The English go on undaunted, and their losses include only two noblemen, a knight, and

> Davy Gam, esquire;
> None else of name; and of all other men
> But five and twenty.
> (IV.viii.106-108)

The implication is clear: it is the common Englishman who has fought and won the war, and it is a King, realizing his responsibility to those common men, who has led them.

These are a few of the salient features of the play's nationalistic theme, but there are also a few indications that Shakespeare was not entirely happy with his hero-king presentation. Or to put it another way, Shakespeare the poet rebels against Shakespeare the patriot. Henry, for example, evades responsibility. On the surface, of course, he appears to be taking the whole burden of the war on himself:

> Upon the king! let us our lives, our souls,
> Our debts, our careful wives,
> Our children, and our sins lay on the king!
> We must bear all. O hard condition!
> Twin-born with greatness, subject to the breath
> Of every fool, whose sense no more can feel
> But his own wringing. What infinite heart's ease
> Must kings neglect that private men enjoy!
> (IV.i.236-243)

But this is not quite true. From the beginning he has tried to shift the responsibility for the war: first he cites the Church (I.ii.9 ff.); then he accuses the Dauphin of inciting hostility (I.ii.281 ff.); and Henry says often that he is merely following God's will, that it is a part of the divine plan that he should conquer France. All of this may convince his troops, but it never quite convinces the audience or Henry himself.

In the case of the traitors, Cambridge, Grey, and Scroop, Henry makes them sentence themselves. A trick of this kind is, perhaps, expedient, for Henry can claim it is they who have condemned themselves and thereby obviate any possibility of leniency, but it is a trick Prince Hal would never have stooped to. Henry also evades his quarrel with Williams by passing the glove to Fluellen. He sophistically claims that the Governor of Harfleur will be responsible for whatever damage is done to the town. (III.iii.19 ff.). When Henry prays he seems self-righteous rather than penitent:

> Five hundred poor I have in yearly pay,
> Who twice a day their wither'd hands hold up
> Toward heaven, to pardon blood; and I have built
> Two chantries, where the sad and solemn priests
> Sing still for Richard's soul.
> (IV.i.304-308)

And when Henry answers Williams he does not really

speak to the question (IV.i.150 ff.). All these are perhaps minor points, but they do indicate that Shakespeare refused to make his hero a spotless saint.

The comic scenes here are also revealing in that they are more mechanical than those in *Henry IV*. There, each comic scene made a comment on, contributed to our understanding of, the serious level. They seem now to be inserted merely for relief and amusing effect. The love plot is so much in the background that the final scene, which is the only one devoted to it, seems structurally anomalous. Now and then we see the dirty, ugly side of the war:

> Our gayness and our gilt are all besmirch'd
> With rainy marching in the painful field.
>
> (IV.iii.110-111)

> . . . in a moment look to see
> The blind and bloody soldier with foul hand
> Defile the locks of your shrill-shrieking
>   daughters;
> Your fathers taken by the silver beards,
> And their most reverend head dash'd to the
>   walls.
>
> (III.iii.33-37)

There are Bardolphs to rob churches and Pistols to accept bribes, just as much as there are dear friends to fill the breach on St. Crispin's Day.

The language, though it occasionally rises to heights of oratorical excellence, is not nearly so poetic and powerful as that of the first three plays of the tetralogy. There is a flatness, for example, in a speech like Henry's in IV.i when he speaks to Williams, or in Canterbury's in I.ii, that betrays a certain lack of inspiration. And finally, there is the use of prologues, a device Shakespeare did not normally feel compelled to employ in apology for the limitations of his stage and craft; surely this, if nothing else, betrays the uneasiness Shakespeare the dramatist and poet felt in presenting a patriotic pageant.

Yet, it is the pageant we remember, and a superb one it is. Henry the magnificent symbol rather than Henry the evasive and expedient man is the image which remains dominant. For all its less glorious elements, the primary tone of the play is that of "Cry, 'God for Harry, England, and Saint George!'" (III.i.34). This is what Shakespeare in *Henry V* sets out to create and in the end does. It is a panegyric to patriotism and national pride, and everything else in the play pales beside the resonant strains of

> We few, we happy few, we band of
>   brothers;
> For he to-day that sheds his blood with me
> Shall be my brother; be he ne'er so vile

> This day shall gentle his condition:
> And gentlemen in England now a-bed
> Shall think themselves accurs'd they were
>   not here,
> And hold their manhoods cheap whiles any
>   speaks
> That fought with us upon Saint Crispin's
>   day.
>
> (IV.iii.60-67)

Helen J. Schwartz

SOURCE: "The Comic Scenes in *Henry V*," in *Hebrew University Studies in Literature*, Vol. 4, No. 1, Spring, 1976, pp. 18-26.

[*In the following essay, Schwartz examines the importance of the comic scenes to the play as an epic and contends that these scenes prove the worthiness of the king and his subjects. Schwartz maintains that Shakespeare replaces the Eastcheap gang with more orderly comic characters who can prosper under Henry's command and can contribute to the stability of his rule.*]

The comic scenes in Shakespeare's *Henry V* are often used to support a satiric interpretation of the play, are diagnosed as evidence for an inadequate rendering of an epic intention, or are censured or largely ignored in interpretations of the play as epic. I would argue, however, that these scenes have an integral and important function in the plotting of a national English epic and a drama of an heroic king. Two ingredients are necessary for such a play: subjects capable of glory and a ruler both personally noble and politically effective. J. H. Walter, in his introduction to the Arden edition, has ably argued Henry's qualities as an ideal king: wise in formulating national policy, but also forceful in implementing it. It is my intention to show how the comic scenes give evidence both of Henry's ability as a monarch and of the potential of English subjects to achieve national glory.

The comic scenes produce this effect by several means. Their overall plotting shows the comic figures of misrule controlled and replaced by a new kind of comic figure who serves and thrives under Henry's command. Falstaff, the most lovable of the Eastcheap gang, cannot survive in the world of Henry V after rejection by the newly reformed monarch in *2 Henry IV*. And his cohorts are pushed further and further from power in *Henry V* by the king's just policies as well as by the honesty and bravery of the emergent comic type. The epic evocation of "English Mercuries" in the Prologue to Act II is apparently undercut by the immediately following scene with Pistol and his friends but the eventual predominance of soldiers like Fluellen upholds the truth of epic. Furthermore, parallel episodes show the Eastcheap crew as typical of the English soldier. Finally, the comic Fluellen-Williams episode after Agincourt (IV. vii) parallels and parodies the earlier conspiracy against the king involving Cambridge, Grey and Scroop. The progression from serious threats to parallel comic threats shows that the king has achieved his national policy and increased the stability of his rule.

The first casualty among the figures of misrule is Falstaff. Perhaps it is true, as Mistress Quickly claims, and Fluellen implies (IV. vii), that "the king has killed his heart" (II. i. 92). And we who have seen Falstaff in the two earlier plays may be more saddened than gratified by the report of his deathbed repentings. But there can be no room for the old knight in the world of Henry V or *Henry V* (perhaps because he might steal the show). To Fluellen, one of the new comic type that replaces the Eastcheap gang, Falstaff's death is only matter for a "figure" to compare a modern (and superior) hero to an ancient one: "As Alexander killed his friend Cleitus, being in his ales and his cups; so also Harry Monmouth, being in his right wits and his good judgements, turned away the fat knight with the great-belly doublet: [. . .] I have forgot his name. [. . .] I'll tell you there is good men porn at Monmouth" (IV. vii. 46-53, 55). Falstaff's "discretion" and mercenary motives are no longer good, clean fun; France is not Gadshill, and Pistol lacks Falstaff's wit and perception. When Pistol goes off to France with his friends "like horse-leeches, [. . .] To suck, to suck, the very blood to suck" (II. iii. 58-59), and when he treats his French prisoner this way—"As I suck blood, I will some mercy show" (IV. iv. 68)—he is not viewed tolerantly as Falstaff was in similar situations, but seems more like "the weasel Scot" who might invade a defenceless England "and so [suck] her princely eggs" (I. ii. 170-171).

If the English troops invading France are no better than the Scots provided against by Henry's wisdom, they can hardly be considered the stuff that epics are made of. The introduction of the Eastcheap gang initially supports—in fact, stimulates—such fears about Harry's troops. The first comic scene comes immediately after the description of "English Mercuries" in the Prologue to Act II:

> Now all the youth of England are on fire,
> And silken dalliance in the wardrobe lies:
> Now thrive the armourers, and honour's
>   thought
> Reigns solely in the breast of every man.
>
> (ll. 1-4)

But our first example of these troops is Bardolph, whose face is fiery not from martial zeal but from drink. Then Pistol engages Nym in a fight over the former Mistress Quickly and they are reconciled only when Pistol promises to pay a debt to Nym from his expected war profits; dalliance gives way, but to economic "honour". It seems that the choric evocation of the ideal soldier Henry needs is satirically undercut by the reality. But just as Canterbury's machinations (I. i) seem to undermine the epic promise of the first Prologue, only to be reversed by the kingly decorum and intelligence of Henry in the second scene, so here in the second act our suspicions about Henry's "English Mercuries" are aroused only to be undercut by the subsequent fate of Bardolph, Nym and Pistol.

Furthermore, the actions of other commoners show that the gallants from Eastcheap are the nadir, not the norm, of the Englishman. Parallel episodes show Pistol and his friends to their disadvantage. For example, Nym and Pistol seem more likely to kill or disable each other in a personal quarrel over Mistress Quickly than to kill any Frenchmen (even for mercenary motives). There are two other occasions in the play when it seems that personal quarrels may divert English soldiers from their fight against France. But when Fluellen and Macmorris seem about to fight over the "disciplines of war" and the Irish nation, they break off when their duty as soldiers calls (III. ii); and when Williams and the disguised Henry quarrel before Agincourt, they hold the resolution of their personal differences in abeyance until they have fought the French. But Nym and Bardolph abate their "love quarrel" in the second act only to fight about a debt which the parasite Pistol will repay from profits in France. Ultimately they do go into battle, but at Harfleur it is only the Scylla of Fluellen which drives them to the Charybdis of the Harfleur "breach." Their behaviour also contrasts with the common soldiers'—Bates, Williams, and Court—when they talk fearfully *before* Agincourt though they resolve to fight bravely.

Eventually the brave commoners prevail over the comic figures of misrule. But although the Harfleur encounter between Fluellen and Pistol shows the Welsh captain in control, it appears later that the roles may be reversed. The posturing of Pistol at the "pridge" has taken in Fluellen, and therefore the thieving Bardloph may escape Exeter's sentence if Pistol's intercession with Fluellen succeeds. But though the honest comic soldier may be mistakenly impressed by heroics, he is sure about his military principles: "discipline ought to be used" (III. vi. 59). Furthermore, the English captain, Gower, can see through the likes of Pistol and warns Fluellen: "You must learn to know such slanders of the age, or else you may be marvellously mistook" (ll. 83-85). And these commoners are supported by commanders like Exeter who order thieves hanged and a king like Henry V who reinforces military discipline and justice (ll. 112-120).

Thus, as the play progresses, we see in Henry's army

that the cowardice of Pistol is exposed and that first Bardolph and then Nym are hanged for theft. but it seems that Pistol's mercenary plans find lawful fulfillment in the service of war. He expects the ransom of his French prisoner as a prize (IV. iv). But while the victor crows over his captive, the Boy returns to his duty with the luggage boys, where presumably he is killed in the renewed French attack. It is this same attack which prompts King Henry to kill all the prisoners, including Pistol's. Three significant features emerge from this plotting. First, it shows mercenary motives foiled. Second, we see an important attrition in the Eastcheap group: the Boy has rejected Pistol as a model. Instead he has *chosen* allegiance to duty, not to booty, and thus he is killed by a cowardly enemy, not by his own disciplining colleagues. Third, it is fitting that the cowardly attack of the French should deprive an English coward of his spoils.

Finally, the "aunchient lieutenant" is undone even in his bragging superiority to the Welsh customs of his fellow soldier, Fluellen; he is made to eat the leek and is reprimanded by the Englishman Gower. At the end of the play, Pistol's comic cunning is powerless in Henry's army. He alone survives of the Eastcheap gang, since "Nell [Quickly] is dead i' the spital/Of malady of France" (V. i. 87-88). They are replaced by the dutiful comic characters, just as King Henry V has replaced Prince Hal.

Fluellen, chief among the emergent comic type, is laughable in his preoccupation with the Welsh mystique and the rules of war, but neither obsession works counter to the purpose of the war as the Eastcheap motives do. As we have seen, his preoccupation helps preserve military order, even when he is taken in by Pistol's appearance. His fight with Pistol over the Welsh leek (V. i) has been put off because it was occasioned, as Fluellen says, "in a place where I could not breed no contention with him" (ll. 11-12).

Act IV, scene i. The English camp before Agincourt, with Richard Moore (center) as Pistol, in the 1975 Royal Shakespeare Theatre production of Henry V.

That is, he subordinates private quarrels to the interest of the national quarrel. Finally, his insistence on quiet in the English camp on the eve of Agincourt sets up a comparison between the English camp and that of the Roman Pompey in contrast to the showy noise of the French camp:

> Fluellen: [to Gower] Speak lower. It is the greatest admiration in the universal world, when the true and aunchient prerogatifes and laws of the wars is not kept: if you would take the pains but to examine the wars of Pompey the Great, you shall find [. . .] that there is no tiddle taddle [. . .] in Pompey's camp; I warrant you, you shall find the ceremonies of the wars, and the cares of it, and the forms of it, and the sobriety of it, and the modesty of it to be otherwise.
>
> Gower: Why the enemy is loud; you hear him all night.
>
> Fluellen: If the enemy is an ass and a fool and a prating coxcomb, is it meet, think you, that we should also [be] [. . .]?
>
> Gower: I will speak lower. (IV. i. 65-82)

Though Fluellen's military pedantry is laughable, his intention is not, as Gower's response acknowledges. Furthermore, this speech, coming as it does after the French foppery and internecine backbiting in III.vii and after Erpingham's stoic wit to the king (IV. i. 13-17), shows the relative sobriety of the English camp and undercuts Pistol's braggadocio in the episode immediately preceding the speech quoted above. The realistic conversation with the common soldiers following Fluellen's speech may indicate that while the English are not exactly ancient Romans, their stoic acceptance of duty in the king's cause proves them to be more like Erpingham than like the empty show of the French and of Pistol. King Henry himself tells us exactly how to value Fluellen and his rules of war: "Though it appear a little out of fashion,/There is much care and valour in this Welshman" (IV. i. 84-85).

My final example of the function of the comic scenes deals with the Fluellen-Williams episodes in Act IV. Here we see a comic equivalent of the scene with the traitors Cambridge, Grey and Scroop (II. ii). Henry's handling of the episodes is similar, with his staging of the "commissions"-turned-accusation in the early scene and employment of the glove gambit at Agincourt. But the king's earnest play to unmask treason becomes, in the later scene, a playful resolution of loyal "disloyalty." The private friends of Henry plan public murder of the king; the soldier who commits himself to fight in the national cause voices private reservations about the king's policies. But although Williams pledges to fight the common soldier of Erpingham's company, he will not and cannot fight the king. What would be a point of honour in a private quarrel becomes a public treason when the king is involved.

This contrast is pointed up by the judgements of Fluellen. When asked by the king whether Williams should keep his oath to fight an English soldier, he answers, "He is a craven and a villain else" (IV. vii. 140); when the quarrel is presented as a promise to strike the *king*, he says, "let his [Williams'] neck answer for it, if there is any martial law in the world" (IV. vii. 46-47). Henry rejects the harsh judgement of the loyal Fluellen, just as he has rejected the traitors' harsh advice about the common man who railed against the king. He accepts the justness of Williams' defence:

> King Henry: It was ourself thou didst abuse.
>
> Williams: Your majesty came not like yourself: you appeared to me but as a common man [. . .] and what your highness suffered under that shape. I beseech you take it for your own fault and not mine: *for had you been as I took you for, I made no offence;* therefore, I beseech your highness, pardon me. (IV. vii. 52-60; emphasis added).

Henry knows that Williams is basically loyal and that his comments did not reflect any deep-seated disaffection, as the soldier argues: "All offences, my lord, come from the heart; never came any from mine that might offend your majesty" (IV. vii. 49-51).

Williams, then, parallels both the common man and the traitors in the earlier scene. His challenge, if urged, is as dangerous to the king's life as the planned treason of Cambridge, Scroop and Grey; but Henry's dismissal of Williams is just like his "mercy" to the commoner who was his earlier detractor. Because the king has brought a just order to English society at home and to his troops in France, he can regard such criticism as "little faults" to be "wink'd at" (II. ii. 54, 55).

In conclusion, the comic scenes provide evidence of the worthiness of king and subjects in Shakespeare's English epic. The victory over France owes much to Henry's leadership—in ordering himself, national policy, and military discipline. But much is also owing to the brave and well-disciplined comic characters. Just as Henry represents Britain in his person, so do Henry's four captains—Fluellen, Macmorris, Jamy and Gower—represent the four British races: Welsh, Irish, Scottish, English. None are exactly "English Mercuries," but all are not Pistols. Though the Eastcheapians never seriously threaten the French venture, their control and explusion by the valiant captains represent the symbolic replacement of misrule by order. Henry's influence supports the valour and responsibility of the state at the commoners' level, just as his wisdom has ordered the state at the highest levels of government. As the comic scenes help to show, it is the efforts of loyal soldiers as well as those of an heroic king which achieve "the world's best garden" (Epilogue, 7).

HENRY

Critics have been vastly divided in their responses to Henry. Some scholars, such as **Joseph M. Lenz,** Dorothy Cook, M. M. Reese, and Rolf Soellner, have praised Shakespeare's presentation of Henry as the ideal ruler. Reese declares that Shakespeare carefully directed the dramatic action of the play to portray him as doing everything that the Elizabethan age expected of the perfect king, and Soellner contends that Henry represents Shakespeare's ideal character and that he attempts to paint a sympathetic portrait of his hero. However, most critics, including Norman Rabkin, Hardin Craig, W. L. Godshalk, Roy W. Battenhouse, Marilyn L. Williamson, and Stopford A. Brooke have argued that Henry is far from perfect. Rabkin asserts that although Henry is depicted as an ideal king, he is not flawless, and Craig acknowledges that Shakespeare was conscious to show Henry's humanity. Godshalk examines Henry's inability to accept responsibility for his actions and ways he uses this weakness to his own benefit. Battenhouse maintains that Henry's morality and piety are not deeply held principles, but mere counterfeits of genuine feeling, and Williamson characterizes the king's actions in the "wooing scene" as manipulative, self-justifying, and disingenuous. Still other commentators have focused on particular aspects of Henry's character. Sylvan Barnet analyzes Henry's ambiguity, while **William Babula** and H. M. Richmond detail his development and maturation throughout the play. For further analysis of Henry's character, see the essays by **E. F. C. Ludowyk** and **Robert B. Pierce** in the OVERVIEWS section, the essays by **D. A. Traversi** and **Charles Mitchell** in the KINGSHIP section, and the essay by **Landon C. Burns, Jr.** in the EPIC ELEMENTS section.

Hardin Craig

SOURCE: "Success in the Theater," in *An Interpretation of Shakespeare,* Lucas Brothers, 1948, pp. 116-53.

[In this excerpt, Craig discusses Henry's fulfillment of the qualities of a true king. Craig contends that Shakespeare displayed his hero in the framework of four virtues—Justice, Temperance, Fortitude, and Wisdom—and illustrated these virtues through Henry's conduct. Craig states that while Shakespeare presented a glorified king, he was also careful to show Henry's humanity.]

To understand what it is that Shakespeare has done with his favorite character it is necessary to resort to a common doctrine of the Renaissance, the qualities of the true prince. Normal, moral, efficient manhood seems often to be the commonplace thing. Shakespeare had the task of making his audience realize the significance of normal virtues. Milton had this same demonstration to make in the case of Adam; and Thackeray came near succeeding with it in Henry Esmond. Shakespeare displays his king in the framework of Justice, Temperance, Fortitude, and Wisdom. The idea of the perfect prince or governor was an old one in Shakespeare's day and is still an idea of great importance. *Henry V* illustrates these virtues in the action of the play, not formally in terms of the four Platonic virtues, but essentially in the conduct of the King. No doubt Shakespeare has heightened his effort to exalt the commonplace by his splendid gift of eloquence and his deep appeal to patriotic feeling. These enabled him to cast a light of glory over his hero and his deeds, and Shakespeare uses every occasion to endow his hero with his own knowledge about life. He had learned the fundamental importance and the wide appeal of human nature, or humanity. He therefore loses from beginning to end no opportunity to show how human his hero is.

Shakespeare begins the play of *Henry V* with his usual ideational clarity. The dialogue between the Archbishop of Canterbury and the Bishop of Ely (I, i) brings out the kingly accomplishments of the new monarch. Henry V, we are given to understand, has the qualities of a real king as the Renaissance understood the matter. He is a scholar—knows divinity, commonwealth affairs, war, and policy. When he speaks we discover that he is an orator. The second scene of the first act reveals the new king's careful sense of justice. He investigates his claim to the French crown and gets advice from the best authorities, and in this area of justice, the particular field of kings, one sees him strong, not only in distributive justice, but in corrective justice. He punishes the traitors, Scroop, Cambridge, and Grey, displaying, as he does so, natural, righteous indignation. His judgment is in the form of an invective (II, ii, 79 ff.).

The brilliant assault on Harfleur (III, i) shows King Henry's courage and his mastery of the psychology of combat (ll. 5-17):

> But when the blast of war blows in our
>   ears,
> Then imitate the action of the tiger;
> Stiffen the sinews, sumon up the blood,
> Disguise fair nature with hard-favour'd rage;
> Then lend the eye a terrible aspect;

Let it pry through the portage of the head
Like the brass cannon; let the brow
   o'erwhelm it
As fearfully as doth a galled rock
O'erhang and jutty his confounded base,
Swill'd with the wild and wasteful ocean.
Now set the teeth and stretch the nostril
   wide,
Hold hard the breath and bend up every
   spirit,
To his full height.

Henry's courage is, however, properly tempered with prudence, so that it is true fortitude. He would rather not fight at Agincourt, because he is ill-prepared to do so; but, if he has to fight, he will fight bravely and in the wisest way (III, vi, 173-4):

We would not seek a battle, as we are;
Nor, as we are, we say we will not shun it.

Henry V is definitely religious, and no man could show a greater zeal to get God on his side. His private prayer on the night before the battle of Agincourt (IV, i, 306-22) is a model of humility and confession:

O God of battles! steel my soldiers' hearts;
Possess them not with fear; take from them
   now
The sense of reckoning, if the opposed
   numbers
Pluck their hearts from them. Not to-day, O
   Lord,
O, not to-day, think not upon the fault
My father made in compassing the crown!

He has no foolishness in his heart as regards the superiority of kings. He knows, just as Shakespeare knew, that kings are men. In the wise and reasonable words he says to the soldiers while he is walking among them in disguise (IV, i, 103-246) and in the soliloquy that follows, he puts stress, as Shakespeare does elsewhere, on the overwhelming responsibilities of kings. Surely these opinions on kingship which Shakespeare attributes to his great hero at a crisis in his life are very close to Shakespeare's own opinions. The allegiance of his soldiers means merely that the battle in which they are about to engage is a common enterprise, not the King's battle only or mainly. There are moving scenes within the English camp, and in the battle the King shows himself wise, merciful, appreciative of the service of others, and yet stern where sternness is required. The play ends in the glory of national victory, presented, not as conquest, but as justice and the will of God, as if it were regarded as the restoration of a rightful king to his kingdom.

In the last scene of the play we have presented an aspect of Henry V's character for which this play and its predecessors have hardly prepared us. It no doubt fulfilled an ideal of Shakespeare's age to show this king without a trace of sentimentality. He will lay firm hands on that which belongs to him. He loves France so well that he will not part with a village of it. That disposition to claim his rights belonged to him and no doubt made him more attractive to the audience. but his manners are another matter. Although his wooing of the Princess Katherine is a very funny scene, very charming on the stage, one is hardly prepared to see him suddenly become actually bluff and boisterous, qualities admired in King Henry VIII and of course attractive to the Elizabethan audience.

Henry V has in it little dramatic conflict, but is a positive hero play almost epic in its nature. One would not minimize the greatness of Shakespeare's representation or the splendid character of his hero. King Henry V has his personal struggles, which display his courage, his wisdom, his essential democracy, his piety, and his charm. . . .

William Babula

SOURCE: "Whatever Happened to Prince Hal? An Essay on *Henry V*," in *Shakespeare Survey: An Annual Survey of Shakespearian Study and Production,* Vol. 30, 1977, pp. 47-59.

[*In the following excerpt, Babula traces the development of Henry V as he matures throughout the play, transforming from a clever but immature youth to an honest and experienced king. Babula concludes by noting how the maturation of the character of Henry V contributes to the dramatic unity of the play.*]

E. M. W. Tillyard [in *Shakespeare's History Plays,* 1946] is right in his assertion that Shakespeare in *Henry V* was 'jettisoning the character he had created' in the *Henry IV* plays. The Hal that developed out of those earlier histories is not present at the opening of *Henry V.* This does not mean that Shakespeare has now accepted a Henry 'who knew exactly what he wanted and went for it with utter singleness of heart . . .' Nor has he, as Mark Van Doren would have us believe [in *Shakespeare,* 1939], stretched a hero 'until he struts on tiptoe and is still strutting at the last insignificant exit.' Nor, on the other extreme, is Henry the ideal humanistic hero, 'conceived of as beyond the limitations of nature, able to impose the order of philosophy on the protean world of history.' Rather, as H. M. Richmond notes [in *Shakespeare's Political Plays,* 1967], Henry in this play begins as a 'clever young hero masquerading as the ideal king', and ends as 'a mature man'. Thus the process of growth that Henry undergoes in the play is crucial. While this process may render the second tetralogy inconsistent, it gives a marked consistency to the play *Henry V* as it stands alone. For in it Shakespeare has decided to dramatize again the maturation of a ruler. . . .

The play opens with a Chorus that provides part of the context in which the audience sees Henry. In typical epic fashion the poet through his Chorus presents the invocation: 'O for a Muse of fire, that would ascend / The brightest heaven of invention . . .' (Prologue, 1-2). It *sounds* as if we are going to see the epic hero many have seen in Henry V. And there is no reason to doubt this notion as the Chorus turns apologetic:

> But pardon, gentles all,
> The flat unraised spirits that have dared
> On this unworthy scaffold to bring forth
> So great an object: can this cockpit hold
> The vasty fields of France? or may we cram
> Within this wooden O the very casques
> That did affright the air at Agincourt?
>
> (Prologue, 8-14)

The theme is presented as epic but the audience is also reminded that they are seeing an illusion created by art. The Globe, the 'scaffold', this 'cockpit', this 'wooden O' are to be transformed into the vastness of France. A perfect apology for the limitations of the Elizabethan stage? If so, every play would require it to some degree. Or perhaps Shakespeare is introducing the audience to one of his major concerns: the distance between art and reality. In this case it applies to the theatre. It will come to apply, however, to the distance between the art, the words, the rhetoric of Henry and the reality of his actions. There is an art that covers reality in the political world as well as in the playhouse.

As the play proper opens the audience hears of what it is going to see and hear of so much in *Henry V*: the quarrel. In this case the Parliament is contemplating a bill that will strip the Church of its wealth. As Canterbury comments, 'If it pass against us, / We lose the better half of our possession' (I, i, 7-8). The pivot upon which this question rests is the king. Canterbury then begins to heap praise upon this king— a character we have not yet seen in this play. Henry, no longer the riotous prince, is now like a 'paradise'. He can 'reason in divinity', 'debate of commonwealth affairs', and cut 'the Gordian knot' of policy—a reference to Alexander the Great that will rebound ironically later in the play. Yet all of this idealized language can be explained rather cynically. When the Bishop of Ely asks which side is Henry on, Canterbury replies that the king is 'rather swaying more upon our part . . .' (I, i, 73). And certainly it is difficult to miss the suggestion of a bribe when Canterbury explains the king's favor—note the 'for' in particular:

> For I have made an offer to his majesty,
> Upon our spiritual convocation
> . . . to give a greater sum
> Than ever at one time the clergy yet
> Did to his predecessors part withal.
>
> (I, i, 75-6, 79-81)

Could Henry make an unbiased choice? All of the grand-sounding language by which Canterbury describes the king sounds like the epic and idealizing language of the Prologue. In fact it sounds as if the bishop would cover the limitations of the king just as Shakespeare would disguise the limitations of his playhouse. But beneath the language there is an inescapable reality of person and platform.

In the second scene Henry appears for the first time. He sends for Canterbury and requires of him:

> My learned lord, we pray you to proceed
> And justly and religiously unfold
> Why the law Salique that they have in
>   France
> Or should, or should not, bar us in our
>   claim:
> And God forbid, my dear and faithful lord,
> That you should fashion, wrest or bow your
>   reading . . .
>
> (I, ii, 9-14)

One critic [M. M. Reese, in *The Cease of Majesty,* 1961] has commented: 'To consult his spiritual advisers on a matter of this gravity was the correct thing for a king to do . . .' Yet the audience knows that the bishop, to protect Church property, must have the war in France; it is hard to imagine that this politic king does not know the same thing. What he seems to want are the words that will legalize aggression. He also wants to abdicate his responsibility for any of the slaughter to follow.

> For God doth know how many now in
>   health
> Shall drop their blood in approbation
> Of what your reverence shall incite us to.
>
> (I, ii, 18-20)

Verbally Henry pretends to have little to do with what will happen; the active verb 'incite' is given to the bishop—whatever happens will be his fault. It is not a very pleasant situation for Canterbury. This is indeed a politic king but not necessarily an epic hero.

Canterbury then launches upon a 62-line defense of Henry's right to the French throne. No audience simply hearing this complicated and twisting explanation could have much idea what it means. In terms of stage action the king himself seems confused. After he has been told in Canterbury's involved speech that he is the proper heir, he still has to ask: 'May I with right and conscience make this claim?' (I, ii, 96). He does not really understand the basis of his claim and neither could the audience. The bishop assures him, however, by reference to 'the book of Numbers'. The search for authority seems rather desperate. One would hardly think of the book of Numbers as providing 'unhidden passages' through which an English king could claim a French throne.

When Henry resolves to claim the throne, before the French ambassadors enter, he states: 'France being ours, we'll bend it to our awe, / Or break it all to pieces . . .' (I, ii, 224-5). It is the absolute demand of the immature man, the kind of demand we would expect from Hotspur. But when the ambassadors come in and tell Henry the Dauphin rejects all of his claims and has sent over some 'tennis-balls' instead, Henry projects himself as an epic hero—but note how his self-glorification reminds us of Richard II, another sun-king:

> . . . I will rise there with so full a glory
> That I will dazzle all the eyes of France.
> Yea, strike the Dauphin blind to look on us.
>
> (I, ii, 278-80)

It sounds impressive, but Richard II sounded impressive, too. Henry pretends this insult has resolved him when he had already made up his mind to claim France. Also, Henry does to the Dauphin what he did to Canterbury; he takes responsibility from himself and puts it on another. It is the Dauphin who 'hath turn'd his [tennis] balls to gun-stones' (I, ii, 282). It is the Dauphin whose soul 'shall stand sore charged for the wasteful vengeance / That shall fly with them . . .' (I, ii, 283-4). If the audience has put aside the Hal of the *Henry IV* plays, it is seeing a clever, but not necessarily attractive, immature man. . . .

The Chorus then returns to tell the audience to imagine the 'well-appointed king' sailing in epic splendor to France. And quite properly to the epic tone Henry will not accept a compromise with the French; he is not satisfied with the king's daughter Katharine and 'some petty and unprofitable dukedoms'. Instead, the cannon will fire and the siege of Harfleur will continue. Yet even in this epic-sounding Chorus there are certain ambiguities. Is it a positive act for Henry to have left England, 'Guarded with grandsires, babies, and old women' (III, Prologue, 20)? The reference to the cannon by the Chorus seems clearly ironical: 'And down goes all before them' (III, Prologue, 34). It is just not true. Harfleur is not coming down. Once more words are found quite distant from the reality of the situation.

As the scene shifts to before Harfleur the audience hears the rhetorical Henry exhorting his men: 'Once

more unto the breach, dear friends, once more; / Or close the wall up with our English dead' (III, i, 1-2). It may be a compelling statement, but as Richmond notes the attacks repeatedly fail. Also, Henry's own language suggests the distortion of human nature required to carry on these brutal acts:

> Then *imitate* the action of the tiger;
> *Stiffen* the sinews; summon up the blood,
> *Disguise* fair nature with hard-favour'd rage;
> Then *lend* the eye terrible aspect . . .
>
> (III, i, 6-9)

The words in italics all suggest an unnatural making-over of man for war. Yet Henry sees in these men, these 'English dead' a 'noble lustre'. . . .

The scene then shifts back to the central quarrel. Incredibly, Henry, as he speaks to the Governor of Harfleur, is denying responsibility for what will happen in the city. He describes in detail the terrors that will befall Harfleur if it does not surrender, then warns the Governor: ' . . . you yourselves are cause . . .' (III, iii, 19). He also terms the Governor 'guilty in defense'. This is just too much from Henry. Shakespeare makes his own attitude clear when he compares through Henry the war the king is ready to unleash 'to the prince of fiends'. It is a devil that Henry brings. Even more pointed is the irony in Henry's calling his soldiers 'Herod's bloody-hunting slaughtermen' (III, iii, 41). It is impossible to take the allusion as a compliment. More and more the doubts about the validity of Henry's quarrel are growing. Yet, for the first time something seems to be changing. Harfleur surrenders because the Dauphin cannot aid it. But as Henry accepts his prize—consider the rhetoric he employed a moment ago—he seems somewhat deflated and his language reflects this change: 'The winter coming on and sickness growing / Upon our soldiers, we will retire to Calais' (III, iii, 55-6). For the first time Henry stops sounding like an epic hero and starts sounding like an honest man. Rhetoric is put aside. Henry trapped in a discredited war is beginning to mature. . . .

When the French ambassador enters in the same scene it is he who fills the air with the rhetoric of war: 'Our voice is imperial: England shall repent his folly . . .' (III, vi, 31-2). Instead of reacting in kind, as he did when he received the tennis balls, Henry simply asks him to leave the country:

>   Turn thee back,
> And tell thy king I do not seek him now;
> But could be willing to march on to Calais
> Without impeachment . . .
>
> (III, vi, 148-51)

Henry is asking for peace. But almost more important

is his rejection of the epic art associated with the opening prologues. It is, as Henry notes, foolish to admit your weakness to your enemy. But Shakespeare seems to want to make it clear that Henry is no longer covering reality with words. So while the statement may be illogical from a strategical point of view, it is dramatically logical as it shows Henry's maturation. Thus in honesty, without artifice, he comments:

> . . . to say the sooth,
> Though 'tis no wisdom to confess so much
> Unto an enemy of craft and vantage,
> My people are with sickness much
>   enfeebled,
> My numbers lessen'd . . .
>
> (III, vi, 151-5)

This is not the Henry who reminded the audience of Hotspur in the opening scene.

In fact all of the disagreeable elements that Shakespeare associated with the English earlier now begin to pass over to the French. At the moment it is Henry who is seeking peace. Also the petty quarrels are now French petty quarrels. In III, vii, the Constable of France, Orleans, and the Dauphin argue about their armor and their horses. Going the furthest, the Dauphin says of his horse:

> It is the prince of palfreys; his neigh is like the bidding of a monarch and his countenance enforces homage.
>
> (III, vii, 29-31)

This is too much for Orleans but the Dauphin will not be stopped. He declared: 'I once writ a sonnet in his praise and began thus: "Wonder of nature"' (III, vii, 42-3). In fact the Dauphin states: 'My horse is my mistress' (III, vii, 46). The argument begins to parallel that of Nym and Pistol over Nell; only now the question is far more absurd. The mistress in question now becomes a horse. It is the French who are being presented as absurd.

Instead of Henry's rhetoric, the audience hears the bragging of the French who are all impatient for the day when 'by ten / We shall have each a hundred Englishmen' (III, vii, 168-9). Yet it will be the English who will be out on the field of battle first. And now instead of Henry it is the Dauphin who is looked at with suspicion. When he exits the Constable of France calls the Dauphin a braggart who can never do harm. When Orleans says that the Dauphin is valiant, the Constable ironically agrees, for 'he told me so himself' (III, vii, 117). If the audience is watching for parallels it can see one between Pistol and the Dauphin. Gradually Henry is moving away from the unattractive elements in the play. Shakespeare is shifting them to the French.

Yet, petty quarrels continue to plague the English camp. Henry disguises himself with a cloak as a 'gentleman of a company'. Soon he runs into Pistol and though the king shows restraint he does provoke an argument with him when he tells Pistol he is Fluellen's kinsman. It all ends with Pistol's 'The figo for thee, then!' (IV, i, 60). As Henry continues through the camp he meets the positive parallels to Nym, Bardolph, and Pistol in Bates, Court, and Williams. When Henry says, however, the king's cause is 'just and his quarrel honourable' (IV, i, 133), Williams replies, 'That's more than we know' (IV, i, 134). In fact he then goes on to hold the king responsible if the cause is not just:

> But if the cause be not good, the king himself hath a heavy reckoning to make, when all those legs and arms and heads, chopped off in a battle, shall join together at the latter day and cry all 'We died at such a place . . .'
>
> (IV, i, 140-5)

Once more a raw nerve is struck in Henry and in a speech that covers 42 prose lines (IV, i, 154-6), the audience hears him denying responsibility again. He avoids the central issue of the just cause and presents such statements as: 'Every subject's duty is the king's; but every subject's soul is his own.' On stage, though Williams and Bates agree, the speech is hard to follow—recall Canterbury's treatment of the Salic laws. And it just does not answer the question of responsibility that Williams posed. Henry is not yet free of his rhetoric.

In fact, the soldiers continue cynical when Henry tells them the King has said he would not be ransomed. As Williams says:

> Ay, he said so, to make us fight cheerfully: but when our throats are cut, he may be ransomed, and we ne'er the wiser.
>
> (IV, i, 204-6)

This exchange leads to another foolish quarrel and Henry and Williams exchange favors so that they can recognize each other and fight at a more appropriate time. Oddly, it is not Henry, but Bates who stops the quarrel: 'Be friends, you English fools, be friends . . .' (IV, i, 239). As the soldiers exit, Henry in soliloquy, upset by Williams' remarks about the king's responsibility, comments:

> Upon the king! let us our lives, our souls
> Our debts, our careful wives,
> Our children and our sins lay on the king!
>
> (IV, i, 247-9)

Yet the war is his responsibility. It is hard to miss Shakespeare's irony when Henry laments: ' . . . in gross brain little wots / What watch the king keeps to maintain the peace . . .' (IV, i, 299-300). It was Henry who, like Bardolph, stole the *pax* or peace. While Henry is still confined by his rhetoric, he is growing more honest. He is ready to admit that not only is there some doubt about his claim to the French throne, but there is doubt about his right to the English crown. As the scene ends, referring to the murder of Richard II, he prays:

> Not to-day, O Lord,
> O, not to-day, think not upon the fault
> My father made in compassing the crown!
>
> (IV, i, 309-11)

The process may be taking a long time, but Henry is maturing.

I spoke above of the parallel between the Chorus's admission that it was covering a limited stage with devices of art and our sense that Henry may have been doing the same thing in his role as epic king. In the Prologue to Act IV, the Chorus now apologizes for the battle scene:

> . . . O for pity!—we shall much disgrace
> With four or five most vile and ragged foils,
> Right ill-disposed in brawl ridiculous,
> The name of Agincourt.
>
> (IV, Prologue, 49-52)

But this apology does not nearly come up to the apology required. In the Prologue to the play, the Chorus asked the audience 'into a thousand parts divide one man' (l. 24) and thus imagine the large battle. Another apology for technical limitations? Hardly. None of this prepares us for what we are going to see in the only actual battle scene where French and English meet: IV, iv. What Shakespeare has asked us to do is to divide Pistol the coward and a more cowardly Frenchman into a thousand parts to represent the monumental English victory at Agincourt. Pistol takes him prisoner and says he will cut his throat. The Boy translates the French soldier's reply:

> He prays you save his life: he is a gentleman of a good house; and for his ransom he will give you two hundred crowns.
>
> (IV, iv, 47-9)

The offer satisfies Pistol, who states: 'As I suck blood, I will some mercy show' (IV, iv, 68). His words recall his earlier intentions as he left for France: 'To suck, to suck, the very blood to suck' (II, iii, 58). Shakespeare is not limited by his theatre, he has chosen to present Agincourt in the worst way possible. The only hero we see on stage is one whom, as the Boy comments, 'Bardolph and Nym had ten times more

valour than . . .' (IV, iv, 74).

As the French begin to sense defeat, Bourbon urges them on in terms that recall the argument over Nell, the reference to Frenchwomen giving 'their bodies to the lust of English youth . . .' (III, v, 30) and Henry's references to the rape of virgins as he stood outside Harfleur. Orleans says he who will not follow him into battle is

> Like a base pandar, [who will] hold the
>   chamber-door
> Whilst by a slave, no gentler than my dog,
> His fairest daughter is contaminated.
>
> (IV v, 14-16)

Then the battle, if possible, becomes even less attractive. Exeter describes in pathetic terms the deaths of York and Suffolk. Henry is moved almost to tears. But at this very moment Henry learns the French are regrouping and he commands: 'Then every soldier kill his prisoners: / Give the word through' (IV vi, 37-8). Immediately juxtaposed to this act is the French act of brutality: they have slaughtered the boys who were with the luggage. For this, Fluellen explains, 'The king, most worthily, hath caused every soldier to cut his prisoner's throat. O, 'tis a gallant king!' (IV vii, 10-11). The irony seems inescapable. Just as Henry decided to attack France before the insult of the tennis balls, Henry now ordered his massacre before the French carried out theirs. Pistol and the French soldier are not bad 'ciphers to this great accompt'. Once more the reality of the battle has been quite different from the promises of the early Choruses. If we are going to admire the Henry that was maturing before the battle, Shakespeare must extricate him from this degrading turmoil.

But it is not time yet. Fluellen and Gower compare Henry who could 'cut the Gordian knot' and Alexander the Great who comes out in Fluellen's Welsh distortion of big as Alexander the Pig. Both epic heroes are being trimmed down to size. The audience may imagine, however, that Shakespeare is going to compare Henry's victory with Alexander's conquests. But this is hardly the case. There is a comparison, however, as Fluellen states:

> If you mark Alexander's life well, Harry of Monmouth's life is come after it indifferent well . . . Alexander . . . did, in his ales and his angers, look you, kill his best friend, Cleitus.
>
> (IV vii, 34-6, 39-41)

When Gower objects that Henry never killed any of his friends, Fluellen responds with Falstaff:

> Harry Monmouth, being in his right wits and his

good judgments, turned away the fat knight . . .

       (IV, vii, 49-51)

The comparison with Henry presented as coldblooded, can hardly be to his advantage.

In fact, as he enters immediately after this passage he threatens the French prisoners once more: 'We'll cut the throats of those we have . . .' (IV, vii, 66). Yet when the French surrender Henry can take a new tone: 'Praised be God, and not our strength, for it!' (IV, vii, 90). In contrast to his earlier bragging, in contrast to the French bragging, his tone and attitude seem refreshing. But another quarrel, much less important, must be settled as well. Williams and Henry are to meet after the battle. But to avoid insult to the royal person, Henry gives the favor that marks him as Williams' enemy to Fluellen. He is careful, however, that nothing serious should pass and he sends certain lords to 'follow, and see there be no harm between them' (IV, vii, 190). Yet we see on stage another quarrel as Williams recognizes the favor and strikes Fluellen. The audience must by now desire peace on stage. Henry enters to settle the quarrel and tells Williams that he had insulted the king the night before the battle. Williams defends himself, however, by saying it was Henry's fault:

> . . . what your highness suffered under that shape, I beseech you take it for your own fault and not mine . . .
>
>   (IV, viii, 56-8).

And as Henry rewards this fellow the audience feels he is finally beginning to take responsibility. It was his fault. Yet Fluellen's advice to Williams at this point can apply to Henry as well:

> I pray you to serve God, and keep you out of prawls, and prabbles, and quarrels, and dissensions . . .
>
>   (IV, viii, 69-70)

The Prologue to act V presents the conqueror Henry in rather unheroic terms. That is, Henry is no longer a braggart. What follows is his reaction to a triumphal procession:

>   . . . he forbids it,
> Being free from vainness and self-glorious pride;
> Giving full trophy, signal and ostent
> Quite from himself to God.
>
>   (V, Prologue, 19-22)

It is easy to be cynical about this pose, yet it does present us with a Henry who is more humble than the character we experienced at the beginning of the drama. He also becomes more attractive to us when the

Chorus, ignoring real time, now carries Henry back to France—only now he is there for peace and not for war. His new role is juxtaposed to the roles his soldiers still play. The audience watches while the English soldiers continue to argue among themselves. Fluellen, in terms of stage action, had just condemned 'quarrels and dissensions' but now he is ready for another meaningless argument with Pistol about the Welsh and the symbol of their pride, the leek (V, i). Once more there is confusion and dissension on stage when the audience is weary of this kind of thing. We have been overwhelmed with quarrels, debates, and wars; everything should be over. No wonder Henry looks so good in the final act when he brings peace to a play that is itself in turmoil.

Indeed, Henry is removed from the conflicts that take place on stage. Fluellen beats Pistol on the stage for mocking the Welsh, a punishment well earned. In fact, Pistol has been driven out of the army as the worst aspects of Henry's character seem to have been driven out of him. Now Pistol, whom we will hear of no more, comments:

> Old do I wax; and from my weary limbs
> Honour is cudgelled. Well, bawd I'll turn,
> And something lean to cutpurse of quick hand.
> To England will I steal, and there I'll steal:
> And patches will I get unto these cudgell'd scars,
> And swear I got them in the Gallia wars.
>
>   (V, i, 89-94)

He will continue to be a thief, an occupation that Henry has now apparently disavowed. Also throughout the play Pistol's boasting served to parody the epic language of the king and the Chorus. Pistol is going to continue to boast and swagger like a 'turkey-cock'—he is going to present himself as a soldier wounded in the wars—while the audience will see in the next scene a Henry who has put off such swaggering language. Thus Pistol who served in the play as a parallel to Henry, reminding us of the king's limitations, now serves as a contrast to a matured king. Having shown us what Henry is not going to be, he departs forever from Shakespeare's stage. It is the perfect moment to dismiss him.

This time Henry has come not to suck the blood of France but for peace. Yet even this late in the play we are reminded of an earlier Henry. The king tells Burgundy that peace is the French King's responsibility: 'Well then the peace, / Which you before so urged, lies in his answer' (V, ii, 75-6). Will the king accept Henry's 'just demands?' Once again he is avoiding responsibility. But there is a difference. He is now ready to compromise, something a Hotspur could never do. He tells his negotiators:

Kenneth Branagh as Henry V in the 1984 Royal Shakespeare Theatre production.

. . . take with you free power to ratify,
Augment, or alter, as your wisdoms best
Shall see advantageable for our dignity,
Anything in or out of our demands
And we'll consign thereto.

(v, ii, 86-90)

He is much more concerned with wooing Katharine.

Indeed it is in this action, as they are left alone on stage (except for Alice), that the audience really sees a new Henry. The change in Henry is particularly signified by the change in his language. He once spoke in epic rhetoric concerning war, he now speaks in simple prose as he pleads his love. In fact he insists upon an honesty of style; he is not covering anything with art. This is certainly different from the Henry we saw before and from the Chorus who admitted covering reality with art. Now Henry woos:

But, before God, Kate, I cannot look greenly nor gasp out my eloquence, nor I have no cunning in protestation; only downright oaths . . .

(v, ii, 146-9)

Though love is certainly different from war, the audience does see and hear a Henry who seems to have rejected the deceptive arts of rhetoric. For the first time we may be having a fully positive reaction to him. There is no longer a distance between words and reality, a distance we felt so keenly between the words of the Chorus and the realities of the action. No longer does he need the confusing legal language of the bishop; no false claims are being covered up by words. Also all of the imagery of the rape of Frenchwomen, which certainly reflected upon Henry's purposes in attacking France, now only serves as a contrast to his honorable proposal of marriage.

Thus the quarrel is finally resolved with the marriage

of Henry and Katharine—the ending reminds one of the conclusions of various comedies. Peace is the value stressed. Yet there is one final irony that obviously affected the Elizabethan audience. If more and more the audience felt as it watched this play the futility of all 'dissensions', what more support could it require than the Epilogue? Henry dies and leaves both France and England to his son. But the Chorus—now like Henry in the last scene, speaking without art or rhetoric—tells us honestly that:

> Henry the Sixth, in infant bands crown'd King
> Of France and England, did this king succeed;
> Whose state so many had the managing,
> That they lost France and made his England
>   bleed.
>
> (Epilogue, 9-12)

Thus, with no cover of art, the audience is reminded of the uselessness of the entire glorious action. The reality of war is no longer disguised; the Chorus presents it as accomplishing nothing.

Thus the play presents several positive elements in its conclusion. If it began in war, it suggests the value of peace at the end. If it begins with a foolish king, it seems to end with a mature one. If it begins with an artificial language, it ends with an honest one. Thus process and development must be recognized if the play is to be understood. It is as if Shakespeare had decided to redo the education of a prince presented in *1* and *2 Henry IV*. Any inconsistency that Shakespeare may be charged with is historical. That is, he begins in *Henry V* to write about a monarch who resembles the earlier character Hotspur. This is a new play in which a rash, rhetorical, young and foolish king will learn a lesson in moderation. The audience can follow his development as it responds to his language and the language of the Chorus. At the end of the play both king and Chorus eschew the rhetorical language with which they disguised facts. Art has been stripped off and the reality remains. At the close of the play Henry is honest and peaceseeking; he has matured as monarch and man. Thus in *Henry V* we simply do not have Hal. Shakespeare repeats the theme concerned with the education of a prince, but it is a different prince. Overlooking this fact has led many a critic astray who could not locate the Hal of the earlier plays in this one. He is not there. Thus the unity of *Henry V* is internal and does not depend upon a tetralogy for justification. *Henry V* must stand alone if its dramatic unity is to be appreciated.

W. L. Godshalk

SOURCE: "Henry V's Politics of Non-Responsibility," in *Cahiers Elisabethains*, No. 17, April, 1980, pp. 11-20.

[*In the essay below, Godshalk focuses on Henry's tendency to evade responsibility, claiming that this trait "is both his political strength and his personal weakness." Godshalk contends that Henry's political and personal insecurities are the basis for his fear of the responsibilities of kingship.*]

Readers of Shakespeare have been vastly divided in their responses to Henry V. Some have seen him as "an ideal or nearly ideal character", while others have been just as certain that he is a jingoistic warmonger. Alfred Harbage argued [in his edition of *Henry V*, in *William Shakespeare: The Complete Works*, 1969] that the divergent readings were a result of Shakespeare's temporarily inept dramaturgy: "The 'faults' which critics have found in Henry are really the side-effects of Shakespeare's having tried to do too much for him-by conferring upon him incompatible virtues . . . At the same time that he exemplifies Christian virtue, he also exemplifies non-Christian virtu." More recently, Norman Rabkin takes a less critical look [in "Rabbits, Ducks, and *Henry V*," *SQ* 28 (1977)] at these unresolved conflicts in Henry's character, emphasizing the "complementarity" of Shakespeare's concept which requires "that we hold in balance incompatible and radically opposed views each of which seems exclusively true." Multivalence is Shakespeare's dramatic virtue. In the following pages, I do not reject the idea that Henry is a complex character—far from it—but I do isolate one factor of that complexity in an attempt to show how that factor—Henry's inability to accept responsibility—is both his political strength and his personal weakness.

From the beginning of his concept of the character, Shakespeare underlines Henry's tendency to evade responsibility. In *1 Henry IV*, although Hal may come up with some plausible excuses for his inaction, he only fleetingly assumes his role as heir apparent. He may kill Hotspur in true princely fashion, but he allows Falstaff to take the credit and responsibility for the act. The freeing of the Douglas he delegates to his brother John, and he himself retires to the background. At the beginning of Part 2, he has again deserted the court; just as in Part 1, after elaborately promising his father that he has reformed, he returns to the tavern in a playful march. Some critics have been hard put to rationalize these shifts in Hal's behaviour, but I think we can accommodate them if we accept what appears to be the evident fact that Hal has a difficult time handling responsibility. This is not to deny that Hal desires the crown and wishes to be a powerful monarch, but at some level—Shakespeare intimates—Hal is terrified by the dreadful responsibilities of kingship.

At the same time, Hal is a shrewd political manipulator, and although we do not see him in a position of great authority in *1 Henry IV*, we are given ample demonstrations of his power of control. Falstaff tries to manipulate Hal throughout the play, but it is Hal who steals the old man's horse at Gadshill and later forces him to walk to Shrewsbury. Hotspur too is part of Hal's plan. Although Hotspur may well believe that his *roan* shall be his *throne* (II.3.70), Hal informs his father, *Percy is but my factor* (III.2.147), and finally it is Hal who vaults on his horse *like feathered Mercury* and witches *the world with noble horsemanship* (IV.1.104, 110). But perhaps the most interesting and informative example of Hal's ability to control is his brief scene with Francis, where the poor drawer is cruelly and utterly manipulated by Hal's *precedent* (II.4.31). And indeed, it is a precedent for Hal's political career.

The basis for these characteristics, I contend, is insecurity, both political and personal. The political insecurity of the Lancastrian crown is freely admitted by Hal's father and fully illustrated by Shakespeare in the last two acts of *Richard II* and throughout the Henry IV plays. Hal is instructed by Henry to begin a foreign war to help make the crown more secure, *to busy giddy minds/With foreign quarrels* (2 Henry IV, IV.5.213-14). However, Hal's neurotic inability to accept responsibility for that war in *Henry V* indicates a deeper level of insecurity. A close reading of that play with these ideas in mind will suggest the source of Henry's personal insecurity, and it will certainly show us his political genius as he turns his failing into political capital: the subtle politics of non-responsibility are Henry's forte.

The first scene of the play shows us the Archbishop of Canterbury and the Bishop of Ely discussing a *bill* which, if passed, will strip the Church of *the better half* of its possessions (I.1.8). The opposition of the clerics is presented as ironic since the bill would be both politically and morally good for the state. Apparently indifferent, Henry uses the situation to gain certain favours from the Church—*a greater sum/ Than ever at one time the clergy yet/ Did to his predecessors part withal* (79-81). But Henry gets more than a bribe from the embattled clergy. Feeling the need to be absolved from the responsibility of the French war—a war which he is determined to begin—he charges the Archbishop to take extreme care: *For God doth know how many now in health/ Shall drop their blood in approbation/ Of what your reverence shall incite us to* (I.2.18-20). Originally the king had asked Canterbury simply to explain the Salic Law; now quite unexplainably that explanation has become an incitement to war. Henry, of course, realizes that the clergyman has a stake in turning the attention of the state to foreign broyles in order to save the Church's possessions. Using that self-interest, Henry forces responsibility onto the Church. *May I with right and conscience make this claim?* (96), Henry asks, and, taking the hint, Canterbury replies, *The*

sin upon my head, dread sovereign!(97). Although it has been argued that Henry is carefully soliciting advice before making a momentous decision, his insistent demand that the Archbishop take responsibility for the war seems unusual. After a king has freely evaluated the advice of his council, he should assume complete responsibility for his final decision. Henry does not.

Happily for him, yet another scapegoat is available. After determining to bend France *to our awe/ Or break it all to pieces* (1.2.224-5), Henry calls in the messengers from the Dauphin who deliver him a *tun* of tennis balls. The insult—the Dauphin reminds the king of his *wilder days* (267)—provides Henry with another person on whom to place blame for the war. He asks the ambassadors to

> *tell the pleasant prince this mock of his*
> *Hath turn'd his balls to gun-stones; and his soul*
> *Shall stand sore charged for the wasteful vengeance*
> *That shall fly with them: for many a thousand widows*
> *Shall this his mock mock out of their dear husbands;*
> *Mock mothers from their sons.*
>
> (I.2.281-6)

Although Canterbury has already taken the sin of the war on his head, Henry now assures the Dauphin that his ironic gift will make *him* guilty of the Franco— British war which Henry has *already* determined to begin. Henry establishes a cause and effect sequence where none really exists. His anger over the Dauphin's reminder of his *wilder days* is excessive, even childish, but to his own satisfaction, Henry has distributed the blame for his war. He comes away from his first scene smelling, so his thinks, like a lily.

In Henry's next scene, he again places responsibility for his actions on his victims. Using the case of a drunken soldier, he contrives to have the three traitors—Scroop, Cambridge, and Grey—advise him to judicial severity. When Henry offers to have the soldier released without punishment, Scroop advises: *Let him be punish'd, sovereign, lest example / Breed, by his sufferance, more of such a kind* (II.2.45-6). We assume that Scroop's advice issues from a guilty conscience trying to mask itself with strict justice. Henry, it appears, relies on this reaction. A little cat-and-mouse game follows, with Henry's *let us yet be merciful* (47) eliciting a series of admonitions against excessive mercy. In this way, when he hands the men the warrants for their arrest, he can answer their cries for mercy with: *The mercy that was quick in us but late/ By your own counsel is suppress'd and kill'd: / You must not dare, for shame, to talk of mercy* (79-81). The traitors must take responsibility for Henry's lack of mercy, and in gale of self-justification, the king continues his diatribe, especially against his favourite, Scroop, for sixty-two more lines. *This revolt of thine,* he tells Scroop indignantly, *is like / Another fall of man* (141-2). The submerged implication is that Scroop stands in the same relation to Henry as Adam stood to God. Scroop's punishment is as deserved and irrevocable as Adam's; Henry's innocence, as absolute as God's. So Henry implies.

But the situation is much more complicated than the Chorus's easy answer that France had found a *nest of hollow bosoms* which it filled with *treacherous crowns* (II.Chorus.21-2). One of the so-called traitors, Richard Earl of Cambridge has—through Mortimer—a better claim to the throne than Henry. At least, such a case may be argued. Cambridge's enigmatic statement—*For me, the gold of France did not seduce, / Although I did admit it as a motive / The sooner to effect what I intended* (II.2.155-7)—is explained by this fact: Cambridge wants Henry's crown, not the treacherous crowns of France. There is a conspiracy of silence here, for both sides can profit from the pretence that this is a foreign intrigue rather than a native dynastic struggle. Henry gains political sentiment against the underhanded French; Cambridge keeps the Yorkist aspirations quietly alive to be reactivated at a later time. Shakespeare had already treated this reactivation fully in the *Henry VI* plays and perhaps felt that only a subtle allusion to the Yorkist claim was needed here.

We can make two points about this situation. First, Cambridge's conspiracy underlines the political insecurity of Henry's reign. Obviously Henry IV was wrong: the dynastic troubles from the past have not been completely solved by turning the attention of the English toward the conquest of France. Second, Cambridge's claim to the English crown is historically similar to Henry's claim to the French crown. This submerged parallel—Shakespeare does not insist upon it—ironically undercuts Henry's pretensions to France. This subtle point has its more blatant counterpart in the first scene of *King John* where John's judgment of the Faulconbridge case may be applied to his own claim to the English crown. Like John, Henry judges against himself.

As Henry sentences his three former friends to death, he gives them over to God's mercy. God, not he, must take care of the erring sheep. *Touching our person seek we no revenge*, he claims, *But*—and this is an ironic *but* for the first line must sound like a reprieve to the ears of the three traitors—*we our kingdom's safety must so tender, / Whose ruin you have sought, that to her laws / We do deliver you* (174-7). Not only must the traitors condemn themselves, Henry must abjure any personal animosity; the impersonal law is functioning here.

The scene at Southampton is surrounded in the play by two scenes which chronicle the sickness and death of Falstaff. In the scene before Henry's condemnation

of the traitors, Henry himself is held responsible for Falstaff's depression and subsequent degeneration:

Nym. *The king hath run bad humours on the knight; that's the even of it.*

Pistol. *Nym, thou hast spoke the right; His heart is fracted and corroborate.*

(II.1.121-4)

And immediately after Henry finishes denouncing his former friend Scroop, Mistress Quickly describes the serio-comic death of Henry's former friend Falstaff. The ironic contrast is apparent: Henry's bitter denunciation of Scroop may be turned against himself. The juxtaposition of scenes severely qualifies the credibility of Henry's righteous indignation and of his attempts to avoid responsibility for what he has done and is doing.

Before the walls of Harfleur, Henry again exhibits his propensity for evasion. After leading his soldiers to the walls and urging them into the breach, he asks the citizens, *What is't me, when you yourselves are cause, / If your pure maidens fall into the hand / Of hot and forcing violation?* (III.3.19-21). For Henry there seems to be a disjunction between the act of leading soldiers into the breach and the responsibility for what the soldiers do while they are there. In any case, Henry goes on to explain, quite coolly, what will happen if he takes the city by storm. He asks:

What rein can hold licentious wickedness
When down the hill he holds his fierce
   career?
We may as bootless spend our vain
   command
Upon th' enraged soldiers in their spoil
As send precepts to the leviathan
To come ashore. Therefore, you men of
   Harfleur,
Take pity of your town and of your people,
While yet my soldiers are in my command.

(22-9)

Although Henry can justly argue that his *blind and bloody* soldiers (34) will be out of control after a successful siege, he seems morally obtuse when he tries to transfer the blame for the siege onto the citizens of the city. The citizens cannot be faulted (Gentili's statement [in *De Iure Belli*] notwithstanding) for loyally defending their city for the French king. If patriotism is a virtue for the English, it is equally a virtue for the French.

Later, when the tables are turned and Henry is confronted with the main French army, he tries to evade the confrontation, sending Montjoy back to the French king with this message:

tell thy king I do not seek him now,
But could be willing to march on to Calais
Without impeachment; for, to say the sooth,
Though 'tis no wisdom to confess so much
Unto an enemy of craft and vantage,
My people are with sickness much enfeebled, . . .
We would not seek a battle as we are;
Nor, as we are, we say we will not shun it.

(III.6.146-51, 170-1)

If Henry's soldiers are as sick as he claims, this attempt at evasion may be a simple measure of his intelligence. But, given the pattern of Henry's behaviour to this point in the play, we may not be wrong in suspecting that even here a characteristic tactic is at work. Henry does not wish to initiate an action and thus have to assume responsibility for its outcome. The situation is reversed, but Henry's response is predictable.

And as we may expect from Shakespeare's procedure so far, Henry's response to the French challenge is undercut, for the foppish French knights are hardly presented as adequate opponents (i.e., *an enemy of craft and vantage*) for the English. The English are tough professional and conscripted soldiers who know exactly what battle is all about; the French are inexperienced, nervous, impatient—courtiers playing at soldiership. The dramatized contrast serves to question Henry's apparent fears that the battle will be a disaster for his seasoned troops. His *sprezzatura* may be the bravura of an almost sure winner. Or is Henry's admission of weakness merely propaganda so that the French will ride (I am here thinking of Olivier's jingoistic movie version) unsuspectingly into a horrible massacre?

Before the battle, Henry—disguised in Sir Thomas Erpingham's cloak—visits his troops. Shakespeare here dramatizes the Chorus's adulatory *little touch of Harry in the night* (IV.Chorus.47). But the situation, instead of allowing the king to cheer his men warmly and personally in a bad hour, again gives Henry a chance at apologetics. When Michael Williams eloquently maintains that *if the cause be not good, the king himself hath a heavy reckoning to make* (IV.1.135-6), Henry skilfully counters with what appears to be a rather well-prepared argument:

So, if a son that is by his father sent about merchandise do sinfully miscarry upon the sea, the imputation of his wickedness, by your rule, should be imposed upon his father that sent him: or if a servant, under his master's command transporting a sum of money, be assailed by robbers and die in many irreconciled iniquities, you may call the business of the master the author of the servant's damnation. But this is not so: the king is not bound to answer the particular endings

of his soldiers, the father of his son, nor the master of his servant; for they purpose not their death when they purpose their services.

(IV.1.150-63)

This part of Henry's defence, it seems to me, is indefensible. First, Henry does not address himself to William's hypothesis which is that Henry will be guilty if the war is unlawful and his guilt will be increased if certain soldiers are *damned* while participating in an unlawful war. Williams does not argue that the soldiers are not responsible for themselves and their individual crimes. Second, the father and the master are not precisely analogous to the king. Death is inextricably linked to battle; soldiers fight to kill, and Williams has already pointed out to Henry that *few die well that die in a battle; for how can they charitably dispose of any thing when blood is their argument?* (143-6). In contrast, death is not a necessary part of the father's mission or the master's command; the son and the servant are not being sent to kill or be killed.

Henry wishes to have it both ways: *Every subject's duty is the king's; but every subject's soul is his own* (182-4). For the king they must kill without mercy; for themselves they must maintain Christian charity. This separation of political duty from personal morality is undoubtedly an orthodox position for a Tudor apologist, but the sceptical listener will not necessarily accept this kind of immoral orthodoxy. Bates's response, *I do not desire* [the king] *should answer for me* (195), is that of a man who knows how to accept responsibility for his actions.

In the light of our analysis of Henry's inability to accept responsibility, his following soliloquy resounds with irony. *Upon the king!* he exclaims as if in anguish,

but let us our lives, our souls,
Our debts, our careful wives,
Our children, and our sins lay on the king!
We must bear all. O hard condition!

(236-9)

If we may trust the evidence of this soliloquy, Henry has no insight into his evasions. As we have seen, Henry bears nothing; he refuses to. And possibly in his prayer near the end of this scene, we come close to understanding this mysterious inability:

Not to-day, O Lord!
O not to-day, think not upon the fault
My father made in compassing the crown!
I Richard's body have interred new,
And on it have bestow'd more contrite tears
Than from it issued forced drops of
* blood. . . .*

More will I do;
Though all that I can do is nothing worth,
Since that my penitence comes after all,
Imploring pardon.

(298-303, 308-11)

Retaining the usurped throne, Henry obviously feels responsible for his father's usurpation and Richard's inevitable assassination. This guilt is impossible to evade since his *penitence comes after all* and since Henry is not prepared to renounce the fruits of his father's evil—the crown. Henry's earlier savage indignation against Scroop is, at least on one level, a denunciation of his own father's act and Henry's subsequent feelings of guilt. Since he reveals these deep feelings in prayer, I think we can take them at face value; this is not another evasion. Given this central insight into Henry's emotions, we can see why he is forced into elaborate delegations of responsibility. Overwhelmed by guilt from the past, he forces others to take responsibility for the present.

After the battle, Shakespeare returns to Henry's quarrel with Williams over the issue of ransom. Disguised as Erpingham, Henry has committed himself personally to Williams: *Give me any gage of thine, and I will wear it in my bonnet: then, if ever thou darest acknowledge it, I will make it my quarrel* (IV.1.214-16). Now, when Henry hands Fluellen the gage given him by Williams with a cock-and-bull story about Alençon, we are not surprised. Fluellen must take the blow meant for Henry; and after forcing an explanation and an apology from Williams, the king has Exeter fill his glove with crowns. The incident is clearly another manifestation of Henry's passing the buck; he could never claim, *The buck stops here.* We have much more sympathy for the two manipulated soldiers than for the evasive king—even though we now understand more fully his compulsion. The effect of the incident is to question Henry's intention of not allowing himself to be ransomed. After all, he does not keep faith with Williams, and a man who cannot keep faith in small things can hardly be expected to keep faith in large—especially when his life is at the stake.

Henry's final comment at Agincourt, however, may well surprise us. After a brilliant military achievement, he proclaims:

O God, thy arm was here;
And not to us, but to thy arm alone,
Ascribe we all! When, without stratagem,
But in plain shock and even play of battle,
Was ever known so great and little loss
On one part and on th' other? Take it,
  God,
For it is none but thine!

(IV.8.108-14)

That Henry might wish to evade responsibility for dubious achievements such as starting a war, executing a close friend and a claimant to the throne, or getting caught in the field with a weak army, we can understand. But why not take credit for winning a major battle? The question may give rise to a series of conjectures, some perhaps more tenable than others, but I suggest a simple answer in line with our previous analysis. Henry knows—I am not sure how conscious this knowledge is—that to accept responsibility for any victory implies an acceptance of other responsibilities which may lead to less happy consequences. If Henry allows himself to climb on the scale of responsibility once, he may never be able to get off.

Henry ends the play as he began, by distancing himself from the imminent decision. If Henry forces responsibility for the war on Canterbury and on the Dauphin, he commands others to be responsible for the peace that follows. When the French king declares that he is ready to begin negotiating a peace treaty, Henry turns to his entourage:

Go, uncle Exeter,
And brother Clarence, and you, brother
  Gloucester,
Warwick and Huntingdon, go with the king;
And take with you free power to ratify,
Augment, or alter, as your wisdoms best
Shall see advantageable for our dignity,
Any thing in or out of our demands,
And we'll consign thereto.

(V.2.83-90)

While Henry plays with Katherine for a kiss, the negotiations for the marriage are carried on by his surrogates. Somehow this separation of play from work sums up perfectly Henry's inability; like a young child, he desires the candy, but he cannot force himself to mow the grass to earn it. Fortunately for Henry, he is powerful, cunning, and manipulative enough to indulge himself while others assume the sins, take the beatings, suffer death, and, most pathetically, negotiate for his wife.

And so while the serious negotiations go on off stage, Henry plays with Katherine for a kiss, assuring her, when she demurs, that *nice customs curtsy to great kings.* He calls her *Dear Kate* in his most charming *bluff king* manner, and tells her, *You and I cannot be confined within the weak list of a country's fashion: we are the makers of manners, Kate; and the liberty that follows our places stops the mouth of all find-faults, as I will do yours, for upholding the nice fashion of your country in denying me a kiss* (V.2.284-90). In this speech I find a grim irony. After evading responsibility for the butcheries of his conquest of France. Henry as a jest takes responsibility for changing an idle social custom. The French princess may now kiss before she is married. While Henry gains his kiss, the thoughtful reader may well remember his harsh question to the citizens of Harfleur: *What is't to me . . . / If your pure maidens fall into the hand / Of hot and forcing violation?* The memory under-cuts Henry's boyish exuberance in this scene. My reaction is a faint disgust.

Of course, Henry is a good many more things than the passive neurotic that I've sketched here. If he were merely a dodger of responsibility, he would hardly be the successful political and military leader he is in the play. On the contrary, Henry is able to use the politics of non-responsibility with a great deal of acumen. By forcing others to take responsibility for his actions, he walks through the holocaust untar-nished—the perfect Christian king *and* the Machia-vellian manipulator. Henry says it in many ways, but this message is perfectly clear: "Don't blame me! I'm not responsible!"

Joseph M. Lenz

SOURCE: "The Politics of Honor: The Oath in *Hen-ry V*," in *The Journal of English and Germanic Phi-lology*, Vol. 80, No. 1, January, 1981, pp. 1-12.

[*In this excerpt, Lenz studies the role of honor in* Henry V *and the importance the king places on keep-ing his oaths. Lenz asserts that Henry does not make his oaths rashly, but that he is fully aware of their implications. Lenz also focuses on Henry's constant pleas to God for forgiveness and mercy.*]

Henry V begins with the king's resolve to invade France, "by God's helpe," and it closes with his prospective marriage to Katherine, consummating the success of the initial oath:

> Then shall I swear to Kate, and you to me,
> And may our oaths well kept and prosp'rous
>   be!
>
> (V.ii.373-74)

So Henry rounds "the world's best garden he achieved" (Epilogue) with oaths. Although the walled garden symbolizes the order Henry establishes in England, its simple circularity belies the difficulty of his achieve-ment. Henry struggles with disloyal subjects, unwill-ing soldiers, an irreverent French prince, and the memory of his father, all of them posing threats to the crown through their disrespect for oaths and oath-taking. Henry, however, honors his oaths, and by example teaches his subjects, as well as his enemies, to honor theirs. . . .

Shakespeare begins *Henry V* by illustrating that Hen-ry is a man who keeps his word, who takes his oaths

fully aware of their implications. In *Henry V*, the king demands that his bishops ascertain his right to the French throne: "May I with right and conscience make this claim?" (I.ii.96). Only after a long legal discussion and careful thought on the consequences for England does Henry vow:

> Now are we well resolv'd, and by God's
>   help
> And yours, the noble sinews of our power,
> France being ours, we'll bend it to our awe.
>
> (I.ii.222-24)

Difficult to achieve, and prompted by the bishops' desire to evade taxation, this oath may be thought rash. But given the care with which Henry proceeds, he needs only to attempt the deed to fulfill the oath: "Or lay these bones in an unworthy urn, / Tombless, with no remembrance over them" (ll. 228-29). The Dauphin gives Henry more justification when, in the same scene, the Ambassador relays the prince's insult to Henry, which makes it an insult to England. The king reiterates the vow, but now adding the determi-nation of "God's will" to his cause. Henry knows the implications of his oath. He investigates his right, and he provides for the safety of Britain. When he repeats the oath a second time, he utters law: France will be invaded.

As king, Henry V's personal honor is intricately tied to national honor. According to the medieval-Renais-sance concept of monarchy [quoted by E. F. J. Tuck-er, in "The Legal Fiction and Human Reality: Hal's Role in *Henry V*," *ETJ* 26, 1974], the king has two bodies, one "private, mortal, and morally corrupt-ible" and one "public, immortal, and morally incor-ruptible." Even as Prince Hal, Henry keeps his roles of private man and public servant distinct but insep-arable. He admits to using his poor reputation to accent his intended reformation. Further, the mock banishment of Falstaff (*I Henry IV*, II.iv.481) antic-ipates the very language of the actual banishment (*2 Henry IV*, V.v.63). How Henry's public duty alters his private life is illustrated twice in *Henry V*. When the king receives the tennis balls, he expresses a righ-teous indignation. The Dauphin jests at the expense of Henry's wayward youth, but as he will be taught, Henry, now England, cannot stomach such frivolity:

> So get you hence in peace; and tell the
>   Dolphin
> His jest will savor but of shallow wit,
> When thousands weep more than did laugh
>   at it.
>
> (I.ii.294-96)

Henry shows the same stern manner here that he does in his rejection of Falstaff. As Prince Hal he had the leisure to enjoy drink, gaming, and bad companions;

as king his personal reputation must mirror that of his country. Henry again exemplifies his public duty when he condemns the plotters, Cambridge, Scroop, and Grey:

> Touching our person seek we no revenge,
> But we our kingdom's safety most so
>   tender,
> Whose ruin you [have] sought, that to her
>   laws
> We do deliver you.
>
> (II.ii.174-77)

The traitors sought to murder Henry, thus filling their purses with coin and saving France the inconvenience of invasion. They fail to realize that Henry and England are one. Whatever harm comes to Henry also comes to England. The king magnanimously forgives them their affront to his person; but he cannot allow England to bestow the same mercy, and has them executed. With both the Dauphin and the assassins, Henry teaches those who oppose him that they are

dealing with a nation. Henry's honor is England's honor. When someone throws a gauntlet at the king's feet, he may expect five thousand in reply.

The trick, though, is to gain the support of the five thousand. Unlike Richard II and King Lear, who learn too late their responsibility to their subjects, Henry realizes that his power depends upon his subjects' trust in him: "Every subject's duty is the King's" (IV.i.176-77). When Henry tells the aged Thomas Erpingham that a bed holds more comfort than the barren field, the knight replies:

> Not so, my liege, this lodging likes me
>   better,
> Since I may say, "Now lie I like a king."
>
> (IV.i.16-17)

Erpingham feels privileged merely keeping the company of the king. Henry's soldiers owe him their lives; their oaths make it their duty. Henry reinforces that duty by flattering his men's honor. He borrows

Act IV, scene viii. Henry (Alan Howard) and his nobles thank God after the battle of Agincourt in the 1975 production of Henry V.

Erpingham's cloak, he encourages Westmoreland with fame, he allows York the first attack, and he rewards Williams' boldness with a gauntlet filled with coins. His men bear their shields fully aware of personal and national honor.

Henry amends his statement, "Every subject's duty is the King's," with, "but every subject's soul is his own." The king, though, is God's anointed representative on earth. Duty to one's king and responsibility to one's God unite under these circumstances. By binding his subjects to him with sanctified oaths, the king cements their loyalty, for it becomes sinful to disobey. Henry claims that his subjects' sins are their own—that he is not responsible for their salvation (IV.i)—but he does provide a means for salvation. One need only obey the king and honor one's duty to him to please God. The ladder of honor proceeds from personal to national to spiritual. Before the battle of Agincourt Henry describes what those who die for England may expect:

> They shall be fam'd; for there the sun shall
> greet them,
> And draw their honours reeking up to
> heaven.
>
> (IV.iii.100-101)

Again, Falstaff is right, but more so than he is wont to be: honor is indeed air, the air that sustains life eternal. When one gives his word of honor, his oath, he barters with scutcheons and air, worldly and eternal fame. Those who break their word suffer for it, like Hotspur; those who keep it may expect a reward richer than a king's treasury.

We cannot attend to Henry's speeches without remarking the frequency of his pleas to God. In nearly every formal address Henry cites God's will, his forgiveness, his mercy, or simply invokes his name. After Agincourt, the king and his men praise God: "Do we all holy rites: / Let there be sung *Non nobis* and *Te Deum*" (IV.viii.122-23). In fact, Henry proclaims death to all who boast of the victory, "or take that praise from God / Which is his only" (IV.viii.115-16). Such public demeanor is fairly customary, and as [Niccolo] Machiavelli counsels [in *The Prince*, translated by Mark Musa, 1964], most advisable. From his first invocation of "God's will" to back the French enterprise to his singing of the "Te Deum," Henry continually reminds his subjects of the source of his authority and, seemingly, his own belief in that source.

The many roles Henry plays make it difficult to determine exactly what he "really" believes. He acts the parts of king, judge, general, common soldier, suitor, and even prankster. When he does find himself alone, without an audience, on the eve of the battle, he complains of what he sees as the power behind the throne, the pomp, the ritual, the show, the "Ceremony" that makes him different from the "wretched slave." His concern for symbols, however, does lead him to confront that which the symbol represents. Like his early attempt to clear the legal path to the French crown and his later suit to Katherine for her hand, Henry tries to set the record straight with God. Henry, though anointed king and son of a king, is still king by default. His father usurped the crown from Richard II, and the sin haunts Henry V:

> Not to-day, O Lord,
> O, not to-day, think not upon the fault
> My father made in compassing the crown!
>
> (IV.i.292-94)

This is not a sham. The king is caught by the very mythology he has fostered. He has bound his subjects to him with oaths and has sworn victory in France, yet he fears his father's "fault" will mar all and he seeks assurance. Henry numbers those things he has done to pacify God's wrath, but he accepts that retribution shall make its claims. Like Claudius in *Hamlet,* the king cannot part with the profits of the "fault." Henry prays only to delay the penalty, not to dismiss it entirely:

> Though all that I can do is nothing
> worth,
> Since that my penitence comes after
> all,
> Imploring pardon.
>
> (IV.i.303-305)

When we consider that the king accepts the eventual punishment of his family (Lancaster) for Henry Bullingbrook's breach of oath to Richard II, we assume that he shies from further provoking God, and honors the oaths he takes.

Because his father compassed the crown, Henry feels obliged to conduct himself—and England—according to the letter of the law. The loophole in the Salic law makes legal the invasion of France. Cambridge, Scroop, and Grey sentence themselves to death by insisting on absolute justice for the man who railed against the king. Henry demands France's "full accord" with the "tenures and particular effects" of the peace treaty. In each case, a taken or broken oath enforces the law. Henry swears by God's will to win the French throne. He reminds the traitors and his loyal soldiers of their bonds of honor to him. And, to confirm his initial vow, the winning of France, Henry ends the play with the promise of marriage to Katherine, wooing her as a plain soldier who has "only downright oaths, which I never use till urg'd, nor never break for urging" (V.ii.144-46). . . .

FALSTAFF

Although Falstaff never appears in *Henry V*, his absence has a significant impact on the tone of the play. Critics including **John Middleton Murry** have asserted that Falstaff had to be removed from the play in order for Henry to mature into his position as king. Michael Platt explores the absence of Falstaff from the play and Henry's absence from Falstaff's death bed. He maintains that Falstaff was afraid to die, and that this fear is seen in other characters throughout the play. He also contends that Henry, although he never speaks of Falstaff's death, learns from it and teaches his soldiers to imitate Falstaff. Robert F. Fleissner extensively analyzes Mistress Quickly's allusion to Falstaff's dying moments, noting how appropriate it is that Falstaff's death was as complex and dramatic as his life.

John Middleton Murry

SOURCE: "Falstaff and Harry," in *Shakespeare*, Jonathan Cape, 1936, pp. 170-87.

[*In the excerpt below, Murry praises Shakespeare's handling of the death of Falstaff in* Henry V. *He assesses Falstaff's reported death and analyzes the dramatic necessity of removing Falstaff from the play.*]

Falstaff lives in and by a certain inimitable opulence of language. That opulence of language he does not employ in person in *Henry V*. He speaks no word in the play. We hear that he is ill; and we know the reason. 'The King hath killed his heart', says Mistress Quickly. She goes off to tend him. Then she reappears.

> HOST. As ever you came of women, come in quickly to Sir John. Ah, poor heart! He is so shaked of a burning quotidian-tertian, that it is most lamentable to behold. Sweet men, come to him.
>
> NYM. The King hath run bad humours on the knight; that's the even of it.
>
> PIST. Nym, thou hast spoke the right; His heart is fracted and corroborate.
>
> NYM. The king is a good king: but it must be as it may; he passes some humours and careers.
>
> PIST. Let us condole the knight; for, lambkins, we will live.   (II. i. 122-34)

There is no mistaking the meaning. They all agree: Falstaff's heart has been broken by the King. One more scene and he is dead. But, miraculously, to describe his death, the rich rare language that is his,

that is him, suddenly comes from one who never had command of it before. Mistress Quickly has her own way of talking, and a splendid way it is; but now she speaks with a voice not her own.

> PIST. Bardolph, be blithe: Nym, rouse thy vaunting veins: Boy,
>
> Bristle thy courage up; for Falstaff he is dead,
> And we must yearn therefore.
>
> BARD. Would I were with him, wheresome'er he is, either in heaven or in hell!
>
> HOST. Nay, sure, he's not in hell: he's in Arthur's bosom, if ever man went to Arthur's bosom. A' made a finer end and went away an it had been any christom child; a' parted even just between twelve and one, even at the turning o' the tide: for after I saw him fumble with the sheets and play with flowers and smile upon his fingers' ends, I knew there was but one way; for his nose was as sharp as a pen and a' babbled of green fields. 'How now, Sir John!' quoth I: 'what, man! be o' good cheer.' So a' cried out 'God, God, God!' three or four times. Now I, to comfort him, bid him a' should not think of God; I hoped there was no need to trouble himself with any such thoughts yet. So a' bade me lay more clothes on his feet: I put my hand into the bed and felt them, and they were as cold as any stone; then I felt to his knees, and they were as cold as any stone, and so upward and upward, and all was as cold as any stone.
>
> (II. iii. 4-28)

There are moments—and this is one of them—when I think that the most marvellous speech in all Shakespeare. It is wonderful. There is nothing remotely like it in all the literature of the world. How should there be? It is Shakespeare's requiem over the darling of his imagination.

There is no death like Falstaff's: therefore there is no description of a death like his. I cannot think of any other character whom Shakespeare was compelled to kill, as he was compelled to kill Falstaff. It is a quite different act from the killing of Mercutio. Mercutio is merely killed; but Falstaff is degraded. It had to be. Shakespeare could not spare him. Falstaff had to be cast off in order that Prince Hal could get back into history and become the national hero of *Henry V*.

> I am the Prince of Wales; and think not, Percy,
> To share with me in glory any more:
> Two stars keep not their motion in one sphere;
> Nor can one England brook a double reign.
>
> (*H4A*. v. iv. 64-7)

Those are Prince Harry's words to Hotspur before he kills him. Change 'Percy' to 'Falstaff', and they exactly describe the dramatic necessity for the dethroning of Falstaff. Only the order in which the necessity is compulsive is not the historical order, but the imaginative. And the necessity is a symbol of the tension between imaginative reality and historical fact.

Shakespeare was—thank Heaven—not a critical philosopher, but a poet of the human heart. Had he been a critical philosopher, he might have said to himself, 'The orders are different, incommensurable: Falstaff cannot be degraded, neither can he die. His degradation and death are appearance only: crude and clumsy symbols of the discrepancy between Imagination and Reality, between the poet's knowledge and the people's expectation, between the Soul and the Body'. He might have said this and gone on to glorify the warrior king. But he could not. His human heart could not suffer it. He had not *been* Sir John Falstaff for nothing. He stands looking upon him, as Horatio looks upon Hamlet:

> Now cracks a noble heart. Good night,
>   sweet prince;
> And flights of angels sing thee to thy rest!

SOURCES FOR FURTHER STUDY

Literary Commentary

Barnet, Sylvan. "The English History Plays." In *A Short Guide to Shakespeare*, pp. 113-37. San Diego: Harcourt Brace & Company, 1972.

    Analyzes the character of Henry V within the context of the tetralogy (*Richard II*, *1 Henry IV*, *2 Henry IV*, and *Henry V*). Barnet also compares the structure and language of Henry V with the other three plays.

Battenhouse, Roy W. "*Henry V* as Heroic Comedy." In *Essays on Shakespeare and Elizabethan Drama in Honor of Hardin Craig*, edited by Richard Hosley, pp. 163-82. Columbia: University of Missouri Press, 1962.

    Labels *Henry V* a "heroic comedy," claiming that in this work Shakespeare offers a deeply ironical view of history by simultaneously presenting the king as a glorious national hero and as a man motivated by greed.

Berman, Ronald, ed. *Twentieth Century Interpretations of Henry V: A Collection of Critical Essays*. Englewood Cliffs, N. J.: Prentice-Hall, Inc., 1968, 120 p.

    Collection of critical essays from scholars including William Butler Yeats, E. M. W. Tillyard, and Una Ellis-Fermor.

Brennan, Anthony S. "That Within Which Passes Show: The Function of the Chorus in Henry V." *Philological Quarterly* 58, No. 1 (Winter 1979): 40-52.

    Details the role of the Chorus and compares the prologues with the content of each act.

Brooke, Stopford A. "*Henry V.*" In *Ten More Plays of Shakespeare*, pp. 294-313. London: Constable and Co., 1913.

    Asserts that in *Henry V* Shakespeare offers a superbly balanced view of war and patriotism.

Cook, Dorothy. "*Henry V:* Maturing of Man and Majesty." *Studies in Literary Imagination* 5, No. 1 (April 1972): 111-28.

    Dramatizes the theme of individual maturity by demonstrating the king's growing realization of both his responsibility toward his subjects and the necessity of a humble reliance on the will of God.

Coursen, Herbert R., Jr. "*Henry V* and the Nature of Kingship." *Discourse: A Review of the Liberal Arts* XIII, No. 3 (Summer 1970): 279-305.

    Contends that *Henry V* is an ingenious politician who, in the course of becoming a successful monarch, has lost the ability to act as an "average" citizen.

Danson, Lawrence. "*Henry V:* King, Chorus, and Critics." *Shakespeare Quarterly* 34, No. 1 (Spring 1983): 27-43.

    Defends the Chorus against critical controversy.

Dean, Paul. "Chronicle and Romance Modes in *Henry V.*" *Shakespeare Quarterly* 32, No. 1 (Spring 1981): 18-27.

    Examines *Henry V* as both a "chronicle" and "romance" history and studies the relationship between the Chorus and the king.

Fleissner, Robert F. "Falstaff's Green Sickness Unto Death." *Shakespeare Quarterly* XII, No. 1 (Winter 1961): 47-55.

    Comments on the appearance of Falstaff before his death.

Goldman, Michael. "*Henry V:* The Strain of Rule." In *Shakespeare and the Energies of Drama*, pp. 58-73. Princeton, NJ: Princeton University Press, 1972.

    Examines the great speeches of the Chorus and of Henry, commenting on the relationship they create between the actors and the audience and contends that the theme of the play is overcoming limitations by supreme effort.

Ornstein, Robert. "*Henry V.*" In *A Kingdom For A Stage: The Achievement of Shakespeare's History Plays*, pp. 175-202. Cambridge: Harvard University Press, 1972.

    Contends that despite allusions throughout *Henry V* to justice and mercy, Shakespeare presents war as brutal and dehumanizing.

Phialas, Peter G. "Shakespeare's *Henry V* and the Second Tetralogy." *Studies in Philology* LXII, No. 2 (April 1965): 155-75.

Views the nature of kingship and the ideal relation between a ruler and his subjects as the central thematic interests in *Henry V.*

Platt, Michael. "Falstaff in the Valley of the Shadow of Death." *Interpretation: A Journal of Political Philosophy* 8, No. 1 (January 1979): 5-29.

Asserts that Falstaff's death is a central plot point in *Henry V.* The critic notes that of the three instances of men preparing for death, Falstaff's death is the only one from which Henry is absent. Platt discusses Falstaff's final words and analyzes Mistress Quickly's report of his death.

Quinn, Michael, ed. *Shakespeare: Henry V, A Casebook.* London: Macmillan and Co., 1969, 252 p.

Includes excerpts of criticism by Samuel Johnson and George Bernard Shaw as well as full length essays by E. E. Stoll and others.

Rabkin, Norman. "The Polity." In *Shakespeare and the Common Understanding,* pp. 80-149. New York: The Free Press, 1967.

Asserts that the ideal representation of Henry is more of a fantasy than a reality, stating that although Henry is depicted as a wise and fortunate ruler, he is not flawless.

Reese, M. M. "Shakespeare's England: *Henry V.*" In *The Cease of Majesty: A Study of Shakespeare's History Plays,* pp. 317-32. London: Edward Arnold, 1961.

Argues that a true appreciation of Henry V requires that he be judged by Elizabethan rather than modern standards.

Richmond, H. M. "*Henry V.*" In *Shakespeare's Political Plays,* pp. 175-200. New York: Random House, 1967.

Traces the king's development from deceit and hypocrisy in the early scenes to responsibility and humility at the close.

Rossiter, A. P. "Ambivalence: The Dialectic of the Histories." In *Angel with Horns and Other Shakespeare Lectures,* edited by Graham Storey, pp. 40-64. London: Longmans, Green and Co., 1961.

Discusses the relationship between serious and comic elements in Shakespeare's history plays.

Shalvi, Alice. "Studies in Kingship: *Henry VI, Richard III, Richard II, Henry IV, Henry V.*" In *The World and Art of Shakespeare,* edited by A. A. Mendilow and Alice Shalvi, pp. 89-118. Jerusalem: Israel Universities Press, 1967.

Contends that Henry is an ideal king, but because of this fact, there is little tension or development in the play.

Smith, Gordon Ross. "Shakespeare's *Henry V:* Another Part of the Critical Forest." *Journal of the History of Ideas* XXXVII, No. 1 (January-March 1976): 3-27.

Argues that the speeches and characters in *Henry V* reflect the diverse variety of political thought in the Renaissance rather than a narrow Tudor orthodoxy.

Snyder, Karl E. "Kings and Kingship in Four of Shakespeare's History Plays." In *Shakespeare 1964,* edited by Jim W. Corder, pp. 43-58. Fort Worth: Texas Christian University Press, 1965.

Examines the character of kings and kingship in *Richard II, Henry IV, Parts 1 and 2,* and *Henry V.*

Soellner, Rolf. "*Henry V:* Patterning after Perfection." In *Shakespeare's Patterns of Self-Knowledge,* pp. 113-28. Ohio State University Press, 1972.

Argues that Henry V exemplifies the four cardinal virtues—fortitude, justice, prudence, and temperance—which Renaissance Christian humanists held were requisite in a good man.

Walter, J. H. "Introduction to *Henry V.*" In *Shakespeare: The Histories, A Collection of Critical Essays,* pp. 152-67. Englewood Cliffs, N. J.: Prentice-Hall, Inc., 1965.

Discusses the epic elements of *Henry V,* particularly Shakespeare's portrayal of the king as an ideal hero.

Wentersdorf, Karl P. "The Conspiracy of Silence in *Henry V.*" *Shakespeare Quarterly* 27, No. 3 (Summer 1976): 264-87.

Focuses on Henry's discovery of Cambridge, Scroop, and Grey's efforts to secure the crown for Edmund Mortimer.

Williams, Charles. "*Henry V.*" In *Shakespeare Criticism: 1919-1935,* edited by Anne Ridler, pp. 180-88. London: Oxford University Press, 1936.

Contends that in Act IV Henry reveals for the first time that he has embraced the challenges that face him and attains a highly developed sense of honor.

Williamson, Marilyn L. "The Courtship of Katherine and the Second Tetralogy." *Criticism* XVII, No. 4 (Fall 1975): 326-34.

Argues that Henry's wooing of Katherine is consistent with his conduct earlier in *Henry V* and recapitulates a pattern of behaviour that he has demonstrated both in this play and in the Henry IV plays.

Media Adaptations

Henry V. J. Arthur Rank, 1944.

Classic adaptation of the play, distinguished by Laurence Olivier's formal experiment of beginning the drama as a 16th-century performance of the play in the Globe Theatre, and having the stage eventually transform into realistic historical settings. Starring Olivier as Henry. Distributed by Paramount Home Video, Home Vision Cinema. 136 minutes.

Henry V. Cedric Messina; Dr. Jonathan Miller; BBC, 1980.
　　Part of the "Shakespeare Plays" series. Distributed by Ambrose Video Publishing, Inc. 163 minutes.

Henry V. Samuel Goldwyn, 1989.
　　Unrated. Stirring, expansive retelling of the play stressing the high cost of war—showing the ego-mania, doubts, and subterfuge that underlie conflicts. Stars Kenneth Branagh, Derek Jacobi, Alec McCowen, Paul Scofield, and Emma Thompson. Distributed by CBS/ Fox Video, Signals, The Video Catalog. 138 minutes.

KING LEAR

INTRODUCTION

The earliest possible composition date for *King Lear* is 1604, but most scholars believe it was written in 1605 or 1606. The first recorded performance of the play was in December 1606. Two of the earliest printed editions of the play—the First Quarto in 1608 and the First Folio in 1623—differ remarkably in the number of lines and whole passages included or omitted, as well as in assignment of speeches to specific characters. The tale of a legendary king Lyr, or Ler, and his three daughters appears in many English fairytale or folklore versions, as well as in Raphael Holinshed's *Chronicles* (1577, 1587) and John Higgins's *Mirror for Magistrates* (1574). In addition to these sources, Shakespeare was likely familiar with an anonymous play, *The Chronicle History of King Leir*, written sometime in the 1500s and published in 1605. Critics generally agree that Shakespeare derived the Gloucester subplot from Philip Sidney's *Arcadia* (c. 1580).

Shakespeare altered his sources freely, representing the traditional story in a unique way and introducing new characters and dramatic action. But in 1681 his version was eclipsed by Nahum Tate's adaptation. Tate eliminated the Fool and the blinding of Gloucester, introduced a love affair between Edgar and Cordelia, and brought Shakespeare's play to a "happy ending," with Cordelia's forces victorious and Lear restored to his throne. Critics as well as audiences endorsed Tate's changes, and it was nearly 150 years before Shakespeare's *King Lear* was restored to the British stage.

The play's tragic ending has been the focus of critical commentary through the centuries and up to the present. Some scholars have judged it as the natural culmination of Lear's suffering. Others, especially those who regard *Lear* as a pessimistic or nihilistic play, view the ending as proof of their argument. In contrast, critics who claim there is a providential or Christian design in *Lear* contend that the ending underscores the redemptive power of love. Many commentators emphasize the ambiguity of the play's ending, arguing that it reflects neither an optimistic nor a pessimistic view of life, but the mystery of human existence.

Other principal topics of critical debate include the function of the Gloucester subplot, the issue of Lear's madness, and the characters themselves. Earlier commentators tended to disparage the subplot as vulgar or distracting. Modern critics, however, generally view it as an enhancement of the principal plot. There is a broad range of opinion on Lear's madness: when it begins, its extent and effects, and even whether Lear is ever truly insane. The king's misjudgments and his progress toward self-knowledge are also frequent subjects for discussion. Although some commentators have neatly divided the other characters into categories of "good" and "evil," most contemporary scholars emphasize their subtleties and complexities.

PRINCIPAL CHARACTERS

(in order of appearance)

Kent: British nobleman devoted to Lear. The king banishes him when he protests Cordelia's disinheritance, but he continues to be a faithful friend. Disguised as Caius, he serves as Lear's messenger and companion on the heath, and maintains contact with Cordelia and the French king.

Gloucester: British nobleman and father of Edgar and Edmund. Duped by Edmund and initially hesitant to offend his patron, the Duke of Cornwall, Gloucester later aids the king, provoking Cornwall to tear out his eyes.

Edmund: Illegitimate son of the Earl of Gloucester. He schemes to replace his half-brother Edgar as their father's heir and successfully aligns himself with the Duke of Cornwall. He receives a mortal wound at the hands of Edgar, revealing before he dies that he has ordered the murder of Cordelia.

Lear: King of Britain, he gives up his title and authority at the outset of the play. Having divided his kingdom between Goneril and Regan and disinherited Cordelia, Lear is abused by his older daughters. He endures a violent storm on a deserted heath, then a painful but joyous reconciliation with Cordelia and later imprisonment. He dies cradling her body in his arms. (*See* **Lear** *in the* **CHARACTER STUDIES** *section*.)

Goneril: Daughter of Lear and wife of Albany. Lear curses her when she asserts her authority in her own home. Married to a man less ambitious than she, Goneril forms an attachment with Edmund and poisons Regan out of jealousy. She dies at her own hand. (*See* **Lear's Daughters** *in the* **CHARACTER STUDIES** *section*.)

Regan: Daughter of Lear and wife of Cornwall. She readily joins her sister Goneril in a scheme to deprive their father of all the privileges of royalty. Ruthless in pursuit of her ambitions and as vicious as her husband, Regan offers herself to Edmund when she becomes a widow. (*See* **Lear's Daughters** *in the* **CHARACTER STUDIES** *section.*)

Cordelia: Lear's youngest daughter. Disinherited by her father, she marries the King of France and with his help raises an army to invade Britain. She is reconciled with Lear, but her forces are defeated, and she and her father are imprisoned together. She is murdered by a guard. (*See* **Lear's Daughters** *in the* **CHARACTER STUDIES** *section.*)

Albany: British duke and husband of Goneril, who scorns him for his fair-mindedness and lack of personal ambition.

Burgundy: French nobleman who declines to marry Cordelia after Lear has disinherited her.

France: French king who willingly weds Cordelia without a dowry. He sends an army to invade Britain in support of Cordelia and her father.

Edgar: Son of the Earl of Gloucester. Tricked by his half-brother Edmund into fleeing their father's castle, Edmund assumes the role of Poor Tom, a mad beggar. He is eventually reconciled with Gloucester and vanquishes Edmund in a trial-by-combat.

Oswald: Goneril's steward and confidant. Oswald treats Lear with disrespect, is drawn into a brawl with Kent, and, when he attempts to kill Gloucester, is slain by Edgar.

Curan: A courtier who is the first to reveal, in a conversation with Edmund, that the political disputes between Cornwall and Albany may lead to civil war.

Cornwall: British duke and husband of Regan. He rewards Edmund for betraying his father and plucks out Gloucester's eyes for aiding the king. One of his own servants, outraged by the blinding of Gloucester, slays Cornwall.

Fool: The king's jester and companion. His first marked appearance is in Act I, scene iv, and he disappears without explanation at the end of Act III, scene vi. Mingling riddles and jokes, metaphors and maxims, proverbs and old songs, the Fool provides Lear with advice and attempts to ease his suffering. (*See* **Fool** *in the* **CHARACTER STUDIES** *section.*)

Doctor: Attends Lear after he is rescued and brought to the French camp near Dover.

PLOT SYNOPSIS

Act I: In a state room of Lear's palace, Kent and Gloucester discuss the king's intention to renounce his throne and divide his kingdom among his daughters. Lear enters with his daughters and sons-in-law, and announces that he will award the largest share of his kingdom to the daughter who demonstrates she loves him most. First Goneril, then Regan, professes that her love is boundless. Cordelia, however, tells Lear she loves him to the limit of her obligation as his daughter. Enraged, Lear disinherits Cordelia and commands that half of Britain will be ruled by Goneril and her husband Albany, the other half by Regan and her husband Cornwall. Kent bluntly and repeatedly tells Lear that his decision is rash, and Lear banishes him. When the king tells Cordelia's suitors, the Duke of Burgundy and the King of France, that she will have no dowry, Burgundy withdraws his suit, but France declares he will wed her nonetheless.

The scene shifts to Gloucester's castle, where Edmund soliloquizes about his illegitimacy and his intention to supplant his half-brother Edgar as their father's heir. Gloucester enters, and Edmund reveals a letter he claims was written by Edgar which hints at murdering their father. Gloucester laments the present disruption in nature, state affairs, and family relations, then departs. When Edgar enters, Edmund warns him that he should stay away from their father until he can heal the breach between them.

The rest of Act I takes place in various rooms and courtyards of Albany's castle, where Lear and one hundred of his knights have set up residence. Goneril complains to her servant Oswald that her father's men are riotous and insolent. In another room, Kent enters in disguise and offers his service to Lear. The king's Fool urges Lear to moderate his behavior, suggesting that Lear himself is a fool for having given away his authority. Goneril enters and tells her father he must send away fifty of his knights. Insulted and furious, Lear twice invokes a curse on her, charging her with ingratitude and himself with bad judgment. Weeping with rage and fearful of his sanity, he sets off for the castle of Regan and Cornwall.

Act II: Edmund learns that Cornwall and Regan are coming to Gloucester's castle, and that the Dukes of Cornwall and Albany are on the verge of war. He tricks Edgar into fleeing and tells Gloucester that Edgar tried to persuade him to kill their father. Cornwall and Regan arrive, congratulate Edmund on his service to Gloucester, and offer to be his patrons. Outside Gloucester's castle, the disguised Kent encounters Oswald, insulting and then beating him. Cornwall orders Kent to be put into stocks, even though this represents a grave insult to the king whose messenger he is. The setting shifts to a wood, where

Edgar, alone and friendless, decides to adopt the disguise of a mad beggar, Poor Tom. Back in Gloucester's courtyard, Lear has arrived with his Fool and is incensed at the sight of his messenger in stocks; he demands to see Regan and Cornwall, who eventually come and release Kent. Lear complains of Goneril's treatment and curses her again, but Regan defends her sister's behavior. Goneril enters, and the two sisters enforce ever tighter limits on the terms under which Lear may reside with them. Fighting back tears and vowing revenge, Lear rushes out into the stormy night.

Act III: On a deserted heath, a fierce storm rages. Kent confers with a gentleman, sending him off to meet Cordelia and the French forces, then sets out himself to find Lear. He locates the king and his Fool on another part of the heath, and they both urge Lear to seek shelter in a hovel nearby. Meanwhile, at Gloucester's castle, Gloucester tells Edmund that he means to seek out Lear and give him assistance. Before he succeeds, Lear, Kent, and the Fool discover Edgar, disguised as Poor Tom, in the hovel. Edgar raves wildly and rambles in a seemingly unintelligible fashion, while Lear repeatedly inquires if his daughters have driven him to madness. In a room in Gloucester's castle, Edmund shows Cornwall the letter Gloucester has received about the movement of the French forces, and Cornwall rewards him for his treachery by naming him Earl of Gloucester. In a farmhouse near the castle, Lear sets up a mock court of justice to arraign his daughters. Gloucester arrives and instructs Kent to take Lear to Dover, where they'll find assistance. Gloucester returns to his castle and learns that Edmund has informed on him. Cornwall orders that Gloucester be bound, then plucks out one of his eyes. A servant intercedes and draws his sword against Cornwall; Cornwall is wounded and Regan slays the servant. Cornwall plucks out Gloucester's other eye and commands that he be turned out of the castle.

Act IV: Edgar meets blind Gloucester on the heath and agrees to accompany him to a cliff near Dover. In a courtyard of Albany's castle, Goneril and Edmund confer, and she sends him back to Cornwall with a token and a kiss. While Albany accuses Goneril of unnatural behavior toward her father—and she upbraids him as a weakling—they receive word that Cornwall has died of the wound he received in the fight with his servant. At the French camp near Dover, Kent remarks that Lear is too ashamed to see Cordelia, and she consults with a physician about her father's madness. In a room of Gloucester's castle, Regan learns that Oswald bears a letter from Goneril to Edmund and gives him another to deliver from herself. Meantime, in a field near Dover, Edgar persuades Gloucester that he has led him to the edge of a cliff high above the sea. Gloucester throws himself forward and falls to the ground. Edgar, posing now as a passing stranger, assures Gloucester that he has

seen him fall from the cliff-top and land, miraculously, unhurt. Lear enters, raving still about his faithless daughters, and runs off when Cordelia's attendants approach. Next Oswald appears and attempts to kill Gloucester, but Edgar slays him and reads the letters in Oswald's wallet. At the French camp, the sleeping Lear is brought to Cordelia's tent, where he is gently awakened by music and his daughter's kiss. At first believing he is dead and she a spirit, Lear afterwards recognizes her and asks for forgiveness.

Act V: In the British camp, a disguised Edgar gives Albany the letter from Goneril to Edmund that he took from Oswald's body, promising that he will provide proof of its veracity. The British forces speedily overwhelm the French, and Lear and Cordelia are taken prisoners. Albany, congratulating Edmund on his valor, inquires about their safety. Edmund's high-handed response leads Albany to remind him that he is a subject, not an equal. When Goneril and Regan spring to his defense, Albany orders Edmund arrested on a charge of high treason—and impeaches Goneril with him. Regan, complaining that she is unwell, is led away. A trumpet sounds three times to call forth the man who will prove Edmund guilty: Edgar appears and fatally wounds Edmund in armed combat. Minutes pass while Edgar describes to Albany and Edmund how he assumed the role of mad beggar and then came to the aid of his father, who died, he tells them, not half an hour ago. A courtier enters with the news that Goneril has admitted poisoning Regan and then killed herself. Kent enters and inquires after Lear. Edmund admits that he has ordered Cordelia's death, and an officer is dispatched to the prison to countermand the warrant. The order has already been carried out, however, and Lear enters carrying Cordelia's body. In what is perhaps the most heart-wrenching of all Shakespearean scenes, Lear dies cradling his daughter's body in his arms.

PRINCIPAL TOPICS

Double Plot

Commentary on the double plot or subplot in *King Lear* frequently combines discussion of its function in the play with critiques of Gloucester, Edgar, and Edmund. Historically, critics have pointed out the many parallels between the two plots, as well as the verbal echoes and cross-references from one story to the other. But more recently the differences between them have been highlighted by critics who demonstrate the discrepancies in circumstances and themes in the separate tragedies of Lear and Gloucester. In the judgment of most modern critics, the subplot is much more than a repetition of the principal story. They see it as intensifying or heightening the central themes of the play, including the ingratitude of children, disorder in the family, human fallibility, the concept of individual identity, and the notion of spiritual development and rebirth.

Two scenes in the secondary plot have received the most attention: the blinding of Gloucester and his attempt to kill himself. Earlier critics found the blinding scene so vicious that they felt it ought to have taken place offstage. Modern critics, however, generally insist that audiences must experience its full horror to appreciate its implications: the evil that Lear and Gloucester struggle against is nothing short of monstrous. Commentators agree that Gloucester's physical blindness corresponds to Lear's moral blindness. The scene in which Edgar first deludes his sightless father into believing that they are not standing in a flat field but rather on the verge of a steep cliff, and then that he has miraculously survived a plunge from that cliff onto the sands below, has evoked a broad range of responses from critics. Some have interpreted it as the last step in Gloucester's progress toward spiritual renewal. Several others, acknowledging that it is a rather cheap theatrical device on Edgar's part, believe it has an allegorical significance, perhaps imitating Lear's own fall from grace into the abyss of human suffering. Many commentators have noted that the event does produce a miracle, bringing Gloucester to the realization that he must accept his suffering with a stoical or Christian patience.

There is general agreement that Gloucester is portrayed as slower-witted than Lear. Some critics argue that in early scenes he is evidently a very foolish, gullible man. Others see evidence of pride or arrogance in his make-up and emphasize his sensuality. There is a variety of opinion about Edgar's role in the play. For some commentators, he is a means of bringing about certain events and commenting on others—a poetic representation rather than a psychologically realistic figure. He has also been described as an agent of justice or retribution. Many find his chorus-like comments flat and insipid, and they condemn his moralistic speech to the dying Edmund. Gloucester's younger son is frequently associated with malevolent Nature. Edmund's vivacity and brashness in the first half of the play are frequently remarked on, and commentators point out that audiences often find him attractive, even sympathetic. As with many other aspects of the subplot, Edmund's intrigues with Goneril and Regan are not presented in detail; readers and audiences alike are left with only a few clues or hints on which to base any conclusions.

Language and Imagery

King Lear is notable for the relative plainness or simplicity of its language. Compared with other Shakespearean tragedies, the number of extended poetic speeches is meager, and there is a noticeable absence of ornate passages. Some critics believe that this naturalistic or unmannered style emphasizes the limitations of language to express the depths of human feelings. Words are inadequate in the face of the cruelty and suffering that Lear must endure. And the final image of the murdered Cordelia is truly an unspeakable horror.

Many commentators have called attention to several words that appear repeatedly in the play. Among such key-words are "nothing," "fool," and "nature." Each of these has a wide range of meaning or significance. For example, Cordelia's use of the word "nothing" is different from Edgar's. Several critics have pointed out that the word "fool" is associated, on one occasion or another, with every virtuous character in *King Lear*. Others have suggested that a principal issue in the play is the contrast—and close relation—between folly and wisdom. In the judgment of most commentators, "nature" is central to the design of *Lear*. Many critics see the world of the play as comprising several levels of nature. Others focus on the meaning of "natural" and "unnatural" in the *Lear* world, or evaluate the connection between nature and the theme of order and disorder.

Appraisals of imagery patterns in *King Lear*—the form and meaning of particular images or groups of images within the context in which they appear—often highlight recurring images from nature. These images frequently occur in ferocious or violent forms. Allusions to animals emphasize their untamed, savage, or predatory aspects. Such natural elements as the storm appear in their most extreme or turbulent state. For many critics, these associations emphasize the cruelties and unnaturalness of the *Lear* world. Another important set of images in the play relates to sight or vision. These images help underscore the issue of moral and physical blindness in Lear and Gloucester. Yet another set of contrasts is provided by images of clothing and nakedness, which many critics see as a means of highlighting the question of essence or identity.

Love

There is almost a complete absence of passionate or romantic love in *King Lear*. The King of France speaks movingly of this kind of love when he becomes betrothed to Cordelia, but he disappears from the play at the end of the first scene. Edmund's liaisons with Goneril and Regan combine political scheming with eroticism, and they are not central to the dramatic action. Yet many critics assert that love is the principal focus of *King Lear*. The play's emphasis on family relations and love between members of a family has been pointed out by many commentators. Several have noted the importance of the Elizabethan concept of the parallels between the family and the state. This is especially relevant with respect to the issue of the bonds that hold together each of these institutions.

The value of love—its ability to console the suffering, to affirm life, to redeem evil and restore order to nature—is a chief issue in commentary on *King Lear*. The play may be seen as presenting compassion for others as the highest form of love and, indeed, as the chief virtue humanity is capable of attaining. Some have argued that in its fullest manifestation, human love becomes a reflection of divine love, as demonstrated by Cordelia. Her love may be interpreted as infinitely patient, forgiving, and the ultimate source of Lear's spiritual redemption. For some commentators, her love symbolizes God's limitless and redeeming love for erring humanity.

Lear's own conception of love is also a central issue. His use of the love test in the first scene of the play has been variously interpreted as revealing a shallow notion of love or as demonstrating a pathetic need for reassurance. His reaction to Cordelia's refusal to give him a public assurance of her love may be motivated by humiliation, egoism, or genuine dismay by her response. Several critics have seen in Lear's reaction an unnatural possessiveness, an unfatherly wish to have all of a married daughter's love, perhaps even incestuous desire.

Madness

Commentary on the topic of madness in *King Lear* frequently begins by pointing out that in none of the earlier versions of the story is there a suggestion that the king loses his sanity. Shakespeare introduced this element. His first audiences would undoubtedly include people familiar with the earlier dramatization of the Lear story or with the chronicle histories that covered the reign of this legendary king. This background would not have prepared them for the spectacle of a lunatic monarch onstage. Furthermore, madness was generally considered comical, and the image of a man—even a king—"fantastically dressed with wild flowers," as the Folio stage direction indicates, might well have evoked laughter rather than pity. Critics propose that the many references to madness by Kent and Lear himself in the first two acts of the play represent careful preparation for the events of Acts III and IV.

A central issue relating to Lear's madness is the question of when it begins. This question has drawn responses from physicians and psychologists as well as literary critics. Some earlier commentators suggested that Lear shows evidence of insanity in the first scene of the play. They contended that giving up his royal title, challenging his daughters to a love test, and banishing Kent and Cordelia are symptomatic of senile dementia. Most modern critics, however, take a different view of Lear in this scene, fixing the responsibility for his behavior on pride, arrogance, vanity, misjudgment, or some other characteristic. The majority see his madness as progressive: his moments of irrationality in the first two acts represent a prelude to his madness in the scenes on the heath. Many commentators identify Lear's abrupt encounter with Edgar as Poor Tom as the moment at which he loses his hold on sanity. There is a minority, however, who argue that his madness is not fully evident until he appears in Act IV, scene vi.

What drives Lear mad, and what is the dramatic function of his madness? Critics have suggested several causes, including his daughters' ingratitude, his frustration in confronting the lack of justice in the world, and guilt when he realizes the consequences of his actions. A number of commentators have called attention to the correspondence between the storm on the heath and the storm in Lear's mind. Many have also remarked on the theme of "reason in madness," verbalized by Edgar in Act IV, scene vi. And while most critics agree that the reconciliation with Cordelia shows Lear restored to sanity, a few have suggested that he is driven mad once again by Cordelia's murder.

CHARACTER STUDIES

Lear

Lear is the central figure of the play, and evaluations of his character inevitably lead to broader questions. By the same token, discussions of thematic issues nearly always include critiques of the play's protagonist. Considerations of Lear's actions and speculation about his motives necessarily move from the level of a specific personality to issues of universal significance. He raises basic questions about human existence, and the answers—or lack of answers—have universal implications.

One principal issue is whether Lear is a victim of other people or impersonal forces, or responsible for his own tragedy. To what degree does his own nature or temperament determine his destiny and to what degree is it affected by events or other characters? Why does he test his daughters' love in the first scene of the play? Many commentators have asserted that his abdication of rule is a violation of natural order, an act that in itself condemns him. Other critics disagree, arguing that Lear has given appropriate thought to the future of his kingdom under divided leadership. Some critics assert that he places Cordelia in an intolerable situation in the opening scene, while others criticize her response to the conditions he imposes. There is widespread agreement that in this episode and the ones immediately following it, Lear shows a poor understanding of himself and of others. Many scholars find other faults, including egoism, a need for flattery, a rash temperament, and excessive pride.

Beyond what happens to him—or what he is responsible for—in the first two acts of the play, critics have focused on Lear's passage on the heath. What does he learn there? As he rages at the elements, laments his fate at the hands of ungrateful daughters, and consorts with a fool, a professed madman, and faithful followers, does he eventually come to understand himself? Critics are sharply divided on the question of whether Lear achieves self-knowledge or an understanding of his relation to others. Some believe that as he outlasts the physical storm, he endures a passage of emotional anguish leading to comprehension of his own guilt. Others contend that he emerges from the storm with only a limited appreciation of the consequences of his actions.

Commentators look to the final scene of the play for evidence that Lear has achieved spiritual regeneration. There is continuing controversy about the significance of his speeches after he comes on stage bearing Cordelia's body. Only a minority of critics assert that he dies happy, deluded in the belief that his daughter lives. Those who support an optimistic perspective on his tragedy hold that his spiritual journey or Cordelia's self-sacrifice reconcile Lear with an ultimately benevolent universe. Other critics see Lear's ending as uneasy accommodation: evil does not triumph, but neither does good prevail. And some hear Lear's howls as evidence that there is no justice in this world.

The Fool

A great deal of the commentary on Lear's Fool is devoted to an explanation of the cultural and literary heritage that contributed to his creation. The "natural" or simple-minded fool who inadvertently shows wisdom or good judgment is part of this heritage. So is the legendary Lord of Misrule, the ringleader in certain festivals celebrating temporary freedom from the constraints of society's rules and conventions. Other precedents include royal court fools and stage clowns, particularly such Shakespearean clowns as Feste in *Twelfth Night* and Touchstone in *As You Like It*. Critics have suggested that Lear's Fool, like Feste and Touchstone, owes much to the talents of the great Elizabethan comic actor Robert Armin, whose remarkable gifts may have inspired Shakespeare to design parts specifically for him.

In the judgment of many modern commentators, the Fool in *King Lear* is a "wise fool," a commentator on

dramatic events who is impartial yet sympathetic to his master's suffering. His devotion to Lear is frequently remarked on, yet some critics question whether this is an entirely admirable trait. It has been suggested that the Fool's devotion sometimes leads him to errors of judgment. His repeated—perhaps even tiresome—references to Lear's daughters hasten the king's descent into madness, some critics have maintained. The Fool's apparent devotion to Cordelia has also been frequently noted. Commentators have pointed out that he disappears from the play before she reappears, and there is speculation about the complementary roles they play in curing the king's madness.

The Fool's abrupt departure in Act III, scene vi is for some critics an unexplainable mystery. Others link his disappearance with his death; he is perhaps heartbroken by the king's suffering and madness, or he falls a victim to the raging storm. His end is as mysterious as his beginnings: he seems to be a character with no personal history and only minimal motivation.

Lear's Daughters

Cordelia, Lear's youngest daughter and clearly his favorite, appears in just three scenes and speaks only a little more than one hundred lines. The play barely touches on her roles as lover or wife, focusing instead on her relationship with her father. The scene featuring their reconciliation is regularly referred to as one of the most tender and moving in all dramatic literature. Yet commentary on Cordelia generally centers on the first and final scenes of the play.

Why doesn't Cordelia indulge her father and give him the kind of answer to his love test that she surely knows he's looking for? Some critics have defended her as dedicated to truth-telling and reluctant to participate in the hypocritical contest with her sisters. Others have suggested that she is inherently unable to speak freely about an emotion that is so personal. And some propose that she is too rigid in her conviction that participating in the contest will compromise her integrity. There is also the suggestion that speculation about her motives is pointless, for she is not a realistically drawn figure but rather a symbolic one.

In the view of most commentators, Cordelia is a paragon of virtue: selflessly devoted to her father and capable of a love that is endlessly forgiving. Critical disagreement arises over the issue of her role as the agent of Lear's spiritual redemption, and such commentary inevitably focuses on her death. Does her selflessness redeem Lear and purge his suffering and sins? Some commentators, offering a Christian view of the play—although they acknowledge it is set in pre-Christian times—regard Cordelia as a reflection of divine salvation and God's unfailing love for mankind.

Others, less committed to a Christian view of the play, agree that her imperishable spiritual essence has greater significance than her physical death. And many critics associate her murder with the defeat of virtue, seeing it as testimony to the lack of comfort or justice in the universe.

As with Cordelia, more questions have been raised about Goneril and Regan than have been answered. Are they merely versions of the wicked elder sisters of traditional fairy tales, or perhaps one-dimensional emblems of evil from an allegory? What motivates their responses in the first scene of the play: hypocrisy, humiliation, greed? How reliable or accurate are their remarks about Lear at the end of this scene and, more importantly, about the conduct of the king and his entourage of knights? Are their liaisons with Edmund based on love or lust?

Modern commentators generally contend that Goneril and Regan are more than simple portraits of unadulterated evil. Many critics have argued that there is some justification for their complaints about Lear's rowdy knights—and the potential threat they pose to an orderly kingdom. In the first part of *King Lear,* the sisters seems to be rational, even shrewd observers. But several commentators have identified a shift in their behavior before the play reaches its mid-point: from then until the end of the drama, their viciousness intensifies and becomes almost irrational. Most modern analyses of Goneril and Regan emphasize the play's reversal of roles between parents and children, and regard Lear's two older daughters as representatives of a new political order that seeks to replace the old form of royal authority embodied by their father.

CONCLUSION

There is no clearly defined or "exact" meaning of *King Lear.* No reputable modern critic claims to have found answers to the questions the play poses about human nature, universal order, and justice. Nor is there a single, identifiable source of Lear's tragedy, although various commentators have proposed that it may have its origin in human will, divine malice, or cosmic absurdity. Rather than attempting to "explain" the play, Northrop Frye suggests, try to "see something of its dimensions and its scope." *King Lear* has often been described as the Shakespearean tragedy that speaks most directly to twentieth-century readers and audiences. Despite all the commentary about it, words remain inadequate to express its incomparable power and artistry. Confronted by the unspeakable horror of Lear's suffering and Cordelia's death, our own response may be like his: "Howl, howl, howl!"

(See also *Shakespearean Criticism*, Vols. 2, 11, and 31)

OVERVIEW

Northrop Frye

SOURCE: "King Lear," in *Northrop Frye on Shakespeare,* edited by Robert Sandler, Yale University Press, 1986, pp. 101-21.

[In this informal, almost conversational, essay on King Lear*—developed from his lectures to undergraduate students over many years—Frye ranges widely across many aspects of the play as he outlines its tragic vision. He describes the Elizabethan concept of order or hierarchy in nature and the different levels of existence in* King Lear: *the supernatural, the human, physical nature, and the demonic world. Frye also discusses the association of the word "nothing" with loss of identity and remarks on the various meanings of the word "fool" in the play. As he takes up each of these thematic issues, he also offers commentary on Lear, Cordelia, Goneril and Regan, Edmund, and Edgar.]*

The story of Lear is one of a series of legends about the ancient history of Britain, legends that in Shakespeare's day were thought to be genuine history. How they got to be that makes a curious story, but we just have time for its main point. A Welsh priest living in the twelfth century, called Geoffrey of Monmouth, concocted a fictional history of early Britain modelled on Virgil, and according to this Britain was settled by Trojan refugees led by one Brutus, after whom Britain was named. There follows a long chronicle of kings and their adventures, mostly, so far as we can see, gathered out of Welsh legend and historical reminiscence. This is where the story of Lear and his three daughters came from: Lear was supposed to have lived somewhere around the seventh or eighth century before Christ. So, except for *Troilus and Cressida,* which is a very medievalized version of the Trojan War, *King Lear* is the earliest in historical setting of all Shakespeare's plays. It's true that we notice a tendency to mix up various historical periods increasing as Shakespeare goes on. In *Hamlet,* for instance, we seem to be most of the time in Denmark of the Dark Ages, but Hamlet is a student at Wittenberg, a university founded around 1500, and Laertes appears to be going off to a kind of Renaissance Paris. In *King Lear* we find Anglo-Saxon names (Edmund, Edgar, Kent) and Roman ones (Gloucester), and we also have contemporary allusions, including religious ones, of a type that the audience was accustomed to. But still there does seem to be a roughly consistent effort to keep the setting pre-Christian.

There are a lot of advantages here for what is perhaps Shakespeare's biggest dramatic design. First, with a setting so far back in time, the sense of the historical blurs into the sense of the mythical and legendary. The main characters expand into a gigantic, even titanic, dimension that simply wouldn't be possible in a historical context like that of *Henry IV*. Then again, there are certain tensions between a tragic structure and a framework of assumptions derived from Christianity. Christianity is based on a myth (story) which is comic in shape, its theme being the salvation and redemption of man. You can see what I mean by comic: when Dante wrote his poem about hell, purgatory and paradise he called it a *commedia* because it followed the central Christian story, which ends happily for all the people who matter. Tragedy needs a hero of outsize dimensions: you can get this easily in Greek tragedy, where some men can really be descended from gods, and where there's very little distinction between history and legend anyway, but in Christianity there's no hero except Christ who has a divine dimension of any kind. Also, tragedy raises some disturbing questions about what kind of power is in charge of the universe. Christianity has prompt and confident answers, but the more emotionally convincing the tragedy, the more we may feel that the answers sometimes are a bit too pat. We can see this feeling reflected in what people say who are assumed to be living before the coming of Christ.

The very little evidence we have seems to indicate that Shakespeare took more time over *King Lear* than over most of his plays, and the freedom with which he handled a story familiar to his audience is extraordinary. No previous account of Lear suggests that he went mad, or that Cordelia was hanged by her enemies; and the incorporating of the Gloucester-Edgar subplot, as a counterpoint to the main, Lear-Cordelia one, is entirely Shakespeare's. The material seems to have come from Sir Philip Sidney's *Arcadia*, but the source doesn't seem significant. Neither do the books he consulted for the names of the devils inhabiting Poor Tom and the like. There's a Quarto text as well as a Folio one, but the relations between them that an editor has to deal with are just too complex to go into.

When you start to read or listen to *King Lear*, try to pretend that you've never heard the story before, and forget that you know how bad Goneril and Regan and Edmund are going to be. That way, you'll see more clearly how Shakespeare is building up our sympathies in the opposite direction. The opening scene presents first Gloucester and then Lear as a couple of incredibly foolish and gullible dodderers (Gloucester's gullibility comes out in a slightly later scene). Gloucester boasts about how he begot Edmund in a way that embarrasses us as well as Kent, and we feel that Edmund's treachery, whatever we think of it, is at any rate credibly motivated. Even at the end of the play, his simple phrase "Yet Edmund was beloved," meaning that Goneril and Regan loved him at least, reminds us how intensely we can feel dramatic sympathy where we don't necessarily feel moral sympathy.

As for Lear and his dreary love test, it's true that Goneril and Regan are being hypocrites when they patter glibly through the declarations of love they are required to make, but we shouldn't forget that it's a genuine humiliation, even for them, to have to make such speeches. At no time in the play does Lear ever express any real affection or tenderness for Goneril or Regan. Of course loving Goneril and Regan would be uphill work, but Lear never really thinks in terms of love: he talks about his kindness and generosity and how much he's given them and how grateful they ought to feel. He does say (publicly) that Cordelia was always his favourite, and that certainly registers with the other two, as their dialogue afterward shows. But they don't feel grateful, and nobody with Shakespeare's knowledge of human nature would expect them to. Then again, while they're not surprised that Lear acts like an old fool, even they are startled by how big a fool he is, and they realize that they have to be on their guard to stop him from ever having the power to do to them what he's just done to Cordelia. The hundred knights Lear insists on could easily start a palace revolution in such a society, so the hundred knights will have to go.

In the first two acts, all Lear's collisions with his daughters steadily diminish his dignity and leave them with the dramatic honours. They never lose their cool: they are certainly harsh and unattractive women, but they have a kind of brusque common sense that bears him down every time. A hundred knights would make quite a hole in any housekeeper's budget, and we have only Lear's word for it that they're invariably well behaved. If we look at the matter impartially, we may find ourselves asking, with the daughters, what all the fuss is about, and why Lear must have all these knights. When Regan says:

> This house is little: the old man and's people
> Cannot be well bestow'd.
>
> (II.iv. 290-91)

what she says could have a ring of truth in it, if we forget for the moment that she's talking about Gloucester's house, which she and Cornwall have commandeered. Every move that Lear makes is dramatically a flop, as when he kneels to Regan, intending irony, and she says "these are unsightly tricks," which they assuredly are. The same thing is true of some of Lear's allies, like Kent and his quarrel with Oswald that lands him in the stocks. It is not hard to understand Kent's feelings about Oswald, or his exasperation with the fact that Goneril's messenger is treated with more consideration than the king's, but still he does seem to be asking for something, almost as though he were a kind of *agent provocateur*, adopting the strategy of Goneril's "I'd have it come to question."

It is not until the scene at the end of the second act,

with its repeated "shut up your doors," that our sympathies definitely shift over to Lear. Regan says, "He is attended with a desperate train," meaning his fifty (or whatever their present number) knights, but they seem to have sloped off pretty promptly as soon as they realized that they were unlikely to get their next meal there, and Lear's "desperate train" actually consists only of the Fool. When we catch her out in a lie of that size we begin to see what has not emerged before, and has perhaps not yet occurred to them: that "his daughters seek his death," as Gloucester says. It is during and after the storm that the characters of the play begin to show their real nature, and from then on we have something unique in Shakespeare: a dramatic world in which the characters are, like chess pieces, definitely black or white: black with Edmund, Goneril, Regan and Cornwall; white with Lear, Cordelia, Edgar, Gloucester, Kent and eventually Albany.

Perhaps the best way of finding our bearings in this mammoth structure is to look for clues in the words that are so constantly repeated that it seems clear they're being deliberately impressed on us. I'd like to look at three of these words in particular: the words "nature," "nothing" and "fool."

To understand the word "nature," we have to look at the kind of world view that's being assumed, first by Shakespeare's audience, then by the characters in the play. The opening words of Edmund's first soliloquy are "Thou, Nature, art my goddess," and later in the first act Lear, beginning his curse on Goneril, says: "Hear, Nature, hear; dear goddess, hear." It seems clear that Edmund and Lear don't mean quite the same thing by the goddess Nature, but I think Shakespeare's audience would find this less confusing than we do.

At that time most people assumed that the universe was a hierarchy in which the good was "up" and the bad "down." These ups and downs might be simply metaphors, but that didn't affect their force or usefulness. At the top of the cosmos was the God of Christianity, whose abode is in heaven; that is, the place where his presence is. The lower heaven or sky is not this heaven, but it's the clearest visible symbol of it. The stars, made, as was then believed, out of a purer substance than this world, keep reminding us in their circling of the planning and intelligence that went into the Creator's original construction.

God made a home for man in the garden of Eden, which, like the stars, was a pure world without any death or corruption in it. But Adam and Eve fell out of this garden into a lower or "fallen" world, a third level into which man now is born but feels alienated from. Below this, a fourth level, is the demonic world. The heaven of God is above nature; the demonic world of the devils is below it; but the important

thing to keep in mind is that the two middle levels both form part of the order of nature, and that consequently "nature" has two levels and two standards. The upper level, the world symbolized by the stars and by the story of the garden of Eden, was man's original home, the place God intended him to live in. The lower level, the one we're born into now, is a world to which animals and plants seem to be fairly well adjusted: man is not adjusted to it. He must either sink below it into sin, a level the animals can't reach, or try to raise himself as near as he can to the second level he really belongs to. I say "try to raise himself," but he can't really do that: the initiative must come from above or from social institutions. Certain things—morality, virtue, education, social discipline, religious sacraments—all help him to raise his status. He won't get back to the garden of Eden: that's disappeared as a place, but it can be recovered in part as an inner state of mind. The whole picture looks like this to the audience:

1. Heaven (the place of the presence of God), symbolized by the sun and moon, which are all that's left of the original creation.

2. Higher or human order of nature, originally the "unfallen" world or garden of Eden, now the level of nature on which man is intended to live as continuously as possible with the aid of religion, morality and the civilized arts.

3. Lower or "fallen" order of physical nature, our present environment, a world seemingly indifferent to man and his concerns, though the wise can see many traces of its original splendour.

4. The demonic world, whatever or wherever it is, often associated with the destructive aspects of nature, such as the storm on the heath.

When we speak of "nature" it makes a crucial difference whether we mean the upper, human level of nature or the environment around us that we actually do live in. Many things are "natural" to man that are not natural to anything else on this lower level, such as living under authority and obedience, wearing clothes, using reason, and the like. Such things show that the proper "natural" environment for man is something different from that of animals. But when Edmund commits himself to *his* goddess Nature, he means only the lower, physical level of nature, where human life, like animal life, is a jungle in which the predators are the aristocracy. When Lear appeals to the goddess Nature to curse Goneril, he means a nature that includes what is peculiarly natural to man, an order of existence in which love, obedience, authority, loyalty are natural because they are genuinely human; an order in which "art," in all its Elizabethan senses, is practically indistinguishable from nature.

Goneril is being cursed because her treatment of her father is "unnatural" in this context.

But we shouldn't assume that Edmund knows clearly that he is talking about a lower aspect of Nature, or that Lear knows clearly that he is talking about a higher one. Such categories aren't clear yet in a pre-Christian world. In the Lear world there is no actual God, because there is only the Christian God, and he has not revealed himself yet. Very early, when Kent stands out against Lear's foolish decision, Lear says, "Now, by Apollo—" and Kent answers:

> Now, by Apollo, King
> Thou swear'st thy Gods in vain.
>
> (I.i. 160-61)

Lear retorts by calling him "miscreant," unbeliever. A parody of this discussion occurs later, when Kent is in the stocks. And just as the divine world is hazy and mysterious, so is the demonic world. *King Lear* is in many respects the spookiest of all the great tragedies, and yet nothing explicitly supernatural or superhuman occurs in it: there is nothing to correspond to the Ghost in *Hamlet* or the witches in *Macbeth*. Five fiends inhabit Poor Tom, but we don't believe in his devils, and wouldn't even if we didn't know that Poor Tom is really Edgar. To Shakespeare's audience, the Lear world would look something like this:.

1. World of impotent or nonexistent gods, which tend to collapse into deified personifications of Nature or Fortune.

2. Social or human world with the elements the more enlightened can see to be essential to a human world, such as love, loyalty and authority. In particular, the world represented by Cordelia's and Edgar's love, Kent's loyalty, Albany's conscience, etc.

3. World of physical nature in which man is born an animal and has to follow the animal pattern of existence, i.e., join the lions and eat well, or the sheep and get eaten.

4. A hell-world glimpsed in moments of madness or horror.

As an example of what I'm talking about, notice that one of the first points established about Edmund is his contempt for astrology. If we ignore the question of "belief" in astrology, for ourselves or for Shakespeare or his audience, and think of it simply as a dramatic image revealing character, we can see that of course Edmund would dismiss astrology: it has no place in his conception of nature. Astrology was taken seriously in Shakespeare's day because of the

assumption that God had made the world primarily for the benefit of man, and although the original creation is in ruins, we can still see many evidences of design in it with a human reference. The stars in the sky are not just there: they've been put there for a purpose, and that's why the configurations of stars can spell out the destinies of men and women.

Similarly, there are links, however mysterious and fitful, between natural and human events, at least on the top social level. Comets, earthquakes and other natural disturbances don't just happen: they happen at crucial times in human life, such as the death of a ruler. Not necessarily a Christian ruler: there were . . . such portents at the time of the murder of Julius Caesar. So Lear has some ground for expecting that the order of nature around him might take some notice of his plight and of his daughters' ingratitude, considering that he's a king. But one thing the storm symbolizes is that he's moving into an order of nature that's indifferent to human affairs. His madness brings him the insight: "They told me I was everything: 'tis a lie; I am not ague-proof." With his abdication, whatever links there may be between the civilized human world and the one above it have been severed.

It should be clear from all this that the question "What is a natural man?" has two answers. On his own proper human level it is natural to man to be clothed, sociable and reasonable. When Goneril and Regan keep asking Lear why he needs all those knights, the first part of his answer, in the speech beginning "Oh, reason not the need," is a quite coherent statement of the fact that civilized life is not based simply on needs. But in this storm world that Lear is descending into, what is natural man like? Lear has hardly begun to formulate the question when Poor Tom appears as the answer to it. "Didst thou give all to thy two daughters?" Lear asks, still preoccupied with his own concerns. But we're getting down now to the underside of the Goneril-Regan world:

> Poor Tom, that eats the swimming frog, the toad, the tadpole, the wall-newt and the water; that in the fury of his heart, when the foul fiend rages, eats cow-dung for sallets, swallows the old rat and the ditch-dog; drinks the green mantle of the standing pool . . . (III.iv. 132ff.)

The imagery creates a world more nauseating than Hamlet ever dreamed of. "Is man no more than this?", Lear asks. In a way Poor Tom is a kind of ghastly parody of a free man, because he owes nothing to the amenities of civilization. Lear is reminded that he still has at least clothes, and starts tearing them off to be level with Poor Tom, but he is distracted from this. He says in a miracle of condensed verbal power: "Thou art the thing itself." He has started at one end of nature and ended at the other, and now his downward journey has reached a terminus. Perhaps one of Edgar's motives in assuming his Poor Tom disguise was to provide a solid bottom for Lear's descent. Below or behind him is the chaos-world portended by the storm: the world of the furies and fiends that Edgar is keeping Lear protected from, just as he protects Gloucester later from the self-destructive "fiend" that wants to hurl him over a cliff.

The word "nothing" [also appears in] *Richard II,* where it [is] connected with the conception of the king's two bodies [that is, his dual nature as both an individual and an office of state]. In both plays "nothing" seems to have the meaning of being deprived of one's social function, and so of one's identity. A king who dies is still a something, namely a dead king; a king deprived of his kingship is "nothing," even if, or especially if, he still goes on living. That is one thing that the issue of the train of knights is about. They represent, for Lear, his continuing identity as king, even though he has abdicated his powers and responsibilities: he wants both to have and not have his royalty. His daughters do not, at least not at first, want to kill him: they want him to go on living without power, once he has renounced it. Regan says, and may well mean it at this point:

> For his particular, I'll receive him gladly,
> But not one follower.
>
> (II.iv. 293-94)

Such treatment of him is, at least symbolically (and symbolism is immensely important here), what Lear says in another connection is "worse than murder." To kill him would be murder; to let him survive without his identity is a kind of annihilation. Similarly Edgar says, when assuming his Poor Tom disguise: "Edgar I nothing am." He's still alive, but his identity as Edgar is gone, or at least in abeyance.

There is another context, easier to understand, in which the conception of nothing is of great significance. What is the cause of love, friendship, good faith, loyalty or any of the essential human virtues? Nothing. There's no "why" about them: they just are. In putting on his love-test act, Lear is obsessed by the formula of something for something. I'll love you if you love me, and if you love me you'll get a great big slice of England. When Cordelia says that she loves him according to her "bond," she of course doesn't mean anything like Shylock's bond [in *The Merchant of Venice*]: the word for her has more the modern sense of "bonding." Love and loyalty don't have motives or expectations or causes, nor can they be quantified, as in Lear's "Which of you shall we say doth love us most?" Much later in the play, when Cordelia awakens Lear and he finally realizes he is still in the same world, he says:

> I know you do not love me; for your sisters
> Have, as I do remember, done me wrong:
> You have some cause, they have not.
>
> (IV.vii. 73-75)

Cordelia's answer, "No cause, no cause," is one of the supreme moments of all drama. And yet when Cordelia says that, she is saying precisely what she said at the beginning of the play: she will have nothing to do with these silly conditional games. It is characteristic of such relationships that sooner or later they come to focus on some anxiety symbol, which for Lear is the issue of the hundred knights. Pursuing this anxiety drives Lear toward the madness he so much fears, and forces him into those dreadful bargaining scenes that we can hardly bear to reread:

> Thy fifty yet doth double five and twenty,
> And thou art twice her love.
>
> (II.iv. 261-62)

As for "fool," we have first of all Lear's version of the common phrase, used several times by Shakespeare, "all the world's stage":

> When we are born, we cry that we are come
> To this great stage of fools.
>
> (IV.vi. 184-85)

The word "fool" is in course of time applied to practically every decent character in the play. Those who are not fools are people like Goneril and Regan and Edmund, who live according to the conditions of the lower or savage nature they do so well in. But Albany is called a "moral fool" by Goneril because he is unwilling to accept such a world; Kent is called a fool for taking the part of an outcast king. As for the Fool himself, he is a "natural," a word that again evokes the sense of two levels of nature. As a "natural" in this world, he is deficient enough, mentally, to be put in a licensed position to say what he likes. In his kind of "natural" quality there is a reminiscence of a still coherent and divinely designed order of nature, a world in which no one can help telling the truth. In our world, there is the proverb "children and fools tell the truth," and the Fool's privilege makes him a wit because in our world nothing is funnier than a sudden outspoken declaration of the truth.

There is another sense of the word "fool" that seems to be peculiar to Shakespeare, and that is the "fool" as victim, the kind of person to whom disasters happen. Everyone on the wrong side of the wheel of fortune is a fool in this sense, and it is in this sense that Lear speaks of himself as "the natural fool of fortune." . . . [When] Gloucester says:

> As flies to wanton boys are we to th' gods,

A scene from Grigori Kozintsev's 1970 Russian-language version of King Lear, *in which Lear and Cordelia are taken to prison.*

> They kill us for their sport.
>
> (IV.i. 36-37)

he certainly hasn't forgotten that his own plight is the quite understandable result of his own folly, Edmund's treachery and Cornwall's brutality; it doesn't need any gods to explain it. Some nineteenth-century commentators felt that this remark displayed an atheistic pessimism which Shakespeare himself believed in (because they did) and was keeping up his sleeve. I don't know what Shakespeare believed, but he knew what his audience would buy, and he knew they wouldn't buy that. Gloucester is no atheist: he postulates gods, divine personalities, and if he replaced them with a mechanism of fate or destiny he couldn't ascribe *malice* to it. What he feels is that there is some mystery in the horror of what's happened to him that goes beyond the tangible human causes.

Edgar and Albany, on the other hand, are moralists: they look for human causes and assume that there are powers above who are reacting to events as they should. Albany is a decent man, and Goneril a vicious woman, and yet in Goneril's world Albany looks weak and ineffectual. He produces his great melodramatic coup, the letter proving Goneril's intrigue with Edmund, which should overwhelm her with shame and confusion. But Goneril isn't listening: in her world, of course anyone of her social rank who despised her husband would take a lover. It's true that she kills herself when Edmund is fatally wounded, but that too is part of the Goneril ethic. Albany's demonstrations of the workings of providence also get undercut pretty badly. When he hears of the death of Cornwall he says it shows that "justicers" are above, passing over the fate of Gloucester himself and of Cornwall's servant. He sees a "judgement of the heavens" in the deaths of Goneril and Regan: at once Kent enters, inquires for the king, and Albany says, "Great thing of us forgot!" It looks almost as though the memory of the "heavens" had slipped up along with Albany's. Finally, he tries to set up a scene of poetic justice in which:

> All friends shall taste
> The wages of their virtue, and all foes
> The cup of their deservings.
>
> (V.iii. 302-304)

What follows this is Lear's terrible lament over the

dead body of Cordelia, and in the nuclear-bomb desolation of that speech, words like "wages" and "deserving" fade into nothingness. It may be, as some say, that Lear thinks Cordelia is alive again at the end of the speech, but we know that if so he is being mocked with another illusion.

Edgar too, for all his prodigies of valour and fidelity, gets some curiously limp things to say. At the end of the heath scene he makes a chorus comment (which is not in the Folio):

> When we our betters see bearing our woes,
> We scarcely think our miseries our foes.
> 　　　　　　　　　　　　　(III.vi. 105-106)

and so on for another dozen sickening lines. After he strikes down Edmund in the final duel, he remarks that the gods are just, and that Gloucester's blindness was the inevitable result of going into a whorehouse to beget Edmund. (I feel very sorry for Edmund's mother, who seems to me to get a quite undeservedly bad press.) Even though Edmund agrees with the statement, it doesn't make much of a point, as we're explicitly told that Goneril and Regan were "got 'tween lawful sheets." In fact, the whole relation between Gloucester and the Lear tragedies seems to have something of a contrast between an explicable and an inexplicable disaster. The Gloucester tragedy perhaps can—just—be explained in moral terms; the Lear tragedy cannot.

There is a lot more to be said about both Albany and Edgar, and I shall be saying some of it myself in a moment. They are not in the least ridiculous characters, but, like all the virtuous people, they are fools in the sense that a fool is a victim: they utter the cries of bewildered men who can't see what's tormenting them, and their explanations, even if they are reassuring for the moment, are random guesses. In this dark, meaningless, horrible world, everyone is as spiritually blind as Gloucester is physically: you might be interested in looking at the number of references to blindness in the play apart from those connected with Gloucester. The moral for us, as students of the play, is clear enough: we have to take a much broader view of the action than either a fatalistic or a moral one, and try, not to "explain" it, but to see something of its dimensions and its scope.

Many critics of Shakespeare have noticed that there often seem to be two time clocks in the action of his plays, the events in the foreground summarizing slower and bigger events in the background that by themselves would take longer to work out. It's a little like looking at the scenery from the window of a car or train, with the weeds at the side of the road rushing by and the horizon turning slowly. In the foreground action the scene on the heath seems to take place in the same night that begins with Regan and Cornwall shutting Lear out. In the background we pick up hints that Albany and Cornwall are at loggerheads, but are forced to compose their differences and unite against a threatened invasion from France, partly encouraged by Cordelia, although in the foreground action nothing has yet happened to Lear that would justify such an invasion. At the end of Act II we still don't feel that Gloucester's statement "his daughters seek his death" is quite true yet, though they certainly don't care if he does die. But within an hour or two Gloucester's concern for Lear becomes strictly forbidden, and his action in helping the king to get to Dover is, from Cornwall's point of view, the basest treachery. It's not difficult to get all this from the indications we're given. I think there's also a third rhythm of time, if it really is time, in a still larger background.

Before the play begins, we are in roughly the upper world of human nature; not a paradisal state, of course, but a world where there is authority, social discipline, orders of distinction, and loyalty: the conditions regarded as the central ones in the Tudor world. Then the dreaded image of the map appears, with a proposal to carve up the country. . . . By the end of the scene we have the feeling of sliding into a different world, and when Edmund steps forth with his "Thou, Nature, art my goddess," we feel that he's the first person to have recognized this new world for what it is. He's Gloucester's "natural" son, and on this level of nature he's the kind of person who will take command. When the storm begins in Act III it's described in a way that makes it clear that it's more than just a storm. It's an image of nature dissolving into its primordial elements, losing its distinctions of hierarchies in chaos, a kind of crossing of the Red Sea in reverse.

One of the central images of this descent is that of the antagonism of a younger and older generation. "The younger rises when the old doth fall," says Edmund, and Goneril, speaking of Lear, issues a blanket denunciation of old people generally: "The best and soundest of his time hath been but rash." On the other side, Lear appeals to the gods, "If you do love old men," and Gloucester, with a still more futile irony, appeals for help, during the blinding scene, to any "who will think to live till he be old." The principle that made hereditary succession so important in the history plays seems to be extended here, in a world where the honouring of one's parents is the most emphasized of all virtues. Albany regards Goneril's treatment of her father as the key to everything else she does that's wrong:

> She that herself will sliver and disbranch
> From her material sap, perforce must wither
> And come to deadly use.
> 　　　　　　　　　　　　　(IV.ii. 34-36)

The connection between honouring one's parents and long life is, of course, already present in the fifth commandment, though the characters in *King Lear* are not supposed to know that. In any case the principle doesn't work in the post-storm world: Cornwall's servant feels that so wicked a woman as Regan can't possibly live out her full life, and Regan does get poisoned, but then Cordelia is hanged, so that again doesn't prove or explain anything. Wherever we turn, we're up against the ambiguity in all tragedy: that death is both the punishment of the evil and the reward of the virtuous, besides being the same end for everybody. Our moralists, Edgar and Albany, the survivors of the play, actually speak as though the length of human life had been shortened as a result of the play's action. The last four lines, spoken by Edgar in the Folio and by Albany in the Quarto, are:

> The weight of this sad time we must obey,
> Speak what we feel, not what we ought to
>   say:
> The oldest hath borne most: we that are
>   young
> Shall never see so much, nor live so long.
>
> (V.iii. 323-26)

The second line, incidentally, seems very curious. If it's a vindication of the conduct of Cordelia and Kent in the opening scene, it's a bit late in the day; and as a general principle it covers too much ground. When Edmund says, "Legitimate Edgar, I must have your land," he is saying what he feels, and certainly not what he ought to say. Nonetheless, I think it's a very central comment: it points to the fact that language is just about the only thing that fights for genuine humanity in this blinded world.

Let's go back to the conception of the king's two bodies. Lear gives up his second body when he surrenders himself to the power of Goneril and Regan, and consequently, as we said, he no longer has any identity as a king. His loss of identity troubles him, and he says to Oswald: "Who am I?" The question is rhetorical, but Oswald's answer, "My lady's father," has the unusual quality of being both the exact truth and a calculated insult. The next time he asks the question it is the Fool who answers: "Lear's shadow." There follows the expulsion and the storm on the heath, and before long things begin to change in Lear. We notice the point at which he is suddenly conscious of the misery of the Fool, and an even more significant moment when he says: "I'll pray, and then I'll sleep." The prayer is a strange prayer, not addressed to any deity, but to the "poor naked wretches" of his own kingdom. What is happening is that he has lost his identity as a king in the body peculiar to a king, but is beginning to recover his royal nature in his other body, his individual and physical one; not just the body that is cold and wet, but the mind that realizes how many others are cold and wet, starting with the Fool and Poor Tom. To use religious terms, his relation to his kingdom was transcendent at the beginning of the play; now it is immanent. Whatever his actual size, Lear is a giant figure, but his gigantic dimensions are now not those of a king or hero; they are those of a human being who suffers but understands his affinity with others who suffer.

In the mad scenes (which would have to be very carefully staged in Shakespeare's day because there was a tendency to think mad people funny), we get a negative aspect of Lear's new sense of identity with his subjects. He speaks of the endless hypocrisies in the administering of justice, of the sexual pleasure with which beadles lash whores, of the prurience lurking under the prude, of the shame of living in a society where "a dog's obeyed in office." These things are not exactly news to us, but they are new sensations to him. All Poor Tom's fiends of lust and theft and lying sweep through him, but they are not in possession of him: he is . . . absorbing the good and bad of the human nature in his kingdom. He is at the opposite pole from the deposed king who had half expected the storm to take his part:

> Tremble, thou wretch,
> That hast within thee undivulged crimes,
> Unwhipp'd of Justice; hide thee, thou bloody
>   hand . . .
>
> (III.ii. 51-53)

We can summarize all this by saying that Lear has entered a world in which the most genuine language is prophetic language: that is, language inspired by a vision of life springing from the higher level of nature. Albany's providence and Edgar's divine justice make sense as a part of such a vision, though as prophecy in the sense of predicting what is going to happen it may fail. Kent, again, is often prophetic; his fury against Oswald is really a prophetic vision of the kind of thing that such people as Oswald do in the world:

> Such smiling rogues as these,
> Like rats, oft bite the holy cords a-twain . . .
>
> (II.ii. 74-75)

The "holy cords" may be parental or matrimonial: in either case he's dead right about Oswald, as the rest of the play shows. Again, he is someone possessed by a need to have a "master" who represents genuine "authority," as he says to Lear. At the end of the play, when he comes in to "bid my king and master aye good-night," he of course means Lear; when he repeats this a few lines later, a second or two after Lear's death, he may have some intuition about a bigger master who nonetheless includes Lear:

I have a journey, sir, shortly to go;
My master calls me, I must not say no.
                              (V.iii. 321-22)

I don't mean that he is moving toward a specific religious belief, Christian or other; I mean only that his vision of the source of authority and mastery is expanding from its exclusive focus on King Lear.

The audience is apparently expected to recognize a number of Biblical allusions that the characters who make them do not know to be Biblical. Cordelia speaks of going about her father's business, echoing a phrase of Jesus in the Gospel of Luke: had she known of the resemblance she would hardly have made the remark in quite those words. A gentleman says of Lear:

Thou hast one daughter,
Who redeems nature from the general curse
Which twain have brought her to.
                              (IV.vi. 206-208)

He could, theoretically, mean Goneril and Regan, or he could mean Adam and Eve. I'd say that he means Goneril and Regan and has probably never heard of Adam and Eve. At the same time it would be true to say that Adam and Eve brought a general curse on nature, and a bit overblown to say it of Goneril and Regan, except insofar as they are participating in a "second fall of cursed man," [*Henry V*]. The statement is unconsciously prophetic, and the audience picks up more than the speaker is aware of.

Lear on the heath, again, is attended by two bedraggled prophets, the Fool and Poor Tom. The Fool is introduced in the somewhat ambiguous role of keeping Lear amused by repeating incessantly, "You are nothing, nothing, nothing." However unhelpful, it is prophetic enough: it tells Lear the outcome of his journey to Regan and what the next stage of his life will be. Goneril, no devotee of either humour or truth, believes that he is "more knave than fool," because the Fool is a "natural" allied to a level of nature that she does not know exists. On the heath the Fool's role is largely taken over by Poor Tom, although the idiot doggerel that he recites (in the Folio text only) at the end of Act III, Scene ii is still called a "prophecy." As for Poor Tom, a ballad on "Tom o' Bedlam" was collected in the eighteenth century, and may well go back to something very similar extant in Shakespeare's time. The last stanza of the ballad goes:

With an host of furious fancies
Whereof I am commander,
With a burning spear, and a horse of air,
To the wilderness I wander.
By a knight of ghosts and shadows

I summoned am to tourney
Ten leagues beyond the wide world's end,
Methinks it is no journey.

This kind of imagery reminds us of certain primitive poets and magicians, like the "shamans" of central Asia, who go through long initiations that involve journeys to upper and lower worlds. We are now in a world where all knowledge of anything "spiritual" or otherworldly has been degraded to Poor Tom's fiends, his nightmare with her ninefold, his dark tower of Childe Roland, and other phantasms linked to the night and the storm.

Edgar says explicitly that he is trying to "cure" Gloucester's despair, and to lead him to feel that "ripeness is all," that man does not own his life, and must wait until it concludes of itself. Lear has told Gloucester the same thing earlier, and the fact that the mad Lear is in a position to do so says a good deal about the essential sanity of Lear's madness. What Edgar expects to do for Lear by producing his Tom o' Bedlam act is more difficult to say. He seems to be acting as a kind of lightning rod, focussing and objectifying the chaos that is in both Lear's mind and in nature. He's holding a mirror up to Lear's growing madness, somewhat as, to refer to a very different play, Petruchio tries to cure Katharina's shrewishness by showing her in his own behaviour what it looks like [*The Taming of the Shrew*].

The action of the play seems to be proceeding to a conclusion that, however sombre and exhausting, nonetheless has some serenity in it. But just as we seem about to reach this conclusion, there comes the agonizing wrench of the hanging of Cordelia and the death speeches of Lear. Naturally the stage refused to act this down to the nineteenth century: producers settled for another version that married Cordelia off to Edgar. We act the play now as Shakespeare wrote it, but it's still pretty tough even for this grisly century. I said that in the course of the play the characters settled into a clear division of good and bad people, like the white and black pieces of a chess game. The last of the black pieces, Goneril, Regan and Edmund, have been removed from the board, and then comes the death of Cordelia. Part of this is just the principle that the evil men do lives after them, Edmund's repentance being too late to rescind his own order. But there seems to be a black king still on the board, and one wonders if there is any clue to who or what or where he is.

I [have] said [in an earlier lecture] that *Hamlet* was the central Shakespeare play for the nineteenth century; in the twentieth century feelings of alienation and absurdity have arisen that tend to shift the focus to King Lear. All virtuous or evil actions, all acceptances or rejections of religious or political ideology, seem equally absurd in a world that is set up mainly for the benefit of the Gonerils and the Cornwalls. A generation ago this statement would have stimulated arguments about ways and means of changing such a world, but such arguments are not only irrelevant to Shakespeare's play, but avoid one of its central issues. . . .

Perhaps it takes a madman to see into the heart of tragedy, the dark tower of Lear's fury and tenderness, rage and sympathy, scorn and courtesy, and finally his broken heart. I've often come back to the titanic size of Lear, which is not a size of body or ultimately even of social rank, but of language. This seems to put him at an immense distance from us, except that he is also utterly human and recognizable. Perhaps Lear's madness is what our sanity would be if it weren't under such heavy sedation all the time, if our senses or nerves or whatever didn't keep filtering out experiences or emotions that would threaten our stability. It's a dangerous business to enter the world of titans and heroes and gods, but safer if we have as a guide a poet who speaks their language.

To speak of a black king, however metaphorically, is to make an assumption, and to ask what or who it is makes secondary assumptions. Another step takes us into the blind-men-and-elephant routine, where we "identify" the source of tragedy as the consequence of human acts or divine malice or fatality or cosmic absurdity. I also spoke of three important words in the play, "nature," "fool" and "nothing": perhaps I could have mentioned a fourth, "fortune." Fortune in Shakespeare's day . . . was symbolized by a wheel, and there are several powerful images of wheels in this play. In some rural areas at certain times of the year a wheel was made of straw, rolled to the top of a hill, then set on fire and let roll down: the Fool seems to be using this image about Lear's fall from one level of nature to another. Lear himself, waking out of sleep and seeing Cordelia, speaks of himself as bound on a wheel of fire, a spirit tormented in hell, though he soon discovers he isn't. Edmund accepts Edgar's view of him as the nemesis of Gloucester's folly in the phrase "The wheel has come full circle," after which he suddenly changes character. The image is inexact in one essential respect: wheels turn, but they remain wheels. Whatever is turning in *King Lear* also keeps turning *into* other things. The language of definition is helpless to deal with this: the language of prophecy can come closer, because it's more nearly related to the language of madness. At the beginning of the play Lear is technically sane, but everything he says and does is absurd. In his mad scenes his associations are often hard to follow, but his general meaning is blindly clear. The language is a counter absurdity: that is what the play leaves for us, a sense of what we could release if we could speak what we feel.

I keep using the word "prophetic" because it seems to me the least misleading metaphor for the primary power of vision in human consciousness, before it gets congealed into religious or political beliefs or institutions. In the final scenes particularly, we see both what's in front of us, where "all's cheerless, dark and deadly," and the power of language that will not stop expanding, even when it starts to press into the mystery that's blocked off from us by death. We don't know the answers; we don't know that there are no answers. Tragedy forces on us a response of acceptance: we have to say, "Yes, this kind of thing is human life too." But by making that response we've accepted something much deeper: that what is defined or made finite by words becomes infinite through the power of words.

DOUBLE PLOT

William R. Elton claims that the double plot in *King Lear* serves a variety of purposes. The Gloucester subplot, he suggests, serves as a frame for the main story, offering a more prosaic version of Lear's tragedy. It also heightens and enriches the central narrative, Elton argues, intensifying the portrayal of the king's mental anguish through the depiction of Gloucester's physical suffering. He also notes that the contrapuntal movement back and forth between the two plots maintains our interest by featuring diverse characters and events that reflect the central issues in the play. **Ian W. O. House** also remarks on this switching back and forth between the two stories. Whichever way we turn, he points out, we are confronted by the same underlying premise: evil is a permanent element in human existence. House also calls attention to the way that the subplot alternately disturbs and clarifies our comprehension of the main story through alternating contrasts and parallels between the two tragedies. The critic also focuses on the humorous tone of the subplot, commenting that what begins as broad comedy or farce gradually turns into increasingly dark and bitter humor.

Both Jan Kott and Phyllis Rackin have examined the scene in which Gloucester attempts to kill himself. In this episode, Kott speculates, Gloucester becomes Everyman, a figure in a grotesque parable about the blind man who recovers his spiritual sight. Gloucester's actions have meaning "only if the gods exist," Kott declares; otherwise they are only a feeble protest against suffering and injustice. In sharp contrast to this viewpoint, Rackin denies that this is an absurd joke at Gloucester's expense. He truly is saved by a miracle, she asserts, the incomparable devotion of the son he had disowned. Elton notes that Gloucester's suicide attempt comes before Lear and Cordelia's reconciliation. Previously in the play, his tragedy has echoed Lear's, the critic points out, but from this moment to the end of the drama, the order is reversed.

Northrop Frye, Ian House, and Geoffrey Aggeler have all commented on the character and function of Edgar. Frye views him as a moralist. Edgar continually looks for human causes of events, Frye maintains, and assumes that some divine power will shape circumstances in a benevolent fashion, but the views he expresses are consistently undercut by events in the play. House concedes that Edgar's chorus-like speeches may seem smug or self-righteous, but in effect they show him struggling to maintain his courage, his hopes, and his beliefs in the face of grim reality. In House's estimation, Edgar grows in stature as the figure of Edmund diminishes. Aggeler traces a pattern of moral development in Edgar, proposing that although he is naive, self-pitying, and easily manipulated by Edmund in the early scenes, he becomes progressively more effective in helping himself and others. Whereas he's an unconscious catalyst in Lear's regeneration, Aggeler contends, Edgar becomes a purposeful agent in guiding Gloucester toward regeneration and challenging Edmund to a trial by combat. House argues that whereas Edmund is amusing and even attractive in the first part of the play, he eventually displays the hollowness or "banality of evil," and audiences lose interest in him. Richard Matthews, however, finds Edmund in the final scene of the play deeply interesting. Focusing on events after Edgar has mortally wounded his brother, Matthews sees Edmund progressively achieving a sense of his own mortality, a measure of compassion for others, an acknowledgement that his punishment is justified, and a transforming recognition that he was beloved by Goneril and Regan.

Ian W. O. House

"'I know thee well enough': The Two Plots of *King Lear*," in *English*, Vol. 41, No. 170, Summer, 1992, pp. 97-112.

[*House emphasizes the dynamic relation between the main plot and the subplot in* King Lear, *proposing that the differences as well as the similarities between them unsettle and illuminate our understanding of the principal story. As the critic explains, the double plot universalizes the action by shifting emphasis away from individual characters and situations; the effect is more like that of a prism than a mirror, multiplying images rather than giving back a single one. Further, House analyzes the notorious implausibility of dramatic events in* Lear, *arguing that the absurdity is purposeful and heightened by the changes in the humorous tone of the subplot "from farce to melodrama, from domestic tragedy to surrealism." In the course of discussing these issues, the critic provides extended evaluations of Gloucester, Edmund, and, especially, Edgar.*]

Does the subplot of *King Lear* do more than provide parts for actors who would otherwise have been out of work? Why pad out a play with a plot that merely repeats, with whatever incidental variations, the events and themes of the main plot? The two plots are closely similar but have no narrative connexion; Gonerill's opportunism is independent of Edmund's intrigue. . . .

[A. W.] Schlegel, the first critic to comment on the subplot, says: 'Were Lear alone to suffer from his daughters, the impression would be limited to the powerful compassion felt by us for his private misfortune. But two such unheard-of examples taking place at the same time have the appearance of a great commotion in the moral world, [*Lectures on Dramatic Art*]. Is Schelgel right? Surely we do not share Gloucester's view that the divisions spring from eclipses in the sun and moon. Isn't the effect, rather or also, that this evil, of flesh tearing itself ('Is it not as this mouth should teare this hand/For lifting food too't?' (III.4.15)), is a permanent feature of life. . . . ? The universalizing effect happens not only because, statically, we see links between the two plots but because, dynamically, our attention is continually switched. Wherever we turn, whatever the individual characters and circumstances, the same underlying truth is to be discerned. In this way our interest is focused on the situation and is not totally absorbed by the welfare of individual characters. The double plot gives a sense of largeness and completeness, of a world and of time passing rather than the selective events of a cautionary tale.

This cannot, however, in itself be an adequate answer to the charge of redundancy. The effect of something universal—something that is not parochial, transitory, accidental, unrelated to the sorry scheme of things entire—can be achieved by plays that have a single plot. Do not the *Oedipus* of Sophocles or the *Misanthrope* of Molière far transcend the particular circumstances of their protagonists? The principle of artistic economy justifies the subplot only if the universalizing effect in this case could not have been achieved by a single plot.

Some hostile critics suggest that, in *King Lear*, our minds are burdened by plot complications and our emotions are fatigued by an excess of horrors. Margaret Webster, drawing on her large experience as a director, says [in *Shakespeare Today*] that the characters are 'too fierce and full for the space within which they are confined'; they interrupt the main plot and distract us from it. On the other hand, [A. C.] Bradley who agrees in essence with this complaint, far from finding all the characters 'fierce and full', thinks that Gloucester is neither interesting nor distinct [*Shakespearean Tragedy*].

Some reply that the subplot does not distract us but,

by being on a more human scale, makes the main plot more credible and engages our sympathy more readily. Its victims are not 'every inch a king' but ordinarily decent men, however flawed; the hardheartedness of its villain is neither uncaused by anything in nature nor untinged by repentance. The greatness of Lear, the scope and depth of his mind in its many phases, is never more sharply felt than by contrast with the stumblings of Gloucester, *l' homme moyen sensuel* [the average nonintellectual man].

These defences of the subplot as universalizing and human are not wrong, but they tend to be couched in an unilluminatingly general way and they too often involve a reductive approach to the play. It ceases to be a changing experience in which subplot and main plot continuously interact with each other and with us (a dynamic reading) and becomes a static thing in which points of correspondence and divergence can be noted.

As the subplot unfolds, its similarities and differences from the main plot at all levels (narrative, character, theme, genre, tone) shape our response to the main plot and form an integral part of our experience of the play as a whole. Until the blinding of Gloucester the subplot lags behind the main plot, offering at each point an oblique, and even comic, reflection of it. Thereafter the subplot takes the lead, stepping into the uncharted darkness. However grim its story, we are to learn that no worst there is none; Lear's agonies, though also, perhaps, his joys, however transitory or delusive, will outtop Gloucester's.

The subplot is sometimes claimed to simplify the main plot, often converting what is archetypal or philosophical in the Lear plot into physical situations (blindness rather than madness), or morality play (the didactic journey of Gloucester and Poor Tom) or 'medieval' ritual (the fratricidal combat at the end). It seems to me that . . . the Gloucester plot makes the Lear plot look both odder and more normal, makes it more appalling and more affecting.

The subplot both unsettles and clarifies our understanding of the main plot. The fall of Lear and the rise of Edgar are not only two different ways of responding to adversity but also, as we shall see, and linked with that, two different kinds of drama. Shakespeare's detailed craftsmanship in forging links and contrasts and parallels, in exciting our interest and then in switching to another strand of the play, is matched by our sense of a generosity, almost a casualness, in the co-existence of the two stories. They are so different, however similar, in narrative line, in characters and in tone that their relationship is bound to generate a hundred impressions in us. Each goes its way—sometimes with urgent intention, not staying a jot; sometimes labouring and stumbling, inevitably,

but for no compelling reason—to Dover. . . .

No doubt for many in the original audience the effect was enhanced by the fact that they knew the broad development of one of Shakespeare's sources, *The True Chronicle History of King Leir* (though, as it turned out, that knowledge would mislead them), while the narrative of the Gloucester plot was unknown. Yoking the familiar story of Leir with the unfamiliar story of the Paphlagonian King is to put a wild card into the deck. As one story proceeds on its appointed way, modifying its original, another meets it in unpredictable counterpoint until, crushingly, Lear and Cordelia are denied the happiness that would have kept faith with the chronicles and, with qualified optimism, a new ruler emerges from the doom-laden underplot. The play's recurrent concern with recognition ('Do'st thou know me, fellow?' (I.4.26), 'Does any heere know me?' (I.4.223), 'Your name, fair Gentlewoman? (I.4.233), the whole relationship of Gloucester and Edgar, Lear's reunion with Cordelia, . . .) is matched by the fact that the two plots and their characters barely recognise each other. Crucially, in the great meetings between Lear and Edgar, and between Lear and Gloucester, there is ignorance, or shocking disparity between recognition and action, or recognition with heartbreaking indifference: 'I know thee well enough, thy name is Glouster' (IV.6.175). The characters in each story are as deeply mistaken about the significance of the events in the other as they are about the events in their own. Lear is not, as Edgar thinks, 'childed as I fathered' (Q1:III.6.108), for Gloucester's cruelty towards him springs not from malevolence but from ignorance. Similarly, Lear is mistaken when he says:

> 'for Glouster's bastard Son was kinder to his
>   Father,
> Then my Daughters got 'tweene the lawfull
>   sheets.'
>
> (IV.6.114)

The unpredictability of the relationship between the two stories is increased by the fact that *Lear* is, by contrast with, say, *Macbeth* and *Othello,* a play without plot, a causally determined sequence of events. Once Lear has been driven out into the storm and Edmund's intrigues have dispossessed Edgar, almost anything might happen and almost nothing actually does happen. In the background, conventional stage armies are conventionally assembled, but in the foreground of our attention, they are all fools and madmen, absorbing punishment, punchbags, not doers. Indeed, one important function of the subplot is to provide some narrative impulse for a play that would otherwise be devoid of incident for two or three acts. Lear has glimpsed the truth about his daughters before the end of Act I: 'O most small fault, / How ugly did'st thou in *Cordelia* shew?' (I.4.264-5). Once he knows that, he can experience deeper suffering and, possibly, widening circles of enlightenment, but the play does not allow him to act upon his knowledge. It leaves him to howl and to 'crawl toward death'. . . .

The unpredictability, the sense that each plot appears to take its own chances, does not mean that the two plots are not linked with extraordinary craftsmanship. In his first appearance we may think that Gloucester is no more significant than one of those bystanders commonly used at the beginning of plays to create an impression of the main characters before they enter. We cannot notice until the next scene the economy with which Shakespeare unites his two plots by making a principal figure in one an attendant lord in the household of another. Gloucester is created with exactness of implication both about his character and about his fate: 'It did alwayes seem so to us' (3). He is a member of the inner circle, one of the 'gilded Butterflies' who 'Talke of Court newes . . . Who looses and who wins', but he has been kept in the dark about Lear's change of plan and also, as we shall learn, about Lear's 'darker purpose'; he is rooted in a world of 'seemes' and 'appeares' (4); he is behind the times. Edmund, too, is an outsider: a bastard who has been 'out nine years' (31) and who is barely known to Kent. By the end of the scene Kent will have been banished and Cordelia, 'stranger'd with our oath', will have left for France. Almost all the characters of the play are, at some time and in some sense, outsiders, cut off from society by the cruelty of others or by their own folly or inhumanity. But we can have no premonition of the nightmare that awaits the genial courtier, polished in his manners and coarse in his attitudes, or of how soon the language of compliment that is used between the three men will be called into question as 'a glib and oylie Art'.

Gloucester, it seems, is no more than one called upon to do his master's bidding and attend the lords of France and Burgundy: one who will do 'to swell a progress, start a scene or two; / Advise the prince, . . .' But later, when, like Edmund, he is gathered up into the affairs of Regan and Cornwall and then sees the king's servant thrown into the stocks, he reveals a kindliness and prudence that make him more than 'an easy tool; / Deferential, glad to be of use, . . .' A personality is added to a role. This concern for others, whatever the motive, will be his undoing and it is appropriate that it is at this moment that he should begin his transition from comic dupe to tragic victim.

The relationship between the two plots is not only material but also causal and analogical. Causally, Edmund owes his promotion to the lust of Lear's daughters and to the ambition of one of their husbands, while Gloucester's downfall is caused by his

care for Lear and by his desire to keep a foot in that camp and, in its turn, provides the opportunity for Edgar's reconciliation with him. The blinding of Gloucester turns all hearts against those who have also wronged the king. Edgar's assumed madness precipitates Lear's final descent into the madness of obsession: 'Did'st thou give all to thy Daughters?' (III.4.48). Edgar's defeat of Edmund restores the possibility of the right governance of the country.

Analogically, the position is more complicated. Obviously, Lear is like Gloucester in that he suffers for failing to understand the true nature of his children. But he is also like (as well as unlike) Edgar in being mad, naked and an outcast, and he is also like Edmund in that he proposes a redistribution of property on unorthodox lines: 'Where Nature doth with merit challenge' (I.1.52). This last similarity is not farfetched. Edmund's blasphemous invocation of Nature as his goddess links him to Lear, who will call upon the same goddess in his great curse on Gonerill and who has already invoked 'the sacred radiance of the Sunne' (I.1.108). Equally, Edgar is like Cordelia a wronged child and sibling, though he is the victim of intrigue rather than of opportunity and his response ('which makes me bend' (Q1: III.6.107)) is the opposite of her inflexibility. Then again, on his first appearance, it is Edmund who is, for us, similar to Cordelia, the truth-teller. Am I the only person ever to have wondered, on first acquaintance with the play, whether Cordelia would turn out to be a villain, harbouring in her plainness 'more craft, and more corrupter ends'?

The subplot begins to seem not like a looking-glass but like Sir Epicure Mammon's hall of mirrors 'cut in more subtle angles to disperse/ And multiply the figures' [Ben Jonson, *The Alchemist*]. For example, it is often pointed out that whereas Lear's folly receives the mental punishment of madness (*ira furor brevis*), Gloucester's physical sin brings the physical and conventional retribution of blindness. That, however, is not a point to be stressed too heavily, since Gloucester feels fear and despair and the dullness of Lear's sight is not only metaphorical: 'Mine eyes are not o'th'best' (V.3.278). In both plots, as [Ann] Thompson puts it [in "who Sees Double in the Double Plot?"] ideas about distributive justice in families lead to ideas about distributive justice in society. Here again, there may be a difference between Lear's large expressions of concern for the poor naked wretches and Gloucester's practical attempt to relieve the poverty of one beggar; he says, 'Here take this purse' (IV.1.63), before launching into his reflections on distribution and excess. [William R.] Elton invites us to contrast the genuine supernatural of the thunder's 'rumble' with the fraudulent demons of Edgar's 'grumble' in the straw or Cordelia's fidelity to objective truth with Edgar's fidelity to subjective feeling [*King Lear and the Gods*]. It has also been suggested that, while Lear combines Gonerill's selfish wilfulness with Cordelia's courageous advocacy, Gloucester unites Edmund's lust with Edgar's pathos. And so one could go on. These correspondences arise, I think, as two rich plots take their ways; they are important but they do not really show us how our experience of one unfolding plot shapes our experience of the other.

It may be useful, therefore, to show how, in one scene, one aspect of the secondary plot shapes our experience of the play. In the play's second scene, what is this ridiculous business with a letter, and the terrible dispatch of it into Edmund's pocket, and the plan of 'Auricular assurance'? Is this plot going to be comic: Gloucester the foolish *senex* [old man], full of idle and fond superstitions, reflecting Lear's 'infirmity' and 'waywardnesse'? Gloucester's sudden taking against Edgar seems like a broadly comic parallel to Lear's taking against Cordelia, itself a decision so abrupt and startling as to be, at least potentially, comic. Like Lear, too, he believes that we exist and cease to be by the operation of the orbs. Once one knows the play, however, there are terrible premonitions peeping out everywhere in the comedy: 'Let's see: if it bee nothing, I shall not neede Spectacles' (34-5).

Edgar enters. Not merely is it a comedy, however serious, but the stage manager knows it is a comedy: 'Pat: he comes like the Catastrophe of the old Comedie: my Cue is villainous Melancholly with a sign like Tom o' Bedlam' (131). We are encouraged to see Edgar as a pasteboard figure in a low farce, to see him as we shall see him for a great deal of the play, someone who is plasticine in his brother's hands and then a gibbering idiot.

The comic tone of this scene offers relief from the intensity of the Lear scene (audiences always warm to Edmund at this point), throws it into relief, makes us aware of its comic potential, lulls us with the false promise of comfort (our hearts will not be wrung by this plot) and, as comedy always does, sharpens our intellectual awareness (of resemblances and differences). Later we shall know the serious issue of this fooling, when we know that our laughter at 'Nothing like the image, and horror of it' (172) was but a faint glimpse of the 'image of that horror' (V.3.263) of the apocalyptic ending. Edgar's later development needs to be read not only as the flowering of a personality but also as the passage from one genre to another or, perhaps better, to many others.

In the rest of Act I, which is essentially serious, the humour constantly shifts in emphasis and kind: the bluntness of Kent, the derisory subservience of Oswald (whom audiences love to hate), the farcical tripping of Oswald, the corrective satire of the Fool. In this play, comedy and tragedy are sometimes related by appalling juxtapositions but often by constant modulation and interpenetration.

The broadly humorous tone of the subplot is maintained through the spurious duel with its swirl of servants and torches, Edmund's hyperbolic description of his brother's devilry ('Mumbling of wicked charmes, conjuring the Moone') and his histrionic appeal to his father's attention ('Looke Sir, I bleed'). The comedy of Edgar as an evil magician points forward to his later association with devils. On the heath his talk will be full of devils; when his father enters with a torch, he cries, 'This is the foule Flibbertigibbet' (III.4.112); later he will again appear to Gloucester's mind's eye as 'The Fiend, the Fiend' (IV.6.79). This association of Edgar with the devil works partly by contrast; no man is less devilish than Edmund's 'Brother Noble' (I.2.176) with his 'foolish honestie' (I.2.178). But there is another, darker dimension to it that becomes apparent in the storm scenes.

As the links between the two plots multiply, the subplot becomes ever more serious, its humour ever darker. We can no longer enjoy Edmund's satirical hyperbole, which now itself seems 'most savage and unnaturall' (III.3.7), for we know how truly appalling are the events to which he is reacting. . . . From now on, Edmund and his words do not, on the whole, engage our interest. The banality of evil is in his language. We might contrast his resounding boast at the halfway point ('The yonger rises, when the old doth fall' (III.3.25)) with the puzzled and puzzling words with which his brother closes the play:

> The oldest hath borne most: we that are
>   yong
> Shall never see so much, nor live so long.
>   (V.3.324)

Edgar has a bruised sense of the limitations of the young and of the suffering implicit in the fall of the old; his lines respond to the experience we have lived through. Edmund's words reverb a hollowness. This is a degeneration not merely from the braggadocio of his first soliloquy but from its quieter depths. There even his use of 'us' was pregnant: 'Why brand they us/ With Base?' Not a merely self-pitying 'me', but a compassionate and angry 'us'. Edmund knows that there is a whole 'tribe' of people like him. Lear will need a storm to know that he has taken too little care of the poor naked wretches, but Edmund experiences fellow-feeling or solidarity already. There is self-pity here and selfishness too but, implicitly, other possibilities, some ground from which, at the end, he can mean to do good.

Only in the corners and implications of the play do we continue to find an Edmund who is more than an appetite for power and an object of desire. When, with the blinding, the Lear plot reaches out to appropriate the Gloucester plot, Edmund is, in a sense, banished from his own plot. Cornwall says to him: 'the revenges wee are bound to take uppon your Traitorous father, are not fit for your beholding' (III.7.7). Later, Regan says:

> *Edmund,* I thinke, is gone
> In pitty of his misery, to dispatch
> His nighted life: Moreover to descry
> The strength o'th'Enemy.
>
> (IV.5.11)

We do not know whether we discern, through the disingenuousness of Cornwall and his wife, the lineaments of pity.

As Edmund withers, Edgar grows in interest. The stages of his dark journey of the imagination to Dover with his father are marked by many different kinds of comedy from the black farce of the 'fall' from the cliff-top to the chillingly boisterous Mummerzett [a pseudo-rastic dialect] with which Oswald is dispatched, the cheerful melodrama of Edgar's description of the fiend with a thousand noses, and the Beckettian comedy of Lear's boots. Edgar's failure to reveal himself to his father is as comically cruel as Launcelot Gobbo's [in *The Merchant of Venice*]. The comedy does not trivialize, diminish or attempt to dispel human suffering. In some ways it throws it into relief. But it does make us alert to see the absurdity inherent in it and in the pathos of man's punily fist-shaking reactions to it:

> I will do such things,
> What they are yet, I know not, but they
>   shalbe
> The terrors of the earth?
>
> (II.4.278)

The comedy offers us also, as does his disguise to Edgar, a relief for our feelings and even a way of concealing them. But our own laughter may also seem to us outrageous and forbidden; King Lear persuades us of the unplumbed darkness of the human mind not least by showing us the unpredictability and strangeness of our own reactions. A blind old man attempts to commit suicide: we laugh. A man is killed: we laugh. The king is mad: we laugh. It's a mad world, my masters, and a frightening one. The laughing, leering faces of [the French painter Honoré] Daumier rise, unbidden, in my mind.

The comic incongruities of the subplot and its chameleon transformations from farce to melodrama, from domestic tragedy to surrealism, are linked to the implausibility of which it has frequently been accused. How can a father believe that one of his sons would write an incriminating letter to the other while they are living in the same house? Why does Edgar, when on the run, return to the neighbourhood of his father's house? Why does he adopt so many bizarre impersonations? Why does he not reveal himself to his father? . . . Realistic answers to these questions are likely to be helpful in each case and unsatisfing for the totality. The improbabilities of this plot arise from the madness of its world and also from the multiplicity of its dramatic genres; the stuff of many of these genres is, typically, disguise or 'business' with letters.

To think about the impact of implausibility and lunacy it will be helpful to look at a climax where Lear, Gloucester and Edgar come together: all three marry in an instant. Edgar's great cry 'Fathom, and halfe, Fathom and halfe; poore *Tom!*' (III.4.37) is not in the Quarto. It is part of the Folio's systematic tendency to build up the character of Edgar. Edgar's cry here from within the hut, the voice of the storm and of someone wrecked in it, and, therefore, of the tempest in Lear's mind, is chilling. The Fool identifies him straightaway as a 'spirit'. His appearance as the dispossessed madman that Lear has dreaded becoming, with the bitter irony of 'Humh, goe to thy bed and warme thee' (46), turns the King's wits. Lear's obsession now governs him: 'Did'st thou give all to thy Daughters?' (48). The moment is unbearably moving and is also comically grotesque: 'Nay, he reserv'd a Blanket, else we had bin all sham'd' (64). Primal nakedness and civilized prudery about nudity are jarred together. We measure simultaneously the artifice of society and the distance the great king has travelled towards the merely animal. It is a further savage irony that it is the harmless Edgar who pushes Lear over the cliff. The harmless edgar is the most deadly of the play's characters: the murderer of Oswald, the slayer of his brother, the lethal narrator to his father.

Poor Tom makes Lear seem both odder, because Lear is genuinely mad, and relatively normal; we can understand how Lear has been brought to this condition, but why should Edgar have adopted this disguise and why does he enter upon it so wholeheartedly and with, apparently, such appalling indifference for the consequences to others? Why are his speeches about lust and devils so long, so vigorous, so vile? Surely they far exceed the demands of the part he needs to play. In the energy of these speeches, their driving rhythms, their disgusted relish of lubricity, we feel, I think, some release for Edgar and for ourselves. This is the darkness in all of us, even in the best of us. Children and actors know the freedom and confidence and excitement that come from working with a mask. The role of unaccommodated man, which is Edgar's mode of accommodation to this harsh world, protects him but also lays him bare. His nakedness is, and is not, the thing itself; it is both mask and revelation. At some level he knows about 'the sulphurous pit; burning, scalding', and this knowledge may be part of what fits him to be king. . . .

At this profound moment the plots are linked not only by cause but by analogy (and, of course, disanalogy). We have seen Lear as Edmund and still see him as Gloucester; now we see him, he sees himself, as a reflection of Edgar: the demented outcast. Consideration of Edgar's nakedness leads Lear to his insight into the nature of man: 'Unaccommodated man, is no more but such a poore, bare, forked Animall as thou art' (103). This insight, like his later insights into injustice and hypocrisy, is not in itself extraordinary. What makes it extraordinary is the intensity of the language and the fact that it occurs to this man in whom absolute power has given way to absolute need; it is not an intellectual idea but the vision of the whole man. Lear now treats Edgar as his philosopher; the man who has been through the sharpest of all adversities and who expresses in his own body the nature of man must know the cause of thunder and of its moral equivalents, madness and the hard-heartedness of daughters.

The presence of Gloucester makes this a great non-recognition scene as moving as the reconciliation between Lear and Cordelia. If Edgar recognises his father, he does not know the truth about his conduct; Gloucester does not recognise his son and is still misled about his nature; Lear recognises neither of them; no-one recognises Kent. It is the world's midnight, full of 'absence, darknesse, death; things which are not'. In the darkness Gloucester sees: 'Our flesh and blood, my Lord, is grown so vilde, that it doth hate what gets it' (142-3). But his sight is as dull as Lear's. He does not see his loving son, heart-broken: 'Poore Tom's a cold' (144). Like Lear, 'I am almost mad my selfe' (163). At the end he cares for Edgar without recognising him: 'In fellow there, into th' Hovel; keepe thee warm' (171). In its concern for the anonymous other, outcast by madness, it is as touching as Lear's 'Come, let's in all' (172). Edgar has precipitated not only madness but also, through the insight he provokes into the condition of man, fellow feeling.

From now until the end of the play, Edgar will comment frequently, almost like a chorus, upon his own situation or that of others. His continual, and sometimes long-winded, reflections upon his experience can make him seem, despite his lively lunacy, rather priggish. Sometimes his soliloquies seem too naively optimistic or too simple to capture the bitterness and complexity of what we see. . . . Edgar is whistling in the dark; his words demonstrate the inadequacy of language in the face of experience—this experience, which is entirely the creation of words. His use of words to define and contain 'the horror, the horror'

is part of his admirable resilience and perseverance. The words in which he represents his situation to himself are as important in his life's struggle as the masks he wears to meet the faces that he meets.

Through his eyes, untainted by guilt and unclouded by heroics, we can measure the bizarreness of what we see and hear:

> My teares begin to take his part so much,
> They marre my counterfetting.
>
> (III.6.59)

> I would not take this from report,
> It is, and my heart breakes as it.
>
> (IV.6.139)

> O matter, and impertinency mix'd
> Reason in Madnesse.
>
> (IV.6.172)

Most breathtaking of all in its simple enormity is his explanation of his extraordinary attempt to cure his father of his suicidal urge:

> Why do I trifle thus with his dispaire,
> Is done to cure it.
>
> (IV.6.33)

Seldom can a confidence have seemed so unconvincing. We contrast this . . . indirection with Cordelia's straightforwardly loving treatment of Lear and we see to what indirect and crooked paths even a cheerful and frank rationalist (such as the Edgar of his first scene; such as ourselves?) may be driven by the wickedness of the world. It can seem that Edgar is a glutton for his father's punishment, as though

> he hates him
> That would upon the wracke of this tough
>   world
> Stretch him out longer.

It is too easy to say that this concern to preserve his father from suicide is prompted by religious considerations. His attitude towards the prospect of his own death is given by his words to Albany:

> (O our lives sweetnesse,
> That we the paine of death would hourely
>   dye,
> Rather than die at once!)
>
> (V.3.183)

He may even begin to seem like the fiends who fill his conversation and imagination in Acts III and IV. Edgar's warped deeds and words are the converse of, and the necessary response to, the facile words of Gonerill and Regan. Edgar's speeches and conduct are forced from him by the weight of the sad time. In such a time, to speak and act as one feels and as one needs to do in order to survive is to appear a villain and a fool.

On the other hand, Edgar's longer reflections ('When we our betters see bearing our woes (Q1, not in F: III.6.100-13); 'Yet better thus, and knowne to be contemn'd (IV.1.1-9); 'By nursing them my Lord' (V.3.180-220)) seem oddly inadequate to the situations they describe or by which they are provoked. When Lear's words fail to rise to the situation, their failure is transparent; he is reduced to howls or iterations; his aphasia is magniloquence. But the thinness of Edgar's language is the thinness of ours; in the face of the experience that is King Lear we feel that he feels as inadequate as we do. In both cases, Shakespeare's own rhetoric, which creates both the experiences and the inability of the characters to match them with words, is triumphant. . . .

Edgar's imperative . . . is survival: 'Whiles I may 'scape/ I will preserve myselfe' (II.3.5). His method . . . is disguise: as Poor Tom, as the man who goes to the foot of the cliff to rescue Gloucester, as the bumpkin who kills Oswald, as the messenger to Oswald and as the disguised challenger of Edmund. (To this list we might add, parenthetically, his two appearances as a fiend: in Edmund's description of him to Gloucester at the time of his flight and in his own description of Gloucester's cliff-top companion.) His most effective disguise is to be quite openly part of the heath on which he lives; his language is full of ford and whirlpool, of bog and guagmire, of the hawthorn through which the cold wind blows. . . .

Cordelia told the truth openly. Defenceless, she has 'nothing'; she has death. Edgar knows that as himself he is nothing. Only by playing Poor Tom, a part far less openly heroic than Cordelia's, can he be 'something'. To be something, to be able to say 'come on' (V.2.11), is not much, but it may be another quality that fits him to be king.

Although, as he leads his blind father around in Acts IV and V, he may seem to be worse than ever he was, we can also feel that his curve of fortune is beginning to rise. For one thing, he knows the truth about his father. (He would have known it earlier if he had listened: 'I had a Sonne,/ Now out-law'd from my blood; he sought my life' (III.4.163). But children rarely hear what their fathers are saying.) For another, when Gloucester is puzzled about Edgar's changing voice or Edgar calls him 'father', we sense a growing bond between the two. Also, he is now wearing some clothes.

He has learnt to adapt. . . . But he has done so without losing [the] ability to respond to the sufferings of others: 'Who, by the Art of knowne and feeling sorrowes,/ Am pregnant to good pitty' (V.6.219). Edgar unites the plighted cunning of the villains with the human compassion of the good; by sacrificing his identity and by concealing his tears he safeguards his life and, perhaps, some part of his personality. He can emerge in the last scene, triumphant in arms, authoritative and humble. But to bend, however necessary, is to be, to some degree, warped. We sense this deviation from normal human decency in the impassioned play-acting of his mad scenes, in the bizarre treatment of his father, in his own knowledge that he maintained his disguise too long ('Never (O fault!) reveal'd my selfe unto him' (V.3.191)), and in the unyielding judgements he makes as an exchange of charity with his dying brother.

Like history, *King Lear* repeats itself first as tragedy and then as farce. The subplot's comic, domestic, bizarre and didactic transformations of the main plot throw that into relief, show us more clearly what it is, but they also indicate the absurdity latent in the extremism of tragedy. Implausibility or melodrama are *placed*, incorporated into the strengths of the play. The play gives us two outcomes. We that are young may draw some fragile comfort from the story of Edgar, who found 'the happy hollow of a tree' (II.3.2). Bent, he strengthened, warped by his experience, he survives. The cheerful and charming Edgar of his first scene was a passive victim. Now he has killed his father by accident and, in killing his brother, has committed the act that has the primal eldest curse upon it. But he is the man best fitted to be king. He has done what we all need to do: obeyed the weight of the sad time.

LANGUAGE AND IMAGERY

With regard to the style of *King Lear*, Nicholas Brooke has remarked on different rhythms in the dramatic verse. Sometimes these rhythms are broken up and sometimes they are sustained, he notes, but they are always directly related to the alternating crescendos and modulations in the play's dramatic action. Emily W. Leider has called attention to the alternating pattern of plain speech and flattery in *King Lear*, focusing on the connections between words and action in such characters as Lear, Kent, and Cordelia. **George W. Williams** examines the correlation between the external storm on the heath and the storm raging within Lear's mind.

The metaphor of the storm is at the heart of *King Lear*, Williams argues: the warring elements reflect divisions in the family as well as in the kingdom, and the storm represents the process of purgation that Lear must endure. When the king invokes the full fury of the storm in III.ii.1-9 and 14-24, Williams contends, he is calling for the total annihilation of creation. Like Williams, **John C. McCloskey** emphasizes the "unnaturalness" of nature in *King Lear*. McCloskey views the *Lear* world as wild and ferocious, devoid of values and order. He sees a reflection of this collapse into moral disorder in the increasing intensity of animal imagery—early references to animals are relatively nonviolent, but as Lear's suffering deepens they become vicious, even monstrous.

The play's repeated references to "nature" are explored by Northrop Frye and discussed by Nicholas Brooke and G. Wilson Knight. Like William Empson, Frye also evaluates the key-word "fool." Empson provides a detailed explanation of the different ways this word is used throughout the play and applied to many of its characters. Frye, too, remarks that the word "fool" is linked with every virtuous person in *King Lear*, and he further notes its association with victimization through the agency of mysterious, impersonal forces. The importance of the word "nothing" has been pointed out by both Brooke and Frye. Brooke particularly calls attention to the opposition of "nothing" and opulence or luxury. Frye, however, argues that the word variously resonates with such concepts as annihilation of identity and the enigmatic nature of love and loyalty.

George W. Williams

SOURCE: "The Poetry of the Storm in *King Lear*," in *Shakespeare Quarterly*, Vol. II, No. 1, January, 1951, pp. 57-71.

[*Williams focuses on Act III, scene ii of* Lear, *pointing out the correspondence of the storm with Lear's disordered mind, disrupted families, and the divided kingdom. The storm has a restorative effect on Lear, the critic declares, and he must live through it in order "to be cured of evil." Williams reads the language of Lear's speeches evoking the destructive elements in terms of the Old Testament flood and the New Testament concept of the Last Judgment. He also demonstrates the relation between images of animals and warring elements, harsh diction, and the theme of disordered nature.*]

The lines opening the second scene of Act Three of *King Lear,* comprising the king's remarks on the storm, often quoted and admired, and admittedly some of the most important in the play, have never been examined in detail. They are, however, climactic in the play and fundamental to the character of the king, and they exhibit that combination of dramatic and poetic genius which one expects to find in Shakespeare in critical passages. They are, in short, "the very heart of the organism" [G. Wilson knight in *The Shakespearean Tempest*]. The late Harley Granville-

Barker has pointed out [in *A Companion to Shakespeare Studies*] the fusion of the storm in nature and the storm in the protagonist:

Lear—striving (we are given the hint) " . . . in his little world of man to outscorn the to-and-fro-conflicting wind and rain," matching himself against the storm, echoing it in defying it—becomes for us, without ceasing to be himself, a very image of it. He creates it dramatically; but not by detached description, which would merely let us see it through his eyes. He is endued, and he endues, us, with the very spirit of it. He, for the crucial moment, is at one with it, and we with him, and he is to us Lear and the storm too.

This dramatic presentation of the storm without identified and equated with the storm within and, it may be added, with the disruption in the kingdom, requires writing of the highest intensity.

The first speech in the second scene is Lear's (III. ii. 1-9). It is the crowning speech of the first part of the play—in a sense the keystone. Only a few lines later, Lear says, "My wits begin to turn." His speeches in scene ii show the last traces of his already vanishing sanity, and in scene iv he is "far gone, far gone." His prayer in scene iv (28-36) concluding:

Take physic, pomp;
Expose thyself to feel what wretches feel,
That thou mayst shake the superflux to them
And show the heavens more just

is the first step in the regenerative process, showing as it does a sympathy towards man and an incipient willingness to admit an error, but it is also the last sane utterance, if not indeed an expression of a mentality already deranged, and it follows the height of the storm.

The storm of the Third Act is prepared for with the greatest care. At the conclusion of the Second Act there are several references to its approach.

Cornwall. Let us withdraw; 'twill be a storm. (290)
Gloucester. Alack, the night comes on, and the bleak winds
Do sorely ruffle. For many miles about
There's scarce a bush. (303-305)
Regan. Shut up your doors. (307)
Cornwall. Shut up your doors, my lord; 'tis a wild night.
My Regan counsels well. Come out o' th' storm. (311-312)

In scene i of Act Three the clouds continue to gather.

Kent. Who's there, besides foul weather?

Gentleman. One minded like the weather,
  most unquietly.

Kent. I know you. Where's the king?

Gentleman. Contending with the fretful
  elements;

Bids the wind blow the earth into the sea,

Or swell the curled waters 'bove the main,

That things might change or cease; tears his
  white hair,

Which the impetuous blasts, with eyeless
  rage,

Catch in their fury and make nothing of;

Strives in his little world of man to outscorn

The to-and-fro-conflicting wind and rain.

This night, wherein the cub-drawn bear
  would couch,

The lion and the belly-pinched wolf

Keep their fur dry, unbonneted he runs,

And bids what will take all. (1-15)

Kent. Fie on this storm! (49)

This descriptive speech is extremely important to the great storm speech of the following scene, for it suggests in advance the wildness of the night (not realized fully until it appears in Lear), it anticipates the themes he is to develop (the violence of the wind and water, destruction and annihilation), and it emphasizes significantly the unnaturalness of nature. The animal imagery is here, as typically in Lear, very revealing: the implication is clear that the animals mentioned in this passage—wild, ravening, and scavenging at best and here urged by abnormal causes to a state beyond their characteristic wildness—are reacting more reasonably to the storm than is the king. Edgar's lines, "False of heart, light of ear, bloody of hand; hog in sloth, fox in stealth, wolf in greediness, dog in madness, lion in prey" (III. iv. 95-97), may serve as a useful gloss to these allusions. Thus the lion is not the royal figure (is without the majesty and ceremony of kingship) so much as he is the beast of prey; the wolf, by nature greedy, is *belly-pinched,* almost starving; and the bear dam, having nursed her cubs—who like Lear's daughters have taken all from her and yet clamor for more—hungers to feed herself and them. An association is evidently intended. These wild animals in spite of their roughness are, after all, out of the weather under cover from the storm in the same way that Lear's daughters have found shelter from its violence, closing their doors to him as they went. Lear himself points the significance of these references to wild animality in his earlier lines:

No, rather I abjure all roofs, and choose

To wage against the enmity o' th' air,

To be a comrade with the wolf and owl—

Necessity's sharp pinch!

(II. iv. 211-214)

The wolf, symbol of greed, and the owl, of malevolence,

are the evil companions the king expects to meet on the heath. Actually even the most irrational animals have left the barren heath to seek protection, while the king, *unbonneted,* and abandoned by every creature, stands alone against animal nature, human nature, and, as he discovers, cosmic nature, attended only by the pricking wisdom of the Fool.

The unnaturalness and wildness of nature are further indicated in the very winds and seas themselves, which are urged to reverse the order of things prescribed in the creation of the world: "God said againe, Let the waters under the heauen bee gathered into one place, and let the drie land appeare: and it was so" [Genesis i. 9-10]. But the reversion and madness of the elements are equated with the chaotic condition of the king at odds with himself and are described in terms of human physiology to heighten the identification. The *impetuous blasts* are in a state of *eyeless rage* just as Lear is in *high rage;* the image of sight instantly recalls the frequent references to Lear's spiritual blindness and to Gloucester's physical blindness. The correspondence between Lear and the world, the microcosm and the macrocosm, is indicated in the line "striving in his little world of man" and affirmed by Gloucester: "O ruin'd piece of nature! this great world/Shall so wear out to naught" (IV. vi. 137). This anthropomorphic description of the storm winds emphasizes another parallel which is inherent in the Lear-cosmos relation. The correspondence between the microcosm and the macrocosm, macrocosmic violence in terms of the microcosm, suggests additional and amplifying correspondences; the kingdom and the family, the body politic and the body domestic, are caught up in this mesh of interlocking connotations. That these correspondences form an intended extension of relevance Gloucester explains: "These late eclipses in the sun and moon portend no good to us. Though the wisdom of nature can reason it thus and thus, yet nature finds itself scourg'd by the sequent effects. . . . Love cools, friendship falls off, brothers divide. In cities mutinies; in countries, discord; in palaces, treason; and the bond crack'd 'twixt son and father. . . . We have seen the best of our time. Machinations, hollowness, treachery, and all ruinous disorders follow us disquietly to our graves" (I. ii. 112-125). The assimilation of the body politic into the equations between the body domestic or the family, the microcosm, and the macrocosm is suggested in the imagery borrowed from political warfare describing military operations: *to-and-fro-conflicting* and

But yet I call you [elements] servile
  ministers,

That will with two pernicious daughters join

Your high-engender'd battles 'gainst a head

So old and white as this!

(III. ii. 21-24)

The eclipses, the jarring elements, the divided kingdom, the disordered family, the demented Lear are firmly linked together in the system of correspondences. At the same time, however, it must be noted that the storm, a perversion of nature, is yet disorder within order and actually presupposes an order. "The storm suggests, on one level, the victory of a nature hostile to humanity; yet the storm is regularly regarded as a convulsion of nature—a disorder which interferes with but does not destroy an essential order which still *is*. There is chaos in the world; but tragedy sees chaos in perspective; it measures chaos by order. Chaos is irreparable only when it is mistaken for order; when it is felt as disorder, there is still hope. . . . .

The tragic world is a kind of chaos: the disorder within the soul is projected into the larger world" [R. B. Heilman, *This Great Stage*]. The storm is thus the disorder or purgative necessary to the order or health of the king. It can only be meaningful if taken in this sense and understood to be a necessary evil through which he must live so as to be cured of evil.

In the first nine lines of scene ii the storm and the style rise to their greatest pitch. It is in fact only through the rise in the style that the audience comes to feel the full extent of the storm. In these lines Shakespeare reaches the point for which he has been preparing in the preceding two scenes. The report which the Gentleman makes in scene i first announces the condition of the king, at war with himself and the elements. This is followed by a digression of thirty-five lines during which the conversation shifts to the fortunes of Cordelia and the activities of the British dukes. Kent recalls the storm hastily before his exit and immediately in the person of the king it breaks in full fury.

> Blow, winds, and crack your cheeks! rage!
>   blow!
> You cataracts and hurricanoes, spout
> Till you have drench'd our steeples, drown'd
>   the cocks!
> You sulph'rous and thought-executing fires,
> Vaunt couriers to oak-cleaving thunderbolts,
> Singe my white head! And thou, all-shaking
>   thunder,
> Strike flat the thick rotundity o' th' world,
> Crack Nature's moulds, all germains spill at
>   once,
> That make ingrateful man!

The phonetics in these lines is especially remarkable. Most notable is the frequency of fricatives and stops in clusters of onomatopoetic vernacular words chosen to suggest the roughness and harshness of the weather:

> blow, crack, cheek, blow, cataract, spout, drench'd,

steeples, drown'd, cocks, thought-executing, oak-cleaving thunderbolts, singe, shaking thunder, strike (in the Qq, *smite*), thick, crack, spill, make.

The pattern of nasals—

> winds, hurricanoes, drench'd, drown'd, vaunt, cleaving thunder, singe, thunder, rotundity, nature's moulds, germains, make, ingrateful man—

and the pattern of the sibilants—

> winds, cheeks, cataracts, hurricanoes, spout, steeples, cocks, sulph'rous, executing, fires, couriers, bolts, singe, shaking, strike (in the Qq, *smite*), nature's moulds, germains, spill, once—

while not so spectacular are equally present. The combination of a low vowel with a nasal, honored from classical times, occurs most effectively in

> *Vaunt*-couriers to oak-cleaving *thund*erbolts
> Singe my white head! And thou, all-shaking
>   *thund*er,
> Strike flat the thick *rotund*ity o' th' world.

Here the *-und-* group links the three lines inextricably together, providing the equivalent of the continued rumbling of thunder. But after the hissing, the crashing, and the thundering, the passage comes to rest as far as that is possible on the liquids, *moulds, all, spill, ingrateful.* . . .

It is not inappropriate to examine the relationship of the king and the elements at this point as it is revealed in these nine lines and in the following eleven. This tremendous nine-line speech can not be regarded as an accurate though frenzied meteorological report on the state of the weather. Such has already been given by the two faithful retainers at the opening of the Act. These lines are not the statement of one resigned to his fate, for the king is not yet in the purgative stage. If they are regarded as a prayer to the great gods for retribution, serious difficulties are encountered in resolving the imprecations hurled at the elements in the second part of the speech, following the lines of the Fool, and including "I tax you not, you elements, with unkindness. . . ." and "But yet I call you servile ministers. . . ." If these lines again form a prayer they differ strikingly from the more easily recognized prayers, "O heavens, if you do love old men" and "Poor naked wretches." They are in fact much closer to the curses of barrenness which they parallel in thought as well as in tone and mood. The Gentleman explains finally the nature of the king's speech: "Bids the wind blow the earth into the sea,/ Or swell the curled waters 'bove the main" (III. i. 5-6). This bidding can only be equivalent to the command of the king, as when he says: "bid them

[Regan and Cornwall] come forth and hear me,/ Or at their chamber-door I'll beat the drum/ Till it cry death to sleep" (II. iv. 118-120). These wild lines then must be understood as direct orders to the winds, the waves, the thunder, and the lightning. Such an interpretation accords well with what has been seen of the character of the king. The commands of the first nine lines recall those given throughout the earlier part of the play; they are in the same vein. King Lear regards himself still as every inch a king, and shouting his orders to his subordinates, he reveals clearly his proud, arrogant, and stubborn authority. The elements are Lear's servants. But he has given to them, as to Cordelia, Kent, and the Fool, nothing. Here at last the reckoning is made: nothing comes of nothing. From these unfee'd servants Lear no longer receives toadying flattery, he no longer receives even obedience. To a royal philosophy of *quid pro quo* (or *quid pro nihilo*) [something for something (or something for nothing)], the basis of Lear's erroneous sense of values, comes the awakening: "You owe me no subscription." *Nihil pro nihilo* [nothing for nothing]. The first lines of the speech command general destruction in which Lear's white head must perforce be singed. The second group of eleven lines is anti-climactic; the destruction does not occur. The tempest continues, however, to beat down on Lear's unprotected head. The realization develops that the elements are no longer his servants; they are in fact his masters, now servilely and venally colleagued with his daughters. He is no longer a king. He discovers at this moment when the elements do not obey him that they, allies of his ungrateful daughters, have also thrown off the imperial yoke. Instead of responding to his commands immediately, as he remembers later, they turn on him. "When the rain came to wet me once and the wind to make me chatter; when the thunder would not peace at my bidding; there I found 'em, there I smelt 'em out" (IV. vi. 102-105). It is the remarks of the Fool between the two sections of the speech that make this clear: "O nuncle, court holy-water in a dry house is better than this rainwater out o' door." That is to say, voluntary submission to your rebelling daughters is to be preferred to enforced submission to the rebelling of nature, which evidently has no longer any intention of obeying you.

Furthermore, in giving these orders to the elements, Lear is acting in conformity and parallel with Roman and Celtic tradition. These mythologies both state the ancient position of the king as the creator of the weather, especially of the stormy weather. Numa, an early king of Rome, for classical precedent, is recorded to have been able to call on the elements at will. An interesting expression of this tradition is seen earlier in Edmund's deception of his father: "I told him the revenging gods/ 'Gainst parricides did all their thunders bend" (II. i. 47-48). Though Edmund utters this threat as a means of inciting his father's superstitious nature to action against Edgar, it becomes a "bloody instruction" which with typical Shakespearian irony returns to plague him. Edmund, the parricide, like Lear's daughters, is finally stricken down by the forces that league with the gods. Paradoxically, it is his own head which is eventually "singed."

This power of calling on the thunderbolt, which is granted to the king, exalts him to a position equal to that of Jupiter and identifies him with the Thunderer, the Rain-god, and the Hurler of the Lightnings. As Gloucester says, "He holp the heavens to rain" (III. vii. 62). The king-god Lear demands from the heavens, as is his right, a storm, the violence of which can be paralleled only by the turbid violence of his own mind.

The extent of the storm must be absolute and final. This is made clear in the imagery first of *cataracts* and *hurricanoes* in the quotation. The waters loosed on the land are to be poured from the heavens and raised from the deeps: are to be heavenly and earthly. . . . *Cataracts* are descending waters, of the heavens, and *hurricanoes* are rising waters, of the earth.

By pouring down, the cataracts of heaven will cause the steeples to drink: by inundation the rising waters of the sea will cover the cocks. Lear orders a return of the Hebraic deluge with a covering of the land by the water, a return to a state of near chaos, of elemental confusion. The works of man are to be destroyed and even the works of God are to be annihilated. The words of Jehovah announcing the Flood before the building of the ark similarly describe the destruction of His own work: "And I, Beholde, I will bring a flood of waters upon the earth to destroy all flesh, wherein is the breath of life, from under the heauen: and everything that is in the earth shall perish" (Genesis vi. 17).

As the imagery of cataracts and hurricanes has evoked connotations of destruction comparable to that at the time of the Deluge, so the concluding images suggests the ruin of the Last Judgment. Bolts of thunder and lightning are to flatten out the roundness of the earth, Nature's moulds are to be cracked and shattered until they are useless, all germains are to be spilled. Such imagery can indicate only eschatological destruction. [A. C.] Bradley has suggested [in his *Shakespearean Tragedy*] that the theme of the latter day may have been in Shakespeare's mind during the writing of this play, and Lear himself threatens to do undescribable things, the "terrors of the earth." Bradley cites specifically the passages in Matthew and Mark generally titled "the little apocalypse," and it may not be irrelevant to point out that in both these scriptural predictions there are descriptions of the time of the Final Judgment which would set in within the time scheme of this play: "the brother shall deliuer the brother to death, and the father the sonne, and the children shall rise against their parents and shall cause them to die" (Mark xiii. 12). It is not improbable in the light of the importance of the themes of justice and injustice in the play that Shakespeare was thinking in the king's hectic speech in terms of the Day of Judgment when justice shall finally be accomplished in the world. . . .

The reason for this mad ruin is not hard to find: *ingrateful man.* This is a destruction which like the Noachic Deluge and the Final Judgment is sent as a punishment for filial ingratitude, to overcome all "unnaturalness between the child and the parent." Its thunderbolts must destroy and abrogate utterly; its lightnings must eracinate all germens lest they, grown up sinners and ingrates like Goneril and Regan, might make another generation of ingrateful creatures.

Lear's command to Nature in these tremendous lines is for complete destruction and primordial chaos. Miss [Edith] Sitwell has pointed out [in *"King Lear," Atlantic monthly,* May 1950] that "Lear . . . in his prayer to Nature to kill the sources of life in his daughters, struck at the very heart of Nature, disturbing that lake of Darknesse, the original chaos from which all being arose." In his command he wills that all creation tumble again into that lake of chaos in a cataclysmic eruption with the characteristics at once of the original Deluge and of the "abomination of desolation" at the Latter Day.

John C. McCloskey

SOURCE: "The Emotive Use of Animal Imagery in *King Lear*," in *Shakespeare Quarterly,* Vol. 13, No. 3, Summer, 1962, pp. 321-25.

[*McCloskey examines the association of images from the world of "animals, insects, and the more repulsive denizens" of the seas with the shifts in Lear's emotions. The king's selfishness and moral blindness, together with his inability to understand others, lead him into a world of disordered nature, the critic maintains. McCloskey notes that as Lear moves from resentment in Act I to indignation in Act II, and, finally, rage in Act III, the imagery changes to reflect the increasing intensity of his moods and to underscore the theme of unnaturalness.*]

It has been said that we must accept the passionate, irrational King Lear, with his plan for dividing his kingdom, and the devoted yet strangely reticent Cordelia as data not to be inquired into but taken on poetic faith. Yet Lear's "retirement" is a sensible thing in itself. What makes it fraught with tragedy is his misreading of human nature. Had all his children been

like Cordelia, things might have turned out well. And here is the irony—that what is sensible in itself is made a foolish, senseless thing to do by the characters of those involved. Or to put it another way, imperfect, selfish human nature again wrecks ideals.

Consider that Lear is a king who loves his daughters and out of his egoism expects love in return, a king who believes simply that generosity begets gratitude, that children revere and honor their parents, that obedience is of the nature of the filial relation. A king who "hath ever but slenderly known himself", he has not known his courtiers either, for example, Kent. A king who is curiously naive in the ways of human nature, who has no subtlety in human relations, who does not even suspect that power may corrupt and that old age rendered helpless is a thing for contempt. A king who is not wise enough to protect himself but of his own volition throws himself upon the untender mercies of the evil, whom he does not even recognize as evil.

Yet Lear embodies the idealism of fatherly love as Cordelia and Edgar are emblems of filial devotion, Kent of loyal service, the Fool of conscience, and France of true love. But Lear's idealism is tainted by evil, by the moral corruption of self-deluding egoism, while the idealism of the others is not, and the proper end for Lear is, therefore, tragic disaster.

In the chaotic and hostile world into which Lear is precipitated by his acts of misjudgment, self-will, and wrath, the tragic disaster toward which he proceeds and which culminates in madness and death in a world against which he cannot contend, a world wild and ferocious, a world of negated values, moral blindness, and unnaturalness, is expressed to a remarkable degree by images from the padding, stalking, creeping, crawling, slithering world of animals, insects, and the more repulsive denizens of the waters, and the images are evoked to express or to intensify his anger, rejection, indignation, wrath, and vengeance.

The imagery of the lower animals, which suggests the moral derangement of the world in which Lear has hitherto thought himself secure, begins with the cooling of his reception in Goneril's home, when her servant Oswald neglects to answer Lear's question as to the whereabouts of his daughter. This breach of decorum and respect and reverence for authority stirs a mild resentment in Lear, the first stage of the emotional turmoil which brings him at length to madness. His resentment and, perhaps, a touch of proper contempt, the genesis of which is Lear's instinctive awareness of the social disparity between his kingly state and the lowly status of a servant, are expressed in his epithet "mongrel", an image general, colorless, and uncommitted, since the offence is not at the moment identifiable with the attitude of the daughters or the moral problem of the play. When Oswald describes Lear as not the king but "My lady's father", Lear's indignation is spurred, and the imagery becomes more intense and particularized in its connotative derogation as "whoreson dog" and "cur". It is significant that Lear thinks in terms of such lowly, though commonplace images, since he has himself already entered upon his own descent, with the result that eventually his state is reduced as low, in the storm scene on the heath particularly, as that of the animal world in terms of the imagery of which his mind constitutionally reacts.

From the evocation of mere resentment and indignation the imagery becomes grimmer, more serious, and more vividly suggestive of Lear's destitute moral condition and the frightful eventualities of the future. The Fool's bitter statement,

> For you know, nuncle,
> The hedge-sparrow fed the cuckoo so long,
> That it had it head bit off by it young.
> 　　　　　　　　　　　　(I.iv.234-236)

is not only a sharp and crude image of ingratitude, but it is also an image of Lear's own foolishness, his misjudgment, his improvident helplessness, and his egoistic blindness. The imagery implied in the verb "bit off" is by transference an image of human decapitation and a darkly prophetic forewarning of what Lear is to experience from his children. In the image is implicit the lack of gratitude and love and even common humanity which already are Lear's destiny. The image is so proper and so apt in its context that though Lear seems to ignore it, it succeeds immediately in condensing the whole moral problem which enmeshes Lear in its inevitable consequences.

As Lear enters the incipiency of his rage, irritated by Oswald and shocked by the callousness of Goneril, who desiring to teach him what is properly conventional to age refers to his actions as pranks, thus suggesting his senility, and demands that he be shorn of his knights, the imagery changes to correspond with his emotional state—his indignation and his anger at the filial ingratitude of Goneril, this "degenerate bastard". Since the natural order of things is here disturbed, the expression of this state of affairs, which is quite monstrous, receives its correspondency in its figurative presentment of ingratitude as a "hideous seamonster". This is reinforced by an appropriate shift in the imagery, though the correspondence of destructive intent and power is maintained, to "detested kite". For a kite is a falcon-like bird which preys on small quarry, such as is Lear without his kingship, without his power, moving down the scale from greatness.

Shifting from the image of the kite, Lear intensifies his emotion of frustration and rage, which seethes in him against his unnatural daughter Goneril, whom he has just cursed unnaturally, praying nature to make her sterile, by objectifying his rising obsession of ingratitude in the figure of a serpent's tooth. In thus juxtaposing images from the sky and from the crawling earth he suggests, perhaps, his subconscious awareness that both heaven and earth are against him. Having employed the images of sea-monster, kite, and serpent to vivify his referent, he gives further extension to the notion of Goneril's cruelty and sly, cunning nature by additional images from the animal world, "wolvish visage" and "fox", and these images for the first time blend with anger the passion of vengeance, for Lear wrathfully states that when Regan hears of this she will "flay" Goneril's wolvish visage and the Fool states that had one caught a fox like this daughter it would soon to the slaughter.

Now the imagery sinks below the animal stratum to the mollusk, thus intensifying the sense of the moral depths in which Lear, not yet pessimistically, helplessly wanders. The imagery of the snail and the oyster carries to the lowest pitch of figurative expression the blindness of Lear, his lack of judgment, the low order of the ratiocination from which proceeded his initial error. Then the image of the foolishness of Lear is carried upward to the animal stratum once again by "assess". If in this connection it is recalled that the animal stratum is often referred to as "the animal kingdom", the irony of Lear's position is painfully apparent.

Just as Goneril has been reduced in the area of imagery to a correspondence with animals that sting, bite, and destroy, organisms which are feral and inhuman, so her servant Oswald is dehumanized as a rat, a dog, a goose, the latter image being peculiarly appropriate to Oswald, who is remarkably consistent in the traits implicit in this figure.

With the momentary resurgence of Lear's old imperious attitude in his indignation at the stocking of his messenger Kent, the scale of the animal imagery rises from the stupid and compliant goose to horses, dogs, bears, and monkeys, thus suggesting the greater degree of the culpability of Cornwall and Regan by creating imagery belonging to animals on a higher ratiocinative plane and thereby rendering their guilt less excusable. Now again irony is blended explicitly with the imagery which sets forth Lear's moral problem. His imperious indignation, in terms of the imagery, is as cogent as learning secured from an ant. His intensified anger becomes adulterated with helplessness, and his orders to Regan and Cornwall to come forth are as ineffective as the cockney crying to the eels when she put them alive in the pastry. While anger is often imaged forth in feral terms, blindness, stupidity, weakness, and helplessness are presented in images from the still lower stratum of animate things, that of the snail, the oyster, and the eel, and in the appropriateness of the imagery is apparent once again its integral relation to the total structure of the play.

When Lear, having fled to his "Beloved Regan", reflects upon his love and generosity to his daughters which proceeded from his heart and upon the unnatural ingratitude paid him by Goneril in return, the image which externalizes his emotional state of outraged paternal affection mingled with surprise and shock appears in the form of sharp-toothed unkindness, like a vulture, tearing at his heart, and in his rising anger at Regan's rejection of his claims and her injunction to ask Goneril's forgiveness and return to her, this image is reinforced in the collateral one of being struck with a serpent's tongue upon the very heart. In the psychological application of the imagery as expressive of Lear's emotive states at various stages of his mounting tragedy, the images of the wounding of his heart by vultures and serpents mark a crisis in the rising action, for after this there occurs, eventually in the storm scene, the loss of his wits, in other words, an ironic reduction of Lear himself to that unnatural state which is so essential a theme of the entire tragedy. His estrangement from normal human relations, consonant with the above, is further marked, in passionate reaction to Regan's rejection of him, by his refusal of her demand to dismiss fifty of his knights and by his determination, instead, to abjure all roofs and be a comrade with the wolf and the owl. Throughout the imagery runs an intensification of the theme of unnaturalness, the basis of which is, of course, filial ingratitude. Even the Gentleman discussing with Kent the storm on the heath uses imagery similar to Lear's as an atmospheric reinforcement of the psychological mood into which Lear has been precipitated; the stormy night into which Lear has emerged from the previous rejection scene is one from which the cub-drawn bear, the lion, and the belly-pinched wolf flee. Contending with the frightful elements, tearing his hair, striving to outscorn the wind, rain, and night, Lear is pursued by his heart-struck injuries. Also the unnatural cruelty of his pitiful state and the savagery of the night are figured forth, to some degree, in the aforementioned famished bear, fierce lion, and hunger-driven wolf.

The lowly imagery of the louse employed by the Fool, that of a small, wingless, blood-sucking insect, is an ironic image presenting a vivid, concrete manifestation of the contrast between Lear's impotent state and his rather imperial, though helpless, arraignment of the elements which have with his two pernicious daughters joined their battles against so old and white a head as his. The image of the louse is implicative of a descent from elevation, a contrast with the soaring evil of the vulture, and a descent from size, the massive evil of the sea-serpent; considered in its context it is also, in contrast with "head", indicative of a

lack of intelligence and is, therefore, a further indictment of Lear's original irrationality. The imagery of the louse is both a presentment of Lear's impotency, the louse being on a lower level than that of the feral animals, a small wingless thing, almost insignificant though painful, and also a prefiguring of the pelican image which soon intensifies it, the image of a blood-sucking animate thing, implicit in the figure of the louse, having for its referent the daughters who have taken all and, draining his blood from him, seek his death. And in an extension of this idea and a logical transmutation of it, that of flesh feeding on the flesh that begot it, Lear's emotions express themselves in the metaphor of the pelican daughters. So admirable a consistency is there in the images and so vivid a reflection of Lear's psyche that it is evident that the imagery is of the very texture of Lear's psyche itself. Habitually and spontaneously his mind expresses itself in imagery, and when his mind is in a disturbed state the imagery is that of the animal world, or at least the world of animate, sub-human things.

The notion of descent, which inheres in the animal figures, is made explicit by Lear in his assertion that in Edgar's case nothing could have subdued nature to such a lowness but his unkind daughters. Expressive of this and showing the partial correspondency of Edgar's state with that of Lear on the stormy heath are the images employed by Edgar:

> . . . hog in sloth, fox in stealth, wolf in greediness, dog in madness, lion in prey (III.iv.96-98)

With Lear's climactic statement:

> Ha! here's three on's us are sophisticated! Thou are the thing itself: unaccommodated man is no more but such a poor, bare, forked animal as thou art. Off, off, you lendings! (III.iv. 110-14)

the descent is accomplished, and the correspondency of Lear to the animal stratum toward which his psychic tragedy has been tending and in terms of images from which he has characteristically expressed himself is complete. Bereft of reason, mad, tearing off his clothes, Lear is now little better than the beasts. He has reached the bottom of the scale which his imagery has prefigured. The climax of descent in terms of animal imagery, if this is not too paradoxical a statement, coincides with the climax of the play.

When Lear appears at Dover mad, fantastically dressed with wild flowers, some of his imagery corresponds to his state of mind: crow-keeper, mouse, bird, gilded butterflies; this is the innocent, naive imagery of childhood or senility, a harmless, neutral, non-evocative imagery proper to one whose wits are gone. Yet in the subsequent imagery begins his reascent into partial rationality, his progress upward from the animal state with which in the climax he had identified himself. His memory, in the area of his emotions, reasserts itself and with it a reminiscent indignation and anger which bring into prominence once again his obsession of filial ingratitude: "They flattered me like a dog" (IV.iv.98). Blended with it, too, is a critical bitterness which is an image of his renascent awareness of his fallen state. The wren and the gilded fly, the fitchew and the soiled horse become images of copulation and adultery, and in the extension of causes into a relative complexity is suggested not only the advance of Lear's mind in a tentative way toward humanity once again but the substitution of cynicism for the violated and outraged affection which throughout the play had so obsessed him.

Lear's reascent to reason and, therefore, to humanity is arrested by a resurgence of tragedy—the death of Cordelia. The irony of his apparent moral victory in self-recognition, in his awareness of good and evil, and in at least a rudimentary sense of equity and of the real victory of the malevolence of his enemies, carries the essential tensions of the play through to the very end. Lear's reaction against the injustice of Cordelia's death, the needless waste of goodness in the world, his questioning of the *why* of things, are expressed through his characteristic imagery which presents his skepticism in regard to the moral system of the cosmos, an act of ratiocination which is, of course, on a human rather than an animal level:

> Why should a dog, a horse, a rat have life,
> And thou no breath at all?
>
> (V.iii.306-07)

And on the curve of his partial reascent toward reason and humanity, presented in terms of animal imagery to the last, Lear dies.

LOVE

Critics who assert that love is a principal theme of *King Lear* frequently disagree about how it is presented in the play. Many, however, have noted that the drama depicts it in several different forms. **Marilyn Gaull**, for example, argues that *Lear* focuses on two kinds: divine love, which fosters universal order, and erotic love, which inevitably results in chaos and destruction. Cordelia represents divine love, Gaull and many other commentators suggest. John F. Danby sees Cordelia as the only character in the play who understands the right relation between self-love, love of God, and compassionate love for one's fellow human beings.

In the virtual absence of romantic love in the play,

several critics have contended, family love becomes of paramount importance. Thomas McFarland takes this viewpoint and further notes that despite the play's presentation of such commonplace family problems as favoritism toward one child over another, the demands of aging or unworthy parents, and the ingratitude of children, the family is depicted here as the ultimate source of refuge and solace. Robert C. West also emphasizes the importance of the bonds between parents and children in *King Lear*, and highlights the play's focus on compassionate, selfless love for others.

West is also one of several critics who have called attention to the play's seemingly dark view of sex and procreation. Commentators addressing this issue frequently allude to Lear's tirade against sexual generation in Act IV, scene vi, his curses on Goneril in Act I, and the lewd remarks of the Fool and Poor Tom. **Simon O. Lesser**, in a close examination of the play's first scene, proposes that Lear is desperately seeking reassurance that his daughters love him enough to take care of him through the years of physical and mental decline that lie ahead of him. Lesser also evaluates the king's possessive love of Cordelia and the possibility of unconscious sexual desire in both characters.

Marilyn Gaull

SOURCE: "Love and Order in *King Lear*," in *Educational Theatre Journal*, Vol. XIX, No. 3, October, 1967, pp. 333-42.

[*Gaull argues that* King Lear *depicts two kinds of love: divine love, associated with universal order, and erotic love, associated with chaos and destruction. When Lear abdicates his royal responsibilities, the critic asserts, he plunges his kingdom into a state of spiritual and emotional disorder. Gaull suggests that Lear's choice of corrupt, erotic love over divine love results in a transference of sexuality; the king becomes emasculated as he is gradually stripped of the symbols of his traditional role, while at the same time Goneril and Regan increasingly assume masculine attitudes. By contrast, the critic declares, Cordelia adheres to the principle of domestic and political hierarchy, and thus she becomes an agent of divine love in the play.*]

Placing *King Lear* in the intellectual climate in which the play was conceived, one finds a conflict on the thematic level between two kinds of love: divine love, expressed in an ordered cosmic, social, and spiritual hierarchy, and erotic love, a kind of subterranean energy which is the source of chaos, disorder, and destruction. Specifically, when King Lear assumed he could divest himself of responsibility, retiring as any lesser mortal to the obscurity of an "unburdened" old age, he committed an offense against universal order and thereby denied divine love. Then, when he allowed himself to be seduced of his kingdom by Goneril and Regan, he exchanged his role as king for that of love goddess, suffering all the consequences of a submission, however tacit, to the illegitimate order of eros. . . .

[By] appropriating the privileges of position without the responsibilities, by preferring private interest to public obligation, by investing an inordinate amount of power in inferior indivduals, Lear created the conditions for rebellion by those whom he was enjoined to control. By extension, through his failure to be ruled by reason, he alienated himself from divine love and forfeited his sovereignty over his own baser passions. His abdication of responsibility released the destructive energies of eros in the social and political sphere and delivered him and all those upon whom his life impinged into psychological and spiritual chaos.

It is the three exiles in the play, Cordelia, Kent, and Edgar who, by maintaining the three basic relationships of an ordered society, express divine love. Displaced by the collapse of the social and political hierarchy, they are the most evident victims of Lear's truancy. Nonetheless, they continue to articulate and perform the services demanded by universal order. Thus Cordelia demonstrates woman's subordination to her husband; Kent, a subject's subordination to his king; and Edgar, a son's subordination to his father. . . .

Gloucester and Albany may also be considered victims of Lear's truancy, more helpless than the exiles insofar as their fulfilling their roles in the universal order depends upon circumstance rather than a capacity for divine love. But because they are basically good and adapted, however passively, to their roles in the legitimate hierarchy, they cannot survive in the alternative and subversive hierarchy of eros. The gentle and ineffectual Albany allows his wife to dominate him, creating the conditions for his own cuckolding. And Gloucester, who suffers a defect of vision long before his blindness, was never able to distinguish between the legitimate and the subversive order. His acknowledgment at the opening of the play of the position he allowed Edmund, the product of an adulterous union, is an ominous concession to the order of eros which will ultimately betray him. He admits to Kent: "But I have a son, sir, by order of law, some year elder than this, who yet is no dearer in my account: though this knave came something saucily to the world before he was sent for, yet was his mother fair, there was good sport in the making, and the whoreson must be acknowledged" (I, i, 19-26). The desolating consequences of this emotional generosity are summed up by Edgar in the same speech in which he reveals his identity:

The gods are just, and of our pleasant vices

Make instruments to plague us:
The dark and vicious place where thee he
　got
Cost him his eyes.

(V, iii, 172-175)

If the three exiles, Gloucester, and Albany are victims of Lear's truancy, Goneril and Regan are villains for the same reason. In their mismanaged attempts to fill the vacuum created by Lear, they are simply fulfilling another principle of natural law. The chaos which surrounds them arises from the appetitive or erotic instincts by which they are dominated. But, after all, it was these very instincts to which Lear appealed when he invited his daughters' declarations of love, declarations which he made the qualification for possessing his kingdom. A comparison between Lear's overtures and Cleopatra's at the opening of *Antony and Cleopatra* suggests rather strikingly the role Lear had assumed. Like Lear, she asks, "If it be love indeed, tell me how much" (I, i, 14). And this Egyptian love goddess is admonished by Antony in terms peculiarly reminiscent of Cordelia's: "There's beggary in the love that can be reckon'd" (I, i, 15). What I am suggesting is that not only did Lear disregard divine love in favor of the profane but also that it was a profane love which was essentially perverted. This idea seems to be enforced by a fascinating transference of sexuality which gradually emerges in the interaction of Lear and his daughters. Lear's emasculation begins when he places himself in the custody of his daughters thereby forfeiting along with his kingdom his masculine role as superior, ruler, protector, and provider. After Goneril has abused her power over him, he begins to conceive of her as a man, calls her a "degenerate bastard," claims that he is ashamed of her "power to shake [his] manhood," and finally in his madness accuses both her and Regan of not being "men o' their words" (I, iv, 260, 304; IV, vi, 106). Simultaneously, Goneril and Regan assume increasingly masculine attitudes, particularly in their competition for Edmund's affection. Regan's masculinity is most evident in the passage in which, expressing decidedly female jealousy of Goneril, she adopts the spare terms of the battlefront: "I am doubtful that you have been conjunct/And bosomed with her, as far as we call hers" (V, i, 12-13). Goneril, on the other hand, like an intriguing courtier contrives to have her husband murdered so that she might better pursue Edmund. Her attitude reveals the destructive consequences of investing the political power of a legitimate hierarchy in female figures who are adapted to rule only in the subversive hierarchy of eros: "I had rather lose the battle than that sister/Should loosen him and me" (V, i, 18-19).

The Fool and Edmund, initially vagrants or aberrations in the official hierarchy, function as vocal adversaries in the debate between the two major opposing forces of order and chaos. The Fool with his detached and uncompromisingly literal perspective shrewdly if instinctively predicts and interprets the consequences of Lear's action, measuring it against the norms of hierarchy. For example, when Lear asks him "When were you wont to be so full of songs, sirrah?" The Fool replies:

> . . . e'er since thou mad'st thy daughters
> thy mothers; for when thou gav'st them the
> 　rod, and
> put'st down thine own breeches,
> 　Then they for sudden joy did weep,
> 　And I for sorrow sung,
> 　That such a king should play bo-peep
> 　And go the fools among
>
> 　　　　　　　　　　　　(I, iv, 175-182)

The Fool's musical association is a significant one since it is an indication of his affinity with cosmic order, his instinctive harmony with natural law and divine love. Cordelia similarly uses music to restore Lear's rationality, to bring him back in tune with the divine principles of the universal hierarchy.

Finally, Edmund, the child of eros, serves not only as the voice of the anarchical group but also as the source of its daemonic energy. His superior rationality adapts him to his role of leadership, but his abuse of this faculty for self-advancement marks him as the most culpable. His is the only purely volitional offense against natural law. An unregenerate individual with an insight superior to Lear's, Cordelia's, Edgar's, indeed to that of any of the major candidates for heroic stature, Edmund ranks among the great literary villains who before their defeat contrive to express and to expose the great sanative values of the drama. As an illegitimate son, Edmund has no position in the social and political hierarchy, but this same condition eminently qualifies him to lead the subversive hierarchy of eros, chaos, and destruction. Having been indiscriminately admitted to the hierarchy by Gloucester, Edmund becomes an incipient threat to it, manipulating and exploiting it with a dashing expertise. . . .

Ironically, it is by emulating the King that Edmund becomes the ruler of his illegitimate kingdom. He formulates his legal code on the authority of Lear's distortion of natural law: the prerogatives of youth and private interest over age and public responsibility. By the time Edmund articulates the rationale for his treason, he is only interpreting what has been empirically demonstrated by Lear: "The younger rises when the old doth fall" (III, iii, 26). This statement with its Machiavellian disregard of human feeling, its frigid recognition of what the modern temper regards as the inevitable pattern of social evolution, acquires its barb from the ethos of Lear's world. Although

cosmic hierarchy illustrated and natural law proclaimed that age and the fullness of experience were the supreme virtues for wielding power, Lear voted for his own retirement, disqualified himself, relinquished the protection of a position he held by divine right. Then, he appealed to the very order which he had violated:

> O heavens!
> If you do love old men, if your sweet sway
> Allow obedience, if you yourselves are old,
> Make it your cause. Send down, and take my
> 　part.
>
> 　　　　　　　　　　　　(II, iv, 188-191)

The corrective, the re-assertion of natural law in the development of generations, is offered as an admonition by Edgar to his suicidal father:

> A man must endure
> Their going hence, even as their coming
> 　hither:
> Ripeness is all.
>
> 　　　　　　　　　　　　(V, ii, 9-11)

The battle lines between the forces of chaos, a grotesque paradox of the legitimate hierarchy, and the forces of order, assembled in the costumes of fools, beggars, and madmen, are clearly defined when Gloucester moves from the castle, now ruled by Edmund, to the moor, the storm, and the insane court of Lear. It is a powerful confrontation, for Gloucester is appealing to the very source of chaos when, disheartened by what he thinks is Edgar's treachery, he laments to Lear:

> Our flesh and blood, my Lord, is grown so
> 　vile
> That it doth hate what gets it.
>
> 　　　　　　　　　　　　(III, iv, 148-149)

But in this kingdom of the absurd, even this multiple truth is an untruth, or at best a half truth. Fidelity is everywhere evident—in an anonymous retainer, a mad beggar, and an oracular fool. The central and compelling truth distorted beyond recognition is flung at a raging and primordial world by the alienated and insane symbol and minister of virtue, reason, and justice:

> I am the King himself. . . .
>
> Nature's above art in that respect.
>
> 　　　　　　　　　　　　(IV, vi, 84, 86)

Lear's insanity involves his recognition of the emotional basis of his relationship with Goneril and Regan, a love professedly filial but essentially corrupt, profane, erotic. Thus he passes from a fixation on filial ingratitude to one on lechery and adultery. This change is initiated when he meets Edgar disguised as

Tom o'Bedlam and hears his factitious autobiography. Tom attributes his madness, the "foul field" which pursued him, to his life as a foppish courtier seduced by his mistress and corrupted by his passions:

> A servingman, proud in heart and mind, that curled my hair, wore gloves in my cap; served the lust of my mistress' heart, and did the act of darkness with her; swore as many oaths as I spake words, and broke them in the sweet face of heaven. One that slept in the contriving of lust, and waked to do it. Wine loved I deeply, dice dearly; and in woman out-paramoured the Turk. . . . Let not the creaking of shoes nor the rustling of silks betray thy poor heart to woman. Keep thy foot out of brothels, thy hand out of plackets, thy pen from lenders' books, and defy the foul fiend. (III, iv, 85-99)

Lear's response suggests the essential bestiality which he senses he shares with Tom, both exiles from the protective order of society:

> Thou art the thing itself; unaccommodated man is no more but such a poor, bare, forked animal as thou art. (III, iv, 108-110)

The "foul fiends" for Lear are Goneril and Regan who become more explicitly identified with lust and appetitive excess in the mad scenes of Act IV. Vainly grasping the remnants of his royal position, it is with crushing pathos that he confuses the blinded Gloucester with the pagan god of eros: "No, do thy worst, blind Cupid; I'll not love" (IV, vi, 139-140).

It is divine love, the love which created and maintained the cosmic order, embodied in Cordelia, which restores Lear both to his rationality and to his royal position. "Thou has one daughter," says her emissary to the nearly disabled king.

> Who redeems nature from the general curse
> Which twain have brought her to
> (IV, vi, 208-210)

Although her success in restoring Lear will be limited, since the "curse" was essentially self-inflicted, Cordelia is eminently qualified for her task. She comes from a politically ordered kingdom, suggested in the text by France's deserting her to fulfill his first obligation, the reparation of a breach in his own kingdom (IV, iii, 3-6). Her reason for invading England, not "blown ambition" but "love, dear love, and our aged father's right" (IV, iv, 27-29), is one of the only two motives for war sanctioned by natural law. Self-defense, the other motive, is expressed, ironically enough, by her temporary opponent, Albany, exonerating him from a violation of natural law but creating an almost insoluable conflict (V, i, 20-27). While both causes are just, because Lear is too feeble to defend his right and because in the absence of France

there is no military leader qualified to defend it for him, Albany with the advantage of strength succeeds. It is a facet of natural law which modern revolutionaries have espoused: force until right is ready.

Psychologically and emotionally, Cordelia exhibits the internal order of faculties which she expressed in her speech on proportion in the first act. Her response to the news of her father's suffering is described in appropriately political terms, suggesting the correspondent hierarchies in the internal and external kingdom:

> It seemed she was a queen
> Over her passion, who most rebel-like,
> Sought to be king o'er her. . . .
>
> There she shook
> The holy water from her heavenly eyes,
> And clamor moistened: then away she started
> To deal with grief alone.
> (IV, iii, 14-16, 30-34)

Concomitant with this inner control, proportion, and order are Cordelia's clear perspective, her immediate apprehension of the sources of Lear's madness, and her unsuspected power to restore his sanity, his political identity, and his spiritual harmony with the order of the spheres. Thus she prays:

> O you kind gods!
> Cure this great breach in his abused nature.
> Th' untuned and jarring senses, O, wind up
> Of this child-changed father.
> (IV, vii, 14-17)

The cure is affected by three means, each symbolic of one of the major categories in the chain or order of being: sleep induced by herbs, suggesting the subjugation of nature; music, appealing to rationality and the sense of balance; and Cordelia's kiss, symbol of transcendent love.

> O my dear father, restoration hang
> Thy medicine on my lips, and let this kiss
> Repair those violent harms that my two
>   sisters
> Have in thy reverence made.
> (IV, vii, 26-29)

Considering, therefore, Cordelia as symbol of the entire range of hierarchy and order, one ought, it seems to me, to be able to interpret Lear's awakening as a return to a proper relationship with that hierarchy and divine love. But he continues to challenge Cordelia, confessing thereby his failure to recognize the immutable cosmic bonds involved in the familial relationship.

> I know you do not love me; for your sisters
> Have, as I do remember, done me wrong.

You have some cause, they have not.
(IV, vii, 72-74)

Cordelia's response, "No cause, no cause," is less a volitional expression of Christian charity than the acquiescence of a sane and virtuous individual to the very sources of sanity and virtue, an affirmation of what Kent had described as "the holy cords . . . / Which are too intrinse t'unloose" (II, ii, 76-77).

But there is only a momentary stasis, a temporary suggestion of supernal peace before the violence with which the drama concludes. I would like to suggest several reasons why at the end of the drama Lear is subjected to such apparently unaccountable suffering, why he is unable to reclaim his kingdom, and why Cordelia must become the final though potentially most meaningful sacrifice. First, because Lear is redeemed not by the purgatorial experience of his madness but rather by Cordelia's intervention, he acquires only a passive immunity to further suffering. Secondly, he fails to recognize that his previous suffering was self-inflicted, a miscalculation of the responsibilities of his position which allowed the betrayal of Goneril and Regan. Thirdly, his instincts remain escapist, regressive, expressed in his rationalization of their prospective imprisonment. The pastoral withdrawal, the edinic vision which he depicts so lyrically is the ideal of the courtier rather than the vision of a king; it is a return to a lower order of nature, uncorrupted but outside the pale of human achievement:

> . . . Come, let's away to prison:
> We two alone will sing like birds i' th' cage:
> When thou dost ask me blessing, I'll kneel
>   down
> And ask of thee forgiveness: so we'll live,
> And pray, and sing, and tell old tales, and
>   laugh
> At gilded butterflies, and hear poor rogues
> Talk of court news; and we'll talk with them
>   too,
> Who loses and who wins, who's in, who's
>   out,
> And take upon's the mystery of things,
> As if we were God's spies: and we'll wear
>   out,
> In a walled prison, packs and sects of great
>   ones
> That ebb and flow by th' moon.
> (V, iii, 8-19)

Once more Lear disregards that he is by birth and by divine ordination king, God's minister, and executor of law and order in the secular sphere. In his sanguine willingness to adapt to his environment, to adjust to his surroundings, Lear reveals his decidedly terrestial inclinations. Since Cordelia's existence in the political order depends upon Lear's assuming

From Act IV, scene viii, the Doctor, Cordelia, Lear, and Kent.

command of himself and of his kingdom, she is for the second, and final time, a victim of his weakness.

Finally, the kind of love relationships into which Lear entered and the emotional bases on which he entered them suggest a kind of constitutional defect which prevented him from entering the transcendent emotional realm which Cordelia opened to him. This defect is perhaps best formulated in a statement from Saint Augustine's *City of God*, XI, in which appear many of the orthodox principles of cosmic order: we are "endowed with a kind of attraction for our proper place in the order of nature. The specific gravity of a body is, as it were, its love, whether it tends upward by its lightness or down-ward by its weight."

It is somewhat by natural selection that Edgar not simply survives but prevails at the end of the play. On a plane productively human he resolves the major conflict between eros and divine love, between chaos and order. If the sins of the father are truly visited upon the son, as Edgar's suffering at the hands of Edmund would suggest, then he frees himself and his kingdom of the "foul fiend" when he vanquishes his bastard brother, the ruler of the illegitimate order of eros. Moreover, in his guise as Tom o'Bedlam he has been purged in a preventive fashion of both the vice and the consequences of erotic love. But unlike Cordelia he is a terrestial creature committed to a human sphere, the only sphere in which a human being to remain human may work out his salvation. This salvation, earthly perfection, "ripeness" if you like, is made possible by the emotional affinity he shares with Cordelia, divine or transcendent love, and is the basis for the creation of a new and more stable order.

Simon O. Lesser

SOURCE: "Act One, Scene One, of *Lear*," in *College English*, Vol. 32, No. 2, November, 1970, pp. 155-71.

[*Lear desperately seeks reassurance that his daughters will allow him to carry out his plans for his final years, Lesser maintains, and so he stages a "play" in the opening scene that will draw out this response. The critic notes that the king looks chiefly to his favorite, Cordelia, for love and praise. The extraordinary intensity and possessiveness of his love for her makes Lear more vulnerable to disappointment, Lesser argues. In the critic's judgment, Lear's possessiveness has its source in an unconscious sexual desire, which Cordelia is aware of—even as she guards herself against expressing her own excessive, incestuous feelings toward him. Lesser contends that Cordelia resents the hypocrisy of the love-test, is overwhelmed by hatred of her sisters, and is too angry in this first scene "to think clearly or to serve her own interests."*]

What is basically being enacted in Act I, Scene 1, of *Lear* is an unwritten play. The play has no function in terms of the political purposes of the ceremony. The division of the Kingdom, the redistribution of power and Lear's own plans, have all been decided upon in advance. The intention of announcing all these decisions in the course of a play is evidence of the assurance felt by its author, Lear, that it would be performed as planned, that everyone would accept and enact the role assigned him—or, more accurately, *her*. Other than Lear himself, the only characters in the drama he has composed in his mind are his daughters. Kent is an unwelcome intruder.

In terms of state purposes the play is a foolish way for Lear to make his decisions known. But for Lear himself the play has functions of the utmost importance. The King is an old man who, as he himself points out, is preparing for death. As part of that preparation he is doing something which at some level he knows to be dangerous: he is surrendering his power, wealth and state functions to his daughters and their husbands, retaining for himself only the title and honors of a King and a small retinue of

Knights to attend him. He is in effect throwing himself on the mercy of his daughters and their husbands. Moreover, there is every reason to believe that he knows two of these daughters to be cold-blooded, calculating and untrustworthy. As the first speech of the play tells us, he also has, or has had, reservations about the Duke of Cornwall, Regan's husband. Lear is a frightened man. The despotism he displays later on may be in part a way of denying this and proving to himself that he still has authority and power. It is certain that he desperately needs the reassurance his play has been planned to elicit. We of course, whether readers or spectators, can see as Kent does that it is a poor way of eliciting reassurance upon which he can depend.

Intermixed with this need is an equally powerful desire for praise and love. They are of course the proofs Lear seeks that though he is surrendering his prerogatives he need not be afraid—reassurance against feared or already-present feelings of impotence and defenselessness. But we should not overlook his quasi-independent need to be flattered. This need too is understandable. We speak of extreme old age as a second childhood, and it is in childhood that narcissism is strongest. The regressive influence of age adds to Lear's need to be admired.

The burden of satisfying all of these needs—for reassurance, praise and love—falls almost entirely upon Cordelia. She is the heroine of Lear's play. She is given the climactic position in it, and is clearly intended to give a speech which outshines her sisters' speeches in substance and eloquence, a speech which is at once sincere, yet warm, even extravagant, in its declaration of love and approbation. The thirds into which the kingdom is divided are not exactly equal, any more than the halves into which a grapefruit is cut usually are. Cordelia's portion, Lear suggests, is "more opulent" than her sisters'—and really superior to theirs in some small way, I would suspect. It should be stressed, however, that the superiority of her portion is slight. We have every reason to believe Lear's statement that he is making and announcing the division of the kingdom at this time to prevent future strife; and the opening lines of the scene tell us that the portions going to Albany and Cornwall are so well equalized that neither Duke will have cause for envy. We can assume that Lear would not jeopardize his goal of avoiding future war by giving Cordelia a portion notably superior to the others.

The early parts of Scene 1 prepare us for the recognition that Cordelia is Lear's favorite, if not the only daughter he loves. Though he calls his second daughter "Our dearest Regan," both his charge to her to speak and his earlier charge to Goneril are matter-of-fact. There is scarcely a wasted word. Moreover, though both daughters praise him fulsomely, his responses are perfunctory; indeed, both responses give the impression of having been memorized, or composed in a general way, before the ceremony. The text does not support [Samuel Taylor] Coleridge's view that Lear was "duped by [Goneril's and Regan's] hypocritical professions of love and duty. . . ." On the contrary, it is evident—probably even to Goneril and Regan—that Lear is gliding over this part of the ceremony as quickly as possible to get to the part for which the rest is preparation: his favorite's avowal of admiration and love. From "our joy" at the beginning to the hardly impartial suggestion at the end that Cordelia speak in such a way as to merit a "more opulent" third than her sisters, the invitation to her to avow her love has a different ring than the preceeding ones.

Though we may be no better prepared than Lear to recognize it, the very fact that his expectations are focussed so completely upon Cordelia has its dangerous side. She is the daughter whose avowals can quiet his fears, but by the same token she is the one who can disappoint and hurt him most.

This obvious danger is compounded by two others. The first stems from the fact that Cordelia is Lear's youngest—and because he does not want to be reminded of his age may be thought of as more of a child than she is. Though Lear's bid to Cordelia to speak is longer than the bids to Goneril and Regan taken together, it is only three and a half lines in length. Yet in this brief speech Lear twice refers to Cordelia's youth. We may sense that his emphasis on this causes him to think of Cordelia as more obedient and pliant then her sisters, thus heightening the expectations based upon love and his assurance that the love is returned.

The very intensity of Lear's feeling for his youngest daughter is the second factor that makes his situation so dangerous. Unconsciously we may have already sensed that there is a not wholly desexualized—a repressed incestuous—element in Lear's feeling for Cordelia. There is additional evidence of this incestuous element later in the opening scene and elsewhere in the tragedy. For the light it throws upon this element and other feelings of Lear's, what he says when he is most enraged—disappointed and angry at Cordelia and further infuriated by Kent's intervention in her behalf—is particularly revelatory.

Most significant are some blunt words at the very beginning of his tirade against Kent:

> I loved her most, and thought to set my rest
> On her kind nursery.

"Set my rest" may mean not only "find my rest," but also, on the basis of usage in an Elizabethan card game, "stake my all." These words confirm some of the things we have sensed about Lear's feelings toward all three of his daughters. They tell us of course that Cordelia was his favorite and that he wanted to spend all his remaining days with her, but they just as clearly show that he had no confidence in the kindlines of his older daughters. We may feel that if Lear had been in better control of himself, he probably would have spoken less frankly. But the decision referred to should not be dismissed as the product of anger: it was evidently made when Lear was thinking carefully and objectively about his future course. . . .

Later in this outburst there is another remark which in indirect fashion suggests the strength of Lear's love for Cordelia:

> So be my grave my peace, as here I give
> Her father's heart from her!

The words "So be my grave my peace" seem to imply a comparison—probably to some such words as "and not my stay in my youngest daughter's 'nursery'." The pessimism of the words tells us again that Lear had never expected any kindness from his older daughters.

Considered closely, Lear's rage at Cordelia's refusal to accept the part assigned her in his play and his disinheritance of her are also evidence of his love: his fury and punitive behavior stem chiefly from the frustration of hopes too dear to be renounced. More technically, Cordelia's unanticipated behavior thwarts a whole cluster of unconscious, or at any rate unacknowledged, desires. Lear has evidently not even faced his dependency on his youngest daughter, much less specified the needs he expected her "performance" to satisfy. As we shall see, moreover, some of the things Cordelia says in her third and, ironically, most conciliatory speech give it the character of a sexual rejection. A metaphor Lear uses a little later in this outburst suggests that he has understood the speech, or perhaps the entire pattern of her behavior, in this way: "Let pride, which she calls plainness, marry her."

After disinheriting Cordelia Lear speaks harshly about her to the King of France. However, the opening words of France's reply provide further evidence of the intensity of Lear's affection for his youngest daughter just before this turnabout:

> This is most strange,
> That she whom even but now was your best
> object,
> The argument of your praise, balm of your
> age,
> The best, the dearest . . .

The exchanges between Lear and Burgundy and Lear and France dramatically expose the incestuous element in Lear's love. It is perfectly clear that he no longer wants either Burgundy or France to marry Cordelia. His anger is certainly a factor, but his attitude also suggests that, while he was willing to share his favorite daughter with a husband, he is reluctant to let another man possess her to the exclusion of himself. His position is hardly consistent with his disinheritance of his daughter, but he is now dominated by a part of the psyche little concerned with consistency. . . .

Later in the play, when Lear has been subjected to the cruelty of his older daughters and is experiencing the fury of the storm, he speaks again in passion—passion born not only of his anger toward them but also, it may be surmised, toward himself. His last speech before his wits begin to turn shows that incest is very much on his mind. It is the second crime he specifies, and its placement gives it more emphasis than the one mentioned first.

> Let the great gods
> That keep this dreadful pudder o'er our
>   heads
> Find out their enemies now. Tremble, thou
>   wretch,
> That hast within thee undivulged crimes
> Unwhipped of justice. Hide thee, thou
>   bloody hand,
> Thou perjured, and thou simular of virtue
> That art incestuous.
>
> (III ii 49-55)

When Lear and Cordelia are briefly reunited late in the play, his love—their love—reappears in its original intensity, if not in heightened intensity. . . . Lear's speech to Cordelia in V. iii., after their capture by the victorious British forces, is more like the speech of a lover to his beloved than that of a father to his daughter.

Why does not Cordelia, who loves her father, give him the praise and assurances he so obviously needs and is so obviously beseeching? We can perceive several interlocking factors that combine to inhibit her and set her on a mistaken course she can never correct, though she clearly feels a mounting need to assure her father of her love. She is furiously angry at him, we realize, for staging this farcial pageant, which puts a premium on hypocrisy. More obviously she is overcome by hatred of her unscrupulous sisters. She feels that she cannot compete with them in lying and does not want to participate in such a competition. She is revolted by play, players, and author—this last despite her love for her father. She is too completely in the grip of anger and revulsion to think clearly or to serve her own interests. Her initial refusal to say anything when it is her turn to speak is not simply a rebuff but a reprimand, and intended as one.

Her hatred of her sisters noticeably influences her behavior. Her tendency throughout to understate, to confine herself to minimal statements of her love, is clearly born in part of her desire to disassociate herself from her sisters, to show how different she is from them, and, by so doing, to convey her disapproval of them. But her course—it cannot be called a strategy since it is not rationally decided upon—hurts herself, not her sisters. As Lear perceives her behavior, her over-scrupulousness must make her seem dutiful at best, and patently unloving.

Indeed, everything Cordelia does here turns out wrong. Despite her rejection of the part she senses her father wants her to play, she does try to communicate with him. In particular, she tries to remind him of the cold-bloodedness and insincerity of Goneril and Regan, though this is neither necessary nor an acceptable substitute for what Lear wants from Cordelia. Probably because she is angry at him, moreover, her efforts are half-hearted and not well calculated to succeed. In responding to her father's second effort to induce her to speak, she makes a fugitive attempt to explain her recalcitrance. But the very placement of the words, "Unhappy that I am," causes them to be glided over and robs them of emphasis. She hopes that her tight understatements will call attention to the fulsomeness of her sisters' avowals of love. But such comparisons as Lear is capable of making are all to her disadvantage. Her speeches—in particular her "I love your Majesty/According to my bond, no more nor less"—seem meager and devoid of affection.

To be sure, her next speech (97-106) is longer and warmer. Moreover, she is here directly comparing herself with her sisters and more openly trying to warn her father of their hypocrisy. Though she couches what she says about her sisters in interrogative form, she all but declares: "They don't mean what they say. Their protestations to you aren't even consistent with their marriage vows." Cordelia's decision to bring up the conflict between a daughter's obligations to husband and father is not accidental. It is of course on her mind since she senses that she will suffer more than ordinarily from this conflict because of the unspoken demands her father makes upon her. The main determinant of her allusion is her unconscious awareness of the excessive, incestuous element in her father's love. Her fear is intensified, the entire pattern of her behavior suggests, by a more deeply buried realization that she must also be on guard against her love for him. The need she feels to defend herself against the over-strong attachment to her father has a pervasive influence upon her behavior. It is a major cause of her initial refusal to speak and all her subsequent mistakes. Unfortunately, no consideration she could have advanced to explain and justify her behavior could have been more detrimental in its effects. The point she is driven to insinuate does not escape her father. On the contrary, it has a greater impact upon him than is objectively warranted. The way she words her point must also wound Lear. The idea that the man she marries "shall carry /Half my love with him, half my care and duty" is intolerable to him. The word "half" is probably not meant literally, but this makes no difference: Lear cannot brook the idea of there being any limit on his favorite's love for him.

It is inappropriate to appraise Cordelia's conduct in moral terms. On the other hand, it can and should be noted that, allowing for the stress she is under, she behaves like a child, even a spoiled child, during her father's play. If we did not sense this, if we did not perceive that at times both she and Lear act like infants, we could not accept the suffering which they, and we, are later called upon to endure. That Cordelia is capable of acting more maturely and defending her own interests is shown a little later in this scene (225-234) when, while apparently asking her father to limit and specify the offenses responsible for his disfavor, she very effectively clears herself. Here she is buoyed by France's spirited defense and avowal of confidence in her. Earlier her poise had been undermined by the behavior of her father and sisters. When she acts childishly, she is in the grip of such primitive emotions as anger, resentment, and fear—and, what is perhaps more disturbing still, anxiety born of the feeling, in which her own love is a factor, that her father is making inappropriate demands upon her. Nevertheless, the sulkiness and recalcitrance she displays under these pressures are a part of her too and cannot be disregarded. Had she been more comfortable about her own feelings for her father, which however strong were under firm control, and had she been able to face his love for her consciously and calmly, she would have realized that it would never lead to demands she could not readily and guiltlessly satisfy. What her father needed was to be bathed in a protective affection which would obliterate the feeling that he was old and powerless. Cordelia could have avowed her love—avowed it as extravagantly as she sensed her father wanted her to. Facing her own repugnance for the ceremony, and even any slight hypocrisy of which she might be guilty, she could have given Lear the reassurance he so desperately needed. But of course if tragic characters were as rational and controlled as this, and as capable of compromising, they would not be tragic characters and there would be no tragedy.

Lear's daughters know him no less well than he knows them. There is no reason to doubt some of what Goneril and Regan say about him in private. We feel no disposition to question either Regan's statement that he has never sought to know himself or their judgment that what he has just done shows how old age is exacerbating his natural rashness. They are referring specifically to Lear's disinheritance of Cordelia and banishment of Kent, but what they say applies to the whole of his behavior, including his generosity to them. Lack of self-understanding is the key to everything Lear feels and does after Cordelia disappoints him and is a principal cause of the disappointment itself. Lack of self-control is also a factor in his behavior, but if he had had a fuller awareness of his own feelings, he would have had a much better chance of controlling them.

It seems unlikely that Lear ever acknowledged how much fear and anxiety he felt about giving up his power and prerogatives and going forth bare-handed to meet death. It is still less likely that he apprehended the purposes of the play he had written in his mind. He seems blind to the intensity of his need for love and reassurance—and to the fact that the satisfaction of the need hinges almost entirely upon Cordelia. True, he has tried to be fair and has given all of his daughters roles in his play. But he is listening for one voice, one asseveration of love and esteem.

There is no indication that the speeches of Goneril and Regan have any emotional effect upon Lear. Paradoxically, it would have been better for Cordelia if they had buoyed his confidence: there would have been some diminution of the demands upon her. But what Lear wanted was an extravagant affirmation of esteem from Cordelia. We may suppose that he had composed innumerable speeches for her, each more satisfying than the one before in its affirmations of affection and approval.

Cordelia's actual behavior frustrates Lear's desperate need for love, praise and reassurance. The very real dangers of Lear's external situation do much to explain that need, but it is increased by unconscious factors. As has been mentioned, he is more frightened than he is willing to acknowledge—subject to innumerable vague and protean worries. An important function of the Fool—a splinter of Lear himself—is to name many of the anxieties, fears, and insights too painful for Lear to face. The Fool disappears when Lear himself begins to see more fully.

Cordelia denies her father the very things the ceremony was planned to provide. The impact of this is aggravated by other implications and effects of her behavior. First, it is experienced by her father as a rejection of *his* love. The distinction she draws between the love she owes father and husband is probably perceived as a bitter criticism of his love. Whereas acceptance of love, any kind of love, seems momentarily at least to justify it, rejection calls it into question, makes it seem dubious or evil. Cordelia's words and conduct probably make Lear subliminally aware of the not wholly desexualized nature of his feeling for her—and arouse guilt as well as anger. He feels that she is both scolding and rejecting him.

The independence and fastidiousness she displays hurt him for a second reason. They compel him to recognize that she is no longer baby or girl but grown woman. This in turn forces him to face something else he would prefer not to be reminded of, the fact that he is an old man. Her guardedness may also be wounding because it is the first sign of ambivalence he has permitted himself to recognize in someone he has thought of as loving him without reservation. Finally, as A. C. Bradley points out, Cordelia's behavior subjects Lear to public humiliation: he may feel that everyone present, Kent excepted, is aware of the lack of warmth and the criticism he senses in her words. His rage and need to lash out at her is fully understandable.

All the mistakes which account for Lear's later suffering are made while he is in the grip of this rage. He behaves like a child in a tantrum, striking out against those he loves, against his own self-interest, and against anyone who would remind him of the calamitous errors he is making.

Yet Lear knows that he has only one daughter who has a warm and generous nature and loves him. The fact that as he disowns her he invokes not only the sun but Hecate and the night suggests that he half realizes he is doing something evil. His refusal even to listen to Kent when he first tries to speak suggests even more forcibly that subliminally he knows that he is making a mistake.

We have seen how many constituents of Lear's next speech, the one which interrupts Kent's attempt to defend Cordelia, betray Lear's knowledge of the character of his daughters, of their feeling for him, and of his feeling for them. Yet in this very speech he proceeds to divide Cordelia's third of the kingdom between Cornwall and Regan, Albany and Goneril. His prerogatives are also divided between his sons-in-law. He retains only the titles and honors of King and a hundred knights, whom Cornwall and Albany, not he, must sustain. And he announces that he and his knights will divide their time between his older daughters and their husbands, moving monthly from one castle to the other.

His harshness to Kent once he is given a chance to criticize his sovereign's decisions shows us how determined Lear is not to acknowledge what on some level he assuredly realizes—that he has made a whole series of grievous mistakes. We may assume that Lear knows Kent almost as well as he knows his own daughters and is well aware that Kent has served him loyally and zealously and spoken sincerely. At this point Lear is astonishingly like Oedipus—determinedly blind and overcome by fright and anger when anyone tries to tell him what unconsciously or even preconsciously he already knows.

MADNESS

Both **Kenneth Muir** and Enid Welsford have addressed the "reason in madness" theme in *King Lear*. The king's mad speeches are more than mere raving, Muir asserts. Instead they are restatements or amplifications of ideas he has expressed earlier, for example, his attacks on lechery and human justice. Welsford contends that when Lear loses his sanity, he broadens his vision of the world. In the grip of madness, she argues, Lear has a series of profound insights about human society and the way it functions.

Although Muir and **Josephine Waters Bennett** agree that the sudden confrontation with Edgar as Poor Tom pushes Lear over the brink of insanity, they disagree about what has led to this moment. Muir maintains that Lear is driven insane by three shocking incidents: Goneril's charge about the behavior of his knights, the discovery of Kent in the stocks, and Regan's rejection of his appeals to her. Exposure to the storm and physical exhaustion complete the process, Muir asserts. Waters argues that Lear's hold on reality is loosened by a fatal combination of bitterness, resentment, pride, self-pity, and frustration. His desire for revenge, she suggests, reaches manic proportions when he becomes obsessive about his daughters, attempts to tear off his clothes, and falls into a delusion that Poor Tom is an "ancient philosopher." Bennett also notes Shakespeare's careful preparation for the mad scenes, pointing to all the occasions that give the audience or reader cues to what is happening to Lear's mind.

Several critics contend that Lear's madness is not an isolated phenomenon in the play. Muir calls attention to the corresponding frenzy in nature, the lunatic speeches of the Fool, and Edgar's pretended madness. Taken together, he remarks, they exemplify disordered society and the threat to universal order. George W. Williams has demonstrated that the parallel between the external storm and the storm in Lear's mind is underscored by violent imagery in Act III. And William Empson points out that no character who appears onstage during the storm scenes is entirely sane. The horror of madness and its capacity to illuminate human experience, he declares, are vividly dramatized in *King Lear*. For additional commentary on Lear's madness, see the excerpt by **George W. Williams** in the LANGUAGE AND IMAGERY section and the excerpt by **Enid Welsford** in the section on THE FOOL.

Kenneth Muir

SOURCE: "Madness in *King Lear*," in *Shakespeare Survey: An Annual Survey of Shakespearean Study and Production*, Vol. 13, 1960, pp. 30-40.

[*Muir discusses the theme of "reason in madness" in* King Lear *and outlines the king's descent into insanity. Goneril's sharp complaints, Lear's discovery of Kent in the stocks, and Regan's rejection progressively disorder his mind, the critic argues, and the sudden appearance of Edgar as Poor Tom pushes him over the edge. Muir maintains that Lear's subsequent attacks on hypocrisy and worldly justice "show profound insight" into the human condition. However, the critic cautions readers against assuming that these speeches represent Shakespeare's own point of view.*]

There is no madness in the old play of *King Leir,* none in the story of Lear as told by Holinshed, Spenser, in *The Mirror for Magistrates,* or in any other version before Shakespeare's time, and none in Sidney's story of the Paphlagonian King. . . . [M.] Maeterlinck believed that Shakespeare deliberately unsettled the reason of his protagonists, and thus opened

> the dike that held captive the swollen lyrical flood. Henceforward, he speaks freely by their mouths; and beauty invades the stage without fearing lest it be told that it is out of place. [*Life and Flowers*]

[George] Orwell, on the other hand [in his *Selected Essays*], regarded Lear's madness as a protective device to enable Shakespeare to utter dangerous thoughts. . . .

Against Maeterlinck's view it must be objected that the mad scenes of *King Lear* are no more lyrical than the rest of the play; and against Orwell's view of Shakespeare as the subversive sceptic without the courage of his own convictions it must be pointed out that none of his characters should be taken as his own mouthpiece. Ulysses' views on Order [in *Troilus and Cressida*] are shared by Rosencrantz [in *Hamlet*], whom Shakespeare treats with scant sympathy, and considerably modified by the King in *All's Well that Ends Well.* We cannot even be certain that the *Sonnets* are autobiographical. We cannot tell whether Shakespeare was a cowardly sceptic or a natural conformist. His acceptance of the 'establishment' and his criticism of it are equally in character. This is not to say that no point of view emerges from each play and from the canon as a whole; but the point of view is complex, subsuming both the anarchical and the conformist. The Shakespearian dialectic is not a reflection of the poet's timidity but of his negative capability.

In the dialogue with Gloucester in IV, vi, Lear's invective has a double target—the hypocrisy of the simpering dame and the hypocrisy of the law. There is no evidence to show that Shakespeare was sheltering behind a mask. The attack on lechery can be paralleled in the diatribes of Timon [in *Timon of Athens*] and the attack on authority and law is no more extreme than that of the eminently sane Isabella or that of the praying Claudius [both in *Measure for Measure*] who knew that

> In the corrupted currents of this world
> Offence's gilded hand may shove by justice,
> And oft 'tis seen the wicked prize itself
> Buys out the law.

Lest the audience should be tempted to dismiss what Lear says as mere raving, Shakespeare provides a choric comment through the mouth of Edgar:

> O, matter and impertinency mix'd!
> Reason in madness!

Lear's mad speeches, moreover, are all linked with other passages in the play. The revulsion against sex, besides being a well-known symptom of certain forms of madness, is linked with Lear's earlier suspicion that the mother of Goneril and Regan must be an adultress, with Gloucester's pleasant vices which led to the birth of Edmund and ultimately to his own blinding, and to Edmund's intrigues with Goneril and Regan. The attack on the imperfect instruments of justice, themselves guilty of the sins they condemn in others, is merely a reinforcement of Lear's speech in the storm, before he crossed the borders of madness:

> Let the great gods,
> That keep this dreadful pother o'er our
> heads,
> Find out their enemies now. Tremble, thou
> wretch,
> That hast within thee undivulged crimes,
> Unwhipp'd of justice: hide thee, thou bloody
> hand;
> Thou perjur'd, and thou simular man of
> virtue
> That art incestuous: caitiff, to pieces shake,
> That under covert and convenient seeming
> Hast practis'd on man's life: close pent-up
> guilts,
> Rive your concealing continents, and cry
> These dreadful summoners grace.

Here, as in the mad scene, the justice of the gods, from whom no secrets are hid, is contrasted with the imperfections of earthly justice.

One of Lear's first speeches after his wits begin to turn consists of a prayer to 'houseless poverty':

> Poor naked wretches, wheresoe'er you are,
> That bide the pelting of this pitiless storm,
> How shall your houseless heads and unfed
> sides,
> Your loop'd and window'd raggedness,
> defend you
> From seasons such as these? O, I have ta'en

Too little care of this! Take physic, pomp;
Expose thyself to feel what wretches feel,
That thou mayst shake the superflux to
     them,
And show the heavens more just.

It has not escaped notice that Gloucester expresses similar sentiments when he hands his purse to Poor Tom:

          heavens, deal so still!
Let the superfluous and lust-dieted man,
That slaves your ordinance, that will not see
Because he does not feel, feel your power
     quickly;
So distribution should undo excess,
And each man have enough.

This repetition is of some importance since [Levin L.] Schücking has argued [in his *Character Problems in Shakespeare's Plays*] that it is not really consistent with Shakespeare's philosophy to see in the play a gradual purification of Lear's character. Shakespeare, he argues, nowhere associates compassion for the poor 'with a higher moral standpoint'. The point is not whether Lear's pity was intended to arouse the audience's sympathy for him, nor even whether Shakespeare himself agreed with Lear's sentiments, but whether the audience would understand that his newly aroused concern for the poor was a sign of moral improvement. Here, surely, there can be no doubt. Shakespeare's audience was not so cut off from the Christian tradition as not to know that charity was a virtue; and the fact that similar sentiments are put into Gloucester's mouth is a reinforcement of Lear's words. If Lear were mad at this point—and he has not yet crossed the frontier—he would be expressing reason in madness. Even Schücking is constrained to admit that Lear's later criticisms of society show profound insight; but he claims that this does not exhibit a development of Lear's character, because it is dependent on a state of mental derangement. The Lear who welcomes prison with Cordelia

is not a purified Lear from whose character the flame of unhappiness has burnt away the ignoble dross, but a nature completely transformed, whose extraordinary vital forces are extinguished, or about to be extinguished.

But . . . the three moments in the play crucial to [A. C.] Bradley's theory of Lear's development—his recognition of error, his compassion for the poor, and his kneeling to Cordelia—occur either before or after his madness; and Schücking seems insufficiently aware of the 'reason in madness' theme so essential to the play's meaning. . . .

Lear is driven insane by a series of shocks. First, there is the attack by Goneril (I, iv). This makes him angrily pretend not to know her, or to know himself, but at this point it is still pretence:

Doth any here know me? This is not Lear:
Doth Lear walk thus? speak thus? Where are
     his eyes?
Either his notion weakens, or his discernings
Are lethargied.—Ha! waking? 'Tis not so.—
Who is it that can tell me who I am?

Later in the same scene he begins to realize that he has wronged Cordelia:

          O most small fault,
How ugly didst thou in Cordelia show! . . .
          O Lear, Lear, Lear!
Beat at this gate, that let thy folly in,
And thy dear judgement out!

In the next scene he comes to a full recognition of his folly: 'I did her wrong.' All the Fool's remarks in both scenes are designed, not to distract Lear's attention from Goneril's ingratitude, but to remind him of his foolishness in dividing his kingdom and banishing Cordelia. It is arguable that the Fool's loyalty to Cordelia helps to drive his master mad. At the end of the Act Lear has his first serious premonition of insanity:

O, let me not be mad, not mad, sweet
     heaven!
Keep me in temper: I would not be mad!

The second great shock comes in the second act when Lear finds Kent in the stocks. This causes the first physical symptoms of hysteria, which were probably borrowed by Shakespeare from [Samuel] Harsnett's pamphlet on demoniacs or from Edward Jorden's *Brief Discourse of a Disease Called the Suffocation of the Mother* (1603), which shows 'that divers strange actions and passions of the body of man, which in the common opinion, are imputed to the devil, have their true naturall causes, and do accompanie this Disease'. But the symptoms would now be described as 'racing heart' and 'rising blood pressure':

O, how this mother swells up toward my
     heart!
Hysterica passio, down, thou climbing
     sorrow,
Thy element's below. . . .
O me, my heart, my rising heart! but, down!

The third shock, the rejection by Regan, follows immediately. Lear prays for patience; he threatens revenges—the terrors of the earth—on the two daughters; his refusal to ease his heart by weeping is accompanied by the first rumblings of the storm which is a projecting on the macrocosm of the tempest in the microcosm; and he knows from the thunder that what he most feared will come to pass: 'O fool, I shall go mad!' Exposure to the storm completes what ingratitude began.

Lear's identification with the storm is both a means of presenting it on the stage and a sign that his passions have overthrown his reason. He contends 'with the fretful elements';

> tears his white hair,
> Which the impetuous blasts, with eyeless rage,
> Catch in their fury, and make nothing of;
> Strives in his little world of man to out-storm
> The to-and-fro-conflicting wind and rain.

But when Lear makes his next appearance, invoking the storm to destroy the seeds of matter, urging the gods to find out their hidden enemies, or addressing the poor naked wretches, he is not yet wholly mad, though he admits that his wits are beginning to turn. What finally pushes him over the borderline is the sudden appearance of Poor Tom who is both a living embodiment of naked poverty and one who is apparently what Lear had feared to become. Edgar, in acting madness, precipitates Lear's.

> What! have his daughters brought him to this pass?
> Could'st thou save nothing? Didst thou give 'em all? . . .
> Is it the fashion, that discarded fathers
> Should have thus little mercy on their flesh?
> Judicious punishment! 'twas this flesh begot
> Those pelican daughters.

The Fool comments:

> This cold night will turn us all to fools and madmen.

It is in fact the exposure and the physical exhaustion which prevents Lear's recovery from the shocks he has received. He is soon trying to identify himself with unaccommodated man by tearing off his clothes.

The madness of the elements, the professional 'madness' of the Fool, the feigned madness of Edgar, and the madness of the King himself together exemplify the break-up of society and the threat to the universe itself under the impact of ingratitude and treachery. When Gloucester appears, confessing that he is almost mad and that grief for his son's treachery has crazed his wits, only Kent is left wholly sane.

Poor Tom compares himself with emblematic animals—hog, fox, wolf, dog and lion—and Lear contrasts the naked Bedlam, who does not borrow from worm, beast, sheep and cat, with the sophisticated

people who do. Man without the refinements of civilization is 'a poor, bare, forked animal', as man without reason is no more than a beast. But Lear, who has lost his reason, is anxious to discuss philosophical questions with the man he takes for a learned Theban. His first question, 'What is the cause of thunder?', had been a stock one ever since the days of Pythagoras, who had taught, Ovid tells us [in *Metamorphoses*],

> The first foundation of the world: the cause of every thing:
> What nature was: and what was God: whence snow and lyghtning spring:
> And whether *Jove* or else the wynds in breaking clowdes doo thunder.

The storm suggests the question to Lear. . . .

Lear returns again and again to the thing which had driven him mad—his daughters' ingratitude. He asks if Poor Tom's daughters have brought him to this pass; he exclaims:

> Now, all the plagues that in the pendulous air
> Hang fated o'er men's faults light on thy daughters!—

declares that nothing but his unkind daughters 'could have subdu'd nature / To such a lowness'; and inveighs against the flesh which 'begot / Those pelican daughters'.

Just before he was driven out into the storm Lear had declared that he would avenge himself on his daughters:

> I will have such revenges on you both,
> That all the world shall—I will do such things,—
> What they are, yet I know not; but they shall be
> The terrors of the earth.

In the refuge provided by Gloucester Lear begins to brood on his revenge. . . .

Poor Tom in his blanket, and the Fool in his motley, suggest to his disordered mind two robed men of justice, and he imagines—this is his first actual illusion—that he sees Goneril and Regan. When we remember Lear's later attacks on the operations of justice because the judges are as guilty as the criminals they try, the justices in the mock trial of Goneril and Regan—a Bedlam beggar, a Fool, and a serving-man—are at least as likely to deal justly as a properly constituted bench, even though Lear accuses them of corruption in allowing the criminals to escape.

Shakespeare hits on two characteristics of certain kinds

of mental derangement—the substitution of a symbolic offence for a real one ('she kick'd the poor King her father') and the obsession with a visual image. Lear thinks of the 'warped looks' of Regan, though in an earlier scene he had spoken of her 'tender-hefted nature' and of her eyes which, unlike Goneril's, 'do comfort and not burn'. It was the contrast between her beauty and her behaviour when she, like Goneril, put on a frowning countenance, that impressed Lear with her warped looks; and the same contrast makes Lear ask:

> Is there any cause in nature that makes these hard hearts?

The question is an appropriate introduction to the next scene in which we see the tender-hearted Regan assisting at the blinding of Gloucester.

When the imaginary curtains are drawn on the sleeping Lear we do not see him again for nearly 500 lines—about half-an-hour's playing time—but we are prepared for the development of his lunacy by the two short scenes in the middle of the fourth Act. In one of these Kent reveals that Lear refuses to see Cordelia:

> A sovereign shame so elbows him: his own unkindness,
> That stripp'd her from his benediction, turn'd her
> To foreign casualties, gave her dear rights
> To his dog-hearted daughters, these things sting
> His mind so venomously, that burning shame
> Detains him from Cordelia.

It is significant—though I do not remember that anyone has called attention to it—that after the admission at the end of Act I 'I did her wrong', Lear makes no further reference to Cordelia until he recovers his wits at the end of Act IV. The reason for this is partly, no doubt, that the ingratitude of Goneril and Regan drives everything else from his mind; but we may suspect, too, that Lear's sovereign shame prevents him from facing his own guilt. In the other scene (IV, iv) Cordelia describes her mad father,

> singing aloud;
> With burdocks, hemlock, nettles, cuckoo-flowers,
> Darnel, and all the idle weeds that grow
> In our sustaining corn.

The significance of this picture is that Lear has reverted to his childhood. The Doctor . . . prescribes rest for the lunatic king.

> Our foster-nurse of nature is repose,
> The which he lacks; that to provoke in him,
> Are many simples operative, whose power
> Will close the eye of anguish.

In the scene in which the mad Lear meets the blinded Gloucester there is a wonderful blend of 'matter and impertinency'. Even the impertinency has the kind of free association which is often found in the utterances of certain types of lunatics; and precisely because he is mad Lear is freed from the conventional attitudes of society. He is able, at moments, to see more clearly and piercingly than the sane, because the sane buy their peace of mind by adjusting themselves to the received ideas of society. Lear recognizes the way he has been shielded from reality by flattery. He also sees the hypocritical pretensions of society with regard to sex and with regard to its treatment of criminals. And, finally, he sees that human life is inescapably tragic:

> Thou must be patient; we came crying hither;
> Thou know'st the first time that we smell the air,
> We wawl and cry . . .
> When we are born, we cry that we are come
> To this great stage of fools.

When we next see Lear he is awakening from a drugged sleep. The Doctor has given him the repose he needs. The second part of the cure consists of music which . . . was a means of winding up the untuned and jarring senses. The third part of the cure is Cordelia's love. It is characteristic of her that she is eloquent so long as Lear is asleep, and that she falls back into her natural reticence when he awakens. The cure is completed when he kneels to the daughter he has wronged and begs her forgiveness.

Josephine Waters Bennett

SOURCE: "The Storm Within: The Madness of Lear," in *Shakespeare Quarterly*, Vol. 13, No. 2, Spring, 1962, pp. 137-55.

[Bennett focuses on three scenes—III.iv, III.vi, and IV.vi—where, in her estimation, Lear shows unmistakable signs of insanity. She sees the king's obsessive references to daughters, his attempt to tear off his clothes, and his delusion that Poor Tom is an ancient philosopher as clear indications of madness. The chief causes of Lear's insanity, Bennett observes, are his bitter resentment toward his daughters and his inability to put up an effective defense against repeated humiliations. The critic argues that Lear's delusion at the close of the play—that Cordelia is not dead—is an expression of love and hope rather than a sign of madness.]

An understanding of Lear's madness is essential to any serious interpretation of the play and to any

Lear, Kent, the Fool, Edgar (disguised as Poor Tom), and Gloucester on the heath.

understanding of its structure. Yet critics have not agreed about when Lear goes mad, and almost no attention at all has been given to the dramatic function of his madness. . . .

Interpretation of the play has been distorted by too much emphasis on the external conflict, on Lear's helplessness and the inhumanity of his ungrateful daughters; there has been too little attention to Lear's struggle with himself, to the storm within. . . . Let us begin with . . . the three short scenes which exhibit Lear's insanity, its cause in his own character, and its effect on him.

The first of these scenes is III.iv. Like any competent dramatist, Shakespeare makes obvious those matters which an audience must understand in order to follow the play. . . .

Shakespeare's preparation had to be particularly thorough, because this is an innovation, not to be found in any earlier version of the story, and so the audience would not expect it if they were not prepared. Kent plants the idea in the first scene (line 146) when he implies that Lear is mad for disinheriting Cordelia. We see him in a furious rage in I.iv, and at the end of I.v, he expresses the fear,

> O, let me not be mad, not mad, sweet heaven!
> Keep me in temper; I would not be mad!
>> (ll. 40-41)

We do not see him again until II.iv, when he comes upon Kent in the stocks. Here his rising rage, his "hysterica passio" (l. 55), is countered by a real struggle for patience in his interview with Regan. But his daughters are pitiless in their contest to reduce his retinue, and as he goes out into the gathering storm Lear utters what proves to be a prophecy,

> I have full cause of weeping, but this heart
> Shall break into a hundred thousand flaws

Or ere I'll weep. O fool, I shall go mad!
Exeunt.

With the opening of Act III, the suggestions of approaching insanity grow more frequent. In the first scene Kent speaks of Lear's "unnatural and bemadding sorrow" (l. 38). In the second scene, after his invocation of divine justice, when Kent urges him to take shelter in the hovel, Lear replies, "My wits begin to turn" (l. 67). He goes on, however, to speak gentle and sane words to his Fool,

Come on, my boy, How dost, my boy? Art
cold?
I am cold myself. . . .

The statement, "My wits begin to turn", is a cue to the audience, and it is full of irony because it is more true than the speaker realizes; but Lear is still sane, as he is a moment and one short scene later when they reach the hovel and he hesitates to enter. To Kent's urging he replies, "Wilt break my heart?" (III. iv. 4). He is using the storm and his physical misery to counter and control the storm within his mind, fighting grief and rage with physical suffering, and the prospect of shelter threatens to destroy the balance, as indeed it does. He explains to Kent,

But where the greater malady is fixed,
The lesser is scarce felt. . . .
This tempest will not give me leave to
ponder
On things would hurt me more, . . .

(III.iv. 8-25)

His mind is on the brink, wavering between concern for physical suffering, and for others who share it, and self-pity, bitter hate, and longing for revenge, as he has made clear in the same two speeches:

The tempest in my mind
Doth from my senses take all feeling else
Save what beats there. Filial ingratitude, . . .

But I will punish home.
No, I will weep no more. In such a night
To shut me out! Pour on; I will endure.
In such a night as this! O Regan, Goneril,
Your old kind father, whose frank heart gave
all—
O, that way madness lies; let me shun that.
No more of that.

(ll. 12-22)

This is the storm within, which he is controlling precariously with the help of physical suffering inflicted by the cold. But he is on the brink of madness, as the audience has been repeatedly warned. He pauses for a moment to pity those

Poor naked wretches wheresoe'er you are,
That bide the pelting of this pitiless storm, . . .

(ll.28 f.)

He is not mad while he can pity others, and even blame himself:

O, I have ta'en
Too little care of this! Take physic, pomp;
Expose thyself to feel what wretches feel,
That thou mayst shake the superflux to them
And show the heavens more just.

(ll. 32-36)

He is the king, thinking charitably of others, and then, suddenly, one of those "wretches", Edgar disguised as Tom o'Bedlam, appears, and Lear, just controlling his own sanity by thinking of others, suddenly confuses the Bedlam beggar with himself, and he is over the brink.

His first words to Tom, "Didst thou give all to thy daughters? And art thou come to this?", might, by themselves, be taken as no more than bitter irony, but they are in prose and therefore suited to one whose wits are jangled, or fallen out of tune. More important for the audience, however, because more obvious, is Lear's obsessive reiteration, his insistence in the next three speeches on "his daughters", "thy daughters", and when Kent protests, "He hath no daughters, sir", Lear retorts hotly, "Death, traitor! Nothing could have subdued nature to such a lowness but his unkind daughters." This obsession, or *idèe fixe,* is one of the most easily recognized exhibitions of insanity. Lear's four references to Tom's "daughters", in four successive speeches, could hardly fail to convince listeners seeing the play for the first time, that what had been predicted repeatedly as about to happen has now happened: Lear has gone mad. The aimless babble of Tom's attempt to simulate madness contrasts effectively with Lear's fixed idea. However, just to be sure the point is not missed, the Fool is made to remark, "This cold night will turn us all to fools and madmen" (III.iv.75).

Lear's next speech, "What hast thou been?" invites Tom's caricature of a serving man, which ends incoherently and in turn produces Lear's "Is man no more than this? . . ." This speech ends with the second and most striking exhibition of insanity. . . . Lear's attempt to strip is an action which would be recognized by almost anyone as evidence of violent insanity. Who has not heard tales of people suddenly exhibiting this sign of madness? Today we would promptly put in a call to the nearest mental hospital. While this is not the most common manifestation of mental derangement, it is the most dramatic and easily recognized. Following upon the "eminently sane" "Is man no more than this?" and as an eminently logical conclusion, it exhibits just that "matter and imperti-nency mixed" (IV. vi. 171) which is characteristic of much insanity and which Lear exhibits in all three of his mad scenes.

Lear has given two obvious symptoms of mental derangement, but the rule of the theater is that the audience must be told *three* times anything that it must know and remember in order to understand what is to follow. Shakespeare seldom violates this rule. Immediately after the Fool has restrained Lear's effort to tear off his clothes, Gloucester appears to lead Lear to a better shelter. And now he develops the delusion that Tom in his blanket is an ancient philosopher. Beginning with the lines, "First let me talk with this philosopher. What is the cause of thun-der?" (l. 145), he speaks of nothing else. In six speech-es he five times calls Tom his philosopher, a "learned Theban", a "good Athenian". Neither Kent nor Gloucester can get his attention, and Kent explains (to Gloucester and the audience), "His wits begin t'unsettle." Gloucester echoes the thought (to make sure, among other things, that the audience does not miss it), "Thou sayest the King grows mad. . . . I am almost mad myself. . . . Grief hath crazed my wits" (ll. 156-161). . . .

In spite of the preparation for Lear's madness by his own and others' suggestions of it, and in spite of the three clear symptoms of derangement in III.iv, no critic, so far as I can find, has observed that the chief function of this scene at the hovel is to establish that Lear is mad. Even [Samuel Taylor] Coleridge, who does not seem to have felt that the madness must be progressive, says that "this scene *ends* with the first symptoms of positive derangement", and that Lear appears "in full madness in the sixth scene". Those who feel that the insanity must be climactic empha-size Kent's apologetic, "His wits *begin* t'unsettle" (iv.153), and Gloucester's reply, "Thou say'st the king *grows* mad", but at the opening of scene vi, only twenty-five lines later, Kent says, "*All* the power of his wits *have given way* to his impatience." If we are to weigh words and tenses, we cannot ignore Kent's *all* and *have given* while emphasizing *begins* and *grows.*

Whatever readers of the play, and criticism based on reading, may contend, it seems obvious that Shakespeare intended his auditors to understand that Lear goes mad in III.iv and is mad when he appears next in scene vi. If the play is a properly constructed Eliza-bethan tragedy, the climax, or point of no return in the struggle which makes the plot, should come in this scene. Scenes iii, v, and vii bring the Gloucester plot to its climax of horror. Scenes ii, iv, and vi are concerned with Lear. Scene ii shows us his defiance of the storm and his self-pity:

> I am a man

> More sinned against than sinning

> (III. ii. 58-59)

and his premonition of madness: "My wits begin to turn." In the next scene in which he appears we see him go mad, and in the opening of scene vi Kent says that "All the power of his wits have given way to his impatience." The problem is not, therefore, *whether* he is mad in III.iv, but *why* he is mad, and what dramatic purposes are served by the two further ex-hibitions of his madness.

Kent's clear and emphatic assertion that Lear is now completely mad prepares the audience for the unin-hibited exhibition of Lear's inner conflict, and in successive speeches we are shown his pride, his furi-ous desire for revenge, his attempt to use "justice" to get that revenge, and his self-pity. When the Fool proposes his conundrum, "Prithee, nuncle, tell me whether a madman be a gentleman or a yeoman?" Lear understands that the quip is aimed at him and replies proudly, "A king, a king." The Fool supplies the correct answer, but Lear's mind is obsessed with his passionate desire for revenge:

> To have a thousand with red burning spits
> Come hizzing in upon 'em—

> (ll. 15-16)

This furious desire to "punish home", to torture, is as shocking as Lear's earlier cursing of Goneril. It is, in fact, as savage in wish as the blinding of Glouces-ter is in deed. This is the cause of Lear's madness, his bitter, futile resentment, his frustrated will which has driven him to insane hatred.

In the play-within-a-play which follows, the Fool and Edgar humor Lear by acting the parts he assigns to them, but they also comment, in asides, on the pity of Lear's insanity; as when Edgar says, "Bless thy five wits!" and "My tears begin to take his part so much/ They mar my counterfeiting" (i.e. acting the part of judge). Lear's mind fluctuates from ex-citement over the imagined escape of Goneril to the abyss of self-pity in which he imagines his dogs behaving like his daughters,

> The little dogs and all,
> Tray, Blanch, and Sweetheart—see, they bark
> at me.

> (ll. 61-62)

The next moment he is ready to anatomize Regan to find out, "Is there any cause in nature that makes these hard hearts?" Then, forgetting what he is about, he tells Tom, "You, sir, I entertain for one of my hun-dred; only I do not like the fashion of your garments. You will say they are Persian; but let them be changed." This is an echo of his grievance (my hundred), and of his delusion that Tom is an ancient philosopher (end of sc. iv). It serves to remind the audience that he is mad. The reminder is reenforced, a few lines later by Kent's words, "trouble him not; his wits are gone."

This scene gives us, not a further degree of insanity, but a clear exposition of the internal cause of Lear's madness. Balked pride, humiliation, impotence, and self-pity have worn him out and in the midst of this scene he falls asleep out of sheer exhaustion. We do not see him again until IV.vi. . . .

Act IV, scene vi, the third and last of the "mad" scenes, opens with Gloucester's attempted suicide at Dover cliff, and his assertion that he has learned his lesson of patience. Then, in the Quarto, we have the stage direction, "Enter Lear mad." . . .

Lear's first speech is somewhat incoherent. He is under the delusion that he is in command of troops, for his first words are, "No, they cannot touch me for coining: I am the King himself. Nature's above art in that respect. There's your press money" (ll. 83 ff.). He imagines himself handing out coins to pay recruits. The King born (and so a manifestation of nature) is above the art of the coiner. The speech wanders on to the training of recruits to shoot, to the luring of a mouse within range with a piece of cheese, to a challenge to a duel, to an order of battle; finally he approves a soldier's shot and addresses himself to Edgar, "Give the word" (i.e. password). Edgar replies, "Sweet marjoram" and is told, "Pass."

Lear is in a world of his own imagining, and yet he vaguely senses and reacts to the military bustle around him. The blind Gloucester recognizes his voice, but Lear sees only "Goneril with a white beard". This is cruel, coming from the king for whom Gloucester lost his eyes, but there is worse to follow. Lear is still mad and cannot tell his friends from his enemies, yet he has learned one part of his lesson. He has been brought to recognize his physical limitations, for he goes on to say,

> They flattered me like a dog, and told me I had the white hairs in my beard ere the black ones were there. . . . When the rain came to wet me once, and the wind to make me chatter; when the thunder would not peace at my bidding; there I found 'em, . . . They told me I was everything. 'Tis a lie—I am not ague-proof. (ll. 96-104)

This is Lear's second long speech in this scene, and it marks the beginning of his recognition of his true place in the world—his human frailty; so it marks the beginning of his return to sanity. But he is not through with pride yet. Gloucester asks, "Is't not the King?" and Lear replies promptly, "Ay, every inch a king!" He knows himself, and yet, in a deeper sense, he does

not "know himself". In a vague way he has recognized Gloucester, but he speaks without pity or sympathy, not about Gloucester's loyalty and service to his king, but about his youthful fault:

> Adultery?
> Thou shalt not die. Die for adultery? No. . . .
> Let copulation thrive; for Gloucester's
>   bastard son
> Was kinder to his father than my daughters
> Got 'tween lawful sheets.
>
> (ll. 109-115)

This is cruel. Gloucester owed his blindness not only to the treachery of his bastard son, but also to his loyalty to Lear. He had been punished for his adultery, though Lear in his mad state did not know it—but even if we must assume that he did not know of Edmund's treachery, even if he did not know of Gloucester's loyalty, it was unfeeling of Lear to twit his old liege-man on his blindness—a fact which he did see. Gloucester asks, "Doest thou know me?" and Lear replies,

> I remember thine eyes well enough. Doest thou squiny at me? No, do thy worst, blind Cupid; I'll not love. Read thou this challenge; mark but the penning of it. . . . O, ho, are you there with me? No eyes in your head, nor no money in your purse? [i.e. you are a blind beggar.] Your eyes are in a heavy case, your purse in a light one; yet you see how this world goes. (ll. 135-146)

Beginning with the next speech he launches into a tirade against the world, its hypocrisy and injustice, ending,

> Get thee glass eyes
> And, like a scurvy politician, seem
> To see the things thou doest not. Now, now,
>   now, now!
> Pull off my boots. Harder, harder! So.

The action suggested by this speech is that Lear pulls off his boots (the act of disrobing again). A few lines later he has evidently taken off his hat, for he says,

> This' a good block.
> It were a delicate stratagem to shoe
> A troop of horse with felt. I'll put 't in
>   proof,
> And when I have stol'n upon these son-in-
>   laws,
> Then kill, kill, kill, kill, kill, kill!

His hat is not only off, but the lines suggest that he is trying to put it on his bootless foot. The terrible reiteration of "kill" proves to be the last thunder-peal of the storm in Lear's mind. He is certainly mad from his first speech where he imagines that he is with his army, to his exit, running, followed by the attendants Cordelia has sent to find him. Yet he is not so completely insane as he was in the scene where he attempted to try Goneril and Regan before the Bedlam beggar and the Fool as two judges. In IV. vi, even in his first and most incoherent speech to imaginary soldiers he seems to be aware of the military bustle around him, although he misinterprets it. His second speech recalls the storm and shows that he has at least learned that "I am not ague-proof". A little later, when Gloucester asks to kiss his hand, he replies, "Let me wipe it first; it smells of mortality." In lines 173-177 he speaks sanely,

> If thou wilt weep my fortunes, take my eyes.
> I know thee well enough; thy name is
>   Gloucester.
> Thou must be patient. . . .

But he is not yet ready to be patient himself. His resentment breeds distrust and he mistakes Cordelia's officers for enemies and exhibits the typical cunning of a madman in pretending to yield to them, and then suddenly running. One of these gentlemen makes the interpretive comment,

> A sight most pitiful in the meanest wretch,
> Past speaking of in a king!
>
> (ll. 200-201)

By this simple act of running away (in his stocking feet?), Shakespeare invokes our deepest pity for this proud, willful, stubborn, yet helpless old man. . . .

We cannot leave the subject of Lear's madness without considering one more scene. There has been question of whether Lear returns to insanity just before he dies. His delusion that Cordelia still lives, that he can prove it by a looking-glass, a feather, that she has spoken—these things are not evidences of insanity, but of hope and love. Lear is dazed and stunned by his loss. He cannot accept it. His mind struggles against the unbearable truth. Cordelia is the whole world to him now. He replies to Kent at random, and Albany finally says,

> He knows not what he says; and vain it is
> That we present us to him.
>
> (V. iii. 293-294)

It is not that he is insane, but that he has completely forgotten self in his concentration on Cordelia. Nothing else enters his consciousness. When he is told that his two wicked daughters are dead, he replies (sadly, looking at Cordelia), "Ay, so I think". His daughters are all Cordelia. He has forgotten hate and revenge. When he speaks of killing "the slave that was a-hanging thee", there is a flash of the old pride, but it is only in retrospect,

> I have seen the day, with my good biting
>   falchion
> I would make them skip. I am old now,
> And these crosses spoil [i.e. impair] me. Who
>   are you?
> Mine eyes are not o'th'best. I'll tell you
>   straight.
>
> (ll. 277-280)

Here he recognizes Kent, but he has forgotten his servant Caius who served him in his madness. He is preoccupied, and inattentive, rather than insane. He pays no attention to the messenger who announces Edmund's death, nor to Albany's plan for ruling the state (a piece of business which convention required). Albany breaks off, directing attention to Lear, with his "O, see, see!"

Here Lear makes his last speech, which is sane down to the last three lines, and then reason and life slacken the string together:

> And my poor fool is hanged: no, no, no life?
> Why should a dog, a horse, a rat, have life,
> And thou no breath at all? Thou'lt come no
>   more,
> Never, never, never, never, never.
> Pray you undo this button. Thank you sir.
> Do you see this? Look on her! Look her
>   lips,
> Look there, look there—*He dies.*

LEAR

Lear's dual role as monarch and head of a family—illustrating the Renaissance notion of "the king's two bodies"—has been evaluated by Northrop Frye, Marilyn Gaull, Joyce Carol Oates, and Derek Traversi. Frye points out that when Lear gives up his official title, he effectively destroys his identity. Gaull points out that Lear's abdication of his throne and his banishment of Cordelia are offenses against the concept of universal order, and thus they create the conditions for disorder in his kingdom. Oates contends that Lear is caught in the masculine dilemma of preserving both kingship and fatherhood. His personal self is overwhelmed by his official stature, she argues, and as a result he relinquishes both forms of authority. Traversi contends that Lear's dual role sets his personal tragedy against a universal background, with Lear's willful abdication leading to social disorder.

The king's willfulness is the focus of many critics. **William Rosen** sees Lear as proud, authoritative, and convinced that he is infallible. He has no interest in others' points of views, Rosen contends, and refuses to recognize that his own perspective may be limited.

Judd Arnold maintains that in the first part of the play Lear is irrational and irresponsible. John C. McCloskey declares that in the first scene Lear demonstrates egoism and misjudgment. Because of his self-delusion, McCloskey contends, Lear invokes the tragic consequences of his actions. Frye suggests that Lear is not only foolish to give up his identity as king, he is gullible into the bargain. George W. Williams views Lear in the early scenes as proud, arrogant, and stubborn. In contrast, Simon O. Lesser sees Lear in the love test as frightened and anxious, a man preparing for death and desperately in need of love and reassurance. Maynard Mack reminds us that there are no psychological antecedents for Lear's behavior in the first scene: his actions appear to spring from "the bedrock of his personality" and the consequences of his action are both unlooked-for and spectacular.

Lear on the heath, exiled from the world with which he's familiar and which he dominated, is a focus of critical attention. His suffering there draws pity and a broad range of critical interpretation. Rosen maintains that Lear's spiritual stature increases during his passage through this alien world. As he searches for justice and seeks to understand himself, Rosen asserts, he becomes more than an individual: his quest for order and meaning is a universal experience. When Lear learns compassion for others, Rosen declares, he is completely transformed. By contrast, Arnold contends that the king never entirely frees himself from error or attains true self-knowledge. His struggle to do so is admirable, even noble, Arnold acknowledges, but there is no evidence that he ever attains spiritual renewal. Frye believes that Lear changes on the heath and begins to recover his own sense of himself when he first learns to take thought of others. Similarly, Kenneth Muir also holds that Lear's new-found compassion marks a profound step forward in the king's moral development. Unlike Arnold, Muir maintains that before the onset of his madness Lear recognizes that his own actions contributed directly to his tragedy.

The final scene of the play does not support the notion of Lear's spiritual regeneration, Arnold contends, but it does underscore the idea that although good doesn't triumph, neither does evil. William Empson suggests that the deaths of Lear and Cordelia vividly illustrate a central idea in the play: good intentions can become absurdly perverted by one's own nature and by unexpected events. Enid Welsford, too, argues that the deaths of Lear and Cordelia illuminate a principal motif running through *King Lear*: "In this world there is no poetic justice." For additional commentary on the character of Lear, see the excerpt by **Northrop Frye** in the OVERVIEWS section, the excerpts by **George W. Williams**, and **John C. McCloskey** in the LANGUAGE AND IMAGERY section, the excerpts by **Marilyn Gaull** and **Simon O. Lesser** in the

section on LOVE, the excerpts by **Kenneth Muir** and **Josephine Waters Bennett** in the MADNESS section, and the excerpt by **Enid Welsford** in the section on THE FOOL.

William Rosen

SOURCE: "King Lear," in *Shakespeare and the Craft of Tragedy*, 1960. Reprint by Cambridge, Mass: Harvard University Press, 1967, pp. 1-51.

[*Rosen demonstrates how the focus of dramatic interest in* King Lear *shifts from concern with a particular man to such universal issues as justice, order, and meaning in the world. Initially Lear is imperious, vain, and unwilling to consider any perspective other than his own, the critic notes. In subsequent scenes, Rosen asserts, his notions of himself are no longer valid, for the natural order of society has been subverted and Lear's stature has been stripped away. The critic asserts that on the heath, Lear's suffering becomes universalized: his search for justice in a world where there is none is the dilemma we all must face. Although ultimate knowledge and certainty cannot be achieved, Lear's personality is completely transformed, Rosen concludes, for he develops compassion and comes to understand the ties that bind all humanity together.*]

Apart from action, there are two major devices that delineate character on the stage: direct self-characterization—what the hero says of himself—and the characterization of the hero by others. Often Shakespeare anticipates and prefigures the entrance of the tragic hero by having characters talk about him before he actually comes onto the stage; and such a technique is used notably in *Romeo and Juliet, Julius Caesar, Othello, Antony and Cleopatra* and *Coriolanus*. By prefiguring the hero the dramatist imposes upon the audience a certain angle of vision: the playwright provides the audience with a dramatic attitude towards the central figure by having others preview his traits or impart value judgments on him. Thus we actively entertain certain emotions towards the hero before meeting him; and when he does appear, his words and actions are inevitably compared to the brief portrait already sketched for us.

In *King Lear*, though the king's character is not sketched before he appears on stage, he nevertheless comes immediately into a certain frame of reference, not through the technique of prefiguring, but through his own exalted status. For an Elizabethan audience particularly, his figure would expand in minds to encompass a whole context of values. The person of Lear is from the very beginning associated with great honor, for he can be viewed as the highest human embodiment of all the elements which give order and dignity to society: he is king of his family, and he an old man. Hence the respect which he should command is triply compounded. . . .

Certainly "kingship" had an evocative power for Elizabethans. There is divinity that hedges a king—we find this idea reiterated in much of the writing of the age. Furthermore, the correspondence between the power of the king and that of the father was an Elizabethan commonplace illustrating the order of a universe in which, as God governed all, so kings ruled states, and fathers, families. . . . [The] ordered family, the private life of a nation, is a mirroring in miniature of the ordered hierarchy of public society; and analogies between the king and his subjects and the father and his children prevailed.

It is within such a context that we first see King Lear: his figure activates in the minds of an audience patterns of value of which he is the embodiment. His formal entrance highlights all the dignity and authority associated with kingship. The set of notes sounded, the "sennet," ushers in the concrete symbol of royalty, "enter one bearing a coronet"; and the stage directions give the precise order of entrance which accords with the prerogatives of rank: "King Lear, Cornwall, Albany, Goneril, Regan, Cordelia, and Attendants." On the Elizabethan stage this would be a stately procession of splendor, Lear the central figure in a crowded scene. All are Lear's subjects, dependent on him.

Lear's stature is even further magnified in his first extended pronouncement in which he tells of his intentions to divest himself of "rule,/Interest of territory, cares of state" (I.i.50), for we see him in the role of public and private figure at one and the same time. Because he is king, his actions in dividing the realm have public consequences affecting the destiny of the state; as benefactor to his children in this division, his actions affect the private life of the family as well. And yet, though the figure of the king bodies forth the ideal, the highest good of family and nation, it is important to see that in this scene Shakespeare presents his central character as an ironist would; and in this way: that the audience does not fully engage its sympathies with Lear or those who oppose him since the dramatist supports the values which Lear represents while revealing the king's misguided position.

Lear's character is objectively dramatized at the beginning. And in situations that are dramatized rather than narrated, the task of projecting states of mind devolves upon the language itself. In Lear's first lengthy speech, which is balanced and regally formal, Shakespeare has the king dramatically reveal himself as proud, authoritative, at the height of his power, wishing to hear not truth, but flattery:

> Tell me, my daughters,—

> Since now we will divest us both of rule,
> Interest of territory, cares of state,—
> Which of you shall we say doth love us
>   most, . . .

(I. i. 49)

Lear's abdication is thus the occasion for a pageant of flattery: each daughter is to vie with the other in a public display of love. Goneril fulfills his expectations:

> Sir, I love you more than word can wield
>   the matter;
> Dearer than eye-sight, space, and liberty;
> Beyond what can be valued, rich or rare;
> No less than life, with grace, health, beauty,
>   honour;
> As much as child e'er lov'd, or father found;
> A love that makes breath poor, and speech
>   unable:
> Beyond all manner of so much I love you.

(I.i.56)

Shakespeare makes it obvious that Lear already has in mind the kind of answer he expects from his daughters. It is significant that after Goneril's fulsome protestations of love Lear does not evaluate or praise her remarks. He makes no comment at all on her speech. He has heard what he has wanted to hear, and he immediately bestows upon her a share of the kingdom. It is interesting to note that in *The True Chronicle History of King Leir*, when Gonorill proclaims her love for him, Leir comments, "O, how thy words revive my dying soul" (I.iii.54).

Shakespeare reinforces this imperious characteristic of Lear. Again, after Regan's testimony of love, Lear makes no reference to her speech; in *The Chronicle History* he says, "Did never Philomel sing so sweet a note" (I.iii.74). He allots her portion and calls on Cordelia to "Speak." And it is important to observe that in the three instances where Lear asks the daughters to proclaim the extent of their love, he imperiously concludes with the curt, monosyllabic, "Speak." (The Folio omits the concluding "Speak" addressed to Regan.)

Thus, when Cordelia refuses to follow her sisters in answering with "glib and oily art," the stage has been dramatically set for Lear's wrathful indignation.

> *Lear.*   what can you say to draw
>   A third more opulent than your sisters?
>   Speak.
> *Cordelia.* Nothing, my lord.
> *Lear.* Nothing!
> *Cordelia.* Nothing.
> *Lear.* Nothing will come of nothing. Speak
>   again.
> *Cordelia.* Unhappy that I am, I cannot heave

My heart into my mouth. I love your
  Majesty
According to my bond; no more nor less.

(I.i.87)

Lear's real attitude comes out when in thwarted rage he revealingly says to Cordelia: "Better thou/ Hadst not been born than not t' have pleas'd me better" (I.i.237).

The situation presented here is the problem of any human relationship: shall we attempt to understand another, really understand another person, or will we accept him only on our own terms? Shakespeare presents Lear as a powerful king, wilful and unyielding, a man who has no desire to understand others or communicate with them. He has not here the humanity of thinking beyond himself. He hears only what he wants to hear, tinting everything with the color of his own mind. When Cordelia speaks these words:

> Good my lord,
> You have begot me, bred me, lov'd me: I
> Return those duties back as are right fit;
> Obey you, love you, and most honour you.
> Why have my sisters husbands, if they say
> They love you all? Haply, when I shall wed,
> That lord whose hand must take my plight
>   shall carry
> Half my love with him, half my care and
>   duty.
> Sure, I shall never marry like my sisters,
> To love my father all.

(I.i.98)

Lear, expecting an entirely different answer, the kind of satisfying flattery given by the politic Goneril and Regan, makes no attempt to understand what Cordelia is really trying to say, and casts off the person dearest to him.

Though Lear acts in wrathful haste and blindness, his actions are analyzed, his motivation unfolded, that the audience may see and understand his character fully and unambiguously. Lear even explains himself, like an onlooker unfolding the psychology of action. When he shouts to Cordelia, "Better thou/ Hadst not been born than not t' have pleas'd me better" (I.i.237), he is, in a way, impartially describing himself as one who values love only as a means of adding to his own vanity. And in Kent's banishment there is the same self-revelation. In violent outburst Lear says that Kent must be banished because he sought to make the king break his vow and reverse his sentence which "nor our nature nor our place can bear" (I.i.174). Yet such statements cannot be taken as indications of a high degree of self-awareness on the part of the protagonist. They are best viewed as a mode of partial narrative which S. L. Bethell has described as

"appropriate to poetic drama, since it renders the psychological situation clear without transferring attention from the verse to the process of naturalistic induction" [*Shakespeare and the Popular Dramatic Tradition*].

One can say that in the beginning Lear equates "nature" with his own "conception" of himself; that for Lear the natural rights inherent in majesty, fatherhood, and age demand—or, rather, take for granted—the unquestioning and undivided love of children for parent, benefactor and king; the respect of youth for age; and the complete obedience of subject to ruler. Thus, when Cordelia refuses to conform to Lear's own conception of what is natural, the king arbitrarily casts her off as unnatural, disclaiming all "paternal care,/ Propinquity and property of blood" (I.i.115). He banishes Kent because his "nature" allows not the breaking of vows. For Lear, then, nature is not the external world, or reason, but his own image; and he looks out onto a world which must mirror back his own conceptions of loyalty, love, justice, perfection. Proudly independent in the omnipotence of self, he is detached from all, and in his isolation feels no responsibility and kinship towards others. Lear's folly, like that of Oedipus, is one of blindness, the overweening belief in the infallibility of one's own being, the failure to recognize the limitations of mortality. . . .

[This] view is substantiated for us by Lear's friend, Kent, and by his future antagonists, Goneril and Regan. These three appraise him and reach the same conclusions. Kent slightingly calls him "old man," characterizes his actions as "folly" and "hideous rashness." At the end of the scene, when Goneril and Regan review the happenings in businesslike prose, their final judgment of the king, shrewd and incisive, has already been dramatized as truth:

> *Goneril.* You see how full of changes his age is; the observation we have made of it hath not been little. He always lov'd our sister most; and with what poor judgement he hath now cast her off appears too grossly.
>
> *Regan.* 'Tis the infirmity of his age; yet he hath ever but slenderly known himself.
>
> *Goneril.* The best and soundest of his time hath been but rash; then must we look from his age to receive not alone the imperfections of long-engraffed condition, but therewithal the unruly waywardness that infirm and choleric years bring with them.

(I.i.291)

The speeches of Goneril and Regan at the end of this exposition scene attune us to their later treatment of Lear by arousing a state of expectation, of speculation as to how they will curb their father and king, who has given up his power and yet would, as Goneril fears, still "manage those authorities/ That he hath given away!" (I.iii.17)

In analyzing the way in which Shakespeare portrays Lear at the beginning of the play it becomes evident that the audience sees and understands events not primarily through Lear's eyes, thus becoming one with him, sympathizing with his actions, but through the eyes of Kent and Goneril and Regan who interpret him for us. Friend and foes, by agreeing on the folly which impels Lear, formulate a dramatic attitude towards the character.

When next we encounter Lear there begins a shift in the audience's point of view because there is an attendant change of focus. . . . Lear suddenly moves precipitously from an old world of his own conception into a tough new world which stretches him upon its rack. In this new world Lear finds himself a stranger, rejected, and his is a continual battle to maintain self-respect, to hold desperately to the vision of the man he once was. His values—true values—are no longer recognized; and it is this sudden shift into a new world that drastically changes the dramatic point of view towards Lear.

In Lear's act of dividing the kingdom we saw him at the height of his power. From this high point begins a fall which culminates in the stripping of Lear to the very bone in the storm scene on the heath, a stripping of the respect and honor due him as king, father, and old man. And it is this profound respect which he should command, which is his natural and inherent right, that comprises the informing context of values and determines the audience's point of view towards Lear. . . .

The stripping process is the major movement of the first part of *King Lear*. It begins when Lear disinherits himself. With a pointing of a finger to the map before him he divests himself of his lands and retains only the name and honor of king without responsibility or power. Next Lear strips from himself Cordelia, then Kent. We note the further fall of the king and his further dismantling in the colloquy between Goneril and Oswald. When Goneril learns that Lear struck her gentleman for chiding his fool, she tells Oswald that when the king returns from hunting she will not speak to him; Oswald is to tell the king that she is sick. Furthermore, she even instructs the servant to show disrespect to her father and king:

> Put on what weary negligence you please,
> You and your fellows; I'd have it come to question.
> If he distaste it, let him to my sister,
> Whose mind and mine, I know, in that are one,

> Not to be over-rul'd. Idle old man,
> That still would manage those authorities
> That he hath given away!
>
> (I.iii.12)

Goneril, evincing this attitude to Oswald, triply compounds her felony: she is disrespectful to kingship, fatherhood and old age.

The relentless stripping of the king continues. When Lear asks Oswald where Goneril is, Oswald does not answer; he merely departs. And when Lear asks his knight why Oswald did not return when called, the knight reports, "he would not" (I.iv.59). Such an answer is given to the king, and we must remember that he still commands the respect owing to a king, and that here a servant has given him insult. The knight feels impelled to speak out: "to my judgement, your Highness is not entertain'd with that ceremonious affection as you were wont. There's a great abatement of kindness appears as well in the general dependants as in the Duke himself also and your daughter" (I.iv.61). Lear's reply, "Thou but remb'rest me of mine own conception," is a poignant recognition of what is beginning to take place. And immediately after this, when Lear and Oswald meet, and Lear commandingly asks Oswald, "Who am I, sir?" (I.iv.85), Oswald replies with what can only be considered a deliberate insult: "My lady's father." Here the superiority of degrees so central to the Elizabethan conception of an ordered hierarchic society is completely overthrown and the position of king is subverted.

In this same scene the Fool, acting as chorus, focuses attention on these aspects of overturned degree. It is the Fool who gives the king a lesson in government, pointing out his folly in dividing the kingdom: "When thou clovest thy crown i' th' middle, and gav'st away both parts, thou bor'st thine ass on thy back o'er the dirt. Thou hadst little wit in thy bald crown when thou gav'st thy golden one away" (I.iv.175). "Thou art an O without a figure," the Fool tells Lear, "I am better than thou art now; I am a Fool, thou art nothing" (I.iv.212). It is natural that a king should rule a kingdom; it is unnatural for him to give it away. It is natural that a man should ride an ass; it is unnatural that he should carry the ass on his back. This is the complete overturning of what is natural. . . . [An] undivided kingdom symbolized order and due subordination in the realm; with the division of kingdom comes the breaking of all natural bonds, and chaos ensues.

The Fool holds up before Lear the mirror of his follies that he might clearly see his actions and their consequences. In the beginning of the play Kent, Goneril and Regan framed Lear's figure by objectively analyzing him. Now the Fool's utterances help frame the king, and the audience, seeing Lear in terms of the Fool's remarks, quickly perceives the relations between the two. While the Fool is certainly the disinterested truthteller, the "punctum indifferens" of the play, as Enid Welsford tells us in her social and literary history *The Fool,* his truth narrows upon the folly of a king who would give away his titles; of a father who would allow the child to rule him; of a man who deserves to be beaten for being old before his time. The Fool is, as it were, a mirror for magistrates and fathers. But it is to be noticed that Lear does not seem to recognize his own figure in the Fool's mirror. It is we, the audience, who see it far more clearly than Lear. Thus, the audience is drawn into sympathetic participation with Lear because it can see, Lear cannot; it shares the Fool's superior knowledge, unintelligible to Lear for the most part, and recognizes in Lear the collision of opposites: a man who would still cling to the conception of proper place, the values taken for granted before; yet now, in a new world, put in his improper place. And once having entered into Lear's perspective we are forced to look on the world with his eyes.

Though Kent has said to Lear concerning the Fool, "This is not altogether fool, my lord" (I.iv.165), Lear will not recognize the significance of the Fool's wisdom until later, and it will be a self-recognition, not the result of another's explanation, but gained through his own suffering. In Act I, scene iv, Lear does not realize the significance of the Fool's statement: "thou mad'st thy daughters thy mothers; for when thou gav'st them the rod, and puttest down thine own breeches. . . ." No sooner does the Fool say this than his statement is demonstrated: Goneril, the daughter, comes in and reproves the king for what she considers to be his insolent retinue. Here we have an example of the daughter instructing the father. Again we see the stripping of Lear—in this instance, of the dignity and respect which a daughter owes him. Again, the Fool acts as chorus: "May not an ass know when the cart draws the horse?" (I/iv.244)—another reference to the inversion of order: the cart drawing the horse; the daughter applying the rod to the father.

And when the daughter, Goneril, wants to diminish the king further, when she suggests that he reduce the number of his retinue, he breaks forth in impassioned anguish, calling her degenerate bastard, and goes off to his other daughter, Regan, who he thinks will not, could not, be so unkind.

The whittling away of the king's stature continues unabated. When the disguised Kent becomes a messenger for the king and is put into the stocks by Cornwall for striking Oswald, it is a further insult to Lear, and this is pointed out by both Kent and Gloucester. . . . [When] Lear sees his messenger in the stocks, this insult against kingship is the first thing to come to mind: "What's he that hath so much thy place mistook/To set thee here?" "They durst not do't," he cries out. "They could not, would not do't. 'Tis worse than murder/ To do upon respect such violent outrage" (II.iv.12).

But the outrage proceeds. Lear now learns that Cornwall and Regan refuse to speak with him. He still has not attuned himself to the realities of his new world where the inversion of which the Fool speaks has become the norm; and he tries to rationalize and minimize the affront. . . . But when he looks upon Kent in the stocks there can be no doubt of the insult being done himself; and he passionately commands that his servant be released and that Cornwall and Regan be immediately summoned.

In this scene Lear is further degraded. After Regan finally comes, she says to Lear:

> I pray you
> That to our sister you do make return;
> Say you have wrong'd her, sir.
>
> (II.iv.152)

And Lear replies:

> Ask her forgiveness?
> Do you but mark how this becomes the
>   house:
> "Dear daughter, I confess that I am old;
> Age is unnecessary. On my knees I beg
> That you'll vouchsafe me raiment, bed, and
>   food."
>
> (II.iv.154)

The king actually kneels before Regan in enacting the shame that would be his were he to return to Goneril, forced to beg her forgiveness and favors. Here we have a picture of the grandeur that was king, now plundered of dignity, bent at the knees.

A further reminder of his ignominy comes when the trumpet heralds not a person of eminence, but, ironically, Oswald, who brought galling shame upon him. The indignities against Lear are compellingly, mordantly dramatized when, in a stylized manner, the king is forced to turn from one daughter to the other as they relentlessly reduce the number of his followers. What began as a retinue of one hundred for the king is halved to fifty by Goneril; halved to twenty-five by Regan (here Lear cries out, "I gave you all"). And when Lear turns to Goneril with the words:

> I'll go with thee.
> Thy fifty yet doth double five and twenty,
> And thou art twice her love.
>
> (II.iv.261)

the number is further reduced, until Regan divests him of all—"What need one?"

The daughters have finally stripped him of everything: honor, respect, filial devotion, retainers. The dismantling of the king is almost completed; its culmination is to come in the scene on the heath. When Regan says to Lear, "What need one?" he replies in words which show a turning point in his characterization:

> O, reason not the need! Our basest beggars
> Are in the poorest thing superfluous.
> Allow not nature more than nature needs,
> Man's life is cheap as beast's. Thou art a
>   lady;
> If only to go warm were gorgeous,
> Why, nature needs not what thou gorgeous
>   wear'st,
> Which scarcely keeps thee warm. But, for
>   true need,—
>
> (II.iv.267)

If man is stripped of that which gives him dignity—his true need, if he is judged solely by his basic needs, is he no more than an animal? Is it only clothes which make a man, which separate him from the beast? Deprived of the last vestige of outward dignity, Lear asks questions about the status of human values. His speech is an address not only to Regan, but to the world, an agonizing attempt to find universal meaning, universal justice. His particular fate therefore becomes the fate of mankind, and the audience can no longer take an objective view of Lear. To see a man fall from greatness and be reduced to nothingness is an awful spectacle. But when Lear universalizes his particular experience in his address to the world the dignity of all men is at stake. . . . Sympathizing with Lear's values and his precarious position, through his speech we move into his consciousness; we see the world with his eyes, we are committed to his point of view. . . .

The particular experience of Lear achieves its universality when in his speech to Regan he attempts to pierce through superficialities to the realities they disguise, to expose the real as it should be; for in this he presents the universal human desire to find in the world meaning and order. Waging a heroic battle to preserve his self-control and dignity in the face of the abuses which his daughters have heaped upon him, Lear, in his great agony, turns to address the heavens themselves:

> You heavens, give me that patience, patience
>   I need!
> You see me here, you gods, a poor old man,
> As full of grief as age; wretched in both!
> If it be you that stirs these daughters' hearts
> Against their father, fool me not so much

> To bear it tamely; touch me with noble
>   anger,
> And let not women's weapons, water-drops,
> Stain my man's cheeks!
>
> (II.iv.274)

Isolated, forsaken, despairing of men on earth, Lear can only call upon cosmic powers for help. This sense of isolation, of alienation from society, is characteristic of the tragic hero. Lear, like Job, has had his values and beliefs shaken, and finding no comfort or understanding in men of his own society, turns to the heavens. So Job, understood neither by his wife nor the comforters, had only one recourse: he carried on a monologue directed not so much to the comforters as to the heavens above, pleading to see and reason with God.

In this climactic speech Lear's thoughts focus upon the respect due to age and fatherhood. In a previous speech he poignantly summarized all the respect and honor which should have been his by right: "'Tis not in thee," he told Regan,

> To grudge my pleasures, to cut off my train,
> To bandy hasty words, to scant my sizes,
> And in conclusion to oppose the bolt
> Against my coming in. Thou better know'st
> The offices of nature, bond of childhood,
> Effects of courtesy, dues of gratitude.
> Thy half o' th' kingdom hast thou not
>   forgot,
> Wherein I thee endow'd.
>
> (II.iv.176)

Lear therefore bodies forth the traditional values which give order and cohesion to society: the offices of nature, bond of childhood, effects of courtesy, dues of gratitude. No longer, as in the opening scene of the play, is a balanced point of view maintained towards Lear, where the audience is put in the position of his opponents, seeing the events primarily through their eyes. All the former tensions and conflicts are viewed in a new light because they are seen in a new intellectual and emotional perspective: the ideal of objective values, the order and civilized decency which Lear represents. When Goneril and Regan degrade their father, more than an individual is threatened; the civilized values of humanity are imperilled.

The gulf between the real and the ideal, between what Goneril and Regan actually do and what they should do, is so enormous that it tears Lear's reason to shreds, pitching him into insanity. Lear has come to recognize fully what his daughters are doing to him; and after appealing to the gods, he turns upon his daughters in bitterness. Stripped of his authority to command respect, his appeal to natural courtesies unheeded, the broken rhythms and thoughts of his speech reflect his impotency and aching bewilderment:

> No, you unnatural hags,
> I will have such revenges on you both
> That all the world shall—I will do such
>   things,—
> What they are, yet I know not; but they
>   shall be
> The terrors of the earth. You think I'll
>   weep:
> No, I'll not weep.
> I have full cause of weeping; but this heart
>   *(Storm and tempest.)*
> Shall break into a hundred thousand flaws,
> Or ere I'll weep. O, Fool! I shall go mad!
>   (II.iv.281)

The oncoming storm in the macrocosm, indicated by the Folio stage direction, *"Storm and tempest,"* coincides with the storm which is beginning in the microcosm, the seething conflict within Lear's own mind. Driven to the edge of madness, Lear flees to an inhuman nature which is on the very edge of the civilized world. This nature to which he flees is a nature of chaos corresponding to the chaos in himself. Both the macrocosm and the microcosm are rent and in discord, no longer an expression of cosmic harmony and reason. . . .

At the end of Act II the powerful members of the new order retreated "out o' th' storm" and the "wild night" and the doors of the castle were shut behind Lear. At the beginning of Act III, when the action moves to the heath, we feel that we have reached the end of the human world. Nature's bounds are broken. When Kent asks, "Where's the king?" a gentleman paints in words the picture for the audience:

> Contending with the fretful elements;
> Bids the wind blow the earth into the sea,
> Or swell the curled waters 'bove the main,
> That things might change or cease; tears his
>   white hair,
> Which the impetuous blasts with eyeless rage
> Catch in their fury, and make nothing of;
> Strives in his little world of man to out-scorn
> The to-and-fro-conflicting wind and rain.
> This night, wherein the cub-drawn bear
>   would couch,
> The lion and the belly-pinched wolf
> Keep their fur dry, unbonneted he runs,
> And bids what will take all.
>   (III.i.4)

What does the gentleman's speech, which prefigures Lear, stress? We see all civilization a place of storm, with Lear at the center, raging thundering defiance. The king, once regally confident in his own conception of what constituted nature, now is a prey to the

elements. Lear—the gentleman emphasizes—would impose upon nature his puny will; but nature is indifferent. Lear contends with the elements, "That things might change or cease." And the extremes of these two demands—change or complete destruction—give a most revealing insight into the king's condition. His present situation is so intolerable that it must either be temporary or give way to the end of the world.

We are concerned, then, with personality in conflict with the existing universe. Because of this monumental struggle, Lear's spiritual stature is greatly magnified; and because he represents civilized values which are threatened, all men are endangered. If we concentrate on the remarks made about Lear, we see that these form a significant pattern. Kent talks of the "hard rein" which Albany and Cornwall have "borne/ Against the old kind king" (III.i.27); of "how unnatural and bemadding sorrow/ The King hath cause to plain" (III.i.38). Gloucester predicts to Edmund that "These injuries the King now bears will be revenged home" (III.iii.12). To Regan's demand to know why Gloucester sent the king to Dover, he replies, "Because I would not see thy cruel nails/ Pluck out his poor old eyes; nor thy fierce sister/ In his anointed flesh stick boarish fangs" (III.vii.56). Going beyond Act III, we find Albany indicting Goneril:

> Tigers, not daughters, what have you
>   perform'd?
> A father, and a gracious aged man,
> Whose reverence even the head-lugg'd bear
>   would lick,
> Most barbarous, most degenerate! . . .
>   (IV.ii.40)

Cordelia explains her military expedition in this way:

> O dear father,
> It is thy business that I go about;
> Therefore great France
> My mourning and importun'd tears hath
>   pitied.
> No blown ambition doth our arms incite,
> But love, dear love, and our ag'd father's
>   right.
>   (IV.iv.23)

And later, in the French camp, Cordelia speaks these impassioned words in reviewing Lear's experience on the heath:

> Had you not been their father, these white
>   flakes
> Did challenge pity of them. Was this a face
> To be oppos'd against the warring winds? . . .
> 'Tis wonder that thy life and wits at once
> Had not concluded all.
>   (IV.vii.30)

[All these] references to Lear's misfortune direct our attention to the king's value, and this value remains constant; it does not shift according to the point of view of the onlooker. The accidents of personality recede, and we confront not particular man or ideal man, but the image of Lear embodying institutions and obligations necessary to the continuance of a moral society. The opposition between moral systems has brought about this plight of values. While the conscienceless fail to remember obligations, Lear and Gloucester vainly invoke that memory. Instead of holding to the bonds of gratitude, the leaders of the new amoral world greedily batten on others, their abuse finally turning into horrors. And this clash of opposing worlds brings into focus the overriding concern of players and audience alike: once man is free from memory and responsibility, can there be any limits to presumption? At stake is the most pertinent question of all: from this conflict what mode of life will finally prevail? . . .

In his speeches Lear continually refers his own situation to the problem of universal justice. The particular repeatedly gives way to the universal. At one moment he would seek personal recognition from nature's forces, calling upon them to obliterate the world. In this he would find satisfying retributive justice. At another moment he would find the seat of justice, search out the meaning of the universe—but in this too he is thwarted: he can only envision corruption festering everywhere, for his degradation is testimony of a lawless universe:

> Let the great gods,
> That keep this dreadful pudder o'er our
>   heads,
> Find out their enemies now. Tremble, thou
>   wretch
> That hast within thee undivulged crimes,
> Unwhipp'd of justice! Hide thee, thou
>   bloody hand;
> Thou perjur'd, and thou simular of virtue
> That are incestuous! Caitiff, to pieces shake,
> That under covert and convenient seeming
> Has practis'd on man's life! Close pent-up
>   guilts,
> Rive your concealing continents, and cry
> These dreadful summoners grace. I am a man
> More sinn'd against than sinning.
>
> (III.ii.49)

Whenever Lear calls attention to the concern of the moment, it is only briefly; he is continually seeing in the particular a higher meaning. Even when he thinks of simple things, when he asks the Fool, "Where is this straw?" he proceeds to translate the immediate concern into a recognition of values: "The art of our necessities is strange/ And can make vile things precious" (III.ii.70). On the heath Lear continually pushes

his thoughts beyond his present moment to universal questions. He is concerned with the reason, the justice of an event. His terror, for example, is for that which is out of time:

> Thou think'st 'tis much that this contentious
>   storm
> Invades us to the skin—

he tells Kent;

>   so 'tis to thee;
> But where the greater malady is fix'd,
> The lesser is scarce felt. . . .
>
> (III.iv.6)

Serving as a perfect contrast to Lear is the Fool, for the Fool feels terror for that which is in time, for the immediate occasion:

> O nuncle, court holy-water in a dry house is better than this rain water out o'door. Good nuncle, in; ask thy daughters' blessing. Here's a night pities neither wise men nor fools.
>
> (III.ii.10)

For Lear the storm and his own physical hardship are significant only because they reveal the spiritual chaos of the time. The Fool, ever practical, sees only the bare facts.

That Lear now sees more meaning in things than the Fool is a significant reversal of what had previously taken place. Before the heath scene the Fool served as *raisonneur* [reasoner], continually pointing out the significance of happenings of which Lear was hopelessly unaware. Before, the Fool asked questions of Lear; now it is Lear who asks many questions. He wants to know whether Edgar's daughters have reduced him to the level of a beast. He would talk with the disguised Edgar, calling him "philosopher," "learned Theban," "good Athenian" (III.iv). He asks Edgar, "What is the cause of thunder?" (III.iv.160) and "What is your study?" (III.iv.163) And when the Fool sings out the moral of an occasion:

> "He that has and a little tiny wit,—
> With heigh-ho, the wind and the rain,—
> Must make content with his fortunes fit,
> For the rain it raineth every day."
>
> (III.ii.74)

Lear replies, "True, boy"—a remarkable change from his previous reactions to the Fool's utterances. Before the heath scene Lear never recognized the Fool's pointed moralizing. He either threatened to whip the Fool for his words or paid them no heed.

All this points to the significance, in dramatic terms,

of Lear's wanderings on the heath. His is a quest for knowledge and certainty, a journey to find, somehow, a way back to order and civilization. While many critics have treated Lear as the study of the unstoical man, Lear's unstoical conduct must be related to the dramatic movement of the play—his search for justice. Lear repeatedly tries to reconcile himself to the rending occasions. He strives for stoic endurance, for this would lead to freedom from pain and suffering. "You heavens, give me that patience, patience I need!" (II.iv.274) he cries out when his daughters would deprive him of all his retainers. "No, I'll not weep" (II.iv.286) he steadfastly maintains. On the heath, overwhelmed with grief and on the edge of self-pity, he steels himself with these sentiments: "No, I will be the pattern of all patience; I will say nothing" (III.ii.37). "I will endure" (III.iv.18) is his continual resolve.

That Lear does not unalterably continue in these stoic thoughts is to be explained in terms of the dramatic concern of the action: his main preoccupation is with justice, not his physical condition. To accept a stoic morality would involve a hardening to suffering, an attainment of peace through withdrawal and indifference. It would mean the acceptance of Marcus Aurelius' counsel: "When you are grieved about anything external it is not the thing itself which afflicts you, but your judgment about it. This judgment it is in your power to efface" [*Meditations*]. Lear can not do this, for Shakespeare has focused all attention on the problem of man who seeks justice in a world that has no justice. And this is the basis of the dramatic conflict. To argue that Lear is completely unstoical is to give the impression that Shakespeare is advocating in the play a support for stoic conduct: that Lear brings on his misfortunes because he has not the discernment of a stoic. Such analysis neglects dramatic structure and technique and turns drama into moral and philosophical formulas.

Lear's search for values and justice on the heath is also an attempt to regain his identity and once again recognize his former figure. "Who am I?" Lear insistently repeats this question in various ways, endeavoring to clutch at the shadow of his former being. Does this not explain his repeated references to himself as king even in his most desperate moments of madness? When, completely deranged, he makes his appearance late in Act IV, his first words are: "No, they cannot touch me for coining;/ I am the King himself" (IV.vi.83). The blind Gloucester recognizes him by his voice, "The trick of that voice I do well remember./ Is't not the King?" And Lear replies with great majesty in his madness:

> Ay, every inch a king!
> When I do stare, see how the subject quakes.
> I pardon that man's life. What was thy cause?

Adultery?
Thou shalt not die. Die for adultery! No:
The wren goes to't, and the small gilded fly
Does lecher in my sight.

(IV.vi.109)

Completely isolated, alone with himself, speaking to himself, Lear creates his own world where none are guilty, for all are guilty. Yet he must have justice; and in Act III, scene vi, he sits as judge of all humanity. Before the Fool, Edgar, and Kent he arraigns Goneril and Regan in a mad judgment day where he can still demand justice and assert the prerogatives of kingship. Finally, his pathetic statement, "Come, come, I am a king,/ My masters, know you that?" (IV.vi.203) is a desperate attempt to hold on to his identity. . . .

At the beginning of the play Shakespeare portrays Lear as a proud man who lacks the humanity of thinking beyond himself; he even values love only as a means of adding to his own vanity. On the heath there comes to Lear an emotion which has not shown itself in him before: a concern for others. We first see this in Lear's words to the Fool:

> My wits begin to turn.
> Come on, my boy. How dost, my boy? Art
>   cold?
> I am cold myself. Where is this straw, my
>   fellow?
> The art of our necessities is strange
> And can make vile things precious. Come,
>   your hovel.
> Poor Fool and knave, I have one part in my
>   heart
> That's sorry yet for thee.

(III.ii.67)

For the first time Lear reaches out to touch another human being. Seeing the Fool's suffering, he makes a sympathetic connection, "I am cold myself." He notices the Fool's adversity first; and through sympathetic identification he comes to recognize his own condition. In spite of innumerable outward differences, in one respect Lear and the Fool are equals: they share a common fate; and in their humanity they are kin. No longer do we see Lear as proud and vain. He recognizes other human beings and shows compassion for them. When Kent bids him seek refuge in the hovel, Lear would torture himself further by remaining out in the storm; but he shows concern for Kent, counselling him, "Prithee, go in thyself; seek thine own ease" (III.iv.23). And when he does decide to go into the hovel, he bids the Fool enter first, "In, boy; go first." There follow significant statements which show his concern for the sufferings of "poor naked wretches" everywhere:

> Poor naked wretches, wheresoe'er you are,

That bide the pelting of this pitiless storm,
How shall your houseless heads and unfed
　sides,
Your loop'd and window'd raggedness,
　defend you
From seasons such as these? O, I have ta'en
Too little care of this! Take physic, pomp;
Expose thyself to feel what wretches feel,
That thou mayst shake the superflux to them,
And show the heavens more just.

　　　　　　　　　　　　　　(III.iv.28)

Lear's whole personality undergoes a complete transformation. From a desire to find personal vindication
and personal recognition, his thoughts turn to sympathy for each individual being. He approaches the
view that a moral society depends on the recognition
of each man's value. This stress on the responsibility
of one man for all makes Lear one with all humanity
and binds all humanity into oneness. In his speech he
strips away all thoughts of comforts and superficialities to lay bare basic truth, the human condition
which underlies the world of fleeting appearances. In
an unforgettable moment on the heath Lear translates his verbalization of this necessity for bare truth
into a physical act as he asks the tormenting question:

Is man no more than this? Consider him well.
Thou ow'st the worm no silk, the beast no hide,
the sheep no wool, the cat no perfume. Ha! here's
three on's are sophisticated! Thou art the thing
itself; unaccommodated man is no more but such
a poor, bare, forked animal as thou art. Off, off,
you lendings! come, unbutton here. (III.iv.107)

And he tears off his clothes.

Two interpretations may be offered for Lear's action.
First, consider Lear's statement to Regan when she
argued that he had no need of any retainers:

O, reason not the need! Our basest beggars
Are in the poorest thing superfluous.
Allow not nature more than nature needs,
Man's life is cheap as beast's. Thou art a
　lady;
If only to go warm were gorgeous,
Why, nature needs not what thou gorgeous
　wear'st,
Which scarcely keeps thee warm. But, for
　true need,—

　　　　　　　　　　　　　　(II.iv.267)

If man's life is as cheap as beast's, if it is only clothes
which make a man, which separate him from the
beast, then it is unnecessary for man to borrow from
animals the clothes which cover his nakedness. Thus,
one can say that in stripping off his clothes Lear
dramatically acts out his words to Regan. Casting off
his lendings, he makes a radical return to nature,

becoming one with the beasts. And we can only ask:
is this the bare truth about man? Is this reality, naked
man, man as beast?

One can also view Lear's trearing off his clothes as
the stripping away of all the superfluous values by
which he has lived. One can say that he is acting out
his words,

　　　　O, I have ta'en
Too little care of this! Take physic, pomp;
Expose thyself to feel what wretches feel,
That thou mayst shake the superflux to
　them,
And show the heavens more just.

If one views this act of the stripping of clothes as an
act of purgation, a return to essential man, then a
new Lear will emerge from such torments.

These two interpretations have equal validity, for one
is part of the other. What we are concerned with
now, it is quite obvious, is more than the personality
of a particular king; it is a confronting of the universe, and in that crisis, a questioning and a recasting
of one's vision of reality. Previous to the division of
kingdom, reality for Lear consisted of the values in
his mind, and these he imposed upon the external
world. As long as he had power to control nature, he
could project his expectations, and, with a high degree of success, have them realized. But the will to
believe does not constitute reality. Power is accidental and temporary; things can appear to be what they
are not; man can seek more justice in the world than
there is. Consequently, the most urgent problem—
the concern of the greatest works of art—is to learn
to see reality as it is. In tearing off his clothes Lear
divests himself of the husks of appearance, the accidents of power and rank. The reduction to unaccommodated man puts him on an equal basis with all
men; he is, therefore, akin to all men. . . .

Lear's recognition of his kinship with all men makes
him see more sympathy and understanding in the
world than before. Through sympathy he discovers
himself. We have a moral reorientation, a shift from
individual power to the principle of universal justice.
We have a different vision of society, which is now
seen as organic. Each individual is so intimately united to another that the misery of all is the misery of
one. And we approach a recognition that the most
important bonds of society are inner and spiritual,
not merely the external and the formal.

The stripping of Lear suggests even more levels of
significance. It is the culmination of his daughters'
stripping him of honor and dignity, the final dismantling of the king. It suggests that man by himself,
against nature's forces, is insignificant; that he is not

King Lear as played by Edwin Forrest in 1826.

Nevertheless, Lear's insight into truth and happiness is not negotiable in this tough world. He cannot convert his experience into saving advantages. To give the play a Christian interpretation and make of it a divine comedy is to distort the work. By the end of the play Lear's world has narrowed to Cordelia, but she is dead in his arms. "Is this the promis'd end?" (V.iii.263) Kent cries out in anguish; and Edgar joins in, "Or image of that horror?" "Fall, and cease!" is Albany's tortured utterance. Evil is in the world and there is no escape. It is much better, says Kent, that Lear die:

> Vex not his ghost; O, let him pass! He hates him
> That would upon the rack of this tough world
> Stretch him out longer.
>
> (V.iii.313)

In *King Lear* Shakespeare takes us to the edge of the human world to front the terrors of life and the viciousness of man's brutality. He offers no solution to the ungraspable phantom of life. However, in the midst of terror we see the nobility and greatness of man's spirit. Keats gives us one of the most illuminating insights into the nature of tragedy: "The excellence of every art is its intensity, capable of making all disagreeables evaporate, from their being in close relationship with Beauty and Truth. Examine 'King Lear,' and you will find this exemplified throughout . . ." [a letter to George and Thomas Keats]. From the time of Aristotle, men have maintained that great art has a civilizing function: it tells us, like history or science, what is; but even more, it can tell us what ought to be. Lear's suffering, his search for justice and identity, is a facing of the fearful elements of the world. His vision of truth and his complete change of character give us a sense of the nobility of spirit which can transcend the confinements of man's condition. "There lies within the dramatic form," Arthur Miller tells us with great conviction, "the ultimate possibility of raising the truth-consciousness of mankind to a level of such intensity as to transform those who observe it." ["The Family in Modern Drama"].

Judd Arnold

SOURCE: "How Do We Judge King Lear?" in *Criticism*, Vol. XIV, No. 3, Summer, 1972, pp. 207-26.

[Arnold asserts that although other characters in the play—including Edgar, Gloucester, Albany, and Cordelia—are transformed, Lear's own progress toward self-knowledge and spiritual regeneration is never completed. The king is certainly more sinned against than sinning, the critic admits, and he doesn't deserve to suffer as he does.

. . . the measure of all things; that he derives his strength from his dependence on his fellow men. It is a suggestion that all men, at one time or another, are outcasts and wanderers. It is a recognition that man's worth is independent of rank and power. . . .

However, Arnold maintains, Lear's self-righteous, self-pitying temperament is evident throughout the drama, and he never fully apprehends or acknowledges that his egoism and passion for vengeance have contributed significantly to his plight. The critic also shows how the speeches of Lear's "comforters," especially Kent and the Fool, heighten our understanding of the king; and he argues that Goneril and Regan, before their shrewd rationality becomes excessive viciousness, are reasonably concerned about their father "disrupting the order he is supposed to embody."]

As [William] Hazlitt said [in *Characters of Shakespeare's Plays*], final judgments about *King Lear*, its protagonists, or its "effect upon the mind" are "mere impertinence." But we can say something definite about the way Lear is viewed in the play, especially by those who love him best—Cordelia, Kent, the Fool, Gloucester, Edgar, Albany. All come to agree that Lear's spiritual renewal depends on his learning to see himself as more than simply a victim of a loveless universe. Not one of these comforters ever expresses the conviction that Lear achieves such saving insight. Their sense of frustration seems justified by what happens in the play and particularly by the carefully developed contrast between the resolutions of the Lear and Gloucester plots.

Lear's comforters provide a well-developed set of reliable perspectives that are unique in Shakespearean tragedy. . . .

Focusing on these perspectives may not yield any startling new conclusions about the larger meaning of the Lear story. But a full appreciation of what these characters observe and achieve makes some old conclusions questionable. Obviously they lend little support to the view that Lear, through a spiritual regeneration, reveals a purposeful, triumphant providential order. But neither do they illustrate nor declare the "decay and fall of the world" felt in Lear by Professor [Jan] Kott [in *Shakespeare Our Contemporary*], nor the "grim pagan universe annihilating faith in divine justice" that is so painstakingly defined by William Elton [in *King Lear and the Gods*]. Lear's onstage observers would tend to support that critical camp which sees in Lear's story a painful problem. As Richard Sewall puts it: " . . . though the good cannot be said to triumph, neither can evil. . . . If the play denies the comforts of optimism, it does not retreat into cynicism." [*The Vision of Tragedy*]. A more recent critic urges, even though he sees signs of an amoral, even malignant universe in the play, that Lear is primarily a "savage and beautiful confrontation of the ambiguity of human experience [John Rosenberg, in "King Lear and His comforters"]. In learning the offices of love, Lear's servants are ennobled and transfigured and reveal the beauty of the Lear universe. In the dashing of their love-borne hopes for Lear's spiritual rebirth we learn of its terrors.

The problem of perspective in Lear challenges us as soon as the king broaches the love test as an instrument for deciding the division of a kingdom. Should we judge the king by the literal absurdity of the test, and the division itself from the point of view of a conservative Elizabethan who has just lived through the uneasy years prior to the accession of James? Or do we respond to it as to some strange fairy tale existing beyond historical or "realistic" perspectives? . . .

The opening exchange between Kent and Gloucester reveals that the partitioning of the kingdom is already the subject of court gossip. Though Lear is later told by Kent and the Fool that he has made an extraordinary political blunder, everyone seems at least resigned to Lear's retirement. But the immediate response to his subsequent behavior, from the broaching of the love test to the exiling of Cordelia and Kent, is astonishment and outrage. Even Goneril and Regan, who initially maintain their composure and flatter the king, reveal, in their first private moment, surprise and concern:

> *Gon.* You see how full of changes his age is;
> the observation we have made of it hath
> not been little: he always loved our sister
> most; and with what poor judgment he
> hath cast her off appears too grossly.
>
> *Reg.* 'Tis the infirmity of his age; yet he hath
> ever but slenderly known himself.
>
>   (I, 1, 288-94)

The sisters are also disturbed by the treatment of Kent. If we can shed 300 years of viewing Goneril and Regan as simply demonic figures in a morality pattern—the Evil Sisters—we could better appreciate, if not the kindliness of their remarks, at least the sanity of them. They are rationally concerned with preventing an unpredictable old man from courting invasion or in any other way disrupting the order he is supposed to embody. If we view them only as monsters we become less sensitive to the drama of their spiritual disintegration and the extent of Lear's responsibility for it. More important, we feel less strongly the validity of their pointed analysis. Lear's behavior causes it; all other witnesses to his public performance anticipate it. Burgundy, who is in attendance only to exploit opportunity, makes no overt statement of anger. He does, however, make a hasty and politic withdrawal from the uncomfortably strange scene. France speaks directly of the "strange," unnatural behavior of the king and violates diplomatic decorum by chiding his host. Cordelia and Kent lecture Lear at length about his failures as a king, a father and a friend. Cordelia is caught off guard by Lear and fumbles at first. Her first words, uttered as an aside, reflect her confusion and dismay: "What shall Cordelia speak? Love, and be silent" (I, i, 62). Later she expresses a peculiar mixture of love for her parent and contempt for his wayward behavior. Kent leaps to Cordelia's defense and to an impassioned assessment of Lear's "hideous rashness." Kent must be "unmannerly/When Lear is mad" (I, 1, 145-46). He is no more impressed with Lear's grandeur than Cordelia. His self-sacrificing opposition to the king is testament to his love, but his opposition is not to any heroic frenzy but to heart-breakingly shrill, willful senility. His childing, loving question—"What would'st thou do, old man?"—strips Lear of his official dignity and stands as a plaintive rebuke, sadly forced when "majesty falls to folly" (I, 1, 146-49).

The opening scene then is strange and unrealistic. But the "realistic" perspectives of Kent, Cordelia, France, Goneril and Regan remove the scene from the world of fairy tale or wooden allegory and make it a painful, shocking exhibition of the moral and emotional condition of the declining king. The degree to which we surrender to the literal scene and to the harshest judgments of Lear makes, I think, an extraordinary difference in our response to the meaning and dramatic effect of the story which ensues. Ironically, the meanly irrelevant love test Lear contrives out of his self-indulgent folly is, by the very nature of that folly, transformed into the desperately real test of love and service that the rest of the play records. Lear's irresponsibility, his imperviousness to reason, his vicious abuse of Cordelia and Kent make him difficult to love. His performance makes clear that he can be served only by the most selfless devotion. The very order that Lear represents as king depends now on the strength of others to grant it under the most trying circumstances.

The love Lear needs is not easily granted. Obviously, Goneril and Regan are incapable of giving it. They judge, condemn and reject Lear. Cordelia, at the outset, presents a minor problem. She has been held a rendering of moral perfection in an allegorical mold. The psychologizing [Samuel Taylor] Coleridge, however, detected in her "some little faulty admixture of pride and sullenness" and his point has recently been remade by Sears Jayne who calls/attention [in "Charity in *King Lear*"] to her lack of charity. How severely we ought to judge Cordelia is perhaps a moot point. Her refusal to humour her father can be read not only as a measure of sound moral judgment, but also, by what it presupposes about Lear's capacity to heed reason, as a mark of respect. On the other hand, we cannot ignore the well-developed contrast between the responses of Kent and Cordelia to Lear. Cordelia's major speech prior to her departure is full of self-justification and self-congratulation:

> I yet beseech your Majesty,
> (If for I want that glib and oily art

> To speak and purpose not, since what I well
>   intend,
> I'll do't before I speak), that you make
>   known
> It is no vicious blot, murther or foulness,
> No unchaste action, or dishonored step,
> That hath depriv'd me of your grace and
>   favour,
> But even for want of that for which I am
>   richer,
> A still-soliciting eye, and such a tongue
> That I am glad I have not, though not to
>   have it
> Hath lost me in your liking.
>
> (I, i, 223-33)

Kent, however, leaves no doubt that his sole concern is the well-being of the man he has "ever honour'd as my King,/Lov'd as my father, as my master follow'd" (I, i, 140-41). His words are full of astringent instruction, but instruction borne of compassion. He courts death and banishment because

> My life I never held but as a pawn
> To wage against thine enemies; nor fear to
>   lose it,
> Thy safety being motive.
>
> (I, i, 155-57)

Perhaps Shakespeare gives Cordelia no lines in support of Kent—not even a thank you—to heighten the contrast between the responses of the two. Or perhaps we are to understand that she has been rendered heartbreakingly inarticulate by a flood of emotion. Yet after Kent's departure she seems almost grimly composed, makes her self-justifying claims, cooly and bitterly consigns her father to her sister's care and sweeps off to France. All we can note with certainty is that when Cordelia reappears in Act Four, her language suggests that she has arrived at a larger understanding of the selfless offices of love and she says to Kent then: "O thou good Kent! how shall I live and work/ To match thy goodness? My life will be too short, / And every measure fail me" (IV, vii, 1-3).

To feel what nearly every character in the play, except Goneril and Regan, comes to learn about the trials of love and service we must continue to feel how severely Lear tests them. Maynard Mack raises the problem of perspectives on Lear by complaining of a number of productions which "rationalize" the treatment given him by Goneril and Regan [in *"King Lear" in Our Time*].

> Something like a climax in this rationalizing mode was reached in Peter Brook's [Royal Shakespeare Company] production [featuring] Paul Scofield in 1962. There in I, iv, evidently to justify Goneril's complaints about her father's retinue and thus

motivate her insolence to him, Lear's knights literally demolished the set, throwing plates and tankards, upending the heavy table on which presumably the king's dinner was soon to be served, and behaving in general like boors—as if the visible courtesy of their spokesman earlier (I, iv, 54-78), Albany's significant unawareness of what Goneril is complaining about, and Lear's explicit description of his knights:

My train are men of choice and rarest
    parts,
That all particulars of duty know, ...
had no existence in the play.

Mack then accuses the production of depending on "what is called in today's theatrical jargon, the subtext."

The most obvious result of subtextualizing is that director and (possibly) actor are encouraged to assume the same level of authority as the author. The sound notion that there is a life to which the words give life can with very little stretching be made to mean that the words the author set down are themselves simply a search for the true play, which the director must intuit in, through and under them. Once one has done so, the words become to a degree expendable.

Yet there is a good deal of evidence in the words of the text to justify Brook's approach. Time passes between I, i and ii. In that time Lear has apparently been granted his retirement on his own terms. Goneril has apparently had cause to complain that "His knights grow riotous, and himself upbraids us / On every trifle" (I, iii, 7-8). Why should we not believe her? In spite of what Mack says about Albany, the Duke does not seem unaware of a problem. Later he only cautions his wife that she "may fear too far," and to her accusation of his "milky gentleness," "want of wisdom" and "harmful mildness" he responds only with the timorous suggestion that in "Striving to better, oft we mar what's well" (I, iv, 338-56). Lear himself, in such acts as striking Oswald, shows he is at least capable of indecorum. The manner in which he adopts the services of the disguised Kent is suspicious. Earlier he had failed to heed the wisdom of Kent. Now he is cool to the simple offer of honest service. Not until Kent plays Lear's games is he accepted. Oswald enters and is again slapped by Lear. Kent enters the sport and trips Oswald. (It is perhaps to such antics that Edgar later refers when he recounts how Kent "in disguise / Follow'd his enemy king, and did him service / Improper for a slave" (V, iii, 219-21). Only after Kent's delightfully crude gesture does Lear embrace him and then, I suspect, with a schoolboyish glee. My use of the term *schoolboyish* may be my response to an imaginary subtext. But in the light of the succeeding observations of the Fool it is at least defensible. Precisely at this point the Fool begins to lecture the unheeding Lear on his childishness—on his having made his daughters his mothers, on his having put down his own breeches and given them the rod. Lear's on-stage observers at least make credible Goneril's declaration that Lear is "an idle old man, / That still would manage those authorities / That he hath given away. Now by my life, / Old fools are babes again!" (I, iii, 17-20).

It is not surprising that there has been less critical attention given to Lear's errors than to his suffering. His anguish is overwhelming. Goneril's and Regan's rational, self-serving shrewdness quickly gives way to gratuitous viciousness. Their savagery reaches an early climax as they mockingly subject him to public humiliation by stripping him of his remaining privileges and allowing him to flee into the storm. Nothing Lear has done deserves this. So at this stage in the drama those most sensitive to Lear's condition emphasize his undeserved plight. Albany's cautious criticism of his wife gives way to bitter anger. Gloucester is moved to risk his life to solace his king. Kent turns from instructing Lear to anatomizing Lear's tormentors—the "smiling rogues" who "bite the holy chords a-twain" (II, ii, 74-75).

But the more judgmental perspectives on Lear are maintained chiefly by the Fool who knows that Lear's regeneration and his achievement of patience must begin with his understanding of his own guilt, understanding that he must expect neither to exercise an authority he has surrendered nor to receive solace from the monsters he has loosed. Only through such understanding can he master his suffering and escape despair and madness. As long as he continues to lose himself in self-righteous condemnation of others, in judging the world by his daughters, in self-indulgent self-pity and in futile vows of vengeance, he is his own worst enemy. But the self-knowledge and self-possession that Cordelia and Kent initially urged Lear to seek and that the Fool insistently urges on him thereafter prove more than he can master. Those odd moments when he appears on the verge of recognizing his guilt are sadly colored by the terms of his recognition. As his misjudgment of Cordelia begins to dawn on him he still declares himself victim of "small faults" in her which "wrenched" him from the frame of nature and "drew" love from his heart. His cry, "O Lear, Lear, Lear," uttered while beating his head to "let his folly in" and his "dear judgment out," smacks of being a shameless public gesture to solicit pity rather than a declaration of guilt or understanding (I, iv, 279-80). His pathetic lack of self-control is revealed in numerous outbursts such as his response to Goneril's cutting his band of followers. In tears, he flies at her.

Life and death! I am asham'd
That thou hast power to shake my manhood
    thus,

That these hot tears, which break from me
   perforce,
Should make thee worth them. Blasts and
   fogs upon thee!
Th'untented woundings of a father's curse
Pierce every sense about thee! Old fond eyes,
Beweep this cause again, I'll pluck ye out,
And cast you, with the waters that you
   loose,
To temper clay. Yea, is't come to this?
Ha! Let it be so: I have another daughter,
Who, I am sure is kind and comfortable:
When shee shall hear this of thee, with her
   nails
She'll flay thy wolvish visage. Thou shalt
   find
That I'll resume the shape which thou dost
   think
I have cast off forever.

                    (I, iv, 305-19)

He alternately weeps, curses and refuses to weep. He looks forward to what he assumes is a deserved solace from his other daughter, a "kind and comfortable" sort who will express her kind pity in a barehanded flaying of her sister's wolfish visage. And he futilely vows revenge.

The expectation of solace from Regan is a willful refusal to face truth. The Fool tells him so—tells him his brains are in his heels. Kent tells him so from the stocks. Kent's splenetic, insulting (and just) attacks on Cornwall and Regan seem intentionally designed to force them to place him in the stocks simply to demonstrate to Lear the facts of his circumstances. But Lear refuses to accept the truth that Kent reveals. And throughout his ordeal he sees himself only as "So kind a father." He exploits every theatrical device to shame his tormenters—tears, pleas and curses. He throws himself on his knees before Regan and the assembled court expressly to shame her, and even in his mock plea for forgiveness he reveals his self-righteous conviction of his utter guiltlessness: "Dear daughter, I confess that I am old" (II, iv, 155). He plays at patient forgiveness: "You heavens," he pleads, "give me that patience, patience I need!" (II, iv, 273). But he concludes the speech with another impotent vow to vengeance. Even as we are moved by Lear's real suffering and appalled by Regan's insensitivity to it, we can understand her disgust at Lear's "unsightly tricks" and the Fool's almost contemptuous mockery of the king's surrender to his "rising heart": "Cry to it, Nuncle, as the cockney did to the eels when she put 'em i' th' paste alive; she knapp'd 'em o' th' coxcombs with a stick, and cried 'Down, wantons, down!" (II, iv, 120-25).

Lear on the heath is a larger figure. His passion as it is reported and revealed is grand. The image of

him "contending with the fretful elements, . . . striving in his little world of man to outscorn / The to and fro conflicting wind and rain," of enduring what the "cub drawn bear" could not endure suggests none of the weakness so abundantly evident earlier (III, i, 4-14). But the change does not clearly reveal the spiritual growth or understanding that Kent and the Fool had hoped for. The elements he would initially forbear to tax with malignant unkindness, suddenly stand as "servile ministers" of his "pernicious daughters." Self-pity has led him to imagine an abusive cosmos. Lear's ensuing speech to Kent, who hopes to lead him to shelter, is a discouraging one. He mistakes Kent's kindness for fear and assumes the fear must be borne of "undivulged crimes, / Unwhipp'd of Justice" (III, ii, 52-53). In Lear's mind, only he has the strength, the strength of innocence, to brave the storm. He sees himself as, unlike the fearful Kent he imagines, and the world of "wretches" like him, a man more "sinned against, than sinning" (III, ii, 60). The line is richly ironic. Lear is, of course, more sinned against than sinning. No man, and certainly no king, deserves what he has suffered. But his lines reflect also an insensitivity to loving service and a determined refusal to come to terms with his own errors.

As Lear's obsession with his daughters' abuse of him expands to a vision of cosmic malice, his servants' tactics shift. They become less concerned with teaching him his errors and more desperate to reveal through tendered comfort the operative power of love in a world Lear sees as only full of hate. The Fool's ironic and sometimes almost cruel judgments (which remain always love offerings—"labors to out-jest / His heart strook injuries") are tempered by words of simple compassion. When Lear loses himself in cursing the universe, and the despairing wish that the "all-shaking thunder, / Strike flat the thick rotundity o' th' world! / Crack Nature's moulds, all germens spill at once / That makes ingrateful man!" (III, ii, 6-9), the Fool can only plead with Lear to accept physical safety at any cost: "Good Nuncle, in, ask thy daughters blessing" (III, ii, 11-12). But the services and love of the Fool and Kent have little power to instruct or solace Lear.

Then, suddenly, there occurs that grand moment in which Lear breaks through the prison of himself and turns to the shivering Fool: "Poor Fool and knave, I have one part in my heart / That's sorry yet for thee" (III, ii, 72-73). The use of "sorry yet" suggests that all along, even though Lear has not understood the relationship between his failures and his suffering, he has dimly sensed that his egocentric absorption in the abuse to which he has been subjected can lead only to despair and madness. His hovering on the brink of this knowledge, his tortured abortive struggle to achieve patience, makes his condition almost too painful to witness. His surfacing self-knowledge is articulated most fully two scenes later. He repeats his plea to the Fool to take shelter. He refuses to take comfort, himself. He then records his struggle towards patience in words that remind us of all the elements in his own being that have impeded it, and which Kent and the Fool have continually warned him against:

> Thou think'st 'tis much that his contentious
>   storm
> Invades us to the skin: so 'tis to thee;
> But where the greater malady is fix'd,
> The lesser is scarce felt. Thou'ldst shun a
>   bear;
> But if thy flight lay toward the roaring sea,
> Thou'ldst meet the bear i' th' mouth. When
>   the mind's free
> The body's delicate; this tempest in my mind
> Doth from my senses take all feeling else
> Save what beats there—filial ingratitude!
> Is it not as this mouth should tear this hand
> For lifting food to't? But I will punish home:
> No, I will weep no more. In such a night
> To shut me out? Pour on; I will endure.
> In such a night as this? O Regan, Goneril!
> Your old kind father, whose frank heart gave
>   all,—
> O! that way madness lies; let me shun that;
> No more of that.
>
>   (III, iv. 6-22)

The old obsession with "filial ingratitude" oppresses him again. The lust for vengeance is restated. The temptation to pity himself as the "old kind father" with the "frank heart" seeps out again. But then with marvelous clarity he sees that this is the way madness lies. He turns again to the Fool:

> . . . get thee in. I'll pray, and then I'll sleep.
> Poor naked wretches, whereso'er you are,
> That bide the pelting of this pitiless storm,
> How shall your houseless heads and unfed
>   sides,
> Your loop'd and window'd raggedness,
>   defend you
> From seasons such as these? O! I have ta'en
> Too little care of this. Take physic, Pomp;
> Expose thyself to feel what wretches feel,
> That thou mayst shake the superflux to them,
> And show the heavens more just.
>
>   (III, iv. 27-36)

[In *Shakespeare's Doctrine of Nature*, John] Danby calls this the "last and grandest act of Lear's sanity" and upon it rears an argument in favor not only of Lear's spiritual regeneration, but of Shakespeare's commitment to the ideal of Christian communism.

> Charity, repentance, a renewed will to amendment,

an awareness of his neighbors accompanying the new awareness of himself, the falling away of original egocentricity, of anger, revenge, impatience with the heavens—the prayer shows Lear's mind settling itself in its proper frame.

This brief quotation hardly does justice to the sensitivity of Danby's argument. I quote it chiefly as perhaps the strongest declaration of Lear's regeneration on the heath. It is a hopeful moment. But from the views of Kent and the Fool it is a fleeting moment—one in which they can take little comfort.

Their hopes are dashed when Edgar, disguised as a man driven wild by universal corruption, appears on the heath. Lear identifies Mad Tom as another who has "given all to his daughters," and thereby demonstrates his powerlessness to shun the way madness lies. He cannot sustain his charitable vision of the world. The temptation to hate overpowers the instinct to love. To the dismay of Kent and the Fool, the wretched "bare forked animal" preaching the triumphant reign of Satan becomes, for Lear, the "noble philosopher." Gloucester arrives to serve Lear, but his love, like Kent's and the Fool's, is ignored. The promise inspired by Lear's prayer is betrayed by his bitterness, and Kent, even as he thanks Gloucester for trying to comfort the king, is forced to acknowledge that "All the power of his wits have given way to his impatience" (III, vi, 4-5). Lear's self-centered passion dwindles at last into that pathetic, whining mock trial of his daughters and is dissipated at last in exhaustion and sleep. The Fool's last jests about jointstools, a final effort to remind Lear of reality, are unheard. Kent's final plea, "Where is the patience now / That you so oft have boasted to retain?" (III, vi, 58-59), is unheeded. When "oppressed nature sleeps," Kent, Gloucester and the Fool, in what ought to be a stunning visual image of the office of pure compassion, which is all they now have left to offer, take Lear in their arms and bear him at last to shelter. What they have seen is not progress toward intellectual and spiritual regeneration but anguish, the spirit of vengeance and self-pitying passion overwhelming reason.

Gloucester's journey to the heath links the two plots in *Lear* and marks a major shift in the movement of the play. Heretofore, only Kent and the Fool have stood by Lear. Others, responding to the instinct of self-preservation or pride, have withdrawn, weakly acquiesing to the rule of Goneril and Regan. Gloucester's self-sacrificing effort is the first of a series of spiritual triumphs, all initiating in soul-wrenching pity for Lear, all demonstrating that selfishness, whether in Goneril and Regan, or in the greater souls of Gloucester, Edgar and even Edmund, cannot ultimately resist the power of self-sacrificing love which begins to well up almost uncontrollably in individual hearts. . . .

[In Act IV] we watch the progress of Gloucester and Edgar and a series of complementary transformations in others, each of whom learns how to gain his life by giving it in perfect charity. Cordelia reappears in Act Four free of all vestiges of the self-justifying moralist, and sympathetically weeping "holy water from her heavenly eyes" (IV, iii, 31). She is ready to go about her father's business (IV, iv, 23-24). (The allusion to Christ's selfless office is too clear to be argued, I think.) Albany finds the strength to resist his wife and sister-in-law for Lear's sake and recognizes in Cornwall's death that "you are above,/You justicers, that these our nether crimes / So speedily can venge!" (IV, ii, 78-79). Even servants nobly rise up to give their lives for Gloucester. The potential for human renewal, embodied in a series of individual changes, begins to assume a predictable and gratifying shape. Only Goneril and Regan remain impervious to pity, but their condition renders them capable only of self-destruction. In Act Four we see the first stages of their turning on one another. In Act Five, Albany will remind us that their ultimate demise is a "judgment of the heavens" (V, iii, 233). And we will see even Edmund touched by remorse. But by the end of Act Four the major transformations have occurred and are capped by Edgar's parting words to Gloucester who has learned to acknowledge the Gods who had preserved him (IV, vi, 73-74). Edgar's words are: "Bear free and patient thoughts" (IV, vi, 80). They are a benediction following a dramatized sermon. They inform our hopes for Lear.

Precisely at this moment Lear reappears, fantastically dressed, still lost in despair. It is a faith-testing sight. Edgar's new-found equanimity is shattered. He sees

Lear (in wheelchair) and the Fool (Brian Cox and David Bradley) in a 1990 National Theatre production of King Lear.

in Lear anew the evidence of man's fall: "O thou side-piercing sight" (IV, vi, 85). Lear's madness is more frightening than before. Self-pity has given way to an intense, bitter mockery of a worldly hell, a world of cruelty, deception, good and lechery. He focuses, with a metaphoric crudity that reflects and generates disgust, on the image of woman as the emblem of human duplicity.

> Let copulation thrive; for Gloucester's
>   bastard son
> Was kinder to his father than my daughters
> Got 'tween the lawful sheets. . . .
> Down from the waist they are Centaurs,
> Though women all above:
> But to the girdle do the Gods inherit,
> Beneath is all the fiend's: there's hell, there's
>   darkness,
> There is the sulphurous pit—burning,
>   scalding,
> Stench, consumptions; fie, fie, fie! pah, pah!
> Give me an ounce of civet, good apothecary,
> To sweeten my imagination.
>   (IV, vi, 117-33)

Lear's vision of the "great stage of fools" expands. He rages at defied authority and mocked justice. He speaks "matter and impertinency mix'd;/Reason in madness" (IV, vi, 176-77). He insightfully penetrates to the heart of masked corruption. But he reveals his madness in the singleness of a focus that leads to his malevolent outburst implying that the only fulfillment of nature's law is vengeance: "Kill, kill, kill, kill, kill, kill" (IV, vi, 189). Lear is, indeed, "A sight most pitiful" (IV, vi, 205).

If the regenerative movement of the play is to be fulfilled in Lear, it must be fulfilled hereafter. At last it appears it might be. Lear falls asleep again. He reawakens in Cordelia's arms. He is tired and bewildered, his rage expended. He cannot at first believe what he sees.

> Where have I been? Where am I? Fair
>   daylight?
> I am mightily abus'd. I should e'en die with
>   pity
> To see another thus. . . .
> I am a very foolish fond old man,
> Fourscore and upward, not an hour more or
>   less;0
> And, to deal plainly,
> I fear I am not in my perfect mind.
>   (IV, vii, 52-63)

Lear comes closer than ever before to coming to terms with himself—with his loss of judgment, egoism and guilt. He poignantly surrenders his very being to Cordelia: "If you have poison for me, I will drink it.

/ I know you do not love me; for your sisters / Have, as I do remember, done me wrong: / You have some cause, they have not" (IV, vii, 72-74). Yet the confession is as terrible as it is beautiful. To doubt Cordelia's love now is to deny her again. Cordelia, whose absolute love is absolute proof against the spirit of vengeance can offer only her plaintive rejoinder: "No cause, no cause" (IV, vii, 75). The doctor reminds Cordelia and us we still need patience.

> Be comforted, good Madam; the great rage,
> You see, is kill'd in him: and yet it is danger
> To make him even o'er the time he has lost.
> Desire him to go in; trouble him no more
> Till further settling.
>
> (IV, vii, 78-82)

Still, hope inspired by the logic of earlier events soars. It soon fades. Cordelia's army is defeated. We see neither her nor Lear again until they are led on stage as Edmund's prisoners. Lear's words permit a variety of interpretations. Those who urge Lear's regeneration find him, in these desperate straits, making his fullest statement of it.

> Come, let's away to prison
> We two alone will sing like birds i' th' cage:
> When thou dost ask me blessing, I'll kneel
>   down,
> And ask of thee forgiveness: so we'll live.
> And pray, and sing, and tell old tales, and
>   laugh
> At gilded butterflies, and hear poor rogues
> Talk of court news; and we'll talk with them
>   too,
> Who loses and who wins; who's in, who's
>   out,
> In a wall'd prison, pacts and sects of great
>   ones
> That ebb and flow by the moon.
>
> (V, iii, 8-19)

Here is Lear's loveliest and most unequivocal plea for forgiveness. Here there is hope for grace and joy. Here Lear, for the first time, seems free of the "wrack of this tough world." Perhaps, in context, there is a special charity implicit in the lines, a magnanimous effort of the comforted to be the comforter, to put to rest Cordelia's sense of failure borne of her conviction that with "best meaning" she has "incurr'd the worst" (V, iii, 4). Lear's lines could be delivered as a plea or in cavalier tones designed to help Cordelia brave out their torment. Yet it is also true that the lines might suggest the escapist tendencies that caused Lear to give away a kingdom, a blindness to the nature of his captivity and to the danger to Cordelia. Lear's expectation that Cordelia should rejoice in the condition to which he has brought her has its insane side. (What Cordelia thinks is unavailable to us. She is graciously, patiently and frustratingly silent here.) When Lear continues, we find him once again sinking into his old monomaniacal hatreds. To have faith that the "Gods themselves throw incense" upon such sufferers as he and Cordelia is glorious. To see divine justice taking the forms of fire and famine reflects the old tendency to impotent cursing that was symptomatic of his earlier spiritual disintegration. There is justification for terming Lear's great speech, as it has been termed, as the "maundering of a madman." [Betsy Kantor Stuart, "Truth and Tragedy in *King Lear*"]. But even if we give the lines the most positive reading imaginable, we must recognize that Lear's progress toward redemption is emphemeral. Cordelia is hanged. Lear again sinks into obvious madness. Perhaps we may be content that Lear's moment of joy transcends time and beatifies his full experience. But those in the play who hoped for more find little to solace them. They see only failure.

Edgar's last hope for restoring the king to sanity rests upon a final effort to make him acknowledge the good that has continued to serve him in the person of Kent. But Lear can recognize neither the goodness of Edgar nor Kent. He looks dimly up at the figure of his faithful servant and sees only another representative of the world he feels has betrayed him. His response to both good men is: "A plague upon you, murderers, traitors, all!" (V, iii, 269). Kent's attempt to tell Lear how he "from your first of difference and decay, / Have follow'd your sad steps," proves, in Edgar's phrase, "bootless" (V, iii, 288-94). Albany removes all doubt about the king's condition by reminding us all that he "knows not what he says, and vain it is / That we present us to him" (V, iii, 293-94). Kent's abortive effort to effect his restoration to Lear is, for me at least, as painful as Cordelia's death.

The explicitly dramatized purgative and regenerative processes in Edgar, Gloucester and others is not repeated in Lear. His heart does not "burst smilingly." He dies pathetically insisting on signs of life in the inert body of his daughter. He dies cursing a demonic world, unrestored to all who have stood for a world beyond the one which sets him howling. Lear's death cannot erase the beauty of what others achieve; it cannot deny the grandest potentials in human nature or the providential order those potentials suggest. But it leaves those who have magnificently survived the cruelest test of human love with the terrible evidence that such love is heroic precisely because there is no guarantee that it will be rewarded.

THE FOOL

Although Northrop Frye refers to the Fool as a "natural," **Robert Hillis Goldsmith** asserts that Lear's attendant is not a simpleton. Both Goldsmith and **Enid Welsford** identify him as one of Shakespeare's "wise fools." Welsford emphasizes his role as a neutral observer, an authoritative commentator on the sources of Lear's tragedy. Goldsmith distinguishes Lear's Fool from the traditional satirical or ironical fool, pointing to his unflagging devotion to, and sympathy for, the king. Goldsmith argues that the Fool begins the process of restoring Lear's sanity, but lacks the capability to complete his conversion. Welsford suggests that the Fool leaves the stage when Lear, in the throes of madness, himself becomes a "wise fool."

Both Northrop Frye and William Empson have remarked on the number of times the word "fool" appears in *King Lear*. During the course of the play, Frye points out, the word is used in connection with virtually every character, with the exception of Goneril, Regan, and Edmund. In one sense, Frye declares, the word is synonymous in *King Lear* with "victim." Empson sees the word "fool" as a central metaphor for a narrative set in motion by the folly of Lear's abdication. For additional commentary on the Fool in *King Lear*, see the excerpt by **Northrop Frye** in the OVERVIEWS section.

Enid Welsford

SOURCE: "The Court-Fool in Elizabethan Drama," in *The Fool: His Social and Literary History*, Farrar & Rinehart Incorporated, 1936, pp. 243-70.

[*In this excerpt from her classic study of the social and literary tradition of the Fool figure, Welsford describes Lear's Fool as both a commentator on dramatic events and a tragic figure in his own right. He is a "sage-fool" who intuitively knows the truth and doesn't hesitate to speak it, the critic observes, and his focus on the connection between a wise man and a fool underscores Lear's tragedy. In Welsford's judgment, the Fool disappears from the play when the king, in his madness, becomes a "wise fool" himself. Having lost his rational wits, she contends, Lear now sees the truth: that patient acceptance is the only possible response to a world in which there is no guarantee of divine or human justice.*]

[When] Shakespeare made Lear and his Fool companions in misfortune, he may have broken the canons of classical art, but he certainly was not destroying verisimilitude. On the contrary, if he was catering for the popular taste for clownage, he was doing so by creating a figure who was sufficiently life-like to be tragically convincing. The human truth and pathos of the situation is indeed so appealing that it has sometimes distracted attention from the deeper purpose of the dramatist in this juxtaposition of King and Clown. Lear's Fool is not merely a touching figure who might easily have been drawn from life, he is

also the fool of the sottie [Satirical farce], and, although evidently half-witted, is endowed with a penetration deeper and more far-reaching than that superficial sharp-wittedness and gift for smart repartee which went to the making of a successful court-jester. He is in fact the sage-fool who sees the truth, and his rôle has even more *intellectual* than emotional significance. For *King Lear* is not merely a popular play. If it offends against classical decorum, it is nevertheless true to a definitely intellectual tradition and makes use of the conventions of 'fool-literature' which were . . . clerical rather than popular in origin, and were used as the vehicle for a reasoned criticism of life. The Fool, therefore, as I shall endeavour to prove, is here used both as a commentator whose words furnish important clues to the interpretation of a difficult play; and also as a prominent figure caught up into the drama, whose rôle and nature form a vital part of the central tragic theme.

Lear's Fool, like Touchstone [in *As You Like It*] and Feste [in *Twelfth Night*], is an 'all-licensed' critic who sees and speaks the real truth about the people around him. His business, however, is not to deal out satirical commonplaces, but to emphasize one peculiarly dreadful instance of the reversal of position between the wise man and the fool; indeed he labours this point with a maddening reiteration which is only excusable because his tactless jokes and snatches of song spring so evidently from genuine grief. The sorrow underlying his shrewd sarcasm rises to the surface when he interrupts Goneril's plausible scolding to give us a sudden glimpse of the horror lurking behind an apparently ludicrous situation:

> For, you trow, nuncle,
>   The hedge-sparrow fed the cuckoo so long,
>   That it had its head bit off by its young.
> So, out went the candle, and we were left
>   darkling.

When King Lear made his daughters his mothers he committed an act of indubitable folly of which his fool is only too ready to remind him; but the same fool comments on folly of a very different order, when the disguised Kent offers his services to his helpless master:

> FOOL. Sirrah, you were best take my
>   coxcomb.
> KENT. Why, fool?
> FOOL. Why, for taking one's part that's out
>   of favour.

The same point is made even more forcibly when the Fool finds Kent in the stocks:

> KENT. How chance the king comes with so
>   small a train?

FOOL. An thou hadst been set i' the stocks
  for that question,
thou hadst well deserved it.
  KENT. Why, fool?
  FOOL. We'll set thee to school to an ant, to
  teach thee there's no labouring i' the
  winter. All that follow their noses are led
  by their eyes but blind men; and there's
  not a nose among twenty but can smell
  him that's stinking. Let go thy hold when
  a great wheel runs down a hill, lest it
  break thy neck with following it; but the
  great one that goes up the hill, let him
  draw thee after. When a wise man gives
  thee better counsel, give me mine again: I
  would have none but knaves follow it,
  since a fool gives it.

    That sir which serves and seeks for gain,
      And follows but for form,
    Will pack when it begins to rain,
      And leave thee in the storm.
    But I will tarry; the fool will stay,
      And let the wise man fly:
    The knave turns fool that runs away:
      The fool no knave, perdy.

  KENT. Where learned you this, fool?
  FOOL. Not i' the stocks, fool.'

This whole passage proved so puzzling to [Samuel] Johnson—whose mind was not attuned to the nuances and complex ironies of fool-literature—that he wished to straighten out the reasoning by emendation, and in particular to alter the last two lines of the song into:

    The fool turns knave who runs away;
    The knave no fool perdy.

This version does, perhaps, make better common sense, but then is it common sense that the Fool is trying to convey? Dr Johnson might have been saved from his bewilderment if he had used [Erasmus's] *The Praise of Folly* as a commentary; for, in his conversation with Kent, the Fool is being as subtle, ambiguous and volatile as Erasmus himself in his play upon the various meanings and relations of the words 'fool' and 'knave'. Folly is the opposite of wisdom, how *unwise* it is to pursue a policy which in this world of ours must lead you to the stocks. I am only a Fool, but I can teach you better than that. But after all, do I want you to follow my advice? No, let it be followed only by knaves, for it is the advice of a fool— a contemptible vicious being, as all men acknowledge. But who is this Fool who not only desires none but knaves to follow his advice, but also defiantly proclaims that he will himself disregard it:

    I will tarry, the fool will stay

And let the wise man fly.

After all which is which? The knave who runs away, comes out into the open, and is at once seen as the abject contemptible ludicrous creature that he has always really been. The fool is at least true to himself. He has never professed to be wise, he will not now act as though he were worldly wise. If Dr Johnson's reading is accepted the meaning of the passage remains much the same, only it closes with a shrug and a wink instead of on a note of exalted defiance. In both cases the Fool suggests that there is ambiguity in the words wisdom and folly, but that at any rate the Fool would seem to be a man devoid of worldly wisdom. Here the Fool is hinting at thoughts beyond the range of Feste and Touchstone, thoughts which are vitally connected with the central theme of the tragedy.

In treating the Fool as the disinterested truth-teller, the *punctum indifferens* [neutral commentator] of the play, Shakespeare was not making any new departure from his earlier comic method as shown in the handling of Touchstone; and, as a piece of realistic character-drawing, Lear's 'Good boy' with his lovable, sympathetic qualities is only a profounder study of a type already exemplified in the jester of *Twelfth Night*. Nevertheless, Shakespeare's tragic fool differs very profoundly from his comic brethren. In Arden and Illyria [the dramatic settings of *As You Like It* and *Twelfth Night*] it is regarded as a sufficiently good joke that the madman should be the spokesman of sanity, that the ostensible fool should find it so easy to draw out the latent folly of the wise. But Lear's Fool goes further than this. Like others of his profession he is very ready to proffer his coxcomb to his betters, but in doing so he does not merely raise a laugh or score a point, he sets a problem. 'What am I? What is madness?' he seems to ask, 'the world being what it is, do I necessarily insult a man by investing him with motley?'

With this apparently comic question the Fool strikes the keynote of the tragedy of Lear. . . .

It has often been pointed out that Lear has a more passive rôle than most of Shakespeare's tragic characters. Nevertheless he is involved in an event, and his relationship with the Fool is no mere static pictorial contrast, but part of the tragic movement of the play; the movement downwards towards that ultimate exposure and defeat when the King is degraded to the status of the meanest of his servants. We watch the royal sufferer being progressively stripped, first of extraordinary worldly power, then of ordinary human dignity, then of the very necessities of life, deprived of which he is more helpless and abject than any animal. But there is a more dreadful consummation than this reduction to physical nakedness. Lear hardly feels the storm because he is struggling to retain his mental integrity, his 'knowledge and reason', which are not only, as he himself calls them, 'marks of sovereignty', but the essential marks of humanity itself:

O, let me not be mad, not mad, sweet
      heaven!
Keep me in temper, I would not be mad! . . .
O fool, I shall go mad!

Lear's dread is justified, 'sweet heaven' rejects his prayer, and the central scenes on the heath are peopled by a blind, half-crazy nobleman, guided by a naked beggar supposed to be mad, and by an actually mad King served by a half-witted court-jester. . . .

But now that the worst has happened, now that Lear has lost his sanity, he has enlarged his vision. As his wits begin to leave him, he begins to see the truth about himself; when they are wholly gone he begins to have spasmodic flashes of insight in which, during momentary lulls in the storm of vengeful personal resentment, he sees the inner truth about the world. 'Thou wouldst make a good fool', said the Fool to his master at the beginning of his misfortunes, and he spoke as a prophet. In his amazing encounter with the *blind* Gloucester, the *mad* Lear has something of the wit, the penetration, the quick repartee of the court-jester. From the realistic point of view it is no doubt a dramatic flaw that Shakespeare does not account more clearly for the fate of the real man in motley; but his disappearance was a poetic necessity, for the King having lost everything, including his wits, has now himself become the Fool. He has touched bottom, he is an outcast from society, he has no longer any private axe to grind, so he now sees and speaks the truth.

And what is the truth? What does the mad Lear see in his flashes of lucidity? . . . Certainly his vision is a grim one. He sees not one particular event but the whole of human life as a vast sottie:

LEAR. What, art mad? A man may see how
   this world goes, with no eyes. Look with
   thine ears: see how yond justice rails upon
   yond simple thief. Hark, in thine ear:
   change places; and, handy-dandy, which is
   the justice, which is the thief? Thou hast
   seen a farmer's dog bark at a beggar?

GLOUCESTER. Ay, sir.
LEAR. And the creature run from the cur?
   There thou mightst behold the great image
   of authority: a dog's obeyed in office. . . .

      . . . Plate sin with gold,
And the strong lance of justice hurtless
      breaks;
Arm it in rags, a pigmy's straw does pierce it.

None does offend, none,—I say, none; I'll
      able 'em:
Take that of me, my friend, who have the
      power
To seal th' accuser's lips. Get thee glass eyes;
And, like a scurvy politician, seem
To see the things thou dost not.

Already we have watched king and noblemen turned into fools and beggars, now the great reversal of the Saturnalia is transferred from the action of the tragedy into the mind of the tragic hero, who discovers in his dotage, what the evil have known from their cradles, that *in this world there is no poetic justice*:

When we are born, we cry that we are come
To this great stage of fools.

. . . [The] blind Gloucester and mad Lear have come to know that to see truly 'how the world goes' is to 'see it feelingly'. And when the world is seen feelingly, what then? Why then we must be patient. That is all.

'Patience', like 'wisdom', 'folly', 'knavery', 'nature', is one of the key words of this tragedy. As soon as Lear begins to realize the nature of his misfortune, he begins to make pathetic attempts to acquire it, and when his mental overthrow is complete he recommends it as the appropriate response to the misery of life:

If thou wilt weep my fortunes, take my eyes.
I know thee well enough; thy name is
      Gloucester:
Thou must be patient; we came crying
      hither:
Thou know'st, the first time that we smell
      the air,
We wawl and cry.

Edgar takes the same point of view:

What! In ill-thoughts again? Men must
      endure
Their going hence, even as their coming
      hither:
Ripeness is all.

What is meant? Something different from tame submissiveness or cold stoicism, but completely opposed to that restless activity in pursuit of our own ends which Edmund thinks so preferable to passive obedience to fortune or custom. Patience, here, seems to imply an unflinching, clear-sighted recognition of the fact of pain, and the complete abandonment of any claim to justice or gratitude either from Gods or men; it is the power to choose love when love is synonymous with suffering, and to abide by the choice knowing there will be no Divine Salvation from its consequences.

And here, I think, is the solution of the problem set by the Fool; the problem of apparent moral relativity, 'Wisdom and goodness to the vile seem vile, filths savour but themselves', so that Albany and Goneril have not even sufficient common ground to make a real argument possible. Nevertheless, Shakespeare does not allow us to remain neutral spectators of their debate, he insists that although Goneril's case is as complete and consistent as that of Albany it is *not* equally valid, *not* equally true. In the first place Shakespeare's poetry persuades and compels us to accept the values of the friends rather than of the enemies of Lear. Secondly, Shakespeare makes the fullest possible use of the accepted convention that it is the Fool who speaks the truth, which he knows not by ratiocination but by inspired intuition. The mere appearance of the familiar figure in cap and bells would at once indicate to the audience where the 'punctum indifferens', the impartial critic, the mouthpiece of real sanity, was to be found.

Now the Fool sees that when the match between the good and the evil is played by the intellect alone it must end in a stalemate, but when the heart joins in the game then the decision is immediate and final. 'I will tarry, the Fool will stay—And let the wise man fly.' That is the unambiguous wisdom of the madman who sees the truth. That is decisive. It is decisive because, so far from being an abnormal freakish judgment, it is the instinctive judgment of normal humanity raised to heroic stature; and therefore no amount of intellectual argument can prevent normal human beings from receiving and accepting it, just as, when all the psychologists and philosophers have said their say, normal human beings continue to receive and accept the external world as given to them through sense perception. 'They that seek a reason for all things do destroy reason', notes the judicious [Richard] Hooker / [in *The Laws of Ecclesiastical Polity*]; our data, our premises, we must simply receive, and receive not only through our heads but also through our senses and our hearts. To see truly is to 'see feelingly'.

It would seem, then, that there is nothing contemptible in a motley coat. The Fool is justified, but we have not yet a complete answer to his original query: 'What is folly?' Which is the wise man, which is the fool? To be foolish is to mistake the nature of things, or to mistake the proper method of attaining to our desires, or to do both at once. Even Edmund and Edgar, even Goneril and Albany, could agree to that proposition. But have the perfectly disinterested made either of these mistakes and have not the self-interested made them both? The evil desire pleasure and power, and they lose both, for the evil are mutually destructive. The good desire to sympathize and to save, and their desires are partially fulfilled, although as a result they have to die. Nor have the

good mistaken the nature or 'mystery of things' which, after all, unlike Edmund, they have never professed either to dismiss or to understand. It is, indeed, as we have seen, the good who are normal. Lear, in his folly, is not reduced, as he fears, to the level of the beasts, but to essential naked humanity, 'unaccommodated man', 'the thing itself'. It is the evil who 'be-monster' themselves, it is the sight of Goneril which makes Albany fear that

> It will come,
> Humanity must perforce prey on
> itself,
> Like monsters of the deep.

In this connection it is not without interest that the Elizabethan playwrights made conventional use of the inherited belief in thunder as the voice of the Divine Judge, and that the Divine inspiration of madmen has always been a widespread and deeply rooted popular superstition.

Not that I would suggest that this great tragedy should be regarded as a morality play full of naïve spiritual consolation. That Shakespeare's ethics were the ethics of the New Testament, that in this play his mightiest poetry is dedicated to the reiteration of the wilder paradoxes of the Gospels and of St Paul, that seems to me quite certain. But it is no less certain that the metaphysical comfort of the Scriptures is deliberately omitted, though not therefore necessarily denied. The perfectly disinterested choose loving-kindness because they know it to be intrinsically desirable and worth the cost, not because they hope that the full price will not be exacted. It is Kent's readiness to be unendingly patient which makes him other than a shrewder and more far-calculating Edmund. If the thunder had ceased at Lear's bidding, then Lear would not have become a sage-fool. What the thunder says remains enigmatic, but it is this Divine ambiguity which gives such force to the testimony of the human heart. Had the speech of the gods been clearer, the apparently simple utterances of the Fool would have been less profound:

> FOOL. He that has a little tiny wit,
> 　With hey, ho, the wind and the rain,
> 　Must make content with his fortune's
> 　fit,
> 　For the rain it raineth every day.
> LEAR. True, my good boy.

And so we reach the final reversal of values. 'Ay every inch a king', says Lear in his madness, and we do not wholly disagree with him. The medieval clergy inaugurated the Saturnalia by parodying the Magnificat: Shakespeare reverses the process. Lear's tragedy is the investing of the King with motley: it is also the crowning and apotheosis of the Fool.

Robert Hillis Goldsmith

SOURCE: "Shakespeare's Wise Fools," in *Wise Fools in Shakespeare*, 1955. Reprint by Michigan State University Press, 1963, pp. 47-67.

[*Goldsmith calls Lear's jester a "wise fool" and distinguishes him from traditional fools known principally for being half-witted or cunning, satirical or ironical. The Fool's chief characteristic is devotion to the king, the critic declares, and in this steadfastness he demonstrates the virtues of "patience, humility, and love." Goldsmith notes that this devotion sometimes clouds the Fool's reason, a paradoxical situation since the Fool's principal task is to help Lear clarify his own judgment. But nursing the mad king back to sanity is beyond his skills, the critic asserts, and when it becomes apparent that others will take on this responsibility, the Fool departs.*]

The Fool in *King Lear* has become so enmeshed in the play's meaning that it is difficult to disentangle him. Several recent critics have approached the play's theme through the character of the Fool and the concept of wise folly which he brings into the play. One of these . . . critics, William Empson, refers to Lear's Fool as a lunatic ["Fool in *Lear*"]. But is this fool mentally defective? If the Fool and his 'folly' are so important to our full understanding of *King Lear*, then the question is not academic. Except for the bizarre diagnoses of a few scattered writers, the consensus of the critics is that Touchstone, Feste, and Lavache [in *As You Like It, Twelfth Night,* and *All's Well That Ends Well*] are clever artificial fools, not naturals; that they are conscious humorists, not unwitting instruments. However, when they come to examine Lear's Fool, the critics are far from agreed on the state of his mind. The preponderant opinion since the beginning of the nineteenth century seems to have been that this fool is a naive natural or even a half-wit boy. . . .

There is some justification for this reading of the Fool's character in the light of a confused popular tradition. [The court fool] Triboulet was little more than a babbling idiot who belonged successively to two French kings, yet he was endowed by the folk imagination with wisdom and intelligence far beyond the reach of his reason. Popular fancy is constantly distorting and disregarding the facts of history when building its legends. Shakespeare went not to history but to the popular and literary tradition (or to [the Elizabethan Comic actor Robert] Armin, which was the same thing) for the stuff of which he created Feste and Lear's Fool, but the poet refined upon the fool of tradition. Even in conceiving his most ambiguous characters, Shakespeare was ever firm and dramatically sure. Can we say then that in his conception of Lear's Fool the dramatist abandoned his usual methods, that his fool wavered between an unconscious

simpleton and a penetrating, ironical commentator? Since the best and only reliable arbiter in all such matters of interpretation is the text itself, let us turn to it.

Midway through the play, the disguised Edgar addresses the Fool as "innocent" (III, vi, 8). There is little to be gleaned from the context in which the term appears. However, in a passage which closely follows, there are speeches which strikingly contrast the Fool, the crazed King, and the feigned madman:

> FOOL. Prithee, nuncle, tell me whether a
>   madman be a gentleman or a yeoman.
> LEAR. A king, a king!
> FOOL. No, he's a yeoman that has a
>   gentleman to his son; for he's a mad
>   yeoman that sees his son a gentleman
>   before him.
>
> LEAR. To have a thousand with red burning
>   spits
> Come hizzing in upon 'em—
> EDGAR. The foul fiend bites my back.
> FOOL. He's mad that trusts in the tameness
>   of a wolf, a horse's health, a boy's love, or
>   a whore's oath.
>
> (III, vi, 10)

Of the three, the Fool alone speaks to the point, and he speaks the language of proverbial wisdom, the language of [the satirical fool] Marcolf. Edgar has as much and no more reason for calling Lear's Fool an "innocent" as Rosalind has for terming Touchstone a "natural." Both gentlefolk accept the gold coin for a copper penny, for so it passes current. As with the ambiguous title "Fool," the names "Innocent" and "Natural" seem to have been titles of office as frequently as they were descriptive epithets. . . .

Paradoxically, Lear's Fool is nobody's fool. He seldom lapses into nonsense or irrelevance; when he does, he does so to save himself from a beating. The Fool obliquely taunts Goneril: "The hedge-sparrow fed the cuckoo so long / That it had it head bit off by it young" and then skips off into quasi-nonsense: "So out went the candle, and we were left darkling" (*Lear* I, iv, 235). This seemingly irrelevant last line may echo several verses from Spenser's version of the tale of Lear: "But true it is that, when the oyle is spent, / The light goes out, and weeke is throwne away; / So when he had resigned his regiment, / His daughter gan despise his drouping day, / And wearie wax of his continuall stay" ([*Faerie Queene*] II, x, 30). The similarity can hardly be coincidental when both passages refer to Goneril's treatment of Lear. A little further on the Fool makes another sharp thrust at Goneril but immediately blunts its effect with what sounds like the refrain from an old song: "May not an ass know when the cart draws the horse? / Whoop, Jug, I love thee!" (I, iv, 244). If we remember that

"Jug" was not only a diminutive variant for Joan or Jane but was also a cant term for a common trull, we are not at all sure that the exclamation is really pointless. Can it not be that the Fool uses this mock declaration of love and loyalty to Goneril merely to deride those turncoats and time-pleasers who, like Oswald, shift and veer with every wind of favor? Such an interpretation would fit some later speeches of the Fool as well. Certainly he does not expect the loyal Kent to heed his cynical advice to "Let go thy hold when a great wheel runs down a hill, lest it break thy neck with following it" (II, iv, 72). The Fool habitually hides his meaning in metaphor.

Another passage which has troubled the explicators combines paradox, metaphor, and a bit of proverbial lore:

> The codpiece that will house
> Before the head has any,
> The head and he shall louse:
> So beggars marry many.
> The man that makes his toe
> What he his heart should make
> Shall of a corn cry woe,
> And turn his sleep to wake.
>
> (III, ii, 27)

Commentators have noted the obvious reference in the first stanza to the imprudent behavior of beggars and its logical consequences, but they have not always remarked on the relevance of the Fool's gibe to Lear's plight. Furness explains that Lear in preferring Regan and Goneril to Cordelia is like the man who covers the meaner members of his body and leaves his head and heart unprotected and as a result suffers pinching and pain in those very parts he sought to protect. A careful reading of this verse is not only rewarding in itself but will help to throw light upon a sequent passage. As Kent enters, the Fool remarks, "Marry, here's grace and a codpiece; that's a wise man and a fool" (III, ii, 40). Grace is, of course, a gentleman, the King in this instance. Or has he, the wise man, by his irrational behavior toward Cordelia changed places with the Fool? Has he not acted the part of a codpiece covering and protecting those baser parts—his lecherous and ungrateful daughters, Goneril and Regan? The Fool suggests that it may be the King who is the real fool.

So well does he disguise his thoughtful comments in the veiled language of imagery and old songs that he has misled some observers into actually taking him for a fool. Such a misunderstanding does not disturb him any more than it troubles Touchstone. To Kent's grudging admission that "This is not altogether fool, my lord," the Fool responds with characteristic insouciance: "No, faith; lords and great men will not let me. If I had a monopoly out, they would have part

on't. And ladies took, they will not let me have all the fool to myself; they'll be snatching" (I, iv, 166). Critics have been led astray not always by an unperceptive literal-mindedness but sometimes by a desire to superimpose their own patterns on Shakespeare's design. Coleridge speaks of "the overflowings of the wild wit of the Fool" [*Coleridge's Shakespearean Criticism*], and [A. C.] Bradley complains that regarding the Fool in *Lear* as wholly sane "destroys the poetry of the character" [*Shakespearean Tragedy*]. But whose poetry are we here considering—Coleridge's, Bradley's, or Shakespeare's? Shakespeare's conception of the timid but faithful fool, torn from his natural element—the banquet hall—and thrust shivering upon the wild, stormy heath is poetic enough for our imagination, particularly when we remember that the Fool follows his King against the promptings of his own common sense. He gives shrewd advice to others but does not heed it himself. . . .

Many of the Fool's comments betray a shrewd knowledge of the world, not what one would expect from a brilliant half-wit:

FOOL. O nuncle, court holy water in a dry house

The Fool.

is better than this rain water out o' door. Good nuncle, in, and ask thy daughters blessings! Here's a night pities neither wise men nor fools. (III, ii, 10)

The Fool has wit enough to come out of the rain but is restrained by a stronger power—loyalty to his sick King. Which of his five wits does the Fool lack? Certainly he has abundant store of fantasy and imagination—else he would not be constantly speaking in metaphor. His memory is long as we may see from his continual harping upon Lear's past and his injustice to Cordelia. The Fool does not lack common sense. His urging the King to come to terms with his daughters and the shrewd but cynical advice he gives Kent prove that he sees the world as it is. The only one of his faculties about which there may be any doubt is his judgment. We have already noted how his loyalty gets the better of his common sense. That lapse may be construed as a weakness in judgment— if we adopt the point of view of Goneril.

What about the Fool's heckling the King into madness? An anonymous Gentleman tells Kent and us that the Fool "labours to outjest his [Lear's] heart-struck injuries" (III, i, 16). But, these very jests are neither wise nor psychologically sound when applied as remedy for Lear's malady. Nay, even more; they are downright harmful. Professor [Oscar James] Campbell observes that the Fool's "jests, far from mitigating his master's woes, intensify them by forcing the King to realize the depth of his folly" [*The Living Shakespeare*]. The Fool then bears some of the responsibility for driving Lear mad. From this observation, one might argue that Lear's Fool is either malicious or stupidly naive. What then are we to say of the behavior of Kent? No one has seriously questioned his loyalty to his King or his sanity. And yet Kent's rash and headstrong righteousness is equally unwise and injudicious as a physic for Lear's choleric temper. Bradley notes that it is Kent who brings Lear's quarrel with Goneril to a head, and in falling upon the detestable Oswald and beating him, "he provides Regan and Cornwall with a pretext for their inhospitality." Kent therefore must share with the Fool any responsibility for hurrying Lear out of his wits. If Kent demonstrates by his loyal-hearted blundering that he has "more man than wit" (II, iv, 42) about him, then the Fool shows by his probing metaphors that he has no less of either quality. Both the Fool and the loyal Kent are too emotionally attached to the King to be good physicians to his sick mind.

About the Fool's doglike fidelity to Lear, a few further words are needful. Much has been written in praise of his utter, blind devotion to his master. Perhaps, we ought to recall, parenthetically, that the Fool wavers in his loyalty for a long moment and only hurries after his King when commanded by

Goneril: "You, sir, more knave than fool, after your master!" Immediately afterwards he throws off all prudence and sings:

> A fox, when one has caught her,
> And such a daughter,
> Should sure to the slaughter,
> If my cap would buy a halter.
> So the fool follows after.
>
> (I, iv, 337, 340)

The incident should temper but not destroy our belief in the Fool's loyalty. Whether he follows Lear, at first, out of faithfulness or merely from necessity matters little. He follows and stays with his master until forced to drop out of the play. And in remaining by Lear, the Fool violates his own sense of prudence. If this is not devotion, it is the next best thing. Walking clear-eyed into the stormy night and to his probable death on the heath, he comes as close as any fool ever does to the heroic.

With the prophetic sense so often attributed to fools and madmen, Lear's Fool sings a stave and makes a prediction:

> That sir which serves and seeks for gain,
>   And follows but for form,
> Will pack when it begins to rain
>   And leave thee in the storm.
> But I will tarry; the fool will stay,
>   And let the wise man fly.
> The knave turns fool that runs away;
>   The fool no knave, perdy.
>
> (II, iv, 79)

The first part of this jingle is a clear forecast of the course of the play and of the Fool's relation to it. The last two lines, however, have caused some confusion. That eminent rationalist, Dr. Samuel Johnson, solved the problem by emending the text to read: "The fool turns knave, that runs away; / The knave no fool,—." But, although his revision makes easier reading, it is too pedestrian for the Fool's meaning. Johnson's changed reading not only alters the words but rudely violates the character and spirit of Shakespeare's wise fool. . . . The ironical fool is playing ambiguously with the term "fool." The knave who runs away from a friend in adversity is accounted prudent, even wise, in the eyes of the world and such worldings as Goneril, Regan, and Edmund. But he is no more than a fool in the eyes of God, for, as Saint Paul says, "the wisdom of this world is foolishness with God" (I Cor. iii, 18). The Fool emphatically declares that he is no such knave, and we are left to infer that he may be truly wise in the sight of God.

This fool has come a long way from the railing Marcolf and the scheming Cacurgus [in the anonymous

Misogonus]. How far he has progressed beyond his shrewd ancestors and his cunning contemporaries may be seen in the almost contemptuous twist which he gives to the prudential wisdom of Solomon. When he cynically advises Kent: "We'll set thee to school to an ant, to teach thee there's no labouring i' th' winter" (II, iv, 68), he is echoing:

> Go to the ant, thou sluggard;
>   Consider her ways, and be wise:
> Which having no chief,
>   Overseer, or ruler,
> Provideth her bread in the summer,
>   And gathereth her food in the harvest.
>
> (Prov, vi, 6)

But he does not really wish Kent to follow his advice, for as he remarks a little later, "I would have none but knaves follow it, since a fool gives it" (II, iv, 77). He has become a wise fool in the Erasmian or Pauline sense.

The Fool has also become Lear's alter ego, his externalized conscience, or, as he puts it himself, "Lear's shadow" (I, iv, 251). In this role he chides the King:

> FOOL. If thou wert my fool, nuncle, I'd have thee beaten for being old before thy time.
> LEAR. How's that?
> FOOL. Thou shouldst not have been old till thou hadst been wise.
>
> (I, v, 44)

It is his task with his probing, sometimes caustic comments to cut away the cataracts of illusion which cloud Lear's eyes. What though the process be painful! What though the Fool, and later Edgar, must lead the old King through the darkness of unreason! The cure begun by the Fool is completed by Edgar and Cordelia, and Lear sees better through the eyes of a chastened spirit. The Fool's manner grows gentler as the King's madness increases. But it is not his business, nor has he the skill, to nurse the old man back to mental health. And so he goes to bed at noon in the play.

[Harley] Granville-Barker justly warns that the Fool ought not to be "all etherealized by the higher criticism." The actor who plays the role must still "sing like a lark, juggle his words so that the mere skill delights us, and tumble around with all the grace in the world" [*Prefaces to Shakespeare*]. Such is the professional duty of the court and stage fool. But he must be so portrayed that we may perceive the Fool's real wisdom and the central position he takes in the meaning of the play. Shakespeare, by giving him another stanza to sing from Feste's old song, links this fool with the wise fool of comedy but at the same time points up the difference between the two. Lear's Fool has had to learn patience in adversity.

> He that has and a little tiny wit—
>   With hey, ho, the wind and the rain—
> Must make content with his fortunes fit,
>   For the rain it raineth every day.
>
> (III, ii, 74)

Although it would be a mistake to regard Shakespeare's fools as mere personifications of wisdom, it is nevertheless true that each possesses his special virtue. Touchstone, by the air of realism which he breathes into the antique forest of romance, may be said to embody the Aristotelian virtue of truthfulness. Feste, by his advocacy of moderation in loving and laughing, adds to truthfulness the virtue of temperance. He lives in and expresses the golden mean. Lear's Fool, however, transcends his fellows in the quality of his wisdom. He is the supremely wise fool who expresses in his heartfelt devotion to Cordelia and to his king the Christian virtues of patience, humility, and love.

LEAR'S DAUGHTERS

A. C. Bradley and John F. Danby represent the traditional, prevailing view of Cordelia as the ideal female, endowed with tenderness, resolve, dignity, and unfailing love. Marilyn Gaull emphasizes Cordelia's obedient nature and argues that she represents the divine or transcendent love which created and sustains universal order. Danby further asserts that in the love test, Cordelia demonstrates courage, self-confidence, and poise; her self-assurance, he argues, should not be confused with pride, he argues. J. Ginger links Cordelia's actions in Act I, scene i with her penchant for bluntness and honesty. In contrast, Simon O. Lesser judges that her actions in the play's opening scene are influenced by anger toward her father and resentment of her sisters—emotions which impair her judgment and prevent her from giving her father the praise and reassurance she knows that he needs. Lesser detects an incestuous element in the love between Lear and his favorite daughter. Bradley sees personal antagonism toward her sisters in Cordelia's responses to the love test, as well as a touch of pride. But more importantly, he asserts, Cordelia is inherently unable to make a public avowal of her love.

Bradley also asks the question posed by a number of critics: what is the purpose of Cordelia's death? He finds a sense of reconciliation in her murder, emphasizing that the essence of Cordelia remains untouched by death. In Bradley's view, what happens to her is of infinitely less importance than the fact of her existence. Joyce Carol Oates offers a radically different perspective on Cordelia's death, arguing that the play depicts her as the female life-force that threatens patriarchal society and thus must be extinguished.

Cordelia refuses to conform to the subservient role that Lear and his male-dominated world intend her to play, Oates contends, and with her attempt to individualize herself, she becomes a rebellious force aligned with ungovernable Nature.

Oates has a very different view of Goneril and Regan, although she sees them as victims, too, of a patriarchal society. In her judgment, Goneril and Regan actively seek political gain as if they were Lear's rebellious sons testing his power and authority; because they are daughters, not sons, the play treats their ambition as unnatural. **Edwin Muir** focuses on Goneril and Regan as representatives of a new generation of rulers who sincerely believe their youth and strength give them a superior right to govern. He also notes their lack of differentiation or individuality, suggesting that this enhances their roles as mysterious, impersonal forces that Lear is unable to understand. Both Northrop Frye and Judd Arnold suggest that the king's older daughters deserve an objective appraisal. Frye points out that the love test is a public humiliation for them as well as for Cordelia, and that there is evidence in the text to support their complaints about Lear and his knights. Arnold, too, finds their complaints credible; he further proposes that Lear's voluntary abdication has contributed significantly to the sisters' spiritual degeneration, a point of view also expressed by Marilyn Gaull. For further commentary on Cordelia, see the excerpt by **Northrop Frye** in the OVERVIEWS section, and the excerpts by **Marilyn Gaull** and **Simon O. Lesser** in the section on LOVE. For additional commentary on Goneril and Regan, see the excerpts by **Northrop Frye** in the OVERVIEWS section and **Judd Arnold** in the section on LEAR.

A. C. Bradley

SOURCE: "King Lear," in *Shakespearean Tragedy: Lectures on "Hamlet," "Othello," "King Lear," "Macbeth"*, Macmillan and Co. Limited, 1905, pp. 280-330.

[*Bradley's remarks about Cordelia have been frequently cited by subsequent critics, even by those who profoundly disagree with his perspective on Lear's youngest daughter. He views her as a superlative figure who combines many of the individual virtues of Shakespeare's other heroines: a loving nature, a tender heart, resolution, and dignity. In Bradley's judgment, Cordelia ought not to be blamed for her imperfections—touches of pride and personal antagonism, an inability to speak of love, and her insistence on telling the truth rather than showing compassion—for these are all part of Shakespeare's unalterable tragic situation. The critic finds some degree of reconciliation in Cordelia's death. Bradley suggests that although she is an innocent victim, in her spiritual perfection she is beyond the reach of the evils committed by others; she seems not so much deprived of life as liberated from it.*]

The character of Cordelia is not a masterpiece of invention or subtlety. . . . [She] appears in only four of the twenty-six scenes of *King Lear*; she speaks—it is hard to believe it—scarcely more than a hundred lines; and yet no character in Shakespeare is more absolutely individual or more ineffaceably stamped on the memory of his readers. There is a harmony, strange but perhaps the result of intention, between the character itself and this reserved or parsimonious method of depicting it. An expressiveness almost inexhaustible gained through paucity of expression; the suggestion of infinite wealth and beauty conveyed by the very refusal to reveal this beauty in expansive speech—this is at once the nature of Cordelia herself and the chief characteristic of Shakespeare's art in representing it. Perhaps it is not fanciful to find a parallel in his drawing of a person very different, Hamlet. It was natural to Hamlet to examine himself minutely, to discuss himself at large, and yet to remain a mystery to himself; and Shakespeare's method of drawing the character answers to it; it is extremely detailed and searching, and yet its effect is to enhance the sense of mystery. The results in the two cases differ correspondingly. No one hesitates to enlarge upon Hamlet, who speaks of himself so much; but to use many words about Cordelia seems to be a kind of impiety.

I am obliged to speak of her chiefly because the devotion she inspires almost inevitably obscures her part in the tragedy. This devotion is composed, so to speak, of two contrary elements, reverence and pity. The first, because Cordelia's is a higher nature than that of most even of Shakespeare's heroines. With the tenderness of Viola [in *Twelfth Night*] or Desdemona [in *Othello*] she unites something of the resolution, power, and dignity of Hermione [in *A Winter's Tale*], and reminds us sometimes of Helena [in *All's Well That Ends Well*], sometimes of Isabella [in *Measure for Measure*], though she has none of the traits which prevent Isabella from winning our hearts. Her assertion of truth and right, her allegiance to them, even the touch of severity that accompanies it, instead of compelling mere respect or admiration, become adorable in a nature so loving as Cordelia's. She is a thing enskyed and sainted, and yet we feel no incongruity in the love of the King of France for her, as we do in the love of the Duke for Isabella.

But with this reverence or worship is combined in the reader's mind a passion of championship, of pity, even of protecting pity. She is so deeply wronged, and she appears, for all her strength, so defenceless. We think of her as unable to speak for herself. We think of her as quite young, and as slight and small.

'Her voice was ever soft, gentle, and low'; ever so, whether the tone was that of resolution, or rebuke, or love. Of all Shakespeare's heroines she knew least of joy. She grew up with Goneril and Regan for sisters. Even her love for her father must have been mingled with pain and anxiety. She must early have learned to school and repress emotion. She never knew the bliss of young love: there is no trace of such love for the King of France. She had knowingly to wound most deeply the being dearest to her. He cast her off; and, after suffering an agony for him, and before she could see him safe in death, she was brutally murdered. We have to thank the poet for passing lightly over the circumstances of her death. We do not think of them. Her image comes before us calm and bright and still.

The memory of Cordelia thus becomes detached in a manner from the action of the drama. The reader refuses to admit into it any idea of imperfection, and is outraged when any share in her father's sufferings is attributed to the part she plays in the opening scene. Because she was deeply wronged he is ready to insist that she was wholly right. He refuses, that is, to take the tragic point of view, and, when it is taken, he imagines that Cordelia is being attacked, or is being declared to have 'deserved' all that befell her. But Shakespeare's was the tragic point of view. He exhibits in the opening scene a situation tragic for Cordelia as well as for Lear. At a moment where terrible issues join, Fate makes on her the one demand which she is unable to meet. . . . [It] was a demand which other heroines of Shakespeare could have met. Without loss of self-respect, and refusing even to appear to compete for a reward, they could have made the unreasonable old King feel that he was fondly loved. Cordelia cannot, because she is Cordelia. And so she is not merely rejected and banished, but her father is left to the mercies of her sisters. And the cause of her failure—a failure a thousand-fold redeemed—is a compound in which imperfection appears so intimately mingled with the noblest qualities that—if we are true to Shakespeare—we do not think either of justifying her or of blaming her: we feel simply the tragic emotions of fear and pity.

In this failure a large part is played by that obvious characteristic to which I have already referred. Cordelia is not, indeed, always tongue-tied, as several passages in the drama, and even in this scene, clearly show. But tender emotion, and especially a tender love for the person to whom she has to speak, makes her dumb. Her love, as she says, is more ponderous than her tongue:

> Unhappy that I am, I cannot heave
> My heart into my mouth.

This expressive word 'heave' is repeated in the passage which describes her reception of Kent's letter:

> Faith, once or twice she heaved the name of
>   'Father'
> Pantingly forth, as if it press'd her heart:

two or three broken ejaculations escape her lips, and she 'starts' away 'to deal with grief alone.' The same trait reappears with an ineffable beauty in the stifled repetitions with which she attempts to answer her father in the moment of his restoration:

> *Lear.*   Do not laugh at me;
> For, as I am a man, I think this lady
> To be my child Cordelia.
>
> *Cor.*   And so I am, I am.
>
> *Lear.* Be your tears wet? yes, faith. I pray,
>   weep not;
> If you have poison for me, I will drink it.
> I know you do not love me; for your sisters
> Have, as I do remember, done me wrong:
> You have some cause, they have not.
>
> *Cor.*   No cause, no cause.

We see this trait for the last time, marked by Shakespeare with a decision clearly intentional, intentional, in her inability to answer one syllable to the last words we hear her father speak to her:

> No, no, no, no! Come, let's away to prison:
> We two alone will sing like birds i' the cage:
> When thou dost ask me blessing, I'll kneel
>   down,
> And ask of thee forgiveness: so we'll live,
> And pray, and sing, and tell old tales, and
>   laugh
> At gilded butterflies. . . .

She stands and weeps, and goes out with him silent. And we see her alive no more.

But (I am forced to dwell on the point, because I am sure to slur it over is to be false to Shakespeare) this dumbness of love was not the sole source of misunderstanding. If this had been all, even Lear could have seen the love in Cordelia's eyes when, to his question 'What can you say to draw a third more opulent than your sisters?' she answered 'Nothing.' But it did not shine there. She is not merely silent, nor does she merely answer 'Nothing.' She tells him that she loves him 'according to her bond, nor more nor less'; and his answer,

> How now, Cordelia! mend your speech a
>   little,
> Lest it may mar your fortunes,

so intensifies her horror at the hypocrisy of her sisters

that she replies,

> Good my Lord,
> You have begot me, bred me, loved me: I
> Return those duties back as are right fit,
> Obey you, love you, and most honour you.
> Why have my sisters husbands, if they say
> They love you all? Haply, when I shall wed,
> That lord whose hand must take my plight
>   shall carry
> Half my love with him, half my care and
>   duty:
> Sure, I shall never marry like my sisters,
> To love my father all.

What words for the ear of an old father, unreasonable, despotic, but fondly loving, indecent in his own expressions of preference, and blind to the indecency of his appeal for protestations of fondness! Blank astonishment, anger, wounded love, contend within him; but for the moment he restrains himself and asks,

> But goes thy heart with this?

. . . Cordelia answers,

> Ay, good my lord.
> *Lear.* So young, and so untender?
> *Cor.* So young, my lord, and true.

Yes, 'heavenly true.' But truth is not the only good in the world, nor is the obligation to tell truth the only obligation. The matter here was to keep it inviolate, but also to preserve a father. And even if truth *were* the one and only obligation, to tell much less than truth is not to tell it. And Cordelia's speech not only tells much less than truth about her love, it actually perverts the truth when it implies that to give love to a husband is to take it from a father. There surely never was a more unhappy speech. . . .

Cordelia's hatred of hypocrisy and of the faintest appearance of mercenary professions reminds us of Isabella's hatred of impurity; but Cordelia's position is infinitely more difficult, and on the other hand there is mingled with her hatred a touch of personal antagonism and of pride. Lear's words,

> Let pride, which she calls plainness, marry
>   her!

are monstrously unjust, but they contain one grain of truth; and indeed it was scarcely possible that a nature so strong as Cordelia's, and with so keen a sense of dignity, should feel here nothing whatever of pride and resentment. This side of her character is emphatically shown in her language to her sisters in the first scene—language perfectly just, but little adapted to soften their hearts towards their father—and

again in the very last words we hear her speak. She and her father are brought in, prisoners, to the enemy's camp; but she sees only Edmund, not those 'greater' ones on whose pleasure hangs her father's fate and her own. For her own she is little concerned; she knows how to meet adversity:

> For thee, oppressed king, am I cast down;
> Myself could else out-frown false fortune's
>   frown.

Yes, that is how she would meet fortune, frowning it down, even as Goneril would have met it; nor, if her father had been already dead, would there have been any great improbability in the false story that was to be told of her death, that, like Goneril, she 'fordid herself.' Then, after those austere words about fortune, she suddenly asks,

> Shall we not see these daughters and these
>   sisters?

Strange last words for us to hear from a being so worshipped and beloved; but how characteristic! Their tone is unmistakable. I doubt if she could have brought herself to plead with her sisters for her father's life; and if she had attempted the task, she would have performed it but ill. Nor is our feeling towards her altered one whit by that. But what is true of Kent and the Fool is, in its measure, true of her. Any one of them would gladly have died a hundred deaths to help King Lear; and they do help his soul; but they harm his cause. They are all involved in tragedy.

Why does Cordelia die? I suppose no reader ever failed to ask that question, and to ask it with something more than pain,—to ask it, if only for a moment, in bewilderment or dismay, and even perhaps in tones of protest. These feelings are probably evoked more strongly here than at the death of any other notable character in Shakespeare; and it may sound a wilful paradox to assert that the slightest element of reconciliation is mingled with them or succeeds them. Yet it seems to me indubitable that such an element is present, though difficult to make out with certainty what it is or whence it proceeds. And I will try to make this out, and to state it methodically.

(*a*) It is not due in any perceptible degree to the fact, which we have just been examining, that Cordelia through her tragic imperfection contributes something to the conflict and catastrophe; and I drew attention to that imperfection without any view to our present problem. The critics who emphasise it at this point in the drama are surely untrue to Shakespeare's mind; and still more completely astray are those who lay stress on the idea that Cordelia, in bringing a foreign army to help her father, was guilty of treason to her country. When she dies we regard her, practically

From Act V, scene iii, Lear, his daughters, Edmund, Albany, Edgar, Kent, and soldiers.

speaking, simply as we regard Ophelia [in *Hamlet*], or Desdemona [in *Othello*], as an innocent victim swept away in the convulsion caused by the error or guilt of others.

(*b*) Now this destruction of the good through the evil of others is one of the tragic facts of life, and no one can object to the use of it, within certain limits, in tragic art. And, further, those who because of it declaim against the nature of things, declaim without thinking. It is obviously the other side of the fact that the effects of good spread far and wide beyond the doer of good; and we should ask ourselves whether we really could wish (supposing it conceivable) to see this double-sided fact abolished. Nevertheless the touch of reconciliation that we feel in contemplating the death of Cordelia is not due, or is due only in some slight degree, to a perception that the event is true to life, admissible in tragedy, and a case of a law which we cannot seriously desire to see abrogated.

(*c*) What then is this feeling, and whence does it come? I believe we shall find that it is a feeling not confined to *King Lear*, but present at the close of other tragedies; and that the reason why it has an exceptional tone or force at the close of *King Lear*, lies in that very peculiarity of the close which also—at least for the moment—excites bewilderment, dismay, or protest. The feeling I mean is the impression that the heroic being, though in one sense and outwardly he has failed, is yet in another sense superior to the world in which he appears; is, in some way which we do not seek to define, untouched by the doom that overtakes him; and is rather set free from life than deprived of it. Some such feeling as this—some feeling which, from this description of it, may be recognised as their own even by those who would dissent from the description—we surely have in various degrees at the deaths of Hamlet and Othello and Lear, and of Antony and Cleopatra and Coriolanus. It accompanies the more prominent tragic impressions, and, regarded alone, could hardly be called tragic.

For it seems to imply (though we are probably quite unconscious of the implication) an idea which, if developed, would transform the tragic view of things. It implies that the tragic world, if taken as it is presented, with all its error, guilt, failure, woe and waste, is no final reality, but only a part of reality taken for the whole, and, when so taken, illusive; and that if we could see the whole, and the tragic facts in their true place in it, we should find them, not abolished, of course, but so transmuted that they had ceased to be strictly tragic,—find, perhaps, the suffering and death counting for little or nothing, the greatness of the soul for much or all, and the heroic spirit, in spite of failure, nearer to the heart of things than the smaller, more circumspect, and perhaps even 'better' beings who survived the catastrophe. The feeling which I have tried to describe, as accompanying the more obvious tragic emotions at the deaths of heroes, corresponds with some such idea as this.

Now this feeling is evoked with a quite exceptional strength by the death of Cordelia. It is not due to the perception that she, like Lear, has attained through suffering; we know that she had suffered and attained in his days of prosperity. It is simply the feeling that what happens to such a being does not matter; all that matters is what she is. How this can be when, for anything the tragedy tells us, she has ceased to exist, we do not ask; but the tragedy itself makes us feel that somehow it is so. And the force with which this impression is conveyed depends largely on the very fact which excites our bewilderment and protest, that her death, following on the deaths of all the evil characters, and brought about by an unexplained delay in Edmund's effort to save her, comes on us, not as an inevitable conclusion to the sequence of events, but as the sudden stroke of mere fate or chance. The force of the impression, that is to say, depends on the very violence of the contrast between the outward and the inward, Cordelia's death and Cordelia's soul. The more unmotived, unmerited, senseless, monstrous, her fate, the more do we feel that it does not concern her. The extremity of the disproportion between prosperity and goodness first shocks us, and then flashes on us the conviction that our whole attitude in asking or expecting that goodness should be prosperous is wrong; that, if only we could see things as they are, we should see that the outward is nothing and the inward is all. . . .

Edwin Muir

SOURCE: *The Politics of "King Lear,"* Jackson, Son & Company, 1947, 24 p.

[*In the following excerpt from a lecture delivered at the University of Glasgow in April 1946, Muir discusses Goneril and Regan as representatives of a new political order. In the early 1600s, when the play was written, the medieval concept of communal traditions was giving way to modern notions of political rule—ones that emphasized effectiveness rather than principles, the critic observes. With their unconcern for traditional values or customs, Muir explains, Goneril and Regan embody the amorality of* Realpolitik *(politics based on practical factors rather than ethical or moral considerations) and the unscrupulous emphasis on power associated with Machiavellianism (the theory that the attainment of political power is justified by any means). The critic points out their lack of individuality and argues that they are like impersonal forces, beyond human appeal or understanding.*]

King Lear was written round about 1605-6 . . . In the interval between the first and the last of these dates the medieval world with its communal tradition was slowly dying, and the modern individualist world was bringing itself to birth. Shakespeare lived in that violent period of transition. The old world still echoed in his ears; he was aware of the new as we are aware of the future, that is as an inchoate, semi-prophetic dream. Now it seems to me that that dream, those echoes, fill *King Lear* and account for the sense of vastness which it gives us, the feeling that it covers a far greater stretch of time than can be explained by the action. The extreme age of the King brings to our minds the image of a civilization of legendary anti-quity; yet that civilization is destroyed by a new generation which belongs to Shakespeare's own time, a perfectly up-to-date gang of Renaissance adventurers. The play contains, therefore, or has taken on, a significance which Shakespeare probably could not have known, but could only have felt, and without his being aware, he wrote in it the mythical drama of the transmutation of civilization. . . .

Of the great tragedies *King Lear* is the only one in which two ideas of society are directly confronted, and the old generation and the new are set face to face, each assured of its own right to power. *Macbeth* is a drama of murder and usurpation and remorse; it changes the succession of the crown and brings guilt upon the offender, the guilt showing that the old order is still accepted, and the old laws still valid, since Macbeth feels that he has done wrong, both as the killer of a man and the supplanter of a king. But Regan, Goneril and Cornwall never feel they have done wrong, and this is because they represent a new idea; and new ideas, like everything new, bring with them their own kind of innocence. *Hamlet,* although it deals with a dynastic and therefore a political problem, is essentially a personal drama, perhaps the most personal of them all: there is no relationship in *King Lear* so intensely intimate as that of Hamlet to his mother. Lear's own relation to his daughters is most nearly so; yet Goneril and Regan are curiously equal in his estimation, indeed almost interchangeable; he is willing to accept either if she will only take his part against her sister; and as if his rage had blotted out their very names, he confounds them indistinguishably in his curses upon his daughters; so that we feel that daughters have become to him some strange and monstrous species. To Goneril and Regan, on the other hand, he is hardly even a father, but merely an old man who thinks and feels in a way they cannot understand, and is a burden to them. The almost impersonal equivalence of the two women in their father's eyes gives a cast to the play which is not to be found in any of the others, and makes us feel, indeed, that Lear is not contending with ordinary human beings but with mere forces to which any human appeal is vain, since it is not even capable of evoking a response. He, the representative of the old, is confronted with something brand new; he cannot understand it, and it does not even care to understand him.

There is something more, then, than ingratitude in the reaction of Lear's daughters, though the ingratitude, that "marble-hearted fiend", strikes most deeply into his heart. This something more is their attitude to power, which is grounded on their attitude to life. It is this, more than the ingratitude, that estranges Lear from them. His appeals cannot reach them, but, worse still, his mind cannot understand them, no matter how hard he tries. As this attitude of his daughters violates all his ideas of the nature of things, it seems to him against nature, so that he can only cry out against them as "unnatural hags". "Unnatural" is the nearest he can come to a definition of the unbridgable distance that divides him from them; his real struggle is to annihilate that distance, but he never succeeds; in his most intimate conflict with them he never comes any closer to them. When Regan shuts him out in the storm her action is symbolical as well as practical. His daughters are inside; he is outside. They are in two different worlds.

The story of *King Lear* tells how an old man parts his kingdom between his daughters when he feels no longer able to rule. He retains to himself only

> The name and all th' addition to a king,

and leaves to them and their husbands

> The sway, revenue, execution of the rest.

His daughters, having got what they want, that is the power, and not caring much for the name or the addition, turn against him. As daughters, their act is one of filial ingratitude; as princesses and vice-regents, it is an act of "revolt and flying off". These two aspects of their policy are inseparable; in turning against their father they subvert the kingdom; by the same deed they commit two crimes, one private and one public.

But there is a complication. For Goneril and Regan's idea of rulership is different from their father's and so on the anguish caused by their ingratitude is piled the bewilderment of one who feels he is dealing with creatures whose notions are equally incomprehensible to his heart and his mind. In the later stages of the conflict it is the tortures of his mind that become the most unbearable, since they make the nature of things incomprehensible to him, and confound his ideas in a chaos from which the only escape is madness. The note of Lear's tragedy is to be found in another play [*Othello*]:

> Chaos is come again.

The note of the play itself, the summary judgment on the whole action, is expressed in Albany's words:

> If that the heavens do not their visible spirits
> Send quickly down to tame these vile offences,
> It will come,
> Humanity must pertorce prey on itself,
> Like monsters of the deep.

Yet this is the world which Lear's two daughters and Cornwall and Edmund and Oswald freely accept as theirs; it is their idea of a brand new order; and the play therefore deals not only with a conflict between two daughters and their father, and two vice-regents and their king, but with two conceptions of society.

In the new conception of society, that of Goneril and Regan, Nature plays an important part; the number of references to Nature in the play, almost always as images of cruelty or horror, has often been commented upon. [A. C.] Bradley in his book on Shakespearean Tragedy tries to make a list of the lower animals which are mentioned in the drama. . . . "These references are broadcast through the whole play", he says, "as though Shakespeare's mind were so busy with the subject that he could hardly write a page without some allusion to it. The dog, the horse, the cow, the sheep, the hog, the lion, the bear, the wolf, the fox, the monkey, the polecat, the civet-cat, the pelican, the owl, the crow, the chough, the wren, the fly, the butterfly, the rat, the mouse, the frog, the tadpole, the wall-newt, the water-newt, the worm—I am sure I cannot have completed the list, and some of them are mentioned again and again. . . . Sometimes a person in the drama is compared, openly or implicitly, with one of them. Goneril is a kite; her ingratitude has a serpent tooth: she has struck her father most serpent-like upon the very heart: her visage is wolfish: she has tied sharp-toothed unkindness like a vulture on her father's breast: for her husband she is a gilded serpent: to Gloster her cruelty seems to have the fangs of a boar. She and Regan are dog-hearted: they are tigers, not daughters; each is an adder to the other;

the flesh of each is covered with the fell of a beast. . . . As we read, the souls of all the beasts in turn seem to us to have entered the bodies of these mortals; horrible in their venom, savagery, lust, deceitfulness, sloth, cruelty, filthiness" [*Shakespearean Tragedy*].

After looking on this picture of nature, turn to the first speech of Edmund, the mouthpiece of the new generation:

> Thou, Nature, art my goddess; to thy law
> My services are bound. . . .
> Well then,
> Legitimate Edgar, I must have your land:
> Our father's love is to the bastard Edmund
> As to the legitimate. Fine word, 'legitimate'.

Goneril and Regan and Cornwall, though they do not have Edmund's imaginative intellect, worship Nature in the same spirit. For it gives them the freedom they hunger for, absolves them from the plague of custom, justifies them when they reflect that their dimensions are well-compact and their shape true, as if that were all that was needed to make human a creature in human shape. They rely confidently on certain simple facts of nature: that they are young and their father old, strong while he is infirm, and that their youth and strength give them a short-cut to their desires. They are so close to the state of nature that they hardly need to reflect: what they have the power to do they claim the right to do. Or rather the power and its expression in action are almost simultaneous. When Lear pleads with Goneril she replies:

> Be then desir'd
> By her that else will take the thing she begs
> A little to disquantity your train.

Regan says a little later:

> I pray you, father, being weak, seem so.

After Cornwall puts out Gloster's eyes, and Regan stabs the servant who tried to prevent it, he says:

> Turn out that eyeless villain; throw this
>   slave
> Upon the dunghill.

And Regan adds,

> Go thrust him out at gates, and let him
>   smell
> His way to Dover.

The most repulsive thing about these words, apart from their cruelty, is their triteness. The two daughters ignore all the complexities of the situation, and

solve it at once by an abominable truism. They are quite rational, but only on the lowest plane of reason, and they have that contempt for other ways of thinking which comes from a knowledge of their own efficiency. As they are rational, they have a good conscience, even a touch of self-righteousness; they sincerely believe their father is in the wrong and they are in the right, since they conceive they know the world as it is, and act in conformity with it, the source of all effective power. They do not see far, but they see clearly. When they reflect, and take thought for the future, their decisions are rational and satisfactory by their own standards. When Goneril wants an excuse for reducing her father's retinue, she instructs her servant Oswald how to behave towards him:

> Put on what weary negligence you please,
> You and your fellows: I'd have it come to
>   question . . .
> And let his knights have colder looks among
>   you;
> What grows of it, no matter: advise your
>   fellows so:
> I would breed from hence occasions, and I
>   shall,
> That I may speak.

This is a technique which we have seen much practised in our own time.

The members of the new generation are bound together by common interest, since they all wish to succeed in their individual ambitions, which they cannot achieve without help; but their most immediate bond is a common way of thinking, a spontaneous intellectual affinity resembling that of a chosen group to whom a new vision of the world has been vouchsafed. They feel they are of the elect and have the sense of superiority which fits their station. They are irresistibly driven to choose as confederates men and women of their own stamp, even though these are likely in the long run to thwart or destroy them. Having renounced morality as a useful factor in conduct, they judge others with a total lack of moral discrimination, being confined irretrievably to the low plane of reason on which they move. Accordingly Cornwall can say to Edmund:

> You shall be ours;
> Natures of such deep trust we shall much
>   need;
> You we first seize on.

And of honest Kent:

> This is some fellow,
> Who, having been praised for bluntness, doth
>   affect
> A saucy roughness, and constrains the garb

Quite from his nature: he cannot flatter, he;
An honest man and plain, he must speak
    truth:
An they will have it, so; if not, he's plain.
These kind of rogues I know, which in this
    plainness
Harbour more craft and more corrupter ends
Than twenty silly-ducking observants
That stretch their duties nicely.

Lear could not have made these mistakes, for he had some knowledge of the moral nature of men; but Cornwall and Goneril and Regan can and do; for while they have worked out the equation of life with complete satisfaction to themselves, they have done so by omitting the moral factor.

The new generation may be regarded then as the embodiment of wickedness, a wickedness of that special kind which I have tried to indicate. . . .

Shakespeare was acquainted with the Renaissance man, and . . . his plays abound in references to "policy", which stood in his time for what the Germans dignify by the name of *Realpolitik*, that is political action which ignores all moral considerations. . . . It was an age in which Italian princes, and others too, permitted themselves a liberty of action which one would have expected to disrupt or destroy the state; yet it did not. Instead, the subject conformed to a rulership which itself seemed impossible because antisocial; he conformed by becoming the mere instrument of his ruler. The Macchiavellian became a stock figure in later Elizabethan drama; Shakespeare must have met many a man like Edmund who refused to be deprived by the plague of custom. Bradley calls Edmund a mere adventurer, yet afterwards describes him as a consummate politician in the new style. "He acts in pursuance of a purpose", says Bradley, "and if he has any affections or dislikes, ignores them. He is determined to make his way, first to his brother's lands, then—as the prospect widens—to the crown; and he regards men and women, with their virtues and vices, together with the bonds of kinship, friendship, or allegiance, merely as hindrances or helps to his end. They are for him divested of all quality except their relation to his end; as indifferent as mathematical quantities or mere physical agents.

A credulous father and a brother noble,
. . . I see the business,

he says, as if he were talking of x and y [*Shakespearean Tragedy*].

To regard things in this way is to see them in a continuous present divested of all associations, denuded of memory and the depth which memory gives to life. Goneril and Regan, even more than Edmund,

exist in this shallow present, and it is to them a present in both senses of the word, a gift freely given into their hands to do with what they like. Having no memory, they have no responsibility, and no need therefore to treat their father differently from any other troublesome old man. This may simply be another way of saying that they are evil, for it may be that evil consists in a hiatus in the soul, a craving blank, a lack of one of the essential threads which bind experience into a coherent whole and give it a consistent meaning. The hiatus in Lear's daughters is specifically a hiatus of memory, a breach in continuity; they seem to come from nowhere and to be on the road to nowhere; they have words and acts only to meet the momentary emergency, the momentary appetite; their speech is therefore strikingly deficient in imagery, and consists of a sequence of pitiless truisms. Bradley complains of the characters in the play that, "Considered simply as psychological studies few of them are of the highest interest." This is true of Goneril and Regan, for the human qualities of highest interest are left out of them. But this was Shakespeare's intention; he had to interest us in two characters who were both evil and shallow. Their shallowness is ultimately that of the Macchiavellian view of life as it was understood in his age, of "policy", or Realpolitik, whichever we may choose to call it. The sisters are harpies, but as rulers they act in the approved contemporary Macchiavellian convention.

SOURCES FOR FURTHER STUDY

Literary Commentary

Aggeler, Geoffrey. "'Good Pity' in *King Lear*: The Progress of Edgar." *Neophilologus* 77, No. 2 (April 1993): 321-31.

    Follows Edgar's transformation from victim to agent of justice. Initially naive and self-pitying, on the heath Edgar develops the capacity to pity others and learns to temper compassion with reason, Aggeler maintains.

Brooke, Nicholas. "Prologue." In *Shakespeare: "King Lear,"* pp. 9-17. *Studies in English Literature*, No. 13. London: Edward Arnold, 1963.

    An introduction to a book-length treatment of the play's themes and characters. Brooke here reviews the implausibility of the dramatic action and discusses the function of the poetic verse and imagery.

Danby, John F. "Cordelia." In *Shakespeare's Doctrine of Nature: A Study of "King Lear,"* pp. 114-40. London: Faber and Faber, 1949.

    Discusses the allegorical significance of Shakespeare's portrayal of Cordelia.

Dunn, E. Catherine. "The Storm in *King Lear.*" *Shakespeare Quarterly* III, No. 4 (October 1952): 329-33.

Argues that ingratitude is crucial to interpreting the metaphor of the storm in *King Lear*. In Renaissance terms, ingratitude is an "enormous evil," severing ties that hold together families, friends, and society itself, Dunn explains.

Elton, William R. "Double Plot." In *"King Lear" and the Gods*, pp. 267-83. San Marino, CA: The Huntington Library, 1966.

Disputes the opinion that the double plot in *Lear* is confusing or uneconomical. Elton claims that it is an effective means of clarifying the principal dramatic action and serves many different functions.

Empson, William. "Fool in *Lear.*" *Sewanee Review* LVII, No. 2 (April-June 1949): 177-214.

A detailed analysis of the various ways and situations in which the word "fool" is used throughout the play. The word becomes a "key metaphor," Empson maintains, for a tale set in motion by Lear's foolish renunciation of his power.

Frye, Dean. "The Context of Lear's Unbuttoning." *ELH* 32, No. 1 (March 1965): 17-31.

Analyzes the relation between clothing, nature, and artifice in *King Lear*. "Proper clothes" symbolize a well-ordered society and ritual costumes lend meaning to ceremonial roles, Frye proposes.

Ginger, J. "The Worlds of *King Lear.*" *IBADAN* 20 (October 1964): 20-26.

Evaluates the variety of belief systems represented in *King Lear*. The king's faith in the supernatural, Edmund's skepticism, and Goneril and Regan's rationalism are all shown to be invalid philosophies, Ginger declares; in contrast, Cordelia's charity and Edgar's morality suggest "the healing effect of the Christian idea."

Heinemann, Margot. "'Demystifying the Mystery of State': *King Lear* and the World Upside Down." *Shakespeare Survey* 44 (1992): 75-83.

Contends that *King Lear* dramatizes "the breakdown of a social and political system" as well as the conflict between competing political ideologies.

Holly, Marcia. "*King Lear*": The Disguised and Deceived." *Shakespeare Quarterly* XXIV, No. 2 (Spring 1973): 171-80.

Demonstrates that the characters in *King Lear* who assume false identities are those "who see themselves most honestly and clearly."

House, Ian W. O. "'I know thee well enough': The Two Plots of *King Lear.*" *English* 41, No. 170 (Summer 1992): 97-112.

House emphasizes the dynamic relation between the main plot and the subplot in *King Lear*, proposing that the differences as well as the similarities between them unsettle and illuminate our understanding of the principal story. Further, House analyzes the notorious implausibility of dramatic events in Lear, arguing that the absurdity is purposeful and heightened by the changes in the humorous tone of the subplot "from farce to melodrama, from domestic tragedy to surrealism." In the course of discussing these issues, the critic provides extended evaluations of Gloucester, Edmund, and, especially, Edgar.

Hunter, G. K. Introduction to *King Lear* by William Shakespeare, edited by G. K. Hunter, pp. 7-52. Harmondsworth: Penguin Books, 1972.

Examines the close-knit relation between dramatic action in *King Lear* and the competing value systems presented in the play.

Knight, G. Wilson. "*King Lear* and the Comedy of the Grotesque." In *The Wheel of Fire*, pp. 160-76. London: Methuen, 1949.

Argues that a vivid and recurrent emphasis on "the incongruous and the fantastic" is at the core of *King Lear*.

———. "The *Lear* Universe." In *The Wheel of Fire*, pp. 177-206. London: Methuen, 1949.

A wide-ranging analysis of themes and characters in *King Lear*. Knight evaluates the various meanings of "nature" in the play, examines its presentation of divine and human justice, and traces the ways in which several characters learn to accept and endure suffering.

Kott, Jan. "*King Lear*, or Endgame." In *Shakespeare Our Contemporary*," pp. 100-33. London: Methuen, 1967.

Describes *King Lear* as a tragedy of the "grotesque." Kott asserts that the play affirms no absolute values and holds out no hope of consolation or redemption. He also provides an extended comparison of *Lear* and Samuel Beckett's *Endgame*.

Leider, Emily W. "Plainness of Style in *King Lear.*" *Shakespeare Quarterly* XXI, No. 1 (Winter 1970): 45-53.

Examines the relation between language and dramatic action in *King Lear*. Leider refers to the contrast between plain speech and flattery used by other characters, but her principal focus is on the speeches of Lear.

MacIntyre, Jean. "Truth, Lies, and Poesie in *King Lear.*" *Renaissance and Reformation* 6, No. 1 [o.s. 18, No. 1] (February 1982): 39-45.

Evaluates the function of benevolent falsehoods in *King Lear*. MacIntyre shows that Lear and Gloucester, susceptible to flattery and unwilling to hear unadorned truths, are brought to reality through the creative fictions of Kent and Edgar. The essay highlights the effects of Edgar's various disguises and "poetic" styles.

Mack, Maynard. "'We came crying hither': An Essay on Some Characteristics of *King Lear.*" *Yale Review* LIV, No. 2 (December 1964): 161-86.

An explanation for the general reader of why "*King Lear* above all others is the Shakespearean tragedy for our time." Mack focuses on the play's depiction of violence and pain, the "spectacular consequences" of willful action, and the necessity for patient acceptance of suffering and an unintelligible universe.

Matthews, Richard. "Edmund's Redemption in *King Lear.*" *Shakespeare Quarterly* XXVI, No. 1 (Winter 1975): 25-29.

Identifies a profound change in Edmund after he is mortally wounded. From that point on, Matthews argues, Edmund first exhibits compassion for Gloucester, then acknowledges Goneril's and Regan's love for him, and finally acts to save Lear and Cordelia. The critic also provides an overview of previously published commentary on Edmund.

McFarland, Thomas. "The Image of the Family in *King Lear.*" In *On "King Lear,"* ed. Lawrence Danson, pp. 91-118. Princeton: Princeton University Pres, 1981.

Contends that the family is the only refuge and source of consolation in the dramatic world of *King Lear*. Romantic love is virtually non-existent in the play, the critic points out, and in its absence family bonds become of primary importance.

Milne, Evander. "On the Death of Cordelia." *English* VI, No. 34 (Spring 1947): 244-48.

Reviews historical preferences for Nahum Tate's "happy ending." Milne concludes that the play's depiction of the savagery of natural laws would be compromised if Cordelia survived at its close.

Oates, Joyce Carol. "'Is this the promised end?': The Tragedy of *King Lear.*" *Journal of Aesthetics and Art Criticism* XXXIII, No. 1 (Fall 1974): 19-32.

Analyzes "the incompatibility of the visionary and the tragic" in *King Lear* by exploring the play's presentation of women. Oates argues that *Lear* is brutally anti-feminine, particularly in its equation of the female life force with chaotic, ungovernable Nature.

Rackin, Phyllis. "Delusion as Resolution in *King Lear.*" *Shakespeare Quarterly* XXI, No. 1 (Winter 1970): 29-34.

Focuses on Lear's final speech. Although "the passage itself seems to support an optimistic interpretation," the play as a whole "seems to demand the pessimistic one," Rackin notes. Yet in her judgment, Lear's defiance of objective evidence and his belief that Cordelia lives is a supremely creative act, and his death is triumphant.

Reid, Stephen. "In Defense of Goneril and Regan." *American Imago* 27, No. 3 (Fall 1970): 226-44.

A psychoanalytic interpretation of Lear's two older daughters. Reid proposes that until the middle of Act III, Goneril and Regan have no intention of killing their father. But Cordelia's arrival in Britain with the French army reawakens repressed feelings of love, rejection, and resentment toward Lear that erupt in pathological, murderous impulses.

Salingar, Leo. "Romance in *King Lear.*" In *Dramatic Form in Shakespeare and the Jacobeans*, pp. 91-106. Cambridge: Cambridge University Press, 1986.

Examines the play in terms of traditional narrative and stage romances. Salingar demonstrates the "pattern or rhythm of successive waves" of hope and despair in the dramatic action as the play moves back and forth between romance and tragedy. He also calls attention to the romance theme of fathers and daughters.

Traversi, Derek. "*King Lear.*" *Stratford Papers on Shakespeare* 5 (1964): 183-200.

Analyzes both the personal and universal tragedy of *King Lear*. Traversi follows Lear in his two roles as father and king through a pattern of disruption and suffering that culminates in reconciliation. The essay also treats the "parallel story" of Gloucester and argues that the two opposing groups of "good" and "evil" characters mirror aspects of Lear's own nature.

Ventura, Sylvia M. "The Tragedy of *King Lear.*" *General Education Journal* 13 (1967-68): 81-90.

Judges Lear's "tragic flaw" as "pride, compounded by wrath." Although he disrupts order in his kingdom, he ultimately achieves a selfless understanding of his world and thus, Ventura suggests, Lear represents Shakespeare's affirmation of "the nobility of the human soul."

West, Robert H. "Sex and Pessimism in *King Lear.*" *Shakespeare Quarterly* XI, No. 1 (Winter 1960): 55-60.

Maintains that although *King Lear* repeatedly represents the act of sex and procreation as "a kind of dreadful seizure," the play shows that it may be "exalted by the miracle of love." According to West, the dramatic action also affirms the principle of faithful bonds between parents and children.

Media Adaptations

King Lear: An Introduction. BHE Education Ltd., Seabourne Enterprinses Ltd., 1970.

Performances of key scenes, including brief narration. Distributed by Phoenix/BFA Films. 28 minutes.

King Lear. Filmways, 1971.

Peter Brook's effort at updating the drama. Distributed by Nostalgia Family Video, Discount Video Tapes, Inc. 137 minutes.

King Lear. Cedric Messina; Dr. Jonathon Miller; BBC, 1982.
> Part of the "Shakespeare Plays" series. Distributed by Ambrose Video Publshing. 185 minutes.

King Lear. Kultur, 1984.
> Starring Laurence Olivier as King Lear. Distributed by Home Vision Cinema, Kultur Video, Facets Multimedia. 158 minutes.

King Lear. The Cannon Group, Inc.; Menahem Golan; Yoram Globus, 1987.
> Unrated. A loose adaptation from Shakespeare's play. Stars Peter Sellers, Burgess Meredith, Molly Ringwald, Jean-Luc Godard, and Woody Allen. Distributed be Ingram International Films, Cannon Video. 91 minutes.

King Lear. Thames Television, 1988.
> Made-for-British-TV presentation offering a highly edited version of the drama. Distributed by HBO Home Video. 110 minutes.

King Lear, 1991.
> Sound production. Distributed by Bob Jones University Press, Western Publishing Co. 120 minutes.

MUCH ADO ABOUT NOTHING

INTRODUCTION

Scholars agree that *Much Ado about Nothing* was written and first performed sometime between late 1598 and 1599, the year the comic actor Will Kemp, who first played the role of Dogberry, left the acting company that first performed the play. An entry in the Stationer's Register, dated August 4, 1600, includes a reference to the play, ordering that it not be published. Critics have offered several explanations for this entry in the Register, with some maintaining that it reflects official censorship or Puritan pressure, and others stating that it was merely an attempt on the part of the Lord Chamberlain's Men (an acting company with which Shakespeare was associated) to prevent a pirated edition of *Much Ado* from being published.

Evidence indicates that *Much Ado* enjoyed considerable popularity during Shakespeare's day and throughout the seventeenth and eighteenth centuries. The earliest available commentary on a performance of the play appeared in 1613, in the accounts of the Treasurer to King James, Lord Stanhope. In a poetic tribute that appeared in a 1640 edition of Shakespeare's plays, Leonard Digges wrote, ". . . but let *Beatrice* / and *Benedicke* be seene, loe in a trice / The Cockpit, Galleries, Boxes, all are full," attesting to the play's popularity. But it was not until late in the seventeenth century and early in the next that true critical assessments first appeared. In the late seventeenth and early eighteenth centuries, critics identified Ludovico Ariosto's *Orlando Furioso* as one of *Much Ado*'s principal sources and introduced several thematic and technical points—questions regarding how true to life the characters' words and actions are, and examinations of Shakespeare's use of language—that were to become very important in later studies of the comedy. As for Shakespeare's sources for *Much Ado,* the dramatist borrowed from a story in Matteo Bandello's collection of tales, *La prima parte de le novelle* (1554), which Shakespeare knew both in Italian and in French. In *Much Ado,* he tightened the action for dramatic effect, drawing in elements from Ariosto's version of the tale along with some hints from Edmund Spenser's *Faerie Queene* (1590), a major influence upon Elizabethan writers.

Much Ado has been described as a comedy which, despite its surface gaiety and occasional slapstick, is also serious and even profound in its implications. It has also been considered an enjoyable but problematic play. Attempts to assess it have varied, but most commentators have agreed that *Much Ado* is a comedy of manners, a play which gently pokes fun at the manners and conventions of an aristocratic, highly sophisticated society. True to this form, *Much Ado* features instances of eavesdropping, the war of the sexes, mistaken identities, misunderstood communications, and a tangle of subplots all ending in the pairing off of marriageable couples, the downfall of a scheming villain, and the happiness of a wedding dance.

PRINCIPAL CHARACTERS

(in order of appearance)

Leonato: Governor of Messina. The elderly father of Hero, he enters into Friar Francis's plan to, in effect, resurrect his daughter.

Hero: Mild daughter of Leonato. She is unexpectedly slandered at the altar on her wedding day by her betrothed, Claudio.

Beatrice: Niece of Leonato. She contemptuously engages in sharp duels of wit with the alleged woman-hater, Benedick, but eventually agrees to marry him.

Don Pedro: Prince of Aragon. Having defeated his half-brother in a recent military uprising, he is duped by the still-dangerous Don John, and then humbled by Leonato for believing Hero unfaithful.

Don John: Don Pedro's bastard brother. A scheming villain, he is interested in avenging his recent military defeat by quietly making trouble for those chiefly responsible, Don Pedro and Claudio.

Claudio: A young lord of Florence. An unimaginative young soldier, he falls in love with Hero—and is then led to believe the worst about her.

Benedick: A young lord of Padua. One of Don Pedro's soldiers, he is a confirmed bachelor who initially sees in Beatrice only a verbal sparring partner; each tries to outpoint the other in expressing their mutual disdain, though they eventually agree to marry.

Balthasar: Don Pedro's attendant. As Don Pedro and his fellow conspirators set out to trick Benedick into believing Beatrice is in love with him, Balthasar sings the melancholy love song, "Sigh no more, ladies, sigh no more," accompanied by the lute.

Antonio: Brother of Leonato. He joins with his brother in heatedly offering to fight Don Pedro and Claudio for Hero's honor.

Conrade: A follower of Don John who supports Borachio and his master in playing a dastardly trick on Claudio.

Borachio: Another follower of Don John. He conceives the specifics of a scheme for deceiving Claudio and Don Pedro, and then carries out the plan with the approval of Don John.

Margaret: A gentlewoman attending Hero. She is overheard talking with Borachio by Don Pedro and Claudio, who mistakenly think they are overhearing Claudio's betrothed meeting secretly with another man.

Ursula: A gentlewoman attending Hero. She joins Hero in deceiving Beatrice into believing that Benedick loves her.

Dogberry: a constable who loves to hear himself talk, though he mangles the English language in the style of Mrs. Malaprop, from Richard Sheridan's play *The Rivals.*

Verges: A headborough, or police official. Another lover of officious language, he joins with his associate, Dogberry, in a comic interrogation of the arrested villains, Borachio and Conrade.

The Watch: Two foolish men, Hugh Otecake and George Seacole, who are deputies of Dogberry. In the end, they prove essential in proving Hero guiltless of unfaithfulness to Claudio.

Friar Francis: A priest who, with Beatrice, believes in Hero's innocence.

PLOT SYNOPSIS

Act I: After winning a swift military victory over the forces of his bastard brother, Don Pedro, Prince of Aragon, rides to Messina to visit the governor, Leonato. Don Pedro is accompanied by the defeated Don John, with whom he has been reconciled; Don John's followers, Borachio and Conrade; and by two of his most distinguished soldiers, the young lords Claudio and Benedick. Once in Messina, Benedick, a confirmed bachelor, renews his bantering "merry war" of words with Leonato's niece, Beatrice, while the proper Claudio falls in love at first sight with Beatrice's mild-mannered cousin, Hero. Don Pedro, learning of Claudio's love, offers to help the young soldier by

impersonating him at a masked ball and wooing Hero for him. But two eavesdropping servants overhear Don Pedro's offer; one of them reports to Antonio, who reports to Leonato that Don Pedro himself is in love with Hero, while the other servant's more accurate report about the Prince's wooing reaches the treacherous Don John. He sees a golden opportunity to cause trouble for both Claudio and Don Pedro, two of the figures who had been instrumental in his own recent defeat.

Act II: That evening at the masquerade, Don John attempts to arouse Claudio's suspicion that the Prince is wooing Hero for himself. But whatever suspicion is implanted is quickly swept away when Don Pedro appears with Leonato and Hero, who all consent with joy when Claudio proposes to Hero on the spot. Knowing that the wedding cannot be arranged in less than a week, Don Pedro proposes that the group, for amusement, attempt to get Beatrice and Benedick to fall in love—by shaming Benedick about his "contemptible spirit" as a woman-hater, and by insisting that Beatrice, despite her haughty words, really loves him. With this new plot afoot, Don John begins hatching a new plot of his own: to break up the impending marriage of Claudio and Hero. He intends to do this by arranging to have Claudio and the Prince overhear a staged meeting between Borachio and Margaret, and then tricking them into believing that they are overhearing Hero with an unknown lover.

Act III: Seeing Benedick begin to soften toward Beatrice, Don Pedro and his fellow conspirators decide to trick Beatrice, using the same sort of strategy that had worked on Benedick, with Ursula and Hero undertaking the deception. Don John, meanwhile, succeeds in convincing Claudio and Don Pedro of Hero's unfaithfulness. However, two members of the Watch overhear the drunken Borachio describe Don John's trickery to Conrade. Having been told to apprehend all vagrants, the Watch arrest Borachio and Conrade and take them to Dogberry and Verges, their superiors. These two law-enforcement officials bring their prisoners before Leonato, who is on his way to Hero's wedding. But Dogberry's blathering explanation exasperates the Governor, who tells the constable to question the detainees himself while he hastens on to the wedding.

Act IV: At the wedding ceremony, Claudio and Don Pedro accuse Hero of unfaithfulness before the entire congregation, shocking her so that she falls down in a dead faint out of shame. The accusers leave the church. But Friar Francis believes that they are mistaken, and he suggests to Leonato that he let it be known that Hero has died. Aside from Friar Francis, only Beatrice and the church sexton fully believe in Hero's innocence. Seeking an ally to avenge the wrong committed against her cousin, Beatrice finds Benedick nearby. At this moment of crisis, he confesses his love and asks how he may serve her. She commands him, "Kill Claudio," and after some minutes of uncomfortable hesitation he leaves to challenge Claudio to single combat. Meanwhile, Dogberry continues to examine the "false knaves" Borachio and Conrade, whose scheme against Hero is revealed through the sexton's damning testimony.

Act V: Enraged at the accusations of Claudio and Don Pedro, Leonato and Antonio speak sharply to them both, going so far as to challenge Claudio to a duel. After the angry Governor and Antonio leave, Hero's accusers are confronted by Benedick, who also challenges Claudio to single combat, but neither Claudio nor Don Pedro take Benedick seriously. Dogberry and Verges arrive with their prisoners in Leonato's presence, and the true story comes out about the treachery of Don John and his dishonoring of Hero. With their eyes opened to their error, but still believing Hero dead, Don Pedro and Claudio ask Hero's father for forgiveness; Leonato, still not revealing that Hero is alive, forgives them on the condition that Claudio make amends by hanging an epitaph on Hero's tomb, singing aloud a song honoring her, and marrying one of his nieces, allegedly a "copy" of the "dead" Hero. Claudio agrees, and at the wedding that follows he is presented to a masked bride, who is revealed to be Hero. The deceptions of the good conspirators are revealed to Beatrice and Benedick, who wittily agree to marry each other. At this joyous news, a messenger arrives with word that Don John has been captured while fleeing the city. As the play ends, Benedick promises "brave punishments" for Don John and then directs the pipers to strike up a tune for a wedding dance.

PRINCIPAL TOPICS

The War of the Sexes

The differences between men and women—how they relate to each other, misunderstand each other, love and repel each other, is a common theme in motion pictures, comics, television comedies, and world literature. It appears throughout Shakespeare's comedies as well, and *Much Ado* is no exception to the pattern. In *Much Ado,* much of the conflict between the sexes concerns Beatrice and Benedick, with their relentless disdain for each other. Each tries to outduel the other in crafting the most clever and most deflating remark, and the impression is given that their sparring has a long history which precedes the action of the play. The goal of each is not to deliver the most crushing, hot-blooded blast, but to offer the most coolly disdainful remarks possible. In Act I, and in Benedick's absence, Beatrice begins by likening him

to a disease: "God help the noble Claudio, if he have caught the Benedick." The war of the sexes begins in earnest with Benedick's arrival, the two fencing verbally and giving the impression that each considers the other not worth noticing.

In their absence, Don Pedro and the newly betrothed Claudio and Hero decide to give the war an interesting twist by attempting to bring together Beatrice and Benedick as lovers. Their plans succeed, but upon the disgracing of Hero, love faces a cruel ordeal, turning from tenderness to heated, near-frantic rage on the part of Beatrice after Benedick hesitates at her command, "Kill Claudio." Here she turns from employing wit to questioning Benedick's manhood, calling him "Count Comfect, a sweet gallant surely!" In one of the most-often quoted sections of *Much Ado,* she declares, "O that I were a man for his sake, or that I had any friend would be a man for my sake. But manhood is melted into curtsies, valour into compliment, and men are only turned into tongue, and trim ones too: he is now as valiant as Hercules that only tells a lie and swears it. I cannot be a man with wishing, therefore I will die a woman with grieving." This sentiment is one with the words of Balthasar's song, from Act II, scene iii: "Sigh no more, ladies, sigh no more, / Men were deceivers ever / One foot in sea, and one on shore, / To one thing constant never." This song, one of the loveliest in all of Shakespeare's plays, is repeated in several places in Kenneth Branagh's 1993 film version of *Much Ado,* becoming, through repetition, the play's theme.

Appearance vs. Reality

The theme of appearance versus reality has long been considered central to the play's structure and tone. As one can see from the Plot Synopsis, all of the main characters deceive or are deceived by others at some point during the play. On this theme of deception, much critical comment has surrounded the view that the very title of the play contains a key Elizabethan pun, with Shakespeare punning on *nothing* and *noting,* meaning eavesdropping. However, some critics have observed that the key to the play's unity lies in equating *noting* with *observation;* that is, we take note of a situation and make judgments based on our observations. In *Much Ado,* there is a failure, some critics argue, to observe and act sensibly. While critics have often noted that the theme of appearance versus reality is articulated in most of Shakespeare's plays either by circumstances or by deliberate acts of deception by the characters, some commentators maintain that neither pattern pertains to *Much Ado,* as deception and false perceptions are not undone; rather, they are characteristic of the norm of Messina society.

Critics agree that *Much Ado* concerns, in great part,

misunderstandings of various sorts—some deliberate, some unintentional. In terms of this play, the term "love's truth," or "love's faith," has been described by one critic as "the imaginative acting of a lover and the need for our imaginative response to it, the compulsion, individuality, and complexity of a lover's truthful realization of beauty, and distinctions between inward and outward beauty, appearance and reality, and fancy and true affection." Shakespeare's ideas about love's truth inform the structure, characterization, dialogue, and other elements of *Much Ado*. Scholars have written extensively about the common device Shakespeare uses for presenting a lover's imagination, the "play-within-a-play"; and in *Much Ado* this device is used often. Several significant deceptions are carried off by the play-within-a-play, notably the deception of Benedick into believing that Beatrice is in love with him, by the play-acting Don Pedro, Leonato, and Claudio; and the tricking of Beatrice into believing that Benedick is pining for her, by the conspirators Hero and Ursula.

In each of these cases, there must be "much ado" in straightening out the tangled misperceptions each lover holds for the other, but, as critics have noted, it is part of Shakespeare's intent to suggest that those who engage in a quest for love's truth find that the longest course of action, involving "much ado," is often the only one that seems possible to them.

Music and Dance

Critics have long noted the significance of music in *Much Ado*, both in the text itself and in the form of the play. Balthasar's song, "Sigh no more, ladies, sigh no more," has been commented upon often, in part because it is performed in a crucial point in the play, which ends with a wedding dance. Commentators have remarked on similarities between the action of the play itself and a dance, with couples engaging, turning, performing intricate movements together, and retiring.

CHARACTER STUDIES

Beatrice

Scholars have often emphasized that Shakespeare deliberately introduces the sparring mockers, Beatrice and Benedick, before the pallid romantics, Hero and Claudio. Of the first pair, Beatrice appears first and sets the tone for what is to follow. She is any man's match in a war of wit, but knows how to restrain her words in the presence of simple, harmless, and unimaginative men like Don Pedro's Messenger. (Wit, in comedies from the day of Shakespeare through the eighteenth century, means the ability of a person to discern similarities in meaning between like-sounding words and phrases, and then to craft a quick reply in which this connection is made evident.) The impression is given that Beatrice and Benedick have a history together of some sort; perhaps they were at one time interested in each other romantically, but at the time the play opens they are coolly hostile to each other. (This particular interpretation of background was hinted at in Kenneth Branagh's 1993 film production of *Much Ado*, in which Branagh and Emma Thompson star as Benedick and Beatrice.) Something has happened between them to cause this, but that something is never made clear. In any case, what is clear is that Beatrice is not only witty and at least superficially disdainful of men in general (and Benedick in particular), but she can be heatedly passionate, as evidenced by both the words she speaks upon being gulled into believing Benedick is in love with her and the rage she gives vent to after her cousin is humiliated at the altar. For this, for the revelation of her awkward attempt at a poem for Benedick, and for the "pitying" words with which she agrees to marry Benedick at play's end, many scholars agree that Beatrice and Benedick are the only truly three-dimensional characters in *Much Ado*.

Benedick

One of Don Pedro's trusted comrades-in-arms, Benedick possesses a brisk, bouncing nature and ready wit. He is a self-confessed bachelor who would prefer to enjoy life while keeping women at arm's-length—especially Beatrice, for whom he has a particular, antagonistic regard. His disdain for women, it has been suggested, masks his wary respect for Beatrice, with whom he was once involved romantically. As evidence of this, critics note the giddy, schoolboyish behavior Benedick exhibits upon being tricked into believing that Beatrice loves him, rationalizing that Beatrice's scorn is really a facade that covers her deep affection. This new-found passion is put severely to the test after Hero's humiliation and Beatrice commands him, "Kill Claudio." Benedick is torn between his love for Beatrice and loyalty to his army comrade; ultimately, love for Beatrice wins out, and he coldly, insistently challenges Claudio to single-combat. All seems headed for a sad and violent parting between the two friends, until the crucial moment arrives when Borachio and Conrade confess their guilt in shaming Hero. In the end, Benedick is reconciled with Claudio and engaged to Beatrice, with whom he has a final, friendly skirmish of wit. Critics note that when all of the principal characters are on stage together, the major interest of the audience is not the love-at-first-sight relationship that develops between Hero and Claudio, but rather the "merry war" between Beatrice and Benedick.

Hero

In terms of depth and interest, the relationship between Beatrice and Benedick is depicted in a far more compelling manner than is the romance of Hero and Claudio, most critics agree. It has been said often that Hero is for the most part a sweet but colorless young woman who is not so much a three-dimensional character as an entity who exists to fill a place in the drama. She and Claudio mechanically go through the motions of betrothal, with no development of interest, no initial conflict, nor even any wooing on Claudio's part; Don Pedro woos for him. Hero seems less worldly than her cousin, Beatrice, and has little notable to say in the drama. One of the high points of her activity is her gulling of Beatrice in a meant-to-be-overheard conversation with Ursula. At her wedding she is unexpectedly accused of unfaithfulness by Claudio; and then, having recovered from her faint, she is denounced by her own father for shaming him—and it takes some convincing to bring him around to believing in her innocence. Still, Hero goes along with Friar Francis's proposed charade and then obediently enters into marriage with the repentant Claudio. Critics have said that the by-the-numbers romance between this young couple never engages the audience's attention, as does the romance of Beatrice and Benedick—but then, it is never intended to.

Claudio

Claudio is one of the military heroes of Don Pedro's victory over Don John's forces. He is an impressionable, unimaginative young man who is somewhat out of place in the lively, witty society of Messina. He falls in love with Hero upon first laying eyes on her, believes immediately in her unfaithfulness upon witnessing Borachio's deception, immediately agrees to marry another woman sight unseen, and then unapologetically enters into marriage with the "resurrected" Hero. Not surprisingly, critics have described Claudio in terms such as "hateful," "miserable," and the "least amiable lover in Shakespeare." As the editor of The Arden Edition of *Much Ado* has written, "He is doubtless meant for a brave, inexperienced youth, shocked out of romantic devotion by an unsuspected and cunning enemy and, himself a wounded victim, not overblameworthy for his appalling error, and so not disqualified for future happiness. Yet to convey this needs sensitive skill." This sensitive skill is beyond the bounds of patience and skill for many readers and viewers of the play, though critics have taken pains to demonstrate that Claudio is more sinned against than a sinner, and that his coltish inexperience in matters of the head and heart goes far toward excusing the erring decisions he makes.

Dogberry

Dogberry is a figure of fun, one of the several distinguished wise fools encountered in Shakespeare's comedies. He is pompous, given to spouting words he doesn't understand, as when he says that the villainous Borachio should pay for his sins by being "condemned into everlasting redemption"; but he is also one of the few bearers of true knowledge in the play. It is Dogberry who, with the help of the Watch and the Sexton, discovers and reveals Don John's and Borachio's slanderous plot against Hero. Additionally, critics have emphasized Dogberry's pomposity and have faulted productions of the play (including Kenneth Branaugh's 1993 production starring Michael Keaton as Dogberry) that have failed to accurately portray this side of Dogberry's nature.

Don John

Considered one of the more problematic figures in the play, Don John is a snake-in-the-grass. The bastard half-brother of Don Pedro, he is a rebel and presumably a traitor whose armed uprising results not in his deserved death but in an attempted reconciliation between himself and the perhaps overly kind Don Pedro. The latter fails to see that Don John has a deep-seated grudge to destroy the happiness of the principal figures who defeated him: Don Pedro and Claudio. He is thus allowed enough freedom by his captors that he nearly destroys several lives. Interestingly, Keanu Reeves's portrayal of Don John in the Branagh film has been deemed questionable, with one commentator stating that "when he is not curling his lip as a good villain should, he charges about with the same blank expression of unselfconscious stupidity that he brings to all his film efforts." Ironically (and setting aside the critic's personal remarks on Reeves), Don John has been recognized from the earliest days of dramatic criticism as a cardboard villain who announces his intentions as a "plain-spoken villain" to the audience from the start and commits evil for the sake of evil; he is depicted by Shakespeare as just the sort of lip-curling figure with whom Reeves's critics have found fault.

CONCLUSION

Much Ado has been described by critics as an enjoyable but problematic play, with considerable attention paid to various inconsistencies in the plot—for example, Don John's clumsy, unworkable first attempt at making trouble for Claudio and Hero, in Act II, Scene i; the ease with which Don John tricks the same men who had easily defeated him in battle; and Hero's willing marriage to the very man who shamed her, in Act V, Scene iii. Critics also agree that *Much*

Ado is not one of the most popular of Shakespeare's comedies, as it "lacks many of those perpetuating devices that we look for to give us a sense of timeless pleasure," in one critic's words, "of a 'holiday' that is at once a sportive release and also, through lyricism, gives the faintest air of holiday blessedness and calm." In more specific terms, one of Shakespeare's more recent biographers has written, "I cannot help feeling that in *Much Ado about Nothing* some of the prose is on autopilot. The tone for long stretches is an unvaried rapid bird-twitter of verbal sparring that gives one a headache; the characters are not sufficiently characterized by difference of language; and the whole performance is too artificial for my own taste, though it is too clever to be cloying." Still, many readers of Shakespeare's works today would agree that *Much Ado* is one of the foremost comedies of manners in Western literature, one which speaks with wisdom of humanity and the world in which we live.

(See also *Shakespearean Criticism*, Vols. 8, 18, and 31)

OVERVIEWS

Barbara Everett

SOURCE: "Much Ado about Nothing," in *The Critical Quarterly*, Vol. 3, No. 4, Winter, 1961, pp. 319-35.

[*In an excerpt from a general essay on* Much Ado, *Everett illustrates the development by Shakespeare, in his comedies, of certain feelings and attitudes which are a constituent part of his entire dramatic canon, and which tend to be most clearly expressed by the female characters. From Shakespeare's women, the critic argues, come the clearest expressions of humane principle, generous nature, and constancy.*]

Much Ado About Nothing is not, I think, among Shakespeare's most popular comedies. It lacks many of those perpetuating devices that we look for to give us a sense of timeless pleasure, of a "holiday" that is at once a sportive release and also, through lyricism, gives the faintest air of holiday blessedness and calm. It contains no sunlit or moonlit wood where every Jack finds his Jill. No heroine leaps happily into hose to find the sexless and timeless liberty of intellectual sport. There is no "play within a play" to strengthen the artifices that surround it with the solidity of comparative reality, and so to give their happy ending the stamp of truth. If "we did keep time, sir, in our snatches", it is not a snatch of perpetuity that is given in the songs of the play—no *Journeys end in lovers meeting*, nor *It was a lover and his lass*, nor *When daisies pied and violets blue*—but an omen of change:

Men were deceivers ever. The play appears to present, by contrast, a world rather for "working-days" than for "Sundays"; a world that is as formal, and potentially as harsh, as the comic world that probably preceded it, that of *The Merchant of Venice*. But the moneyed, legalistic, and formal world of Venice resolves at last into moonlit Belmont, from which one can see

> the floor of Heaven
> Thick inlaid with patines of bright gold.

The equally and beautifully formal Portia, in whom "The will of a living daughter is curbed by the will of a dead father" ceases to be a "Daniel come to judgment" and becomes a Diana in love, her homecoming heralded by Lorenzo and Jessica with lyrical myths and fables, and herself drawn into a dream from which she "would not be awaked".

Much Ado About Nothing is a play cut off from such pleasant natural resources. It is essentially "inland bred", and relies only on the natural forms of a great house where

> Ceremony's a name for the rich horn,
> And custom for the spreading laurel tree.

"Nature lovers" are offered only the flowers of rhetoric, the pleached arbour of wit, and the "dancing star" of human individuality. Not only the courteous, but the customary, matters in this play: not only the urbane, but the mundane: in fact, it is the unusual fusing of these into one world that is one of the individual characteristics of the play. The chief fact that makes this play unusual and individual (though there are other characteristics, which I shall discuss later, that develop straight out of earlier comedies) is the manner in which "time and place" do *not* "cease to matter", but matter very greatly.

It is not merely that the props of an urban or domestic existence—the window, the arras of a musty room, the church, the tomb, the wedding dress, the nightwatchmen's staves, even the barber's shop—are important "props" in the world of this play. Nor is it merely that "time and place" have a crucial importance in the action:

> What man was he talked with you
>   yesternight
> Out at your window betwixt twelve and
>   one?
> Now if you are a maid, answer to this.

It is rather that the play concerns itself with what can only be called the most mundane or "local" fact in that world of love, in all its forms, that the comedies create: that is, that men and women have a notably different character, different mode of thinking, different system of loyalties, and, particularly, different social place and function. Not only this; but this is the first play, I think, in which the clash of these two worlds is treated with a degree of seriousness, and in which the woman's world dominates.

This is a rash generalisation and objections spring to mind. . . .

Since *The Merchant of Venice* is the first play in which there appears a comic heroine who is also a great lady, one watches with interest to see what part the dominating Portia will play, how she will handle her subjection to the "will of a dead father", and whether she will prove to "fit her fancies to her fathers will" better than does Hermia. She and Bassanio equally "give and hazard all they have"; but it is, at least nominally, a man's world that they give themselves up to:

> her gentle spirit
> Commits itself to yours to be directed,
> As from her lord, her governor, her king.
> Myself and what is mine to your and yours
> Is now directed.

Portia is the salvation of the play; her wealth, her wits, and her pleading of a feminine quality of mercy—deeply Christian in its language and connotation, but allied too to that quality of compassion that is reserved for the women in the comedies—defeat the harshly logical and loveless intellectualism of Shylock. But they do so in masculine disguise, in a masculine court of law, and at the service of a chivalric friendship between men whose values Portia and Nerissa gaily, but seriously, at the end of the play. They lose, as women, the rings they have gained as men; the loyal and unhappily solitary friend Antonio is the peacemaker, being "bound again, His soul upon the forfeit" for the marriage, and is still in some sense master of the play.

It is here that the world of *Much Ado About Nothing* begins. There is no symbolic Antonio to keep the balance; the situation works itself out on its own resources. It does this by the characteristic of the play which has been sometimes regarded as a most happy accident of careless genius—the displacement of Claudio and Hero by Benedick and Beatrice as the play's dominating figures, in the course of what is "logical and necessary" in its action. This is brought about by allowing, more distinctively and fully than in any earlier comedy, a dance and battle—(a "merry war" in which not every "achiever brings home full numbers") of two worlds, which it is a gross, but serviceable, generalisation to call the "masculine" and the "feminine" worlds. And this in itself is achieved by the creation of a peculiarly social and domestic

context—rarified, formal, and elegant, but still suggesting a social reality that makes the character of the sexes distinct. The sense of place, in its importance to the play, I have mentioned earlier; the sense of time has also an unusual function. One need only reflect on the obvious difference of age between Claudio and Hero, and Benedick and Beatrice—who play lightly with the idea of an obstinate, and therefore time-tried, celibacy; and ask oneself in what earlier comedy there is any differentiation other than that of Youth and Age. One can contrast, also, the references to past and future time that occur in earlier comedies with those in *Much Ado About Nothing*. "'A killed your sister", in *Love's Labour's Lost,* or Helena's memory of "schooldays' friendship, childhood innocence", or Titania's memories of the sport on the Indian shore—all quoted above—have all, to varying degrees, an exquisite stylisation, an emblematic quality, that prevents their giving another temporal dimension to the play; they are an inset, not a perspective; an intensification of or contrast with the present, not an evocation of the past. But the causal, continual and colloquial harking-back in *Much Ado About Nothing* has a quite different effect.

> O, he's returned, and as pleasant as ever he was . . .

> He set up his bills here in Messina, and challenged Cupid at the fight; and my uncle's fool, reading the challenge, subscrib'd for Cupid, and challenged him at the birdbolt . . .

> They never meet but there's a skirmish of wit between them . . .

> In our last conflict four of his five wits went halting off . . .

> Indeed, my lord, he lent it me awhile; and I gave him use for it, a double heart for his single one . . .

> I have heard my daughter say she hath often dreamt of unhappiness, and waked herself with laughing . . .

One can, if one likes, play the same game with references to the future, contrasting *Love's Labour's Lost's*

> You shall this twelvemonth term from day to day
> Visit the speechless sick, and still converse
> With groaning wretches . . .

with *Much Ado About Nothing's*

> O Lord, my lord, if they were but a week married, they would talk themselves mad. . . .

I will live in thy heart, die in thy lap, and be
buried in thy eyes; and, moreover, I will go with
thee to thy uncle's. . . .

This easy, humorous, and conversational manner, that
refers to a past and future governed by customary
event and behaviour, and that carries a sense of habitual reality in a familiar social group, gives the play
the quality that it would be certainly unwise to call
"realism"; it is an atmosphere easier to feel than to
define. It is one of ennobled domesticity, aware of,
touched by, and reflecting events in the outside world,
but finally providing its own rules and customs: it is,
in fact, a world largely feminine in character.

Into this world, at the beginning of the play, come
the warriors, covered with masculine honours, cheerful with victory, and heralded importantly by a messenger. They even bring their own style of figured
public rhetoric with them:

He hath borne himself beyond the promise of his
age, doing in the figure of a lamb the feats of a
lion. . . .

The fashion of the world is to avoid cost, and you
encounter it. . . .

I had rather be a canker in a hedge than a rose in
his grace; and it better fits my blood to be disdained
of all than to fashion a carriage to rob love from
any. . . .

The "most exquisite Claudio", the "proper squire", is
the flower of such a world; the plot that concerns
him, and that seems at first to dominate the play, can
be seen as the survival of all that is most formal, and
least flexible, in the earlier comedies: a masculine game
of romantic love with a firm—and sensible—business
basis, the whole governed by an admirable sense of
priorities in duty:

I look'd upon her with a soldier's eye . . .
But now I am return'd, and that war-thoughts
Have left their places vacant, in their rooms
Come thronging soft and delicate desires,
All prompting me how fair young Hero is,
Saying I lik'd her ere I went to wars. . . .

If modern sentimentalism makes one dislike the foun-
dation to Claudio's case—female good looks plus
paternal income—it is as well to remember that it is
an attitude embedded in all the comedies to date,
whenever they touch on realism, and shared not only
by Bassanio but—even though half-mockingly—by
Benedick: "Rich she shall be, that's certain . . . fair,
or I'll never look on her".

The beginning of the play, then, presents, in a social

context, a company of young bloods, headed by the
noble Don Pedro, who all hold together with a cheerful masculine solidarity. The "sworn brothers" are
companions-in-arms, and if one deserts, there is cause
for lamentation: "I have known when he would have
walked ten mile afoot to see a good armour, and now
will he lie ten nights awake carving the fashion of a
new doublet". If Claudio dramatically distrusts Don
Pedro at first—

Let every eye negotiate for itself,
And trust no agent; for beauty is a witch
Against whose charms faith melteth into
blood. . . .

then the discovery of his mistake only strengthens
his later trust in, and solidarity with, Don Pedro; and
this trust is implicit even in the terms of his first
doubt, which still postulates a male world of "negotiation" and "agents", against the hypnotic and possibly devilish enemy, Woman. Claudio's world, and
Claudio's plot, are never "reformed"—in a dramatic,
or moral sense—because they neither can nor need be
changed; the simple course of loving, mistaking, and
winning again, written from a specifically masculine
point of view (again using the word masculine in its
idiosyncratic sense here) that is half romance and half
business, is a necessary backbone to the play, and
holds the comedy together:

Look, what will serve is fit: 'tis once, thou
lovest;
And I will fit thee with the remedy.

And though Hero is in the course of it "killed, in
some senses", as Dogberry might have said, she also
gets her place in the world, and all is well. A comedy
of romance needs something stable, limited, and cir-
cular, in which ends match beginnings, and in Claudio it gets this:

Sweet Hero, now thy image does appear
In the rare semblance that I loved it first . . .
Another Hero!
Nothing certainer. . . .

But, if this world is not 'reformed', it is to a large
extent displaced; and the moment of that displacement is not hard to find:

Don Pedro: Myself, my brother, and this
grieved Count
Did see her, hear her, at that hour last night
Talk with a ruffian at her chamber
window . . .

Exeunt Don Pedro, Don John, and Claudio.

Benedick: How doth the lady?

Left on stage we have a fainting and dishonoured girl; her wholly doubting and wretched old father, held to her only by paternal obligation; a wise and detached old Friar; and the dishonoured girl's cousin, in a rage of loyal devotion that is familial, sexual, and instinctual. One cannot help asking what the young, witty and independent soldier Benedick is doing in that gallery. He has broken the rules of the game, and entered upon a desertion far more serious than Claudio's ever appeared: he is crossing the boundaries of a world of masculine domination. How serious the desertion is, is indicated by his comic—but only partly comic—exchange with Beatrice, at the centre of their professions of love, that follow immediately on the church scene:

> *Ben:* Come, bid me do anything for thee.
> *Beat:* Kill Claudio.
> *Ben:* Ha! Not for the wide world.
> *Beat:* You kill me to deny it. Farewell.

"Kill Claudio" has become such a famous line that perhaps something of its importance, underlying its comic gesture of an unfeasible rage, has been lost. A pacific, sensible and level-headed bachelor is being forced toward a decision of alarming significance; and he accepts it. Beatrice's taunt "You dare easier be friends with me than fight with mine enemy" colours the whole of the end of the play, and produces the peculiar dramatic and psychological complexity of the sense of the challenge. In it, three characters, once a joint group of young men exchanging cheerful and witty backchat, begin to speak and think in two different worlds. Don Pedro's and Claudio's return to the old game between themselves—perfectly in place an hour earlier—becomes curiously embarrassing by the degree to which it can take no account of the dramatic change in Beatrice and Benedick's status, their siding with what the audience knows to be truth, or rather, a truer game than Don Pedro's and Claudio's:

> *Don Pedro:* But when shall we set the savage bull's horns on the sensible Benedick's head?
>
> *Claudio:* Yea, and text underneath, there dwells Benedick the married man?
>
> *Benedick:* Fare you well, boy: you know my mind. I will leave you now to your gossip-like humour; you break jests as braggarts do their blades, which God be thanked, hurt not. My lord, for your many courtesies I thank you. I must discontinue your company. Your brother the bastard is fled from Messina. You have among you killed a sweet and innocent lady. For my Lord Lackbeard there, he and I shall meet; and till then, peace be with him. (*Exit*).
>
> *Don Pedro:* He is in earnest . . . What a pretty

Title page of Much Ado About Nothing *taken from the First Folio (1623).*

thing man is when he goes in his doublet and hose and leaves off his wit!

It is not sufficient to say simply that this effect is gained by some "change" in Benedick's—the witty Benedick's—character. It is rather that our own attitude has changed in the course of the play, so that something developing under the agency of the "important" characters has relieved them of their importance. Certain qualities, certain attitudes that have been found, in the earlier comedies, mainly confined to the women's and fools' parts, have here come into their own.

The plays have such artistic continuity that it is almost impossibly difficult to distinguish certain attitudes and feelings, and call *this* a specifically "feminine" attitude, or *that*, one belonging to a "fool" or "clown"; and the more mature the play, the more danger of falsifying there is. Perhaps it is merely possible to indicate certain speeches of Beatrice which do cohere into an attitude that utilises a "fool's" uncommitted wit and detached play of mind, together with a clown's grasp of earthy reality, yet committed in such a new way that they are given the effect of a female veracity against a masculine romanticism or formality.

> Yes, faith; it is my cousin's duty to make curtsy, and say 'Father, as it please you'. But yet for all that, cousin, let him be a handsome fellow, or else make another curtsy and say, 'Father, as it please me'.

The whole game of romantic passion was never glossed more conclusively than by her foreboding "I can see a church by daylight"; nor the silliness of romantic jealousy than by her sturdy description of Claudio as "civil as an orange, and something of that jealous complexion"; nor the game of formal, courteous and meaningless proposals—(Don Pedro's "Will you have me, lady?") than by her: "No, my lord, unless I might have another for working-days: your Grace is too costly to wear every day". (Certainly, Don Pedro does prove to be a costly guest, since he all but causes the death of his host's daughter.) The beautiful and formal scene that the men have arranged for the uniting of Claudio and Hero—"his Grace hath made the match, and all Grace say amen to it!" begins to be disarranged by Beatrice's detached sense ("Speak, Count, 'tis your cue") and she hastily has to give her "merry heart" the fool's harmless part in the play: "I think it, poor fool, it keeps on the windy side of care". But the rising flight of her impertinence, which provokes Leonato to bustle her off the scene ("Niece, will you look to those things I told you of?") is not unacquainted with "care" Don Pedro's kindly and polite.

> out of question, you were born in a merry hour

is met by her

> No, sure, my lord, my mother cried; but then there was a star danced, and under that was I born.

However light the reference, one goes back to the lamenting Adriana, out of place in a play of brisk farce; or the surprising seriousness of the reference in *Love's Labour's Lost* to Katharine's sister—

> He made her melancholy, sad and heavy,
> And so she died . . .

or the equally surprising seriousness of Titania's loyalty:

> But she, being mortal, of that boy did die . . .
> And for her sake I will not part with
> him. . . .

The liaison of Claudio and Hero draws the "fools"

Benedick and Beatrice into the play; and it is Beatrice who first here begins to show in her apparently detached wit, only partially revealed in her sparring with Benedick, the depth that the occasion demands. Marriage is seen here not as a witty dance of "wooing, wedding and repenting", but as the joining of Beatrice's "cousins", and her remarks have greater and more dangerous point. It is not surprising that on her exit Don Pedro sets afoot his second piece of matchmaking, since Beatrice patently needs a master. "We are the only love-gods."

It is only at the crisis of the play, in the church scene, that this dogged, loyal, and irrational femininity that characterises Beatrice comes into its own. The still hesitating and just Benedick is swept into her degree of belief simply by her obstinate passion of loyalty:

> Is 'a not approved in the height a villain that hath slandered, scorned, dishonoured my kinswoman? O that I were a man! What! bear her in hand until they come to take hands, and then with public accusation, uncovered slander, unmitigated rancour—O God that I were a man! I would eat his heart in the market-place.

Certainly her storms are comic; nevertheless our own sense at the end of the play of the limitations of the romantic background, and critics' unanimous conviction that Benedick and Beatrice "take over the play", is largely summed up by her own "Talk with a man out at a window! A proper saying!" and the comparative shallowness of the romanticism of the main plot very neatly and adequately summed up in her voluble harangue:

> Princes and Counties! Surely, a princely testimony, a goodly count, Count Comfect; a sweet gallant, surely! O that I were a man for his sake! or that I had any friend would be a man for my sake! But manhood is melted into curtsies, valour into compliment, and men are only turned into tongue, and trim ones too. He is now as valiant as Hercules that only tells a lie and swears it. I cannot be a man with wishing, therefore I will die a woman with grieving.

This is simultaneously a remarkable picture of a woman in a state of outraged temper, and an excellent piece of dramatic criticism. For Benedick, this is "Enough. I am engaged." The fools of the play have become the heroes.

To use the word "fools" is perhaps incautious: since, for one thing, Benedick's and Beatrice's speeches are characterised by a degree of sophistication and self command; and for another, the play itself has an excellent collection of clowns who do, noticeably, help to bring about the dénouement and save the day. But if one is attempting to explain the feeling of maturity and development that Beatrice and Benedick bring into the play, then it becomes apparent that a part of their strength comes from Shakespeare's drawing on resources of feeling expressed, in earlier comedies, as much by witty jesters and innocent clowns, as by the kind of sophisticated commentators that one finds in Berowne and Rosaline. The sense of wisdom that they give is best glossed, perhaps, by Blake's "If the fool would persist in his folly, he would become wise". . . .

Benedick and Beatrice are a delightful lesson in how the fool can "Serve God, love me, and mend". This they do by "persisting in their folly", in order to "become wise".

Their attitude at the beginning of the play is the comic stance of self-consciousness. Both gain dignity by an intellectual independence—by "sitting in a corner and crying Heigh-ho!" while they watch "everyone going to the world". This intellectual independence is largely a full and mocking knowledge—especially, at first, on Beatrice's side—of the physical realities underlying romantic aspirations. "But, for the stuffing . . . well, we are all mortal." Over and over again, "my uncle's fool" takes the place of Cupid. "Lord! I could not endure a husband with a beard on his face: I had rather lie in the woollen. . . . " Mars as well as Cupid falls: the heroic warrior, who has done good "service" is "a very valiant trencherman; he hath an excellent stomach . . . (and is) a good soldier—to a lady". Yet the very intellectual detachment that gives a jester his dignity is the power to see general truths; and what is true of "mortals" must therefore be true also of Benedick and Beatrice, who are intellectually and dramatically joined to the hero and heroine of the main plot, by being friend and cousin to them, and by understanding—therefore sharing—their folly. Benedick's *ubi sunts* for bachelors derive their humour from the steadily-increasing knowledge that he is, like Barkis, going out with the tide: "In faith, hath not the world one man but he will wear his cap with suspicion? Shall I never see a a bachelor of three score again? . . . Like the old tale, my lord: It is not so, nor 'twas not so, but indeed, God forbid it should be so!" Like Falstaff, Benedick is comic by being both actor and critic, and knows which way "old tales" go; and though he may cast himself as bachelor, "he never could maintain his part but in the force of his will". Benedick and Beatrice are "fooled" and "framed" by the dramatist even before they are "fooled" by the trick played on them by Don Pedro and the others; their detached intelligence is, by definition, an understanding of the way their "foolish" desires will go. "Shall quips and sentences and the paper bullets of the brain awe a man from the career of his humour? No: the world must be peopled."

Thus, when Benedick and Beatrice do "run mad", they suffer—like Falstaff in love—a loss of dignity the more marked by contrast with their intellectual detachment earlier. Benedick searching for double meanings, and Beatrice nursing a sick heart, a cold in the head, and a bad temper, are as "placed" within the others' play as are the clowns in *Love's Labour's Lost* or *A Midsummer Night's Dream*, attendant on the critique of their superiors. It is, of course, the church scene, and all that follows, that changes this, and shows their double "folly" coming into its own. Beatrice is loyal to Hero simply by virtue of an acquaintance with common sense physical realities—"Talk with a man out at a window! A proper saying!"—and by a flood of intuitive, irrational, and "foolish" pity and love, that instinctively recognizes the good when it sees it—good in Benedick, or in Hero; and Benedick is drawn to her, here, through very similar feelings. "Lady Beatrice, have you wept all this while?" In the professions of love that follow Benedick's opening, there are touches of great humour; but the scene is a serious one, nevertheless. Both Benedick and Beatrice gain a new and much more complex equilibrium and dignity; both pledge themselves by their "soul" to Hero's cause, and hence to each other. To be intelligent is to be aware "that we are all mortal"; and to be mortal is to be a fool; and therefore intelligent men are most fools; but to be a fool, in a good cause, is to be wise. This is an old paradox that echoes through and through Shakespeare's comedies, and after.

Because Beatrice and Benedick are "too wise to woo peaceably", they continue to bicker comfortably through the rest of the play, as though enjoying the mutual death of their individuality:

Two distincts, division none.

Like Theseus' hounds, the quarrels of all the players grow, finally, into:

Such gallant chiding . . .
So musical a discord . . .
Matched in mouths like bells, each under
  each.

An unlyrical play grows into a new and interesting harmony, as all the forms of folly in the play find "measure in everything, and so dance out the answer":

Come, come, we are friends. Let's have a dance ere we are married, that we may lighten our own hearts and our wives' heels.

We'll have dancing afterwards.

First, of my word; therefore play, music.

Though the play can be summed up by the image of

the dance, it is also a battle, in which certain things are lost. Hero's "death" is an illusion, but other things do seem to die out of the comedies: part of an old romantic ideal, and a sense of easy loyalty between young men. Rosalind's "Men have died from time to time, and worms have eaten them, but not for love . . ." and Antonio's bitter, though mistaken, reflections on friendship, both represent a kind of feeling that can be seen to emerge with some clarity in *Much Ado.* Some more important things take the place of what is lost, all perhaps developing out of the sense of that loss; a wisdom, balance, and generosity of mind and feeling, largely expressed through the women's rôles.

This paper has itself probably been unwise, unbalanced and ungenerous in all that it has omitted. I have concentrated only on certain elements in *Much Ado About Nothing* that interest me, and may have distorted them in the process. My intention has not been to present Shakespeare as an earnest—though early—leader of the feminist movement, but only to suggest the development, through the comedies, of certain feelings and attitudes which are a constituent part of the plays as a whole, but which do tend to be most clearly expressed through the women in them. In Messina, Arden, and Illyria the expression of humane principle, of generous and constant feeling, comes principally from the women—whether we choose to see them as symbols merely of an area of the mind possessed by both sexes in common, or whether we see Shakespeare creating a world in which some kind of distinctively female rationale is able to have full play, and to dominate the action. When, in tragedy, the action moves on to the battlements of civilisation, and beyond, the difference of the sexes becomes of minor importance, and the rôle of the women diminishes; they become little more than functions of the hero's mind, barely aware of the area in which that mind operates. Ironically, the heroic qualities which make the woman's stature minor by comparison can be seen as developing through and out of qualities confined largely to the women in the "mature" comedies; the values that are proved by their success in the comedies come to stand the proof of failure in the tragedies. Something of the tragic heroes' passionate constancy and painful knowledge, and something of the sane and honourable happiness that is felt most sharply in the tragedies by its absence, is first developed in the secure limitations of the "mature" comedies, and is chiefly expressed through the talkative and intelligent women who guide events and guard principles. So *Much Ado About Nothing* can be seen to have a certain aptness of title. The small world that it presents with such gaiety, wit, and pleasurable expertise, is perhaps relatively a "nothing" in itself; but a certain amount of the interest and delight it produces comes from the awareness that much can be held in little, and that in "nothing" can "grow . . . something of great constancy".

John Crick

SOURCE: "'Much Ado About Nothing'," in *The Use of English,* Vol. XVII, No. 3, Spring, 1966, pp. 223-27.

[*In the following excerpt, Crick offers a general discussion of* Much Ado, *focusing upon the characters, theme, and language of the play. He depicts the play as one concerned primarily about the potential for evil existing in people who have become self-absorbed in a society that reflects and supports that self-absorption.*]

'The fable is absurd', wrote Charles Gildon in 1710, and most of us would agree. Yet there is the effervescent presence of Beatrice and Benedick and the engaging stupidity of Dogberry and Verges to assure us that all is not dross. Coleridge was convinced that this central interest was Shakespeare's own, his motive in writing the play, and the 'fable' was merely a means of exhibiting the characters he was interested in. This may have been the attitude of audiences in Shakespeare's time: as early as 1613, the play was referred to as 'Benedicte and Betteris'. Can we summarise the play in this way: a few good acting parts standing out against the unsatisfactory background of a preposterous Italian romance? I think not.

Most of the play's critics have seized on the apparent absence of any unifying dramatic conception: the play fluctuates uneasily, it is said, between tragedy, romance, and comedy and never establishes a convincing dramatic form for itself. In these circumstances there are too many inconsistencies of plot and character and, in particular, in the presentation of Claudio and Hero: they begin as the hero and heroine of a typical italianate romance and, under the growing dominance of Beatrice and Benedick in the play, become—rather unconvincingly—the perpetrator and victim respectively of a nearcriminal act. Beatrice and Benedick throw the play off its balance.

It is a truism criticism should be concerned with what a work of art is, and not with what it ought to be. In the case of *Much Ado,* however, it is one worth remembering, for preconceptions about form, plot, and character, and the other components of a play, have so often obscured what is unmistakably there, and shows itself in the very first scene of the play: the precise delineation of an aristocratic and metropolitan society. This is done with a thoroughness and depth which is beyond any requirement of a romantic fable in the tradition of Ariosto and Bandello, and beyond the demands of a plot merely intended to exhibit the characters of Beatrice, Benedick, Dogberry and Verges, in the way that Coleridge suggested.

The opening scene of the play establishes for us the characteristic tone of Messina society. Don John's rebellion has been successfully put down and the victors are returning to Messina with their newly-won honours. It is significant that, in spite of the fact that Don John still exists to cause trouble, there is no serious discussion of the reasons for or consequencies of the rebellion. War is regarded as something that might deprive society of some of its leading lights—Leonato asks the messenger 'How many gentlemen have you lost in this action?'—and enhance the status of others. The messenger informs us that no gentlemen 'of name' have been lost, and Claudio and Benedick have fought valiantly and achieved honour. War is a gentlemanly pursuit, a game of fortune—nothing more.

This first conversation of the play has a studied artificiality which seems to bear out this reading of the situation. The language is sophisticated and over-elaborate, as if it has been cultivated as an end in itself, and not as a vehicle for the discussion of serious matters. Leonato's sententiousness may be that of an old man; yet it fits naturally into the play's elaboration of words:

> 'A victory is twice itself when the achiever brings home full numbers.' 'A kind overflow of kindness: there are no faces truer than those that are so washed. How much better is it to weep at joy than to joy at weeping!'

Even the messenger—a person of humble origin, we presume—has caught the infection and uses euphuistic phraseology:

> 'He hath borne himself beyond the promise of his age, doing, in the figure of a amb, the feats of a lion: he hath indeed better bettered expectation than you must expect of me to tell you how.'

> 'I have already delivered him letters, and there appears much joy in him; even so much that joy could not show itself modest enough without a badge of bitterness.'

This initial impression—of ornate language as the normal conversational mode in upper-class Messina society—is confirmed by the rest of the play: there is an abundance of antitheses, alliterations, puns, euphuisms, repetitions and word-patterns. The imagery has a similar artificiality and tends to consist of the prosaic and the conventional, rather than the striking. Prose, rather than verse, is the natural medium for conventional talk and ideas, and it is therefore not surprising that there is far more prose in *Much Ado* than is normal in a Shakespearean comedy.

In such a society, Beatrice and Benedick are naturally regarded as prize assets. They, too, relish talking for effect—although they do it with far more wit and vigour than the others, whose speeches are usually lifeless and insipid. If Don John's rebellion has not been taken seriously, as we suspect, it is probably because the 'merry war' between Beatrice and Benedick is of far more interest to a fashionable society which, as such societies do, regards a war between the sexes as a subject of perennial fascination. Beatrice, as Benedick says, 'speaks poniards' and 'every word stabs; and yet no harm is done. No Messina gentleman is likely to be deprived of his life by 'paper bullets of the brain'. Yet, one of the play's ironies is that it leads us to doubt this: considerable damage is done by the mere power of words. (It is another of the play's ironies that Beatrice's 'Kill Claudio'—an unusually straightforward command—is motivated by charitable feelings.) Hero—the main victim—comments on this power: 'one doth not know How much an ill word may empoison liking'. . . .

Where Messina conventions are fallible—and Beatrice as a woman, in a predominantly masculine ethos of courtship, games and war, is particularly qualified to speak here—is in questions of love, marriage, and the relationship between the sexes. Beneath her raillery, Beatrice shows a realistic and discriminating attitude to the subjects. She won't accept the choice of others for a husband, ironically remarking, 'Yes, faith; it is my cousin's duty to make curtsy and say, "Father, as it please you." But yet for all that, cousin, let him be a handsome fellow, or else make another curtsy, and say "Father, as it pleases me"'; she rejects romantic notions of the opposite sex—'Lord, I could not endure a husband with a beard on his face'; and, by implication, she won't accept a business marriage. (Benedick's attitude to marriage is similarly realistic—'the world must be peopled'). Hers is a sane perspective on events, an application of generosity and sympathy in a society dominated by ultimately inhuman standards. Her feminine charity triumphs, as Portia's mercy does in *The Merchant of Venice*. Benedick becomes acceptable to her when he symbolically joins his masculine qualities to her feminine principles by taking up, however reluctantly, her attitude to Claudio, and thus shows himself to be, in her eyes, of a finer 'metal' than the average Messina male. Ironically, the plotting which separated Claudio and Hero brings them together, their true feelings breaking through their conventional jesters' roles, and it is Beatrice's clear-sightedness which triumphs over all the pattern of misunderstandings, deceptions, and self-deceptions which make up the play. (This patterned and stylised aspect of the play is very marked in the plot, characterisation, and language: consider, for example, the balancing of the two scenes in the church; the characterisation in pairs: the artificiality of the masque and the mourning scene; and the rhetorical devices of most of the language.)

The incapacity of Messina society is also exposed, at another level, by Dogberry and Verges. Dogberry, like his superiors, adopts the mode of language and behaviour he conceives to be fitting to his position. When it comes to a real-life drama, he is as patently useless as Claudio. He displays condescension towards Verges and all the pompousness of authority: 'I am a wise fellow, and, which is more, an officer, and, which is more, a householder. . . .' Claudio, too, has 'every thing handsome about him'. Dogberry has caught the Messina infection of pride and self-centredness, that self-centredness which makes Leonato—the perfect host at the beginning of the play—wish Hero dead because of the way in which she has shamed him. (Isn't there something more than just a resemblance of name between him and Leontes and Lear?)

Essentially, the play is, I believe, about the power for evil that exists in people who have become self-regarding by living in a society that is closely-knit and turned in on itself. The corruption is usually that of town and city life. (Significantly, Shakespeare's story does not fluctuate between town and country as Bandello's does.) A moral blindness is generated that, if not evil itself, is capable of evil consequences. The agency of evil in this play is not outside, but within. The ostensible villain of the piece—Don John—is a mere cardboard figure who, excluded from a world of flatteries and courtesies, has resorted to 'plain-dealing' villainy. He may be an early sketch for Iago and Edmund but he lacks their intelligence and flair, and Shakespeare has wisely kept him within the narrow bounds appropriate for comedy. The real orgin of the crime is not jealousy, sexual or otherwise, but blind, consuming egotism which expresses itself in a studied artificiality, and at times flippancy, of both language and attitude. Later, Shakespeare was to take the same theme and mould it into tragedy. In the world of Othello, Lear, and Gloucester, the consequences of pride and self-centredness are catastrophic. The ultimate is perhaps *King Lear*—another 'much ado about nothing'—where Lear, like Claudio, could say 'Yet sinned I not but in mistaking'.

Kenneth Muir

SOURCE: "Maturity: *Much Ado About Nothing*," in *Shakespeare's Comic Sequence*, Barnes & Noble Books, 1979, pp. 68-81.

[*In the following excerpt, Muir offers a general historical and literary assessment of* Much Ado.]

The date of *Much Ado about Nothing* can be fixed with unusual accuracy. It was performed while Kemp (who played Dogberry) was still a member of Shakespeare's company, but too late for Francis Meres to know of its existence when he listed Shakespeare's plays in *Palladis Tamia*. So 1598 was the date of its first performance; and it was printed, probably from Shakespeare's manuscript, two years later.

It is hardly anyone's favourite comedy and it is not so frequently performed as *As You Like It* or *Twelfth Night*, doubtless because the main plot is so much less interesting than the underplot. The Hero–Claudio plot, written mainly in verse, is combined with the Beatrice–Benedick plot, written mainly in prose. In our degenerate days it is natural for audiences to prefer prose to verse, but it is possible that Shakespeare, towards the end of the sixteenth century, went through a phase when he thought that the increasing subtlety of his actors demanded a style nearer to colloquial speech—some of Shylock's best speeches, all of Falstaff's, most of Beatrice, Benedick and Rosalind are in prose.

The plots are linked together in various ways. The bringing together of Beatrice and Benedick is a means of passing the time between the day of Hero's betrothal and her marriage; Benedick is chosen by Beatrice to avenge her cousin's honour; and Benedick is a close friend of Claudio's, so that Beatrice's demand poses a favourite problem—posed earlier in *The Two Gentlemen of Verona*—of Love versus Friendship.

The play is also unified by imagery. As in *Macbeth*, the dominating image is one of clothes, and the most frequent figure of speech is antithesis. Clothes are used as a symbol of the difference between appearance and reality, and hence of hypocrisy. In the first scene, for example, Beatrice says that Benedick 'wears his faith but as the fashion of his hat'; Benedick calls courtesy a turncoat; in the second act Benedick says that Beatrice is the infernal Ate in good apparel; and Beatrice asks if Pedro has a brother since 'Your Grace is too costly to wear every day'. Benedick contrasts the amorous Claudio with the man as he used to be:

> I have known when he would have walk'd ten mile afoot to see a good armour, and now will he lie ten nights awake carving the fashion of a new doublet. (II.iii.18ff.)

Pedro has a speech in Act III on Benedick's fancy for strange disguises. Borachio has a long dialogue with Conrade, apparently irrelevant to the matter in hand, on the subject of fashion:

> *Bor.* Thou knowest that the fashion of a doublet, or a hat, or a cloak is nothing to a man.
>
> *Con.* Yes, it is apparel.
>
> *Bor.* I mean the fashion.
>
> *Con.* Yes, the fashion is the fashion.

Bor. Tush, I may as well say the fool's the fool. But seest thou not what a deformed thief this fashion is . . . Seest thou not, I say, what a deformed thief this fashion is, how giddily 'a turns about all the hot bloods between fourteen and five and thirty, sometimes fashioning them like Pharaoh's soldiers in the reechy painting, sometime like god Bel's priests in the old church window, sometime like the shaven Hercules in the smirched worm-eaten tapestry, where his codpiece seems as massy as his club?

Con. All this I see; and I see that the fashion wears out more apparel than the man. But art not thou thyself giddy with the fashion too, that thou hast shifted out of thy tale into telling me of the fashion?

Bor. Not so neither.

(III.iii.108ff.)

The climax of the many references to appearance and reality is the scene in church, when Claudio repudiates his bride. Hero is compared to a rotten orange, 'but the sign and semblance of her honour', blushing like a maid, although she is immodest:

O, what authority and show of truth
Can cunning sin cover itself withal!
Comes not that blood as modest evidence
To witness simple virtue? Would you not
  swear,
All you that see her, that she were a maid
By these exterior shows? But she is none.
Out on thee! Seeming! I will write against it:
You seem to me as Dian in her orb,
As chaste as is the bud ere it be blown;
But you are more intemperate in your blood
Than Venus, or those pamp'red animals
That rage in savage sensuality.

(IV.i.34-9, 55-60)

In a later speech Claudio drops into the favourite figure of antithesis, a figure most apt for the contrast between appearance and reality:

O Hero, what a Hero hadst thou been,
If half thy outward graces had been placed
About thy thoughts and counsels of thy
  heart!
But fare thee well, most foul, most fair!
  Farewell,
Thou pure impiety and impious purity!

(IV.i.99-103)

The two plots are linked together in another way. It has often been observed that the over-all theme of the play (as Masefield put it) is 'the power of report, of the thing overhead, to alter human destiny'. It is true that the complications of the play are all due to overhearing, although it could be argued that Claudio

might, even without the detective work by the watch, have learnt his mistake, and Beatrice and Benedick might have allowed their unconscious love for each other to rise into consciousness. But there are at least seven examples of rumour in the course of the play:

1. In the second scene Antonio tells Leonato:

The Prince and Count Claudio, walking in a thick-pleached orchard, were thus much overheard by a man of mine: the Prince discovered to Claudio that he loved my niece your daughter, and meant to acknowledge it this night in a dance.

In this case, the servant had misheard, for Pedro had offered to pretend to be Claudio, to woo Hero for him.

2. In the next scene Borachio has overheard, correctly, that Claudio hoped to marry Hero, and that Pedro was going to woo for him.

3. In the scene of the dance there are a whole series of misunderstandings, partly owing to the fact that the characters are masked:

(a) Hero, instructed by her father, apparently thinks that Pedro is wooing for himself, but it is not explained what her reactions are when he pretends to be Claudio, as this takes place off stage.

(b) Don John, for reasons which are never explained, thinks that Pedro woos for himself.

(c) Benedick thinks that Beatrice does not recognise him, and she calls him the Prince's Fool.

(d) Borachio pretends that Claudio is Benedick, and tells him that Pedro is wooing Hero for himself; and this, in spite of their previous arrangement, is forthwith believed by Claudio.

(e) Benedick, who is not aware of the arrangement between Pedro and Claudio, naturally believes that Pedro has wooed for himself.

The purpose of all these confusions—and their improbability is not so apparent in performance, is to soften up the audience, so that they are willing to accept as plausible Don John's deception of Pedro and Claudio.

4. In the third scene of Act II, Benedick overhears that Beatrice is dying of love for him, and he promptly decides that her love must be requited.

5. In the first scene of Act III, Beatrice hidden by the woodbine coverture, overhears that Benedick is in love with her. She forthwith decides to return his love:

Derek Jacobi as Benedick and Sinead Cusack as Beatrice in Terry Hand's 1982 Royal Shakespeare Company production.

What fire is in mine ears? Can this be true?
Stand I condemn'd for pride and scorn so
　　much?
Contempt, farewell! and maiden pride adieu!
No glory lives behind the back of such.
And Benedick, love on; I will require thee,
Taming my wild heart to thy loving hand;
If thou dost love, my kindness shall incite
　　thee
To bind our loves up in a holy band;
　　　For others say thou dost deserve, and I
　　　Believe it better than reportingly.
　　　　　　　　　　　　　　(III.i.107-16)

She uses, as Petruchio does, the image of the tamed hawk.

6. Borachio is overheard making love to Margaret, whom the watchers think is Hero; and Borachio, telling the tale of his deception of Pedro and Claudio to Conrade, is overheard by the Watch. This leads to his arrest, and the acquittal of Hero.

7. On the Friar's advice, a report is circulated that Hero is dead, so as to cause Claudio to feel remorse. This remorse becomes overwhelming when it is proved that she was falsely accused. But it is typical of Claudio's self-centredness that when he hears that Hero was innocent he is more concerned about his own feelings than about her supposed death. And when he agrees to marry her cousin he has the significant lines:

I do embrace your offer; and dispose
For henceforth of poor Claudio.

The plots, then, are linked together structurally, imagistically and thematically, so that complaints about lack of unity have little justification. There remains the feeling of many readers that the two plots don't really harmonise since the main plot is largely conventional—depending on the convention employed by Shakespeare in *Othello* and *Cymbeline* that the calumniator of female chastity is *always* believed, though in real life he would not be—and the sub-plot is much more realistic. Moreover, Hero is a nonentity and Claudio is a cad; whereas Beatrice and Benedick (though absurd) are attractive figures to whom an audience warms.

There are several possible answers to these complaints. The first answer is one that has to be made over and over again to Shakespeare's armchair critics: that his plays were meant to be acted, not read, and that the test we should apply should be a theatrical one— Does it work in the theatre? The convention of the calumniator believed always *does* seem to work. We may think Claudio is a credulous fool, but Pedro's equal credulity prevents us from having too harsh an opinion of him.

Nor is it unusual in Shakespeare's plays for him to present his characters on different levels of reality. It has often been noticed that Katherine and the scenes in which she appears are much more vital than those relating to the wooing of Binaca. Just as in painting, an artist will relegate some figures to the background, and just as a photographer will keep his central theme in sharp focus, while the rest of his composition may be comparatively blurred, so the dramatist can vary his treatment of characters in the same play.

The characters in this play range from the purely conventional to the purely human. Don John (for example) announces himself as a villain, a true example of motiveless malignity, who does evil for the sake of evil. Although we could (I suppose) ascribe his villainy to the results of his bastardy, it is not really possible to regard him as anything but a conventional stage villain. Or consider Margaret. At one point in the play she is apparently the mistress of the debauched Borachio, who for some unexplained reason is willing to pretend she is Hero, and call Borachio Claudio (unless this is a textual error). At another point in the play, she is a witty lady-in-waiting, on almost equal terms with Beatrice and

Hero. She cannot be present in the church scene—if she had been she would have exposed Borachio's plot—though it is quite unnatural that she should not be present. When Leonato says that Margaret was hired to the deed by Don John, Borachio protests that she is completely innocent:

> No, by my soul, she was not;
> Nor knew not what she did when she
>   spoke to me,
> But always hath been just and virtuous
> In anything that I do know by her.
>
> (V.i.286-9)

In the next scene, she engages in a witty exchange with Benedick; and at the end Leonato says (in relation to the slander of Hero)

> But Margaret was in some fault for this,
> Although against her will, as it appears.

Leo Kirschbaum, in *Character and Characterisation in Shakespeare*, argues that psychologically the two Margarets are completely incompatible. She is a flat character; but in the course of performance we do not notice the discrepancies, and Shakespeare was not troubled by the difficulties his readers might encounter.

Hero and Claudio are more realistically presented, but they are still conventional figures, and this prevents us from being too involved emotionally at Hero's distresses. Indeed, the audience is never in doubt that things will come right in the end. The very title of the play *Much Ado about Nothing* tells them as much. The chief song has as its refrain,

> Converting all your sounds of woe
> Into hey nonny-nonny.

Borachio, moreover, has been arrested by the watch before the church scene; and it is only the loquaciousness of Dogberry which prevents the slander from being exposed before the marriage scene. So the audience knows that Hero's name will eventually be cleared.

Dogberry is, indeed, a masterly character, one which is beautifully functional, but which is much more than functional. He has to be pompous, loquacious, fond of long words, very much on his dignity, semi-literate, and a bungler; otherwise he would get at the truth much sooner, and Leonato would not hasten to get rid of him on the morning of the marriage. On the other hand, he has to have some glimmerings of intelligence, or he would not have eventually arrived at the truth. On this functional basis, Shakespeare creates a wonderful portrait of a Jack-in-office, much less competent than Verges, whom he bullies and despises. He is the true ancestor of Mrs Malaprop, but much more plausible than her, who having been brought up as a lady would not be likely to make such absurd mistakes. All Dogberry's mistakes, taken individually, are the sort of mistakes one still hears from local politicians in England. Dogberry uses *desartless* for *deserving*, *senseless* for *sensible*, *decerns* for *concerns*, *odorous* for *odious*, *aspicious* for *suspicious*, *comprehended* for *apprehended*. Shakespeare may have known such a man; but he had probably read a book by his acquaintance William Lambard, on the duties of constables, so that one gets a curious mixture of Elizabethan practice with the wildest fantasy. Funny as the Dogberry scenes are, they are best played without too much farcical business; for as with all the best comic characters, there is an element of pathos about Dogberry, as when he is called an ass by one of his prisoners:

> Dost thou not suspect my place? Dost thou not suspect my years? O that he were here to write me down an ass! But, masters, remember that I am an ass; though it not be written down, yet forget not that I am an ass. No, thou villain, thou art full of piety, as shall be proved upon thee by good witness. I am a wise fellow; and, which is more, an officer; and, which is more, a householder; and, which is more, as pretty a piece of flesh as any is in Messina; and one that knows the law, go to; and a rich fellow enough, go to; and a fellow that hath had losses; and one that hath two gowns, and everything handsome about him. Bring him away. O that I had been writ down an ass! (IV.ii.69ff.)

For a modern audience, the rejection of Hero in church makes it difficult to retain any sympathy for Claudio. Prouty seeks to defend him by suggesting that it was merely a marriage of convenience. Since Hero was not a virgin, her father had broken a contract, and a public exposure was therefore permissible. This is all very well. But there is one line only in Claudio's part to suggest that he was thinking of Hero's dowry. His first question to Pedro, when he reveals that he is thinking of the marriage is 'Hath Leonato any son, my lord?' Otherwise Claudio is presented as an abnormally shy, sentimental lover.

Shakespeare had to have a public repudiation. There were theatrical necessities for it—one has only to think what the play would be like without this climactic scene. There were also perfectly good dramatic reasons for a public repudiation. Claudio's action has to seem so atrocious that Benedick—his bosom friend—is willing to challenge him to a duel. The repudiation, and the following scene between Beatrice and Benedick, are a means of showing the innate good sense of Beatrice, her warm-heartedness and intuitive understanding; and they are a means of precipitating the confession of love.

The Mueschkes make the good point that the theme of the play is Honour: 'Honour is the warp of the three hoaxes [perpetrated in the course of the play], hearsay is the weft, and illusion spins the web.' They go on to suggest that

> The repudiation scene, examined with the courtly code of honour in mind, is much more than a *coup de théâtre*. In terms of Renaissance mores, it is a scene of poignant disillusionment and despair. In the conflict between appearance and reality, between emotion and reason, tension increases when lover turns inquisitor and father turns executioner. Here, in a conflict between good and evil, truth clashes with error in a charged atmosphere of contradictory moods and shifting relationships while the outraged moral sense oscillates between absolute praise and absolute blame. Here, when malice triumphs, shame so submerges compassion and slander, mirage, and perjury are accepted as ocular and auditory proof. Incensed by defiled honour, men argue in absolutes shorn from any rational mean, and under the aegis of the courtly code act and react with prescribed cruelty.

In other words, Shakespeare's aim is to criticise the accepted code of honour; and (it may be argued) when Beatrice demands that Benedick should challenge Claudio she also is enslaved by the conventional code. For if Benedick kills Claudio, it will prove only that he is a more accomplished swordsman; and if Claudio kills Benedick it will do nothing to prove the guilt of Hero. It is the dim-witted watch, and the pompous self-important Dogberry who restore Hero's reputation. As St Paul says: 'God hath chosen the foolish things of the world to confound the wise; and God hath chosen the weak things of the world to confound the things which are mighty; and base things of the world and things which are despised, hath God chosen, yea, and things which are not, to bring to nought things that are.'

The behaviour of Claudio—and, indeed, of Pedro—in the scene of the challenge exhibits once again the limitations of the code. Their treatment of Leonato is bad enough, but their light-hearted ragging of Benedick shows a callousness to the memory of Hero, and cannot quite be expiated by the ritual mourning which follows the revelation of her innocence.

Beatrice and Benedick are obviously the two characters who are most vital and real—the ones who are the least conventional. Least conventional in a double sense: in the way they are drawn, and in their reacting against the romantic conventions of the society in which they live. They alone, of the characters in the play, are three-dimensional.

Superficially, it might seem that Beatrice and Benedick who detest each other are tricked into loving each other by overhearing that each is dying for love of the other. But it is fairly obvious that they are in love with each other from the start: that is the reason why they are continually attacking each other. Beatrice and Benedick have several reasons for not admitting to their love. Both (it is clear) are unwilling to make themselves ridiculous, and they are too intelligent and unsentimental to indulge in the gestures of conventional romantic love. It is possible (as Prouty suggests) that they are equally in revolt against marriages of convenience. Beatrice, moreover, thinks of Benedick as a philanderer. When Pedro says 'you have lost the heart of Signior Benedick', Beatrice replies:

> Indeed, my lord, he lent it me awhile; and I gave him use for it, a double heart for his single one; marry, once before he won it of me with false dice, therefore your Grace may well say I have lost it.

The speech is rather obscure; but it seems to imply that Benedick at one time had made love to Beatrice, and she felt his intentions were not serious. Both are proud and apparently self-sufficient. Benedick boasts, not very seriously, of the way women fall in love with him; but he declares to others that he will die a bachelor, and to himself:

> One woman is fair, yet I am well, another is wise, yet I am well; another virtuous, yet I am well; but till all graces be in one woman, one woman shall not come in my grace.

> (II.iii.31 ff.)

Beatrice similarly says:

> He that hath a beard is more than a youth, and he that hath no beard is less than a man; and he that is more than a youth is not for me, and he that is less than a man I am not for him. Therefore I will even take sixpence in earnest of the berrord, and lead his apes into hell.

> *Leon.* Well, then go you into hell?

> *Beat.* No; but to the gate, and there will the devil meet me, like an old cuckold, with horns on his head, and say 'Get you to heaven Beatrice, get you to heaven; here's no place for you maids'. So deliver I up my apes and away to Saint Peter for the heavens; he shows me where the bachelors sit, and there live we as merry as the day is long.

> (II.i.31-41)

It was speeches like this that so shocked Gerard Manley Hopkins that he called Beatrice vain and unchaste. Beatrice does not talk like a mid-Victorian lady, but there is not the faintest suggestion in the play that she is unchaste, and few will agree with Hopkins's epithet 'vile'. Nor, I think, is Beatrice vain; but she is proud. It has been suggested that Hero's lines describing her cousin—

> Nature never framed a woman's heart
> Of prouder stuff than that of Beatrice.
> Disdain and scorn ride sparkling in her eyes,
> Misprising what they look on; and her wit
> Values itself so highly that to her
> All matter else seems weak. She cannot love,
> Nor take no shape nor project of affection,
> She is so self-endeared—

> (III.i.49-56)

are based on a character representing pride in *The Faerie Queene*. But we must remember that Hero is deliberately exaggerating, as she knows that Beatrice is overhearing her. The lines cannot be taken as an accurate portrait. Yet both Beatrice and Benedick are absurd in their self-sufficiency. *Much Ado about Nothing* may be regarded as a subtler version of *The Taming of the Shrew*, transposed from farce to high comedy—and, of course, Benedick needs to be tamed as well as Beatrice. As we have seen, Katherina's violence is at least partly due to the fact that she hates equally the artificialities of romantic love and the humiliations of marriages of convenience, in which she is bound to suspect that the suitor is after her fortune—as indeed Petruchio admits from the start. But the struggle between the Shrew and her tamer is carried out in terms of farce. In *Much Ado*, Beatrice, instead of being physically violent, is aggressive with her tongue, and she chooses as her victim the man she really loves. She is cured and tamed, not by physical violence and semi-starvation, but by hearing the truth about herself, and about Benedick. The irony is that Hero and the others who talk about Benedick's love for her think they are lying, although they are telling the truth; and Pedro and Claudio think they are lying when they speak of Beatrice's love for Benedick.

By the end of the play we realise that all the characters in the play, except the Friar, have been laughed at: the watch for their stupidity, Dogberry for his self-important illiteracy, Leonato for being more concerned with his own honour than with his daughter's life, Claudio and Pedro for their credulity in being deceived by an obvious villain, for the cruelty of their code of honour, and for their failure to recognise that Beatrice and Benedick are in love; Beatrice and Benedick for their pride and self-sufficiency. It is not only Dogberry who should ask to be writ down as an ass.

Bernard Shaw has pointed out how much the witty repartee depends on style. The passage occurs in a review of a performance of the play in 1898:

Shakespear shews himself in it (sc. *Much Ado*) a commonplace librettist working on a stolen plot, but a great musician. No matter how poor, coarse, cheap, and obvious the thought may be, the mood is charming, and the music of the words expresses the mood. Paraphrase the encounters of Benedick and Beatrice in the style of a bluebook, carefully preserving every idea they present, and it will become apparent to the most infatuated Shakespearean that they contain at best nothing out of the common in thought or wit, and at worst a good deal of vulgar naughtiness . . . Not until the Shakespearean music is added by replacing the paraphrase with the original lines does the enchantment begin. Then you are in another world at once. When a flower-girl tells a coster to hold his jaw, for nobody is listening to him, and he retorts, 'Oh, youre there, are you, you beauty?' they reproduce the wit of Beatrice and Benedick exactly. But put it this way. 'I wonder that you will still be talking, Signior Benedick: nobody marks you.' 'What! my dear Lady Disdain, are you yet living?' You are miles away from costerland at once. When I tell you that Benedick and the coster are equally poor in thought, Beatrice and the flower-girl equally vulgar in repartee, you reply that I might as well tell you that a nightingale's love is no higher than a cat's. Which is exactly what I do tell you, though the nightingale is the better musician.

Don John (Keanu Reeves), flanked by Conrade (Richard Clifford, left) and Borachio (Gerard Horan), in Kenneth Branagh's 1993 film adaptation of Much Ado About Nothing.

Shaw, of course, exaggerates, because he was campaigning for Ibsen. It was only in his later years, after all his plays had been written, that he confessed that his own masters were Verdi, Mozart and Shakespeare; and by a curious irony his own plays are being performed now, not for their ideas, but for their style.

In all love comedies the union of the hero and heroine must be delayed by obstacles of one kind or another—'The course of true love never did run smooth.' The obstacles can be external, as for example the opposition of parents who have other plans for their children. Or they may be psychological, the unwillingness of one or other to marry. In Congreve's masterpiece, *The Way of the World,* Millamant is afraid that (as so often in her society) marriage will destroy his love for her. And when she is finally cornered, she tells her lover:

> I shall expect you shall solicit me, as though I were wavering at the gate of a monastery, with one foot over the threshold . . . I should think I was poor if I were deprived of the agreeable fatigues of solicitation.

Then she lays down an elaborate list of conditions for her surrender, including the provisos that she shall not be called such names as 'wife, joy, jewel, spouse, sweetheart, and the rest of that nauseous cant in which men and their wives are so fulsomely familiar . . . Let us be very strange and well bred, as strange as if we had been married a great while, and as well-bred as if we were not married at all.' Millamant, like Beatrice, uses her wit as a shield, because she is in fact very vulnerable and sensitive. In a great modern comedy, Shaw's *Man and Superman,* it is the woman who chases the man, chases him halfway across Europe in a motorcar; in *Much Ado* both the hero and the heroine apparently wish to remain single, and the marriage at the end is a satisfactory one because it fulfils their unconscious wishes. A modern dramatist has written a sequel to *Much Ado* in which Beatrice and Benedick, after their marriage, continue to fight each other as they had done before. But the continuation of the merry war (as Shakespeare calls it) does not mean that their marriage would not be a success. They will enjoy the wise-cracks, and use them as a private method of courtship, long after Claudio and Hero have exhausted the pleasures of romantic hyperbole. (Indeed, if one were to treat the matter realistically—and it would be perverse to do so—one could imagine Hero reminding Claudio too often of the way he repudiated her in church.) . . .

The climactic scene in the play is the one in which Benedick and Beatrice first confess their love for each other. Hero has been repudiated in church by the man she was to marry. Hero faints. In this situation the behaviour of Beatrice and Benedick is contrasted with that of the other characters. Whereas Leonato behaves like an hysterical old fool, first believing that Hero is guilty and wishing that she would die, and later uttering threats against the Prince and Claudio, Beatrice and Benedick are concerned for Hero. Beatrice knows instinctively that she is innocent, and Benedick asks some of the questions which the audience are waiting to be asked. (No one, however, seems to realise that Don John's story of a thousand secret encounters can scarcely be true, since Beatrice and Hero, until this last night, have shared a bed.) The Friar puts forward his plan of pretending that Hero has died, and suggests that the wedding-day is but postponed. Benedick naturally suspects that Don John is at the bottom of the plot to defame Hero, since Claudio and Pedro are honourable men. Everyone leaves the church, except Benedick and Beatrice, who is still weeping for her cousin.

Since they learned that they were loved by the other, Beatrice and Benedick have not met in private, and the audience have been waiting for their meeting for about half an hour of playing-time. In the scene which follows, Benedick is forced to choose between love and friendship. After he has promised to do anything in the world for Beatrice, and she asks him to kill Claudio, he first exclaims 'Not for the wide world'. When John Gielgud and Peggy Ashcroft appeared on Broadway, one of the critics regarded the production as a failure—though it was the best I have ever seen—because the audience laughed at this point. The critic thought the audience laughed because it was obvious that Gielgud's Benedick would not hurt a fly, let alone his friend. But although the scene as a whole is a poignant and dramatic one, there are several lines which are intended to be funny, and this is surely one of them. It is right that the audience should laugh when Benedick offers to do anything that Beatrice wants and refuses the very first thing she asks.

APPEARANCE VS. REALITY

The theme of appearance versus reality has been deemed central to the structure and tone of *Much Ado.* Reflecting on the numerous instances of deception in *Much Ado,* Barbara K. Lewalski has observed, "mistake, pretense, and misapprehension are of the very substance of life in Messina." Reflecting on the numerous instances of deception in *Much Ado,* John Dover Wilson has asserted, "Eavesdropping and misinterpretation, disguise and deceit—sometimes for evil ends, but generally in fun and with a comic upshot—such are the designs in the dramatic pattern of *Much Ado.*" While critics have often noted that the theme of appearance versus reality is articulated in most of Shakespeare's plays either, by circumstances or by deliberate acts of deception by the characters, Elliot

Krieger has maintained, "*Much Ado about Nothing* fits neither pattern, for the series of deceptions that compose the plot, although created by the characters, are lived through *en route* to other deceptions, and are not overcome; false perception characterizes rather than disrupts the norm of the society depicted in the play." All of the main characters deceive or are deceived by others at some point during the play, and critics agree that the successful resolution of the play, to a great extent, concerns the stripping away of illusions that otherwise distort characters' knowledge of themselves and reality. Michael Taylor has addressed the theme of the out-of-balance self-image in *Much Ado*, a work in which the individual who insists upon self-autonomy—Don John—is defeated by the allied "forces of social stability," represented by Dogberry, Verges, the Watch, Hero, and her friends.

In essays on *Much Ado*, the term "love's truth," or "love's faith," refers to the ability of a lover's imagination to transform the surface appearance of a loved one's words or character to recognize and embrace the true inner being. Of the scholars who have written about love's truth in the play, **John Russell Brown** has written one of the key short studies. Brown and other scholars—notably Charles Cowden Clarke, Harold C. Goddard, Walter N. King, Janice Hays, and Arthur Kirsch—have written extensively about the common device Shakespeare uses for presenting a lover's imagination, the "play-within-a-play"; in *Much Ado* this device is used several times. Several notable deceptions are carried off in these plays-within-a-play, including the false conversations by Claudio, Leonato, and Don Pedro which lead Benedick to believe Beatrice is in love with him; and the meant-to-be-overheard conversation between Hero and Ursula which leads Beatrice to believe Benedick loves her. In both of these cases, there is "much ado" in straightening out the tangled misperceptions each lover holds for the other; but, as Brown demonstrates in the excerpted essay below, "to those who are engaged in the quest for love's truth, the longest course is often the only one which seems possible to them. It will ever be 'Much Ado.'"

John Russell Brown

SOURCE: "Love's Truth and the Judgements of *A Midsummer Night's Dream* and *Much Ado About Nothing*, in *Shakespeare and His Comedies*, second edition, Methuen & Co Ltd., 1962, pp. 82-123.

[*In the following excerpt of his commentary on "love's truth," originally published in 1957, Brown argues that one major idea—the ability of a "lover's imagination" to "amend" mere appearances and "recognize inward truth and beauty"—informs and controls the separate plots, characterizations, and relationships of* Much Ado.

Significantly, in light of this central theme, Brown reconsiders Claudio as not a weak character, but one who "is interesting—and actable—in his own right." He adds that "unless we 'imagine no worse' of Claudio than he is represented as thinking of himself. . . Much Ado *will never be for us the lively and human comedy which Shakespeare intended."*]

Shakespeare's ideas about love's truth—the imaginative acting of a lover and the need for our imaginative response to it, the compulsion, individuality, and complexity of a lover's truthful realization of beauty, and the distinctions between inward and outward beauty, appearance and reality, and fancy and true affection—are all represented in *Much Ado About Nothing*; they inform its structure, its contrasts, relationships, and final resolution; they control many of the details of its action, characterization, humour, and dialogue. Indeed, in fashioning these elements into a lively, dramatic whole, Shakespeare achieved his most concerted and considered judgement upon love's truth.

His device for presenting a lover's imagination, the play-within-the-play, is used repeatedly in *Much Ado*; almost every development of the action involves the acting of a part and an audience's reaction to it. The relationship of Benedick and Beatrice (the outstanding characters by whose names the play was sometimes known) is radically altered by two such play-scenes. First Pedro, Leonato, and Claudio simulate a concern for Beatrice whom they represent as pining for love of Benedick, and then Hero and Ursula 'play their parts' (III. ii. 79), simulating a like concern for Benedick and his 'cover'd fire' (III. i. 77) of love for Beatrice. These two performances are far from convincing to our eyes—at one point Leonato seems to 'dry' in his performance—but nevertheless they convince their intended audiences. At the close of the first, Benedick seriously announces 'This can be no trick', and brings our laughter on himself (II. iii. 228-9); we have seen Claudio's amused relish in his own performance, and yet to Benedick 'the conference was sadly borne' (II. iii. 229). Beatrice, likewise, feels a 'fire' in her ears, and believes the fiction 'better than reportingly' (III. i. 107-16). The 'shadows' have been accepted as 'truth' because they have had audiences whose imaginations were ready to 'amend' them.

This response is surprising to the characters concerned and perhaps to their audience, for hitherto Shakespeare has presented Benedick and Beatrice as gay, light-hearted critics of every illusion. Benedick delights in being an 'obstinate heretic in the despite of beauty' (I.i. 236-7) and when Claudio affirms that Hero is the 'sweetest lady', he coolly replies:

I can see yet without spectacles and I see no such matter. (I. i. 191-2)

Beatrice likewise takes pleasure in distinguishing good parts from ill in Benedick, Don John, the prospect of Hero's marriage, and in marriage itself; and when she is complimented for apprehending 'passing shrewdly' she thanks her own wit:

> I have a good eye, uncle; I can see a church by daylight. (II. i. 85-6)

Both are convinced of the folly of love on proof of their own observation; for Beatrice men are clearly made of earth and it is therefore unreasonable to 'make an account' of oneself to a 'clod of wayward marl' (II.i. 62-6), and for Benedick man is clearly a fool when he 'dedicates his behaviours to love' (II.iii. 7-12).

But there are some signs which might prepare us for the double *volte-face*. Although Beatrice professes to scorn Benedick, he is the first she inquires after when news comes of the soldiers' return, and in the masked dance they are drawn together, recognizing each other behind visors. For his part, Benedick is strangely insistent about the outward beauty of Beatrice; if she were not 'possessed with a fury' she would excel Hero as the 'first of May doth the last of December' (I.i. 193-5), and again, using clothes as a symbol for mere appearances, she is the 'infernal Ate in good apparel' (II.i. 263-4). To say truth, these wise ones—in spite of sharp eyes and shrewd tongues, in spite of challenging Cupid and scorning matrimony—these wise ones have failed to see or understand their own inward qualities. To see everything except the force of a lover's imagination, to understand everything except the reason why women will make account of themselves and men will become fools, is to be blind in the affairs of love; without this insight, a good eye, even if its owner distinguishes outward from inward beauty, can only see love as the 'silliest stuff'.

After the two play-scenes, Shakespeare causes the seemingly irrational power of their imaginations to be manifested beyond all doubt. The eyes, understanding, and tongue of the 'sensible' Benedick are all affected; he no longer thinks that Beatrice is possessed of a fury but sees 'marks of love' in her manner and 'double meanings' in her curtest message (II. iii. 254-71). When he is taunted by those to whom he had previously boasted of his wisdom, he finds that his tongue dare not speak that which his 'heart thinks' (III. ii. 14 and 73-5); his old role will not answer the truth of his newly awaked imagination. Beatrice also feels that she is out of all good 'tune', but the mere name of Benedick can cause her to disclose, unintentionally, her heart's concern (III. iv. 43 and 77-8). At the beginning of the play we may have laughed with Benedick and Beatrice at their own witticisms and the absurdities of other people; now we laugh *at* Benedick and Beatrice themselves, at the same time as we feel for them; we laugh at their over-confidence

and subsequent surprise and discomfiture.

The pattern of the play as a whole becomes clearer when these two lovers are compared with Claudio and Hero. Whereas Benedick thinks he sees and understands everything, Claudio is afraid to trust his judgement and must, to his own embarrassment, ask others for confirmation. Conditions are against certainty; he had noticed Hero on his way to the wars but it is only when he sees her for a brief moment on his return that he feels 'soft and delicate desires', all prompting him 'how fair young Hero is' (I. i. 299-307). His 'liking' is sudden and seems to be 'engender'd' solely 'in the eyes', to be 'fancy' and not the affection of 'true' love. Because of the attraction of Hero's outward beauty he can say 'That I love her, I feel', but since he can only guess at her inward beauty he is unable to add 'That she is worthy, I know' (I. i. 230-1). Hero is to be a 'war bride'; Claudio must trust his eyes and sudden intuition.

His lack of certainty is not only contrasted with Benedick's confidence but also with Don Pedro's; although he scarcely knows that Hero is Leonato's daughter, this prince forcefully affirms her worth and readily—perhaps too readily, for he is not asked to do so much—offers to assume Claudio's part in 'some disguise' and woo her in his name. Immediately after this proposal, Claudio's uncertainty is still further contrasted with Antonio's ready certainty; this old man quickly concludes, from events that merely 'show well outward' (I.ii. 8), that Pedro intends to woo on his own account.

Pedro's wooing of Hero in Claudio's name is another of the 'plays' within this play, and those who overhear it react in significantly varied ways. Benedick is convinced that Pedro woos for himself—he has not yet felt the force of a lover's imagination and could not be expected to distinguish true from false fire. And on the malicious suggestion of Don John and his followers, Claudio comes to think so too. If he had relied on his own eyesight he might have distinguished Pedro's assumed manner from 'love's truth', but his uncertainty leads him to accept another's interpretation and to give way to his fears:

> 'Tis certain so; the prince wooes for himself. . . .
> Therefore all hearts in love use their own tongues;
> Let every eye negotiate for itself
> And trust no agent; for beauty is a witch
> Against whose charms faith melteth into blood. . . .
>
> (II. i. 181ff.)

By means of this play-scene Shakespeare has ensured that, when Pedro drops his disguise and the matter is cleared up, we know that Claudio realizes the deceitfulness of appearances and yet dares to marry Hero on the evidence of his eyes alone.

At this stage we know as little about Hero as Claudio does, but at their betrothal it seems as if her modesty matches his. Unlike Benedick, Claudio will not readily trust 'mere words', and so when Beatrice urges him to speak his happiness, he excuses himself with:

> Silence is the perfectest herald of joy: I were but little happy, if I could say how much. (II. i. 316-18).

Hero, likewise, needs to be prompted by Beatrice, and then speaks in private to Claudio alone.

The contrast between the two pairs of lovers is now clear: Benedick and Beatrice think that they know everything and consequently misjudge in the affairs of love; Claudio and Hero believe they know very little and consequently they are hesitant. Claudio's fears have caused him to misjudge once, but nevertheless he is prepared to venture.

Immediately this main contrast has been established, the action of the comedy quickens and yet another play-within-the-play is prepared. In the wars which had brought the young men to Messina Don Pedro had defeated his bastard brother, Don John, and now one of John's followers, Borachio, conceives a plan to dishonour the victor. The plan is approved and Borachio undertakes to persuade Margaret, Hero's waiting-gentlewoman, to impersonate her mistress and talk with him at the bride's chamber window—

> there shall appear such seeming truth of Hero's disloyalty that jealousy shall be called assurance and all the preparation overthrown. (II. ii. 49-51.)

We do not see this played upon the stage but we know that Claudio must witness Hero's 'chamber-window entered, even the night before her wedding-day' (III. ii. 116-17). He will not know that it is Margaret's for he is only sure of the outward beauty of Hero and this Margaret may simulate by her clothes. Nor can he judge the performance by the 'truth' of its action, for the situation it portrays presupposes that Hero does not know a lover's imagination; Margaret's action will be convincingly false. Against such testimony Claudio knows no defence; it answers his worst fears and seems to offer outward proofs where most he lacked them.

When he is assured that Hero will be proved dishonest he swears

> If I see any thing to-night why I should not marry her tomorrow, in the congregation, where I should wed, there will I shame her. (III. ii. 127-30.)

He chooses to denounce her at the wedding ceremony because there mere words are to stand for deepest thoughts and bridal garments for inward beauty: it will enable Claudio to say effectively that which he can scarcely think. His choice is not due to heartlessness as Beatrice too readily assumes, but to the uncertainty he had always striven against, to the purity of his ideal, and to the blind, destructive rage of his disappointment in which he can pity but not feel for Hero.

In the event Claudio can scarcely bring himself to say the necessary words. When he is asked by the friar if he comes-'to marry this lady', he can only answer 'No', and he does not say even this forcefully; Leonato takes it as a jest and lightly corrects the friar, 'To be married *to* her: friar, *you* come to marry her'. The ceremony proceeds and, when Hero has formally avowed her intention, the friar asks an inescapable question:

> If either of you know any inward impediment why you should not be conjoined, I charge you, on your souls, to utter it. (IV. i. 12-14.)

But once more Claudio evades the issue with 'Know you any, Hero?', and when Hero replies 'None, my lord' he still hangs back. The friar has to ask directly 'Know you any, count?', and even then Claudio is silent. At this *impasse* Leonato speaks for him: 'I dare make his answer, none', and with confident assertion Claudio breaks his reserve and blurts out his passion, exclaiming not against Hero, but against treacherous appearances and false confidence. So haltingly and indirectly he comes, with Pedro's support, to his true theme, and in quickly enflamed language renounces and shames Hero:

> . . . Would you not swear,
> All you that see her, that she were a maid,
> By these exterior shows? But she is none:
> She knows the heat of a luxurious bed;
> Her blush is guiltiness, not modesty.
>
> (ll. 32-43)

He is hardly to be understood and Hero asks how she had ever 'seem'd' otherwise than sincere and loving. On this cue Claudio is more explicit, exclaiming on the outward beauty that had deceived him:

> Out on thee! Seeming! I will write against it:
> You seem to me as Dian in her orb,
> As chaste as is the bud ere it be blown;
> But you are more intemperate in your blood
> Than Venus, or those pamper'd animals
> That rage in savage sensuality.
>
> (ll. 57-62)

He catechizes Hero only to receive further proof of

her guilt and he leaves the church resolving never to listen to imagination and never to think that outward beauty can betoken grace.

To examine Claudio's denunciation in detail is to realize part of the judgement lying behind this play. It is basically the same as that presented with tragic intensity in Othello's denunciation of the 'fair devil', Desdemona; both lovers know the 'chaos' which comes when they may no longer look for agreement between inward and outward beauty, and as Othello's forced politeness breaks down in a cry of 'goats and monkeys', so Claudio only finds his voice to denounce the hidden, 'savage sensuality' (IV. i. 62). But not having Othello's confidence in his own power, Claudio does not wish to destroy Hero; he leaves her in impotency and sorrow. The details of Claudio's denunciation—the fearful hesitancy with which he begins, and the remembrance and honour for Hero's outward beauty with which he continues and concludes—are surely meant by Shakespeare to be signs of his great inward compulsion and of his sorrow; it is strange and 'pitiful' to see a lover helplessly vilifying the 'Hero' whom he loves.

When Hero swoons even her father believes that she is guilty, but Beatrice, who in friendship trusts inward promptings, and the Friar, who is greater in experience and wisdom, both believe her innocent. At length they all agree to hide her away from 'all *eyes*' (l. 245), and, saying that she is dead, to maintain a 'mourning ostentation'. The Friar believes that by these means Claudio's intuitions of her inward beauty will grow in power and outlast the mere 'fancy' engendered by her outward beauty:

> When he shall hear she died upon his words,
> The *idea* of her life shall sweetly creep

Leonato, Don Pedro, Claudio, and Benedick (Andrew Cruikshank, Leon Quartermaine, Erick Lander, John Gielgud) in Gielgud's 1950 Shakespeare Memorial Theatre staging.

Into his study of *imagination*,
And every lovely organ of her life
Shall come apparell'd in more precious habit,
More moving-delicate and full of life,
Into the *eye and prospect of his soul*,
Than when she lived indeed; . . .

                                  (IV. i. 225ff.)

If Claudio has truly loved, he will, in due time, believe this inward vision, even against firm outward evidence of her guilt.

In order to compare the two stories of this comedy still further Shakespeare boldly followed these scenes with a dialogue between Benedick and Beatrice. When these lovers are alone together they do not abate one jot of their accustomed sagacity and wit; they are, as they learn to say later, 'too wise to woo peaceably' (V. ii. 73-4). Benedick avows his love for Beatrice and in the same breath asks if that is not 'strange' (IV. i. 269-70). Beatrice likewise confesses that she is stayed in a happy hour for she was 'about to protest' that she loved him (ll. 285-6). But words, even riddling ones like these, are the easier part of their love. Beatrice, believing that Hero has been wronged, takes Benedick's offer of service at face value and bids him 'Kill Claudio'. She makes this terrifying request in few words but when she is refused she vents her scorn of mere words in many:

   . . . manhood is melted into courtesies, valour
into compliment, and men are only turned into
tongue, and trim ones too: . . . (ll. 321ff.)

At length Benedick can put a solemn question, asking

Think you *in your soul* the Count Claudio hath
wronged Hero?

and he receives as solemn an answer:

Yea, as sure as I have a thought or a soul.
                            (ll. 331-3)

If Benedick truly loves he must—as Claudio must—believe his lady's 'soul' against all outward testimony; he had called her inward spirit a 'fury', but, if he has truly looked upon her with a lover's imagination, he will have seen the beauty of that spirit and will now trust and obey—and will challenge Claudio. The twin stories of *Much Ado About Nothing* turn on the same point; the very wise and the very uncertain must both learn to trust inward qualities, mere nothings to some other eyes; through a lover's imagination each must recognize inward truth and beauty, and must speak and act from a convinced heart.

These scenes in the church might have been unbearably pathetic had not Shakespeare already informed us that Borachio's plot had already been discovered. The device used to this end, the introduction of Constable Dogberry and the men of his watch, also contributes to presenting and widening the underlying theme of the whole play. Dogberry is a great respecter of words—of long words, defaming words, and the phraseology of official regulations—but he respects them only with respect to himself; he interprets the regulations for his own peace of mind and uses words for the little that they mean to himself not for what they mean to others. His watch are 'most senseless and fit' men (III. iii. 23), self-respecting like himself but without his pretensions. By a stroke of irony Shakespeare has directed that Borachio, 'like a true drunkard', tells all to Conrade within their hearing. There is no play-acting in this scene; Borachio tells how the 'fashion of a doublet . . . is nothing to a man' (ll. 125-6) and how the 'appearance' of Hero's guilt has deceived the prince and Claudio. When hidden truth is made so plain, the action of the play must seem as good as over, but Dogberry goes with the news to Leonato, and between the one's busy concern to prepare for his daughter's wedding and the other's happy concern to speak in polite and noble words, the message is never truly delivered. It is still further delayed when Leonato asks Dogberry to act as Justice of the Peace and examine the villains in his place. The Constable's pleasure in his new and elevated role almost perverts justice, but the sexton prompts him in his part and is soon running to inform Leonato.

The comedy moves towards its close but several threads of its pattern are yet to be drawn into place. In his grief Leonato protests that counsel is 'profitless As water in a sieve' (V. i. 4-5); a man who has suffered inwardly as he has suffered must needs rage in his grief, although at other times he may have 'writ the style of gods' (V. i. 37). When Don Pedro and Claudio enter, he and Antonio pretend that Hero is dead indeed and so over-act their parts—it is a fiction they come close to believing—that they nearly involve themselves in a duel. But the prince and Claudio wish to avoid all speech and contact with them; they do not rage in their grief, but having lost all hope and confidence are 'high-proof melancholy'. They welcome Benedick's company so that his wit may beat away their care, but witty words no longer 'suit' their thoughts and the jests go awry, and, before leaving them, Benedick challenges Claudio to a duel for Hero's honour. When Dogberry enters with his prisoners Pedro has the patience and assumed good humour to hear him, but he is cut short by Borachio's confession:

I have deceived even your very eyes: what your
wisdoms could not discover, these shallow fools
have brought to light. . . . (V. i. 238ff.)

At this point the focus returns to Claudio. Borachio's

words run 'like iron' through his blood; he is silent as he remembers Hero's true beauty, but his heart is overcharged and must be uttered in soliloquy:

Sweet Hero! now thy image doth appear
In the rare semblance that I loved it first.
(ll. 259-60)

This image springs to his mind from the knowledge of Hero's innocence, not from the sight of her outward beauty, but it is important to notice that the image is identical with the beauty he had seen at first. Dramatic interest is forcefully focused on Claudio by his silence and then by his abrupt soliloquy; by these means Shakespeare emphasizes an important turning-point in the action of the play; Claudio realizes that his love for Hero had been true affection all the time, not mere fancy.

Claudio still believes Hero is dead and when he is again confronted by Leonato he knows 'not how to pray his patience'; yet he 'must speak', asking penance for his sin which lay entirely in 'mistaking' (V. i. 281-5). He is asked to write an epitaph for Hero and next morning to marry Leonato's niece. Here again Shakespeare introduces a daring contrast, for Benedick is also writing verses—to Beatrice. He who had been so sure of his tongue is now at his wits' end to fit his lover's imagination to the 'even road of a blank verse' (V. ii. 34). On the other hand, Claudio now seems uncritical of his own utterance, presenting his finished, but not very polished, verses at Hero's tomb, and trusting that they will speak for him when he is 'dumb' (V. iii. 10).

The comedy is now at its end. Claudio is so hopeless of seeing beauty in love again that he swears to accept the 'penance' of his unseen bride 'were she an Ethiope' (V. iv. 38), and is thereupon, beyond all his hopes, reunited with Hero. Benedick and Beatrice, at the very door of the church, are unwilling—be it through shame or lack of confidence—to assume their 'unreasonable' roles in public. But when Beatrice is shown verses written by Benedick, and Benedick others written by Beatrice, the unreasonable imagination of their love is made evident; their own handwritings appear as strange evidence 'against' their hearts (V. i. 91-2). To prevent yet more ado, Benedick 'stops her mouth' with a kiss; he is now confident in his new role:

since I do purpose to marry, I will think nothing to any purpose that the world can say against it; . . . for man is a giddy thing, and this is my conclusion. . . . (ll. 106-11.)

The joy of the lovers is so complete that it must be expressed forthwith in the harmony of a dance, before the marriage ceremony, and certainly before they

spare a thought for Don John, whose deceit was the occasion of so much of their trouble.

Much Ado has been more adversely criticized for its structure than any other of Shakespeare's comedies. This has been largely due to critics who, judging by the 'humanity' of individual characters, have thought that Shakespeare lost interest in the Claudio-Hero story in order to enjoy creating Benedick and Beatrice. But *Much Ado* is, in fact, the most intellectually articulated of the comedies and will not betray its secret to this piece-meal criticism. Its structure depends almost entirely on one central theme, a theme which had already influenced parts of earlier comedies, that of appearance and reality, outward and inward beauty, words and thoughts—in short, the theme of love's truth. When this theme is recognized, the relationships and contrasts between the two main stories, which Shakespeare has been at pains to establish, are at once apparent and the play's structural unity vindicated. Then Claudio is seen as a purposeful contrast to Benedick and a character who is interesting—and actable—in his own right.

The theme of *Much Ado* may be simply stated, but its presentation is so subtle that the width and wisdom of Shakespeare's vision can only be suggested. This may best be done, in this comedy as in others, by relating the various characters to each other as the action of play directs. Leonato is one who ordinarily is 'no hypocrite, but prays from his heart' (I. i. 152-3), but he is not always patient enough to disentangle the words and actions of others, and, in sorrow, becomes ludicrously pathetic as the man who can only talk. Margaret, the young waiting-woman, is one who takes pleasure in assuming more apprehension than her experience can lay claim to. Don Pedro is rightly confident in judging Hero's inward worth, but his readiness to speak for Claudio is misjudged and his confidence in assessing the scene acted by Margaret and Borachio is probably culpable, for only a lover who could recognize Hero's inward qualities could possibly judge rightly. Dogberry's self-concerned respect for mere words and for his new and dignified role painfully prolongs the misunderstandings of others; yet he has the wit not to 'like' Borachio's look (IV. ii. 46-7) and blunderingly justice is done. The watch discover the malefactors by chance, but their simple good sense not to trust the words of those who have confessed themselves to be villains—they command them 'Never speak' (III. iii. 188)—prevents still further deceit. Benedick and Beatrice, trusting their eyes, judgements, and power of speech too much, are taught, through the good offices of their friends, to recognize and give sway to their imaginations; so Benedick is 'converted' (II. iii. 23) and finds beauty where he had previously seen a 'fury' and Beatrice learns to look as 'other women do' (III. iv. 92). But even when they are brought, through mutual trust of their own 'souls', to admit their love to each other, it again needs the offices of friends before they will admit the folly of their love to the world. Claudio, fearing, with good enough reason, to trust his eyes alone, is an easy prey to his prince's enemies, and accepts outward proof of inward guilt. In so doing he brings suffering on his lady and on himself, but in the end their love is justified by his imaginative recognition of the 'sweet idea' of Hero's true beauty. Both pairs of lovers take a long road to the same conclusion; in retrospect easier ways recommend themselves, but it is part of Shakespeare's wisdom to suggest that, to those who are engaged in the quest for love's truth, the longest course is often the only one which seems possible to them. It will ever be 'Much Ado'.

It is, perhaps, also a part of Shakespeare's wisdom that the success of *Much Ado* should depend largely on the way in which we receive it, that it should be capable of different, and sometimes destructive, interpretations. The acceptance of 'love's truth' always depends on the imagination of its audience, and the 'truth' of this play is no exception. Even the realization of the main theme of appearance and reality can only explain the dramatic structure, it cannot ensure the play's success. Unless we 'imagine no worse' of Claudio than he is represented as thinking of himself, unless we have the readiness and imagination to 'amend' the shadows of love's truth which are presented on the stage, *Much Ado* will never be for us the lively and human comedy which Shakespeare intended. But given this imaginative response, the implicit judgement of the play and the wisdom of the ideals informing it will, even in our delight, shape our own beings and bring to them something of the life-enhancement inherent in this work of art.

MUSIC AND DANCE

Critics have long noted the presence of music in *Much Ado*, both in the text itself and in the form of the play. The play concludes with a dance; and Balthasar's song, "Sigh no more, ladies, sigh no more," has been commented upon often, in part because it is performed in a crucial point in the play. (Balthasar's song was, in fact, assigned a prominent, recurring role in Kenneth Branagh's film adaptation of the play.) Several important critics have written about the importance of music in *Much Ado*, including Bernard Shaw, **W. H. Auden**, and **Paul N. Siegel**; while composer Hector Berlioz based one of his most accomplished works on the play. Of music in *Much Ado*, Shaw wrote sourly that "comparatively few of Shakespear's admirers are at all conscious that they are listening to music as they hear his phrases turn and his lines fall so fascinatingly and memorably; whilst we all, no matter how stupid we are, can understand his jokes and

platitudes, and are flattered when we are told of the subtlety of the wit we have relished, and the profundity of the thought we have fathomed." Writing fifty years after Shaw, Auden seeks to show how Balthasar's song contributes to the dramatic structure of *Much Ado*, while Siegel illustrates the affinities between the plot of *Much Ado* and the movements of a formal dance.

W. H. Auden

SOURCE: "Music in Shakespeare," in *The Dyer's Hand and Other Essays*, Random House, Inc., 1962, pp. 500-27.

[*In the following excerpt from an essay originally published in* Encounter *in 1957, Auden (a major twentieth-century poet) demonstrates how Balthasar's song in Act II, Scene iii of* Much Ado *contributes to the dramatic structure of this work in two ways; by marking the moment when Claudio's "pleasant illusions about himself as a lover are at their highest"; and by suggesting to Benedick, through the song's message, an image of Beatrice as well as a dark sense of "mischief" ahead.*]

The called-for songs in *Much Ado About Nothing* . . . illustrate Shakespeare's skill in making what might have been beautiful irrelevancies contribute to the dramatic structure.

> *Much Ado About Nothing*
>
> Act II, Scene 3.
>
> Song. Sigh no more, ladies.
>
> Audience. Don Petro, Claudio, and Benedick (in hiding).

In the two preceding scenes we have learned of two plots, Don Pedro's plot to make Benedick fall in love with Beatrice, and Don John's plot to make Claudio believe that Hero, his wife-to-be, is unchaste. Since this is a comedy, we, the audience, know that all will come right in the end, that Beatrice and Benedick, Claudio and Hero will get happily married.

The two plots of which we have just learned, therefore, arouse two different kinds of suspense. If the plot against Benedick succeeds, we are one step nearer the goal; if the plot against Claudio succeeds, we are one step back.

At this point, between their planning and their execution, action is suspended, and we and the characters are made to listen to a song.

The scene opens with Benedick laughing at the thought of the lovesick Claudio and congratulating himself on being heart-whole, and he expresses their contrasted states in musical imagery.

> I have known him when there was no music in him, but the drum and the fife; and now had he rather hear the tabor and the pipe.... Is it not strange that sheeps' guts should hale souls out of men's bodies?—Well, a horn for my money when all's done.

We, of course, know that Benedick is not as heart-whole as he is trying to pretend. Beatrice and Benedick resist each other because, being both proud and intelligent, they do not wish to be the helpless slaves of emotion or, worse, to become what they have often observed in others, the victims of an imaginary passion. Yet whatever he may say against music, Benedick does not go away, but stays and listens.

Claudio, for his part, wishes to hear music because he is in a dreamy, lovesick state, and one can guess that his *petit roman* as he listens will be of himself as the ever-faithful swain, so that he will not notice that the mood and words of the song are in complete contrast to his daydream. For the song is actually about the irresponsibility of men and the folly of women taking them seriously, and recommends as an antidote good humor and common sense. If one imagines these sentiments being the expression of a character, the only character they suit is Beatrice.

> She is never sad but when she sleeps; and not even sad then; for I have heard my daughter say, she hath often dream'd of happiness and waked herself with laughing. She cannot endure hear tell of a husband. Leonato by no means: she mocks all her wooers out of suit.

I do not think it too far-fetched to imagine that the song arouses in Benedick's mind an image of Beatrice, the tenderness of which alarms him. The violence of his comment when the song is over is suspicious:

> I pray God, his bad voice bode no mischief! I had as lief have heard the night-raven, come what plague could have come after it.

And, of course, there is mischief brewing. Almost immediately he overhears the planned conversation of Claudio and Don Pedro, and it has its intended effect. The song may not have compelled his capitulation, but it has certainly softened him up.

More mischief comes to Claudio who, two scenes later, shows himself all too willing to believe Don John's slander before he has been shown even false evidence, and declares that, if it should prove true, he will shame Hero in public. Had his love for Hero been all he imagined it to be, he would have laughed in Don John's face and believed Hero's assertion of her innocence, despite apparent evidence to the contrary, as immediately as her cousin does. He falls into the trap set for him because as yet he is less a lover than a man in love with love. Hero is as yet more an image in his own mind than a real person, and such images are susceptible to every suggestion.

For Claudio, the song marks the moment when his pleasant illusions about himself as a lover are at their highest. Before he can really listen to music he must be cured of imaginary listening, and the cure lies through the disharmonious experiences of passion and guilt.

Paul N. Siegel

SOURCE: "The Turns of the Dance: An Essay on *Much Ado About Nothing*," in *Shakespeare in His Time and Ours*, University of Notre Dame Press, 1968, pp. 212-26.

[*In the following essay, Siegel illustrates the affinities between* Much Ado *and "a formal dance in which couples successively part, make parallel movements and then are reunited." The critic demonstrates how love itself, within the context of this play, might be likened to a dance, in which there is an unending succession of dancers who complete their movements with each couple united as they ought as the musicians strike up music for a new dance, the wedding dance.*]

Much Ado About Nothing is like a formal dance in which couples successively part, make parallel movements and then are reunited. Although some of the figures performed in this dance have been noted, the dance as a whole, with its various advances, retreats, turns and counter-turns, has not been described.

As the music strikes up in the dance scene of the second act, Beatrice says to Benedick, "We must follow the leaders," but she adds, "Nay, if they lead to any ill, I will leave them at the next turning" (II. i. 157-160). Beatrice and Benedick repeat the steps of Hero and Claudio in the dance of love which Beatrice describes with light-hearted gaiety (II. i. 72-84), but with variations of their own. Don Pedro not only presides over the dance and directs it, but he also offers to woo Hero for Claudio and suggests the stratagem to make Beatrice and Benedick fall in love with each other. If they succeed in this stratagem, he says, "we are the only love-gods" (II. i. 403). His brother Don John, however, is an opposing force which seeks to get in the way of the dancers and to disturb the harmony of the dance. As Don Pedro leaves the stage, telling Leonato, Claudio and Hero how he will bring about the match between Benedick and Beatrice, Don John, sick with hatred in the presence of the happiness of Claudio and Hero, about to be married, enters and says to his tool Borachio, "Any bar, any cross, any impediment will be medicinable to me. . . . How canst thou cross this marriage?" (II. ii. 4-8). Although both Don Pedro and Don John use the language of plotters—they will "practice on" Benedick, says Don Pedro to his confederates (II. i. 399), and Don John tells Borachio (II. ii. 53-54) "Be cunning in the working this"—Don Pedro's plot is benevolent while Don John's is malevolent.

Each succeeds, but there is a greater force at work which reunites Claudio and Hero in a strengthened unity at the conclusion of the play, when they join Benedick and Beatrice—ironically brought together by Don John's plot as well as by Don Pedro's—in the dance that signalizes the close. Don John's plot not only fools Don Pedro and Claudio but almost causes bloodshed when Leonato and Benedick disregard Friar Francis' wise advice. Instead of letting time and remorse work on Claudio, as this man of God suggests, they challenge him; it is not until foolish Dogberry exposes Don John and his accomplices that they realize their error. In setting right their blunders, Dogberry furthers the purpose of nature, which is itself animated by love—the love of God pervading creation—and which is engaged in a cosmic dance.

Benedick and Beatrice have followed in the steps of Claudio and Hero in falling in love, but in their preliminary estrangement they have also set a pattern. The "skirmish of wit" (I. i. 64) in which they engage in the masked dance scene causes some real wounds. Probably since Hero, informed of Don Pedro's intention to woo her, knew him despite his mask and since Ursula recognized Antonio as well, Margaret and Beatrice, in keeping with the method of repetition so noticeably employed in the play, should also be portrayed as recognizing the masked gentlemen speaking to them in much the same way that the queen and her ladies are aware of the identities of the masked gentlemen in a similar scene in *Love's Labor's Lost*. When Beatrice is informed by Benedick that a gentleman whom he refuses to name has charged her with being disdainful and with having borrowed her wit from a collection of humorous tales, she surmises that the unnamed gentleman is Benedick. When her interlocutor professes not to know Benedick, she replies, it would seem with veiled irony, "I am sure you know him well enough" (II. i. 138) and charges Benedick in turn with being the Prince's fool, with his only gift consisting of "devising impossible slanders" (II. i. 142-143). This gift of devising impossible slanders seems to be an allusion to what he has just said about her. So Benedick also tells himself a little later that her statement that he is the Prince's fool is a slander emanating from "the base (though bitter) disposition of Beatrice" (II. i. 214-215). In the fencing match between them, that is, the sword dance which is a feature of this masque, each is wounded by an identical thrust.

Jest as Benedick may, he has been hurt: "She speaks poniards, and every word stabs" (II. i. 255-256). The hurt inflicted by the words of each is a prefiguration of the much more grievous hurt inflicted by Claudio, who "killed" Hero "with his breath" (V. i. 272). "Sweet Hero, she is wronged, she is slander'd, she is undone," bitterly exclaims Beatrice (IV. i. 314-315), bidding Benedick fight her "enemy." So Don Pedro tells Benedick after the dance, "The Lady Beatrice hath a quarrel to you. The gentleman that danced with her told her she is much wronged by you" (II. i. 243-245). Benedick is later to act as Beatrice's champion in her quarrel with Claudio, but now he announces, "I would not marry her though she were endowed with all that Adam had left him before he transgressed" (II. i. 260-262). So Claudio publicly refuses to marry Hero, the heiress of her wealthy father, returning to Leonato what he calls with bitter irony the "rich and precious gift" (IV. i. 27) he has received from him. Following the suggestion of Don John that "it would better fit your honor to change your mind" (III. ii. 118-119), Claudio is revenging himself by this public disgrace of Hero; similarly Benedick, ruminating over

Act V, scene iv. Antonio, Claudio, Hero, Beatrice, Benedick, Friar Francis, Leonato, and Don Pedro.

Beatrice's slur upon him, had exclaimed, "Well, I'll be revenged as I may" (II. i. 217-218).

Claudio's misapprehension that Hero has been unfaithful to him has been prefigured by his misapprehension that the Prince has deceived him by wooing Hero for himself; both false appearances and the instigation of Don John have misled him in each instance. His first misapprehension comes in the masked dance scene, his brief separation from his partner coinciding with the disengagement of Benedick and Beatrice. Benedick jests at the sulking of the jealous Claudio—"Alas, poor hurt fowl! Now will he creep in sedges" (II. i. 209-210)—but immediately reveals his own hurt: "But, that my Lady Beatrice should know me, and not know me! The Prince's fool! Ha!"

When Claudio, however, rejoins Hero after his brief separation from her, Benedick and Beatrice remain apart. "Come, lady, come," says Don Pedro (II. i. 285-286), as Benedick leaves upon Beatrice's entrance, "you have lost the heart of Signior Benedick." "Indeed, my lord," replies Beatrice, "he lent it me awhile, and I gave him use for it, a double heart for a single one. Marry, once before he won it of me with false dice; therefore your Grace may well say I have lost it" (II. i. 287-291). Her words have been mystifying to the commentators. Is she saying that Benedick had once wooed her and gained her heart? This would be contrary to everything we learn of the two of them in the play, for the whole point of Don Pedro's efforts to make a match between them is that it seems impossible that they fall in love with each other. Is she merely speaking "all mirth and no matter" (II. i. 344)? It would appear that her joking must have some subject. Perhaps the suggestion that she is referring to a game played with cards and dice is the most acceptable.

In any event it is significant that her reference to a previous exchange of hearts, however lightly uttered, parallels Claudio's recital of how taken he was by Hero before he went to war and is echoed immediately afterwards in Claudio's statement that Hero has whispered to him that he is "in her heart" and in his words to her, "Lady, as you are mine, I am yours. I give away myself for you and dote upon the exchange" (II. i. 319-320). The repetition of motifs is continued in the conversation which follows. When Beatrice, looking at the happy couple, gayly exclaims, "Good Lord, for alliance! Thus goes everyone in the world but I, and I am sunburnt. I may sit in a corner and cry 'Heigh-ho for a husband!'" Don Pedro responds in the same vein, "Lady Beatrice, I will get you one." So had he got Hero a husband. When Beatrice turns his statement around with "I would rather have one of your father's getting. Hath your Grace ne'er a brother like you?" Don Pedro replies, "Will you have me, lady" (II. i. 330-338)? His question, laughingly asked to minister to her wit, repeats his wooing of

Hero on behalf of Claudio, which had been mistaken for a wooing for himself.

Don Pedro does get Beatrice a husband. Benedick and Beatrice go as goes everyone in the world, more specifically as Claudio and Hero have gone. In response to Benedick's question in the opening scene "But I hope you have no intent to turn husband, have you?" Claudio had replied, "I would scarce trust myself, though I had sworn the contrary, if Hero would be my wife" (I. i. 197-198). Benedick retorted with a scoff at those who give up their bachelorhood, but he himself, although he indeed swore the contrary, came to do the same. In his very scorn for Claudio's blindness, he revealed the inclination which, like Claudio, he had felt before going to the wars, but which he is resisting: "There's her cousin, and she were not possessed with a fury, exceeds her in beauty as the first of May doth the last of December" (I. i. 192-195).

The comedy lies in Benedick's repeating Claudio's behavior immediately after he laughs at it. "I do much wonder," he says (as we await with gleeful expectation the plot against him) "that one man, seeing how much another man is a fool when he dedicates his behaviors to love, will, after he hath laughed at such shallow follies in others, become the argument of his own scorn by falling in love; and such a man is Claudio" (II. iii. 7-12). Undoubtedly, he is to make a marked pause after the phrase "falling in love" so that the audience may mentally supply his name before he applies his observation to Claudio. He mocks at Claudio, who had previously enjoyed only martial music, for being entranced by the music of the lute—"Is it not strange that sheep's guts should hale souls out of men's bodies?" (II. iii. 59-60)—but he himself will soon yield to the sweet harmony of love, composing songs, albeit, since he was "not born under a rhyming planet," (V. ii. 40-41) halting ones. So too he follows Claudio's behavior in paying new attention to his personal appearance and in mooning about in the melancholy induced by love.

Repetitive as their behavior is, however, there is variation. Claudio is the tongue-tied, timid lover who needs the Prince to do his wooing for him. There are no love scenes between him and the demure Hero. Each can speak well enough with others, Claudio engaging in repartee with Benedick and Hero joining in the fun at the expense of Beatrice, but in each other's presence they are mute. When Don Pedro informs Claudio that he has won Hero for him, Claudio can only say "Silence is the perfectest herald of joy. I were but little happy if I could say how much" (II. i. 318-319). Beatrice pushes the overwhelmed Claudio and the modest Hero into their proper positions. "Speak, Count, 'tis your cue," she tells Claudio and then, having elicited from him his few fervent words of love, she turns to Hero, saying,

"Speak, cousin; or (if you cannot) stop his mouth with a kiss and let not him speak neither" (II. i. 316, 321-323).

Benedick and Beatrice, a highly loquacious pair, do not love in this fashion. Benedick, who, after having been taken in by Don Pedro's plot, resolved "I will be horribly in love with her," (II. iii. 244) is as extravagant in his professions of love as he had been in his professions of misogyny. Beatrice, for her part, is as witty as ever, although now she fences with a buttoned foil. Her progress of love parallels his. As he had revealed an inclination toward her, she had revealed an inclination toward him in her eagerness to make him the subject of conversation and in her Freudian slip in the dance scene, "I am sure he is in the fleet; I would he had boarded me" (II. i. 148-149): "board" not only means "accost," with the implication that she would have repulsed him, but is also capable of a sexual significance. She, as he did, eavesdrops on a conversation whose participants tell each other gleefully in asides that the plot is working and make use of the same figures of the trapped bird and the hooked fish. With comic repetition, each, formerly high-spirited, becomes woebegone in the pangs of love, he pretending to the Prince and Claudio that he has a toothache, she pretending to Hero and Margaret that she has a cold. "I shall see thee, ere I die," Don Pedro had said to Benedick, "look pale with love" (I. i. 249-250). It was more true than Leonato's "You will never run mad, niece" after Beatrice had said of Benedick, "He is sooner caught than the pestilence, and the taker runs presently mad" (I. i. 87-88). "No, not till a hot January," had replied Beatrice. She might better have said not till the springtime, the season for the madness of love, that "ecstacy" (II. iii. 157) from which Leonato is to state she is suffering.

Beatrice duplicates not only Benedick's behavior. Just as Benedick repeats Claudio's actions, she repeats those of Hero, who, lessoned by her father, had replied to Don Pedro's wooing in proper decorous fashion, making light of it, as a lady should, only to accept the suit he had pressed on behalf of Claudio. So Beatrice, after keeping up her defenses, permits herself to be won, although protesting to the end that she is unwounded and unyielding. Margaret, it, may be said, takes Beatrice's place in the dance. Struck by Margaret's jests, flying thick as arrows, Beatrice asks her caustically how long it has been that she has professed herself a wit. "Ever since you left it," retorts Margaret. "Doth not my wit become me rarely?" (III. iv. 69-70). Thus the dance of love is an unending succession of dancers in which the erstwhile jester becomes the subject of fresh jests by one who is as yet heart-whole and able to cavort gaily around the disconsolate lover.

As Beatrice is in the dumps, Hero is getting dressed for the marriage ceremony. Unexpectedly, however, Beatrice has the company of Hero in her melancholy, as Benedick had found himself hurt at the same time as Claudio. "God give me joy to wear it," says Hero of her wedding gown, "for my heart is exceeding heavy" (III. iv. 24-25). Her heaviness of spirits is a premonition, such as is Antonio's melancholy at the beginning of *The Merchant of Venice* and Hamlet's misgivings before the duel, of the blow she is about to receive. Unknown to her, Don John's plot has succeeded, just as, unknown to Beatrice, Don Pedro's plot has succeeded.

There are a number of echoes from one plot to the other. "I pray God his bad voice bode no mischief," says Benedick sourly of Balthasar's song, which has just won Don Pedro's commendation (II. iii. 82-84). "I had as live have heard the night raven, come what plague could have come after it." Mischief is indeed afoot, for Don Pedro and Claudio are about to practice their deception on him. We are reminded, however, of the kind of genuine disaster supposed to be presaged by the raven's cry that is to be brought about by another enacted deception when Don Pedro says immediately after, "Dost thou hear, Balthasar? I pray thee get us some excellent music; for tomorrow night we would have it at the Lady Hero's chamber window" (II. iii. 86-89). Benedick, wondering if he has been tricked, is dissuaded of it by the gravity of Leonato's demeanor: "Knavery cannot, sure, hide himself in such reverence" (II. iii. 24-25). "Knavery" is a word that is more readily applied to the other plot. The deception of Benedick successful, Don Pedro and Claudio congratulate themselves and eagerly await the outcome of the deception of Beatrice. "Hero and Margaret have by this played their parts with Beatrice," says Claudio (III. ii. 78-79)—and just then Don John, who is using Margaret to play another part, enters to tell him that his Hero is "every man's Hero," that she has been playing a part with him. And when Margaret is teasing Beatrice as Hero is preparing for the wedding, she remarks on Beatrice's observation that she cannot smell Hero's perfumed gloves because she is "stuffed," that is, has a head cold, "A maid, and stuffed! There's goodly catching of cold" (III. iv. 64-66). The jesting allegation contained in the double entendre "stuffed" is shortly to be made with deadly earnestness about Hero.

With the marriage ceremony disrupted, it is now Benedick and Beatrice who are united and Claudio and Hero who are separated. Benedick and Beatrice, on overhearing how their pride was condemned, had learned their lessons and sacrificed their egoism to give themselves to each other. As Benedick said "Happy are they that hear their detractions and can put them to mending" (II. iii. 237-238). So Claudio does "penance" for his "sin" (V. i. 282-283). It is a venial sin, for he sinned only in "mistaking." Yet, in not trusting to the heart's promptings but to the false knowledge of the senses, he has sinned against love. Beatrice, strong and loyal in her friendship, trusts despite all evidence to what her heart tells her: "O, on my soul, my cousin is belied!" (IV. i. 147). To Benedick's question "Think you in your soul the Count Claudio hath wronged Hero?" she replies, "Yea, as sure as I have a thought or a soul" (IV. i. 331-334). Beatrice's heart-felt conviction is sufficient for Benedick, believing in her as he does. Claudio, however, has to learn how to give himself wholeheartedly without regard to the impressions of the senses.

This he does in the final scene, when he atones for the wrong he had done Hero by keeping his contract with Leonato and marrying her supposed cousin without seeing her face. The final scene, which may be regarded as a highly patterned wedding masque, is a repetition of the previous marriage scene, to which Claudio and Don Pedro came pretending that they were in earnest before they threw off the mask to unmask, as they thought, the guilty Hero. So Leontes and Antonio come to the second marriage ceremony "with confirmed countenance," (V. iv. 17) with steady faces in pretended earnest, as they play out their little fiction that the disguised Hero is Antonio's daughter. When his bride removes her mask, Claudio finds to his joy that she is Hero herself—or rather, "another Hero," (V. iv. 62) the Hero of his false imaginings, "every man's Hero," having died. So too Beatrice, in response to Benedick's "Which is Beatrice?"—an echo of Claudio's "Which is the lady I must seize upon?—removes her mask to reveal herself. In this masquerade, unlike the dance scene of the second act, which the scene recalls, every one finds his true love.

Before the happy union of both couples is completed, however, there is a final turn by Benedick and Beatrice which repeats in a lighter, quicker tempo the previous turn by Claudio and Hero: it seems for a moment as if the marriage between them that was about to have taken place is not going to take place after all, as the two continue their fencing until the end, with each thrust being parried and met by an answering thrust.

Benedick. Do you not love me?

Beatrice.   Why, no; no more than reason.

Benedick. Why, then your uncle, and the Prince, and Claudio
Have been deceived—they swore you did.

Beatrice. Do not you love me?

Benedick.   Troth, no; no more than reason.

Beatrice. Why, then my cousin, Margaret, and

Ursula
Are much deceived; for they did swear you did.

Benedick. They swore that you were almost sick for me.

Beatrice. They swore that you were well-nigh dead for me.

Benedick. 'Tis no such matter. Then you do not love me?

Beatrice. No, truly, but in friendly recompense.

                                    (V. iv. 77-83)

The revelations that have just taken place are here lightly glanced at: Leonato and the Prince and Claudio, says Benedick, were deceived in believing that Beatrice loved Benedick (just as they were deceived in believing that Hero did not love Claudio); it was given out, says Beatrice, that Benedick was well-nigh dead (just as it was given out that Hero was indeed dead). From this it seems that, having been talked into love, Benedick and Beatrice may talk themselves out of it although their repartee may also be taken as the teasing of two people who are sure of each other. However, Claudio produces a love sonnet that Benedick has written and Hero produces a love sonnet that Beatrice has written. "A miracle!" exclaims Benedick. "Here's our own hands against our hearts" (V. iv. 91-93). It is a miracle rather less wonderful than the resurrection of Hero. The near-rejection of Beatrice is linked with the repudiation of Hero when, Benedick stating to Claudio that he had thought to have beaten him but, since they are about to become kinsmen, will let him live unbruised, Claudio retorts, "I had well hoped thou wouldst have denied Beatrice, that I might have cudgeled thee out of thy single life. . . . " (V. iv. 114-118).

Here we have an amusing turn-about: Benedick had acted as Hero's champion out of love for Beatrice and Claudio now would act as Beatrice's out of love for Hero. Just as in the concluding fencing between Benedick and Beatrice, there is a moment in the final scene when it seems as if the exchange between Benedick and Claudio may become serious. Claudio having made a jest about the prospect of horns for Benedick, Benedick replies with a taunt about the horns of Claudio's father implying that Claudio is both a calf and a bastard. Claudio's "For this I owe you" (V. iv. 51)—that is, I will repay you for this—is an echo of Benedick's statement immediately before expressing pleasure that he will not have "to call young Claudio to a reckoning" (V. iv. 9). But the proposed duel turns into an exchange of wit, and the threats become pleasant banter. In the final harmony love and friendship are reconciled. "Come, come, we are friends," says Benedick.

Beatrice at the beginning of the play had said of Benedick, "He hath every month a new sworn brother. . . . He wears his faith but as the fashion of his hat; it ever changes with the next block" (I. i. 73-77). Ironically, Benedick is to quarrel with his friend Claudio as a result of his love for Beatrice. Benedick's calling Claudio a villain is the counterpart of Claudio's calling Hero a wanton. Benedick's inconstancy in friendship illustrates the truth of the conclusion to which he comes in justifying his change of mind about marriage: "man is a giddy thing" (V. iv. 107-108). To be sure, this inconstancy is the result of his admirable wholeheartedness in love, but his initial recoil in dismay after his lover's offer to do any thing at all for Beatrice is answered by her curt "Kill Claudio" and his plaintive entreaty "Beatrice," (IV. ii. 291-315) five times overborne by Beatrice's furious tirade (the last time he is not even allowed to complete the second syllable), have their comic aspect as an exhibition of the power of love. The vagaries of love induce the most ridiculously inconsistent behavior; men are, as Balthasar sings just before Benedick is made to turn to Beatrice and Claudio is about to be made to turn away from Hero, "One foot in sea, and one on shore,/ To one thing constant never" (II. iii. 66-67).

When Benedick challenges Claudio, neither Claudio nor Don Pedro believe that he can be serious but at length perceive that he is really in earnest: "As I am an honest man, he looks pale. Art thou sick, or angry?" (V. i. 130-131). Early in the play in response to Don Pedro's "I shall see thee, ere I die, look pale with love," Benedick stated: "With anger, with sickness, or with hunger, my lord, not with love" (I. i. 251-252). Don Pedro did indeed live to see the merry Benedick look pale, first with love-melancholy and then with anger, but, as Claudio says (V. i. 199), "for the love of Beatrice" in each case.

Benedick's challenge came just after Claudio had been challenged, first by Leonato and then by his rather comically irate brother Antonio, who, after having counseled patience to Leonato, outdid him in his fury. Wearied by the effort he had made to exercise forbearance with the two fuming old men and dejected by this sequel to his repudiation of Hero, Claudio welcomed Benedick, thinking that his wit would raise his spirits. Instead, he was greeted with another display of anger and another challenge. The scene falls within the pattern formed by a number of scenes in which Benedick mocks Claudio first when he is lovelorn and then when he is jealous and next Claudio in turn mocks Benedick when Benedick himself becomes lovelorn. When one's spirits are low, the other's are high. In the challenge scene, although Claudio is shaken up by his encounter with Leonato and Antonio, he is determined to be merry and meets Benedick's equally determined quarrelsomeness with sallies of wit. It is only at the end that they are in tune with

each other, each happy in his approaching marriage. The turns have been completed, each couple is united and the two couples are joined together in love and friendship, as the pipers strike up the music for the dance that precedes their joint marriage.

BEATRICE AND BENEDICK

Most critics concur that Shakespeare's depiction of the relationship between Beatrice and Benedick far surpasses that of Hero and Claudio in depth and interest. Scholars have often emphasized the fact that Shakespeare deliberately introduces the theme of the sparring mockers Beatrice and Benedick before the theme of the pallid romantics Hero and Claudio; and further, that when all of the principal characters are on stage together, the audience is drawn not to the tame love-at-first-sight relationship that develops between Hero and Claudio, but rather to the "merry war" between Beatrice and Benedick. Commentators have also noted that while the romance of Hero and Claudio is based on the outer senses, Beatrice and Benedick place more value in each other's inner attributes. A key scene often held up for examination is Act IV, Scene i, beginning where Beatrice, alone with Benedick, commands her suitor to "Kill Claudio—and then, enraged by Benedick's hesitation, declares, "Oh, God, that I were a man! I would eat his [Claudio's] heart in the market place." "It is untrue to say that Beatrice and Benedick steal the limelight from them because Claudio and Hero never held it," John Crick has written. "Hero is far too nebulous a figure, and Claudio is made unattractive from the start." However, John Dover Wilson has contended that "the Hero-Claudio plot, on the whole, is quite as effective as the Beatrice-Benedick one, which is to some extent cumbered with dead wood in the sets-of-wit between the two mockers." Nevertheless, what Kenneth Muir has written of Beatrice and Benedick is undeniable: "They alone, of the characters in the play, are three dimensional." **Bernard Shaw** would disagree though, for he found them—contrary to widespread critical judgment—to be repellent individuals who use their wit indiscriminately. Shaw adds that they are perceived as charming only because of Shakespeare's inflated reputation and skillful use of language. Scholar **Denzell S. Smith** perceives the two as essentially realistic individuals whose personalities change during the course of the play; he explains why Beatrice's command to kill Claudio is important, concluding that it marks the play's high point in the development of the characters of Beatrice and Benedick. For additional commentary on the character of Beatrice, see the essays by **Barbara Everett** and **John Crick** in the OVERVIEWS section and the essay by **John Russell Brown** in the APPEARANCE VS. REALITY section. For additional commentary on Benedick's character, see the **Crick** and **Brown** essays.

Bernard Shaw

SOURCE: *"Much Ado About Nothing,"* in *Shaw on Shakespeare: An Anthology of Bernard Shaw's Writings on the Plays and Production of Shakespeare,* edited by Edwin Wilson, 1961. Reprint by Books for Libraries Press, 1971, pp. 141-58.

[*In the following review, originally published in the Saturday Review (London) on February 26, 1898, Shaw (an Irish dramatist and critic who regularly attacked what he considered Shakespeare's inflated repuation as a dramatist) focuses upon Beatrice and Benedick as figures who are—contrary to popular perception—coarse individuals who use their wit indiscriminately. Shaw adds that they are perceived as charming only because of Shakespeare's enchanting language. Shaw's remarks upon the musical nature of the play coincide with remarks made by W. H. Auden in 1957 on* Much Ado.]

Much Ado is perhaps the most dangerous actor-manager trap in the whole Shakespearean repertory. It is not a safe play like *The Merchant of Venice* or *As You Like It,* nor a serious play like *Hamlet.* Its success depends on the way it is handled in performance; and that, again, depends on the actor-manager being enough of a critic to discriminate ruthlessly between the pretension of the author and his achievement.

The main pretension in *Much Ado* is that Benedick and Beatrice are exquisitely witty and amusing persons. They are, of course, nothing of the sort. Benedick's pleasantries might pass at a sing-song in a public-house parlor; but a gentleman rash enough to venture on them in even the very mildest £52-a-year suburban imitation of polite society today would assuredly never be invited again. From his first joke, "Were you in doubt, sir, that you asked her?" to his last, "There is no staff more reverend than one tipped with horn," he is not a wit, but a blackguard. He is not Shakespear's only failure in that genre. It took the Bard a long time to grow out of the provincial conceit that made him so fond of exhibiting his accomplishments as a master of gallant badinage. The very thought of Biron, Mercutio, Gratiano, and Benedick must, I hope, have covered him with shame in his later years. Even Hamlet's airy compliments to Ophelia before the court would make a cabman blush. But at least Shakespear did not value himself on Hamlet's indecent jests as he evidently did on those of the four merry gentlemen of the earlier plays. When he at last got conviction of sin, and saw this sort of levity in its proper light, he made masterly amends by presenting the blackguard *as* a blackguard in the person of Lucio in *Measure for Measure.* Lucio, as a character study, is worth forty Benedicks and Birons. His obscenity is not only inoffensive, but irresistibly entertaining, because it is drawn with perfect skill, offered at its true value, and given its proper interest, without any complicity of the author in its lewdness. Lucio is much more of a gentleman than Benedick, because he keeps his coarse sallies for coarse people. Meeting one woman, he says humbly, "Gentle and fair: your brother kindly greets you. Not to be weary with you, he's in prison." Meeting another, he hails her sparkingly with "How now? which of your hips has the more profound sciatica?" The one woman is a lay sister, the other a prostitute. Benedick or Mercutio would have cracked their low jokes on the lay sister, and been held up as gentlemen of rare wit and excellend discourse for it. Whenever they approach a woman or an old man, you shiver with apprehension as to what brutality they will come out with.

Precisely the same thing, in the tenderer degree of her sex, is true of Beatrice. In her character of professed wit she has only one subject, and that is the subject which a really witty woman never jests about, because it is too serious a matter to a woman to be made light of without indelicacy. Beatrice jests about it for the sake of the indelicacy. There is only one thing worse than the Elizabethan "merry gentleman," and that is the Elizabethan "merry lady."

Beatrice and Benedick, from Act IV, scene i.

Why is it then that we still want to see Benedick and Beatrice, and that our most eminent actors and actresses still want to play them? Before I answer that very simple question let me ask another. Why is it that Da Ponte's "dramma giocosa," entitled *Don Giovanni,* a loathsome story of a coarse, witless, worthless libertine, who kills an old man in a duel and is finally dragged down through a trapdoor to hell by his twaddling ghost, is still, after more than a century, as "immortal" as *Much Ado?* Simply because Mozart clothed it with wonderful music, which turned the worthless words and thoughts of Da Ponte into a magical human drama of moods and transitions of feeling. That is what happened in a smaller way with Much Ado. Shakespear shews himself in it a commonplace librettist working on a stolen plot, but a great musician. No matter how poor, coarse, cheap, and obvious the thought may be, the mood is charming, and the music of the words expresses the mood. Paraphrase the encounters of Benedick and Beatrice in the style of a bluebook, carefully preserving every idea they present, and it will become apparent to the most infatuated Shakespearean that they contain at best nothing out of the common in thought or wit, and at worst a good deal of vulgar naughtiness. Paraphrase Goethe, Wagner, or Ibsen in the same way, and you will find original observation, subtle thought, wide comprehension, far-reaching intuition, and serious psychological study in them. Give Shakespear a fairer chance in the comparison by paraphrasing even his best and maturest work, and you will still get nothing more than the platitudes of proverbial philosophy, with a very occasional curiosity in the shape of a rudiment of some modern idea, not followed up. Not until the Shakespearean music is added by replacing the paraphrase with the original lines does the enchantment begin. Then you are in another world at once. When a flower-girl tells a coster to hold his jaw, for nobody is listening to him, and he retorts, "Oh, youre there, are you, you beauty?" they reproduce the wit of Beatrice and Benedick exactly. But put it this way. "I wonder that you will still be talking, Signior Benedick: nobody marks you." "What! my dear Lady Disdain, are you yet living?" You are miles away from costerland at once. When I tell you that Benedick and the coster are equally poor in thought, Beatrice and the flower-girl equally vulgar in repartee, you reply that I might as well tell you that a nightingale's love is no higher than a cat's. Which is exactly what I do tell you, though the nightingale is the better musician. You will admit, perhaps, that the love of the worst human singer in the world is accompanied by a higher degree of intellectual consciousness than that of the most ravishingly melodious nightingale. Well, in just the same way, there are plenty of quite second-rate writers who are abler thinkers and wits than William, though they are unable to weave his magic into

the expression of their thoughts.

It is not easy to knock this into the public head, because comparatively few of Shakespear's admirers are at all conscious that they are listening to music as they hear his phrases turn and his lines fall so fascinatingly and memorably; whilst we all, no matter how stupid we are, can understand his jokes and platitudes, and are flattered when we are told of the subtlety of the wit we have relished, and the profundity of the thought we have fathomed. Englishmen are specially susceptible to this sort of flattery, because intellectual subtlety is not their strong point. In dealing with them you must make them believe that you are appealing to their brains when you are really appealing to their senses and feelings. With Frenchmen the case is reversed: you must make them believe that you are appealing to their senses and feelings when you are really appealing to their brains. The Englishman, slave to every sentimental ideal and dupe of every sensuous art, will have it that his great national poet is a thinker. The Frenchman, enslaved and duped only by systems and calculations, insists on his hero being a sentimentalist and artist. That is why Shakespear is esteemed a mastermind in England, and wondered at as a clumsy barbarian in France.

Denzell S. Smith

SOURCE: "The Command 'Kill Claudio' in *Much Ado About Nothing,*" in *English Language Notes,* Vol. IV, No. 3, March, 1967, pp. 181-83.

[*In the essay below, Smith explains why Beatrice's command "Kill Claudio" is important, concluding that this command represents "the climax of the development of Beatrice's and of Benedick's character." He notes that, first, the command indicates that both Beatrice and Benedick have reached a point at which neither is as self-centered as they had been at the beginning of the play. Secondly, the command indicates that the two are no longer a pair of duelists in frothy wit, but have become more serious individuals. Thirdly, because it represents the union of Beatrice and Benedick, the command stands at the climax of the plot of* Much Ado. *Finally, the command emphasizes that honor and truth must be inextricably bound up with love. In commanding Benedick to kill Claudio, Beatrice causes the most confusion in the plot than has occurred to this point in the play.*]

After each has been tricked into believing the other to be in love, Beatrice and Benedick do not confront each other privately until Hero has been slandered at the altar. Their confrontation results in a confession of love that, because of the slander, is at once followed by Beatrice's famous command "Kill Claudio" (IV.i.291). Nearly all critics of the play assert that the command is important, but the reason for its importance is seldom stated. Hardin Craig, for example, claims that the command is "a famous climax in both character and plot," but does not explain why. Several reasons can be offered.

First, the command shows Beatrice and Benedick as now less selfish than they were. Benedick's profession of love brings from her not a desire for her self-satisfaction, but rather a desire for satisfaction of Hero's wrongs. She subordinates her interests to Hero's, just as Benedick subordinates his desires to Beatrice's. Second, the command shows that Beatrice and Benedick are now more serious than they were. Rather than jest about serious problems as they did at the play's beginning, they now are engaged with them. Third, Beatrice's engagement with Hero's problem at once puts the new love relationship on a serious level—serious because the slander of Hero is serious, serious because of the possible outcome

of a duel between two competent soldiers, and serious because both lovers regard the duel as a test of Benedick's love. Fourth, the command also shows the intensity of their love. Beatrice asks her newly-professed lover the utmost favor: to place his love for her above that of his long-established friendship with Claudio. Benedick is not only to prefer Beatrice to Claudio, but is to become the revenger who will place himself outside of God's law and outside of his country's law—the revenger who wreaks his vengeance even on his best friend. The extremity of the command is startling. Finally, the command shows Beatrice's acceptance of her womanliness, of the necessity for her at times to admit her physical weakness and to place her trust and confidence in Benedick. For these reasons we can say that the command "Kill Claudio" is the climax in the development of Beatrice's and of Benedick's character.

The command is also a climax of plot because it

Beatrice, played by Emma Thompson, gives Benedick, portrayed by Kenneth Branagh, the command to "Kill Claudio" in Branagh's 1993 film.

exemplifies the union of Beatrice and Benedick. Their story is traditionally comic. Two eligible and comely young people affectedly place themselves in the extreme position of flouting their natural desires, and the stock situation typically ends with the couple falling in love, thus exposing themselves temporarily to the ridicule of those who rightly thought their original position untenable. The extremity of the command, the trust Beatrice shows in asking it, and the choice of lover over friend that Benedick makes in accepting it show the real unity of the lovers. Second, the command is climactic for the plot because it links the major plot with one of the minor plots. Before the command, the actions of Beatrice and Benedick did not affect the Hero-Claudio story. After the command, Benedick's challenge entangles him with the main plot. That the duel does not take place does not detract from the entanglement. The command is climactic, third, because of its surprise. Who would expect that, at the first private meeting of newly professed lovers, such a command would be made and obeyed? Fourth, the command causes greater plot confusion than has occurred before in the play. At the play's beginning no one was estranged, but Don John and his henchmen soon estrange themselves and cause the estrangement of Hero from Claudio, of Hero from her father, of Don Pedro from Leonato and Antonio, of Claudio from Leonato and Antonio, and of Beatrice from Claudio and Don Pedro. Benedick is the only character of importance who is not estranged. After the altar scene he is concerned about Hero's well-being, but he suggests that Claudio and Don Pedro, otherwise honorable and wise, have been tricked. Beatrice's command estranges him from the two men who have his "inwardness and love" (IV.i.247). Only reconciliations follow this high point of confusion. Finally, one of the intents of the Beatrice-Benedick plot has been to show that love is necessary to life. The command makes clear that love is a powerful agent for virtue, since it works to secure honor and truth. If Beatrice is right in her conviction about Hero's innocence (and we as audience know she is), the trial by arms will result in the triumph of good over evil. Dishonor and misunderstanding destroy love; honor and truth foster it.

HERO AND CLAUDIO

For years, critics of *Much Ado* have examined the reason why the Hero-and-Claudio plot seems so colorless alongside the romance of Beatrice and Benedick. **John Wain** explains why and how, to his understanding, the Hero-and-Claudio plot fails to come to life, despite Shakespeare's craftsmanship. In further explanation, scholars have said that with Messina being a society of wit, the conventional Hero and Claudio are in a setting in which their shortcomings, particularly Claudio's, stand out. In this context, **John**

Crick seeks to show how Hero and Claudio exist in a society in which their conventionality stands out as dullness and where Claudio's shortcomings are brought to the fore. Critics agree that Claudio's high point in the play comes at a low point in the portrayal of his character: when he accuses Hero of being a wanton in the presence of her father and the entire wedding party. Feminist criticism has focused upon this particular scene, with scholar **S. P. Cerasano** contending that *Much Ado* "implicitly dramatizes the plight of women and slander within the actual legal structure" of the play's society. For additional commentary on the character of Hero, see the essays by **Barbara Everett** and **John Crick** in the OVERVIEWS section and the essay by **John Russell Brown** in the APPEARANCE VS. REALITY section. For additional commentary on Claudio's character, see the **Crick** and **Brown** essays.

John Wain

SOURCE: "The Shakespearean Lie-Detector: Thoughts on 'Much Ado about Nothing'," in *The Critical Quarterly*, Vol. 9, No. 1, Spring, 1967, pp. 27-42.

[In the excerpt below, Wain (a prolific English author of contemporary fiction and poetry and a critic who beleives that in order to judge the quality of literature the critic

Hero and Claudio in Act V, scene iv.

must make a moral as well as an imaginative judgment)
explains why and how, to his understanding, the Hero-
and-Claudio plot failed to live, despite the craftsmanship
of Shakespeare.]

Why did the Hero-and-Claudio plot go so dead on its
author? The answer is not easy to find. Because it is
not, *per se*, an unconvincing story. Psychologically, it
is real enough. The characters act throughout in consistency with their own natures. Hero, her father
Leonato and his brother Antonio, are all perfectly
credible. Don John, though he is only briefly sketched
and fades out early from the action, is quite convincing in his laconic disagreeableness, a plain-spoken
villain who openly wishes others harm. Conrade and
Borachio, mere outlines, are at any rate free of inherent contradictions; so is Margaret. None of these
characters presents any major difficulty. It begins to
look as if the trouble lay somewhere in the presentation of Claudio.

This young man, according to the requirements of
the story, has only to be presented as a blameless
lover, wronged and misled through no fault of his
own; convinced that his love is met with deception
and ingratitude, he has no choice but to repudiate the
match; later, when everything comes to light, the
story requires him to show sincere penitence and
willingness to make amends, finally breaking out into
joy when his love is restored to him. On the face of
it, there seems to be no particular difficulty. But
Shakespeare goes about it, from the start, in a curiously left-handed fashion. First we have the business
of the wooing by proxy. Claudio confesses to Don
Pedro his love for Hero, and Don Pedro at once
offers, without waiting to be asked, to take advantage
of the forthcoming masked ball to engage the girl's
attention, propose marriage while pretending to be
Claudio, and then speak to her father on his behalf.
It is not clear why he feels called upon to do this, any
more than it is clear why Claudio, a Florentine, should
address Don Pedro, a Spaniard, as 'my liege' and treat
him as a feudal overlord. Doubtless we are supposed
to assume that he is in Don Pedro's service. It is all
part of the *donnée*. There cannot be much difference
in age between them, and Don Pedro is represented
throughout as a young gallant, of age to be a bridegroom himself.

The scene is perfunctory, and carries little conviction;
it seems to have been written with only half Shakespeare's attention. Why, otherwise, would he make
Claudio bring up the topic with the unfortunate
question, 'Hath Leonato any son, my lord?' as if his
motives were mercenary. Don Pedro seems to fall in
with this suggestion when he replies at once that 'she's
his only heir'. This is unpromising, but worse is to
come. Immediately after the conversation between
them, we have a short scene (I, ii) whose sole purpose

seems to be to provide the story with an extra complication—one which, in fact, is never taken up or
put to any use. Antonio seeks out his brother Leonato; he has overheard a fragment of the dialogue
between Claudio and Don Pedro, and evidently the
wrong fragment, so that he believes the prince intends to woo Hero on his account. Leonato wisely
says that he will believe this when he sees it; 'we will
hold it as a dream till it appear itself'; but he does say
that he will tell Hero the news, 'that she may be
better prepared for an answer'. Apart from confusing
the story, the episode serves only to provide an awkward small problem for the actress who plays Hero.
When, in the masked-ball scene in II, i, she finds
herself dancing with Don Pedro, and he begins at
once to speak in amorous tones, is she supposed to
know who he is? Since she has been told that Don
Pedro intends to woo her, she can hardly fail to guess
that he will seek her out; presumably she is ready to
be approached by him; does she intend to consent?
There is no coldness or refusal in her tone, no hint
of disappointment at not being approached by Claudio; she is merely gay and deft in her answers. It is
a small, obstinate problem that is in any case hardly
worth solving; on the stage, most producers cut out
the scene where Antonio makes his mistake, and this
is certainly what I should do myself. But it is hardly
a good beginning.

Claudio is then convinced, by the unsupported assertion of Don John, that the prince has doubled-
crossed him, that he made his offer merely to get
Claudio to hold back while he went after the girl
himself. If Claudio were a generous character we
should expect him to put up some resistance to the
story; he might say something like, 'I have the
prince's own word for it that he would act on my
behalf; we have been comrades in arms, he wishes
me well and I trust him; I know him better than to
believe he would stoop to this'. In fact, he believes
the story straight away, with a depressing, I-might-
have-known-it alacrity.

> 'Tis certain so; the Prince woos for himself.
> Friendship is constant in all other things
> Save in the office and affairs of love;
> Therefore all hearts in love use their own
>   tongues.
> Let every eye negotiate for itself,
> And trust no agent; for beauty is a witch
> Against whose charms faith melteth into
>   blood.
> This is an accident of hourly proof,
> Which I mistrusted not. Farewell, therefore,
>   Hero.

Benedick, who has heard the rumour and sees no
reason to disbelieve it, now enters and tells Claudio
the unwelcome news again, in no very gentle manner;

when Claudio goes off to nurse his grievance, Benedick looks after him with 'Alas, poor hurt fowl! Now will he creep into sedges'. This, though unconcernedly genial, is a contempt-image: Claudio has no more spirit than a dabchick.

At the next general muster of the characters (II, i) Claudio appears with a sour expression that makes Beatrice describe him as 'civil [Seville] as an orange', an image that later recurs in his bitter speech of renunciation at the altar ('Give not this rotten orange to your friend'). When the misunderstanding is abruptly removed, and he is sudenly thrust into the knowledge that Hero is his after all, he is understandably speechless and has to be prompted by Beatrice, who, like Benedick, seems to have a slightly contemptuous attitude towards him.

Claudio is now launched on felicity, yet he has so far been given no memorable lines, has shown no gaiety or wit, and we know nothing about him except that he has a tendency to believe the worst about human nature. He has been brave in battle—offstage, before the story opens—but all we have seen is the poor hurt fowl creeping into sedges. Why Shakespeare treated him like this, when it was important to win the audience's sympathy for such a central character, I cannot say. But it is clear that, for whatever reason, Shakespeare found him unattractive. Already the altar scene, at which Claudio must behave with cold vindictiveness, is casting its shadow before.

The trick is played; the victims are planted, the charade is acted out, Don Pedro and Claudio believe that Hero is false and vicious. What, one wonders for the second time, would be the reaction of a generous young man, with decent feelings and a tender heart? There are several possibilities; he could seek out the man who had stepped into his place and challenge him to a duel; or he could take horse and gallop out of town within that hour, leaving the wedding-party to assemble without him and the girl to make her own explanations. What he actually does is to get as far as the altar and then launch into a high-pitched tirade in which he not only denounces Hero but sees to it that her father is made to suffer as much as possible.

In all this, there is no psychological improbability. Such a youth would in all likelihood behave just in this way, especially if he were a Renaissance nobleman, touchy about his honour. Claudio's basic insecurity, already well demonstrated in the play, would naturally come out in vindictiveness if he thought himself cheated. The story, qua story, is perfectly credible. The reason we do not believe it is simply that it is put into an artificial idiom. If Shakespeare had told this story in the same swift, concrete, realistic prose with which he presented the story of Beatrice and

Benedick, it would be perfectly convincing. But he has, for some reason, written consistently poor verse for the characters to speak, mishandled the details (we will come to that in a moment), and in general made such a poor job of it that everyone feels a blessed sense of relief when Leonato, Friar Francis and Hero take their departure, and the stage is left to Beatrice and Benedick. How reviving it is, to the spirits and the attention, to drop from the stilted heights of Friar Francis's verse, full of lines like

> For to strange sores strangely they strain the
> cure,

to the directness and humanity of

> —Lady Beatrice, have you wept all this
> while?
> —Yea, and I will weep a while longer.

The tinsel and the crape hair are laid aside with the attitudinizing and the clumping verse; we are back in the real world of feeling. Shakespeare obviously shares this relief. His writing, in this wonderful scene in which Benedick and Beatrice admit their love, has the power and speed of an uncoiling spring.

But to come back to Claudio. His vindictiveness towards Hero and her father is not in the least unconvincing; it springs from exactly that self-mistrust and poor-spiritedness which we, and some of the other characters in the play, have already noticed. The question is, why are they there? Why does Shakespeare give this kind of character to Claudio, when he could easily have made him more sympathetic?

The answer, as so often, lies in the exigencies of the plot. Claudio has to humiliate Hero publicly, has to strike an all but killing blow at her gentle nature, for the same reason that Leontes has to do these things to Hermione. In each case, the woman has to be so emotionally shattered that she swoons and is later given out as dead. So that Shakespeare had no alternative but to bring the whole party to the altar and let Claudio renounce his bride before the world. This, I believe, is the central spot of infection from which the poison pumped outwards. Having to make Claudio behave in this way, Shakespeare could feel no affection for him. And he had, as I remarked earlier, no gift for pretending. If he disliked a character, one of two things happened. Either, as in the case of Isabella in *Measure for Measure*, his pen simply ran away with him, providing more and more repulsive things for the character to say; or it refused to work at all. In *Much Ado* it was the second of these two fates that befell Shakespeare. As the play went on, he must have come to dread those scenes in which he would have to introduce Claudio. It became harder and harder to think of anything to make him say. Perfectly good opportunities presented themselves and were refused; he just *could* not try hard. The Shakespearean lie-detector was at work. Think, for instance, of the closing scenes of the play's last act. Claudio, however heartless he may have been, has here several golden opportunities to redeem himself. Shakespeare has only to show him as genuinely penitent, give him some convincing lines to say, and we shall begin to feel sorry for him, to look forward with pleasure to the time when his happiness is restored. In fact, nothing of the kind happens. In spite of the harm done to the play by Shakespeare's true opinion of Claudio, he cannot help showing that opinion. In the scene (V, i) where he and Don Pedro are confronted by Leonato and Antonio, he appears as having disengaged himself, emotionally, from the whole situation.

> Don Pedro.   Nay, do not quarrel with us, good
>   old man.
>
> Antonio.   If he could right himself with
>   quarrelling,
> Some of us would lie low.
>
> Claudio.   Who wrongs him?

An unfortunate question from one in his position; and it would be difficult, to say the least, for an actor to speak it in a tone of kindly innocence. It comes out inevitably with a hard, sneering edge.

That scene develops interestingly, bearing out the view that the story in itself was not repugnant to Shakespeare; he found plenty of interest in it. Antonio, a very minor character whose general function in the play is simply to feed the plot, suddenly comes to life in this scene. Leonato, knowing that his daughter is not really dead yet unable to keep down his anger at the sight of the two smooth young gallants who have brought such sorrow on his grey hairs, begins to rail at Claudio and the prince, whereupon Antonio, catching his mood and feeling it more deeply—for we have no reason to suppose that he is in the secret—begins to rage and threaten, becoming more and more beside himself while his brother, alarmed at the passion his own words have set in motion, plucks at his sleeve with 'Brother—' and 'But, brother Antony—'. 'Do not you meddle; let me deal with this', cries the enraged old gentleman. The whole tiny episode is splendidly alive and convincing. But that life does not reach as far as Claudio. He says nothing until the two old men withdraw and Benedick comes onstage. Then he at once begins his accustomed teasing. He has it firmly in his head that Benedick is there to provide sport, either by his own wit or by providing a target for the infinitely more clumsy jokes that occur to himself or Don Pedro. Lightly dismissing the grief and anger of the previous encounter with,

'We had lik'd to have had our two noses snapp'd off with two old men without teeth', he challenges Benedick to a wit-contest, and in spite of Benedick's fierce looks and reserved manner, goes clumping on with jokes about 'Benedick the married man' until he is brought up sharply by an unmistakable insult followed by a challenge. He can hardly ignore this, but his is a mind that works simply and cannot entertain more than one idea at a time. He can change, when something big enough happens to make him change, but he cannot be supple, cannot perceive shifts in mood. Even after Benedick has challenged him, he cannot get it clear that the time for teasing is over; he keeps it up, woodenly enough, right up to Benedick's exit. So unshakable is his conviction that Benedick *equals* mirth and sport.

Psychologically this is exactly right. Shakespeare saw clearly what kind of person Claudio would have to be, if he were to behave in the way called for by the plot. What depressed him, inhibiting his mind and causing him to write badly, was the iron necessity of making such a man—cold, proud, self-regarding, inflexible—the hero of the main story in the play.

We see this more and more clearly as the last act unfolds. In Scene iii, when Claudio, accompanied by the prince and 'three or four with tapers', comes to do penance at Hero's tomb, Shakespeare shies away from the task of putting words into his mouth. Instead, he makes the scene a short formal inset; Claudio recites a few stiff, awkward rhymes and then a song is sung. The song has merit; the scene, lit by tapers and with a dramatic solemnity, is effective on the stage; but Shakespeare has missed the chance of bringing Claudio nearer to a humanity that would help us to feel for him. It is too late for that; the case is hopeless.

The characters then go home (evidently they are no longer houseguests at Leonato's) and put on 'other weeds' for the marriage of Claudio and the supposed daughter of Antonio, which he has agreed to with the words,

> I do embrace your offer, and dispose
> For henceforth of poor Claudio.

Arriving there, they find Benedick waiting with Leonato. Incredible as it may seem, Claudio again begins his clumsy pleasantries about Benedick's marriage ('we'll tip thy horns with gold', etc. etc.). Neither the challenge, nor the sobering effect of the occasion, nor the fact that he is newly come from the tomb of Hero, can make him forget that Benedick's presence is the signal for an outbreak of joshing. Shakespeare knows that this is the kind of man he is, and with his curious compulsive honesty he cannot help sharing that knowledge with us, whatever it may do to the play.

The cost is certainly great. Antonio goes off to fetch the girls, and brings them in wearing masks. Here, obviously, is an excellent opportunity for Shakespeare to give Claudio some convincing lines. When he is at last confronted with the girl he is to marry instead of Hero, there is plenty that even the most ordinary writer could make him say. He can speak, briefly but movingly, about his love for the dead girl, and his remorse; he can declare his intention of doing everything in his power to bring happiness into the family that has been plunged into misery through his error; he can thank the good fortune that has made him happy, even in this misery, by uniting him to a girl closely related to his love and closely resembling her. Then the unmasking and the joy. It is not my intention to try to take the pen out of Shakespeare's hand and write the play myself; I give these simple indications merely as a way of showing that it is not in the least difficult to imagine an effective speech that Claudio might make at this point in the action—how he might, even now, show some saving humanity.

What Shakespeare actually does is to give him the one line,

   Which is the lady I must seize upon?

This, coming as it does at a crucial moment, has a strong claim to be considered the worst line in the whole of Shakespeare. It is the poet's final admission that Claudio has imposed his ungenerous personality on the story and ruined it beyond repair. After that, there is nothing for it but to get the unmasking scene over as quickly as possible and hurry on to the marriage of Beatrice and Benedick. Hero unmasks, and Claudio utters two words, 'Another Hero!' before the action sweeps on and everyone turns with relief to the sub-plot. . . .

The Hero-and-Claudio plot, we have now established at perhaps tedious length, is a ruin. And what ruined it, in my opinion, was the pull towards psychological realism that seems to have been so strong in Shakespeare's mind at this time. Certainly this made the character of Claudio unworkable, and once that was hopeless it was all hopeless. Because the plot demanded that Claudio should behave ungenerously to a girl he was supposed to love, because Shakespeare could not stick to the chocolate-box conventions but had to go ahead and show Claudio as a real, and therefore necessarily unpleasant, youth, the contradictions grew and grew until they became unsurmountable.

John Crick

SOURCE: "'Much Ado about Nothing'." in *The Use of English*, Vol. XVII, No. 3, Spring, 1966, pp. 223-27.

[*In the excerpt below, Crick addresses Hero and Claudio as a conventional hero and heroine in an unconventional society, a milieu in which Claudio's shortcomings are brought to the fore.*]

Conventional people and societies often relish the unconventional as a safety-valve for repressed instincts. In a society such as Messina's, where the instincts for life are in danger of being drained away in small talk, Beatrice and Benedick offer this outlet. Their conventional role is to appear unconventional. Where the normal fashionable marriage is based on economic interests, and is ironically the end-product of romantic notions of love centred on physical appearance, a 'partnership' of antagonisms and verbal bombardments will offer a vicarious satisfaction to onlookers. Beatrice and Benedick know this and, like court jesters, give society what it wants, until it has to be jolted out of its complacency when near-tragedy strikes. . . .

Against this background are presented the conventional hero and heroine—Claudio and Hero. It is untrue to say that Beatrice and Benedick steal the limelight from them because Claudio and Hero never hold it. Hero is far too nebulous a figure, and Claudio is made unattractive from the start. He is a typical young gentleman of Messina society—'a proper squire', as Don John says—with an ear and eye to fashion. His romantic notions of the opposite sex— 'Can the world buy such a jewel?'—are grounded in a realisation of the economic basis of fashionable marriages in Messina society—'Hath Leonato any son, my lord?'—(In Bandello, Leonato is poor). We are reminded of Bassanio's 'In Belmont is a lady richly left And she is fair . . .' in *The Merchant of Venice*. The shallowness of Claudio's attitude to life is betrayed by his every action. He leaves the wooing of Hero to Don Pedro, and then abandons the courtship with inordinate haste, taking a mere eleven lines to convince himself of the truth of Don John's allegation against Don Pedro, even though the latter has 'bestowed much honour' on him. He is merciless and revengeful when his pride has been wounded by the supposed betrayal, and punishes Hero and her father with sadistic exuberance in the 'wedding scene'—'a rotten orange', he calls Hero. He refuses to abandon his normal flippancy when faced by an angry Benedick in the scene where the latter challenges him. Even when he knows he has done wrong, he refuses to admit his full guilt—'yet sinned I not but in mistaking'. He is willing to accept another marriage offer without a moment's hesitation, perhaps spurred on by the knowledge that the girl is another heir; and his mourning for Hero is very formal and ritualistic, and couched in artificial terms and rhyming verse which has a false ring. Significantly, whereas Bandello emphasises the hero's repentance, this is made a minor affair in Shakespeare, and I can see no evidence for

W. H. Auden's view, expressed in an *Encounter* article, that Claudio 'obtains insight into his own short-comings and becomes, what previously he was not, a fit husband for Hero'. Such a character is incapable of development for Shakespeare offers him as a postulate, a representative type.

In Claudio, therefore, the worst aspects of Messina society are revealed: its shallowness, complacency, and inhumanity. There is nothing absurd about Beatrice's 'Kill Claudio'; in terms of the situation that has been revealed to us, the reaction is a natural one.

S. P. Cerasano

SOURCE: "'Half a Dozen Dangerous Words'," in *Gloriana's Face: Women, Public and Private, in the English Renaissance*, edited by S. P. Cerasano and Marion Wynne-Davies, Harvester Wheatsheaf, 1992, pp. 167-83.

[*In the essay below, Cerasano focusses on Claudio's treatment of Hero to illustrate how, during the course of* Much Ado, *"Shakespeare reveals that maintaining one's reputation is more complex than simply managing to avoid slander." The critic holds that the play "implicitly dramatizes the plight of women and slander within the actual legal structure." Cerasano also seeks to demonstrate that "the language of slander is shown to be a fabrication of the social and sexual values which are mirrored and married (literally and figuratively) in the cultured discourse of the play."*]

In Act III, scene i of *Much Ado About Nothing*, Hero tries to encourage Beatrice's love for Benedick by staging a conversation with Ursula which she expects Beatrice to 'overhear'. During their discussion Hero dismisses the possibility of confronting Beatrice openly with Benedick's passion because Beatrice cannot be trusted to respond positively. She 'turns every man the wrong side out', Hero decides; therefore, since the match between the would-be lovers cannot end happily, Hero teasingly suggests that Benedick should be encouraged to fight against his love and ultimately to reject Beatrice. In aid of this course of action Hero contrives a plot:

> And truly I'll devise some honest slanders,
> To stain my cousin with, one doth not know
> How much an ill word may empoison liking.
>   (III. i. 84-6)

Hero's playful proposal to employ 'honest slander' brings ironic repercussions for her later in the play, for it is the 'dishonest slander' that poisons Claudio's affections, disrupts Hero's marriage, prompts Leonato's rejection of his daughter, and requires finally that Hero 'die', only to return to marry the man who

earlier mistakenly condemned her to death by destroying her reputation. In this way, the possibilities presented by Hero's love game initiate the makings of a more serious matter. In the course of the play Shakespeare reveals that maintaining one's reputation is more complex than simply managing to avoid slander. The private language of 'honest slander' raised by women like Hero in order to unite lovers becomes, in the mouths of men like Don John, a publicised 'dishonest slander' by which relationships and particularly the women involved in them, can be destroyed. Moreover, *Much Ado* implicitly dramatises the plight of women and slander within the actual legal structure. Although several critics comment that the play seems to lack a final trial scene in which to absolve Hero and set things right (as, for example, occurs in *Measure for Measure*) the causes and circumstances of slander—namely, the use and abuse of language—are put on trial publicly in the church scene and tested implicitly throughout the play. Finally, the language of slander is shown to be a fabrication of the social and sexual values which are mirrored and married (literally and figuratively) in the cultured discourse of the play.

The adjudication of slander suits in the Renaissance has been described by some critics (Lisa Jardine and Valerie Wayne, for instance) as following a well-established procedure and offering the possibility for the offended party to find justice under the law. Although they do not imply, for a moment, that a slander suit was a *pro forma* matter, their examples, being drawn from records of the consistory courts (which were ecclesiastical courts), do not reflect the enormous changes in the way slander was conceptualised and adjudicated during the sixteenth century. Throughout the Middle Ages, slander was construed by the Church courts as the telling of lies. It was treated as a spiritual offence and the guilty party was sentenced to do penance, which could take a variety of forms including 'humiliating [public] apology'. This conception of slander was consistent with the type of court which was addressing the offence, and the penalty was consistent with the sort of compensation that the Church courts could legally extract. Although slander was treated as a sin (capable of being ameliorated through holy acts), at some unspecified time before 1500 the courts began to allow a fee to be substituted for penance. Consequently, a blurring of the distinction between the spiritual and the civil spheres of redress occurred, and this confusion overshadowed the litigation surrounding slander suits throughout the sixteenth century.

A further move from spiritual to civil in slander cases occurred with the decline of the local and ecclesiastical courts in the first half of the sixteenth century. Slander thus became actionable in the common law courts. However, the common law courts had inherited the ecclesiastical precedent that slander was a 'spiritual offence', which fell slightly outside the judicial domain that the civil law was best able to adjudicate. There was no debate among the courts at Westminster, all of which acknowledged that the telling of lies was morally wrong; but the courts were bound to specific modes of redress. [Slander could not be treated as an action of trespass in the common law courts unless 'damages' could be assessed.] Restricted to this criteria, the courts did not consider slander as assault, and they were reluctant to award damages for 'evanescent or indirect harm', although that was the type of damage slander most often caused.

But the complications do not stop here. As a result of Henry VIII's break with the Church the ecclesiastical courts gradually began to vanish, and as they did slander suits lost their natural legal venue. In addition, there was a growing awareness that slander constituted not only a moral offence but a breach of the peace, sometimes instigating violence. In recognition of these realities the common law courts eventually found themselves in the unhappy business of trying to deal with slander in a purely civil context. By 1550 slander had become part of the everyday business of common law, in particular of the Court of King's Bench. Before long—and owing in part to the allegations of conspiracy frequently accompanying slander charges—the equity courts also became involved. The Court of Star Chamber, in which assault was integral to the pleadings, became steeped in slander suits. And because of its lower costs and its tradition of expediency, the Court of Requests started to deal with slander on a regular basis. By Shakespeare's day at least three major courts were forced to decide large numbers of cases, although the legal mechanisms through which they operated were ill-suited to deal with the charges at issue.

The judicial precedent established by the common law courts meant that the legal atmosphere was, in some ways, inhospitable to any claimant, and doubly inhospitable to claims by women. Perhaps the latter fact is not surprising, given the well-documented tendencies towards cultural misogyny, as well as women's general disadvantages under the law at the time. Women could not, for instance, plead for themselves without a male guardian. Yet the serious difficulty in adjudicating slander suits resided in the ephemeral nature of verbal assault. Proving that a statement was slanderous was contingent upon issues involving personal identity, and determining tangible damages caused further problems. Both factors were difficult to address and complicated to adjudicate. Then, as now, the textbook definition was clear enough. Slander was:

> a malicious defamation . . . tending either to blacken the memory of one who is dead, or the reputation

of one who is alive, and thereby expose him to public hatred, contempt and ridicule.

Commonly, name-calling was the precipitating activity in slander suits, such as that exemplified in the case in which Thomas Lancaster told 'diverse persons' that John Hampton was a 'cosening knave'. Given the necessity of showing that Hampton had somehow suffered damages, the outcome of the lawsuit depended upon evidence demonstrating that Lancaster had wilfully spread false information about Hampton with the intention of destroying his reputation; and further, that damage to Hampton's professional or personal status (his marriage, for example) had ensued as a result of Lancaster's rumour. The usual insults for which people brought suit—'drunkard', 'quarreller', 'lewd liver', 'notorious thief', 'beggar' or 'runnegate'—might be distasteful; but legal retribution was impossible without demonstrable evidence that harm had been done. And the legal process of proving that the verbal assault had taken place, such as Lancaster really calling Hampton 'a cosening knave', was often circuitous. Unless the defendant had made some egregious comments in public or performed activities such as singing songs or reciting rhymes before a large audience of reliable citizens, showing that the slanderous situation had indeed transpired was difficult. Reliable evidence had to include a number of witnesses, frequently living at a distance, who could 'document' a rumour as it spread.

Therefore, even a cursory reading of cases in a common law court, such as the Court of Requests, shows that it was easy to be violated by verbal abuse but difficult to succeed in pressing charges. Plaintiffs did sometimes manage to extract public apologies and monetary redress for their 'damages'. However, the law was fundamentally incapable of remedying losses to one's reputation. As a result, the courts do not seem to have been consulted because litigants could expect their public images to be restored through legal action. In part, the courts acted as verbal boxing rings, mediating the hostility between litigants and providing a stage whereon actors such as Thomas Lancaster and John Hampton could each audition for the role of victim, more sinned against than sinning. If, in the end, Lancaster was found guilty of slandering Hampton, then Hampton 'succeeded' in court but also had to cope with any residual damage to his reputation. If, on the other hand, Lancaster was found innocent, then he had essentially been slandered by Hampton who, by bringing charges, had implied that Lancaster was a slanderer and a criminal.

Considering the propensity of Elizabethans to take charges of slander to court, this background would have been familiar to the audience of *Much Ado About Nothing*, even though it is almost entirely unfamiliar to most twentieth-century audiences. Likewise, it is important for us to understand that the subordinate position of women during the Renaissance made them especially vulnerable to verbal abuse. Women were expected to be 'chaste, silent, and obedient', and the high social value placed upon women's chastity left them deeply susceptible to claims of whoredom. In fact, virtually all slander suits involving women called into question their sexual morality. A typical case occurred in rural Shropshire in the early seventeenth century; C.J. Sisson later identified it as a provincial version of *The Old Joiner of Aldgate*. In this situation two young men, Humphrey Elliot and Edward Hinkes, were charged with performing 'scandalous and infamous libelous verses, rhymes, plays, and interludes' about Elizabeth Ridge, a young woman of the same village. According to Elizabeth's account the young men hoped to characterise her as 'vile, odious, and contemptible' and, through social pressure, to force her to marry one of them. Moreover, Elizabeth laid the charge that the men conspired against her 'out of a most covetous & greedy desire to gain' her father's sizeable estate, to which she was the sole heiress. Elizabeth Ridge's reasons for taking legal action centred upon the damage done to her reputation, as did Hampton's in the former example. However, the concept of reputation was complicated by gender issues. Like other women Elizabeth was concerned that once she was labelled a 'fallen woman', no man would want to marry her. As a young woman in a small rural village she might well have perceived the opportunities for a suitable match to have been few and far between. Also, the close-knit nature of village life would have ensured that the slanderous rumours spread to most of the inhabitants of the village by the time the case came to trial. On top of these events—by which a young woman like Elizabeth Ridge would have felt violated anyway—there were the further harrowing experiences of undergoing the process of law and of demonstrating that harm had arisen. As a single woman she could not show loss of or damage to her marriage; as a young woman of her class, not engaged in meaningful work or a trade, she could not claim 'damage' to her professional life; as a woman, denied full status as a citizen, she could not easily assert that her public presence had been 'damaged'. If a woman was called a 'whore', she had little compensation to look forward to. Not surprisingly, given the personal costs involved, no woman felt that she could afford to ignore a public allegation such as slander. Even the young Elizabeth I, about whom rumours circulated to the effect that she was pregnant by Thomas Seymour in 1548-9, felt obligated to set the record straight. On 23 January 1549 she wrote to the Lord Protector:

> My lord, these are shameful slanders . . . I shall most heartily desire your lordship that I may come to the court after your just determination that I may show myself there as I am.

At the same time women had to face the fact that the law was particularly inept to assist them in reclaiming such an intangible commodity as reputation, and that the potential consequences of slander for them were vastly different from those for men. The potency of language as it related to sexual status was clearly in the control of men like Elliot and Hinkes, and the process of the law favoured men, whether they were plaintiffs charging other men or defendants against complaints brought by women.

For Renaissance women, reputation, that which was synonymous with a 'good name' or a 'bad name', defined identity in an ideological, as well as in a legal, sense. A 'fair name' was essential in order for a woman to maintain her 'worthiness'; and as a woman was treated as the property of her father, husband or guardian, her name was treated as property which could be stolen, usurped or defiled. In *As You Like It*, for instance, Duke Frederick warns Celia that Rosalind 'robs thee of thy name' (I. iii. 76). Related to the theme of property was an economic discourse that determined the value of a woman's name, and it was always the 'fair name' that was stolen, for the 'black name' could only be 'bought' (suggesting prostitution): 'she hath bought the name of whore, thus dearly' (*Cymbeline*, II. iv. 128). Moreover, reputation could be 'disvalued' (see, for instance, *Measure for Measure*, v. i. 220). Nor was a woman's name her own property to 'sell' as she thought fit. A woman's reputation belonged to her male superior, who 'owned' her and to whom she could bring honour or disgrace. In so far as a woman was 'renamed' when she was slandered and her identity thus altered, her husband lost his good name and was rechristened with abuse—slandered by association. If the characterisation of a woman as 'loose' was true, that was all to the worse. In articulating the dual sense of *name*, signifying both 'reputation' and 'a malicious term', and in describing his wife's effect on his reputation, Frank Ford rails to the audience of *The Merry Wives of Windsor*:

> See the hell of having a false woman: my bed shall be abused, my coffers ransacked, my reputation gnawn at, and I shall not only receive this villainous wrong, but stand under the adoption of abominable terms, and by him that does me this wrong. Terms! Names! Amaimon sounds well; Lucifer, well; Barbason, well: yet they are devils' additions [names], the names of fiends. But cuckold? Wittol? Cuckold! The devil himself hath not such a name. (II. ii. 280-89)

The comic overtones of Ford's tirade are balanced, however, by the more severe associations of a bad name with prostitution. When Othello upbraids Montano, he remarks:

> The gravity and stillness of your youth

The conclusion of Kenneth Branagh's 1993 film: Hero and Claudio are reconciled, and all has been set right.

The world hath noted, and your *name* is
    great
In mouths of wisest censure [judgement]:
    what's the matter,
That you *unlace your reputation* thus,
And *spend your rich opinion* [reputation], for
    the name
Of a *night-brawler?*
               (II. iii. 182-7; emphasis added)

M. R. Ridley glosses 'unlace' as 'not the simple "undo" . . . but the stronger hunting (and carving) term'. The 'undoing' of Montano is suggestive of a literal 'gutting' of his personal value. Othello implies that his unwillingness to 'unlace' himself and 'spend' his rich opinion is a sign not only of Montano's weakness but of his sexual vulgarity. Montano loses his reputation to a 'night-brawler', the disclosure of which costs him dearly in excess of what he has already 'spent' for sexual favours. For the Elizabethans the rhetoric was pungent. Privileging 'dishonour in thy name' makes 'fair reputation

but a bawd', and slander creates 'the wound that nothing healeth' (*The Rape of Lucrece*, ll. 621-3, 731). The language of a sullied reputation—whether or not that reputation belonged to a man or a woman—was constantly associated with female sexuality gone amiss, as if no Montano would ever go astray were it not for the presence of a bawd to tempt him and rob him of his wealth.

The church scene in *Much Ado About Nothing* is replete with just these sorts of legal and ideological associations. As its opening Claudio first breaks the terms of the pre-marital agreement that Don Pedro had arranged for him. He then explicitly rejects Hero and openly refuses to accept her as his property: 'There, Leonato, take her back again' (IV. i. 30). After Claudio's dispossession of Hero he calls her 'rotten orange' (IV. i. 31) and 'an approved wanton' (IV. i. 44), but he waits until he has dissociated himself from her completely so that her reputation and moral state cannot sully his own. In a particularly brutal and unambiguous manner he states that he does not wish:

'to knit my soul/To an approved wanton' (IV. i. 43-4). Claudio's choice of language identifies Hero with prostitution, a suggestion that acts as a powerful verbal cue inciting the other men in the scene to join in his abuse of her. Don Pedro casts her as 'a common stale [whore]' (IV. i. 65). Leonato declares that she is 'fallen' (IV. i. 139), her very flesh is 'foul-tainted' (IV. i. 143), that her sin 'appears in proper nakedness' (IV. i. 175). To destroy Hero's identity further, Claudio attempts to reduce her image, her very being to 'nothingness':

> Would you not swear,
> All you that see her, that she were a maid,
> By these exterior shows? But she is *none*:
> (IV. i. 37-40; emphasis added)

In Claudio's eyes Hero has dissolved from a façade of 'seeming' to 'none' ('no one'—that is, nothingness). The tactics that reduce Hero's status and deny her humanity creep in throughout Claudio's speech in this scene. His language becomes increasingly insidious as he first appeals to the others (primarily the men) to believe that Hero bears a false front, and then turns directly against Hero herself. Intriguingly, he tries to make her name potent and worthless at the same time:

> HERO: O God defend me, how am I beset!
> What kind of catechizing call you this?
>
> CLAUDIO: To make you answer truly to your name.
>
> HERO: Is it not Hero? Who can blot that name
> With any just reproach?
>
> CLAUDIO: Marry, that can Hero;
> Hero itself can blot out Hero's virtue.
> (IV. i. 77-82)

While Hero seeks an explanation as to 'who' ('what person') can blot her name with just cause, Claudio replies that 'Hero itself' can stain her honour. On his rhetorical terms, she cannot possibly win. But whether he means that her tainted name 'itself' can dishonour Hero, or whether she is being symbolically reduced to a genderless object ('Hero *itself*'), Claudio's response is tempered with the sexual values of his society. He would not call a man 'wanton' because it is so explicitly a male term of opprobrium for a woman.

When Claudio slanders Hero in such an extreme manner his rhetoric has the effect of uniting part of the male community behind him, with the exception of Benedick (who, with Beatrice, stands outside the rhetorical and social codes to which Claudio and the others subscribe) and the Friar (who immediately takes steps to attempt to turn slander to 'remorse': (IV. i. 211). Nevertheless, Leonato, Don Pedro and Don John all take an active verbal role in Hero's persecution, knowing that Claudio's slander could well lead to grievous injury. Leonato, in fact, demands Hero's extinction, even her death, as a justifiable retribution for her presumed digression and for jeopardising his name. When Hero swoons, Leonato responds:

> O Fate, take not away thy heavy hand!
> Death is the fairest cover for her shame
> That may be wished for. . . .
>
> Do not live, Hero, do not ope thine eyes;
> For did I think thou wouldst not quickly die,
> Thought I thy spirits were stronger than thy shames,
> Myself would on the rearward of approaches
> Strike at thy life.
> (IV. i. 115-17; 123-7)

Slander and death are familiar bedfellows throughout Shakespeare's plays. The slandered victim, spoken of in terms that relate to discredit, sexual defilement and disease, was finally described as an outcast. Slander, popularly thought of as 'the transient murderer', if not actually the cause of literal death, was thought to lead to public alienation and metaphorical death. As Antony succinctly points out concerning his political opponents:

> These many men shall die; their names are prick'd.
>
> He shall not live. Look, with a spot I damn him.
> (*Julius Caesar*, IV. i. 1, 6).

The urgency of the Friar's proposal to turn slander into remorse recognises the price Hero will have to pay for Claudio's slander. Her alternatives are to be reborn ('a greater birth': IV. i. 213) and to begin anew with a pure reputation (possibly to be slandered again at some future time) or to be hidden away 'in some reclusive and religious life' (IV. i. 242). But finally, the Friar urges that death and resurrection is the best course—'Come, lady, die to live' (IV. i. 253)—regardless of the fact that Hero initially 'died upon his [Claudio's] words' (IV. i. 223) and that Claudio makes no attempt to repair her shattered emotions at the end of the scene, simply going off and leaving her for dead.

In describing the violation of Hero as the conspiracy of 'eyes, tongues, minds, and injuries' (IV. i. 243), Friar Francis reminds us of the other ways in which those in Messina are slandered and violated, and of the covert strategies that stand in the way of the characters' ability to negotiate meaningful interactions. Chief among these undercurrents is that presented by the atmosphere of Messina itself, an environment which revolves around tale-telling, eavesdropping and spying, all purportedly performed in the name of some legitimate purpose. From the opening of the play, where Beatrice asks for 'news' of Benedick, the characters seem caught up in a web of gossip and surface appearances. Marriages are arranged by proxy, while men and women woo and wed behind masks—literal face-coverings and social expectations alike. This tendency towards doubling encourages naive young men like Claudio to cling to the traditional male sphere of war in public, and to accept the less-than-gratifying pose of Petrarchan lover in his private life.

As long as conversations are witty and frivolous, Messina's social code is attractive; but as soon as serious issues are at stake, the community opens itself up to misrepresentation and slander. As much as Hero is slandered by Claudio's words she is also slandered by his eyes, by his predisposition to distrustfulness, and by his need to spy on her in order to test her virtue. And because the men in Messina are so willing to accept what they (mis)perceive and (mis)hear, they easily become impulsive and abusive. Leonato and Claudio will trust each other through a process of male bonding, but they will equally trust impersonal and unsubstantiated 'report'. As a result, they condemn Hero on the basis of slight evidence without allowing her to defend herself. The natural tendency of the residents of Messina is towards gullibility, inconstancy, unpredictability and slander; and also towards giving short shrift to personal identity, individual circumstances or motivations, patience and constancy.

DOGBERRY

Constable Dogberry is considered one of the most beloved characters in all of Shakespeare's works. But critics have not devoted the intensive studies of his character as they have of other principal characters in *Much Ado*. **James Smith** has written one of the more short studies of Dogberry, emphasizing that the wordy constable, far from being mere comic relief, mirrors the values of his betters in Messina society, with their emphasis upon superficiality and appearance above all. Critics agree that, despite their stupidity, Dogberry and his companions, Verges and the Watch, are key to the resolution of the play for their role in divulging the truth about Don John's plot against Hero. **Anthony B. Dawson** demonstrates the significance of Dogberry as an interpreter and conveyer of messages crucial to the play's outcome; he also

compares Dogberry with Bottom, from *A Midsummer Night's Dream*.

James Smith

SOURCE: "'Much Ado about Nothing': Notes from a Book in Preparation," in *Scrutiny*, Vol. XIII, No. 4, Spring, 1946, pp. 242-57.

[*In the following excerpt, Smith seeks to refute Samuel Taylor Coleridge's claim that Dogberry is a dispensable figure in* Much Ado, *and that the play lacks a unified design. The critic contends that Shakespeare's treatment of the constable and his associates is closely linked to his depiction of Messina and its inhabitants, which embody absurdity, shallowness, irresponsibility, and immaturity.*]

Coleridge chose *Much Ado* as an illustration of his famous 'fourth distinguishing characteristic' of Shakespeare, in accordance with which 'the interest in the plot' in the latter's plays 'is always in fact on account of the characters, not *vice-versa* . . . the plot is a mere canvass and no more'. And he went on to exemplify: 'Take away from *Much Ado* . . . all that which is not indispensable to the plot, either as having little to do with it, or, at best, like Dogberry and his comrades forced into the service, when any other less ingeniously absurd watchmen and night-constables would have answered the mere necessities of the action;—take away Benedick, Beatrice, Dogberry, and the reaction of the former on the character of Hero,—and what remains?' The implication is nothing, or almost nothing; so that the play as a whole has no purpose—that it has no unity and, failing to show even a thwarted striving towards unity, is most conveniently for the critic resolved into its elements.

As Coleridge's sharp distinction between plot and character would now no longer be accepted, it becomes at least possible that his judgment on *Much Ado* should be modified—perhaps, indeed, reversed. Antecedently, this would seem probable; for whatever they have said or written, post-Coleridgeans have not, perhaps, ceased to enjoy the play as a whole: at least they have not been reduced to reading it as some of Dickens's novels are read, with a methodical skipping of scenes or chapters. Are they not to be held more justified in their practice than in their theory? The best way to attack this problem is perhaps to consider one by one the elements which Coleridge claims to have isolated from the plot and from each other, asking whether in fact they can be so isolated: whether they or the plot do not succumb to the operation or, if they survive it, whether they are not maimed thereby.

And first of Dogberry: though with regard to him, it

is indeed difficult to maintain the detachment desirable in an analysis. Let us begin however by noting that, though he and his fellows are at times styled malaprops, the term is not altogether happy. Mrs. Malaprop is not a character who, on a second reading of *The Rivals,* gives any great if indeed any pleasure; for her pride in 'the derangement of epitaphs' is a foolish pride that the reader, for discretion's sake, prefers to ignore. Mrs. Quickly of *The Merry Wives,* with her 'alligant' and 'alicholy', has perhaps something of the same pride—though having other things too, she does not prove quite so embarrassing on continued acquaintance; and in any case, rather than painfully aping, she is probably lazily echoing her superiors. As for the Mrs. Quickly of the historical plays, she is another person: with her 'Arthur's bosom', she gives expression, as best she may, not to a selfish foolishness but to a charitable concern for souls—at least, for one soul; arriving in a moment of illumination, or perhaps at the end of a train of thought, at a striking conclusion about the state of the blessed.

Dogberry and his fellows, of from time to time the victims of syllables like Mrs. Malaprop, are more frequently and more significantly, like the second Mrs. Quickly, the victims of ideas. When Verges speaks of 'suffering salvation body and soul', and Dogberry of being 'condemned into everlasting redemption', it is impossible they are being deceived merely by similitude of sounds. Rather, they are being confounded by ideas with which, though unfitted to do so, they feel it incumbent upon themselves to cope. Such utterances are of a piece with Dogberry's method of counting; with his preposterous examination of Conrad and Borachio, in which condemnation precedes questioning; with his farewell of Leonato, to whom, in an endeavour to conserve both their dignities, he 'humbly gives leave to depart'; with his desire 'to be written down an ass', in which the same sense of his own dignity is in conflict with, among other things, a sense that it needs vindication. It is not Mrs. Malaprop, but rather Bottom, who comes to mind here: Bottom who, like Dogberry, is torn between conflicting impulses—whether those of producing his interlude in as splendid a manner as possible, while at the same time showing as much deference as possible to the ladies; or of claiming as his own the 'most rare vision' which, as a vision, certainly had been his, while for its rarity it seemed such as could not rightly belong to any man.

In thus addressing themselves to intellectual or moral feats of which they are not capable, Bottom, Mrs. Quickly and Dogberry do of course display a form of pride. Given his attitude towards Verges:

> a good old man, sir, hee will be talking as they say, when the age is in, the wit is out, God helpe us, it is a world to see . . .

Dogberry's pride needs no stressing. It is however no longer a foolish pride; or if foolish, then not with the folly of Mrs. Malaprop, but rather of all the protagonists of drama, comic or tragic, who measure themselves against tasks which ultimately prove too much for them. Perhaps with justice it is to be classified as a form of *hybris,* a comic *hybris;* and if so, then some kind of essential relation between the Dogberry scenes and the tragically inclined scenes of the main plot is immediately suggested.

The suggestion is strengthened, once Dogberry's strength rather than his weakness, his triumphs rather than his failures, are considered. For he has established himself as Constable of Messina, not only to the content of his subordinates, but with the tolerance of his superiors. In this respect he is no longer to be compared with Bottom—who, it is to be feared, would never gain a firm footing, however humble, at the court of Theseus—but with Falstaff, a character of greater importance. Unlike Bottom, Dogberry and his companions have taken fairly accurate measure both of themselves and of those who surround them; so that, if swayed by *hybris* in a certain degree, they take care that this degree shall fall short of destructive. For example, they are quite clear 'what belongs to a Watch': they will 'sleep rather than talk'; rather than bid a man stand against his will, they will let him go and thank God they are rid of a knave; rather than take a thief, they will 'let him shew himselfe for what he is', and steal out of their company. In short, they will exert themselves, or fight, no longer than they see reason: to adapt Poins's words. Indeed, in this matter they are more consistent than Falstaff, who, in dismissing Prince Henry as 'a Fellow, that never had the Ache in his shoulders', is for once allowing himself to be puffed up by *hybris.* In his boasts to Shallow, Falstaff betrays not a little of a Bottom-like recklessness:

> Master *Robert Shallow,* choose what Office thou wilt in the Land, 'tis thine . . . Boote, boote, Master *Shallow,* I know the young King is sick for mee . . .

And discomfiture of course follows. Whereas Dogberry has perfectly accommodated himself to those on whom he depends, making their ideals his own. His list of qualifications is revealing:

> I am a wise fellow, and which is more, an officer, a householder, and which is more, as pretty a peece of flesh as any in Messina, and one that knowes the Law, goe to, and a rich fellow enough, goe to, and a fellow that hath had losses, and that hath two gownes, and everything handsome about him.

It needs little acquaintance with the Leonato circle to realize that for them too it is a principal concern that everything, as far as possible, shall remain 'handsome about them'. . . .

[Fortune] shall not be impaired, social position shall be safeguarded; this would seem to be the prime occupation of society in Messina. Obviously, it is an important occupation; but equally obviously, it has no claims to be considered as unique. To fill up the gap, war is allowed of as a diversion for males and, for both the sexes, games and small talk. Thus, though not active about things of great importance nor, it would appear, importantly active about anything, society in Messina manages to keep up the appearance of great activity.

Such a society has the merit of being a society, that is, a more or less stable organization of human beings for common ends; and *ex hypothesi*, it is charming on the surface. For appearances lie on the surface. Yet for that reason they may be hollow; and there is a danger that faculties, exercised exclusively on appearances, may incapacitate themselves for dealing with, or even for recognizing, substance, when on occasion this presents itself. Something of the kind would seem to have happened to Pedro, Leonato, Claudio and their like; who when faced with the substance of Hero's grief, display an incompetence as great as that of any Dogberry; give rein to a *hybris* which is, perhaps, greater. For it is inconceivable that any but the most pampered and therefore the most spoilt members of a society should, in circumstances of such distress, show themselves as immune as they do from self-questioning, as free from misgiving. *Hybris* on this scale is of course tragic; but, it may be suggested, *hybris* on this scale is also ridiculous—indeed, unless the ridiculous aspect is first acknowledged, the tragic may escape acknowledgement altogether. For human vanity alone constitutes a strong temptation to discount it as preposterous. The figures of Dogberry and his kind are necessary in the background, to reduce the figures in the foreground to the required proportions—to the proportions of apes (as Isabella says, in *Measure for Measure*), apes for whom no tricks are too ferocious, too fantastic. Coleridge's isolation of Dogberry from the main plot is perhaps the effective reason for his dismissal of that plot as a 'mere canvass'; and if so, this of itself suggests that the isolation is not to be justified. But there is the further point: because of the same isolation, Coleridge dismisses Dogberry as 'ingeniously absurd'. Undoubtedly he is: but also, he is relevantly absurd—relevantly absurd to the main plot, and to life such as the main plot renders it. And finally, Dogberry is relevant not only for his absurdity, but for the limitations placed on this absurdity by his persistent if purblind prudence, but the steady if myopic eye which he keeps fixed on appearances—on his office as constable, on his comfort, on the main chance. This immediately establishes his commensurability with the figures of

the main plot; who like him, take care not to prejudice what is comfort in their eyes.

Having perhaps established this point, we may allow ourselves to go even further than Coleridge in separating Dogberry and the rest from what he called the 'mere necessities of the action'. 'Any other watchmen', he says, 'would have served the latter equally well'; whereas now it would seem clear that, in all probability, they would have served it better. Few if any other watchmen would have taken stock of themselves as frankly as Dogberry; they would not therefore appear guilty of an inconsistency, as Dogberry's assistants seem to be, in arresting the swashbucklers Conrad and Borachio. For they have just declared an intention to attempt no such thing. Or perhaps this inconsistency is due, not to the watchmen, but to the swashbucklers; who indeed, from this point in the play onwards, show a remarkable meekness. But the matter is hardly worth discussing; nor, perhaps, whether the carelessness involved on the author's part is to be described as positive or negative.

Anthony B. Dawson

SOURCE: "Much Ado about Signifying," in *Studies in English Literature*, Vol. 22, No. 2, Spring, 1982, pp. 211-21.

Michael Keaton as Dogberry and Ben Elton as Verges in Kenneth Branagh's 1993 motion picture production of Much Ado.

[*Below, in an excerpt from a larger essay, Dawson examines Dogberry's role in interpreting and expressing messages. The critic also offers an interesting comparison of Dogberry with Bottom, from* A Midsummer Night's Dream.]

Dogberry and Bottom make an interesting contrast. Bottom is involved in drama, he seeks to play all roles, he is transformed in the course of a metadrama which reflects the concern of *A Midsummer Night's Dream* with metamorphosis and the art of the drama. His blithe unawareness of the conditions and constraints of theatrical "reality" (in contrast to, say, Puck's very sharp awareness) is a large part of his humor. Dogberry, on the other hand, is involved in investigation, in seeking out the truth. His language is peppered with malapropisms, which distort language as, analogously, Bottom distorts dramatic conventions, and which reveal Dogberry's proud concern with language just as Bottom's theatrical bravado reveals his egotistical interest in the drama. Dogberry, again like Bottom, is blithely unaware of his humorous incompetence. Thus, at the very core of what makes each of them funny we can perceive the central concerns of the plays they inhabit.

The gap between Dogberry's professional involvement with investigation, with clues that lead to truth, and his evident failure to master the relations between reality as he perceives it and language (his malapropisms frequently mean the opposite of what he "means"), is central to the comic irony of the play as a whole. It is precisely gaps between modes of interpretation which give structure to the plot and fascinate both the characters and the audience. Language is central to interpretation, both as a model for it, and as the *medium* in which it is carried out. This double function is one of the sources of confusion and uncertainty in the play.

Dogberry's speech on being called an ass offers an illustration:

> Dost thou not suspect my place? Does thou not suspect my years? O that he were here to write me down an ass! But, masters, remember that I am an ass. Though it be not written down, yet forget not that I am an ass. No, thou villain, thou art full of piety, as shall be proved upon thee by good witness. I am a wise fellow; and which is more, an officer; and which is more, as pretty a piece of flesh as any is in Messina. . . . Bring him away. O that I had been writ down an ass! (IV.ii.73-86)

The humor in the substitution of "suspect" for "respect," "piety" for "impiety," is itself a sign of insufficient control over the process of signification; but this failure of control becomes most explicit and most humorous in the play with the word and concept "ass" and the application of that word to Dogberry.

Again a contrast with Bottom is instructive. In keeping with the codes of *A Midsummer Night's Dream*, Bottom is turned literally (or should we say, "theatrically," as part of the show) into an ass. Here, in order to bring out the analogous asininity of Dogberry, a linguistic rather than a theatrical code is invoked. In both plays, too, an ironic truth is discovered in asininity, in *A Midsummer Night's Dream* as a result of Bottom's dream (I am thinking of the underlying sense of value, of concord generated out of discord, that ultimately emerges from his dream and his hilariously confused discourse about it); in *Much Ado* as a result of the success of Dogberry's investigation. In the speech under discussion, Dogberry's syntax and the oppositions he creates ("I am an ass . . . I am a wise fellow"), leave us momentarily uncertain whether he truly understands the word "ass." We know he does, but the syntax works against our accepting the fact—"yet forget not that I am an ass." Alternatively, one could say that the word Dogberry misunderstands in "am"; he uses it as if it could have only one kind of locutionary force, or only one tone (as in "So I'm an ass, am I?") or one meaning ("he says I am"). Just as we have to supply the right word in order to get the humor of "Dost thou not suspect my place," so we have to supply the right construction in the sentences that follow. In order to laugh, we have to remind ourselves of what Dogberry "really" means, and at the same time be aware of the appropriateness of what he actually says. Hence the simple correlation, ass-Dogberry, is complicated by a series of interpretative interventions on our part, a series which goes something like this: he is saying he's an ass; he doesn't mean what he says; this is not because he doesn't understand the word "ass" or the word "am," but because he lacks the linguistic power to achieve control over his meaning; nevertheless, what he is saying is *true;* in fact saying it shows him to be an ass. Thus the process of signification itself, so crucial to this play, is brought into humorous relief, exactly as in *A Midsummer Night's Dream* the process of dramatic representation is highlighted by Bottom's transformations.

The distinction between spoken and written language is another of Dogberry's concerns. The exaggerated respect of the unlettered for the written word is part of what is behind Dogberry's desire to be *written*. But beyond that, he alludes to the primacy of writing in the law, and by extension in culture in general. "It is written" is the mark of cultural validity. To become part of a text is to become official; to be writ down an ass would, ironically, fix Dogberry, making him an ass for all time. This, of course, is exactly what Shakespeare has done, though in a slightly different sense than that Dogberry has in mind when he seeks his own textualization.

The problem of the transference of messages is raised

most cunningly within the play in the scene in which Dogberry comes with his report to Leonato just before the wedding. The audience cannot help feeling tantalized here, knowing the importance of Dogberry's message and yet becoming increasingly aware of the fact that Dogberry does not realize its importance, and is probably ignorant of what the real crime, and hence the real message, is. As we watch, we begin to realize that he will not be able to get the message across to Leonato in time to prevent the breaking of the nuptial—except by chance, through some random statement that Leonato will suddenly be able to perceive as significant. But the more Dogberry rambles on, the more likely Leonato is to dismiss him; as an audience we are thus caught in a squeeze, knowing that Dogberry has to be allowed to ramble in order to stumble into revealing the crime and yet realizing that Dogberry's vice of rambling is likely to lead to his quick dismissal. Wanting the message to come through, we are yet caught between the logic of that desire and our enjoyment of the comedy of misinterpretation. The difficulty of getting the message across thus enters directly into our response—we are teased, desiring the discovery and resisting it at once.

SOURCES FOR FURTHER STUDY

Literary Commentary

Allen, John A. "Dogberry." *Shakespeare Quarterly* XXIV, No. 1 (Winter 1973): 35-53
> Emphasizes the important role played by Dogberry in *Much Ado*. The critic holds that Dogberry is at the pivot point of dramatic action in the play, and is far more than simply a figure of fun.

Barish, Jonas A. Barish. "Pattern and Purpose in the Prose of *Much Ado about Nothing*." *Rice University Studies, Renaissance Studies* 60, No. 2 (Spring 1974): 19-30.
> Illustrates how Shakespeare varies and manipulates the word patterns in *Much Ado* to imply differing uses of these patterns and differing attitudes toward them, to make them active elements in the play's progress.

Branagh, Kenneth. Introduction to *Much Ado about Nothing*, by William Shakespeare, pp. vi-xvi. New York: W. W. Norton & Co., 1993.
> Concerns the question, "Why film *Much Ado about Nothing*?"—to which Branagh replies that "it speaks loudly and gloriously about love, one of humankind's permanent obsessions. The cruelty of it, the joy of it. The question of tolerance in love and the danger of judging others. The cost of the ambiguous maturity that people like Hero and Claudio enjoy. The loss of innocence; the power of lust; our obsession with sex

and the flesh. The persistent presense of sheer, unmotivated evil in the world as provided by the Iago prototype Don John."

Hartley, Lodwick. "Claudio and the Unmerry War." *College English* 26, No. 8 (May 1965): 609-14.
> Intriguing study of how Claudio, unlike Benedick, fails in the skill of turning easily from soldier to lover and back, in tune with the courtly tradition. Instead, he is simply an unimaginative soldier, uncomfortable in the "merry war" of love.

Hays, Janice. "Those 'Soft and Delicate Desires': *Much Ado* and the Distrust of Women," in *The Woman's Part: Feminist Criticism of Shakespeare*, edited by Carolyn Ruth Swift Lenz, Gayle Greene, and Carol Thomas Neely, pp. 79-99. Urbana: University of Illinois Press, 1980.
> Examines *Much Ado* for its treatment of what Hays calls a theme addressed several times in Shakespeare's plays: the sexual distrust of women, and their subsequent testing and vindication.

Hockey, Dorothy C. "Notes Notes, Forsooth. . . ." In *Shakespeare Quarterly*, Vol. VIII, No. 3 (Summer 1957): 353-58.
> Finds in the play's title a clue to understanding the apparent "inartistic disharmony" in *Much Ado*. Observing that commentators have long taken for granted Richard Grant White's suggestion that *nothing* and *noting* (or eavesdropping) constitute an Elizabethan pun, Hockey demonstrates that the key to the play's thematic unity lies in connoting *noting* with *observation*. "We note a situation; we take note of a situation—we see and hear, then judge and act accordingly," she writes. "*Much Ado* is a comedy of mis-noting in this common sense," being a play having much to do with human frailty: "the inability to observe, judge, and act sensibly."

Knight, G. Wilson. "The Romantic Comedies." In *The Shakespearian Tempest*, 1932. Reprint. New York: Oxford University Press, 1940, pp. 75-168.
> Draws attention to the play's complex patterns of imagery. Knight especially notes recurring references to birds, "sweet nature," music, and dance, which he claims are closely bound with Shakespeare's treatment of love in the play, and references to "fierce beasts," darkness, and foul weather, which provide a contrasting mood.

Leggatt, Alexander. "*Much Ado about Nothing*." In his *Shakespeare's Comedy of Love*, pp. 151-83. London and New York: Methuen and Co., 1974.
> Demonstrates that in *Much Ado* Shakespeare attempted to combine the "range and fluidity" of *The Merchant of Venice* with the "harmony of disparate elements" that distinguishes *A Midsummer Night's Dream*.

Lewalski, B. K. "Love, Appearance and Reality: Much

Ado about Something." *Studies in English Literature, 1500-1900* VIII, No. 2 (Spring 1968): 235-51.

Reviews the influence of Neoplatonic and Christian concepts on Shakespeare's treatment in this comedy of the problem of appearance versus reality, and of love's ability to distinguish between the two and stimulate a heightened awareness in individuals. Lewalski also compares the lovers in *Much Ado* with those who appear in Baldassare Castiglione's *The Courtier.*

Pettet, E. C. "Shakespeare's Detachment from Romance." In his *Shakespeare and the Romance Tradition*, pp. 101-35. Reprint. 1949. Brooklyn, N.Y.: Haskell House Publishers, 1976.

Argues that *Much Ado* reflects Shakespeare's growing dissatisfaction with the traditional formulae for romantic comedy. Pettet regards the dominance of the Beatrice-Benedick "entanglement" over the Hero-Claudio story as the most telling sign of Shakespeare's shift in interest away from the love romance."

Rowse, A. L. "*Much Ado about Nothing, 1599.*" In *Prefaces to Shakespeare's Plays*, pp. 126-31. London: Orbis, 1984.

Focuses primarily upon the main characters—Beatrice and Benedick, Hero and Claudio, Dogberry and Verges, and Don John—and Shakespeare's use of source material. Rowse deems *Much Ado* "a prime example of Shakespeare's comedy according to his specification: the ingredients—romance, the comedy of high life counterpointed by that of low life, courtly sophistication contrasted with rustic simplicity. The grandees were to be laughed with, the people to be laughed at."

Taylor, Michael. "Much Ado About Nothing': The Individual in Society." *Essays in Criticism* XXIII, No. 2 (April 1973): 146-53.

Addresses the theme of the out-of-balance self-image in *Much Ado*, a work in which the "forces of social stability ally themselves to bring about the comic defeat of the rebellious spirit." This rebellious spirit, claims the critic, is personified by Don John: a figure similar in some ways to John Milton's Satan (in *Paradise Lost*), whose insistence upon self-autonomy is so complete that he is only in his element among "toadies and parasites like Conrade and Borachio." Taylor demonstrates how such a rebellious spirit is thwarted in its self-centered desires.

Media Adaptations

Much Ado about Nothing. International Film Bureau, 1974.

Educational video which offers performances of two scenes from the play: Benedick's and Beatrice's declarations of mutual love, and Benedick's attempts to write a sonnet. Distributed by International Film Bureau, Inc. 12 minutes.

Much Ado about Nothing. BBC, 198?

Television adaptation of *Much Ado* and part of the series "The Shakespeare Plays." Distributed by Ambrose Video Publishing, Inc.

Much Ado about Nothing. Renaissance Films, 1993.

Motion picture version of the comedy, starring Kenneth Branagh, Emma Thompson, Denzel Washington, Michael Keaton, and Keanu Reeves. Distributed by Columbia Tristar Home Video. 110 minutes.

RICHARD III

INTRODUCTION

Although *Richard III* was first published in 1597, most scholars believe that this play about the rise and fall of a wicked king was written several years earlier, probably in 1592 or 1593, and first performed shortly afterward. Evidence shows that it was popular from the beginning: The Elizabethan actor Richard Burbage achieved distinction playing Richard III, and the character's final line—"A horse! A horse! My kingdom for a horse!"—was already famous by the early 1600s when Richard Corbet (1618 or 1621) wrote a poem about the play. It is also believed that Elizabethan audiences would have appreciated the patriotic speech given by Richmond (who becomes King Henry VII) in the last act.

Early critical assessment of *Richard III* was mixed. Sir William Cornwallis (1600) and William Winstanley (1660), for example, objected to Shakespeare's portrayal of King Richard as "a monster." In contrast, poet John Milton (1650) argued that the character in the play was "true to his historical counterpart." Today, most scholars contend that Shakespeare based the drama and its characters primarily on Edward Hall's *The Union of the Two Noble and Illustre Famelies of Lancastre and Yorke* (1548)—a work that relies both on fact and fiction to tell the history of King Richard III's family (the House of York) and its long power struggle (known as the Wars of the Roses) with King Henry VII's family (the House of Lancaster). A secondary source was probably Raphael Holinshed's *Chronicles of England, Scotland, and Ireland* (1587). In turn, each of these works was based upon Thomas More's witty and ironic *Historie of King Richard the Thirde* (published around 1513). In this account, More used a dry, almost humorous tone to describe Richard as hunchbacked, tyrannical, and evil.

Shakespeare's play varies from its sources in numerous ways but two are of particular importance: First, although Shakespeare borrowed Thomas More's ironic narrative tone, he placed it in Richard's mouth, so that the character becomes a complex, semicomical villain who laughs at himself and others even while he is plotting to do harm.

Richard III also functions as a sequel to Shakespeare's trilogy of plays—*Henry VI*, parts one, two, and three—which brings us to the second of Shakespeare's significant modifications: In *Richard III*, Margaret, widow to Henry VI (a Lancastrian king who was murdered by Richard in *Henry VI*, part three), remains in England where the play is set rather than sailing home to France as she did according to history. Onstage, Margaret voices her opinion on the action in the play, and predicts doom and misery as her revenge on Richard and his supporters. In doing so, Margaret serves the same function in the drama as a chorus would. Individual choric figures or a chorus are sometimes used to describe events which occur before the beginning of the play or to comment on the action of the play as it unfolds.

Richard's complexity and Margaret's presence have generated much critical discussion regarding the play's themes of sin and divine retribution. Richard's coronation comes toward the end of a period of bloody civil strife known as the Wars of the Roses, and some critics argue that his wickedness functions as divine punishment against the warring parties, as well as a method of cleansing England for a new era of peace. Other critics have focused on Margaret and her importance to the development of the play, as her curses on each guilty character are fulfilled.

PRINCIPAL CHARACTERS

(in order of appearance)

Richard: Duke of Gloucester, later King Richard III. He is the title character of the play as well as the scheming younger brother of King Edward IV and George, Duke of Clarence. (*See* **Richard** *in the* **CHARACTER STUDIES** *section.*)

George, Duke of Clarence: Brother of King Edward IV and Richard. He is imprisoned in the Tower of London after Richard turns the king against him, and is assassinated on orders from Richard after the king decides to pardon him.

Sir Robert Brakenbury: Lieutenant of the Tower of London. He is in charge of the Tower prison, where first the Duke of Clarence and later King Edward's two young sons are imprisoned.

Lord Hastings: Lord Chamberlain. He is assassinated for refusing to support Richard's ambition to be king.

Lady Anne: Widow of Edward, Prince of Wales, who was the son and heir of King Henry VI. She hates

Richard for murdering her husband and father-in-law, but Richard charms her into marrying him. As Richard's unhappy queen, she dies after he tires of her. (*See* **Lady Anne** *in the* **CHARACTER STUDIES** *section.*)

Queen Elizabeth: Formerly Lady Grey, she is the wife of King Edward IV and mother of Edward, Prince of Wales, and Richard, Duke of York, the king's two young heirs. She hates Richard for murdering her brother and her sons; nevertheless, he convinces her to consider him as a suitor in marriage to her daughter Elizabeth. (*See* **Queen Elizabeth** *in the* **CHARACTER STUDIES** *section.*)

Earl Rivers: Queen Elizabeth's brother. Richard has him assassinated.

Lord Grey: Queen Elizabeth's son from a previous marriage. Richard has him assassinated.

Marquess of Dorset: Queen Elizabeth's son from a previous marriage. He joins the Earl of Richmond's side after Richard is crowned king.

Duke of Buckingham: Richard's co-conspirator. He helps Richard become king, but falls out of favor when he balks at murdering Edward IV's two young heirs. He joins the Earl of Richmond's side against Richard, but is later captured and executed. (*See the* **Duke of Buckingham** *in the* **CHARACTER STUDIES** *section.*)

Stanley, the Earl of Derby: He is the Earl of Richmond's stepfather, and therefore distrusted by Richard, who takes Stanley's son, George, as hostage, hoping thus to insure that Stanley won't dare to fight on Richmond's side.

Margaret: Widow of King Henry VI who was murdered by Richard. She predicts revenge for herself and destruction for King Edward IV's family and supporters. (*See* **Margaret** *in the* **CHARACTER STUDIES** *section.*)

Sir William Catesby: A supporter of Richard. He is sent to find out whether Hastings will support Richard's coronation.

King Edward IV: King of England. The king is ill at the beginning of the play, and dies shortly after he is told that his pardon for his brother the Duke of Clarence came too late to save him from execution.

Duchess of York: Mother of King Edward IV, George the Duke of Clarence, and Richard. She mourns the deaths of King Edward and Clarence, and curses Richard for his wickedness.

Richard, Duke of York: The younger son of King Edward IV and thus second in line to the throne when the king dies. He is imprisoned in the Tower by his ambitious uncle Richard, Duke of Gloucester, who later has him murdered.

Edward, Prince of Wales: Young son and heir of King Edward IV. He is imprisoned in the Tower of London by his ambitious uncle Richard of Gloucester, along with his younger brother, the Duke of York. Later both children are murdered on Richard's orders.

Lord Mayor of London: The leader of the citizens of London. After the death of King Edward IV, Richard and Buckingham fool the Lord Mayor into believing that Richard deserves to become king.

Sir James Tyrrel: An assassin. He is recruited by Richard to arrange for the murder of the two young heirs of Edward IV.

Henry, Earl of Richmond: Later, King Henry VII. He is a Lancastrian who raises an army to defeat King Richard III and his reign of tyranny.

Ghost of Edward, Prince of Wales, son of Henry VI: One of Richard's earlier victims. He haunts King Richard on the night before his battle with Richmond.

Ghost of King Henry VI: A Lancastrian king defeated by Richard's family, succeeded by Richard's brother King Edward IV, and murdered by Richard. His ghost (and all the other ghosts of people whom Richard has murdered) haunts Richard on the night before his battle with Richmond.

PLOT SYNOPSIS

Act I: The Wars of the Roses are for the moment over, the Yorkists have beaten the Lancastrians, and Yorkist Edward IV is now king of England. But his youngest brother, Richard of Gloucester (self-described as deformed, unfit for peace, "subtle, false, and treacherous"), decides to cause trouble. He convinces the king that their brother, George, Duke of Clarence, is dangerous and should be jailed. Richard then tells Clarence that Queen Elizabeth, Edward IV's wife, is responsible for his imprisonment. When he hears that the king is seriously ill, Richard plots to have Clarence killed so that there will be fewer encumbrances to his own succession to Edward's throne. Next, he encounters Lady Anne (widow of Henry VI's son Prince Edward whom Richard and his brothers killed) mourning over the coffin of her father-in-law, Henry VI (whom Richard murdered). At first Anne curses Richard, but eventually he charms her into accepting his ring.

Later, Richard publicly accuses Queen Elizabeth of having turned the king against not only Clarence, but against himself and Lord Hastings. Margaret (widow of Henry VI) appears and curses Richard. In prison, Clarence is stabbed by Richard's hired assassins and drowned in a cask of malmsey wine.

Act II: The dying King Edward insists that the queen and her followers reconcile with Richard and his followers, and each group at least pretends to do so. When Richard announces that Clarence has been killed in his prison cell in the Tower, the king is horrified, for although he had called for Clarence's execution, he later revoked that order. Richard claims that the revocation came too late. Meanwhile, the Duchess of York mourns the death of her son Clarence, as do his two young children. The queen enters, weeping because King Edward has just died. Arrangements are made to send for his young heir, Prince Edward, so that he may be crowned king immediately. Citizens of the kingdom discuss the king's death and worry about the fate of the country. News arrives for the queen that her ally Sir Thomas Vaughan, her brother Lord Rivers, and her son Lord Grey have been imprisoned by Richard and his right-hand man, Buckingham. Fearing for their own lives, the queen and her youngest son, Richard, the Duke of York, flee to sanctuary.

Act III: Young Prince Edward arrives in London, escorted by Richard of Gloucester and Buckingham. He asks for his mother, the queen, and for his brother, the Duke of York, and is told that they "have taken sanctuary." Buckingham summons York to join Edward in London. On the pretext of keeping them safe until Edward's coronation, Richard lodges the two children in the Tower. For the moment, Richard is their Lord Protector, but he plans to usurp Edward's right and become king himself. To that end, he sends his ally Catesby to find out whether Hastings can be trusted to support him in his bid for the throne. But Hastings remains loyal to Prince Edward. Meanwhile, Rivers, Grey, and Vaughan, the queen's allies, are executed by Richard's supporters. In London, a council including Richard, Buckingham, Hastings, and Stanley meets to set the date for Edward's coronation. Without warning, Richard accuses Hastings of treason and orders his execution. Later, Richard instructs Buckingham to suggest to the Mayor and the citizens of London that the two young princes are illegitimate and thus not fit to rule England and that the former King Edward IV was immoral and illegitimate himself. Buckingham returns to report that the citizens are hesitant to endorse Richard as their king. With Buckingham's help, Richard stages a scene where he seems virtuous and unwilling to accept the crown; the citizens

are thus duped into begging him to be king.

Act IV: The Duchess of York, Queen Elizabeth, her son the Marquess of Dorset, and Anne (who is now Richard's wife) try to visit the two young princes in the Tower but are stopped by Brakenbury on orders from Richard. When Anne is called to Westminster to be crowned King Richard's queen, she goes reluctantly. The women are outraged that Richard has usurped Prince Edward's crown. Elizabeth sends her son Dorset to the Earl of Richmond where he will be safe from Richard. Now that he is king, Richard wants to be rid of the two young princes, who pose a threat to his right to rule. But when he asks Buckingham to have them killed, Buckingham hesitates. Instead, Richard recruits Tyrrel to arrange the murder. Seeking to secure his reign further, he instructs Catesby to spread the rumor that Anne is seriously ill: he plans to dispose of her so that he can marry his brother Edward's daughter Elizabeth. Later, when Richard snubs Buckingham, his former right-hand man realizes that his life is now in danger, so he flees Richard's court and joins Richmond. Tyrrel brings the news that the princes have been executed. Pleased, Richard goes to woo his brother's daughter, Elizabeth. His wife, Anne, has died, so nothing can stop him from marrying Elizabeth. Queen Elizabeth and the Duchess of York weep over the death of their loved ones at Richard's hands. Margaret appears, reminding them that her curses have thus been fulfilled. Although Queen Elizabeth is disgusted when Richard tells her he wants to marry her daughter, she agrees to speak to her daughter on his behalf. Stanley warns Richard that Richmond is on his way to England to claim the crown. Distrusting Stanley, who is Richmond's stepfather, Richard holds his son George hostage. Messengers arrive, telling Richard that rebellions are starting up against him throughout the country and that Buckingham has been captured. Richard prepares to leave for Salisbury to battle Richmond.

Act V: On the way to his execution, Buckingham repents of the evil he has done in support of Richard. Meanwhile, both Richmond and Richard arrive on Bosworth Field, and each sets up his camp. Night falls, and Richard is visited in his tent by the ghosts of those he has murdered. They curse him, condemning him to die on the battlefield. The same ghosts visit Richmond and promise him victory. Morning comes, and each of the two leaders encourages his troops before going into battle. When next we see Richard, he has lost his horse and has been fighting on foot. Richard and Richmond fight, Richard is killed, and Richmond, the victor, accepts the crown of England. As Henry VII, he promises to bring peace to the bloodied nation by marrying Edward IV's daughter Elizabeth, thus joining the House of Lancaster (red rose) with the House of York (white rose).

PRINCIPAL TOPICS

Succession

In Act II, scene iii, of *Richard III* a group of English citizens worries over what will become of the nation now that King Edward IV has died and his heir, Edward, Prince of Wales, is still a child. The citizens know that a Protector will be appointed to govern for Prince Edward until he is old enough to rule by himself. They also know that several of the child's uncles are vying with one another to be Protector, and the citizens are frightened that the inevitable power struggle will throw the country into turmoil. They have already endured chaotic years during the Wars of the Roses, as the Houses of York and Lancaster have fought back and forth for England's throne, and they long for peace and order. Unfortunately, they get Richard instead.

The question of succession, or the order according to which a person lawfully and rightfully becomes monarch, was of much concern to the citizens of England during Shakespeare's time since their aging queen—Elizabeth I—was unmarried and had no heirs. Further, although Elizabeth was England's lawful queen, she had already weathered several challenges to her power, including those from Philip II of Spain, who had sent his Armada in 1588 in hope of defeating her; and from Mary, Queen of Scots, a relative whom Elizabeth finally had to execute in 1587. Thus a play about an ambitious nobleman determined to become king was very relevant to Shakespeare's audience.

Richard is a usurper: he becomes king illegally and he knows that if he doesn't at least *appear* to be England's lawful ruler, then there will be endless challenges to his power. The string of murders which Richard commits before and after he becomes king can be seen as attempts to legitimize his rule.

Of the three brothers—King Edward IV; George, Duke of Clarence; and Richard, Duke of Gloucester—Richard is the youngest and farthest from succession to the crown. Clarence is before him and could also become Protector of Edward's heir, the Prince of Wales, should King Edward die. So when the king falls seriously ill, Richard plots to have Clarence die first—thus removing in one stroke a possible Protector and a potential claimant to the throne.

Richard's next move is to make certain that he alone becomes Protector to his nephew, the Prince of Wales. He eliminates Rivers, who is the prince's uncle on his mother's side, and also murders Lord Grey, the prince's half-brother. (The prince's remaining half-brother, the Marquess of Dorset, escapes to join the Earl of Richmond.)

Once Richard becomes unchallenged Protector, it is easier for him to take the throne for himself. He murders Hastings because that nobleman has sworn to remain loyal to Prince Edward's right to the throne. Then, by suggesting that the Prince of Wales and his younger brother, the Duke of York, are illegitimate and therefore unqualified for succession, Richard and Buckingham convince the citizens that Richard is the only one left who by lineage and virtue deserves to be king.

Even after Richard becomes king, he knows that his power is vulnerable to challenge as long as the Prince of Wales and the Duke of York remain alive; although imprisoned and thus hidden from sight, these two rightful heirs to King Edward can still serve as a rallying point for dissatisfied or ambitious subjects. So Richard adds the two young princes to his list of victims.

Still, Richard does not feel secure. He imprisons Clarence's son because that child has a better claim to the throne than he, and he marries Clarence's daughter to a commoner to destroy any possibility of royal claimants coming from that line. Finally, Richard hears that his enemy the Lancastrian Earl of Richmond intends to marry Edward IV's daughter Elizabeth and thus unite the royal families of York and Lancaster. Richard hopes to forestall this union and strengthen his own claim by marrying King Edward's daughter himself, which is why in Act IV, scene iv, he tries to convince Queen Elizabeth to consent to such a marriage.

Richard's attempts to legitimize his power through bloodshed fail when he is killed in battle by the Earl of Richmond, who begins a new line of succession—the Tudors—and is crowned Henry VII.

Language: Oaths, Curses, and Prophecies

Language is a potent weapon in *Richard III*, particularly as a source of retribution. Prophecies and curses are delivered and fulfilled. Oaths that are made but later broken cause disaster. Curses, prophecies, and false or imprudent oaths indeed occur so frequently and are so powerful in *Richard III* that they profoundly affect the play's outcome.

As early as Act I, scene iii, Margaret influences the action by cursing virtually every principal character in the play. She prays for the death of King Edward as well as his heirs and for a life of misery for Queen Elizabeth. She curses Hastings and Rivers with early death, and Richard with sleepless nights and ruin. She finishes by prophesying that Buckingham will be betrayed by Richard: "O Buckingham, take heed of yonder dog!/ Look when he fawns, he bites; and when he bites/ His venom tooth will rankle to the death." By the end of the play, nearly all of Margaret's predictions and curses have been carried out.

Ironically, many of the characters bring destruction upon themselves by reinforcing Margaret's curses with their own false oaths and self-curses. For example, in Act IV, scene iv, Richard swears to Queen Elizabeth that he loves her daughter, and he supports this oath with a self-curse that is meant to take effect if his oath proves false: "God and fortune, bar me happy hours!/ Day, yield me not thy light, nor, night, thy rest!" Richard's oath is indeed false: he does not love Elizabeth's daughter but hopes to marry her to consolidate his power. His self-curse—ruin and sleepless nights—is identical to Margaret's curse in Act I, and by the end of the play, it is fulfilled.

Dark Comedy

A persistent thread of comedy runs through *Richard III*. Since the play is mostly about treachery and vengeance the comedy it contains is appropriately dark, consisting of dramatic irony as well as parody. Some of the humor comes from Richard's self-ridicule, but much of it comes when he mocks the confidence which others mistakenly place in him.

Dramatic irony occurs when the audience understands the real significance of a character's words or actions but the character or those around him or her do not. Richard's sympathetic comments to his brother Clarence as he is being taken to prison (Act I, scene i) result in dramatic irony because we know from the start that Richard is responsible for having Clarence jailed. Dramatic irony occurs again, in Act III, scene ii, when Catesby suggests that Richard should be crowned king in lieu of the Prince of Wales, and Hastings declares: "I'll have this crown of mine cut from my shoulders/ Before I'll see the crown so foul misplac'd." We already know from Richard's conversation with Buckingham one scene earlier that Hastings will indeed lose his head if he opposes Richard. Both of these incidents are intended to make us smile—although perhaps grimly—at Richard's trickery and his victims' naïveté.

Parody is the use of exaggerated imitation to ridicule someone or something that was meant to be taken seriously. Richard mocks both himself and Anne when he parodies a preening lover in Act I, scene ii, after Anne—against all odds—accepts his ring: "I'll be at charges for a looking-glass,/ And entertain a score or two of tailors/ To study fashions to adorn my body." Part of the humor comes from Richard's ability to laugh at himself.

Richard's most triumphant parody occurs when he fools the citizens of London into petitioning him to be their king. By imitating a holy man (which he most certainly is not) and appearing reluctant to accept the crown, Richard succeeds in getting the power he wants.

CHARACTER STUDIES

Richard

The opening couplet in *Richard III* ("Now is the winter of our discontent/ Made glorious summer by this son of York") and the final line of Act V, scene iv ("A horse! A horse! My kingdom for a horse!"), are probably the most famous lines in the play; appropriately, they are also the first and the last words that Richard speaks. Richard is the energizing force of the play. He is responsible for most of the play's dark comedy—which usually occurs when he is mocking himself or ridiculing his victims. He has been called a Machiavel (one who views politics as amoral and that any means, however unscrupulous, can justifiably be used to achieve political power) because of his ruthless drive for power. Almost as soon as he appears onstage he tells us that he is "determined to prove a villain" and mentions the traps he is setting against his own brothers (Act I, scene i). He describes himself as "deform'd, unfinish'd," and so unpleasant to look at that dogs bark at him, and he blames his wickedness on his physical appearance.

Richard does not announce his intention to become king until Act III, scene i, but his plots and murders lead in that direction, and in Act IV he is crowned. A focus of debate has been whether Richard controls events or whether he is simply a divine instrument meant to clear England of the corruption of civil war so that the country can begin afresh. In either case, toward the end of the play Richard has lost his sense of humor and control. "I have not that alacrity of spirit/ Nor cheer of mind that I was wont to have," he declares in Act V, scene iii. The night before battle, he is tormented by sleeplessness and haunted by the ghosts of those he has murdered. The following day he is himself killed in battle by Richmond.

A significant source of controversy is the apparent contradiction between Richard's monstrous behavior and his continuing attractiveness to audiences. One argument suggests that he is not meant to be a realistic character but a melodramatic, comic villain whose extreme antics make us laugh. A somewhat different view is that Richard's witty dialogue and his ability to mock himself make him appealing.

It has also been argued that—with the exception of

the two young princes—Richard's victims are not as innocent as they seem but are instead hypocrites who know they are being used and who try unsuccessfully to use Richard. According to this view, Richard is simply more clever than is anyone else in the play at getting what he wants.

Lady Anne—and the Theme of Wooing

Anne first appears in Act I, scene ii, sadly following the coffin of her father-in-law, Henry VI. She laments King Henry's death and curses his murderer, Richard. She also places a curse on any woman who would marry Richard—thus, ironically—cursing herself.

When Richard enters and tries to take over the funeral procession, Anne reacts in disgust. She calls him a "foul devil" and begs for lightning to strike him dead. But Richard is persistent: he flatters Anne and makes excuses for his crimes, claiming he loves her and inviting her to kill him with his own sword. Eventually, Anne relents. "I would I knew thy heart," she tells him, and agrees to accept his ring.

Some critics acknowledge how implausible this scene may appear, but attempt to show the means by which Richard successfully woos Anne into becoming his wife. Richard carefully listens to Anne, observing her changing emotions. He adapts his arguments to these changes, eventually winning her sympathy. Richard plays upon Anne's grief and skillfully manipulates her. Some critics argue that, in addition to being in mourning, Anne is susceptible to Richard's advances simply because she behaves as women were expected to do at the time.

When Anne appears for the next and last time (Act IV, scene i), she has married Richard and is miserable. She recalls the curse she had made on any woman "mad" enough to become his wife and bitterly regrets that "Within so small a time, my woman's heart/ Grossly grew captive to his honey words,/ And prov'd the subject of mine own soul's curse." When called away to Westminster to be crowned Richard's queen, she goes unwillingly. In Act IV, scene ii, Richard starts the rumor that Anne is seriously ill. In Act IV, scene iii, he briefly mentions that she has died.

Traditionally, Anne has been regarded as weak and vain for being fooled by Richard's flattery. More recently, it has been pointed out that Richard approaches her when she is grieving, so she is vulnerable to his persistent demands. It has also been suggested that since Richard is brother to the king, Anne certainly cannot kill him and has little choice but to accept him. Although her appearance in the play is fairly brief, Anne's role is important for providing us with an early and revealing glimpse of Richard's cunning and persuasiveness.

Queen Elizabeth

Queen Elizabeth's presence in three out of the play's five acts spotlights Richard's ruthless quest for the throne, for as the king's wife and the mother of the king's heir, she has a direct interest in whether or not Richard will succeed. As early as Act I, scene i, he is spreading lies about her influence over the king, and it is clear that there are two factions at court—Elizabeth with her relatives and supporters, and Richard with his henchman Buckingham. The queen first enters in Act I, scene iii, voicing her fears about the king's illness to her brother, Lord Rivers, and her two older sons, Lord Grey and the Marquess of Dorset. She knows that if the king dies, her young son Edward, Prince of Wales and heir to the throne, could be placed under Richard's protection, "a man," she tells her sons and brother, "that loves not me, nor none of you"; indeed, Richard appears shortly afterward and insults her.

In Act II, scene i, Elizabeth and her followers reconcile with Richard at the king's request. By Act II, scene ii, the king is dead, and the distraught queen agrees with Richard that the Prince of Wales should be brought to court. By Act II, scene iv, the queen's situation has worsened, for Richard has imprisoned Rivers and Grey, and holds the Prince of Wales in his custody. Elizabeth realizes that Richard now controls the government: "Ay me! . . ." she cries, "Insulting tyranny begins to jut/ Upon the innocent and aweless throne." She flees with her youngest son, York, into sanctuary, but Richard and Buckingham order York to be brought back to London to "lodge" in the Tower with the Prince of Wales (Act III, scene i), and in Act IV, scene, i, Elizabeth is barred from visiting them.

Elizabeth's final and most famous encounter with Richard occurs in Act IV, scene iv, when she apparently agrees to convince her daughter to marry him. This scene has been described as a battle of wits between Richard and Elizabeth, and it is not clear who wins. It has been pointed out that Elizabeth never explicitly states that she will tell her daughter to marry him. Instead she asks a question, "Shall I go win my daughter to thy will?" and ends by telling Richard, "I go. Write to me very shortly,/ And you shall understand from me her mind." Later in Act IV, scene v, we are told that she has promised her daughter to the Earl of Richmond. Has Elizabeth been weak-willed and inconsistent, or has she finally outwitted Richard?

Duke of Buckingham

As Richard's co-conspirator, Buckingham's role in the

play is an important one. Richard calls him "My other self" (Act II, scene ii), and uses him as an advisor and a spy.

Buckingham's first appearances in the play (Act I, scene iii and Act II, scene i) give no indication that he is anything other than a minor character; at this point, Richard refers to him merely as one of several "simple gulls" or fools whom he is deceiving (Act I, scene iii). But once King Edward dies, Buckingham's role gains prominence. In Act II, scene ii, he schemes to place the king's heir (Edward, Prince of Wales) in Richard's power by fetching the child to London without the protection of his mother or her followers. When Elizabeth flees to sanctuary with her youngest son (the Duke of York), Buckingham takes it upon himself to order the child back to London (Act III, scene i).

In Act III, scene v, Buckingham reveals that he is nearly as good an actor as Richard is. "I can counterfeit the deep tragedian," he says, as he and Richard prepare to fool the Mayor of London into believing that Richard is a good man who has been cruelly betrayed. "Ghastly looks/ Are at my service like enforced smiles," he insists, "And both are ready in their offices/ At any time to grace my stratagems." He proves his point well in scene vii when he helps Richard stage so convincing a performance of humility and royal worth that the citizens of London beg Richard to become king.

Buckingham, however, falls short of being Richard's "other self" when it comes to murdering the two young princes. In Act IV, scene ii, Richard, newly crowned, first hints then bluntly states that he wants Edward's heirs killed. Buckingham's reply—"Your Grace may do your pleasure"—doesn't satisfy Richard, who wants an accomplice to a crime this heinous. Buckingham's next attempt to postpone making a decision only infuriates Richard, who mutters "High-reaching Buckingham grows circumspect." Later, when Buckingham tries to bargain with Richard over the princes' murder, the king rejects him.

Buckingham's hesitation costs him his life. Although like Richard, he has been described as a Machiavel, ultimately he is no match for his deceitful king.

Margaret

Margaret, the bitter Lancastrian queen and widow of Henry VI, appears in only two scenes, but her influence is felt throughout the play. She first enters in Act I, scene iii, speaking—as she often does—in asides. An aside occurs when a character talks to the audience and is not overheard by the other characters onstage. In this instance, Margaret comments to the audience on the bickering occurring between her Yorkist enemies—Elizabeth and her followers on one side, and Richard

and his on the other. When Margaret finally speaks directly to these characters, she curses them, foretelling misery to Elizabeth and death to Rivers and Hastings, but reserving her most virulent warnings for Richard.

By the time she appears again (Act IV, scene iv) most of her prophecies have been fulfilled. She exults in her revenge and teaches Elizabeth and the Duchess of York how to curse Richard, who has become, as Margaret had predicted, an enemy to all of them.

When *Richard III* is produced onstage, Margaret's role is frequently left out on grounds that the language in her scenes is too formal and repetitive to sound relevant to modern audiences. On the other hand, Margaret provides useful background information on Richard's grim quest for power. Her predictions and ghostlike presence ("Here in these confines slily have I lurk'd/ To watch the waning of mine enemies." Act IV, scene iv) reinforce the theme of divine retribution in the play, as do the characters' recollections of her prophecies when they are led to their executions: in Act III, scene iv, for example, Hastings laments, "O Margaret, Margaret, now thy heavy curse/ Is lighted on poor Hastings' wretched head." Likewise Buckingham in Act V, scene i, cries "Thus Margaret's curse falls heavy on my neck."

CONCLUSION

In *Richard III*, the role of Richard is the central focus: critics debate whether this ruthless, compellingly witty character has control of the people and events around him or whether he functions instead as an instrument of divine retribution. But there are other issues that scholars examine with equal care in this rich, early play of Shakespeare's. Of interest, for example, is the play's imagery (in particular the vivid pictures presented in Clarence's undersea dream the night before his murder), as well as the playwright's inclusion of Margaret as an agent of prophecy and the general attitude toward women expressed in the play. All in all, *Richard III* continues to be one of Shakespeare's most popular plays, in large measure thanks to Richard's dazzling wickedness.

(See also *Shakespearean Criticism*, Vols. 8 and 14)

OVERVIEWS

E. M. W. Tillyard

SOURCE: "Richard III," in *Shakespeare's History Plays*, Chatto & Windus, 1944, pp. 198-214.

. . . I [have] put the theme of *Richard III* partly in terms of God's intentions. As it is usual to put it in terms of Richard's character, I had better expand my thesis. But it is a delicate matter. People are so fond of Shakespeare that they are desperately anxious to have him of their own way of thinking. A reviewer in the *New Statesman* was greatly upset when I quoted a passage in *Measure for Measure* as evidence that Shakespeare was familiar with the doctrine of the Atonement: he at once assumed I meant that Shakespeare believed the doctrine personally. And if one were to say that in *Richard III* Shakespeare pictures England restored to order through God's grace, one gravely risks being lauded or execrated for attributing to Shakespeare personally the full doctrine of prevenient Grace according to Calvin. When therefore I say that *Richard III* is a very religious play, I want to be understood as speaking of the play and not of Shakespeare. For the purposes of the tetralogy [Shakespeare's four plays: *1 Henry VI, 2 Henry VI, 3 Henry VI,* and *Richard III*] and most obviously for this play Shakespeare accepted the prevalent belief that God had guided England into her haven of Tudor prosperity. And he had accepted it with his whole heart, as later he did not accept the supposed siding of God with the English against the French he so loudly proclaimed in *Henry V*. There is no atom of doubt in Richmond's prayer before he falls asleep in his tent at Bosworth. He is utterly God's minister, as he claims to be:

> O Thou, whose captain I account myself,
> Look on my forces with a gracious eye;
> Put in their hands thy bruising irons of
>   wrath,
> That they may crush down with a heavy fall
> The usurping helmets of our adversaries.
> Make us thy ministers of chastisement,
> That we may praise thee in the victory.
> To thee I do commend my watchful soul,
> Ere I let fall the windows of mine eyes.
> Sleeping and waking, O, defend me still.
>
> [V.iii. 108-17]

In the same spirit Shakespeare drops hints of a divine purpose in the mass of vengeance that forms the substance of the play, of a direction in the seemingly endless concatenation of crime and punishment. In *3 Henry VI*, York at Wakefield, Young Clifford at Towton, Warwick at Barnet, and Prince Edward at Tewkesbury die defiantly without remorse. In *Richard III* the

great men die acknowledging their guilt and thinking of others. Clarence, before his murderers enter, says:

> O God, if my deep prayers cannot appease
>   thee,
> But thou wilt be aveng'd on my misdeeds,
> Yet execute thy wrath in me alone:
> O spare my guiltless wife and my poor
>   children.
>
> [I.iv. 69-72]

Edward IV, near his death, repents his having signed a warrant for Clarence's death and while blaming others for not having restrained him blames himself the most:

> But for my brother not a man would speak,
> Nor I, ungracious, speak unto myself
> For him, poor soul. The proudest of you all
> Have been beholding to him in his life;
> Yet none of you would once plead for his
>   life.
> O God, I fear thy justice will take hold
> On me and you and mine and yours for this.
>
> [II.i.126-32]

The Duchess of York, who once rejoiced when her family prospered, now in humility acknowledges the futility of ambitious strife.

> Accursed and unquiet wrangling days,
> How many of you have mine eyes beheld.
> My husband lost his life to get the crown,
> And often up and down my sons were
>   toss'd,
> For me to joy and weep their gain and loss.
> And, being seated and domestic broils
> Clean overblown, themselves, the
>   conquerors,
> Make war upon themselves: blood against
>   blood,
> Self against self. O, preposterous
> And frantic outrage, end thy damned spleen.
>
> [II.iv. 55—64]

All this penitence cannot be fortuitous; and it is the prelude to forgiveness and regeneration. But the full religious temper of the play only comes out in the two great scenes in the last third of the play: the lamentations of the three queens after Richard has murdered the princes in the Tower, and the ghosts appearing to Richard and Richmond before Bosworth. These are both extreme and splendid examples of the formal style which . . . should be considered the norm rather than the exception in the tetralogy. Both scenes are ritual and incantatory to a high degree, suggesting an ecclesiastical context; both are implicitly or explicitly pious; and both are archaic, suggesting the prevalent piety of the Middle Ages. The incantation takes the form not only of an obvious antiphony, like Queen Margaret's balancing of her own woes with Queen Elizabeth's—

> I had an Edward, till a Richard kill'd him;
> I had a Harry, till a Richard kill'd him;
> Thou hadst an Edward, till a Richard kill'd him;
> Thou hadst a Richard, till a Richard kill'd him—
>
> [IV.iv.40-3]

but of a more complicated balance of rhythmic phrases and of varied repetitions, as in the Duchess of York's self-address:

> Blind sight, dead life, poor mortal living ghost,
> Woe's scene, world's shame, grave's due by life usurp'd,
> Brief abstract and record of tedious days,
> Rest thy unrest on England's lawful earth,
> Unlawfully made drunk with innocents' blood.
>
> [IV.iv.25-9]

The piety in this scene is implicit rather than explicit, and the two passages just quoted will illustrate it. Queen Margaret is thinking of Richard's crimes and the vengeance he will incur, yet by repeating a phrase in four successive lines she expresses unconsciously the new and fruitful unity that God is to construct out of Richard's impartial wickedness. The Duchess's mention of England's *lawful* earth is in itself an assertion of the principle of order and an implicit prayer for a juster age. The medievalism and its accompanying suggestion of piety comes out in Margaret's great speech to Elizabeth, itself an example of incantation and antiphony. She refers to her prophecies made earlier in the play and now fulfilled.

> I call'd thee then vain flourish of my fortune.
> I call'd thee then poor shadow, painted queen;
> The presentation of but what I was;
> The flattering index of a direful pageant;
> One heav'd a-high, to be hurl'd down below;
> A mother only mock'd with two sweet babes;
> A dream of what thou wert, a breath, a bubble,
> A sign of dignity, a garish flag,
> To be the aim of every dangerous shot;
> A queen in jest, only to fill the scene.
> Where is thy husband now? where be thy brothers?
> Where are thy children? wherein dost thou joy?

> Who sues to thee and cries 'God save the queen'?
> Where be the bending peers that flatter'd thee?
> Where be the thronging troops that follow'd thee?—
> Decline all this and see what now thou art:
> For happy wife a most distressed widow;
> For joyful mother one that wails the name;
> For queen a very caitiff crown'd with care;
> For one being sued to one that humbly sues;
> For one that scorn'd at me now scorn'd of me;
> For one being fear'd of all now fearing one;
> For one commanding all obey'd of none.
> Thus hath the course of justice wheel'd about
> And left thee but a very prey to time;
> Having no more but thought of what thou wert
> To torture thee the more being what thou art.
>
> [IV.iv.82-108]

The speech takes us back to the Middle Ages; to the laments of the fickleness of fortune, to the constant burden of *Ubi sunt* [Where are (those who were before us?)], and to the consequent contempt of the world. . . .

The scene of the ghosts of those Richard has murdered follows immediately on Richmond's solemn prayer, quoted above. It is essentially of the Morality pattern. [A Morality was a medieval play depicting the virtues and vices.] Respublica [the State] or England is the hero, invisible yet present, contended for by the forces of heaven represented by Richmond and of hell represented by Richard. Each ghost as it were gives his vote for heaven, Lancaster and York being at last unanimous. And God is above, surveying the event. The medieval strain is continued when Richard, awaking in terror, rants like Judas in the Miracle Plays [medieval religious plays] about to hang himself. The scene, like Richmond's prayer and his last speech, is very moving. It may have issued from Shakespeare's official self, from Shakespeare identifying himself with an obvious and simple phase of public opinion. But the identification is entirely sincere, and the opinion strong and right, to be shared alike by the most sophisticated and the humblest. The scene becomes almost an act of common worship, ending with Buckingham's assertion:

> God and good angels fight on Richmond's side;
> And Richard falls in height of all his pride.
>
> [V.iii. 176-7]

And just because he participates so fully, because he

holds nothing of himself back, Shakespeare can be at his best, can give to his language the maximum of personal differentiation of which he was at the time capable. This differentiation he achieves, not as in some of the other great places in the play by surprising conjunctions of words or new imagery but by subtle musical variations within a context of incantation. He seems indeed to have learnt and applied the lessons of [the Elizabethan poet Edmund] Spenser. At the same time the substance of what each ghost says is entirely appropriate to the speaker and by referring back to past events in the tetralogy serves to reinforce the structure of the plot. There may be better scenes in Shakespeare, but of these none is like this one. Of its kind it is the best.

That the play's main end is to show the working out of God's will in English history does not detract from the importance of Richard in the process and from his dominance as a character. And it is through his dominance that he is able to be the instrument of God's ends. Whereas the sins of other men had merely bred more sins, Richard's are so vast that they are absorptive, not contagious. He is the great ulcer of the body politic into which all its impurity is drained and against which all the members of the body politic are united. It is no longer a case of limb fighting limb but of the war of the whole organism against an ill which has now ceased to be organic. The metaphor of poison is constantly applied to Richard, and that of beast, as if here were something to be excluded from the human norm. Queen Margaret unites the two metaphors when she calls him "that poisonous bunch-back'd toad" and that "bottled spider," the spider being proverbially venomous.

In making Richard thus subservient to a greater scheme I do not deny that for many years now the main attraction of the play has actually been Richard's character in itself, like Satan's in [John Milton's] *Paradise Lost.* Nor was this attraction lacking from the first. Indeed it antedates the play, going back to More's *History of Richard III,* which was inserted with trifling modifications into Hall's chronicle and repeated thence by Holinshed. Shakespeare in singling out Richard III and later Henry V for special treatment as characters is not therefore departing from tradition but following closely his own main teacher of the philosophy of history, Hall.

One would like to think of Shakespeare hailing More (through Hall) as a kindred spirit and using his charm as an inspiration. Actually, though Shakespeare accepts More's heightened picture of Richard as an arch-villain, he can very coolly reject the episodes of which More made much. He quite omits Edward's wonderful speech on his deathbed and the most moving scene of all, the Archbishop persuading Queen Elizabeth to give up her younger son out of sanctuary. It may be however that More's abundant sense of humour encouraged Shakespeare to add to Richard that touch of comedy that makes him so distinguished a villain. His aside after he has gone on his knees to ask his mother's blessing is very much in More's spirit:

> *Duch.* God bless thee, and put meekness in
> thy mind,
>   Love, charity, obedience, and true duty.
> *Rich.* Amen; and make me die a good old
> man.
>   That is the butt-end of a mother's blessing:
>   I marvel why her grace did leave it out.
>   [II.ii. 107-11]

A number of people have written well on the character of Richard: in one place or another all has been said that need be said. It remains now to think less in terms of alternatives and to include more than is usually done in Richard's character, even at the sacrifice of consistency. [Essayist Charles] Lamb, for instance, who in his brief references raised most of the pertinent questions, wants to exclude the melodramatic side:

> Shakespeare has not made Richard so black a monster as is supposed. Wherever he is monstrous, it was to conform to vulgar opinion. But he is generally a Man.

Actually Shakespeare was already at one with vulgar opinion and willingly makes him a monster. But only in some places; in others he keeps him human. Similarly we need not choose between Richard the psychological study in compensation for physical disability and Richard the embodiment of sheer demonic will, for he is both. It is true that, as Lamb notes, Richard in the allusions to his deformity

> mingles . . . a perpetual reference to his own powers and capacities, by which he is enabled to surmount these petty objections; and the joy of a defect *conquered,* or *turned* into an advantage, is one cause of these very allusions, and of the satisfaction, with which his mind recurs to them.

But [critic Edward] Dowden [in *Shakespeare: His Mind and Art*] also is right when he says of Richard that

> his dominant characteristic is not intellectual; it is rather a daemonic energy of will. . . . He is of the diabolical class. . . . He is single-hearted in his devotion to evil. . . . He has a fierce joy, and he is an intense believer,—in the creed of hell. And therefore he is strong. He inverts the moral order of things, and tries to live in this inverted system. He does not succeed; he dashes himself to pieces against the laws of the world which he has outraged.

It might be retorted that the above distinction is superfluous, because an extreme manifestation of demonic will can only arise from the additional drive set in motion by an unusual need to compensate for a defect. But the point is that Shakespeare does actually make the distinction and that Richard, within the limits of the play, is psychologically both possible and impossible. He ranges from credibly motivated villain to a symbol, psychologically absurd however useful dramatically, of the diabolic.

This shift, however, is not irregular. In the first two scenes, containing his opening soliloquy, his dealings with Clarence, his interruption of the funeral of Henry VI with his courtship of Ann Nevil, he is predominantly the psychological study. Shakespeare here builds up his private character. And he is credible; with his humour, his irony, and his artistry in crime acting as differentiating agents, creating a sense of the individual. After this he carries his established private character into the public arena, where he is more than a match for anyone except Queen Margaret. Of her alone he is afraid; and her curse establishes, along with the psychologically probable picture just created, the competing and ultimately victorious picture of the monstrosity, the country's scapegoat, the vast impostume of the commonwealth. She makes him both a cosmic symbol, the "troubler of the poor world's peace," and sub-human, a "rooting hog," "the slave of nature and the son of hell." She calls on him the curse of insomnia, which later we find to have been fulfilled. Clearly this does not apply to the exulting ironic Richard: *he* must always have slept with infant tranquillity. Thus Margaret's curse is prospective, and though he continues to pile up the materials for the construction of his monstrosity, it is the credible Richard, glorying in his will and his success in compensating his disabilities, who persists till the end of the third act and the attainment of the throne. Thenceforward, apart from his outburst of energy in courting Queen Elizabeth for her daughter's hand, he melts from credible character into a combination of sheer melodrama villain and symbol of diabolism. His irony forsakes him; he is unguarded not secretive in making his plans; he is no longer cool but confused in his energy, giving and retracting orders; he *really* does not sleep; and, when on the eve of Bosworth he calls for a bowl of wine because he has not "that alacrity of spirit nor cheer of mind that I was wont to have," he is the genuine ancestor of the villain in a nineteenth century melodrama calling for whiskey when things look black. Then, with the ghosts and his awakening into his Judas-like monologue, psychological probability and melodramatic villainy alike melt into the symbol of sheer denial and diabolism. Nor does his momentary resurrection at Bosworth with his memorable shout for a horse destroy that abiding impression. That a character should shift from credible human being to symbol would not have troubled a generation nurtured on Spenser. Richard in this respect resembles one of

Spenser's masterpieces, Malbecco, who from a realistic old cuckold is actually transformed into an allegorical figure called Jealousy.

Finally we must not forget that Richard is the vehicle of an orthodox doctrine about kingship. It was a terrible thing to fight the ruling monarch, and Richard had been crowned. However, he was so clearly both a usurper and a murderer that he had qualified as a tyrant; and against an authentic tyrant it was lawful to rebel. Richmond, addressing his army before Bosworth, makes the point absolutely clear:

> Richard except, those whom we fight against
> Had rather have us win than him they follow.
> For what is he they follow? truly, gentlemen,
> A bloody tyrant and a homicide;
> One rais'd in blood and one in blood
>   establish'd;
> One that made means to come by what he
>   hath
> And slaughter'd those that were the means to
>   help him;
> One that hath ever been God's enemy.
> Then if you fight against God's enemy,
> God will in justice ward you as his soldiers;
> If you do sweat to put a tyrant down,
> You sleep in peace, the tyrant being slain.
>   [V.iii.243-9, 252-6]

And Derby, handing Henry the crown after the battle, calls it "this long-usurped royalty."

I have indicated in outline the course of the play: the emerging of unity from and through discord, the simultaneous change in Richard from accomplished villain to the despairing embodiment of evil. Shakespeare gives it coherence through the dominant and now scarcely human figure of Queen Margaret: the one character who appears in every play [of the tetralogy]. Being thus a connecting thread, it is fitting that she give structural coherence to the crowning drama. As Richard's downfall goes back to her curse, so do the fates of most of the characters who perish in the play go back to her curses or prophecies in the same scene, I.3. Nor are her curses mere explosions of personal spite; they agree with the tit-for-tat scheme of crime and punishment that has so far prevailed in the tetralogy. She begins by recalling York's curse on her at Wakefield for the cruelty of her party to Rutland and the penalty she has paid; and then enumerates the precisely balanced scheme of retribution appointed for the house of York:

> If not by war, by surfeit die your king,
> As ours by murder, to make him a king.
> Edward thy son, which now is Prince of
>   Wales,
> For Edward my son, which was Prince of

Wales,
Die in his youth by like untimely violence.
Thyself a queen, for me that was a queen,
Outlive thy glory like my wretched self.

[I.iii.197-203]

Curses on minor characters follow, but Richard, as befits, has a speech to himself. His peculiar curse is the gnawing of conscience, sleeplessness, and the mistake of taking friends for enemies and enemies for friends. I have spoken of the sleeplessness above, how it could not apply to the Richard of the first three acts. Similarly it is not till Bosworth that the curse of thinking his enemies friends comes true. We are meant to think of it when Richmond says in lines quoted above that "those whom we fight against had rather have us win than him they follow." The man with the best brain in the play ends by being the most pitifully deceived. For a detailed working out of the different curses I refer the reader to A. P. Rossiter's study of the play. But it is worth recording that Margaret in her last lines before she goes out unconsciously forecasts the larger theme of the plays. Talking of Richard she says:

Let each of you be subject to his hate,
And he to yours, and all of you to God's.

[I.iii.302-3]

Margaret does not realise that this grouping of Yorkists against Richard will unite them to the Lancastrians similarly opposed, and that the just vengeance of God had even then given way to his mercy.

In style the play is better sustained than its predecessor. There is less undifferentiated stuff, and the finest pieces of writing (as distinguished from the finest scenes) are more dramatic. The quiet concentration of the Duchess of York's last words to Richard is beyond anything in the other three plays:

Either thou wilt die, by God's just
   ordinance,
Ere from this war thou turn a conqueror,
Or I with grief and extreme age shall perish
And never look upon thy face again.
Therefore take with thee my most heavy curse;
Which, in the day of battle, tire thee more
Than all the complete armour that thou
   wear'st!
My prayers on the adverse party fight;
And there the little souls of Edward's
   children
Whisper the spirits of thine enemies
And promise them success and victory.
Bloody thou art, bloody will be thy end;
Shame serves thy life and doth thy death
   attend.

[IV.iv.182-95]

Richard's plotting with Buckingham and his acquisition of the throne though strongly organised must have tired Shakespeare. There are even signs of strain in the last stage of the process when Richard appears between the two bishops; the verse droops somewhat. After this (and it is here that Richard begins his change of nature) the vitality flags, except in patches, till the great scene when the three queens get together to join in lamentation. The courting of Elizabeth for her daughter is a prodigious affair, but not at all apt at this point. It leads nowhere; for in the very next scene (IV. 5) Elizabeth is reported to have consented to her daughter's union with Richmond. Are we to think, with E. K. Chambers [in *Shakespeare, a Survey*], that Elizabeth had outwitted Richard and had consented, only to deceive? This is so contrary to the simple, almost negative character of Elizabeth and so heavily ironical at Richard's expense that I cannot believe it. A better explanation is that Elizabeth was merely weak and changeable and that Richard's comment on her as she goes from him, having consented,

Relenting fool and shallow, changing woman,

[IV.iv.431]

was truer than he thought, forcasting the second change. It is fitting that Richard, having been so often ironical at the expense of others, should himself be the occasional victim of the irony of events. Even so, the scene is far too elaborate and weighty for its effect on the action. Indeed I suspect an afterthought, a mistaken undertaking to repeat the success of the earlier scene of courtship. It would have been better to have gone quickly on to the great finale of the ghosts and Bosworth, to that consummate expression, achieved here once and for all, of what I have ventured to call Shakespeare's official self.

A. C. Hamilton

SOURCE: "The Resolution of the Early Period: *Richard III*," in *The Early Shakespeare*, The Huntington Library, 1967, pp. 186-202.

[*Hamilton demonstrates how* Richard III *"combines the genres of history play and tragedy," pointing out that if we look at the play's action through Richard's eyes, we see the history of his political progress; on the other hand, Margaret turns the play into a tragedy as each of her curses are fulfilled. Finally, Hamilton observes that the momentum of the play is toward Richard's isolation, since everyone connected with him is destroyed by him; moreover, it is Richard's isolation which eventually results in his own destruction.*]

Richard III, in its Quarto title "The Tragedy of King Richard the Third," combines the genres of history play and tragedy. [In drama, a tragedy recounts the significant events or actions in a protagonist's life which, taken together, bring about the catastrophe.] The demands of history itself upon the history play cause no opposition between the two genres: the strong Lancastrian bias of the age allowed the historical Richard to be as great a villain as the imagination of a tragic dramatist could desire. [John] Milton [in *Eikonoklastes,* 1650] rightly praises Shakespeare both for being "so mindfull of *Decorum*" in portraying Richard as a tyrant who counterfeits religious faith, and also for not "departing from the truth of History, which delivers him a deep dissembler, not of his affections onely, but of Religion." As the stage history of the play demonstrates and any reading confirms, Richard is the greatest of Shakespeare's historical characters. He embodies all the qualities of the political characters in the *Henry VI* plays who manipulate events to fit their own desires. [*Henry VI,* parts one, two, and three, are three plays by Shakespeare which precede *Richard III.*] He gathers within himself Joan's duplicity, Eleanor's aspirations, Winchester's pride, Buckingham's and Somerset's ambition, Margaret's and Suffolk's scheming, Clifford's revengeful fury, and, above all, York's intense passion. He stands—or crouches—as the final expression of one who uses time and opportunity to dominate his environment, overcoming for a season the adversity of circumstance, fortune, and fate by sheer human will. If, at his insistence, we look at the play from his perspective, we see a history play that shows his political triumphs, until the final moment brings his faltering before Richmond.

Early in the play, however, Margaret opposes Richard; she ensures that his history play becomes a tragedy, the climax to the tragic form that emerges in the *Henry VI* plays. After the opening scene in *1 Henry VI* sets the stage for a tragedy with the funeral of Henry V, the action in that play turns to historical events; Salisbury's "woeful tragedy" (I.iv.77) is only an episode in the war with France, and the tragedy of Talbot is only one consequence of dissension in England. *2 Henry VI* contains the "tragedy" (III.ii.194) of Gloucester's death and his enemies' "plotted tragedy" (III.i.153), which ends in chaos with York's first claim to the crown. *3 Henry VI* leads quickly to "The True Tragedie of Richard, Duke of Yorke" (the play's Quarto title) and concludes with the brutal murder of Henry and his son. In *Richard III*, the tragic form encompasses the whole play and all the major characters. At the height of the action, Margaret feeds upon the fall of her enemies:

> So now prosperity begins to mellow
> And drop into the rotten mouth of death.
> Here in these confines slily have I lurk'd
> To watch the waning of mine enemies.
> A dire induction am I witness to,

The royal children and their murderers.

> And will to France, hoping the consequence
> Will prove as bitter, black, and tragical.
> (IV.iv.1-7)

She is the instrument through which the historical events in Richard's reign, including finally Richard himself, become an "induction" [prologue] leading to a catastrophe that proves "bitter, black, and tragical."

Richard III differs from the earlier history plays in its source. More's *Historie of King Richard the Thirde* had already transformed mere chronicle event into a literary tradition with considerable dramatic potentiality. Shakespeare knew More through Hall, [in *The Union of the Two Noble and Illustre Famelies of Lancastre and Yorke,* 1548] and he may have known also the dramatic treatments in Thomas Legge's *Richardus Tertius* (1579) and the anonymous *True Tragedie of Richard the Third* (1594). The tradition needed only one further transformation to achieve in *Richard III* one of the most popular plays on the English stage, second perhaps only to *Hamlet.*

The place of Shakespeare's play within this tradition can be quickly indicated. More describes Richard as an absolute villain:

> Richard duke of Gloucester . . . was in witte and courage egall with the other [Clarence], but in beautee and liniamentes of nature far underneth bothe, for he was litle of stature, eivill featured of limnes, croke backed, the left shulder muche higher than the righte, harde favoured of visage, such as in estates is called a warlike visage, and emonge commen persones a crabbed face. He was malicious, wrothfull and envious. . . . He was close and secrete, a depe dissimuler, lowlye of countenaunce, arrogante of herte, outwardely familier where he inwardely hated, not lettynge to kisse whom he thought to kill, dispiteous and cruell, not alwaie for eivill will, but ofter for ambicion and too serve his purpose, frende and fooe were all indifferent, where his avauntage grewe, he spared no mannes deathe whose life withstode his purpose. He slewe in the towre kynge Henry the sixte, saiynge: now is there no heire male of kynge Edwarde the thirde, but wee of the house of Yorke: whiche murder was doen without kyng Edward his assente.

As a historian, More cannot crown his villain by accusing him of Clarence's death. He admits that "of these poinctes there is no certentie, and whosoever divineth or conjectureth, may as wel shote to fer as to shorte" (sig. AAii). To answer these conjectures, Shakespeare shows how Richard plans that murder, persuades the king to condemn Clarence, and hires the murderers. What the historian does not deny, the dramatist, being "mindfull of *Decorum*," supplies, in order that from the beginning his villain may be guilty of an offense that "hath the primal eldest curse upon't—/ A brother's murder."

To More's discussion of Edward's possible implication in his brother's death Hall adds the moral lesson:

> . . . what a pernicious serpent, what a venemous tode, & what a pestiferous Scorpion is that develishe whelpe, called privye envye? Agaynst it no fortres can defend, no cave can hyde, no wood can shadow, no foule can escape, nor no beaste can avoyde, her poyson is so stronge, that never man in authoritie coulde escape from the bytyng of her tethe, scrachyng of her pawes, blastyng of her breath, defoulynge of her tayle.

> Wherefore, let every indifferent persone, serche Histories, rede Chronicles, looke on aucthores, aswell holy as prophane, and thei shall apparauntly perceive, that neither open warre, daily famyne, or accustomed mortalitie, is not so muche an enemie, nor so great a malle to destroye, and suppeditate high power and nobilitie, as is roted malice, inwarde grudge, and dissimuled hatred. (sigs. Rriv^v-R[r]v^r])

In place of this moral abstracted out of the chronicles, Shakespeare offers an image in which "that develishe whelpe, called privye envye" is embodied in Richard.

Earlier dramatic treatments follow More in displaying Richard as the Senecan tyrant [Seneca, a Roman statesman, author, and philosopher of the first century A.D., is famous for nine melodramas which had a great influence on tragic drama in Elizabethan England]. The dramatic limitations of this form show clearly in the *True Tragedie*, where Richard declares: "I hope with this lame hand of mine, to rake out that hatefull heart of Richmond, and when I have it, to eate it panting hote with salt, and drinke his blood luke warme" (ll. 1979-81). Felix E. Schelling [in his *Elizabethan Drama: 1558-1642*] believes that Shakespeare continues the line of *Tamburlaine* [a play by Christopher Marlowe, 1590] by a "concentration of interest in the heroic dimensions of a unified personality, the master passion of which carries the auditor's sympathies with it." Yet Shakespeare's hero differs radically from Marlowe's. In place of one

> Threat'ning the world with high astounding terms,
> And scourging kingdoms with his conquering sword
>
> (Prologue, *Part I*)

he offers one whose victories are shameful—over the simple, believing Clarence, a woman's captive heart, two innocent babes, the trusting Hastings, a gullible commons, and a "Relenting fool, and shallow, changing woman" (R.III IV.iv.431). Tamburlaine's relentless ranting here changes into the direct speaking voice of one who can say to the brother whose death he arranges because of his name:

> Alack, my lord, that fault is none of yours:
> He should, for that, commit your godfathers.
> O, belike his Majesty hath some intent
> That you should be new-christ'ned in the Tower.
>
> (I.i.47-50)

Since the plot leads to Clarence's death by being "new-christ'ned" in a malmsey-butt, murder has become matter for a brutal jest. Richard's tone ranges from the vigor of "Chop off his head" (III.i.193) to the sanctimonious "O, do not swear, my lord of Buckingham" (III.vii.220), from the Faustian [from Christopher Marlowe's play *Doctor Faustus*] cry, "Have mercy, Jesu!" (V.iii.178) to the heroic "A horse! a horse! my kingdom for a horse!" (V.iv.13), or to the quiet thrust of his insolent question, superbly timed to shatter the peace of soul for which the dying Edward yearns: "Who knows not that the gentle Duke is dead?" (II.i.79).

Shakespeare displays Richard's character in the second scene, the wooing and winning of Anne. We know that she was fifteen when she first married Henry VI's son in December 1470, that after her husband's death in the following May she was disguised as a kitchen maid by Clarence in an effort to gain Warwick's estates, and that she was found by Richard, who placed her in sanctuary until the king let him marry her. Shakespeare knows only the curious fact that Richard married her the year after he murdered her husband. Accordingly, he invents the scene in which Richard woos her as she attends the funeral of Henry VI, also one of his victims. The scene proves startling from the outset. In his opening soliloquy, Richard scorns Mars [the Roman god of war] for having smoothed his wrinkled front and capering nimbly into a lady's chamber, while he himself in his deformity must remain, as Mars had been, "wrinkled" and "grim-visag'd":

> And therefore, since I cannot prove a lover
> To entertain these fair well-spoken days,
> I am determined to prove a villain
> And hate the idle pleasures of these days.
>
> (I.i.9, 28-31)

In the closing soliloquy to this opening scene he refers to his "deep intent" (l. 149) in causing Clarence's death, which we take to be his chance at the throne if the king and his brothers' children should die. Instead of saying so, however, he adds surprisingly: "For then I'll marry Warwick's youngest daughter" (l. 153). Though he hints at having "another secret close intent" (l. 158) in marrying her, that intent, as it turns out, is to prove a villain by proving a lover.

Richard's seduction of Anne is a triumph, as he realizes in mock wonder. No lover's triumph is more complete:

> What! I that kill'd her husband and his
>   father—
> To take her in her heart's extremest hate,
> With curses in her mouth, tears in her eyes,
> The bleeding witness of my hatred by;
> Having God, her conscience, and these bars
>   against me,
> And I no friends to back my suit at all
> But the plain devil and dissembling looks,
> And yet to win her, all the world to
>   nothing!
> Ha!
>
> (I.ii.230-238)

The wooing is meant to shock, even as it shocks Richard himself.

> Was ever woman in this humour woo'd?
> Was ever woman in this humour won?
>
> (ll. 227-228)

he asks us; yet he need not pause for an answer. In literature, at any rate, no other woman has been wooed and won by her husband's murderer while she attends the funeral of her husband's father, who was also murdered by him. Anne's yielding cannot be explained by fear, or by her desire for him, or by a sense of guilt because her beauty drove him to murder, or by her not being deceived but cunningly deceiving him. Moral or psychological "explanation" only lessens the scene's dramatic impact. Anne's submission becomes ours: with her we recognize the reasons to curse Richard, yet we find our horror replaced by fascination. All the world loves a lover, especially if he is also a villain who makes evil attractive. Her yielding defines the kind of world we must accept, with its outrage of all human feelings, its perversion of love and marriage, and its human weakness when self is divided against self.

Yet the scene's final dramatic impact lies not in Anne's submission but in Richard's triumph. In the opening soliloquy, where he scorns lovers who trip into "a lady's chamber" (I.i.12), the suddenness of transition to the lines:

> And leave the world for me to bustle in!
> For then I'll marry Warwick's youngest
>   daughter
>
> (ll. 152-153)

astonishes us, and perhaps Richard himself. In his soliloquies and asides throughout the play he reveals himself so intimately that we become his accomplices: in sharing his keen delight in villainy, we share his guilt. No other dramatic character, except possibly Hamlet, appeals on quite the same level in being both intimate and archetypal. If his villainy were less monstrous, if we knew less about him, or even if he took himself seriously, he would become a monster. Instead, he invites our delight in his villainies and browbeats us into accepting him. Yet here we achieve less than full intimacy: he plays a trick on us, and on himself, by proving such a successful lover. His trick is to provide the delight for which we come to the theater, the enjoyment of a moral holiday staged by a consummate actor who always plays his part and plays it perfectly. Hence the delighted surprise with which he trips nimbly into a lady's chamber. The scene takes us into Richard's mind, where all the significant dramatic action takes place.

While the play's significant action occurs internally as our dramatic interest focuses upon Richard's mind, the external action is controlled by Margaret. Her role is to project the play as a historical tragedy. She remains at the English court, contrary to historical fact, in order to revile those who have offended against her. In the scene that follows Richard's seduction of Anne, our attention turns from Richard to Margaret, whose railing causes him and the others to attack her.

Ironically, he teaches her how to curse when he claims that York's curses

> from bitterness of soul
> Denounc'd against thee are all fall'n upon
>   thee;
> And God, not we, hath plagu'd thy bloody
>   deed.
>
> (I.iii.179-181)

In amazement, she learns that curses are effective:

> Did York's dread curse prevail so much with
>   heaven
> That Henry's death, my lovely Edward's
>   death,
> Their kingdom's loss, my woeful
>   banishment,
> Should all but answer for that peevish brat?
> Can curses pierce the clouds and enter
>   heaven?
> Why then, give way, dull clouds, to my
>   quick curses!
>
> (ll. 191-196)

She rails no longer and curses each in turn. Each has brought her curse upon himself by wronging her. In effect, she writes the complots of the tragedies that each then acts out to fulfill her word. Edward, Elizabeth, Rivers, Grey, Hastings, the young Edward, Buckingham, and finally Richard—all suffer and "die the thrall of Margaret's curse" (IV.i.46). They exist upon the level of her dreams to become what she wishes. In *2 Henry VI*, the banished Suffolk wishes "would curses kill" (III.ii.310); now they do, and the action of the play shows how her words become deeds. Within the play, the entire action becomes a play directed by her. Although Richard bustles in the world, dominating it for the present moment through his intelligence and will, he is her chief actor. She is the Past, the present witness to previous wrongs, and her curses determine the future. Allegorically, she is Conscience, Revenge, or one of the Destinies, with the difference that she is involved herself in the guilt, revenge, and fate that she brings on others.

The play is organized into rituals of grief. Elizabeth defines the ritual when she bewails the death of the king. In her agony of grief, she is ready to "join with black despair against my soul / And to myself become an enemy." To the Duchess of York's question, "What means this scene of rude impatience?" she replies, "To make an act of tragic violence" (II.ii.36-39). The play is composed of such acts of tragic violence. *1 Henry VI* has only Talbot's lament upon the death of his son; *2 Henry VI* has Gloucester's lament, Margaret's and Suffolk's lament upon his exile, and Clifford's lament upon the death of his father; and *3 Henry VI* has York's raging when Margaret goads him

to "rude impatience," Henry's lament on the molehill, joined by the laments of the father who has slain his son and of the son who has slain his father, and finally Henry's raging against Richard. In *Richard III*, every character except Richmond laments, and entire scenes are organized into rituals of lamentation.

There is even a competition in weeping. When Elizabeth bewails the death of her husband, the Duchess of York lays claim to having greater cause to grieve,

> Thine being but a moiety of my moan—
> To overgo thy woes and drown thy cries,
>
> (II.ii.60-61)

while Clarence's children refuse to join Elizabeth's lament because she did not weep for their father's death. She responds that she needs no help in weeping, for her tears alone can drown the world. Then their voices join in a three-part ritual of lament:

> *Eliz.* Ah for my husband, for my dear Lord
>   Edward!
> *Child.* Ah for our father, for our dear Lord
>   Clarence!
> *Duch.* Alas for both, both mine, Edward and
>   Clarence!
>
> *Eliz.* What stay had I but Edward? and he's
>   gone.
> *Child.* What stay had we but Clarence? and
>   he's gone.
> *Duch.* What stays had I but they? and they
>   are gone.
>
> *Eliz.* Was never widow had so dear a loss.
> *Child.* Were never orphans had so dear a
>   loss.
> *Duch.* Was never mother had so dear a loss.

This triple threnody [a song of lamentation for the dead] concludes with the Duchess of York's lament for them all:

> Alas! I am the mother of these griefs!
> Their woes are parcell'd, mine is general.
> She for an Edward weeps, and so do I:
> I for a Clarence weep, so doth not she.
> These babes for Clarence weep, and so do I:
> I for an Edward weep, so do not they.
> Alas, you three on me, threefold distress'd,
> Pour all your tears! I am your sorrow's
>   nurse,
> And I will pamper it with lamentation.
>
> (II.ii.71-88)

Such scenes may be compared to the complaint scenes that are a vehicle for Lucrece's curses and laments in her poem [Shakespeare's *The Rape of Lucrece*], and to a similar competition in weeping between her father and Collatine. They are even closer to similar scenes in [Shakespeare's] *Titus Andronicus* that contain a dramatic gathering of rituals of lament.

Lamentation rises to a lyrical climax in a later scene when the Duchess of York, Elizabeth, and Margaret gather to mourn. Elizabeth, who has learned of the murder of her children, wails:

> Wilt thou, O God, fly from such gentle
>   lambs
> And throw them in the entrails of the wolf?
> When didst thou sleep when such a deed was
>   done?
>
>   (IV.iv.22-24)

Margaret responds, "When holy Harry died, and my sweet son" (l. 25), and the Duchess of York laments that she is the chronicle of all their woe. When they sit together, Margaret claims the seniority of her griefs and catalogs their woes:

> I had an Edward, till a Richard kill'd him;
> I had a husband, till a Richard kill'd him:
> Thou hadst an Edward, till a Richard kill'd
>   him;
> Thou hadst a Richard, till a Richard kill'd
>   him.
>
>   (ll.40-43)

Elizabeth's overwhelming grief, which leads her to cry out for "my tender babes! / My unblown flowers, new-appearing sweets!" (ll. 9-10), is modulated with both the quietness of the Duchess of York, who has long been overwhelmed by grief, for

> So many miseries have craz'd my voice
> That my woe-wearied tongue is still and
>   mute,
>
>   (ll. 17-18)

and Margaret's joy in their grief:

> O upright, just, and true-disposing God,
> How do I thank thee that this carnal cur
> Preys on the issue of his mother's body.
>
>   (ll. 55-57)

Though such formalized scenes are often omitted in modern productions as being too stylized for our taste, they shape the play into a tragic history.

The story of Hastings, as one "act of tragic violence," illustrates some features of the play as a historical tragedy and distinguishes it from the earlier history plays that have similar stories of Talbot, Gloucester, and York. For although Shakespeare follows More closely in telling Hastings' story, he adds ironic humor.

Hastings' innocent remark on Richard's cheerful look, "There's some conceit or other likes him well" (III.iv.51), provides a broadly comic touch, for the "conceit" is the means of chopping off his head. Ironically, in his refusal to support Richard's claim to the throne, he pronounces his own doom:

> I'll have this crown of mine cut from my
>   shoulders
> Before I'll see the crown so foul misplac'd.
>
>   (III.ii.43-44)

In his later remark, "God knows I will not do it to the death" (l. 55), he speaks more truly than he knows.

Such ironic comedy changes the significance of his fall. More, seeing in it an example of "the vayne surety of mans mynde so neare hys death," comments: "O lorde God the blyndnesse of our mortal nature, when he most feared, he was in moste suretye, and when he reconed hym selfe moste surest, he lost his lyfe, and that within two houres after" (sig. C[C]iii^{r-v}). In the play, Hastings himself recognizes how "too fond" (III.iv.83) he has been, repents that he triumphed over his enemies while he felt secure in grace, and then interprets his own tragedy:

> O momentary grace of mortal men,
> Which we more hunt for than the grace of
>   God!
> Who builds his hope in air of your good
>   looks
> Lives like a drunken sailor on a mast,
> Ready with every nod to tumble down
> Into the fatal bowels of the deep.
>
>   (ll. 98-103)

Through these lines his earlier affability toward Richard—"I thank his Grace, I know he loves me well . . . His gracious pleasure" (ll. 15-18)—gains new meaning. Just before the blow falls, he speaks of "The tender love I bear your Grace" (l. 65):

> His Grace looks cheerfully and smooth this
>   morning . . .
> I think there's never a man in Christendom
> Can lesser hide his love or hate than he;
> For by his face straight shall you know his
>   heart. . . .
> Marry, that with no man here he is
>   offended;
> For, were he, he had shown it in his looks.
>
>   (ll. 50, 53-55, 59-60)

Here we see him hunting for the grace of a mortal man, as he builds his hope in air of Richard's good looks.

Hastings' moral state is central to the play. Margaret speaks of her murdered son as

now in the shade of death,
Whose bright out-shining beams thy cloudy
    wrath
Hath in eternal darkness folded up,
                                    (I.iii.267-269)

Elizabeth of her dead husband in "his new kingdom of ne'erchanging night" (II.ii.46), Richard of the dead Clarence as one "who I indeed have cast in darkness" (I.iii.327), and Margaret of Elizabeth's dead sons as having their "infant morn" dimmed to "aged night" (IV.iv.16). Elizabeth sees herself wrecked by Richard,

in such a desp'rate bay of death,
Like a poor bark, of sails and tackling reft,
Rush all to pieces on thy rocky bosom.
                                    (ll. 232-234)

In his dream Clarence falls "overboard / Into the tumbling billows of the main" (I.iv.19-20). The play shows the world poised to fall "into the fatal bowels of the deep"; for the bonds between earth and heaven are broken when a "foul devil" (I.ii.50) becomes "the Lord's anointed" (IV.iv.150).

Prayers to God are for revenge, not mercy. Elizabeth accuses God of throwing "gentle lambs . . . in the entrails of the wolf" and sleeping while evil is done. The apocalyptic imagery of harvest, coming darkness, and chaos rises to a scream in Margaret's curse:

But at hand, at hand,
Ensues his piteous and unpitied end.
Earth gapes, hell burns, fiends roar, saints
    pray,
To have him suddenly convey'd from hence.
Cancel his bond of life, dear God, I pray,
That I may live and say "The dog is dead."
                                    (IV.iv.73-78)

Movement within this world is downward: Clarence's dream anticipates his descent into hell, Margaret interprets Elizabeth's state as "One heav'd a-high to be hurl'd down below" (l. 86), the death that threatens Stanley's son is a "fall / Into the blind cave of eternal night" (V.iii.61-62). The movement suggests a world ready for the Last Judgment. England becomes "this slaughterhouse" (IV.i.44), and Hastings prophesies for his country "the fearfull'st time to thee / That ever wretched age hath look'd upon" (III.iv.106-107). When Buckingham "pleads" with Richard to assume the throne because England is "almost should'red in the swallowing gulf / Of dark forgetfulness and deep oblivion" (III.vii.128-129), he mocks the truth. That final shouldering is left to Richard, his high shoulder being the symbol of his malignancy.

The hell that each character inhabits is a mental state. Its chief lyrical statement in the play, Clarence's dream,

has three stages: first the blow of being shouldered into the ocean by Richard, then the pain of drowning when the waters smother his soul within him, and finally the "tempest to [his] soul" (I.iv.44) when he enters hell to be accused by those against whom he has sinned:

With that, methoughts, a legion of foul
    fiends
Environ'd me, and howled in mine ears
Such hideous cries that, with the very noise,
I trembling wak'd, and for a season after
Could not believe but that I was in hell,
Such terrible impression made my dream.
                                    (ll. 58-63)

The first stage of his dream, that of being knocked overboard by Richard, is the "real" world of historical event where Richard arranges Clarence's death and the deaths of the others who stand between him and the throne. The second stage, the agony of death, is the demonic world that Richard creates, expressed in the imagery of drowning. The third stage, the tempest to the soul, is the state of despair, the private hell into which the characters fall under the burden of guilt. Edward on his deathbed seeks to reconcile opposing factions at the court, in order that "more at peace my soul shall part to heaven" (II.i.5); but the news of Clarence's death leaves him to die with his soul "full of sorrow" (l. 96), fearing God's justice. Elizabeth resolves to "join with black despair against my soul / And to myself become an enemy." Each character dies weighed down by guilt.

One by one, those who stand between Richard and the crown—Clarence, Edward, Rivers, Grey, Vaughan, Hastings, the two princes, Margaret, Elizabeth, the Duchess of York, Anne, and Buckingham—make an "act of tragic violence." Together they are an "induction" to the thirteenth fall, a catastrophe that proves "bitter, black, and tragical": the death of Richard. The whole movement of the play effects his gradual isolation, the cutting away of all supporting human relationships. By the end he stands alone; but, being unsupported, he falls. The tragic irony of his actions is that those who stand in his way support him: after they fall, he must fall.

Richard's fall has two stages: In the first he confronts the lamenting women, the Duchess of York and Elizabeth. Earlier in the scene, Elizabeth begs Margaret:

O thou well skill'd in curses, stay awhile
And teach me how to curse mine enemies!
                                    (IV.iv.116-117)

Margaret teaches her, even as she was taught:

Forbear to sleep the nights, and fast the

days;
Compare dead happiness with living woe;
Think that thy babes were sweeter than they
   were,
And he that slew them fouler than he is.
Bett'ring thy loss makes the bad-causer
   worse;
Revolving this will teach thee how to curse.

                              (ll. 118-123)

Then Elizabeth, in turn, teaches the Duchess of York to curse. Up to this moment, the Duchess has submitted patiently to her sorrow, reduced almost to silence, seeing in herself

Dead life, blind sight, poor mortal living
   ghost,
Woe's scene, world's shame, grave's due by
   life usurp'd,
Brief abstract and record of tedious days.

                              (ll. 26-28)

Now she asks, "Why should calamity be full of words?" (l. 126), and Elizabeth replies:

Windy attorneys to their client woes,
Airy succeeders of intestate joys,
Poor breathing orators of miseries,
Let them have scope; though what they will
   impart
Help nothing else, yet do they ease the
   heart.

                              (ll. 127-131)

The Duchess now prepares to forgo her patient resignation and make her "scene of rude impatience":

If so, then be not tongue-tied. Go with me,
And in the breath of bitter words let's
   smother
My damned son that thy two sweet sons
   smother'd.
The trumpet sounds; be copious in exclaims.

                              (ll. 132-135)

When Richard enters, she forces him to stand and "patiently hear my impatience" (l. 156). Her curses determine the shape of his future actions:

Therefore take with thee my most grievous
   curse,
Which in the day of battle tire thee more
Than all the complete armour that thou
   wear'st!
My prayers on the adverse party fight;
And there the little souls of Edward's
   children
Whisper the spirits of thine enemies
And promise them success and victory.

Bloody thou art; bloody will be thy end.
Shame serves thy life and doth thy death
   attend.

                              (ll. 187-195)

Now, when Richard triumphs over Elizabeth, as earlier he triumphed over Anne, the parallel only reinforces the contrast. Before, he needed only to flatter Anne; now he must curse himself and so swear away his future:

As I intend to prosper and repent,
So thrive I in my dangerous affairs
Of hostile arms! Myself myself confound!
Heaven and fortune bar me happy hours!
Day, yield me not thy light; nor, night, thy
   rest!

                              (ll. 397-401)

The triple curse upon him by Margaret, his mother, and himself begins its fulfillment in his dream before the final battle.

This dream marks the start of the second, and final, stage of his fall. The ghost of each of his victims urges him to "despair and die" (V.iii.120 ff.): that is, to despair at the moment of death and be eternally damned. Hall, worrying over Richard's fate after death, ends his story with " . . . but to God whiche knewe his interior cogitacions at the hower of his deathe I remitte the punyshment of his offences committed in his lyfe" (sig. [KKv]). If Richard repents at the last moment and so escapes hell, history provides a poor example for posterity. Holinshed [in his *Chronicles of England, Scotland, and Ireland,* 1587] reproduces Hall's remark almost exactly, adding hopefully that if it happened that God did punish Richard severely, "who shall be so hardie as to expostulate and reason why he so dooth." Obviously, this answer does not satisfy. Shakespeare answers the question through the cry of the ghosts, "despair and die," ten times repeated. Yet each cry leaves a gap between "despair" and "die," affording that moment in which he could repent. But the ghost of Buckingham, who had helped Richard rise to the throne, now assures his fall:

O, in the battle think on Buckingham,
And die in terror of thy guiltiness!
Dream on, dream on of bloody deeds and
   death;
Fainting, despair; despairing, yield thy
   breath!

                              (V.iii.169-172)

Buckingham's curse gives Richard no instant for repentance; it dooms him, as he dies, to despair, and while he despairs, to die. He does dream on of bloody deeds and death: "Give me another horse. Bind up my wounds" (l. 177). That final Faustian cry, "Have mercy, Jesu!" comes, as with Faust, too late; for when he awakes and dismisses his dream—"Soft! I did but dream" (l. 178)—he is damned. In the final battle he asks only for a horse, and the kingdom that he is willing to give in exchange is greater than he knows.

LANGUAGE: OATHS, CURSES, AND PROPHECIES

As many critics have observed, *Richard III* is filled with oaths, curses, and prophecies. E. M. W. Tillyard argues that they are an expression of the play's theme of divine retribution, where the punishment of the feuding families, the destruction of Richard, and the final union of the houses of Lancaster and York are predestined. Margaret, who dispenses a significant portion of the curses and prophecies against the other characters in the play, is described by A. C. Hamilton as the "present witness to previous wrongs" and the embodiment of destiny and revenge.

Critics such as **Frances Shirley** and **David Bevington** have pointed out that the other characters inadvertently help to fulfill Margaret's prophecies by making false or imprudent oaths and thus cursing themselves: When, for example, Richard swears by his success as a king and warrior that he means well to Elizabeth and her family, his false oath turns into a self-curse, and he dies on the battlefield.

Both Karl Weber and **Kristian Smidt** assert that dreaming is closely related to prophecy in *Richard III*. Smidt remarks that the Duke of Clarence's undersea dream predicts his murder and subsequent drowning in the butt of malmsey. Weber maintains that Clarence's dream foreshadows the rest of the play.

Smidt further argues that Richard manufactures dreams and prophecies as a means to control other characters, and while not a genuine prophet, Richard is sufficiently confident and forceful to make his words come true.

Frances Shirley

SOURCE: "Shakespeare's Use of Oaths," in *The Triple Bond*, edited by Joseph G. Price, The Pennsylvania State University Press, 1975, pp. 118-36.

[*In this excerpt, Shirley comments on the seriousness in Elizabethan society of making oaths or swearing and how this is revealed in Shakespeare's* Richard III. *When characters in the play swear to the truth of something that they know is false, their oaths become self-curses which destroy them. So for example in Act IV, scene iv, when Richard swears that he loves Queen Elizabeth's daughter,* he stakes this lie with his success as a king and as a warrior, and consequently he fails at both. Shirley observes that the results of broken oaths are made all the more significant in the play when connected with Margaret's curses on Richard and his followers.]

Out of the pattern of Margaret's cursing seems to grow a predilection for a kind of self-curse is ironically carried out as people break faith and the larger curse is fulfilled. Richard's "so thrive I in my enterprise / . . . As I intend more good to you and yours" (IV.iv.236-37) and Hastings's "So prosper I as I swear perfect love!" (II.i.16) are preludes to eventual destruction. Boyle [Robert Boyle in *A Free Discourse Against Customary Swearing and A Dissuasive from Cursing*, 1695] and others comment on the practice, and Falstaff [a comical character in several of Shakespeare's plays] occasionally uses the same formula, but it seems less meaningful separated from Margaret's imprecations.

Richard himself seems unbothered by conscience or curse until that moment in act V when his control slips, although we have heard that he is a troubled sleeper. Part of our fascinated horror steams from his ability to dissemble. It has been suggested that men swear because they are at a loss for words, but this is certainly not the case with a man who can persuade the mourning Lady Anne of his love. In that scene, his oaths are reserved for threatening the corpse-bearers.

Nor can one say that Richard's oaths always give credence to lies, for he may use them with true statements. As old Margaret lashes out, he seems the soul of compassion: "I cannot blame her. By God's holy Mother, / She hath had too much wrong." This obvious truth is probably calculated to remove doubt from his hypocritical statement of repentance (I.iii.306-7).

Richard meets a temporary match in Queen Elizabeth, however, as he woos her daughter. In a combat of wits, he swears by everything from his anachronistic George to God Himself. Her premise, "If something thou wouldst swear to be believ'd, / Swear then by something thou hast not wrong'd" leads her to reject each oath, cataloguing his evil deeds in the process. Finally, he slips into another of the self-curses, soon to be fulfilled:

> Myself myself confound!
> Heaven and fortune bar me happy hours!
> Day, yield me not thy light, nor, night, thy
>   rest!

There is more, and this turn from the usual pattern of swearing seems to soften Elizabeth's resolution (IV.iv.166-401 *passim*).

Shakespeare matches Richard's oaths to the man.

Sometimes they are as unthinking as his rashest actions, more often as considered as his carefully planned moves to the throne. Sir Thomas More seems to have started the tradition that he swore by Saint Paul, and Shakespeare, like Holinshed, followed it. But the careful reservation of "zounds" ["by God's wounds"—a strong oath] for Richard, Buckingham, and the Murderers is Shakespeare's own.

It is with the Murderers that we have a last example of the way oaths and conscience can be used to form a distinguishing vignette when a lesser dramatist might have created two mere functionaries. The Second Murderer, more sensitive to good and evil, must be reminded of the reward. For an instant he gathers himself together: "Zounds, he dies! I had forgot the reward." "Where's thy conscience now?" he is asked, and he replies cavalierly, "O, in the Duke of Gloucester's purse." He adds, scoffingly, "I'll not meddle with it; it makes a man a coward . . . a man cannot swear, but it checks him" (I.iv.128-31, 137-39). The Folio's replacement of "Zounds" with "Come" is certainly less effective in showing this man's temporary surface callousness, for when he denigrates conscience he touches on the swearing that has probably just given him a twinge.

David Bevington

SOURCE: "'Why Should Calamity Be Full of Words?': The Efficacy of Cursing in *Richard III*," in *Iowa State Journal of Research*, Vol. 56, No. 1, August 1981, pp. 9-21.

[*Bevington examines the power of curses in* Richard III—*in particular, the effectiveness of self-cursing in the play. He remarks that many of Richard's victims—Lady Anne, for example—begin by cursing themselves, and that Richard successfully avoids either cursing himself or being cursed by others until the close of Act IV, at which point he has become king and is desperately trying to hold onto power. Like his victims, the self-curses he resorts to are fulfilled. Bevington concludes that in the world of* Richard III, *people's words become instruments of divine justice that can turn against them.*]

"Why should calamity be full of words?" asks the Duchess of York in IV.iv of *Richard III,* thereby posing a question that seems central to Shakespeare's conception of rhetoric in this early historical play. What is the efficacy of language, and more precisely what is the efficacy of the language of cursing, in *Richard III*? Queen Elizabeth, for her part, having seen the downfall of her kindred and the catastrophic rise of Richard of Gloucester, is not sure that cursing can accomplish anything more than to offer emotional relief to the speaker. In answer to the Duchess of York's question, "Why should calamity be full of words," Elizabeth offers this sad tribute to the purgative value of lamentation and cursing:

> Windy attorneys to their clients's woes,
> Airy succeeders of intestate joys,
> Poor breathing orators of miseries,
> Let them have scope! Though what they will impart
> Help nothing else, yet do they ease the heart.
>
> (IV.iv.126-31)

She is prepared, in other words, to join the Duchess in cursing the new king of England who has killed her kindred and her children, even though she doubts that much can come of it other than letting herself go.

Elsewhere in the play, too, speakers express scepticism as to the efficacy of cursing. In I.iii when Queen Margaret curses her enemies and prophesies their ruin, she offers to exempt Buckingham from her malediction since he is guiltless of any wrong against her house. Buckingham remains notwithstanding ungrateful and unimpressed. To her assurance that he is not "within the compass of [her] curse," Buckingham curtly rejoins, "Nor no one here; for curses never pass/ The lips of those that breathe them in the air" (I.iii.284-85). Margaret of course believes otherwise: "I will not think but they ascend the sky,/ And there awake God's gentle-sleeping peace," she retorts. Attitudes in this play toward the efficacy of cursing cover the whole range of possibilities, from Buckingham's jaded rationalism to the naive faith of Clarence's children, who, confronted with the news of their father's death, have no doubt as to what will happen: "God will revenge it, whom I will importune/ With earnest prayers all to that effect" (II.ii.14-15). They believe not only in God's sure and swift justice, but in their own ability to move God through imprecation. (Sadly enough, we realize, they are misinformed as to the true cause of their father's death and are sure that not Richard but King Edward will have to pay the reckoning.)

The question of the efficacy of cursing becomes, then, a matter of debate, one that is related to the conception of providential justice in the play. Do curses and prayers have an effective power over destiny? Does the actual pronouncing of certain words form a part of the process by which events are fulfilled? Are the curses spoken by Margaret and others necessary to the completion of the acts of which they speak? Why should Margaret, herself guilty of heinous atrocities in the Yorkist-Lancastrian wars, be able to move God to action by her entreaties? Are her prayers as effective as those of Clarence's innocent children? Can there be any power in Margaret's words, or is she merely a prophetess of what must be? If the latter, why does God choose such a guilt-ridden railer as his spokesman?

In this analysis I should like to focus on Richard of Gloucester's own attitudes toward these questions. I should like to examine his studious attempts to avoid, first of all, the curses of others, including Margaret, and second, the self-cursing to which his victims fall unwittingly prone. I should then like to examine the process by which Richard does in fact fall prey both to the curses of others (in particular, his mother) and to self-cursing, despite his efforts to escape such entrapments. This reversal seems to me, in fact, an integral part of the *peripeteia* [dramatic reversal] of *Richard III* and leads toward Richard's *anagnorisis* or discovery—too late for him, of course—as to the true nature of imprecatory language.

Before looking at Richard himself, let me first survey the tragic careers of his chief victims, in order to formulate the pattern against which Richard's actions are to be properly understood. That pattern seems generally to require both the pronouncement of a curse by some other character and the pronouncement of a self-curse by the person in question, though both events need not always be shown and may in some instances have occurred prior to the commencement of the play. The pattern completes itself in the recollection of self-cursing after the fatal events have come to pass, a recollection that is usually accompanied by an acknowledgment of the justice of God's wrath.

The Lady Anne is the first of Richard's victims to curse herself. Even before Richard has approached her with his outlandishly successful wooing, even as she is escorting the dead body of her father-in-law, Henry VI, to burial with tears in her eyes, Anne pronounces her own doom. She begins by cursing the murderer of her father-in-law and her husband, Prince Edward, but then turns to cursing Richard's offspring and any woman who could make the fatal error of marrying such a monster:

> If ever he have child, abortive be it,
> Prodigious, and untimely brought to light,
> Whose ugly and unnatural aspect
> May fright the hopeful mother at the view,
> And that be heir to his unhappiness!
> If ever he have wife, let her be made
> More miserable by the life of him
> Than I am made by my young lord and thee!
>
> (I.ii.21-28)

The audience is aware of the irony in this self-cursing, even though the wooing itself has not yet commenced, since Richard has previously confided to us his intention of winning Anne for his wife. He has also anticipated for us the point of this self-cursing, namely that we, knowing beforehand the enormity of her betrayal of self, see Anne going willfully to her own destruction. As Richard sardonically puts it:

> What though I kill'd her husband and her
>   father?
> The readiest way to make the wench amends
> Is to become her husband and her father,
> The which will I.
>
> (I.i.154-57)

Or as he exults afterwards:

> What? I, that kill'd her husband and his
>   father,
> To take her in her heart's extremest hate,
> With curses in her mouth, tears in her eyes,
> The bleeding witness of my hatred by,
> Having God, her conscience, and these bars
>   against me,
> And I no friends to back my suit withal,
> But the plain devil and dissembling looks?
> And yet to win her! All the world to
>   nothing!
>
> (I.ii.230-37)

Anne's self-cursing has served, then, as a means of emphasizing her awareness of the moral consequences of her fall. Like Eve, she has been armed with knowledge of good and evil, and yet has chosen evil because she is prone to flattery and deception.

Anne's self-cursing also serves as anticipation of her recognition of the justice of her fall. As she reluctantly prepares, in IV.i, for the unwelcome coronation in which she is to play the role of queen, she recalls her earlier words that have led to her present misery:

> O, when, I say, I look'd on Richard's face,
> This was my wish: "Be thou," quoth I,
>   "accurs'd
> For making me, so young, so old a widow!
> And, when thou wed'st, let sorrow haunt
>   thy bed;
> And be thy wife—if any be so mad—
> More miserable by the life of thee
> Than thou hast made me by my dear lord's
>   death!"
>
> (IV.i.70-76)

Although she alters the circumstance of this recollection, thinking of herself as having said directly to Richard the words she actually spoke in soliloquy before his entrance, Anne does repeat the substance of her earlier statement and reports almost word for word the crucially operative phrase: "And be thy wife—if any be so mad—/ More miserable by the life of thee/ Than thou hast made me by my dear lord's death!" Shakespeare is unafraid of repetition in such circumstances; it is a part of the copiousness, subtly altered by *variatio*, that goes to make up the "fullness of words" of which the Duchess of York spoke.

Prince Edward as played by Lena Ashwell.

Buckingham's career follows a similar pattern, even though he is manifestly more guilty than Anne of sinful conduct. First there is Margaret's warning, offered in a friendly spirit since Buckingham has done her no wrong. "O Buckingham, take heed of yonder dog," she admonishes him. "Look when he fawns, he bites; and when he bites,/ His venom tooth will rankle to the death./ Have not to do with him, beware of him;/ Sin, death, and hell have set their marks on him,/ And all their ministers attend on him" (I.iii.288-93). Buckingham predictably fails to heed the warning, despite Margaret's further insistence that Richard will one day "split [Buckingham's] very heart with sorrow" and Buckingham will "say poor Margaret was a prophetess" (I.iii. 299-300). Like Anne, Buckingham proceeds to cursing of himself having been granted a full knowledge of the consequences. In the presence of the dying King Edward, who repeatedly adjures his courtiers not to dally before their king "Lest he that is the supreme King of kings/ Confound your hidden falsehood, and award/ Either of you to be the other's end" (II.i.13-15), Buckingham calls down upon himself his own well-deserved destiny. Turning to Queen Elizabeth, with whose kindred he has been factious, he solemnly intones:

> Whenever Buckingham doth turn his hate
> Upon your Grace, but with all duteous love
> Doth cherish you and yours, God punish me
> With hate in those where I expect most love!
> When I have most need to employ a friend,
> And most assured that he is a friend,
> Deep, hollow, treacherous, and full of guile
> Be he unto me! This do I beg of God,
> When I am cold in love to you or yours.
>
> (II.i.32-40)

It is hardly surprising, perhaps, that Buckingham immediately proceeds to violate this oath by conspiring with Richard to deny Prince Edward the throne, since Buckingham (as we have seen) has already expressed his conviction that oaths are but idle speeches going no further than the lips of those who utter them. As Richard's chief supporter and henchman, moreover, he is most like Richard in his delight and ability in using rhetoric and double entendre to deceive others. He is the practiced Machiavel, able to "counterfeit the deep tragedian,/ Speak and look back, and pry on every side,/ Tremble and start at wagging of a straw;/ Intending deep suspicion, ghastly looks/ Are at my service, like enforced smiles" (III.v.5-9). [A Machiavel is one who views politics as amoral and that any means, however unscrupulous, can justifiably be used in achieving political power.]

In his downfall, however, Buckingham learns—too late for him—the true efficacy of the words spoken not only by Margaret but by himself. Noting that his arrest has appropriately fallen on All Souls' Day, he draws the necessary conclusion:

> Why, then All-Souls' day is my body's
>   doomsday.
> This is the day which, in King Edward's time,
> I wish'd might fall on me, when I was found
> False to his children and his wife's allies;
> This is the day wherein I wish'd to fall
> By the false faith of him whom most I trusted;
> This, this All-Souls' day to my fearful soul
> Is the determin'd respite of my wrongs.
> That high All-Seer which I dallied with
> Hath turn'd my feigned prayer on my head
> And given in earnest what I begg'd in jest.
> Thus doth he force the swords of wicked men
> To turn their own points in their masters'
>   bosoms.
> Thus Margaret's curse falls heavy on my neck:
> "When he," quoth she, "shall split thy heart
>   with sorrow,
> Remember Margaret was a prophetess,"
> Come, lead me, officers, to the block of shame;
> Wrong hath but wrong, and blame the due
>   of blame,
>
> (V.i.12-29)

Again we see Shakespeare's conscious rhetorical repetition of the operative words. What seemed before to Buckingham empty speech has now become confirmation of a providential pattern, by which men are fully warned and then brought low through their own devisings; their own swords are turned against their own bosoms. The curse is efficacious not as magic but as prophecy of a just process in which wicked men undo themselves. The prophetess Margaret goes unheeded at first, like Cassandra, because men are too often blind to their own weaknesses and to the omnipresence of a providential force that will exact punishment for sin. Buckingham is like Richard in his calculated villainy, but differs importantly from him (as do virtually all of Richard's victims) in his free acknowledgment of the justice of divine retribution: "Wrong hath but wrong, and blame the due of blame." Rather than complain at the seeming injustice of his being betrayed by his former ally, he bends his last thoughts to the acknowledgment of a divine necessity in what has happened. Even Buckingham, then, the most seemingly unregenerate of Richard's onetime cohorts, participates in a kind of spiritual *anagnorisis* [dramatic discovery or recognition] that, as we shall see, is denied solely to the play's protagonist.

Clarence's sorrow for his own wrongdoing is so eloquently dramatized in his great jail scene that it scarcely needs elaboration here. His swearing and forswearing have all taken place before the commencement of *Richard III*, and the recollection of these events in I.iv by a man about to die serves to heighten the emphasis on contrition as a means of appeasing God's just wrath. One aspect of the scene, however, requires some analysis here, and that is the extent of emphasis on perjury. The first ghost whom Clarence encounters in his dream, renowned Warwick, asks the pointed question: "What scourge for perjury/ Can this dark monarchy afford false Clarence?" (II.50-51). The charge is telling enough, since Clarence is guilty of having solemnly engaged himself to Warwick's daughter before switching perfidiously back again to the Yorkist side. Next the ghost of Edward, the Lancastrian Prince of Wales, takes up a similar cry: "Clarence is come—false, fleeting, perjur'd Clarence,/ That stabb'd me in the field by Tewkesbury" (II.55-56). Edward too had reason to hope better of Clarence, in view of Clarence's brief Lancastrian alliance. By taking up both sides of the Lancastrian–Yorkist struggle, in fact, Clarence had of necessity perjured himself toward both sides. It is this treachery that the second murderer holds up to Clarence as the cause of his imminent execution: "And that same vengeance doth [God] hurl on thee,/ For false forswearing and for murder too" (II.204-05). Clarence protests rightly enough that his own crimes will not excuse those of his executioners, but he also possesses the philosophical perspective necessary to realize that God's justice is at work even through evil agents. Early in the play, then, we are shown the moralized form of *anagnorisis* to which most of the flawed characters, though not Richard, will be subjected.

Other characters can be dealt with more briefly. Hastings' career fully exemplifies the pattern we are exploring here. He is cursed by Margaret for having been present at the murder of her son Rutland, but plainly indicates by his contemptuous reply to her that he has not yet learned to take prophecy seriously: "False-boding women, end thy frantic curse,/ Lest to thy harm thou move our patience," he retorts (I.iii.246-47). He proceeds to curse himself in the presence of the dying King Edward by swearing an end to his hatred of the queen's allies. The hollowness of this oath becomes the subject of much double-entendre in the bitterly ironic scenes preceding Hastings' arrest, for it is the news of the execution of Rivers, Vaughan, and Grey that persuades Hastings of Richard's continued affection and trust toward him. He is unwilling to see the resemblance between his own plight and that of his enemies, despite Derby's warning that "The lords at Pomfret, when they rode from London,/ Were jocund, and suppos'd their states were sure" (III.ii.83-84); Hastings is blinded by his own overconfidence and obsessive desire for revenge at any cost. And it is this desire for revenge, and his consequent perjury, that necessitate (as he perceives it) the just anger of the Almighty:

> I now repent I told the pursuivant,
> As too triumphing, how mine enemies
> Today at Pomfret bloodily were butcher'd,

And I myself secure in grace and favor.
O Margaret, Margaret, now thy heavy curse
Is lighted on poor Hastings' wretched head!
                                                (III.iv.88-93)

Again, like Buckingham, and others, Hastings expresses no resentment or sense of injustice at the fact of Richard's triumph over him but focuses instead on his realization that Richard's villainy has paradoxically served a just cause as far as Hastings is concerned. Once again the swords of wicked men have turned their own points into their masters' bosoms.

In a similar fashion, the queen's kindred, Rivers, Grey, and Vaughan, are cursed by Margaret for being accessories to Rutland's death, forswear and perjure themselves in the presence of both their temporal and eternal king, and concede at the time of their arrest the appropriateness of their doom (though they also protest that their deaths will be "guiltless" and "unjust," III.iii). They ask only that God hear their prayers as well, and carry out justice on Richard and Buckingham according to Margaret's prophecy as he has done in their own case.

King Edward IV, too, is cursed by Margaret. His crimes have for the most part been committed in *Henry VI, Part III*, but we are shown the scene of his recognition in which he confesses his perjured ingratitude toward his brother Clarence and laments, as he is led away to his death chamber, "O God, I fear thy justice will take hold/ On me, and you, and mine, and yours for this" (II.i.132-33).

What these various case histories suggest is that, in this play, self-cursing is essential to the process by which divine providence works its justice upon individuals. The pronouncement of a curse by Margaret or some other person does not in itself have a causative or magical function; it is rather a form of warning, so that the individual may see that he is fairly appraised of the consequence of his perjuries. Self-cursing is a still more heightened manifestation of this necessary foreknowledge on the part of the one who is to perpetrate evil, and is even, in a metaphorical sense, a form of contract signed between the individual and his destiny. The evil deeds range from Anne's betrayal of no one other than herself, to Hastings' vengeful conspiracy against his political enemies, to Buckingham's cool practice of political murder in the presumably safe knowledge that oaths are no more than empty words spoken to deceive. In virtually every case, an essential part of the spiritual fall is the committing of perjury, and an essential part of spiritual recognition is the acknowledgment of the perjury and the acceptance of its consequences.

Let us now turn to Richard of Gloucester, himself. What I want to illustrate here is the way in which his response to cursing and self-cursing differs at every turn from the responses of his victims, no matter how wicked some of them may have been. Richard does his best to avoid being cursed by others, including Margaret, and manages for a long time to avoid a direct pronouncement in his presence of such a curse. He is especially clever at avoiding self-cursing, until the moment of inevitable reversal finally arrives. And his belated recognition of the consequences of cursing and self-cursing brings with it not acquiescence but despair. The "coward conscience" he has despised in others becomes in him not a teacher but a nemesis.

First, let us look at the attempts of other characters to curse Richard to his face. Of course he is cursed in his absence by many persons in the play, increasingly so as the play goes on, but we also see that he goes to extraordinary lengths to avoid being cursed directly to his face. It is as though he is far more aware than the others of the dangers of hearing a curse pronounced on him. This difference is in fact wholly understandable. The others, no matter how guiltily involved, are to a greater or lesser extent blinded to their own failings and thus are in no position to understand what cursing can mean for them; or, like Buckingham, they simply do not believe in the power of cursing. Richard, whose evil is wholly without pretense or illusion, knows that his utterances are calculatedly insincere, and yet at the same time entertains a superstitious fear of cursing. He is a deliberate villain, then, who adopts quasilegalistic means to avoid exposing himself to liability of outright perjury.

This tactic first manifests itself in I.iii when Queen Margaret concludes her litany of curses by turning, suitably enough, to the greatest troublemaker of them all, Richard himself. When Richard chides her for cursing in turn Edward IV, Edward V, Queen Elizabeth, Rivers, Dorset, and Hastings, and bids her be done with her "charm"—suggesting that Richard views her as indeed a witch whose potent evil is to be avoided—she retorts with her strongest curse of all:

> And leave out thee? Stay, dog, for thou shalt
>   hear me.

(Note that the phrase "Stay dog," suggests that Richard is trying to sneak away.)

> If heaven have any grievous plague in store
> Exceeding those that I can wish upon thee,
> O, let them keep it till thy sins be ripe,
> And then hurl down their indignation
> On thee, the troubler of the poor world's
>   peace!
> The worm of conscience still begnaw thy
>   soul!
> Thy friends suspect for traitors while thou
>   liv'st,

> And take deep traitors for thy dearest
>   friends!
> No sleep close up that deadly eye of thine,
> Unless it be while some tormenting dream
> Affrights thee with a hell of ugly devils!
> Thou elvish-mark'd, abortive, rooting hog,
> Thou that wast seal'd in thy nativity
> The slave of nature and the son of hell!
> Thou slander of thy heavy mother's womb,
> Thou loathed issue of thy father's loins,
> Thou rag of honor, thou detested—
>   (I.iii.214-32)

And at this point Richard interrupts with her name, "Margaret." She, thrown off her stride, replies "Richard!" He responds "Ha!" and she replies in turn, "I call thee not."

> *Richard.* I cry thee mercy then, for I did
>   think
> That thou hadst call'd me all these bitter
>   names.

> *Queen Margaret.* Why, so I did, but look'd
>   for no reply.
> O, let me make the period to my curse!

> *Richard.* 'Tis done by me, and ends in
>   "Margaret."

And Queen Elizabeth ends this colloquy by observing to Margaret,

> Thus have you breath'd your curse against
>   yourself.
>   (I.iii.234-39)

Richard has thus deflected Margaret's anger onto Queen Elizabeth and with a shystering quibble has avoided the "period" to Margaret's curse. It is a paltry quibble, of curse, but it does strongly suggest Richard's interest in avoiding by whatever means the technical and legal fact of a curse that would otherwise light on him and name him culprit. Another ironic effect of this exchange is that Margaret herself has now unwittingly joined those who have cursed themselves.

A further instance of this cunning evasion occurs when Richard encounters his mother, the Duchess of York, for the first time in the play. She has already indicated, in her conversation with her grandchildren, the son and daughter of Clarence, her realization that Richard is a vicious deceiver and a grievous cause of shame to her. She represents then, to Richard, a very real danger, a person against whom he cannot readily proceed because she is his mother, and yet one who knows him for what he really is—unlike Anne, Hastings, Queen Elizabeth, and the rest, who are to a greater or lesser extent fooled by Richard's histrionic ability.

The Duchess of York possesses, moreover, a potent weapon for those believing in, or superstitiously fearful of, the power of cursing: a mother's blessing or her curse.

In this context, then, let us examine their first colloquy. It occurs after the death of Edward IV, when the peers of the realm are gathering to jockey for position. Richard comes in with Buckingham, Derby, Hastings, and others, sees his mother, and adopts as his first order of business the asking of her blessing:

> *Richard.* Madam, my mother, I do cry you
>   mercy;
> I did not see your Grace. Humbly on my
>   knee
> I crave your blessing.   [*Kneels.*]
>
> *Duchess of York.* God bless thee; and put
>   meekness in thy breast,
> Love, charity, obedience, and true duty!
>
> *Richard.* Amen!—[Aside] And make me die a
>   good old man!
> That is the butt-end of a mother's blessing;
> I marvel that her Grace did leave it out.
>   (II.ii.104-11)

I do not want to read this exchange with too serious a tone on Richard's part; Sir Laurence Olivier, for example, delivers Richard's aside in a mocking tone, and I would agree that a sardonic and even flippant air is more dramatically suitable than genuine concern or alarm. I would argue, however, that the sarcasm masks but does not entirely conceal an awareness on Richard's part that a mother's curse is something well avoided.

In fact, throughout the period of Richard's ascendancy to power, Richard never adopts Buckingham's easy—and fallacious—assumption that oaths "never pass/ The lips of those that breathe them in the air." Although Richard is utterly Machiavellian in his manipulation of rhetoric, he does not fall into the self-cursing by which the others seal a contract of perjury until late in the play. In the presence of the dying Edward IV, while Buckingham, Hastings, and others use such phrases as "So thrive I and mine," "and so swear I," and "whenever I . . . God punish me . . . This do I beg of heaven," Richard is conveniently absent. Entering a short while later in the same scene, he employs a far safer form of hypothetical statement:

>   if any here,
> By false intelligence, or wrong surmise,
> Hold me a foe;
> If I unwittingly, or in my rage,
> Have aught committed that is hardly borne
> By any in this presence, I desire

To reconcile me to his friendly peace.
                                 (II.i.54-60)

Not, "May God punish me," or "This do I beg of heaven," but "I desire to reconcile me." Richard is lying, of course, but he is not signing a contract for perjury.

The odd fact is that Richard, quite unlike his later counterparts Iago and Edmund, with whom he is so often compared, is a superstitious man. He fears omens and prognostications, even if he also acts as though he will be able to circumvent those omens by the sheer force of his own wit.

Despite Richard's cleverness in avoiding for a long while the actual formulation of a curse upon himself by others or by himself, he does ultimately capitulate on both scores: he submits to the curses of his mother, and he does contractually tie his whole success to the performing of vows he does not in fact intend to honor. How and why do these crucial reversals occur?

They come about in IV.iv, after Richard has become king, and importantly just after he has committed his most unforgivable crime, the murder of the two young princes. It is just at this point that Richard's sure control of his world begins to falter. He recalls the prophecy uttered by Henry VI that Richmond will be king, and he becomes obsessed, like Macbeth, with a plot to kill this rival and thereby alter destiny itself. He broods over the fact that he has recently visited a place called Rouge-mont, in Exeter—a name of ominous import to his superstitious mind in view of a prophecy, uttered by an Irish bard, that he will not live long after having beheld Richmond (IV.ii.95-107). These divine prognostications are quite unlike those afforded Richard's victims; those persons receive warnings which they might have heeded, and later realize their mistake, whereas Richard's prognostications take the form of the announcement of unavoidable doom which Richard may try to evade by prevarications and desperate cover-up murders but which will ultimately spell his doom. That is why we can say that his credence of dreams and omens is merely superstitious in him, whereas in his victims the final acknowledgment of the truth of prophetic utterance is a sign of spiritual discovery.

Richard is then indeed superstitious and fearful of prophetic utterance, unlike the suave and assured Buckingham earlier in the play. And perhaps it is this growing fear that most of all renders Richard incapable of fending off his mother's curse as he had earlier deflected Margaret's curse with a quibble. The Duchess of York, stung into speech by the deaths of her grandchildren, resolves at last to be "copious in exclaims" and to say what must now be said. Accompanied by Queen Elizabeth, she interrupts Richard on his expedition against Buckingham, in order to arraign Richard on charges of having murdered his own kinsmen. His response is, naturally, another attempt at evasion, although of a rather desperate and crude sort: he orders his trumpets and drums to flourish and strike so that the effective words cannot be heard: "Let not the heavens hear these tell-tale women/ Rail on the Lord's anointed. Strike, I say!" (IV.iv.150-51). The Duchess is not to be denied her speech on this occasion, however, and finally the awful words are spoken:

> Therefore take with thee my most grievous
>   curse,
> Which, in the day of battle, tire thee more
> Than all the complete armor that thou wear'st!
> My prayers on the adverse party fight;
> And there the little souls of Edward's
>   children
> Whisper the spirits of thine enemies
> And promise them success and victory.
> Bloody thou art, bloody will be thy end;
> Shame serves thy life and doth thy death
>   attend.
>
> (ll.188-96)

The language of this curse meaningfully anticipates that of the ghosts who visit Richard in his tent on the night before Bosworth Field.

The pattern of Richard's reversal cannot be completed by the Duchess' cursing, however. He must also curse himself. This he does in a desperate attempt to win from Queen Elizabeth an agreement that he be permitted to marry her daughter. The wooing scene is often compared with the earlier wooing of the Lady Anne, and indeed Richard afterwards thinks he has won this suit also because he is once again dealing with a "Relenting fool, and shallow, changing woman" (l.431). In fact, however, Queen Elizabeth remains in control throughout. What she finally exacts from Richard is the self-cursing he has never before uttered. First, he ties his whole military enterprise to the performance of his vows:

> Madam, so thrive I in my enterprise
> And dangerous success of bloody wars,
> As I intend more good to you and yours
> Than ever you or yours by me were harm'd!
>
> (ll.236-39)

And when this oath will not serve, since, as Queen Elizabeth acidly observes, Richard has already profaned everything else by which a man might swear, he finally throws his spiritual welfare and his very life into the bargain:

> As I intend to prosper and repent,
> So thrive I in my dangerous affairs
> Of hostile arms! Myself myself confound!

> Heaven and fortune bar me happy hours!
> Day, yield me not thy light, nor, night, thy
>   rest!
> Be opposite all planets of good luck
> To my proceeding, if, with dear heart's love,
> Immaculate devotion, holy thoughts,
> I tender not thy beauteous princely daughter!
>
> (ll.397-405)

What more binding or appropriate contract for perjury could providence require? Like Doctor Faustus, Richard has seen the dire warning—*Homo, fuge* [O man, flee!]—and yet has, as it were, set his hand to paper using his own heart's blood.

I should mention that this pattern of cursing and self-cursing appears nowhere in Shakespeare's possible sources or analogues. In *The True Tragedy of Richard III*, Richard sends Lovell as ambassador to Queen Elizabeth to gain her consent to the marriage of her daughter. In the Latin *Richardus Tertius* Richard woos the Lady Elizabeth for himself. In neither instance does he commit himself to any sort of contract for perjury. The earlier scene of Margaret's cursing and the round of self-curses pronounced by Buckingham, Hastings, and the rest in the presence of the dying King Edward, are both absent from Edward Hall's *Union of the Two Noble Families* and its incorporated reprinting of Thomas More's *Life of Richard III*. More reports merely that in Edward's presence "as by their words appeared, each forgave other, and joined their hands together, when as it after appeared by their deeds their hearts were far asunder." [Source titles and quotes are from Geoffrey Bullough, III, *Narrative and Dramatic Sources of Shakespeare*.]

Let me conclude by observing that Richard's *anagnorisis* is wholly unlike that of any of his victims or former partners. In a sense, he learns little in the dream sequence when he is visited in turn by the ghosts of his victims, for he has always been conscious of his own villainy and wary of the consequences of cursing. The dream sequence is more a fulfillment and choric repetition of what he has feared than a healthful revelation to Richard of God's justice. At no time does he indicate a new awareness of what providence has been intending. What he realizes instead is that "coward conscience" has the power to inflict itself on one who had wanted to believe himself free of its strictures. The theme of conscience's relevation to him is "Perjury, perjury, in the highest degree,/ Murder, stern murder, in the direst degree" (V.iii. 196-97), for which he must despair and die. Forced at last to judge himself by the standards embodied in those words, and obliged to concede their absolute truth, he perceives himself cut off from the curative process of penance and so goes to his death (like Macbeth) in a desperate resolve to fight the odds he now knows to be insuperable.

Shakespeare's attitude toward the power of language in this early play thus tempers concern and even pessimism with a final affirmation in the triumph of truth. Throughout the early history plays he shows us how language can be manipulated for evil purposes, not only in Richard of Gloucester, but in Joan of Arc, Suffolk, Richard Plantagenet, the Bishop of Winchester, and many others. One the other hand, we also sense the vibrant power of language to invoke patriotic and moral responses, as in the ringing recital of Lord Talbot's titles, and in Henry of Richmond's oration to his army at Bosworth Field. Certainly in *Richard III* it becomes apparent at last that curses and prayers do not merely vanish into air once they are spoken, as Buckingham avers. Instead, as he himself later acknowledges, a person's words, like his deeds, become swords which an all-seeing God turns against their masters' bosoms. "Wrong hath but wrong, and blame the due of blame."

Kristian Smidt

"Plots and Prophecies—*The Tragedy of King Richard the Third*," in *Unconformities in Shakespeare's History Plays*, The Macmillan Press Ltd., 1982, pp. 53-71.

[*In this excerpt, Smidt focuses on prophecies in* Richard III*. She points out that while Richard is not a real prophet, he invents prophecies in order to control other characters in the play. Further, Richard is so confident in his own abilities that when he tells us what he plans to do, we know that he is likely to succeed. On the other hand, Smidt argues that Margaret's curses are powerful enough to work as genuine prophecies, without her having to act upon them. Finally, Smidt observes that dreams, prayers, and blessings in the play are often prophetic.*]

Shakespeare made liberal use of prediction in all his history plays, but never as much as in *Richard III*. This play is a web of stated intentions, curses, prophecies, and dreams, and practically all expectations are punctually fulfilled. A. P. Rossiter [in his "The Structure of Richard the Third"] and Wolfgang Clemen [in his "Anticipation and Foreboding in Shakespeare's Early Histories"] have both admirably explored this aspect of the play, but it will still bear further scrutiny.

Only two minutes after Richard, Duke of Gloucester, has entered solus he informs us that he is 'determined to prove a villain', and, he goes on,

> Plots have I laid, inductions dangerous,
> By drunken prophecies, libels, and
>   dreams,
> To set my brother Clarence and the King
> In deadly hate the one against the other;
>
>   (I.i.32-5)

Richard's 'plots', 'prophecies', and 'dreams' in themselves foreshadow the mode of the remainder of the play. His pretended prophecy that a certain 'G' will be the murderer of King Edward's heirs proves more true than the victims of the deceit, Clarence and Edward, suspect, but Richard knows already, and we know, that the G stands for Gloucester and not for George. He speaks the truth though with forked tongue. And he never keeps his audience in the dark.

Richard is himself no prophet. But he is a man of iron will and unscrupulous performance coupled with exceptional gifts of persuasion and dissimulation. What he resolves to do he does, and his confidence in telling us of his intentions leaves no room for doubt that they will be carried out successfully. We know before the event that Clarence will be imprisoned and murdered (I.i.32-40, 119-20), that Richard will marry Anne (I.i.153), that he will have his revenge on Rivers, Vaughan, and Grey (I.iii.332), that something will be done 'To draw the brats of Clarence out of sight' and to get rid of the princes in the Tower (III.v.106-8, IV.ii.61), that he will do away with Anne and woo Elizabeth (IV.ii.57-61). All this is revealed in soliloquies, and Richard further confides in us about the success of his undertakings (IV.iii.36-43). In addition, of course, he conspires with Buckingham and his more inferior associates and gives instructions to his hired assassins on two occasions. We know what will happen to Hastings if he does not fall in with Richard's plans, and we know exactly what lies and pretences Richard will use to gain the support of the citizens of London for his coronation. Practically all the plot of the play until near the end of the fourth act is contained in Richard's stated intentions.

These intentions are for the most part reinforced by Margaret's curses and prophecies, since Richard turns on those of his own side and consequently his enemies are hers. In the great cursing scene of Act I, Margaret predicts no fewer than thirteen misfortunes relating to King Edward, his son, Queen Elizabeth, her children, Rivers, Hastings, Richard, and Buckingham. There is even a certain amount of detail in her curses: King Edward is to die 'by surfeit' and the Prince of Wales by 'untimely violence', the queen is to outlive her glory and her children and see another 'decked in [her] rights'. 'The day will come', Margaret warns Elizabeth,

>   that thou shalt wish for me
> To help thee curse this poisonous bunch-
>   backed toad.
>
>   (I.iii.244-5)

As for Richard, she is unsparing in her depiction of punishments for him, especially, as Tillyard points out, the curse of insomnia:

If heaven have any grievous plague in store
Exceeding those that I can wish upon thee,
O let them keep it till thy sins be ripe,
And then hurl down their indignation
On thee, the troubler of the poor world's
     peace!
The worm of conscience still begnaw thy
     soul!
Thy friends suspect for traitors while thou
     liv'st,
And take deep traitors for thy dearest
     friends!
No sleep close up that deadly eye of thine,
Unless it be while some tormenting dream
Affrights thee with a hell of ugly devils!
                                        (I.iii.216-26)

Margaret's curses are no mere displays of clairvoyance but obviously potent agents in bringing about the events which she prophesies, and as they come to pass this is recognised in turn by the victims—all but Richard. As Grey goes to his execution at Pomfret he remarks to Rivers,

Now Margaret's curse is fallen upon our
     heads,
When she exclaimed on Hastings, you, and I,
For standing by when Richard stabbed her
     son.
                                        (III.iii.14-16)

Similarly Hastings, Queen Elizabeth, and Buckingham all remember her words in their hour of distress, and Margaret herself tots up the score of her victories in the great lamenting scene of Act IV.

Margaret is the chief and most vociferous but by no means the only prophet and author of curses in the play. She herself is first prompted by Richard's reminder of his father's curse denounced against Margaret at the time of his death (I.iii.173-95). If 'York's dread curse prevail[ed] so much with heaven', then she must try the same means of revenge. The Duchess of York and Elizabeth take a lesson from Margaret, and the duchess utters violent imprecations against Richard to which Elizabeth says amen (IV.iv.188-98). Anne in the second scene of the tragedy curses the murderer of her husband and father-in-law and prays to God to revenge King Henry's death. Unwittingly she involves herself in her baneful wishes by hypothetically including the wife of the murderer. She remembers this when her misery is complete, just as Buckingham in the reconciliation scene swears an oath which recoils on himself and remembers it on the day of his execution. Even Richard, in the second wooing scene, swears against himself and is probably too sceptical to realise that his maledictions will be most precisely honoured:

Myself myself confound!

Heaven and fortune bar me happy hours!
Day, yield me not thy light, nor, night, thy
     rest!
                                        (IV.iv.399-401)

After his night of agony and confused awakening, the sun 'disdains to shine' on him on the day of battle. Vaughan and Hastings before being beheaded foretell the downfall of their judges. The ghosts, of course, add their full share of cursing. And Richmond, on Bosworth field, prays that he and his forces may be God's 'ministers of chastisement'.

Prayers are mostly for chastisement and revenge, and blessings are as rare in *Richard III* as imprecations are plentiful. Clarence prays for his wife and children, the hoodwinked mayor invokes God's blessing on Richard when the latter agrees to accept the crown, Dorset exits to Brittany with the Duchess of York's benediction (she also rather futilely sends her good wishes with Anne and Elizabeth), Stanley blesses Richmond 'by attorney' from his mother, and of course the ghosts whisper encouragements to Richmond in his sleep. But the only time Richard talks of blessings is when he hypocritically craves one of his mother and makes fun of her admonishments (II.ii.106-11).

Dreams are almost as important as curses and prayers and equally prophetic. Richard uses invented dreams to set Edward against Clarence, Clarence appropriately dreams of drowning and of being tormented in hell, Stanley dreams symbolically of being executed by Richard along with Hastings, and Richard and Richmond dream on the eve of battle of defeat and victory. Hastings sceptically laughs at Stanley's being so simple as 'to trust the mockery of unquiet slumbers' (III.ii.27) but learns to his cost that Stanley was right. And Richard, who is outwardly the least superstitious of all the characters in the play, is plagued nightly after Margaret's curse by the phantom horrors it promises. As Clemen remarks, [in his "Anticipation and Foreboding in Shakespeare's Early Histories"]. 'There is the feeling of fear and uncertainty running like a keynote through almost all the scenes of the play and finding expression in various characters and ways.' So general is the mood of fearsome divination that even the anonymous citizens in II.iii, commenting on the death of King Edward, are inspired with prophetic forebodings.

DARK COMEDY IN *RICHARD III*

A number of critics have examined the types of comedy present in *Richard III* and have speculated about why so much of it exists in what is otherwise a grim play. **William E. Sheriff** points out that although there are no scenes that contain "outright comedy," there are many which become comedic as the result of dramatic irony. (Dramatic irony occurs when the audience understands the real significance of a character's words or actions but the character or those around him or her do not.) Thus Richard's commiseration with Clarence as he is being led to prison in Act I, scene i, becomes comedic because Richard has just informed us that *he* is responsible for having Clarence jailed in the first place. Sheriff suggests that such humor is there to lighten what would otherwise be dry history already well-known to its Elizabethan audience.

Ronald Berman looks at the "tough, cynical, and realistic wit" of both Richard and Buckingham and concludes that while these two characters deservedly pay for their cruel self-centeredness with their lives, in the meantime they serve to illustrate certain qualities of the individual as opposed to those of society. A. P. Rossiter also takes up this issue of society versus the individual to argue that Shakespeare wrote *Richard III* as a comic history in order to express life's ambiguities rather than simply to reproduce the Tudor idea of social and historical order.

John W. Blanpied contends that Richard employs parody to control others by keeping them guessing and to hold off at least temporarily Margaret's fatal prophecies. (Parody is the use of exaggerated imitation to ridicule someone or something that was meant to be serious.)

William E. Sheriff

SOURCE: "The Grotesque Comedy of *Richard III*," in *Studies in the Literary Imagination*, Vol. V, No. 1, April, 1972, pp. 51-64.

[*Sheriff discusses Richard's wittiness and his comedic use of dramatic irony and inversion—or saying one thing and meaning its opposite. Sheriff contends that Shakespeare made Richard appealingly funny so that his audience would remain interested in what might otherwise be a "cold-blooded" history play about Richard's accession to the throne. Sheriff further argues that Shakespeare then turned Richard into a humorless character during the last two acts of the play so that his audience would not be troubled when Richard is finally destroyed on Bosworth Field.*]

The life of Richard III had received impressive treatment in the century before Shakespeare's presentation of the man. His wickedness was held to be fact, especially as the sixteenth-century chroniclers added to each other's accounts. But Richard as a potential comic villain, a grotesque figure of diabolic wit, playing a "game" of evil action is only hinted in the chronicles and is largely Shakespeare's invention. It is Shakespeare who gives us the psychological complexity of

evil and humor that is Richard in the first three acts of *Richard III*. Then the man changes, and Act IV gives us a tyrant, who lacks a twisted humor and displays too openly the evil that wit used to hide. The change is perhaps most apparent in the second wooing scene.

But why the comic at all in Shakespeare's Richard? It is true there are no scenes in the play one can call outright comedy. But there are many scenes that take on comic overtones because of the insight we have into Richard's intent and the resultant dramatic irony. [Dramatic irony occurs when the audience understands the real significance of a character's words or actions but the character or those around him do not] Shakespeare chose to use the comic to emphasize the demonic in Richard.

The element of the grotesque in this play depends on irony, which Hardin Craig [in "Shakespeare and the History Play"] sees as operating at all levels. The entire bloody career of Richard is ironic: it stopped the York succession, settled the family feud, and ended the hundred years of strife. Therefore, it is more than fitting that Shakespeare made effective use of irony in this play. The comedy and irony strengthen the drama and give reassurance of a happy ending. Since the Elizabethans knew that Richard would receive his just reward, they could enjoy what Brander Matthews [in *Shakespeare as a Playwright*] calls the "sardonic humor" of the first three acts. In his life Richard had been much like a character out of the old morality play, a figure who properly received his comedown at the end. [A morality play is a medieval drama in which abstract vices and virtues are presented in human form.] Samuel Johnson [in "General Observations on the Plays of Shakespeare"] saw in *Richard III* traces of the puppet plays in which the Devil was "lustily belaboured by old Vice." The best recent treatment of Richard as a Vice character is that by Bernard Spivack. By "a characteristic medievalism," says Spivack, [in *Shakespeare and the Allegory of Evil*] "destructive forces were always dramatized as grotesque or ludicrous figures." To him Richard is the Vice Deceit, who seeks "the appreciation of the audience for his dexterity."

In an excellent chapter on "Gothic Drama" [in his book *English Drama from Early Times to the Elizabethans*] A. P. Rossiter constantly shows the parallel treatment of the grotesquely comic and the sacred in Gothic art. In the works of Grunewald, Bosch, and Breugel, he notes, there is a reflection of the same medieval aspect of life as seen in the cycle plays and other forms of drama. I should like to suggest that it would be rewarding to picture Richard as a Gothic gargoyle, comic in his grotesqueness, diabolic in his leer, reminding one of hell. He poses as a Christian, prayer book in hand, between two bishops, as he plans the slaughter of innocents. He is a complete inversion of Christian discipleship. It is only by a Providence of which he has no comprehension, and quite beside his intent, that even this apostate can serve as an instrument of divine vengeance, a scourge of God to rid England of her sin. Irony becomes a necessity, for we must know the intent of Richard while those about him do not. His wit is needed to fulfill his purpose, but when that has fulfilled the limited role allowed it by Providence, his wit is shown to be myopic and inadequate. Therefore, when England has been properly scourged, his wit fails him, and he falls prey to Richmond, who arrives to right the state.

Richard is neither the tragic hero of classical stature nor completely static, for he undergoes a noticeable change when he drops his twisted comedy. He develops from a confident doer of evil to a confused and unsuccessful Machiavel [one who views politics as amoral and that any means, however unscrupulous, can justifiably be used in achieving political power] without hope. That he is conscious himself of this development I hope to show in an analysis of the play.

I particularly agree with Louis Cazamian [in *The Development of English Humor*] that Richard is a conscious actor—we know from his soliloquies that he is "clearly conscious of his inner being." Still why the need for the comic in such a portrayal? What appears to have been missed in the various commentaries, although one or two have hinted at it, is that Richard finds a perverse happiness in his diabolic scheming. There is little humor in the early soliloquy of *III Henry VI* and in the opening soliloquy of *Richard III;* instead, there are present the self-searching utterances of an unhappy man. Richard has little of worth to the world. He is brave, but so are most of those about him. He has no beauty, not even a pleasant appearance—and Shakespeare is presenting him to an age that believed the inner self to be reflected in outer appearance. The one pleasing quality he does possess is his wit, in which he has complete confidence. Since he cannot play the game of the world about him, he will use his wit to play his own hellish game. Yet, to those outside his private world he will appear to be engaged in their game. He will even play the Christian, the loving brother, and the protecting uncle. He will even play husband and father to the woman whose husband and father he has destroyed. He will also stand outside both worlds and comment upon the roles he plays in both; he will move both sides of the chessboard. Ironically, he will checkmate himself, for once he wins the crown he has no where else to go. The goal he set to be reached at the end of the game is won, and there is nothing else.

Up to this moment he is happy as he successfully makes one move after the other. Acting the role is pleasant: he puns more than any other character in the play. He cannot refrain from using double meanings that show his confidence and that congratulate himself on his own brilliance. The beauty of it is that we appreciate his accomplishment and are compelled to admire him even though the role he plays and the action it occasions are destructive. Shakespeare, however, removes any guilt we may feel in finding Richard sympathetic by presenting a different man in the final two acts. The irony in such a performance is almost unlimited, as it works on such a multiplicity of levels that it even includes the audience in the irony of being caught as both victor and victim in the same game Richard plays.

The wordplay of the opening soliloquy gives a hint (I.i.1-41). "This sun of York" is often seen as a triple pun on Edward IV as the son of York with a sun on his badge and as the brightest sun of the party in power. I suggest further wordplay in its being reflexive—that is, in also standing for Richard himself. Then his "winter of discontent" is over, and he will commence his glorious summer. Such a reading gives the subtle meaning of dissembling: he will show a merry front to the world that at the moment dances to "delightful measures." We are prepared for the role he will play before he openly informs us of it. He will make his own world and laws. Therefore, his mode of comedy will not be that of others, and we can accept it as comedy on those grounds. When Clarence arrives on the scene, Richard commands his thoughts to dive down to his soul. From this moment forward, we know his soul to be unlike any other encountered in the play.

The opening scene shows the inverted world of Richard in action. Clarence is on his way to the Tower; Lord Hastings has just been released. Both men speak their troubled minds to the man who ironically will have them destroyed in the Tower. Within ten lines of his decisive soliloquy Richard is already playing his hellish game and thoroughly enjoying the position he maintains. He says to Clarence, "Oh, belike His Majesty hath some intent / That you shall be new-christened in the Tower" (I.i.49-50), which is an excellent example of what Wolfgang Clemen [in "Anticipation and Foreboding in Shakespeare's Early Histories"] was referring to when he spoke of the dramatic irony helping to "build up this dense tissue of foreboding hints." Further, it reassures the reader or spectator that Richard is in earnest in the role he has created, and that he is eager to plunge into it. He immediately implants in Clarence's mind the idea that it is the queen, and not the king, who has caused his arrest and the imprisonment of Lord Hastings. Then he cannot resist applauding himself for his cleverness. He adds, "We are not safe, Clarence, we are not safe" (I.i.70). Who cannot be fascinated with such a mind?

When Clarence is out of hearing Richard remarks, "I

do love thee so / That I will shortly send thy soul to Heaven. / If Heaven will take the present at our hand" (I.i.118-20). Here he begins his pose as Christian; it is good that the righteous should go to Heaven, and his own curious kind of divine providence will "help" them to their destiny. Those he loves most, brothers and nephews, should be helped along to their glory.

The following scene has occasioned more comment than any other in the play, for in it Shakespeare has stretched probability to its furthest limits. His own invention, the Richard–Anne wooing scene, has often been criticized for its artificiality. The scene can be found justifiable on the grounds that it furthers the characterization of Richard, showing the lengths to which he will go in order to obtain his aims. Shakespeare realized we had to put up with this fellow until we had him seated on the throne in order for the play to sustain interest. A cold-blooded approach to the throne, with no humor in Richard's character and, as a result, less interest, would have repeated the pattern of so many of the contemporary history plays. If Richard as a hero-villian could be made a fascinating one, what better characterization than to place him in a ludicrous situation which he could master with his particular bent of wit? Ignoring the conventional garden setting for courtly wooing, Shakespeare brilliantly uses Richard's role of inversion. He has the monstrous Richard propose to Anne over the coffin of her father-in-law who has been slain by his hand. The point to be emphasized here is that the ritual is a mockery, in that the symbol of creation (marriage) is enacted over the symbol of destruction (the coffin). Furthering his pose as a Christian, Richard asks for charity after Anne has called him a "minister of Hell." He calls those who bear the corpse of the man he has slain "villains" and swears "by Saint Paul" to make corpses of those who disobey him (I.ii.46, 36, 41). Richard's observance of ritual prepares us for this inversion of spiritual values in Act III where he appears between two bishops with a prayer book in his hands.

Ritual, or not, the scene stands on its own merits in the overall structure of the play. Richard's qualities of deception, persuasion, and daring break forth. As if he were making a test run for his later great experiment on the court, he here moves carefully, calculates the counter-move of his opponent, and moves again. Where most suitors would have shrugged and laughed off defeat, Richard in full confidence continues his "attack," coming in from this side and that until Anne accepts the ring.

A point often overlooked in this famous scene is that Anne does not completely reverse her position. She accepts the ring with the statement "To take is not to give" (I.ii.203). The "boon" he requests of her after this line is to allow him to see to the burial of Henry

VI, and this she agrees to, thankful that he has become so penitent. He then requests she bid him farewell, and her reply is guarded:

> 'Tis more than you deserve.
> But since you teach me how to flatter you,
> Imagine I have said farewell already.
>
> (I.ii.223-25)

Her immediate exit does not allow us further insight into her mind, nor is it necessary. We need not waste sympathy upon her, for she has been taught how to flatter Richard, and to marry him is to accept his world. She does not appear again until Act IV when Shakespeare commences his change in Richard's character, and at that point we see her as a sympathetic person.

At Anne's exit Richard cannot help praising himself; he has been observing himself in this challenging situation, and he is pleased with the result:

> Was ever woman in this humor wooed?
> Was ever woman in this humor won?
> I'll have her, but I will not keep her long.
>
> (I.ii.228-30)

He scorns Anne for her fickle memory, that she has so soon forgot that "sweeter and lovlier gentleman, / Framed in the prodigality of nature" (I.ii.243-44), her husband that he stabbed at Tewkesbury. He becomes engrossed in his role and his success; he will study fashions and adorn his body.

In Act I, scene iii Richard expands his game to include the entire court. The absent King is sick and represented by Queen Elizabeth, who denounces Richard before his entrance ("A man that loves not me, nor none of you") and concludes "I fear our happiness is at the highest" (I.iii.13, 41). Upon this note enters the deceitful Richard, telling Hastings and Dorset that those who have spoken ill of him do him wrong:

> Because I cannot flatter and speak fair,
> Smile in men's faces, smooth, deceive, and cog,
> Duck with French nods and apish courtesy,
> I must be held a rancorous enemy.
>
> (I.iii.47-50)

He receives no favorable welcome from Queen Elizabeth, but when Queen Margaret enters and listens to the wrangle in the background, she gives choric comment on the dissension within the York party, until she steps forward to accuse them all of evil. Her curses include the entire court, but she particularly turns upon Richard. Her invective foreshadows his gnawing conscience and his tormenting dreams. However, at this point Richard begins again his play of wit:

Q. Margaret. Thou loathèd issue of thy
  father's loins!
       Thou rag of honor! Thou detested—
Gloucester. Margaret.
Q. Margaret.   Richard!
Gloucester.   Ha!
Q. Margaret.   I
  call thee not.
Gloucester. I cry thee mercy, then, for I had
  thought
       That thou hadst called me all these
  bitter names.
Q. Margaret. Why, so I did, but looked for
  no reply.
       Oh, let me make the period to
  my curse!

                              (I.iii.232-38)

He has befuddled her by such interruption, and her
spell upon her listeners is broken. Queen Elizabeth
remarks that Margaret has breathed her curse upon
herself. We have another example of Richard's capacity to invert.

Queen Margaret's exit ironically gives Richard a chance
to be penitent in a move parallel to the one he has
made with Anne in the preceding scene. He regrets
any part he had in the wrongs done to Margaret and
asks God's pardon for all who helped to create her
misery:

Gloucester. God pardon them that are the
  cause of it!
Rivers.   A virtuous and a Christianlike
  conclusion,
       To pray for them that have
  done scathe to us.
Gloucester. So do I ever—[*Aside*] being well
  advised.
       For had I cursed now, I had
  cursed myself.

                              (I.iii.315-19)

The pose of the Christian that Richard mockingly
adopts remains with him until his coronation. In his
soliloquy after the court departs to attend the sick
king he says:

But then I sigh, and with a piece of Scripture
Tell them that God bids us do good for evil.
And thus I clothe my naked villainy
With old odd ends stolen out of Holy Writ,
And seem a saint when most I play the
  devil.

                              (I.iii.334-38)

He does not stop at stealing from the Holy Scriptures; he swears "by God's holy mother" (I.iii.306)
(perhaps a joke at Margaret) in pretending repentance;

and later he will use a prayer book to further his
ends. Against the background of his "repentance" in
this scene, the two murderers enter, and Richard
arranges the death of his brother Clarence.

The following scene, which concerns the legendary
vat-drowning of Clarence, is one of the most grimly
ironic in the play. Inversion has followed Clarence to
the Tower, and the scene is full of Christian sermon-
izing which Clarence never thinks to apply to himself after he has related his ominous dream of death
and damnation to Brakenbury.

The Christian references which set *Richard III* somewhat apart from the *Henry VI* trilogy continue in the
next act. Edward opens the first scene as a "peacemaker," who having done a "good day's work" (II.i.1)
is ready to meet his Redeemer. But although his actions have produced outward unity, the "peace" he
has created is not much different from that which
Richard approves and preaches. He has "set [his]
friends at peace on earth" (II.ii.6) and Clarence has
drowned in a butt of malmsey wine. His request that
the court not "dissemble" (8) ironically recalls Richard's more outrageous preaching and mockery of
spiritual values.

Richard arrives on the reconciliation scene in full
command of his role:

I do not know that Englishman alive
With whom my soul is any jot at odds
More than the infant that is born tonight.
I thank my God for my humility.

                              (II.i.69-72)

To an audience that has just witnessed the murder of
Clarence, the irony in Richard's words is dramatically effective. He manages to convince the king that it
was through the king's order that Clarence was executed. The king laments the times and ironically echoes his slain brother in the fear of divine vengeance:
"O God, I fear Thy justice will take hold / On me,
and you, and mine, and yours for this" (II.i.131-32).
The inverted values have involved the king, too: his
earlier warning to Rivers and Hastings is now directed at himself.

Act III concentrates on Richard's quick moves to
attain the throne after the death of Edward IV. In
seven fast-moving scenes which reflect the swiftness
of the thought that lies behind the action, the young
princes are secured in the Tower, Lord Hastings is
executed, and Richard is requested to take the throne.
Richard relies on only one man, and that man is
Buckingham, who according to the chronicles [Raph-
ael Holinshed's *The Chronicles of England, Scotland,
and Ireland*] was not as eager as he appears in Shakespeare's play to be involved with Richard's schemes.

In the first scene Buckingham continues the irony of the inversion by lecturing Cardinal Bourchier that he is "Too ceremonious and traditional" (III.i.45) in insisting on sanctuary for the children. The Cardinal allows his mind to be overruled by Buckingham's logic, although he knows and has stated that it would be a deep sin to violate such sanctuary as the widow and the child have taken. Richard preaches to the prince that the youth's years have not yet exposed him to the world of deceit, to which the prince's response is, "may God keep me from false friends" (III.i.16). Later in an aside Richard informs us that "like the formal vice Iniquity / I moralize two meanings in one word" (III.i.82-83). His talk with the other nephew results in his being outwitted by a very young child. When the princes have been led to the Tower, Buckingham asks if Richard does not think the lad was incensed by his mother to make scornful remarks, and Richard, almost tossing the boy aside as being of no consequence, replies:

> No doubt, no doubt. Oh, 'tis a parlous boy—
> Bold, quick, ingenious, forward, capable.
> He is all the mother's from the top to toe.
>
> (III.i.154-56)

A subtle change is beginning to take place in Richard's character. However, to the casual observer he is much the same as before. Hastings, still taken in by Richard, observes three scenes later:

> I think there's never a man in Christendom
> That can less hide his love or hate than he,
> For by his face straight shall you know his
>   heart.
>
> (III.iv.53-55)

But Richard must resort to an obvious lie when he shows his withered arm, which all present know to have been a disfigurement from birth, and declares it to be the result of the witchcraft of Queen Elizabeth and Jane Shore. Since Shakespeare chose to present the historical scene as it was represented in the chronicles, he also had to make the decision to show Richard as being reduced to theatrics and open falsehood to gain his ends. The diabolic figure of brilliant wit of the opening scenes of the play has given way to a ruthless monster, confident in his ability to make his victims accept his pretenses, however illogical. He now dares to say:

> If! Thou protector of this damnèd strumpet,
> Tellest thou me of "if"? Thou art a traitor.
> Off with his head! Now, by Saint Paul I
>   swear,
> I will not dine until I see the same.
>
> (III.iv.76-79)

The strawberry incident in this scene also contains comic irony. Edward Dowden [in *Shakespeare: A Critical Study of His Mind and Art*] remarks on the cynical humor throughout this conference, mainly in the manner in which Ely's strawberries are reserved until the head of Hastings is off. Charles Forker [in "Shakespeare's Chronicle Plays as Historical-Pastoral"], speaks of Richard's "little reign of terror" in the scene and the contrast between the emblematic goodness of the garden and the withered arm of Richard. Again we have inverted value in that Richard will not partake of the garden until Hastings is executed.

Two rascals—one a master and the other his disciple—produce the humor of the remainder of the act as they play together the game of double meanings, mock innocence, and false piety. As with the capers of Volpone and his servant Mosca [two characters in Ben Jonson's play *Volpone*], the comedy consists in the outrageously successful gulling of dupes. The play of deceit is introduced by Buckingham, who like Mosca has learned well from his master. Richard's failure to comprehend fully his lesson could be ominous for him, for when Richard next tries to manipulate Buckingham, the servant is shrewd enough to know when to stop.

The fifth scene shows Richard lecturing Buckingham on the arts of dissembling before the mayor and Catesby arrive. Then his old comic inversion shows again. Viewing the head of Hastings, he laments:

> So dear I loved the man that I must weep.
> I took him for the plainest harmless creature
> That breathed upon this earth a Christian;
> Made him my book, wherein my soul
>   recorded
> The history of all her secret thoughts.
>
> (III.v.24-28)

He has slain his confessor on earth. Successful with the mayor, Richard dives once more to hellish depths. He instructs Buckingham to spread rumors that Edward's children are bastards and that his mother had committed adultery. Brothers and nephews have been sacrifices in his black ritual; motherhood means little to him. We are quite prepared for his final act to gain the throne—his use of the church and its holy vows.

The prayer book scene should be seen in relation to the entire play: this is Richard's great moment. If he can carry off the role of the devout contemplative before the mayor and the citizens, the throne is his. The situation is critical, as Buckingham explains. Few of the citizens are in favor of Richard as their king—only ten shouted in his favor when Buckingham informed them of the illegitimacy of the young princes. Therefore, the scene with the prayer book is crucial in his career.

In comparing the speeches of Buckingham and Richard, one can see that the wit of the latter far exceeds that of the former. Buckingham's lines sound prepared, rehearsed, and ritualistic. Richard's lines are studiously spontaneous, flexible, and loaded with comic overtones. He is the comedian of the first act again, as he wins the crown. When Buckingham, in the name of England, offers him the throne, Richard is ostensibly the wooed instead of the wooer. Playing the "maid's part" (III.vii.51) as instructed by Buckingham, he gives over thirty lines of humble reasons why he cannot entertain such a thought. But in his humility he manages to produce three valid reasons why he both stays to listen to the argument and why he cannot accept the crown. He brings up the obstacle of the princes and their royal line before Buckingham does. When the charge of bastardy removes this obstacle, there is nothing for him to do as a devout and humble leader of his people but accept the crown.

The opening scene of Act IV initiates the action that results in the destruction of Richard. Lord Stanley comes to fetch Anne for the coronation, and Queen Elizabeth sends Dorset to Richmond. The next scene presents the changed Richard. It is almost a shock to find his wit overshadowed by his insecurity and his lack of humor. He is directly involved as an open participant in the reality of the court and can no longer remain hidden behind his brilliant cleverness. The first indication of this remarkable change is seen during his attempts to enlist Buckingham's aid in the murder of the princes. His innuendoes no longer carry effectiveness; he must speak openly. Shocked, Buckingham leaves the presence of the king but returns later to request the Earldom of Hereford promised to him earlier. The king repeatedly ignores the request and finally snaps, "I am not in the giving vein today" (IV.ii.119). Comedy occurs in a Machiavel's petulance exposing his true feelings. How foolish to act in anger. It forewarns Buckingham, who fearfully leaves the court. The Machiavel has blindly endangered himself.

When Tyrrel tells Richard of the murder of the princes, Richard prepares to court the young Elizabeth as a "jolly thriving wooer" (IV.iii.43). But the comedy has grown more complex. In the face of Queen Elizabeth's and the Duchess's accusations Richard cries:

> A flourish, trumpets! Strike alarum, drums!
> Let not the Heavens hear these telltale
>   women
> Rail on the Lord's anointed. Strike, I say!
> (IV.iv.148-50)

The Machiavel is now afraid of the Heavens, and his fears overcome him. He cannot fight with witty words; he must drown out their words with the noise of battle.

The direct coaxing of Elizabeth by Richard is not

historical fact, although Holinshed has a thorough discussion of how Richard's messengers, "being men both of wit and grauitie, so persuaded the queene with great and pregnant reasons, & what with faire and large promises, that she began somewhat to relent," and finally to give in to Richard's wish that she allow her five daughters to leave sanctuary and be placed in the custody of the "rauenous woolfe." However, not only the public but the young lady herself so loathed the idea of her marriage to the king, that even with Anne out of the way, the historical Richard postponed his courtship until "he were in more quietnesse" (*Chronicles*, III.431).

Why does Shakespeare invent an incident and present it at some length? He gives it more than two hundred lines, some forty more than he gave to the earlier wooing of Anne. It is my opinion that he wished to balance the presentation of his characterization of Richard; that is, whereas he first convinced us of the powers of this monstrous comedian, he now wishes to destroy that image in order that the entire concept of Richard's character can be shattered on Bosworth Field without regret on the part of the spectator. The qualities we found fascinating in Richard, his brilliant wit, his corrupt sense of humor, his ability to stand outside the scene and watch himself, are missing in his encounter with Queen Elizabeth, and we are in this manner prepared for the concluding act of the play. Early in his confrontation with Queen Elizabeth it is she who takes over the lead from Richard, and it is in her lines we find double meanings (IV.iv.216-34). A few speeches more and we find that she has got to the heart of the matter; she recognizes that his soul is of another world (IV.iv.256-60). It is now Richard who is befuddled. He says, "Be not so hasty to confound my meaning," and later, "Come, come, you mock me. This is not the way / To win your daughter" (IV.iv.261, 284-85). At this point the dialogue reverts to Senecan stichomythia. We have a lecture on the religion of Richard revealed through Queen Elizabeth's questions and parries, until the moment arrives where she takes over Richard's lines and completes them in the masterful manner in which he completed those of Queen Margaret in Act I:

> K. Richard. Now, by my George, my Garter,
>   and my crown—
> Q. Elizabeth. Profaned, dishonored, and the
>   third usurped.
> K. Richard. I swear—
> Q. Elizabeth.   By nothing, for this is no
> oath.
>
> . . . . .
>
> K. Richard. Now, by the world
> Q. Elizabeth.   'Tis full of thy foul
> wrongs.

Richard III as played by Edwin Booth in 1872.

K. Richard. My father's death—
Q. Elizabeth.   Thy life hath that
   dishonored.
K. Richard. Then, by myself—
Q. Elizabeth.   Thyself thyself
   misusest.
K. Richard. Why then, by God—
Q. Elizabeth.   God's wrong is
   most of al!

                              (IV.iv.366-68, 374-77)

It is the comedy of a Machiavel who has been over-matched—and by a woman.

His deterioration of wit is seen sharply in the remainder of the scene:

K. Richard.   Some light-foot friend post to
   the Duke of Norfolk—
Ratcliff, thyself, or Catesby—where is he?

Catesby.   Here, my lord.

K. Richard.   Fly to the Duke. [To Ratcliff]
   Post thou to Salisbury.
When thou comest thither—[To Catesby]
   Dull unmindful villain,
 Why stand'st thou still, and go'st not to the
   Duke?

Catesby.   First, mighty sovereign, let me
   know your mind.
 What from your Grace I shall deliver to
   him.

K. Richard.   O true, good Catesby, bid him
   levy straight.
The greatest strength and power he can
   make,
And meet me presently at Salisbury.
                              (IV.iv.440-50)

Then when Ratcliff wishes to know what he should do at Salisbury, Richard has forgotten he had told him to go there. He explains by saying, "My mind is changed, sir, my mind is changed" (IV.iv.456). And this line becomes ironic wordplay without his knowing it, the greatest irony of all for a man who has taken such pleasure in his own wit. Richard has developed from the brilliant comical villain of the first act to the befuddled, tragical murderer who blindly slays five "Richmonds" at Bosworth Field before being destroyed by the real Richmond.

The conclusion leaves us with comedy in two senses, neither of which was anticipated when the play began. First, as we have seen in the cases of Elizabeth and Buckingham, Richard, the deceiver, in the end has been deceived himself. His too confident trust in

opportunism has caused his ultimate downfall. Disorder of the magnitude of his operation requires machinations of too obvious a nature, which he foolishly undertakes—it is the comedy of the guller being gulled. Second, we have the comedy of England's return to normalcy; the tyranny of Richard is overcome as others cease scrambling with each other for power and unite against the tyrant for a natural ordering of things.

In general the comedy of *Richard III* is different from that in the *Henry VI* trilogy where several characters were given comical treatments in various degrees. In *Richard III* the comedy is centered around the murderous king. Forker remarks that Richard "turns the acquisition of power into a monstrous private joke," and the enormity of the act in its macabre nature may have attracted Shakespeare to focus his growing ability with comedy on the one man. The comedy supports and furthers his dramatic themes dealing with weakness in high places and the dangers to the state which result, and as the dramatist developed in his handling of the English history play genre, he obviously became more adept at using comic elements to enrich his work. He dared to portray his most wicked king as his most comic king.

John W. Blanpied

"The Dead-End Comedy of *Richard III*," in *Time and the Artist in Shakespeare's English Histories*, Associated University Presses, 1983, pp. 85-97.

[*Blanpied asserts that Richard himself, behaving like an actor or clown, is responsible for the comedy in* Richard III. *The critic contends that for the first three acts, Richard is in control: He keeps us entertained and is able to hold off the grim, inevitable history represented by Margaret's prophecies. Blanpied also asserts that two incidents threaten Richard's comedy. One is Clarence's vivid nightmare in Act I, scene iv, which stops being a threat once Clarence is dead and unceremoniously shoved into a cask of malmsey wine. The other is the murder of the two young princes, and Blanpied points out that this grim scene occurs in Act IV, after Richard's power to attract us has begun to disintegrate.*]

Richard is a great role, as Richard himself was the first to discover in his coming-out soliloquy in *3 Henry VI*. All his predecessors—in Shakespeare, Marlowe, More, and elsewhere—are superseded by the way theatricality is built into his character. He is "sent" into the "world," incomplete: he is not of it, has no fixed identity, no "character" but the unique freedom of the self-creating actor. It is painful—he can see that the world that rejects him is not worth having, that worldly power is a sham and worldly attachments worse than nothing—but it is also exhilarating because he alone stands undetermined by that world's laws and rhythms. In fact, he can create himself by mocking down the world. That will be his plot, the action through which he will become a character. He is not born into this plot, this role; he creates them. He creates "history" by showing how lifeless and manipulable, how insubstantial it is in the hands of a mocking artist.

His first soliloquy in *3 Henry VI* is the *locus classicus* [Classical source] of machiavellian theatrics: energetic performing power, the proliferation of selves through dissembling roles, in the service of an ultimate goal, the crown. But the machiavel [one who views politics as amoral and that any means; however unscrupulous, can justifiably be used in achieving political power] itself is a role in *Richard III*. It is played by Buckingham, Richard's "other self," who has mastered the "deep tragedian's" arsenal of effects as a means toward the end of worldly power. In his opening monologue Richard himself does not allude to the crown; he mentions it only glancingly after meeting Clarence, and not at all in his exuberance after seducing Anne. For two acts he scarcely considers the ends of acting. Foremost in the dramatic persona comes the self-delighting antic [Clown], for whom the world is so corrupt and stupid that the satisfactions to be gained in mocking it cannot compare with those of regarding himself, his own audience, in a glass, and descanting on his own deformity. With Buckingham, then, he begins to play for power; but even then we watch the antic playing the machiavel:

> My other self, my counsel's consistory,
> My oracle, my prophet, my dear cousin,
> I, as a child, will go by thy direction.
>
> (2.2. 151-153)

The self-delighting antic is invisible to Buckingham. In Richard he really sees himself.

The antic thrives on absolute antithesis. Richard would "undertake the death of all the world" (1. 2. 123), wants "the world for me to bustle in" (1. 1. 152), "all the world to nothing!" (1. 2. 237). It is idle to wag a finger at this anarchic individualism as if it were an embarrassment. It is his study, his pride, his art, to create himself in radical opposition to the world— meaning "history," the sum-total of everyone else's experience; to perfect himself in opposition to everything that is not himself. Such rigorous economy surely masks a powerful fantasy, bound to be exposed sooner or later, but for awhile it pleases us to be engaged by Richard's sheer performing verve. And besides, coming fresh from the clamor of *Henry VI*, we must welcome a theatrical mode that presents such deftly vivid distinctions. Probably no play was ever before pitched to its audience with such subtly knowing calculation as is *Richard III* in its opening gesture. The cool precision of Richard's rhetorical stance disavows bombast, sentimentality, vagueness; it asserts dry clarity. It gives enough of a "character" to seem fascinating, not so much as to muddy our immediate perception, or disturb the grounds of our engagement. It offers, in other words, a uniquely theatrical gratification.

The opening is a masterful tease, a great theater game; the speech is a wonderful blend of self-disclosure and self-concealment, or so it seems. Richard is bored, an unemployed actor in "this weak piping time of peace"; therefore, since he cannot have war and cannot enjoy lust, "I am determined to prove a villain." This is a coldly aesthetic aim, and curiously abstract, as if the nature of the villainy were unimportant. Like Iago, that other trickster, he is something of a *bricoleur* [jack-of-all-trades], working from available materials: if they are rotten to begin with, what can he do? At least he will make the rottenness intelligible, answerable, by shaping it as his opposition, his Not-me. He does not say "I am a villain," but "I will try myself out in the role of 'villain.'" We respond first to the fiction of intimate disclosure, privileged confidence. We respond second to the thinly hidden "self," the perhaps tortured and suffering self, seeking compensatory gratification for psychic damage, or at least a kind of suffering we can only faintly perceive. Yet the tone is cool and elegant, the theater game superb, and safe. He "reveals" a dramatic persona exclusively to us, while being sure to suggest an underlying character only slightly deployed in this action, and not accountable to it. He implies in his performing verve that his energies derive from a source other than "history," "this breathing world." He is somehow autonomous, independent, unfathomable. Yet that hidden character may be a dramatic persona, too, glimpsed "behind" the first one. Our emerging doubts about the authenticity of a "self" within these roles constitutes a third line of awareness.

Tamburlaine is obviously [Elizabethan playwright Christopher] Marlowe's darling, his speech strong because it is Marlowe's, and he consumes the world because it is so shadowy to begin with. But Richard is autonomous and self-creating (with a hint of something cogent underneath) and the world he encounters is highly organized and operates on iron and distinctive laws. Indeed, the antithesis between Richard and the "world" takes the overdetermined and fantastical form of two opposing modes of drama.

Richard's is obvious enough—a highly personal mode of aggressive mimicry, the assumption of others' voices, masks, stances, in order to mock them down. He specializes in parody—thrives on others' hypocrisy, pries open dissociations, exposes the passive will beneath aggressive language, leads his victims to the destruction, the punishment, the negation, they secretly desire. He perfects himself through furious activity, but success depends on his remaining, though Crookback and prominent, invisible. ("I would I knew thy heart," says Anne; "'Tis figured in my tongue," he replies. Unlike Tamburlaine, his tongue is not gorgeous or Senecan, except in mockery. He is always ironic, his voice never his "own" except, perhaps, in soliloquy, though even this is a cool illusion.)

The world that Richard opposes is the radical reduction of historical experience in the *Henry VI* plays (where no such clearly defined world exists) into a Providential drama of the most static, mechanical, and impersonal kind:

> That high All-seer which I dallied with
> Hath turned my feigned prayer on my head
> And given in earnest what I begged in jest.
>
> (5. 1. 20-22)

This is Buckingham, but it could be almost any of Richard's victims. Distinctions among them are tenuous, ghostly—feigned. What gives this world its peculiar unity, its definition as a play (that is, as shaped rather than "natural") is Margaret, who appears as its spokesman, and in a sense as Richard's rival dramatist. Not that she creates anything personally; her function is to reveal God's play, which she does through curses and prophecies. She appears only twice, the first time to announce the plot as a series of providential reprisals, the second to recapitulate and confirm the plot:

> Edward thy son, that now is Prince of
> Wales,
> For Edward our son, that was Prince of
> Wales,
> Die in his youth by like untimely violence!
>
> (1. 3. 198-200)

(Never mind that the violence is "like" only in being "untimely": her vision, like her speech, makes distinctions only between "mine" and "thine.")

> Thy Edward he is dead, that killed my
> Edward;
> Thy other Edward dead, to quit my
> Edward. . . .
>
> (4. 4. 63-64)

"Here in these confines slily have I lurked," she intones, "witness" to the "dire induction" of events inexorably coming to pass. She uses the theatrical metaphor to suggest that a superior play has fulfilled itself through Richard, the scourge-of-God. What she "witnesses" is a parodic morality play in her own image: barren (gutted by a lifetime of brutality and suffering), external, mechanical, empty of personality and motivation, its single causative principle a reflex quid-pro-quo reaction, action itself conceivable only

as crime, and the past *(Henry VI)* reduced to a series of crimes to be harvested in the present. The present is All Soul's Day, Judgment Day, the day when history itself is brought to an end. Margaret, in other words, "witnesses" a play about the end of playing.

What makes her so pat a rival to Richard is her very gratuitousness, her ghastly detachment, her disembodied instrumentality. Her entire character is emptied into her function as Prophet, and she is uniquely impotent as a character, incapable of acting (in either sense of the word), of withholding or deploying a "self" or of influencing any action. (All Richard's victims pay tribute to her power, but after the fact: they are all very eager to read their fates in her table of curses, to see the world in her quid-pro-quo terms. Clarence alone—whom she doesn't curse—experiences guilt and terror internally, rather than homiletically.) Margaret, in other words, is archetypal, Richard existential. She is (or has become) her function, bound to her language. But Richard, essenceless, has no language of his own, only parodies others', turning it back murderously upon them:

QUEEN MARGARET
[after sixteen lines of cursing]
   thou detested—

RICHARD
  Margaret.

MARGARET
  Richard!

RICHARD
    Ha!

MARGARET
    I call thee not.

RICHARD
  I cry thee mercy then; for I did think
  That thou hadst called me all these bitter
  names.

MARGARET
  Why, so I did, but looked for no reply.
  O, let me make the period to my curse!

RICHARD
  'Tis done by me, and ends in "Margaret."
                (1. 3. 232-38)

Margaret has, undeniably, a kind of brute theatrical force, though it derives from—it consummates—the tradition of declamatory assertiveness so prominent in the *Henry VI* plays, and which we discovered to be the manifestation of the self-paralyzing will that emerged as "history": the dissociation of men from their own experience. In its helplessness, its mindlessness, and its deep antipathy toward acting, Margaret's theater-mode radically opposes Richard's, but they are yoked together. Margaret's curses have a potential power to anyone secretly sharing her outright belief in magical language—which means everyone but Richard. Buckingham, the pragmatist, knows that "curses never pass / The lips of those that breathe them in the air" (1. 3. 284-85), and yet the future ghost, witness of the inexorable justice of the "high All-Seer," admits that "My hair doth stand on end to hear her curses" (303). Richard, at this, makes a truly strange response: is it simply perverse (to keep Elizabeth and the others off balance) or is it perversely nonironic (thereby unbalancing us)? In either case, by voicing a humane sympathy for Margaret as crazed victim of the past rather than its prophet, he undercuts her authority:

> I cannot blame her. By God's holy Mother,
> She hath had too much wrong, and I repent
> My part whereof that I have done to her.
>
> (1. 3. 305-7)

Part of our pleasure comes from the obvious pretense that Richard is the underdog, triumphing against overwhelming odds, "all the world to nothing." He counts the obstacles between him and the crown. But they all come down quite readily, and in fact he never does seem to sweat until after he has the crown, never seems passionate or panicky in his operations. Not only is he not an underdog, but even the scrupulously overdetermined structure of antitheses, of matched opposites, is spurious: the manifestation of a fantasy of power. It is not just that his victims are willingly victimized, though that is true, but also that their willingness traps Richard into a reflexive role of easy mastery that gradually hardens into a kind of slavishness. In working the ironic fulfillment of the peers' dissembling vows—"So thrive I mine!" and so forth—Richard seems to fulfill his own role in Margaret's program as "hell's black intelligencer; / Only reserved their factor to buy souls / And send them thither" (4. 4. 71-73). It is precisely the pallid ease, however, with which these "souls" first dissemble and then, reflexively, suffer their reversals, that as characters makes them so shadowy, such parodic play figures, and hence such contemptible victims. Richard knows this—that is why the machiavel, who values the world he scorns, is a second-rate role. One may even imagine a Richard nauseated by his victims' compulsive will to be used, to be "shadows." Just this kind of puppetry provoked his dramatic insurgence in the first place (in *3 Henry VI*, 3. 2), and now it appears that all his fiercely cool manipulating energy is bound to the ultimately futile activity of making shadows of shadows.

But the play's structure is so clear, so welcome, and so brilliantly exploited for three acts by Richard that it frees our responses for pleasure in his nimbleness, and we accede to fictions we would find suspect anywhere but in a comedy. *Richard III* is not quite a comedy, but neither is it a tragedy. Typically a Shakespearean comedy proliferates confusion of plot and character with the implied promise of a wondrous resolution that delightfully enlarges the field of play in the end. *Richard III* generates the confusions, the contradictions, and through the dazzling con-man artistry of Richard seems to promise (like Falstaff [a comic character found in several of Shakespeare's plays], caught between his wit and his grossness) a marvelous payoff. But it is a pseudocomedy, dead-end comedy. Behind the fiction of Richard versus the World lies the myth of Richard's centrality, a center of power. The struggle is a fantasy; Margaret is a fantastic opposite, Richard's victims are ghosts, and the scenes of encounters are setups, discrete occasions for Richard's mastery of shadows all-too-willing to disappear.

> This is the day wherein I wished to fall
> By the false faith of him whom most I
> trusted.
>
> (5. 1. 16-17)

Behind the antithetical structure is a solipsistic need for full control.

I do not speak of *Richard's* need, for that would presume a psychologically complete character, whereas I think we are merely teased by the theatrical gestures of one. But through Richard—through the myth of his centrality and coherence—a fantasy of power is played out. For credibility, it needs the pseudocomic antithetical structure. Yet this structure, and hence Richard's control, are twice severely threatened. The first occasion is Clarence's account of his dream (1. 4). Unlike Stanley's dream of the wild boar (3. 3) with its obviously flat significations, and certainly unlike Richard's ghostly visitation before Bosworth, Clarence's dream narrative gives form to an unrestrained and continuous flow of feeling. It takes its form not from a convention of moral allegory—the homiletic acceptance of one's guilt because one is found out by the cosmic polygraph—but as images vulcanized from a psyche beset by guilt and terror. The sea-vision is wondrous and ambiguous, and the stifled soul rendered with bodily directness:

> 　　　　　　　　　　　　often did I strive
> To yield the ghost; but still the envious
> flood
> Stopped in my soul, and would not let it
> forth
> To find the empty, vast, and wand'ring air,
> But smothered it within my panting bulk,
> Who almost burst to belch it in the sea.
>
> (1.4. 36-41)

Temporarily the speech is the speaker, just as the

dream was the dreamer and not a discrete part in a morality. In its organic unity, and consequently in its dramatic potency, this language opposes itself both to Richard's parodic style and to the rhetorically demonstrative styles of his victims. This alternative is the rare and momentary surfacing, into haunting lyrical images, of a flow of dramatic energy that usually lies concealed within the forms it empowers, but which here, under pressure of obliteration, reveals itself. In other words, the dream narrative suggests a kind of recreative power language might have, but which is systematically smothered in *Richard III*. It does not recur. Clearly it is a kind of language that Richard cannot pervert through parody, and so it makes an independent bid for our attention and engagement that must be suppressed. Richard had warned the murderers not to let Clarence talk; now he must be both stabbed *and* drowned. The need to suppress him speaks for itself.

Clarence personally makes no special claims on us—only his voice—and Richard in the next scene performs upon Edward and the court politicians—newly "reconciled" in peace and love—with such brilliantly extravagant virtuosity that the threat seems to be turned aside. The other challenge to his control of the comic structure comes later: the murder of the young princes. Here, the play's chief way of dealing with the threat of emotional impact is to distance us from the murders. Tyrrel is hired by Richard and in turn hires Dighton and Forrest, whose account of the murder Tyrrel relays in a highly mannered monologue. This comes at a time when Richard's control, both over his own persona and over others, is disintegrating, and it shows him, now king, insulated from the world rather than bustling in it. It presses in on him, visible and immobile at the center, and his agents enact his will badly or not at all. In short, though the play maneuvers to intercept the threat of our engagement in the pathos of the princes, it also pulls away from Richard. In serving his interests—in responding to the need for central control—it exposes the nature of those interests. As in the *Henry VI* plays, but with much steeper articulation, we are disengaged and left to look with chill regard upon the helpless course of the last two acts.

It is not the "success" of Margaret's play of retributive justice—nothing due its power or authority either as drama or as idea—that leads to the debacle of the ending, but the failure of Richard's play: its internal collapse. His compulsive drive toward individuation, the clear antithetical form, has been a continuing testament to his control, but it leads ironically to a high degree of visibility. He uses up the "world"—that is, those shadows who would rather succumb to Margaret's "justice" than incriminate Richard by acting a shrewd audience. He wins the crown, that symbol of the summit of individuation. But then as a

Self, rather than an exploiter of others' selfabnegations, Richard turns out to have very little force or coherence. To act directly, visibly, through one's agents, is quite different from acting invisibly through the secret wills of others.

The interview with Queen Elizabeth crystallizes Richard's exhaustion. The scene parodies his seduction of Anne, which of course was a virtuoso performance, brisk and graceful in its immaculate control. Never, before or after, was it clear that Richard really needed Anne for worldly ambitions; the success itself was certainly the point. By contrast stands his *need* for Elizabeth, which keeps him visible as an actor striving but unable to deploy himself in credible shapes of language, figured in his tongue. Moreover, he is (as artist) faced with disintegrating materials. Dissociated from his true object—Elizabeth's unseen, unknown daughter—he is forced to improvise, in Elizabeth, an agent. But he has already used her up; except for her daughter, she has nothing left to lose, to masquerade. Now it is he (as before it was Anne) who labors after a shifting target, while Elizabeth, relentlessly ironic, leads him through a mocking chase after a suitable "title" for his wooing. "There is no other way, / Unless thou couldst put on some other shape, / And not be Richard that hath done all this" (4. 4. 285-87). As the antic, Richard *has* been able to reshape himself convincingly, in role after role, throughout the play. But the strenuous effort of this interview brings him nothing but himself, "Richard that hath done all this"—that is, the historical Richard that presumably underlay his antic character all along. The disclosure leads directly into a display of incoherence among his followers, "songs of death" from the filed, then to Bosworth and Richmond.

This progress toward dramatic exhaustion, the drama's mortification by the "fixed future" of history, magnifies that in *2 Henry VI* where York bid to refashion "history" in his own image and ended up as its fodder. When men fail to re-create they become creatures of the chaos that, in the histories, wears the face of an orthodoxy that is both blindly aggressive and profoundly passive. Margaret's confidence is born out by the clanking machinery of the final act: the parade of ghosts declaiming Richard's outstanding debts, the reflex-insurgence of a faceless Richmond (Henry Tudor, materializing from overseas—i.e., "out there" again), the colorless correct oration of this blank hero to his troops (which exactly reverses the bookkeeping logic of Margaret's play, as in "If you do fight against your country's foes, / Your country's fat shall pay your pains the hire"), and finally the summary perfection of his closing choric speech. In other words, though Richmond thematically supersedes Margaret as the Nemesis figure, dramatically the last act recapitulates the salient features of her world-theater: strictly sequential, reactive, depersonalized, boasting off-stage authority, asserting no intrinsic force or presence. Such drama depends upon the validity of an orthodox context of belief; it would cast *us* as upholders of such a convention, repositories of its authority. If we are even half-willing to play such a role, it must be because Richard as a credible dramatic force has failed. The paralysis of his waking soliloquy shows this. It is not just that he suffers despair, but that he has no means to express his terror other than the frantic manipulation of conventional tropes [figures of speech]:

> What do I fear? Myself? There's none else
>   by.
> Richard loves Richard: that is, I am I.
> Is there a murderer here? No. Yes, I am:
> Then fly. What, from myself? . . .
>   (5. 3. 183-86)

His charismatic resurgence of energy in the end—his colorfully vicious oration and the dead-end heroics in battle—only underscores the way he has lapsed into the predetermined, the "historical" role as villain.

Richard's dramatic style, by which he remains invisible among his fellows, binds him to them as a parasite on shadows. For three acts he draws blank checks on our all-too-willing credulity. He "stays alive" theatrically so long as he does not succumb to that "historical" character that lies waiting for him like a net under an aerialist. We sustain him with our credulity, hoping that he will dance something new into being, trying to forget the dreary net beneath. The net is the orthodox providential structure of the play; Richard defies it and we cheer, but at last there is nowhere to go, no real risks have been taken and nothing new been produced, and it claims him. Curiously, the historical figure he becomes in his fall is a denial of history, at least of a meaning to history that Shakespeare has been seeking. His fall proclaims the triumph of the More-Holinshed-Tudor myth of history—of that monolithic image of the providence-driven past that Shakespeare has been resisting. Now it looks as if Shakespeare has, like Richard, been operating on the ghostly Providence all along, as his secret security, and so has been binding his powers to it.

Peter Brook, writing of Grotowski [in *The Empty Space*], states that "the act of performance is an act of sacrifice, of sacrificing what most men prefer to hide—this is [the actor's] gift to the spectator." All the signs of such a sacrifice are in Richard's attitudes toward us—the seeming disclosure of original pain, the teasing possibility of a "moral sentience" that in defeat would make him tragic. Like any actor, but magnified, Richard seems powerful because he seems to fetch some "terrific" energy from outside the play's fictional domain and his function in it. Such an "outside" is, paradoxically, an "inside"—an interior and independent "self" that sets him apart from his fictive fellows (to whom this "self" is a ghost, invisible), and that brings him thrusting directly into our presence, a delight and a menace. When it becomes clear that Richard's is only an illusion of such energy, that it is reflected from the fictive world he mocks, that he is its antitype, and that he has no reservoir of secret strength to spend in our presence—that "he" has never been among "us" at all—then he loses his privileged power of ghostliness and becomes an interesting dramatic fiction: netted, and now either edible or analyzable. And indeed, Richard's sacrificial gestures in our direction have been ruses; the parody of intercourse enacted with Anne has been enacted with us as well. He does offer, however, no small attraction—the fantasy (which we may share for a while) of ever-expanding power exercised from an ever-unbroached, unimplicated center, requiring no relinquishing of the gratified self. It is the child's Superman vision projected into a real political world (and no doubt the idea of the artist as superman tempted Shakespeare no less than Marlowe in the brave new theater world of the early 1590s). At the center sits a hypothetical "self," extending control through murderous performance, sustaining itself on our consenting credulity, meanwhile acting to cancel all bonds, to sedate all live engagement, to gather an emptied world all to himself to bustle in. When Richard does disintegrate he discloses no hidden "self," but a set of stunted potentialities: a lack of bustle. Nothing has been sacrificed, and nothing, no "self," created.

What of our role in all this? We are flattered perhaps to analyze our responses in terms of a double-gratification: we enjoy a moral holiday in Richard's antics, and then, William Toole writes [in "The Motif of Psychic Division in *Richard III*"], "as the play progresses this faculty [moral judgment] is reawakened and we find the appropriateness of what happens to Richard appealing to our moral instincts." But I suspect our participation in the play is more complicated than this; that this is a kind of rationalized fiction of what really happens. The play inescapably mirrors its audience. The offer of a "sacrifice" by an actor to a spectator is obviously a two-way gesture, frightening as well as exhilarating to the spectator. Something is being required of us too, taken from us in exchange. At the most obvious level we are put under an obligation to think and feel in certain ways, to care, to pay attention, to keep a trust; our freedom is restricted, we are fixed and identified in a special relationship. More profoundly, it is likely that such an exchange in the theater activates its primitive powers to disturb us fundamentally. If we look we lose ourselves because we see something magical. Like Pentheus in *The Bacchae* [a play by the Greek tragedion Euripides] we both want to look and are afraid, afraid perhaps that looking in itself will entail *our* sacrifice.

We mirror Richard's sham sacrifice, his sham openness. As he pretends to reveal, we pretend to look, to protect what we see. The play becomes a screen where we and Richard are immensely pleased to enact a restricted fiction about history. We reflect his disengagement, his self-protectiveness; in the end, our cover blown, we are expelled from the fictional space, the place of spurious magic. But we leave secretly relieved, glad not to have been asked to be more deeply moved. On the other hand, neither have we been bedazzled by the claims of the theater, and we may be sorry after all to have gotten off so well intact. Richard's own refusal to relinquish control of the play's action has kept us, in turn, free of any real responsibility of feeling for him. When he does at last lose control, he does not gain new power, there is no release of energy (as in *Richard II,* or in any of the tragedies) because there has been nothing growing and seeking the sacrificial action. In the fantasy of control that we share with Richard and with the latent performing mode of the play lies a fear of being changed, of participation in the other, the Not-me. In this mode, the object of acting is to stop others' acting; to murder the bonds of breath as Richard instructs Buckingham to "murder thy breath in middle of a word." Buckingham acts (in 3. 3) to conjure support from London crowds for the murder of Hastings. In truth *we* are the prize, to control us the object of the larger performance. But we are approached by a villain, the machiavel's instructor, smiling, with murder figured in his tongue: we must be sedated. Yet moral recoil is hardly warranted here, for we have shared in the process, playing our own self-protective, hence manipulating part, aggressive in our nodding passivity, refusing to mingle breath, to recreate; smiling back at the dancing clown while holding tight to our net.

WOOING

An episode in Richard III that has caused much controversy is Act I, scene ii, where Richard successfully woos Lady Anne over the corpse of her father-in-law, Henry VI, whom Richard himself has recently murdered. Nineteenth-century critics found Anne's acquiescence incredible and Shakespeare's invention of the scene inappropriate.

On the other hand, several twentieth-century critics have defended the scene as realistic or have acknowledged its importance to the themes of the play. Harold F. Brooks, for example, remarks that Richard's "breathtaking impudence" is supported by historical accounts of him at the time, and that the scene provides an effective counterpoint to Richard's later negotiations with Queen Elizabeth for her daughter's hand in marriage. **Denzell S. Smith** contends that the scene

proves Richard's fitness as "God's scourge" against a nation mired in civil war. In wooing Anne, Smith asserts, Richard displays his skill at manipulating people by staying one step ahead of them and by playing many different roles. **Donald R. Shupe** draws upon psychology to demonstrate that the scene is a realistic encounter between two different personality types. And Irene G. Dash argues that in submitting to Richard, Anne is simply behaving according to Elizabethan society's expectations of women. Rejecting any explanations for Anne's submission, A. C. Hamilton observes that in demonstrating for us Richard's villainy, the scene is not meant to be realistic; it is meant to shock us, and it succeeds.

Denzell S. Smith

SOURCE: "The Credibility of the Wooing of Anne in *Richard III,*" in *Papers on Language and Literature,* Vol. VII, No. 2, Spring, 1971, pp. 199-202.

[*Smith acknowledges that Richard's success in wooing Anne has been regarded by many as "incredible" and that the scene in which it occurs has been called too brief to be realistic. Smith argues, however, that the scene becomes believable as Richard tailors his words and actions to the changes in Anne's emotions, allowing her to exhaust her anger and appealing to her "vanity and responsibility" so that he wins her sympathy.*]

That Richard even considers wooing Anne, whose husband, Edward the Prince of Wales, and father-in-law, King Henry the Sixth, he has killed, seems effrontery enough, but that he accosts her as the sole mourner in the funeral procession of the dead King and moves her from intense hatred of him to acceptance of his suit in a brief scene of 193 lines seems to many readers incredible. A stylized compression of time cannot justify the scene, since the length of time represented by it is no more than the time needed to play it. Thus the question of its realism cannot be dismissed.

As one of its main points, the scene demonstrates Richard's near-diabolical powers. As Richmond is God's minister, so Richard is God's scourge, and his ability to succeed with Anne suggests greater than mortal powers. As a lover, Richard obviously should be at a disadvantage. Ten of the forty-one lines of his opening soliloquy explain why he cannot "prove a lover." He is "curtail'd of . . . fair proportion," "cheated of feature," and "deformed, unfinish'd . . . scarce half made up." "Deformed" Richard, therefore, has "determined to prove a villain," and the remainder of scene one exemplifies his aptness for his chosen vocation when he dissembles before his brother Clarence, whom he has had jailed. His villainy exemplified, Richard assures his audience that he must marry Anne, not for love but "for another secret close intent"; the "secret," which he does not reveal, is that Clarence appropriated the fortune of Anne, the daughter of Warwick the kingmaker, and that Richard will get this fortune if he does away with Clarence and marries Anne. What could better exemplify Richard's audacious self-confidence than to have him woo this particular woman at this particular time? And what could better suggest his near-diabolical powers than to have him succeed in that endeavor he is physically most unsuited for, so unsuited that he claims it to be the very motive of his villainy?

The trick is to persuade the auditors that Richard does succeed. Shakespeare makes the success credible through the obvious rhetorical device of forceful and emotional argument, but, more significant, rather than giving Richard but one role or *ethos* for Anne to evaluate, Shakespeare gives Richard seven. Not only does Richard suit his arguments to each role, but he changes his pose to accord with the natural progression of Anne's emotions.

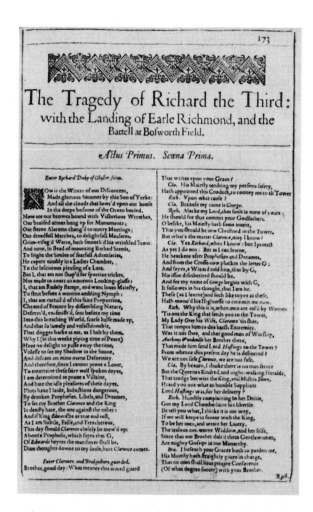

The title page of Richard III *taken from the First Folio (1623).*

Richard, in the second scene, first appears in the role of the strong, dominating man as he opportunistically seizes the initiative when he encounters the funeral procession (33-42). Just as Anne has finished cursing the murderer of Edward and Henry and considerately has told the pallbearers to rest, Richard enters and twice repeats her command to set down the corpse. He does not gainsay her, he does not stop the procession, but he takes the power from her as he forces others to do what she really wants done. When Anne vigorously condemns him, he changes his role to that of the pleader (49-82). He asks her to be charitable by permitting him a chance to acquit himself. When she continues to rant, he next becomes the innocent (89-108). He tells an outright lie when he denies he slew her husband, and he refuses to answer her charge that he killed the king by explaining instead why he attacked Queen Margaret. He piously asserts that the king is better off in heaven than on earth. To this Anne can only respond that Richard is "unfit for any place but hell." Her answer provides Richard with his cue for assuming a new role, that of the brazen lover (110-37), for he replies that the fittest place for him is her bedchamber. As lover, Richard dwells on his desire for her, returning compliment for insult and tenderness for scorn. These appeals to her vanity are immediately followed by his claim that her beauty was the cause of his acts, an obvious appeal to her vanity which also shifts the guilt to her. He soon softens his pose to that of the fond delinquent who now deserves favor (138-71). That Richard's arguments have some effect is indicated by her silence, although she has a chance to reply (171), and since he has her scorn but not her remonstrance, this role is succeeded naturally by his humble and penitent role (172-210). He offers her his life in an argument by alternatives which reiterates the appeal to her vanity and her responsibility. Kill me or take me up, he says as he bares his breast and hands her his sword,

> for I did kill King Henry—
> But 'twas thy beauty that provoked me.
> Nay, now dispatch; 'twas I that stabb'd
> young Edward—
> But 'twas thy heavenly face that set me on.
> [179-82]

His earlier appeal to her charity bears fruit, for she refuses to kill him and, after her rage, refuses to command him to kill himself. Richard pursues the initiative he has held from the beginning and gets her to accept his ring. When he succeeds in his suit, he parts from her as the repentant (211-25) who, having "most cause to be a mourner," will bury the king before keeping his assignation with her.

Richard assumes these roles so that his posture at every turn is adapted to the natural progression of Anne's emotions. He manipulates her by permitting her first to attack him violently, as she must, by taking advantage of her natural pause as her temper runs its course so that he speaks more and she less, and by causing her to waver through the boldness of his argument and thus to succumb. He stays one step ahead of her in this natural sequence. Through an ingenious variety of roles supported by appropriate arguments. Richard responds to and helps bring about a natural—and therefore credible—emotional sequence in Anne.

Donald R. Shupe

SOURCE: "The Wooing of Lady Anne: A Psychological Inquiry," in *Shakespeare Quarterly*, Vol. 29, No. 1, Winter, 1978, pp. 28-36.

[*Shupe applies psychological theories to the wooing of Anne in* Richard III *to prove that the scene is a realistic one. Using a scale called "Mach IV" (which rates people according to their level of Machiavellian tendencies) Shupe concludes that Richard has a "High Mach" personality and is thus able to manipulate people coolly and ruthlessly, while Anne, who responds emotionally and ethically, has a "Low Mach" personality and is therefore easily manipulated by him.*]

Early in *Richard III*, Richard, as part of his plot to win the throne, decides to marry the Lady Anne. He undertakes her wooing at what would appear to be the least propitious moment for such an enterprise, during the funeral procession for her father-in-law, Henry VI, whom Richard has murdered. Richard, already responsible for the death of her husband, could hardly be surprised at the storm of vituperation Anne pours forth when he accosts the procession. Yet, less than 180 lines after Anne's "Avaunt, thou dreadful minister of hell!" (I. ii. 46), she takes leave of Richard with the friendly and playful ines: "But since you teach me how to flatter you. / Imagine I have said farewell already" (ll. 223-24). During this time span Richard has maneuvered, lied, cajoled, chastised, flattered, and even offered up his own life to Anne.

Despite the considerable virtuosity of Richard's performance, the wooing scene has often been questioned on grounds of credibility. At best the scene has great difficulties; and an actor portraying Richard is virtually assured that his performance will be evaluated, at least in part, in terms of his success in making the scene persuasive.

In his *Shakespeare on the Stage*, William Winter said, "Edwin Booth was the only actor I ever saw who made absolutely credible the winning of *Lady Anne*; and, as nearly as I can ascertain, from careful study and inquiry, he was the only actor of *Richard* who ever accomplished that effect." Either this represents

an overly critical view of the scene's difficulty or our standards for the scene have changed—or, perhaps, the quality of acting has improved—because many modern critics regard the wooing scene as at least potentially credible. For example, Wolfgang Clemen [in his *A Commentary on Shakespeare's* Richard III] believes that "Given a good performance, we are convinced, and only when the scene is read or subsequently analysed does it seem illogical." Similarly, a reviewer [Arnold Edinborough] of the 1967 Stratford, Ontario production of *Richard III* said that the director's "interpretation even made the wooing of Lady Anne feasible, and put the play into a meaningful perspective for our times." Even though the wooing scene is now frequently viewed as credible, however, modern critics still express reservations about it in psychological terms. Thus, for example, Clemen says:

> Anne's acquiescence following the dialogue between herself and Richard is bound to seem psychologically implausible according to modern standards, and critics have regarded the scene as no more than a brilliant bout of verbal fencing. But within a psychologically improbable framework Shakespeare has succeeded in achieving an effect both dramatically skilful and even humanly convincing.

The question I wish to raise is whether the wooing scene is indeed psychologically implausible by modern standards.

Richard is a Machiavellian personality type. [Machiavellianism represent the view that politics is amoral and that any means, however anscrupulous, can justifiably be used in achieving political power.] In order to obtain the throne, he is willing to lie and murder without qualm. He is cunning, ruthless, and capable of vast deception; at the same time, he is cool, aloof, and unresponsive to demands for justice and fair play. This picture of Richard is consistent with the findings of modern research concerned with the Machiavellian personality.

Stimulated by an interest in the nature of the successful manipulator, psychologist Richard Christie [with Florence L. Geis in *Studies in Machiavellianism*] has developed a scale based on statements contained in Machiavelli's *The Prince* and the *Discourses,* a scale he calls the Mach scale. One version of this scale (Mach IV) contains twenty statements, and a given subject is asked to rate the extent of his agreement or disagreement with each. The following is a sampling of the statements:

> One should take action only when sure it is morally right. Never tell anyone the real reason you did something unless it is useful to do so. It is wise to flatter important people It is hard to get ahead

without cutting corners here and there.

The "High Mach" personality type tends to disagree with the first statement above and agree with the others. Most of Christie's research has involved subjects, usually college students, who, having responded to the statements, have then been divided on the basis of the median score into High and Low Mach groups. The two groups are then subjected to some experimental treatment, often an interpersonal game situation. The difference between Richard III and a college student who scores above the median on Christie's Mach scale may be of great magnitude, of course. But Christie's experimental findings nevertheless illuminate important aspects of Richard's personality.

Subjects who score as High Mach personality types tend to manifest a disparaging, hostile, and cynical view of people and are surprisingly candid about themselves. Richard's scornful treatment of others, consistent with the High Mach type, hardly needs to be documented from the play. And his candor about himself is remarkable for its directness: "I am determined to prove a villain" (I. i. 30). If we extend our analysis of Richard's self-disclosure back to his role in *3 Henry VI,* we find such statements as the following:

> Why, I can smile, and murder whiles I smile,
> And cry 'Content!' to that which grieves my
>   heart,
> And wet my cheeks with artificial tears,
> And frame my face to all occasions.
>
> . . . . .
>
> I can add colors to the chameleon,
> Change shapes with Proteus for advantages,
> And set the murderous Machiavel to school.
>   (III. ii. 182-85, 191-93)

Even by self-definition, Richard is a High Mach type.

The candor of the High Mach only applies, of course, when there are no reasons for dissembling. For instance, in an experiment by Ralph V. Exline, ["Visual Interaction in Relation to Machiavellianism and an Unethical Act"] in which subjects were goaded into cheating by a confederate of the experimenter and were later confronted by the experimenter for dishonesty (often with threats of intervention by the "Dean" or "Honor Council"), High Mach personality types looked the experimenter in the eye more frequently while denying the cheating and confessed to cheating less often than did Low Mach personality types.

The following is a list of behaviors research has shown to be characteristic of High Machs, all of which are exemplified by Richard in the wooing scene.

(1) The High Mach improvises innovatively. Richard chastises, lies, and denies; then he confesses, but in doing so blames his crimes on his love for Anne. He parries rancor with flattery; he soothes; he is vulgar, sweet, and kind; he offers his life to Anne, and when she refuses to dispatch him he offers to kill himself at her command. In quick succession Richard tries tack after tack with incredible facility.

(2) The High Mach takes risks. We develop such great respect for Richard's virtuosity that, even had Anne taken him up on the offer of his life, we would have expected him adroitly to sidestep and turn the occasion to his advantage. Nevertheless, we must not forget that, because of the untimely occasion, the entire situation is fraught with great risk for Richard.

> What? I that killed her husband and his
>   father
> To take her in her heart's extremest hate,
> With curses in her mouth, tears in her eyes,
> The bleeding witness of my hatred by,
> Having God, her conscience, and these bars
>   against me,
> And I no friends to back my suit at all
> But the plain devil and dissembling looks?
>   (ll. 230-36)

(3) The High Mach keeps cool and avoids becoming emotionally involved. The wooing scene is highly emotional, but it is Anne who charges the atmosphere, not Richard; he maintains a steady coolness. His responses to Anne's most vindictive curses are matter of fact, light, and flattering.

> RICHARD
>   Why dost thou spit at me?
> ANNE
>   Would it were mortal poison for thy sake!
> RICHARD
>   Never came poison from so sweet a place.
> ANNE
>   Never hung poison on a fouler toad.
>   Out of my sight! Thou dost infect mine
>   eyes.
> RICHARD
>   Thine eyes, sweet lady, have infected mine.
>   (ll. 144-49)

Anne is confused by Richard's behavior. She curses him, he responds with flattery; she professes hate, he vows love. Anne has every reason to hate him, but he doesn't react properly; he can't be convinced. Her confusion culminates with the pathetic "I would I knew thy heart" (l. 192). The Machiavellian personality type is at best in situations of confusion and ambiguity: "It is as if the high Machs took advantage of the general confusion produced by ambiguity to be slightly more Machiavellian than might have been astute when others had fewer distracting concerns" [Richard Christie and Florence L. Geis]. Richard's behavior creates confusion and ambiguity and thus provides an atmosphere conductive to his own ends.

Anne's behavior in the wooing scene is consistent with that of Low Mach personalities who "personalize the situation and respond primarily from an emotional-ethical orientation. They become so engrossed with the particular person or content they are dealing with that they get carried away and neglect to manipulate, implicitly assuming that fair play will prevail" [Christie and Geis]. Except for the coyness of her final remarks in the scene, Anne engages in no manipulations. She is highly emotional, deeply involved in Richard as a person; and she is quite caught up in the notions of justice and fair play.

What happens, then, when High meets Low? "High Machs manipulate more, win more, are persuaded less, persuade others more . . ." [Christie and Geis]. Highs make out better in interpersonal bargaining when three conditions are met: (a) when the interaction is face-to-face with the other person; (b) when there is latitude for improvisation; and (c) when the situation allows the arousal of emotions (for instance, when the stakes are high). In thirteen studies in which all three of these conditions were met, Richard Christie and Florence L. Geis report that High Machs won out in all but one case. Clearly these three conditions are met in the wooing scene.

The success of the High Mach is not simply a result of his innovative and manipulative abilities; it stems in large part from his singular dedication to the achievement of an end. He may *act* emotional or concerned, but this never interferes with his clear pursuit of an objective. He knows "how to push the limits of the possible without breaking them [Christie and Geis]." The Low Mach, on the other hand, is easily distracted and disadvantaged by his belief that fair play and reciprocity will be observed: " . . . in the process of ongoing, face-to-face interaction in which participants must follow the action and improvise responses in context, without time for private reflection, low Machs can get 'carried away' in going along with others [Christie and Geis]."

Contrary to the widely-held belief that the scene is psychologically implausible, then, we find that a psychological analysis of the personalities of Anne and Richard adds credibility and indicates again that Shakespeare was an astute observer of human qualities and relationships. Shakespeare created a scene in which a High Mach personality is involved in bargaining with a Low Mach personality, and the scene includes those conditions that research has shown will benefit the success of the High Mach personality. The high emotionality of the scene, stemming from Anne's intense

hatred, has for some, no doubt, detracted from the plausibility of Richard's success. Yet is is within situations of high emotionality that the High Mach has greatest advantage.

A number of research studies have supported a two-component theory of emotion. According to this theory, in order for a person to experience emotion, two conditions must be satisfied: (a) the person must be physiologically aroused, and (b) the situation must be such that an emotional label can be attached to this arousal. If a person is physiologically aroused, say through injection of a drug, but the situation is not one the individual can label as emotion-arousing, he may feel *as if* he were emotional but not actually experience emotion. If the person is in an emotional situation but no physiological changes occur, he does not experience emotion. Similar physiological symptoms can lead to different emotional states, depending entirely upon the situation in which the individual finds himself. Thus emotions such as fear, hate, love, or joy may stem from the same or similar physiological changes, with the distinct emotion experienced depending upon the situation and a person's interpretation of it.

The wooing scene opens with the funeral procession for Anne's father-in-law. Anne is physiologically aroused and a label is easily at hand for this arousal: grief, in combination with hatred for the person responsible for the grief. Anne therefore experiences emotion. As Richard enters, Anne can easily attach the label "hatred" to her arousal and experience that emotion. If we hypothesize that later in the scene as Anne is softening toward Richard she is still physiologically aroused, what emotion would she then experience? The dead Henry has been temporarily forgotten, and Richard has diffused her intense hatred. Is it possible for a new emotional label to be attached to her feelings at that point? Could she then experience attraction for Richard—even love?

Elaine Walster [In "Passionate Love"] has developed a theory of love, based on the two-component theory of emotion, which may answer this question.

> We would suggest that perhaps it does not really matter how one produces an agitated state in an individual. Stimuli that usually produce sexual arousal, gratitude, anxiety, guilt, loneliness, hatred, jealousy, or confusion may all increase one's physiological arousal, and thus increase the intensity of his emotional experience. As long as one attributes his agitated state to passion, he should experience true passionate love. As soon as he ceases to attribute his tumultuous feelings to passion, love should die.

It is certainly not uncommon in literature for the

emotions of fear, hate, love, and jealousy to be close-ly associated, one leading to another. Walster quotes an intriguing remark from the work of an early psy-chologist, H. T. Finck: [in *Romantic Love and Person-al Beauty*]

> Love can only be excited by strong and vivid emotion, and it is almost immaterial whether these emotions are agreeable or disagreeable. The Cid wooed the proud heart of Diana Ximene, whose father he had slain, by shooting one after another of her pet pigeons. Such persons as arouse in us only weak emotions or none at all, are obviously least likely to incline us toward them. . . . Our aversion is most likely to be bestowed on individuals who, as the phrase goes, are neither 'warm' nor 'cold'; whereas impulsive, choleric people, though they may readily offend us, are just as capable of making us warmly attached to them.

Providing support for this theory is an unpublished study in which male subjects, who were led to be-lieve they would soon receive electrical shock and were therefore presumably aroused because of this expectation, rated an attractive young woman to whom they were introduced as more likable and friendly than did a control group of subjects not expecting to receive electrical shock. The results sug-gest that an individual physiologically aroused may attribute his arousal, at least in part, to his reaction to another person.

But this does not explain why Anne later in the scene is sufficiently attracted to Richard to accept his ring rather than remaining repulsed by him; for repulsion is also an aroused reaction. To explain Anne's attrac-tion toward Richard we must assume that repulsion is no longer a viable emotion toward a person who responds with flattery and vows of love, as Richard does. An important indicator is Anne's "I would I knew thy heart" (I. 192). At this point, Anne is con-fused (which, according to Walster, may also lead to arousal), and from this moment on her arousal may be attributed to attraction toward Richard.

The key to the credibility of this scene is its height-ened emotionality. Heightened emotion is not only a condition advantageous to the success of the Machi-avellian but also a condition necessary for the final change in Anne's attitude from repulsion to attrac-tion. Consequently, the brevity of the wooing scene does not detract from its credibility but in fact adds to it: a continued state of arousal for Anne would be untenable if the scene were more prolonged.

Part of what makes Anne's conversion credible and the whole scene psychologically plausible is Anne's refusal to take Richard's life or order him to take his own. The competing psychological theories of cognitive dissonance and of self perception both lead

to the same conclusion: that in light of Anne's refusal, her change in attitude is not only possible but likely.

The first theory postulates, among other things, that two incongruent attitudes (or a behavior and an atti-tude which are incongruent) will create a state called "cognitive dissonance." The discomfiture of cognitive dissonance motivates an individual to resolve an in-congruity through attitude change. This theory has shown great power, not only in enabling us to inter-pret and predict some rather unusual laboratory find-ings, but also in explaining the day-to-day rationaliza-tions people engage in when justifying decisions.

Cognitive dissonance occurs for Anne between her two speeches in the following exchanges:

> RICHARD
>   Thine eyes, sweet lady, have infected mine.
> ANNE
>   Would they were basilisks to strike thee
>   dead!
> RICHARD
>
>   . . . . .
>
>   Lo, here I lend thee this sharp-pointed
>   sword,
>   Which if thou please to hide in this true
>   breast
>   And let the soul forth that adoreth thee,
>   I lay it naked to the deadly stroke
>   And humbly beg the death upon my knee.
>   Nay, do not pause: for I did kill King
>   Henry—
>   But 'taws thy beauty that provokèd me.
>   Nay, now dispatch: 'taws I that stabbed
>   young Edward—
>   But 'twas thy heavenly face that set me on.
>   Take up the sword again, or take up me.
> ANNE
>   Arise, dissembler: though I wish thy death,
>   I will not be thy executioner.
>   (II. 149-50, 174-86)

If Anne could bring herself to kill Richard, her atti-tudes, feelings, and behavior would be consonant and no cognitive dissonance would occur; but she cannot, nor can she directly order him to kill himself. Cog-nitive dissonance is therefore created, and Anne's attitude toward Richard must change to resolve this dissonance. As Richard says, she must "Take up the sword again, or take up me."

Daryl Bem [in "Self-Perception Theory"] has proposed a self-perception theory that explains many of the find-ings in the studies of cognitive dissonance, and does so without recourse to the hypothetical "dissonance reduction." When an individual makes a statement in a context that is free from force or inducement, we tend to credit him with the stated belief. If the individual is induced to make the statement, however, by being coerced or rewarded in some manner, we question whether the statement reflects his true attitude. According to Bem's theory, the individual proceeds in the same way; he observes his behavior and its context, and he formulates his attitudes accordingly. Anne's refusal to kill Richard or command him to kill himself in a context where such an action seems justified would suggest to observers that she is not so unfavorably disposed toward him. According to Bem's theory, Anne would soon come to the same conclusion herself on the basis of the same evidence.

RICHARD

Most critics agree that Richard is a Machiavellian villain (Machiavellianism is a precept that considers politics amoral and claims that any means, however unscrupulous, are justified in achieving and holding onto power). They also agree that he is witty—frequently poking fun at himself as well as at his victims. But critics are divided on the nature of Richard's wickedness, on his motives, and ultimately, on his purpose in the play.

Francis Fergusson asserts that Shakespeare was not interested in exploring the psychological state of the historical Richard, but in creating a Richard for the stage who is an irresistible comic villain. **Morton J. Frisch** acknowledges that Richard is a fascinating character who attracts us "almost against our will." But Frisch chooses to examine Richard's motives and state of mind, and remarks that Richard's quest for power is pointless because he has no idea what he wants to do with power once he gets it. In a similar vein, Janette Dillon focuses on Richard's solitariness: She observes that he is isolated by choice because he is egotistical, ambitious, and ruthless, but that he is also forced into isolation through a "physical deformity which sets him apart from others."

Speaking from an economic rather than a psychological point of view, **Paul N. Siegel** calls Richard a businessman who makes frequent references to money and business on his way toward making himself king.

Finally, both E. M. W. Tillyard and Murray Krieger consider Richard an instrument rather than an instigator of the action in the play. Tillyard describes him as an agent of divine retribution whose crimes unite a divided England against a common enemy, while Krieger suggests that Richard functions as a "purge," clearing out England's guilty past to make way for the future. Krieger further argues that we are charmed by Richard and unsympathetic to most of his victims because they are hypocrites who are nearly as

ambitious as he is. For further analysis of the character of Richard, see the essay by **Frances Shirley** in the section on LANGUAGE: OATHS, CURSES, AND PROPHESIES; and the essay by **William E. Sheriff** in the section on DARK COMEDY.

Paul N. Siegel

SOURCE: "Richard III As Businessman," in *Shakespeare Jahrbuch*, Vol. 114, 1978, pp. 101-06.

[*In this excerpt, Siegel closely examines Richard's speeches and concludes that Richard uses the vocabulary of business in any endeavor he undertakes, whether it be planning the assassination of his brother Clarence or seeking Queen Elizabeth's blessing to marry her daughter.*]

Richard is very much of the new capitalist world. He uses the language of business and displays its attitudes throughout. Much attention has been paid to the stylization of the play's dialogue, with its stychomythia in the wooing scene of Anne, its ritualistic curses of Margaret, its chorused laments of the three queens, but little notice has been taken of what Charles Lamb called the "sprightly colloquial" language of Richard, which acts as a counterpoint to this stylization. It is a colloquial language that often recalls the contemporary turns of phrase expressing the values of our own business civilization.

We might begin by looking at a line of images which can be called that of "the peddler and his packhorse." In his soliloquy at the end of the first scene of the play, Richard says that Edward "must not die/Until George be packed with post horse up to heaven" (I,4,145 f.). He regards Clarence as a bale of goods which he will sling over a horse's back and ship express from the kingdom of England to the kingdom of heaven. Richard's quick mind then leaps ahead to his plans after Clarence and Edward are dead, but he stops himself with the jocular reminder: "But yet I run before my horse to market. / Clarence still breathes, Edward still lives and reigns; / When they are gone, then must I count my gains." (I, 1, 159-161) "I run before my horse to market" was a proverbial phrase meaning "I'm running ahead of myself in my eagerness" or, as Kittredge glosses it [in his *The Complete Works of Shakespeare*]. "I count my chickens before they're hatched." The packhorse has to take one's goods to the market before one can make his profit. Only then, when one has carried out his plans, can he sit down to total up what he has made. The image of the peddler and his packhorse is used again when Richard says to Queen Elizabeth of his labors in behalf of her husband Edward "I was a packhorse in his great affairs" (I, 3, 121) and also, a little later, when he says in disclaiming any desire to be king, "I had rather be a peddler." (I, 3, 148) It is an image which seems to spring naturally to his lips.

Richard also frequently uses financial and monetary terms. "Repaired with double riches of content" (IV, 4, 319), "advantaging their loan with interest / Of ten times double gain of happiness" (IV, 4, 323 f.), "go current from suspicion" (II, 1, 96)—that is, pass as genuine currency without being suspected of being counterfeit—these are but a few examples. In addition to these uses of such terms and subsequent ones I shall cite, I have counted eight others. . . .

When Richard wishes to entice Elizabeth to marry her daughter to him, he tells her that, after having conquered Buckingham, he will to her daughter "retail my conquest won, / And she shall be sole victoress." (IV, 4, 323 f.) "Retail", derived from the earlier meaning (*OED* 1) [*OED* stands for *Oxford English Dictionary*] "to sell (goods, etc.) in small quantities", signifies (*OED* 2) "to recount or tell over again", suggesting not only relating in detail but counting and recounting money. Richard is, therefore, promising Elizabeth's daughter the joys of gaining all of England, which he represents as something to be counted out bit by bit.

Richard uses not only monetary terms but business language. He greets the men he has hired to kill Clarence with "How now, my hardy stout-resolved mates! / Are you now going to dispatch this thing?" and sends them off with "about your business straight. Go, go, dispatch." (I, 3, 339 f., 353 f.) "Dispatch" was a word with business connotations. One of its meanings was (*OED* I, 3) "to dismiss (a person) after attending to him or his business; to settle the business and send away". This was easily extended to (*OED* I, 4) "to get rid of or dispose of (any one) by putting to death; to make away with, kill". Richard is playing on the word: the murder of Clarence is just a little business matter to be speedily taken care of. Clarence may try to talk them out of it, but the professional killers, enterprising free-lance forerunners of Murder, Incorporated, know their jobs (after all, "business is business") and will not allow themselves to be diverted. The word "business" in "about your business straight" suggests the same coldbloodedness as in Edmund's words in calculating his course, "A credulous father, and a brother noble . . . I see the business" ([*King Lear*] I, 2, 195-198).

Richard is twice referred to by other characters as a business agent. Buckingham, urging him before the citizens to rule in his own stead, not as the lord protector of the boy king, tells him to take on "the charge and kingly government of this your land; / Not as protector, steward, substitute, / Or lowly factor for another's gain." (III, 7, 130-133) "Steward" meant, of course, the business manager of an estate, and "factor" meant the business agent acting in behalf

of his principal. Richard, despite his public professions, was really not content to be either, but the irony is that in the last analysis a business agent is all that he is: Margaret, reciting the many deaths of guilty persons that have already occurred, says, "Richard yet lives, hell's black intelligencer, / Only reserved their factor to buy souls / And send them thither." (IV, 4, 71-73) He is the business agent of hell, buying souls and shipping them off to it.

As a businessman, Richard is, to use the language of Babbitt, a "real hustler," a "gogetter." [George Babbitt is an American businessman in Sinclair Lewis's novel *Babbitt*.] He displays enormous energy from the time in *3 Henry VI* he says that he is as one "lost in a thorny wood" from which he will "hew" his "way out with a bloody axe" (III, 2, 174-181) until the time of his last battle when he dashes frantically about calling "A horse! / My kingdom for a horse!" (V, 4, 7) Hustle and bustle characterize his behavior throughout. "Delay leads impotent and snail-paced beggary" (IV, 3, 53)—inactivity is invariably followed by bankruptcy—he exclaims, calling forth to combat. On the eve of his last battle, he says, in an attempt to regain his old zest, "Tomorrow is a busy day." (V, 3, 18) And before entering the final fray he cries out, "Come, bustle, bustle, / Caparison my horse." (V, 3, 290) His underlings in their way speak his language. "Tut, tut, my lord, we will not stand to prate. / Talkers are no good doers," says the First Murderer (I, 3, 349 f.), assuring him that they will not allow Clarence to engage them in conversation and move their pity. "Talk is cheap" and "time is money."

Richard's energy is the energy of the bourgeoisie. "The bourgeoisie," says *The Communist Manifesto*, "has disclosed how it came to pass that the brutal display of vigor in the Middle Ages, which reactionists so much admire, found its fitting complement in the most slothful indolence. It has been the first to show what man's activity can bring about . . . Constant revolutionizing of production, uninterrupted disturbance of all social conditions, everlasting uncertainty and agitation distinguish the bourgeois epoch from all earlier ones." The word "business," it may be pointed out, is derived from "busyness."

With Clarence dead, says Richard, "God take King Edward to his mercy / And leave the world for me to bustle in!" (I, 1, 151 f.) The world which had been rejected by medieval otherworldliness as one of the three great temptations—"the world, the flesh, and the devil"—he welcomes as his sphere of activity, gladly relinquishing an alleged heaven to Edward. In response to Gratiano's attempt to joke away Antonio's melancholy by telling him that he has too great care for the things of this world, Antonio replies, "I hold the world but as the world, Gratiano—/ A stage where every man must play a part" (I, 1, 75-78)—a theatre with the ephemerality of the theatre in contradistinction to the eternity of heaven. But for Richard this world is all. The bourgeoisie, says *The Communist Manifesto*, "has drowned the most heavenly ecstacies of religious fervor . . . in the icy water of egotistical calculation."

Morton J. Frisch

SOURCE: "Shakespeare's Richard III and the Soul of the Tyrant," in *Interpretation: A Journal of Political Philosophy*, Vol. 20, No. 3, Spring, 1993, pp. 275-84.

[*Frisch contrasts Richard's lust for control over other people with Caesar's ambition for greatness. He contends that unlike Caesar, Richard is not interested in the well-being of his country, in building empires, or even in achieving glory for himself. Instead, Frisch observes, Richard wants power for its own sake, and when he finally becomes king, his motivation is reduced to securing his power by killing anyone who might question his right to rule. Frisch further suggests that as the play progresses, it becomes apparent that "Richard does not really know what he wants. He does not know his own mind."*]

Caesar's many successes . . . did not divert his natural spirit of enterprise and ambition to the enjoyment of what he had laboriously achieved, but served as fuel and incentive for future achievements, and begat in him plans for greater deeds and a passion for fresh glory, as though he had used up what he already had. What he felt was therefore nothing else than emulation of himself, as if he had been another man, and a sort of rivalry between what he had done and what he purposed to do.

Plutarch, *Caesar*, LVIII.3.

Shakespeare's Richard III differs from the tyrant Socrates describes in Plato's *Republic* in that he has an attractive quality about him, attractive in the sense of fascinating. There is something in the character of Richard which cannot fail to attract us almost against our will, which is all the more incredible since Richard from the outset is "determined to prove a villain" (I.i.30). The wonderfully versatile power of his mind, his talent for equivocation and ambiguity are objects of sheer fascination. Shakespeare has performed the extraordinary feat of presenting the serpentine wisdom of the tyrannic soul in such a way that it cannot fail to excite our sensibilities. In the satisfaction we receive in contemplating the character of Richard, in the various situations in which Shakespeare has shown him, it is almost as if we lose sight of the cold-blooded, calculating tyrant whose ugly soul is overshadowed and even to some extent obscured by the marvelous play of his intellect. But whatever plausible

appeal Richard may have had because of the brilliant qualities of his mind dissipates when he orchestrates the murder of his young nephews.

Shakespeare delineates the character of the tyrannic soul in his characterization of Richard III in a more direct way than the Platonic dialogue does, for here we see the tyrant in action. Shakespeare was able to write a play in which the tyrannic soul becomes a reality rather than something which is merely the subject of conversation. The tyrant as an idea is a perfect example of limitless self-love. Richard prides himself most on his ability to deceive, to dissemble, although he is not nearly as effective on this score as he has led himself to believe. He conceives of himself, in the third part of *Henry VI*, the play which precedes this one, as someone who can prove his superiority to Machiavelli, who can accomplish feats which no one else would even attempt, so much so that the impossible becomes plausible (*3 Henry VI* III.ii.193). It seems reasonable to assume that Richard is not ignorant of the fact that Machiavelli, who teaches rather than practices the tyrannical art, the art of deception, is more capable of dissimulation than others and therefore must be regarded as a most serious competitor for the tyrant. Richard's willingness to take on Machiavelli can therefore be understood as a challenge to the philosopher's reputed superior knowledge of political practice.

It is only too clear that the consciousness of power attending the working out of Richard's schemes is the inexorable guide of his political existence. He is driven by the restless desire of power after power, but the pleasure for him is in the pursuit rather than the mere possession of power. He is less attracted to kingship by the prospect of achieving anything with the kingship than by the exciting problems anticipated for its acquisition. Perhaps the most revealing confrontation in the entire play is that between Richard and the young Prince Edward. Edward, when he learns that he along with his younger brother is being sent to the Tower of London, indicates his unpleasant feelings about that place and asks whether Caesar had built it. He remarks, almost as an aside, that Caesar's fame has outlived his death and that death therefore makes no conquest of this conqueror (III.i.68-69, 87-88). It is obvious what the praise of Caesar implies. Caesar appears to be a model for Edward, and by bringing in Caesar, Edward introduces the thought of loftier motives than kingship or kingly power to someone whose soul has been consumed in his passion for securing the kingship. The problem for Richard is that his passion for power has nothing further to satisfy itself once he secures the throne. Richard is not like Caesar. He has no grand vision of empire as Caesar had. He even has no interest in regaining territories in France lost by his brother's predecessor on the throne, Henry VI. But Edward says that, if he lives long enough to be king, he will recover England's ancient right in France again (III.i.91-92).

There is certainly no reason for thinking that Richard would have been satisfied with performing the mundane tasks of rule upon receiving the crown. He was not unaware of the fact that "the golden yoke of sovereignty" imposes "a world of cares" and a "burden" on someone like himself who has little or no interest in assuming those cares and burdens (III.vii. 145, 222, 228). But nevertheless his action is animated by his obsession for securing the English crown which he looks upon as "the high imperial type of this earth's glory" (IV.iv.245). It comes best into view in his remark that "what other pleasure can the world afford [than] to command, to check, to o'erbear? [Therefore] I'll make my heaven to dream upon the crown" (*3 Henry VI* III.ii.147, 166, 168). Prince Edward draws Richard's attention to some larger motive than the passion for kingly power by alluding to Caesar's grand vision of empire, thus moving from the petty end of Richard to the grand end of Caesar. But Richard does not leave further avenues for his lust for power beyond securing the kingship. No other pleasure comes nearer to divinity for him than this kind of pleasure. He does not have the vision to move on to greater goals.

The episode between Richard and the young Prince Edward needs further elucidation. It is quite possible that Edward's statement about Caesar creates the shadow of a doubt in Richard's mind as to his inflated opinion of his own superiority. We sense something important about the fact that Richard does not hesitate to proclaim his superiority to Machiavelli, but not to Caesar. No difference between Richard and Caesar is more telling than that which is revealed in Richard's speech to his army before the final battle at Bosworth Field. He refers to "these bastard Bretons, whom our fathers have in their own land beaten, bobb'd, and thump'd, and, in record left them the heirs of shame," but never once does he consider the possibility of regaining England's lost territories in France (V.iii. 334-36). It is Edward's concentration on militaristic honor that leads him to emphasize a return to France. It is not impossible that Edward, after recovering England's lost territories in France, would have harbored hopes of conquering all of France, thus securing the union of France and England under the crown of England. He clearly has a vision which could easily transform itself into imperialism.

Edward is devoted to militaristic honor and hence to foreign war and conquest. He has presumably read Caesar's *Commentaries,* an account which, in his opinion, would make Caesar's fame immortal. He even goes so far as to suggest that it is the wit and wisdom encapsulated in those commentaries which make Caesar's valor live (III.i.86). Caesar's greatness will be admired and praised by many generations after his death. It goes without saying that Shakespeare made Richard III immortal, but Caesar made himself immortal first through his exploits and then through his commentaries. Caesar evidently wanted to be remembered long after his death. It is for this reason that he was constantly seeking to outdo his past accomplishments with greater and greater deeds, but the highest part of his greatness was his commentaries. His greatness is more spectacular because of his commentaries. Caesar did not need a Shakespeare to embellish his greatness. Richard receives his fame at the hands of Shakespeare, the fame of infamy, but an infamy which becomes a substitute for oblivion. The young Prince Edward's praise of Caesar makes Richard appear low.

The contrast between Richard and Caesar is perhaps nowhere more clearly seen than in reading Plutarch's characterization of Julius Caesar. Plutarch says that Caesar competed with himself to outdo himself, driven by his "plans for greater deeds [than he had already accomplished] and a passion for fresh glory, as though he had used up what he already had. What he felt was therefore nothing else than emulation of himself, as if he had been another man, and a sort of rivalry between what he had done and what he purposed to do" (Plutarch, *Caesar,* LVIII.3). Shakespeare's Richard, by way of contrast, means to prove himself to himself by overpowering others, but apparently lacks that further incentive to compete with himself, to outdo himself. He soliloquizes in order to assure himself of his own superiority. His recurrent soliloquies (with the exception of the last) can be construed therefore as exercises in self-assurance in order to reinforce his sense of his own absolute worth. He is absolutely convinced in his own mind that he will be able to capture the English throne no matter how difficult that task might be, but altogether missing is the incentive or the will to compete with himself by establishing any further goals beyond that. The securing of the English throne somehow marks the limit of his aspirations. He lacks the incentive or the desire to set new goals for himself. He is constrained by the narrowness of his vision.

It is true that Richard thinks he can accomplish almost anything, but only within the narrow confines of maneuvering his way to the crown. He has no interest in the burdens of statecraft or the pursuit of empire. Richard gives us to understand that he has the power of going to any length in contriving anything, employing only speech, only persuasion (*3 Henry VI* III.ii.182-93). He accomplishes feats which no one else would even think of attempting, like wooing Lady Anne in the presence of the corpse of her murdered husband's murdered father, both of whom he had admittedly murdered. Who would ever think that she could be maneuvered into the intolerable position of having to live with a second husband responsible for her first husband's death? He glories in the sweetness of his triumph over Anne. But he overestimates his own abilities, for his deceitfulness and deviousness are rather transparent to those who know him well. He may be able to break down the walls of Anne's restraint, but the former Queen Elizabeth is not taken in by the pretense of his profession of love for her daughter, the Princess Elizabeth. She feigns a reluctant acquiescence to his proposal of marriage to her daughter which has Richard convinced that he has won her support. It would be fair to assume that Richard deceives himself into thinking that Elizabeth is convinced of his sincerity. He appears to have no sense of his own limitations. He cannot see himself correctly.

Richard hardly ever lets his conscience get the better of him, but his conscience asserts itself in his sleep when the spirits of those he has murdered or arranged to have murdered appear to him in a dream. This cold, unmoving rock of a man, claiming as he does that he fears neither heaven nor hell, finally dissolves under the pressure of conscience, brought on by the burden of a troubled soul (V.iii.179-204). He claims that he is not touched by conscience, but the moment he is willing to admit that his "coward conscience" inspires him with fear, he does not seem to be the same Richard as before (V.iii.179). There is a decided difference in tone, for Richard is only Richard without a conscience. But even before this admittedly frightful encounter, Lady Anne, now his wife, reveals that she had never spent a restful night in his bed without being awakened by his frightful or timorous dreams (IV.i.82-84). We are left wondering whether he had had previous encounters with the conscience he scorns and despises in the timorous dreams which only his wife is able to bring to our attention. The former Queen Margaret, addressing Richard earlier in the play, prophesizes that "no sleep [will] close that deadly eye of thine unless it be while some tormenting dream affrights thee with a hell of ugly devils," but we are given no more information than that (I.iii.225-57). It seems not improbable at all that Richard is plagued nightly after Margaret's curse by the tormenting dreams she prophesizes, for when contemplating the murder of the young princes, he refers to them as "foes to my rest and my sweet dream's disturbers" (IV.ii.72). What might have caused him to sleep uneasily was the anxiety brought about by his memory of the prophecies of Henry VI and a bard of Ireland that Richmond would be "likely in time to bless the regal throne" (*3 Henry VI* IV.vi.74), and that he would not live long after he saw Richmond (IV.ii.94-96, 104-5).

Richard successfully conceals his nightmares for a long time. He rarely mentions his troubling dreams prior to the one nightmare which almost completely unnerves him. One may surmise that he suppresses them, but whatever one's conclusion on that, it seems evident that he does not tell us everything that goes on in his thoughts. The dark shadow of guilt, dimly perceived in the deepest recesses of his soul, does not appear to surface until toward the end of the play. He does not have to face up to the horror of his catalogue of crimes until the visitation of the spirits of his victims at that time. He awakens to conscience only after he is cursed by the ghosts of his murdered victims.

Richard seems willing to acknowledge the power of conscience as he attempts to defy it, for in his remarks to his retinue made shortly after his dream, he says that "conscience is but a word which cowards use, devised at first to keep the strong in awe" (V.iii.310-11). He had never dreamed it possible that his conscience could get under his skin, but he is evidently intimidated by the power of conscience. By his own admission, he is at war with his conscience. Conscience is a diabolical enemy to be overcome. The action of the play moves between Richard's announcement in the opening scene of his determination to prove himself a villain and the eventual realization, after the ghosts of those murdered ones appear to him in a dream, that he is a villain (V.iii.192). The promise that he made to himself to prove himself a villain, the desire for his own perfection as a villain, has been fulfilled. It is a moment of frightened self-awareness in which he confesses to himself that he hates himself for the hateful deeds he has committed (V.iii.190-91). He is stricken with remorse. He almost completely loses his presence of mind, crying to Jesus for mercy (V.iii.179). Richard, who refuses to recognize the existence of conscience, gives himself over to the terrible tortures of conscience, but one cannot say that he was restrained by conscience.

It can be shown that the love of honor is a possible remedy for the misuse of political power, for the desire for recognition makes it possible for rulers to perform selfless acts for selfish reasons; but it is not a sufficient corrective, since the appeal to honor must be perfected by being in the service of something far more exalted than honor. We are led to reflect on the possibility of Richard III becoming a beneficent tyrant, but there is absolutely no suggestion that he could have become that, inasmuch as he reveals a remarkable indifference to honor and praise and therefore lacks the incentive to measure up to some standard of praise. He apparently has no need for recognition from others. It seems evident that there is no potential for goodness in Richard Plantagenet. It would be accurate to say that Shakespeare's characterization of Richard goes a long way toward showing the impossibility of transforming the soul of the tyrant into something fine. One cannot fancy Shakespeare, from the standpoint from which he viewed the actions of the unjust tyrannical soul, holding the view that the correction of tyranny is possible through

A William Blake drawing of Richard and the ghosts (Act V, scene iii).

the conversion of the tyrant from badness to goodness. Shakespeare did not consider Richard perfectible, his last soliloquy notwithstanding.

Richard III is the only one of Shakespeare's kings explicitly associated with Machiavelli. Machiavelli may not be Shakespeare's model of a philosopher, but he is the only philosopher to whom Richard could conceivably relate. Richard knows without having to be reminded that he is not a philosopher in spite of his offer in *3 Henry VI* to take Machiavelli to school. It can hardly be said that he is reflective. We obviously cannot take seriously Buckingham's characterization of Richard as someone bent on meditation and contemplation in the interest of his soul rather than having an interest in wordly pursuits, for that is simply a ploy to feign a reluctance on Richard's part to accept an offer of the crown (III.vii.72, 74, 76). It is not the contemplative life to which Richard turns. The most that we can expect from him in a reflective posture is that he derives delight from contemplating his shadow in the sun, his own projected image of himself (I.i.25–26; ii.267–68). The fact that he mentions Machiavelli does not prove that there is anything philosophic in him, but it should not surprise us that practitioners of politics are for the most part defective in theoretical understanding.

We are always confronted with tyrants and, incredible as it may seem, they continue to be a subject of peculiar fascination and attractiveness by virtue of their remarkable capacity for ruse and deception. Richard wishes to prove himself best, but only to his own satisfaction. He is not at all concerned with being admired or praised by others. Self-admiration or self-satisfaction does not have to be confirmed by the admiration of others, but without the acclaim of others, Richard can only prove himself best to himself by overpowering others. The intensity of his will to power is clearly manifested in his remark that, if the crown were further off than it is, he would still pluck it down, but more than that the very impossibility of the enterprise becomes a supreme challenge to him (*3 Henry VI* III.ii.194–95). It is hardly necessary to say that the work of the true statesman is to raise politics to its highest possible level, but Richard does not possess the moral equipment necessary to make Englishmen good citizens of England, inasmuch as he cannot be presumed to be guided by any concern with the common good. His statement that he is "unfit for state and majesty" is truer than he realizes (III.vii.204). This greatest of English tyrants attempts in Machiavellian fashion to set aside the moral order of the world through a policy of ruse, treachery, and murder. His ruthless statesmanship, a calculated ruthlessness characteristic of Machiavelli, succeeds in acquiring kingly power, and in preserving it for so short a time, but his vow to outdo Machiavelli never comes to pass. It appears to be a vauntingly ambitious claim to a superiority which could not be achieved, for he has hardly been crowned before his house of cards begins to collapse. He cannot maintain the sover-eignty he has so recently acquired (IV.ii.60–61). There is no indication that Richard could ever rule England.

Richard III is the most exclusively political of Shakespeare's history plays. The tragic history of Richard III is not simply the tragic history of England consumed in a civil war, the War of the Roses, England's greatest disaster, but an attempt to sharpen our sense of the potential for tragedy in political life through the depiction of the actions of an unjust tyrannical ruler. The murder of the young princes, a deed which is unqualifiedly evil, exceeds the greatest cruelties of the War of the Roses and shows how ugly or deformed a tyrant's soul can be. Shakespeare does not say so in so many words, but it would be reasonable to assume that he believed that the responsible exercise of political power, the rule of wisdom with its very strict standards, is seldom available to political society. The rule of wisdom is very difficult to achieve. Henry V represented England's finest hour, but in a very short time, the horror of the War of the Roses, culminating in the tyranny bred by these civil dissensions, and the resurrection of that regime out of the long madness that had scarred England, would be succeeded only by a future fraught with uncertainty. It would seem that the potentiality for absolute evil in human affairs is too great to expect a transformation of the harshness of political life.

There is simply no sufficient explanation for the villainy of Richard, inasmuch as he is not really interested in being burdened with the responsibilities of a sovereign. He proves indifferent to the responsibilities of power other than its retention. One would be hard pressed therefore to argue that his villainy derives mainly from his desire to reign as king. Richard is much more of a schemer than an opportunist. He has an irresistible impulse to manipulate. It would seem that villainy has become an end in itself, that is, that the means to an end which is not really an end has supplanted the end and become an end in itself. It seems almost impossible to suppose that what Richard has in mind is simply to prove himself a villain, to live for nothing except the need to assert himself violently, unless of course it is intended as a test of his mettle. But there can be little doubt that Richard is much happier when he is seeking the throne than after he possesses it, for what gives him most pleasure is the expectation of a satisfaction which is always and essentially in the future rather than the reality of that satisfaction. We can say therefore that the pursuit is more enjoyable for him than the attainment of the end, but that enjoyment ceases once the object of the pursuit is obtained. It is not hard to understand that the motivation which had spurred Richard on to his course of action is no longer there once he becomes king. Richard of Gloucester plotting to take the throne is in his element, but as king he is reduced to merely securing his position. He cannot enjoy his power.

But however we are to understand Richard's motives, it is certainly most significant that, when he realizes that he is a villain, he is appalled at the very thought. The nightmare has now fully invaded his consciousness. In the most astounding of turnabouts, he faces up to his own villainy in his monologue after his dream, but it is too late to seek his own salvation. Richard is what he is by virtue of the character of his actions. He does not have the means to correct himself. He defined himself with precision earlier on when he said, "I am in so far in blood that sin will pluck on sin" (IV.iv.63–64). He is imprisoned by his own treachery. His astonishing statement that he hates himself must be taken at its face value, although nothing in his previous experience can account for the sentiment he now experiences. He apparently does not like what he sees in himself. He is not even sure of his villan's role any more. It almost borders on self-contempt. It certainly seems that his conscience takes the heart out of him, but it would be a gross overstatement to say that Richard is repentant. It would be more accurate to say that he is ambivalent, for he both affirms and denies his guilt virtually in the same breath.

Richard, for some reason that we never learn, blurts out that he hates himself for the hateful deeds he has committed. It is at first impossible to believe that one who is so apparently convinced of his own superiority would ever experience such a sudden change of attitude toward himself. We have no indication from any of his previous remarks that he ever entertained any misgivings concerning his conduct, but this in no sense implies that he did not harbor some silent doubts. Why should the mere appearance of apparitions in a dream induce him to change his estimate of himself, unless of course they were in fact conjured up by his own imagination in order to create a confrontation with himself? Richard might have intended to seek from such a confrontation an exoneration of his consciousness of his own guilt. By concealing, or leaving to inference, this side of Richard, Shakespeare leaves to be figured out the reasoning by which he led himself to think of himself as deeply immoral. His reasoning remains unknown to us, leaving us wondering what he had in mind. It is altogether possible that Shakespeare wanted to tell us that conscience is a force to be reckoned with in a conscience-ridden world, and that even someone as impervious to conscience as Richard cannot extricate himself altogether from that moral consciousness. We are confronted with a tyrant who, at least momentarily, is out of heart with tyranny, who has just declared that he hates himself for the hateful deeds he has committed. Shakespeare's play shows that a tyrant who lacks both goodness and conscience, one could even say that goodness goes against his grain, nevertheless recognizes himself as a hateful creature, because he does not know how to be altogether evil.

Richard's greatest passion as it appears is to manipulate or overpower others. It hardly needs to be said that it is in the nature of the desire for power that it can never be fulfilled. The desire for power must feed upon more power. The pursuit can be satisfying only as long as the end recedes, and unless the end is continuously redefined, the pursuit will be over and the satisfaction will cease. Richard thought that he wanted to become king, but what he really wanted was to prove himself capable of becoming king. The effort is everything for him; the result is inconsequential. The pursuit of power or the tyrant's activity has no end other than more power, which is precisely Richard's problem. There is a certain reasonableness in Richard's actions, inasmuch as it is not unreasonable for a prince of the realm to think in terms of his possible succession to the throne, but that is where his reasonableness ends, for the objective itself is unimportant to him. Shakespeare demonstrates, through his treatment of tyranny, a clear awareness of the delusions of power, that there is no inherent satisfaction in satisfying the desire for more, since there is no end in view. The end is endless.

We have seen that Richard is more interested in proving himself capable of becoming king than in performing the role of a ruler, but more than that he is unable to see that he was striving for something that he never really wanted. He only thought that he wanted to be king. It is conceivable that his wish to be king is simply a projection of his youthful wish for his father, the Duke of York, to become king. In the third part of *Henry VI*, the young Richard tries to convince his father to seize the crown, saying: "And, father, do but think how sweet it is to wear a crown," and only after his father's death does he say that he would make his heaven to dream upon the crown (*3 Henry VI* I.ii.28–29; III.iii.168). There can be little doubt that Richard thinks he wants the crown, but he can have been projecting what was originally a wish for his father without giving little more than a thought to what is actually involved in performing the functions of kingship. He has no interest in that kind of thing, but he never abandons his youthful addiction to the crown. Shakespeare seems merely to attempt to show that Richard seeks to be king, but in the course of the play it becomes quite clear that Richard does not really know what he wants. He does not know his own mind.

It must above all be emphasized that, from Shakespeare's point of view, the soul of the tyrant, given its highest expression in this play, represents the darker side of human nature, exhibiting qualities residing in the human character itself. It is even conceivable that the gulf which separates Richard Plantagenet from the rest of the world is not as great as might be imagined at first appearance. Shakespeare's absorption in the character of Richard which emerges from the soliloquies he has written for him reveals a remarkable sensitivity to that possibility. Richard represents a disposition by no means uncommon if we are to take seriously Socrates' remark that "surely some terrible, savage and lawless form of desires is in every man, even in some of us who seem to be ever so measured" (Plato, *Republic*, 572b). It would seem as though Shakespeare wanted to show utter depravity as it might be experienced in a human soul, the soul of a tyrant; revealing the inadequacy of the tyrant's conception of what constitutes human happiness, and all that this implies for the human condition. It would be a real question for Shakespeare whether everyone seeks to have more, to overreach others, as his later contemporary, Thomas Hobbes, was to maintain.

THE WOMEN IN *RICHARD III*: ANNE, THE DUCHESS OF YORK, ELIZABETH, AND MARGARET

Critics have studied the women in *Richard III* for their significance both as individuals and as a group. **Madonne M. Miner**, for example, focuses on the play's misogyny (the hatred of women), stating that Richard continually blames women instead of accepting the guilt which is really his own. Miner and **Irene G. Dash** also discuss the women's role as "ciphers" or "nonpersons," especially after they become widows and their sole source of power and of social identity—their husbands—is gone. Both critics note a positive element of women's fate in the play: Through their adversity, the women eventually identify with each other and unite against Richard.

Taken individually, the four women each pose certain problems for critics. E. M. W. Tillyard regrets that Shakespeare included the scene (Act IV, scene iv) in which Richard asks for Queen Elizabeth's blessing to marry her daughter. Tillyard states that Elizabeth's weak submission to Richard serves no purpose, coming as it does toward the end of the play. In contrast, Dash and Stephen L. Tanner contend that Elizabeth does not submit, but in fact wins this battle of wits, and Tanner maintains that her victory signals Richard's fall from power.

Lady Anne has also been criticized for submitting to Richard. David Bevington refers to Richard's "outlandishly successful" wooing of Anne, and regards her acquiescence as an enormous "betrayal of self." While Dash defends Anne's behavior, observing that she had little choice but to submit to King Edward's brother, she also describes Anne as the most conventional and "self-deprecating" woman in the play.

David Ritchey calls Margaret "a formidable and warlike creature." Harold F. Brooks comments that Margaret appears in all three of the *Henry VI* plays and is important as a connecting link between them and *Richard III*, and as an embodiment of vengeance against Richard. Dash states that Margaret is often left out of productions of *Richard III*, and Dash argues that this omission "affects the total impact of the play," for Margaret's speeches emphasize her own anomalous position as Henry VI's widow and prophesy the fate of the other women in the play.

The Duchess of York—Richard's mother—has not received as much critical attention as have the other women in the play. A. C. Hamilton and Madonne M. Miner, however, both discuss the scene (Act IV, scene iv) in which Margaret and Elizabeth teach the Duchess how to curse so that she can condemn her son. Hamilton remarks that before this scene, the Duchess had been mostly quiet—resigned to her misery. For further analysis of the character of Margaret, see the essay **Frances Shirley** in the LANGUAGE: OATHS, CURSES, AND PROPHESIES section; and the essay by **A. C. Hamilton** in the OVERVIEWS section. For further analysis of the character of Anne, see the essays by **Denzell S. Smith** and **Donald R. Shupe** in the WOOING section.

Madonne M. Miner

SOURCE: "'Neither Mother, Wife, nor England's Queen': The Roles of Women in *Richard III*," in *The Woman's Part: Feminist Criticism of Shakespeare*, edited by Carolyn Ruth Swift Lenz, Gayle Greene, and Carol Thomas Neely, University of Illinois Press, 1980, pp. 35-55.

[*Miner addresses the misogyny that occurs in* Richard III *and how it affects Anne, Margaret, the Duchess of York, and Queen Elizabeth. The critic points out that women are used as "scapegoats." Miner also observes that in the play women are dependent upon men for their roles in life, so that when Richard kills King Henry VI and his son, Edward (in an earlier play), Margaret ceases to be a wife, mother, or queen. Miner further remarks that Richard debases women by misusing the metaphors of pregnancy and birth. Miner concludes by asserting that there is a positive aspect to* Richard III: *after suffering injustice from Richard, the women draw closer to one another.*]

Richard III opens with a soliloquy, in which Richard, Duke of Gloucester, distinguishes time past, time present, and what he perceives to be time future:

> Grim-visaged War hath smoothed his
>   wrinkled front,
> And now, instead of mounting barbèd steeds
> To fright the souls of fearful adversaries,
> He capers nimbly in a lady's chamber
> To the lascivious pleasing of a lute.
>
> . . . . .
>
> Why, I, in this weak piping time of peace,
> Have no delight to pass away the time.
>
> . . . . .
>
> And therefore, since I cannot prove a lover
> To entertain these fair well-spoken days,
> I am determinèd to prove a villain.
>   (I.i.9-13, 24-25, 28-30)

Out of step with his time, Richard determines to force it into closer conformity with his own nature. Implicitly, the quality of the present which Richard finds so onerous is its femininity; present days belong to "wanton ambling nymphs," not to marching warriors, not to hunchbacked younger brothers. The opposition between war and peace is expressed as opposition between male and female; "male" is associated with "bruisèd arms," "stern alarums," and "barbèd steeds," and "female" with "merry meetings," "delightful measures," and "sportive tricks." It makes no difference whether we agree or disagree with Richard's sexual collocations; what is of importance is Richard's exclusive identification with one side of the

antithesis and his determination to obliterate those who represent the opposite—those who, according to the imagery of Richard's soliloquy, are women.

In addition to introducing the poles of opposition in *Richard III*, Gloucester's opening soliloquy also introduces a tactic that Richard employs throughout: an allocation of guilt along sexual lines so that women are invariably at fault. Within the soliloquy it is apparent that women are to blame for effacing the countenance of "Grim-visaged War" and, immediately following the soliloquy, Richard explains to brother Clarence that women are to blame for other things as well. Even though Richard has just told us that he has spun "inductions dangerous" so as to set Clarence and Edward "in deadly hate the one against the other," when Clarence enters, under guard, Richard maintains that women are at the root of his woes:

> Why, this it is when men are ruled by
>   women.
> 'Tis not the king that sends you to the
>   Tower.
> My Lady Grey his wife, Clarence, 'tis she
> That tempers him to this extremity.
>   (I.i.62-65)

Richard's allegation not only deflects suspicion from himself and onto Elizabeth, but also tends to unite the two brothers against an intruder (the sister-in-law, the "Other"). While challenging bonds of marriage, Richard appears to be reaffirming bonds of consanguinity. Clarence catches the impulse of Richard's comment and carries it yet further, naming Mistress Shore as another female force undermining the throne; if one woman is not to blame, another may be found. Clarence cites Shore's intervention in favor of Hastings and Richard agrees: "Humbly complaining to her deity / Got my Lord Chamberlain his liberty" (I.i.76-77). Obviously, according to Richard, when prostitutes capture the ear of kings, when wives wield more power than brothers, the time is out of joint.

In the subsequent exchange with Anne, who follows the corpse of her father-in-law Henry to Chertsey, as in that with Clarence, Richard directs culpability from himself and onto the female figure. He greets the recently widowed woman as "sweet saint" (I.ii.49), and bolsters this greeting with a string of compliments, to which she responds with curses. When Anne charges him with the slaughter of her father-in-law, Henry VI, and her husband, Edward, Richard initially scrambles for a surrogate (blaming Edward IV and Margaret) but then hits upon a far more effective line, accusing Anne as the primary "causer" of the deaths:

> Your beauty was the cause of that effect;
> Your beauty, that did haunt me in my sleep

To undertake the death of all the world,
So I might live one hour in your sweet
    bosom.

(I.ii.121-24)

Thus, Anne is responsible; her beauty serves as incentive for murder. Richard, of course, lies; he kills Edward and Henry so as to come closer to the throne, and he woos Anne for the same reason. By the end of the scene, however, this hunchbacked Machiavellian is able to acknowledge his role in the murders of Edward and Henry, to offer Anne his sword to use against him, and to smile in the knowledge of his victory as she refuses to take vengeance.

Nay, do not pause, for I did kill King
    Henry,
But 'twas thy beauty that provokèd me.
Nay, now dispatch; 'twas I that stabbed
    young Edward,
But 'twas thy heavenly face that set me on.
Take up the sword again, or take up me.

(I.ii.179-83)

By focusing on her beauty, Richard insists that Anne fit the very flat definition of "womankind" he articulated in his opening soliloquy—a definition that divides the world into male and female provinces, denying the latter any possibility of communion with emblems (such as swords) of the former. Focusing upon Anne's guilt, Richard deflects responsibility from himself, and constructs a bond of alliance between Anne and himself, against the House of Lancaster, rendering her powerless.

While the exchange between Richard and Anne may be the most dramatic example of Richard's aptitude with respect to sexual dynamics and the allocation of guilt, it is by no means a final example. Another variation occurs in Act III, scene iv, when Richard determines to weed out the ranks of those in opposition to his coronation. Because Hastings is involved with Mistress Shore, all Richard need do is accuse Shore, implicate Hastings (guilt by association) and be rid of him. Thus, in the midst of an assembly meeting, Richard draws forth his withered arm and announces: "And this is Edward's wife, that monstrous witch, / Consorted with that harlot strumpet Shore, / That by their witchcraft thus have markèd me" (III.iv.69-71). Hastings's reply, "If they have done this deed, my noble lord" (72), is twisted by an enraged Richard into unimpeachable evidence of guilt: "If! Thou protector of this damnèd strumpet, / Talk'st thou to me of ifs? Thou art a traitor. / Off with his head!" (73-75). In spite of the incredible and illogical nature of Richard's accusation (his arm has always been withered; the association of Elizabeth and Mistress Shore as conspirators is extremely unlikely), it holds: Hastings loses his head on the basis

of his involvement with a woman. Although the dynamics in the three examples cited above vary considerably, in each instance Richard blames women in order to benefit himself and, in so doing, he creates or destroys associational bonds between men.

If, in the scenes above, Richard is able to manipulate women and blame so as to cut or spin associational threads, his tailoring skills appear yet more impressive when he sets himself to matchmaking—an activity which appears to encourage the reduction of female status from "person" to "thing exchanged." As Lévi-Strauss observes in *Structural Anthropology*, marriage functions as the lowest common denominator of society; based as it has been on the exchange of a woman between two men, marriage brings together two formerly independent groups of men into a kinship system. Richard takes advantage of these associational possibilities, but, interestingly enough, the impulse behind his marital connections most often appears to be one of destruction rather than creation; society is wrenched apart rather than drawn together. We see Richard play the role of suitor twice, with Lady Anne and with Queen Elizabeth (whom he approaches to request the hand of her daughter Elizabeth). To be sure, in formulating his marital plans, Richard approaches women—an eligible widow and a widowed mother—but in both cases, Richard actually focuses on men behind the women. Before meeting Anne en route to Chertsey, he reveals his designs on her:

For then I'll marry Warwick's youngest
    daughter.
What though I killed her husband and her
    father?
The readiest way to make the wench amends
Is to become her husband and her father.

(I.i.153-56)

"To make the wench amends"? Such, of course, is not the actual motivation behind Richard's system of substitution; he realizes that in order to substantiate his claims to the position previously held by Henry VI, it is politic to align himself with Henry's daughter-in-law. Further, maneuvering himself into Anne's bedchamber, Richard moves closer to replacing Edward, former occupant thereof, and former heir to the throne. Thus, after killing Anne's "husband and father," Richard can assume their sexual and political roles. Finally, Richard's speech clarifies the function of women in the marital game: whether the game be one of exchange or one of substitution, the female serves as a piece to be moved by *others,* and a piece having value only in *relation* to others.

Political values, however, like those of the stock market, fluctuate wildly, and by Act IV, Richard (now king) recognizes that Anne has outlived her usefulness to him. After instructing Catesby to rumor it abroad that Anne is "very grievous sick," Richard ruminates alone: "I must be married to my brother's daughter, / Or else my kingdom stands on brittle glass. / Murder her brothers and then marry her!" (IV.ii.58-60). As in his earlier choice of bride, Richard here pursues a woman from whom he has taken all male relatives; although not fully responsible for the death of Elizabeth's father, Richard conspires to lessen the natural term of Edward's life, and he employs more direct measures with respect to Clarence (Elizabeth's uncle) and the two princes (Elizabeth's brothers). However, not all possible rivals have been obliterated: Richmond also seeks the hand of Edward's daughter, and Richard's awareness of a living male rival sharpens his desire to legitimize his claim:

> Now, for I know the Britain Richmond aims
> At young Elizabeth, my brother's daughter,
> And by that knot looks proudly on the
>   crown,
> To her go I, a jolly triving wooer.
>
> (IV.iii.40-43)

Elizabeth, of course, has been a loose end; with the young princes dead ("cut off") she remains the only legitimate possibility of access to the throne. By tying his own knots, Richard plans to exclude Richmond from making any claims to the kingdom. In sum, Richard woos both Anne and Elizabeth because of the position they occupy with respect to men. However, in proposing marriage (which might lead to a bonding of male to male through female), Richard does not seek a union *with* other men but rather *replaces* them by assuming their roles with respect to women.

In considerations of the way Richard employs women as scapegoats and currency, younger female figures have received most attention. However, when we consider how Richard uses women as ciphers, three older women—Queen Elizabeth, Margaret, and the Duchess of York—step, reluctantly, into the foreground. All of these women suffer, on one level, a loss of definition at the hand of Richard. Caught in a society that conceives of women strictly in relational terms (that is, as wives to husbands, mothers to children, queens to kings), the women are subject to loss of title, position, and identity, as Richard destroys those by whom women are defined: husbands, children, kings. Early in the play, Queen Elizabeth perceives the precarious nature of *her* position as her husband, King Edward, grows weaker and weaker. "The loss of such a lord includes all harms" (I.iii.8), she tells her son Grey. Elizabeth's words find verification not only in later scenes, but also, here, before Edward's death, in the figure of Margaret, England's former queen. Margaret, hiding in the wrings, listens as Richard taunts Elizabeth and accuses her of promoting her favorites. When Elizabeth replies, "Small joy have I in being England's Queen" (109), Margaret

can barely restrain herself; she says in an aside: "As little joy enjoys the queen thereof; / For I am she, and altogether joyless" (154-55). Margaret's aside pinpoints the confusion that results when women must depend upon men for identity and when Richard persists in removing these men. Is a woman to be considered "queen" after her "king" has been killed? Does one's title apply only as long as one's husband is alive? And, after her husband's death, what does the "queen" become? Margaret serves, of course, as model for the women of *Richard III;* she enters in Act I and shows Elizabeth and the Duchess of York what they have to expect from the future; like her, they are destined to years of sterile widowhood. But the women of York do not yet perceive Margaret's function; with Richard, they mock her and force her from the stage. Before leaving, however, Margaret further clarifies her relationship to Elizabeth by underlining the similarity of their woes:

> Thyself a queen, for me that was a queen,
> Outlive thy glory like my wretched self!
> Long mayst thou live to wail thy children's
>   death;
>
> . . . . .
>
> Long die thy happy days before thy death,
> And, after many length'ned hours of grief,
> Die neither mother, wife, nor England's
>   Queen!
>
> (I.iii.201-3, 206-8)

Alive—but neither mother, wife, nor England's queen: the description may apply to Margaret, Elizabeth, and the Duchess. Only a very short time elapses between the day of Margaret's curse and the day Elizabeth suffers the death of her lord. Addressing the Duchess, the twice-widowed woman cries: "Edward, my lord, thy son, our king, is dead! / Why grow the branches when the root is gone? / Why wither not the leaves that want their sap?" (II.ii.40-42). Elizabeth's questions forecast her upcoming tragedy.

Not only does Richard subvert the role of queen, he also undermines roles of mother and wife. For example, while the death of Edward robs Elizabeth of a husband, it robs the Duchess of York of a son. Having lost son Clarence earlier, the Duchess's "stock" suffers a depletion of two-thirds. She turns to Elizabeth, commenting that years ago she lost a worthy husband,

> And lived with looking on his images;
> But now two mirrors of his princely
>   semblance
> Are cracked in pieces by malignant death,
> And I for comfort have but one false glass
> That grieves me when I see my shame in
>   him.

Thou art a widow, yet thou art a mother
And hast the comfort of thy children left.

(II.ii.50-56)

Stressing Elizabeth's yet-current claim to motherhood, the Duchess appears to abjure her own; it is as if she no longer wants to assume the title of mother if Richard is the son who grants her this right; accepting "motherhood" means accepting responsibility for "all these griefs," for the losses sustained by Elizabeth and by Clarence's children.

It is not enough for one mother to abandon her claim to the title of mother; Richard pursues a course of action that eventually forces Elizabeth to relinquish her claim also (note that as the play proceeds, Elizabeth comes to bear a closer resemblance to Margaret). The process leading to Elizabeth's forfeiture of her title is more complicated than that of the Duchess and is accomplished in a series of steps: Buckingham and Richard override maternal authority and, parenthetically, the right of sanctuary, by "plucking" the Duke of York from the sheltering arms of his mother; Brakenbury, under order from Richard, denies Elizabeth entrance to the Tower, thereby denying her right to see her children; Richard casts doubt on the legitimacy of Edward's marriage to Elizabeth, and hence, on the legitimacy of her children; Richard preys upon Elizabeth to grant him her daughter in marriage while Elizabeth knows that to do so would be to sentence her daughter to a living death.

As this process is set in motion, the "Protector" refuses to grant Elizabeth her status as mother; as it comes to a close, Elizabeth freely abjures her motherhood in an attempt to protect her remaining child. Up until the murder of her sons, Elizabeth insists, often futilely, upon her maternal rights. When, for example, Brakenbury refuses to admit her to the Tower, she protests violently upon the grounds of familial relation: "Hath he set bounds between their love and me? / I am their mother; who shall bar me from them?" (IV.i.20-21). Almost as if she were determined actively to dispute Richard's allegations that her children are illegitimate, Elizabeth reiterates, time and time again, the status of her relationship and that of her children to Edward. After the deaths of young Edward and Richard, however, Elizabeth is forced to perform an about-face. Because of Richard's manipulations, a "mother's name is ominous to children"; hence, she must deny her title of mother in order to express her genuine identity as a mother concerned for her children's welfare. She dispatches her son Dorset to France—"O Dorset, speak not to me, get thee gone!" (IV.i.38)—and expresses her willingness to deny the legitimacy of young Elizabeth's birth to save her from marriage to Richard.

And must she die for this? O, let her live,

And I'll corrupt her manners, stain her
  beauty,
Slander myself as false to Edward's bed,
Throw over her the veil of infamy;
So she may live unscarred of bleeding
  slaughter,
I will confess she was not Edward's daughter.

(IV.iv.206-11)

It is the love of a mother for her daughter which prompts Elizabeth's offer; she willingly renounces her titles both of wife and legitimate mother.

In the examples cited above, Richard's general course of action is such to encourage women to abandon traditional titles, to de-identify themselves. Richard more specifically encourages this cipherization by confounding the integrity of titular markers: that is, by juggling titles without regard for the human beings behind these titles (although Richard does not restrict himself to female markers, females suffer more grievously from these verbal acrobatics than do males, who may draw upon a wider range of options with respect to identifying roles). Richard's changing choice of title for his sister-in-law Elizabeth most clearly exemplifies his policy of confoundment. Richard's first reference to Elizabeth occurs in a conversation with Clarence, in which Richard promises that he will employ any means to procure his brother's freedom: "And whatsoe'er you will employ me in, / Were it to call King Edward's widow sister, / I will perform it to enfranchise you" (I.i.108-10). Several things are happening here. First, as the wife of Edward, Richard's brother, Elizabeth is Richard's sister (sister-in-law); she need not solicit the title from Richard, although Richard certainly implies that it is his prerogative to grant or withhold the title at will. Second, the title Richard actually bestows on Elizabeth is "King Edward's widow," an equivocation of marvelous subtlety; Elizabeth *is* the widow of Grey but Richard's phrasing makes it possible to read this description as a prediction: Elizabeth will wear weeds again. And finally, when Richard and Elizabeth meet in the following scene, it is Elizabeth who twice addresses Richard as "Brother Gloucester"; Richard refuses to call her anything, because, at this time, he has nothing to gain by doing so. Later, in Act II, following the convenient demise of Edward IV, Richard, as if to ensure a smooth transference of power, attempts to placate Elizabeth: he calls her "sister." In Act IV, however, after Richard has approached Elizabeth for the hand of young Elizabeth, he calls her "mother": "Therefore, dear mother—I must call you so—/ Be the attorney of my love to her" (IV.iv.412-13). The exchange between Richard and Elizabeth also supplies a rather startling example of Richard's indifference to the human beings who actually give substance to the titles he juggles with such apparent ease. Richard insists that he will provide substitutes for the children Elizabeth has lost at his hand:

> To quicken your increase I will beget
> Mine issue of your blood upon your daughter.
> A grandam's name is little less in love
> Than is the doting title of a mother.
>
> (IV.iv.297-300)

Focusing exclusively upon a "grandam's *name*" and the "*title* of a mother," Richard attempts to obscure the very real difference between these two positions; he attempts to confound all meaning attached to female position markers—a policy in keeping with his determination to confound women altogether.

Given Richard's perception of woman as enemy, as "Other," we should not be surprised that the action of the play depends upon a systematic denial of the human identity of women. Richard's apparently successful attempts to obscure Elizabeth's titular "sense of self" and Elizabeth's rejection of both her own identity and that of her daughter exemplify, on one level, the progression of women in *Richard III*: from mother to nonmother, wife to widow, queen to crone. However, this "progression" does not take into account a less obvious and more positive progression of women from a condition of bickering rivalry to a condition of sympathetic camaraderie. In the midst of loss, the women turn to each other. Thus, an interesting, but generally ignored, countermotion of interaction *among* women is introduced; having been reduced to the condition of nothing, Margaret, Elizabeth, and the Duchess evidence a new humanity, a humanity apparent nowhere else in the play. We need only explore the progression in the four scenes in *Richard III* in which women confront each other (I.iii; II.ii; IV.i; IV.iv) to see this countermotion. Act I, scene iii, opens with Elizabeth and Richard at each other's throat; with the entrance of Margaret, however, Richard is able to direct all hostility toward her. Even Elizabeth joins with crook-backed Gloucester in condemning the widow of Lancaster; angry words fly across the stage. When Elizabeth applauds Richard for turning Margaret's curse back on herself, Margaret chides the "poor-painted queen":

> Why strew'st thou sugar on that bottled
>   spider
> Whose deadly web ensnareth thee about?
> Fool, fool, thou whet'st a knife to kill
>   thyself.
> The day will come that thou shalt wish for
>   me
> To help thee curse this poisonous bunch-
>   backed toad.
>
> (I.iii.241-45)

Margaret's prediction proves true, but the women must suffer first.

If the preceding scene depicts the hostility between women of different Houses, Act II, scene ii, depicts hostility between women of the same House. Instead of coming together in sympathy upon learning of the deaths of Clarence and Edward, the women of York and the children of Clarence engage in a chorus of moans, each claiming the greater loss. An appalling absence of empathy characterizes this meeting. A few lines may serve to indicate the mood of the entire scene:

> DUCH. O, what cause have I,
>   Thine being but a moi'ty of my moan,
>   To overgo thy woes and drown thy cries!
> BOY. Ah, aunt, you wept not for our father's
>   death.
>   How can we aid you with our kindred
>   tears?
> DAUGHTER. Our fatherless distress was left
>   unmoaned;
>   Your widow-dolor likewise be unwept!
> ELIZABETH. Give me no help in lamentation;
>   I am not barren to bring forth complaints.
>
> (II.ii.59-67)

Obviously, the tendency here is away from commiseration and toward a selfish indulgence. It is not until Act IV, scene i, that a reversal of this tendency begins to make itself felt, the result of the women's sympathy as their position continues to erode. Elizabeth, the Duchess of York, Anne, and Clarence's daughter meet en route to the Tower to greet the young princes. When Elizabeth is denied visitation privileges, the Duchess and Anne support her maternal rights. Even when Stanley announces that Anne is to be crowned queen, the bond of sympathy between Anne and Elizabeth is not destroyed. Given her history of suffering, Elizabeth can respond now with feeling to Anne as Margaret could not when she was replaced by Elizabeth. When the new queen expresses her wish that the "inclusive verge of golden metal" were "red-hot steel to sear me to the brains," Elizabeth attempts to console her: "Go, go, poor soul! I envy not thy glory. / To feed my humor wish thyself no harm" (IV.i.63-64). The Duchess of York adds her blessing also: "Go thou to Richard, and good angels tend thee!" (92). How different from the feeling of Act II, scene ii! Even though this union of sympathy may not generate any practical power (Richard continues to confound the women) it does prompt a revision in our responses to them: they attain a tragic dignity.

The most moving example of women-aiding-women, however, occurs in Act IV, scene iv, where the women of York join Margaret of Lancaster in cursing Richard. This union is achieved only gradually. Old Queen Margaret enters alone and withdraws to eavesdrop on Elizabeth and the Duchess of York, who sit down together to lament the death of the princes and lament their uselessness: "Ah that thou wouldst as soon afford a grave / As thou canst yield a melancholy seat" (IV.iv.31-32). When Margaret comes forward and joins the two women on the ground, she first claims that her griefs "frown on the upper hand" and it seems the scene will be a reiteration of the earlier contest.

> If sorrow can admit society,
> Tell o'er your woes again by viewing mine.
> I had an Edward, till a Richard killed him;
> I had a husband, till a Richard killed him.
> Thou hadst an Edward, till a Richard killed
>   him;
> Thou hadst a Richard, till a Richard killed
>   him.
>
>   (IV.iv.38-43)

The Duchess, catching the rhythm of Margaret's refrain, interrupts in order to wail a few lines of her own. Margaret, however, regains voice, reminding the Duchess that it is her womb that has bred the cause of all their sorrows: "From forth the kennel of thy womb hath crept / A hellhound that doth hunt us all to death" (IV.iv.47-48). These words signal a reversal in the dynamics of the scene; no longer willing to recognize the legal ties to men which prohibit a communion between women of different parties, these women join together in sorrow, in suffering; it is easy enough to imagine the three of them, seated on the earth, hand in hand. The Duchess abandons her competition with Margaret for the title of most grief-stricken, and turns, in commiseration, to her: "O Harry's wife, triumph not in my woes! / God witness with me I have wept for thine" (59-60). Elizabeth, too, moves toward Margaret, admitting that the prophesied time has come for her to request Margaret's help in cursing the "foul bunch-backed toad" (81) Richard. Thus, the exchange among the women leads to the decision to arm themselves (to assume a male prerogative) with words; Margaret provides lessons in cursing and the Duchess suggests that they smother Richard in "the breath of bitter words" (133); no longer wasted or feeble words—instead, the women now use words as weapons. Accordingly, when Richard enters a short while after Margaret's departure, Elizabeth and the Duchess verbally accost and accuse him. Unaccustomed to such noise, an indignant Richard commands: "Either be patient and entreat me fair, / Or with the clamorous report of war / Thus will I drown your exclamations" (152-54). Richard's response to these insistent female voices is worthy of note as it reiterates the alliance of Richard with war and against women, and as it serves as summary statement of Richard's policy with respect to women—they must be silenced. The Duchess, however, finds voice, and her final words to Richard take the form of a curse; she turns against her own House, prays for the adverse party, and damns her son Richard to a death of shame. Her ability to do so with such

strength is surely a result of the communion of sympathy shared by the three women. If, in previous scenes, a meeting of women merely leads to angry words and altercation, the meeting of Act IV, scene iv, leads to the formation of bonds among the women against a single foe. When the progression of female characters is charted on this level, it becomes apparent that they do not deserve the a priori dismissal they too frequently receive. Although attenuated by Richard, women take on an emotional solidity, a roundness of true humanity.

A consideration of birth metaphor clarifies, yet further, the paradoxically double presentation of women in *Richard III*; specifically, perversion of birth metaphors suggests the negative condition of women [. . .] (from mother to nonmother, etc.), while the persistence and importance of these metaphors suggest the very positive condition of women [. . .] (as individuals having considerable power and human value). Although examples of the birth metaphor are so numerous as to render selection a problem, three categories may be arbitrarily distinguished: metaphor as descriptive of the condition of the times; as descriptive of Richard's activities and of Richard himself from the perspective of other characters; and as descriptive of Richard's mind as revealed in his own comments.

As mentioned previously, Richard "declares war" on the present time in his opening soliloquy; the extent to which he realizes this declaration may be felt in comments made by other characters throughout the play about the changed condition of the times—comments which most often work through a distortion of imagery usually associated with birth. When a group of citizens gathers to discuss the recent death of Edward and the probable confusion that will result, one compares his apprehension of ensuing danger to the swelling of water before a boisterous storm (II.iii.42-45). Although "swelling" is not, by any means, a term associated exclusively with pregnancy, it almost always conveys a feeling of pregnant expectation. Here, and at all other times throughout *Richard III*, that which is expected, that which swells the body, is something ominous, something negative. This consistently pejorative use of the term "swelling" stands in contrast to a possible positive application of the word: that is, swelling as indicative of a generous fertility. A similarly pejorative application of usually positive terms occurs in the speech of Elizabeth when she, like the citizens, is informed of Edward's death. Refusing all offers of sympathy from others, she cries: "I am not barren to bring forth complaints. / All springs reduce their currents to mine eyes, / That I . . . / May send forth plenteous tears to drown the world" (II.ii.67-68, 70). Two aspects of Elizabeth's choice of metaphor are worthy of note. First, the widow asserts her fertility, but a fertility that gives birth to complaints, instead of children. Second, the "children" that Elizabeth does produce assume the shape of tears, tears which, under normal conditions, might function as springs of life. Given the corruption of conditions under Richard, however, Elizabeth sends forth her tears to destroy life, "to drown the world."

Examination of Richard's specific activities reveals more explicitly his perversion of regenerative processes. When the thugs employed to murder Clarence attempt to convince him that Richard is the father of this deed, Clarence shakes his head in disbelief: "It cannot be, for he bewept my fortune / And hugged me in his arms and swore with sobs / That he would labor my delivery" (I.iv.247-49). While Clarence assumes that Richard will "deliver" him from prison, to freedom, Richard intends to deliver Clarence from prison to death. Thus, Richard reverses the normal delivery process; instead of drawing Clarence forth from the womb, two midwives push him back into a yet darker womb (specifically, into a butt of malmsey). The speech of Tyrrel, another murderer employed by Richard, provides a second commentary on Richard's activities. Having commissioned the execution of the young princes, he tells the king: "If to have done the thing you gave in charge / Beget your happiness, be happy then, / For it is done" (IV.iii.25-27). "The thing" given in charge is the murder of two children; once more, begetting and killing are conjoined. The comments of Margaret and the Duchess affirm this unnatural conjunction, transferring it to the literal level: Richard's unnatural birth. Margaret attacks Richard as "Thou slander of thy heavy mother's womb! / Thou loathèd issue of thy father's loins!" (I.iii.230-31). Similarly, because of son Richard, the Duchess of York cries out against her own womb, revealing an extreme of female debasement and acceptance of guilt: "O my accursèd womb, the bed of death! / A cockatrice hast thou hatched to the world, / Whose unavoided eye is murderous" (IV.i.53-55). Richard, forcing an association of the womb with "the bed of death," succeeds, at least *partially,* in debasing the value of women, these creatures with wombs.

One final category of defective birth imagery is that employed by Richard in describing his own activities. After the general altercation of Act I, scene iii, for example, Richard steps off alone and comments: "I do the wrong, and first begin to brawl. / The secret mischiefs that I *set abroach* / I lay unto the grievous charge of others" (I.iii.323-25, emphasis added). Or, just a short time later, when Edward, unaware of Richard's expeditious execution of Clarence, informs his court that peace has been made "between these swelling wrong-incensèd peers," Richard replies: "A blessèd *labor* my most sovereign lord" (II.i.52-53, emphasis added). But undoubtedly the most graphic of the many examples of debasement of the language of birth occurs in Act IV, scene iv, as Richard encourages

Elizabeth to allow him to right previous wrongs by marrying her daughter. When Elizabeth protests, "Yet thou didst kill my children," Richard counters: "But in your daughter's womb I'll bury them, / Where in that nest of spicery they will breed / Selves of themselves, to your recomforture" (IV.iv.423-25). Richard will bury old Elizabeth's children in young Elizabeth's womb? Could Richard hit upon a line of argument any more perversely unnatural? Up to this point, most birth metaphors have been constructed so as to suggest that the womb breeds no good (as, for example, that the Duchess's womb breeds a cockatrice); here, Richard forces the metaphor to work in reverse as well: the womb serves as tomb, functioning as both sprouting ground and burial plot. In forcing this perverse alliance of terms, Richard reaffirms, on a linguistic level, the impulse behind all of his activities with respect to women—the impulse to silence, to negate. Yet, paradoxically, the persistence with which Richard acts upon this impulse gives the lie to the possibility of its fulfillment: Richard's *need* to debase birth imagery implies that women (those capable of giving birth) have a power which finally cannot be devalued or eliminated; further, his repeated attempts, on a larger level, to rob women of their identity as mothers, wives, or queens, are doomed to frustration in that he cannot rob women of their identity as creative, regenerative human beings.

Richard III opens with a series of complaints directed, implicitly, against women. It is women who tame "Grim-visaged War," who caper to lutes, who play Love's games—and who govern the times. *Richard III* ends with a series of scenes on the battlefield; men engage in combat with men, and women are nowhere to be found (the last female on stage appears in Act IV). On one level, the process of the play is one of denial and deflation; as Richard destroys husbands, kings, and children, as he confounds traditionally stable sources of identity and subjects women to an unnatural association with the forces of death, he suggests that women are without value—or, even worse, that they are destructive of value. But a reading of *Richard III* on just this one level does an injustice to the play; running parallel to the process described above is a counterprocess, one that insists upon the inherently positive value of women. We see evidence of this counterprocess in the progression of women from a condition of rivalry, battling amongst themselves, to a condition of camaraderie, sympathizing with each other, and in the persistence of the attack that Richard feels compelled to wage, both in life and in language, against these powerful foes. Even Richmond's final speech contributes to our sense of the invincibility of these females; after describing the bloody hatred between brothers which has divided England, Richmond proposes a reunification through his conjunction with the young woman Elizabeth. Hence, the argument of *Richard III* moves in two directions. The first insists that women are purely media of exchange and have no value in themselves; the second, overriding the first, insists that even when used as currency, women's value cannot be completely destroyed.

Irene G. Dash

SOURCE: "The Paradox of Power: The *Henry VI-Richard III* Tetralogy," in *Wooing, Wedding, and Power: Women in Shakespeare's Plays*, Columbia University Press, 1981, pp. 155-207.

[*In her examination of the powerlessness of women in* Richard III, *Dash focuses primarily upon Margaret, Anne, and Elizabeth. She describes Margaret as "dynamic," remarking also that she is the least conventional of the three women and the character most often left out of productions of the play. Dash describes Anne, by contrast, as more compliant and more typically "feminine" in her obedience to Richard. Finally, she asserts that Elizabeth, who at first seems somewhat lackluster, grows more complex in Act IV, after Richard has murdered her young sons and she has asked Margaret to teach her how to curse her enemies. At this point, Dash compares the two wooing scenes, observing that where Anne falls victim to Richard's clever words, the more experienced Elizabeth turns the tables on him.*]

In *Richard III*, four widows walk the stage: Margaret, Elizabeth, the Duchess of York, and Anne. If women are confused by the meaning of power when they are young, being wooed or acting as wives to men of power, they realistically discover its meaning when they become widows. They learn that their husbands were not only the source of their power, but worse still, of their identity. How does a woman cope with this discovery, this becoming a nonperson? Shakespeare offers four versions in *Richard III*, from the simple acceptance of her status by the Duchess of York to the anxious search for new patterns by Elizabeth, who first entered this tetralogy when, as a widow suing for rights to her husband's lands, she discovered her powerlessness for the first time. Saved by her wit and beauty, she then moved from powerlessness to power. Like Margaret earlier, she became a queen and the mother of princes. When, in *Richard III*, the pattern repeats itself, Elizabeth seeks more substantial answers.

Her experience continues to mirror Margaret's despite deviations. Elizabeth's husband, instead of being murdered by Richard, dies, his illness aggravated by Richard's histrionics. Instead of losing one son and heir to the throne, she loses two. Instead of being childless at the end of the play, she remains a mother with surviving children. Instead of being a widow of a defeated monarch, she is widow of a man who was

in power. But it little matters. Like Margaret, Elizabeth too loses power, discovering the strength of the patriarchal system. Finally, near the play's close, she seeks alternatives. Shakespeare offers a tentative glimpse at women supporting women, women relying on women, women bonding—even if in bitterness—with women.

To do this, the dramatist alters history and creates one of the most interesting studies in the play—he retains Margaret. Historically, she never returned to England after the deaths of her son and husband. Moreover, she died before the time of the action of this play. According to the chronicles, she roamed the French court, a woman in mourning for the rest of her life:

> And where in the beginning of her tyme, she lyved like a Quene, in the middel she ruled like an empresse, toward thende she was vexed with troble, never quyet nor in peace, & in her very extreme age she passed her dayes in Fraunce, more lyke a death then a lyfe, languishyng and mornyng in continuall sorowe, not so much for her selfe and her husbande, whose ages were almost consumed and worne, but for the losse of prince Edward her sonne (whome she and her husband thought to leve, both overlyver of their progeny, and also of their kyngdome) to whome in this lyfe nothyng could be either more displeasant or grevous.

Shakespeare not only brings her back to England but gives her an important role in the play. She acts as narrative voice; she is seer and sibyl [a female prophet], predicting the doom of those responsible for the deaths of her son and husband; but she is also a dynamic woman, an anomalous character, roaming the palace of a rival monarch, expressing her opinions in positive language, sneering at York's unattractive progeny who now control power. Having lost all, she fears no one.

Margaret, who weaves in and out of this tetralogy [*Henry VI*, parts 1-3, and *Richard III*], the only woman character whose growth we observe from youth to old age, may also have challenged Shakespeare as a creative artist. Knowing that she walked through the court in France, a person in constant mourning, he might have wanted to project this image on the stage. Would such a woman have learned anything? Would she have grown? How might she have handled life, alone, in a hostile environment? Finally, has she made any breakthrough in self-knowledge; did she learn anything about herself as a woman?

Before she enters, Shakespeare introduces her principal antagonist, Richard, the title character. He defines the power and powerlessness of women in the first scene of *Richard III*. Introduced in soliloquy, he confides his plans to reach the throne despite the mass of relatives standing between him and his objective. "I am determined to prove a villain" (I.i.30), he proclaims, baring his plot to frame his brother Clarence. When the latter enters, en route to prison, Richard immediately blames a woman for Clarence's present fate. "Why, this it is, when men are rul'd by women" (62), Richard asserts, implying Queen Elizabeth's evil influence on Edward. Misogyny runs wild, for Clarence easily agrees, adding Mistress Shore's name to those who "rule" the King. Before the scene closes, a third woman is mentioned. Richard, again in soliloquy, admits,

> . . . I'll marry Warwick's youngest daughter.
> What though I kill'd her husband and her
>   father?
> The readiest way to make the wench amends
> Is to become her husband and her father.
>
> (I.i.153-56)

Moments later Anne, the play's third widow, walks on following the coffin of King Henry, her father-in-law, and taking it to burial. Asking the pall bearers to "set down" their "honorable load" (I.ii.i), Anne delivers a long set speech of mourning explicitly cursing the murderer, Richard. She then orders the pall-bearers to resume the trek to the place of burial. Richard, unobserved, interferes, countermanding her order. "Stay, you that bear the corse, and set it down" (33). At their attempt to continue, Richard threatens with his sword. They obey. Graphically, this scene illustrates Richard's power and Anne's powerlessness. Helpless to challenge him physically, she attempts to disarm him with words. She seeks to force her will. Scorn, hatred, vehemence, curses: all fall from her lips. Little anticipating the aim of his confrontation, she is astonished and completely bewildered when Richard offers marriage.

Historically, Richard pursued Anne for two years before winning her. Shakespeare compresses this into one scene, choosing a moment when she is most confused and emotionally most unstable. In a long protracted courtship, their debates—her responses to his persistent claims—would have to be developed so that the many variables in personality could influence the decision. When compressed into a single scene, his duplicity and her confusion must be apparent at once. Some critics believe that the scene offers an opportunity to prove Richard's extraordinary ability. More recently critics have become aware of the psychological vulnerability of a person at a time of emotional crisis such as the loss of a husband and a father-in-law.

First Richard tries flattery, but Anne resists, assuring him that she would scratch her beauty with her nails (I.ii.126) if she thought it were the cause of the death of her husband or father-in-law. Then Richard, the consummate actor, offers her his sword and "lays his breast open" for her to kill him. He challenges her in

a style that she cannot fathom. Untrained in the use of the sword, unwilling to take a human life, Anne reacts as a normal human being might, especially someone who has not been initiated into the games of war and murder. Although Richard continues "Nay, do not pause: for I did kill King Henry—/ But 'twas thy beauty that provoked me" (179-80), she drops the sword. But Richard's words are really superfluous. All of her training as a woman assures him success. Men are trained to kill. Woman are not. Here, against a defenseless person, in a time of uncertain peace, to kill the brother of the King would be insanity as well as suicide.

Richard then poses a false dichotomy for her: "Take up the sword again, or take up me" (I.ii.183). He leaves her no option; she must either kill him or accept him as her husband. Caught between suspicion and her training as a woman, Anne can do no more than say, "Arise, dissembler! Though I wish thy death, / I will not be thy executioner" (184-85). Still she does not acquiesce to marriage. The key interchange between them occurs moments later when Richard offers "Then bid me kill myself" (186) but refuses to accept her words, "I have already" (187). Instead, he then questions the honesty of her original intention. "That was in thy rage. / Speak it again" (187-88) he challenges, promising to kill himself for love. Anne's agonized words, "I would I knew thy heart" (192) are spoken by many of the characters throughout the play. No one knows Richard's "heart"—his intention—until it is too late. For a woman being wooed, however, the price is particularly high—not friendship or allegiance, but marriage.

Although Richard congratulates himself on his success—"To take her in her heart's extremest hate, / With curses in her mouth, tears in her eyes" (I.ii.231-32)—Shakespeare here creates a situation in which a manipulative liar has the best chance of success, a moment when his prey is most confused. Richard's timing, audacity, overwhelming flattery, and histrionics with the sword are beyond Anne's ability to cope. She belongs with such characters as Ophelia [from Shakespeare's play *Hamlet*], who is conforming, obedient, docile, "feminine." Historically, having resisted Richard for two years, she may have had more of the strength of Margaret or an Elizabeth. She may also have had as few options as they did, being sought by the persistent brother of the King. But rather than repeat a pattern already twice told, Shakespeare creates another type of woman, caught in a different situation, and reacting on a level not yet dramatized in this tetralogy. The man she must confront is the man who boasted in the previous play:

> Why, I can smile, and murther whiles I

smile,

. . . . .

Deceive more slily than Ulysses could,

. . . . .

Change shapes with Proteus for advantages,

. . . . .

Can I do this, and cannot get a crown?
Tut, were it farther off, I'll pluck it down.
                    (*3 Henry VI,* III.ii.182-95)

Richard applies his abilities, skills, and techniques to convince Anne.

Critics have been harsh in their evaluation of her. August W. Von Schlegel, the nineteenth-century German scholar, writes that "Anne disappears without our learning anything further respecting her: in marrying the murderer of her husband she had shown a weakness almost incredible." William Richardson, in the eighteenth century, concludes that "She is represented by Shakespeare of a mind altogether frivolous; incapable of deep affection; guided by no steady principles of virtue . . . ; the prey of vanity, which is her ruling passion." As Richardson continues, he not only says that Richard understands her perfectly but that she is a character of "no rational or steady virtue, and consequently of no consistency of character." He even suggests that it is "resentment, rather than grief, which she expresses." Georg Gervinus, the nineteenth-century German literary historian, offers a more balanced appraisal, however, when he writes, "We must take into account extraordinary degree of dissimulation, which deceives even experienced men," nothing also how stereotypical a portrait Shakespeare creates in Anne by having her delight in saving "such a penitent."

Anne appears in only one other scene, and that without Richard. Now married, she hopes to visit her nephews—the heirs apparent—held in the tower by her husband. Unlike her historical prototype, she admits:

Lo, ere I can repeat this curse again,
Within so small a time, my woman's heart
Grossly grew captive to his honey words,
And prov'd the subject of mine own soul's
  curse.

                              (IV.i.77-80)

She is self-deprecating, and blames herself for her fate. Her conventionality is perhaps best testified to by the fact that she survives in all versions of the play. In Colley Cibber's version, Richard even tries to tempt her to commit suicide. In a recent production at the Cort Theatre starring Al Pacino, she appears so cold, self-righteous, and vindictive that audiences applaud Richard's success. There, although the text that remains is Shakespeare's, the cuts are reminiscent of Cibber's popular eighteenth-century work.

On the other hand, the one woman who most frequently disappears from productions is the one who challenges Richard, the least conventional woman— Margaret. Cibber set the pattern in 1700 when he eliminated her from his text. Since then, his version with its heavy emphasis on the male "star" role has seldom left the stage. But even when Shakespeare's text is used, Margaret frequently disappears or loses most of her lines. For example, in a Phelps 1845 prompt-book, she no longer functions as an individual, cursing the many members of the court, but acts rather as a choral voice of doom. Very similar cutting appears in a 1964 typescript of the play. She is also absent from Laurence Olivier's film version and from the Pacino 1979 production. Comparing the Cibber version with Shakespeare's play, Arthur Colby Sprague writes that:

the more obviously memorable episodes . . . have
survived. . . . But Margaret is gone and Clarence
and Hastings and Edward: the price paid for
compactness was high. It is a version . . . which
does best when it keeps to surfaces and shallows;
an opportunist version, cunning, prosaic and vulgar.

Many productions of *Richard III,* like Olivier's and Pacino's mentioned above, follow Shakespeare's text but also take their cues for cutting from Cibber. It is perhaps difficult for audiences to realize how deeply eighteenth-century changes—perhaps because they reflect attitudes toward women that still exist—continue to intrude on, shape, and gently distort the text.

Margaret's absence necessarily affects the total impact of the play; her entrance, in Act I, scene iii, offers a welcome antidote to Richard's swaggering triumph with Anne. Listening to Queen Elizabeth and Richard arguing, Margaret, once again, as she did so long ago in *1 Henry VI* speaks in asides. This time, however, her asides are not the questions of a young virgin but the bitter comments of an old woman. She listens to the conversation of those in power. To Elizabeth's "Small joy have I in being England's Queen" (109), Margaret mutters to herself:

And less'ned by that small, God I beseech
  him!
Thy honor, state, and seat is due to me.
                              (I.iii.110-11)

At once we are reminded that Margaret is a deposed queen. We wonder at her presence in this court. Commenting on Richard's words, but still speaking in aside, she exclaims:

Hie thee to hell for shame, and leave this
    world,
Thou cacodemon, there thy kingdom is.

(142-43)

Only the audience hears her; nevertheless, her lines establish her strange position. What is she doing at the court, this woman, so unafraid of Richard who, in asides, tells us of the murder of Henry in the tower and the killing of her son Edward? When she speaks aloud, Margaret pierces the false veneer of Richard, but also reveals antagonism for the woman who has made her a shadow, a nonbeing, the woman who is Queen. Although Richard reminds Margaret that she is "banished on pain of death" (166), she dismisses the threat, challenging him to enforce it. "I do find more pain in banishment / Than death can yield me here by my abode" (167-68). He then pursues another direction. Always aware of his audience, the people around him on the stage, he attacks Margaret for the murders of York and Rutland. As a result the squabbling members of the court unite against her. Aware of Richard's technique, she taunts:

What? were you snarling all before I came,

. . . . .

And turn you all your hatred now on me?

(187-89)

She then curses each of them. Still wrestling with the patriarchal values she has absorbed, she first curses the Queen, her alter ego in this strange arrangement where kings are murdered to make way for kings but queens in number are permitted to survive. Listing the parallels between them, Margaret wishes the other woman a fate like her own:

Though not by war, by surfeit die your king,
As ours by murther, to make him a king!
Edward thy son, that now is Prince of
    Wales,
For Edward our son, that was Prince of
    Wales,
Die in his youth by like untimely violence!

(I.iii.196-200)

She keeps returning to her role of mother.

Long mayst thou live to wail thy children's
    death,
And see another, as I see thee now,
Deck'd in thy rights as thou art stall'd in
    mine!

(203-5)

Finally, she condemns Elizabeth to a fate too familiar to women.

Long die thy happy days before thy death,
And after many length'ned hours of grief,
Die neither mother, wife, nor England's
    queen!

(206-8)

In this long passage, Margaret details her own life as queen. Unlike the curses one might choose for a man, those chosen for Elizabeth have a different emphasis—not death but life continued after joy has passed.

When the bitter woman fails to stop her cursing, Richard interrupts. In verbal battle, she responds, wishing him a fate more heinous than the others. Her curse concludes with "Thou detested—." Never one to refuse a challenge, Richard quickly interjects the word "Margaret." But she is not to be deflected from her purpose. Her sentence continues, ending with "Richard!" Elizabeth, although she bears no love for Richard, is still a victim of that minority status psychology that mandates she express her deepest contempt for another woman. "Thus have you breath'd your curse against yourself" (239), she mocks. Her words are hardly worth including in this exchange except to remind us of the difference between the two women—the sibyl-like, intense, passionate Margaret, and the more pedestrian, rational Elizabeth.

Finally, Cassandra-like, Margaret warns the one person exempt from her vengeance to beware of Richard:

Have not to do with him, beware of him;
Sin, death, and hell have set their marks on
    him,
And all their ministers attend on him.

(I. iii. 291-93)

But Buckingham rejects her warning. Nevertheless, he shudders at her curses. Ironically, she is attacked as being a witch and a lunatic although her listeners recognize the core of truth in her words. During this scene Dorset, the new young lord who is Elizabeth's son, warns "Dispute not with her, she is lunatic" (253). Buckingham expresses the impact of the curses for all of them, "My hair doth stand on end to hear her curses" (303).

When her curses come true, she believes her mission is completed. But Shakespeare suggests that one possibility lies ahead—women extending their hands to each other in support—creating bonds with each other, rather than living in separate isolated worlds, connected only with the men whom they have wed. Entering in Act IV, scene iv, Margaret, in soliloquy, mutters "So now prosperity begins to mellow" (IV. iv. 1). Still bitter, overflowing with anger and hatred, she plans to go to France, hoping the lives of those who robbed her of son and husband will prove "bitter, black, and tragical" (7). She is a figure from the revenge tragedy of the period, asking right for right and Plantagenet for Plantagenet. It is only after the Duchess of York exclaims

> O Harry's wife, triumph not in my woes!
> God witness with me, I have wept for thine
> (IV. iv. 59-60)

that Margaret explains herself to them: "I am hungry for revenge" (61). She prays for Richard's end. Aware of her anomic position, Margaret returns to the theme of displacedness—"Thou didst usurp my place"—and to the role of childlessness and widowhood. She cannot establish a bond with any woman—not lend support, or seek help, or accept friendship.

"Vain flourish of my fortune" (IV. iv. 82), she had called Elizabeth. Detailing its meaning, the displaced Queen recognizes the role she played, "One heav'd a-high, to be hurl'd down below" (86). She knows now that she was merely

> The flattering index of a direful pageant;
>
> . . . . .
>
> . . . a bubble;
> A queen in jest, only to fill the scene.
> (85-91)

She then enumerates the functions of a queen, listing the bending peers and thronging troops that followed her and Elizabeth when each was Queen. This speech, by the dramatist who later was to list the many roles of man as he progressed from infancy to old age, vibrates with the emptiness of a woman's roles. "Vain flourish of my fortune," Margaret had repeated. It is a line that many older women might speak, watching young women seeking success in the world and misreading their husbands' glories for their own.

Although Margaret's words are full of venom, hatred, and disappointment, Elizabeth seeks to create some bond, some tenuous connection, with this other woman. The scene marks a shift in attitude and is the first in which these women finally speak to each other as equals. Frequently referred to as the scene of the wailing women, it is also the beginning of mutual supportiveness. "My words are dull, O, quicken them with thine!" (124), Elizabeth begs, asking Margaret for instruction in cursing.

> Think that thy babes were sweeter than they were,
> And he that slew them fouler than he is.
> (IV. iv. 120-21)

The older woman offers a basic premise that provides strength for Elizabeth's next encounter.

Clues to a sometimes ambiguous exchange between characters frequently appear in the sequential arrangement of Shakespeare's scenes. Moments after Margaret's advice to Elizabeth, Richard enters and asks for Elizabeth's daughter's hand in marriage. Uncle Richard, murderer of the young woman's brothers, now King, anticipates success. In the debate between them, Elizabeth has her first opportunity to apply her newly learned lesson. Questions rather than answers characterize most of her replies. "Shall I be tempted of the devil thus?" (418), she asks. "Ay, if the devil tempt you to do good" (419), Richard sanctimoniously replies. "Shall I forget myself to be myself" (420), she continues. "Ay, if yourself's remembrance wrong yourself" (421), he answers. When she seems to equivocate, Richard simply carries on as best he can, picking up what he thinks are hints of affirmation. Even Elizabeth's "Yet thou didst kill my children" (422) fails to daunt him. He offers what he considers a perfectly logical response:

> But in your daughter's womb I bury them;
> Where in that nest of spicery they will breed
> Selves of themselves, to your recomforture.
> (IV. iv. 423-25)

This speech, so ugly in its lasciviousness, reflecting the character of the man who is speaking, must be answered without disgust by a mother. Again Elizabeth resorts to a question, rather than an answer. "Shall I go win my daughter to thy will?" (426). Has she finally fooled Richard? Immediately after her departure, he gloats, "Relenting fool, and shallow, changing woman" (431).

She should not fool us. We have heard her scene with Margaret. We have listened to her first words to Richard in this encounter—"For my daughters, Richard, / They shall be praying nuns, not weeping queens" (201-2)—and we have seen her pity for Anne. The choice of a convent for her grows not from religious conviction—we have not heard any deep expressions of religious faith from Elizabeth—but from the wish to give her daughters control over their own bodies. Elizabeth has expressed herself on this subject from the time of her first appearance in *3 Henry VI*.

When one compares Anne's response to Richard with Elizabeth's series of rhetorical questions topped by the instruction: "Write to me very shortly, / And you shall understand from me her mind" (428-29), one realizes Shakespeare's artistry. Richard, thinking that he is repeating an earlier wooing scene, assumes a repetition of that success—this time with far less effort than in his encounter with Anne. Because of his misogyny, he fails to hear the nuances that separate the responses of the women. He forgets the differences between them: one a young, unwordly heiress, the other a mature woman who has lived a varied existence. Finally, he has figured without understanding the impact of the death of one's child on a parent. The superb manipulator of people, Richard fails to read a woman accurately, because he fails to understand her feelings toward herself and her children.

To an extent, then, Elizabeth has triumphed. She has begun to understand the meaning of power and the necessity for choosing one's language with care, for restraining one's words, refraining from cursing. She has learned that she must function alone, leading, not leaning. In this her first test after her encounter with Margaret and her awareness of the role of queen as shadow, she has begun to understand the limits of power for a woman. She succeeds in fooling Richard, but had he not lost his life in battle, she probably would have been powerless against him. Her daughter, instead of becoming a nun, marries Richard's victorious adversary: Richmond, later Henry VII. Thus, she too becomes a queen, wearing the borrowed robes of power.

The women in these plays, queens and duchesses, wives of men of political strength, seek to exert power but discover its elusiveness. Margaret Fuller writes: "A profound thinker has said 'No married woman can represent the female world, for she belongs to her husband. The idea of Woman must be represented by a virgin.'" Perhaps the Queen in Shakespeare's audience believed this. The women in these plays, however, demonstrate the powerlessness of women whether virgins, wives, or widows. Fuller herself countered the argument by blaming marriage and "the present relation between the sexes, that the woman *does* belong to the man, instead of forming a whole with him."

This chapter opened with references to power and to women's powerlessness in a society where sexual politics is so pervasive that women have internalized the message. Shakespeare illustrates this by revealing the minority psychology of the women. They scorn other women, attempt to imitate men, and tend to believe in their own inferiority. The men too believe the women inferior to them, whether the women are selfconfident and challenge male power, or whether they acquiesce, seeking to appease male anger. The stereotypes do not exist solely among the characters in the plays, but appear also in the world outside the plays—in the criticism and productions. We read of Margaret's unwomanly strength, and of Richard's womanly guile. A recent critic describes the character's histrionic talents and sensitivity to people and atmosphere: "His awareness of other people has, in the best Hitlerian manner, an almost *feminine* subtlety. The list of roles he assumes is endless" (italics mine). On the basis of evidence within the plays, one

might have expected a different conclusion. For—as well as Richard—York, Edward, Buckingham, and Warwick have been the supreme manipulators, men of guile, organizing behind the scenes and plotting insurrection. Misogyny persists.

Optimistically, Fuller recommends that women not be influenced by men because they fail to see the entire picture. She instructs women to look within themselves to find their own "peculiar secret." This means rejecting the stereotypes and accepting their own strengths. Margaret, struggling with the concept that strength is "masculine," is vulnerable to the attack of "unwomanliness." Elizabeth, perhaps discovering her own "peculiar secret," tries to establish a bond of friendship or support with the woman she had scorned. But learning to curse is hardly a start on the path to understanding that the stereotypes (for "maleness" strength, courage, and initiative; and for "femaleness" docility, passivity, and weakness) must be denied if women are to gain power, not over the lives of others, but over their own lives. Shakespeare dramatizes the reality that women cannot do this alone. These plays reveal the limited world that exists as long as people believe that power belongs to men and powerlessness to women, refusing to recognize "the benefits . . . the world would gain by ceasing to make sex a disqualification for privileges and a badge of subjection."

SOURCES FOR FURTHER STUDY

History

Richards, Jeffrey. "The Riddle of Richard III." *History Today* 33, No. 8 (August 1983): 18-25.

>   Attempts to distinguish fact from fiction regarding the reign of Richard III. Richards concludes that King Richard III "was an efficient but unlucky and ultimately unhappy ruler."

Literary Commentary

Berman, Ronald. "Anarchy and Order in 'Richard III' and 'King John.'" *Shakespeare Survey* 20, edited by Kenneth Muir, pp. 51-9. Cambridge: Cambridge University Press, 1967.

>   Contends that *Richard III* and *King John* differ from Shakespeare's other history plays in the "cynical and realistic wit" of some of their major characters. Berman sees both plays as a struggle between individual pragmatism and historic order.

Brooks, Harold F. "'Richard III,' Unhistorical Amplifications: The Women's Scenes and Seneca." *Modern*

Language Review 75, Pt. 4 (October 1980): 721-37.

Suggests that when Shakespeare wrote the scenes for the wooing of Anne and the mourning of Margaret, Elizabeth, and the Duchess of York, he was strongly influenced by the tragedies of the Roman playwright Seneca.

Dillon, Janette. "'I am myself alone': *Richard III.*" In her *Shakespeare and the Solitary Man*, pp. 49-60. Totowa, N.J.: Rowman and Littlefield, 1981.

Describes Richard as "trapped between voluntary and involuntary types of isolation." Dillon sees the close of the play as the triumph of the social order over the "anarchic solitary" individual.

Fergusson, Francis. "Richard III." In *Shakespeare: The Pattern in His Carpet*, pp. 51-6. New York: Delacorte Press, 1970.

States that the character of Richard himself is the source of the play's energy and that Shakespeare drew upon history as well as upon classical and medieval drama to portray Richard as a heartless and comical villain.

Gurr, Andrew. "Richard III and the Democratic Process." *Essays in Criticism* XXIV, No. 1 (January 1974):39-47.

Argues that Richard was not defeated by ghosts or by his own conscience but by Stanley's decision to fight for Richmond and thus to exercise his natural "democratic right" to choose a good ruler.

Heilman, Robert B. "Satiety and Conscience: Aspects of Richard III." *The Antioch Review* XXIV, No. 1 (Spring 1964): 57-73.

Remarks that Richard is not a stereotypical villain but a complex enough character to be regarded as a precursor to Shakespeare's later, tragic hero Macbeth.

Kott, Jan. "The Kings." In his *Shakespeare Our Contemporary*, translated by Boleslaw Taborski, pp. 3-46. London: Methuen & Co. Ltd., 1965.

Discusses the kings in Shakespeare's history plays. Kott observes that Richard III first controls the pace and direction of history but is later destroyed by it.

Krieger, Murray. "The Dark Generations of *Richard III.*" *Criticism* 1, No. 1 (Winter 1959): 32-48.

Maintains that Richard is not completely in control of events in the play. Krieger asserts that Richard functions as a "purge" to rid England of a wicked past and as a "scourge" to punish those who are as guilty as he is, and that in this way the play resembles a Greek tragedy.

Muir, Kenneth. "Image and Symbol in Shakespeare's Histories." *Bulletin of the John Rylands Library* 50 (1967-1968): 103-23.

Observes that in addition to the frequent use of animal imagery in *Richard III* ("dog," "toad," etc.),

there are also numerous images taken from drama, and that Richard himself plays roles.

Neill, Michael. "Shakespeare's Halle of Mirrors: Play, Politics, and Psychology in *Richard III.*" *Shakespeare Studies* 8 (1980): 99-129.

Analyzes the theatrical imagery in *Richard III* as well as the frequent references to mirrors and reflections. Neill points out that this play is greatly concerned with "self": England divided against itself in civil war, Richard creating himself king, and Buckingham betraying himself.

Ritchey, David. "Queen Margaret (*Richard III*): A Production Note." *North Carolina Journal of Speech and Drama* 7, No. 2 (1973): 37-41.

Identifies three interpretations of Margaret's role (as a chorus pointing to the past and predicting the future; as a defeated Lancastrian wanting retribution against the Yorkists; and as a ghost) and the difficulties they pose to productions of *Richard III.*

Rossiter, A.P. "Angel with Horns: The Unity of *Richard III.*" In *Angel with Horns and other Shakespeare Lectures*, edited by Graham Storey, pp. 1-22. London: Longmans, 1961.

Examines the apparent disunity between the dire pronouncements of vengeance in the play and Richard's wicked but appealing buffoonery. Rossiter contends that the play is not a cut-and-dried "moral history"; instead it is a "comic history" presenting the ambiguities and contradictions of human lives.

Shaw, George Bernard. *Shaw on Shakespeare*, edited by Edwin Wilson, pp. 164-75. Freeport, New York: E.P. Dutton, 1961.

An anthology of Shaw's critical reviews of productions of *Richard III*, as well as Shaw's letter to an actor urging him to play the part of Richard.

Tanner, Stephen L. "Richard III versus Elizabeth: An Interpretation." *Shakespeare Quarterly* XXIV, No. 4 (Autumn 1973): 468-72.

Asserts that, contrary to what Richard and some critics believe, Elizabeth wins the verbal battle with Richard over whether he will marry her daughter.

Velz, John W. "Episodic Structure in Four Tudor Plays: A Virtue of Necessity." *Comparative Drama* VI, No. 2 (Summer 1972): 87-102.

Calls *Richard III* a one-man play whose "action is a series of . . . self-contained encounters with the protagonist. . . ." Velz explains that this format occurred because small Tudor acting companies had to double up on minor parts, and argues that Shakespeare turns this to his advantage in *Richard III.*

Weber, Karl. "Shakespeare's *Richard III*, I.iv.24-33." *Explicator* 38, No. 3 (Spring 1980): 24-6.

Suggests that Clarence's vivid "undersea" nightmare in Act I "foreshadow[s] the rest of the play," as each image in the dream represents "the fate of England under Richard's rule."

Wilson, John Dover. Introduction to *Richard III*, by William Shakespeare, edited by John Dover Wilson, pp. vii-xlv. Cambridge: Cambridge University Press, 1954.
    Overview of *Richard III*, with information on the play's composition date, sources, style, and critical reception.

Media Adaptations

Richard III. London Film Productions, Ltd., 1955.
    Critically acclaimed motion picture version of the history play, featuring Laurence Olivier, John Gielgud, Ralph Richardson, and Claire Bloom. The film was produced and directed by Laurence Olivier. Distributed on video by Embassy Home Entertainment, 1985. 138 minutes.

Richard III. International Film Bureau, 1974.
    Covers two scenes from the play: Richard's "winter of our discontent" soliloquy and his wooing of Lady Anne. Distributed by International Film Bureau, Inc. 12 minutes.

Richard III. BBC, Time-Life Television, 1982.
    Televised performance of the history play, part of the "Shakespeare Plays" series. Distributed by Time-Life Video. 228 minutes.

Richard III. MGM/UA, 1996.
    Motion picture set in an imaginary England during the 1930s, capturing the political atmosphere—one of instability and tyranny—of the time period. Ian McKellen, who wrote the screenplay, plays Richard III. The film also stars Annette Bening as Queen Elizabeth, Jim Broadbent as Buckingham, Robert Downey, Jr. as Rivers, Nigel Hawthorne as Clarence, Kristin Scott Thomas as Richard's wife, Anne, and Maggie Smith as the Duchess of York. Directed by Richard Loncraine. Distributed by MGM/UA Home Video. 100 minutes.

THE TAMING OF THE SHREW

INTRODUCTION

Shakespeare is thought to have written *The Taming of the Shrew* between 1590 and 1594, although the only version that has survived is the one published in the First Folio in 1623. It appears to have been staged several times during Shakespeare's lifetime at both the Globe and the Blackfriars theaters, and a sequel written by John Fletcher between 1604 and 1617 attests to its popularity. It was also produced in 1633 at the court of Charles I.

The play has a complex structure. It begins with a two-scene "Induction" or introductory segment, which concerns an elaborate practical joke played by a nobleman on a drunken tinker. At the end of the Induction the various characters settle down to watch a play. This "play within a play," which in turn consists of a main plot and a complex subplot, constitutes the main action of *The Taming of the Shrew*.

Shakespeare appears to have drawn on many sources in writing the play. The character of the "shrew"—a word used to indicate an opinionated, domineering, and sharp-tongued woman—is found in the folklore and literature of many cultures. The earliest example in English drama is thought to be the character of Noah's wife in the medieval mystery plays. In the sixteenth century shrewish wives were featured in a number of plays, many of which depicted cruel physical punishments for the shrew. The principal source of the Bianca-Lucentio subplot is George Gascoigne's play *Supposes* (1566). Gascoigne's play was itself derived from an Italian play, Ludovico Ariosto's *I Suppositi* (1509), and many of its elements can be traced back to the classical Latin comedies of Plautus and Terence. As for the Induction, the story of a poor man tricked into thinking he is a nobleman was common in Europe and Asia in the sixteenth century, and is at least as old as the story of the Caliph Haroun Al Raschid and the beggar Abu Hassan in *The Arabian Nights*. In addition, an anonymous play entitled *The Taming of a Shrew* and published in 1594 is generally thought to be either a pirated copy of Shakespeare's play or an inaccurate copy of an earlier play that may have been another source for Shakespeare's version. While the action of *The Taming of a Shrew* is very close to that of Shakespeare's play, both the language and the names of the characters are different. One interesting difference between the two plays concerns the Induction. In Shakespeare's play as we have it, the characters in the Induction are not mentioned in the text after the end of Act I, scene i. In *A Shrew*, on the other hand, the story line of the Induction is brought to a conclusion at the end of the play. Some modern productions of Shakespeare's *Shrew* incorporate material from *The Taming of a Shrew* in order to complete the story introduced in the Induction. Others eliminate the Induction altogether.

PRINCIPAL CHARACTERS

(in order of appearance)

In the Induction:

Christopher Sly: A poor tinker (traveling mender of housewares). As a practical joke, a Lord and his attendants try to convince him that he is really a nobleman who has been suffering from insanity. The play that constitutes the five acts of *The Taming of the Shrew* is put on for Sly's entertainment. He comments once on the play at the end of Act I, scene i, then disappears from the text.

Hostess: Ejects Sly from the tavern at the beginning of the play.

Lord: Returning from a hunt, he finds Sly drunk and asleep. As a practical joke, he and his men try to convince Sly he is a nobleman. The Lord arranges for the players to present the play that constitutes the main action of *The Taming of the Shrew*.

First and Second Huntsmen: Two of the Lord's huntsmen who are with him when he discovers Sly.

Servants: The Lord's attendants, who join in his practical joke on Sly.

Players: A group of traveling actors who arrive at the tavern. The Lord, who has seen them perform before, asks them to put on a play.

Barthol'mew: The Lord's page (a young male attendant). On the Lord's orders, he dresses like a woman and pretends to be Sly's loving and obedient wife.

Messenger: Announces that the play is about to begin.

In Acts I-V:

Lucentio: Son of a wealthy Pisan merchant, he comes

to Padua intending to study, but immediately falls in love with Bianca, whom he sees in the street. He pretends to be a schoolmaster named Cambio in order to gain access to Bianca, and eventually elopes with her.

Tranio: Lucentio's servant, he assists Lucentio in plotting the latter's elopement with Bianca. On Lucentio's orders, Tranio pretends to be Lucentio while Lucentio is pretending to be Cambio. As Lucentio, Tranio presents himself as a suitor for Bianca's hand and is selected by her father to marry her.

Baptista: A wealthy Paduan merchant with two daughters, Katherina and Bianca. He decides that he will not allow Bianca to marry until a husband is found for Katherina.

Gremio: An elderly man; one of Bianca's suitors. In Act III, scene ii, he tells Lucentio and Tranio about Petruchio's scandalous behavior during the marriage ceremony between Petruchio and Katherina.

Katherina: The "shrew" of the title, and Baptista's elder daughter, known in Padua for her hot temper and sharp tongue. She marries Petruchio and is "tamed" by him, becoming an obedient wife. At the end of the play she delivers a lecture on wifely obedience to the other brides. (*See* **Katherina** *in the* **CHARACTER STUDIES** *section.*)

Hortensio: Another of Bianca's suitors, and a friend of Petruchio's. Hortensio pretends to be a music teacher named Litio (sometimes spelled "Licio" in order to see Bianca. When he discovers her flirting with "Cambio," he abandons his suit and marries a wealthy widow after visiting Petruchio in the country to obtain tips on controlling a woman.

Bianca: Baptista's younger daughter, she initially appears quiet and submissive. However, she skillfully intrigues with Lucentio, with whom she eventually elopes, and in the final scene of the play refuses to come when her husband calls her.

Biondello: Another of Lucentio's servants, who is aware of Lucentio and Tranio's ploy of changing identities but is not immediately told of the reason for it.

Petruchio: A wealthy gentleman from Verona whose father has recently died. He comes to Padua to visit his friend Hortensio and to look for a wealthy bride. He marries Katherina and undertakes to transform her into a compliant wife. (*See* **Petruchio** *in the* **CHARACTER STUDIES** *section.*)

Grumio: Petruchio's servant. He often misunderstands, or pretends to misunderstand, Petruchio's commands,

with comic results. In Act IV, scene I, he recounts the various mishaps that befell him, Katherina, and Petruchio on their way to Petruchio's country house. Later, he teases Katherina when she asks for food.

Curtis: One of the servants at Petruchio's country house. Grumio tells him about the journey from Padua to the country house. Later, Curtis tells the other servants about Petruchio's odd behavior in the marriage chamber.

Nathaniel, Joseph, Nicholas, Philip, Walter, Sugarsop: Servants at Petruchio's country house.

Pedant: An elderly scholar from Mantua, persuaded by Tranio to pose as Lucentio's father.

Tailor and Haberdasher: Summoned by Petruchio to make new clothes for Katherina.

Vincentio: Lucentio's father. On his way to Padua to visit Lucentio, he becomes the butt of a joke initiated by Petruchio and taken up by Katherina. On his arrival in Padua, he is nearly thrown into prison when Tranio, the Pedant, and Biondello all insist he is an imposter.

Widow: Hortensio marries her when he gives up his suit for Bianca. In the final scene of the play, she quarrels with Katherina and refuses to come when Hortensio summons her.

PLOT SYNOPSIS

Induction: Christopher Sly, a drunken tinker, is expelled from a tavern and falls asleep on the ground. He is discovered by a Lord and his huntsmen. The Lord orders his men to dress Sly in fine clothes and put him to bed in the best chamber. When Sly awakes, Lord and servants conspire to convince him that he is really a nobleman. The Lord's page (a young male attendant) dresses like a woman and pretends to be Sly's wife. After some initial confusion, Sly appears convinced that he is a nobleman. He is told that a comedy will be played for him to aid his recovery. Sly will comment briefly on the play at the end of Act I, scene 1, then disappear from the text.

Act I: Sly's play begins: Lucentio, son of a wealthy Pisan merchant, and his servant, Tranio, arrive in Padua, where Lucentio intends to study. They overhear Baptista announcing that he will not allow his younger daughter, Bianca, to marry until a husband is found for his elder daughter, Katherina. From the remarks of Bianca's suitors, Hortensio and Gremio, and Katherina's angry reaction to them, it appears that Bianca is perceived as sweet-natured and mild, while Katherina is considered a "shrew"—a stubborn, domineering, and sharp-tongued woman. Baptista exits with his daughters after announcing that he will hire schoolmasters for them. Lucentio tells Tranio that he has fallen in love with Bianca. They plan that in order to gain access to Bianca, Lucentio will pretend to be a schoolmaster, while Tranio will pretend to be Lucentio and present himself as another suitor for Bianca. Petruchio and his servant, Grumio, arrive in Padua from Verona. Petruchio tells Hortensio that he has come to Padua to find a wealthy wife. Hortensio tells him about Katherina, warning him that while she is wealthy and beautiful she is shrewish in temperament. Petruchio insists that he cares nothing for looks, youth, or manners, so long as his bride is rich. Hortensio decides to assume a disguise and asks Petruchio to introduce him to Baptista as Litio, a music teacher. Gremio enters with Lucentio, whom he presents as Cambio, a schoolmaster for Bianca. Tranio also enters, dressed as Lucentio, and reveals his intention to woo Bianca.

Act II: Katherina beats Bianca, whose hands are tied. When Baptista scolds Katherina, she accuses him of favoritism. Petruchio presents his suit for Katherina and offers "Litio" (Hortensio) as a music teacher for her. Baptista welcomes Petruchio but expresses doubt that he will find Katherina to his liking. Gremio presents "Cambio" (Lucentio) as a schoolmaster, while Tranio, introducing himself as Lucentio, asks to be admitted among Bianca's suitors. Baptista and Petruchio quickly agree on terms for Katherina's hand. In their first meeting, Katherina responds to Petruchio's compliments by telling him to leave. Their ensuing exchange of insults soon turns to sexual innuendo. When Baptista enters with Gremio and Tranio, Katherina denounces Petruchio as "one half lunatic / A madcap ruffian and a swearing Jack." Petruchio, however, insists that they have reached an agreement to marry on the coming Sunday, and Baptista agrees to the marriage. Baptista immediately turns to the matter of a match for Bianca, settling on "Lucentio" (Tranio) when he offers the largest dower (her inheritance should she be widowed). However, he stipulates that Lucentio's father must first guarantee the dower. Tranio resolves to find an old man to pose as Lucentio's father.

Act III: "Cambio" and "Litio" take turns tutoring Bianca. While pretending to translate a passage from Ovid, "Cambio" reveals his identity to Bianca; Bianca responds by the same method, telling him, "presume not . . . despair not." On Katherina's appointed wedding day Petruchio first is late, then appears wearing tattered and mismatched clothing and riding a broken-down nag. While Petruchio and the others go off in search of Katherina, Tranio tells Lucentio of his plan to have someone pose as Lucentio's father, while Lucentio suggests that he may elope with Bianca.

Gremio enters and reports on the wedding ceremony: Petruchio swore at and struck the priest, threw wine in the sexton's face, and kissed the bride noisily. The wedding party enters. Although Katherina wants to stay for the banquet, Petruchio draws his sword, announces that he will protect his property, and forces her to leave with him immediately.

Act IV: Petruchio and Katherina arrive at Petruchio's country house after various mishaps along the way. Petruchio finds fault with everything the servants do, cursing and beating them and refusing to let Katherina eat supper because, he says, the meat is overcooked. After Katherina and Petruchio exit to the bridal chamber, one of the servants reports that Petruchio is "making a sermon of continency" to Katherina, while she sits bewildered, "as one new risen from a dream." In a soliloquy, Petruchio compares his treatment of Katherina to the taming of falcons, which were left hungry and deprived of sleep until they became docile. He decides that he will keep her from sleeping by complaining all night. Meanwhile, in Padua, "Lucentio" (Tranio) convinces "Litio" (Hortensio) to abandon his suit after they find Bianca flirting with "Cambio" (Lucentio). Hortensio tells Tranio he will marry a wealthy widow. Tranio tells Bianca and Lucentio that Hortensio will go to Petruchio's "taming school" to learn to control the widow. By a clever ploy, Tranio persuades an aged Pedant (scholar) to pose as Lucentio's father. Back at Petruchio's house, Hortensio is visiting. Petruchio invites Katherina to eat with them, but insists that she thank him before allowing her to eat. A tailor and a haberdasher arrive with new clothes Petruchio has ordered for Katherina, but he finds fault with everything they offer and despite Katherina's protests sends the men away. After announcing that they will leave for Padua immediately he begins talking nonsense, saying they will mount their horses and go on foot and claiming that it is morning when it is afternoon. When Katherina corrects him, he states that before they go to Padua, "It shall be what a' clock I say it is." Back in Padua, Tranio, the Pedant, and Baptista agree to meet at Lucentio's lodgings to seal Bianca's betrothal. Meanwhile, on their way to Padua, Petruchio and Katherina argue about whether the sun or the moon is shining. Petruchio insists they will not continue to Padua until she agrees with him. Katherina gives in, saying, "What you will have it nam'd, even that it is, / And so it shall be so for Katherine." Hortensio tells Petruchio that "the field is won." They encounter an old man, whom Petruchio addresses as a young woman. Katherina follows Petruchio's lead, calling the old man a "budding virgin." When Petruchio then corrects her, she begs pardon for her "mad mistaking." The old man turns out to be Lucentio's father, Vincentio, and they all continue to Padua together.

Act V: Lucentio and Bianca sneak off to be married.

Katherina, Petruchio, and Vincentio arrive at Lucentio's lodgings. The Pedant and Vincentio argue violently over which of them is Lucentio's father, and Vincentio is in danger of being arrested until Lucentio and Bianca, newly married, arrive on the scene, explain the deception, and beg pardon of their fathers. They all exit, and Katherina wants to follow; but Petruchio first obliges her to kiss him in public. At the wedding banquet, the men place bets as to which of them has the most obedient wife. All three send for their wives, but only Katherina obeys. Petruchio sends her to bring the other wives. The men concede the bet to Petruchio, but he insists on a further demonstration. He tells Katherina to take off her cap and stamp on it, which she does, then orders her to tell the women their "duty" to "their lords and husbands." Katherina responds with a long speech in favor of wifely obedience. Petruchio praises and kisses her, and they go off to bed as the other men congratulate Petruchio on having tamed his "shrew."

PRINCIPAL TOPICS

Gender Roles

Nearly all critical commentary on *The Taming of the Shrew* deals to some extent with the play's treatment of gender roles: that is, what it has to say about socially accepted definitions of appropriate male and female behavior. On the surface, the play appears to confirm a very traditional view that men should dominate women and that women should submit to male authority. All of the characters except Katherina agree throughout the play that her initial rebellious, self-assertive, "shrewish" behavior is not acceptable. In the end, Kate has apparently come round to this position as well, giving a long speech proclaiming the rightness of male dominance and female submissiveness.

Until fairly recently, few people challenged this view of the play. In fact, the play knew centuries of popularity with audiences who found Petruchio's "taming" of Katherina both inoffensive and amusing. In the late nineteenth century, however, commentators began to express uneasiness with the way Katherina is treated, and directors began to experiment with various "ironic" readings of the plays. In the twentieth century, debate over the play's attitude toward gender roles has produced a wide variety of interpretations.

The play's treatment of gender goes well beyond its basic plot. Unlike most playwrights who wrote plays about "shrews" in the early modern period, Shakespeare suggests possible motivations for Katherina's shrewishness: her father clearly favors her sister, Bianca; the prospective suitors are shallow and rude; father and suitors alike tend to treat marriage as a purely commercial transaction. Katherina's relationship with Petruchio is complex. Their early verbal exchanges suggest a certain equality of intelligence. Although the text of the play leaves room for a wide variety of theatrical interpretations of the relationship, the traditional and most common approach emphasizes a strong sexual attraction between Katherina and Petruchio as well as a growing comradeship. Moreover, although Petruchio seeks to control Katherina, he appears to admire and value her spirit.

The relationship between the play's main plot, subplot, and Induction also affects its depictions of gender roles. A struggle for power between men and women is introduced as an issue from the beginning of the play, when, in the Induction, a woman—the Hostess—ejects a drunken Christopher Sly from the tavern. In the course of the Lord's practical joke, one of his young male attendants dresses like a woman and pretends to be Sly's noble, soft-spoken, and obedient wife. The practical joke itself can be seen as a parallel to Petruchio's efforts to reform Katherina, as both involve attempts to transform one sort of character into another. For some critics, the Lord's inability to effect a convincing change in Sly's character contrasts with Petruchio's "successful" transformation of Katherina in the main plot. For others, however, the obvious artificiality of both Sly's transformation into a nobleman and the page's transformation into a woman are meant to indicate that Katherina's transformation is equally artificial.

Critics' examinations of these various aspects of the play have led to no consensus as to the play's attitude toward gender roles. A number of critics continue to maintain that the play ultimately accepts and reinforces male dominance of women. Many of these critics also argue, however, that while accepting male dominance the play emphasizes the need for mutual affection, cooperation, and partnership in marriage. Another view maintains that Katherina's final speech should be read ironically, with the implication that she will pretend to defer to Petruchio in public while ruling the household in private. Yet other commentators argue that the play ultimately undermines male dominance of women by showing this dominance to be artificial and illogical. Directors of modern productions of *The Taming of the Shrew* have also offered a wide variety of interpretations of this issue.

Appearance vs. Reality

Confusion between appearance and reality is a principal source of humor in *The Taming of the Shrew*. In the Induction, Sly is misled by carefully orchestrated appearances into believing that he is really a wealthy nobleman rather than a poor tinker. The subplot like-wise depends on the confusion of appearance and reality as various characters practice elaborate deceptions. Hortensio pretends to be the music teacher Litio. Lucentio poses as the schoolmaster Cambio. He and Bianca use Latin lessons as a cover for their courtship, and they deceive her father by eloping on the eve of her planned betrothal to another man. Lucentio's servant, Tranio, pretends to be his master and persuades an elderly scholar to pose as his master's father.

In the main plot, the difficulty of distinguishing between appearance and reality is emphasized in various ways. Petruchio's servant Grumio often misinterprets his master's instructions, with comic results. More crucially, Petruchio's strategy in dealing with Katherina often involves replacing the most apparent of realities with something more to his own liking. "Say that she rail, why then I'll tell her plain / She sings as sweetly as a nightingale," Petruchio resolves before his first meeting with Katherina. Although she insists she wants nothing to do with him, he tells her father they have agreed to be married. At his country house and on the road back to Padua he insists that it is morning when it is afternoon and that the moon is shining in broad daylight. When Katherina finally gives in to him, her surrender is signaled by her acceptance of his version of reality, in defiance of appearance: "What you will have it nam'd, even that it is, / And so it shall be so for Katherine."

The various deceptions in the Induction and the subplot seem to poke fun at social distinctions, suggesting that the difference between a servant and a master, or between a poor Latin teacher and a wealthy merchant's son, is merely a matter of appearance. This idea is echoed in the main plot by Petruchio when he appears at his wedding in rags and says of Katherina, "To me she's married, not unto my clothes," or when he tells Katherina not to worry about the way she is dressed because "'tis the mind that makes the body rich."

The theme of appearance and reality is also related to the play's treatment of gender roles. Some commentators maintain that Petruchio transforms Katherina by refusing to accept her appearance of shrewishness as reality. Instead, he sets up a sort of alternate reality, insisting that she is really lovable and obedient until she accepts his view of her identity. Other people argue, however, that the continual confusion of appearances and reality in the play undermines the concept of male dominance. They suggest that with so much deception going on in the play, the audience should be suspicious of taking Katherina's transformation at face value. Perhaps she is merely pretending to give in to Petruchio. Or perhaps—as other critics have maintained—male supremacy itself is shown to be merely an illusion.

Games and Role-Playing

Closely related to the theme of appearance versus reality is the play's emphasis on games and role-playing. It has been suggested that Petruchio treats social conventions—including the conventions governing relations between men and women—as a sort of game. The airy cynicism with which he discusses his search for a wife contrasts with both Lucentio's romanticism and Baptista's businesslike materialism. He treats the marriage ceremony itself as a joke, arriving late and poorly dressed, insulting the clergy, and forcing the bride to leave early. He seems to welcome Katherina's "shrewishness" as an interesting challenge, and compares his efforts to "tame" her to a sportsman's taming of a hawk. According to this view, Petruchio's strategy in "taming" Katherina is to convince her to join in this game with him. This strategy seems particularly clear during the journey back to Padua in Act IV, when Katherina finally decides to go along with Petruchio's assertions contrary to fact and joins him in pretending that the aged Vincentio is a young woman. Katherina's final speech to the other wives is then seen as marking her agreement to play the role of obedient wife, secure in the knowledge that she and her husband both know this is merely a role.

Role-playing and play-acting also figure prominently in *The Taming of the Shrew*. The play-within-a-play structure emphasizes to the audience that what they are about to see is a performance—not reality, but someone's interpretation of reality. Many of the characters "become" actors in the play: Tranio plays the role of Lucentio, Lucentio poses as Cambio, Hortensio poses as Litio, and so on. Thus, for instance, a single actor might appear as one of the "players" in the Induction, as Tranio at the beginning of Act I, and later as Tranio-playing-Lucentio. Petruchio himself often seems to be playing an exaggerated role for Katherina's benefit. Recently, several critics have pointed out that Shakespeare also draws attention to the Elizabethan practice of using boys to play women's parts. This is especially true in the Induction, where the page Barthol'mew pretends to be Sly's wife.

Critics draw widely different conclusions from the play's emphasis on its own theatricality. Some suggest that it points up the extent to which the ability to lead a happy and productive life depends on one's ability to adapt to the roles one is required to play in society. Others argue that the play's treatment of role-playing undermines social conventions—particularly those governing relationships between men and women—by suggesting that they are merely artificial "roles" that people feel obliged to accept.

Imagery

Of particular importance in *The Taming of the Shrew* is Shakespeare's use of animal and other types of imagery in portraying various characters' attitudes toward other characters, toward women in general, and toward marriage.

The play is especially rich in animal imagery, beginning with the traditional use of the word "shrew" to describe a willful and quarrelsome woman. When Katherina and Petruchio first meet, their rapid exchange of insults is rife with references to animals, as is the exchange of jests by the wedding guests in the final scene of the play. Dogs and horses figure prominently in the play, and several characters are compared to animals. In Act IV, Petruchio likens his handling of Katherina to the methods used in taming hawks.

In many cases, the use of animal imagery to describe a character is clearly demeaning, as when Gremio refers to Katherina as a "wild-cat" (I.ii.196), or Hortensio describes Bianca as a "proud disdainful haggard [untamed hawk]" (IV.ii.39). In other cases, the effect is more complex. While some critics see Petruchio's use of animal imagery in referring to Katherina as indicative of a desire to subdue and control her, others have argued that Petruchio's likening of Katherina to a falcon, for instance, reflects a recognition that a successful marriage requires two minds working in partnership.

Much of the play's animal imagery is also part of the imagery of games and sport. Early in the Induction the Lord arrives from hunting, and subsequently hunting is used to typify both the pursuit of women by the play's various suitors, and the behavior of women toward each other.

Clothing and entertaining, particularly dining, also figure prominently in the play. Petruchio's strategy for subduing Katherina involves both his refusal to dress as expected when he arrives at their wedding poorly dressed, and his refusal to allow Katherina to purchase the clothes she wants. Clothing is also important to the various deceptions in the Induction and the subplot. At various points in the play, Katherina's exclusion from or participation in banquets or dinner parties becomes an issue. Petruchio prevents her from taking part in the banquet at her own wedding, and later allows her to join him and Hortensio at dinner only after she has thanked him for providing food. Towards the end of the play he threatens to keep her from Bianca's wedding banquet unless Katherina kisses him in public. Finally, it is at that banquet that Katherina makes the public display of obedience that convinces the other guests that she has truly been "tamed."

CHARACTER STUDIES

Katherina

Katherina is established as a "shrew"—a loud, unmanageable, bad-tempered woman—by her own behavior and by the comments of other characters, who repeatedly characterize her as ill-tempered and unreasonable. Unlike the stock character of the shrew found in many plays from Shakespeare's time, however, Katherina emerges as a complex individual who engages the audience's sympathy and concern. Baptista's obvious preference for her sister, Bianca, his crassly materialistic approach to his daughters' marriages, and the shallowness and rudeness of the Paduan suitors suggest possible reasons for Katherina's shrewish behavior. Her "shrewish" remarks are generally also clever and to the point, suggesting that she is more intelligent than most of the other characters in the play. Moreover, despite her shrewishness she is capable of concern for others, repeatedly trying to shield the servants from Petruchio's violent displeasure.

Katherina first appears in Act I, scene i, where she vigorously protests both Baptista's decision not to allow Bianca to marry until a husband is found for Katherina, and the insulting remarks of Gremio and Hortensio. This leads Tranio, who is looking on with Lucentio, to comment that she is "stark mad or wonderful froward [disobedient, unmanageable]." After Baptista and his daughters leave, Hortensio and Gremio continue to comment on Katherina's bad temper and the near-impossibility of any man agreeing to marry her.

At the beginning of Act II, Katherina enters with Bianca, whose hands are tied, and strikes her when she denies any preference for either of her suitors. When Baptista scolds her for her behavior toward her sister, Katherina accuses him of favoritism. Later in the same scene, in her first meeting with Petruchio, she meets his initial overture with hostility and insults. He responds with sexual innuendos. After he makes a particularly obscene remark, she strikes him. When her father enters, she denounces Petruchio as "one half lunatic" and responds to his insistence that they have agreed to be married on Sunday by commenting, "I'll see thee hang'd on Sunday first." But when Petruchio claims that she is only pretending to oppose the marriage and Baptista agrees to the match, she exits without saying anything further.

In Act III, when Petruchio at first fails to show for his wedding, Katherina complains bitterly: not only has she been forced against her will to accept "a madbrain rudesby full of spleen," but now she is being made a fool of. She exits weeping. Reporting on Petruchio's outrageous behavior during the marriage ceremony, Gremio remarks that in response to the groom's behavior the bride "trembled and shook." Nonetheless, when Petruchio insists that they leave immediately after the ceremony, Katherina resists, first entreating Petruchio to stay, then firmly refusing to leave. When Petruchio insists on his right to make her leave and threatens violence against anyone who tries to stop them, she goes with him without further comment.

At the beginning of Act IV, Grumio reports on his trip to Petruchio's country house with Petruchio and Katherina. After Katherina's horse fell on her, Petruchio began to beat Grumio, and Katherina "waded through the dirt to pluck him off." Grumio's account leads Curtis to remark that Petruchio "is more shrew than she." When at the country house Petruchio upbraids and strikes the servants, Katherina defends them and urges him to be patient. After the couple retires to their chamber, Curtis tells the other servants that Petruchio is lecturing his bride on self-restraint, while she "Knows not which way to stand, to look, to speak, / And sits as one new-risen from a dream." In subsequent scenes, Petruchio repeatedly imposes his will despite Katherina's resistance and verbal protests. In Act IV, scene v, as they return to Padua for Bianca's wedding, Katherina again contradicts Petruchio, saying that the sun is shining when he has commented on the brightness of the moon. When he refuses to go on unless she agrees with him, she gives in, only to have him insist that it is indeed the sun. Commenting that "the moon changes even as your mind," Katherina gives in, agreeing to call it whatever he chooses. Hortensio tells Petruchio that "the field is won." Katherina's acceptance of Petruchio's will at this point is generally seen as a turning point in their relationship, although critics have offered varying opinions as to Katherina's mood at this point as well as the meaning of this turning point. When the travelers meet Vincentio on the road, Katherina easily falls in with Petruchio's joke of addressing the old man as if he were a young woman.

In Padua, as the Bianca-Lucentio subplot comes unraveled, Katherina wants to follow the other characters to see the outcome. Petruchio insists that she first kiss him publicly, and after a brief resistance, she complies. At Bianca's wedding banquet, Katherina becomes involved in an argument with the Widow when the latter refers to Katherina's reputation as a shrew. Later, when Petruchio, Lucentio, and Hortensio place bets on their respective wives' obedience, Katherina is the only wife to come when summoned. She obediently brings in the other wives, and when Petruchio tells her to take off her cap and stamp on it, she complies. When Petruchio orders her to instruct the other wives on their duty to their husbands, Katherina responds with a long speech advocating wifely obedience. Emphasizing the "painful labor" a husband takes on to ensure the security of his wife, she states that wives owe husbands a "debt" of "love, fair looks, and true obedience." She remarks that women are "soft" and "weak," and urges them to give up their pride, "for it is no boot" [there is no remedy]. In her final words in the play, she offers to place her hand under Petruchio's foot, to "do him ease."

Directors and actresses have adopted a variety of approaches to Katherina's final speech, depending on their interpretation of the play's meaning. Sometimes it is delivered ironically, as if Katherina does not mean what she says and is either humoring Petruchio or treating his wager as a joke. When the speech is delivered seriously, the tone adopted may vary from one of joyful acceptance to one of despair and resignation.

Petruchio

The traditional interpretation of the character of Petruchio sees him as a romantic and dashing figure, sweeping Katherina off her feet with his manly energy, intelligence, and determination. His displays of violence and bad temper are then presented as merely a ploy, intended either to show Katherina the absurdity of her own violence and bad temper, or to shock her out of her habitual contrariness. While this remains the most common dramatic interpretation of the role, more recently literary critics and some productions of the play have portrayed Petruchio as a less than ideal man. These interpretations present his violent, domineering, and frequently unreasonable behavior as an intrinsic part of his character, rather than as an affectation assumed for Katherina's benefit. They also tend to stress the crudity of many of his comments about marriage and about Katherina.

Petruchio first appears at the beginning of Act I, scene ii, when he and his servant, Grumio, arrive in Padua from Verona to visit Petruchio's friend Hortensio. Petruchio is quickly involved in a heated misunderstanding with Grumio and ends up wringing the servant's ear. When Petruchio tells Hortensio he has come to Padua to seek a wife, Hortensio tells him he knows of a woman who is very wealthy, but shrewish. Despite warnings from both Hortensio and Gremio about Katherina's temperament, Petruchio insists that he will woo her, claiming that wealth is his sole requirement in a wife and that he will not be frightened off by mere noise.

In Act II, Petruchio presents himself to Baptista as a suitor for Katherina. At Hortensio's request, he also introduces Hortensio as Litio, a music teacher, leading Baptista to engage Hortensio to instruct his daughters. Brushing aside both Baptista's invitation to dinner and the older man's doubts about Katherina's acceptability, Petruchio immediately opens negotiations about the amount of money to be settled on Katherina. He and Baptista swiftly reach agreement. When Baptista stipulates that Petruchio must first obtain Katherina's love, Petruchio replies that "that is nothing," adding that he is "as peremptory as she proud-minded" and predicting that she will "yield" to him. When Hortensio enters bleeding and reports that Katherina has broken the lute over his head, Petruchio calls her "a lusty wench" and expresses eagerness to meet her.

In a soliloquy in Act II, scene i, just before his first meeting with Katherina, Petruchio describes his plan for dealing with her. Whatever she does, he will act as if she has done the opposite: If she is verbally abusive, he will praise her sweet voice; if she refuses to speak, he will applaud her eloquence; if she refuses to marry, he will ask her to set a date. When Katherina enters, they become embroiled in an exchange of insults that soon turns to sexual innuendo. When she strikes him after he makes a particularly obscene comment, Petruchio threatens to strike her back if she hits him again. Despite Katherina's hostility when Baptista returns Petruchio says they have agreed to marry. When Katherina protests, Petruchio claims they have agreed that she will continue to behave shrewishly "in company." Baptista agrees to the marriage.

On the day appointed for the wedding, Petruchio arrives late and dressed in rags, defending his inappropriate attire by saying that Katherina is marrying him, not his clothes. His behavior at the ceremony, which takes place off-stage, offends Gremio, who subsequently describes it: Petruchio swore in church, struck the priest, guzzled the wine and threw the remainder in the sexton's face, and kissed the bride noisily. After the ceremony, Petruchio insists that he and Katherina must leave immediately. He overrides Katherina's objections by announcing that he "will be master of what is [his] own" and pretending to protect her against the others' desire to detain her.

When Petruchio and Katherina arrive at his country house at the beginning of Act IV, Petruchio verbally abuses and beats the servants and sends the dinner back uneaten, telling Katherina it is burned and bad for their health. In the bridal chamber, he treats her to a lecture on self-restraint. In his second soliloquy, Petruchio likens Katherina to a wild falcon that must be prevented from eating and sleeping until it is tamed. Subsequently, he repeatedly frustrates Katherina's needs and desires, all the while insisting that he does so for her own good.

He also insists that Katherina agree with him even when he contradicts the most obvious realities, leading even his friend Hortensio to comment on his unreasonableness. Late in Act IV, as Katherina and Petruchio prepare to return to Padua for Bianca's wedding, he argues with Katherina about the time of day, insisting that they will not leave until "It shall be what a'clock I say it is." Later, on the road to Padua, he repeatedly changes his opinion as to whether the sun or the moon is shining and refuses to continue until Katherina agrees with him. Her eventual statement that "What you will have it nam'd, even that it is" is usually regarded as marking her capitulation to Petruchio. When they meet Vincentio on the road, Katherina plays along with her husband's joke when he pretends to think the old man is a young woman.

Through the remainder of the play Petruchio repeatedly tests Katherina's compliance. When they reach Padua, he threatens to return home unless she kisses him in the street. At Bianca and Lucentio's wedding banquet, a number of the other guests imply that Petruchio has failed to get control over Katherina. Petruchio proposes a wager on which of the three new wives—Katherina, Bianca, or the widow Hortensio has married—is most obedient. When Katherina is the only one of the three wives to come when summoned, Petruchio sends her to fetch the other wives, then tells her to take off her cap and stamp on it. Finally, he orders her to "tell these headstrong women / What duty they do owe their lords and husbands." At the end of Katherina's long speech in favor of male authority and female obedience, Katherina offers to place her hand under her husband's foot, to "do him ease." Petruchio praises her, kisses her, and takes her off to bed, suggesting as they leave that Hortensio and Lucentio have a hard road before them in their marriages.

Critical commentary and productions of the play reflect a wide diversity of opinion regarding both the nature of Petruchio's treatment of Katherina and his reasons for it. Motivations ascribed to his character range from love for Katherina to a will to dominate, from self-interest to a simple enjoyment of a challenge. Similarly, a wide variety of interpretations have been put forward regarding the dynamics of his relationship with Katherina. Some see him as bullying his wife into submission; others claim that he insightfully leads her to an acceptance of her "true" nature and of her rightful role in society. Still others claim that in the course of the play, Katherina and Petruchio negotiate a mutually acceptable mode of co-existence within the limits imposed by their society.

CONCLUSION

Like Shakespeare's other plays, *The Taming of the Shrew* lends itself to a variety of interpretations, both on stage and in the field of literary criticism. Moreover, modern interpretation of the play is complicated by the centrality to the play of issues that are hotly debated in our own time—in particular, the question of what roles men and women can and should play in society and in relationship to each other. Is Petruchio a loving husband who teaches his maladjusted bride to find happiness in marriage, or is he a clever bully who forces her to bow to his will? Does Katherina's acquiescence in playing the part of obedient wife reflect a joyous acceptance of her assigned role as a married woman and the beginning of a fulfilling partnership with her husband? Does it, instead, mean that she has learned to play the obedient wife in public so as to get her own way in private? Or does it reflect the defeat of a spirited and intelligent woman forced to give in to a society that dominates and controls women and allows them only very limited room for self-expression? Our own answers to these questions may have less to do with the play itself than with our attitudes towards the issues and ideas it explores.

(See also *Shakespeare Criticism*, Vols. 9, 12, and 31)

OVERVIEWS

Ruth Nevo

SOURCE: "'Kate of Kate Hall,'" in *Comic Transformations in Shakespeare*, Methuen, 1980, pp. 37-52.

[*Nevo provides an overview of the action and structure of* The Taming of the Shrew, *concentrating on the relationship between Katherine and Petruchio. Citing with approval Michael West's observation that Shakespeare's focus here is not "women's rights" but "sexual rites," Nevo sees the play as a rollicking depiction of the battle between the sexes. Kate, she suggests, is shown to be so fearful of not being loved, and so accustomed to being told she is unlovable, that she has come to behave as if it were true. Petruchio appears as a master psychologist whose "instructive" and "liberating" methods free Kate from her mistaken idea of her identity and enable her to find her true self. Rather than breaking Kate's spirit, Nevo argues, Petruchio uses his superior will and intelligence to convince Kate to enter into an alliance with him. For further commentary on the relationship between Katherine and Petruchio, see in particular the excerpts by H. J. Oliver in this section and in the section on Petruchio, the excerpts by George Hibbard, Coppélia Kahn, and Shirley Nelson Garner in the section on Gender, Robert Ornstein's excerpt on Katherine, and Ralph Berry's discussion in the section on Games and Role-Playing.*]

A more gentlemanly age than our own was embarrassed by *The Shrew*. G. B. Shaw announced it 'altogether disgusting to the modern sensibility'. Sir Arthur Quiller-Couch of the New Shakespeare [1928], judged it

> primitive, somewhat brutal stuff and tiresome, if not positively offensive to any modern civilised man or modern woman, not an antiquary. . . . We do not and cannot, whether for better or worse, easily think of woman and her wedlock vow to obey quite in terms of a spaniel, a wife and a walnut tree—the more you whip 'em the better they be.

It will be noticed, however, that Q's access of gallantry causes him to overlook the fact that apart from the cuffings and beatings of saucy or clumsy *zanni* which is canonical in Italianate comedy, no one whips anyone in *The Taming of the Shrew*, violence being confined to Katherina who beats her sister Bianca, and slaps petruchio's face. Anne Barton [in *The Riverside Shakespeare*, 1974] has done much to restore a sense of proportion by quoting some of the punishments for termagent wives which really were practised in Shakespeare's day. Petruchio comes across, she says,

> far less as an aggressive male out to bully a refractory wife into total submission, than he does as a man who genuinely prizes Katherina, and, by exploiting an age-old and basic antagonism between the sexes, manoeuvres her into an understanding of his nature and also her own.

Ralph Berry reads the play rather as a Berneian exercise in the Games People Play, whereby Kate learns the rules of Petruchio's marriage game, which she plays hyperbolically and with ironic amusement. 'This is a husband-wife team that has settled to its own satisfaction, the rules of its games, and now preaches them unctuously to friends.' [See Berry's excerpt in the section on Games and Role-Playing below.] In our own day, the wheel, as is the way with wheels, has come full circle and the redoubtable feminist, Ms Germaine Greer, has found the relationship of Kate and Petruchio preferable to the subservient docility of that sexist projection, the goody-goody Bianca [in *The Female Eunuch*, 1970].

With all this fighting of the good fight behind us, we may approach the play with the unencumbered enjoyment it invites. As Michael West has excellently argued [in an article in *Shakespeare Studies*, 1974], 'criticism has generally misconstrued the issue of the play as women's rights, whereas what the audience delightedly responds to are sexual rites'. Nothing is more stimulating to the imagination than the tension of sexual conflict and sexual anticipation. Verbal smashing and stripping, verbal teasing and provoking and seducing are as exciting to the witnessing audience as to the characters enacting these moves. It is easy to see why *The Shrew* has always been a stage success,

Frontispiece from the 1838 edition of the Kemble-Garrick version of The Shrew.

and so far from this being a point to be apologized for it should be seen as exhibiting Shakespeare's early command of farce as the radical of comic action, a mastery temporarily lost as he struggled to absorb more rarefied material in *The Two Gentlemen* and only later recovered. The mode, however, of the sexual battle in *The Shrew* is devious and indirect and reflects a remarkably subtle psychology. Petruchio neither beats his Kate nor rapes her—two 'primitive and brutal' methods of taming termagant wives, but neither is his unusual courtship of his refractory bride simply an exhibition of cock-of-the-walk male dominance to which in the end Katherina is forced to submit. Michael West's emphasis upon wooing dances and the folklore of sexual conquest is salutory, but Petruchio's conquest of Kate is far from merely a 'kind of mating dance with appropriate struggling and

biceps flexing'. Nor is she simply 'a healthy female animal who wants a male strong enough to protect her, deflower her, and sire vigorous offspring'.

Only a very clever, very discerning man could bring off a psychodrama so instructive, liberating and therapeutic as Petruchio's, on a honeymoon as sexless (as well as dinnerless) as could well be imagined. Not by sex is sex conquered, nor for that matter by the witholding of sex, though the play's tension spans these poles. Christopher Sly, one recalls, is also constrained to forgo his creature comforts, a stoic *malgré lui* [French: in spite of himself], and thereby a foil and foreshadower of the self-possessed Petruchio.

In the Induction, the page Bartholomew plays his part as Lady Sly to such effect that Sly pauses only to determine whether to call the lovely lady 'Al'ce madam, or Joan madam?' (Ind.ii.110) or plain 'madam wife' before demanding 'Madam, undress you, and come now to bed' (Ind.ii.117). Bartholomew must think fast, of course, and does: '[I] should yet absent me from your bed', he says, lest '[you] incur your former malady', and hopes that 'this reason stands for my excuse' (Ind.ii.124). Sly clearly has his own problems: 'Ay, it stands so that I may hardly tarry so long. But I would be loath to fall into my dreams again. I will therefore tarry in despite of the flesh and the blood' (Ind.ii.125-8). But Christopher Sly's 'former malady' is, of course, an imposed delusion: it is not as an amnesic lord that he is himself but as drunken tinker. Katherina's, we will finally learn to perceive, was self-imposed, and requires the therapies of comedy— 'which bars a thousand harms and lengthens life'—not the tumbling tricks of a 'Christmas gambold' for its cure. This lower level functions as foil to the higher yardstick and guarantor of the latter's reality.

The play's formal *telos* [Greek: ultimate end] is to supply that which is manifestly lacking: a husband for the wild, intractable and shrewish daughter of Baptista. But how shall Katherina herself not perceive that this husband is sought in order to enable her younger sister to be happily married to one of *her* numerous suitors? The situation of inflamed and inflammatory sibling rivalry which the good signor Baptista has allowed to develop between these daughters of his is suggested with deft economy. Her very first words:

> I pray you, sir, is it your will
> To make a stale of me amongst these mates?
> (I. i. 57-8)

speak hurt indignity, an exacerbated pride. Her response when Baptista fondles and cossets the martyred Bianca:

> A pretty peat! it is best

Put finger in the eye, and she knew why.

(I. i. 78-9)

indicates her opinion that if Bianca is long suffering she is also extracting the maximum benefit and enjoyment from that state. Nothing that Baptista says or does but will be snatched up and interpreted disadvantageously by this irascible sensitivity:

> Why, and I trust I may go too, may I not? What, shall I be appointed hours, as though (belike) I knew not what to take and what to leave? Ha!

(I. i. 102-4)

These first glimpses already invite us to infer some reason for the bad-tempered, headstrong, domestic tyranny Kate exercises, but when we find her beating her cowering sister, screaming at her for confidences about which of her suitors she most fancies, and turning on her father with

> What, will you not suffer me? Nay, now I
>   see
> She is your treasure, she must have a
>   husband;
> I must dance barefoot on her wedding-day,
> And for your love to her lead apes in hell.
> Talk not to me, I will go sit and weep,
> Till I can find occasion of revenge.

(II. i. 31-6)

we surely do not require inordinate discernment to understand what ails Katherina Minola. It is a marvellous touch that the pious Bianca, defending herself from the wildcat elder sister (with no suitor), says:

> Or what you will command me will I do
> So well I know my duty to my elders.

(II. i. 6-7)

Bianca, it may be supposed, is not the only younger sister who has got her face scratched for a remark like that.

All of Padua, we are given to understand, is taken up with the problem of finding someone to take his devilish daughter off Baptista's hands, leaving the field free for the suitors of the heavenly Bianca. And this is precisely a trap in which Kate is caught. She has become nothing but an obstacle or a means to her sister's advancement. Even the husband they seek for her is in reality for the sister's sake, not hers. When she says: 'I will never marry' it is surely because she believes no 'real' husband of her own, who loves her for herself, whom she can trust, is possible. How indeed could it be otherwise since patently and manifestly no one does love her? Because (or therefore) she is not lovable. And the more unlovable she is the more she proves her point. Katherina of Acts I and

II is a masterly and familiar portrait. No one about her can do right in her eyes, so great is her envy and suspicion. No one can penetrate her defences, so great her need for assurance. So determined is she to make herself invulnerable that she makes herself insufferable, and finds in insufferability her one defence. This is a 'knot of errors' of formidable proportions and will require no less than Petruchio's shock tactics for its undoing.

The undoing begins with the arrival of Petruchio, to wive it wealthily in Padua. No doubts are entertained in Padua about the benefits of marriage where money is, but it will be noted that no one is banking on a rich marriage to save him from the bankruptcy courts. All the suitors are wealthy; Lucentio, potentially at least. The contrast that Shakespeare sets up between Petruchio and Lucentio is an interesting ironic inversion of that obtaining in the Terentian tradition. In Terence the second (liaison) plot entailed tricky stratagems for acquiring money in order to buy (and keep) the slave girl. The main (marriage) plot on the other hand hinged upon the fortunate discovery of a true identity, which meant both legitimizing the affair and acquiring the dowry. Here, in the case of Bianca and Lucentio the mercenary mechanics of match-making are masked by Petrarchan ardours on Lucentio's part (or Hortensio's, until the appearance of the widow):

> Tranio, I burn, I pine, I perish, Tranio,
>
> . . . let me be a slave, t' achieve that maid
> Whose sudden sight hath thrall'd my
>   wounded eye.

(I. i. 155; 219-20)

and by angelic docility on Bianca's part; while Petruchio's affairs are deromanticized by the unabashed, unmasked worldliness of his motivation:

> I come to wive it wealthily in Padua;
> If wealthily, then happily in Padua.

(I. ii. 75-6)

and the formidable temper of Kate.

To Petruchio's incontinent and precipitate request to draw up the 'covenant' between them, Baptista demurs:

> Ay, when the special thing is well obtain'd,
> That is, her love; for that is all in all.

(II. i. 128-9)

and the reply is unequivocal:

> Why, that is nothing; for I tell you, father,
> I am as peremptory as she proud-minded;
> And where two raging fires meet together,

They do consume the thing that feeds their
    fury.
Though little fire grows great with little wind,
Yet extreme gusts will blow out fire and all;
So I to her, and so she yields to me,
For I am rough, and woo not like a babe.

                                        (II. i. 130-7)

And again: 'For I will board her, though she chide as
loud / As thunder when the clouds in autumn crack'
(I. ii. 95-6). Final recognitions will reverse these evaluations: the nakedly mercenary relationship will prove
itself productive of affection and of spirit as well as
sheer animal spirits; the romantic will prove hollow,
its Petrarchanism a mere mask.

In *The Shrew*, Shakespeare's characteristic handling of
multiple levels is already to be discerned. The main
protagonists are the agents of the higher recognitions,
the middle groups function as screens on which are
projected distorted mirror images of the main couples—images in a concave mirror; while the lower
orders ridicule the middle by the parody of imitation, and act as foils for the higher by providing a
measure of qualitative difference.

Though *The Shrew* fails to integrate Christopher Sly
satisfactorily and indeed abandons him altogether
after Act I, such a function for him, as I have already indicated, is adumbrated. Shakespeare, it seems,
felt more comfortable with the playlet-within-the-
play of *Love's Labour's Lost* and *A Midsummer Night's
Dream* for his clowns, or with the parenthetic internal comment of a cunning and a foolish servant
combination like Grumio/Tranio or Launce/Speed
than with the clown-frame, to which he does not
return. But the flurry of disguisings and contrivings,
'supposes' and role-playings in Baptista's middle-class
household, resolved finally by nothing more complex than natural selection and substantial bank
balances, do set off admirably the subtler, more
complex and interiorized transformations of the
Petruchio-Katherina relationship.

Petruchio's first speech in reply to Katherina's haughty insistence on her full name, is richly expressive:

    You lie, in faith, for you are call'd plain
        Kate,
    And bonny Kate, and sometimes Kate the
        curst;
    But Kate, the prettiest Kate in Christendom,
    Kate of Kate-Hall, my super-dainty Kate,
    For dainties are all Kates, and therefore,
        Kate,
    Take this of me, Kate of my consolation—
    Hearing thy mildness prais'd in every town,
    Thy virtues spoke of, and thy beauty
        sounded,

    Yet not so deeply as to thee belongs,
    Myself am mov'd to woo thee for my wife.

                                        (II. i. 185-94)

Ironic, mocking, amused and appreciative, it invites
us to infer a certain relief, to say the least. Though he
has stoutly affirmed his priorities:

    Be she as foul as was Florentius' love,
    As old as Sibyl, and as curst and shrowd
    As Socrates' Xantippe, or a worse . . .

    I come to wive it wealthily in Padua;
    If wealthily, then happily in Padua.

                                        (I. ii. 69-71; 75-6)

the spirited, bonny dark lass Baptista's terrible daughter turns out to be cannot but cause him a lift of the
heart. She, for her part, does not of course respond
immediately to his good-humoured teasing, but we
may surely assume a certain vibration to be caused
by this note of a tenderness which her obsessive fear
of not finding has consistently put out of court. But
she has built up sturdy bastions and will certainly
not imitate her conciliatory sister. Combat is her
chosen defence, and that these two are worthy opponents the set of wit which follows shows. Then comes
the cut and thrust of the clash between her proud-
mindedness and his peremptoriness. She misses no
ploy, is outrageously provocative and brazenly impo-
lite, verbally and even physically violent. He trips
her up with a bawdy pun, she dares him to return a
slapped face, and it is by no means certain to anyone
that he will not. His strategy of mock denial:

    'Twas told me you were rough and coy and
        sullen,
    And now I find report a very liar;
    For thou art pleasant, gamesome, passing
        courteous . . .

                                        (II. i. 243-5)

contains an infuriating sting in its tail:

    But slow in speech, yet sweet as spring-time
        flowers.

                                        (II. i. 246)

so that she is criticized for being what she most prides
herself on not being, and consoled by being told she
is what she most despises. Again:

    Why does the world report that Kate doth
        limp?
    O sland'rous world! Kate like the hazel-twig
    Is straight and slender, and as brown in hue
    As hazel nuts, and sweeter than the kernels.
    O, let me see thee walk. Thou dost not halt.

                                        (II. i. 252-6)

And poor Kate must be beholden to him for patronizing defence against the alleged detractions of a despised world, and finds herself judiciously examined for faults much as if she were a thoroughbred mare at a fair. It is no wonder that in reply to his

> Father, 'tis thus: yourself and all the world,
> That talk'd of her, have talk'd amiss of her.
> If she be curst, it is for policy,
> For she's not froward, but modest as the
>   dove;
> She is not hot, but temperate as the morn;
> For patience she will prove a second Grissel,
> And Roman Lucrece for her chastity;
> And to conclude, we have 'greed so well
>   together
> That upon Sunday is the wedding-day.
>
>   (II. i. 290-8)

she can only splutter 'I'll see thee hanged on Sunday first'; a response which is immediately interpreted by Petruchio, for the benefit of the spectators, as a secret bargain between lovers:

> 'Tis bargain'd 'twixt us twain, being alone,
> That she shall still be curst in company.
> I tell you 'tis incredible to believe
> How much she loves me. O, the kindest
>   Kate,
> She hung about my neck, and kiss on kiss
> She vied so fast, protesting oath on oath,
> That in a twink she won me to her love.
> O, you are novices! 'tis a world to see
> How tame, when men and women are alone,
> A meacock wretch can make the curstest
>   shrew.
>
>   (II. i. 304-13)

Round one thus ends indeed with 'we will be married a'Sunday'.

Sunday, however, brings not the marriage that has been prepared for in the Minola household, but a mummer's carnival. Petruchio arrives inordinately late, and in motley. Of the uproar he produces in the church we hear from Gremio, in a lively description containing the shape of things to come:

> Tut, she's a lamb, a dove, a fool to him!
> I'll tell you, Sir Lucentio: when the priest
> Should ask if Katherine should be his wife,
> 'Ay, by gogs-wouns,' quoth he, and swore so
>   loud
> That all amaz'd the priest let fall the book,
> And as he stoop'd again to take it up,
> This mad-brain'd bridegroom took him such
>   a cuff
> That down fell priest and book, and book
>   and priest.

> 'Now take them up,' quoth he, 'if any list.'
> *Tranio*   What said the wench when he rose
>   again?
> *Gremio*   Trembled and shook; for why, he
>   stamp'd and swore
> As if the vicar meant to cozen him.
> But after many ceremonies done,
> He calls for wine. 'A health!' quoth he, as if
> He had been aboard, carousing to his mates
> After a storm, quaff'd off the muscadel,
> And threw the sops all in the sexton's face . . .
>
> This done, he took the bride about the neck,
> And kiss'd her lips with such a clamorous
>   smack
> That at the parting all the church did echo.
>
>   (III. ii. 157-73; 177-9)

All of this is prologue to the first open clash of wills between these fiery newly-weds. He will instantly away, she 'will not be gone till I please myself':

> The door is open, sir, there lies your way;
> You may be jogging whiles your boots are
>   green.
>
>   (III. ii. 210-11)

> Father, be quiet, he shall stay my leisure.

> Gentlemen, forward to the bridal dinner.
> I see a woman may be made a fool,
> If she had not a spirit to resist.
>
>   (III. ii. 217; 219-21)

This is Petruchio's cue:

> They shall go forward, Kate, at thy
>   command.
> Obey the bride, you that attend on her.
>
> But for my bonny Kate, she must with me.
> Nay, look not big, nor stamp, nor stare, nor
>   fret,
> I will be master of what is mine own.
> She is my goods, my chattels, she is my
>   house,
> My household stuff, my field, my barn,
> My horse, my ox, my ass, my any thing;
> And here she stands, touch her whoever
>   dare,
> I'll bring mine action on the proudest he
> That stops my way in Padua. Grumio,
> Draw forth thy weapon, we are beset with
>   thieves;
> Rescue thy mistress if thou be a man.
> Fear not, sweet wench, they shall not touch
>   thee, Kate!
> I'll buckler thee against a million.
>
>   (III. ii. 222-3; 227-39)

And he snatches her off, sublimely indifferent to anything she says, insisting upon his property rights, benignly protective, mind you, of his bonny Kate, turning all her protests to his own purposes and depriving her of any shred of self-justification by his indignant defence of her.

Stage-manager and chief actor, master of homeopathy—'He kills her in his own humour' as Peter says—Petruchio's play-acting, his comic therapy, provides the comic device. One of a long line of Shakespearean actor-protagonists he holds the mirror up to nature, and shows scorn her own image. The tantrums that she has specialized in throwing he throws in super-abundance, forcing her to see herself in the mirror he thus holds up.

Grumio's tale of the saga of the journey:

> . . . hadst thou not cross'd me, thou shouldst have heard how her horse fell, and she under her horse; thou shouldst have heard in how miry a place, how she was bemoil'd, how he left her with the horse upon her, how he beat me because her horse stumbled, how she waded through the dirt to pluck him off me; how he swore, how she pray'd that never pray'd before; how I cried, how the horses ran way, how her bridle was burst; how I lost my crupper, with many things of worthy memory, which now shall die in oblivion, and thou return unexperienc'd to thy grave.
>
> (IV. i. 72-84)

prepares for the continuing hubbub in the Petruchean dining-hall. That Petruchio's strategy has the additional advantage of an austerity regime as far as food and sleep and 'fine array' is concerned is all to the good. Petruchio is canny and will leave no stone unturned. Also, he has tamed hawks. But it is not physical hardship which will break Kate's spirit, nor does he wish it, any more than a spirited man would wish his horse or his hound spiritless. And Petruchio, we recall, wagers twenty times as much upon his wife as he would upon his hawk or his hound. Significantly, Kate's recurrent response to his carrying on is to fly to the defence of the cuffed and chivvied servants. Crossing her will, totally and consistently, under the guide of nothing but consideration for her desires, confuses and disorients her, as she complains to Grumio:

> What, did he marry me to famish me?
> Beggars that come unto my father's door
> Upon entreaty have a present alms,
> If not, elsewhere they meet with charity;
> But I, who never knew how to entreat,
> Nor never needed that I should entreat,
> Am starv'd for meat, giddy for lack of sleep,
> With oaths kept waking, and with brawling
>   fed;

> And that which spites me more than all
>   these wants,
> He does it under the name of perfect love;
>
> (IV. iii. 3-12)

Katherine gets the point, but fails to get from Grumio even one of the mouth-watering items from a hearty English menu with which he tantalizes her. When she, listening hungrily to Petruchio's 'sermon of continency', and knowing not 'which way to stand, to look, to speak,' is 'as one new-risen from a dream', she might well rub her eyes and say, with Christopher Sly, . . . 'do I dream? Or have I dream'd till now?' (Ind. ii. 69).

What subtle Dr Petruchio has done is to drive a wedge into the steel plating of Kate's protective armour, so that he speaks at once to the self she has been and the self she would like to be; the self she has made of herself and the self she has hidden. The exchange of roles, with herself now at the receiving end of someone else's furies, takes her, as we say, out of herself; but she also perceives the method of his madnesses. Petruchio's remedy is an appeal to Kate's intelligence. These are not arbitrary brutalities, but the clearest of messages. And they are directed to her with undivided singleness of purpose.

In Act IV the remedy comes to fruition and Kate enunciates it:

> Then God be blest, it [is] the blessed sun,
> But sun it is not, when you say it is not;
> And the moon changes even as your mind.
> What you will have it nam'd, even that it is,
> And so it shall be so for Katherine.
>
> (IV. v. 18-22)

And then it is enacted, with considerable verve, as she addresses Vincentio, on cue from Petruchio, as 'young budding virgin, fair, and fresh, and sweet' and then promptly again, on cue, undoes all. Kate has yielded to a will stronger than her own and to an intelligence which has outmanoeuvred her, but the paradoxical, energizing and enlivening effect of the scene is that the laughter is directed not against her as butt or victim, but, through her prim performance, towards the disconcerted Vincentio. The *senex* [Latin: old man] is made fun of, in effect, by a pair of tricksters in some subtle alliance with each other not clear to him, but clear to the audience. Partly this response is structured by New Comedy paradigms. As Grumio puts it in Act I: 'Here's no knavery! See, to beguile the old folks, how the young folks lay their heads together!' (I. ii. 138-9). But mainly I believe it is due to our sense of liberation from deadlock. Petruchio has enlisted Kate's will and wit on his side, not broken them, and it is the function of the final festive test to confirm and exhibit this. It is also to be noted that the arrival in Padua of Vincentio 'exhausts' Lucentio's wooing devices, just as Petruchio's taming device exhausts its function; and it is a dexterous turn of composition which balances the mock nonrecognition of Vincentio on the way to Padua, and his encounter with his Mantuan proxy, with the unmasking and recognition of the true Katherina, and the true Bianca, at the banquet.

That Kate is in love by Act V, is, I believe, what the play invites us to perceive. And indeed she may well be. The man she has married has humour and high spirits, intuition, patience, self-command and masterly intelligence; and there is more than merely a homily for Elizabethan wives in her famous speech:

> A woman mov'd is like a fountain troubled,
> Muddy, ill-seeming, thick, bereft of beauty,
> And while it is so, none so dry or thirsty
> Will deign to slip, or touch one drop of it.
> Thy husband is thy lord, thy life, thy
>   keeper,
> Thy head, thy sovereign; one that cares for
>   thee,
> And for thy maintenance; commits his body
> To painful labor, both by sea and land;
> To watch the night in storms, the day in
>   cold,
> While thou li'st warm at home, secure and
>   safe;
> And craves no other tribute at thy hands
> But love, fair looks, and true obedience—
> Too little payment for so great a debt.
>   (V. ii. 142-54)

She wins her husband's wager but the speech bespeaks a generosity of spirit beyond the call of two hundred crowns. We have just heard Bianca snap at Lucentio mourning his lost bet: 'The more fool you for laying on my duty', and it seems that the metamorphosis of folly into wisdom which the comic action performs makes an Erastian reversal. More fool the Paduans indeed, in their exploitative hypocrisies and meannesses, than this madcap pair. . . .

H. J. Oliver

SOURCE: An introduction to *The Taming of the Shrew*, Oxford at the Clarendon Press, 1982, pp. 1-75.

[*Oliver suggests that understanding* The Taming of the Shrew *is made difficult by a contradiction between the genre of the play and Shakespeare's development of Katherina's character. The play, he points out, is a farce, and a farce can succeed only when the characters are so flat and unrealistic that the audience does not feel obliged to take them seriously. Oliver suggests that in creating the character of Katherina, Shakespeare could not resist the temptation to investigate what might make a woman a shrew. Because Katherina is a realistic and sympathetic character, Oliver argues, the audience cannot but feel uncomfortable with Petruchio's treatment of her. Oliver's view of the play contrasts with that of Nevo, above. For further commentary, see in particular the excerpts by George Hibbard, Coppélia Kahn, and Shirley Nelson Garner in the section on Gender Roles, Robert Ornstein's excerpt on Katherina, Oliver's own comments in the section on Petruchio, and Ralph Berry's discussion in the section on Games and Role-Playing.*]

Literary tradition perhaps prepared Shakespeare's audience, going to *The Taming of the Shrew,* to expect a farce; the Induction certainly did not invite them to become deeply involved with the characters of the inset play; the very costume worn by the boy playing Katherine may have identified her as nothing but a shrew: in short, there may have been as much likelihood of the audience's sympathizing with Katherine, when she first appeared on the stage, as there is of a twentieth-century music-hall audience's feeling sorry for a mother-in-law. The very first words addressed to Kate also take it for granted that she has no humanity: Gremio's reply to Baptista's invitation to court his elder daughter is 'To cart her rather. She's too rough for me'—which virtually calls Kate to her face a prostitute; Hortensio classes her among 'devils'; Tranio can believe only that she is 'stark mad, or wonderful froward'; Gremio brands her a 'fiend of hell'. Yet already a modern audience, at any rate, has made a mental reservation. Kate's own first words, to her father, 'I pray you, sir, is it your will / To make a stale of me amongst these mates'—with their resentment at Gremio's insult and their feeling that a father might well resent it too—seem reasonable enough and, what is more, deserving of sympathy.

That, in brief, is the main problem in understanding or interpreting the play. It is as if Shakespeare set out to write a farce about taming a shrew but had hardly begun before he asked himself what might make a woman shrewish anyway—and found his first answer in her home background. Just as, later, his portraits of Capulet, Lady Capulet, and the Nurse were to serve to arouse pity for the young Juliet, tragically thrown back on her own resources, so here the sketches of the spoilt younger daughter and of the father lacking in discernment (but perhaps not in good will—one may agree with R. B. Heilman that Baptista is not the villain of the piece) help the audience to understand what Baptista does not—and *tout comprendre, c'est tout pardonner.* We sympathize with Katherine—and as soon as we do, farce becomes impossible. . . .

[In] *The Taming of the Shrew* [Shakespeare] was dramatizing material from unrealistic literature that was perfectly acceptable on the level of the Punch and Judy show but ran the risk of embarrassing as soon as it rose above that level. We may laugh at Punch's hitting Judy on the head in the puppet play but it is not so easy to laugh at Petruchio's taming of Katherine. As M. R. Ridley put it [in *William Shakespeare. A Commentary,* 1936] if it were all farce 'our subtler feelings would lie contentedly quiescent. . . . But Shakespeare, being Shakespeare, cannot restrain his hand from making Petruchio more of a man, and Katharine more of a woman, than from the artistic point of view was wise; and so Petruchio's bullying of Katharine, funny though it would be if they were mere marionettes, and effective and indeed salutary though it is in its results, leaves a slightly unpleasant taste in the mouth. It is not necessary to agree with this in detail—for example, about Petruchio—in order to agree with it in general. In other words, Shakespeare was already too good a dramatist for the material he was dramatizing: characterization and farce are, finally, incompatible.

Finding itself in this dilemma, the average audience seems to decide to get as much enjoyment as it can from the farce—trying, as it were, to keep its sympathy with Katherine in a state of suspense (paradoxically, a suspension of belief, in the interests of enjoying what is not to be believed). And on the level of farce, *The Taming of the Shrew* is, generally, superb; and in so far as one can put sympathy aside and watch the taming of Kate as one might watch the taming of a falcon or wild beast (although even that presents problems to an audience more sensitive than Shakespeare's to cruelty to animals), one can 'enjoy' Petruchio.

Ann Thompson

SOURCE: An introduction to *The Taming of the Shrew,* by William Shakespeare, Cambridge University Press, 1984, pp. 1-41.

In a review of the stage history of The Taming of the Shrew, *Thompson suggests that the play has always "been disturbing as well as enjoyable" and that its "'barbaric and disgusting' quality has always been an important part of its appeal." Until the middle of the nineteenth century, she points out, the play was almost always produced with considerable modifications to Shakespeare's text. Many of the changes increased the roughness of Petruchio's behavior, while others, often in the same version, "softened" the play, making it explicit that Katherina is in love with Petruchio and that Petruchio's domineering behavior is only a ploy. More recently, as women's rights have become an issue, directors have tended to give their productions an ironic tone. Usually this is done by making it appear that Katherina's submission is not to be taken seriously, although sometimes productions go to the other extreme and imply that Katherina has been*

brainwashed. Thompson concludes that contemporary social and political attitudes will continue to color productions of the play.]

When the Royal Shakespeare Company staged *The Shrew* in Stratford in 1978, Michael Billington, reviewing the production in *The Guardian* on 5 May, was very anxious to let his readers know that, although he had found the evening theatrically successful in many ways, he had not enjoyed himself at all. He had in fact found the experience so distasteful that he ended by advocating censorship, questioning 'whether there is any reason to revive a play that seems totally offensive to our age and our society' and recommending that 'it should be put back firmly and squarely on the shelf'. Nevertheless he praised the director, Michael Bogdanov, for the honesty of his approach to this 'barbaric and disgusting' play: 'Instead of softening its harsh edges like most recent directors, he has chosen to emphasize its moral and physical ugliness.' This 'ugliness' is particularly apparent to modern audiences, especially when, as on this occasion, the play is performed in modern dress, but the stage history of the play shows that its 'barbaric and disgusting' quality has always been an important part of its appeal and that from the very beginning it has been disturbing as well as enjoyable. In what follows, given the limitations of space, I intend to concentrate on this problem and to examine how adapters and directors have dealt with it. This inevitably involves a stress on the taming plot to the exclusion of the rest of the play, but such an imbalance is not inappropriate since the Induction and the sub-plot were entirely banished from the stage for a hundred years while Garrick's *Catharine and Petruchio* was preferred; even now when they are performed they are often ignored by reviewers, whereas the crises of the taming plot, especially the wooing scene (2.1) and the last scene, are usually described in detail. . . .

Alone among Shakespeare's plays, *The Shrew* provoked a theatrical 'reply' in his lifetime in the form of Fletcher's *The Woman's Prize, or The Tamer Tamed,* written and performed around 1611, a sequel in which Petruchio, now a widower, marries again and is himself tamed by his second wife. In writing this sequel Fletcher was in effect putting the play into its traditional context of the war of the sexes, a context in which normally, as in the stories of Boccaccio and Chaucer, a story about a husband outwitting or triumphing over his wife is capped or balanced by one in which a wife outwits her husband, the overall moral being that, despite a theoretical and practical male supremacy, the best marriages are those based on equality and mutual respect, as Fletcher claims in his epilogue:

The Tamer's tam'd, but so, as nor the men
Can find one just cause to complain of,
    when

They fitly do consider in their lives,
They should not reign as Tyrants o'er their
    wives.
Nor can the Women from this president
Insult, or triumph; it being aptly meant,
To teach both Sexes due equality;
And as they stand bound, to love mutually.

If played straight, with a minimum of interpretative direction, Shakespeare's play contains no such indication of a comfortable, egalitarian compromise but rather leaves its audience with the impression that a woman's role consists in graceful submission. Perhaps this is one reason why, despite a long and vigorous stage tradition, it has probably been played straight less often than any other play in the canon. From *The Taming of a Shrew* in 1594 up to the 'free adaption' made by Charles Marowitz in 1975 it has been constantly altered and adapted. Until the middle of the nineteenth century the adaptations involved drastic cutting and wholesale rewriting, whereas in more recent times the overt meaning of the text has been undercut or contradicted by details of performance and stage business—what Michael Billington calls 'softening the edges'.

Of course, the adaptation has not all been in one direction. Many version have actually played up the brutality, a tradition which began as early as *A Shrew* with its stage direction *Enter Ferando [Petruchio] with a peece of meate uppon his daggers point* in the equivalent of 4.3, where the author apparently draws on Marlowe's *Tamburlaine* (Part 1, 4.4) to emphasise the savagery. In the late seventeenth century, John Lacey's *Sauny the Scott, or The Taming of the Shrew* (c. 1667), which supplanted Shakespeare's text on stage until it was replaced in 1754 by David Garrick's version called *Catharine and Petruchio*, inserts an additional scene in which the husband pretends to think that his wife's refusal to speak to him is due to toothache and sends for a surgeon to have her teeth drawn. This episode is repeated with relish in the eighteenth century in James Worsdale's adaptation, *A Cure for a Scold* (1735). In Garrick's version, which held the stage until the mid nineteenth century, we find an ominous addition to the dialogue when one of Petruchio's servants says his master 'shook his Whip in Token of his Love' (p. 24). When John Philip Kemble performed Garrick's text in 1788 he wrote the words 'whip for Petruchio' opposite the hero's entrance in the wedding scene, and it is possible that Garrick also used a whip from this point. At all events it became an almost obligatory stage property for countless subsequent productions.

Curiously, we find that this exaggeration of the play's brutality is often being done at the same time as an attempt is made to soften it, illustrating the thoroughly ambiguous appeal of the whole business. The role of Katherina is constantly adjusted: she is given more motivation for her behaviour in accepting Petruchio in the first place, and her major speech in the last scene is cut, rewritten or apologised for. Even *A Shrew* motivates her somewhat clumsily by giving her an aside in the wooing scene:

> *She turnes aside and speakes*
> But yet I will consent and marrie him,
> For I methinkes have livde too long a maid,
> And match him too, or else his manhoods
>   good.
>
> (scene v, 40-2)

Thus it is made explicit that (a) Katherina can see some positive advantage in marrying Petruchio, and (b) she is going to relish competing with him. It is interesting that Garrick's additions to this scene are very similar: his Catharine also has an aside in the midst of the insults:

> A Plague upon his Impudence! I'm vexed—
> I'll marry my Revenge, but I will tame him.
>
> (p. 14)

Then at the end of the scene she confirms this hint of a reversal of roles and adds further motivation in her closing soliloquy:

> Sister *Bianca* now shall see
> The poor abandon'd *Cath'rine*, as she calls
>   me,
> Can hold her Head as high, and be as proud,
> And make her Husband stoop unto her Lure,
> As she, or e'er a Wife in *Padua*.
> As double as my Portion be my Scorn;
> Look to your Seat, *Petruchio*, or I throw you.
> *Cath'rine* shall tame this Haggard;—or if she
>   fails,
> Shall tye her Tongue up, and pare down her
>   Nails.
>
> (pp. 16-17)

What Garrick has done here is to transfer some of Petruchio's taming rhetoric ('stoop unto her Lure', 'tame this Haggard') to Catharine in an attempt to redress the balance between them. . . .

Garrick's treatment of the heroine's big speech is also interesting. Catharine speaks the first nineteen lines of the speech (as written by Shakespeare) with a few brief interruptions from Petruchio ('Why, well said *Kate*') and Bianca ('Sister, be quiet—'), but then Petruchio makes his own submission:

> Kiss me, my Kate; and since thou art become
> So prudent, kind, and dutiful a Wife,
> *Petruchio* here shall doff the lordly Husband;
> An honest Mask, which I throw off with
>   Pleasure.

Far hence all Rudeness, Wilfulness, and
  Noise,
And be our future Lives one gentle Stream
Of mutual Love, Compliance and Regard.

(p. 56)

Finally, Petruchio '*Goes forward with* Catharine *in his Hand*' and delivers the next section of her speech himself (Shakespeare's 5.2.155-64), ending the play on the statement that women are 'bound to love, to honour and obey', significantly altered from Shakespeare's 'bound to serve, love and obey'. When Kemble played Garrick's text he restored these lines to Catharine, but the general effect either way was that the play as staged made a gesture towards an ethic of balance or equality between the sexes which is simply not present in the original text.

Garrick's version (which omits the Induction altogether and disposes of the sub-plot by presenting Bianca as one 'new-married to *Hortensio*' at the beginning) proved so popular that the full text had to wait for performance until 1844, in England and 1887 in the United States. It was in fact the last of Shakespeare's plays to be restored to the stage in its original form when J. R. Planché produced it in an Elizabethan style for Benjamin Webster at the Haymarket Theatre, London, in 1844. It is interesting that when Augustin Daly did stage the original play in New York in 1887, despite much publicity about the fullness and purity of the text, his two major alterations (apart from some cutting and considerable rearrangement) were in the wooing scene and the last scene. In both cases he followed Garrick, inserting Katherina's threat to tame Petruchio in 2.1 and Petruchio's promise to 'doff the lordly Husband' in 5.2. He cut Katherina's speech as Garrick had done and he ended the play on the same line, though Katherina spoke it, as she had done in Kemble's production.

Since the late nineteenth century the movement for the liberation of women has done for *The Shrew* what reaction to the anti-semitism of our time has done for *The Merchant of Venice:* turned it into a problem play. It is no longer fashionable to rewrite the text or interpolate lines, so modern directors and reviewers have had to grapple with the 'barbaric' original delivered more or less as it stands. (Film directors, however, have allowed themselves more liberty with the text: Sam Taylor's 1929 film uses Garrick's version and Franco Zeffirelli's 1966 one modernises freely and adds some new dialogue.) As in earlier centuries, the tone of the play has proved to be difficult, and the last scene in particular has become something of a touchstone for the liberal (or otherwise) sympathies of all concerned since at least 1897, when George Bernard Shaw wrote

> No man with any decency of feeling can sit it out

in the company of a woman without being extremely ashamed of the lord-of-creation moral implied in the wager and the speech put into the woman's own mouth.

Several directors have tried to overcome the problem by insisting on a jolly, farcical atmosphere throughout, but Katherina's final speech is simply too long and too serious to be buried under a welter of comic stage business, and has even been thrown uncomfortably into relief by such attempts. This apparently happened when Edith Evans played Katherina in 1937 and again when Peggy Ashcroft played her in 1960. When performed relatively seriously the play has inevitably provoked topical references, especially in the 1920s and 30s and again in the 1970s and 80s. When Eileen Beldon played Katherina in modern dress in 1928, for example, she is said to have delivered her speech with 'a beautiful sincerity', but one reviewer was moved to comment

> It was, I thought, a severe criticism of the modern dressing that while one was listening to the lady announcing her shame, one's mind instantly reverted to the proposal that the word 'obey' should be abolished from the Marriage Service.

When Sybil Thorndike gave a similarly 'sincere' performance in 1927, *The Stage* commented on her 'air of conviction' in the last scene

> which would obviously not commend itself to the out-and-out feminists of the Women's Federation League or the generality of the shingled and Eton-cropped sisterhood.

And one mid-1930s reviewer came up with an interesting explanation for the great popularity of the play in the years immediately preceding the First World War:

> That *The Taming* was presented [at Stratford] for eight years in succession from 1909 onwards may perhaps be accounted for in some measure as being due to the activities of the vote-hungry viragoes who from 1910 to the eve of the War were breaking windows, setting fire to churches, chaining themselves to railings, and generally demonstrating their fitness to be endowed with Parliamentary responsibility. Katherina's 'purple patch' concerning the duty of women . . . was a smashing rejoinder to the militant Furies who were making fools of themselves in the ways indicated.

A different kind of topical reference was evoked in 1939 when the *Glasgow Herald*'s reviewer commented on Wolfit's production, 'If the whip and starvation business has a distasteful touch, it has also the saving grace of being applied with an un-Nazi sense of fun.' The play seems to have been 'saved' by a sense of fun rather frequently in the 1970s, as for example in 1973 when, despite a serious programme note by the well-known feminist Germaine Greer, most critics found Clifford Williams's production farcical and jolly, and one newspaper headlined its review 'And never a whisper of Women's Lib'.

As in earlier centuries, the play is still 'softened' by careful, but by now more subtle, adjustments in the wooing scene and the last scene. Twentieth-century actresses restricted to the authentic text in the wooing scene have often motivated Katherina by making it abundantly obvious that she falls in love with Petruchio at first sight. Sometimes, however, it has been difficult for reviewers to agree on whether this happened or not. Janet Suzman's 1967 performance, for example, was apparently ambiguous in this scene, with some reviewers convinced that she was attracted to Petruchio from the beginning but others claiming that love blossomed out of initial antipathy. If Kate does fall in love in the wooing scene (2.1), the director and actress can achieve the same effect as earlier generations achieved by interpolating lines; it may undermine the tension of the next two acts but it helps to make the taming process more tolerable for the audience. At the same time, it has often seemed necessary for Katherina to undercut her speech in the last scene in some way. When Mary Pickford played the part in the 1929 film version of the play (the first sound film of any of Shakespeare's plays) we are told that 'the spirit of Katherina's famous advice to wives was contradicted with an expressive wink', beginning (apparently) a new tradition of ironic or ambiguous performances. These could be executed with varying degrees of good humour: when Sian Phillips played the role in 1960 'her delivery of the concluding sermon on how good wives should submit to their husbands was made with tongue slightly in cheek', a limited qualification of a basically generous submission, but when Joan Plowright played it in 1972 one reviewer commented

> I certainly didn't believe a word of it [the final speech] when uttered by Joan Plowright with a slightly sarcastic inflection to her voice which undermines totally any possible virtue the entire exercise might have had—that the two in the end find real love and understanding.

The nadir of bitterness and resentment was perhaps reached in Paola Dionisotti's performance in 1978:

> Kate's famous speech . . . is delivered in a spiritless, unreal voice and received without much appreciation by the men, and with smouldering resentment by the women. The main feeling is of shame—and that the systematic deformation of Kate's character (the deformity of submission on top of spite) is being revenged in the weariness and boredom of the men. When Petruchio says 'we'll to bed' it sounds as if they have been married for

years. It is an interesting and courageous (not to say feminist) way to interpret the play.

This was another time when the critics disagreed. Michael Billington wrote that Dionisotti delivered the speech 'with a tart, stabbing irony' (*The Guardian*, 5 May 1978), but I saw this production three times myself and agree with the *TLS* reviewer, Lorna Sage, that the tone was 'spiritless' and 'unreal'. Many reviewers felt on this occasion that it might have been more logical not to present Shakespeare's text at all (one review was headlined 'The Shaming of the True'), but to put on an adaptation such as that of Charles Marowitz (1975), in which the text is cut, rearranged and interspersed with scenes from a modern courtship in order to transform it into a treatise on sadism and brainwashing. In this version Petruchio drives Katherina mad and finally rapes her. She enters in the last scene wearing 'a shapeless institutional-like garment' and delivers her speech 'mechanically' and as if she has 'learnt it by rote'.

Of course not all modern Katherinas have been bitter, but it has often seemed the case that a straightforward and apparently sincere delivery of the final speech has provoked as much topical thoughtfulness in reviewers (and presumably audiences) as the more subversive mode. Barbara Jefford apparently 'comes as near as any Katherina ever will to making the final abject speech of the changed shrew sound plausible', while Jane Lapotaire 'gives the speech full value, touches us deeply, and leaves us to sort out our feelings about women's lib as best we may'. Vanessa Redgrave's performance seems to have been a complex one, enabling one reviewer to remark

> The delicious touch of irony which she adds to this speech amplifies the suggestion that she submits to Petruchio, not because woman must submit to man as her natural master, but because she loves him.

Another critic thought, however, that 'she shows us a woman discovering that the delivery of a grovelling and submissive speech can actually give her a special new sensual kick'. Obviously the interpretation of this speech can lie as much in the mind of the reviewer as in the intention of the director or the performance of the actress.

Thus throughout its stage history *The Taming of the Shrew* has probably received fewer completely straight performances than any other Shakespearean play of comparable popularity on the stage. The apparently unrelieved ethic of male supremacy has proved unpalatable, and generation after generation of producers and directors have altered and adapted the text in more or less flagrant ways in order to soften the ending. Of course, responses to the play are bound to be affected by the status of women in society at any given time and by the way that status is perceived by both men and women. Reading through the reviews, one sees the play acting as a kind of litmus paper, picking up worried and embarrassed reactions from men who were probably just as committed to male supremacy as they take the play's hero to be but whose methods of oppressing their women were less obvious and more socially acceptable. Productions of the play have frequently attracted whatever thoughts were in the air on the perennially topical subjects of violence and sexual politics, and this tendency can hardly fail to increase in our own time. The play may indeed become less popular on the stage than it has been in previous centuries as it becomes, rightly, more and more difficult to put on productions of it which are simply rollicking good fun.

GENDER ROLES

Since Katherina's shrewish behavior constitutes the central problem of the play, it is not surprising that most critical commentary on *The Taming of the Shrew* deals to some extent with its vision of the relative roles of men and women. Until well into the nineteenth century, audiences and critics alike seem to have accepted at face value what appears to be the play's central assumption about gender roles: that male dominance and female submission constitute the right and natural relationship between the sexes. In this context, Petruchio's "taming" of Katherina was generally seen as innocent fun. By the end of the century, however, critics were beginning to show an element of discomfort with the relationship between Petruchio and Katherina. The Irish playwright and critic Bernard Shaw, writing in 1897, described the last scene of the play as "altogether disgusting to modern sensibility." He found the concept of male domination implicit in the wager and explicit in Katherina's final speech so offensive that no man "with any decency of feeling" could watch the scene "in the company of a woman without feeling extremely ashamed."

Subsequently, many critics have sought to defend *The Taming of the Shrew* against charges of sexism by contending that the play takes a tongue-in-cheek view of traditional gender roles. In the 1950s, critics such as Nevill Coghill, **Harold C. Goddard** [in the section on KATHERINA], and Margaret Webster argued that Katherina's submission is not to be taken seriously. In this view, the audience is meant to perceive that Katherina will dominate the marriage by allowing Petruchio an outward show of mastery. More recently, several commentators have suggested that the play ultimately undermines conventional social and gender roles. In an article excerpted below, **Coppélia Kahn** argued that Petruchio's exaggerated

behavior and irrational demands dramatize the absurdity of the concept of male superiority. Karen Newman, in an article published in 1986, pointed out that the play continually draws parallels between the theatrical role-playing of the stage and the real-life role-playing of social superiors and inferiors and of dominant husbands and obedient wives. In this way, she argued, it reveals that these real-life roles are not inherent in the nature of the individuals who play them, but rather are imposed by social and cultural constraints. In making a similar argument about the impact of the play, both Michael Shapiro and Juliet Dusinberre (1993) focused on the Elizabethan practice of using boy actors in female roles. By frequently calling attention to this practice, both critics suggested, the play underlines the artificiality of conventionally "feminine" behavior.

Many critics, however, reject an ironic reading of Petruchio's subduing of Katherina. In 1951, George Ian Duthie maintained that *The Taming of the Shrew* reaffirms the Elizabethan view that a husband stands in relation to his wife as a king to his subjects. In a 1960 article, Derek Traversi asserted that the play defends the view that there is a "right" order of things according to nature requiring that women be subject to their husbands. Many of these critics have emphasized the "gentleness" of Petruchio's behavior in comparison to the brutality displayed in earlier "shrew-taming" plays. In 1963, **Cecil C. Seronsy** (in the section on APPEARANCE VS. REALITY) suggested that Petruchio draws Katherina into enthusiastic acceptance of the role of obedient wife by "supposing" the existence in her of the qualities he desires and gradually assimilating her to the image he has willed. **Margaret Loftus Ranald** (in the section on IMAGERY) claimed that Shakespeare's use of images drawn from falconry portrays a model of matrimony based on "mutuality, trust, and love." Five years later, Marianne L. Novy suggested that by presenting conventional gender roles as a game, Petruchio makes it possible for Katherina to participate with him in developing a mutually satisfying accommodation to the rules of society. The complementarity of the relationship between Katherina and Petruchio is also stressed by **Ruth Nevo** (in the OVERVIEWS section) and **Joan Hartwig** (in the section on IMAGERY). Some commentators, however, see the relationship in a less positive light. In her article excerpted below **Shirley Nelson Garner** argued that the humor of the play rests on a misogynistic joke, and that it portrays marriage as an institution that can work only at the expense of woman's independence of thought, speech, and action. **H. J. Oliver** (in the OVERVIEWS section and the section on PETRUCHIO) and **Robert Ornstein** (in the section on PETRUCHIO) also maintain that Katherina is forced into a submission that diminishes her character.

A number of commentators have related the play's treatment of courtship and marriage to social concerns and cultural practices current in England at the time the play was written. In the section below, **George Hibbard** relates the play to various Elizabethan views of marriage. **Irving Ribner**, in a 1967 essay (in the APPEARANCE VS. REALITY section), saw the play as ridiculing two common Elizabethan views of relationships between men and women, one based on romantic love and the other based on domination of one partner by another. Work on this topic has also been done by such critics as Carol Heffernan (1985) and Linda Boose (1994).

George R. Hibbard

SOURCE: "'The Taming of the Shrew': A Social Comedy," in *Shakespearean Essays*, edited by Alwin Thaler and Norman Sanders, The University of Tennessee Press, 1964, pp. 15-28.

[*Hibbard suggests that* The Taming of the Shrew *contrasts opposing views of marriage that co-existed in Elizabethan England. He asserts that in the last decades of the sixteenth century, the tradition of parents arranging their children's marriages was being challenged, while a new ideal of mutual love between partners was taking root. The* Shrew *satirizes the old, mercenary order, Hibbard maintains, especially in the scene where Baptista appears to auction off Bianca to the highest bidder. But it also rejects the romantic view of marriage depicted in the Bianca-Lucentio subplot in favor of matches such as Katherina and Petruchio's, based on "real knowledge and experience." The critic calls attention to the directness and honesty of the conflict between the latter couple and contrasts it with Bianca and Lucentio's reliance on ploys and deceptions. For another view of the play's treatment of Elizabethan marriages, see the essay by Irving Ribner in the section on Appearance vs. Reality.*]

A case, of sorts, can be made out for the view that *The Shrew* is designed to bring out and contrast the two opposed attitudes to marriage that existed at the time when it was written: the idea of marriage as a purely business matter, which may be called realistic since it corresponds to the facts, and the idea of it as a union of hearts and minds, which may be called romantic. That some kind of contrast is intended is evident from the conduct of the two plots, which alternate with each other in a regular and contrapuntal fashion until the final scene, where they come together and are rounded off. In this reading of the play the realistic attitude is embodied in Petruchio who makes no secret of his mercenary intentions. To Hortensio, who asks him why he has come to Padua, he replies:

Antonio, my father, is deceased,

And I have thrust myself into this maze,
Haply to wive and thrive as best I may.
[I. ii. 54-6]

A few lines later he clinches the matter when, having said that the age and appearance of the lady are of no importance so long as she is rich, he adds:

I come to wive it wealthily in Padua;
If wealthily, then happily in Padua.
[I. ii. 75-6]

He plainly belongs to the old conservative school of thought, and his views on wives and their place are in keeping. In III. ii, having married Katharina, he pretends to defend her against her friends and kinsmen, ostensibly telling them but in fact telling her:

Nay, look not big, nor stamp, nor stare, nor fret,
I will be master of what is my own.
She is my goods, my chattels, she is my house,
My household stuff, my field, my barn,
My horse, my ox, my ass, my any thing.
[III. ii. 228-32]

The words are substantially a version of the tenth commandment and they serve as a forcible reminder of the weight of authority and tradition behind the attitude to woman which they express. In accordance with this same body of ideas, Petruchio feels that his wife should be in complete subjection to him; uses the appropriate means to subdue her to his will; and having achieved this purpose, explains its significance to Hortensio in V. ii by saying:

Marry, peace it bodes, and love, and quiet life,
An awful rule and right supremacy;
And, to be short, what not, that's sweet and happy.
[V. ii. 108-10]

In contrast to this story, in which the woman is treated as a chattel, enjoys none of the pleasures of courtship and is humiliated and subdued, there runs alongside it the tale of Bianca. She enjoys the pleasures of being wooed by no fewer than four men, of making her own choice from among them, of deceiving her father, of stealing a runaway marriage, of having it approved of by both the fathers concerned, and, most important of all, of continuing to get her own way with her husband after marriage as well as before it.

Put in these terms, *The Shrew* looks like an argument for the romantic attitude. But this conclusion only has to be stated for it to be found unacceptable. The scenes involving Petruchio and Katharina have much more vitality than those involving Bianca. We are left at the end with the conviction that the arranged match is a far more durable and solid thing than the romantic one. The most eloquent speech in the whole play is Katharina's, extolling the principle of male dominance and female subjection as a law of nature, and it follows on Petruchio's triumph over Lucentio in the matter of the wager. The main interest of the play is in Petruchio and Katharina, not in the rest.

Does this mean, then, that Shakespeare has come down on the side of the arranged marriage and the old order? In general terms it would seem unlikely, for in his subsequent comedies love is the central value. More to the point, however, such an inference will not square with the evidence of the second half of II. i, which is a pointed and effective piece of comic satire on the marriage market. In the first half of the scene Petruchio has wooed Katharina and the match between them has been fixed. Petruchio makes his exit saying:

> Father, and wife, and gentlemen, adieu,
> I will to Venice—Sunday comes apace—
> We will have rings, and things, and fine
>   array,
> And kiss me, Kate, we will be married o'
>   Sunday.
>
> [II. i. 321-24]

The way is now open for Baptista to dispose of his younger daughter and he wastes no time in setting about it. The scene that follows, between him and Gremio and Tranio, is conducted on a blatantly commercial level. Baptista's opening words, referring to the match that has just been concluded between Katharina and Petruchio, set the tone:

> Faith, gentlemen, now I play a merchant's
>   part,
> And venture madly on a desperate mart.
>
> [II. i. 326-27]

Tranio catches the allusion at once, and endorses it by saying:

> 'Twas a commodity lay fretting by you,
> 'Twill bring you gain, or perish on the seas.
>
> [II. i. 328-29]

Both of them regard Katharina as a questionable piece of goods that Baptista has done well to get off his hands. At this point Gremio puts in his claim for the hand of Bianca and Tranio promptly asserts his counterclaim. Both begin by saying that they love her, but the statement really amounts to nothing—in any case Tranio is only standing in for Lucentio—and Baptista immediately brings the whole thing down to

the only terms that matter when he stops the incipient quarrel with the words:

> Content you, gentlemen, I will compound
>   this strife.
> 'Tis deeds must win the prize, and he, of
>   both,
> That can assure my daughter greatest dower,
> Shall have Bianca's love.
>
> [II. i. 341-44]

The dower involved here is the money the husband assured to his wife on marriage, in order to provide for her widowhood if he should die before her. It was an essential part of the marriage contract in Shakespeare's England. *Deeds* in this context mean, not the service with which the lover of romance won his lady, but property and cash. There is surely a pun on the sense of *title-deeds*. Bianca's fate is to be settled by an auction, not by a knightly combat. Gremio makes his bid; Tranio puts in a better; Gremio increases his offer; Tranio outbids him once more, and actually uses the word "out-vied" to describe his success. The satire is unmistakable. It is clinched by Baptista's weighing of the two offers and settling, with a careful proviso, for the higher. Turning to Tranio, he says:

> I must confess your offer is the best,
> And, let your father make her the assurance,
> She is your own—else, you must pardon me,
> If you should die before him, where's her
>   dower?
>
> [II. i. 386-89]

But, being a good business man, he keeps the second customer in reserve. If Tranio's father fails to back up his son's offer, Bianca will be married to Gremio after all.

The scene leaves one in no doubt about the play's attitude to the marriage market. With it in mind, it is now possible to go back to the two contrasted plots and to consider them afresh. The fundamental difference between them in terms of their construction has been well analyzed by Bertrand Evans, who shows that while the Bianca story is developed through an intricate series of deceptions and disguises, there is no deception whatever in the Katharina-Petruchio story. Petruchio is told in no uncertain terms about Katharina's character before he meets her, and he, in turn, tells her, at their first meeting in II. i, that he intends to tame her. To use Evans's own words:

> *The Taming of the Shrew*, then, is unique among Shakespeare's comedies in that it has two distinct plots, one relying mainly on discrepant awarenesses, the other using them not at all.

This contrast is more than a matter of the mechanics

of plotting and of exploiting two different kinds of awareness in the audience. It is functional, springing from the contrasted characters of those involved in the two actions and from the antithetical attitudes to life and marriage that are presented through them.

Viewed in relation to the characters of the sisters, the two plots develop along the same lines, each containing a complete reversal. At the opening Bianca appears to be everything that the age thought a girl ought to be, obedient to her father, submissive to her elder sister, modest, unobtrusive and quiet. Katharina is her opposite, disobedient to her father, tyrannical towards her younger sister, aggressive, rebellious and noisy. In each case, however, these initial impressions are misleading. As the play goes on the two girls change places, as it were, until, at the end of it, Katharina is revealed as the perfect wife and Bianca as the difficult and troublesome one. Each has, in fact, shown herself as she really is. Nor has the change been an arbitrary one; it has been implicit from the beginning, where there are clear indications that things are not as they seem. Baptista's initial offer in I. i to allow Gremio and Hortensio to court Katharina, if they wish, terrifies Gremio. His answer is an outraged recoil:

> To cart her rather: she's too rough for me . . .
> There, there, Hortensio, will you any wife?
>
> [I. i. 55-6]

Carting was, of course, the punishment inflicted on harlots. As well as being treated like a chattel by her father, Katharina is being grossly insulted by the old pantaloon. Her vigorous complaint to Baptista is fully justified:

> I pray you, sir, is it your will
> To make a stale of me amongst these mates?
>
> [I. i. 57-8]

Stale has a double meaning. Primarily in this context it signifies "a laughing-stock," but it also carries the sense of "whore." Katharina is a woman of independent spirit revolting against a society in which girls are bought and sold in marriage. Moreover, the word *mates*, which she uses of Gremio and Hortensio, is also carefully chosen. It means "vulgar fellows of no real worth," and its accuracy is borne out by their reactions to her contempt and her threats. "From all such devils, good Lord deliver us!" says Gremio, to which Hortensio adds, "And me too, good Lord!" [I. i. 66, 67]. They are both poor-spirited creatures, with no vigour or masculinity about them. Instead of standing up to Katharina, they are cowed by her. And she knows it. As Petruchio shrewdly remarks in II. i, "If she be curst it is for policy" [II. i. 292]. Her shrewishness is not bad temper, but the expression of her self-respect. Indeed, it even looks like a deliberately adopted form of self-defence, a means of testing the

quality of the men she meets, in order to ensure that she has some say in the matter of marriage and is not sold off to a wealthy milksop. She is certainly not opposed to the prospect of marriage. The opening of II. i makes this plain enough, for in it she ill-treats Bianca for being so successful with men, and, when her father seeks to restrain her, she cries out in a jealous fury:

> What, will you not suffer me? Nay, now I
>   see
> She is your treasure, she must have a
>   husband,
> I must dance bare-foot on her wedding-day
> And for your love to her lead apes in hell.
>
> [II. i. 31-4]

She detests the idea of being an old maid and of her younger sister preceding her in marriage. She is attached to traditional notions of order and fitness. Provided that she can find a man who will stand up to her and earn her respect, she is ready and even eager to marry. Her subsequent behaviour, including her final speech, is all of a piece with her character and attitude as revealed in these two appearances and in the analogy drawn by Petruchio at the end of IV.i between the process by which he tames her and the methods used to tame a haggard, for the Elizabethans believed that falcons and the like were really of an affectionate nature and could be brought to love the man who trained them. Gervase Markham, for example, after listing the various kinds of hawks, adds these words: "all these Hawkes are hardy, meeke, and louing to the man" [in his *Country Contentments*]. Moreover, in his subsequent directions for training them, he lays great stress on kindness, writing as follows:

> All Hawkes generally are manned after one manner, that is to say, by watching and keeping them from sleep, by a continuall carrying of them vpon your fist, and by a most familiar stroaking and playing with them, with the Wing of a dead Foule or such like, and by often gazing and looking of them in the face, with a louing and gentle Countenace, and so making them acquainted with the man.

"Hardy (i.e. bold), meeke, and louing to the man" is a very accurate description of Katharina's real character.

At this stage in the action it is not yet clear what Bianca's nature is. We still do not know whether Katharina's hearty dislike of her is the result of jealousy, or whether it rests on other and more creditable grounds. Her role so far has been a passive one, thogh it is already evident that she is her father's favourite and knows that she can rely on his support. In III. i, however, she appears in a new situation, and much that has hitherto been obscure ceases to be so. Alone with two of her suitors, Lucentio, disguised as a teacher of Latin, and Hortensio, disguised as a teacher of music, Bianca discards the submissive mask she has worn in the presence of her father and shows her true disposition. As the two lovers dispute over which of them shall give his lesson first, she asserts her authority, saying:

> Why, gentlemen, you do me double wrong,
> To strive for that which resteth in my
> choice:
> I am no breeching scholar in the schools,
> I'll not be tied to hours nor 'pointed times,
> But learn my lessons as I please myself.
> And to cut off all strife, here sit we down:
> Take you your instrument, play you the
> whiles—
> His lecture will be done ere you have tuned.
>   [III. i. 16-23]

The kitten shows her claws. She is in complete control of the situation enforcing her will on both men, and she remains in control of it for the rest of the play. Her refusal in V. ii, after she has married Lucentio, to come at his bidding is already implicit in this scene.

The differences between the two sisters are more than differences of character, they also have a representative quality which is reflected in the way the two plots are conducted. In a society where the subjection of women is taken for granted two courses are open to the woman who does not accept this assumption: she can either resort to open revolt, or she can take the more devious, and usually more effective, line of apparent acquiescence and submission as a means to getting her own way through deception, intrigue and petticoat government. Katharina and Bianca embody these two different kinds of reaction to the existing situation; and so do the two plots, the one proceeding openly through a conflict of wills and tempers, the other moving to its end through a complicated tangle of misdirection and disguises. *The Taming of the Shrew* is an incisive piece of social criticism as well as an amusing play.

The scope of this criticism is widened and enriched by Shakespeare's presentation and handling of the men. Here again the main instrument is contrast. As I have pointed out, the men of Padua, with whom Lucentio may be included though he comes from Pisa, are a poor-spirited lot, content to play the marriage game along the conventional lines of dowries and intrigue. Petruchio, however, is something quite different. From the moment that he enters the play, at the opening of I. ii, his masculinity is emphasized. He is violent and aggressive, thoroughly enjoying the row with his servant, Grumio. He is always frank and honest, with himself as well as with others. He resorts to no subterfuges, but states his motive in coming to Padua so openly and unashamedly that it sounds like a challenge to instead of an acceptance of, the conventions:

> I come to wive it wealthily in Padua;
> If wealthily, then happily in Padua.

He bursts in on the intrigues rather like an Elizabethan buccaneer descending on a civilized but effete Mediterranean city. He brings a breath of fresh air with him; his very language is boisterous and blustering. . . .

Petruchio's other great asset is his confidence in himself and his sportsman's love of risk. Audacity is the keynote of his wooing. Recognizing Katharina's spirit he deliberately engages her, through his calculated familiarity and impudence, in a battle of wits that leads on to a physical struggle and a battle of wills. She cannot resist the challenge he throws down; and the whole affair is conducted like a game within the limits supplied by certain rules which are tacitly accepted by both. She oversteps those rules when she strikes him, but the warning he gives: "I swear I'll cuff you, if you strike again" [II. i. 220], is enough to make her realize that the rules must be kept. Neither of them must injure the other's self-respect and, once he has released her, there must be no further resort to direct physical force. The engagement—in the military as well as the marital sense of the word—that follows is really a process by which each of them comes to know and to appreciate the other fully. And it is very significant that although they are married in III. ii they do not seem to go to bed together to consummate their marriage until the very end of the play, by which time they are allies and lovers, for Katharina has kissed Petruchio in the street at the end of V. i.

It is their knowledge of, and their trust in, each other, which have grown out of experience, that give this pair such an advantage over the other two pairs at the end of the play. Hortensio and his widow do not know one another, nor do Lucentio and Bianca. How should they? Hortensio has married on the rebound, and Lucentio's wooing of Bianca has been conducted in terms that allow of no real engagement of heart or head. The stratagems that have led to his success have not been his own but Tranio's. It is Tranio who gets rid of Hortensio as a rival wooer, who instructs the Pedant in his part and who tells Lucentio when and how to steal the marriage. Lucentio is depicted throughout as a man besotted by love of a rather fanciful kind and, consequently, incapable of initiating any action. The brittle, bookish, artificial style of his language as a lover is an effective criticism of his shortcomings as a man. He has nothing of Petruchio's independence, self-reliance and grasp on essentials. His lyrical description of Bianca in V. i. when he refers to her as "the wished haven of my bliss" [V. i. 128], is a convincing proof that he has not so much as noticed the pointers to her true nature which are set out so clearly in III. i.

That *The Shrew* is a gay, high-spirited, rollicking play, full of broad farcical scenes and richly comic narrative passages is self-evident. What I have tried to show is that it also has a serious side to it. Underneath the comic exaggeration it is basically realistic. It portrays the marriage situation, not as it appeared in the romances of the day, but as it was in Shakespeare's England. And the criticism it brings to bear on it is constructive as well as destructive. Baptista, the foolish father who knows nothing about his daughters yet seeks to order their lives, is defeated all along the line. So is Gremio, the old pantaloon, who thinks he can buy a wife. The play's disapproval of the arranged match, in which no account is taken of the feelings of the principals, could not be plainer. Within the framework of marriage as it existed at the time, it comes out in favour of the match based on real knowledge and experience, over against the more fanciful kind of wooing that ignores facts in favour of bookishly conventional attitudes and expressions of feeling. Paradoxically enough it is Katharina and Petruchio, for each of whom it is the other, as the other really is, that matters, who embody the new revolutionary attitude to marriage, rather than Lucentio and Bianca.

Coppélia Kahn

SOURCE: "'The Taming of the Shrew': Shakespeare's Mirror of Marriage," in *Modern Language Studies*, Vol. V, No. 1, Spring, 1975, pp. 88-102.

[*Kahn interprets* The Taming of the Shrew *as a farce that relies on exaggeration to at once indulge and undermine the male fantasy of mastery over women. Shakespeare, she asserts, set out to write a comedy that would both critique and celebrate marriage and resolved this apparent contradiction through an ironic portrayal of Katherina in the final scenes of the play. Kahn compares Petruchio's violence and Katherina's shrewishness, remarking that while society accepts the violence of men as normal male behavior, it condemns forceful self-assertion by women, even when it serves as a psychological defense or arises from real provocation, as it does in the play. The critic further notes that Petruchio's view of Katherina as his property and his comparison of her to a hawk that must be tamed by deprivation are devastating evidence that "male supremacy in marriage denies women's humanity." She adds that Petruchio's attempt to make Katherina see the world through his eyes emphasizes the absurdity of the principle of male dominance. On the road back to Padua, Kahn suggests, Katherina adopts a pose of submissiveness that her husband correctly understands as a signal for compromise. From this point on, Katherina*

develops a practice of "satirical exaggeration" that allows Petruchio to appear dominant, yet still permits her to retain a small measure of psychological independence.]

As Robert Heilman demonstrates [in an article in *Modern Language Quarterly*, 1966] the taming is best viewed as a farce which "carries out our desire to simplify life by a selective anesthetizing of the whole person; man retains all his energy yet never really gets hurt." Farce, according to Heilman, deals with people as though they lack normal physical, emotional, and moral sensitivity, and are capable only of mechanical responses. In making Kate react almost automatically to the contradictory kinds of treatment Petruchio administers (flattery before the wedding, and force afterwards), Shakespeare molds her to the needs of the farce. In the first three acts, before the taming begins in earnest, she is portrayed in terms of her resistance to male efforts to dispose of her in marriage. Our strongest impression of her is that she fights back. But though she declares she'll see Petruchio hanged before she marries him, marry him she does, and though she flatly refuses to obey his first command to her as a wife, she exits mutely with him at the end of Act III. Contrary to our expectations, she doesn't retaliate with all the shrewish weaponry said to be at her disposal. In the end, as I shall show, she subverts her husband's power without attempting to challenge it, and she does so in a gamesome spirit, without hostility or bitterness. Thus Shakespeare allows the male to indulge his dream of total mastery over the female without the real-life penalties of her resentment or his guilt.

But the farce has another purpose which Heilman and other critics fail to see. It exaggerates ludicrously the reach and force of male dominance and thus pushes us to see this wish for dominance as a childish dream of omnipotence. In short, the farce portrays Petruchio's manliness as infantile. A 1904 editor of the play [R. Warwick Bond] roundly declared, "It will be many a day . . . ere men cease to need or women to admire, the example of Petruchio." How pitiable that we should still need and admire it, almost seventy years later. That we do is revealed by the prevailing tendency of criticism to justify Petruchio's methods in Petruchio's terms, endorsing that version of masculinity which the farce undercuts as well as indulges. Though it has long been recognized that Shakespeare gives Kate's "shrewishness" a psychological and moral validity lacking in all literary predecessors, critics still argue that Petruchio's heavy-handed behavior is merely a role briefly assumed for a benign purpose. They claim that he is Kate's savior, the wise man who guides her to a better and truer self, or a clever doctor following homeopathic medicine. They have missed the greatest irony of the play. Unlike other misogynistic shrew literature, this play satirizes not woman herself in the person of the shrew, but *male attitudes toward women.* My purpose is to reveal the ways in which Shakespeare puts these attitudes before us.

Long before Petruchio enters, we are encouraged to doubt the validity of male supremacy. First of all, the transformation of Christopher Sly from drunken lout to noble lord, a transformation only temporary and skin-deep, suggests that Kate's switch from independence to subjection may also be deceptive and prepares us for the irony of the dénouement. More pointedly, one of the most alluring perquisites of Sly's new identity is a wife, and his right to domineer over her. As Scene 1 of the Induction begins, Sly suffers public humiliation at the hands of a woman when the Hostess throws him out of her alehouse for disorderly conduct. After he awakens from his sleep in the second scene, it is the tale of his supposed wife's beauty and Penelope-like devotion and patience that finally tips the balance, convincing him that he really is the aristocrat of the servants' descriptions. . . .

The humor lies in the fact that Sly's pretensions to authority and grandeur, which he claims only on the basis of sex, not merit, and indulges specifically with women, are contradicted in his real identity, in which he is a woman's inferior. Similarly, as I shall argue later, Petruchio seems to find in Kate the reflection of his own superiority, while we know that he is fooled by a role she has assumed.

In the main play, the realistic bourgeois ambiance in which Kate is placed leads us to question the definition of shrewishness which the characters take for granted. In medieval mystery plays and Tudor interludes, shrews were already married to their pusillanimous husbands and were shown as domestic tyrants. Male fears of female freedom were projected onto the wife, who was truly a threatening figure because she treated her husband as he normally would have treated her. When the husband attempted rebellion, he usually lost. Shakespeare departs from this literary tradition in order to sketch Kate as a victim of the marriage market, making her "the first shrew to be given a father, to be shown as maid and bride" [according to M. C. Bradbrook in an article in *Shakespeare Jahrbuch*, 1958]. At her entrance, she is already, for her father's purpose, that piece of goods which Petruchio declares her to be after the wedding. Baptista is determined not to marry the sought-after Bianca until he gets an offer for the unpopular Kate, not for the sake of conforming to the hierarchy of age as his opening words imply, but out of a merchant's desire to sell all the goods in his warehouse. His marketing technique is clever: make the sale of the less popular item the prerequisite of purchasing the desirable one. As Tranio sympathetically remarks after Kate's marriage is arranged, "'Twas a commodity that lay fretting by you" [II. i. 328]. Knowing that

Gremio and Hortensio are interested only in Bianca, Baptista tactlessly invites them to court Kate, and does so in her presence. The two suitors then begin to insult her. Gremio refers to her as a prostitute by offering to "cart" her through the streets, a punishment for prostitutes, instead of to court her. When she indignantly asks her father, "Is it your will, sir, to make a stale of me amongst these mates?" [I. i. 57-8], she is only reacting to the insult and aptly characterizing her situation as that of a whore being loosed to anyone who'll have her for the best price.

That money, not his daughter's happiness, is Baptista's real concern in matchmaking becomes evident when Petruchio brusquely makes his bid for Kate. Previously, Petruchio's desire to marry solely for money, even though he had inherited his father's fortune, was comically exaggerated. The rhetorical expansiveness of his speech made humorous the profit motive which Baptista takes seriously:

> . . . if thou know
> One rich enough to be Petruchio's wife—
> As wealth is burden of my wooing dance—
> Be she as foul as was Florentius' love,
> As old as Sibyl, and as curst and shrewd
> As Socrates' Xanthippe or a worse,
> She moves me not, or not removes, at least,
> Affection's edge in me, were she as rough
> As are the swelling Adriatic seas.
> I come to wive it wealthily in Padua;
> If wealthily, then happily in Padua.
>
> [I. ii. 66-76]

Both Petruchio and Baptista pretend to make Kate's love the ultimate condition of the marriage, but then Petruchio simply lies in asserting that she has fallen in love with him at first sight. Her father, though he doubts this far-fetched claim ("I know not what to say" [II. i. 318]) claps up the match anyhow, for on it depends Bianca's match as well. Both marriages provide insurance against having to support his daughters in widowhood, promise grandsons to whom he may pass on the management and possession of his property, and impart to his household the prestige of "marrying well," for the wealth of the grooms advertises Baptista's own financial status. Petruchio's and Tranio / Lucentio's frequent references to their respective fathers' wealth and reputations remind us that wealth and reputation pass from father to son, with woman as mere accessory to the passing. . . .

Even the Bianca plot emphasizes heavily the venal aspects of marriage, though it is usually characterized as romantic, in contrast to the realism and farce of the taming. In Act II, scene 1, Baptista awards Bianca to Tranio / Lucentio solely because he offers more cash and property as "widowhood" (that is, claims to have more total wealth) than Gremio does. As George

Hibbard has shown, the scene satirizes the hard-headed commercial nature of marital arrangements. Baptista's chivalric "'Tis deeds must win the prize" [II. i. 342] puns on title deeds to property, and the length and specificity of each suitor's inventory of wealth calls inordinate attention to the fact that dutiful, submissive Bianca, courted in high-flown style by the ardent Lucentio, is still a piece of property, to be relinquished only with the guarantee that Baptista will profit if the groom expires. Always the clever businessman, Baptista accepts Lucentio's bid pending his father's assurance of his fortune, but keeps Gremio in reserve should the deal fall through.

It is time to turn with Kate from the father to the husband. From the moment Petruchio commands his servant "Knock, I say" [I. ii. 5], he evokes and creates noise and violence. A hubbub of loud speech, beatings, and quarrelsomeness surrounds him. "The swelling Adriatic seas" and "thunder when the clouds in autumn rack" [I. ii. 74, 96] are a familiar part of his experience, which he easily masters with his own force of will or physical strength. Like Adam, he is lord over nature, and his own violence has been well legitimized by society, unlike Kate's, which has marked her as unnatural and abhorrent. But let us examine the nature of Petruchio's violence compared to Kate's.

The hallmark of a shrew is her scolding tongue and loud raucous voice—a verbal violence befitting woman, since her limbs are traditionally weak. It is interesting that Kate is given only twelve lines in her entrance scene, only five of which allude to physical violence:

> I' faith, sir, you shall never need to fear:
> Iwis it [marriage] is not halfway to her heart.
> But if it were, doubt not her care should be
> To comb your noddle with a three-legged
>   stool
> And paint your face and use you like a fool.
>   [I. i. 61-5]

Here she threatens Hortensio in response to his greater threat, that no man will marry her. These lines have a distinctly defensive cast; Kate refers to herself in the third person, and denies any interest in a mate because two prospective mates (Hortensio and Gremio) have just made it clear that they have no interest in her. Kate's vision of breaking furniture over a husband's head is hypothetically couched in the subjunctive. Yet later Tranio describes her speech in this scene as "such a storm that mortal ears might hardly endure the din" [I. i. 172-73]. Throughout the play, this kind of disparity between the extent and nature of Kate's "shrewish" behavior and the male characters' perceptions of it focuses our attention on masculine behavior and attitudes which stereotype women as either submissive and desirable or rebellious and shrewish. Kate is called devil, hell, curst, shrewd (shrewish), and wildcat, and referred to in other insulting ways because, powerless to change her situation, she *talks* about it. That her speech is defensive rather than offensive in origin, and psychologically necessary for her survival, is eloquently conveyed by her own lines:

> My tongue will tell the anger of my heart,
> Or else my heart, concealing it, will break,
> And rather than it shall I will be free
> Even to the uttermost, as I please, in words.
>   [IV. iii. 77-80]

Though she commits four acts of physical violence onstage (binding and striking Bianca, breaking a lute over Hortensio's head, hitting Petruchio and then Grumio), in each instance the dramatic context suggests that she strikes out because of provocation or intimidation resulting from her status as a woman. For example, the language in which her music lesson with Hortensio is described conveys the idea that it is but another masculine attempt to subjugate woman. "Why, then thou canst not break her to the lute?," asks Baptista. "I did but tell her she mistook her frets / And bowed her hand to teach her fingering," replies Hortensio [II. i. 147, 149-50]. Later Petruchio explicitly attempts to "break" Kate to his will, and throughout the play men tell her that she "mistakes her frets"—that her anger is unjustified.

On the other hand, Petruchio's confident references to "great ordnance in the field" and the "Loud 'larums, neighing steeds, trumpets' clang" of battle [I. ii. 203, 206] bespeak a lifelong acquaintance with organized violence as a masculine vocation. The loud oaths with which he orders his servants about and startles the priest in the wedding service are thus farcical exaggerations of normal masculine behavior. In its volume and vigor, his speech suggests a robust manliness which would make him attractive to the woman who desires a master (or who wants to identify with power in its most accessible form). Grumio characterizes his master in terms of his speech, in lines which recall the kind of speech attributed to Kate:

> O' my word, and she knew him as well as I do,
> she would think scolding would do little good upon
> him. She may perhaps call him half a score of
> knaves or so—why, that's nothing. And he begin
> once, he'll rail in his rope-tricks. I'll tell you what,
> sir, and she stand him but a little, he will throw
> a figure in her face and so disfigure her with it
> that she shall have no more eyes to see withal
> than a cat. You know him not, sir.
>
>   [I. ii. 108-16]

If Petruchio were female, he would be known as a shrew and shunned accordingly by men. Behavior desirable in a male automatically prohibits similar behavior in a female, for woman must mold herself to be complementary to man, not competitive with him. Indeed, if manhood is defined and proven by the ability to dominate, either in battle or in the household, then a situation which does not allow a man to dominate is existentially threatening. When Petruchio declares, "I am as peremptory as she proud-minded" [II. i. 131], he seems to state that he and his bride-to-be are two of a kind. But that "kind," bold, independent, self-assertive, must only be male. Thus his image of himself and Kate as "two raging fires" ends on a predictable note:

> And where two raging fires meet together
> They do consume the thing that feeds their
> 　fury.
> Though little fire grows great with little
> 　wind,
> Yet extreme gusts will blow out fire and all.
> So I to her, *and so she yields to me,*
> For I am rough and woo not like a babe.
> 　　　　　　[II. i. 132-37; emphasis mine]

His force must necessarily triumph over Kate's because he is male and she is not. Those critics who maintain that his is acceptable because it has only the limited, immediate purpose of making Kate reject an "unbecoming" mode of behavior miss the real point of the taming. The overt force Petruchio wields over Kate by marrying her against her will in the first place, and then by denying her every wish and comfort, stamping, shouting, reducing her to exhaustion, etc., is but a farcical representation of the psychological realities of marriage in Elizabethan England, in which the husband's will constantly, silently, and invisibly, through custom and conformity, suppressed the wife's.

At the wedding in Act III, scene [2], Petruchio's behavior travesties the decorum, ceremony and piety which all those present feel ought to accompany a marriage. It is calculated to deprive Kate of the opportunity to enjoy the bride's sense of triumph, of being the center of admiration and interest; to humiliate her in public; to throw her off her guard by convincing her he is mad; and to show her that now nothing can happen unless and until her husband pleases. The final effect of the wedding scene, however, is less comical than the rhetorically delightful accounts of Petruchio's off-stage antics. When all the trappings are stripped away (and they are, by his design), the groom is simply completing the legal arrangements whereby he acquires Kate as he would acquire a piece of property. When he declares he'll "seal the title with a lovely kiss" [III. ii. 123], he refers not just to Kate's new title as his wife, but also to the title-deed which, sealed with wax, passed to the purchaser in a property transaction. (The pun recalls Baptista's "deeds," a similar play on words discussed above.) Tranio remarks of Petruchio, "He

hath some meaning in his mad attire" [III. ii. 124], and he is right. When Petruchio says "To me she's married, not unto my clothes" [III. ii. 117], he assumes a lofty morality, implying that he offers Kate real love, not just its worldly show. This moralistic pose becomes an important part of his strategy in Act IV when he claims to do nothing that isn't for Kate's "good." But in the brutally plain statement he delivers at the conclusion of the wedding scene, he momentarily drops this pose:

> She is my goods, my chattels; she is my
> 　house,
> My household stuff, my field, my barn,
> My horse, my ox, my ass, my anything.
> 　　　　　　　　　　　　[III. ii. 230-32]

His role as property-owner is the model for his role as husband; Kate, for him, is a thing. Or at least she will become a thing when he has wrenched unquestioning obedience from her, when she no longer has mind or will of her own. It is impossible that Shakespeare meant us to accept Petruchio's speech uncritically: it is the most shamelessly blunt statement of the relationship between men, women, and property to be found in the literature of this period. After the simple declarative statements of possession, quoted above, which deny humanity to Kate, the speech shifts to chivalric challenges of imaginary "thieves" who would snatch her away. Is she goods, in the following lines, or a medieval damsel?

> 　　　　　　　　　　. . . Touch her
> 　whoever dare,
> I'll bring mine action on the proudest he
> That stops my way in Padua. Grumio,
> Draw forth thy weapon, we are beset with
> 　thieves.
> Rescue thy mistress, if thou be a man.
> 　　　　　　　　　　　　[III. ii. 233-37]

The point is that Petruchio wants to think of her in both kinds of terms. The speech concludes grandly with the metamorphosis of Petruchio into a knight-errant:

> Fear not, sweet wench; they shall not touch
> 　thee, Kate.
> I'll buckler thee against a million.
> 　　　　　　　　　　　　[III. ii. 238-39]

The modulation of simple ownership into spurious chivalry reveals the speaker's buried awareness that he cheapens himself by being merely Kate's proprietor; he must transform the role into something nobler.

Petruchio's thundering oaths and physical brutality reach a crescendo at his country house in Act IV, when he beats his servants, throws food and dishes on the floor, stomps, roars and bullies. These actions are directed not against his bride but at his servants, again in the name of chivalry, out of a fastidious devotion to his bride's supposed comfort. But his stance is rooted realistically in his status as lord of a manor and master of a household which is not Kate's but his. He ordered her wedding clothes, chose their style and paid for them. Kate wears them not at her pleasure but at his, as Grumio's jest succinctly indicates:

> *Petruchio.* Well, sir, in brief, the gown is not
>   for me.
> *Brumio.* You are i' th' right, sir; 'tis for my
>   mistress.
>
>   [IV. iii. 155-56]

In the famous soliloquy which opens "Thus have I politicly begun my reign" [IV. i. 188-211], Petruchio reduces Kate to an animal capable of learning only through deprivation of food and rest, devoid of all sensitivity save the physical. The animal metaphor shocks us and I would suggest was meant to shock Shakespeare's audience, despite their respect for falconry as an art and that reverence for the great chain of being emphasized by E. M. W. Tillyard. I suppose Kate is actually being elevated in this speech, in view of previous references to her as her husband's horse, ox, and ass, for a falcon was the appurtenance of a nobleman, and a valued animal. But the blandness of Petruchio's confidential tone, the sweep of his easy assumption that Kate is not merely an animal, but *his* animal, who lives or dies at his command—has a dramatic irony similar to that of his exit speech in the wedding scene. Both utterances unashamedly present the status of woman in marriage as degrading in the extreme, plainly declaring her a sub-human being who exists solely for the purposes of her husband. Yet both offer this vision of the wife as chattel or animal in a lordly, self-confident tone. Urbanity is superimposed on outrage, for our critical scrutiny.

Shakespeare does not rest with showing that male supremacy in marriage denies woman's humanity. In the most brilliant comic scene of the play (IV. 5), he goes on to demonstrate how it defies reason. Petruchio demands that Kate agree that the sun is the moon in order to force a final showdown. Having exhausted and humiliated her to the limit of his invention, he now wants her to know that he would go to any extreme to get the obedience he craves. Shakespeare implies here that male supremacy is ultimately based on such absurdities, for it insists that whatever a man says is right because he is a man, even if he happens to be wrong. In a male-supremacist utopia, masculinity might be identical with absolute truth, but in life the two coincide only intermittently.

Why does Kate submit to her husband's unreason? Or why does she *appear* to do so, and on what terms? On the most pragmatic level, she follows Hortensio's advice to "Say as he says or we shall never go" [IV. v. 11] only in order to achieve her immediate and most pressing needs: a bed, a dinner, some peace and quiet. Shakespeare never lets us think that she believes it right, either morally or logically, to submit her judgment and the evidence of her senses to Petruchio's rule. In fact, the language of her capitulation makes it clear that she thinks him mad:

> Forward, I pray, since we have come so far,
> And be it moon or sun or what you please.
> *And if you please to call it a rush-candle,*
> Henceforth I vow it shall be so for me. . . .
> But sun it is not when you say it is not,
> *And the moon changes even as your mind.*
>
>   [IV. v. 12-15, 19-20; emphasis mine]

At this point, Hortensio concedes Petruchio's victory and applauds it; Petruchio henceforth behaves and speaks as though he has indeed tamed Kate. However, we must assume that since he previously donned the mask of the ardent lover, professing rapture at Kate's rudeness, he can see that she is doing the same thing here. At their first meeting he turned the tables on her, praising her for mildness and modesty after she gave insults and even injury. Now she pays him back, suddenly overturning his expectations and moreover mocking them at the same time. But he is not fooled, and can take that mockery as the cue for compromise. It reassures him that she will give him obedience if that is what he must have, but it also warns him that she, in turn, must retain her intellectual freedom.

The scene then proceeds on this basis, each character accepting the other's assumed role. Kate responds to Petruchio's outrageous claim that the wrinkled Vincentio is a fair young maiden by pretending so wholeheartedly to accept it that we know she can't be in earnest. She embroiders the fantasy in an exuberant declamatory style more appropriate to tragedy than comedy:

> Young budding virgin, fair and fresh and
>   sweet,
> Whither away, or where is thy abode?
> Happy the parents of so fair a child!
> Happier the man whom favorable stars
> Allots thee for his lovely bedfellow!
>
>   [IV. v. 37-41]

Her rhetoric expresses her realization that the power struggle she had entered into on Petruchio's terms is absurd. It also signals her emancipation from that struggle, in the terms she declared earlier: " . . . I will be free / Even to the uttermost, as I please, in words" [IV. iii. 79-80].

Of course, a freedom that exists only in words is ultimately as limited as Petruchio's mastery. Though

Kate is clever enough to use his verbal strategies against him, she is trapped in her own cleverness. Her only way of maintaining her inner freedom is by outwardly denying it, which thrusts her into a schizoid existence. One might almost prefer that she simply give in rather than continue to fight from such a psychologically perilous position. Furthermore, to hold that she maintains her freedom in words is to posit a distinction without a difference, for whether she remains spiritually independent of Petruchio or sincerely believes in his superiority, her outward behavior must be the same—that of the perfect Griselda, a model for all women. What complicates the situation even more is that Kate quite possibly has fallen in love with her tamer, whose vitality and bravado make him attractive, despite his professed aims. Her failure to pursue her rebellion after the wedding or in the country house supports this hypothesis as does the tone of her mockery in Act IV, Scene 5, and thereafter, which is playful and joyous rather than bitter and angry as it was in the first three acts. . . .

In the last scene, Shakespeare finally allows Petruchio that lordship over Kate, and superiority to other husbands, for which he has striven so mightily. He just makes it clear to us, through the contextual irony of Kate's last speech, that her husband is deluded. As a contest between males in which woman is the prize, the closing scene is analogous to the entire play. It was partly Petruchio's desire to show his peers that he was more of a man than they which spurred him to take on the shrew in the first place. Gremio refers to him as a Hercules and compares the subduing of Kate to a "labor . . . more than Alcides' twelve" [I. ii. 255-56]. Hortensio longs but fails to emulate his friend's supposed success in taming. Lucentio, winner in the other wooing context, fails in the final test of marital authority. Petruchio stands alone in the last scene, the center of male admiration.

As critics have noted, the wager scene is punctuated by reversals: quiet Bianca talks back and shrewish Kate seems to become an obedient wife. In a further reversal, however, she steals the scene from her husband, who has held the stage throughout the play, and reveals that he has failed to tame her in the sense he set out to. He has gained her outward compliance in the form of a public display, while her spirit remains mischievously free. Though she pretends to speak earnestly on behalf of her own inferiority, she actually treats us to a pompous, wordy, holier-than-thou sermon which delicately mocks the sermons her husband has delivered to her and about her. It is significant that Kate's speech is both her longest utterance and the longest in the play. Previously, Petruchio dominated the play verbally, and his longest speech totalled twenty-four lines, while Kate's came to fifteen. Moreover, everything Kate said was a protest

against her situation or those who put her in it, and as such was deemed unwomanly, or shrewish. Petruchio's impressive rhetoric, on the other hand, asserted his masculinity in the form of command over women and servants and of moral authority. Now Kate apes this verbal dominance and moralistic stance for satirical effect.

In content, the speech is thoroughly orthodox. Its sentiments can be found in a dozen treatises on marriage written in the sixteenth century. . . . Kate offers them with complete seriousness, straightforwardly except for a few verbal ironies, such as the reminder of her husband's rhetorical patterns in "thy lord, thy life, thy keeper, / Thy head, thy sovereign" [V. ii. 146-47], which echoes his "my goods, my chattels; . . . my house, / My household stuff, my field, my barn, / my horse, my ox, my ass, my anything." The grave moral tone of the speech, as I have noted, comes from Petruchio also, but its irony emanates primarily from the dramatic context. First, it follows upon and resembles Kate's rhetorical performance on the road back to Padua. It is a response to her husband's demand that she demonstrate her obedience before others, as she did then before Hortensio, and as such it exceeds expectations once more. It fairly shouts obedience, when a gentle murmur would suffice. Having heard her address Vincentio as "Young, budding virgin," we know what she is up to in this instance. Second, though the speech pleads subordination, as a speech—a lengthy, ambitious verbal performance before an audience—it allows the speaker to dominate that audience. Though Kate purports to speak as a woman to women, she assumes the role of a preacher whose authority and wisdom are, in the terms of the play, thoroughly masculine. Third, the speech sets the seal on a complete reversal of character, a push-button change from rebel to conformist which is, I have argued, part of the mechanism of farce. Here as elsewhere in the play, farce has two purposes: it completes the fantasy of male dominance, but also mocks it as mere fantasy. Kate's quick transformation perfectly fulfills Petruchio's wishes, but is transparently false to human nature. Towards the end of her lecture, Kate hints that she is dissembling in the line "That seeming to be most which we indeed least are" [V. ii. 175]. Though she seems to be the most vocal apologist for male dominance, she is indeed its ablest critic.

On one level, the dénouement is the perfect climax of a masculine fantasy, for as Kate concludes she prepares to place her hand beneath her husband's foot, an emblem-book symbol of wifely obedience. On a deeper level, as I have tried to show, her words speak louder than her actions, and mock that fantasy. But on the deepest level, because the play depicts its heroine as outwardly compliant but inwardly independent, it represents possibly the most cherished male fantasy of all—that woman remains *untamed*, even in her subjection. Does Petruchio know he's been taken? Quite probably, since he himself has played the game of saying-the-thing-which-is-not. Would he enjoy being married to a woman as dull and proper as the Kate who delivers that marriage sermon? From all indications, no. Then can we conclude that Petruchio no less than Kate knowingly plays a false role in this marriage, the role of victorious tamer and complacent master? I think we can, but what does this tell us about him and about men in general?

It is Kate's submission to him which makes Petruchio a man, finally and indisputably. This is the action toward which the whole plot drives, and if we consider its significance for Petruchio and his fellows we realize that the myth of feminine weakness, which prescribes that women ought to or must inevitably submit to man's superior authority, masks a contrary myth: that only a woman has the power to authenticate a man, by acknowledging him *her* master. Petruchio's mind may change even as the moon, but what is important is that Kate confirm those changes; moreover, that she do so willingly and consciously. Such voluntary surrender is, paradoxically, part of the myth of female power, which assigns to woman the crucial responsibility for creating a mature and socially respectable man. In *The Taming of the Shrew*, Shakespeare reveals the dependency which underlies mastery, the strength behind submission. Truly, Petruchio is wedded to his Kate. . . .

Shirley Nelson Garner

SOURCE: "*The Taming of the Shrew:* Inside or Outside of the Joke?" in *"Bad" Shakespeare: Revaluations of the Shakespeare Canon*, edited by Maurice Charney, Fairleigh Dickinson University Press, 1988, pp. 105-19.

[*Unlike the majority of contemporary critics, who argue on various grounds that* The Taming of the Shrew *subverts or critiques traditional gender roles, Garner contends that the play's assumptions about women and sexuality are fundamentally misogynistic, and that it is directed towards an audience that believes it is both right and necessary that men should exercise control over women. In developing her argument, Garner examines the attitudes about women expressed both in the Induction and in the main part of the play. In particular, she looks closely at the language and imagery used to describe Katherina. Garner also analyzes the character of Petruchio and the methods he uses to subdue Katherina.*]

If you had grown up hearing that Shakespeare is the greatest writer in the English language (or at least one of the two or three greatest) and that he is a "universal" poet, who speaks across time and national (even cultural) boundaries, you—especially if you were a woman student—would be shocked to study him in a college or university in the 1980s and to read *The Taming of the Shrew* for the first time. My own students—particularly my women students, though sometimes the men in my classes as well—often exclaim in dismay, "I can't *believe* Shakespeare wrote this!" A graduate student, rereading the play with only a faded memory of having read it before, commented that it was commonly her experience now to read something that she had once enjoyed only to find it disappointing. That was what happened when she read *Taming of the Shrew*, and it gave her a sense of loss. Reading the play from a woman's perspective, she could not help but be a "resisting reader." Even if teachers of literature offer an ingenious reading of the play, their students will probably not be seduced into a very happy view of it. They will know in their hearts that—at the least—there is something wrong with the way Kate is treated. And they will be right.

I am not sure that anyone except academics who have invested much—perhaps all—of their professional lives in studying Shakespeare would need to debate whether *Taming of the Shrew* is good or bad. The best that can be said for the play is [as Peter Berek concludes in an essay in *"Bad" Shakespeare*, ed. Maurice Charney, 1988] that it shows Shakespeare had suppler attitudes toward gender than his contemporaries and that it "may have been a valuable, even necessary, stage in moving toward his astonishing expansion of the possibilities of gender roles." This argument makes the play *interesting*, but it does not make it *good*.

The Elizabethans probably considered the play "good." Attesting to the popularity of its main idea, numerous shrew-taming stories exist as well as another version of the play, evidently, acted close to the time of Shakespeare's *Taming of the Shrew*. The values that underlie the story are obviously those of a patriarchal society, in which the desirability of male dominance is unquestioned. When patriarchal attitudes are called into question, as they have been in our time, it becomes a more delicate matter to put an "uppity" woman in her "proper" place—on the stage or off—and she becomes a less easy mark for humor. *Taming of the Shrew* read straight, then, must seem less "good."

Interpretations of the play that stress its farcical elements or view the ending as ironic are often efforts, I think, to keep the play among the "good," to separate Shakespeare from its misogynist attitudes, to keep him as nearly unblemished as possible. These efforts to preserve *Taming* suggest that in our time it has become one of the problematic plays in Shakespeare's canon. They demonstrate how relative to time and place are the ideas of "good" and "bad." What I wish to argue here is that no matter how you read the ending, no matter how you define the genre of the play, it is still a "bad" play. . . . [It] is clear that some people still like the play, still count it among the "good," or "more good than bad." This fact suggests that "good" and "bad" are also relative to the pleasures of the particular members of an audience. I would also argue that whether you see the play as "good" or "bad" depends on where you see yourself in terms of the central joke. If you can somehow be "in" on it, the play will undoubtedly seem better than if you cannot be.

The central joke in *The Taming of the Shrew* is directed against a woman. The play seems written to please a misogynist audience, especially men who are gratified by sexually sadistic pleasures. Since I am outside the community for whom the joke is made and do not share its implicit values, I do not participate in its humor. Because the play does not have for me what I assume to be its intended effect, that is, I do not find it funny, I do not find it as good as Shakespeare's other comedies.

The Induction makes immediately clear the assumptions about women and sexuality that are at the core of *Taming*. When a Lord, a character named only according to his rank, imagines and creates for Christopher Sly a world like his own (though more romantic), the "woman" he peoples it with suggests a sixteenth-century ideal: gentle, dutiful, utterly devoted to her husband. He directs his servingman to tell Bartholomew, his page, how to play the part of Sly's wife:

> Such duty to the drunkard let him do
> With soft low tongue and lowly courtesy,
> And say, "What is't your honor will
>   command
> Wherein your lady and your humble wife
> May show her duty and make known her
>   love?"
> And then, with kind embracements, tempting
>   kisses,
> And with declining head into his bosom,
> Bid him shed tears, as being overjoyed
> To see her noble lord restored to health
> Who for this seven years hath esteemed him
> No better than a poor and loathsome beggar.
>
>   (2.114-23)

Surface manner, "With soft low tongue and lowly courtesy," defines inner character, marks the "lady" as "feminine." The importance of soft-spokenness as an essential attribute of femininity is suggested by King Lear's lament over his dead Cordelia: "Her voice was ever soft, / Gentle and low, an excellent thing in woman" (5.3.274-75). In a culture that tended to see things in opposition, to split mind and body, virgin and whore, the quiet woman represented the positive side of the opposition. The woman who spoke up or out, the angry woman, represented the negative side. At a moment when Hamlet feels the greatest con-

tempt for himself, he mourns that he "must, like a whore, unpack . . . [his] heart with words / And fall a-cursing like a very drab" (2.2.592-93). When Bartholomew appears dressed as a lady and Christopher Sly wonders why the page addresses him as "lord" rather than "husband," Bartholomew answers:

> My husband and my lord, my lord and
>   husband,
> I am your wife in all obedience.
>
>   (Ind. 2.106-7)

The male fantasy that underlies this exchange is that a wife will be subject, even subservient, to her husband in all matters.

More subtly suggested as attractive in the Induction is a notion of sexuality associated with the violent, the predatory, the sadistic. The Lord immediately directs that the drunken Christopher Sly be carried to bed in his "fairest chamber," which is to be hung round with all his "wanton pictures" (Ind. 1.46-47). After Sly is promised all the requisites for hunting, including hawks that "will soar / Above the morning lark" and greyhounds "as swift / As breathèd stags, . . . fleeter than the roe" (Ind. 2.43-48), he is offered the most desirable paintings. The movement from hunting to the predatory sexuality imaged in the pictures makes obvious the association between hunting and the sexual chase. Sly is promised by the Second Servingman:

> Adonis painted by a running brook
> And Cytherea all in sedges hid,
> Which seem to move and wanton with her
>   breath
> Even as the waving sedges play with wind.

And the other men join in the game, revealing their own erotic fantasies:

> *Lord.* We'll show thee Io as she was a maid
> And how she was beguiled and surprised,
> As lively painted as the deed was done.
> *Third Servingman.* Or Daphne roaming
>   through a thorny wood,
> Scratching her legs that one shall swear she
>   bleeds,
> And at that sight shall sad Apollo weep,
> So workmanly the blood and tears are
>   drawn.
>
>   (Ind. 2.50-60)

Suggestions of violence, particularly of rape, underlie all of these images. The figures the paintings depict are among the familiar ones in Ovid's *Metamorphoses*: Adonis, the beautiful, androgynous youth gored to death on a wild boar's tusks; Io, a maid Zeus transformed into a heifer in order to take her; and Daphne, who was changed into a laurel tree to prevent Apollo's raping her. The images of violence intensify, as though each character's imagination sets off a darker dream in another. Interestingly enough, the story of Adonis is drawn the least bloody though it is inherently more so. It is Daphne, the innocent virgin, who bleeds. It would seem that the most predatory and sadistic impulse calls forth the most compelling eroticism for those who participate in the shared creation of these fantasies.

It is appropriate that *The Taming of the Shrew* is acted for the male characters of the Induction, for its view of women and sexuality is attuned to their pleasure. Underlying the notion of heterosexual relationships in *Taming*, especially marriage, is that one partner must dominate. There can be no mutuality. The male fantasy that the play defends against is the fear that

a man will not be able to control his woman. Unlike many of Shakespeare's comedies, *Taming* does not project the fear of cuckoldry (though perhaps it is implicit), but rather a more pervasive anxiety and need to dominate and subject. In taming Kate, Petruchio seems to give comfort to all the other men in the play. Before Hortensio marries the Widow, he goes to visit Petruchio, to see his "taming school," which Tranio describes to Bianca:

> Petruchio is the
> master,
> That teacheth tricks eleven and twenty long
> To tame a shrew and charm her chattering
> tongue.
>
> (4.2.56-58)

However pleasant the idea of a "taming school" may

From Act III, scene ii, Petruchio and Katherina at the Baptista house.

be for men, the attitude it implies toward women is appalling.

From the outset, Kate is set up so that her "taming" will be acceptable, will not seem merely cruel. This strategy serves as a means to release the play's misogyny just as madness allows Hamlet, Othello, and Lear to castigate the women who love them—their mothers, daughters, lovers, wives—and rail against them and women in general in shocking ways. In the play's only soliloquy, Petruchio delineates his plan to subject Kate:

> Thus have I politicly begun my reign,
> And 'tis my hope to end successfully.
> My falcon now is sharp and passing empty,
> And till she stoop she must not be full
>   gorged,
> For then she never looks upon her lure.
> Another way I have to man my haggard,
> To make her come and know her keeper's
>   call,
> That is, to watch her as we watch these kites
> That bate and beat and will not be obedient.
> She eat no meat today, nor none shall eat.
> Last night she slept not, nor tonight she shall
>   not.
> As with the meat, some undeserved fault
> I'll find about the making of the bed,
> And here I'll fling the pillow, there the
>   bolster,
> This way the coverlet, another way the
>   sheets.
> Ay, and amid this hurly I intend
> That all is done in reverent care of her,
> And in conclusion she shall watch all night.
> And if she chance to nod I'll rail and brawl
> And with the clamor keep her still awake.
> This is a way to kill a wife with kindness,
> And thus I'll curb her mad and headstrong
>   humor.
> He that knows better how to tame a shrew,
> Now let him speak—'tis charity to show.
>   (4.1.182-205)

Petruchio's stringent mode is just that used to tame hawks; it might well come from a manual on falconry. The notion behind this central metaphor of the play is that a shrewish woman is less than human, even less than a woman, so may be treated like an animal. Only the audience's acceptance of this premise allows them to feel the play as comic.

Critics' efforts to dismiss the play's harsh attitude toward women, to disclaim its cruelty, have led them to emphasize that *Taming* is a farce and not to be taken with the kind of seriousness that I am taking it. In other words, to pay attention to its cruelty, to give credence to its misogyny, is to misread its genre. Though *Taming* does not feel to me like farce, I do not wish to argue about its genre. Accepting it for the moment as farce, I would ask rather: Could the taming of a "shrew" be considered the proper subject of farce in any but a misogynist culture? How would we feel about a play entitled *The Taming of the Jew* or *The Taming of the Black*? I think we would be embarrassed by anti-Semitism or racism in a way that many of us are not by misogyny. I do not think critics could imagine writing about those fictitious plays a sentence comparable to this written of *The Taming of the Shrew* [by Robert B. Heilman, in an introduction to *The Taming of the Shrew*]: "Once she [Kate] was naturally and unquestionably taken to be a shrew, that is, *a type of woman widely known in life* and constantly represented in song and story [*italics mine*]."

To be sure, Kate is an angry woman. She threatens violence to Hortensio; ties Bianca up and strikes her; breaks a lute over Hortensio's head when he, in disguise, is trying to teach her to play it; beats Grumio; and strikes Petruchio. Yet what is said about her makes her worse than angry. When Hortensio refers to her as "Katherine the curst," Grumio echoes him and makes clear how intolerable a "shrewish" woman is to the men in the play:

> Katherine the curst!
> A title for a maid of all titles the worst.
>   (1.2.128-29)

Gremio refers to her at various moments as a whore (1.1.55), a "fiend of hell" (1.1.88), and a "wildcat" (1.2.196). The other men repeat his sentiments. "Shrewd," "curst," "froward," Kate is mainly noticeable for her "scolding tongue." Many of the impressions of Kate are rendered through Gremio and Hortensio, who are the most threatened by her. Gremio insists that no man would marry her, only a devil would, and asks incredulously, "Think'st thou, Hortensio, though her father be very rich, any man is so very a fool to be married to hell?" When Hortensio affirms that there are "good fellows in the world" who will marry her for enough money, Gremio replies, "I cannot tell, but I had as lief take her dowry with this condition, to be whipped at the high cross every morning" (1.1.123-34). Hortensio confesses to Petruchio that though Kate is young, beautiful, and well brought up,

> Her only fault—and that is fault enough—
> Is that she is intolerable curst!
> And shrewd and froward, so beyond all
>   measure
> That were my state far worser than it is,
> I would not wed her for a mine of gold.
>   (1.2.87-91)

Even Baptista accuses Kate of having a "devilish spirit" (2.1.26).

We come to understand, perhaps, that Kate does not deserve this kind of denunciation, that the male characters rail so against her because she refuses to follow patriarchal prescriptions for women's submission to men. When Bianca, so praised and desired for her "beauteous modesty" (1.2.233-34), rejects Hortensio, he immediately denounces her as a "proud disdainful haggard" (4.2.39). This sudden reversal suggests that the men see women only in relation to male desires and needs and describe them accordingly. Yet we only glimpse the way their bias works. Shakespeare does not reveal it so obviously as he does in, say, *Antony and Cleopatra*, where the men who degrade and insult Cleopatra are clearly threatened by her and jealous because she is able to seduce Antony away from them.

Shakespeare also adumbrates circumstances that account for Kate's anger. The preference of everyone around her, including her father, for a quiet woman (in other words, a woman without any spirit) is enough to provoke her. She undoubtedly understands the high value placed on women's silence, which Lucentio reads, in Bianca for example, as a sign of "maid's mild behavior and sobriety" (1.1.70-71). She, of course, understands Bianca's competitiveness with her, which is acted out with passive aggression: "Her silence flouts me and I'll be revenged" (1.1.29). She also chafes at her certain sense that she is men's possession, a pawn in the patriarchal marriage game. She reproaches Baptista about Bianca:

> Now I see
> She is your treasure, she must have a
>   husband;
> I must dance barefoot on her wedding day,
> And, for your love to her, lead apes in hell.
> Talk not to me; I will go sit and weep
> Till I can find occasion of revenge.
>
> (2.1.31-36)

Though Baptista tells Petruchio that he must obtain Kate's love before he will give his permission for the two to marry (2.1.128-29), when it comes down to it, Kate is simply married off, bargained over like a piece of goods:

> *Baptista.* Faith, gentleman, now I play a
>   merchant's part
> And venture madly on a desperate mart.
> *Tranio.* 'Twas a commodity lay fretting by
>   you;
> 'Twill bring you gain or perish on the seas.
> *Baptista.* The gain I seek is quiet in the
>   match.
>
> (2.1.319-23)

She is not a woman to accommodate easily an economy that makes her a possession of men, in which a husband can say of a wife:

> I will be master of what is mine own.
> She is my goods, my chattels; she is my
>   house,
> My household stuff, my field, my barn,
> My horse, my ox, my ass, my anything.
>
> (3.2.229-32)

Shakespeare also allows Kate to claim her anger and gives her a moving explanation of her outspokenness:

> My tongue will tell the anger of my heart,
> Or else my heart, concealing it, will break,
> And rather than it shall I will be free
> Even to the uttermost, as I please, in words.
>
> (4.3.77-80)

Yet what is said or shown to extenuate Kate does not weigh heavily enough to balance the condemnation of her, which is an effort to prepare us to accept Petruchio's humiliation of her as a necessity, or "for her own good."

Kate and Petruchio are both strong-willed and high spirited, and one of Petruchio's admirable qualities is that he has the good sense to see Kate's passion and energy as attractive. When he hears of her tempestuous encounter with Hortensio, he exclaims:

> Now, by the world, it [sic] is a lusty wench!
> I love her ten times more than e'er I did.
> O how I long to have some chat with her!
>
> (2.1.160-62)

Presumably Petruchio puts on an act to tame Kate; he pretends to be more shrew than she (4.1.81). As one of his servants says, "He kills her in her own humor" (4.1.174). But Kate's "shrewishness" only allows Petruchio to bring to the surface and exaggerate something that is in him to begin with. When we first see him, he is bullying his servant—wringing him by the ears, the stage direction tells us—so that Grumio cries, "Help, masters, help! My master is mad" (1.2.18). It surprises only a little that he later hits the priest who marries him, throws sops in the sexton's face, beats his servants, and throws the food and dishes—behaves so that Gremio can exclaim, "Why, he's a devil, a devil, a very fiend" (3.2.154). When he appears for his wedding "a very monster in apparel," we learn that his dress is not wholly out of character; Tranio tells Biondello:

> 'Tis some odd humor pricks him to this
>   fashion,
> Yet oftentimes he goes but mean-appareled.
>
> (3.2.72-73)

The strategy of the plot allows Petruchio "shrewish" behavior; but even when it is shown latent in his character and not a result of his effort to "tame"

Kate, it is more or less acceptable. Dramatically, then, Kate and Petruchio are not treated equally.

In general, whatever is problematic in Petruchio is played down; whereas Kate's "faults" are played up. For example, we tend to forget how crassly Petruchio puts money before love at the beginning of the play since he becomes attracted to Kate for other reasons. He speaks frankly:

> I come to wive it wealthily in Padua;
> If wealthily, then happily in Padua.
>
> (1.2.4-75)

And Grumio assures Hortensio in the most negative terms that money will be Petruchio's basic requirement in a wife:

> Nay, look you sir, he tells you flatly what his mind is. Why, give him gold enough and marry him to a puppet or an aglet-baby or an old trot with ne'er a tooth in her head, though she have as many diseases as two-and-fifty horses. Why, nothing comes amiss so money comes withal.
>
> (1.2.76-81)

No one in the play speaks against this kind of materialism; indeed, it seems to be the order of the day.

Kate's humbling begins from the moment Petruchio meets her. Petruchio immediately denies a part of her *self*, her identity as an angry woman. Just as the Lord of the Induction will make Christopher Sly "no less than what we say he is" (Ind. 1.71), so Petruchio will begin to turn Kate into his notion of her. Yet because her will and spirit meet his, the absurdity of his finding Kate "passing gentle" (2.1.235-45) and his elaboration of that idea is more humorous than not. It is when Petruchio begins to give Kate ultimatums, which I know he can and will enforce, that the play begins to give me a sinking feeling:

>   Setting all this chat aside,
> Thus in plain terms: your father hath consented
> That you shall be my wife, your dowry 'greed on,
> And will you, nill you, I will marry you.
>
> . . . . .
>
> For I am he am born to tame you, Kate,
> And bring you from a wild Kate to a Kate
> Conformable as other household Kates.
>
> (2.1.261-71)

The reason I begin to lose heart at this point is that I am certain Kate will not be able to hold her own against Petruchio. The lack of suspense is crucial to my response. I know that an angry woman cannot survive here. When I read or see *Macbeth* or *The Merchant of Venice*, though I know the witches' prophecies will come true to defeat Macbeth and that Portia will trick Shylock out of his pound of flesh, I always feel the power of the contest. But not in *Taming*.

After Kate and Petruchio are married and go to Petruchio's house in act 4, the play loses its humor for me. The change in tone follows partly from the fact that Petruchio's control over Kate becomes mainly physical. In Padua, the pair fights mainly through language, a weapon that Kate can wield as well as Petruchio. When Kate strikes Petruchio in the city, he swears he will hit her back if she does it again (2.1.218). Though he deserves slapping in the country, she cannot risk that there. While Petruchio never strikes her, he tries to intimidate her by hitting the servants and throwing food and dishes at them. The implication is that if she does not behave, he will do the same to her. Petruchio's physical taming of Kate is objectionable in itself; it is particularly humiliating because it is "appropriate" for animals, not people. Petruchio's description of his plan to tame Kate has no humor in it; related in soliloquy, it has the sound of simple explanation.

Kate's isolation in the country among Petruchio and men who are bound to do his bidding creates an ominous atmosphere. Her aloneness is heightened by the fact that even Grumio is allowed to tease her, and her plight becomes the gossip of Petruchio's servants. Her humiliation has a sexually sadistic tinge since there is always the possibility that Petruchio will rape her, as he threatens earlier:

> For I will board her though she chide as loud
> As thunder when the clouds in autumn crack.
>
> (1.2.93-95)

Petrucho's notion of sexual relations here is worthy of Iago, who says of Othello's elopement, "Faith, he tonight hath boarded a land carack" (*Othello* 1.2.49). Grumio immediately tells Hortensio, "'A my word and she knew him as well as I do, she would think scolding would do little good upon him. . . . I'll tell you what, sir, and she stand him but a little, he will throw a figure in her face and so disfigure her with it that she will have no more eyes to see withal than a cat" (1.2.107-14). He suggests that Petruchio can out-scold and outwit Kate, but he also implies, through particularly violent imagery, that Petruchio will use force if necessary. Petruchio even tells Baptista, "I am rough and woo not like a babe" (2.1.137).

When we hear that Petruchio is in Kate's bedroom "making a sermon of continency to her" (4.1.176), I imagine that he is obviously acting contrary (his favorite mode), preaching abstinence when he might be expected to want to consummate his marriage. I have also wondered whether we are supposed to imagine that Kate has hoped to please him by offering herself sexually. Or does she actually desire him? Is the play reinforcing the male fantasy that the more a man beats and abuses a woman the more she will fawn on him? But the episode is probably related mainly to assure us that Petruchio does not rape Kate, since we have been led to think he might. A play within a play, *The Taming of the Shrew* is enacted to crown Christopher Sly's evening. I think it is intended to have the same salacious appeal as are the paintings proposed for his enjoyment.

Kate and Petruchio's accord is possible only because Kate is finally willing to give up or pretend to give up her sense of reality—which *is* reality—for Petruchio's whimsy. He will do nothing to please Kate until she becomes willing to go along with him in everything, including agreeing that the sun is the moon. When she will not, he stages a temper tantrum: "Evermore crossed and crossed, nothing but crossed!" (4.5.10). Eager to visit Padua, she gives over to him in lines that can only be rendered with weariness:

> Forward, I pray, since we have come so far,
> And be it moon or sun or what you please.
> And if you please to call it a rush-candle,
> Henceforth I vow it shall be so for me.
>
> (4.5.12-15)

What follows is one instance after another of Petruchio's testing Kate's subjection to him.

One of the most difficult aspects of the play for me is the way the women are set against each other at the end. Kate and Bianca have been enemies from the beginning, but now the Widow takes sides against Kate, calling her a "shrew" (5.2.28). Kate's famous speech on wifely duty is addressed to the widow as a reproach. The men use their wives to compete with each other:

> *Petruchio.* To her, Kate!
> *Hortensio.* To her, widow!
>
> (5.2.33-34)

Betting on whose wife is the most obedient, the men stake their masculinity on their wives' compliance. A friendly voice will be raised against this kind of wager in *Cymbeline*, but not here. Only the Widow and Bianca, who will subsequently become "shrews," demur. When Kate throws her cap under foot at Petruchio's direction, the Widow remarks, "Lord, let me never have a cause to sigh / Till I be brought to such a silly pass"; and Bianca queries, "Duty call you this?" When Lucentio reproaches Bianca for costing him

five hundred crowns, she replies, "The more fool you for laying on my duty" (5.2.123-29). Though the Widow and Bianca are hateful characters, I find myself in sympathy with them. The ending of the play simply goes awry for me.

Kate's final speech may be taken straight, as a sign that she has "reformed"; or it may be taken ironically, as though she mocks Petruchio. The happiest view of it is that Kate and Petruchio perform this final act together, to confound those around them and win the bet. Even if we accept this last interpretation, I cannot take pleasure in Kate's losing her voice. In order to prosper, she must speak patriarchal language. The Kate we saw at the beginning of the play has been silenced. In one sense, it does not matter whether she believes what she is saying, is being ironical, or is acting: her words are those that satisfy men who are bent on maintaining patriarchal power and hierarchy. For them, Kate's obedience, in Petruchio's words, bodes

> peace . . . and love, and quiet life,
> An awful rule and right supremacy;
> And . . . what not that's sweet and happy.
>
> (5.2.108-10)

For Kate, it means speaking someone else's language, losing a part of her identity. She no longer engages in the high-spirited play of wit that was characteristic of her when Petruchio first met her (2.1.182-259).

If I stand farther back from the play, it seems even less comic. It is significant that *Taming* is a play within a play: "not a comontie a Christmas gambold or a tumbling trick" or "household stuff," but "a kind of history" (Ind. 2.137-42). It seems to carry the same weight as *The Murder of Gonzago* in *Hamlet* or the rustics' dramatization of *Pyramus and Thisbe* in *A Midsummer Night's Dream*. The pithy truth that *Taming* contains implies a kind of heterosexual agony. It is noticeable that just before the play begins, the Induction calls attention to the fact that the Page, though pretending to be a woman, is actually a man. Convinced that he is a lord and that the Page is his wife, Sly wants to take his "wife" to bed. The Page begs off, claiming the physicians have said that lovemaking would be dangerous for Sly, and adds: "I hope this reason stands for my excuse." Picking up the double meaning attendant on the similarity of pronunciation between "reason" and "raising," Sly continues the phallic pun: "Ay, it stands so that I may hardly tarry so long" (Ind. 2.125-25). The source of Sly's desire is ambiguous: Is it the woman the Page pretends to be, or is it the man the Page reveals he is? Perhaps they are the same: a man in drag. In any case, the breaking of aesthetic distance here asks us to recognize that we are watching a homosexual couple watch the play. From their angle of vision, *Taming* affirms how problematic heterosexual relations are, especially marriage. The fault would seem to lie with women, who are all "shrews" at heart. If a man aspires to live in harmony with a woman, he must be like Petruchio (a comic version of Hotspur) and able to "tame" her. If he is gentle, like Lucentio, he will undoubtedly become the victim of a shrewish wife. This is not a happy view of women; it is an equally unhopeful vision of love and marriage.

Even though there may be ambiguities at the conclusion of Shakespeare's comedies, they are most joyous when couples join with the prospect of a happy marriage before them. In order for marriage to be hopeful in Shakespeare, women's power must be contained or channeled to serve and nurture men. When it is—in *As You Like It, Twelfth Night,* or *A Midsummer Night's Dream*—the comic ending is celebratory. When it is not, in *The Merchant of Venice* or *Love's Labor's Lost,* the tone of the ending is less buoyant, even discordant. In *Love's Labor Lost,* when women remain in power and set the terms of marriage, it is implied that something is not right. Berowne comments:

> Our wooing doth not end like an old play;
> Jack hath not Jill. These ladies' courtesy
> Might well have made our sport a comedy.
> (5.2.872-74)

When the King insists that it will end in "a twelve-month and a day," after the men have performed the penances their ladies have stipulated, Berowne replies, "That's too long for a play." The final songs contain references to cuckoldry, and their closing note is on "greasy Joan" stirring the pot. What is different about the movement toward a comic ending in *Taming* is that women are set ruthlessly against each other, Kate's spirit is repressed, and marriage is made to seem warfare or surrender at too high a price.

Taming is responsive to men's psychological needs, desires, and fantasies at the expense of women. It plays to an audience who shares its patriarchal assumptions: men and also women who internalize patriarchal values. As someone who does not share those values, I find much of the play humorless. Rather than making me laugh, it makes me sad or angry. Its intended effect is spoiled. It is not only that I do not share the play's values, but also that I respond as a woman viewer and reader and do not simply respond according to my sense of Shakespeare's intention or try to adopt an Elizabethan perspective (assuming I *could*). I stand outside of the community the joke is intended to amuse; I sympathize with those on whom the joke is played.

I understand that within the tradition of shrew stories, Shakespeare's version is more generous of spirit

and more complex than other such stories. But *Taming* seems dated. I think that it is interesting historically—in tracing a tradition, in understanding sixteenth-century attitudes toward women—and that it is significant as part of Shakespeare's canon, as any work of his is. But limiting its importance this way, I imply that I find it less good than many of his comedies. And I do. If I went to see it, it would be out of curiosity, to find out how someone in our time would direct it.

Shakespeare continually depicts in comedy an infertile world in which lovers are separated; the task of the play is to restore the world by bringing lovers together. In several instances, he presents characters who are "man-haters" or "woman-haters" and unites them. Benedick and Beatrice, Hippolyta and Theseus are examples; Kate and Petruchio are forerunners of these couples. Interestingly enough, Shakespeare never again shows a woman treated so harshly as Kate except in tragedy. I think that Shakespeare either began to see the world differently or that he recognized the story of Kate and Petruchio did not quite work. Most significantly, he obviously enjoyed portraying witty women characters, and he must have seen that it was preferable to leave their spirits untamed.

APPEARANCE VS. REALITY

Contradictions between appearance and reality constitute a central issue in *The Taming of the Shrew* and figure in many discussions of the play's other themes and of the development of its characters. In 1963, **Cecil C. Seronsy**, in an essay excerpted below, asserted that its structural unity derives from the playwright's ingenious development of the theme of "supposes." Petruchio, the critic contended, succeeds in transforming Katherina by "supposing" that her appearance of shrewishness does not represent her "real" nature. Seronsy links this theme of transformation in the main plot to the string of deceptions in the subplot and the failure of the other bridegrooms to effect similar transformations in their brides. Four years later, **Irving Ribner** examined the play's use of contrasts between appearance and reality as part of his argument that in the play Shakespeare critiques two common Elizabethan views of courtship and marriage. In this essay, also excerpted below, Ribner traced the theme of "deceptive identities" in the Induction, the subplot, and the main action of the play. In the end, he contended, both the "romantic" marriage of Lucentio and Bianca and the more traditional, male-dominated relationship of Petruchio and Katherina are shown to be illusions.

Other critics who have addressed this theme in depth include Maynard Mack and Sears Jayne. In a 1962 essay, Mack asserted that Petruchio imitates Katherina's rude and willful behavior so that she may see for herself the effect it has on others. At the same time, the critic argued, Petruchio thrusts on Katherina the likeness of a modest, well-behaved young woman, so that she may recognize "what she may become if she tries." Four years later, Jayne interpreted the dramatic events following the opening scenes of the play as Sly's wish-fulfilling dream. This approach to the play, he suggested, helps explain the Induction's emphasis on dreaming, the many instances of pretense and supposing throughout the comedy, and "the extraordinarily close connection" between what Petruchio accomplishes and what the tinker himself wants: financial security and domination over women.

Discrepancies between appearance and reality also play important roles in the analyses of **Harold Goddard** (in the section on KATHERINA), **George R. Hibbard** (in the GENDER ROLES section) and **Richard Henze** (in the section on GAMES AND ROLE-PLAYING). For a brief discussion of the relationship between the theme of appearance versus reality and the play's use of clothing images, see the excerpt from **Norman Sanders**'s essay in the section on IMAGERY.

Cecil C. Seronsy

SOURCE: "'Supposes' as the Unifying Theme in 'The Taming of the Shrew," in *Shakespeare Quarterly*, Vol. XIV, No. 1, Winter, 1963, pp. 15-30.

[Seronsy asserts that the structural unity of The Taming of the Shrew *derives from Shakespeare's ingenious development of the theme of "supposes," which he found in the source of his subplot. The fullest expression of this theme is in the main action, he maintains, where with unusual insight Petruchio supposes qualities in Katherina that no other character, possibly not even she, has ever suspected existed. His "shrew-taming" method enables him to recover Katherina's "real nature." In developing his argument, the critic examines parallels and contrasts between the failure of the "apparent" tutors Hortensio and Lucentio to mold their brides and the success of Petruchio, the "real" teacher of the play, in transforming Katherina.]*

I believe that the unity of Shakespeare's comedy goes much deeper than the mere fitting and joining of the various plots, and I question whether the shrew theme is the principal instrument of this organization of parts. Instead, the subplot, with its theme of "supposes" which enters substantially into both the shrew action and the induction, appears to offer a better explanation—one which will account in large measure for Shakespeare's superior handling of all three elements of the plot. If one is to judge by the way the subplot has in most discussions been somewhat lightly dismissed or at least has been given relatively little

emphasis, the likelihood appears that the full significance of the idea behind "supposes", with its possibilities for dramatic enlargement, has been overlooked. There is no reason to assume that the word "supposes" itself must be limited now or in sixteenth-century usage to mean only "substitutions" of characters for one another in a mere mechanical routine of outward disguise. For Elizabethans it had substantially the same values in meaning as it has for us: "supposition", "expectation", "to believe", "to imagine", "to guess", "to assume". If we keep before us this wider sense of the word, it is not difficult to see how it becomes a guiding principle of Petruchio's strategy in winning and taming the shrew, and it may well be the key to what Mark Van Doren notes as our secret occupation in observing the stages by which Petruchio and Katherina "surrender to the fact of their affection" [in *Shakespeare*, 1939].

The subplot goes back to George Gascoigne's *The Supposes*, a translation in 1566 of Ariosto's *I Suppositi* . . . . Shakespeare . . . greatly enlarges upon the game of "supposes" even in the very plot of that name derived from Gascoigne. Although Baptista in his first speech makes it clear that old Gremio and Hortensio are Bianca's only suitors, which in itself proves to be a false supposal, Shakespeare, by risking the disguising of Hortensio with all its entailing inconsistencies in plot, may have wanted to place him in a parallel situation with the other serious suitor Lucentio as a supposed tutor in order to compound the mischief, even though Hortensio does not remain long in the field and at the end of the lesson scene already gives clear signs of relinquishing his suit. (Gremio, as the *old* suitor, is obviously too much a traditionally stock comic character out of Roman comedy to enter this competition.) Both serious young rivals, Lucentio and Hortensio, deliberately make themselves supposed tutors, producing a situation that does not exist in either *A Shrew* [a play similar to Shakespeare's printed in 1594] or *The Supposes* and thereby sustaining interest and some suspense in the subplot until the shrew-taming plot gets under way. It is this circumstance more than any other that makes Shakespeare's sub-plot so much more lively and interesting than its counterpart in *A Shrew*. And it is this emphasis upon the school administered by two lovers, supposed tutors, that by a comic irony prepares the way for the "taming school" to come, administered by Petruchio, not supposed a teacher at all. Petruchio turns out to be a real tutor, to whom Hortensio himself goes to school, as does even Lucentio in the last act of the play. And Bianca, the ready scholar in the supposed school under the direction of the two rivals, contrasts sharply with Katharina who repulses her tutor. Yet finally Bianca, supposedly mild and tractable, also in a sense goes to school, to her sister Katharina, supposed intractable, to learn obedience. It is this fine joining of the two plots, along lines suggested by the "supposes" theme, which is missed entirely by *A Shrew*. And with it is missed this delightfully ironic turn at the close of Shakespeare's play. There is some significance too in the way Petruchio is made to link the two plots together by his sponsoring Hortensio as supposed tutor, just as Gremio sponsors Lucentio, while we are shortly to see Petruchio himself engaging in a game of "supposes" that goes much deeper than theirs. In Petruchio's "taming" of Katharina we see this game most triumphantly played.

Both Petruchio and Katharina in the process of learning from each other make subtle adjustments in attitude. His motive for marriage is at first wealth, yet, while that remains an important consideration, he comes to see that she possesses other qualities which make her worth the trouble of winning over. These evidences of Katharina's real nature as against her supposed temperament, are present in the first scene with her father. Petruchio sees these traits and hits

upon a novel method of bringing them into realization. One of Shakespeare's happiest strokes . . . is to exhibit Petruchio's own system of tutoring and thus closely relate the themes of shrew-taming and supposes. Petruchio's method is to suppose (and he is correct) or assume qualities in Katharina that no one else, possibly even the shrew herself, ever suspects. What he assumes as apparently false turns out to be startlingly true. His "treatment" is a steady unfolding of her really fine qualities: patience, practical good sense, a capacity for humor, and finally obedience, all of which she comes gradually to manifest in a spirit chastened but not subdued. There can be no question about the justice of his tactics, if measured by the end product, for he enables her first to see herself as others see her, and then, her potentiality for humor and self-criticism having been brought out, she is able to discover in herself those qualities he is so sure she possesses. He is a superb teacher whose method is not unknown to many another teacher. And, since

From Act III, scene ii, Petruchio and Katherina and others, including Tranio, Baptista, and Grumio.

his system of make-believe is a profounder one than that effected in the more conventional, superficial, and mechanical disguises of the inherited subplot, there emerges a lively and pointed contrast between the two sets of complications. For, whereas in the subplot, although the theme of supposes is to some extent already enriched and deepened in Shakespeare's play, supposition is still based for the most part upon intrigue and the purely physical circumstances of name, situation, and the like, here in the shrew plot the supposition represents a deeper, more conscious effort, the will to believe and make real and establish beyond cavil what everyone else fails to see. The distinction is one between outer circumstance and inner conviction, a kind of triumph of mind or personality over a world of stubborn outward "fact" not quite so real as had been supposed. . . .

At her very first appearance (I. i) Katharina makes it clear that she will resist all attempts to make her anything other than what she thinks she is. Assumed to be a shrew, she will not change; so great is the power of suggestion upon her. She will not be made a "stale amongst these mates" [I. i. 58], though Hortensio punningly tells her that no mates are possible unless she becomes gentler and milder. She bitterly resents being "appointed hours" on what proves, however, to be a false supposition about her powers: "as though, belike, I knew not what to take, and what to leave, ha?" [I. i. 103-04]. All this whets our interest in Petruchio's forthcoming tactics of transforming her. In the following scene Baptista has almost given up hope that Katharina will ever marry, "Supposing it a thing impossible" [I. ii. 123], as Hortensio says, but this turns out to be a false "suppose". On the other hand, Petruchio at that moment is just as confident that he can woo and tame her, and thereby accomplish the supposedly impossible. He who has heard the stormy sea raging like a lion and the thunder of artillery on the field of battle is not to be daunted by "a little din" [I. ii. 199] coming from a woman's tongue. His method begins to take shape even before he meets her: he will suppose the shrew's raging as negligible or non-existent simply by refusing to hear it. Soon he will meet her and then proceed from this negative mode of not positing (or supposing) *bad* traits in her to the positive supposing of such *good* traits in her as gentleness, good humor, patience, and obedience, which have not yet come to the surface. Already he seems to have an insight, lacking in her father, her sister, and others, into the potential existence of these finer qualities in Katharina.

This sharper insight emerges in (1) his first visit to Baptista and (2) his first interview alone with Katharina, both in Act II. For in his opening speech to the father, still having not yet seen the daughter (note how skillfully suspense is accumulated by allowing the audience to watch the building up of Petruchio's design), he asks [II. i. 42-3], "Pray, have you not a daughter / Call'd Katharina, fair and virtuous?" He goes on to extol the young woman for her reported beauty, wit, affability, bashful modesty, and mildness—purely fictionalized qualities as yet, so far as anyone knows. His humor is to proceed with her *as if* these *were* existent traits in her, as indeed in the testing they later prove to be. He jauntily assures Baptista that the obtaining of his daughter's love will be no task at all, and when he hears Hortensio's account of Katharina's striking him with the lute, he interprets even this action favorably, as a sign of her being "a lusty wench" and he longs "to have some chat with her" [II. i. 160, 162]. All her actions, whether or not objectionable, are to be assimilated into the image he wills and imposes. And, when alone, waiting for her to appear, he announces in soliloquy his plan of winning her by contraries, by playing a calculated game of supposes [II. i. 170-80]:

> Say that she rail; why then I'll tell her plain
> She sings as sweetly as a nightingale;
> Say that she frown; I'll say she looks as clear
> As morning roses newly wash'd with dew:
> Say she be mute and will not speak a word;
> Then I'll commend her volubility,
> And say she uttereth piercing eloquence:
> If she do bid me pack, I'll give her thanks,
> As though she bid me stay by her a week:
> If she deny to wed, I'll crave the day
> When I shall ask the banns and when be
>   married.

Then immediately upon her coming to him, he puts his system of make-believe to work. He assumes familiarity by addressing her as "Kate" and smothers her angry remonstrances by adding that his "Kate" is "plain", "bonny", "sometimes Kate the curst" [II. i. 186], but "pretty" withal, "super-dainty", and possessed of mildness. Then follows the punning wit-combat, from which it is clear that he has taken her measure, most certainly as she has not his. In this exchange the many mutual animal epithets that fly between them are a key to the extent of this understanding of one another. Her attributions are most often wrong, his are right. Thus, her "asses are made to bear, and so are you" is an inappropriate judgment proved wrong in the sequel; his "women are made to bear, and so are you" is gentler, more playful, and more nearly valid, to say the least [II. i. 199, 200]. He is far from being the "jade" she calls him; and it can be held that more truly she buzzes like a bee, as he says, than that he acts like the buzzard (a useless hawk or stupid person), as she supposes. For him, Katharina is a "slow-wing'd turtle" and a "wasp". For her, Petruchio is a "coxcomb" and a "craven". The point here is not that Katharina comes off the worse in this wit-combat; indeed she carries on the battle on pretty equal terms with him. It is simply that in the choice and manipulation of epithets Shakespeare subtly suggests two sets of suppositions: Petruchio's, whose distortions and exaggerations are deliberate and cannily near the truth; and Katharina's, which are tinged with anger and show wrong judgment.

Petruchio next boldly exhibits to her his strategy of "supposes", which she has not yet grasped. This he does by presenting a fine series of contrasts between unflattering reports he has *heard* of her, though for the most part deliberately "supposed" (she is rough, sullen, frowning, limping), and what he has supposedly *found* in her (she is pleasant, gamesome, courteous, soft, affable, straight as the hazel-twig—indeed all the things he wants her to be, and which she is, in fact, capable of becoming). And after commending her as a very Diana, he announces that it is his destiny to tame her. By thus making veritable destiny out of his expectations, his "supposes", he is asserting the triumph of mind and character. This is reflected in his reply to the returning Baptista's asking him how successful he has been in his suit [II. i. 282-83]: "How but well, sir? how but well? / It were impossible I should speed amiss." He has, he says, found the daughter modest, contrary to all reports, and he has concluded in agreement with her, though that agreement is wholly his own "suppose", that Sunday will be their wedding-day. When at this point others in the company intervene on behalf of the now faintly protesting shrew, who is by this time clearly losing the fight, Petruchio "supposes" himself her defending champion against interlopers. Meanwhile, the game of supposes goes on merrily in the other plot, where at the end of the act, Tranio, disguised as Lucentio, has apparently won the field in behalf of his master, and now, being required to produce a father and prove his claim of supposedly great possessions, wittily says [II. i. 406-07], "I see no reason but supposed Lucentio / Must get a father, call'd 'supposed Vincentio'." The motif of "supposes" in both plots has thus been firmly established by the end of Act II.

When Katharina next appears (III. ii) she still fails to see Petruchio's game as she waits for him to arrive at the wedding, falsely supposing him to be fickle, a mere jester, and a bitter one at that. When he does come late before the assembled wedding party dressed in the most outlandish way, he acts *as if* he cannot understand why they frown at him, *as if* they saw [III. ii. 96] "some comet or unusual prodigy". But we see something real behind all this strange pretense in his declaration [III. ii. 117]: "To me she's married, not unto my clothes". It is as though the "suppose" he adopts serves to point up the reality that lies behind appearance and as though he here is whimsically rebuking them all for mistaking the shadow for the substance. Then, despite his unaccountably rude behavior in church, particularly his conduct towards the priest, and possibly on account of it, Katharina

remains quiet throughout, and we see that his "suppose" is gradually becoming reality, as evidenced in his reference to her [III. ii. 195] as "this most patient, sweet, and virtuous wife".

Although by her compliance she has born out his hard-worked hypothesis at this point, she makes, shortly after this, a last serious attempt at a showdown, when her temper flares up at his insistence, against her inclination, upon not staying for the wedding feast. For a moment he relaxes the reins by letting her think she is gaining the ascendance, and then in mocking yet basically sound supposal of her independence of others, he orders her to command that the feast is to proceed. But the bride-who-is-to-be-obeyed has falsely supposed that she is not to be commanded by her husband, and Petruchio pulls in the reins, asserting his prerogative as master and ordering her to accompany him. Finally, at the close of the scene, he once again becomes her supposed champion, this time as her rescuer from supposed "thieves", and encourages her against a supposed fear of them. It is all a masterpiece of imposed superior will.

The game goes on in Act IV with the arrival of the newly-wedded couple at the country house. Petruchio's good-humoredly bidding Katharina to be merry at a moment when she is tired and oppressed by the cold, uncomfortable journey thither, his rejection of the meat brought in to the hungry wife on the ground that he acts thus only out of solicitude for her against "choler", his reported sermon to her on continency in the bedchamber, as if she needs to be guarded against the supposed raging passions of a body already worn out with hunger and fatigue—these are all pieces of the same device he continues to employ, all supposedly "done in reverend care of her" [IV. i. 204], as he himself puts it, and all comprising, as he later confides in soliloquy [IV. i. 208], "a way to kill a wife with kindness." Even though the shrew has not yet been wholly tamed, his supposal of patience in her has led her a little earlier [IV. i. 156] to counsel this very virtue in him when he strikes the servant. She has already learned enough of that virtue which he so ardently and uncompromisingly supposes in her to begin teaching it to him.

With Tranio's announcement to Bianca in the following scene that Hortensio, heretofore supposed Licio the music teacher, having removed himself as a rival, is now intent upon winning and mastering a wealthy widow, and for that purpose has gone to Petruchio's country house, to his "taming school", the two plots are neatly brought together again. Even the servant Grumio has learned something of his master's technique, as we see (IV. iii) when he alternately offers, then withdraws her food, as if acting out of regard for her good. Petruchio, with his newly-arrived "pupil" looking on, further displays his technique in the scene with the haberdasher and tailor, when he denies Katharina the cap and gown on a trumped-up supposal that these items are unbecoming to her.

Petruchio's triumphant strategy reaches its climax on their return trip to Padua. Here his unyielding supposal converts the sun to the moon and then reverses itself, to all of which Katharina dutifully assents, while he protests that it is *he* [IV. v. 10] who is "evermore cross'd and cross'd". Next, on meeting Lucentio's real father, who is soon to encounter an impostor disguised as himself, Petruchio "disguises" the old man by sheer supposal as a young girl, then returns him to his identity as an old man. To all of this the erstwhile shrew assents, being now completely converted to her husband's supposal of things, no matter whither it leads. She now sees as he sees, and in a triumph of comic reversal she responds with a humor that redeems her from the hint, dangerously close, of abject submission. This comes first in her well-known speech of acquiescence [IV. v. 19-22]:

> But sun it is not, when you say it is not;
> And the moon changes even as your mind.
> What you will have it named, even that it is;
> And so it shall be so for Katharine.

But her master-stroke comes when, in addressing the old man "restored" to his true identity by Petruchio's whim, with still finer humor she neatly ties together *both* of her husband's two feats of make-believe in a delightful, less commonly noticed pun (italics mine). Petruchio had told her earlier in the scene [IV. v. 6-7], during the sun episode,

> Now, by my mother's *son,* and that's myself,
> It shall be moon, or star, or what I list.

Now she brilliantly concurs [IV. v. 45-9] in his reversal of the old man's identity with

> Pardon, old father, my mistaking eyes,
> That have been so bedazzled with the *sun*
> That everything I look on seemeth green:
> Now I perceive thou art a reverend father;
> Pardon, I pray thee, for my mad mistaking.

The field is now won for Petruchio, as Hortensio has already perceived. It may not be altogether fanciful to see an allusion to Katharina's gradually-won perception of things, her buoyant self-discovery, in the line "That everything I look on seemeth green". In this final encounter, she enjoys more than a half-share of the honors as the two of them enter into full partnership.

The final scene of the play presents a shrew not only tamed but enthusiastically joining her husband in the game of showing the others a profitable example of what wifely obedience can be. Victory has crowned a method in which nearly all expectations, or suppositions, have been reversed except Petruchio's. Hortensio and Lucentio, supposed masters of their wives, are not masters after all. Apparently Hortensio's apprenticeship in Petruchio's taming school did not last sufficiently long, nor was it thoroughgoing enough. Bianca and the Widow, supposedly sweet and accommodating, offer more than a trace of shrewishness themselves, whereas Katherine, the supposed shrew, is really the obedient and understanding wife. Petruchio has made of his supposal, originally fictive but later supported by an insight into the real truth of his wife's nature, a triumphant fact. The other husbands, acting on probability, on the apparently predictable outcome, find their suppositions faulty. Petruchio's is a triumph of the imagination, of a well-worked-out hypothesis, and Theseus' comment on the artisans' play in *A Midsummer Night's Dream* [V. i. 211-12] applies with equal truth to the psychological facts here: "The best in this kind are but shadows; and the worst are no worse, if imagination amend them." . . .

Irving Ribner

SOURCE: "The Morality of Farce: *The Taming of the Shrew*," in *Essays in American and English Literature Presented to Bruce Robert McElderry, Jr.,* edited by Max F. Schulz with William D. Templeman and Charles R. Metzger, Ohio University Press, 1967, pp. 165-76.

[*In* The Taming of the Shrew, *Ribner maintains, Shakespeare presents two views of marriage and ridicules both by placing them within the dramatic context of the Induction. The critic argues that the principal issue confronting Sly is "the identity of women and the true nature of the seemingly dutiful and loving wife." This theme of deceptive identity recurs throughout the Bianca-Lucentio subplot, Ribner remarks, and is most fully developed in the central action, where the effect of Petruchio's "shrew-taming" is to confuse Katherina about appearance and reality. The critic sees in the final scene of the play only an apparent return to reality. In its presentation of the Widow and Bianca as the real shrews and Katherina as "the trained dog or hawk of her master," he contends, this episode continues to offer a conventional Elizabethan view of marriage as filtered through Sly's perspective. The play's conclusion, the critic asserts, is as fanciful and idle as the tinker's sojourn in the Lord's bed chamber.*]

At the heart of Shakespeare's *Taming of the Shrew* is a coarse medieval antifeminist joke which has come down to us in several versions, the most interesting perhaps being the mid-sixteenth century ballad, *A Merry Jest of a Shrewd and Curst Wife Lapped in Morel's Skin for her good behaviour.* . . . Implicit in this story of wife-beating and submission is the notion of woman as subordinate to her husband, as much his property as the old plowhorse, Morel, in whose raw skin the errant wife of the ballad is finally wrapped. It is a view of woman . . . which Petruchio himself in Shakespeare's play clearly proclaims:

> She is my goods, my chattels; she is my
> house,
> My household stuff, my field, my barn,
> My horse, my ass, my anything
> [III. ii. 230-32]

Most critics of the play have taken these lines as an expression of Shakespeare's moral attitude, and there is usually the lame apology that he is merely expressing the common Elizabethan view for the delight of an audience to whom it was more congenial than it may be to most of us today. Geoffrey Bullough, for instance [in *Narrative and Dramatic Sources of Shakespeare, Vol I*, 1957], tells us that Shakespeare's play is "as much a social comedy preaching the subjection of women as was *A Shrew*, but its effect is more witty and civilized."

With the material of his crude ballad source Shakespeare combined the Bianca-Lucentio subplot which he took from George Gascoigne's *Supposes*. . . .

In adapting Gascoigne's early play, itself based upon a sophisticated Italian original and written for an Inns of Court audience, Shakespeare emphasized even beyond anything in his source the tradition of elegant Petrarchan love-making in which Gascoigne's story had its origins. Shakespeare removes the pregnancy of Gascoigne's heroine which is an essential part of his plot, so as to suggest a more elevated kind of love-making in which the lady's chastity must always be preserved and which must culminate in marriage. In Shakespeare's subplot the woman is not her husband's chattel to be beaten into submission by him, but a goddess upon a pedestal to be worshiped. Love is not entirely a matter of legal possession secured by marriage contracts; it is an all-embracing passion which makes the lover the slave of his mistress and which consumes him utterly until he is united with the object of his desires:

> Tranio, I burn, I pine, I perish, Tranio
> If I achieve not this young modest girl.
> [I. i. 155-56]

This, of course, is at the opposite extreme from Petruchio. The usual explanation is that the subplot was intended as a contrast which by its very absurdity enforces the contrary view of domestic felicity in the Petruchio-Kate relationship. And this view is usually regarded as fully vindicated by the supposed victory in the contest of wives with which the play ends.

Those who take this final scene in literal terms as a vindication of Petruchio's view of marriage tend to ignore the animal context in which the scene is cast. Petruchio bets upon his wife as he would upon a hawk or a hound, and his victory is that of any good trainer of dogs.

Those who might be tempted to take the Bianca-Lucentio relationship as representing a more refined view of marriage closer to Shakespeare's heart must be reminded that this marriage is based entirely upon deception and that, in spite of Lucentio's Petrarchan protestations, Shakespeare to emphasize its essential crassness must reduce it before it can be concluded to crude commercial terms not unlike those in which Petruchio courts his Kate. The supposed Lucentio, who is really Tranio in disguise, bids like a merchant against Gremio for the prize [II. i. 363 ff.]. If Petruchio is cast as the animal trainer, these lovers are reduced at last to traders at a horse sale. Bianca is merely the "commodity" which Baptista awards to the highest bidder, pending a binding legal guarantee of his bid:

> I must confess your offer is the best;
> And, let your father make her the assurance,
> She is your own; else you must pardon me.
> [II. i. 386-88]

To see in either of these love relations Shakespeare's view of marriage we must conclude that he saw the most vital of all human relations either as the act of buying an animal or as the act of beating one into submission.

But the real key to Shakespeare's moral commentary on marriage may perhaps be found in the third story with which Shakespeare combined these two. This is the old *Arabian Nights* tale of "the sleeper awakened," a folklore motif which has come down to us in many versions. What is significant about it is that it poses again the problem of the relation of appearance to reality, and this questioning of the very nature of reality in Shakespeare's play . . . is a framework in which the other two plots are set. The relations of Katherine to Petruchio and of Bianca to Lucentio are both seen as a kind of play within a play—a fantastic performance staged before an old man rendered incapable of distinguishing the true from the false. The Christopher Sly induction is absolutely essential to *The Taming of the Shrew* because it furnishes the frame of reference in which the other two plots are to be seen, and in this perspective the wooing of Kate is as absurd as the wooing of Bianca. We do not have, as some suppose, a presentation of two views of marriage, the one finally to be judged more valid than the other; we have the holding up to ridicule of two views of marriage, and as the Petruchio-Kate relation receives the greater dramatic emphasis, it is the one found most wanting.

At the same time that the Christopher Sly induction introduces its confusion between appearance and reality it relates this theme to the problem of courtship and marriage, for the most prominent thing about which Sly is confused is the identity of woman and the true nature of the seemingly dutiful and loving wife. Throughout the performance before them Sly in reality will be sitting next to Bartholomew the page who will seem to him to be the model of the loving wife ready to serve her supposed husband with

> What is't your honour will command,
> Wherein your lady and your humble wife
> May show her duty and make known her
>   love?
>
> [Induction i. 115-17]

As the play within this play opens Bartholomew appears to Sly to be all that Katherine will become as the result of her taming:

> My husband and my lord, my lord and
>   husband,
> I am your wife in all obedience
> [Induction ii. 106-07]

And the theater audience's sense of Sly's delusion will prepare it to see Petruchio's supposed victory as the same kind of delusion. When the Bianca-Lucentio subplot is introduced, again the theme of false identity appears. This entire subplot will depend upon confusion of persons. Lucentio will assume the disguise of his servant, wooing under false pretense, and when he has won his lady the final scene will reveal her not as the meek young girl he had fallen in love with, but rather as a wife as willful and as disobedient as her sister Katherine had seemed at the play's beginning. The subplot consists, of course, of a whole set of "supposes" and these are linked thematically to the induction as they are to the main plot, for Christopher Sly is as uncertain of reality and of his own identity as are the characters he is watching. Only the theater audience knows the truth, and this awareness causes it to see the self-delusion of Shakespeare's characters.

The taming of Katherine in Shakespeare's source consisted essentially of the beating of a wife into submission. In Shakespeare's play this physical element is greatly toned down, although elements of it survive. What we have instead is, in fact, the teaching of Katherine to question reality and to accept falsehood as truth, just as it is accepted by Christopher Sly. A few illustrations may suffice.

Petruchio's initial approach to Baptista is one of pretending to believe what the audience knows is false. He describes Katherine as we have already been made to see in a previous scene that she is not:

> . . . hearing of her beauty and her wit,
> Her affability and bashful modesty,
> Her wondrous qualities and mild behaviour
> [II. i. 48-50]

And as an opening gift he presents Baptista with a teacher to instruct Katherine, who we know is not "Licio, born in Mantua" as Petruchio calls him [II. i. 60], but simply the disguised Hortensio.

This deliberate pretense that falsehood is truth is maintained in his first encounter with Katherine herself:

> . . . I find you passing gentle.
> 'Twas told me you were rough and coy and
>   sullen,
> And now I find report a very liar;
> For thou art pleasant, gamesome, passing
>   courteous
>
> [II. i. 242-45]

The treatment of Katherine in Petruchio's house is largely a matter of his denying what she knows to be true until she herself is confused about reality, and this process of confusion is only completed upon the road to Padua when she is ready to agree that the sun is the moon and that a withered old man is a fair young girl, just as Christopher Sly believes that the page beside him is a loving wife.

The process of taming thus becomes a denial of truth and a destruction of that power of reason which separates man and woman from the lower animals. That its final effect is to reduce the tamed wife to the level of an animal is made clear by the very soliloquy in which Petruchio compares his "politic reign" as husband to the taming of a hawk by its master:

> My falcon now is sharp and passing empty;
> And till she stoop she must not be full-
>   gorged,
> For then she never looks upon her lure.
> Another way I have to man my haggard,
> To make her come and know her keepers'
>   call,
> That is, to watch her, as we watch those
>   kites
> That bate and beat and will not be obedient
> [IV. i. 190-96]

The animal terms of Petruchio's courtship have, in fact, been made clear from the beginning. At the end of their first encounter, he pretends to examine Kate in the terms with which a would-be purchaser would survey a horse:

> Why does the world report that Kate doth
>   limp?

O sland'rous world! Kate like the hazel twig
Is straight and slender, and as brown in hue
As hazelnuts, and sweeter than the kernels.
O, let me see thee walk: thou doest not halt
[II. i. 252-56]

Limping is a defect one looks for in horses, not in wives. To be "brown in hue" can be meritorious only in horses, for Elizabethan women were prized for the whiteness of their skins, darkness in complexion being, in fact, regarded as a sign of a lecherous disposition. When Petruchio asks that his prospective bride be paraded before him like a horse in a ring, we are being well prepared for the crude animalism of the wife-contest of the play's final scene.

In *The Taming of a Shrew* the Christopher Sly framework is maintained throughout the play, and the final scene is a return to reality in which we find Sly again a beggar out on the street. He then announces to the tapster that he has learned how to tame a shrew and will go home to practice his lesson upon his own wife. This is a fitting conclusion for the medieval antifeminist joke which is the substance of this play. Why this final episode is not in Shakespeare's play has been the subject of much debate. I do not think it necessary to suppose, as some have done, that our text represents a shortened version or is in some way corrupt. Richard Hosley has shown by an examination of all Elizabethan induction plays [in an article in *Studies in English Literature, 1500-1900*, 1961] that Shakespeare's failure to complete his was no way unusual. The answer may be that for Shakespeare to have ended his play as *A Shrew* ends might have destroyed the effect of his work which he had been building toward from the very beginning.

The complications of Shakespeare's play actually are over at the end of the first scene of the fifth act. The second scene is a kind of epilogue which serves a function similar in the total structure to what might have been served by the concluding element of the Christopher Sly story which Shakespeare omitted. It is the same kind of final summing up of the play's moral content. It is Shakespeare's substitute for a return to reality—a return to a reality which is not reality at all. The characters of the play have now seemingly abandoned their disguises, and in the contest of wives which is the chief substance of the scene we are to see what has been the result of all the action of the play—the revelation of what a true, dutiful and loving wife should be.

And what do we find? Bianca and the widow are themselves revealed as shrews and Kate is revealed as the trained hawk or dog of her master. Is this reality? By his constant stressing of false appearance Shakespeare has led us to the point where this final revelation seems as much a fancy and an idle dream as

Sly's stay in the lord's palace. We continue to see in this final scene a vision of domestic felicity such as might be seen by a beggar disguised as a lord, incapable of distinguishing man from woman and uncertain even of his own identity. Rather than the crude return to reality at the end of *The Taming of a Shrew* Shakespeare gives us a seeming return to reality which is merely the embracing by Petruchio, Lucentio and the rest of an absolute delusion. We continue to the very end of the play to see a conventional Elizabethan statement about marriage through the eyes of a Christopher Sly.

It is thus not necessary for us to forgive Shakespeare for presenting an outmoded view of marriage and to say that the play is redeemed in spite of this by its exuberance, farce, or comic characterization. The play actually ridicules two views of man's relation to woman, and in this ridicule there is important moral commentary. It is this moral commentary, in fact, which holds together the separate parts of the play and makes of it the delightful experience which it is.

GAMES AND ROLE-PLAYING

Critics have long noted the play's emphasis on role-playing; in 1839, for instance, Hermann Ulrici asserted that both the Induction and the main action of *The Shrew* dramatize the principle that people should accept the roles in life "which nature has assigned" them. More recently, Charles Brooks (1960) suggested that Katherina learns to play the role of the obedient wife not only as a way to ensure domestic harmony but also as a means by which she and Petruchio can amuse themselves at the expense of others. **Richard Henze**, in a 1970 article excerpted below, interpreted *The Shrew* as "a dramatic exploration of the nature of role playing in comedy and in life." Under Petruchio's expert direction, the critic argued, Katherina learns to play a variety of parts so proficiently that her role in her marriage becomes indistinguishable from her role in life. Two years later, Ralph Berry proposed that while the drama may be, in essence, "a fairly brutal sex farce," it is also a subtle portrayal of two people coming to terms with the "rules of the game" played between men and women. Alexander Leggatt, in a 1974 article excerpted here in the section on Petruchio, focused on the importance of literary and social conventions in the play, especially those of education, sport, and playacting. The lesson for Katherina, as well as for the audience, he asserted, is that humans are essentially conventional creatures for whom "order and pleasure are inseparable." Leggatt also suggested that the play's continual evocation of sports, particularly hunting, helps the audience to view the action as a game and thus makes Petruchio's often brutal treatment of Katherina seem more acceptable. In 1979, Marianne L. Novy suggested that games and role-playing help Katherina to come to terms with a social order that insists on male dominance and female submission.

Some critics, however, reject the concept that game-playing softens the impact of Petruchio's methods for either Katherina or the audience. **H. J. Oliver** (in the OVERVIEWS section and the PETRUCHIO section), rejected suggestions that Katherina and Petruchio are "playing a game" and contended that Katherina is a very real loser in her relationship with her husband. **Shirley Nelson Garner** (in the GENDER ROLES section) on the other hand, allowed in a 1988 essay that a joke lies at the center of the play. She argued, however, that this central joke is essentially misogynistic, and that the play is designed to amuse and entertain men who take pleasure in the subjugation of women.

Richard Henze

SOURCE: "Role Playing in *The Taming of the Shrew*," in *The Southern Humanities Review*, Vol. 4, No. 3, Summer, 1970, pp. 231-40.

[*Henze regards* The Taming of the Shrew *as a "dramatic exploration of the nature of role playing in comedy and in life." Under Petruchio's expert direction, the critic claims, Katherina learns to play a variety of parts so proficiently that her role in the marriage pageant becomes indistinguishable from that in life. On the other hand, Henze contends, Sly, Lucentio, Bianca and other characters share an inability to play multiple parts, and thus each of them has only a limited capacity to adapt to changing circumstances. Katherina's essential shrewishness, as well as Petruchio's inherent crudeness, do not change, the critic argues; rather, they become acceptable qualities because each of them is able to play, respectively, obedient wife and loving husband—complementary roles that foster harmony in their relationship.*]

The relationship between induction and play proper in *The Taming of the Shrew* has always been considered one of the play's principal problems, made more vexing by the lack of an epilogue to tie up the lordship of Sly. Various critics, reacting in various fashion, have suggested that an epilogue was never necessary, that an epilogue was lost, and that an epilogue should be recreated when the play is staged. Perhaps more important than the speculation about a possible epilogue, however, has been the attempt by recent critics who regard the play as an artistic success to show that the induction, even without an epilogue, does have a clear relationship to the rest of the play, and that the play and induction have a common unifying theme. Richard Hosley, for example [in his introduction to the Pelican edition, 1964] recognizes

parallels of appearance and reality between induction and play, and Cecil Seronsy says that the success of *The Shrew* "lies chiefly in the union of the three strands, in their having a fundamental likeness, the game of supposes or make believe"; all three plots involve "the inter-play of love and illusion, and transformation on varying levels." As far as I can determine, however, no one has fully heeded Sly's lady's suggestion that comedy is a kind of history and, therefore, that life is sometimes a kind of comedy, and treated the entire play, including the induction, as a dramatic exploration of the nature of role playing in comedy and in life. That I want to do in this paper. I intend to show that Petruchio teaches Kate that, as Jaques says in *As You Like It,*

> All the world's a stage
> And all the men and women merely players.
> They have their exits and their entrances,
> And one man in his time plays many parts
> 　　　　　　　　　　　　(II.vii.139-141)

and that he then, like an expert director, trains Kate to play roles so expertly that one cannot separate Kate's part in the pageant from Kate's function in life.

Jaques' metaphor of the World as a stage was, by the Renaissance, a commonplace idea that Shakespeare might have encountered in dozens of different places. The world was considered God's theater where men play their parts in the drama of life. . . .

In his training of Kate, Petruchio proves the metaphor by playing a series of parts, as buyer, wooer, tamer, and husband, and by directing Kate in roles as wooed maiden, wife with jealous husband, wife with tyrannous husband, and finally obedient wife with loving husband. Like Petruchio, Kate plays each part more subtly than the last until she performs so well that one, like the Lord with the actor in the induction, cannot separate actor from role:

> This fellow I remember
> Since once he play'd a farmer's eldest son.
> 'Twas where you woo'd the gentlewoman so
> 　well.
> I have forgot your name; but sure that part
> Was aptly fitted and naturally perform'd.
> 　　　　　　　　　　　　(Ind.i.83-87)

So one tends to forget that it is the shrew who is playing the obedient wife at the end of *The Taming of the Shrew* exactly because the part is so naturally performed that the shrew is the obedient wife.

Before Petruchio succeeds in turning Kate into an expert actress, however, the Lord fails to make Sly a convincing actor. After the Lord finds Sly in the gutter, he decides to help Sly play the part of a Lord:

What think you? If he were convey'd to bed,
Wrapp'd in sweet clothes, rings put upon his
    fingers,
A most delicious banquet by his bed,
And brave attendants near him when he
    wakes,
Would not the beggar then forget himself?
                                            (Ind.i.37-41)

The hunters assure the Lord that the beggar will:

> 2. *Hunt.* It would seem strange unto him
>   when he wak'd.
> *Lord.* Even as a flatt'ring dream or worthless
>   fancy.
>
>   (Ind.i.43-44)

However quickly the beggar forgets himself, and Sly decides rather quickly that he is a lord indeed, we do not forget that the beggar is only a beggar. However real Sly is to himself as lord, he is not a real lord to us; his part is not "aptly fitted and naturally perform'd" (Ind.i.87) as an effective player's part should be. Sly has sufficient imagination to think himself a lord when he sees the obvious evidence; he does not have sufficient imagination to project that image so that the audience will find it credible; he remains, consistently, Christopher Sly. Even if the Lord were not to tell us, we, like Hippolyta watching Bottom's Pyramus, would find Sly's lordship a jest.

The Taming of the Shrew, acted by the players welcomed by the Lord, begins as part of that jest and as a play, a pretense, within the pretense of Sly's role as lord. But where Sly's transformation remains a jest because of Sly's inability to play aptly a lord, *The Taming of the Shrew* becomes more than a joke; it acquires substance and meaning in spite of its apparent repetition of the medieval jest about the crude taming of a shrewish wife; and it acquires that meaning not just because Bianca is wooed and won nor because Kate is tamed, but because Kate is able to become, under Petruchio's direction, a versatile, expert actress in the pageant of life, able to play her part in a comedy of marital harmony so well that one can use the role partly to characterize the person who plays it. While watching a jest, on the other hand, one remembers all too well, even if one is not directly reminded, that the subject of the jest is being forced to play a part for which, in Sly's case especially, he may be ill-suited. That distinction between a practical joke and the comedy of life is evident not only in the contrast between Sly and Kate, who is very well-suited for her role as the obedient wife at the end of the play, but also in the contrast between Kate and Vincentio as a fair, fresh maiden and that between Kate and Bianca, the modest, shy, dutiful daughter, for all too clearly Vincentio is not a fair, fresh maiden, and Bianca, intent on playing her joke

on both Hortensio and her father, is not modest, shy, or dutiful. Kate plays her obedient wife part, on the other hand, so well that one cannot say for sure whether or not she is an obedient wife at heart; one can only say that she plays the part well enough to encourage us to imagine that she is obedient indeed. With the final success of Kate as actress and Petruchio as director, the movement of the play from jest to "a kind of history" is completed.

What Petruchio does, then, both during the wooing of Kate and the taming of Kate, is, like the Lord with Sly, to place his subject in a pageant where she will need an actor's ability to assess her role and decide how to play it. Unlike Sly, who remains a simple tinker because he lacks that ability, Kate finally learns, under the direction of Petruchio, to alter her role as the pageant of marriage and life requires.

Petruchio begins his wooing pageant by studying his role:

> I will attend her here,
> And woo her with some spirit when she
>   comes.
> Say that she rail; why, then I'll tell her plain
> She sings as sweetly as a nightingale.
>   (II.i.169-172)

Petruchio has exactly the tact that Luciana, in *The Comedy of Errors* recommends to Antipholus of Syracuse: "'Tis holy sport to be a little vain / When the sweet breath of flattery conquers strife" (III.ii.27-28); but Petruchio's words here point out more than his ability to flatter; they indicate as well his ability to play a part for the sake of effect.

Petruchio's wooing of Kate depends heavily on irony. He finds her "passing gentle," "pleasant, gamesome, passing courteous" (II.i.244-247), although he must admit that she is "as brown in hue / As hazelnuts" (II.i.256-257). The tone is gently mocking, not harsh; the language is nearly lyrical; the pose as complimentary lover is obviously a pose. Yet the very indirectness of the approach, the fact that it depends on Petruchio's ability to deliberately play the part of lover, indicates the nature of Petruchio's treatment of Kate throughout the play; he plays roles that allow her, as a fellow actress in the pageant of life, to play a complementary role as courted maiden or to misinterpret her role and disrupt the play.

Part of Petruchio's success in his role as wooer can be attributed to his willingness to allow Kate to play face-saving roles that preserve the pageant of wooing in spite of Kate's inability at the time to play the part of courted maiden. She is allowed the role of shy maiden who hides her affection in public beneath shrewishness:

'Tis bargain'd 'twixt us twain, being alone,
That she shall still be curst in company.
I tell you 'tis incredible to believe
How much she loves me.

(II.i.306-309)

Even in this allowance, however, Petruchio is beginning his instruction of the novice actress by pointing out to her that she may play multiple apparently contradictory roles as shrew and affectionate but modest maid without damage to her self as long as she recognizes that they are roles in a pageant.

Having completed the wooing of Kate, in which Petruchio plays roles of eager lover, tactful flatterer, and honest critic, he begins her taming: "For I am he am born to tame you, Kate" (II.i.278). Petruchio now overplays the possessive husband:

I will be master of what is mine own.
She is my goods, my chattels; she is my
    house,
My household stuff, my field, my barn,
My horse, my ox, my ass, my anything!

(III.ii.231-234)

The very exaggerated misapplication of the anti-coveting commandment indicates the zest with which Petruchio can play a part; the same energy he applies to his roles as tamer, wooer, and finally affectionate husband. Because Petruchio plays contradictory roles with equal effectiveness, we cannot say simply that Petruchio is a possessive husband or a tamer or a wooer any more than we can say that Kate is simply obedient or shrewish or that Baptista is simply mercenary when he holds his auction: "I play the merchant's part / And venture madly on a desperate mart" (II.i.328-329). We can say, however, that Petruchio plays each part quite well, that the roles are "aptly fitted and naturally perform'd."

On his wedding day, Petruchio plays yet another part, that of the lord turned into beggar, the reverse of Sly's role in the induction. As Tranio says, "He hath some meaning in his mad attire" (III.ii.126). That meaning is partly to point out to Kate that

To me she's married, not unto my clothes.
Could I repair what she will wear in me
As I can change these poor accoutrements,
'Twere well for Kate and better for myself.

(III.ii.119-122)

In one sense, Petruchio can repair what Kate will have in him; he can change his role from tamer to trusting husband as she changes her role from shrew to trusting wife; and that alteration can be about as easy for an expert actor like Petruchio as changing external clothing. In another sense, however, Petruchio cannot

"repair what she will wear in me / As I can change these poor accoutrements," for beneath the parts that Petruchio plays is a rather crude quality that one may perhaps define as Petruchio himself; a Petruchio who can beat his servant and a priest, who can get vulgarly drunk, who can wear rags on his wedding day without embarrassment, who can whip a horse in the mud and curse his servants, is a Petruchio who could stand refinement. But one can accept that crudeness, as one can accept Kate's shrewishness that remains her definitive quality in spite of her apparent reformation, if that crudeness or shrewishness is sufficiently disguised by roles that permit harmonious human relationships. Petruchio may be crude and an acceptable husband if he plays the part of husband well enough. Kate may be a shrew and a desirable wife if she plays well enough the obedient and affectionate wife. It is to Petruchio's credit that he recognizes in Kate the role-playing capability that she does not herself recognize. . . .

Petruchio overcomes Kate's fear, not only of playing a role other than that of shrew, but of playing the role of wife:

Kath. Husband, let's follow, to see the end of
    this ado.
Pet. First kiss me, Kate, and we will.
Kath. What, in the midst of the street?
Pet. What, art thou asham'd of me?
Kath. No, sir, God forbid! but asham'd to
    kiss.
Pet. Why then, let's home again. Come,
    sirrah, let's away.
Kath. Nay, I will give thee a kiss. Now pray
    thee, love, stay.
Pet. Is not this well?

(V.i.147-154)

This is well. With Kate and Petruchio now playing their parts well, they are able to follow cues like expert actors on a stage. While the audience watches, Kate comes at her husband's command, tramples her cap underfoot, and fetches in her reluctant prey. The beggars have forgot themselves, but they, unlike Sly, change roles willingly and successfully. When her husband plays the role of hunter and sends for her, Kate willingly plays the part of falcon and swoops after the game. Then she plays the role of ideal wife, just one part of many that she may be called upon to play if all the world is a stage and men and women merely players; but implicit in her speech, in spite of its possible irony, is Kate's trust that Petruchio would "commit his body / To painful labour both by sea and land, / To watch the night in storms, the day in cold" (V.ii.148-150) for her if he did not have the money, property, and servants that he does have. That role he is potentially capable of playing; that much he has taught her.

As the "comonty" presented to Sly becomes "a kind of history" of a complicated relationship between man and woman, it escapes the bounds of pretense that the induction first established and becomes a comic image of life. The speech by Kate at the end of the play is a serious statement echoing the homilies, themselves a large segment of Elizabethan life, and boding peace, love, quiet life, "an awful rule, and right supremacy, / And, to be short, what not that's sweet and happy" (V.ii.109-110). As the end of the play becomes serious business, the action that has accomplished that end becomes itself more serious, hardly a joke pointing out how one may wish things were. The way to a quiet life is Petruchio's way, the play indicates, not Lucentio's or Hortensio's. Lucentio gets a hypocritical goddess; Hortensio gets a mean, rich widow; Petruchio gets a wife. As Kate kisses Petruchio once again, the kiss, that has been important throughout the play, again provides the counter image to the falcon taming. It is an image of marital agreement, of affection, and of trust, an image of a relationship between husband and wife both playing roles proper for comedy.

Once one has in mind the fact that the play is about the comedy of life, the parallels between induction and play proper become obvious. The problem that Lucentio, Hortensio, Bianca, and the widow all have in common is the problem exactly of Sly, an inability to shift roles easily as the pageant of life and human relationships requires. Just as Sly is always a simple tinker whatever the surroundings, so Lucentio is always the same Lucentio, a fairly weak-kneed, imprudent young fellow too much afflicted by love-in-idleness and repent-at-leisure. Bianca, whatever the modest exterior, is too consistently the hypocritical vixen. Hortensio is consistently second-fiddle; the widow, what we see of her, mean and self-contained. All four, unable to play the varied roles that life requires, are incapable of reacting to cues that would permit a peaceful pageant. They are actors who ignore all but their own roles, who fail to see the unity, scope, and meaning of the play, who ignore the fact that actors need other actors. Kate, on the other hand, heeds the cue to play an obedient wife. In heeding that cue she is, in effect, an obedient wife: one's part in the theater of the world is one's function in life; but more important, she is effectively acting out a role in a play that she and Petruchio play together, the pageant of marriage. . . .

IMAGERY

The prevalence of animal imagery in *The Taming of the Shrew*, particularly imagery having to do with falconry and hunting, has been interpreted in various ways. **Margaret Loftus Ranald** examines Shakespeare's use

of falconry images, while **Joan Hartwig** evaluates the play's many references to horses. In particular, the two critics focus on ways in which the relationship between Katherina and Petruchio is likened to that between a master and his hawk or his horse. While both writers concede that these images suggest a desire on the part of Petruchio for absolute control over his wife, they go on to argue that these images are used in the play to dramatize the desirability of partnership and cooperation in marriage.

Many other critics refer to animal or hunting imagery in developing their interpretations of the play. **George Hibbard** (in the GENDER ROLES section), states that Katherina's true nature is shown to be like that usually ascribed to falcons, "bold," "meek," and "loving." Alexander Leggatt suggests that the play's many references to hunting help to render Petruchio's sometimes brutal treatment of Katherina more acceptable to an audience. Katherina's "taming," the critic argues, is made to seem part of "a game—a test of skill and a source of pleasure"—in which "cruelty and violence are acceptable, even exciting." Other commentators, however, see the play's animal imagery in a less positive light. **Irving Ribner**, for instance (in the section on APPEARANCE VS. REALITY), finds the comparisons of Katherina to various animals demeaning. **Coppélia Kahn** (in the GENDER ROLES section), argues that while Katherina's comparison to a falcon may indicate that Petruchio values her, it still reduces her to the status of an animal and a possession.

Images having to do with clothing and various forms of entertainment also figure prominently in *The Taming of the Shrew*. **Norman Sanders** examines Shakespeare's use of these images in the play, suggesting that by depriving Katherina of food and appropriate clothing, Petruchio drives home to her the social and personal implications of her rejection of the accepted order. Sanders also briefly examines the function of references to music in the play.

Norman Sanders

SOURCE: "Themes and Imagery in *The Taming of the Shrew*," in *Renaissance Papers*, April, 1963, pp. 63-72.

[*In the following excerpt, Sanders focuses on the importance in the play of clothing and images related to household management. By disrupting the conventions of dining and proper attire, the critic suggests, Petruchio drives home to Katherina the social and personal implications of her disorderly behavior. In both the main action and in the subplot, the critic maintains, clothing becomes indicative of the discrepancy that can exist between a person's appearance and his or her true identity. The critic also comments briefly on the symbolic significance of music in the play and on Shakespeare's use of imagery to achieve dramatic unity.*]

Dining and entertainment are traditionally and theatrically symbols of concord, amity and respect; and thus it is that Kate's first lesson is given in a travesty of a feast. She is first dragged away from the wedding banquet where, as Petruchio says, the "honest company . . . Dine with my father, drink a health to me" (III.ii.192-95). The entertainment she experiences at her new home is rather different. Grumio enters to set the scene of the journey from which the guests are to be received: a journey of tired jades, lost cruppers, burst bridles, and foul ways, with the travellers mere pieces of ice in a cold world. The reception is equally calamitous: there is "no man at the door" to hold a stirrup or take a horse, "no regard, no attendance, no duty," and no meeting in the park by the "loggerheaded and unpolished grooms." And, as the scene proceeds, the music accompanying the meal becomes snippets of old ballads, the washing of the hands a slapstick routine, and the dishes are used as aggressive weapons on "heedless joltheads and unmannered slaves." The food itself is burnt and dried, mere overcooked flesh that "engenders choler, and planteth anger." By Petruchio's report Kate's bed of rest after the journey is to be of a piece with her other entertainment:

> Last night she slept not, nor tonight she shall
>   not:
>   . . . some undeserved fault
> I'll find about the making of the bed
> And here I'll fling the pillow, there the
>   bolster,
> This way the coverlet, another way the
>   sheets.
>
>   (III.iii.191-95)

Later, at a less "formal" level of entertainment Grumio is to drive home the lesson, only to be followed by Petruchio with the rituals of dining, and a speech which demands for its true effect that the meal he has prepared himself be either microscopic or quickly taken away from her.

But although by such inverted domestic rites Kate is shown the social implications of her disorder, it is by sartorial imagery that she is shown the personal ones. For clothes can be a measure of either the inward man or of the deception he practises on others or on himself. Kate's persecution of Bianca early in the play takes this form in Bianca's plea:

>   but for these other gawds,
> Unbind my hands, I'll pull them off myself,
> Yea, all my raiment, to my petticoat.
>   (II.i.3-5)

Once the wedding is planned, Petruchio (as well he

might) sees his preparations in terms of garments: "I will unto Venice to buy apparel 'gainst my wedding day . . . I will be sure my Katherine shall be fine . . . We will have have rings and things and fine array" (II.i.307-16). Bianca will not dance barefoot but will help dress her sister's chamber. However, when the day arrives this normality is transgressed by means of clothes. Biondello heralds Petruchio's and Grumio's approach in a long verbal *tour de force* describing "a monster, a very monster in apparel." Petruchio's attire is called a shame to his estate and an "eyesore to our solemn festival." But as Tranio observes he "has some meaning in his mad attire." His dress is a parallel to Kate's equally "mad" attitude which only Petruchio sees as being something which is donned but not so easily doffed as his outlandish garb.

> To me she's married, not unto my clothes.
> Could I repair what she will wear in me
> As I can change these poor accouterments,
> 'Twere well for Kate and better for myself.
>
>   (III.ii.116-19)

The clothes imagery becomes physical comedy in the scene with the tailor and haberdasher. Petruchio states normal practice again.

> And now, my honey love,
> Will we return unto thy father's house
> And revel it as bravely as the best,
> With silken coats and caps and golden rings,
> With ruffs and cuffs and fardingales and
>   things;
> With scarfs and fans and double change of
>   brav'ry.
>
>   (IV.i. 52-57)

But at the end of the scene, by sheer verbal pyrotechnics, he has reduced the topic of clothes and their maker to "a rag, a remnant" and mere "masquing stuff"; and he can universalise his lesson.

> Our purses shall be proud, our garments
>   poor,
> For 'tis the mind that makes the body rich;
> And as the sun breaks through the darkest
>   clouds
> So honor peereth in the meanest habit.
> What, is the jay more precious than the lark
> Because his feathers are more beautiful?
> Or is the adder better than the eel
> Because his painted skin contents the eye?
> O no, good Kate.
>
>   (IV.i.172-79)

When in the final scene it is Kate's cap that Petruchio orders her to throw as a bauble under foot, it becomes for the audience a symbol of her new realisation of what she has been but is no longer.

In the Bianca/Lucentio plot, too, clothes are used as a means of deception and the theme runs as a more conventional commentary on the more complex deceptions practised by Kate and Petruchio. Tranio takes his master's "colored hat and cloak" as a sign of his assumption of Lucentio's rôle, and puts on his "apparel and countenance." Vincentio is to notice first Tranio's attire when they first meet: "O fine villain! A silken doublet! a velvet hose! a scarlet cloak! and a copatain hat!" (IV.iv.63-64). Lucentio will put on a further change and go disguised "in sober robes, / To old Baptista" as a pedant. A true Pedant, in his turn, is clothed as it becomes him to pretend he is Vincentio; and Hortensio plays his part as a musician.

While the images of clothes and household management are used as a means of showing Kate's adjustment to society, it is the imagery of music which conveys the degree and implications of her maladjustment in the main sections of the play. I need not dwell on this, for Mr. T. W. Herbert and Mrs. T. R. Waldo have presented all the pertinent evidence in an interesting article on the subject [*in Shakespeare Quarterly*, 1959]. Although their principal aim was to prove Shakespeare's sole authorship of the play, they do make some points material to my case. They point out that man's adjustment to nature and society was frequently seen in terms of musical harmony, the cosmic expression of which was the music of the spheres; and they gather together those allusions in the play which show Kate as "anti-musical," allusions which culminate with a visual impact when she breaks the lute over Hortensio's head. However, I think we may go further and notice that while Bianca, seen by Lucentio as "the patroness of heavenly harmony," is contrasted with her sister in that she "taketh most delight / In music, instruments, and poetry," we are given a hint of her married frowardness by her rejection of music in the scene with Hortensio, and her willing association with dalliance and disguise. Thus it is ironical that whereas Kate, who at first "chides as loud / As thunder when the clouds in autumn crack," is taught to sing as sweetly as the nightingale; it is Bianca who finally causes her husband to lament of her "it is harsh hearing when women are froward."

One final point might be made about the conscious artistry and essential unity of the play. In the induction scenes all of the themes and images are mooted: from the harsh sound of hounds and hunting horns to the Lord's assurance that if Sly would have music "twenty caged nightingales do sing"; from the cold bed of rejection on which Sly sleeps so soundly to the luxurious bed of acceptance in which he wakes. The water, the conserves, the sack and costly raiment all make their appearance, and are offered to the tinker as he sits like Kate on her wedding night like one "new risen from a dream." Here we find too the wife who is no wife and absents herself from her husband's bed; but who is to all appearances a humble wife ready to show her duty and make known her love with kind embraces. And finally the Lord's whole action is like that of Petruchio an experiment in the manipulation of a human personality: for Sly, like Kate, is "monstrous"—though it is with ale rather than pride. It is for this reason too that, while admitting the final scene in *The Taming of a Shrew* has some attractive features, I think Shakespeare knew what he was about when he allowed Sly's "flattering dream or worthless fancy" to pass early and without note into the certainly not profound but nevertheless assured comedy of Kate's reformation.

Margaret Loftus Ranald

SOURCE: "The Manning of the Haggard: or *The Taming of the Shrew*," in *Essays in Literature*, Vol. 1, No. 2, Fall, 1974, pp. 149-65.

[*Ranald suggests that in* The Taming of the Shrew *Shakespeare examines three types of marriage common in Elizabethan England. She contends that the play's falconry imagery is used to present the relationship of wife to husband as being similar to that between a falcon and its keeper. Petruchio uses the methods of hawk-taming, she argues, in order to bring Katherina under his control without breaking her spirit.*]

The Taming of the Shrew is, in George Hibbard's phrase [in *Tennessee studies in Language and Literature* 2, 1946], "a play about marriage in Elizabethan England," and also unique in the Shakespearean comic canon in dealing with the behavior of husband and wife after the marriage ceremony. At the same time it also offers a distinctly subversive approach to an antifeminist *genre*, that of the wifebeating farce. In this play Shakespeare has skillfully remolded his material to portray an atypical Elizabethan attitude towards marriage through the development of a matrimonial relationship in which mutuality, trust, and love are guiding forces.

Shakespeare's method at this early stage of his career makes use of the familiar device of contrast. He takes the three most frequent matrimonial situations of Elizabethan England, and indeed any time and place: a marriage arranged by parents for economic gain, marriage to a widow for her money, and a marriage of compatibility and equality. This last, the marriage of Kate and Petruchio, at first seems to be one based on economics, but by the end of the play it is shown to be the model for the others, and indeed the only one that is for more than "two months victuall'd." The play then is Shakespeare's comment on that traditionally male-oriented view of marriage which requires the molding of a wife, by force if necessary, into total submission to her husband. In *The Taming of the Shrew*, however, the action shows the failure of what would then have been considered "proper" marriages and the boisterous success of the relationship of equality between the sexes personified by Kate and Petruchio.

The imagery and method of the taming need exploration as contributing to the development of this theme, and they represent an amalgam of two approaches, those of falconry and the conduct books of Elizabethan England. Petruchio follows the principles and uses the imagery of hawk-taming while following the letter of the conservative English conduct books, but subverting their repressive intent. The principles of the conduct books and the legal position of women in Elizabethan England are developed along with the principles of training and skill by which one subdues a hunting bird, and the result is a completely different view of the "oeconomie" of matrimony. . . .

Petruchio rejoices in Kate's faults. She will be a haggard worth the taming, a good hawk for his hand:

> I am as peremptory as she proud-minded;
> And where two raging fires meet together
> They do consume the thing that feeds their fury.
> Though little fire grows great with little wind,
> Yet extreme gusts will blow out fire and all;
> So I to her, and so she yields to me,
> For I am rough and woo not like a babe.
> (II.i.132-38)

And further, he is a fit husband for her:

> For I am he am born to tame you Kate,
> And bring you from a wild Kate to a Kate
> Conformable as other household Kates.
> (ll. 278-80)

Thus at the very beginning of the play, Petruchio sees the essential similarity between the two of them. He willingly undertakes the task of taming in full knowledge of its challenging difficulty, as a falconer brings a difficult hawk to submission. Consequently the imagery of much of the play indicates a perception of the matrimonial state as similar to the compact between falcon and keeper. The falcon must be taught obedience to her master, but at the same time her wild and soaring nature must be preserved. This is a cardinal principle of hawk-taming. The bird must retain her hunting instinct; otherwise she is useless. But she must be taught to exercise her wild nature on command, to hunt under the government of her keeper/master. Accordingly, the hawking passage of IV.i.193 ff. is extremely important, as also is the image of Bianca as a "proud, disdainful haggard" (IV.ii.39).

Hortensio cannot remain with a woman who will be "ranging" abroad to cast "wand'ring eyes on every stale" (III.i.90), or lure of dead prey. This comment also gives a clue to the revelation of the shrewish Bianca beneath the appearance of conformity. But Petruchio operates differently from the moneyminded Hortensio and the swooning-romantic Lucentio. He has the patience to tame his wild bird without breaking her spirit, perceiving the advantages that will accrue to him in training a good hunting hawk. While Hortensio will seek easier game and marry a wealthy widow, only to find himself discomfited, and Lucentio will find himself married to a shrew, Petruchio will preserve Kate's witty and independent nature so that in partnership they may hunt down pretension and falsehood in others.

Thus the hawking imagery carries more weight than the mere suggestion that wives and falcons are more tractable when half starved. Its real value lies in emphasizing the fact that the taming of a wild, mature falcon aims at achieving mutual respect between bird and keeper. As a result of this battle of wills, the bird learns her function and purpose, and the keeper learns that he must continually work to preserve the bird's obedience. Kate and Petruchio develop similar attitudes toward each other, and implicit in this image is that of marriage as a partnership, neither party in full control of the other, yet each owing something to the other: respect and consideration on the part of the man, and obedience and respect on the part of the woman. As the falconer never asks the impossible of his bird, as he cherishes, feeds, and keeps it, not attempting irrevocably to alter its nature, so too should a husband behave toward his wife, taking care never to lose her friendship. And, to carry the analogy with falconry further, the keeper must expect his bird to be moody and unpredictable, and he must never relax his vigilance, for he can never be sure that he is in complete control of his hawk. Finally, the compact between master and falcon is basically a voluntary commitment. When it soars, waiting for its prey, the bird is capable of flying away free, and only the kindness of the keeper and the consequent gratitude or indebtedness of the bird can keep it under control. So too with Kate and Petruchio. . . .

Joan Hartwig

SOURCE: "Horses and Women in *The Taming of the Shrew*," in *The Huntington Library Quarterly*, Vol. 45, No. 4, Autumn, 1982, pp. 285-94.

[*Pointing out that women are compared to horses in many English Renaissance texts, Hartwig suggests that Petruchio's "taming" of Katherina is made to suggest the training of a horse to respond to its rider's commands. The critic also examines the English practice during Shakespeare's time of punishing shrewish women by forcing them to parade in public wearing a "scold's bridle," a device that forced a painful metal gag into their mouths. In contrast with such brutal methods, Hartwig argues, Petruchio's methods seem gentle and reasonable, and they result in a "complementary relationship" that benefits both man and wife.]*

In a 1534 treatise on husbandry, attributed to Sir Anthony Fitzherbert, after discussing the benefits of keeping horses, cows, and sheep together in one pasture in order to get the most even grazing, the author begins a list of the properties "that a good horse hath." Of the fifty-four properties listed, two are like a man: "to have a proude harte" and "to be bolde and hardy." Then follow properties that resemble a badger, a lion, an ox, a hare, a fox, an ass, and finally the ten "properties of a woman":

> The fyrst is, to be mery of chere; the seconde, to be well paced; the thyrde, to haue a brode foreheed; the fourth, to haue brode buttockes; the fyfthe, to be harde of warde; the syxte, to be easye to lepe vppon; the .vii. to be good at a longe iourneye; the .viii. to be well sturryne vnder a man; the .ix. to be alwaye besye with the mouthe; the tenth, euer to be chowynge on the brydell.

Fitzherbert is quite serious about his list of properties, but it is amusing to note that the ten properties like a woman exceeds all other categories in length, and that the list begins briefly, but honorifically, with how a good horse is like a man and ends more prolixly and bawdily with how that same horse is like a woman.

That a good horse is well esteemed, as is a valued wife, may be inferred from Master Ford's expression of jealous mistrust: "I will rather trust . . . a thief to walk my ambling gelding, than my wife with herself" (*The Merry Wives of Windsor:* II.ii.272-75). When Hortensio and Gremio agree to find a husband for Kate in *The Taming of the Shrew* so that they may both pursue Bianca, Gremio voices his willingness to pay for such a man in this measure:

> I am agreed, and would I have given him the best horse in Padua to begin his wooing that would thoroughly woo her, wed her, and bed her, and rid the house of her. (I.i.139-42)

All these remarks share an assumption that a woman and a horse are commodities to be bought and sold. Petruchio's initial offer to marry Kate could not be more explicit in treating her as an object of sale:

> As wealth is burden of my wooing dance—
> Be she as foul as was Florentius' love,
> As old as Sibyl, and as curst and shrewd
> As Socrates' Xanthippe, or a worse,

> She moves me not, or not removes, at least,
> Affections' edge in me, were she as rough
> As are the swelling Adriatic seas.
> I come to wive it wealthily in Padua—
> If wealthily, then happily in Padua.

> (I.ii.66-74)

Grumio's following remark—"Why, give him gold enough and marry him to a puppet or an aglet-baby or an old trot with ne'er a tooth in her head, though she have as many diseases as two and fifty horses"— specifically links the sale of Kate with the purchase of horses. And Kate's father, following the conclusion of Petruchio's arrangement for the impending wedding and his departure to Venice "to buy apparel 'gainst the wedding-day," says: "Faith, gentlemen, now I play a merchant's part / And venture madly on a desperate mart" (II.i.328-29). Tranio's and Gremio's bidding for Bianca in such a mass of detailed wealth— "Tyrian tapestry . . . ivory coffers . . . six score fat oxen . . . houses . . . two thousand ducats by the year . . . argosies" (II.i.348-82)—sounds very much like the bidding at a horse auction.

Even in Petruchio's hasty wooing of Kate they jest about their relationship in terms of the copulation of horses. When Petruchio asks her to sit on him, she replies, "Asses are made to bear, and so are you." Petruchio returns, "Women are made to bear, and so are you," to which Kate responds, "No such jade as you, if me you mean" (II.i.200-203). Hardly the enthusiasm of Cleopatra's imagination when she pictures Antony on horseback and wishes herself the horse—"O happy horse, to bear the weight of Antony!" (*Antony and Cleopatra:* I.v.21), but the association between women and horses is Kate's immediate thought as well. Petruchio concludes their wooing scene that employs other animal and insect analogies (the turtledove, the buzzard, the wasp, the cock, the crab) with remarks about her "princely gait" and with the assertion that "I am he am born to tame you, Kate, / And bring you from a wild Kate to a Kate / Conformable as other household Kates" (II.i.261, 278-80). To the buyer of horses, the gait of the horse as well as his general conformation is of utmost importance. The wildness of Kate is associated more specifically with the horse than with the other animals mentioned. Petruchio later has a long passage that evokes an analogy with taming a hawk (IV.i.177-83), but even this passage ends with reference to controlling a horse—"And thus I'll *curb* her mad and headstrong humor." Therefore, his method of taming his shrew quite appropriately corresponds with the taming of horses in the Renaissance.

Training the horse to obey his rider's signals is known as the "manage." Although today the terms of manage are usually gentle, using the hands on the reins, pressure from the legs, and placement of body weight as aids to signal the horse of its rider's wishes and reserving the spurs, whip, and voice commands for unusual circumstances, in Shakespeare's day harsher methods were employed, as Gardiner's remarks to the Lord Chancellor make clear:

> For those that tame wild horses
> Pace 'em not in their hands to make 'em
>   gentle,
> But stop their mouths with stubborn bits and
>   spur 'em
> Till they obey the manage.
>
> *(Hen VIII: V.ii.21-24)*

Shakespeare does not always suggest approval of such measures, but in *The Taming of the Shrew* Petruchio's harsh treatment of Kate is not out of line, if we view his taming of her as analogous to the taming of a horse, bringing both into the control of the rider.

The manage includes many movements besides the normal gaits, halts, and turns, and there were different ideas of the sequence in which these movements should be taught to the horse. Of general acceptance, however, was the idea that a horse must first be "paced" and then taught to "stop." In other words, the horse must learn to travel smoothly at the desired gait and at the rider's signal and then to stop in a disciplined way. Gervase Markham [in *Cavelarice or the English Horse man,* 1607] describes the "stop" as "a suddaine and firme setting downe of all his foreleges together without any further motion." Similarly, D. H. Madden [in *The Diary of Master William Silence,* 1907] describes the "stop" as essential to another stage of teaching the manage, the "career," a fast run of eighty or one hundred yards: "the essential characteristic of the career, wherein it differed from the ordinary gallop, was its abrupt ending, technically known as 'the stop,' by which the horse was suddenly and firmly thrown upon his haunches."

Petruchio's treatment of Kate in his house and on the road back to Padua resembles the kind of exactitude and repetition of exercises that a rider requires when training his horse in the manage, including the precise stop as Petruchio requires Kate to assess the sun as moon and Vincentio as a young maiden.

Grumio's description to Curtis of the journey from Padua to Verona is not only an illustration of Petruchio's being "more shrew than she"; it is a picture of inept horsemanship and manage.

> Thou shouldst have heard how her horse fell, and she under her horse; thou shouldst have heard in how miry a place; how she was bemoiled, how he left her with the horse upon her, . . . how I cried, how the horses ran away, how her bridle was burst.
> (IV.i.64-71)

This passage recalls Biondello's earlier description of the horse upon which Petruchio arrives for the wedding, as unsound and diseased (III.iii.47-60). Both of these passages present horses and riders in discord with each other, and thus counter the more usual image where a horse and rider in concord exemplify the harmony of man and nature.

A further aspect of the literal association between horses and women has to do with the condition that Kate herself embodies—that of the shrew or scold. Petruchio has not heard of Kate's reputation, but Hortensio assures him that she is "renowned in Padua for her scolding tongue" (I.ii.98), and the audience has enough evidence early in the play to see how she came by her reputation. In two essays in *The Reliquary* (1860 and 1873), Llewellynn Jewitt describes the bridles that were common in the cure of scolds, variously called the "brank," the "Scold's Bridle," or the "Gossips' Bridle":

> The Brank consisted of a kind of crown, or framework, or iron, which was locked upon the head; and it was armed in front with a gag, a plate, or a sharp-cutting knife or point, which was placed in the poor woman's mouth, so as to prevent her moving her tongue—or it was so placed that if she did move it, or attempt to speak, it was cut in the most frightful manner. With this cage upon her head, and with the gag firmly pressed and locked against her tongue, the miserable creature whose sole offending perhaps was that she had raised her voice in defence of her social rights, against a brutal and besotted husband, or had spoken honest truth of some one high in office in her town, was . . . led by a chain, by the hand of the bellman, . . . through all the principal streets of the town, for an hour or two, and then brought back bleeding, faint, ill, and degraded. Let them fancy all this, and then say whether it is not indeed a happy thing that our lot is cast in better days than those in which such disgusting public punishments could be asked for by husbands, or neighbours; inflicted by the authorities and tolerated by the people themselves.

Mrs. Eliza Gutch [*Country Folk-lore*] records more recently (1893) the practice of "wife-selling" which requires the wife to be led into the marketplace "with a halter round her neck." These literal representations of the associations assumed by English folk between women and horses from ages past make Petruchio's harsh treatment of Kate seem mild by contrast.

The "taming-school" of which Petruchio is the master and Hortensio the somewhat awed witness does effect the desired transformation in Kate by teaching her the discipline of "curbing" her will to her master's signals. His control, as she asserts in her final speech, must depend upon "honest will" rather than

An engraving of scene ii of the Induction, featuring Christopher Sly.

upon whimsy or tyranny, as some of Petruchio's stratagems may seem at the time he produces them. But seen from the metaphorical analogue of taming the wild horse to graceful "manage," his insistence on her submission seems quite reasonable.

In contrast, the apparent humanistic training of Bianca by her disguised suitors in music, Greek and Latin, and in poetry does not humanize Bianca in the least. She becomes, when released to be herself, the stubborn and willful wife; whereas Kate's apparently brutal treatment releases her into a gracefully obedient and respectful wife. Lucentio and Hortensio disguise themselves in order to tutor Bianca, and Petruchio disguises himself in order to instruct Kate. But whereas the former disguises, which present the young admirers as different people, are donned to insinuate them into where they are forbidden, Petruchio dons his disguise—changes in manner and clothing which do not change his identity—in order to lead Kate out of her father's and of her own self-inflicted prison. Lucentio and Hortensio change their outward identity

to manipulate within the status quo, but Petruchio changes himself psychologically into manic tyrant in order to change the situation, the institution of marriage, and the bride into realities that do not depend upon social prescription. He hints at his more human form of realism when others protest that his "unreverent robes" ill befit the occasion of a wedding. Petruchio challenges the entire social structure when he asserts, "To me she's married, not unto my clothes" (III.ii.113).

The final contest of wills between Petruchio and Kate defines the matter more explicitly. Kate wishes to follow the quarreling relatives "to see the end of this ado," but Petruchio demands a kiss. She says, "What, in the midst of the street?" And he, "What, art thou ashamed of me?" Kate's careful response is "No sir, God forbid, but ashamed to kiss." Yet when Petruchio threatens a return to Verona, she concedes to the man rather than to fear of social judgment.

The symbolic associations of the horse and rider figure

are several throughout history, but the horse as appetite and passion and the rider as mind, reason holding the body under control, is an analogy pervasive from early times. Beryl Rowland, in a study of the horse and rider figure in Chaucer's works [in *The University of Toronto Quarterly* 35, 1966], observes that "under the influence of the Christian Church the significance of the figure appears to harden: the horse is equated with the body or with Woman, the evil repository of sex; the rider is the soul or Man." Rowland continues:

> The less alarming analogy whereby the woman is the horse to be bridled and controlled by man is so commonplace as to become proverbial. . . . So fundamental is the analogy in our thinking that token symbols such as the bridle, harness, collar or saddle-girth are often substituted, and the symbolism persists even today in the marriage ceremony in which the ring is the halter used by the groom to harness his bride.

When the rider is able to keep his mount under his control, both the horse and rider are figures of nobility. The complementary relationship that accrues honor to both is what Petruchio and Kate have achieved at the end of the play. Even the wager that the three newly-wed husbands make on their wives resembles wagers commonly made on the performances of horses by their proud owners. That Kate wins the wager for Petruchio is no surprise, since she has learned the "manage" well. Her recognition that acceptance of her husband as her "lord" and her "sovereign" allows her to realize herself fully may seem too "conformable" for modern sensibilities. Yet the final lines of her speech recall the metaphor that has been operative throughout the play. The hand placed below the foot to "do him ease" suggests the image of a rider ready to mount his horse, using the hand instead of stirrup to ease him into the saddle. We might be reminded of the Dauphin's praise of his palfrey:

> The dull elements of earth and water never appear in him, but only in patient stillness while his rider mounts him. . . . 'Tis a subject for a sovereign to reason on, and for a sovereign's sovereign to ride on; and for the world, familiar to us and unknown, to lay apart their particular functions and wonder at him. (*Hen V:* III.vii.20-37)

So Kate, as she accepts Petruchio for her sovereign, transforms from unhappy shrew into graceful woman, creating "wonder" in her world.

KATHERINA

Many different interpretations of Katherina's character

have been put forward on stage and by the critics. An account of the various stage interpretations of her character can be found in the excerpt by **Ann Thompson** in the OVERVIEWS section.

One popular view sees Katherina as a miserable and maladjusted woman at the beginning of the play who by its end has been transformed into a happy wife who has learned to accept joyfully her appointed role in society. Many twentieth-century critics, including **Harold Goddard** as well as **Ruth Nevo** and **H. J. Oliver** (in essays excerpted in the OVERVIEWS section), have suggested that Shakespeare provides psychological insight into the reasons for Katherina's shrewishness, showing her to suffer from her father's open preference for her underhanded younger sister. Goddard characterized Katherina as a "cross child . . . starved for love" who is restored by Petruchio to her "natural self," which is "lovely and sweet." A number of other critics, including **George R. Hibbard** (in the GENDER ROLES section), see Katherina's "true" character as loving and amenable. Others see her as a forerunner of Shakespeare's later, more attractively drawn comic heroines, such as Rosalind in *As You Like It* and Beatrice in *Much Ado about Nothing*. Like them, these critics point out, Katherina possess a keen wit, a passionate nature, and a strong will. **Kenneth Muir** suggested that Katherina's initial hostility toward Petruchio is caused in part by a fear that he is only interested in her money. "Unconsciously," the critic wrote, "she wants to submit and to accept her femininity." Katherina's adjustment to an acceptable social role was also stressed by **Richard Henze** (in the GAMES AND ROLE-PLAYING section) as well as **Cecil C. Seronsy** (in the APPEARANCE VS. REALITY section).

A rather different interpretation also common on stage is that Katherina is not really "tamed" at all. Rather, she learns to humor Petruchio's need to feel that he is in control; she plays the obedient wife in public so as to exercise control at home. This view, an example of which can be found in the piece by Harold Goddard below, was especially popular among critics during the 1950s. **Coppélia Kahn** (in the GENDER ROLES section), also argued that Katherina's acceptance of the role of obedient wife is more apparent than real. Katherina's exaggerated portrayal of the obedient wife, Kahn contended, is meant to indicate both to the audience and to Petruchio that while she will submit outwardly to achieve a peaceful home life, psychologically she retains her independence. Kahn conceded, however, that this is a hollow victory; regardless of whether she really believes in Petruchio's superiority, she has tacitly agreed to tailor her behavior to his wishes.

Robert Ornstein, on the other hand, suggested that Katherina's initial shrewishness and her submission to Petruchio are motivated by her fear of remaining lonely and unmarried. Never particularly "independent" or "strong-minded," Katherina in his view submits entirely to Petruchio's "bullying." Ornstein characterized as "demeaning" both Petruchio's treatment of her and the view of women she expresses in her final speech.

Harold C. Goddard

SOURCE: "'The Taming of the Shrew,'" in *The Meaning of Shakespeare*, The University of Chicago Press, 1951, pp. 68-73.

[*Goddard believes the "subterranean" meaning of* The Taming of the Shrew *is that Katherina will have the upper hand in her marriage to Petruchio. Unless one sees the play in this light, he argues, or accepts it as merely a farce, it is an intolerable expression of the principle of male superiority, and there is no evidence anywhere in Shakespeare's other works that he held such a view of human relations. Goddard claims that Katherina's shrewishness is only superficial, the result of Baptista's unfair partiality toward Bianca and his neglect of his elder daughter. By wisely and lovingly treating her as if she were "a cross child who is starved for love," Petruchio transforms her back to her original good-tempered self. Arguing that the Induction supports this analysis, Goddard suggests that Petruchio, like Sly, is duped into believing "that he is a great lord—over his wife."*]

We must never for a moment allow ourselves to forget that *The Taming of the Shrew* is a play within a play, an interlude put on by a company of strolling players at the house of a great lord for the gulling of Christopher Sly, the drunken tinker, and thereby for the double entertainment of the audience. For the sake of throwing the picture into strong relief against the frame—an in a different sense in the case of *The Murder of Gonzago* in *Hamlet*—the play within the play is given a simplification and exaggeration that bring its main plot to the edge of farce, while its minor plot, the story of Bianca's wooers, goes quite over that edge. But, even allowing for this, the psychology of the Katharine-Petruchio plot is remarkably realistic. It is even "modern" in its psychoanalytical implications. It is based on the familiar situation of the favorite child. Baptista is a family tyrant and Bianca is his favorite daughter. She has to the casual eye all the outer marks of modesty and sweetness, but to a discerning one all the inner marks of a spoiled pet, remade, if not originally made, in her father's image. One line is enough to give us her measure. When in the wager scene at the end her husband tells her that her failure to come at his entreaty has cost him a hundred crowns,

> The more fool you for laying on my duty,
> [V. ii. 129]

she blurts out. What a light that casts back over her previous "sweetness" before she has caught her man! The rest of her role amply supports this interpretation, as do the hundreds of Biancas—who are not as white as they are painted—in real life.

[There] is everything to indicate that Kate's shrewishness is superficial, not ingrained or congenital. It is the inevitable result of her father's gross partiality toward her sister and neglect of herself, plus the repercussions that his attitude has produced on Bianca and almost everyone else in the region. Kate has heard herself blamed, and her sister praised at her expense, to a point where even a worm would turn. And Kate is no worm. If her sister is a spoiled child, Kate is a cross child who is starved for love. She craves it as a man in a desert craves water, without understanding, as he does, what is the matter. And though we have to allow for the obvious exaggeration of farce in his extreme antics, Petruchio's procedure at bottom shows insight, understanding, and even love. Those actors who equip him with a whip miss Shakespeare's man entirely. In principle, if not in the rougher details, he employs just the right method in the circumstances, and the end amply justifies his means.

It is obvious that his boast at the outset of purely mercenary motives for marrying is partly just big talk—at any rate the dowry soon becomes quite subsidiary to Kate herself and the game of taming her. In retrospect it seems to have been something like love at first sight on both sides, though not recognized as such at the time. Whatever we think of Petruchio's pranks in the scenes where farce and comedy get mixed, there is no quarreling with his instinctive sense of how in general Kate ought to be handled. When a small child is irritable and cross, the thing to do is not to reason, still less to pity or pamper, or even to be just kind and understanding in the ordinary sense. The thing to do is to take the child captive. A vigorous body and will, combined with good humor and a love that is not expressed in words but that makes itself felt by a sort of magnetic communication, will sweep the child off his feet, carry him away, and transform him almost miraculously back into his natural self. . . . This is precisely what Petruchio does to Kate (and what Shakespeare does to his audience in this play). She is dying for affection. He keeps calling her his sweet and lovely Kate. What if he is ironical to begin with! The words just of themselves are manna to her soul, and her intuition tells her that, whether he knows it or not, he really means them. And indeed Kate is lovely and sweet by nature. (She is worth a bale of Biancas.) What girl would not like to be told, as Petruchio tells her, that she sings as sweetly as a nightingale and has a countenance like morning roses washed with dew? She knows by a perfectly sound instinct that he could never have thought up such lovely similes to be sarcastic with if he considered her nothing but a shrew. There is a poet within him that her beauty has elicited. What wonder that she weeps when the poet fails to appear for the wedding! It is not just humiliation. It is disappointed love.

And Kate is intelligent too. She is a shrewd "shrew." You can put your finger on the very moment when it dawns on her that if she will just fall in with her husband's absurdest whim, accept his maddest perversion of the truth as truth, she can take the wind completely out of his sails, deprive his weapon of its power, even turn it against him—tame him in his own humor. Not that she really wants to tame him, for she loves him dearly, as the delightful little scene in the street so amply proves, where he begs a kiss, begs, be it noted, not demands. She is shy for fear they may be overseen, but finally relents and consents.

> Kath.: Husband, let's follow, to see the end
> 　　of this ado.
> Pet.: First kiss me, Kate, and we will.
> Kath.: What! in the midst of the street?
> Pet.: What! are thou ashamed of me?
> Kath.: No, sir, God forbid; but ashamed to
> 　　kiss.
> Pet.: Why, then let's home again. Come,
> 　　sirrah, let's away.
> Kath.: Nay, I will give thee a kiss; now pray
> 　　thee, love, stay.
> Pet.: Is not this well? Come, my sweet Kate.
> Better once than never, for never too late.
> 　　　　　　　　　　　　　[V. i. 142-50]

How this little scene is to be fitted into the traditional interpretation of the play it is hard to see.

Everything leads up to Kate's long lecture at the end on the duty of wives to their lords. What fun she has reading it to those two other women who do not know what every woman knows! How intolerable it would be if she and Shakespeare really meant it (as if Shakespeare could ever have meant it!), though there is a deeper sense in which they both do mean it. . . . The self-styled advanced thinkers of our day, who have been for obliterating all distinctions between the sexes and leveling them to a dead equality, are just lacking enough in humor to think Kate's speech the most retrograde nonsense, as indeed it would be if it were the utterance of a cowering slave.

Though actresses in the past have edged in the direction of this interpretation of Kate, a triumph still remains for one who will go the whole distance and find in her a clear first draft and frank anticipation of Beatrice [in *Much Ado about Nothing*]: Petruchio, too, must be made fine and bold, not just rough and bold, or crude and bold. And as for Bianca, you can pick up a dozen of her in the first high school you happen

on, any one of whom could act her to perfection by just being herself. . . .

In the Induction to *The Taming of the Shrew*, Christopher Sly the tinker, drunk with ale, is persuaded that he is a great lord who has been the victim of an unfortunate lunacy. Petruchio, in the play which Sly witnesses (when he is not asleep), is likewise persuaded that he is a great lord—over his wife. Sly is obviously in for a rude awakening when he discovers that he is nothing but a tinker after all. Now Petruchio is a bit intoxicated himself—who can deny it?—whether with pride, love, or avarice, or some mixture of the three. Is it possible that he too is in for an awakening? Or, if Kate does not let it come to that, that *we* at least are supposed to see that he is not as great a lord over his wife as he imagined? The Induction and the play, taken together, do not allow us to evade these questions. Can anyone be so naïve as to fancy that Shakespeare did not contrive his Induction for the express purpose of forcing them on us? Either the cases of Sly and Petruchio are alike or they are diametrically opposite. Can there be much doubt which was intended by a poet who is so given to pointing out analogies between lovers and drunkards, between lovers and lunatics? Here surely is reason enough for Shakespeare not to show us Sly at the end when he no longer thinks himself a lord. It would be altogether too much like explaining the joke, like solving the equation and labeling the result ANSWER. Shakespeare wants us to find things for ourselves. And in this case in particular: why explain what is as clear, when you see it, as was Poe's Purloined Letter, which was skilfully concealed precisely because it was in such plain sight all the time?

Kenneth Muir

SOURCE: "*The Taming of the Shrew*," in *Shakespeare's Comic Sequence*, Barnes and Noble, 1979, pp. 22-8.

[*Disagreeing with the views of critics who find Petruchio's behavior offensive, Muir argues that Katherina is a much happier woman at the end of the play than she is at the beginning. He cites as evidence performances in the role of Katherina by several of the best-known actresses of the twentieth century, who, he reports, clearly "enjoyed themselves in the part." Katherina's initial hostility toward Petruchio, he suggests, is a result of pride and of fear that he is a fortune-hunter: "Unconsciously," he writes, "she wants to submit and accept her femininity." Muir also argues that Katherina's speech in favor of wifely obedience should not be taken seriously, but rather as a parody of obedience.*]

Petruchio's methods of taming Katherina have aroused the horror of many modern critics. Sir Edmund Chambers, for example, said [in *Shakespeare: A Survey*, 1925] that 'you can hardly refuse to shed a tear for the humiliation of Katherine' and that she 'stands for all time as a type of the wrongs done to her much-enduring sex'. John Masefield declared [in *Shakespeare*, 1911] that Katherina was 'humbled into the state of submissive wifely falsehood by a boor' and her sermon to the other wives is 'melancholy claptrap'. Sir Arthur Quiller-Couch [in the New Cambridge edition, 1928] thought that 'any modern civilised man', reading the play, would find the whole Petruchio business tedious, and 'to any modern woman' it would be offensive as well.

It is true that Petruchio's avowed motive—and his actual motive at the beginning of the play—is to wed a rich wife; and apparently he does not mind about her character or appearance:

> Be she as foul as was Florentius' love,
> As old as Sibyl, and as curst and shrewd
> As Socrates' Xanthippe or a worse . . .
> I come to wive it wealthily in Padua;
> If wealthily, then happily in Padua.
>
> (I.ii.67-9, 73-4)

His method of taming Katherina is that of a bully. He uses his superior physical strength. He arrives at the wedding in absurd clothes in order to humiliate his bride; he misbehaves atrociously during the actual ceremony; he boorishly refuses to stay for the marriage feast; he uses the methods of a hawk-tamer by starving his wife; instead of consummating the marriage he preaches Katherina a sermon on continence; he tantalises her by refusing to let her have the fashionable clothes she covets; he makes her say things they both know to be false; he makes a wager on her obedience, which he wins; and in the end she preaches to the other wives on the necessity of slavish obedience. A high-spirited girl has been tamed by brutal and shameful methods into accepting slavery.

Such is the complaint of some modern critics; but, of course, such an interpretation of the play is absurd. The play is a farce and Shakespeare wrote it nearly three centuries before Nora slammed the door at the end of *A Doll's House* [a nineteenth-century play by Henrik Ibsen]. On the stage, as Chambers and Quiller-Couch reluctantly admit, the play is not offensive: it is funny. The account given in the last paragraph omits some important aspects of the taming process. Apart from anything else, it is apparent that the 'high-spirited girl' at the beginning of the play is, whatever the reasons, impossible to live with. Miserable herself, she does her best to make others miserable. At the end of the play she appears to be much happier. The four best Katherinas I have seen in the last fifty years—Sybil Thorndike, Edith Evans, Peggy Ashcroft and Vanessa Redgrave—are not exactly submissive in temperament and they all enjoyed themselves in the part. Dame Edith played it in two different ways. On

the first occasion, fresh from her triumphs in the Comedy of Manners, she played Katherina almost in the manner of a Restoration heroine and her final speech of submission was delivered ironically with a conspiratorial leer to the women in the audience. 'Men like to think they are our lords and masters', she implied, 'and I don't mind humouring them, children as they are; but, as you all realise, I can do what I like by giving Petruchio, this overgrown schoolboy, an illusion of authority.' I thought at the time that this way of delivering the speech was out of period and that Shakespeare cannot have intended it. But it has since been pointed out that Vives in *The Instruction of a Christian Woman* had remarked that 'a good woman by lowly obeisance ruleth her husband', so that Dame Edith's interpretation may well have been right. The second time she played the part, she presented Katherina as a problem child, jealous of her sly and popular sister, hating the idea of a marriage of convenience, with its sordid mercenary basis, and not being able to find a man she could respect. She is attracted by Petruchio's virility and she submits to him only because she loves him. Dame Peggy Ashcroft and Vanessa Redgrave likewise made it plain that they had fallen in love and that they unconsciously wish to submit.

It is worth noting that Germaine Greer is one of the few women who have written in defence of Petruchio. She maintains in *The Female Eunuch* that Kate

> has the uncommon good fortune to find Petruchio who is man enough to know what he wants and how to get it. He wants her spirit and her energy because he wants a wife worth keeping . . . she rewards him with strong sexual love and fierce loyalty.

Her submission is 'genuine and exciting because she has something to lay down, her virgin pride and individuality'. Petruchio is 'both gentle and strong' and Kate's address to the other wives at the end of the play 'is the greatest defence of Christian monogamy ever written'. It is surely not so much a defence of Christian monogamy as of the principle, derived from the Bible and universally accepted in the sixteenth century, of wifely obedience. As we have seen, Luciana had expressed the same ideas in *The Comedy of Errors*. We cannot know for certain whether Shakespeare himself accepted this view of marriage. It was, perhaps, somewhat undercut by the sex of the reigning monarch; but there are survivals of the subordination theory when the great heiress Portia surrenders to Bassanio, even though she soon reasserts her authority. The increasing independence of the comic heroines, who all outshine the men they are destined to marry, makes it difficult for us to imagine that their submission will be more than a formality; and in the love scenes of the final plays we are conscious of the complete equality of Florizel and Perdita, of Ferdinand and Miranda. In both cases love's service is perfect freedom.

Although Miss Greer possibly romanticises the qualities of Petruchio, Katherina is not really reduced to servitude and no audience imagines that she is. Nor do they really believe that Petruchio is a fortune-hunter, even though he starts with that ambition; and if we examine his behaviour throughout the play, we can see that those critics who write him off as a vulgar bully have missed a great deal. As soon as he hears of Katherina's reputation for shrewishness, his fortune-hunting fades into the background and he feels challenged by the task of taming her. He calls the task one of Hercules's labours. In the first wooing scene, although he indulges in plain-speaking about her reputation, he makes her know that he admires her beauty and spirit. He calls her bonny Kate, the prettiest Kate in Christendom and super-dainty Kate. At the end of the scene he speaks of

> this light, whereby I see thy beauty,
> Thy beauty that doth make me like thee well.

And, clearly, the attraction is mutual. She is attracted by his virility and humour; he is attracted by her beauty and wildness. In some ways the wooing resembles that of Beatrice and Benedick who are likewise individualists, distrusting equally the conventions of romantic love and the unromantic realities of marriages of convenience. All through the play we can see that Katherina's knowledge of her sister's character and the humiliation she feels that a husband must be found for her before Bianca can marry, drive her into impossible behaviour. At the same time she wants a husband, while doubting whether any man she respects will want to marry her, even with a dowry to sweeten the bargain. Those critics who find her degraded in Act V tend to ignore the much worse degradation of her situation in Act I.

Her violence towards Petruchio and her attempts to dominate are, at least in part, a means of testing him. Unconsciously she wants to submit and to accept her femininity, but she is prevented at first by her pride and by the fear that Petruchio is mainly interested in her dowry. After she has been starved and prevented from sleeping, she is willing to agree that the sun is the moon; but her relief at her own submission can be gauged from the way in which she joins in the joke:

> Be it moon, or sun, or what you please;
> And if you please to call it a rush-candle,
> Henceforth I vow it shall be so for me
>
> . . . . .
>
> Then, God be bless'd, it is the blessed sun;

> But sun it is not, when you say it is not;
> And the moon changes even as your mind.
>   (IV. v. 13-15, 18-20)

Anyone who heard Dame Edith Evans's address to old Vincentio as—

> Young budding virgin, fair and fresh and
>   sweet,
> Whither away, or where is thy abode?
> Happy the parents of so fair a child;
> Happier the man whom favourable stars
> Allots thee for his lovely bed-fellow—
>   (IV.v.36-40)

must have been convinced that Katherina had learned to laugh.

As G. R. Hibbard points out in his admirable introduction to the play, [in the New Penguin edition, 1968] Petruchio by his outlandish behaviour has been holding up a mirror wherein his wife can see herself. In this distorting mirror she sees how impossible her own behaviour has been. Her realisation of this can be glimpsed in her sympathy with the servant who has been unjustly struck by Petruchio (IV.i.142) and with the cook (IV.i.154). Once Katherina decides to adopt the role of the obedient wife, she plays it with zest, exaggerating and parodying it as Petruchio had parodied the role of despotic husband. This, as we have seen, is apparent in her address to Vincentio; and there is nothing improbable in the assumption that her speech to the other wives is a deliberate exaggeration, as when she urges them to place their hands below their husbands' feet. The marriage, despite appearances, is based on love, mutual respect, and a kind of equality.

Robert Ornstein

SOURCE: *"The Taming of the Shrew,"* in *Shakespeare's Comedies: From Roman Farce to Romantic Mystery*, University of Delaware Press, 1986, pp. 63-72.

[Ornstein argues that far from being "an independent, strong-minded woman," Katherina takes a highly conventional view of woman's place in society and of her own identity. Pointing to evidence in the text that Katherina's primary goal in life is marriage, he suggests that her fear of remaining unmarried motivates both her initial shrewish behavior and her relatively easy surrender to Petruchio. Rejecting the assertions of other critics that the relationship between Petruchio and Katherina is one of mutuality and respect, he points out that Petruchio repeatedly "tests" Katherina's obedience even after she has stopped fighting him. Concluding with an analysis of Katherina's speech in favor of wifely obedience, the critic suggests that her words demonstrate "a demeaning view of her sex."]

If Kate were an independent, strong-minded woman, Petruchio's bullying would not so completely destroy her will. He is able to reduce her to abject submission because she is never unconventional or genuinely rebellious. Rather than a free spirit, she is a prisoner of insecurities that make her more sympathetic and more psychologically complex than the heroine of *A Shrew*. [a similar, anonymous play published in 1594]. She does not lash out against men because she refuses to accept the role and destiny society allots to women. Although she jeers at Petruchio's wooing, and once attempts to strike him, and swears she will see him hanged before she will marry him, she is silent when Petruchio and her father agree to the match and is wretched at the thought that Petruchio will not come to the church to marry her. Love and marriage are what she wants, and fearing that she will not be loved, she behaves in a way that makes men aviod rather than reject her. She lashes out at Bianca because she has suitors, and she complains that Bianca is her father's favorite although her behavior makes it impossible for Baptista to be close to her. Acutely self-conscious and always ill at ease, she fears that the world is pointing and laughing at her, that she will be alone and miserable while her sister is married and happy; the intensity of that fear provokes the rage that makes her a wretched outcast. And yet marriage is always on her mind: she lays hands on Bianca to make her tell which suitor Bianca loves best. It is not astonishing that Kate is so well-behaved at her wedding, even though Petruchio is an offensive lout, because marriage gives her all that she wishes—esteem, a place in society, perhaps even love. And therefore she wants to enjoy all the traditional pleasures of the wedding ceremony and the feast with family and friends. She is ready to be like other brides and other wives, but he wants something more special in a spouse and therefore the taming will proceed despite Kate's reasonableness.

Even after his insulting bully-boy conduct at the wedding, Petruchio might still turn from a frog—or perhaps a toad—into a prince of a fellow when Kate, delighted to have a husband, kisses him. When they do kiss, however, Petruchio does not reveal the true refinement and sensitivity that he hid beneath a facade of crudeness. He is the same as before, the same as he will always be: once a frog, always a frog. For only one brief moment are he and Kate equal partners in a witty charade. When, on the road back to Padua, she joins with him in pretending that Vincentio is a fair maiden rather than an old man, they both enjoy the role-playing. But as R. B. Heilman notes [in his introduction to the Signet Classic Shakespeare edition], this mutuality does not last. When, in the next scene, Kate refuses to kiss Petruchio in the street, he cracks the whip again, threatening to drag her away from the wedding feast for her sister as he had dragged her away from her own wedding feast.

Dressed in suitable garb, Petruchio seems on his good behavior at the feast. But when Lucentio speaks of friendship and good cheer, he mutters, "Nothing but sit and sit and eat and eat." What a bore civility is. To relieve the tedium he quickly baits Hortensio about his bride, the Widow; and he shows that he is quite willing to banter with someone else's wife though he tolerates no back talk from his own. Her education complete, Kate is silent but not more confident or social. She does not join in the conversation until the Widow's sparring with Petruchio opens up the old wound of her self-consciousness. Baited by Petruchio, the Widow refers to Kate's shrewishness. When Petruchio says that Hortensio is afraid of his wife, the Widow answers:

> He that is giddy thinks the world turns
> round.
> *Pet.* Roundly replied.
> *Kate.*   Mistress, how mean you that?
> *Wid.* Thus I conceive by him.
> *Pet.* Conceives by me! how likes Hortensio
> that?
> *Hort.* My widow says, thus she conceives her
> tale.
> *Pet.* Very well mended. Kiss him for that,
> good widow.
> *Kath.* "He that is giddy thinks the world
> turns round":
> I pray you, tell me what you meant by that.
> *Wid.* Your husband, being troubled with a
> shrew,
> Measures my husband's sorrow by his woe:
> And now you know my meaning.
> *Kate.* A very mean meaning.
> *Wid.*   Right, I mean you.
> *Kate.* And I am mean indeed, respecting you.
>   (5.2. 20-33)

Kate's temper is beginning to boil, and Petruchio, the famed teacher of good manners is delighted, not horrified. "To her, Kate," he yells. . . .

Petruchio suggest the wager that will confirm his genius at wife-taming. He knows that Kate will obey his commands and, like a trained hawk, show her aggressive spirit when let fly. Bianca leaves the table when Petruchio threatens to "have at her for a bitter jest or two"; naturally, she is not eager to return and replies to Lucentio's summons that she is busy and cannot come. The Widow suspects rightly that "some goodly jest" is in hand and also refuses to return. At Petruchio's summons, Kate immediately returns to the table and goes off again to fetch the other women, by force if necessary. Although Kate wins the wager for Petruchio, he would have her perform one additional trick to "show more sign of her obedience" by stepping on her cap at his command. The Widow and Bianca are appalled by this display of something Bianca hesitates to call "duty." To Lucentio's complaint that she has made him lose five hundred crowns, she replies, "The more fool you for laying on my duty," as indeed he is. The wish is father to the critical thought that Kate's early tantrums express an intrinsic honesty while Bianca's amiableness and dutifulness are proof of a simpering, scheming hypocrisy. Other evidence, I imagine, are her love of music and poetry and her attractiveness to many suitors. The final revelation of the hardness and latent shrewishness of her nature is presumably her refusal to return to the wedding table, where she has been baited by her brother-in-law on her wedding day while her bridegroom sat silent. If her anger at her husband's wager on her obedience is reprehensible, we must rejoice in Ophelia's submission to Polonius's dictates and idealize Helena's willingness to be humiliated by Bertram. . . .

Kate offers no metaphysical justification for wifely obedience; instead she dwells on the natural superiority of men (who are spoken of as "prince," "lord," "king," "governor," "head," and "sovereign") to women, who are described as "muddy," "ill-seeming," "thick," "froward," "sullen," "peevish" and "sour" when they disobey their husbands, to whom they owe all. Kate also reminds the brides that they are "unable worms" with soft and weak bodies.

This is not the speech of woman who has blossomed under her husband's tutelage and can confidently enjoy her femininity. Of course, some suggest that Kate speaks these lines with a knowing wink or smile to assure an audience that she does not mean what she says. No doubt the speech can be made comic by a wink or a sly manner of delivery—almost any speech can—but ironic subtlety is not Kate's distinguishing characteristic, and these lines are too earnest and weighted with conviction to be a clever gambit. She means what she says; she takes pride, if not pleasure, in stooping to Petruchio's whistle, especially when she proves herself more valuable and praiseworthy than the other wives, who have the ease and confidence she lacks. She must take a demeaning view of her sex or be oppressed by the realization of her singularly demeaning marriage.

PETRUCHIO

A key question in interpreting *The Taming of the Shrew* is whether Shakespeare presents Petruchio as an admirable character or as an offensive one. Closely related is the matter of his motives for wanting to marry Katherina and his goals in "taming" her. Productions of the play have differed widely in their answers to these questions, as have the critics.

Many writers point to Petruchio's energy, imagination, and firmness of purpose as qualities that make him an attractive character. Others, such as **Cecil C. Seronsy** (in the section on APPEARANCE VS. REALITY), regard him as an exceptionally perceptive man able to recognize possibilities in Katherina's character that no one else in the play suspects. Most modern critics, like Alexander Leggatt and **H. J. Oliver** interpret Petruchio's outrageous behavior as a role he assumes in order to shake Katherina out of her shrewishness. Leggatt portrays Petruchio's treatment of Katherina as an attempt to make her a willing participant in his "game." Similar analyses were developed in the early 1970s by **Richard Henze** (in the section on GAMES AND ROLE-PLAYING) and Ralph Berry. Oliver rejects this interpretation, arguing that Petruchio's methods are often unjustifiably harsh and that while Petruchio admires Katherina's spirit he is seriously intent on dominating and controlling her. Critics such as **Coppélia Kahn** and **Shirley Nelson Garner** (in the GENDER ROLES section) point out that Petruchio's violent and willful behavior is not limited to the "taming" process, but is demonstrated in the play well before he meets Katherina. Petruchio,

An engraving of Act IV, scene i, featuring Katherina and Petruchio.

they argue, is even more "shrewish" than Katherina, but his behavior is considered acceptable and even praiseworthy because he is a man.

Petruchio's motives have also been the subject of critical debate. In an essay published in 1897, the Irish dramatist Bernard Shaw praised Shakespeare's creation of Petruchio as a realistic portrait of a man motivated by a desire to "make himself rich and comfortable." Many other commentators, however, such as **Kenneth Muir** and **Harold Goddard** (in the section on KATHERINA), see Petruchio as being motivated by a genuine affection and admiration for Katherina. **George R. Hibbard** (in the GENDER ROLES section), in a 1964 essay suggested that Petruchio is at least partially motivated by "his sportsman's love of risk." Michael West, on the other hand, in an article published in 1974, saw the attraction between Katherina and Petruchio as primarily sexual. More recently, critics such as Kahn and Garner have characterized Petruchio as motivated by a desire to assert his manhood by dominating his wife.

H. J. Oliver

SOURCE: An introduction to *The Taming of the Shrew*, Oxford at the Clarendon Press, 1982, pp. 1-75.

[*In the following excerpt, Oliver analyzes Petruchio's suitability for the task of "taming" Katherina. The critic rejects readings that see Petruchio as motivated by love as well as evaluations that suggest Katherina and Petruchio are merely "playing a game." Instead, Oliver emphasizes Petruchio's superior maturity and experience and his ability to make a plan and stick to it as the primary reasons for his success. The critic also suggests that Petruchio's treatment of Katherina is at times so harsh that it would have won sympathy for Katherina even from an Elizabethan audience hardened to plays about "shrew-taming."*]

[Petruchio], of course, is the 'right' man for the task—and it is difficult to understand the objections to Peter Alexander's statement [in *Shakespeare's Life and Art*, 1939] that the story is, among other things, a variation on 'the perilous maiden theme, where the lady is death to any suitor who woos her except the hero, in whose hands her apparent vices turn to virtues'. As Curtis infers, hearing of Petruchio's behaviour, 'he is more shrew than she' (4.1.75); or as Grumio puts it, 'an she knew him as well as I do, she would think scolding would do little good upon him' (1.2.107-8); as Peter sums it up, 'he kills her in her own humour' (4.1.168) (and not, surely, as the sentimental modern orthodoxy believes, by *burlesquing* her behaviour, so that she sees herself as others see her, and finally 'sees the joke', but by standing

over her and proving that with him shrewishness simply will not work).

For his role as tamer, he has all the necessary attributes. For example, he is mature: 'Yet you are withered', Kate taunts him, and he replies ''Tis with cares' (2.1.238)—and although in most modern productions Kate is played by a sophisticated actress in her twenties or thirties, Shakespeare may well have thought of her as about sixteen. She is older than Bianca—but then on the evidence of other Shakespeare comedies Bianca would be thought marriageable at fourteen—and Kate's tantrums as well as Petruchio's treatment of them may seem rather more credible if she, too, in her own way is a spoilt child. However that may be, she certainly thinks of Petruchio, in the line just quoted, as older than she is. He also claims—and there is no reason to doubt the claim—a wide range of dangerous experience:

> Have I not in my time heard lions roar? . . .
> Have I not heard great ordnance in the field . . .
> And do you tell me of a woman's tongue . . . ?
> Tush, tush, fear boys with bugs!

—and Grumio adds 'For he fears none' (1.2.196-206).

In the tradition of the best tamers, he is quite without sentiment:

> I come to wive it wealthily in Padua;
> If wealthily, then happily in Padua
>
> (1.2.74-5)

and insists that his prospective father-in-law come to the point:

> Then tell me, if I get your daughter's love,
> What dowry shall I have with her to wife?
>   (2.1.118-19).

It is apparently not even beneath his dignity to bargain with Bianca's wooers that if they want Katherine out of the way, they shall pay the expenses of his courtship of her.

If he lacks sentiment, however, he is certainly capable of appreciating strength in a woman's character, including strength of resistance, and when he hears of Kate's breaking of the lute over Hortensio's head proclaims:

> Now by the world, it is a lusty wench;
> I love her ten times more than e'er I did.
> O how I long to have some chat with her!
>   (2.1.159-61).

Love, of course, has nothing to do with the case, and there is no place for love in a farce; but he does admire, and he welcomes the challenge of prospective strong opposition. Kate is like him in that respect: the implication of their first meeting and its prolonged and rather tedious exchange of insults is that she is at least interested in him, almost in spite of herself, and welcomes his un-Hortensio-like refusal to cower.

Petruchio has one other quality invaluable in a tamer—the ability to make a plan, and to keep to it. Just before their first meeting he announces, in soliloquy, his proposed strategy of calculated opposition:

> Say that she rail, why then I'll tell her plain
> She sings as sweetly as a nightingale . . .
> If she deny to wed, I'll crave the day
> When I shall ask the banns, and when be
>   married
>
> (2.1.169-79);

he tells her to her face what he proposes to do:

> For I am he am born to tame you, Kate,
> And bring you from a wild Kate to a Kate
> Conformable as other household Kates
>
> (2.1.275-7)

and then, again in soliloquy, when the programme is in operation, explains exactly how he is carrying out the plan 'to man my haggard' (4.1.175-98). Nothing is accidental, nothing unpredicted; and Hazlitt summed it up perfectly when he said that 'There is no contending with a person on whom nothing makes any impression but his own purposes, and who is bent on his own whims just in proportion as they seem to want common sense. With him a thing's being plain and reasonable is a reason against it. . . . The whole of his treatment of his wife at home is in the same spirit of ironical attention and inverted gallantry.'

Katherine learns that it is no use hitting him, as she might hit Hortensio, for 'I swear I'll cuff you if you strike again' (2.1.222); it is no use being shrewish when he has announced that it is their agreement that she shall be so in public; it is no use refusing to go with him after the wedding when he pretends that he is rescuing her from those who might help her to stay; it is no use claiming to be the injured party when he thanks the wedding guests who 'have beheld me give away myself / To this most patient, sweet, and virtuous wife' (3.2.193-4); it is no use complaining that food is denied when it is said to be bad for her health. Petruchio's campaign has already passed the point of possible failure when the assurance is given, in 4.1.68-70, that for the first time she was more concerned with somebody else—Grumio—than with herself ('how she waded through the dirt to pluck him off me'); and soon afterwards she is seen trying to defend the servants from her husband's (feigned) anger.

Lynn Fontanne and Alfred Lunt as Kate and Petruchio, in a 1935 production of The Taming of the Shrew.

There is nothing to warrant an assumption that—at this stage, at any rate—Katherine and Petruchio are merely 'playing a game'. She *is* being *tamed*, and the spectacle would be acceptable if, but only if, Katherine had no feelings and the audience had no concern for *her*. In fact, however, Shakespeare sometimes dramatizes Kate's genuine distress. No modern playgoer can fail to sympathize with her, part of the time at least, and—difficult as such questions are—it is not easy to believe that the Elizabethan audience was always on Petruchio's side.

A crucial scene is the wedding. Katherine's words when her bridegroom does not appear for the ceremony are bound to arouse compassion:

> No shame but mine . . .
> Now must the world point at poor
>   Katherine
> And say 'Lo, there is mad Petruchio's wife,
> If it would please him come and marry her'
>
> (3.2.8-20).

Tranio is embarrassed ('Patience, *good* Katherine . . .'); and Baptista for once shows fatherly understanding:

Go, girl, I cannot blame thee now to
　weep,
For such an injury would vex a very
　saint,
Much more a shrew of thy impatient
　humour.

They are both further concerned—not least for Katherine—when Petruchio arrives in his disarray ('See not *your bride* in these unreverent robes'). Most significantly of all: Gremio admits, in his account of the riotous marriage ceremony, that Katherine is 'a lamb, a dove' compared with Petruchio, and confesses 'I seeing this came thence *for very shame*'. If even Gremio can be ashamed, the audience cannot fail to be so too; it will feel that this is indeed 'a way to *kill* a wife', and not 'with kindness'. The world of farce—for all the broad humour of Petruchio's antics—has been left behind, and Katherine has long ceased to be merely the subject of an experiment.

The audience's disquiet will probably continue in the scenes at Petruchio's house, when she is not only denied food but also allowed to be the victim of mockery by the very servants; and there will not be general agreement with the attempts by some twentieth-century critics to 'save' her by saying that she 'enjoys the game' in Act 4 Scene 5 when she declines any longer to have an opinion different from her husband's. The mood is rather weary resignation:

　. . . be it moon, or sun, or what you please;
　And if you please to call it a rush-
　　candle,
　Henceforth I vow it shall be so for me
　　　　　　　　　　　　(ll. 13-15).

Petruchio's victory, if it is a victory, is a very poor one indeed—and to say this is not to agree for one minute with H. C. Goddard's desperate claim that 'the play is an early version of *What Every Woman Knows*—what every woman knows being, of course, that the woman can lord it over the man so long as she allows him to think he is lording it over her'. (As R. B. Heilman nicely put it [in a 1966 article in *Modern Language Quarterly*], 'After three centuries of relative stability, then, Petruchio has developed rather quickly, first from an animal tamer to a gentleman lover who simply brings out the best in Kate, and then at last to a laughable victim of the superior spouse who dupes him'.) In fact, Katherine never 'lords it' over Petruchio; in nearly every sense that matters she loses; and Goddard admits that his main reason for interpreting the play in this way is to bring it 'into line' with the other comedies because otherwise it would be 'an unaccountable exception' and a regression. It is not a regression but a young dramatist's attempt, not repeated, to mingle two genres that cannot be combined. . . .

SOURCES FOR FURTHER STUDY

Literary Commentary

Berry, Ralph. "The Rules of the Game." In *Shakespeare's Comedies: Explorations in Form*, pp. 54-71. Princeton, NJ: Princeton University Press, 1972.

　Argues that while The *Taming of the Shrew* may be, in essence, a "brutal sex farce," it is also a subtle portrayal of two people coming to terms on the rules of the games played between men and women.

Boose, Linda. "*The Taming of the Shrew*, Good Husbandry, and Enclosure." *Shakespeare Reread: The Texts in New Contexts*, edited by Russ McDonald, pp. 193-225. Ithaca: Cornell, 1994.

　Relates the play's treatment of social and sexual hierarchy to socioeconomic changes and class conflict in early modern England.

Bradbrook, Muriel C. "Dramatic Role as Social Image: A Study of *The Taming of the Shrew*." *Shakespeare Jahrbuch* 94, (1958): 132-50.

　Examines Shakespeare's adaptation of the traditional roles associated with characters in earlier treatments of the shrew story, focusing in particular on his development of the characters of Katherina and Petruchio.

Brooks, Charles. "Shakespeare's Romantic Shrews." *Shakespeare Quarterly* 11, No. 3 (Summer, 1960): 351-6.

　Compares Katherina and Bianca with other Shakespearean female characters.

Coghill, Nevil. "The Basis of Shakespearian Comedy." *Essays and Studies* 3 (1950): 1-28.

　One of the first essays to argue that Katherina, not Petruchio, is the one who succeeds in mastering "the art of practice of matrimony."

Dusinberre, Juliet. "*The Taming of the Shrew*: Women, Acting, and Power." *Studies in the Literary Imagination* 26, No. 1 (Spring, 1993): 67-84.

　Points out ways in which the play calls attention to the Elizabethan practice of using boy actors in female roles and examines the effect of this practice on the play's portrayal of gender relations.

Duthie, George Ian. "Shakespeare and the Order-Disorder Antithesis" and "Comedy." *Shakespeare*, pp. 39-56, 57-88. London: Hutchinson's University Library, 1951.

　Interprets *The Taming of the Shrew* in terms of Elizabethan notions of a divinely ordered hierarchy of creation.

Greer, Germaine. "The Middle-Class Myth of Love and Marriage." *The Female Eunuch*, pp. 195-215. New York: McGraw-Hill, 1970.

Briefly discusses *The Taming of the Shrew* in the context of changing ideas about the nature of marriage in late sixteenth-century England.

Heffernan, Carol F. "*The Taming of the Shrew:* The Bourgeoisie in Love." *Essays in Literature* 12, No. 1 (Spring, 1985): 3-14.

Analyzes the play's portrayal of the values of the emergent middle class and its critique of the materialistic nature of Elizabethan marriage arrangements.

Heilman, Robert B. "The 'Taming' Untamed, or, The Return of the Shrew." *Modern Language Quarterly* 27, No. 2 (June, 1966): 147-61.

Argues against twentieth-century interpretations of *The Shrew* that turn this "free-swinging farce" into "a brittlely ironic comic drama."

Jayne, Sears. "The Dreaming of 'The Shrew'." *Shakespeare Quarterly* 17, No. 1 (Winter, 1966): 41-56.

Regards the dramatic events of *The Taming of the Shrew* from Act I, scene ii, onwards as Sly's wish-fulfilling dream.

Leggatt, Alexander. "The Taming of the Shrew." In *Shakespeare's Comedy of Love*, 41-62. London: Methuen, 1974.

Notes that although Petruchio appears to challenge orthodox notions of propriety with his eccentric behavior, he ultimately teaches Katherina to appreciate social amenities and to value "peace . . . and love, and quiet life" (V, ii, 108). In addition, the critic calls attention to the many images drawn from sport, especially such blood sports as "hunting and hawking," associated with Petruchio's taming of Katherina.

Mack, Maynard. "Engagement and Detachment in Shakespeare's Plays." *Essays on Shakespeare and Elizabethan Drama in Honor of Hardin Craig*, edited by Richard Hosley, pp. 275-96. Columbia: University of Missouri Press, 1962.

Examines the psychological process by which Petruchio tries to change Katherina's view of her own identity.

Newman, Karen. "Renaissance Family Politics and Shakespeare's *The Taming of the Shrew.*" *English Literary Renaissance* 16, No. 1 (Winter, 1986): 86-100.

Argues that by emphasizing its own theatricality, *The Taming of the Shrew* undermines Elizabethan social and gender roles by revealing them to be artificial.

Novy, Marianne L. "Patriarchy and Play in *The Taming of the Shrew*," in *English Literary Renaissance* 9, No. 2 (Spring, 1979): 264-80.

Examines the relationship between game-playing and the play's reaffirmation of male authority in the play.

Ranald, Margaret Loftus. "The Performance of Feminism in *The Taming of the Shrew.*" *Theatre Research International*, n.s. 19, No. 3 (Fall, 1994): 214-25.

Provides a brief review of the play's performance history, focusing in particular in how the relationship between Katherine and Petruchio has been portrayed.

Shapiro, Michael. "Framing the Taming: Metatheatrical Awareness of Female Impersonation in *The Taming of the Shrew.*" *The Yearbook of English Studies* 23 (1993): 143-66.

Looks at how the Elizabethan use of boy actors in female roles might have affected audience perception of the play's female characters.

Shaw, Bernard. "Chin Chon Chino." *The Saturday Review* 84, No. 2193 (November 6, 1987): 488-90.

Praises the play as a "realistic comedy" but finds the final scene deplorable.

Traversi, Derek. "'The Taming of the Shrew.'" *William Shakespeare: The Early Comedies*, pp. 14-22. London: The British Council, 1960.

Maintains that *The Taming of the Shrew* defends the view that male domination of women is ordained by nature.

Ulrici, Hermann. "Criticisms of Shakspeare's Drama: 'Much Ado about Nothing'—'Taming of the Shrew'." *Shakspeare's Dramatic Art: And His Relation to Calderon and Goethe*, translated by A. J. W. Morrison, pp. 289-99. London: Chapman Brothers, 1839.

Notes relationships between the Induction and the main body of the play.

Webster, Margaret. "The Early Plays." *Shakespeare without Tears*, pp. 135-58. New York: Whittlesey House, 1942.

Sees the play as depicting an ideal couple's negotiation of a "marriage of true minds."

West, Michael. "The Folk Background of Petruchio's Wooing Dance: Male Supremacy in 'The Taming of the Shrew.'" *Shakespeare Studies: An Annual Gathering of Research, Criticism, and Reviews* 7 (1974): 65-73.

Examines similarities between the play and folk traditions of courtship in arguing that the principal source of the play's "imaginative appeal" is its lusty depiction of the rites of sexual initiation.

Media Adaptations

Kiss Me Kate. MGM, 1953.

Film version of the 1948 Cole Porter musical based on *The Taming of the Shrew*. Two divorced actors can't separate their real lives from their stage lives after they are engaged to play Katherina and Petruchio in a production of Shakespeare's play. Distributed by MGM/UA Home Entertainment, Facets Multimedia, Inc. 110 minutes.

Kiss Me Petruchio, New York Shakespeare Festival, 1982.
Documentary on the New York Shakespeare
Festival's production of *The Taming of the Shrew*.
Distributed by Films Inc. Video, Professional Media
Service Corp., 58 minutes.

The Taming of the Shrew. Pickford Corporation, Elton
Corporation, United Artists, 1929, re-edited 1966.
Earliest film version, an early talkie featuring the
only pairing of real-life couple Mary Pickford and
Douglas Fairbanks. Distributed by Nostalgia Family
Video, Critics' Choice Video. 66 minutes.

The Taming of the Shrew. Columbia, 1967.
A lavish screen version, starring Elizabeth Taylor
and Richard Burton and directed by Franco Zeffirelli.
Distributed by Columbia Tristar Home Video, The
Video Catalog, PBS Video. 122 minutes.

The Taming of the Shrew. International Film Bureau, 1974.
Presents two scenes from the play: Petruchio vows
to marry Katherina, and he begins the process of
"taming" her. Distributed by International Film
Bureau, Inc. 13 minutes.

The Taming of the Shrew. NET, 1980.
Performance by the American Conservatory Theatre
at the Geary Theatre in San Francisco. Distributed
by WNET/Thirteen Non-Broadcast. 120 minutes.

The Taming of the Shrew. Cedric Messina, Dr. Jonathan
Miller, BBC, 1981.
Stars John Cleese and Sarah Badel. Distributed by
Ambrose Video Publishing, Inc. 127 minutes.

THE TEMPEST

INTRODUCTION

Critical consensus places the composition of *The Tempest* sometime in the years 1610-11. Its first recorded performance was before King James I on November 1, 1611, making it one of the last, if not the last, drama that Shakespeare produced without the help of a collaborator.

Although regarded as one of the dramatist's most original works, *The Tempest* is said to have been influenced by a number of texts, including Michel de Montaigne's essay "Of the Cannibals" (translated into English in 1603), Sylvester Jourdain's *A Discovery of the Bermudas* (1610), *A true Declaration of the estate of the Colony in Virginia* (1610), as well as other accounts of exploration and discovery in the New World. In terms of plot, several possible sources have been put forth, though none contain more than scant resemblances to Shakespeare's play. Thus, many scholars agree with the assessment of Frank Kermode that the genesis of *The Tempest* is in no single work, but in a body of formal literature and folklore that typically features a magician, a lovely young princess, and a group of stranded courtiers and commoners.

The work is said to be of a piece with Shakespeare's other late plays, which, though comedies, are not without tragic elements and dark undertones. This facet of the play was less frequently noted by early commentators, who stressed both the play's imaginative singularity and depth of observation. However, *The Tempest*'s intermingling of moods has led many recent critics to focus on the complexities and ambiguities of the work. An example of such criticism is that of the play's central character, Prospero, a somewhat mysterious figure who supports many shades of interpretation. Prospero is a magician and the originator of the action in the play. The forces that motivate Prospero include revenge against those who have usurped his power, as well as reconciliation, which is symbolized by the union of Ferdinand and Miranda. Analysis of these motivating factors is central to the critical thought regarding the thematic structure of *The Tempest*.

Additionally, *The Tempest* is thought to confront the question of the effects of colonization and civilization on human nature in relation to the Christian theme of redemption.

PRINCIPAL CHARACTERS

(in order of appearance)

Alonso: King of Naples. He had helped Antonio to seize the dukedom of Milan from Prospero, but over the course of the play grows repentant for his actions.

Sebastian: Alonso's traitorous brother. He plots to kill Alonso while on the island, and so take the throne of Naples, but is foiled by Prospero's servant, Ariel.

Antonio: Brother to Prospero and usurper of the dukedom of Milan. He urges Sebastian to murder Alonso in his sleep.

Ferdinand: Son of King Alonso and heir to his throne. After being tested by Prospero he is granted permission to marry Miranda.

Gonzalo: Trusted advisor to Alonso, he is sympathetic to the plight of Prospero.

Prospero: Former Duke of Milan. He is a powerful magician who uses his control over the spirit Ariel to create a tempest that brings Alonso and his entourage to the island. He seeks retribution for the treachery that these men have visited upon him. (See **Prospero** *in the* **CHARACTER STUDIES** *section*.)

Miranda: Daughter of Prospero. Completely educated by her father on the island; innocence is her defining quality. She falls in love with Ferdinand. (See **Miranda** *in the* **CHARACTER STUDIES** *section*.)

Ariel: A spirit of the air. Bound to Prospero, who has freed him from imprisonment, he seeks his freedom from the magician in exchange for serving him faithfully during the course of the play. (See **Ariel** *in the* **CHARACTER STUDIES** *section*.)

Caliban: The misshapen offspring of a devil and the witch Sycorax. He is the recalcitrant slave of Prospero, who uses him to perform menial labor. (See **Caliban** *in the* **CHARACTER STUDIES** *section*.)

Trinculo: Alonso's jester. He falls in with Caliban and Stephano in a comical plot to wrest power from Prospero.

Stephano: Butler to King Alonso, and a drunk. He

plans a conspiracy to take over the island with the help of Caliban and Trinculo.

PLOT SYNOPSIS

Act I: While traveling at sea King Alonso of Naples and several members of his court, including his brother Sebastian, his son Ferdinand, his advisor Gonzalo, and Duke Antonio of Milan are caught in a powerful storm and shipwrecked on a tropical island where Prospero and his daughter, Miranda, live. Meanwhile, Prospero relates to his daughter the tale of their exile on this island. Twelve years ago, Prospero, then Duke of Milan, saw his rule usurped by his brother Antonio, who, with the aid of King Alonso, set him and his young child adrift at sea. Both would have died had Alonso's kind counsellor, Gonzalo, not equipped their boat with provisions, including Prospero's magic books and wand. The currents brought them to the island, which once belonged to the now-dead witch Sycorax. The only inhabitants they encountered were Caliban, Sycorax's grotesquely malformed son, and Ariel, a spirit of the air long since imprisoned in a tree by Sycorax. Prospero endeavored to educate Caliban, teaching him language and attempting to instill moral character, but failed in the latter. And, after Caliban's failed effort to rape Miranda, Prospero was forced to reduce him to a slave, assigning him the tasks of chopping wood and finding fresh water. The magician freed Ariel from his prison, but then placed the spirit in his service, exploiting his powers over the air and sea. Anxious to earn his full freedom, Ariel serves his master dutifully, creating the tempest at sea and leading the shipwrecked voyagers to safety on the island. While all survive the storm, Prospero sees that they are splintered into groups, leaving each to believe that the others have perished. Ferdinand is separated from the rest and drawn by the song of Ariel to Prospero's cave. Miranda, upon seeing the prince (the first man aside from her father and Caliban that she has ever beheld) immediately falls in love. Prospero does not disapprove of this, as it is part of his plan, but treats the boy with mock circumspection before Miranda. Claiming that Ferdinand must be tested, Prospero enslaves the boy with his magic.

Act II: King Alonso and his counselors Sebastian, Antonio, and Gonzalo appear in another part of the island; unable to locate Ferdinand, they believe that he is dead. Gonzalo attempts to change the subject and delivers a speech on his ideal commonwealth. A discussion ensues, but is cut short by the appearance of Ariel, who puts all save Sebastian and Antonio to sleep. The two speak of murdering Alonso in order to take his kingdom, but Ariel puts an end to the conspiracy by awaking the king's venerable advisor.

Nearby, a drunken Trinculo runs across Caliban. After some deliberation the jester decides to climb under Caliban's cloak as protection against an approaching storm. Soon after, Stephano, also drinking, encounters the pair hidden under the cloak and mistakes them for some strange monster. Later recognized by Trinculo, the trio fall to drinking together. Caliban, overcome by the "celestial liquor," claims his everlasting subservience to Stephano. The three then set off, with Caliban singing of his newfound freedom.

Act III: Miranda stops to speak to Ferdinand, now engaged in gathering logs to prove his worthiness. While Prospero watches unseen, both declare their love for one another. Meanwhile, a new conspiracy is being hatched on the island. Caliban urges his drunken companions to kill Prospero, allowing Stephano to become king of the island and to take Miranda as his queen. The ever vigilant Ariel learns of the plot. Elsewhere, Prospero (kept invisible by magic) creates an illusory banquet, mocking Alonso and his company. Soon Ariel appears in the form of a harpy and causes the banquet to vanish. He taunts the king and his fellows and reproves them for their crimes against Prospero and Miranda. Alonso, frightened by the prospect that his betrayal has been found out, runs away, followed by the others.

Act IV: Prospero's trial of Ferdinand is now over. He releases the prince from his spell and again calls on Ariel, this time to create a magical betrothal masque for the young lovers. Thus appear the spirits Iris, Juno, and Ceres with a gathering of nymphs, who dance and sing along. Prospero becomes suddenly troubled as he recalls the conspiracy of Caliban, Stephano and Trinculo. He ends the masque and forms a plan to punish the plotters. Ariel disappears briefly only to return laden with fine clothes that Prospero directs him to hang on a line. Caliban and the others, all of whom are drenched, happen upon the garments. As they put on the clothes, Ariel and the spirits under his direction change shape into a pack of dogs and chase them away.

Act V: Prospero, fully outfitted in the robes of his dukedom, determines to relinquish his magical powers by breaking his magic wand and throwing his books into the sea. But first he instructs Ariel to bring Sebastian, Antonio and the others before him. Holding them in an enchanted circle, he greets the honorable Gonzalo, rebukes Sebastian for his treacherous actions, and orders Antonio to relinquish control of the dukedom of Milan and return the seat to its rightful owner. Meanwhile, King Alonso has grown repentant and Prospero shows him his son and Miranda playing a game of chess. Ariel again appears, this time with the ship's Master and Boatswain who tell those gathered that their ship is intact and ready to set sail for Italy. Ariel again disappears and returns with Caliban, Stephano, and Trinculo, all of whom are still drunk and bruised from their exploits. To all, Prospero offers forgiveness for their treacheries. He will forsake his magic and accept his place as Duke of Milan. As his final act, he releases Ariel from servitude and speaks the epilogue to the play, bidding the audience for applause.

PRINCIPAL TOPICS

Magic

Magic has a strong presence throughout *The Tempest* and pervades nearly every action in the play. While this quality informs the work with a fairy tale atmosphere, it is important to recognize that in Shakespeare's time the topic of magic was treated with more seriousness than in our own. Some Renaissance scholars, such as Henry Cornelius Agrippa (of whose writings Shakespeare may have been cognizant), possessed much expertise in the subject of magic and wrote books describing the different sources of magical power. In simple terms, Shakespeare's audience would have been aware of two types of magic, the white (good) and the black (evil). In this scheme Prospero likely would have been deemed a theurgist, or practicer of white magic—a force derived from divine sources and dealing in the control of natural elements. This form of magic is said to have affinities with the natural sciences, as in the study of alchemy (the forerunner of modern chemistry). The other form of magic, black magic, is only tangentially related to the action of *The Tempest*. It was supposed to come from demonic sources, such as those that might have been wielded by Caliban's mother, the witch Sycorax.

Prospero and his servant, Ariel, are the two principal workers of magic in *The Tempest*. Both possess powers of illusion and deception. Under Prospero's orders, Ariel creates a powerful tempest at the beginning of the play that appears to destroy Alonso's ship and strand all of its passengers on the island. By the end of the play, however, the Boatswain exclaims that the ship "Is tight and yare bravely rigg'd, as when / We first put out to sea." Likewise, Prospero uses magic to separate and confuse the new inhabitants on the isle and to convince each that the others were surely killed in the storm. Prospero's manipulation of others through magic points to one of the important motifs in the work, the contrast between appearance and reality. Thus, as the illusions are lifted at the end of the play, Shakespeare invokes the theme of disenchantment, and places reality aright. These effects are particularly revealed in the characters of Caliban, who appears to have reached a level of disillusionment by rejecting his previously slavish

behavior, and Alonso, in his newfound remorse for his past evil actions toward Prospero. Another significant critical application of this topic is a comparison of Prospero's magical powers to the work of an artist (i. e. Shakespeare) and his manipulation of reality through art. Many biographical explanations of *The Tempest* equate Prospero with Shakespeare and claim that the play represents Shakespeare's farewell to drama. Evidence for such an interpretation relies on the fact that Prospero consistently manipulates scenes and events in the play: he stages masques, orchestrates illusions, directs the actions of his fellows on the island, and finally, in the epilogue to the work, addresses the audience, asking for applause—, "But release me from my bands / With the help of your good hands: / Gentle breath of yours my sails / Must fill, or else my project fails, / Which was to please." Prospero's "project" therefore becomes the same as Shakespeare's, the entertainment (and perhaps instruction) of his audience. His magical manipulations are thus aligned with Shakespeare's own artistic endeavors in creating the play.

Order and Structure

Critics have over the centuries been very interested in the structure of *The Tempest,* noting that, in a manner quite uncharacteristic of him, Shakespeare closely adhered to the classical concept of the unities of time and space in that play. The action takes place entirely on the tropical island that is home to Prospero, Miranda, Ariel, and Caliban, and its duration is only a few hours—approximately as long as a theatrical performance of *The Tempest* would take. The only other play in which Shakespeare observed the classical unities rule is the early *Comedy of Errors,* and his reasons for this late departure from his usual practice have remained somewhat mysterious. Various theories have been advanced by critics in this regard: some, for example, contend that Shakespeare wanted to prove to his detractors, like Ben Jonson, that he could indeed write a tightly unified play; others suggest that the play might be a very early and immature work in which Shakespeare conformed to the unities out of inexperience; still others view the play as Shakespeare's farewell to the theater in which he wanted to portray a perfectly ordered, balanced world as a sort of final vision. In this latter biographical interpretaion, the dramatist is linked with the character of Prospero, an artificer and magician, through whom Shakespeare comments on his own role as an artist and arranger of reality.

Most scholars, however, have focused on Shakespeare's skillful use of order and structure in *The Tempest* as a means of advancing the themes of reconciliation, restoration of order, and forgiveness in the play. *The Tempest*'s strong use of symmetry, contrast, and parallelism in charactrization and structure neatly contributes to the idea of order achieved by the end, with characters commenting upon each other (for example, Ariel on Caliban, and Propsero on Gonzalo) and various scenes inviting parallels that ultimately contribute to harmony. Many commentators have also called attention to Shakespeare's handling of time in the play. All scenes are based firmly in the present, with the past referred to only to illuminate the present, and the hoped-for future presented as an offshoot of the present. With so much emphasis on the now, the theme of the need to seize the opportunity to bring about forgiveness and reconciliation while the moment is right is highlighted through Shakespeare's masterful handling of order and structure in the play.

Music and the Masque

The Tempest is one of Shakespeare's most musical plays and is filled with more songs and music than any other of his dramas. Much of this music comes in the form of Ariel's songs, which are scattered throughout the play, but music is also an integral part of the betrothal masque that Prospero throws in celebration of Miranda's and Ferdinand's love. In Shakespeare's time music was commonly associated with celestial harmony, a theory that derives in part from the writings of Aristotle and the ideas of Medieval Christian commentators on his work. According to this theory, the planets, the moon, the sun, and the stars were said to orbit the earth in perfect crystalline spheres that produced a kind of beautiful music, representing the sanctity of the heavens. This blissful harmony is said to relate to the theme of reconciliation that informs *The Tempest*. While the play opens with its characters in a state of conflict, primarily involving Prospero's desire to revenge the usurpation of his dukedom, the motion of the play is toward reconciliation in the next generation. Prospero's feud with King Alonso is overcome by the love of Miranda and Ferdinand and their political squabbling is ended by the joining of their children in marriage.

Music is further related to the theme of reconciliation in the betrothal masque of Ferdinand and Miranda. While Shakespeare's presentation of this masque in Act IV, scene i, seems a bow to its vogue at the time that *The Tempest* was written, it nevertheless represents several integral thematic aspects of the play. In Shakespeare's time the masque—a stylized production consisting of song, dance, music, and mythology designed as a courtly entertainment—had reached a high point of popularity. This masque in *The Tempest* invokes the mythological figures of Iris, Juno, and Ceres, the last of whom, a classical goddess of fertility, places a blessing on Miranda and Ferdinand. It also invokes Shakespeare's theme of life as an illusion and the transience of worldly things. As the masque

ends, Prospero tells Ferdinand, "Yea, all . . . shall dissolve / And, like this insubstantial pageant faded, / Leave not a rack behind. We are such stuff / As dreams are made on, and our little life / Is rounded with a sleep."

CHARACTER STUDIES

Prospero

Prospero is the central force behind the entire action of *The Tempest*, and remains the only character (except for his servant, Ariel) who is aware of everything that takes place over the course of the play. Prospero first appears in Act I, scene ii, in the role of father and educator to his daughter, Miranda, at which time he relates the tale of his lost dukedom and his lust for revenge. Yet he does not reveal his plan to Miranda; instead, he sends her to sleep (to spare her innocence) before conversing with Ariel about what should be done with the victims of the recent shipwreck. His tone changes somewhat when he speaks to Ariel, as he uses coercion and threats to assure that his bidding is done. Likewise, he treats the slave, Caliban, with a heavy hand; while he once had hopes of educating the creature, he appears to have long since given up in that endeavor. He remains Machiavellian in his behavior even after Miranda awakes and beholds Ferdinand. Feigning skepticism, he reveals in an aside his pleasure that the two have met and fallen in love.

In the first scene of Act III, Prospero appears to soften slightly as he witnesses the growing love of Miranda and Ferdinand. Still, he has more important business that requires his attention and he achieves it through Ariel, who carries out his whims in punishing Alonso, Sebastian, Antonio, and later Caliban and his companions. Here Prospero uses his skill in magic to achieve his ends. He instructs Ariel to create the masques—a mock banquet for the king, with illusory delights, and a betrothal masque for Ferdinand and Miranda—while he stands back from the action.

By the opening of Act V, Prospero has for the most part achieved his goals. He speaks with confidence, "Now does my project gather to a head / My charms crack not; my spirits obey." With the conspirators brought before him, Prospero takes his pleasure in reprimanding them and in demonstrating his victory. But first he decides to abjure his magical powers, "I'll break my staff / Bury it certain fadoms in the earth, / and deeper than did ever plummet sound / I'll drown my book." He no longer needs the assistance of magical powers and will return to oversee his dukedom in Milan. Ariel can be set free and Caliban can once again be sole ruler of the island.

While his initial motivation is highly charged by a desire for revenge, the final note of Prospero's character is one of mercy and forgiveness. Generally he is perceived as wise, benevolent, and just. His role in the play as a magician and an artificer of the plot give him an almost god-like quality, since he controls the other characters' perceptions of reality and metes out punishment and reward as he sees fit. Likewise, Prospero plays the role of ruler in the microcosmic society on the island. His word becomes law, though many seek to depose him. Still, he appears fair in his dealings with others, expresses his fatherly love for Miranda, and appears more eager to set things right than to harshly discipline those who have wronged him. Additionally, in his final plan, which brings his daughter and Alonso's son, Ferdinand, together, he demonstrates a movement toward reconciliation rather than revenge.

Ariel

Ariel makes his first appearance midway through Act I, scene ii, as he is called upon by Prospero to do his bidding. Obedient without being sycophantic, Ariel expresses his confidence and pride in his magical skill which has brought King Alonso and his followers to the island. A spirit of the air possessing the ethereal qualities of that element, Ariel desires, above all, his own freedom, which he hopes to bring about by serving his master well. Still, he is anxious to see the day of his release. He asks Prospero after completing a task, "Is there more toil? Since thou dost give me pains / Let me remember thee what thou hast promis'd, / Which is not yet perform'd me." The promise is that of liberty, which Prospero assures him will soon come to fruition, but quiets the restless spirit by reminding him of his former imprisonment in a "cloven pine" at the hands of the witch Sycorax. Thus admonished, Ariel continues in his chores by enchanting young Ferdinand with his songs, including the lyric beginning "Full fadom five thy father lies," which convinces the prince that his father, King Alonso, was drowned in the tempest. This is, of course, only the first of Ariel's actions used to deceive the newcomers to the island.

Ariel again proves himself an able servant in the opening scene of Act II, when he awakens Gonzalo in time to forestall the conspiracy of Sebastian and Antonio as they plot to murder their king. Likewise, he warns his master of the parallel conspiracy brewing with the drunken Caliban, Trinculo, and Stephano in the following act. Act III, scene iii, bears further witness to Ariel's powers of illusion as he helps Prospero create a magical banquet for Alonso, Antonio, and Sebastian. Causing the banquet to disappear with a clap of his wings, he rebukes the "three men of sin."

In Act IV, Ariel once again serves his master faithfully by presenting the masque in honor of Miranda and Ferdinand, and later doling out Prospero's punishment to Caliban and his fellow conspirators. The last act of the play finds Ariel once again at Prospero's side. He runs the last of his errands, bringing all of the other characters in turn before the magician, who finally grants him his only request, freedom.

The spirit Ariel is, by most accounts, benevolent like his master. Though an otherworldly creature, he is charged with no religious significance. Neither angel nor demon, he is morally neutral. His only defining characteristic is his elemental quality that predisposes him toward the liberty and freedom of the air. His magical powers also seem to derive from the air and range from a control over that element—including the ability to become invisible and to change his appearance—to the power of enchantment with his mesmerizing voice. Overall, Ariel deals in illusion and, although he can appear menacing, his actions never directly cause any physical harm.

Caliban

While primarily an actor in the comic subplot that mimics the more serious affairs that occur on the island, Caliban is, from a thematic standpoint, one of the most important characters in the play. He is first introduced in the second scene of Act I, in which he appears in all his bitterness as the slave of Prospero, forced to stack his wood. Contrasted to Ariel, who is a being of the sky, Caliban is presented as a vile creature of low cunning, associated with earth. He is bestial in appearance and manner, and forever disobedient and rebellious to his master. Caliban tells Prospero how greatly he regrets having revealed all of the island's secrets, while the magician reproves him for having attempted to rape Miranda. Caliban's response is typical of his amorality, "O ho, O ho! would't had been done! / Thou didst prevent me; I had peopled else / This isle with Calibans." Prospero now uses Caliban as a menial slave, though once he had attempted to educate the creature. Caliban's thoughts on this effort at enlightenment are readily seen from his own words, "You taught me language; and my profit on't / Is, I know how to curse. The red plague rid you / For learning me your language!"

Caliban appears again in Act II, scene ii. He is happened upon by Trinculo, then Stephano and, after some physical comedy and the imbibing of some wine, he declares his eternal allegiance to the latter. While the three fall in together, some distinction can be made between Caliban and the king's jester and butler in terms of language. While Caliban often speaks in verse, Stephano's and Trinculo's discourse is in prose. This fact becomes more readily apparent in the second scene of Act III. While Caliban has since launched a plot to assassinate Prospero, he reveals his lyrical connection to the island and his closeness to its beauty: "Be not afeard; the isle is full of noises, / Sounds and sweet airs, that give delight, and hurt not. / Sometimes a thousand twangling instruments / Will hum about mine ears; and sometimes voices, / That, if I then wak'd after long sleep, / Will make me sleep again . . . ."

Act IV, scene i, finds Caliban's hoped-for conspiracy (and freedom) put to an end by Prospero and Ariel. While Caliban attempts to keep Trinculo and Stephano in check, they become distracted by the glittering clothes that Ariel has placed before them. Caliban responds to their dalliance, "I will have none on't: we shall lose our time, / And all be turn'd to barnacles, or to apes / With foreheads villainous low." He is right, and the trio of inebriated conspirators is chased from the stage by Ariel's spirits in the form of wild hounds. All three reappear in the only scene of Act V, herded before Prospero by Ariel. Prospero grants Caliban pardon for his thoughts of treachery and the slave laments his failure. Caliban's final words imply that he has learned somewhat of a lesson, but ring with irony considering his past actions, "I'll be wise hereafter, / And seek for grace. What a thrice-double ass / Was I, to take this drunkard for a god, / And worship this dull fool!"

Caliban has traditionally been described as amoral, bestial, and recalcitrant, yet has attracted a great deal of attention for his seemingly incongruous knowledge and appreciation of natural beauty. Completely uncivilized, he is said to represent the state of man prior to society. His character comes from reports of wild men in the New World that Shakespeare would most certainly have heard. As such, he is neither good nor evil because his motivations lie outside the moral codes of the Europeans. In his rebellion he likewise evinces his antipathy for the rules of civilized men, and he longs instead for freedom outside the mores of society and for the peace and beauty of his tropical island.

Miranda

Miranda, like the other major characters in *The Tempest*, first appears in Act I, scene ii, but is involved very little in the action of the play itself. She is approximately fifteen years old at the time the drama unfolds, and has lived on the island for the past twelve years with only her father, Ariel, and Caliban as companions. She asks her father to put an end to the storm that he has called, fearing that someone might be hurt. Prospero assures her that no harm will be done, and then, at her request, tells her the story of his former life as Duke of Milan as well as the tale of how they came to the island. Miranda is intelligent

and inquisitive by nature, but until this point was never allowed this knowledge of her past. Instead she was quieted by her father with the words "Stay: not yet." In her reaction to Prospero's story she demonstrates her compassion, innocence, and limitless capacity for awe at the world around her. This is nothing, however, when compared to her response to the appearance of Ferdinand, who is brought before her and her father by Ariel. Her words reveal her inexperience, "What is 't? a spirit? / Lord, how it looks about! Believe me, sir, / It carries a brave from. But 'tis a spirit." Prospero assures her it is not. She continues, "I might call him / A thing divine; for nothing natural / I ever saw so noble." She instantly falls in love with Alonso's son, who returns these feelings. And, despite Prospero's fatherly jibes at her innocence of worldly things, events unfold exactly as he has planned.

Miranda does not appear again until Act III, in which she and Ferdinand declare their love. Miranda offers to bear some of the logs that Prospero has engaged the youth to stack, but he declines, declaring that he labors willingly for one as beautiful as she. Inexperienced and innocent, Miranda represents boundless love unfettered by self-consciousness or the conventions of society. She agrees to be his wife if he will be her husband, and under the watchful eyes of Prospero the match is nearly complete. Prospero only has to grant his blessing, which he does in Act IV, scene ii, by holding a betrothal masque in honor of their love.

The last glimpse into Miranda's character comes in the final scene of the drama as Prospero reveals her and Ferdinand playing chess to Alonso and the others gathered. The lovers quarrel over the game lightly, but their love is certain. Miranda accuses, "Sweet lord, you play me false." Ferdinand denies this accusation, and she responds, "Yes, for a score of kingdoms you should wrangle, / And I would call it fair play." Then, upon seeing the courtiers before her, she once again expresses the limitless awe and wonderment that are among her defining qualities, "O wonder! / How many goodly creatures are there here! / How beauteous mankind is! O brave new world, / That has such people in 't!" Prospero, in reply, comments with his characteristically disillusioned voice that highlights her unfamiliarity with worldly matters, "'Tis new to thee."

CONCLUSION

The Tempest, like many of Shakespeare's plays, has continued to elicit a broad range of scholarly interpretations and has eluded any conclusive judgments as to its dominant themes or the nature of its characters. The work is, however, generally regarded as a complex combination of romance, comedy, and tragedy that highlights many of Shakespeare's characteristic concerns with the nature of dramatic art, Christian themes of reconciliation and forgiveness, and the perils of human interaction in society. *The Tempest* is also seen by many as the culmination of the dramatist's later work, and has been compared in terms of its intricacy and depth with Shakespeare's comedy *The Winter's Tale* and his tragedy *King Lear*.

(See also *Shakespearean Criticism*, Vols. 8, 15, and 29)

OVERVIEWS

Frank Davidson

SOURCE: "*The Tempest*: An Interpretation," in *JEGP: Journal of English and Germanic Philology*, Vol. LXII, 1963, pp. 501-17.

[*In the following essay, Davidson surveys various twentieth-century critical interpretations of* The Tempest, *including biographical theories that view the work as an allegory of Shakespeare's life and as his farewell to the stage; thematic speculations that emphasize the prevalent theme of reconciliation; and social/political criticism—such as that of Northrup Frye, who suggests that the drama is about the evolution of a new social order. Davidson goes on to formulate his own interpretation of the play based on its adherence to the Renaissance ideals of political and natural order and its emphasis on the importance of reason in ordering society and restraining human passions.*]

I

Twentieth-century critics have left us a great variety of sometimes conflicting views on the meaning of Shakespeare's *The Tempest*. They have for the most part, however, been acute in their observations and have, even in their disagreements, bequeathed us a wealth of penetrating comment and points of view on a labyrinthine piece of dramatic art. Some, more objective than others in their approach, have been disturbed by interpretations which seem to have no basis within the framework of the play itself. E. E. Stoll, for example, [in *PMLA* XLVII (1932)], wearied, it seems, by the insistence that Shakespeare was dramatizing, in a part of *The Tempest* at least, events of his own life, or writing an allegory, contends that the critic should be a "judge, who does not explore his own consciousness, but determines the author's meaning or intention" from what the play actually says.

This discussion will attempt to restate and examine

briefly meaning ascribed to *The Tempest* by several of these critics of renown of the present century and to follow with an interpretation of the play based on philosophical and psychological thinking of the Tudor era and justified, I hope, by the work itself.

II

For E. K. Chambers *The Tempest* [in *Shakespeare: A Survey*, n.d.] is a "dream" or "fairy tale," the protagonists of which are "imagined beings, taken partly from folk-belief, and partly from literature, to be the symbols of forces dimly perceived by the poet as ruling that life, which is itself, after all, in another degree, but such stuff as dreams are made on." In his consideration of Prospero's dissolution of the hymeneal revels enacted for Ferdinand and Miranda, he follows Ulrici, Dowden, and others, interpreting the action as Shakespeare's farewell to the stage. Sir Arthur Quiller-Couch finds in *The Tempest* a subject which, he remarks, constantly engaged Shakespeare's "mind towards the close of his life: *Reconciliation*, with pardon and atonement for the sins or mistakes of one generation in the young love of the children and in their promise. This is the true theme of *Pericles, Cymbeline, The Winter's Tale, The Tempest*, successively." Stoll agrees with Chambers that the play is a fairy tale, a "sort of glorious fairy-tale," he calls it, "precious not . . . because of the structure or situations, but because of the characters, the poetry and the rich and dreamy spirit which for the most part informs it." He is conscious of a "tendency to reverie" in the play, of a "change in his [Shakespeare's] imagery," of outlines that "tend to become vast, vague and wavering, as in a dream," and of some profound thought on "the end, not only of man's work but of Nature's, and of life as a dream, and death as a sleep." He is at total variance with Chambers with reference to any biographical interpretation. Hardin Craig, [in *An Interpretation of Shakespeare*, n.d.] like Stoll, looks at the play objectively but stresses more than do the other critics the fact that it is stage drama. In support of his view he directs attention to some significant facts unmentioned by Stoll: that "Prospero has committed error, has suffered wrongs, has striven against them, even has some struggles, often overlooked, on the island." *The Tempest*, he says, represents "Man moving toward the realization of the greatest Renaissance ideal," having "grown on the one side into a competent man of action, and on the other into a man of self-command." [In *Six Plays of Shakespeare*, n.d.,] G. B. Harrison follows the lead of Chambers and Stoll in viewing the play as a fairy tale and that of Quiller-Couch in assigning as theme, "reconciliation; wrongs committed in one generation . . . set right in the happiness of the next." Donald Stauffer [in *Shakespeare's World of Images*, 1949] interprets the play as one of "moral ideas," which "grow from age and experience and self-discipline and resignation, almost from disillusion." Prospero's 'nobler reason' is for him "no scientific rationality, but an ethical control over passion." Northrop Frye rules out allegory and argues [in *The Tempest*, The Pelican Shakespeare, 1949] that *The Tempest* is about a "dissolving society" and a "new kind of social order" that moves "not out of the world, but from an ordinary to a renewed and ennobled vision of nature." Prospero, he explains, "takes the society of Alonso's ship, immerses it in magic, and then sends it back to the world, its original ranks restored, but given a new wisdom. . . ." He touches on the biographical theory and sees possibilities in it without subscribing to it. Frye's is a beautiful piece of exposition, persuasive and charmingly lucid. Mark Van Doren warns the reader [*A Midsummer Night's Dream, As You Like It, Twelfth Night, The Tempest*, The Pocket Library, n.d.] that "*The Tempest* is a composition about which we had better not be too knowing"; that "it seems to order itself in terms of meanings" which are not "self-evident," but which are subject to a variety of interpretations, even contradictory ones, and of which even "the wildest is more or less plausible." He accepts the "reconciliation" theme mentioned by Quiller-Couch and Harrison but associates with it a theme of "separation." He touches upon the biographical theory but lends it no credence.

Any of the preceding views, except perhaps the biographical, may be to an extent justified by the lines of the play. Three, however, those of Frye, Stauffer, and Craig, provide some very pertinent observations not included in the others. Frye almost induces belief in his theme of a new society. He finds arguments for it in the compassion of Prospero, in the reconciliation of implacable enemies through the marriage of their children, and in the fact that most of the characters find themselves, "when no man was his own." Prospero, however, is so much the center of the action from beginning to end, he so dawrfs the other characters, that the social aspect dwelt upon by Frye is but vaguely defined. Stauffer is aware not only of moral ideas in the play, but of moral ideas which are the outgrowth of "age, experience, self-discipline, resignation, almost disillusion" and which anticipate "*ethical control over passion*" (italics added). Craig particularizes more than does Stauffer the experience, the self-discipline, and their results. For him, as we have noticed, "Prospero has committed error, has suffered wrongs, and has struggled against them, even has some struggles, often overlooked, on the island" and under the discipline imposed by these conflicts, has moved toward "*the realization of the greatest Renaissance ideal*" (italics added).

III

In content as well as in period *The Tempest* is, as Craig implies, Renaissance drama. It reflects such

inherited classical theories and faiths and philosophies of sixteenth-century Western Europe as natural differentiation in degree and in duties of rulers and subjects ("specialty of rule" Ulysses called it in *Troilus and Cressida*); zeal for learning; the relative importance of speculative and practical living and a morality and psychology based upon convictions about the rationality, the passionate nature, and the free will of man.

Although Craig does not identify the "error" with which he charges Prospero, there can be hardly a doubt that he has in mind the cause of Prospero's failure as a Duke, a type of error of which the Renaissance took cognizance. As Frye correctly observes, Prospero "appears to have been a remarkably incompetent ruler of Milan." The obsession or passion with which Shakespeare endowed him would, for an Elizabethan, have made him so, for he devoted himself to speculative studies, "neglecting worldy ends, all dedicated / To closeness" (I.ii.89-90), and by this immoderate inclination contributed to the defection of his brother, the loss of his dukedom, the exile of himself and Miranda, and the conflict that enmeshed him after he was forced by circumstance to care for himself and his daughter on a practically uninhabited island. "The government," he tells Miranda, while acquainting her with his former situation as Duke,

> 　　　　　　　　I cast upon my brother,
> And to my state grew stranger, being transported
> And rapt in secret studies . . .
>
> I, thus neglecting wordly ends, all dedicated
> To closeness and the bettering of my mind . . .
>
> 　　　　　　　　in my false brother
> Awaked an evil nature . . .
>
> 　　　　　　　Me, poor man, my library
> Was dukedom large enough.
>
> 　　　　　　　　　　　(I.ii.75-110)

His error is evident in his words. His lack of any practical interest in the affairs of his people, his passion for a meditative and private life, and his delegating the actual operation of governing to a kinsman, as did Lear (in itself a perversion of nature), would have proved an almost insurmountable barrier for any sixteenth-century European ruler.

Study was, however, though insufficient in itself, an asset for the gentleman of the time, and for princesses as well, as Henry VIII demonstrated, and Prospero, too; for instruction in the liberal sciences would, says Sir Thomas Elyot, "prepare the mynde and make it apte to receive vertue." But, Elyot goes on to say, the governor should be "neyther by study withdrawen from affaires of the publike weale, nor by any busyness utterly pluckyd from Philosophy and any other noble doctrynes." John Lyly voices a similar thought, pointing out that there is an active life "which is about ciuill function and administration of the common weale," and a speculative, "which is continuall meditation and studie. . . . If this actiue life be without philsophie, it is an idle life, or at the least a life euill imployed which is worse: if the contemplatiue lyfe be seperated from the Actiue, it is vnprofitable." Prospero's error helps to explain the presence of Ariel and Caliban in the play and to prepare for the climax.

On the island, to which Providence has guided him, Prospero, the scholar, dedicated to closeness, is forced to employ that function of the rational soul which, to this time, he has neglected—the active. Through the kindness of Gonzalo, he still has his books and he still uses them, but he must divide his time now between speculative and practical concerns. He discovers two inhabitants on the island, Ariel, whom he releases from imprisonment, a delicate spirit, brave, adaptable to a variety of visible forms as well as to invisibility, freedom-loving, accommodated to any of the four elements, and Caliban, a creature of earth, offspring of a witch and the devil, whom he attempts to instruct in the manners of human life. The former, Prospero detains as servant in spite of protest; the latter, subsequent to his kind treatment and its ingratitude, he shuts in a cavern and assigns menial tasks—a rebellious slave. Neither of these beings is human. Ariel, who, it must be remembered, acts only on Prospero's bidding, can, under his direction, perform rationally (I.ii.207-208) but lacks human affection (V.i.19); Caliban is without reason and acts from instinct. But both act. Chambers speaks of Ariel, as from one point of view, "the agent and minister of an inscrutable Providence," which Ariel demonstrates himself to be (III.iii.60-75), with his adeptness at working with sensory objects—seas, shores, creatures, winds—through which, according to him, Providence operates to maintain order and justice in the world. Stoll treats Ariel and Caliban in considerable detail. Somewhat contemptuous of those critics who have a "taste for an inner meaning, biographical or symbolical," he likens Ariel to Puck "in the enjoyment of his own performances and of his effects on mortals" and speaks of him as "more ethereal . . . than the fairies," representing "*a power of nature, like wind or water, harnessed for a time to man's service* [italics added], and delighting in it, yet ever ready to break loose." Caliban is for Stoll "a mooncalf," "the perfect brute," who "fits perfectly into the dramatic scheme as the creature of earth—both a parallel and a contrast with the spirit of the air. . . ." The two, he significantly remarks, constitute a "state of nature—Prospero and Miranda as human figures coming in between." Stoll lays great stress upon his point that

these two figures are "not single abstractions personified, but many-sided conceptions, incarnated," "developments out of popular superstitious conceptions, which are concrete," both closely associated with nature. Of their growth in the poet's mind, he explains that

> there was of course a guiding thread of thought, or a germinal idea—the spirit of the air in the one case, the spawn of the earth in the other—but that worked darkly under cover. Guided by touch and instinct, the poet, when consciously active at all, was intent upon the life and shape of the imagined creature, not on a meaning within it. (Or rather upon both, for this meaning—this germinal idea—is simple and inherent, not arbitrary and external . . . and the creature and its meaning are one.)

One may gladly accept all this and then, making an additional observation, point out a "guiding thread of thought, or germinal idea" in each of these nonhuman creatures that is different in some respects from those that have been suggested and more in keeping with Prospero's necessity, in his isolation, to be practical as well as informed. His volitions, it may be noted, are transformed to deeds by Ariel and Caliban on his requests and demands. The "germinal idea" for each of the two figures seems to have been drawn from the psychology well known to the period.

Briefly, one basic concept in Elizabethan psychology was that man possesses three souls—a vegetative, which he has in common with plants and the lower animals and whose functions are nourishment, growth, and reproduction; a sensible, which he shares with lower animals and whose chief function is, through affections and passions, to stimulate beast or man to activity; and a rational, which is peculiar to man and whose chief functions are to know, to speculate, and to will.

As the sensible soul, seat of the passions, was the one most closely associated with motion, it naturally became the agent of Prospero's activity, and at two levels: the basically physical or vegetal, and the mental and spiritual. Castiglione defines man's position with reference to these levels and points out two types of man's government of the active agents at the two levels, suggesting in terms of body, desire, soul, and reason, a relationship such as in *The Tempest* exists between Prospero and Caliban on the one hand and between Prospero and Ariel on the other, the former that of master and slave, the latter that of prince and subject according to laws.

Significant to any satisfactory interpretation of Caliban perhaps are this basic psychological concept of the souls and their functions; the necessity Prospero is under, after he reaches the island, to act; and his two admissions concerning his relations with Caliban:

first, that he and Miranda have subjected themselves in a measure to Caliban, have come to depend upon him for building fires, fetching wood, and performing other menial services that profit them (I.ii.311-13), and second, that he acknowledges "this thing of darkness" his (V.i.275-76). It would seem that Shakespeare, in Prospero's concession of dependence on and ownership of the creature, is suggesting that the "germinal idea" for Caliban is the brute body, responding to sensory and sensual instincts and desires, and operating at the subsistence and reproductive level of life; that, in contrast, the "germinal idea" for Ariel is the spirit of the sensible soul, acting, though dissentingly at times, in the elemental world of nature under the instruction of a rational soul to the attainment of personal and universal justice. In other words, Caliban and Ariel are attributes of Prospero, practical aspects of himself of which he was hardly conscious during his strictly speculative years. Each would be free; that was the rational soul's dilemma. Caliban speaks of a time when he was his "own king" (I.i.342). His attempted rape of Miranda is representative of the flesh's natural procreative urge, an instinct whose lustful, insidious propensities Prospero has not been conscious of in himself until after his banishment and which he finds "abhorrent," "capable of all ill," and amenable to "stripes . . . not kindness." The rational soul's necessitated employment of the vegetative for practical ends has given Prospero a peep at the "unweeded garden / That grows to seed"; at that dark aspect of nature to which the bastard Edmund pledged himself in "Thou, Nature, art my goddess."

With reference to such an interpretation of Caliban and Ariel as I have attempted here, there may be pertinency in Francis Bacon's observation:

> For the sensible soul—the soul of brutes—must clearly be regarded as a corporeal substance, attenuated and made invisible by heat; a breath . . . compounded of the natures of flame and air, having the softness of air to receive impressions, and the vigour of fire to propagate its action; . . . clothed with the body, and in perfect animals residing chiefly in the head, running along the nerves, and refreshed and repaired by the spirituous blood of the arteries. . . . [T]his soul is in the brutes the principal soul, the body of the brute being its instrument whereas in man it is itself only the instrument of the rational soul, and may be more fitly termed not soul, but spirit.

Professor Stoll, persevering and right as he is against a critic's reading his own impressions into *The Tempest* or any other literary work, does recognize that Shakespeare could "forget himself to the point of . . . entering into the soul of a phenomenon of nature" and giving it reality.

IV

I have observed above that *The Tempest* is Renaissance drama in that it reflects among other characteristics of the time, some of the closely related political, ethical, and psychological views. I have stated one of the basic principles featured in that psychology—old as Plato and new as Spenser—and have tried to show its applicability to an identification of Ariel and Caliban. Another basic belief, likewise significant to an interpretation of the play and incorporated in many of the sixteenth-century works on moral philosophy, is, that for man's attainment of the highest good in life, the *summum bonum*, obedience to natural order is essential. Just as

> The heavens themselves, the planets, and this centre
> Observe degree, priority, and place,
> Insisture, course, proportion, season, form,
> Office and custom, in all line of order . . .
> (*Troilus and Cressida* I.iii.85-88)

so man, for his felicity, must "observe degree, priority, and place" of subject and ruler, of child and parent, of youth and age, of passion and reason.

Perversions of natural order such as Ulysses sets forth in *Troilus and Cressida* (I.iii.101-24) develop into a pattern in *The Tempest*, bringing complications and distress. Twelve years before the opening incident of the action Antonio, brother and subject of Prospero, had, with the aid of Alonso, King of Naples, seized power in the dukedom of Prospero and set him and his baby daughter adrift upon the sea in the rotten carcass of a tub. Prospero speaks of Antonio as an "unnatural" brother. The first incident of the play ties in with this recollected earlier one and reveals the contemptuous behavior, during a shipwreck ("degree being vizarded") of sailors toward a king's councilor and toward the king himself. In rapid succession then come the demands of a servant, Ariel, for his freedom from his master; the defiance of a master by a slave, who claims ownership of the island on which they live; the plotting of Antonio and King Alonso's brother, Sebastian, to assassinate the king and seize Naples (a duplication in many respects of the conspiracy that unseated Prospero); Miranda's taking issue with her father concerning a lover; and the fomenting of a conspiracy by Caliban and two drunken sailors against Prospero. All these revolts, save that of Ariel, who can act under the direction of reason (I.ii.206-208), originate in uncontrolled passions: ambitious desire, anger, hatred, youthful love, cupidity.

Passions were not looked upon as evil in themselves by Elizabethans, except among the stoics; they were, however, when out of control, considered dangerous to both body and mind. One of man's greatest conflict was, at least in theory, that between his reason and his passions, and this conflict, according to Francis Bacon, became a theme even better adapted to artistic than to philosophical treatment. It is basic to the struggle in the second book of *The Faerie Queene*, where, up to the close of Canto v, Sir Guyon contends against Furor, and, through the remainder of the book, against Acrasia or concupiscible desire. Shakespeare makes the passions an active force in his tragedies, and in *The Tempest* he employs them as chief contender against Prospero.

The lines of *The Tempest* are interlaced with the diction of the contemporary psychology in its treatment of the reason and the passions. There are words, phrases, clauses that speak of the restraint of this enemy: "be patient"; "Be collected"; "music crept by me upon the waters, / Allaying both their fury and my passion"; "The white cold virgin snow upon my heart / Abates the ardor of my liver." Many expressions reflect the effects of the uncontrolled passions: "I'm out of patience"; "being transported / And rapt"; "beating my mind"; "amazement"; "infect his reason"; "a fever of the mad"; "tricks of desperation"; "immitigable rage"; "At the first sight / They have changed eyes"; "My spirits, as in a dream, are all bound up"; "madness"; "Their great guilt . . . / Now 'gins to bite the spirits"; "I have made you mad"; "ecstasy"; "anger so distempered"; "vexed"; "my beating mind"; "a madness held me"; "they devour their reason." Other passages indicate a return to a normal state of mind after the working of a passion: "their rising senses / Begin to chase the ignorant fumes that mantle / Their clearer reason"; "Their understanding / Begins to swell, and the approaching tide / Will shortly fill the reasonable shore / That now lies foul and muddy"; "their senses I'll restore."

Even the title of the play is not so much concerned with the sea storm Prospero raises as with the passions he stirs in his guests and in himself, passions that in his twelve years of isolation may have shown calm at the surface but which now, as he faces his foes, mount high again. In the books of philosophy and psychology of the day a not unusual symbol for the passions is a tempest.

Incidents of the play as well as the diction and the title speak of the passions. Prospero lectures Ferdinand on continence in love after the lovers, with his consent, have plighted troth, and predicts dire calamities if his exhortation goes unheeded (IV.i.14-24; 50-54). The scene is echoed in the wedding masque (IV.i.96-97) when Iris speaks of the "vows . . . no bedright shall be paid / Till Hymen's torch be lighted." Both Stoll and Frye are perplexed by Prospero's seemingly unnecessary admonition. Stoll associates it with a "measure of ugliness and horror, cynicism and grossness" to be found in the late comedies of Shakespeare, and asks, "Why

should he [Prospero] warn Ferdinand, about to be left for a moment with Miranda, not to break her virgin-knot, and then, the next moment, harp on the subject again?" Frye attributes Prospero's moments of anger to the "nervous strain of dealing with such characters" as those about him and states that "in his fussing over protecting Miranda from the obviously honorable lover, there is a touch of the busybody." Elizabethan psychology would have supported neither of the critics, as it leaves no doubt about the danger of concupiscible pleasures. When Prospero warns Ferdinand, "Do not give dalliance / Too much the rein" (IV.i.51-52), he is not speaking grossly and is not a busybody.

Passions of grief and remorse are vigorously presented in III.iii of *The Tempest*. Ariel appears to Alonso, Sebastian, and Gonzalo as a harpy, reminds the first three of their sins, informs them that he has made them mad, proclaims himself and his aids ministers of fate, and warns that

> The powers, delaying not forgetting, have
> Incensed the seas and stones—yea, all the
>   creatures
> Against your peace.
>
> (III.iii.73-75)

Alonso, grieving the disappearance of his son, whom he has given up for dead (III.iii.7-10), imagines that he hears the billows, the winds, the thunder accusing him of the evil he has done Prospero (III.iii.95-102) and reminding him that because of his misdeeds he now suffers the loss of his son. Sebastian and Antonio are in a frenzy. Gonzalo, seeing that "All three of them are desperate," requests that someone with suppler joints than his, "follow them swiftly, / And hinder them from what this ecstasy / May now provoke them to" (III.iii.107-109). Shakespeare had used the passions of grief and anger very effectively as a cause of Lear's madness and, in *The Tempest,* shortly before Gonzalo beseeches someone to follow the desperate trio, has Prospero, a ware of what has occurred, reflect;

> And these mine enemies are all knit up
> In their distractions.
>
> (III.iii.89-90)

v

Prospero, as has been noted, while informing Miranda of his past, assumed some of the blame for his disaster, attributing it in part to his immoderate zeal for speculative learning to the neglect of his active duties as a ruler. Linked with his intemperate behavior was a selfpride, which characterizes him through most of the play: "Prospero the prime Duke," he boasts to his daughter, "being so reputed / In dignity, and for the liberal arts / Without a parallel" (I.ii.72-74). His sensitivity displays itself in his susceptibility to feelings of resentment, anger, and revenge. In the wrongs done him by his brother and in the challenges to his authority by Ariel and by Caliban, he is hurt most by their ingratitude; in each instance he lays great stress upon his own kindnesses to these betrayers of his trust and tenderness, and on each occasion gives way to anger, just as he does when his daughter, attempting to argue a point with him about her lover, draws the quick, sharp rebuke, "my foot, my tutor?" (I.ii.469) and the more vehement reproof, "one more word / Shall make me chide thee, if not hate thee" (I.ii.475-76). To Ferdinand he appears "crabbed" and "composed of harshness" (III.i.8-9). When he suddenly remembers that Caliban and the sailors are moving against him, his passion is such as to alarm Ferdinand and Miranda. To the former's observation, "Your father's in some passion / That works him strongly," the latter replies that "till this day" she has not seen him "touched with anger so distempered" (IV.i.143-45). Prospero, noting their concern, confesses vexation, and requests, "Bear with my weakness, my old brain is troubled. / Be not disturbed with my infirmity" (IV.i.159-60). He will take a turn or two, he says, "to still my beating mind."

The revenge motif in *The Tempest* has never had the attention it deserves. Stoll attributes the scenes involving Prospero's anger to "the poverty of the plot," and observes that "No obstacles opposing his omnipotence from without, one must be raised up within." Stoll seems unaware of the tension building up from the *protasis* of the second scene of the play to the moment when this man who, as scholar, had been "trasported and rapt in secret studies" must make a momentous decision. "The drama," says Stoll "is indeed seldom performed: there is too little suspense, and the conjuring tricks pall upon us." Craig comes nearer the mark in his assertion quoted above that "Prospero . . . even has some struggles, often overlooked, on the island." Miss Campbell takes cognizance of the vengeance motif but only to point out how Shakespeare transformed to comedy an impending tragedy of revenge. Frye seems to be quite conscious of the dark strain in the play but lets it pass with the observation that "Like Hamlet, Prospero delays revenge and sets up a dramatic action to catch the conscience of a king. . . ." It should be noted that the revenge motif carries into the secondary action as Caliban urges Stephano to avenge the wrongs Prospero has done him (III.ii.61-62). Desire for vengeance has apparently lain dormant in Prospero through the years of his banishment, and now, with the sudden advent of his foes, the great wrong of twelve years before is stirringly present again, arousing the passions and stimulating the will to action. Tensions begin

building in the first act, when Prospero insists that his daughter be alert to the situation they face. "The hour's now come," he says; "The very minute bids thee ope thine ear. / Obey, and be attentive" (I.ii.36-38). After outlining for her the significant events of the unfortunate past, he comes again "to the present business / Which now's upon's, without the which this story / Were most impertinent" (I.ii.136-38). He must seize upon the moment or his "fortunes / Will ever after droop" (I.ii.183-84). The suspense intensifies in Act III when Prospero announces concerning his enemies, "They now are in my power," and mounts to a climax at the close of Act IV:

> At this hour
> Lie at my mercy all mine enemies.
> Shortly shall all my labours end. . . .

VI

The Tempest is not mere spectacle or story of a magician's supernatural dominance of men and spirits. Nor does it lack suspense. The conflict that makes drama is present in Prospero, and its resolution comes, not so much of physical, as of moral and mental travail. The two functions of the rational soul, speculative and practical, at last fuse. The former has prepared "the mynde and [made] it apte to receive vertue"; the latter wills and acts virtuously. "Degree" is preserved; reason, the distinctive attribute of man, triumphs over passion. When Ariel, who lacks human sympathy but who recognizes suffering when he sees it, reports the sorrowful plight of Gonzalo and the penitence and grief of Alonso, the "enemy . . . inveterate," Prospero meets the challenge. "Shall not myself," he asks,

> One of their kind, that relish all as sharply,
> Passion as they, be kindlier moved than thou art?
> Though with their high wrongs I am struck to the quick,
> Yet with my nobler reason 'gainst my fury
> Do I take part. The rarer action is
> In virtue than in vegeance.
>
>   (V.i.22-28)

So the conflict ends. Prospero has achieved virtue, and the virtue seems to be *magnanimity,* "the wonderful effects" of which, "appear principally in three points," the second of which is "dutie towards enemies, against whom generositie will in no wise suffer a man to practise or consent to any wickednesse. . . .

A note has sounded throughout the play, however, of a force superior to and within whose compass man's reason and virtue operate. At the end of the first scene, when death seems imminent to members of the court party, Gonzalo exclaims, "The wills above be done!" Near the close of the play he gives credit to the "gods" for having brought him and his party to the island, and with his comment raises the question whether all the events of the past twelve years have not been parts of a Providential plan. Between these two pronouncements Prospero makes acknowledgment to "Providence divine" for having brought him and his daughter safely ashore, Ariel associates the "powers" with the maintenance of justice in the world, and Ferdinand lays claim to Miranda through "immortal Providence." Relative to this "Providence" with its continuity and greatness, man, even with his reason, "is such stuff / As dreams are made on, and [his] little life / Is rounded with a sleep."

Another repetitive note in the play is freedom. The word "liberty" accompanies Ariel's first appearance, and the last command he receives opens the final line of the drama, "Be free." Just before his release, however, Prospero requests he set Caliban and his companions free. Ferdinand can find liberty even in confinement if, from his prison, he may see Miranda daily, and he compares his willingness to be her husband to that of bondage to be free. The freedom of Ariel and Caliban, as we might expect, follows closely Prospero's liberating himself from the passion that has ridden him and his finding his true self in the rule of reason. The relations of the servant and of the slave to Prospero change with this event; they are no longer in revolt. Caliban's sense of values, for instance, is transformed to such a degree that he can exclaim, "How fine my master is!" and wonder at his own asininity of a moment before in mistaking Stephano for a god. In brief, master, servant, and slave, each finds his freedom in the degree or specialty of rule that nature assigns him.

Frye thinks that Prospero shows little promise of being a better Duke after his return to Milan than he was before leaving it. This view comes perhaps of the statement made by Prospero near the close of the drama, "Every third thought shall be my grave," as if he plans to be again the purely meditative man. The implication of Frye's thinking is that Prospero has learned from his long experience little of lasting worth for a ruler. We must remember, however, that he will reoccupy Milan through conquest; he has conquered himself and his political foes. His prospective mediation is certainly not unusual for his day or for his immediate situation. Having proved the power of reason concerning a passion closely aligned with life, he can now exercise that power to promote serenity of mind in the contemplation of death, a subject which seems to have haunted Elizabethan thought. Frye's prediction is not so well based as Craig's: that Prospero, having achieved virtue and restored himself to power, will, upon his return to Milan, attend to practical affairs of state without abandoning study and meditation; " . . . the Renaissance," he says, "put no premium on ignorance."

MAGIC

The magical atmosphere Shakespeare creates in *The Tempest* is one of the play's defining qualities and, according to critics, this element of magic pervades many of the primary themes in the work. While the topic allows for a wide range of interpretation, it is most often associated with the opposing forces of illusion and reality and the theme of reconciliation. **Robert Egan** discusses this point by equating Prospero's magic with the artist's molding of reality into something that more closely resembles his moral vision. Thus, Prospero manipulates the natural world as a means to reform, punish, and instruct the other inhabitants of the island, from Caliban to Alonso. Barbara Traister also emphasizes the qualities of the magician as artist, in this case as a director in control of the action. Not only does Prospero manage his fellow players by enchanting them, he also manipulates others through the presentation of scenes and illusions, such as the masques. Here again, he uses magic as a form of moral instruction. Traister also discusses Prospero's final renunciation of magical powers, concluding that, in choosing to abjure sorcery, Prospero decides to again confront a long-neglected worldly reality. In this sense, as many other commentators have observed, *The Tempest* allows the magician/artist to briefly suspend the exigencies of the real world in order to effect a thematic change. Prospero transforms the mood of revenge and conspiracy into one of hope and reconciliation. Thus, as **Frances Yates** argues, Prospero's magic derives from good and compassionate sources, which, if not divine, are at least benevolent.

Robert Egan

SOURCE: "This Rough Magic: Perspectives of Art and Morality in *The Tempest*," in *Shakespeare Quarterly*, Vol. XXIII, No. 2, Spring, 1972, pp. 171-82.

[*In the following essay, Egan interprets Prospero's magic in* The Tempest *as an indicator of the play's theme of the possible moral rejuvenation of mankind. Prospero, as an artist/magician and the ultimate ruler of the island, usurps the role of God by forcefully projecting his moral vision on all of the other characters in the play, including the indigenous creatures Ariel and Caliban and the shipwrecked nobles from Italy. According to Egan, this vision lacks the elements of love and forgiveness necessary for it to succeed in a real human society. Prospero's 'rough magic,' based on the desire for vengeance, however, is transformed by the end of the drama into a moral system tempered by charity and in*

From Act III, scene i of The Tempest.

keeping with the Christian belief in a shared love for all humanity.]

Is the knowing all? To know, and even happily, that we meet unblessed; not in some garden of wax fruit and painted trees, that lie of Eden, but after, after the Fall, after many, many deaths. Is the knowing all? And the wish to kill is never killed, but with some gift of courage one may look into its face when it appears, and with a stroke of love—as to an idiot in the house—forgive it; again and again . . . forever?

Arthur Miller, *After the Fall*

Whether or not *The Tempest* was chronologically the last of Shakespeare's plays is a debatable and ultimately an irrelevant question. The Bard's farewell to the London stage before serenely tottering off to Stratford is a cliché requiring little attention; quite obviously, it takes the play for something far slighter than it is. Nevertheless, there is an unmistakable sense of finality permeating the work. Themes and their variations from throughout the Shakespeare canon

seem to draw together here. The characters include a hero more sinned against than sinning, a pair of young and innocent lovers, a guilt-ridden King, a faithful old Counsellor, a machiavellian usurper, a swaggering braggart, and a fool—all central character types of the tragedies, histories, and comedies, recapitulated and condensed in this most compact and precisely ordered of Shakespeare's plays.

More specifically, *The Tempest* deals centrally with ideas and concepts of at to a far greater extent than any of the plays before it. All its events and circumstances are either the direct result or the consequence of Prospero's "Art". We have seen a poet and painter discourse on their crafts (which are for sale to the highest bidder) in *Timon,* the poet Gower has presented *Pericles,* and the art of Julio Romano has been a significant factor in the denouement of *The Winter's Tale.* But here, for the first and last time, the artist is hero and protagonist, and his principal meditations, decisions, and actions are couched in terms of his art. We may well look, then, for implications of some final statement or pronouncement by Shakespeare upon his own art. First, however, we must examine the art of Prospero in detail, evaluating its meaning through the forms it takes, the intentions on which it is founded, and the ends it accomplishes.

I

The least likely place to begin the investigation of a play is at its end, but the Epilogue of *The Tempest* offers us, through an unusual and unconventional view of the art of the play as a whole, an illuminating insight into the role of art within the play. Nearly all other Shakespearian epilogues declare or assume the termination of the play-world, calling their audiences back to an extra-theatrical norm of reality by requesting applause. This pattern is surprisingly consistent, whether couched in the utilitarian prose of the Dancer in *2 Henry IV* or the finely wrought verse of Puck. The most concise and representative example is the Epilogue of *All's Well That Ends Well,* spoken by the King:

The King's a beggar, now the play is done.
All is well ended if this suit be won,
That you express content; which we will
  pay,
With strife to please you, day exceeding day.
Ours be your patience then, and yours our
  parts.
Your gentle hands lend us, and take our
  hearts.

The first line dominates those that follow; it leaves no doubt that the play-world's standards of identity and reality have come to an end and bear no relevance to the present situation. The speaker is no longer the King but an actor. The play, its events, and its characters are offered simply as "our parts", objects of artifice for the pleasure and approval of the audience.

The Epilogue of *The Tempest*, however, specifically does away with this perspective, purposefully eliminating any barrier between the play-world and the real:

> Now my charms are all o'erthrown,
> And what strength I have's mine own,
> Which is most faint: now, 'tis true,
> I must be here confin'd by you,
> Or sent to Naples. Let me not,
> Since I have my dukedom got,
> And pardon'd the deceiver, dwell
> In this bare island by your spell;
> But release me from my bands
> With the help of your good hands:
> Gentle breath of yours my sails
> Must fill, or else my project fails,
> Which was to please. Now I want
> Spirits to enforce, Art to enchant;
> And my ending is despair,
> Unless I be reliev'd by prayer,
> Which pierces so, that it assaults
> Mercy itself, and frees all faults.
>   As you from crimes would pardon'd be,
>   Let your indulgence set me free.

The opening three lines lead us to expect a conventional declaration by an actor who is only an actor, the "charms" of his art "o'erthrown". Yet such an expectation is deliberately undercut: it is still Prospero who speaks—from the island, not from the stage—and the play has yet to reach a conclusion. Moreover, its final event, the impending return to Naples, is charged to the members of the audience. It is their "spell" (Epilogue. 8) that holds him confined; their hands must release him and their "gentle breath" (Epilogue. 11) supply the "auspicious gales" which he has promised Alonso (V.i.314). In effect, they are invited to enter the play-world and assume a role, through their applause, as a moving force in its culmination.

This is not simply a metaphoric request for applause; without such participation by the audience, Prospero's "project fails" (Epilogue. 12)—that same project we have watched evolve through the play and "gather to a head" (V.i.1) in the fifth act. An appeal for applause is thus delivered, but it is spoken from within the play; while in previous epilogues the speaker stepped out of his dramatic context to address the audience in its own sphere of reality, Prospero brings the audience into the play. Here and here alone in Shakespeare, the play's art has no terminal boundaries but rather subsumes the "real", extra-theatrical world of its spectators, supplanting their sense of reality with its own.

What is the nature of this art, powerful enough to encompass the play's audience, and what is the "project" in which their participation is ultimately required? We shall return to the full significance of the Epilogue later; but meanwhile, on the most immediate level, we know Prospero's art to be that of a formidable magician—a demiurge, in effect, since he can control and order all the elements to the extent of raising a storm which splits a vessel and shipwrecks its passengers without "so much perdition as an hair / Betid" (I.ii. 30-31) to them or to the ship itself. Miranda associates his abilities with a "god of power" (10); and indeed, his "so potent Art" (V.i.50) seems almost blasphemously close to godhead when he recalls rifting "Jove's stout oak / With his own bolt" (45-46) and even raising the dead. Yet these are not powers naturally accruing to him; they were gained by years of seclusion and study (which cost him his dukedom), and they are embodied not in Prospero himself but in such objects as his books, his staff, and his magic garment. Without his books, says Caliban, "He's but a sot, as I am" (III.ii.91). Prospero himself perceives this separation of his artistic function from his identity as a man to the extent that he can, in putting off his garment, say, "Lie there, my Art" (I.ii.25).

A more specific dimension of his art is its consistent preoccupation with mimesis, particularly mimesis of a dramatic kind. Even the storm was a "spectacle" (I.ii.26): it was "Perform'd to point" (194) by Ariel, and all its lightnings and thunderclaps were in fact only semblances, as they did no harm. (One is reminded of W. B. Yeats's ultimate image of art in "Byzantium": "An agony of flame that cannot singe a sleeve.") His subject spirits are never what they seem, but continually assuming roles and guises. Ariel plays a seanymph and a harpy, and his lesser cohorts appear variously in "urchin-shows" (II.ii.5) as apes, hedgehogs, adders, and hunting dogs. Ariel, in fact, offers Prospero the services of himself and "all his quality" (I.ii.193); we recall that contemporary actors referred to their profession as "the Quality". Prospero's remarks, after the banquet has been removed from before the Court party, might well be those of a director or stage manager congratulating his performers on a job well done:

> Bravely the figure of this Harpy has thou
> Perform'd, my Ariel; a grace it had
>   devouring:
> Of my instruction hast thou nothing bated,
> In what thou hadst to say: so, with good life
> And observation strange, my meaner
>   ministers
> Their several kinds have done.
>
>   (III.iii.83-88)

Finally, the masque presented in the fourth act is

overtly an exercise of dramatic art. It is evident, therefore, that a considerable portion of Prospero's art involves the dramatic medium. We should, however, be careful to avoid any immediate identification of Prospero with Shakespeare, or even with the playwright in general. For Prospero is not a mere representative figure or allegorical cipher; he is a fully rounded character and, potentially, a tragic protagonist. As such, he is representative only in the broad sense that Lear and Hamlet are. To understand his full significance we must focus our attention on the terms of the play itself before inferring any outside implications. Prospero is a magician as well as a dramatist—both are facets of the same "Art"—and a man as well as an artist.

II

What, then, are the ends toward which he employs his art; what, in other words, is the substance of his "project"? We can begin with his relationship to Caliban, who, while the most "monstrous" character of the play, is in effect the lowest common denominator of all its characters—indeed, of all humanity. He is the amoral, appetitive, suffering Self in all of us, ever in search of freedom to satisfy all its hungers—visceral, sexual, and emotional—and ever ready to follow any "god" who promises such freedom. Prospero's general method of dealing with this essence of fallen man is to check his degeneracy with verbal chastisement and physical pain—the "urchin-shows" of apes and adders—and to draw him up toward a state of fulfillment and moral regeneration. He teaches him how "To name the bigger light, and how the less" (I.ii.337), and, through Miranda, how to speak. Moreover, besides specifically indicating the path to reformation, he shows him visions of some indistinct, heavenly ideal to spur him on further:

> and then, in dreaming,
> The clouds methought would open, and
>   show riches
> Ready to drop upon me.
>
> (III.ii.138-140)

Thus Prospero has employed his art to expose and chastise Caliban's faults, lead him to goodness, and depict images of what he should be. This specifically moral function is the basic pattern of almost all his artistic endeavors. He shipwrecks the Court party with the specific intention of subjecting Alonso, Antonio, and Sebastian to an ordeal of self-knowledge and purgation through the performance of his spirits. Ariel confronts them point-blank with their guilts—"You are three men of sin"—and leaves them with only two alternatives for the future: "Ling'ring perdition" or "heart-sorrow/ And a clear life ensuing" (III.iii.53,77,81-82). Ferdinand, too, undergoes a separate, punishing trial to rid him of his own

"Caliban" qualities and to purify his love. Again, the ordeal culminates in a mimetic vision of the ideal which Prospero intends for him to assume: the masque of chastity.

Prospero's project, then, is no less than to purge the evil from the inhabitants of his world and restore them to goodness. Thus his relation to the rest of the characters—manipulating their lives, judging their flaws, and setting standards of goodness for them—is, again, close to godhead. Through Ariel he equates himself with the "Destiny, / That hath to instrument this lower world / And what is in't" (III.iii.53-55); and Ferdinand, in the presence of "So rare a wonder'd father and a wise" (IV.i.123), thinks himself in Paradise. Such overt and implied resemblances have led some critics into mistaking Prospero for a figuration of God the Father. But it is precisely this assumption of god-like powers and responsibilities by one who is in no way superhuman that precipitates the central problem of the play. Prospero's artistic powers, being capable of great evil as well as great good, place him in a perilous position. The line between theurgy and necromancy could be thin at times, and the mage could easily cross it unawares. We need only remind ourselves that "*prospero*" is the Italian for "*faustus*". In order to fulfill the responsibilities he has assumed—before he can presume to influence others with his art—it is imperative that Prospero himself have a comprehensive and flawless moral vision of his world. He must perceive not only what is evil in men and what, ideally, they should be, but also what men are, and what relationship he, as a man, bears toward them. Without such a clarity of vision, the exercise of his art may result in corruption for himself and chaos for those around him.

III

Our first insight into the moral vision on which his art is based emerges through his own narration (I.ii) of his first contact with evil in the world. We learn that, in the course of the "secret studies" through which his art was acquired, he "grew stranger" to his dukedom: rejected the everyday realities of statecraft for the ideal realm in his books. Being totally unaware or unsuspecting of the temptations of worldly power, he left the manage of his state to his brother, assuming that, since he reposed in Antonio an absolute love and a "confidence sans bound," his love and confidence would naturally be returned. Instead, however, it "Awak'd an evil nature," the throne was seized, and Prospero was cast away. His reaction to this eruption of evil is marked not simply by bitterness but by a pronounced incredulity "That a brother should / Be so perfidious!" He was, and is still, unable to conceive of the contradiction between what a brother should be and what his brother was. Similarly, he cannot accept the fact that his own officers supported the usurper: that any evil could exist in the world as he knew it without being "new created / . . . or chang'd . . . / Or else new form'd".

But primarily his amazement centers on the fact that his brother should have acted contrary to all logical and ideal norms of brotherhood—that his own kind could return hate where love was owed. The lapse of time has brought him no new understanding of this. He cannot even cope with its memory, and the increasing frustration of his failure to do so emerges in his irrational, peevish demands that his daughter attend him. He ignores Miranda's simple but overwhelming bit of realism:

> I should sin
> To think but nobly of my grandmother:
> Good wombs have born bad sons.

Such an acknowledgement of evil as part of the natural condition of man is unacceptable to Prospero. His years of seclusion in his library have instilled in him a moral perspective rooted not in the real world but in the ideals of his art. Significantly, he still prizes his volumes above his dukedom, and insists on judging the real world by their rigid moral absolutes. If his brother acted contrary to the ideal of a brother, then his brother was not a brother but some alien, inhuman thing of evil, to be dealt with as an enemy. In short, he rejects the sinner with the sin.

The dangerous short-sightedness of this view is self-evident, and it is further revealed in the history of his relationship to Caliban. Initially recognizing Caliban as a human creature, he accepted him totally and afforded him all the "human care" ideally due to a fellow being. He trusted him, like Antonio, sans bound, giving him the run of his cell and the unguarded company of his daughter, without a thought of any evil he might do. Then, when the inevitable assault (Caliban being Caliban) occurred, he relegated Caliban to the status of an entirely inhuman creature, unable to connect his evil with any species but that of a devil-begotten, "poisonous slave," an "earth," a "filth" who deserved "stripes . . . , not kindness." As he overlooks Miranda's explanation of Antonio's evil—that good wombs have born bad sons—he misses the full implications of his own comparison of Ferdinand to Caliban: that Caliban's evil is an essentially human characteristic. There is a Caliban in the best of men; his presence and even his birthright must be recognized if he is to be effectively dealt with; for if left to run entirely at large he will inevitably perpetrate evil, and if disowned and repressed he will prove a greater threat by rebelling outright.

Of course, Prospero has not, at this point in the play, permanently disowned his affinity with either Antonio or Caliban. His ultimate intention, as his arrangement of the love between Ferdinand and Miranda indicates, is to reunite himself with all his enemies and so restore a harmony and order to his world in which, presumably, Antonio and Caliban will have their places. First, however, that world must be altered by his art to fit the letter of his moral vision. Alonso, Sebastian, and Antonio must all either assume a clear life or suffer lingering perdition; there is no middle ground. His faulty moral perception will not permit him to acknowledge as natural and human any being with the least taint of evil; he will accept nothing short of a world where all brothers are entirely trustworthy and all monsters entirely harmless: a prospect similar in scope and impossiblity to Gonzalo's island commonwealth (II.i.139-160). But Gonzalo never mistakes his vision for more than a utopian reverie. Prospero, on the other hand, intends to eliminate, by force if necessary, all elements of humanity which will not conform to his vision.

Here, then, is the central and potentially tragic flaw in Prospero's awareness. He has, in a very real sense, confused his role as an artist with that of a god, forgetting his humanity in the process. In presuming to substitute his own sense of morality for cosmic law he has designated to himself a higher order of being and the authority to damn and destroy his fellow men: in effect, he has usurped the divine prerogative of vengeance. Thus his project is threatened with failure on two counts. His artistic ideal of a perfect world, given the nature of post-Lapsarian humanity, can never be realized. Meanwhile he is in constant danger of mistaking his own passionate resentment of the wrongs he has suffered for righteous indignation, thereby perverting his own goodness and wreaking havoc on those over whom he has power. This element of vindictiveness and vengeful passion is never far from him, and it threatens constantly to overwhelm the nobler ends of his project. It accounts for the hint of sadistic relish with which he devises and threatens new forms of punishment for Caliban, and it is even more evident in his reactions to the ordeal of the Court party in the third act. He derives an obvious pleasure from their "disractions" and rejoices not so much that his art has attained its end, in showing them their evil, as simply that they are now in his power. He still refers to them, significantly, as "mine enemies", and clearly has no intention yet of terminating their "fits" (III.iii.88-93).

IV

Ferdinand is the one character whose moral regeneration Prospero undertakes without the danger of giving way to motives of revenge, not only because Ferdinand has never wronged him, but also because he comes closest, with Miranda, to fulfilling Prospero's standard of goodness. Through the innate innocence and nobility of his nature he responds ideally to nurture, and in the betrothal of Ferdinand and Miranda Prospero sees the first concrete realization of the moral order he intends to impose on his world. He is, of course, overlooking the obvious fact that these are, even within the terms of the play, two remarkably good young people, and their goodness can hardly be established as a norm of humanity in general. Nevertheless he celebrates their union with a masque which, besides depicting the specific ideal of chastity he wishes to impress on them, constitutes an ultimate mimetic image of the world he means to forge through his art. As such, it is worth close consideration.

The playlet centers on Iris, Ceres, and Juno, anthropomorphic embodiments of a nature which substantiates and rewards the human values of Prospero's moral system: theirs is a world from which all that is less than flawless, let alone evil, is rigidly exorcised. But the goddesses are being played by spirits who are, in fact, elemental creatures of nature—the real nature surrounding Prospero—and they are compelled, possibly against their wills, to enact a natural order which is not their own, but Prospero's "pathetic fallacy". Moreover, the chief details in Iris' opening description of the masque's landscape include "cold nymphs", "dismissed" and "lass-lorn" bachelors, vineyards which bear no fruit but are "pole-clipt", and a "sea-marge" that is "sterile and rocky-hard" (IV.i.60-70). This is a world not simply ordered and controlled but gelded of all that is spontaneous and primal, leaving only that which is cold, hard, and sterile. The culminating dance of nymphs and reapers brings to mind a similar pastoral vision, the sheep-shearing scene of *The Winter's Tale* (IV.iv.). There, however, we had the earthly, mildly ribald merriment of the Clown and his two girl-friends, along with a dance of satyrs. But none dance in Prospero's pastoral that are not "properly habited" (IV.i.138: stage direction).

Clearly, this vision fragments and distorts the realities of human experience. Venus and Cupid have been denied their rightful place in the pantheon, and the generative, sexual impulse they represent is strictly expelled from the world of the masque. Under such circumstances, the goddesses' invocations of "Earth's increase" and "foison plenty" seem as unlikely as that "Nature should bring forth, / Of its own kind all foison, all abundance" (II.i.158-159) on Gonzalo's island. There is no fertility or natural regeneration where the nymphs are cold and the bachelors lass-lorn. Ceres' "rich leas" are nullified by her pole-clipped vineyard and sterile sea-marge. Like Gonzalo's plantation, the "latter end" of Prospero's commonwealth "forgets the beginning" (II.i.153-154).

The entire masque, then, is overtly artificial and calculatedly unconvincing: a "vanity" of his art in a far more serious sense than he means the term. As such,

it points up the basic flaw in his artistic and moral perspectives. His moral system is clearly at odds with human reality, and the artistic embodiment of that system, therefore, has no viable connection with reality. Not that the specific moral ideal set forth in the masque, premarital chastity, is in itself fallacious, but Prospero has set himself a greater goal than the depiction of an ideal. He means his art to encompass and directly influence reality. In his remarks to Ferdinand and Miranda (IV.i.13-23) he draws no distinction between the order of the masque's world and that of the world outside it. On these terms, as a comprehensive image of the real world, the masque is bound to fail. Since it ignores the realities of post-Lapsarian existence, it is incapable, as art, of comprehending or coping with the propensity for evil in fallen man. The events of the play rapidly make this as clear to Prospero as it is to us. The wide disparity between the play-world of his art and the real world he inhabits is immediately revealed by an abrupt intrusion of extra-theatrical reality; the morally precise nature of Ceres, Juno, and Iris is belied by the approach of true naturals, Caliban, Stephano, and Trinculo, bent on rape and murder. His art-work cannot co-exist with such reality, but "heavily" vanishes "to a strange, hollow, and confused noise". Patently, his art has failed to come to terms with the nature of things as they are.

Perceiving this, Prospero addresses Ferdinand in what amounts to an epilogue: the "Our revels now are ended" speech. It is unfortunate that this passage, out of its context, has come to be misinterpreted as the central statement of *The Tempest*. In fact, it amounts to a bitter testament of nihilistic despair on Prospero's part, antithetical to the sense of affirmation the play ultimately achieves. It begins, as do the other epilogues in Shakespeare (and as the epilogue at the end of this play does not) by acknowledging the termination of the masque's play-world; it is an "insubstantial pageant" with a "baseless fabric". But Prospero goes on to imply that since his art-work has proved baseless, so any attempt to order reality through art must ultimately fail, since reality itself is only a fading illusion. Thus, while he has recognized the failure of his art, he has not yet discovered the cause of this failure: the flawed moral perspective on which his art is based. His vision is still as disastrously short-sighted as it was in his initial confrontations with Antonio and Caliban. Since reality will not conform to his concept of reality, he assumes that reality is unreal; that all the world and all humanity amount to no more than a flawed image which will fade into ultimate sleep—ultimate nothingness.

Retaining his serious misconception of himself as god rather than man, he assumes the right to condemn as unregenerate and destroy all that will not fit his moral code:

> A devil, a born devil, on whose nature
> Nurture can never stick; on whom my pains,
> Humanely taken, all, all lost, quite lost;
>   . . . I will plague them all,
> Even to roaring.
>
>   (IV. i. 188-190, 192-193)

Caliban is not a devil—thoroughly evil and unredeemable—but a type of humanity. Prospero has earlier denied the humanity of the Court party in the same way, calling them "worse than devils" (III.iii.36), and it is no coincidence that Stephano and Trinculo initially revealed their distorted perceptions by mistaking each other for devils (II.ii.90, 99). Prospero is committing the same error in a far graver sense: despairing in the nurture of Caliban, he despairs of the redemption of the low nature in all men; and, turning from despair to rage and vengeance, he resolves to "plague them all", to strike out at all whose evil qualities have frustrated him. As he summons hounds named "Fury" and "Tyrant" (IV.i.257), revelling in the pain of the clowns and exulting in the fact that "At this hour / Lies at my mercy all mine enemies," his spirits become his "goblins," and he himself threatens to become a satanic personification of revenge. Tragic chaos impends.

Disaster is averted, however, by the action of Ariel, who intervenes not as a *deus ex machina* but as an advocate on behalf of Prospero's own "nobler reason" (V. i. 26). The climactic crisis of the play passes in less than fifteen lines, as Prospero undergoes a brief but intensely meaningful psychomachy. Having described the whereabouts and miseries of the Court party (and it was after a similar description of Caliban and his confederates that Prospero called up Fury and Tyrant), Ariel checks the momentum of Prospero's passion by charging him with the central moral obligation he has hitherto ignored in his artistry:

>   Your charm so strongly works 'em,
> That if you now beheld them, your affections
> Would become tender.
> PROS.   Dost thou think so, spirit?
> ARI.   Mine would, sir, were I human.
> PROS.   And mine shall.
>
>   [V.i.17-20]

Good or evil, flawed or perfect, they are human—as he is—and on this basis alone he is bound to commiserate with them, to forgive them, and ultimately to accept them:

> Hast thou, which art but air, a touch, a feeling
> Of their afflictions, and shall not myself,
> One of their kind, that relish all as sharply
> Passion as they, be kindlier mov'd than thou

> art?
> Though with their high wrongs I am struck to th'quick,
> Yet with my nobler reason 'gainst my fury
> Do I take part: the rarer action is
> In virtue than in vengeance.
>
>   [V.i.21-28]

As an artist, he must limit his ends to the revelation of truth and self-knowledge; as a man, he can presume no further:

>   they being penitent,
> The sole drift of my purpose doth extend
> Not a frown further. . . .
>   . . . they shall be themselves.
>
>   [V.i.28-30, 32]

His moral vision is completed with the discovery and acceptance of this one truth: the overriding necessity for recognition and acceptance of one's own kind—in short, for love. This has been the element missing in his art: the flaw which rendered the masque of the goddesses inadequate. Only through unconditional forgiveness and acceptance of human nature, after all that can be done to reform it, can an art be capable of comprehending and dealing with the realities, good and evil, of the world. Prospero, then, finds himself as an artist as well as a man. What he rejects in the "elves of hills" speech is not his art *in toto*, but his "rough magic": that aspect of his art by which he presumed to rise to a Jove-like stature over other men, refusing to forgive them or accept their kinship as fellow beings until he had made them over in the image of his own faulty moral perspective. In drowning his book he does away not with the essence of his art but with that same volume that he has prized above his dukedom—above the society of his fellows: his blind absorption in the ideal to the exclusion of the real and the human. Far from the end of his artistic powers, this marks the point at which his art truly begins to function effectively.

The ultimate end of his artistic project, the restoration of order and harmony to the real world, starts to materialize as he frees and formally forgives each of his enemies. The simple act of forgiveness might seem too pat a solution of the play's central problem if its difficulty were not made absolutely clear. As Prospero's confrontation with the evil in human nature was first represented by his alienation from his brother, his acceptance of that nature is affirmed in Antonio's pardoning:

>   Flesh and blood,
> You, brother mine, . . .
>   . . . I do forgive thee,
> Unnatural though thou art.
>
>   [V.i.74-75,78-79]

The words come haltingly. Prospero must force himself to forgive by sheer strength of will, repeating his pardon twice during the scene as if to convince himself, and emphasizing each time his detestation of the "unnatural" evil he accepts as "flesh and blood". Having done so, however, he can proceed toward the completion of his project by presenting his most successful single art-work: an image of moral perfection that is at once ideal and real. With a gesture of dramatic art, he draws aside the curtain to reveal Ferdinand and Miranda.

Thus order is restored to the world of the play. Prospero regains his dukedom, the reformed Alonso finds his son, and the perpetuation of order is insured by the betrothal of the lovers. But Prospero is now too wise to trust wholly in a "brave new world". He is aware that the preservation of order will continue to require the forgiveness of evil, and he affirms this on a broadly representative scale by reacknowledging his responsibility for, and even kinship with Caliban: "this thing of darkness I / Acknowledge mine". And even here, at the lowest level of human nature, forgiveness sparks hope as Caliban resolves to "be wise hereafter / And seek for grace". Antonio, of course, remains ominously silent, but it is the very presence of his unreformed evil that underlines the triumphant order which has been achieved in its spite. Each other character has found himself through Prospero's art "When no man was his own," and Prospero himself is no exception: his has been the last and greatest self-discovery.

V

The play, as we have seen, does not end here, and Prospero's project is as yet incomplete. The artistic and moral vision of the masque was invalidated by its irrelevance to the outside world, proved by the violent non-correspondence of the three rebels to the three goddesses. By the same token, the ultimate ratification of the vision which Prospero has discovered and Shakespeare developed—for certainly Shakespeare speaks with Prospero at this point—must come from outside the world of *The Tempest*. The art of Shakespeare as well as of Prospero will prove a vanity unless the audience assumes its validity by participating in a cognate act of the love and recognition which are the essence of that art. In the Epilogue, then, Prospero brings the spectators into the play in order to place them in circumstances exactly parallel to the moment of his own climactic decision, charging them with the same responsibility. As Ariel reminded him that the courtiers were "Confin'd together" and could not budge "till your release" (V.i.7, 11), so Prospero must be "confin'd" until the spectators "release" him (Epilogue.4,9). As he has "pardon'd the deceiver" (7), they must set him free by their "indulgence" (20).

The Epilogue thus serves as a bridge between play and audience: a transitional link between art and reality. By the use of overtly religious terms such as "prayer", "Mercy", and "indulgence" in the last five lines, Shakespeare links his artistic vision with the orthodox principle of Christian charity. If his audience will make his vision their own—and it is an unprecedented testament of faith in his art that he terms its success dependent on such total acceptance—they will be participating in an act of prayer, which will bring down mercy and redemption on both the prayer and the prayed-for. Thus he endows his play's vision of love with the universal validity associated by his contemporary audience with the theological framework of their cosmos. His art passes beyond the moral spectrum of his play and merges with that of the world surrounding it, as Prospero, Shakespeare, and the audience unite in a recognition, acceptance, and celebration of their shared humanity.

Frances A. Yates

SOURCE: "Magic in the Last Plays: *The Tempest*," in *Shakespeare's Last Plays: A New Approach*, Routledge & Kegan Paul, 1975, pp. 85-106.

[*In the following excerpt from a lecture originally delivered in 1974, Yates examines the nature of Prospero's magic in* The Tempest *by relating it to the writings of Henry Cornelius Agrippa, a Renaissance expert on the subject. She calls the magic "intellectual and virtuous," the kind that Agrippa described in his* De occulta philosophia. *According to Yates, Prospero's intentions with his magical powers are good and aimed at the moral reform of the individual in society. In addition, she hints at Prospero's role in foreshadowing the scientific revolution of the seventeenth century by noting his similarities to John Dee, an eminent mathematician and a contemporary of Shakespeare.*]

To treat of magic, or the magical atmosphere, in Shakespeare one ought to include all the plays, for such an atmosphere is certainly present in his earlier periods. In the Last Plays this atmosphere becomes very strong indeed and, moreover, it becomes more clearly associated with the great traditions of Renaissance magic—magic as an intellectual system of the universe, foreshadowing science, magic as a moral and reforming movement, magic as the instrument for uniting opposing religious opinions in a general movement of Hermetic reform. . . .

[*The Tempest* is] the supreme expression of the magical philosophy of the Last Plays. . . .

First, let us consider the textual history of *The Tempest*. Like all Last Plays, except *Pericles* and *Henry VIII*, it seems to have had a first appearance around

1610-11, or at least a play called *The Tempest* was performed at court in 1611. Unlike *Cymbeline* and *The Winter's Tale* it was apparently not seen by Simon Forman at about that time, so we do not have his plot summary to compare with the play as we have it. Like *The Winter's Tale*, it was one of the plays by Shakespeare which were performed by the King's Men before Princess Elizabeth and her betrothed in 1612. Like all Last Plays except *Pericles* it was first printed in the First Folio of 1623 where it is the first play in that famous volume.

Thus the history of *The Tempest* follows the familiar pattern and there is room for an earlier version of the play to have been revised to suit performance before Princess Elizabeth and the Palatine. This has in fact been suggested in critical discussions of the play, summed up by Frank Kermode in his introduction to the Arden edition, where it is pointed out that the masque in the play, which is evidently a nuptial masque, was perhaps added to an earlier version to make it suitable for performance before the princely pair. Thus, *The Tempest*, as we have it, would enter that atmosphere of masque and pageantry surrounding the wedding of Princess Elizabeth which is central for the understanding of *Cymbeline* and which Foakes has detected in *Henry VIII*. I would further suggest that the emphasis on chastity before marriage in *The Tempest*, where it is so marked a feature of Prospero's advice to the young prince, should be compared with the treatment of the same theme in *Philaster*, the play by Beaumont and Fletcher performed before Elizabeth and the Palatine at the same time, in which the overtures made before marriage to his betrothed by the Spanish prince, seem to be a mark of the impurity of a Spanish match. Prospero is perhaps emphasising that his daughter is *not* making a Spanish match.

The themes of *The Tempest* connect with the Last Play themes as a whole. There is a young generation, Ferdinand and Miranda, the very young princely pair, and an older generation, Prospero and his contemporaries, divided by bitter wrongs and quarrels but brought together at the end in the magical atmosphere of reconciliation. *The Tempest* fits very well into our general historical approach to the Last Plays with its argument that these 'reconciliation through a younger generation' themes belong into an actual historical situation in which Prince Henry and his sister were seen as hopeful figures of this kind. Prince Henry being now dead, only a daughter and her lover represent the young generation in *The Tempest*. Miranda has no brother. Nor indeed have Perdita or Marina. Only Imogen has brothers, and *Cymbeline* was not performed after the death of Prince Henry and before Frederick and Elizabeth, as were *The Winter's Tale* and *The Tempest*.

We have now to think about magic in *The Tempest*.

What kind of magic is it? This is a problem which has been considerably discussed in recent years and I am not bringing forward any very new or startling discovery in observing that Prospero, as a magus, appears to work on the lines indicated in that well-known textbook of Renaissance magic, the *De occulta philosophia* of Henry Cornelius Agrippa. Frank Kermode was a pioneer in pointing to Agrippa as a power behind Prospero's art in his introduction to *The Tempest* in the Arden edition, first published in 1954. Prospero as a magus, says Kermode, exercises a discipline of virtuous knowledge; his art is the achievement of 'an intellect pure and conjoined with the powers of the gods without which [and this is direct quotation by Kermode from Agrippa] we shall never happily ascend to the scrutiny of secret things, and to the power of wonderful workings'. In short, Prospero has learned that 'occult philosophy' which Agrippa taught and knows how to put it into practice. Moreover, like Agrippa, Shakespeare makes very clear in *The Tempest* how utterly different is the high intellectual and virtuous magic of the true magus from low and filthy witchcraft and sorcery. Prospero is poles apart from the witch Sycorax and her evil son. Indeed, Prospero as the good magus has a reforming mission; he clears the world of his island from the evil magic of the witch; he rewards the good characters and punishes the wicked. He is a just judge, or a virtuous and reforming monarch, who uses his magico-scientific powers for good. The triumph of a liberal and Protestant Reformation in *Henry VIII* has its counterpart in *The Tempest* in the triumph of a reforming magus in the dream world of the magical island.

Prospero's magic is then a good magic, a reforming magic. But what exactly is the intellectual structure or system within which his magic works? Here we have to turn to Agrippa's definitions which can be simplified, rather drastically, as follows.

The universe is divided into three worlds: the elemental world of terrestrial nature; the celestial world of the stars; the supercelestial world of the spirits or intelligences or angels. Natural magic operates in the elemental world; celestial magic operates in the world of the stars; and there is a highest, religious, magic which operates in the supercelestial world. The lofty religious magus can conjure spirits or intelligences to his aid. The enemies of this kind of magic called it diabolical conjuring, and indeed the pious believers in it were always aware of the danger of conjuring up evil spirits, or demons, instead of angels. Prospero has the conjuring power, and he performs his operations through the spirit, Ariel, whom he conjures. Of the two branches, Magia and Cabala, set out in Agrippa's handbook of Renaissance magic, Prospero would seem to use mainly the Cabalistic conjuring magic, rather than the healing magic of Cerimon, or the profound natural magic which pervades *The Winter's Tale*.

It is inevitable and unavoidable in thinking of Prospero to bring in the name of John Dee, the great mathematical magus of whom Shakespeare must have known, the teacher of Philip Sidney, and deeply in the confidence of Queen Elizabeth I. In his famous preface to Euclid of 1570, which became the Bible of the rising generations of Elizabethan scientists and mathematicians, Dee sets out, following Agrippa, the theory of the three worlds, emphasising, as does Agrippa, that through all the three worlds there runs, as the connecting link, number. If I may paraphrase what I have myself said elsewhere, Dee was in his own right a brilliant mathematician, and he related his study of number to the three worlds of the Cabalists. In the lower elemental world, he studied number as technology and applied science. In the celestial world his study of number was related to astrology and alchemy. And in the supercelestial world, Dee believed that he had found the secret of conjuring spirits by numerical computations in the tradition of Trithemius and Agrippa. Dee's type of science can be classified as 'Rosicrusian', using this word, as I have suggested that it can be used, to designate a stage in the history of the magico-scientific tradition which is intermediate between the Renaissance and the seventeenth century.

The commanding figure of Prospero represents precisely that Rosicrucian stage. We see him as a conjuror in the play, but the knowledge of such a Dee-like figure would have included mathematics developing into science, and particularly the science of navigation in which Dee was proficient and in which he instructed the great mariners of the Elizabethan age.

Now, if the first version of *The Tempest* appeared around 1611, the date at which Shakespeare chose to glorify a Dee-like magus is significant. For Dee had fallen into deep disfavour after his return from his mysterious continental mission in 1589, and he was completely cast off by James I after his accession. When the old Elizabethan magus appealed to James in 1604 for help in clearing his reputation from charges of conjuring devils, James would have nothing to do with him, in spite of his earnest protests that his art and science were good and virtuous and that he had no commerce with evil spirits. The old man to whose scientific learning the Elizabethan age had been so deeply indebted was disgraced in the reign of James and died in great poverty in 1608.

Seen in the context of these events, Shakespeare's presentation of a scientific magus in an extremely favourable light takes on a new significance. Prospero is far from diabolic; on the contrary, he is the virtuous opponent of evil sorcery, the noble and benevolent ruler who uses his magico-scientific knowledge for good ends. Prospero might be a vindication of Dee, a reply to the censure of James. And the contemporary scientists and mathematicians who were working in the Dee tradition were to be found, not in the circle of the King, but in that of his son, Prince Henry. The Prince was eager to build up a navy, as Dee used to advise Elizabeth to do, and he patronised and encouraged scientific experts like William Petty who built for him his great ship, the *Royal Prince*. Mathematicians and navigators of the Elizabethan age, Walter Raleigh and his friend Thomas Hariot, were imprisoned by James in the Tower, but were encouraged by Prince Henry. Thus here the line of inquiry which seeks to establish that Shakespeare's Last Plays belong in the atmosphere and aspirations surrounding the younger royal generation makes contact with this other line of inquiry into the magico-philosophical influences in the plays. Prospero, the magus as scientist, would belong with Prince Henry and his interests, and not with those of his unscientific father with his superstitious dread of magic.

Thus I am suggesting new contexts in which to see *The Tempest*. This play is not an isolated phenomenon but one of the Last Plays, and other Last Plays breathe the atmosphere of learned magic, the medical magic of Cerimon in *Pericles*, the deep Hermetic magic of *The Winter's Tale*, the incantatory singing of *Henry VIII*. All such magics connect with one another and belong to the late period of Renaissance magic. *The Tempest* would be one of the supreme expressions of that vitally important phase in the history of the European mind, the phase which borders on, and presages, the so-called scientific revolution of the seventeenth century. Prospero is so clearly the magus as scientist, able to operate scientifically within his world view, which includes areas of operation not recognised by science proper.

There is also, and this is very important, the element of moral reform in Prospero's outlook and aims, the element of Utopia, an essential feature of the scientific outlook of the Rosicrucian period, in which it was seen to be necessary to situate the developing magico-scientific knowledge within a reformed society, a society broadened by new moral insights to accept the broadening stream of knowledge. Prospero as scientist is also Prospero the moral reformer, bent on freeing the world of his island from evil influences.

Finally, we should see *The Tempest* in the context of *Henry VIII*, in which the reforming conciliatory themes of the Last Plays are presented through real historical personages. Henry VIII is seen as the monarch of the Tudor imperial reform, casting out vices in the person of Wolsey, and presenting a Reformation, originally Protestant, but in which the old hardness and intolerance has been done away in an atmosphere of love and reconciliation.

From these various lines of approach, *The Tempest*

would now appear as the corner-stone of the total edifice of the Last Plays, the play presenting a philosophy which connects with all their themes and reflects a movement, or a phase, which can now be more or less identified among the currents of European intellectual and religious history. It is the Rosicrucian movement, which was to be given open expression in the manifestos published in Germany in 1614 and 1615.

In my book, *The Rosicrucian Enlightenment,* I have argued that this movement was connected with the currents stirring around the Elector Palatine and his wife. These were ostensibly Protestant, as befitted the head of the Union of German Protestant Princes, but drew on Paracelsist alchemy and other Hermetic influences for spiritual nourishment. The manifestos envisage a general moral and religious reform of the whole world. These strange hopes were to be extinguished in utter disaster, with the brief reign in Prague in 1619-20 of the 'Winter King and Queen' and the subsequent total defeat and exile of the unfortunate pair. Thus ended in ignominy and confusion the movement which had been building up around them in London, a movement very much weakened by the death of Prince Henry. Not only their own party in England but many in Europe had fixed their hopes on these two. And it would be wrong to say that all came to an end with the disaster, for the movement lived on, taking other forms, and leading eventually to important developments.

Shakespeare has often been derided for his absurd geographical error in giving a 'sea coast' to Bohemia in *The Winter's Tale,* but may his object have been to provide a setting for the frightful storm in which the infant Princess arrives in Bohemia? Shakespeare took the name 'Bohemia' from Greene's novel, *Pandosto,* the plot of which he was adapting. Yet there is something strangely prophetic in his choice of a story about Bohemia, foreshadowing the terrible tempest of the Thirty Years' War which would break out in Bohemia following the shipwreck of the Winter King and Queen. Is it possible that Shakespeare may have known more of what was going on in Bohemia than do critics of his geographical ignorance? Might he, for example, have had some contact with Michael Maier, Paracelsist doctor and Rosicrucian, who was moving between Prague and London in the early years of the century, linking movements in England with movements in Germany and Bohemia?

A main feature of the 'new approach' to Shakespeare's Last Plays presented here has been the argument that the hopes of a younger generation which the plays seem to express may allude to hopes in relation to a real historical generation, Prince Henry, and, after his death, Princess Elizabeth and her husband. Taken at its face value, this argument would amount to yet another 'topical allusion' detected in the plays, a type of investigation which has been very much used and abused. Even if the topical allusion to the younger royal generation is fairly substantially based, what does it amount to in relation to Shakespeare's genius, to the understanding of his mind and art? Topical-allusion hunting for its own sake is but an empty sport unless it can open doors to new approaches to matters more profound.

And it is precisely this, or so I believe, that this topical allusion can do. The other new approach attempted has been to the thought of the Last Plays, to the philosophy of nature with religious and reforming undercurrents, with association with scientific movements of the kind propagated by John Dee, with spiritual and mental enlightenment. And it is just such a movement as this which seems to have been associated in German circles with the Elector Palatine and with his disastrous Bohemian enterprise.

The German Rosicrucian movement was certainly not newly invented in connection with the Elector Palatine and his wife. It was something already in existence with which they, or the movement associated with them, became somehow involved. There are various influences from England on the movement which I have tried to bring out in my book, influences from Philip Sidney's mission to Germany and to the imperial court, influences from visits of the Knights of the Garter, influences from John Dee's sojourn in Bohemia. The second Rosicrucian manifesto of 1615 has included in it a discourse on secret philosophy which is based on Dee's *Monas hieroglyphica.* The works of the Englishman, Robert Fludd, a leading exponent of Rosicrucian philosophy, were published at Oppenheim, a town in the territory of the Elector Palatine. And, most curious of all from the theatrical point of view, there appears to have been an influence of English actors, or of plays acted by travelling English actors in Germany, on the ideas and modes of expression of the Rosicrucian publications.

The man known to be behind the movement, Johann Valentin Andreae, states in his autobiography that in his youth, around 1604, he wrote plays in imitation of English comedians, and at about the same time he wrote the first version of his strange work, *The Chemical Wedding of Christian Rosencreutz,* first published, in German, in 1616. This is a mystical romance reflecting ceremonial of orders of chivalry in a setting which I believe I have identified as the castle and gardens of the Elector Palatine at Heidelberg, reflecting his court there and the presence in it of his English wife, the Princess Elizabeth. Andreae's style in all his writings is dramatic, infused with theatrical influences. The story of Christian Rosencreutz and his Order, told in the manifestos (which were not actually written by Andreae though inspired by him), is said to be a fiction or a play. And the mysterious doings in the castle grounds in *The Chemical Wedding* include a play, the plot of which is given as follows (I quote from the résumé of it in my book):

> On the sea-shore, an old king found an infant in a chest washed up by the waves: an accompanying letter explained that the King of the Moors had seized the child's country. In the following acts, The Moor appeared and captured the infant, now grown into a young woman. She was rescued by the old king's son and betrothed to him, but fell again into the Moor's power. She was finally rescued again but a very wicked priest had to be got out of the way. . . . When his power was broken the wedding could take place. Bride and bridegroom appeared in great splendour and all joined in a Song of Love:

> This time full of love
> Does our joy much approve. . . .

The plot reminds one of the plots of Last Plays, with shipwrecked infants who grow up to have adventures in which evil influences are surmounted, stories reflecting a passage of time from an older generation to a younger, and ending in general love and reconciliation. And, if I am right in my suggestions, this play described in *The Chemical Wedding* is supposed to be enacted in a setting reflecting the court of the Elector Palatine and the Princess Elizabeth at Heidelberg. It is as though Shakespearean dramatic influences in London at the time of their wedding were being reflected back to them through a mystical haze. The extremely simple plot of the comedy described in *The Chemical Wedding* is punctuated by Biblical allusions, as though the fiction had some reference to the religious problems of the day.

This is only one example of the curious reflections of plays, perhaps of plays staged by English players in Germany, in the German Rosicrucian literature. Was there some connection between players and Rosicrucian ideas? Ought we to look for light on Shakespeare in these directions? Did the Last Plays deliver a message the meaning of which we have lost? Are the connections between the Last Plays and the new generation of Prince Henry and his sister much more than topical allusions in the ordinary sense? Might they introduce us to ways of unravelling Shakespeare's position in the religious, intellectual, magical, political, theatrical movements of his time? Or, more than that, might they help us to penetrate to Shakespeare's inner religious experiences?

A French writer who has made a study of the Rosicrucian literature in relation to Shakespeare thinks that *The Chemical Wedding* reflects rituals of initiation through enaction of the mystery of death. He believes that some of Shakespeare's plays—he mentions particularly Imogen's death-like sleep and resurrection in *Cymbeline*—reflect such experiences, conveyed through esoteric allusion in the imagery. He sees influences of 'spiritual alchemy' in the imagery of *Cymbeline*. The Rosicrucian method of using the play or the fiction as the vehicle through which to indicate an esoteric meaning would also be Shakespeare's method. I mention Arnold's book here not because I think it reliable as a whole, or in detail (it is not), but because the general drift of his comparative study of Rosicrucian literature and of Shakespeare may not be altogether wide of the mark.

Shakespeare died in 1616 and so did not live to hear the news of the events of 1620, the defeat at the Battle of the White Mountain, the flight of the Winter King and Queen of Bohemia, the outbreak of the Thirty Years' War. Perhaps that was the terrible storm which he prophetically dreaded.

ORDER AND STRUCTURE

Perhaps the most important critical observation in regard to *The Tempest*'s structure is that of its adherence to the classical principles of unity. The entire movement of the play is supposed to occur over the course of just a few hours—probably not much longer than the drama would actually take to perform—on or near the small tropical island that has been Prospero's and Miranda's home for the past twelve years. In 1710 Charles Gildon was one of the first to comment on this (for Shakespeare) unusual observance of the unities of action and time. Critics have since noted that this was the dramatist's first and only use of strict adherence to the unities; yet why he choose to form his final play in this manner remains somewhat of a mystery. **Ernest Gohn** argues that Shakespeare's adoption of these principles is reflected in the theme of urgency that sets the tone for the play. In contrast, Rose Zimbardo concerns herself with the struggle between order and chaos in the work. Her interpretation privileges Prospero as an artist who seeks to impose form on the universe through his art. Less concerned with unity than with the overall structure of the play, **Burton Weber** sees in the work a strong symmetry in which one character or set of characters balances and comments upon the other. The result is the creation of a microcosm of society within the bounds of a piece of art, which allows Shakespeare to explore the interplay of good and evil and the equilibrium that modern civilization achieves between the two.

Ernest Gohn

SOURCE: "*The Tempest: Theme and Structure*," in *English Studies*, Vol. 45, No. 2, pp. 116-25.

[*In the following essay, Gohn discusses Shakespeare's use—hitherto unpredecented in his plays—of the classical unities of time and place in* The Tempest. *He argues that the work's structural unity, with action occurring as it does over the course of approximately three hours, is reflected in a thematic emphasis on the present. Gohn's analysis continues by relating this dramatic sense of urgency and preoccupation with the "now" in the play to its themes of hoped-for redemption and reconciliation.*]

Critics have spent so much time on character-analysis—and upon possible biographical, allegorical, and symbolic implications of *The Tempest*—that they have overlooked the great emphasis put on the sense of the present in the play. But it is an emphasis which we cannot ignore: such words and phrases as 'now', 'at this moment', 'at this instant' echo and reinforce one another throughout the play. Furthermore, the episodes of the play are usually conceived in a present which is a crucial nexus uniting the past to the future: the past is relevant only as it affects the present, the future only as it grows out of the present. The past is defined as that which occurred years ago in Milan, the future as that which will take place after the characters leave the island.

Shakespeare no sooner finishes his brief opening shipwreck scene than be begins to emphasize the crucial quality of the present. Prospero assures Miranda, who has been moved to pity by the sight of the wreck, that all he has done in raising the storm has been done in care of her, who is ignorant of what she and her father are. But now "Tis time', says Prospero, 'I should inform thee farther' (I, ii, 22-23). Prospero's care for his daughter, which has led him to raise the storm, is, then, intimately related to the time at which Miranda must learn of her past: he repeats, 'For thou must now know farther' (I, ii, 33). Prospero has at times in the past started to tell his history to her, but in the past he has always stopped, 'Concluding, "Stay, not yet" ' (I, ii, 36). At this moment, however, 'the hour', 'the very minute' (I, ii, 36-37) has come. Miranda must know of her origins before she can take her place in Prospero's present scheme. As he assures her later in the midst of his narrative:

> Hear a little further,
> And then I'll bring thee to the present
>   business
> Which now's upon 's, without the which
>   this story
> Were most impertinent.
>
>   (I, ii, 135-38)

To Miranda, the 'present business' which is 'now' upon them must refer to the storm she has just witnessed. To Prospero, also, the shipwreck seems to be the 'present business'; but he evidently has more in mind, for when Miranda asks him his reason for raising the tempest, he replies in most general terms, terms which neither she nor the audience can understand until the play is over:

> Know thus far forth.
> By accident most strange, bountiful Fortune,
> Now my dear lady, hath mine enemies
> Brought to this shore. And by my prescience
> I find my zenith doth depend upon
> A most auspicious star, whose influence
> If now I court not, but omit, my fortunes
> Will ever after droop. Here cease more
>   questions.
>
>   (I, ii, 177-84)

Prospero's storm is merely the first phase of a larger sense of the moment which he 'now' courts, a sense which includes everything in the play. It is, one supposes, to keep his larger scheme secret that he carefully sends Mirando to sleep before he calls for Ariel: 'I am ready now' (I, ii, 187).

Ariel's interview with Prospero is, of course, mainly further exposition: we learn how Ariel has acted as Prospero's agent in creating the shipwreck and in disposing the various groups about the isle; we also learn of Ariel's imprisonment by Sycorax (the pre-Prospero history of the island). But between these two bits of exposition, we are again recalled to the sense of the present, made vivid by the pressure of time: 'The time 'twixt six and now / Must by us both be spent most preciously' (I, ii, 240-41). In this instance, Prospero's 'now' is that moment at least 'two glasses' after noon. But in Ariel's slight attempt at rebellion and in its happy resolution ('That's my noble master! / What shall I do? Say what. What shall I do?'—I, ii, 299-300), we realize that for Ariel, as for Prospero, the 'present business' is 'now' in another sense. Having performed his duties in this scheme of Prospero, he will be free. He had asked for his liberty 'Before the time be out' (I, ii, 246), but in his glad acceptance of Prospero's promise, we cannot help but think for Ariel the present is the larger action in which he must play his part.

Having been sent off by Propero's whispered command, Ariel returns, leading Ferdinand onstage. Ferdinand's passion has been allayed by Ariel's song, which, he recognizes, is 'no mortal business' (I, ii, 406). Prospero has thus prepared Ferdinand for the transcendant experience which he is now to have. Ferdinand 'now' (I, ii, 407) hears the music above him, and Prospero immediately directs Miranda to look at what she first thinks is a spirit. That Shakespeare's young lovers love at first sight is certainly no news, but in no other play is the event revealed so dramatically in the present, in a moment so pregnant. Miranda thinks that Ferdinand must be something divine, Ferdinand that Miranda must be a goddess.

They have, as Prospero recognizes, changed eyes 'at first sight' (I, ii, 440), but the intensity of the present is revealed must fully in their mutual wonder. As they recognize their humanity, Miranda reveals that this is the 'first' (I, ii, 445) man that she ever sighed for; Ferdinand ignores Prospero's ungentle tone to propose marriage immediately. It is a 'swift business' (I, ii, 450) which causes Prospero to impose the test on Ferdinand. As the scene ends, Miranda comforts Ferdinand by assuring him that her father's nature is gentler than it has just appeared: 'This is unwonted / Which now came from him' (I, ii, 497-98). Something about *this* occasion makes him act in a manner unusual to him.

As Shakespeare turns to the shipwrecked crew in Act II, we soon discover that for them, too, the present is of peculiar significance. Gonzalo immediately recognizes the miraculous quality of their preservation and, joined by Adrian though ridiculed by Antonio and Sebastian, extols the idyllic quality of the island. He is most amazed, however, that their clothes are 'now' (II, i, 68, 97) still as fresh as when they first put them on in Africa for the marriage of Claribel who 'now' (II, i, 98) is Queen at Tunis. Gonzalo's moralizing does not ease the sorrow of Alonzo; rather, it stimulates lamentation for what he had done in the past that has occasioned the sorrow of the present. (Ironically, he does not realize how right he is, in a sense of which he is yet ignorant.) After Gonzalo's description of the ideal commonwealth—the possibilities of their present predicament now so obviously contrary to what they had known in the past in Milan and Naples—Ariel sends them all, except Sebastian and Antonio, to sleep.

For these men, left awake to do the wicked plotting which so explicitly reproduces the earlier plot against Prospero, the memory of the past stimulates the action of the present. Like Prospero, they see an occasion not to be missed. As Antonio begins to prod Sebastian.

> The occasion speaks thee, and
> My strong imagination sees a crown
> Dropping upon thy head.
>
> (II, i, 207-9)

Sebastian is 'standing water', but Antonio will teach him 'how to flow' (II, i, 221-22). As Antonio proceeds to be more explicit, he says 'what's past is prologue, what to come, / In yours and my discharge' (II, i, 253-54). This murder must be performed now. If it were death that 'now' (II, i, 261) had seized the sleepers, they would be no worse off than they are 'now' (II, i. 262). In the past Prospero's servants were Antonio's fellows; 'now' (II, i, 274) they are Antonio's men. Alonzo would be no better than the earth he lies upon, 'If he were that which now he's like,

that's dead' (II, i, 282). Ready to carry out their treachery, they draw their swords, when Ariel enters to sing in Gonzalo's ear. If the sleepers are not kept living, Prospero's 'project' will not succeed (II, i, 299). In his song Ariel warns Gonzalo that conspiracy has taken this opportunity ('His time'—II, i, 303). The conspirators are about to 'be sudden' (II, i, 306) but Gonzalo awakes, saying 'Now good angels / Preserve the King!' (II, i, 306-7). Even Sebastian's lying explanation for their drawn swords stresses the present— 'Even now we heard a hollow burst . . . ' (II, i, 311). In this episode we again see the overwhelming relevance of action in the present. For Antonio and Sebastian, the present moment (not before or later) is the occasion to carry out their evil purposes. They are stopped only by the timely appearance of Ariel. The Antonio-Sebastian-Alonzo subplot is thus intimately a part of Prospero's larger project—his conduct of the 'present business' which is the major concern of the play. Were the conspirators to succeed now, Prospero's unique opportunity for reconciliation with Alonzo would be lost. A lesser, evil instant would destroy the larger, good instant.

When we next see the court party, they are weary from their fruitless search for Ferdinand, and, stopping to rest, Alonzo will 'no longer' (III, iii, 8) keep hope for his flatterer. Antonio and Sebastian see in the abandonment of hope and in the weariness the possibility of another attempt on the king's life. They agree to take the 'next advantage' (III, iii, 13), which will be 'tonight, / For now they are oppressed with travel' (III, iii, 14-15). But at this moment Prospero again intervenes, this time with the dumb-show banquet. Sebastian will 'now' (III, iii, 21) believe in unicorns and in the phoenix; Gonzalo recognizes that if the reported this 'now' (III, iii, 28) in Naples, he would scarce be credited, although stories which had seemed unbelievable in his youth are 'now' (III, iii, 47) vouched for by travellers. As they approach the table to eat, Ariel appears in the guise of a harpy, the banquet suddenly vanishes, and Ariel delivers the speech which Prospero has commanded. In this speech Alonzo and his followers are first accused of evil, then reminded of their powerlessness ('Your swords are now too massy for your strengths'—III, iii, 67). But Ariel's most important business is to recall their treachery to Prospero in the past, again bringing the past into the context of the crucial present. The powers have delayed, not forgotten (III, iii, 73). Alonzo is promised punishment in the future, a punishment to be avoided only by repentance. Prospero compliments Ariel on his performance and observes that his enemies are 'now' (III, iii, 90) in his power. As Prospero goes off to join Miranda and Ferdinand, Alonzo recalls his early sin. For him, Ariel's speech, with its references to Providence, Fate, Prospero, and foul deeds is the moment of moral awakening, although at this point it drives him to despair instead of repentance.

As Gonzalo observes, after Alonzo and the others have run off:

> Their great guilt,
> Like poison given to work a great time after,
> Now 'gins to bite the spirits.
>
> (III, iii, 104-6)

They must be stopped from the suicide to which they are 'now' (III, iii, 109) provoked.

Following his formal gift of Miranda to Ferdinand (in the course of which Ferdinand promises not to violate her chastity, as he hopes for long life with 'such love as 'tis now'—IV, i, 25), Prospero calls for Ariel so that he can present the masque. Ariel asks, 'Presently?' and Prospero replies, 'Aye, with a twink' (IV, i, 42-43). Ariel promises to fulfill the task

> Before you can say, 'come', and 'go',

Breathe twice and cry, 'so, so'.

(IV, i, 44-45)

Ariel is not to approach until Prosporo calls for him, but it is after only six lines that Prospero bids, 'Now come, my Ariel!' (IV, i, 57). As the masque ends with a dance, Prospero suddenly recalls the Caliban-Stephano-Trinculo conspiracy, the 'minute' (IV, i, 141) of whose plot has come. Again, that is, Prospero recalls the importance of the moment: there is a minute for Alonso, for Ferdinand, and even for Caliban. We recall that from his first meeting with Stephano and Trinculo, Caliban, having discovered that they were not plaguing spirits, had perceived them as agents through whom to effect his own liberation. As Prospero breaks up the entertainment, the revels 'now' (IV, i, 148) are ended. When Caliban approaches the cell, he, too, is aware of the precious quality of the moment: 'We are now near his cell' (IV, i, 195). Caliban's urgency can only be increased as Stephano and Trinculo are

Miranda, Prospero, Ariel, and Caliban.

beguiled by the trumpery; Caliban will have none of it, for 'we shall lose our time' (IV, i, 248). The plotters being chased away, Prospero knows he is in absolute control:

> At this hour
> Lie at my mercy all mine enemies.
> Shortly shall my labors end . . .
>
> (IV, i, 263-65)

The enemies are in Prospero's power, but as Shakespeare approaches his fifth-act denouement [the final explanation or outcome of the plot] he maintains the emphasis on the present. The act opens with Prospero's assertion that 'Now' his project gathers 'to a head' (V, i, 1). He asks Ariel the time and learns that it is the sixth hour, 'at which time' (V, i, 4) Prospero had promised their work would cease. Ariel tells Prospero how he had left the court party mourning—if Prospero 'now' (V, i, 18) beheld them, he would be moved. While Ariel goes to release Alonzo and the others, Prospero abjures his rough magic; he will break his staff as soon as he has commanded some heavenly music, which 'even now' (V, i, 52) he does. Ariel brings in the distracted party, whose charms are dissolving 'apace' (V, i, 64); as Prospero reminds them of their past sins, their understanding grows. It will 'shortly' be clear that 'now' (V, i, 81-82) is muddy. Ariel is asked to fetch Prospero's Milanese garments 'quickly' (V, i, 86). Knowing that he will 'ere long' (V, i, 87) be free, Ariel can sing that he will live merrily 'now' (V, i, 93); he is then sent to bring the boatswain and the master to Prospero 'presently' (V, i, 101). Prospero, clad in his ducal robes, then reveals himself to the others, reassuring them that a living prince does 'now' (V, i, 109) speak to them. Alonzo immediately resigns the dukedom and entreats pardon, and Prospero embraces Gonzalo. Prospero could cause the disgrace of Sebastian and Antonio, but 'at this time' (V, i, 128) he will remain silent. Alonzo, thinking that the loss of his son is irreparable, laments, and Prospero reveals the living presence of Ferdinand, whom Alonzo greets, 'Now all the blessings / Of a glad father compass thee about' (V, i, 179-80). Miranda's response to the brave new world now revealed to her echoes the immediacy of her response to Ferdinand. Learning that Miranda is Prospero's daughter, Alonzo would ask her pardon, but Prospero, his purpose now accomplished, has no more use for the past:

> Let us not burden our remembrance with
> A heaviness that's gone.
>
> (V, i, 199-200)

As we approach the end of the play, we find that even the minor characters have experienced the suddenness of events. The master and boatswain had 'even now' (V, i, 232) been awaked and had been brought from the ship 'on a trice' (V, i, 238). Sent to free Caliban and his companions, Ariel drives them in only three lines later. Stephano (who is drunk 'now'—V, i, 278) and Trinculo are recognized by the court party, and Prospero acknowledges Caliban as his; the three are ordered to trim the cell, as a condition of their pardon. From the events of the day, even Caliban seems to have learned something: he immediately assents to Prospero's command (instead of cursing) and promises to be wise 'hereafter' (V, i, 294). The play ends with Prospero's promise to tell the others his story and with his final command to Ariel. The auspicious gales provided, Ariel will then be free. . . .

When Prospero reveals his identity to Alonzo, Sebastian, and the others, he does not tell them, though they ask, how he came to be lord of the isle,

> For 'tis a chronicle of day by day,
> Not a relation for a breakfast, nor
> Befitting this first meeting.
>
> (V, i, 162-64)

The play that Shakespeare has usually written is a chronicle of day by day: an event happening at a particular time causes another event at some subsequent time. *The Tempest* is not such a play. Except for the few details which he has told Miranda in the first act—and the added hints we get from the scenes with Ariel and Caliban—we in the audience know no more of the story of Prospero than does Alonzo. At the end of other plays, notably *Hamlet*, Shakespeare has one character promise to tell the ignorant and amazed auditory what has happened—as Prospero promises at the end of *The Tempest*. The difference is that we in the audience already know what Horatio will tell the others—in fact, we now some things about Hamlet of which Horatio is probably ignorant. In *The Tempest* we do not know. We can assume that Shakespeare considered such knowledge irrelevant to his play, that the tale of Prospero on the island is nonessential; for Shakespeare is here not interested in the sequence of day by day, but in the now which can redeem the past.

If this reading of *The Tempest* is correct, we can find a reason for Shakespeare's use of unity in this play, a reason which is, moreover, essential for our understanding of the play. What we perceived in the foregoing discussion is the great emphasis which Shakespeare puts on the idea of the present in *The Tempest*. If this play is, like the other romances, about reconciliation, it is about reconciliation *now*, within the few hours which Prospero must seize. Unlike Leontes, Prospero does not need time to repent. Rather, he needs to grasp the moment in which he can offer money, can stay his fury, can effect the awakening of Alonzo's conscience, can restore his daughter to her proper place among mankind. To tell this story, incorporating such themes, Shakespeare used the form most likely to create this sense of the urgency of the moment. He wrote a unified play.

Burton J. Weber

SOURCE: "The Ordering of *The Tempest*," in *Wascana Review*, Vol. 10, No. 1, Spring, 1977, pp. 3-20.

[*In the following essay, Weber outlines the "elaborate and symmetrical structure" of* The Tempest, *contending that characters, both in groups and as individuals, are contrasted with one another in order to dramatize Shakespeare's theme of civilization's effects on human beings. In this scheme, Weber explains, Ariel and Caliban represent aspects of human behavior outside the bounds of civilized society. They are in turn compared to the human characters in the play who represent the virtues and vices of civilized man. Thus, Prospero personifies intellectual virtue; Sebastian and Antonio intellectual evil; Gonzago embodies emotional goodness; Stephano and Trinculo demonstrate emotional vice. These symmetries are likewise played out in the drama's minor characters, including Miranda and Ferdinand, who represent potential for good among the young in society.*]

Friends and foes of *The Tempest* agree on its stylized characterization. The richness of the play lies more in the arrangement than in the fulness of its characters, and through the play's elaborate and symmetrical structure Shakespeare makes a coherent and systematic statement about civilization. The characters of *The Tempest* are repeatedly dichotomized. Nonhuman characters are contrasted with human ones, virtuous secondary characters with evil ones, central characters who are tested with central characters who are reformed. These dichotomies focus on the question of how the virtues of civilization may be attained and its evils rejected. Not only are characters divided into groups, however, but within the groups characters are systematically contrasted—Ariel with Caliban, Prospero with Gonzalo, Antonio and Sebastian with Stephano and Trinculo, Ferdinand with Miranda, and even Alonso with the boatswain. These contrasts analyze the effects of civilization in terms of man's two constituents, mind and body.

The fact that Ariel and Caliban are not human beings makes them easy symbols for the faculties divorced from society's nurture, and Shakespeare heightens this symbolic potentiality by suggesting the imperviousness of the pair to training: Ariel is forgetful (1.2.260-263) and "nurture" cannot "stick" on Caliban (4.1.188-190). That the pair represent spirit and body is an obvious enough conclusion. Ariel, airy thought, is devoid of feelings. He knows how Prospero would react to a moving sight but is not himself moved—his "affections/Would become tender . . . were [he]

human" (5.1.17-20)—and when he imitates Ferdinand's mourning gestures and likens the sighing Ferdinand to a man blowing on porridge (1.2.221-224), his behaviour, which would be callous in a human being, shows his incapacity to feel. Caliban, the earthy body, is devoid of mind. For convenience' sake he is given the capacity of speaking, but that capacity is distinguished from human rationality by Caliban's inability to know good from evil (1.2.353-355, 360-362).

These characters reveal the natural strengths and weaknesses of the faculties. The mind loves to range—Ariel's songs are all symbolic, and the one he sings about himself deals with roaming (5.1.88-94)—but the mind's chief asset is formal morality. Ariel possesses principles, for he voluntarily opposes Caliban and voluntarily defends Prospero (3.2.43, 113); his contractual relationship with Prospero (1.2.245-250) suggests his sense of legal obligation. Ariel's morality makes it appropriate that he take, as he does, the role of moral expositor and agent: in the wedding masque he announces Ferinand's test of chastity (4.1.88-101) and in "full fadom five" the regeneration of Alonso (1.2.399-407); he descends like a harpy to punish the noble conspirators (3.3.53ff) and runs in a dog-pack to punish the base ones (4.1.255ff). The body's parallel to the mind's joy in knowing is the delight of the senses. Caliban shows this delight not only in his taste for filberts and scamels (2.2.167-172) but in that touching responsiveness to music (3.2.133-141) which makes it impossible to view him as simply an embodiment of evil. As to the mind's morality, the body's parallel is what could be called love, the instinctive desire to serve. Caliban is likened to a dog in this respect: he was at first the pet of Prospero, who "strok[ed]" him (1.2.333-335), and finding a new master, he licks his shoes (3.2.22).

The faculties' potentialities for evil are treated through the parallel desires of Ariel and Caliban for an illegitimate freedom. Ariel's desire to break his contract (1.2.242-246) represents the mind's proud desire to be free of its recognized obligations. Caliban's sexual (1.2.348-352) and wrathful (3.2.86-89) yearnings represent the lust of the flesh, and the fact that liquor produces Caliban's cry of freedom (2.2.178-185) reinforces the idea that the body longs for a release from inhibitions. That these two evils are distinct is suggested by Ariel's inability to perform Caliban-like deeds: he was "too delicate/To act her [Sycorax's] earthy and abhorr'd commands" (1.2.272-273). The inherent tendency to evil accords with conventional theology, and Shakespeare evokes this theology in his parallel early histories of Ariel and Caliban—stories which are not formal allegories but factual details carrying analogical overtones. Prospero's release of Ariel from the spell which Sycorax had cast but which she herself could not undo (1.2.274-293) recalls Christ's ability to free men from otherwise-inevitable damnation. Ariel's grumbling, then, is like a proud man's refusal to acknowledge God's gift, an act like Satan's initial refusal to serve. Caliban's parentage—the fact that he is the offspring of a wicked woman and a devil (1.2.263-270)—recalls the inherited curse upon man's flesh.

Ariel and Caliban, by defining man's natural endowment, serve as bases for measuring society's influence on men. The virtuous secondary characters show what perfection civilization can bring men to. Prospero clearly stands at the top of the play's moral ladder, and Prospero's endorsement places Gonzalo there with him: Prospero's initial praise (1.2.160-168), repeated to and by Ariel (5.1.15,) is summed up in his address to Gonzalo, "Holy Gonzalo, honourable man" (5.1.62). Shakespeare makes religion the source of civilization's perfecting power; both the virtuous characters are notably pious. Prospero conquers the pride natural to the mind by meditating on the *de contemptu* theme—that is of course the point of "Our revels now are ended" (4.1.148-158). His religion is—as befits his significance—formal and intellectual: religious meditation figures in the plans he makes for his life in Milan (5.1.310-311). Gonzalo's piety is shown early in his trusting but resigned prayer, "The wills above be done! but I would fain die a dry death" (1.1.66-67). In his final summarizing tribute to the providence which has brought good out of evil (5.1.201-213), Gonzalo, though admirably reverent, is factually inaccurate: Sebastian and Antonio have "found . . . [them]selves" in a way which ironically undercuts Gonzalo's optimism. Gonzalo's religiousness is emotional rather than rational.

Prospero embodies intellectual, Gonzalo emotional virtue. Prospero does not lack feeling, and Shakespeare is careful to distinguish him from the men of intellectual evil, the callous Antonio and Sebastian; his harsh treatment of the mourning Ferdinand is accounted for in an aside (1.2.453-455), lest it be mistaken for such coldness as the courtiers display toward the mourning Alonso. But Prospero is clearly a man in whom mind pre-dominates. At the important moment when, having his "enemies" at his "mercy" (4.1.262-263), he pardons them, he is shamed into pity by the hypothetical pity of a creature inherently incapable of emotion (5.1.21-24), and then he acts not by feeling but by a rational ethical principle (5.1.27-30). As Prospero is not devoid of feeling, so Gonzalo is not empty of mind. So much attention has been paid to Shakespeare's source for Gonzalo's utopia (2.1.139-165) that its nature has been neglected: Gonzalo is giving a gentlemanly dissertation on a classical theme. He has a gentleman's [sic] learning, then, but that learning is contrasted with intellectual accomplishment. Gonzalo knows poetry and fabling Plato—imaginative and therefore emotional writing. The difference between this learning and rational knowledge

is suggested by the difference between the rule of the island which Gonzalo imagines and the conscious control and learned means of Prospero's actual governance. Gonzalo's strength is emotional, and in this he is the complement of Prospero: at the moment when he is mastered by Prospero's learned magic, Gonzalo is Prospero's instructor, teaching him with his tears how to weep for pity (5.1.62-64),

The virtuous secondary characters indicate that civilization can develop the natural strengths of the faculties. Prospero's esoteric knowledge is the development of the mind's delight in learning, but Prospero's knowledge is less important than his ethical perfection. The point of his control of the island is not that he allegorically represents God but that as an ethical man he models his rule on God's, with of course such qualifications as distinguish human from divine prerogatives. Like God, he teaches and tries, he imposes reformative punishments, and he controls the unreformable. Gonzalo has Caliban's sensory perceptiveness: he is accurate (1.2.218-219) when he says that the courtiers' garments are unstained by the storm (2.1.55-68), and therefore his praise of the green island (2.1.51) can be trusted. But in Gonzalo, perceptiveness is enriched by a religious sense of gratitude: his praise of the island is part of his tribute to God's mercy (2.1.1-8). The desire to serve which Caliban displays reaches full development in Gonzalo's love for Alonso. Gonzalo empathizes with his master's suffering (2.1. 137-138), humbly babbles about utopia in order to distract him (2.1.138, 165), and disinterestedly persists in the face of rebukes (2.1.9, 102-103, 166). That Gonzalo saves Alonso through a dreamed warning (2.1.295-302) is symbolically appropriate: the non-rational imagination does the protecting, rather than the reason which would cause an intellectual man to stand guard.

The virtuous characters also prove that civilization can overcome men's natural weaknesses. Prospero triumphs over pride when he gives up his magical power and forgives the enemies he has conquered. In the first he contrasts with the ambitious Antonio and Sebastian; in the second he does more than simply subdue wrong feeling, for the echoes of a revenger's tragedy make Prospero a potential scourge, tyrannical avenger of an ambitious tyrant. Gonzalo's moral triumph comes when he, like Prospero, has his enemies within his power; he overcomes the lust of the flesh by loving rather than hating them. By their mockery, Antonio and Sebastian do succeed in angering Gonzalo, for though he is not overcome by wrath (2.183-184), he must be angry since Antonio does try to mollify him (2.1.181). Yet when Alonso and the courtiers go mad, Gonzalo protects his enemies equally with the master he loves (3.3.104-109).

The aristocratic and the base plotters sit at the foot

of the ladder which Prospero and Gonzalo have climbed. Shakespeare indicates that the four belong in the same moral class by paralleling their stories. By attributing irreligiousness to them, he marks their distance from the men whom civilization has perfected. In the place of Prospero's intellectual belief, Antonio has a philosophic atheism which he successfully teaches to Sebastian (2.1.270-275). In place of Gonzalo's pious feelings, Stephano and Trinculo have a reverence for sack: their bottle is the bible they swear on, kiss, and reinterpret (2.2.121, 131, 143-144; the image occurs to Stephano independently of Caliban's belief that sack is "celestial" [2.2.117-127]). The twin actions which involve these two pairs of plotters fall into four sections: and exposition, a fatal error, a climactic reversal of fortune, and a denouement. The expositions prove that civilization can aggravate the natural weaknesses of men and deprive them of even their natural strengths. The rest of the actions—tragedies of purgation without the morally triumphant close—prove that civilization's destructiveness can be irreversible and therefore absolute.

Sebastian and Antonio embody intellectual evil. In the expository scene in which they greet the island, they reveal the desiccation of the feelings which are not their dominant attribute. At the point at which Gonzalo demonstrates his loving empathy for Alonso ("It is foul weather in us all, good sir,/When you are cloudy"), Sebastian and Antonio demonstrate their callousness in puns and pantomime ("Fowl weather"—looking up; "Very foul"—wiping away an imaginary dropping) (2.1.137-138). When Alonso in his grief rebukes Gonzalo, "Prithee, peace," Sebastian's punning simile, "He receives comfort like cold porridge" (2.1.9-10), recalls Ariel's metaphor for the sighing Ferdinand: the courtiers have made themselves as unfeeling as a creature inherently emotionless. The pair also show that they have lost the mind's natural insight and morality. The sneers which they direct at Gonzalo's reference to the *Aeneid* (2.1.71-84) expose their shallow learning. Modernists, they have only heard about the *Aeneid*, not studied or even read it, and therefore they do not know where Carthage was, and do not know that Aeneas and Dido had both been literally widowed (they ignorantly suppose that by "widow" Gonzalo alludes to Dido's desertion, and they refer to the jocular use of "widower" for a deserting husband). The courtiers reveal their depravity by their disgust at Gonzalo's supposed euphemism ("Good Lord, how you take it!"): they think Aeneas a knave and Dido a whore, and scorn anyone who believes in heroism or tragedy. The faults of the pair are acquired, not natural: they have been hardened by courtly nonchalance and stultified by courtly Machiavellianism. Gonzalo's reference to their boredom points to the former (2.1.177-179), and the courtiers' unsavory similes for the island (2.1.41-47) suggest that cultivated aloofness has cost them their

responsiveness to beauty. Doctrinaire materialism accounts for the sneers which they direct at Gonzalo's belief in natural innocence (2.1. 150-162). That accepting the fashionable doctrine has impoverished their minds is suggested by the fact that in laughing at the word "innocent," Sebastian simple-mindedly restricts its meaning to physical virginity ("No marrying 'mong his subjects?"), and that in laughing at the word "idle" ("all idle; whores and knaves"), Antonio blindly refuses to believe in a goodness which is as evidently present in Gonzalo as it is evidently absent in himself.

Stephano and Trinculo embody emotional evil. In the expository episode in which they greet the island, they reveal the dullness of the wits which are not their chief attribute. The pair ridicule Caliban for his credulity concerning them (2.2.137-146), but both of them cling stubbornly to a credulous first impression of him. Trinculo, having concluded that Caliban is a fish, decides upon second glance that he is an odd fish, "Legg'd like a man! and his fins like arms!" (2.2.24-35). Stephano, having concluded that Caliban (with Trinculo) is a monster, decides upon further contact that he is an odd monster, "a most delicate monster" with "Four legs and two voices" (2.2.58-96). The commoners also reveal that they have lost the body's natural strengths, sensitivity and love. In the sights of the island Trinculo can find only reminders of city ugliness: "yond same black cloud . . . looks like a foul bombard that would shed his liquor," "I will here shroud till the dregs of the storm be past" (2.2.20-22, 41-42). For music, Stephano has only the tavern songs he rightly calls "scurvy" (2.2. 43-56). As for the desire to serve, that quality has given way to self-assertion. Both Trinculo and Stephano dream of the independence they can gain by displaying Caliban (2.2.28-34, 69-72), and Trinculo soon proceeds to a more direct assertiveness: "A most scurvy monster! I could find in my heart to beat him,—" (2.2.155-156). The pair's faults are of course acquired; dullness and self-assertion are the proverbial results of drinking, and the pair's degraded taste is directly linked with the tavern. The commoners' drunkenness typifies lower-class life in the city in the way that the courtly code typifies the aristocracy: Stephano and Trinculo are, like Antonio and Sebastian, representatives of civilization.

The plotters' fatal errors take the form of decisive yieldings to their characteristic weaknesses. The courtiers' plot is an act of pride, a violation of "conscience," the mind's inherent morality (2.1.270-275), in the interest of ambition (2.1.285-289). The act is significant for Sebastian because it is his first deadly sin, for Antonio because it repeats and propagates his earlier crime. The difference between the two is suggested not only in the temptation scene itself, where Antonio persuades Sebastian, but at the beginning of the episode, when Ariel's music brings sleep to the company. At that point Sebastian speaks comfortingly to Alonso (2.1.188-191)—not out of duty, for he has disrespectfully berated him (2.1.124-131), nor out of love, for he has callously blamed Ferdinand's death on him (2.1.119-123), but out of politeness: lacking virtue and love, Sebastian is at least conventional. Antonio, on the other hand, soothes Gonzalo and Alonso (2.1.181, 191-193) because he has just thought of murdering them in their sleep: he is already a criminal. The commoners' plot contrasts with the aristocrats' in its motivation. Stephano desires Miranda (3.2.101-105), and his willingness to beat Trinculo (3.2.74-75) suggests that he approves of Caliban's cruel wrath: the commoners yield to the lust of the flesh. The distinction between Antonio and Sebastian is mirrored in the distinction between Stephano and Trinculo. Stephano is the leader, passing upon the plot and inducing Trinculo to follow him (2.2. 104-110). He is analogous to Antonio, who is the most devout materialist and the first to practise the creed; Stephano is the bearer of the butt and the first and greatest imbiber (2.2.115-125, 3.2.1-3).

The next stages in the actions, the reversals of fortune, are presented in parallel symbolic scenes. The banquet and the line-tree episode allegorically show the moral consequences of the plotters' fatal errors. The banquet symbolizes the mind's fulfillments (the communion table is the probable source of the symbol), the garments on the line-tree the fulfillments for the body (clothes make the body splendid). The way in which Sebastian and Antonio approach the banquet typifies their crime. When the magical servants vanish, Sebastian says, "No matter, since/They have left their viands behind; for we have stomachs.—/Will't please you taste of what is here?" (3.3.40-42). Men interest Sebastian only in so far as they are of service to him; he is glad not to have to share with others even what is theirs; and his virtuous words are only hollow gestures of politeness (he offers the banquet only in order that he himself may eat). The immorality, self-interest, and virtuous facade characterize the courtiers' pride. Similarly, the way in which Trinculo and Stephano approach the clothing symbolizes passional sinning: covetousness is suggested by Trinculo's "we know what belongs to a frippery," gluttony by his "put some lime upon your fingers" (the image is drawn from bird-catching), wrath by Stephano's "by this hand, I'll have that gown," and lust by his "Mistress line, is this not my jerkin?" (that "line" and "jerkin" are obscene is clear from the subsequent joke about loss of hair) (4.1.225-226, 245-246, 227-8, 235-238). These sins are tied to the plot against Prospero by the repeated references to matters associated with kingdom: royal robes, exploration, patronage, banishment (4.1.222-223, 236-238, 241-244, 250-252). The snatching of the banquet and driving away of the looters thus indicate that because of their

plots, the plotters have lost those fulfillments appropriate for their natures.

The purgative panishments [sic] visited upon the sinners are also richly symbolic. First of all, the agents of punishment serve to distinguish kinds of evil. Ariel's guise as a harpy, here reminiscent of a Fury, characterizes the aristocratic plotters: the airy soul receives an airborne and divine avenger. The spirits' guise as hunting dogs fits the base plotters: the earthy body receives a mundane retribution. Furthermore, the agents of punishment are tied to the preceding episodes of judgment. Harpies, of course, snatch banquets, and hunting dogs pursue foxes, which symbolize theft and therefore typify the looters. The linking suggests that the connection between sin and suffering is not casual but intrinsic. As to the punishments themselves, the madness visited upon the aristocrats is both abstractly appropriate as a punishment for spiritual sin (it is a mental torment) and concretely appropriate as the revenge which conscience takes for its violation. The commoners' cramps and "pinch-spot[s]" are also abstractly appropriate, physical punishments for sins of the flesh, and they are concretely appropriate, symptoms of the diseases that result from the abuse of the body. Prospero connects the two kinds of punishment when, having seen the commoners "pinch-spotted" (4.1. 260-261), he refers to the courtiers' madness as "inward pinches" (5.1. 77). The linking suggests that the two sorts of punishment are parallel and alike in purpose.

The expositions in the two actions define civilized evil. The middle sections pose the question of whether this evil can be cured. The answer which the endings give has already been foreshadowed. The mania of Antonio and Sebastian is contrasted with Alonso's melancholia: Alonso blames himself (3.3. 95-102), but Sebastian and Antonio attack the avenging spirits, taking them for persecuting "friend[s]" (3.3.102-103). Apparently suffering is not going to cause the two courtiers to question and change themselves. The obliviousness of Stephano and Trinculo is contrasted with the anxiety of Caliban. Caliban fears that he and his companions will be changed to geese or to apes "With foreheads villainous low"—to animals emblematic of stupidity; and he foresees and fears Prospero's pinches (4.1.247-248, 232-234). He thus shows an awareness of the superiority of mind and susceptibility to correction which are lacking in the two greedy commoners. They, apparently, are beyond redeeming.

The denouements show, then, that civilized evil can be unreformable. It is true that Sebastian reproves Stephano's thievery, and that he calls the restoration of Ferdinand "A most high miracle" (5.1.298-299, 177). The rest of his behaviour, however, proves that the former statement is not a sign of reborn morality;

and the latter is not a sign of empathy towards Alonso, for Sebastian is contrasted with Gonzalo, who at this point is too choked with emotion to speak (5.1.200-201). Both statements are like Sebastian's unfelt words of comfort earlier, simply politeness. The comments which Antonio and Sebastian make about Caliban (5.1.263-266), reminiscent of their earlier jokes about the island, prove that the pair have not abandoned their courtly nonchalance. More important, they have not gained in insight or morality. Sebastian is dumbfounded at being caught by Prospero: "The devil speaks in him" (5.1.129). His surprise shows that he has no truer estimate of his intellectual place than he had when he sneered at Gonzalo's supposed errors. The reference to the devil also recalls Sebastian's attitude to the avenging spirits; it proves that he feels no guilt. Antonio's responses are the same as Sebastian's; he is both too surprised and too resentful to speak. When Prospero says, "I do forgive/Thy rankest fault,—all of them," he comments on Antonio's surprise, stressing the fact that Antonio has been found out; when he "require[s]" the dukedom, he comments on Antonio's resentment, chastizing his immorality. The commoners emerge no better than the aristocrats. Punishment has not made Stephano and Trinculo any wiser, and since the mind is not their dominant attribute, it is only fitting that they should prove even duller than the stultified courtiers. When Prospero accuses Stephano, "You 'ld be King o' the isle, sirrah?" Stephano replies, "I should have been a sore one, then" (5.1.187-288). He is not alert enough to be startled by Prospero's knowledge, and his joke shows that not only does he feel no guilt, but he does not even recognize the seriousness of the charge. Punishment has not restored the commoners' sensivity or love, either. The pair moan about pickled meat and cramps (5.1.282-286), their minds as confined to the tavern as ever. Stephano enters attacking his betters, and though Trinculo realizes that there has been a hitch ("here's a goodly sight." 5.1. 259-260), he does not recognize his master. The failure to love is as central for the commoners as the failure to be moral for the aristocrats, and that failure is epitomized in the drunken battle address which opens the episode: "Every man shift for all the rest, and let no man take care for himself; for all is but fortune" (5.1.255-257). The opening clauses tell what Trinculo and Shephano should have learned; the misplacings show that they have not learned it; and the last clause proves that the pair do not blame themselves for their pains, and therefore cannot change (it is parallel, thus, to Sebastian's refusal of guilt, "The devil speaks in him").

In the denouements the four representatives of civilized evil are contrasted with the characters who represent the natural faculties. While Antonio and Sebastian show their irremediable pride, Ariel completes his service (5.1.20-242), and while Stephano and Trinculo demonstrate their incurable lust, Caliban learns to love: he is awed by his master, and he comes to serve him willingly (5.1. 262-263, 294-295). Furthermore, Ariel recognizes and honors a moving situation when polite Sebastian and silent Antonio are not touched by Ferdinand's restoration, and Caliban overcomes his credulous worship of Stephano (5.1.295-297) when the besotted Stephano cannot see the difference between Prospero's mind and his: the depraved men have less emotion than an unfeeling spirit and less thought than an unreasoning animal. Because they cannot be reformed, the plotters become prisoners: Antonio and Sebastian are held in mental bonds, restrained by Prospero's threats to reveal their plot (5.1.126-129), and Stephano and Trinculo are put in the custody of Caliban (5.1.291-292), placed in physical restraint. Meanwhile the non-human characters are freed. Ariel of course is released (5.1. 317-318), and Caliban in the end ceases to be a slave, becoming, like Gonzalo, a willing servant. The contrasts emphasize that civilized vices are more pernicious than man's natural limitations, and more dangerous.

By showing the contrary potentialities in civilization, the secondary characters raise the question of how its positive results may be attained and its negative ones avoided. The central characters provide the answers. The first set of these characters are Ferdinand and Miranda. In pairing them, Shakespeare utilizes an old idea about the difference between men and women, though he does not apply this idea systematically or even refer to it symbolically. The difference between the two lovers is allegorized in their wedding masque, in which the motif of the union of the sky and the earth appears twice: the sky is represented by Juno and by the nymphs who symbolize the water evaporated from the springs, the earth by Ceres and by the reapers who symbolize the land which receives the rain (4.1.60-86, 128-138). The lovers contrast like airy Ariel and earthy Caliban. The two of them prove that education can set men climbing toward the rung reached by Prospero and Gonzalo.

Ferdinand needs a corrective education. His primary danger—Prospero's treatment suggests—is aristocratic pride. Prospero charges Ferdinand with attempted usurpation (1.2.455-459), and he captures him in a way which anticipates the arraignment of the proud nobles in the banquet episode. Prospero disarms Ferdinand with a spell (1.2.475-476) in the way that Antonio and Sebastian are later disarmed (3.3.66-68), and he accuses him of a guilt (1.2.472-474) which is like that of the melancholy Alonso. Since, as the aside indicates, Prospero's words are not to be taken at face value, what is suggested is what is later made explicit, that as an intellectual courtier Ferdinand is liable to the sin of pride, but that he has not yet embraced that sin: Prospero is trying rather than punishing him (4.1.5-7). Desiccation is Ferdinand's secondary danger. When he tells Miranda that though he has "ey'd" many women "with best regard" and listened to them with "too diligent ear," he has never loved any with "full soul" (3.1.39-46), Ferdinand shows that he has been practising Sebastian's courtly formality and detachment.

Miranda needs maturing rather than correcting. A woman of feeling, she is already like Gonzalo and unlike Caliban: her reaction to the shipwreck proves the first ("O, I have suffered/With those that I saw suffer!" 1.2.1-15), and her indignation at Caliban's attempted rape suggests the second (1.2.353-364). She needs, however, a proper object for her love. Her child-like devotion to her father shows in her sighing response to his description of their exile, "Alack, what trouble/Was I then to you!" (1.2.151-152). Prospero's desire to transfer her affections accounts for the magician's formula with which he enhances her first glimpse of Ferdinand: "The fringed curtains of thine eye advance/And say that thou seest yond" (1.2.411-412). Miranda's immaturity of mind—it is not her dominant attribute—is suggested by her passiveness to Prospero's teachings ("More to know/Did never meddle with my thoughts," 1.2.21-22).

The trial which strengthens Ferdinand against his pride is the central part of his education. As antidote to the ambition which leads Antonio and Sebastian to seek kingship, Prospero humbles Ferdinand to the antithetical rank of slave: Ferdinand notes the antithesis (3.1.59-63). In accepting the humiliation willingly (3.1.1-15) Ferdinand matches Prospero's voluntary surrender of power. The importance of the trial is proved by the fact that through it Ferdinand wins Miranda's hand (4.1.1-8); Ferdinand's emotional education, though more complicated, is less important. Prospero's first task there is to rouse Ferdinand's quiescent feelings. He awakens him as he awakens Alonso, with grief, then turns grief to consolation (1.2.390-396) and consolation to love (1.2.488-496): the sequence is a natural one, though magic speeds the pace. The new emotions enable Ferdinand to distinguish his love for Miranda from his previous courtly dallying (3.1.37-48), but Prospero is then careful to see that Ferdinand does not give way to excess. The Anacreontic portion of the wedding masque (4.1.88-101) repeats the lesson Prospero gives in his curse ("If thou dost break her virgin-knot . . ." 4.1.13-23). There Prospero elaborates Ferdinand's own oath to Miranda ("O heaven, o earth . . . if [I speak] hollowly, invert/What best is boded me . . ." 3.1.68-73); he distinguishes sacramental sexuality from animal lust, giving specific meanings to the cherishing and honorable love which Ferdinand has sworn.

The central part of Miranda's education is the trial which teaches her to leave her father and cleave to the husband who is her rightful master. Prospero tries Miranda by commanding her to cleave to her father and leave her lover (not speak to him); he commands childishness in order that Miranda may outgrow it by disobeying, and this of course she does (3.1.36-37, 57-59). At the same time, she takes the proper reverent attitude toward Ferdinand, refusing at first meeting the place of goddess (1.2.424-431), and taking thereafter the place of servant: she tries to carry Ferdinand's logs (3.1.23-25), she pledges to "be [his] servant" (3.1.83-86). Prospero also strengthens Miranda's judgment. Having told her about Antonio's treachery and usurpation, Prospero then accuses Ferdinand of like crimes. The accusations have moral significance, but not as descriptions of Ferdinand's present moral state; and the purpose of Prospero's repeated injunctions, "Speak not you for him: he's a traitor" and "What!/An advocate for an impostor!" (1.2.463, 479-480), must be to force Miranda to judge Ferdinand on her own. By her Platonic defence of him, her rejection of Prospero's rebuttal, and her trust in her own decision (1.2.460-462, 481-486; 3.1.48-57), Miranda achieves the independence of mind which Prospero intends.

The four evocative lines (5.1.172-175) which are their contribution to the play's climactic discovery summarize the lovers' state. Miranda's "you play me false" is a reminder—unintentional on her part—of the attempt of Stephano to play her false, and Ferdinand's "not for the world" is a parallel and equally unintentional reminder of Antonio's desire for kingdom. The reminders point up the lovers' goodness. The opposite of Stephano's wrath and sensuality is Miranda's declaration of forgiving love: "Yes, for a score of kingdoms you should wrangle,/And I would call it fair play." Ferdinand's principled "I would not for the world" is the opposite of Antonio's immoral ambition. That the pledges are contained in teasing and banter makes the virtue sound effortless: the lovers' education has started them well. But the reminders also suggest the youthful innocence of the pair: as they do not know of the incidents to which they accidentally refer, so they do not see the evils in the world around them. Education prepares them for struggles in a world which as yet seems new and brave.

Alonso is given more weight than Ferdinand and Miranda. In the discovery to which The Tempest builds, the focus is on the joyful discoverer, not on the objects discovered. Furthermore, Ferdinand and Miranda must share attention with one another, while Alonso is paired with a figure who does not demand equal attention, the boatswain. King and boatswain constitute the second set of central characters. They prove that when a man has fallen off the ladder and landed with Antonio or Stephano, repentance can start him upward again. By the prominence given to Alonso, Shakespeare implies that of the two means whereby civilization's potentiality for good may be realized, repentance is the more important. He thus forestalls the optimistic conclusion that education can eliminate man's frailty and render penitence unnecessary.

Alonso's story contains no exposition. His nature is defined by his partnership with Antonio in the overthrow of Prospero, and the introduction of Antonio and Sebastian serves to suggest what Alonso was like before the shipwreck. Alonso's action falls into three sections, a change of heart which contrasts with the fatal error of Antonio and Sebastian, a change of mind which contrasts with the courtiers' reversal of fortune, and a denouement in which Alonso's redemption[sic] is demonstrated.

Alonso's reactions to the supposed death of Ferdinand constitute the first stage of his development. The loss of his son is retribution for Alonso's callousness to Miranda (3.371-72) and gives him an opportunity for the reawakening of the feelings which are not his dominant capacity. He responds properly, resembling the emotional Gonzalo in his cry of grief, "O thou mine heir/Of Naples and of Milan, what strange fish/Hath made his meal on thee?" (2.1.107-109). The next stage is more important, for it involves the king's main flaw. The madness visited upon Alonso punishes his deposition of Prospero (3.3.68-70, 72-75), and it offers him the opportunity to cure his pride. Alonso accepts, showing the "heartsorrow" which Ariel recommends (3.3. 75-82) by admitting his sin: "the thunder . . . pronouc'd/The name of Prosper: it did bass my tresspass" (3.3.95-102). In both these stages, Alonso is contrasted with Antonio and Sebastian in a way which demonstrates the resonance of contrite acts—a resonance by which Shakespeare validates the religious views he assigns to Prospero and Gonzalo. In the first episode, it is suggested that Alonso might not have grieved for his son, for Sebastian is not moved either by the loss or by the grief of his kindred. That Alonso does grieve is only a small step toward virtue, for callousness is the lesser of his faults; yet the behaviour of Antonio and Sebastian suggests that this act averts further and serious sin. Ferdinand's loss and Alonso's grief give the two courtiers the chance to soften their hearts (Antonio has as much reason to feel compassion as Gonzalo does, and Sebastian has more); once they refuse the opportunity, they fall into a fatal worsening of their major weakness, pride. In the second episode, Alonso's wonder at the gestures of the magical servants (3.3.36-39) connects him with the admiring Gonzalo (3.3.28-34) and shows that his affections have been reawakened. His hesitancy to eat (3.3.42) indicates that if he is not a man of clean conscience, he is no longer a man of pride: his hesitancy is contrasted with Gonzalo's innocent confidence (3.3.43-49), but it is also contrasted with the aggressive selfishness of Sebastian. That there is a connection between the awakening of feeling and the cessation of pride is suggested by Alonso's final gloomy pronouncement,

"I feel/The best is past" (3.3. 49-52). Moved by the loss of his son. Alonso sees the vanity of seeking kingdoms, and is thus diverted from his former ends. In this progress, Alonso is contrasted with Antonio and Sebastian. The courtiers, having refused earlier to be moved, greet the banquet with cold wit ("A living drollery," 3.3.21-27), and they approach it with proud possessiveness. At the end of the episode the three men are accused together (3.3.53-58), but Antonio and Sebastian, not having made the preparatory changes, reject the accusation; only Alonso, prepared, accepts and is reformed. Virtue, Shakepeare suggests, is cumulative [sic].

The denouement shows Alonso's restoration. By voluntarily returning Prospero's dukedom and by begging Miranda's pardon (5.1.118-119, 196-198), Alonso repents and cures his two weaknesses. The less important of these weaknesses is given an extended treatment, a treatment reminiscent of the emotional education of Ferdinand. Having awakened Ferdinand's feelings, Prospero cautions him against an excess, sensuality; so, having softend Alonso, Prospero warns against an excess of grief, the excess the king displays when he moans that his sorrow is beyond the cure of patience. Prospero recommends a religious patience to Alonso (5.1.141-144) as earlier he extols the "sanctimonious ceremonies" of marriage, and as he tries Ferdinand's purity, so he makes a brief trial of Alonso's empathy, not restoring Ferdinand until Alonso has grieved for Prospero's "lost" daughter (5.1.144-152). In his final regenerate state, Alonso is likened through his piety to the men of virtue. The events which Sebastian attributes to diabolic power Alonso thinks an "oracle" must explain (5.1.242-245); and he says "Amen" (5.1.204) to Gonzalo's praise of providence. Alonso is contrasted with the men of intellectual evil. His return of Prospero's dukedom is of course the opposite of the courtiers' reluctance, and when the king expresses his love for Ferdinand and Miranda, "Let grief and sorrow still embrace his heart/That doth not wish you joy!" (5.1.214-215), his curse falls upon the unmoved courtiers.

If Alonzo's story is compressed by the omission of its beginning, the boatswain's is compressed by the omission of its middle. It contains a beginning which likens the boatswain to Stephano and Trinculo, and an end which shows his redemption. When the other mariners think of praying, the boatswain thinks of drinking (1.1.51-52), and in this he is like the bottle-worshipping commoners. His bawling, repeatedly chastized (1.1.15, 40-41, 43-45), identifies him as a man of emotional excess, and the rebellion which constitutes the fatal error of Stephano and Trinculo has its parallel in the boatswain's lack of devotion to the king: "Good, yet remember whom thou hast aboard," says Gonzalo, and the boatswain replies, "None that I love more than myself" (1.1. 19-20).

Shakespeare takes pains to make the boatswain memorable, tagging him with Gonzalo's many-times-repeated joke about the drowning mark (1.1.28-33, 46-48, 58-60); the tag recalls him four acts later (5.1.216-218). When he re-enters, he is a changed man. His precise speech is antithetical to his earlier bawling, and his reverence for the court is the reverse of his earlier lack of love: "The best news is, that we have safely found/Our King, and company" (5.1.221-222). His new piety associates him with the virtuous characters and dissociates him from the base plotters; as Gonzalo notes, the boatswain is no longer a "blasphemy" who "swear[s] grace overboard" (5.1.218-220). The explanation for his transformation—the middle of the batswain's story—is only narrated (5.1.230-240), but that narration connects the boatswain's punishment with the punishment of Stephano and Trinculo in the same way that the king is connected with Antonio and Sebastian. The boatswain was "clapp'd under hatches"—trapped, as the commoners are hunted; and he was subjected to roaring, shrieking, howling, jingling chains,/And mo diversity of sounds, all horrible"—to the delirium of disease as the commoners are subjected to its cramps and pustules.

As as example of penitence, the physical boatswain contributes one final touch to the play's systematic explanation of how the virtues of civilization may be attained. As a balance to the intellectual Alonso, he fills the final place in the symmetrical structure of *The Tempest*.

MUSIC AND THE MASQUE

Many critics have commented that music and spectacle inform *The Tempest* to an extent unequalled in any of Shakespeare's earlier plays. Related to the magical atmosphere in the play, music foregrounds the work, setting its mood and reiterating many of its themes. On this point, **Theresa Coletti** observes that music is an "evocative symbol of magic in the play" and argues that it structures the work and its meaning. For Coletti this meaning is rooted in harmony and feeds into the play's reconciliation theme. David Lindley makes a similar assertion about the importance of order and harmony in the work, but (in keeping with a recent critical trend of looking for grim meaning in the drama) examines the problematic nature of music in *The Tempest*—seeing it as a means of deception and a source of dramatic tension. Lindley relates music and the masques, in addition, to the darker aspects of theme in the play. Both masques—one for the betrothal of Miranda and Ferdinand, and one the banquet laid out for Alonso, Sebastian, and Antonio—prove illusory. While the first is brought abruptly to an end by the conspiracy of Caliban, the second is designed from the outset to frustrate. Lind-

ley thus notes Shakespeare's tendency to turn what is ostensibly celebratory into something dark and malignant. Clifford Davidson likewise discusses the darker overtones of Prospero's masques, seeing their surface splendor as only a thin veneer that fails to hide bleaker realities.

Theresa Coletti

SOURCE: "Music and *The Tempest*," in *Shakespeare's Late Plays: Essays in Honor of Charles Crow*, edited by Richard C. Tobias and Paul G. Zolbrod, Ohio University Press, 1974, pp. 185-99.

[*In the following essay, Coletti analyzes music as "the medium through which order emerges from chaos" in* The Tempest. *Perhaps more pervasive in this work than in any other of Shakespeare's plays, music is, according to Coletti, a structural principle that suggests the thematic struggle between harmony and disorder and the difficulty of achieving the former over the latter. By comparing Shakespeare's use of music in* The Tempest *with that in an earlier work,* As You Like It, *Coletti explains how music sets both tone and theme, and maintains that the play represents Shakespeare's most extensive use of the medium to highlight themes of freedom, forgiveness, and human redemption.*]

The vital center of *The Tempest* is its music. Pervading and informing the action of the play, music is always sounding, always affecting and shaping the lives of the characters. Often directionless and ambiguous in its meaning, the music of *The Tempest* provides a context for Prospero's magical machinations and becomes, through the course of the play, a powerfully evocative symbol of this magic. In *The Tempest* music is the medium through which order emerges from chaos; it is the agent of suffering, learning, growth, and freedom.

Critics who have noted the pervasiveness of music, songs, and musical allusions in Shakespeare's drama have often attempted to extrapolate from the canon of his work and posit a distinct philosophy of music which they insist he was trying to communicate in his plays. This is most easily accomplished by rather vague references to Renaissance ideas of divine harmony and the "music of the spheres," that macrocosmic heavenly order of which this worldly microcosm was thought to be a reflection. It has also been pointed out that during the Renaissance, music came more and more to be associated with a "rhetoric of emotion," a kind of language of the heart in which man could express his inmost feelings and communicate them to others. Though neither of these notions can account for our experience of a play as musically rich as *The Tempest*, together they can provide us with helpful tools for understanding how Shakespeare employed music in his drama. For from ideas of order we can derive principles of structure, and if there is a providential design in *The Tempest,* it is certainly an artistic and a musical one. Furthermore, this design manifests itself in the manner in which it speaks to deep human feelings; it is meaningful in the extent to which it can express the "language of the heart." In *The Tempest* these two modes of interpretation form a unity from which music emerges as an emotional and philosophical idea. . . .

If we want to examine music as an informing idea in *The Tempest,* we can begin by looking at a play with which it has many affinities, *As You Like It.* One can view *The Tempest* and *As You Like It* as companion plays in more than one sense. In terms of plot they share many common elements. Each begins *in medias res* [in the middle of the story's action]; Duke Senior and Prospero have both been deposed before the plays' actions begin. Each drama presents a principal figure whose machinations orchestrate events to bring about a desired end; Rosalind wishes to win Orlando and Prospero to recover his dukedom. Both plays juxtapose groups of good and bad characters; there are the evil-doers and the victims of evil. The primary actions of *The Tempest* and *As You Like It* unfold in artificial worlds where the old exigencies of court life do not obtain. Prospero's island and the Forest of Arden become places of self-discovery where new standards of behavior are learned. Each play's deepest concern is with the process of recognition of error and regeneration, and finally, each abundantly employs music as a vehicle for commenting upon this process or for helping to bring it into being.

As You Like It is richer in music than the plays that preceded it. From his experience with the earliest comedies Shakespeare had probably learned the value of music as an important dramatic device. Here the songs are more carefully integrated, reinforcing and illuminating the themes of the play. The first song, "Under the greenwood tree" (II, v. 1), portrays the life of the exiles in the Forest of Arden and focuses their dramatic situation. Cast from their position of security at court, the new inhabitants of Arden are learning that nature supplies a home that is in many ways far superior to the one they have left behind: "Here shall he see no enemy / But winter and rough weather" (II, v. 6-7). A musical statement of one of the themes of the play, the beneficent effect of nature on man, the song also reveals the character of its two singers, Amiens, the cheerful exile, and Jaques, the melancholy cynic. This is a fine instance of music as dramatic economy. Simultaneously fulfilling two functions, the song delineates the import of the play's action and displays antithetical responses to it.

The placement of the songs in *As You Like It* also intensifies the play's dramatic movement. "Blow, blow, thou winter wind" (II, vii, 174) repeats the theme of the first song, but it is more caustic, more explicit in its comment. The implications of this song, which contrasts winter's natural violence with the violence that human beings inflict upon each other, are undercut by its dramatic position. Coming directly after Orlando carries in his faithful but debilitated servant Adam, the song becomes an ironic comment upon itself, for we have just seen an example of friendship that is not "feigning," of loving that is not mere "folly." We have also discovered that Duke Senior's attachment to Orlando's father survives in his kindness to the son. Like Jaques' misanthropic speech on the ultimate insignificance of human life, the song makes a point which the events of the play qualify, and the agent of this qualification is the very benignity of nature itself.

One final instance of the use of music in *As You Like It* is worth nothing. While perhaps bearing no explicit relationship to the progress of the plot or the nature of character, the song "It was a lover and his lass" (V, iii, 5) has an evocative power that imbues the entire conclusion of the play. Celebrating a life of love and springtime, the song by contrast reminds us of the winter of exile and misfortune that has just passed. It looks ahead to the marriages that are about to take place and brings a sense of freshness to inform the repentance that Duke Frederick and Oliver experience. More atmospheric than thematic, this song suggests a new order of living and being; it transcends the events of the play to provide a context that expresses their fullest meaning. In this sense it comes closer than any other song in the play to the use of music that Shakespeare employs in *The Tempest.*

This brief discussion of *As You Like It* illustrates how important to a drama music and song can be. Taken together, the songs of *As You Like It* form more than a decorative enhancement of the action. Amiens' simplicity and energetic gaiety are so closely connected to its progress that it is very difficult to imagine the play without him or his songs. The music of *As You Like It* moves with the play as an analogous structure of mood and motive. It does not, however, become the structural principle of the play itself. This is where *The Tempest* takes its crucial departure from a play with which it otherwise shares many similarities.

The difference between the two plays is, of course, the chronological fact of twelve or thirteen years. Historical considerations of dramatic presentation—the acquisition by the King's Men of the Blackfriars Theatre—can, in part, account for the unique use to which music was put in *The Tempest.* But the deepest distinctions between *The Tempest* and *As You Like It* are those that point to profounder questions of ethics and the nature of freedom and responsibility. The answers supplied by *As You Like It* are essentially

Ferdinand and Miranda watch Prospero's masque.

those of the comic vision—that human nature is susceptible to goodness and that man, if not perfectible, is at least reformable. But Shakespeare's romances follow the writing of the tragedies, and they are caught in a delicate balance between the affirmation of the earlier plays and the dark and ponderous probings of *Macbeth* and *King Lear*. And if they are able to sustain or even suggest a positive vision, it is only after an excess of suffering and the painful passage of time.

The divergent attitudes toward time that *As You Like It* and *The Tempest* reveal are perhaps a key to understanding the very different roles that music takes in each of these plays. In one sense, time seems to be of little significance in *As You Like It*. Duke Senior and his company regret their unfortunate exile, but the Forest of Arden has a medicinal effect that tempers the burden of the past and makes the present livable, even enjoyable. The future, too, looms in their consciousness as neither a promise nor a threat. There is in the play, however, the repeated appearance of what

I call "the salutary moment," those unique instants when men and women fall in love and when wrongdoers recognize their errors and seek forgiveness. This is the "love at first sight" of Rosalind and Orlando, of Celia and Oliver. It is also the instantaneous conversion of Duke Frederick by his encounter with a religious hermit and the quick reformation of Oliver when saved from the devouring jaws of a lion by the intervention of his brother. Time, then, in *As You Like It* is fragmented and dispersed; it is important insofar as it coincides with certain significant incidents. Helen Gardner, speaking of the "unmeasured time" of this play, points out that comedy by its very nature makes use of changes and chances which are not really events but "happenings." Comedy exploits adaptability; it tests a character's willingness to grasp the proper moment and fashion it to his own end. Briefly, it dramatizes Rosalind's advice to Phoebe: "Sell when you can, you are not for all markets" (III, v, 60). This *carpe diem* attitude toward living, which depends on the coincidence of situation and desire, posits a sense of time that locates value in the particular moment. Time's effect, then, is not cumulative but instantaneous; it is not the fulfillment of destiny but life lived "as you like it."

I stated earlier that the music of *As You Like It* formed a structure analogous to the movement of the play, and I think my point is reinforced if we notice that the songs tend to embody this special "momentary" quality as well. They either occur in relatively short scenes devoted to the consciousness of "having a song" (II, v; IV, ii; V, iii), or they exploit a significant movement by providing an ironic or thematic comment (II, vii; V, iv). The possible exception is "It was a lover and his lass" (V, iii), the import of which has already been discussed.

If the musical instances in *As You Like It* parallel in theme and tone the movement of the play, the music of *The Tempest* orchestrates its developing action at every point. The songs of *As You Like It* are largely situational; for the most part, they do not require a comprehensive view of the drama to render them meaningful. They do not depend upon time as a moving force that brings events and feelings to a certain issue. Time, however, is of utmost importance in *The Tempest*. Prospero has four hours to complete his magic revels; this sense of time (and timing) thus makes *every* moment meaningful. An intution of urgency, a recognition of catastrophe just barely avoided, imbues our experience of *The Tempest*. Our perception of time in the play includes both a sense of the "proper moment" and a feeling of necessary duration. Ariel saves Gonzalo and Alonso from the swords of Antonio and Sebastian in "the nick of time," but Alonso saves himself by enduring a period of suffering. And I think, too, we can see how the shape of time in *The Tempest* is largely coextensive with its music. For music informs the play not only as an agent of the "proper moment"; it also directs and integrates all of the play's moments into the total vision that is the play. *The Tempest* could not exist without its music, whether it is the strange and solemn airs that accompany the magic banquet, the sprightly singing of Ariel, or the drunken cavorting of Caliban, Stephano, and Trinculo. All of these bear an intimate relationship to each other; all relate to Prospero's one significant action—his effort to recover his dukedom and to bring his enemies to a recognition of their past and their errors.

Ultimately one's view of the importance of music in *The Tempest* will depend upon what one thinks the play's dramatic import finally is. If one believes that Prospero's island is an harmonious one where redemptive grace allays and triumphs over evil, one is apt to find its music symbolic of a celestial concord which will eventually obtain on earth. It is true that *The Tempest's* music revolves around the opposition of concord and discord and that the agents of these two modes of being respond (or do not respond) to it in their respective ways. But rather than seeing the play as the victory of harmony over disorder, I think *The Tempest* suggests how very difficult it is to bring order into being and that order, once achieved, is indeed a fragile thing, precariously balanced between the violent past from which it has emerged and the threatening future which may consume it. Music, then, assists at the birth of this tentative order, and Prospero's music must be considered in terms of both the extensions and limitations of his art.

The first song of the play is Ariel's "Come unto these yellow sands" (I, ii, 375), which he sings to a grieving Ferdinand. The tempest has finally subsided, and Ariel's song celebrates the simplicity of the calm earth into which Ferdinand has been transported. As an invitation to the dance, "then take hands," the song looks ahead to that moment at the end of the play when all of its characters are joined inside Prospero's magic circle. The magic which Prospero had used to invoke the tempest now enchants Ferdinand, drawing him further into the island and toward Miranda. This is the first crucial step toward their marriage, which will in part resolve the parental strife that had been Prospero's cause for raising the tempest. One critic has suggested that this song is the musical counterpart of the sweet-singing Sirens' invitation. "The island has all the magical charms of Circe's island: strangers from afar have been lured to it and Prospero provides a magical banquet and charms his visitors by music's powers, so that they are no longer able to obey their reasoning powers." Here Prospero's more benevolent powers replace the lust and destruction of the Sirens, and the music leads Ferdinand, not to an easy satisfaction, but to a test of discipline and faithfulness. Ferdinand's response to the song, "Where should this music be? I' th' air or th' earth?" (I, ii, 388), establishes the magical quality of this island, where the very air is music. W. H. Auden has written that "the song comes to him as an utter surprise, and its effect is not to feed or please his grief, not to encourage him to sit brooding, but to allay his passion, so that he gets to his feet and follows the music. The song opens his present to expectation at a moment when he is in danger of closing it to all but recollection."

As Ferdinand follows this elusive music, Ariel begins his second song, "Full fathom five thy father lies" (I, ii, 397). Probably no song of *The Tempest* is so well remembered and perhaps no other is thematically so important. Ferdinand is made to believe that his father is dead; similarly, Alonso will believe that Ferdinand is dead, and in that belief he will undergo the madness, the "sea change" of grief and humility, from which he will emerge transformed. The poetry of the song transports Alonso from the world of mutability and flux to a kind of permanence. His bones and eyes become coral and pearls; the "sea" gives form to what was subject to decay. Thus the song reminds us that the life of Milan—the disordered world of usurpation and potential tyranny—is now under the shaping influence of Prospero's art. Ferdinand reacts to the song not with grief but with awe: "This is no mortal business, nor no sound / That the earth owes" (I, ii, 407-408). The music, in the play's first triumph over history, moves Ferdinand to accept his past and leads him to the future—and Miranda.

The swift agent of Prospero's well-timed music, Ariel plays a "solemn strain" (II, i, 178) that lulls the Milan travelers to sleep. Gonzalo, in his simplicity and warm-heartedness, submits most easily, but Alonso soon follows. Sebastian and Antonio, however, are significantly exempted from the effect of the music. Prospero's magic has no power over them. Their own imperviousness to this music, their inability to hear it, contrasts sharply with Caliban, who, even in his vile earthiness, is subject to the music's seduction. "The isle is full of noises," he tells Stephano and Trinculo, "Sounds and sweet airs that give delight and hurt not" (III, ii, 132-133). When Sebastian and Antonio plot to take the lives of Alonso and Gonzalo, Prospero's music urgently intervenes. Ariel sings a warning song, "While you here do snoring lie" (II, i, 290), into Gonzalo's ear, and the sleepers awake. The music that had induced their slumber becomes the agent of their deliverance; Alonso and Gonzalo escape catastrophe.

One of the primary distinctions to be made about music in *The Tempest* is, of course, that there is Ariel's music and there is Caliban's music. And while there is that moment when Caliban seems to come close to understanding both of these musical languages, he remains, for the most part, on the side of the raucous and the bawdy. This is the music of Stephano and Trinculo as well. Stephano's first two songs, "I shall no more to sea" (II, ii, 41) and "The master, the swabber, the boatswain, and I" (II, ii, 45), are indeed the "scurvy tunes" that he calls them. The songs are a kind of comic diversion and an introduction to the buffoonery of the three that is to follow. Their lustiness and earthiness offers a clear antithesis to the obedient chastity of Ferdinand and Miranda, who are learning that fulfillment must be by desert and not demand.

Caliban, now under the influence of his new god "sack," raises his own voice in song. His "Farewell master" (II, ii, 173) and "No more dams I'll make for fish" (II, ii, 175) signalize his revolt from Prospero. The latter song ends with a call for freedom, reminding us, perhaps, of Ariel's behest early in the play that Prospero release him. Ariel must work for his freedom; Caliban expects his to fall into his lap. It is important, too, I think, and perhaps ironically

significant that the only two characters in the play who *ask* for freedom are the non-human ones, while all the other characters are very much involved in a struggle to be free from history, from each other, and from themselves. Caliban's "scurvy song" heralds the delusion he is about to come under in thinking Stephano and Trinculo the vehicle through which his freedom may be realized. Together the comrades plot to kill Prospero and take the island, and they seal their bargain with their song "Flout 'em and scout 'em" (III, ii, 118). Caliban remarks, "That's not the tune" (121), and Ariel enters with his tabor and pipe and a wholly different kind of music. This evokes different responses from the three; Stephano thinks it the devil, Trinculo expresses penitence, but Caliban counsels them not to fear this intervention. Curiously, the two scenes of the drunken songs frame the scene of log-bearing Ferdinand, engaged in his trial to prove to Prospero his fitness for Miranda. Ferdinand's sobriety in performing his task and his willingness to accept control and responsibility—his efforts to bring about his own freedom—are thrown into relief by this contrast with desire run wild. This reminds us that Prospero's attempt to bring a new order into being is threatened on all sides by strongly motivated self-satisfaction and potential anarchy.

Ariel's music, then, has intervened a second time to hinder the enactment of a plot hatched to assassinate a ruler. Similarly, shortly after the maneuvers of Stephano, Trinculo, and Caliban to do away with Prospero, we see Antonio and Sebastian once again involved in machinations to kill their king. Again Ariel interrupts, this time with "solemn and strange music" (III, iii, 18), and he produces the dance of the strange shapes and their banquet. Alonso and Gonzalo admire the apparition, calling it "harmony" and "sweet music." Antonio and Sebastian, still beyond the pale of the island's music, can only relate the phenomenon to mundanities of geography and travelers' tales. Gonzalo thinks the shapes' "manners" more gentle than human kind, while Sebastian wants to eat the food they have placed in front of him. Like Stephano, Trinculo, and Caliban, his earthly-mindedness has no access to the beauty that affects Gonzalo and Alonso.

Ariel enters again, this time disguised as a harpy, and the banquet disappears. He explains to them the initial effect and purpose of his music: "you 'mongst men / Being most unfit to live, I have made you mad" (III, iii, 57-58). Ariel reminds them of their deposition of Prospero and promises them "lingering perdition" unless they are able to experience "heart's sorrow / And a clear life ensuing" (82). Ariel is telling the representatives of Milan that they must submit to the music of the island and endure the pain that the achievement of freedom involves or continue to be agents of chaos and evil. This is the point where the powers and limitations of Prospero's art merge. While it is true that the play has revealed that there are those amenable to order and those that are not, Prospero can only use his music to bring his captives to a consciousness of their own disordered, threatening behavior. His music cannot perform that transformation by itself. As Ferdinand had to choose whether or not he would undergo the ordeal of log-bearing, Alonso must choose whether or not he will repent. In doing so he must experience a depth of despair as a necessary prelude to his recovery: "My son i' th' ooze is bedded; and / I'll seek him deeper than e'er plummet sounded / And with him there lie mudded" (III, iii, 100-102).

Perhaps the most magnificent use of music in *The Tempest* is that which introduces and informs the masque that Prospero produces as a wedding blessing for Ferdinand and Miranda. The song "Honour, riches, marriage, blessing" (IV, i, 106) looks forward to the happy union of the couple. Yet while the song of Juno and Ceres bespeaks a life of plenty, this is not the same kind of richness that Gonzalo had envisioned when he dreamed of his ideal commonwealth: "Bourn, bound of land, tilth, vineyard, none; / . . . all men idle, all" (II, i, 148, 150). Juno and Ceres sing of the bounty that is the result of cultivation: "Barns and garners never empty, / Vines with clust'ring bunches growing" (111-112). This copiousness is the result of dedicated work, of nature and nurture, and the dance which concludes the masque is one of nymphs and "August-weary" reapers. We should remember, too, that Prospero's magic is also the outcome of his hard "labours." If we would chide Gonzalo for his innocent simplicity in imagining a golden world, the masque song balances his dream with one that must admit the necessity of the human work that brings work that brings fruitfulness and bounty.

This masque is perhaps revelatory of Prospero's imaginative desire to see order and goodness, but it expresses this goodness as the result of meaningful human effort. The frailty of this vision, however, shows itself by rapidly dissolving as Prospero remembers Caliban's "foul conspiracy" against his life. Jan Kott has called this play "the great Renaissance tragedy of lost illusions," and while one may hesitate to see it as the dark and murky drama which he thinks it is, one must, I think, give credence to the sense of incompleteness that emerges as the play comes to a close. For there are gaps, empty spaces in our perception of the human lives we have seen portrayed, which we suspect even Prospero's finest magic and greatest music cannot touch. His famous "Our revels now are ended" speech (IV, i, 148) seems, in fact, to point to the limitations of the musically enchanted spectacle he has produced. Just how fragile it really is is evidenced by its ambiguous effect on Prospero himself. For he has yet to be reminded by Ariel that "the rarer action" is

one of loving forgiveness, and there is that crucial moment when it seems as if his "nobler reason" will be as baseless as the fabric of his vision. When "the insubstantial pageant" fades, what is left is Prospero and his beating mind.

His labors however, are not without positive issue. Prospero's music had made Alonso and his company mad, yet that madness was a necessary prelude to their recognition of guilt and repentance. If Prospero's music led the shipwrecked travelers to an awareness of their own history, it also provided a vehicle through which this awareness—this madness—could be healed. They enter Prospero's magic circle to a "solemn air . . . the best comforter / To an unsettled fancy . . ." (V, i, 58-59). Yet if they have attained a freedom from madness, it is a freedom that must accept the burden of responsibility for its past and future. In this context, Ariel's final song, "Where the bee sucks, there suck I" (V, i, 87), is significant. One critic has suggested that this song, which is about Ariel's freedom, is really a lyric coda to the entire play, celebrating the attainment of freedom on the part of all who have been involved. I think the song has a different and greater function. As it suggests Ariel's approaching happiness, it points to the world beyond the play, the world which must remain that of our imaginings. And in going beyond the world of the play, we must inevitably consider not only the "cowslip's bell" and the merry summer that Ariel looks forward to with delight, but also Milan and the world to which the reinstated Prospero must return. Ariel's song most poignantly reminds us that his freedom is not the freedom of a Prospero or an Alonso, that only a spirit can be free to the four elements. For the court of Milan freedom must now reside in responsible action emerging from the recognition of the pain of history.

Throughout *The Tempest* Prospero's art—his music—had been the measure of the shaping influence he had on the lives of other people. Its power finally, I think, must be as tentative as the conclusion to which it brings us. It has united Ferdinand and Miranda and created a new future for Alonso, but Antonio is still trapped in vile self-seeking, and the cases of Sebastian and Caliban are questionable. Music has helped to bring about some order in what had been chaos, some concord from what had been discord. But Prospero breaks his staff and drowns his book, and thus he abandons his music as well. There is the suggestion, I think, that from now on the attainment and preservation of freedom and forgiveness will be a thoroughly human effort in which music can no longer intervene.

PROSPERO

While Prospero is clearly the central figure in *The*

Tempest and orchestrates much of its action, the question of whether he should be viewed with sympathy has divided critics. In the nineteenth century, Charles Cowden Clarke contended that Prospero is by nature "a selfish aristocrat" whose rule of the island "stops only short of absolute unmitigated tyranny." Denton J. Snider focused on Prospero more as an allegorical figure, a symbol of "creative Imagination" and a poet, or possibly Shakespeare himself, "grasping and arranging the pure forms of his own poetic art." This view foreshadows many of the critical concerns regarding Prospero in the twentieth century. E. K. Chambers's perception reflects Snider's and that of other biographical commentators who interpret Prospero's surrender of his magic at the end of *The Tempest* with Shakespeare's farewell to dramatic art. Colin Still's 1921 assessment of the play highlights its allegorical aspects, and places Prospero in the role of God as punisher and redeemer of humanity. Dover Wilson complicates this reading by describing the darker elements in Prospero's character, including his overall irascibility. The latter half of the twentieth century has witnessed a continuation of a broad range of interpretation of Prospero's character. He has often been associated with the themes of reconciliation and enlightenment (both spiritual and political) by such critics as Robert Speaight, Stephen Orgel, and D. G. James. According to Speaight, Prospero plays a quasi-priestly role in reconciling spiritual and temporal values in *The Tempest*. Orgel focuses on Prospero's magical guise as a deceiver and manipulator, arguing that by relinquishing his power to mislead he acknowledges his kinship with humanity. In James's assessment, Prospero represents a conflict of interest between public and private lives and stresses the interdependency of the spiritual and temporal realms. A similar line of interpretation appears in the criticism of Neil Wright, who explores Prospero's role as a poet who uses his art to elevate the human soul. Karol Berger has noted that Prospero's use of magic figures prominently in the play's development of the theme of the dangers, both to oneself and to others, of retreating into oneself. Prospero's characterization as mirrored in his relations with Ariel and Caliban has been the subject of a recent study by **Ian Ferguson.**

Ian Ferguson

SOURCE: "Contradictory Natures: The Function of Prospero, His Agent and His Slave in *The Tempest*," in *Unisa English Studies*, Vol. XXVIII, No. 2, September, 1990, pp. 1-9.

[*In the following essay, Ferguson investigates the contradictory qualities of Prospero's character as they are borne out by his interaction with the other characters in* The Tempest, *especially with Caliban and Ariel. According*

to Ferguson, Prospero is essentially a ruler, now dressed as an artist and a director, who has abdicated his power without fully accepting moral responsibility for his actions. Prospero's endeavors throughout the play are bent on revenge and the restoration of his lost worldly power. His activities are thrown into dramatic relief, however, by his subjects Ariel and Caliban. These two characters, contends Ferguson, are symbolic of the "wild man," a figure common in Medieval literature, who personifies the "inescapable irrationality inherent in civilized man." Prospero's subjugation of these two almost ironically results in his own education, as he learns the value of forgiveness, compassion, and freedom from those to whom he has so long failed to grant mercy.]

The generally accepted belief that *The Tempest* is Shakespeare's last complete play has led to numerous ingenious (and frequently sentimental) readings of the text. It is widely regarded as Shakespeare's farewell to the stage with Prospero's famous speech on mutability as the centrepiece to support such an interpretation. Yet, it is seldom that artists consciously sum up their careers in so obvious a way. Even Kurosawa's *Dreams,* while focusing on images and incidents that have stimulated that director's films, can hardly be regarded as his farewell to the medium. As an artist matures and grows older the themes and images that inform his earlier work are frequently revised and transformed. I do not believe that the energy that generates works of art is simply cut off in a conscious decision to write (or paint) no more. Artists are too tenacious and hardy to be so easily persuaded by mortality to sum up their art in a final, complete and irrevocable statement. In the case of Shakespeare his concern with the nature and function of kingship, his use of the masque elements in, for example, the final scene of *As You Like It,* as well as his exploration of the relationships between generations are gathered together in the last five plays. Just as Kurosawa in our time has set out to examine the images and thoughts that have inspired his films, so Shakespeare has taken images and ideas from earlier plays and transmuted them into a vision made richer by a lifetime's experience.

Scholarly research has established the strong influence of the masque form on *The Tempest* and this has stimulated the critical desire to give the characters a fixed allegorical meaning. What that allegory is, however, is frequently disputed. Prospero has, in different interpretations, been equated with Shakespeare, God and the Spirit of the Renaissance. Similarly Ariel has been called the spirit of Imagination or the Poetic Inspiration.

Not surprisingly such 'definitive' readings are unsatisfactory and perhaps the most significant point about *The Tempest* is that it is singularly enigmatic and eludes the critical urge to apply fixed didactic meanings to it. As Marsh has pertinently observed [in *The Recurring Miracle,* 1962]:

> . . . I find it the most puzzling of all Shakespeare's plays, and the one about which generalizations are least satisfactory.

The richness of the text is beyond dispute. It has provoked readings that satisfy our contemporary views of society and, although these may not be reconcilable with Jacobean sensibility, they are in our terms all of a piece. Recently, for instance, a critic [Neil Viljoen, in *Ear: The English Academy of Southern Africa Review* 5 (1988)] has asserted:

> I believe that Caliban must be seen as a victim of imperialism, as a victim of a rapist society and in establishing a socio-political framework for *The Tempest* I have shown that the play deliberately makes a social and political statement, that that is part of its intention, in so far as intentionality can be established.

The problem here is that in Shakespeare's age imperialism was not the bogey that it has become in the dying years of the twentieth century. That Shakespeare's plays are for all time need not be disputed here but it is, I believe, essential that we should not apply political codes that do not accord with seventeenth-century perceptions, for example:

> Alonso's daughter, Ferdinand's sister, Claribel, was married to (I use the phrase deliberately) the King of Tunis. Europe is married to Africa, suggestive of the Old World married to the New. Claribel, light, has been married to a King of darkness. There is comment to this effect in the play. It was, I think quite obviously, a politically motivated marriage. And I wonder if that is not a kind of rape.

This observation misses the point that Tunis is, in *The Tempest,* closely associated with the ancient city of Carthage. Far from being part of the New World, Tunis is, in the minds of the characters and the contemporary playgoer, associated with the Classical Age. The New World for Shakespeare was the Bermudas and the Americas. Furthermore the comparison of Claribel with 'the widow Dido' suggests the instability of love, the fragility of vows of constancy and the nature of betrayal. Although this theme is but lightly touched on in *The Tempest* it remains a potent undercurrent. Prospero excludes Venus and Cupid from participation in the masque, and the discovery of Ferdinand and Miranda playing chess is accompanied by accusations of cheating. Although the charge is delivered jocularly and with affection, it contains a note of dissonance:

> MIR. Sweet lord, you play me false.

> FER.   No, my dearest love,
> I would not for the world.
> MIR. Yes, for a score of kingdoms you should wrangle,
> And I would call it fair play.
>
>   (V.i.172-5)

One senses that the return to Naples and Milan will not automatically confer a permanent and ideal happiness on the young couple. The political world demands recognition, and idealism can cruelly deceive.

In proposing a reading, however tentative, of *The Tempest* it is perhaps wisest to begin at a point at which most critics are in agreement, namely, that Prospero is central to the play. He is, as Frank Kermode notes in his introduction to the Arden edition of the play, 'a masque presenter'. Furthermore, an examination of the structure of the play reveals that Prospero (and his familiar Ariel) are the only two characters who are aware of all the events of the afternoon's business. The others are only allowed knowledge of their particular dilemma and until the last scene do not know that they are not the sole survivors.

Prospero is the director of the action, a character within the play and also the 'presenter' of the masque. The text of the play is studded with reminders that Prospero manipulates the action of the play and that the present moment we are watching blurs the boundaries between our time and the fictional time of the play:

> The hour's now come,
> The very minute bids thee open thine ear
>   (I.ii.36-37)

> Now does my project gather to a head:
> My charms crack not; my spirits obey; and time
> Goes upright with his carriage.
>
>   (V.i.1-3)

The play concludes when the 'time' of the action dissolves into the time of the play's completion and the audience releases the characters and is, in turn, released from the spell of the masque play:

> Now my charms are all o'erthrown
> And what strength I have's my own.
> Which is most faint now, 'tis true
> I must be here confin'd by you,
> Or sent to Naples.
>
>   . . . . .
>
>   Now I want
> Spirits to enforce, art to enchant. . . .
>   (*Epilogue* 77.1-5 and 13-14)

The reiteration of the word 'now' reinforces the fact that the action of the play and the length of performance are the same and that we, the audience, are an essential part of the meaning of the play. In this the play observes the form and function of a masque. It is important that we should examine the nature, not merely the form of the masque. The masque element of the play is present, partly, in the elaborate stage directions that suggest the need to ensure that the play is performed with the elaborate effects that are typical of the seventeenth-century masque.

The masque is a complex and sophisticated form of theatre and, although in the Caroline period it became essentially spectacle, in Shakespeare's day it was an intricate structure as reliant on text as it was on ingenious theatrical devices. *The Tempest* was written when the architect Inigo Jones and the writers Jonson and Daniel held equal sway in the creation of court entertainment. The content and form of the masque have been admirably researched by Stephen Kogan who states [in *The Hieroglyphic King,* 1986]:

> . . . the entire form seems poised between the extremes of harmony and conflict. Shakespeare reflects this tension in his masque-like play *The Tempest,* which similarly moves between the language of ethereal visions and the language of politics and struggle.

The political element found in the masques of the period is dramatically presented in the juxtaposition of usurpation and inheritance on the island, as well as in the account of events some sixteen years earlier. Prospero's desire for revenge for the wrongs he has endured in the past also serves to introduce a sense of mutability, the insubstantiality of our world in relation to eternity, and the transitory nature of performance is directly associated with human life:

> Our revels now are ended. These our actors
> As I foretold you, were all spirits, and
> Are melted into air, into thin air:
> And, like the baseless fabric of this vision,
> The cloud-capp'd towers, the gorgeous
>   palaces,
> The solemn temples, the great globe itself,
> Yea, all which it inherit, shall dissolve,
> And, like this insubstantial pageant faded,
> Leave not a rack behind.
>
> (IV.i.148-56)

The insubstantiality is stressed by the use of 'were all spirits and this insubstantial pageant faded'. Even as he speaks, Prospero's conjuring and the actions of the world dissolve and pass. 'The great globe itself is a common iconic image for the world and was frequently used by Shakespeare in plays as different in kind as *King Lear* and *As You Like It:*

> This wide and universal theatre
> Presents more woeful pageants than the scene
> Wherein we play.
>
> (*As You Like It* II.vii.137-9)

While in *King Lear* man's existence is seen as a part in a play:

> When we are born, we cry that we are come
> To this great stage of fools.
>
> (IV.vi.183-4)

Throughout *The Tempest* the association of audience and performer is stressed through the insistence on our time and that of the players being one.

It is, however, the dichotomy evident in the language and themes of the play, that is largely responsible for the puzzling (and fascinating) spell that the play has cast on both literary critics and theatre directors who all struggle to make complete sense of the play. These conflicting elements are also strongly reflected in the characterizations of Prospero, Ariel and Caliban.

The Tempest opens with a vividly dramatic stage effect, a storm at its height. The language reveals, with Shakespeare's characteristic economy, aspects of character; the King and Ferdinand are at prayer, whereas the 'villains' of the play respond with violence and inappropriate pride:

> SEB. A pox o' your throat, you bawling,
> blasphemous, uncharitable dog!
>
> (I.i.40)

and,.

> ANT. Hang, cur! hang, you whoreson,
>   insolent noisemaker.
> We are less afraid to be drowned than thou
>   art.
>
> (I.i.43-5)

It remains for that 'noble Neapolitan, Gonzalo' to attempt to introduce a note of optimism and uneasy jocularity:

> I have great comfort from this fellow:
>   methinks
> he hath no drowning mark upon him; his
>   complexion is perfect gallows.
>
> (I.i.28-30)

The desperation of the drowning mortals is followed immediately by our first sight of Prospero and Miranda on 'the uninhabited Island' that is Prospero's small kingdom. Coleridge's observation is dramatically very pertinent:

Exquisite judgement—first the noise and confusion—then the silence of a deserted island—and Prospero and Miranda.

Apart from establishing Miranda's compassion and her horror at the probable fate of those aboard the threatened galleon, Shakespeare reveals that this Tempest initially registered by the play-goer as a realistic storm—the diction of the mariners is an accurate response to a violent hurricane at sea—is the product of Prospero's thought and not the actual predicament of 'mortality set among the terrors of natural existence'. The action of *The Tempest* is determined and governed by the 'beating' of Prospero's mind. Herein lies the richness and sophistication of Shakespeare's concept and it is in accord with the particular demands of the masque form. Robert Uphaus has asserted [in *Beyond Tragedy,* 1981]:

> Because Prospero is, *among other things,* an artist who has staged a tempest within a play called *The Tempest,* it seems fair to assume that the play is also a kind of psychodrama with the characters and events of the play acting out facets of Prospero's mind. (my emphasis)

While this view is couched in contemporary terms that would have had little meaning for Shakespeare, it does accord with one of the functions of the masque, the assertion of the power and function of kingship.

In the reign of James I great emphasis was placed upon the function and obligations of the king. James expressed the moral duties of the ruler in his treatise *The Basilican Doron,* the 'kingly gift' is in effect a testament of royal doctrine for the instruction of the young Prince Henry. The duty of obligation is clearly a matter of prime consideration:

> But as yee are clothed with two callings, so must ye be alike carefull for the discharge of them both: that as ye are a good Christian, so ye may be a good King, discharging your office . . . in the poynts of justice and acquitie: which in two sundry waies ye must do: the one, in establishing, and executing (which is the life of the lawe) good lawes among your people: the other, by your behaviour in your owne person . . . consider first the true difference betwixt a lawfull good King, & an usurping Tyrant: . . . The one acknowlegeth himself ordeined for his people, having received form God a burthen of government whereof he must be countable. The other thinketh his people ordeyned for him a praye to his appetites, as the fruites of his magnanimitie; and therefore, as their endes are directly contrarie, so ar their whole actions. . . .

In King James's political speeches this moral and godly function of the ruler is stressed and he spoke constantly of the necessity for the king to abide by 'the fundamental laws of the kingdom'.

The concern for the principles of kingship and the relationship between God's justice and earthly law inform the masques of the Stuart court and also find expression in the poems of state, most particularly Jonson's *Panegyre on the Happie Entrance of James . . . To His first high Session of Parliament:*

> . . . reverend Themis did descend
> Upon his state; let downe in that rich chaine
> That fasteneth heavenly power to earthly
>   raigne.
>
> (11.20-2)

In keeping with Shakespeare's concern for the function and purpose of kingship which formed a major theme not only in the history plays but also in the great tragedies, *The Tempest* deals, although more obliquely, with the moral function of kingship. Prospero is not an ideal king although he is a magus, a man of learning. His deposition and exile at the hands of his brother, Antonio, are the result of his own abdication from responsibility:

> I, thus neglecting worldly ends, all dedicated
> To closeness and the bettering of my mind
> With that which, but by being so retir'd,
> O'er-priz'd all popular rate, in my false
>   brother
> Awak'd an evil nature; and my trust,
> Like a good parent, did beget of him
> A falsehood in its contrary, as great
> As my trust was. . . .
>
> (I.ii.89-96)

Here Prospero indicates that his sense of injury is great, but fails to acknowledge his own abdication from responsibility. One of the chief characteristics that marks Prospero is a sense of resentment for injury to his authority. As the Duke of Milan he should not have 'neglected worldly ends'. Furthermore, his wounded self-esteem is reflected in his previous speech when he refers to his brother's 'parasitic' theft of power:

> . . . he was
> The ivy which had hid my princely trunk,
> And suck'd my verdure out on't.
>
> (I.ii.85-7)

The image conveys the draining of power and vitality of which his brother, Antonio, is undoubtedly guilty. However, the image would have suggested more to Shakespeare's audience drawing as it does on a picture, epigram and moral published in *Theater of Fine Devices.* Within the iconological meaning of the ivy sapping the strength of the oak is a secondary meaning which stresses Prospero's almost petulant sense of the personal injustice dealt him by the usurper. The motto attached reads:

> Ungratefull men breed great offence
> As persons voyd of wit or sence.

This moral is amplified by the verse that follows the simple woodcut illustration:

> The Oke doth suffer the yong Yvy wind
> Up by his sides till it be got on by,
> But being got aloft it so doth bind
> It kils the stocke that it was raised by;
> So some proves so unthankfull and unkind,
> To those on whom they chiefly do rely
> By whom they first were called to their
> state
> They be the first (I say) give them the
> mate.

Although Antonio is culpable as a usurper who has broken the bonds of duty between king and subject as well as flouted the ties of blood (as Macbeth had also done), it is significant that Prospero feels indignation and injury when he has himself undervalued the high office to which he is divinely appointed. Earlier in the same scene he comes closer to a recognition of his abrogation of duty:

> The government I cast upon my brother,
> And to my state grew stranger, being
> transported
> And rapt in secret studies.
>   (I.ii.75-77)

His use of the verb 'cast' suggests a degree of careless disregard for the divinely imposed responsibilities of kingship. Disturbingly in the final lines of the play it appears that Prospero has still not acquired the understanding of the duties owed, in Jacobean terms, by the ruler:

>   . . . in the morn
> I'll bring you to your ship, and so to
> Naples.
> Where I have hope to see the nuptial
> Of these our dear-belov'd solemnized;
> And thence retire me to my Milan, where
> Every third thought shall be my grave.
>   (V.i.306-311)

Prospero's search for knowledge would have been regarded in the seventeenth century as laudable and proper, but his failure to act as the 'politic father of his people' planning their 'careful education' would have been seen as a dereliction of duty. Prospero shows little inclination for this responsibility of government and the playgoer realizes that he has mistaken the defeat of Antonio and Sebastian for penance.

However, Prospero does advance in moral understanding if not in political acumen. Initially, and for the greater part of the play, he is afflicted with a 'nausea' for the human condition. This affects even his tenderness for Miranda, who although he tells her she was 'a cherubin', he also sees as burdened with human emotions, most specifically that of love:

> Poor worm, thou art infected!
> This visitation shows it.
>   (III.i.31-2)

Prospero's character vacillates between affection and disgust with the human condition. Finally, it is this 'nausea' that Prospero conquers and through the Christian virtues stressed by King James (as well as by the writers of court masques) he achieves a common humanity, one which accepts the limitations of that humanity:

> Though with their high wrongs I am struck
> to th'quick,
> Yet with my nobler reason 'gainst my fury
> Do I take part: the rarer action is
> In virtue than in vengeance: they being
> penitent,
> The sole drift of my purpose doth extend
> Not a frown further.
>   (V.i.25-30)

Recognition of virtue leads him to abjure his magic powers thus placing himself once more within the structure of human society. Finally, in the Epilogue he accepts the need for Divine Providence:

>   Now I want
> Spirits to enforce, Art to enchant;
> And my ending is despair,
> Unless I be reliev'd by prayer,
> Which pierces so, that it assaults
> Mercy itself, and frees all faults.
>   (*Epilogue*. 77.13-18)

The growth of understanding is most palpably demonstrated in his recognition of the 'hag-seed' 'on whose nature'/ Nurture can never stick':

>   . . . this thing of darkness I
> Acknowledge mine.
>   (V.i.275-6)

The contradictory elements that Prospero embodies are also evident in Shakespeare's portrayal of Ariel and the slave, Caliban. Both of these figures are, I believe, derived from the same source, the medieval icon of the 'wild man'. This is more evidently true in Shakespeare's portrayal of the 'salvage and deformed slave' Caliban, who has been bewitched by Prospero's initial kindness into abdicating his own position on the island:

> When thou cam'st first,
> Thou strok'st me and made much of me;
>   would'st give me
> Water with berries in't; and teach me how
> To name the bigger light and how the less,
> That burn by day and night: and then I
>   lov'd thee,
> And show'd thee all the qualities o'th'isle.
> The fresh springs, brine-pits, barren place
>   and fertile:
> Curs'd be I that did so!
>
>   (I.i.334-41)

Caliban demonstrates a naïve susceptibility to the attentions of men which he mistakes for affection not once, but twice, on both occasions disastrously in terms of his own well-being. His infatuation with Stephano leads him to betray once again the secrets of the island and to seek revenge on Prospero through a man of lower order:

> I'll show thee the best springs; I'll pluck thee
>   berries;
> I'll fish for thee, and get thee wood enough.
> A plague upon the tyrant that I serve!
> I'll bear him no more sticks, but follow thee,
> Thou wondrous man.
>
>   (II.ii.160-64)

Caliban is not governed by any understanding of social codes and his nature responds purely to the pleasure principle and the desire to possess his own kingdom:

> PROS. . . . thou didst seek to violate
> The honour of my child.
> CAL. O ho, O ho! would't had been done!
> Thou didst prevent me; I had peopled else
> This isle with Calibans.
>
>   (I.ii.349-53)

In his definitive study of the wild man in art and literature [*The Wild Man: Medieval Maths and Symbolism*, 1980], Timothy Husband has observed:

Prospero and Miranda watch the storm.

The wild man, a purely mythic creature, was a literary and artistic invention of the medieval imagination. . . . By every account the wild man's behaviour matched his primitive surroundings. Strong enough to uproot trees, he was violent and aggressive, not only against wild animals but also against his own kind.

The figure of the wild man arises from the need to explain and define an inescapable irrationality inherent in civilized man:

The wild man . . . served to counterpoise the accepted standards of conduct in society in general. If the average man could not articulate what he meant by 'civilized' in positive terms, he could readily do so in negative terms by pointing to the wild man.

By the sixteenth century the iconographic image of the wild man was a commonplace in English literature and plays a significant role in both poetry and drama. The portrayal of the wild man is fairly constant in his appearance which gives us, in Spenser's description, a strange figure devoid of the niceties and refinements of civilized living:

His wast was with a wreath of yuie greene
  Engirt about, ne other garment wore:
  For all his haire was like a garment seene;
  And in his hand a tall young oake he bore,
  whose knottie snags were sharpened all
    afore.
And beath'd in fire for steele to be insted.
But whence he was, or of wombe ybore,
Of beasts, or of the earth, I have not red
But certes was with milke of Wolves and
  Tygres fed.

(Spenser: *The Faerie Queene*,
Book IV, Cant. VII.7)

The figure of the wild man appears in theatre as early as 1515 in the masqye-type play *The Place Perilous*. The most important early use of this figure occurs, however, in the dumb show prologue to *Gorbuduc* (1561):

Firste the Musicke of violenze began to play, durynge whiche came vppon stage six wilde men clothed in leaues.

He also serves a vital function in Spenser's highly emblematic poem, *The Faerie Queene*, where the two distinct personalities of the wild man are portrayed. Initially the view is one akin to the Caliban figure:

It was to weet a wilde and saluage man,
  Yet was no man, but onely like in shape
  and eke in stature higher by a span,
  All ouergrowne with haire, that could

awhape
An hardy hart, and his wide mouth did
  gape
With huge great teeth, like to a tusked
  Bore
For he liu'd all on rauin and on rape
Of men and beasts; and fed on fleshly gore,
The signe whereof yet stain'd his bloudy lips
  afore

His neather lip was not like man nor beast,
  But like a wide deepe poke, downe hanging
    low,
  In which he wont the relickes of his feast,
  and cruellspoyle, which he hadspard, to
    stow:
  And ouer it his huge great nose did grow,
  Full dreadfully empurpled all with bloud;
  And downe both sides two wide long ears
    did glow,
  And raught downe to his waste, when vp
    he stood,
More great then th'eares of Elephants by
  Indus flood.

(Spenser: *The Faerie Queene*,
Book IV, Cant. VII. 5-6)

Significantly, it is only Caliban who truly appreciates the beauty of the island. Prospero regards it merely as a place of exile in which he practises his 'rough magic' and longs for a return to Milan. Gonzalo's description of an ideal commonwealth is little more than an optimistic attempt to come to terms with the fickleness of Fortune. Nonetheless, his view that 'Nature should bring forth, / Of its own kind, all foison, all abundances' is echoed in the masque that Prospero conjures up to express his hope for a fruitful and blessed future for Miranda and Ferdinand:

Earth's increase, foison plenty,
Barns and garners never empty;
Vines with clust'ring bunches growing;
Plants with goodly burthen bowing;
Spring come to you at the farthest
In the very end of harvest!

(IV.i.110-115)

Although the magic figures of Juno, Ceres and Iris give their benediction, we realize that it is an ideal vision that can at best be only fleetingly achieved in the 'real' world of politics and social structures. Very few of the characters are conscious of the magical harmony of the island and most concentrate on the disagreeable qualities of mires and foul-smelling pools. However contradictory the idea may appear, the 'salvage' is the one figure who is most conscious of the 'qualities' of the island. Caliban hears the music and dimly perceives a beauty and meaning beyond his reach:

Be not afeard; the isle is full of noises,
Sounds and sweet airs, that give delight, and
  hurt not.
Sometimes a thousand twangling instruments
Will hum about mine ears; and sometime
  voices,
That, if I then had wak'd after long sleep,
Will make me sleep again: and then, in
  dreaming,
The clouds methought would open, and
  show riches
Ready to drop upon me; that, when I wak'd
I cried to dream again.

(III.ii.133-41)

In these lines we are reminded of Bottom and his confused perception of beauty that will forever be beyond his comprehension:

I have had a most rare vision. I have had a dream, past the wit of man to say what dream it was. Man is but an ass if he go about to expound the dream. . . . The eye of man hath not heard, the ear of man hath not seen, man's hand is not able to taste, his tongue to conceive, nor his heart to report what my dream was! (*A Midsummer Night's Dream* IV.i.198-204)

Importantly, however, the difference between Bottom and the island 'salvage', lies in the way Caliban is manipulated by the beauty that can make him 'sleep again' or weep 'to dream again' While Bottom, a 'hard-handed' man 'of Athens', confuses the various senses the 'salvage and deformed' Caliban perceives the magic in terms of a harmony and order that his nature cannot possess. That the supernatural element is divine is suggested in Shakespeare's use of the conventional emblem, common in the fifteenth and sixteenth centuries, of the cloud that parts to reveal God's generosity symbolized in the hand offering assistance or in the gift of a cornucopia of plenty. In his portrayal of Caliban, Shakespeare perceives the violence and the anarchic nature of the wild man, but he also allows him a perception of beauty from which civilized man is partly excluded. The dichotomy, striking in that it echoes the civilized Prospero's own contradictions, embodies the dual image of the wild man as perceived in late medieval and post-medieval myth and symbol:

As both myth and symbol . . . the wildman could be at once savage and sublime, evoke fear and admiration, and represent man's antithesis and ideal.

One characteristic of the wild man that is most fully portrayed in Caliban is his passionate response to music. It is, perhaps, this capacity for appreciation that allows us to accept Caliban's 'repentance' and

belated recognition of degree in human society:

. . . I'll be wise hereafter,
And seek for grace. What a thrice-double ass
Was I, to take this drunkard for a god,
And worship this dull fool!

(V.i.294-97)

That he should 'seek for grace' allows the possibility of redemption and endorses the view held by St Augustine and subsequent religious writers:

What is true for a Christian beyond the shadow of a doubt is that every real man, that is, every mortal animal that is rational, however unusual to us may be the shape of his body, or the color of his skin or the way he walks, or the sound of his voice, and whatever the strength, portion or quality of his natural endowments, is descended from the single first-created man. . . . God is the Creator of all; He knows best where and when and what is, or was, best for Him to create, since He deliberately fashioned the beauty of the whole out of both the similarity and dissimilarity of its parts.

The promise of salvation, or at least the hope of redemption through a search for spiritual grace, is not confined to Caliban but embraces mercy and redemption for Prospero in the religious sense. The disturbing element of his political naïveté remains constant by the end of the play. For Caliban the conclusion of the play offers the potential of salvation for a different order of creation than that of human society, the 'spawn' of the witch Sycorax. It is the belief in salvation that is the play's chief concern, similar to that expressed by the medieval poet, Heinrich von Hesler in *Apokalypse*:

Werden sulle, daz sie genesen
Order sie suln vorlorn wesen
Oder mit dem Tuvele hin gen
Daz muz an Goter guaden sten.

(Whether they will be saved or
lost and go with the devil, that
will have to be left to the mercy
of God.)

Although the portrayal of Caliban owes much to the emblem of the Wild Man it is also important that we should remember that he is the child of the witch Sycorax who, like Prospero, was initially cast away on the island where she died leaving her son the island inheritance:

This island's mine, by Sycorax my mother,
Which thou tak'st from me.

(I.ii.333-4)

The conflicting elements of personality that are evident

in Prospero are also revealed in the commentary on the 'foul witch' whose life was spared 'for one thing she did'. The information that even a creature dedicated to evil—as surely as Prospero is a devotee of 'white' magic—hints at the mercy that must be extended to any creature that acts for the good of man rather than for his downfall.

The most important completely supernatural creature on the island is Ariel who, like Caliban, exhibits characteristics typical of the wild man concept. Ariel is protean and his appearances are calculated to inspire delight (the 'water nymph') or, alternatively, terror (the figure of the 'harpy'). Although he possesses magical powers, he is nonetheless only an agent and was initially subject to the powers of Sycorax who confined him in 'a cloven pine'. He is similarly and most unwillingly the agent of Prospero who keeps him in thrall by the memory of his 'dozen years' of imprisonment and by the threat of further confinement:

> If thou more murmur'st, I will rend an oak,
> And peg thee in his knotty entrails, till
> Thou hast howl'd away twelve winters.
>
> (I.ii.294-6)

Prospero rules his agent and his slave most tyrannically, threatening Caliban with physical pain and Ariel with imprisonment. Each is terrorized by what he most fears and in this respect Prospero is ruthlessly efficient.

Ariel's inability to initiate magic in spite of his supernatural powers of transformation is akin to the wild man's capacity to alter his appearance while exhibiting no further power:

> In early medieval times the wild man was universally thought of as a giant, but as giganticism became equated with irredeemable stupidity, the wild man's scale reduced as a matter of self-preservation. . . . By the late Middle Ages, many depictions show the wild man reduced to Lilliputian scale, disporting among the leaves and tendrils of plants.

By the sixteenth century we find the converse of the Caliban-type wild man existing side-by-side with the ogre-like representation. The violent and deformed 'salvage' who threatens Britomart in Spenser's *The Faerie Queene* has an opposite manifestation in Book VI of that poem:

> O what an easie thing is to descry
>   The gentle bloud, how euer it be wrapt
>   In sad misfortunes foule deformity,
>   And wretched sorrowes, which haue often
>   hapt?

> For howsoeuer it may grow mis-shapt,
>   Like this wyld man, being vndisciplynd,
>   That to all vertue it may seeme vnapt,
>   Yet it will shew some sparkes of gentle
>   mynd,
> And at the last breake forth in his owne
>   proper kynd.

> That plainely may in this wyld man be red,
>   Who though he were still in this desert
>   wood,
>   Mongst saluage beasts, both rudely borne
>   and bred,
>   Ne euer saw faire guize, nelearned good,
>   Yet shewd some token of his gentle blood,
>   By gentle vsage of that wretched Dame.
>   For certes he was borne of noble blood,
>   How euer by hard hap he hether came;
> As ye may know, when time shall be to tell
>   the same.

(Spenser: *The Faerie Queene*, Book VI Cant. V. 1-2)

The delicacy and 'gentle blood' of the wild man is also a trait of Ariel which is contradicted by that spirit's coldness. If Caliban represents uncontrolled emotions Ariel is detached from human concerns, although he is capable of objectively reminding Prospero of his human responses:

> ARI. . . . Your charm so strongly works 'em
> That if you now beheld them, your affection
> Would become tender.
> PROS.   Dost thou think so, spirit?
> ARI. Mine would, sir, were I human.
> PROS.   And mine shall
> Hast thou, which art but air, a touch, a
>   feeling
> Of their afflictions, and shall not myself,
> One of their kind, that relish all as sharply
> Passion as they, be kindlier mov'd than thou
>   art?
>
> (V.i.17-24)

It is Ariel's relationship with air which has provoked the critical view that equates him with the imaginative qualities of man. In *The Recurring Miracle* Derek Marsh cautiously states that Ariel represents 'something like the imagination of man'. However, there is an element that is disturbingly hedonistic and self-centred in Ariel. The use he intends to make of his freedom from servitude is entirely governed by pleasure and a search for a permanent summer:

> Where the bee sucks, there suck I:
> In a cowslip's bell I lie;
> There I couch when owls do cry.
> On the bat's back I do fly
> After summer merrily.

461

Merrily, merrily shall I live now
Under the blossom that hangs on the bough.
                              (V.i.88-94)

In this he exhibits a kinship with the gentle wildman of the late medieval period:

Je viz cellon que ma aprins nature
sans soucy nul tousjours joyeusemant

. . . . .

En (ce) croux ci fois moy ébergement
Quant a viandes soueves nullement
ne en fort breuvages nen prond point
  deplesance
De froiz fruitage me repes seullement
Et ainsy ai, Dieu mercy, souffisance.

(I live according to what Nature has taught
  me
Free from worry, always joyously.

. . . . .

In a hollow tree I make my home.
I do not delight in fancy food
Or in strong drink.
I live upon fresh fruit alone,
And so I have, thank God, enough.)

The function of both Ariel and Caliban lies in their ability to instruct the human Prospero to express worthy emotions and demonstrate a capacity for generosity and forgiveness. In so doing they achieve their freedom and allow Prospero to return to worldly concerns conscious of the need for forgiveness and mercy if man is to be more, and express more, than brutish appetite. It is a lesson as appropriate for the twentieth century as it was for the seventeenth.

ARIEL

Commentary on Ariel has tended to speculate about his nature and to suggest possible sources for his original and unique characterization. In 1811 August Wilhelm Schlegel was the first to identify Ariel with the element of air, contrasting him with Caliban, who is linked with the lower element of earth. And, while Schlegel was careful not to reduce Ariel or any other characters in the play to simple allegory, symbolic studies of this creature have abounded in modern criticism. John Ruskin looked at the political and social aspects of Ariel's character in 1862, maintaining that the spirit's freely-rendered labor is the source of his contentment and eventual freedom. E. K. Chambers continues the allegorical tradition in the

twentieth century, locating Ariel as "the spirit of poetry" in his interpretation of the play. Likewise, Ariel is sometimes seen as a personification of human consciousness. His continual pleading with Prospero for his freedom, in this reading, helps bring about the magician's realization of the need for mercy and forgiveness. Several commentators, however, have found these and other allegorical explanations of Ariel's character unconvincing and instead have focused on uncovering Shakespeare's sources for Ariel. **W. Stacy Johnson**, for example, locates the origins of the creature in a variety of contexts, favoring one which places him in a Neoplatonic conception of reality, which allows for the existence of benevolent spirits in the natural world. This possibility simplifies the character by avoiding any spiritual complications associated with either divine or demonic realms. By contrast, **Clifford Davidson** emphasizes that Ariel is not a purely benevolent creature and that his motivation is Prospero's threats of punishment more than a yearning for freedom. For further analysis of Ariel's character, see the essay by **Robert Egan** in the MAGIC section; and the essay by **Ian Ferguson** in the PROSPERO section.

W. Stacy Johnson

SOURCE: "The Genesis of Ariel," in *Shakespeare Quarterly*, Vol. 11, No. 3, July, 1951, pp. 205-10.

[*In the following essay, Johnson surveys the many possible sources for the character of Ariel, including the Bible, books of Renaissance magic, and works on demonology. From these he arrives at a definition of the creature that synthesizes both Medieval and Neoplatonic conceptions of spirits, but favors the latter by placing Ariel in the category of a spirit-agent that draws power from natural elements (in this case the air), rather than labeling him as a demonic or angelic being. Thus, Ariel has powers over natural forces, allowing him to conjure the tempest that brings Alonso, Antonio, Ferdinand, and the others to the island. In terms of his motivation, Ariel also appears to be more a fantastic creature from folklore bent on achieving his personal freedom than an abstract being with religious overtones and purely good or evil intentions.*]

As the sole agent of Prospero's magic in *The Tempest*, the spirit Ariel is a crucial figure for any analysis of the play. He has been called a personification of fancy, of art, of the airy element in which he exists; but each of these interpretations derives from an allegorical reading which is not yet convincingly established on grounds of plain evidence. What kind of spirit is Ariel, and how would Shakespeare's audience see a character functioning as he does? In answering these questions on the basis of the Renaissance background, the scholar may begin to graps the magic concept which is basic to Shakespeare's drama.

The Renaissance background of any occult or supernatural manifestation is a complex one. In general the various attitudes of Shakespeare's contemporaries toward the spirit world can be reduced to two main traditions: the medieval orthodox one, largely embodied in popular witch lore, which holds that all magical and miraculous powers are due directly either to God's or to Satan's hand; and the one involved in Neo-Platonic philosophy and in such occult pursuits as alchemy and cabalism, holding that magic may properly be practiced as an incidental means of the wise man ascending toward spiritual unity with the divine. These two concepts modify each other to some extent and are often blurred, particularly in popular writings; but the basic difference remains. The esoteric works of scholarly occultists exalt a magic in harmony with divine and natural law, but the popular works of priests and controversialists—like the *Malleus Maleficarum* and King James's *Daemonologie*—condemn all magic as either spurious or inspired by Satan. Even Wierus and Reginald Scot, skeptical of witches' and sorcerers' powers, make little distinction between scholar-magician and black witch. For a follower of the Neo-Platonist Iamblichus, or for such a learned spirit-raiser as the famous Dr. John Dee (who was a favorite of Elizabeth) there might be neutral and even rational spirits, useful in good faith. But for King James the magician-conjured spirit is diabolical.

Ariel functions primarily as a benevolent rather than a diabolical spirit, although he is capable of chastising the evil and rebellious: he appears in thunder to Alonso, Sebastian, and Antonio, and he frustrates poor Caliban's scheme for revenge. But he has served the witch Sycorax as a familiar, and it may be that he is a neutral agent of the magician who controls him. The problem as to whether he is a demon, angel, or symbolic creation can best be approached not according to his motivation, since he is represented as being subordinate to Prospero's will, but according to his name, manner of performance, and status *as* an elemental servant. The first possible key is the spirit's name, and this leads directly into the other aspects of his nature.

The name's form is that of an angelic epithet, with the *-el* (God) ending. Emile Grillot de Givry remarks that the sorcerer's black books, which took on particular interest for learned men of the Renaissance, are filled with invocations of angels and of God by various words, of which there are "seventy-two divine names, all ending in *el*." The use of these names by sorcerers and occultists probably derives from medieval Jewish demonology, in which Ariel is a spirit of the waters. This name, as well as other similar ones, may have come into Renaissance magic through the cabala; and while *Ariel* is not commonly mentioned in spirit invocations, the variant *Uriel* is often used: Uriel was the favorite spirit of Dr. Dee, about whom Shakespeare—like all England—undoubtedly knew. Abel Lefranc, in his "L'origine d'Ariel," reports having found Shakespeare's very figure in a book written for magicians of the highest order, the *Steganographia* of Trithemius. This work, according to Lefranc, names the seven angels who control the seven planets of astrology and, subordinate to these angels, twenty-one "spiritus subjecti per quos nunciantur arcana." The idea that magic works through the controlling of spirits who direct natural phenomena (in the cabala, angels who animate both celestial and earthly elements) is in Renaissance occultism a commonplace. But Lefranc emphasizes the fact that in that order of spirits which is said by Trithemius to serve the magician ("per quos intentionis nostrae operamur effectum") appears a spirit called Ariel, one of the three placed under Zachariel, governor of Jupiter; and he goes so far as to suggest that the *Steganographia* is the direct source for Shakespeare's character.

The argument for Ariel as this kind of agent could agree with W. C. Curry's idea of the spirit as a rational Platonic demon, able to carry out general commands through his own devisings, but not such evil commands as those of Sycorax. This idea would place Ariel essentially outside the orthodox perspective of Christian angel and devil. The fact is that this play, like those with classical settings, has no explicit Christian elements, referring only to the gods and spirits of classicism and folklore; but, intended or not, this omission of the Christian trimmings is appropriate in a play about a hero-magician on a fantastic island, written during the reign of a king who abhorred magic. At any rate, even if Shakespeare did not read Trithemius, as one may reasonably doubt, the concept of *natural* "angels" or spirits who control the elements and can be in turn controlled by man, who are Neo-Platonic demons partly translated into Hebrew-Christian terms (their names ending in *-el*), certainly bears a relationship to the Shakespearian concept.

Another suggestion is that Ariel's name comes from the Bible, Isaiah xxix. The Geneva Bible (London, 1594) uses the term *altar* in the chapter, but it adds this prominent gloss:

> The Ebrewe word Ariel signifieth the Lyon of God and it signifieth the Altar, because yᵉ Altar seemed to devour the Sacrifice that was offered to God. . . .

And *Ariel* rather than *altar* is employed in the Bishops' Bible. This chapter contains, along with the name, several curiously suggestive phrases. To Ariel it is said (I quote the Geneva text), "thou . . . shalt speak out of the ground, and thy speech shall be as out of the dust: thy voice also shall be out of the ground like him that hath a spirit of divination." There is something here reminiscent of the strange voices and spirits on Prospero's island, although this parallel alone must seem far-fetched. But again, "thou shalt bee visited of the Lorde of hostes with thunder, and shaking, and a great noyse, a whirlewind, and a tempest, and a flame of devouring fire." The impression of this is strikingly like that made by Ariel's tempest-raising, when the spirit "flam'd amazement," appeared as "lightnings . . . dreadful thunder-claps . . . fire and cracks / Of sulphurous roaring" (I.ii. 198-204), as well as of his later manifestation in thunder (III.ii.53 ff.). This same chapter speaks of hungry and thirsty men who dream they eat and drink and awake to find their viands gone (8), just as Alonso's company is amazed to see its magic banquet disappear; and finally there is a "spirite of slumber" which "shuts up your eyes" (10), reminding the reader of Prospero's causing Miranda to sleep and Ariel's making all of Alonso's party, save Sebastian and Antonio, drowsy. There is of course no parallel of meaning between this chapter and the play, but the similarity in imagery and incident makes some relationship—perhaps even a sub-conscious one on Shakespeare's part—quite possible.

Whatever its direct source, the appropriateness of the name certainly dictates its choice for this creature of air. According to the Neo-Platonism of Iamblichus the airy spirit is not only rational but is "composed of a 'spiritual matter' . . . merely an organic part of the universe." The aerial as contrasted with the celestial spirit is sublunar, and thus corruptible; he is an administrant of natural processes, and he can be controlled by a wise man. But sublunar spirits may be further subdivided, and the aerial spirit made only a particular elemental kind. In general the fourfold division of the elements—fire, water, earth and air—is accepted in magical writings. Agrippa holds that there are four such elements, that each has three manifestations, and that each element in its pure manifestation is unmixed and incorruptible; no magician can succeed without grasping this elemental nature. However, Thomas Vaughan insists that there are only two elements, earth and water, and that air is "a certain miraculous hermaphrodite, the cement of two worlds and the medley of extremes," where all of nature is represented in "innumerable magic forms," in which the invisible species of all things are contained; he quotes Agrippa in calling air "corpus vitae spiritus nostri sensitivi," "The body of life of our sensitive spirit," and he says mysteriously, "I should amaze the reader if I did relate the several offices of this body, but it is the magician's back door and none but friends come in at it." Both these views, particularly Vaughan's, suggest possible bases for Shakespeare's use of a spirit whose element is air.

A contemporary of Shakespeare who is particularly concerned with the subject of spirits, Randall Hutchins, holds that

> We who are formed in nature are sometimes lords over nature, and we effect operations so marvelous, so unexpected, and so difficult, that even the very Manes obey them, the stars are disturbed, the divine powers are won over, the elements become our servants.

Since this is true, he argues, it is likely that immortal spirits can perform greater works. And he believes that such spirits may be evoked by magic means. Evil forces in particular, may be either controlled or diabolically wilful; the spirits of the air are among these.

> Nor certainly should it be otherwise thought than that evil demons agitate the very bowels of the earth and arouse resounding tempests in the air, since in it some of them have their seat, as is by all means the case and obviously apparent. Witnesses to this are: Hermis Trismegistus, in *Ad Asclepium* near the beginning, and Peucer in his book on divination by dreams, where he declares that demons form various phantoms and portents like meteors in the air, portray representations of armies in conflict, reproduce blares of trumpets, clashes of arms, sounds of blows, cries of wailing, and applause of the victors, make forms of animals in the air from the confluence of gathered clouds and passage of light scattered from the sky.

The aptness of this and similar passages in giving a background for Ariel's exploit is apparent. Hutchins' work, the *Tractatus de spectris,* attempting to refute both the Roman Catholic view that specters are spirits of the dead and the "atheistic" one that they are hallucinations only, shows respect for the opinions of Neo-Platonic philosophers *and* of magicians. But Hutchins identifies elemental demons as exclusively bad specters. Dealing explicitly with "aerial spirits," he says

> Such can descend to lower regions quicker than thought and, having taken on bodies from the denser air, appear visibly at times. . . . These spirits often disturb the air, stir up tempests and thunders. They do not retain one form, but take on various forms, and change these according to the manifold variety of attitudes they encounter, when either evoked by the incantations of witches or impelled by seditious influences to do harm.

And the association of aerial beings with tempest-raising and with such "influences" is not peculiar to this treatise. Robert Burton, in his "Digression of the Nature of Spirits," not only distinguishes between aetherial (celestial or angelic) and sublunary or natural spirits, but definitely divides the latter according to elements. He calls these devils, reflecting the orthodox translation of demons into Christian imps.

His "aerial spirits . . . are such as keep quarter most part in the aire, cause many tempests, thunder, and lightnings, tear Oakes . . . Counterfeit Armies in the air, strange noyses . . . and cause whirlewindes on a sudden, and tempestuous stormes. . . ." Like Bodin, Burton believes that the tempests of the sea are usually brought about by such spirits rather than by natural means. The fact that the main function of aerial spirits in this long passage and in Hutchins is the raising of tempests, resulting in "shipwracks" (and since they are spoken of as devils, their work is parallel to that of tempest-raising witches), is surely significant, particularly in conjunction with Burton's statement that these aerial creatures are those "that serve Magicians," the very spirits who performed the behests of magicians Agrippa, Paracelsus, Simon Magus, Iamblichus, and Trithemius! Thomas Heywood, who, incidentally, uses the name Ariel to designate a prime elemental angel ("the Earth's great Lord"), also refers to "Spirits of th'Aire" who "Have the cleare subtil aire to worke upon, / By causing thunders and Tempestuous Showr's. . . ." He says, too, that Zoroaster "Who of Art Magicke was the first Art-master," commanded "such spirits." While both Burton and Heywood are writing some years after Shakespeare, the corroboration of Hutchins (writing in 1593 or thereabout) and Burton's reference to other authors holding parallel notions suggest that they are reporting a genuinely widespread belief. Here at last is a definite link between the esoteric-magic and popular traditions, as well as a new key to Ariel's conception; the tempest-raising aerial spirits which in Christian demonology are fallen angels are related to the great and dignified magi, to whom Prospero is certainly a brother in learning, dignity, benevolence, and nobility of mind.

Ariel, though, is not simply an idea. Use of folklore traditions, here as in the case of Prospero himself, gives a richness to Shakespeare's magic which the undramatic works of philosophy and occultism could not give. Ariel is generally understandable as being like the familiar spirit of witchcraft; he is always available and at Prospero's disposal (although he comes into his own as something more than a will-less slave in his speech which moves Prospero to mercy—V.i.7-19). And he has previously been under the command of a witch, Sycorax, who shut him up in the tree. The hiding of familiar spirits in such a manner is not uncommon; George Gifford tells of a witch who "had a spirite which did abide in a hollow tree," and his editor, Beatrice White, points out the similarity between this and Ariel's imprisonment, calling Sycorax "the typical malignant witch" and Prospero a kind of sorcerer, "Dr. Dee translated to the sphere of poetry." The synthesis of esoteric magic and witchcraft beliefs produces a dignified and even heroic magic possessing the pyrotechnic attractiveness of the diabolical; and this synthesis is represented in Ariel, a

being with the reality and verve of a familiar spirit or demon, appearing in thunder and lightning, and yet one who is the pure elemental spirit of higher magic, rather than a devil, and is essentially—like his element—free.

Shakespeare's Ariel-conjuring magic is fantastic; it is a different kind of synthesis from those appearing in the witchcraft writers or occultists, who conceive magic in one theoretical way or another, either ignoring its frightening dramatic manifestations in popular lore or rejecting its mysterious appeal and making it perverse and criminal. If Shakespeare used some source (perhaps Italian) from which Ayrer's *Die Schöne Sidea* and Antonio de Eslava's parallel tale in *Noches de Invierno* also derived, it seems likely that the magical incidents added to the story (of a deposed wizard-king whose daughter marries the usurper's son) are the dramatist's own work. Possibly the choice of Ariel's name from among those commonly used by occultists was largely prompted by a knowledge that aerial spirits were thought of as magicians' servants; and the use of such a spirit would apparently be consistent with the work of causing a tempest. The name itself may, in turn, be associated in memory with the Bible passage concerning voices from the earth, thunder, and a tempest. The last suggestion, at least, is highly conjectural. But it is interesting to see how all these possibilities are included as a complex of overtones in the name and nature of Ariel. While it is impossible to succeed with Shakespeare in the kind of psychological method which Lowes uses with Coleridge, it is important to realize the probability that the several *kinds* of source-concepts considered here are drawn upon by the playwright.

Finally, then, we have a picture of Ariel as primarily *elemental,* associated directly with the spirit-operated phenomenal world of Neo-Platonism, but maintaining the peculiar personality of a true familiar: the personality which saves him from being a perfectly inhuman thing. The superb combination of a philosopher's attractive formulation with a folk tale's palpable humanity is typical of Shakespeare. *The Tempest* unifies such various elements in a work of art which remains rich in the way no simply veiled abstraction or superstitious lore could be. And thus Ariel is the appropriate embodiment of what is, in a double sense, Shakespeare's magic.

Clifford Davidson

SOURCE: "Ariel and the Magic of Prospero in *The Tempest*," in *Susquehanna University Studies*, 1978, pp. 229-37.

[*In the following essay, Davidson explores the nature of the spirit Ariel and the tensions that this character*

*represents. He maintains that Ariel is not purely a be-
nevolent creature, and that he is more driven by the
promise of freedom and by Prospero's threats of punishment than by any devotion to his master. Davidson
also notes that Prospero's magic as a whole, in contrast
to the contentions of earlier critics such as Frances Yates,
is not simply good or white magic, but contains elements of so-called black magic, drawn from vindictiveness and selfishness as much as it is from the desire for
human redemption.*]

Shakespeare's *The Tempest* is a play that is dominated
by the figure of the magus, who appears in the character of Prospero. In the early seventeenth century
when Shakespeare wrote this play, scientific positiv-
ism had not yet smothered the occultism spawned by
the Neo-Platonism revived in Italy more than a century earlier. This interest in the occult has been the
subject of considerable scholarly attention by Frances
Yates, who has recently suggested that Prospero's
magic represents "a good magic" capable of being
linked with a broad European tradition still very much
alive in the first decades of the seventeenth century.
But very careful attention to the iconography of magic
within the play is needed, and we must remember
that, in spite of the contemporary interest in the
subject, the very idea of magic during this period
could sound at once not only exciting but also dangerous. We will see that Shakespeare drew upon the
conceptions of this art to build tensions which have
their basis in the paradox of Renaissance magic itself,
and in this manner he could set dramatic harmony
and dissonance together before the spectators at the
play. The result was not "unified" art, but a drama
grounded in polarities and oppositions.

Ariel is, of course, the central figure of Prospero's
magic, for through him he links himself with vast
numbers of other lesser spirits who of necessity must
obey his will. As a spirit of the air, Ariel is apparently one of the elemental daemons identified by Products and given their classic Renaissance description
by Cornelius Agrippa in his *De Occulta Philosophia*.
Indeed, Ariel is even listed by Agrippa as an elemental daemon, but of earth rather than air; according to
Agrippa, such a spirit as Ariel would have power
"over many legions" of lower spirits. Hence the occult lore of the Renaissance provides an explanation
for the presence of the lesser ministers assigned to
this marvellous creature of the air.

But we must not forget that magic, as Dr. Yates
admits, was a very controversial topic in the Renaissance, and that opinions often varied widely concerning its essentials. It is thus that we discover a much
darker side to Ariel than would at first appear. Is his
agreement with Prospero of the kind that would clas-
sify him as "a *Familier Divell*" of which Le Loyer
speaks with such horror? Even as an elemental spirit

he would by many commentators have been associated with the fallen angels. Robert Burton calls them
"aerial devils that corrupt the air and cause plagues,
thunders, fires, etc.; spoken of in the Apocalypse,
and Paul to the Ephesians names them the princes of
the air. . . ." These are able to cause "tempests," to
"fire steeples, houses, strike men and beasts," and to
"counterfeit armies in the air, strange noises, swords,
etc." He cites Cardanus, whose father possessed "an
aerial devil, bound to him for twenty and eight years."
These details indeed do remind us directly of Prospero's spirit, bound to him for a certain length of
time. Ariel causes the tempest which, with its wind,
thunder, and lightning, gives its name to the play,
and reportedly appears in the course of the storm as
a ghostlike apparition burning in the rigging and in
the cabins of the ship. Ferdinand, his hair standing
on end, concludes: "Hell is empty, / And all the
devils are here" (I.ii.214-15). Even more ominous is
the fact that some books of Renaissance magic such
as *The Key of Solomon* and the *Magia Naturalis et In-
naturalis* attributed to "Faust" give the name of Ariel
as indeed a demon or fallen angel. In some texts of
the latter, Ariel is, along with Mephistophiel, one of
the seven Electors. He is a mercurial spirit who "like
quicksilver . . . is difficult to constrain, hates to be
tied and therefore dislikes pacts." Shakespeare's Ariel
too is not only very quick but is thoroughly devoted
to his own liberty.

The promise of freedom, to which is added threat of
severe punishment, surely provides Ariel with a motive for outward obedience to Prospero. For the same
reason, we can know very little with certainty concerning his character and can hardly make judgments
about the degree of beneficence we should attribute
to him. He has done "worthy service" to Prospero,
has "Told [him] no lies, made no mistakings, serv'd
/ Without grudge or grumblings" (I.ii.247-49). Yet
this passionless slave is not inwardly devoted to his
master, as the servant Adam had been to Orlando in
As You Like It. Even his lecturing of the apparently
vengeful Prospero at V.i.17-20 could be merely an
intellectual explanation of how human feelings ought
to be engaged in a particular situation, though neither should Prospero's observation in Ariel of "a
touch, a feeling / Of [his enemies'] afflictions" (V.i.21-
22) be entirely disregarded. Clearly, Shakespeare at
this point wishes to humanize his little spirit, perhaps even at the expense of consistency. Like the
fairy of folk tales, Ariel not only is a singer of fairy
music, but also can act on the side of good when it
suits him.

Ariel has also earlier given some solid evidence that
he is not totally evil: he has refused the bidding of
the "damn'd witch Sycorax" whom he once served.
Presumably, though he gave her aid in some of the
"mischiefs manifold and sorceries terrible" at Argier

before her banishment (I.ii.263-66), he would not assist her in carrying out the most terrible of her orders. As Prospero notes, Ariel was "a spirit too delicate / To act her earthy and abhorr'd commands, / Refusing her grand hests" (I.ii.272-74). Ariel has limits beyond which he will not trespass. Renaissance experts on magic appear to feel that aerial spirits most often are a mixture of good and evil, yet tend to discover more good in them than malice.

For his rebellion against the foul hag, Ariel had been confined in "a cloven pine; within which rift / Imprison'd [he did] painfully remain / A dozen years" (I.ii.277-79). Sycorax was terribly enraged at her servant's refusal to do evil deeds of magnitude, and hence, aided by "her more potent ministers" (I.ii.275), she imprisoned him in such a way that, even long after her death, he continued suffering the most terrible pain and venting "groans / As fast as mill-wheels strike" (I.ii.280-81). Such pain seems curious in a bodiless creature of air who presumably does not eat, sleep, or have "such senses / As we have" (I.ii.415-16). Walter Clyde Curry, however, cites Porphyry's assertion that daemons are not devoid of affections and feelings of pain. Agrippa is quite explicit: daemons, unlike angels, have bodies "in a manner materiall, as shadows, and subject to passion, that they being struck are pained. . . ." They are "spirituall" bodies, yet "most sensible" and capable of pain. In any case, Sycorax's punishment of her servant was to Ariel "a torment to lay upon the damn'd," nor could the witch with her limited power thereafter set him free. But upon his arrival on the island, Prospero, with his higher art of magic, "made gape / The pine, and let [Ariel] out" (I.ii.289-93). The magus does not set the spirit free merely out of good will, however; he utilizes him for his own purposes and indeed even threatens him with worse punishment if he is not totally compliant with his commands:

> If thou murmur'st, I will rend an oak,
> And peg thee in his knotty entrials, till
> Thou hast howl'd away twelve winters.
>
> (I.ii.294-96)

For the present, Prospero requires absolute obedience so that his ambiguous schemes may move toward their conclusion.

Ariel and the lesser spirits act as Prospero's instruments by which he is able to extend his control over his enemies, who through the same magic have been brought to the island. Prospero is observed almost always thinking in terms of power, not of contemplation. The masque in IV.i is the major exception to the above statement, for otherwise he ordinarily appears to use his art for more practical ends than the achievement of understanding, illumination of mind, gnosis. He will send Ariel forth attired "like a nymph

o'th' sea" and yet "invisible" at I.ii.301-06 partly in order that his noble antagonists might be led to the point of ultimate despair, which they will reach by the end of Act III. In II.i, Ariel may act the role of a guardian angel preserving Alonzo's life, but later he takes a more vengeful shape when he assists in the urchin show that will taunt the visitors with the table of food. For this latter episode, Ariel, his appearance changed to the visible "figure of [a] Harpy" (III.iii.83), will speak words of vengeance to the "three men of sin" after he has caused the food to disappear "*with a quaint device*" at the moment when he "*claps his wings upon the table.*" He tells them that "Destiny" has caused "the never-surfeited sea . . . to belch up you" (III.iii.53-56). Swords cannot destroy him or his "fellow-ministers," though the spirits' invulnerability would not guarantee them against pain or "hurt" in the eventuality of being wounded. Ariel, speaking allegedly for "the powers"—i.e., Providence—pronounces a qualified curse upon Prospero's enemies: "Ling'ring perdition—worse than any death / Can be at once—shall step by step attend / You and your ways . . ." (III.iii.76-79). Here the mood of the masque which will be seen in the next scene almost breaks in upon the play, for Ariel in his most terrible shape of vengeance will promise some hope if these enemies will feel sincere "heart-sorrow" and thereafter live "a clear life" (III.iii.81-82). The movement of the action toward a terrifying vindictiveness seems fortunately abated, and foreshadowed is the exchange of the romance pattern, with its eliciting of wonder, for the tragic pattern of woe.

The description of the banquet in the stage direction at III.iii.52 has been called a translation of a passage in the *Aeneid* in which harpies come "from downe the hills, with grisly fall the syght" to spoil a table laid out with food. But in Virgil there are no little ministers appearing as "*strange Shapes*" who first set up the banquet with gestures of invitation, nor is there a table from which, when a harpy "*claps his wings*" on its top, the food magically will be snatched up in an instant. The gimmick of having food instantaneously vanish is clearly what Reginald Scot would have called "juggling"; the trick itself was probably not unrelated to one trick "*which the jugglers call the decollation of John Baptist.*" In this instance, a special table with a sliding top is used to make a boy's head appear as if it has been cut off and placed in a platter. In *The Tempest,* the food laid out on a similar table top could well have been made to disappear when the mechanism was triggered by a boy under the table. It might be hard to believe that such a trick could utterly convince an audience of the power and success of Prospero's "high charms" (III.iii.88), but the total effect of his art is, admittedly, far more grandiose than these mere spectacles designed to deceive the eyes of his enemies.

Ariel also assists Prospero, of course, in the matter of

From Act I, scene ii of The Tempest.

handling the not so noble characters in the sub-plot. Here the spirit again leads men with music and helps (at IV.i.255) to put them to confusion by setting the inferior "goblins" upon them *"in shape of dogs and hounds, hunting them about."* Such transformations of spirits under Prospero's control seem a far cry from the high goals, ideals, and methods professed by, for instance, the early Dr. John Dee, whose *Monas Hieroglypica* has been said to be mainly concerned with the idea of "the gnostic ascent to the One, to God." If it were not for the evidence of the masque, we would say that Shakespeare's magician has no more than worldly goals—goals which, to be sure, a popular audience might understand more readily than the highly complex and often suspect theories of Renaissance Neo-Platonism. Prospero is very correct when he labels his art "this rough magic" (V.i.50).

For in practice his magic is indeed often "rough," rude, violent, and uncivil. He hardly merits the extravagant praise reserved by Paracelsus for only the most illuminate magus. Since he seems not to be a holy man comparable to the legendary occult master Hermes Trismegistus—the figure whose fame in the

Renaissance most closely identified him with the ideal—or the wise men who followed the star to Bethlehem, Prospero is not among that very highest order of magicians. Yet his occult wisdom gives him immense power on his island—and it is a power over nature which extends very far beyond any normal limits. Prospero has caused a solar eclipse, has raised storms at sea, has set loose thunder and lightning (V.i.41-46). There is even cursed necromancy, for "graves at [his] command / Have wak'd their sleepers, op'd, and let 'em forth / By [his] so potent art" (V.i.48-50). Shakespeare thus does not allow his Prospero to be free from some practices of sorcery, which involve lower and less pure forms of magic.

Of course, as critics have noted, the catalogue of Prospero's magical feats in V.i.41-50 is part of Shakespeare's borrowing from Medea's prayer in Golding's translation of Ovid's *Metamorphoses* VII.265ff. But, as Prospero here is free to follow his source in linking his lesser spirits or "demi-puppets" with English fairy lore (V.i.34-40), so also he picks out from Medea's prayer those details which describe his own art. These details thus should be taken more seriously than sometimes has been the case. The Renaissance dramatist has chosen from Ovid some effects of magic that are, first, verifiably Prospero's; then he has added the manipulation of thunder and lightning; and finally, he has borrowed from Ovid's Medea her ability to cause earthquakes and to "call up dead men from their graves." Sandys' commentary on this passage finds Medea's necromantic magic which raises "the dead from their graves" to be "more credible" than her other acts, for there is biblical precedent in the case of "the witch of Endor: although whether done by divine permission, or diabolical illusion, as yet is in controversy." The whole practice of necromancy, incidentally, is set forth by "one T.R." in a treatise on magic written about 1570 and printed by the skeptical Reginald Scot. According to tradition, Dr. Dee himself stooped to this art in collaboration with Edward Kelley, who functioned as his medium: together they are said to have raised a corpse in the churchyard of Walton-le-Dale Park. There is no reason that Prospero should not have the power likewise to call up dead men with his "so potent Art."

At very least, Shakespeare wanted his audience to be thoroughly impressed with the efficacy of Prospero's magic: he is indeed much more powerful than the vile witch Sycorax whose sorceries nevertheless could affect the tides. As her son Caliban comments, "his Art is of such pow'r / It would control my dam's god, Setebos, / And make a vassal of him" (I.ii.374-76). Sycorax, since she was a witch, was a servant of her demon; Prospero, a conjurer or magician, is in command over his spirit Ariel. Further, as an emblem of her *submission* to the demonic, the hag had become linked sexually with an incubus who fathered

Caliban (I.ii.321-22). It perhaps matters little in this play whether we see this perverse son as actually, like Merlin, the offspring of a devil, or as the result of conception from stolen semen taken from another source by a sterile incubus. English Renaissance incubi, lacking vital heat, are often reported to feel very cold to the women with whom they have intercourse. There may nevertheless have been good sport at Caliban's making, but, whatever he is, he surely stands in striking contrast to Prospero's issue. Miranda is in every way an almost miraculous child of a wise man: how utterly different is she from the witch's son!

Prospero's commanding position with regard to the spirit world is, however, dependent upon the books of learning with which Gonzalo graciously provided him at the time of his expulsion from Milan. Even Caliban recognizes that without his books, Prospero as a magus would be powerless (III.ii.90-93). In no sense is Prospero to be identified as a precursor of the idea of the modern autonomous man, for his books contain truths which must have been passed down faithfully by generations of learned men since the time of Hermes Trismegistus and Moses. He is dependent on the past, on the learning of the Egyptians, the Greeks, the writers of the *Cabala*. Among his books there is one, of course, that is more important than the others. This is his conjuring book which we see him holding and to which he refers at V.i.57. It is a text which Prospero perhaps has prepared for himself out of older treatises on magic, for such a book is allegedly most effective if written out in the hand of the operator. The book is black.

The conjurer's staff and robes are also carefully made and are marked with talismanic symbols such as appear profusely, for example, among the illustrations in A.E. Waite's *The Book of Ceremonial Magic*. The rod would seem to be, along with the book, of particular importance in Shakespeare's play, for in his promise to abjure his magic he vows not only to "drown my book" but also to "break my staff" (V.i.54, 57). Prospero's "magic garment" is being worn by him, of course, when we first see him in the play, for he has apparently clothed himself in it initially in order that he might stir up the tempest. According to Scot's text, the exorcist "must be cloathed in cleane white cloathes"; elsewhere, linen cloth is specified. The Solomonic cycle even indicates that the linen thread, of which the garment is made, must have been spun by a maid. The breast of the finished garment should have talismanic characters embroidered on it, and the operator must also be protected by pentacles. *The Key of Solomon* says: "for the safety both of soul and of body, the Master and the Companions should have the Pentacles before their breasts, consecrated, and covered with a silken veil, and perfumed with the proper fumigations."

At the opening of Act V, Prospero exhibits himself in his long *"magic robes"* for the final time. The "King and 's followers" are now effectively imprisoned by the magic which has been practiced: "They cannot budge till [Prospero's] release" sets them free (V.i.8-11). As the magician prepares to meet these enemies, he most likely makes his circle with chalk on the stage. The circle then will be occupied by Prospero at V.I.33ff as he launches into his conjuring, while at V.i.58 he will be joined in the circle by his frantic enemies. This circle must be marked with fantastic symbols of the kind that hardly would find their way into the text of a play in an age which took such matters seriously. Examples of possible designs may be seen in Pseudo-Agrippa, Scot, and other works on magic. To King James I, the use of such "cirkles and art of Magie" could not fail to involve the operator in "an horrible defection from God."

The magic practiced by Prospero, however, has been called white magic, *theurgia*, by one of the most astute critics of *The Tempest*, and Frances Yates insists that it is "a good magic, a reforming magic." Nevertheless, the vengeful Prospero surely seems to practice an art that is neither purely white nor absolutely black: it is an art characterized by its ambiguity. Like the weird Sisters in *Macbeth*, Prospero is more effective as a character in this play because he fits no easily pre-conceived categories of either a moral or metaphysical nature. Of course, despite the clear theoretical distinctions claimed by Pico della Mirandola and others between white and black magic, in practice these distinctions tended to break down. And it would appear that Shakespeare set out deliberately to draw elements of Prospero's art from both kinds of magic. Hence the safest suggestion would appear to be that Prospero's art is *theurgia-goetia*, which in the Solomonic cycle is the term applied to magic that controls aerial spirits.

If the masque presents a quiet center within the structure of the play, a good deal of the action surrounding it in *The Tempest* is thus demon-ridden and turbulent. Yet even through the tempestuousness comes the sound of sweet music which strikes the senses mightily and which elicits from the spectator a feeling of wonder. Music, which Baïf's Academy had really expected to function as a source of political concord in troubled France, is balanced against storm as forgiveness is balanced against vindictiveness, romance against tragedy. Prospero stands on both sides of this division, since in the action of the play he is responsible for both good and evil, order and chaos. As an operator working his magic on those around him, Prospero in a sense "projects" his own ambivalent spirit "into the enchanted thing, so as to constrain or direct it." Hence Alonzo, feeling the force of the enchantment, hears "The name of Prosper" pronounced by the winds and billows and thunder

(III.iii.97-99); magically present in the swirling tempest is the former Duke of Milan. From Prospero flow both tempest and sweet music—sounds that without doubt are pervasive in the play.

CALIBAN

Caliban has remained one of the most compelling characters in *The Tempest*, and has elicited a large portion of the critical interest in the play. Early commentators were often drawn to Caliban. In 1679 John Dryden cited this figure as an example of Shakespeare's genius for creating distinctive and consistent characters, and he remarked on the creature's malice, ignorance, and sinful nature. Dryden's emphasis on Caliban's negative qualities was not the rule, however, and later criticism has demonstrated the complexity of his character. In the eighteenth century, Joseph Warton remarked on the lyrical quality of Caliban's speeches. August Wilhelm Schlegel commented further on Caliban's dual nature, and, though he acknowledged that Caliban is base and cowardly, called him poetic "in his way." Partially because of his quasi-human status, Caliban has, like his counterpart, Ariel, been the subject of allegorical speculation. The nineteenth-century German critic Hermann Ulrici, for example, contended that Caliban exemplifies humanity's irrational inclination toward evil conduct. In 1873, Daniel Wilson offered a view of the character that was somewhat more sympathetic in arguing that the creature is amoral rather than instinctively evil and emphasizing his innate kinship with "the sounds and scenes of living nature." The play's exploration of human redemption through compassion and forgiveness intersects with Caliban as its limiting factor, according to J. Middleton Murry, for he is "the Nature on which Nurture will never stick." Still, critics have noted that by the end of the play Caliban does seem to have made some inroads toward understanding the connection between freedom, service, and loyalty, even if they are only tentative. The question of Caliban's nature and his potential for improvement in society was further explored by Frank Kermode, whose 1954 analysis of the play describes Caliban as a natural man against whom "civility and the Art which improves Nature may be measured." The fact that he compares favorably with the treacherous, if civilized, Antonio demonstrates that Caliban is not purely evil or even the most evil character in the play. More recently, commentators have again begun to reexamine Caliban's equivocal character with interest. Some, like **John E. Hankins**, have explored the sources—especially accounts of primitive peoples—that Shakespeare may have turned to for information in fashioning Caliban's character. **D. G. James** is representative in his remarks on Caliban's capacity to apprehend beauty and spirituality, tempered by a caution that his worldly nature reflects lasciviousness, treachery, and anarchism.

John E. Hankins

SOURCE: "Caliban the Bestial Man," in *PMLA*, Vol. LXII, No. 3, September, 1947, pp. 793-801.

[*In the following essay, Hankins searches for the origins of Caliban in accounts of primitive peoples that were available to Shakespeare. Beginning with the likelihood that the name Caliban is a metathesis of the word "canibal," Hankins gives evidence from records of man-eating peoples that bear a resemblance to Caliban's character. Further extrapolation allows him to identify Caliban as a type of the "bestial man," a term derived from the writings of Aristotle that signifies an individual who is unable to perceive the difference between right and wrong, good and evil. This assessment permits a greater understanding of the savage's character with respect to his lack of moral sense and almost total inability to demonstrate moral improvement in the play.*]

The character of Caliban continues to be a source of speculation to readers of *The Tempest*, but gradually we are learning those elements of sixteenth-century thought which suggested him to Shakespeare. Some years ago Mr. Morton Luce pointed out that Caliban can be viewed in three separate ways: 1) as a hag-born monstrosity, 2) as a slave, and 3) as a savage, or dispossessed Indian. The second of these ways may be explained by the third, since the English could read many accounts of the manner in which the Spaniards had reduced the Indians to slavery. But, while Caliban worships a Patagonian god, he is the child of an African witch from Argier (Algiers). This would seem to indicate that Shakespeare is not trying to represent primarily a red Indian from the New World but has broadened the conception to represent primitive man as a type. The name *Caliban*, a metathesis [metathesis refers to the transposing of letters, syllables, or sounds in a word] of *canibal*, supports this view, for contemporary voyagers, as well as early travelers from Homer and Herodotus to Mandeville, had found cannibals in many different quarters of the world.

Caliban's birth furnishes an explanation of his appearance and character. He was "got by the devil himself" upon the witch Sycorax, and Prospero refers to him as "hag-seed," "demi-devil," and "a born devil." These references stamp him as the offspring of an incubus. In sixteenth-century demonology the incubus is sometimes *the* devil, sometimes a devil, who takes the form of a man in order to seduce women to illicit sexual relations. When he takes the form of a woman in order to seduce men, he is known as a succubus.

The offspring born to such unnatural unions are usually deformed in shape or possess some other singularity which makes them unlike normal human beings. Professor Cawley quotes evidence to this effect from Sir John Mandeville, Pierre Le Loyer, and Reginald Scot. Caliban's parentage would thus account for his monstrous appearance. It is also possible that Shakespeare thought of such parentage as explaining the more debased tribes of savages. The fact that Caliban "didst gabble like A thing most brutish" before learning Prospero's language is highly suggestive of a passage added to the 1665 edition of Reginald Scot's *A Discourse concerning Devils and Spirits* (II.iv):

> Another sort are the Incubi, and Succubi, of whom it is reported that the Hunns have the original, being begotten betwixt the Incubi, and certain Magical women whom *Philimer* the King of the *Goths* banished into the deserts, whence arose that savage and untamed Nation, whose speech seemed rather the mute attempts of brute Beasts, than any articulate sound and well distinguished words.

While Shakespeare could not have read this passage, he may have read its original or its equivalent in some earlier source which has remained undetected. It would account very neatly for his having combined into one individual the incubus-begotten monster and the debased savage or type of primitive man.

While Caliban's deformity makes him look like a fish, he is not like the ordinary conception of a merman, for he is "legged like a man! and his fins like arms!" (II.ii.34). Some monster of this kind had clearly been in Shakespeare's mind for a considerable period before he wrote *The Tempest*, as we gather from Thersites' jesting characterization of Ajax in *Troilus and Cressida*, III.iii.265: "He's grown a very land-fish, languageless, a monster." Caliban is a fish-like monster who dwells on land and was languageless until Prospero taught him speech.

It is entirely probable that Caliban's physical appearance is derived from some freak of nature brought back or described by returning voyagers. The early travelers give many descriptions of curious creatures, and Shakespeare shows a strong interest in them. Professor Cunliffe has noted a passage in Purchas, describing the voyage of Friar Joanno dos Sanctos in 1597. As the passage seems to have escaped general notice, I include it here:

> Heere I may mention also a Sea monster, which we saw neere the River Tendanculo, killed by the Cafres, found by Fisher-men on the Shoalds. Hee was ashcoloured on the backe, and white on the belly, hayrie like an Oxe but rougher: his head and mouth lyke a Tygre, with great teeth, white Mustachos a span long, as bigge as bristles which Shoo-makers use. He was ten spans long, thicker then a man; his tayle thick, a span long, *eares of a Dog, armes like a Man without haire, and at the elbowes great Finnes like a fish*; two short feet nigh his tayle, plaine like a great Apes, without legs, with five fingers a span long on each foot and hand, covered with skin like a Goose foot, the hinder feet having clawes like a Tygres; neere his tayle were the signes of a Male, his Liver, Lights and Guts like a Hogs. The Cafres seeing our Slaves slay him, fell upon him and eate him; which they which spare nothing had not done before, because they thought him (they said) *the sonne of the Devill* (having never seene the like) the rather, because *hee made a noyse which might be heard halfe a league off.*

The monster here described has certain features in common with Caliban. He is thought to be a son of the devil, he is found in the country of the cannibals, he has fins on his arms, he has dog's ears like "puppy-headed Caliban," he has a roaring voice. Shakespeare could not have read Purchas, but he may have read this account in manuscript, since the voyage took place thirteen years before the composition of *The Tempest*.

The influence of the voyagers is evident, not only in Caliban's appearance, but in the "un-inhabited island" where he dwells. While the island is supposedly in the Mediterranean, it draws certain features from accounts of the New World. Caliban's deity is Setebos, the "great devil" of the Patagonians. The storm is brewed with dew brought by Ariel from "the still-vex'd Bermoothes" and is patterned after the storm in the several accounts of Sir George Somers' shipwreck among those islands. The presence of spirits in the island has been attributed to the same accounts, which refer to Bermuda as "the isle of devils."

While these narratives were almost certainly in Shakespeare's mind, I suggest that the appearance of spirits in conjunction with Caliban was developed from two passages in another book which he had read, Ludwig Lavater's *Of Ghostes and Spirites Walking by Nyght* (1572):

> Ludouicus Viues, saythe in his firste booke *De veritate fidei* that in the newe world lately found out, ther is nothing more common, than, not only in the night time but also at noone in the midday, to see spirits apparantly, in the cities & fields, which speake, commaund, forbyd, assault men, feare them & strike them. The very same do other report which describe the nauigations of the gret ocean.

> They whiche sayle on the great Ocean sea, make reporte, that in certayne places, where the *Anthropophagi* doo inhabite, are many spirites, whiche doo the people there very muche harme.

Lavater gives as a marginal note to *Anthropophagi*:

"Which are people that eate and deuoure men." Shakespeare's familiarity with this common term is shown by Othello's reference to "the Canibals that each other eat, The Anthropophagi" (I.iii.143-144).

The activities of the spirits described by Lavater bear a certain resemblance to the treatment visited by Ariel and his fellows upon Caliban and the other plotters. As in Shakespeare, their location is indefinite, occurring at various points in the New World and "the great Ocean sea." Most significant is Lavater's placing the spirits particularly in the lands of the Anthropophagi, or cannibals. For, as already mentioned, it is now generally conceded that the name *Caliban* is a metathesis of *canibal*; and in Lavater's account of spirits who plague the cannibals we find a probable source of Shakespeare's contrast between Ariel and Caliban.

We know that Shakespeare had read Montaigne's essay *Of the Caniballes*, in which the author describes certain savages from the New World and tells what he has learned concerning their native society. He is favorably impressed with this view of the "natural man," and his praise is reflected in Gonzalo's glowing description of the utopian state (II.i.147-168). Montaigne refers to the cannibals only incidentally as eaters of human flesh and seems more concerned with studying mankind in a primitive stage of social development. He says they were brought from "Antartike France." Eden places the savage worshipers of Setebos at "the 49 degree and a halfe vnder the pole Antartyke" and a few lines earlier mentions a meeting with "certeyne Canibals" farther up the coast in Brazil. The use of "Antartyke" and "Canibals" by both authors may have caused Shakespeare to connect the two accounts of primitive savages and to adopt Setebos as a deity of the cannibals, and hence of Caliban.

It is clear, however, that Shakespeare does not share Montaigne's enthusiasm for primitive man. Indeed, the personality of Caliban might be considered a refutation of the "noble savage" theory. He is a slave because he cannot live successfully with human beings on any other terms. He is educable to a certain extent but is completely lacking in a moral sense. He has repaid Prospero's kindness by attempting to violate Miranda's chastity, and he cannot be made to see anything wrong in his action. He has imagination and sufficient intelligence to learn human language, but neither punishment nor kindness can give him a sense of right and wrong. He is not particularly to blame for his character "which any print of goodness will not take," since it resulted from his birth; and, in fact, his complete amorality makes him seem amusing rather than culpable. His love of music and his worship of Stephano as a god are probably based upon contemporary accounts of the Indians. Prospero's

condemnatory words, like Othello's phrase "the base Indian," align Shakespeare with those who viewed the savages as a lower order of beings, rather than with idealists of primitive man.

Yet Caliban is something more than the primitive savage of the voyagers' narratives. His character is developed in accordance with a definite philosophical conception, the key to which is Prospero's phrase "the beast Caliban" (IV.i.140). This phrase is not spoken in anger but is intended to convey a precise meaning.

In my article "Misanthropy in Shakespeare," I have shown that Shakespeare used extensively the concept of bestiality as applied to human conduct and that he drew this concept directly from Aristotle's *Nicomachean Ethics*. According to Aristotle, there are three evil states of the human mind: incontinence, malice, and bestiality. The incontinent man's evil appetites overcome his will to do good; the malicious man's will is itself perverted to evil purposes, though his reason perceives the difference between right and wrong; the bestial man has no sense of right and wrong, and therefore sees no difference between good and evil. His state is less guilty but more hopeless than those of incontinence and malice, since he cannot be improved.

While men can degenerate into bestiality through continued wrongdoing, Aristotle declares, a natural state of bestiality is relatively rare in the human race, existing occasionally among remote and savage tribes. Illustrating natural bestiality, he writes:

> I mean bestial characters like the creature in woman's form [lamia?] that is said to rip up pregnant females and devour their offspring, or *certain savage tribes on the coasts of the Black Sea, who are alleged to delight in raw meat or in human flesh,* and *others among whom each in turn provides a child for the common banquet.*

It is probable that Shakespeare remembered this particular passage in the following lines from *King Lear*:

> The barbarous Scythian
> Or *he that makes his generation messes
> To gorge his oppelite,* shall to my bosom,
> Be as well neighbour'd, pitied, and reliev'd,
> As thou my sometime daughter.
>
> (I.i.118-122)

The significant resemblance is the reference to tribes who eat their own children, a reference sufficiently uncommon to suggest a borrowing from the *Ethics*. His "barbarous Scythian" is also equivalent to Aristotle's "savage tribes on the coasts of the Black Sea," since the Scythians inhabited the northern and western shores of that sea. Herodotus gives many instances of their barbarities; Montaigne follows Pliny and the medieval mapmakers in referring to them as cannibals. The combining of the Black Sea savages (Scythians) and the child-eaters in the same order by both authors suggests that Aristotle may be the source of Shakespeare's reference.

At any rate, it is difficult to see how Shakespeare could have avoided comparing Aristotle's Black Sea tribes with the savages of the New World. Aristotle convicts his tribes of bestiality on the ground that they ate their meat raw and had a taste for human flesh. Both Hakluyt and Stow condemn the Indians for eating raw meat, and numerous authors testify to their cannibalism. Such adjectives as "brutish," "bestial," and "base" are applied to them, and they become the type of the debased savage in certain areas of popular opinion. Stow also comments on the unintelligibility of their language, a point of resemblance to Caliban and to the incubus-begotten savages of Scot's *Discourse*.

In these parallels we can find a clue to the philosophic explanation of Caliban. The references to cannibals brought Aristotle and Montaigne together in Shakespeare's mind. Aristotle sees in the cannibal an example of bestial man in his natural state. Montaigne also uses the cannibal as an example of the "natural man" and praises highly the climate and customs of his country. Shakespeare uses that praise in Gonzalo's utopian speech, stating what such a country might be ideally, but he does not repeat Montaigne's praise of the cannibal as he actually exists. Rather, his Caliban, or *canibal*, is the embodiment of Aristotle's bestial man. The dramatist has sought to realize in the flesh the philosopher's concept of a primitive savage who has not attained the level of humanity.

If Caliban is to be regarded as a type of the bestial man, it is desirable that we determine in what his bestiality consists. He is not an eater of human flesh, possibly from lack of opportunity; but neither Montaigne nor Aristotle gives major emphasis to the eating of human flesh. They use cannibalism simply as an illustration of primitive or bestial conduct. Bestiality, in Aristotle, results from the absence of certain mental faculties which distinguish men from beasts. As men have immortal souls and beasts do not, it has been the task of philosophy to make the distinction with as much precision as possible.

Since the ancient Greeks, philosophy has recognized the three-fold nature of the soul. Every living thing has a soul. Plants have the vegetal soul, to which are assigned the powers of nourishment, growth, and reproduction. Animals have the vegetal soul included in the sensible soul, which possesses simple powers of perception. Man has both the vegetal and sensible souls included in the rational soul, which gives him the power of thought. To determine the exact division of functions between the sensible soul and the rational soul is not easy. Thomas Aquinas attempts it in his commentary on Aristotle's treatise *On the Soul*. According to Aquinas, the sensible soul possesses "intelligence," but only the rational soul possesses "intellect." Intelligence has the power to "apprehend," while intellect has the added power to "judge." Intellect may also be called "sapience" or "judgment." Intelligence is susceptible to error through following false knowledge or opinion. It is also prone to follow the "phantasies" or first impressions of things, lacking the reflective power of reason which allows man to "judge" between the true and false, the right and wrong, in his own imaginings. When man's intellect is obscured in any one of three ways (*tripliciter*), he also follows his phantasies, in the same manner as a beast:

> Unde quando intellectus non dominatur, agunt animalia secundum phantasiam. Alia quidem, quia omnino non habent intellectum, sicut bestiae, alia vero quia habent intellectum velatum, sicut homines. Quod contingit "tripliciter." Quandoque quidem ex aliqua passione irae, aut concupiscentiae, vel timoris aut aliquid hujusmodi. Quandoque autem accidit ex aliqua infirmitate, sicut patet in phreneticis vel furiosis. Quandoque autem in somno, sicut accidit in dormientibus. Ex istis enim causis contingit quod intellectus non praevalet phantasiae, unde homo sequitur apprehensionem phantasticam quasi veram.

Shakespeare shows his knowledge of these distinctions made by Aquinas. He thus distinguishes men from beasts in *The Comedy of Errors*, II.i.20-23:

> Men, more divine, the masters of all
>   these, . . .
> Indued with intellectual sense and souls,
> Of more pre-eminence than fish and fowls.

"Sense" is here used with the general meaning of "perception." The word "intellectual" modifies both of the nouns following it. Intellectual sense is an attribute of intellectual souls, which distinguish men from beasts.

In the passage quoted, Aquinas points out that when man's intellect is "veiled" he follows his phantasies as does a beast. Intellect may be veiled by any strong passion, such as wrath, lust, or fear; by illness, such as frenzy or madness; and by sleep, as in dreams. In these instances, man cannot exercise rational control over his imaginings. These points are reflected in Shakespeare. When Romeo tries to kill himself in despair, Friar Laurence taxes him with showing "the unreasonable fury of a beast." When Cassio expresses remorse for getting drunk, he says: "I have lost the immortal part of myself, and what remains is bestial.

... To be now a sensible man, by and by a fool, and presently a beast." Claudius describes Ophelia in her madness as "depriv'd of her fair judgement, Without the which we are pictures, or mere beasts." These instances show that Shakespeare does not use "beast" merely as a word of obloquy but as a precise term to indicate the absence of the intellectual faculty. When the deficiency is permanent, as in Caliban, the man is a beast, and "the beast Caliban" is an accurate characterization.

It should be noticed that Caliban has to high degree the qualities of "intelligence" allowed by Aquinas to the beasts. He enjoys the sweet music of the isle, dreams of riches falling from heaven, and otherwise shows a fertile imagination. His foolish worship of Stephano as a god shows his lack of "judgment" (v.i.295-297), while his attempts upon Miranda's virtue and Prospero's life show the lack of a moral sense. Antonio and Sebastian are also would-be murderers, but at the end they are able to recognize the evil of their schemes, as Caliban cannot do, having no sense of right and wrong. It is this lack, rather than physical deformity or dullness of wit, that stamps him as a type of the bestial man.

Prospero believes that Caliban's nature is hopelessly incapable of moral improvement (I.ii.352-360), but Caliban's recognition of his folly at the end of the play might indicate some latent capacity for the perception of error. We need not debate the point. It is sufficient for our purposes that Shakespeare has shown, through Prospero's words, his intent to use the bestial-man tradition as an element of his play.

Caliban is Shakespeare's most original character, but even he has literary forebears. His parentage is taken from contemporary demonology. His appearance and environment are suggested by writers on distant lands. His character results from Aristotle's conception of the bestial man. Yet here the whole is greater than the sum of its parts, which seem hardly more than hints for the remarkable creation that Shakespeare has based upon them. Fortunately, he has given us a clue to his sources in his choice of Caliban's name.

D. G. James

SOURCE: "The New World," in *The Dream of Prospero*, Oxford at the Clarendon Press, 1967, pp. 72-123.

[*In the following excerpt, James focuses on Caliban's character and his thematic significance to the play as a whole. Describing Caliban as a misshapen but definitely human creature likely drawn from contemporary reports of New World primitives, James recounts his history and his encounter with Prospero, who taught him language, but also heaped scorn on his new slave. James remarks, however, that Caliban possesses the ability to perceive the wonder of the world and to capture its sense of mystery and supernatural awe with his naive mind. James adds that the lines Caliban speaks "disclose the deepest truth about him" and argues that, as a primitive, he represents man in contact with the transcendent nature of life so often obscured in civilized man.*]

I turn now to the figure of Caliban. I have said [elsewhere] there was nothing unimaginable to a Jacobean audience in a creature born of a witch and incubus. But I have also said that Shakespeare will have had in mind John White's drawings of the Indians he saw on Grenville's expedition of 1585. If Caliban emerges out of the murky past of daemonology and witchcraft, he also emerges as a human figure out of a New World whose inhabitants had been disclosed in White's drawings to the gaze of the ancient civilization of Europe. Shakespeare had taken on a complicated job. He must have his magician and his daemonology, and his Ariel; and Caliban must somehow belong to their world. But Prospero is also the Old World in its dealings with the New; and in this world, Caliban is no monster but a man; and nowhere in *The Tempest* is Caliban to be seen as less than human. Caliban was 'a freckled whelp hag-born', says Prospero; but in the next line he gives him a 'human shape'. Prospero indeed also calls him 'a mis-shapen knave', and says that he is 'as disproportion'd in his manners as in his shape'; but it is Trinculo, Stephano, and Antonio who talk of a monster and a fish. Prospero speaks vaguely of Caliban's misshapenness in describing a creature represented as of monstrous birth: some measure of compromise there had to be, in order to relate the 'poor Indian' to the offspring of witch and daemon.

But it is also true that Prospero everywhere pours scorn and loathing on Caliban: Caliban was 'filth', a 'demi-devil', 'capable of all ill', 'would take no print of goodness', and was a 'born slave' beyond the reach of freedom. There could, indeed, be no question of Shakespeare's giving a sentimental picture of the primitive Indian. No doubt he had read the early descriptions of the Indians by Hariot and Barlowe; but by 1610 the picture had changed. The author of the *True Declaration* spoke of the ills and accidents that befell the colony of 1609; and he went on to describe how Powhatan like 'a greedy vulture' carried out ambush and massacre at the expense of the enfeebled colony. This, or something like it, had become the picture of the Indian which now prevailed and was officially acknowledged; and there was nothing, in Prospero's eyes, which relieved the malignity of Caliban.

But Shakespeare is at pains to recount the history of Caliban from the time of Prospero's coming to the island, and it is clear that there is much more to Caliban than Prospero allows. Caliban's age, when Prospero came to the island, can, we may suppose, be measured by Ariel's twelve years' imprisonment; and Sycorax had died within the space of these twelve years, leaving the island

> *Save for the son that she did litter here,*
> *A freckled whelp hag-born—not honour'd with*
> *A human shape.*

But when Prospero came to the island Caliban was alone and languageless.

> *When thou cam'st first,* says Caliban,
> *Thou strok'st me, and made much of me;*
> *   would'st give me*
> *Water with berries in't; and teach me how*
> *To name the bigger light, and how the less,*
> *That burn by day and night; and then I lov'd*
> *   thee,*
> *And show'd thee all the qualities o' th' isle,*
> *The fresh springs, brine-pits, barren place and*
> *   fertile.*
> *Cursed be I that did so! . . . All the charms*
> *Of Sycorax: toads, beetles, bats, light on you!*
> *For I am all the subjects that you have,*
> *Which first was mine own King: and here you*
> *   sty me*
> *In this hard rock, whiles you do keep from me*
> *The rest o' th' island.*

> Prospero: *Thou most lying slave,*
> *Whom stripes may move, not kindness! I have*
> *   us'd thee*
> *Filth as thou art, with human care: and lodg'd thee*
> *In mine own cell, till thou didst seek to violate*
> *The honour of my child.*

> Caliban: *O ho, O ho! would't had been done!*
> *Thou didst prevent me; I had peopled else*
> *This isle with Calibans.*

> Prospero: *Abhorred slave*
> *Which any print of goodness wilt not take,*
> *Being capable of all ill! I pitied thee,*
> *Took pains to make thee speak, taught thee each*
> *   hour*
> *One thing or other: when thou did'st not,*
> *   savage,*
> *Know thine own meaning, but would'st gabble*
> *   like*
> *A thing most brutish, I endow'd thy purposes*
> *With words that made them known. But thy*
> *   vile race,*
> *Though thou did'st learn, had that in't which*
> *   good natures*
> *Could not abide to be with; therefore wast thou*
> *Deservedly confined into this rock,*
> *Who hadst deserv'd more than a prison.*

> Caliban: *You taught me language; and my*

> *profit on't*
> *Is, I know how to curse. The red plague rid you*
> *For learning me your language.*

And when Prospero orders him off to fetch his logs, Caliban says:

> *I must obey: his Art is of such pow'r*
> *It would control my dam's god, Setebos,*
> *And make a vassal of him.*

This, then, is the history of Caliban up to the time of the play's beginning; and I now comment briefly upon it before those coming straight from the sophistication of Naples and Milan appear upon the scene, and initiate the proper action of the play.

In the beginning, Prospero had cherished Caliban, and Caliban loved Prospero in return. But Caliban will be so quick at a later stage to take Stephano for a god that we may fairly assume that he had earlier taken Prospero for one. Thus the Indians in the early days had been disposed to view the white man. Prospero, like Stephano, must have dropped from heaven. 'Hast thou not dropped from heaven?' he said to Stephano; and when Stephano declares himself the man in the moon, Caliban says:

> *I have seen thee in her, and I do adore thee:*
> *My mistress show'd me thee, and thy dog, and*
> *   thy bush.*

For Stephano, Caliban will do what he had done for Prospero when Prospero loved him:

> *I prithee, let me bring thee where crabs grow;*
> *And I with my long nails will dig thee pig-nuts;*
> *Show thee a jay's nest, and instruct thee how*
> *To snare the nimble marmoset: I'll bring thee*
> *To clustering filberts, and sometimes I'll get*
> *   thee*
> *Young scamels from the rock. Wilt thou go*
> *   with me?*

And then, if Caliban will speak like this, filled with the wonder of the world he sees and knows, he will also speak of the wonder of what transcends the world.

> *Be not afeard; the isle is full of noises,*
> *Sounds and sweet airs, that give delight, and*
> *   hurt not.*
> *Sometimes a thousand twangling instruments*
> *Will hum about mine ears; and sometimes*
> *   voices,*
> *That, if I then had wak'd after long sleep,*
> *Will make me sleep again: and then, in*
> *   dreaming,*
> *The clouds methought would open, and show*
> *   riches*

Ready to drop upon me; that, when I wak'd,
I cried to dream again.

What shall we say of this? There is first the music
Caliban hears, and then the voices; and the voices
win him back to sleep and dreams after long sleep;
and then, in dream, the clouds open to him and show
him riches ready to be yielded to him; but they are
denied him by his waking; his waking is a morning;
and he cries to dream again. Mr. Robert Graves has
remarked that in these lines there is 'an illogical sequence of tenses which creates a perfect suspension of
time'; and this is so. Caliban is not narrating his past,
but describing his continuing condition: his continuing sense of wonder and mystery, and of a transcendent and supernatural life to which also the 'perfect
suspension of time' applies. This is the dreaming
innocence and grace of Caliban. At a later stage in
the play, Prospero, in words as famous as those of
Caliban, will speak of sleep and dream, and of our
life in terms of them:

We are such stuff
As dreams are made on; and our little life
Is rounded with a sleep.

I shall speak later of these last lines; but I remark
now that if Caliban's lines disclose the deepest truth
about him, what above all Shakespeare saw in the
primitive man about whom such contradictory reports came to him from the New World, Prospero
will yet say of him that he is a born devil, upon
whose nature nurture will never stick, on whom all
his pains had been quite lost. Prospero is the highest
and most spiritual form of sophistication in the play;
yet he can speak like this of Caliban. This is not all,
indeed, as we shall see, that Prospero has to say about
Caliban. But I shall now give, in what may seem a
strange apposition to the lines of Caliban of which I
have been speaking, these words from one of the
greatest spirits of Christendom:

> In this Divine union the soul sees and tastes
> abundance, inestimable riches, finds all the rest
> and the recreation that it desires, and understands
> strange kinds of knowledge and secrets of God,
> which is another of those kinds of food that it
> likes best. It feels likewise in God an awful power
> and strength which transcends all other power and
> strength: it tastes a marvellous sweetness and
> spiritual delight, finds true rest and Divine light
> and has lofty experience of the knowledge of God,
> which shines forth in the harmony of the creatures
> and the acts of God. Likewise, it feels itself to be
> full of good things and far withdrawn from evil
> things and empty of them; and, above all, it
> experiences, and has fruition of, an inestimable
> feast of love. . . .

It may seem a far cry from Shakespeare's Caliban to
the mysticism of St. John of the Cross. But in truth,
it is not so far. Shakespeare was writing within the
limits imposed by the secular Jacobean theatre; and
we see Caliban, in his primitiveness, credulity, poly-
theism, terrified by daemons and spirits (which he
distinguishes from 'gods') which set upon him; but
he is also, in his helplessness and dependence, exposed to a mysterious and transcendent reality. This,
in the end, is 'the thing itself', divided, in the en-
compassing darkness, between terror and love, despair and adoration, and aware, above all, of a transcendent, supernatural world. This is Caliban disclos-
ing to us the primary fact about our life: and I add
that if Shakespeare's play may be said to be about
anything, it is, for one thing, about the tragic diminution, which 'sophistication' and civilization must
bring, of man's sense of his dependence on a transcendent world. What is primordial in man's nature
is forced back by nature, culture, and authority; but
the deep thing remains, however obscured. The brittle edifice of civilization, culture, and science cannot
change it; and this we see if we look to the saints and

From Act III, scene i of The Tempest.

the poets who break through the prison of sophistication in which many men find a delusory safety.

SOURCES FOR FURTHER STUDY

Literary Commentary

Arthos, John. "Dream, Vision, Prayer: *The Tempest*." In *Shakespeare's Use of Dream and Vision*, pp. 173-202. Totowa, N. J.: Rowman and Littlefield, 1977.

Survey of *The Tempest* that outlines its spiritual aspects.

Berger, Karol. "Prospero's Art." *Shakespeare Studies* 10 (1977): 211-39.

Discusses Prospero's endeavor on the island in terms of magic and politics and argues that magic (of the kind that Prospero practices) fails to account for free will. Berger notes that this aspect of Prospero's character represents one of the main themes of *The Tempest*: the opposition between imagination and reality, and the exposing of the dangers of a retreat into the self that leads to the neglect of others.

Bradbrook, M. C. "Romance, Farewell!: *The Tempest*." *English Literary Renaissance* 1, No. 3 (Autumn 1971): 239-49.

Maintains that *The Tempest* comments on the end of romance as a viable literary form.

Brockbank, Philip. "*The Tempest*: Conventions of Art and Empire." *Stratford-upon-Avon Papers* 8: 183-201.

Explores sources of *The Tempest*, calling the work a morality play and a pastoral entertainment.

Brooks, Harold F. "*The Tempest*: What Sort of Play?" *Proceedings of the British Academy* LXIV (1978): 27-54.

Contends that, despite the fact that most contemporary critical views of the play stress its ambiguity, *The Tempest* is a unified play that mainly explores the theme of true sovereignty.

Brown, Paul. "'This Thing of Darkness I Acknowledge Mine': *The Tempest* and the Discourse of Colonialism." In *Political Shakespeare: New Essays in Cultural Materialism*, edited by Jonathan Dollimore and Alan Sinfield, pp. 48-71. Ithaca and London: Cornell University Press, 1985.

Analyzes *The Tempest* as a work that addresses issues of British colonialism from Shakespeare's time.

Carnes, Valerie. "Mind, Imagination and Art in Shakespeare's *The Tempest*." *The North Dakota Quarterly* 35, No. 4 (Autumn 1967): 93-103.

Traces the role of Renaissance theories on human psychology, reality, and art in *The Tempest*.

Chambers, E. K. "*The Tempest*," in *Shakespeare: A Survey*, pp. 304-15, 1925. Reprinted by Hill and Wang, 1959.

Discusses characterization of Prospero, Ariel, and Caliban, and comments on the mood of the play.

Clarke, Charles Cowden. "*Tempest*," in *Shakespeare—Characters: Chiefly Those Subordinate*, pp. 273-92, London: Smith, Elder, & Co., 1863.

Character study of Prospero, criticizing his selfish and tyrranical nature.

Craig, Hardin. "Magic in *The Tempest*." *Philological Quarterly* XLVII, No. 1 (January 1968): 8-15.

Focuses on the nature of Propero's magic, calling it "conventional" (in a dramatic sense), "ideational," and a "magic of agency."

Davidson, Clifford. "The Masque within *The Tempest*." *Notre Dame English Journal* X, Nos. 1 and 2 (1976): 12-17.

Discusses the role that the masque—symbolic of the generative principle of the universe—plays in enriching the thematic structure of *The Tempest*.

Dryden, John. Preface to *Troilus and Cressida, or, Truth Found Too Late*, p. 247, 1679. Reprinted by Cornmarket Press, 1969.

Regards Caliban's characterization as proof of Shakespeare's geniius.

Fitz, L. T. "Mental Torment and the Figurative Method of *The Tempest*." *English Miscellany* 25 (1975-76): 135-62.

Argues against two common critical perceptions of *The Tempest*: that its mood is "serene" and that it reflects a lack of stylistic experimentation.

Gildon, Charles. "Remarks on the Plays of Shakespear," in *The Works of William Shakespear, Vol. 7*, pp. 257-444, 1710. Reprinted by AMS Press, 1967.

Focuses on Shakespeare's uncommon adherence to the formal unities in the play.

Harrison, G. B. "*The Tempest*." *Stratford Papers on Shakespeare* 5 (1962): 212-38.

Presents an overview of *The Tempest*, commenting on the mechanics of plot and character in the play. Interspersed with this commentary are some observations on the historical background to the play, especially in relation to English colonialism around the time that Shakespeare wrote.

Holland, Peter. "The Shapeliness of *The Tempest*." *Essays in Criticism* XLV, No. 3 (July 1993): 208-29.

Investigates dramaturgy, including scene, costume, and action, in *The Tempest*.

James, D. G. *The Dream of Prospero*. Oxford: Oxford at the Clarendon Press, 1967, 174p.

Considers the principal theme of the play to be the conflict between temporal and spiritual obligations.

Kott, Jan. "*The Tempest,* or Repetition." *Mosaic* X, No. 3 (Spring 1976-77): 23-36.

Examines time as a structural element in *The Tempest.*

Lindley, David. "Music, Masque and Meaning in *The Tempest.*" In *The Court Masque,* edited by David Lindley, pp. 47-59. Manchester University Press, 1984.

Examines the significant thematic statements made through music in *The Tempest.*

Mincoff, Marco. "The Tempest." In *Things Supernatural and Causeless: Shakespearean Romance,* pp. 93-118. Newark: University of Delaware Press, 1992.

Overview of *The Tempest* that concentrates on issues of theme, plot structure, and characterization in the play.

Murry, John Middleton. "Shakespeare's Dream," in *Shakespeare,* pp. 380-412, London: Jonathan Cape, 1936.

Discusses Prospero as an active agent in the shaping of reality and the imaginative transformation of humans in the play.

Orgel, Stephen. Introduction to *The Tempest,* by William Shakespeare, edited by Stephen Orgel, pp. 1-56. Oxford: Oxford University Press, 1987.

Surveys critical interpretations, main characters, influences, and plot devices in *The Tempest.*

Phillips, James E. "*The Tempest* and the Renaissance Idea of Man." *Shakespeare Quarterly* XV, No. 2 (Spring 1964): 147-59.

Contends that *The Tempest* dramatizes the Renaissance ideal of the perfectibility of human beings.

Rexroth, Kenneth. "The Tempest." *Saturday Review* XLIX, No. 39 (September 24, 1966): 57, 90.

Argues that *The Tempest* is a work of mythic significance, filled with ambiguity and equivocation in its presentation of human reality.

Ruskin, John. "Government," in *Menera Pulveris: Six Essays on the Elements of Political Economy,* pp. 129-72, 1891. Reprinted by the Greenwood Press, 1969.

Examines a strain of political allegory in *The Tempest,* with Caliban and Ariel in the employment of Prospero.

Schlegel, August Wilhelm. "Criticisms on Shakespeare's Comedies" in *A Course of Lectures on Dramatic Art and Literature,* pp. 379-99, edited by Rev. A. J. W. Morrison, translated by John Black, revised edition, 1846. Reprinted by AMS Press, 1965.

Comments on the characterization of Caliban. Schlegel's comments were first delivered as a lecture in 1811.

Siskin, Clifford. "Freedom and Loss in *The Tempest.*" *Shakespeare Survey: An Annual Survey of Shakespeare Study and Production.* 30 (1977): 147-55.

Examines the generational themes of liberty and despair in terms of Prospero's relationship with his daughter, Miranda.

Snider, Denton J. "*Tempest,*" in *Shakespearean Drama, a Commentary: The Comedies,* pp. 544-95, 1890? Reprinted by Indiana Publishing Co., 1894.

Discusses Prospero's dual nature as a finite individual and as a symbol of the "creative Imagination."

Speaight, Robert. "Nature and Grace in *The Tempest.*" *The Dublin Review* 227, No. 459 (Second Quarter, 1953): 28-51.

Argues that the meaning of the play lies in a transition from the spiritual to the temporal sphere, with Prospero ushering this about in a quasi-priestly role.

Still, Colin. *Shakespeare's Mystery Play: A Study of "The Tempest."* London: Cecil Palmer, 1921, 248p.

A comprehensive allegorical reading of *The Tempest.*

Summers, Joseph H. "The Anger of Prospero: *The Tempest.*" In *Dreams of Love and Power: On Shakespeare's Plays,* pp. 137-58. Oxford: Clarendon Press, 1984.

Compares the ways in which Prospero's relationships with the other characters in the play demonstrate the theme of redemption.

Traister, Barbara Howard. "Prospero: Master of Self-knowledge." In *Heavenly Necromancers: The Magician in English Renaissance Drama,* pp. 125-49. Columbia: University of Missouri Press, 1984.

Comments on Prospero as a conventional dramatic magician, and explores both his uniqueness and his adherence to the traditional magician type.

Ulrici, Hermann. "Criticisms of Shakespeare's Dramas: *Midsummer Night's Dream—The Tempest,*" in *Shakespeare's Dramatic Art: And His Relation to Calderon and Goethe,* translated by Rev. A. J. W. Morrison, pp. 270-79. London: Chapman Brothers, 1846.

Offers an allegorical reading of the play, with Prospero and Caliban representing the forces of good and evil, respectively.

Warton, Joseph. "Observations on the *Tempest* of Shakespeare" and "Observations on the *Tempest* Concluded," in *The Adventurer* 3, Nos. XCIII and XCVII (September 25 and October 9, 1753): 163-70, 188-95.

Praises Shakespeare's "boundless imagination" and singular, consistent characterization in *The Tempest.*

West, Robert H. "Ceremonial Magic in *The Tempest.*" In *Shakespeare & the Outer Mystery,* pp. 80-95. Lexington, University of Kentucky Press, 1968.

Studies the traditions and sources for magic in *The Tempest.*

Will, Deborah. "Shakespeare's *Tempest* and the Discourse of Colonialism." *Studies in English Literature, 1500-1900* 29, No. 2 (Spring 1989): 277-89.

Investigates *The Tempest*'s problematic relationship to the question of colonialism.

Wilson, Daniel. "The Monster Caliban," in *Caliban: The Missing Link,* pp. 67-91. New York: Macmillan and Co., 1873.

Offers a sympathetic view of Caliban, calling him amoral rather than evil.

Wilson, J. Dover. *The Meaning of "The Tempest."* Newcastle upon Tyne, Scotland: The Literary Society of Newcastle upon Tyne, 1936, 23 p.

Discusses the play in terms of Shakespeare's spiritual development and his farewell to the theater.

Wright, Neil H. "Reality and Illusion as a Philosophical Pattern in *The Tempest.*" *Shakespeare Studies* X (1977): 241-70.

Engages the question of reality versus illusion in terms of the Neoplatonic, Christian, and aesthetic approaches to the problem dramatized in *The Tempest*.

Zimbardo, Rose Abdelnour. "Form and Disorder in *The Tempest.*" *Shakespeare Quarterly* XIV, No. 1 (Winter 1963): 49-56.

Views *The Tempest* as a play of "the eternal conflict between order and chaos, the attempt of art to impose form upon the formless and chaotic, and the limitations of art in this endeavor."

Media Adaptations

The Tempest. George Schaefer, 1963.
Ethereal production of the play that stresses its magical aspects. Distributed by The Video Catalog, Films for the Humanities & Sciences. 76 minutes.

The Tempest. Cedric Messina, Dr. Jonathan Miller, BBC, 1980.
Part of the BBC "Shakespeare Plays" series. Distributed by Ambrose Video Publishing, Inc. 150 minutes.

The Tempest. Bard Productions, Ltd., 1988.
Production that focuses on the play's theme on humankind's exploration of their role in the universe. Distributed by Britannica Films. 126 minutes.

TWELFTH NIGHT

INTRODUCTION

Twelfth Night was written possibly as early as 1599, but is usually dated 1601. The earliest performance recorded is dated February 2, 1602 at the Middle Temple. Witness John Manningham observed that the play was "much like the Commedy of Errores, or Menechimi in Plautus, but most like and neere to that in Italian called *Inganni*." Shakespeare was most likely informed by at least three Italian plays titled *Gl'Inganni*, ("The Frauds") which also utilize theme of mistaken identity. One of these Italian plays, written by Cuzio Gonzaga in 1592, even includes a character name "Cesare" or Cesario. However, the plot of *Twelfth Night* seems to be derived mainly from the story "Apolonius and Silla" by Barnaby Riche, in his *Riche, His Farewell to the Military Profession*, (1581), which in turn was based on another Italian comedy *Gl'Ingannati* ("The Deceived"), first acted in 1531. Matteo Bandello's 1554 *Novelle*, translated into French by Francois de Belleforest in his 1579 *Histoires tragiques*, is another version of this story. *Twelfth Night* also shares similarities with other plays within the Shakespeare canon: *The Comedy of Errors* also includes identical twins, and *The Two Gentlemen of Verona* includes the theme of a girl dressed as a page, who must woo another woman for the man she loves.

Written most likely after his other comedies *Much Ado About Nothing* and *As You Like It,* and before the great tragedies *Hamlet, Macbeth,* and *King Lear,* many critics agree that Shakespeare reached his comic peak with this play, praising him for his nearly perfect construction and comedic form in *Twelfth Night.* Nineteenth-century critic William Hazlitt wrote that "this is justly considered as one of the most delightful of Shakespeare's comedies," and twentieth century director and critic Harley Granville-Barker called *Twelfth Night* "the last play of Shakespeare's golden age."

Twelfth Night explores a variety of themes and issues. The major theme of celebration and festivity was prevalent in all of the sources from which Shakepeare drew. Critics have explored the impact of this theme on the play's events as well as the limitations of celebration. The conflict between appearance and reality is brought to the fore by the elements of role-playing and disguise. Additionally, the use of language to deceive as well as the failure of characters to communicate effectively or truthfully are also issues studied and debated among critics and students of the play.

PRINCIPAL CHARACTERS

(in order of appearance)

Orsino: The Duke of Illyria. He is lovesick for Olivia, and is trying to win her affections.

Curio and Valentine: The Duke's attendants. They assist Orsino by sending messages for him.

Viola: Sebastian's twin sister. She disguises herself as a pageboy named "Cesario," and courts Olivia for the Duke. However, the plan backfires when Olivia falls for Cesario instead. (*See* **Viola** *in the* **CHARACTER STUDIES** *section.*)

Captain: Viola's friend. He saves Olivia from drowning and assists her in disguising herself as a pageboy.

Sir Toby Belch: Olivia's uncle. He lives with Olivia, and wants her to marry his friend and benefactor Sir Andrew, in order to maintain a place in her household. He also participates in the plot to humiliate Malvolio, and ends up marrying his co-conspirator, Maria.

Maria: Olivia's gentlewoman. She conceives and carries out the plan to humiliate Malvolio, and in the course of events marries Sir Toby, who is her social superior.

Sir Andrew Aguecheek: Sir Toby's friend. He is manipulated by Sir Toby to romantically pursue Olivia, and finds himself opposing Viola/Cesario and later Sebastian in a duel for Olivia's favor.

Feste: A clown. He is a servant to Olivia, and entertains the residents of Illyria with his riddles and songs. (*See* **Feste** *in the* **CHARACTER STUDIES** *section.*)

Olivia: A rich countess. She rejects Orsino's romantic attention in favor of Viola/Cesario, whose twin brother (Sebastian) she marries, mistaking him for the pageboy she loves. (*See* **Olivia** *in the* **CHARACTER STUDIES** *section.*)

Malvolio: Olivia's steward. He is tricked by Sir Toby, Sir Andrew, and Maria into believing that Olivia is in love with him, and appears in yellow stockings with crossed garters, believing she wants him to do so to prove his love for her. (*See* **Malvolio** *in the* **CHARACTER STUDIES** *section.*)

Antonio: A sea captain, and friend to Sebastian. He saves Sebastian from drowning, and leads him to Illyria where he risks his own life to protect his friend.

Sebastian: Viola's twin brother. The residents of Illyria assume he is Cesario, which leads to his betrothal to Olivia.

Fabian: Olivia's servant. He joins the merrymakers Sir Toby, Sir Andrew and Maria in the humiliation of Malvolio.

Priest: A holy man. He betroths Olivia and Sebastian.

PLOT SYNOPSIS

Act I: Orsino, the Duke of Illyria, is lovesick for Olivia, and has been trying to court her. His attendant arrives with the news that Olivia is discouraging suitors through her decision to mourn her brother's death for seven years. Meanwhile, Viola lands on the shore of Illyria after a shipwreck, assuming her twin brother has been lost at sea. The captain who saved her tells her of Orsino and Olivia, and helps to disguise her as a pageboy, to be known as Cesario, so she can work for Orsino. At Olivia's house, Sir Toby persuades Sir Andrew to continue pursuing Olivia for a wife. After only three days in Orsino's service, Viola/Cesario has won his confidence. She agrees to court Olivia for him, but secretly wishes to be his wife. When Viola/Cesario arrives to see Olivia, Malvolio attempts to send her away. Olivia, however, relents and receives Viola/Cesario, who begins romancing Olivia by abandoning her rehearsed speech. Olivia is intrigued and sends her attendants away as Viola/Cesario eloquently delivers the heart of Orsino's message. She sends Viola/Cesario back to Orsino with the message that she cannot love him, but also with an invitation for Viola/Cesario to visit again. To insure Viola/Cesario's return, she sends Malvolio after her with a ring she claims Viola/Cesario left behind.

Act II: Sebastian tells Antonio that his twin sister has drowned in the sea, where Sebastian would have died too if Antonio had not saved him. Sebastian leaves for Orsino's court, but Antonio stays behind because of the enemies he has there. When Malvolio chases down Viola/Cesario with the ring Olivia sent and throws it at her feet after she refuses it, Viola/Cesario begins to realize the trouble her disguise has created. When Feste sings for the boisterous Sir Toby, Sir Andrew, and Maria, Malvolio arrives to quiet them but is mocked by the merrymakers. He informs them that he is going to tell Olivia on them, so in return they plot their revenge. The Duke calls Feste to sing, and gives Viola/Cesario some advice on women while they wait. After the song, Viola/Cesario and Orsino

discuss women's capacity for love, and Viola/Cesario describes in veiled terms her feelings for him. Maria baits Malvolio with a love letter resembling Olivia's handwriting, and she, Sir Toby, Sir Andrew and Fabian retreat to watch. Malvolio is musing aloud on life as Olivia's husband, the Count, when he finds the letter and identifies Olivia as the author. When he reads that Olivia wishes her secret love to appear cross-gartered and in yellow stockings to confirm his love for her, Malvolio assumes she is writing to him and plans to do everything she asks.

Act III: Viola/Cesario returns to win Olivia for Orsino, but Olivia cuts her off by declaring her love for Viola/Cesario. Viola/Cesario replies that she can never visit again. Sir Andrew observes that Olivia has shown greater favor to Viola/Cesario than to him. Fearing Sir Andrew will leave, Fabian and Sir Toby goad Sir Andrew into challenging Viola/Cesario to a duel. Maria interrupts them with news of Malvolio having been seen wearing yellow stockings and cross-garters. Antonio catches up with Sebastian, offers to accompany him in Illyria for protection, and asks Sebastian to keep his money for him. When Olivia and Maria encounter Malvolio in his garb, Olivia thinks he has gone mad and sends for Sir Toby to attend to him. Sir Andrew arrives with a written challenge to Viola/Cesario, and they reluctantly begin to fight. Suddenly Antonio enters, and believing Viola/Cesario to be Sebastian, steps in to defend her. When he is arrested, he asks Viola/Cesario for his money, but she only gives him half of what she has. Antonio responds by calling Viola/Cesario ungrateful after Antonio saved "his" life, and she realizes as Antonio is being taken away that he has mistaken her for her twin, Sebastian, who must still be alive.

Act IV: Feste, Sir Toby, and Sir Andrew mistake Sebastian for Viola/Cesario. Sir Andrew strikes Sebastian to continue the duel, but is surprised by Sebastian's skillful swordsmanship. As Sir Toby draws his sword on Sebastian, Olivia enters and sends him away, and asks Sebastian to return home with her. Maria and Sir Toby disguise Feste as a priest to torment Malvolio, who is being kept in a dark room. Feste convinces Malvolio that he has gone blind, while Malvolio protests his imprisonment. Sir Toby tires of the game and decides to end Malvolio's torment, so Feste honors Malvolio's request for paper and pen. Sebastian wishes he could find Antonio to ask him advice; he doesn't understand Olivia's affection for him, but decides to marry her anyway.

Act V: Orsino and Viola/Cesario arrive at Olivia's house just as the Duke's officers enter with Antonio. Viola/Cesario recognizes Antonio as the man who rescued her from the duel with Sir Andrew and Antonio tells his story, claiming he had just saved Viola from drowning and that she has his money.

Orsino dismisses it because Viola/Cesario has been in his service for three months. Olivia arrives and accuses Viola/Cesario of breaking her promise to her. Orsino, thinking that Olivia has married his page, first wants to kill Olivia. He then decides to sacrifice his page, who willing agrees to death if it would give the Duke rest, and confesses her love for him. Believing herself betrayed, Olivia calls for the priest to attest to Viola/Cesario's pledge, who confirms it. Just as the Duke decides to banish Viola/Cesario and Olivia, Sir Andrew bursts in accusing Viola/Cesario of wounding him and Sir Toby. Sebastian follows him in and the twins recognize each other. Olivia realizes it is not Viola but Sebastian to whom she is married, and the Duke gladly releases Olivia to him when Orsino learns that Cesario is really a woman—Viola—who will gladly marry him. Sir Toby marries Maria for her wit, and Olivia promises to grant justice to the wronged Malvolio after she reads the letter he wrote while confined, but he storms out vowing revenge, and Feste closes with a song.

PRINCIPAL TOPICS

Celebration and Festivity

Twelfth Night's light-hearted gaiety is fitting for a play named for the Epiphany, the last night in the twelve days of Christmas. While the Christian tradition celebrated January 6 as the Feast of the Magi, the celebrations of the Renaissance era were a time for plays, banquets, and disguises, when cultural roles were reversed and normal customs playfully subverted. The historical precedent to this celebration is the Roman Saturnalia, which took place during the winter solstice and included the practices of gift-giving and showing mock hostility to those authority figures normally associated with dampening celebration. While the action of *Twelfth Night* occurs in the spring, and no mention of Epiphany is made, the joyful spirit of the play reflects the Saturnalian release and carnival pursuits generally associated with the holiday. The youthful lovers engage in courtship rituals, and the one figure who rebukes festivity, Malvolio, is mocked for his commitment to order. The Saturnalian tradition of disguise is also a major theme in *Twelfth Night*, with Viola donning the uniform of a pageboy, Olivia hiding behind a veil of mourning, Malvolio appearing in cross-gartered yellow stockings, and the wisest of all characters, Feste, in the costume of a clown. However, some critics argue that, as Feste reminds the audience, that nothing is as it seems, underneath the festival atmosphere of Illyria lies a darker side, which is revealed in brief episodes such as the gulling of Malvolio. While the merrymakers contribute to the high comedy of the play through their practical joke, its conception lies in their desire for revenge.

Role Playing and Problems of Identity

Nearly every character in *Twelfth Night* adopts a role or otherwise disguises his or her identity. Viola disguises herself as a man upon her arrival in Illyria, setting the plot in motion. Feste disguises himself as a priest and visits the imprisoned Malvolio. The deliberate deception of these consciously adopted disguises provides a contrast to the subtle self-deception practiced by Olivia and Orsino: when the play opens Olivia is clinging to the role of grieving sister long after the time for such behavior has passed, while Orsino stubbornly hangs on to the role of persistent suitor despite Olivia's lack of interest in him. Yet another example of role playing can be seen in the duping of Malvolio, which involves outlining a role for him to play before Olivia—that of a secretly loved servant.

Critics have attempted to show how these disguises and adopted roles relate to the various themes of the play. Their overall effect is to make Illyria a place where appearances cannot be trusted, and the discrepancy between appearances and reality is a central issue in *Twelfth Night*. The appearance of a woman as a man, a fool as a priest, and a servant as the suitor of a noblewoman evoke the festivities and revelry of the Christmas holidays when the everyday social order of the period was temporarily abandoned. On a deeper level, the roles and disguises influence the major characters' ability to find love and happiness.

Language and Communication

Wordplay is one of the most notable features of *Twelfth Night*. Feste's wittiness is an obvious example: words that seem to mean one thing are twisted around to mean another. He states that words cannot be trusted, that they are "grown so false I am loath to prove reason with;" yet he skillfully uses words for his own purposes. Viola, too, demonstrates a talent for wordplay in her conversations with Orsino, when she hints at her feelings for him, and with Olivia, when she makes veiled references to her disguise. In these instances, the listener must look beneath the surface meaning of the words being used to discover their true import. Thus, language contributes to the contrast of illusion and reality in the play.

Commentators have also examined how the written messages in *Twelfth Night* also contribute to the theme of language and communication. When the play begins, Orsino and Olivia are engaged in a continuing exchange of messages that state and restate their stubbornly held positions which lack any real emotion to back them up. Another formal message, in the form of a letter, dupes Malvolio into believing that Olivia loves him. In these instances, formal messages convey no truth, but serve only to perpetuate the fantasies of the characters in the play. Malvolio's message to Olivia is an exception: while he is imprisoned, Malvolio pleads his case passionately to her in a letter. This instance of true communication provides a contrast to the self-indulgent fantasizing of Olivia and Orsino.

CHARACTER STUDIES

Viola and Olivia

The principal scenes shared by Olivia and Viola begin with scene v in Act I, when the two women meet face to face. Viola has heard of Olivia from the captain and Orsino, but meets her for the first time when she arrives with Orsino's message. From early in the conversation, Viola/Cesario matches Olivia in wit, and wins an audience with her, even though Olivia has heard Orsino's message before. Yet she is intrigued with Viola/Cesario's bold style, and responds to Viola/Cesario's request to lift her veil. Viola/Cesario encourages Olivia to not leave her beauty in the grave but to embrace love while she is young and have children to carry it on. When Olivia starts asking questions of Viola/Cesario, it becomes clear that her energies have shifted from maintaining her refusal of Orsino, to learning more about the page who is such an eloquent gentleman. When in Act II, scene ii, Viola/Cesario receives the ring from Malvolio that Olivia claims she left, Viola begins to realize the futility of the love triangle her disguise has created: "My master loves her dearly; And I, poor monster, fond as much on him; And she, mistaken, seems to dote on me. What will become of this?"

Olivia continues to pursue Viola/Cesario, and Viola continues to deflect her attentions. When Olivia encounters Sebastian in Act IV, scene i, she asks him back to her house and he goes. When he seems amenable to her affections, she wastes no time in finding a priest to officiate the fledgling commitment between them. This, however, creates a problem when Olivia meets Viola/Cesario again in the final act, and Viola/Cesario acts surprised at Olivia's familiar tone. Viola confesses that she loves the Duke, so Olivia, feeling betrayed and not wanting to be taken for a fool, brings out the priest to vouch for their vows. The confusion clears when Sebastian arrives on the scene, and Olivia realizes that she is indeed betrothed—to a real man—and Viola is freed from her disguise and is engaged to marry the Duke.

The comparison of Viola and Olivia has engaged critics in frequent debate. Viola and Olivia, whose names are essentially anagrams of each other, are parallel characters in many ways; however, Viola is generally regarded as the principle character. The women begin the play in similar circumstances: Olivia disguises herself behind a veil of mourning, and Viola dresses as a pageboy. They both have also recently lost brothers; however each woman approaches those situations differently. While Olivia chooses to waste her youth engaged in a meaningless ritual of mourning, languishing in exquisite self-denial, Viola continues to hope for her brother's welfare, but chooses to get on with the business of living. Furthermore, it is Viola, some critics argue, who possesses the ability to see past the masks of the other characters, and who encourages Olivia to drop the veil and seize love while she is young. Olivia recognizes the value in this and does so, in a misdirected way at first, but with happy results at the end. Viola's arrival in Illyria is key to the action of *Twelfth Night*; without the insights she shares with Olivia and Orsino on love and life, the lovesick Duke and the stubborn object of his affections may have otherwise simply grown old and died in a stalemate. Furthermore, Viola becomes interchangeable with Olivia to the Duke, when he abruptly ends his pining for Olivia when he learns that Viola is a woman and accepts her in place of Olivia as a wife.

Malvolio

Olivia's steward Malvolio, whose name literally means "ill-wisher," first appears in Act I, scene v, with his lady Olivia. His disposition is in direct opposition with Feste the clown, as Feste softens Olivia with his wit. Malvolio, however, is not won over. His insults to the clown prompt Olivia to declare "O, you are sick of self-love, Malvolio, and taste with a distemper'd appetite."

Malvolio is the center of the subplot which develops in Act II, scene iii, as Feste, Sir Andrew, Sir Toby and Maria are participating in revelry. Malvolio interrupts the merriment to say that if they cannot be quiet they will have to leave. The merrymakers mock and disregard Malvolio, so he vows to tell Olivia of the disruption their festivities are causing. In revenge, the four merrymakers devise a plan to make Malvolio look foolish in Olivia's eyes by capitalizing on his oversized ego.

In the fifth scene of Act II, Maria writes a letter supposedly from Olivia and drops it in Malvolio's path. He is letting his mind wander to the preferential way Olivia treats him, and contemplating himself in the role of her husband, the Count. Suddenly he spies the letter and reads the cryptic message. His vanity identifies him as the object of Olivia's secret love, as he "crushes" the letters M.O.A.I. to fit his name. The letter asks its subject to appear smiling in yellow stockings and crossed garters which Malvolio does at the first chance he gets to see Olivia, in Act III, scene iv. She thinks he has gone mad and sends for Sir

Toby to look after him. The merrymakers torment Malvolio further in Act IV, scene ii, by disguising Feste as a priest, who convinces Malvolio that he has gone blind. Sir Toby finally decides to end the game, and Feste grants Malvolio's request for pen and paper, which Malvolio uses to record the injustices done to him for Olivia to read. When he finally gets an audience with her in the final act she promises Malvolio that he will be both "plaintiff and the judge Of thine own cause," but Malvolio storms out declaring "I'll be reveng'd on the whole pack of you!"

Critics often note that the character of Malvolio stands in stark contrast to the atmosphere of gaiety that pervades the play. In a society where sensual indulgence is encouraged, Malvolio stands for law and order and is vilified for his position. He is fighting a losing battle, as Sir Toby points out in Act II, scene ii, "Dost thou think, because thou art virtuous, there shall be no more cakes and ale?"—in other words, "do you think that your attitude of righteousness will stop us from partying?" He has been compared by some scholars to the Puritans of Elizabethan times for his somber attitude and his crushing of the message in the letter to fit his fantasies, much like the Puritans bent the Biblical text to suit their own purposes. It is often noted that, because of his dissimilarity to the rest of the characters, Malvolio's presence in the play is critical. He plays the defender of the rules meant to be broken, in order to provide a scapegoat for the pranks of the merrymakers. Without the tension his character creates, the comic possibilities of the play would be severely diminished. Malvolio's punishment is particularly fitting because it exploits his own character defects. It is his own vanity that delivers him into the hands of the merrymakers and overcomes his rational restraint. Thus Malvolio is tricked into appearing opposite of his true nature: the consummate killjoy is smiling and dressed like a clown.

Feste

Feste the clown is the perpetrator of folly in *Twelfth Night* and the polar opposite of his colleague, Malvolio, Olivia's other servant. Feste's function in this society is to be an objective observer and commentator, and in so doing reveal the ridiculousness in the others' behavior. In first appearance, in Act I, scene v, he convinces Olivia that it is foolish to mourn her brother's death when his soul is in heaven. Later, in Act II, scene iv, Feste sings for Orsino, who requests a silly love song. Feste, however, perhaps to poke fun at Orsino's excessive lovesickness performs a melodramatic song about a lover who died alone for an unrequited love. The Duke in response briskly dismisses him. When Feste, dressed as Sir Topas, a priest, visits Malvolio in his confinement in Act IV, scene ii,

he tries to convince Malvolio that he is blind, and that things are really quite different from the way Malvolio perceives them. In the final act, Feste summarizes the play with a song.

Commentators point out that, paradoxically, the character designated as a fool is the one who grasps the simple truths behind the action, which is that appearance does not always reflect reality. Feste observes of himself *"culcullus non facit monachum"* [the cowl does not make the monk]; that's as much to say as I do not wear motley on my brain"—in other words, "the way I dress does not define me; while I may look stupid, my mind is quite sharp." When first encountering Feste in Act III, scene i, Viola is one of the few characters to appreciate the depth of his insight when she observes, "This fellow is wise enough to play the fool, And to do that well craves a kind of wit."

CONCLUSION

Twelfth Night is most often praised by critics for its comedic form and artistic unity. Its interrelated themes are complex and intriguing, and have inspired many controversial and contradicting theories. Some view it as Shakespeare's farewell to comedy, and note that its melancholy undertone foreshadow his great tragedies. However, most twentieth-century critics agree that festivity and Saturnalian pursuits lie at the heart of this play.

(See also *Shakespearean Criticism*, Vols. 1 and 26)

OVERVIEW

Harley Granville-Barker

SOURCE: "Preface to *Twelfth Night*" in *Prefaces to Shakespeare, Vol. VI*, B.T. Batsford Ltd., 1974, pp. 26-32.

[*In an essay originally published in 1912, Granville-Barker offers his vision for* Twelfth Night *as a director, beginning by describing what he believes was Shakespeare's intention for the set and how he may have written some parts such as Feste and Maria for specific actors. Barker also discusses the way he thinks Shakespeare constructed the play, suggesting that he may have originally intended a different outcome, and that on the Elizabethan stage, Viola/Cesario would have been played by a young boy, not a girl. He describes the casting choices Shakespeare may have made for other characters, including Sir Toby, Sir Andrew, Fabian, Feste and Antonio and in conclusion, describes the prose and verse of the play, defending his position that Elizabethan prose should be spoken quickly.*]

[*Twelfth Night*] is classed, as to the period of its writing, with *Much Ado About Nothing, As You Like It,* and *Henry V.* But however close in date, in spirit I am very sure it is far from them. I confess to liking those other three as little as any plays he ever wrote. I find them so stodgily good, even a little (dare one say it?) vulgar, the work of a successful man who is caring most for success. I can imagine the lovers of his work losing hope in the Shakespeare of that year or two. He was thirty-five and the first impulse of his art had spent itself. He was popular. There was welcome enough, we may be sure, for as many *Much Ado's* and *As You Like It's* and jingo history pageants as he'd choose to manufacture. It was a turning point and he might have remained a popular dramatist. But from some rebirth in him that mediocre satisfaction was foregone, and, to our profit at least, came *Hamlet, Macbeth, Lear,* and the rest. *Hamlet,* perhaps, was popular, though Burbage may have claimed a just share in making it so. But I doubt if the great heart of the public would beat any more constantly towards the rarer tragedies in that century and society than it will in this. To the average man or play-goer three hundred or indeed three thousand years are as a day. While we have Shakespeare's own comment even on that 'supporter to a state,' Polonius (true type of the official mind. And was he not indeed Lord Chamberlain?), that where art is concerned 'He's for a jig, or a tale of bawdry, or he sleeps.'

Twelfth Night is, to me, the last play of Shakespeare's golden age. I feel happy ease in the writing, and find much happy carelessness in the putting together. It is akin to the *Two Gentlemen of Verona* (compare Viola and Julia), it echoes a little to the same tune as the sweeter parts of the *Merchant of Venice,* and its comic spirit is the spirit of the Falstaff scenes of *Henry IV,* that are to my taste the truest comedy he wrote.

There is much to show that the play was designed for performance upon a bare platform stage without traverses or inner rooms or the like. It has the virtues of this method, swiftness and cleanness of writing and simple directness of arrangement even where the plot is least simple. It takes full advantage of the method's convenience. The scene changes constantly from anywhere suitable to anywhere else that is equally so. The time of the play's action is any time that suits the author as he goes along. Scenery is an inconvenience. I am pretty sure that Shakespeare's performance went through without a break. Certainly its conventional arrangement into five acts for the printing of the Folio is neither by Shakespeare's nor any other sensitive hand; it is shockingly bad. If one must have intervals (as the discomforts of most theatres demand), I think the play falls as easily into the three

divisions I have marked as any. [Intervals after II, iii and IV, i.]

I believe the play was written with a special cast in mind. Who was Shakespeare's clown, a sweet-voiced singer and something much more than a comic actor? He wrote Feste for him, and later the Fool in *Lear.* At least, I can conceive no dramatist risking the writing of such parts unless he knew he had a man to play them. And why a diminutive Maria—Penthesilea, the youngest wren of nine—unless it was only that the actor of the part was to be such a very small boy? I have cudgelled my brains to discover why Maria, as Maria, should be tiny, and finding no reason have ignored the point.

I believe too (this is a commonplace of criticism) that the plan of the play was altered in the writing of it. Shakespeare sets out upon a passionate love romance, perseveres in this until (one detects the moment, it is that jolly midnight revel) Malvolio, Sir Toby and Sir Andrew completely capture him. Even then, perhaps, Maria's notable revenge on the affectioned ass is still to be kept within bounds. But two scenes later he begins to elaborate the new idea. The character of Fabian is added to take Feste's share of the rough practical joke and set him free for subtler wit. Then Shakespeare lets fling and works out the humorous business to his heart's content. That done, little enough space is left him if the play is to be over at the proper hour, and, it may be (if the play was being prepared for an occasion, the famous festivity in the Middle Temple Hall or another), there was little enough time to finish writing it in either. From any cause, we certainly have a scandalously ill-arranged and ill-written last scene, the despair of any stage manager. But one can discover, I believe, amid the chaos scraps of the play he first meant to write. Olivia suffers not so much by the midway change of plan, for it is about her house that the later action of the play proceeds, and she is on her author's hands. It is on Orsino, that interesting romantic, that the blow falls.

> Why should I not, had I the heart to do it,
> Like to the Egyptian thief at point of death,
> Kill what I love?—a savage jealousy
> That sometime savours nobly.

On that fine fury of his—shamefully reduced to those few lines—I believe the last part of the play was to have hung. It is too good a theme to have been meant to be so wasted. And the revelation of Olivia's marriage to his page (as he supposes), his reconciliation with her, and the more vital discovery that his comradely love for Viola is worth more to him after all than any high-sounding passion, is now all muddled up with the final rounding off of the comic relief. The character suffers severely. Orsino remains a finely interesting figure; he might have been a magnificent one. But there, it was Shakespeare's way to come out on the other side of his romance.

The most important aspect of the play must be viewed, to view it rightly, with Elizabethan eyes. Viola was played, and was meant to be played, by a boy. See what this involves. To that original audience the strain of make-believe in the matter ended just where for us it most begins, at Viola's entrance as a page. Shakespeare's audience saw Cesario without effort as Orsino sees him; more importantly they saw him as Olivia sees him; indeed it was over Olivia they had most to make believe. One feels at once how this affects the sympathy and balance of the love scenes of the play. One sees how dramatically right is the delicate still grace of the dialogue between Orsino and Cesario, and how possible it makes the more outspoken passion of the scenes with Olivia. Give to Olivia, as we must do now, all the value of her sex, and to the supposed Cesario none of the value of his, we are naturally quite unmoved by the business. Olivia looks a fool. And it is the common practice for actresses of Viola to seize every chance of reminding the audience that they are girls dressed up, to impress on one moreover, by childish by-play as to legs and petticoats or the absence of them, that this is the play's supreme joke. Now Shakespeare has devised one most carefully placed soliloquy where we are to be forcibly reminded that Cesario is Viola; in it he has as carefully divided the comic from the serious side of the matter. That scene played, the Viola, who does not do her best, as far as the passages with Olivia are concerned, to make us believe, as Olivia believes, that she is a man, shows, to my mind, a lack of imagination and is guilty of dramatic bad manners, knocking, for the sake of a little laughter, the whole of the play's romantic plot on the head.

Let me explain briefly the interpretation I favour of four or five other points.

I do not think that Sir Toby is meant for nothing but a bestial sot. He is a gentleman by birth, or he would not be Olivia's uncle (or cousin, if that is the relationship). He has been, it would seem, a soldier. He is a drinker, and while idleness leads him to excess, the boredom of Olivia's drawing-room, where she sits solitary in her mourning, drives him to such jolly companions as he can find: Maria and Fabian and the Fool. He is a poor relation, and has been dear to Sir Andrew some two thousand strong or so (poor Sir Andrew), but as to that he might say he was but anticipating his commission as matrimonial agent. Now, dull though Olivia's house may be, it is free quarters. He is, it seems, in some danger of losing them, but if only by good luck he could see Sir Andrew installed there as master! Not perhaps all one could wish for in an uncle; but to found an interpretation of Sir Toby only upon a study of his

unfortunate surname is, I think, for the actor to give us both less and more than Shakespeare meant.

I do not believe that Sir Andrew is meant for a cretinous idiot. His accomplishments may not quite stand to Sir Toby's boast of them; alas! the three or four languages, word for word without book, seem to end at 'Dieu vous garde, Monsieur.' But Sir Andrew, as he would be if he could—the scholar to no purpose, the fine fellow to no end, in short the perfect gentleman—is still the ideal of better men than he who yet can find nothing better to do. One can meet a score of Sir Andrews, in greater or less perfection, any day after a west-end London lunch, doing, what I believe is called, a slope down Bond.

Fabian, I think, is not a young man, for he hardly treats Sir Toby as his senior, he is the cautious one of the practical jokers, and he has the courage to speak out to Olivia at the end. He treats Sir Andrew with a certain respect. He is a family retainer of some sort; from his talk he has to do with horses and dogs.

Feste, I feel, is not a young man either. There runs through all he says and does that vein of irony by which we may so often mark one of life's self-

William Evans Burton and his wife as Sir Toby Belch and Maria in 1852.

acknowledged failures. We gather that in those days, for a man of parts without character and with more wit than sense, there was a kindly refuge from the world's struggle as an allowed fool. Nowadays we no longer put them in livery.

I believe Antonio to be an exact picture of an Elizabethan seaman-adventurer, and Orsino's view of him to be just such as a Spanish grandee would have taken of Drake. 'Notable pirate' and 'salt-water thief,' he calls him.

> A bawbling vessel was he captain of,
> For shallow draught and bulk unprizable;
> With which such scathful grapple did he
>   make
> With the most noble bottom of our fleet,
> That very envy and the tongue of loss
> Cried fame and honour on him.

And Antonio is a passionate fellow as those west countrymen were. I am always reminded of him by the story of Richard Grenville chewing a wineglass in his rage.

The keynotes of the poetry of the play are that it is passionate and it is exquisite. It is life, I believe, as Shakespeare glimpsed it with the eye of his genius in that half-Italianised court of Elizabeth. Orsino, Olivia, Antonio, Sebastian, Viola are passionate all, and conscious of the worth of their passion in terms of beauty. To have one's full laugh at the play's comedy is no longer possible, even for an audience of Elizabethan experts. Though the humour that is set in character is humour still, so much of the salt of it, its play upon the time and place, can have no savour for us. Instead we have learned editors disputing over the existence and meaning of jokes at which the simplest soul was meant to laugh unthinkingly. I would cut out nothing else, but I think I am justified in cutting those pathetic survivals.

Finally, as to the speaking of the verse and prose. The prose is mostly simple and straightforward. True, he could no more resist a fine-sounding word than, as has been said, he could resist a pun. They abound, but if we have any taste for the flavour of a language he makes us delight in them equally. There is none of that difficult involuted decoration for its own sake in which he revelled in the later plays. The verse is still regular, still lyrical in its inspiration, and it should I think be spoken swiftly . . .

I think that all Elizabethan dramatic verse must be spoken swiftly, and nothing can make me think otherwise. My fellow workers acting in *The Winter's Tale* were accused by some people (only by some) of gabbling. I readily take that accusation on myself, and I deny it. Gabbling implies hasty speech, but our ideal

was speed, nor was the speed universal, nor, but in a dozen well-defined passages, really so great. Unexpected it was, I don't doubt; and once exceed the legal limit, as well accuse you of seventy miles an hour as twenty-one. But I call in question the evidence of mere policemen-critics. I question a little their expertness of hearing, a little too their quickness of understanding Elizabethan English not at its easiest, just a little their lack of delight in anything that is not as they thought it always would be, and I suggest that it is more difficult than they think to look and listen and remember and appraise all in the same flash of time. But be all the shortcomings on one side and that side ours, it is still no proof that the thing come short of is not the right thing. That is the important point to determine, and for much criticism that has been helpful in amending what we did and making clearer what we should strive towards— I tender thanks.

The Winter's Tale, as I see its writing, is complex, vivid, abundant in the variety of its mood and pace and colour, now disordered, now at rest, the product of a mind rapid, changing, and over-full. I believe its interpretation should express all that. *Twelfth Night* is quite other. Daily, as we rehearse together, I learn more what it is and should be; the working together of the theatre is a fine thing. But, as a man is asked to name his stroke at billiards, I will even now commit myself to this: its serious mood is passionate, its verse is lyrical, the speaking of it needs swiftness and fine tone; not rush, but rhythm, constant and compelling. And now I wait contentedly to be told that less rhythmic speaking of Shakespeare has never been heard.

CELEBRATION AND FESTIVITY

The themes of celebration and festivity were inherent in Shakespeare's sources; the incorporation of the Twelfth Night holiday was probably suggested by the Italian play *Gl'Ingannati*, which contained a reference to La Notte di Beffania, the Epiphany. However, recent criticism has reached past the surface gaiety suggested in the title, and delved into themes behind the temporary release of a celebration. The topics of madness and self-deception were first introduced in the late nineteenth century by the French critic E. Montegut, who saw *Twelfth Night* as a carnival farce (a farce is a humorous drama which relies more heavily on improbable situations and coarse wit than on character and plot development). During that same time, Frederick Furnivall developed a companion theory to Montegut's carnival madness: he noted the "shadow of death and distress across the sunshine" of the play, triggering a continuing stream of criticism in that vein. Continuing in the theme put forth by Furnivall, twentieth-century critic **Thad Jenkins Logan** discusses the dark side of festivity, demonstrating that by abolishing limits of festivity in the stage world of Illyria, the audience will grow in its understanding that in reality, festivity taken to its extreme breaks down and creates an unsafe atmosphere for its participants.

Recent commentary has also focussed on the two titles of the play (*Twelfth Night* or *What You Will*). **Michael Taylor** demonstrates how the actions of various characters support both titles of the play: some point towards the passive acceptance of festivity's role in shaping events, while others embody the active stance suggested by "what you will." Maurice Charney uses Robert Herrick's 1648 poem, "Twelfe night, or King and Queene," to illustrate the festive atmosphere of Twelfth Night Renaissance celebrations.

Michael Taylor

"'Twelfth Night' and 'What You Will,'" in *Critical Quarterly*, Vol. 16, No. 01, Spring, 1974, pp. 71-80.

[*Taylor compares the passive posturing of Orsino, who reflects the acceptance of events shaped by a carefree or festive approach, to the more active stance of Viola, who aptly captures the essence of the subtitle 'What You Will'. Olivia and Orsino both retreat from reality in their respective emotional indulgences: Orsino's in unrequited love and Olivia's in grief for her brother. The critic contends that Malvolio, however, believes he can change his reality through sheer force of will and therefore also acts according to the subtitle in his quest for greatness.*]

Although the exact chronology of Shakespeare's plays is still in dispute, on the available evidence most commentators think *Twelfth Night* to be the last of the Romantic Comedies, close in time to *Hamlet*. The piquancy of this association has not gone unnoticed, and there is occasionally an anachronistic ring to critical judgements on *Twelfth Night*, caught best by the one that thrusts Hamlet's greatness upon Malvolio. Yet the dilemma which confounds the tragic protagonist appears also to disturb the equanimity of those in the comedy who, like him, balk at what seem to them excessively difficult situations, and who, like him also, are unable to end their troubles simply by opposing them. Even in indulgent Illyria, retreat into langour or knock-about-comedy does not muffle entirely the clamorous demands from the real world for decisions to be made and actions taken. Over the play hangs Sir Toby's great question, 'Is it a world to hide virtues in?' (I.3.117-118).

In many ways, of course, Illyria, unlike Hamlet's Denmark, offers its aristocratic inhabitants a life freed from the obligation to exercise their virtues. The kind of licence that the play's main title conveys can be enjoyed at its most untrammelled in the simple indulgences of the sub-plot. Although Sir Toby has as much contempt for his drinking companion, Sir Andrew Aguecheek, as he has for his puritan enemy, Malvolio, Sir Andrew's naive conception of the good life lies at the heart of their activity: 'it rather consists of eating and drinking' (II.3.10-11). If it were not for Maria, who hatches the plot against Malvolio, the sub-plot would have little to offer other than the spectacle of aimless roistering. Despite Sir Toby's noisy contempt for 'the modest limits of order' (I.3.8), or his lack of respect for place, persons and time (to echo Malvolio's accusation), his belligerent claim to the hedonistic life does not amount to very much. The festive spirit, given free reign on Twelfth Night, depends here, as elsewhere in the play, upon an essential passivity on the part of its adherents.

Passivity in the guise of a carefree enjoyment of the good things of life may be more tolerable than in the form it takes with Orsino, whose contribution to a Twelfth Night philosophy has nothing to recommend it. Of all Shakespeare's romantic heroes his role must surely be the most difficult for any actor to make attractive. Supine in his passion, Orsino conducts his love-affair with Olivia through emissaries, Valentine initially, and then Viola as Cesario. This leaves him free to contemplate the tyrant sway of his 'love-thoughts' from which in fact he longs to escape, or says he does: 'And my desires, like fell and cruel hounds/E'er since pursue me' (I.1.23-24). Unable to act, he cannot take responsibility for his own feelings, as his figure indicates, divorcing himself from them as though they were external agents sent to plague him. He seems no more able to translate words into deeds than Olivia's other suitor, Sir Andrew, whom he also resembles, though on a more highly poetic plane, in his vacillation and instability of opinion. In the space of some ninety lines in Act II, Orsino moves from a conception of himself as devoted to the 'constant image of the creature/That is beloved' (II.4.18-19) through an attack on the inconstancy of men's affections when compared with women's (II.4.32-34) to an attack on women's inconstancy in love when compared with men:

> Alas, their love may be called appetite,
> No motion of the liver but the palate,
> That suffers surfeit, cloyment, and revolt.
> (II.4.96-98)

Orsino's patronizing regret, here, for the crudity of women's love for men not only contradicts his recent opinion as to 'giddy and unfirm' masculine fancies, but does so in language which cannot but remind us of the play's opening lines, where he appeals on his own behalf for a medicinal 'surfeiting' in order that his 'appetite may sicken and so die' (I.1.3). 'Surfeit, cloyment, and revolt', in fact, constitute the cycle from whose paralyzing influence Orsino escapes only in his marriage to Viola.

Subject to every fleeting whim, what can someone like Orsino *do*? He cannot do much more than talk about what he might do, or, at best, demand that others do urgently for him what he can only urgently demand them to do. 'Be clamorous and leap all civil bounds' (I.4.20) he urges Viola, for (in a pophetic line) 'It shall become thee well to act my woes' (I.4.25). 'What shall I do?' (V.1.109) he asks Olivia, whose reply nicely balances courtesy and contempt: 'Even what it please my lord, that shall become him' (V.1.110). Although his question may not be so inane as Sir Andrew's 'What is "pourquoi"? Do, or not do?' (I.3.83), between them they voice in comic fashion the alternative which faces Hamlet: do, or not do. In both their cases (unlike his), any attempt to take decisive action is doomed to be comically ineffectual. When Orsino discovers that Olivia believes herself to be in love with Cesario he indulges his fury in self-dramatization and empty threats:

> Why should I not, had I the heart to do it,
> Like to th'Egyptian thief at point of death,
> Kill what I love?
>
> (V.1.111-113)

Such bombast circumstance gives way to a recognition of impotence (though still phrased bombastically): 'Live you the marble-breasted tyrant still' (V.1.118).

Indolence, passivity and impotence are constitutive of a Twelfth Night philosophy: care must be, indeed, the enemy of this life. With Viola's entry onto *Twelfth Night's* stage, the emphasis shifts temporarily (to return each time she returns) to a meaning of the play's sub-title 'What You Will' which offers itself as a genuine alternative to the main title. She supplies what those idling through an Illyrian Twelfth Night lack: direction, willed purpose, persistence and decisiveness. 'I'll serve this duke' (I.2.55) she says when we meet her first, indicating how much more than simply an Orsinian lament was her original question: 'And what should I do in Illyria?' (I.2.3). In her disguise as Cesario, she obeys Orsino's instructions to the letter, much to Malvolio's discomfiture. 'He's fortified against any denial' (I.5.138-139) Malvolio complains to an intrigued Olivia, 'He'll speak with you, will you or no' (I.5.147-148). How much her purposefulness becomes her is indicated, of course, in Olivia's admiring, 'You might do much' (I.5.263). In these circumstances, Viola's perplexity over Olivia's continued rejection of Orsino's suit does not extend beyond herself. We can see quite clearly why her active involvement in Illyrian affairs should in a trice break down Olivia's self-denying and artificial barriers against natural feeling. 'Even so quickly may one catch the plague?' (I.5.281) wonders Olivia. In these circumstances, even so.

Having caught it Olivia does not retire into sweet beds of flowers, even though she suffers the same treatment from Viola that she has been according Orsino. Her resilience here does not come as a total surprise to us, for she has displayed, from the outset, her own brand of willed purpose. In her misplaced determination to mourn her brother's death for seven years, we acknowledge a strength of will, however perverse. Valentine's caustic account to Orsino of her decision grasps its comic impropriety:

> But like a cloistress she will veiled walk,
> And water once a day her chamber round
> With eye-offending brine: all this to season
> A brother's dead love, which she would keep
>   fresh
> And lasting in her sad remembrance.
>
> (1.1.29-33)

Valentine reduces Olivia's daily expression of devotion to an unthinking exercise in the art of sad remembrance, as mechanical as watering flowers, except that the salt in Olivia's tears hurts her eyes. His metaphor from preserving meat, the ambiguity in 'eye-offending' and his pointed use of the transferred epithet ('a brother's dead love') tell us why Olivia might well have to strain hard for her tears. Her persistence is unnatural and foolish, a stubborn exertion of the misdirected will.

A determination to pursue a course of action, no matter how fatuous, obviously provides no real alternative to an indulgence of inertia. Olivia's activity in memory of her dead brother resembles Orsino's languor in behalf of love: each a retreat from reality. In Shakespeare's presentation of Malvolio (whose name means 'bad will'), his conviction that reality can be transformed by an exercise of the will overwhelms all his notions of social decorum and subdues his common-sense. Malvolio has no intention of hiding *his* virtues, for he is, in Maria's words, 'the best persuaded of himself; so crammed as he thinks, with excellencies that it is his grounds of faith that all that look on him love him' (II.3.136-139). Maria's trick against him exploits this supreme conceit, relying on Malvolio's strength of will to pursue inanity to excess and surfeit. Her letter cleverly appeals to his 'blood' and 'spirit', askin him to inure himself 'to what thou art like to be, cast thy humble slough and appear fresh' (II.5.135-137). Unlike Orsino, Malvolio finds nothing difficult nor distasteful in the activities demanded of him, despite their demeaning tricks of singularity:

> Be opposite with a kinsman, surly with servants.
> Let thy tongue tang arguments of state; put thyself
> into the trick of singularity.... Remember who
> commended thy yellow stockings and wished to
> see thee ever cross-gartered. (II.5.137-141)

Malvolio's performance exceeds expectation. Only a man blindly convinced of his own worth, assured that in no circumstances can he possibly appear ridiculous, could parade himself in this manner. Arrogantly self-willed, Malvolio, more extremely than Olivia, brings the notion of self-assertion in the play's sub-title into greater disrepute than Sir Toby the license implicit in 'Twelfth Night'. The letter speaks to his deepest convictions about himself, especially in one of its last injunctions: 'Go to, thou art made, *if thou desir'st to be so*' (II.5.142-143) [my italics], releasing in him a flood of 'wills':

> I will be proud, I will read politic authors, I will baffle Sir Toby, I will wash off gross acquaintance, I will be point-devise, the very man. (II.5.148-150)

Such a rhapsody, despite his insistence on Jove's benign intervention, places Malvolio squarely in the second and third of the three categories of greatness the letter describes: 'Some are born great, some achieve greatness, and some have greatness thrust upon 'em' (II.5.132-134).

Thad Jenkins Logan

SOURCE: "*Twelfth Night*: The Limits of Festivity" in *Studies in English Literature, 1500 to 1900*, Vol. 22, No. 2, Spring, 1982, pp. 223-38.

[*Logan explores the darker side of the carnival atmosphere of* Twelfth Night, *arguing that in the night world of the play, festivity has lost its innocence. He identifies the theme of the main plot as sexual, and the subplot, revelry, explaining that sexuality and revelry are the "two faces of the Saturnalian experience." The critic contends that the characters of the play are able to lose themselves in festivity because they, with the exception of Feste and Malvolio, are young and wealthy and literally carefree. Malvolio plays the parental role, and true to the reversal which underlies Saturnalian festivity, is imprisoned, just as those natural impulses of restraint are locked up and ignored during the pursuits of pleasure. Feste links the plots and suggests through his melancholy songs that festivity isn't as satisfying as it appears. Logan maintains that in* Twelfth Night, *love has nothing to do with personality and that Shakespeare intends to demonstrate to his audience through removing natural limits in the stage world that Saturnalian festivity taken to its final extreme is not reconcilable with social or moral norms, and results in violence and indiscriminate passion.*]

In *Twelfth Night* Shakespeare presents us with a world given over to pleasure, intoxication, and freedom. Any accurate interpretation must acknowledge the thematic importance of festivity, and critics like Barber, Leslie Hotson, L. G. Salingar, and John Hollander have provided valuable insights in this respect. Yet none of these critics has dealt quite adequately with the particular nature of festivity in this play, and my concentration on the dark side of the carnival world of *Twelfth Night* should be viewed as a supplement to their interpretations. It is clear that festive experience permits of distinctions: a New Year's Eve party, a Christmas dinner, and a wedding are all festive occasions, but constitute different experiences. Similarly, from a point of view of structure, the formal features which lead Barber to characterize a comedy as "festive" may be discovered in many plays, but crucial differences among the plays exist within that framework. The experience of *Twelfth Night* is very different from that of *As You Like It* or *Midsummer Night's Dream*, plays in which a critic may find similar dramatic elements and a number of formal analogues; I conceive the identifying, distinctive experience of *Twelfth Night* to be a function of the nature of festivity in that play. As its title suggests, the world of this play is a night world, and festivity here has lost its innocence.

Leslie Hotson has noted [in *The First Night of Twelfth Night*, 1954] that the subtitle "what you will" recalls the motto of the Abbaye de Thélème: "fay ce que vouldras." The phrase suggests that a fundamental concern of the play is what [David Horowitz, *Shakespeare: An Existential View* (London: Tavistock, 1965)] has called "multiple pleasures and wills to pleasure." Jan Kott, in a brilliant though idiosyncratic assessment of *Twelfth Night*, asserts that sex is the theme of the play ["Shakespeare's Bitter Arcadia," in *Shakespeare Our Contemporary*, 1964]; this is accurate enough but it is incomplete, since the secondary plot is highly significant in terms of stage time, and that plot is not primarily centered on sexuality, but on a set of drives that have to do with food, drink, song, dance, and fun. "Revelry" is probably as good a term as any to describe these particular sorts of pleasure, and I will use it in this essay to refer specifically to them. The relationship between the two plots is, in part, dependent on the fact that revelry and eroticism are closely allied; they are the two faces of Saturnalian experience. *Twelfth Night*, then, is an anatomy of festivity which focuses in the main plot on sexuality and in the sub-plot on revelry; the subtitle implies that these are what we, the audience, want.

It is crucial to recognize that the play makes an appeal to our own drives toward pleasure, toward liberation from the restraints of ordinary life. This is not, finally, an immoral play, but its authentic morality can only be discovered if we are willing to make a descent into the night world: its meaning remains opaque if we insist on seeing at every moment in every play a conservative, Apollonian Shakespeare. (We will do well to remember that Dionysus is the presiding genius of the theater.) *Twelfth Night* is not an enticement to licentious behavior, but it is an invitation to participate imaginatively in a Saturnalian feast.

A pervasive atmosphere of liberty and license is established by the opening scenes. The first thing we recognize about Illyria is that it is a world of privilege and leisure in which the aristocracy are at play. Goddard, whose vision of the play is in many ways similar to my own, calls Illyria "a counterfeit Elysium" [in *The Meaning of Shakespeare*, 1954], and characterizes its citizens as parasitical pleasure-seekers, partly on the grounds that any aristocratic society is founded on "the unrecognized labors of others". Certainly, there are only two characters in the play who seem to have any work to do: they are Feste and Malvolio, whose positions in the social world will be discussed at greater length; for most of the characters, leisure is a way of life. There are no rude mechanicals here. Sir Toby, Sir Andrew, and Maria are clearly not members of the lower class, although the conventions of comedy and Shakespeare's usual practices have sometimes led directors to make that mistake about them. That the characters of the sub-plot are themselves members of the aristocracy is a significant feature of this play. Olivia and Orsino are at the very top of the social hierarchy; they are young, rich, elegant, and fashionable. The captain who rescues Viola suggests something of their éclat in his initial description of Orsino [quotations from *The Riverside Shakespeare* (1974)]:

> And then 'twas fresh in murmur (as you
> know,
> What great ones do, the less will prattle of)
> That he did seek the love of fair Olivia.
>
> (I.ii.32-34)

Even the shipwrecked twins are well-off; Sebastian is amply provided for by the doting Antonio upon his arrival in Illyria, and Viola has somehow emerged from the sea with enough gold to pay the captain "bounteously."

The wealth and social position of the characters are important in several ways and should be established clearly in production; besides setting the action in a framework of aristocratic values, pleasures, and mores, they contribute a great deal to a sense of liberation and license. Characters are, in part, free to pursue "what they will" because they can afford to do so. The financial conditions upon which Illyrian revelry depends are made explicit by Sir Toby: "Let's to bed, knight. Thou hadst need send for more money" (II.iii.182 and 183). Along with economic freedom, the social status of the main characters allows them to pursue pleasure according to their fancy. Orsino is attended by courtiers who provide him with music, and presumably with "sweet beds of flow'rs," on command; Olivia speaks to Cesario/Sebastian from a position of power, arranging rendezvous as she chooses. Her disorderly kinsman and his guest may be threatened by her displeasure, but they are apparently in no danger from any sort of civil authority; in the brawl that follows the practical joke played on Viola and Sir Andrew, it is only the outsider, Antonio, who is arrested.

Political power is, in fact, vested in Orsino; as the Duke of Illyria, he might be expected to function as the parent-figure in Northrop Frye's model of the structure of comedy ["The Mythos of Spring: Comedy" in *Anatomy of Criticism,* 1957]. From his first speech, however, it becomes clear that Orsino is not going to embody principles of law, order, and restraint in this comic world. In fact, there are no parents at all in Illyria, as Joseph Summers cogently noted [in "The Masks of Twelfth Night" in *The University of Kansas City Review,* 1955]. Here, the social order is in the hands of youth, and wealth and power are at the service of youth's pursuit of pleasure.

It is Malvolio, of course, who fills the dramatic functions of the senex and the blocking figure, but what is curious about Malvolio in this respect is that he is a servant of Olivia. In a comic world noticeably lacking parents, Malvolio becomes a parent figure insofar as he performs some characteristic parental roles: it is he who tells the revellers to be quiet and go to bed. Yet Malvolio is a remarkably ineffective blocking figure; he shows himself powerless to control Sir Toby and Maria, much less to inhibit the actions of the lovers. The figure who stands for law and order in this play is not only made the butt of practical jokes, but is, in the structure of the play's society, only an employee. As such, he has no real authority: his "parenting" may be made use of by Olivia when it is convenient, and dispensed with when it is not. No one is morally or legally compelled to obey Malvolio; certainly no one is inclined to do so, nor is anyone inclined to share his stolid, earnest, workaday consciousness.

In the course of the play, the sort of consciousness that Malvolio embodies is literally locked away in the dark. His imprisonment is a striking emblem of the psychic reversal that underlies Saturnalian festivity: impulses that are normally repressed are liberated, while the controls of the super-ego are temporarily held in check. What gives Illyria its distinctive atmosphere is our sense that in this world such a reversal is a way of life. For most of the characters, everyday is holiday. Festivity is the norm here, and misrule is the order of the night.

The audience of *Twelfth Night* participates imaginatively in an experience of psychic liberation, but does not share the "madness" of the Illyrians; in Freudian terms, our ego and super-ego continue to function normally. There are modes of awareness available to us that are not available to the characters (we hold, for example, the keys to all riddles of identity in this play), and we retain an integrity of consciousness that the characters do not. Freud, of course, conceived of art as a transformation of unconscious fantasy material into a publicly acceptable form; while a Freudian theory of art tends to be limited and reductive, it provides a useful model for an audience's experience of *Twelfth Night*. Fantasies of love and anarchy, given free in Illyria, are presented on the stage, made present for our contemplation as well as our imaginative participation. It is as though we are allowed to be at once asleep and awake; our own fantasies, "what we will," are newly discovered to us. The sorts of things we learn about the night-world of the psyche are profoundly disturbing. Festivity turns out to be fraught with dangers and complications: Eros mocks the individual; Dionysis is a god of pain as well as a god of pleasure.

According to Leslie Hotson, for Shakespeare and his original audience "what the Dalmatian-Croatian *Illyria* brought to mind was thoughts of wild riot and drunkenness." In the sub-plot of *Twelfth Night*, as in the Bacchic rites, what riot and drunkenness lead to are violence and cruelty. Among all Shakespeare's comedies, it is only in *Twelfth Night* and *As You Like It* that there is literally blood on the stage. It is characteristic of the violence in the former play to be artificial in the sense of being invented by the characters themselves rather than necessitated by the movement of the plot or brought in from outside the comic world by a villain. In *As You Like It*, for instance, violence is created by the wicked Duke Frederick or by the encounter of man and nature. Because the violence of *Twelfth Night*, at least that which we see on the stage, is directly or indirectly effected by an appetite for diversion, there is always an element of superfluity about it that is curiously disturbing; it is like the underside of play. Violence in this play is optional, chosen, "what we will."

Freud has taught us that cruelty is the genesis of practical jokes. Whether or not Malvolio deserves his treatment at the hands of Maria, it seems to me that her sadistic impulses towards him are obvious. Once he has been gulled into smiles and yellow stockings, her response to him is "I can hardly forbear hurling things at him" (III.ii.81). Her "sportful malice" creates a web of illusion that is, up to a point, very funny indeed. Yet from the moment Malvolio cries out "they have laid me here in hideous darkness" (IV.ii.29 and 30), he begins to claim a share of the audience's sympathy. His plight is too close to our own nightmare fears, his language too evocative, for us to feel quite comfortable laughing at him. The feeling that the joke has gone too far is voiced by Sir Toby: "I would we were well rid of this knavery"

(IV.ii.67-68). The game threatens to come real: "We shall make him mad indeed," objects Fabian, to which Maria responds, "The house will be the quieter" (III.iv.133-34). She has, she says, "dogg'd him like his murtherer" (III.ii.76-77), and she is in earnest in her perpetration of psychic violence. That Maria bears the name of the Virgin is another example of the reversal characteristic of Saturnalian festivity.

Once Malvolio has fallen prey to the machinations of the revellers and to his own fantasies, Sir Toby's idea of a good time is to set Cesario and Sir Andrew at one another. He does not, of course, expect blood to be spilled—certainly not his own—but he has not reckoned with encountering the energies of Sebastian. Energy is precisely what he does encounter, however, and it leaves him and his companion broken and bloody. The play discovers to us the fact that festive revelry is likely to unleash psychic forces that are not easily controlled. In the metaphoric language of stage action, the wounded revellers function both in terms of myth and in terms of quotidian experience: in one sense, they are suffering the predictable consequences of a drunken brawl; in another, they remind us that the rites of Bacchus culminate in bloodshed.

There is within the play world one character who provides an ironic commentary on revelry, who seems to know that the pursuit of pleasure can be destructive, and who leads the audience toward a recognition of the emptiness of festive excess. Paradoxically, this is Feste the jester, whose name and office closely associate him with the festive experience. Festivity, as I have suggested, is the conceptual and experiential link between the sub-plot and the main plot; similarly, Feste acts in the play as a link between different sets of characters, moving freely from one group to another, like the spirit of festivity incarnate in the world of Illyria. But oddly, festivity itself, as incarnate in Feste, seems to participate in the principle of reversal characteristic of the play, and hover on the verge of becoming its opposite.

As Feste moves through the world of Illyria, he challenges our assumptions about festivity and foolery; he suggests not only that the fool is the only sane person in this world, but also that festivity is not as satisfying an experience as we might imagine. All three of his songs direct our attention to aspects of experience we might prefer to forget: death, the swift passage of time, and the fact that, on the whole, life is likely to bring us more pain than pleasure. Feste does not often amuse us, or the other characters; we do not often laugh with him—he does not give us occasion to do so. He seems to be, on the whole, rather an unhappy fellow. He is first discovered to us as an employee who may be dismissed; like Malvolio, Feste is a professional. Festivity is work for him, and it is evidently work which has become tiresome. He appears on stage as though he is returning from a long absence; his first words are "Let her hang me!" in response to Maria's scolding that his absence has displeased Olivia. It is easy to imagine Feste played as though he were disillusioned, cynical, and bored. Olivia herself calls him "a dry fool," says he grows dishonest, and tells him "your fooling grows old, and people dislike it" (I.v.110). Feste is distanced from the other inhabitants of Illyria because he is immune to the lures of drink, love, fantasy, and the distortions they create: he seems to have known these things and come out the other side. The festive experience is his trade; it holds no mysteries for him, and no delights.

Feste and Malvolio are, as we might expect, antagonists. They quarrel early in the play, and in the last scene Feste recalls that quarrel, taking special pleasure in Malvolio's humiliation and the part he has played in it. There seems to be a good deal of personal

thus the whirligig of time brings in his reveng⎯ (V.i.376, 377). The experience of dislike is not a common one in Shakespeare's comedies, and its appearance here is disturbing. Feste also does not like Viola, who makes a serious mistake about his nature; "I warrant thou art a merry fellow, and car'st for nothing." His response is a cold one: "Not so, sir, I do care for something; but in my conscience, sir, I do not care for you. If that be to care for nothing, sir, I would it would make you invisible" (III.i.26-30). The straightforward statement of dislike, of a motiveless personal hostility, sounds a new note in the comic world; it is, of course, Feste who at the end of the play will lead us out of that world.

There is a similar moment of "dis-integration" when Sir Toby reveals his true feelings about Sir Andrew: "Will you help?—an ass-head and a coxcomb and a knave, a thin-fac'd knave, a gull!" (V.i.206-207). There is never much sense of a human community established in *Twelfth Night*. Friendship is not a significant

From Act V, scene i, the Duke, Viola, Antonio, Olivia, the priest, and officers and attendants.

structural feature of the main plot, as it is in *Midsummer Night's Dream* and *As You Like It*. The revellers' fellowship is broken by the end of the play, and they do not participate in the happy ending. We are, admittedly, told that Sir Toby has married Maria, but we do not see them together on stage at the end. Antonio, so far as we can tell from the script, is never released from arrest, and Malvolio leaves the stage in anger. Critical notions that the end of the play is a vision of harmony and communal integration seem to me totally unjustified. A social community based on charitable love is never created in *Twelfth Night;* here, erotic love does not become a figure for charity, and marriage does not symbolize a universal harmony.

"What is love?" asks Feste. The conclusions we are led toward by the action of *Twelfth Night* are not, on the whole, happy ones. Sexuality in Illyria is mysterious and illusive. "What are we? What would we?" are questions the play sets for its audience. In Feste's lyric, love is the immediate gratification of desire: "Then come kiss me sweet and twenty." The play, however, begins with a stalemate: desire is frustrated, and fantasies conflict. Orsino wants Olivia, Olivia "will admit no kind of suit." It is the characteristic situation of courtly love; the roles Olivia and Orsino choose to play are familiar ones. In the course of the play, Shakespeare leads us from conventional modalities of love to a discovery of other erotic truths. This discovery is effected by the relationship of the four lovers as it is played out in the stage-world.

Part of the extraordinary appeal of Viola and Sebastian (and they have been almost as attractive to critics as to the characters in the play) comes from their air of innocence. Both Olivia and Orsino explicitly use the word "youth" on almost every occasion when they speak to or about Cesario. The twins bring a special vernal quality into the play; it is their appearance that breaks the stalemate established in the first scene. They are, in a sense, the green world. A significant number of critics assume that they teach Olivia and Orsino the meaning of love, and redeem the world into which they enter. I believe that such an interpretation does not sufficiently acknowledge our experience of the erotic aspects of the play. It is important, first of all, to notice that both Viola and Sebastian are androgynous.

Throughout the play we are compelled to pay attention to Viola's shifting sexual identity. We see her first as a girl, and watch her make decisions about how to present herself to the world; the idea of disguise thus becomes prominent, and entails the awareness that we ordinarily determine gender by dress, by appearance. The possibility of disguise suggests that there is something arbitrary about identity, and a disguise that involves a change of gender similarly suggests that our apprehension of sexual identity is mutable and susceptible to illusion. After her first scene, Viola never again appears to us as anything but a boy; unlike Rosalind, she does not re-assume her "woman's weeds" at the end of the play. A number of lines in the play draw attention to her disguise. The most notable is Orsino's description:

> Diana's lip
> Is not more smooth and rubious; thy small
>   pipe
> Is as the maiden's organ, shrill and sound,
> And all is semblative a woman's part.
> (I.iv.31-34)

A modern audience perceives this as a moment in which Orsino is close to discovering the "truth" about Cesario; Shakespeare, however, must have written the lines assuming that Orsino would deliver them to a boy disguised as a girl disguised as a boy. Viola, in fact, seems to be both a boy and a girl, and is romantically involved with both a man and a woman.

Sebastian also combines characteristics of both genders. Although I have remarked on his energy, Sebastian says of himself (on parting with Antonio), "I am yet so near the manners of my mother, that upon the least occasion more mine eyes will tell tales of me" (II.i.40-42). In relation to both Antonio and Olivia, Sebastian takes a passive, classically feminine role; he enjoys their attentions, and allows them to present him with lavish gifts. Now in one sense Antonio is a nurturing parent-figure, and again the principle of reversal is operative; the parent is subservient to the child: "If you will not murther me for my love," cries Antonio, "let me be your servant" (II.i.35-36). Antonio not only speaks to Sebastian like a doting parent, however, but also like a lover. Against Sebastian's wishes, he has followed him to Illyria:

> I could not stay behind you. My desire
> (More sharp than filed steel) did spur me
>   forth,
> And not all love to see you (though so much
> As might have drawn one to a longer
>   voyage)
> But jealousy what might befall your travel.
> (III.iii.4-8)

Like Viola, Sebastian is involved in erotic relationships with both a man and a woman.

The twins' androgyny may be, as some critics have suggested, related to their youth and innocence, but it also makes any romantic relationship into which they enter suspect. As soon as Viola/Cesario becomes an object of desire, we are drawn into the night world. Insofar as Viola is a girl, her encounters with Olivia inevitably suggest lesbianism; insofar as Cesario is a boy, all his relations with Orsino suggest homosexuality. Barber, in attempting to deal with this issue, assures us that "with sexual as with other relations, it is when the normal is secure that playful aberration is benign [in *Shakespeare's Festive Comedy,* 1959]." Undoubtedly, but what sexual relation can we perceive as normal in Illyria?

What we see on stage in the course of the play is a delirious erotic chase; Viola pursues Orsino who pursues Olivia who pursues both Viola and Sebastian, who is pursued by Antonio. Salingar has noted [in "The Design of *Twelfth Night*" in *Shakespeare Quarterly,* 1958] that "the main action of *Twelfth Night,* then, is planned with a suggestive likeness to a revel." Indeed. And the sort of revel it is most like is an orgy. Ordinarily, sexual experience is private, and involves two partners. In orgiastic experience, the number of possible sexual partners is multiplied, and distinctions of gender become less important. On the stage, we see Sebastian erotically linked with Antonio and Olivia, Orsino with Cesario and Olivia, Viola with Orsino and Olivia, Olivia with Viola and Sebastian. For the spectators of this "whirligig," and for the characters caught up in it, the complexities of eroticism in Illyria are dizzying.

There never is, needless to say, a real orgy; the playwright is in control of the revels, after all, and the comedy ends in marriage; sexual energy is channelled into appropriate social institutions. In Barber's words, "delusions and misapprehensions are resolved by the finding of objects appropriate to passions." Well, yes. Orsino marries Cesario, who loves him, and Olivia marries a man. But by this time passions have so slipped their moorings in terms of objects of desire (who, for example, does Olivia love?) that this finding of objects appropriate to passions seems rather like a game of musical chairs. My point is that the marriages at the end of *Twelfth Night* do not convince us that sexuality is ever ordered and controlled with regard to the individual in society.

In the final scene Olivia and Orsino claim their partners. There is no doubt, from an audience's perspective, who is in control here: Olivia and Orsino are older and they possess social status that the twins do not; they further control the scene in the special theatrical sense of having most of the lines. Olivia has already, by the last scene, engineered a marriage with the complaisant Sebastian. Having effected her own wedding by sheer force of will, it is Olivia who moves at the end of the play to arrange the betrothal of Viola and Orsino:

> My Lord, so please you, these things further
>   thought on,
> To think me well a sister as a wife,
> One day shall crown th' alliance on't, so

> please you,
> Here at my house and at my proper cost.
>
>   (V.i.316-19)

Orsino embraces her offer, and takes Viola's hand. It is important to remember that if we saw this scene in a theater, we would see him take Cesario's hand; the actor is still dressed as a boy, as he is some moments later when Orsino leads him from the stage.

Throughout the play, Olivia and Orsino are self-absorbed, self-willed and self-indulgent creatures: there is no evidence that they change significantly as a result of their encounters with the twins. Orsino's last words, like his first, are about himself: "But when in other habits you are seen, / Orsino's mistress, and his fancy's queen" (V.i.387-88). He is still speaking of "fancy." Orsino's anagnorisis seems to involve only the recognition that if he cannot have Olivia he may as well take Cesario: "I shall have share in this most happy wrack" (V.i.266). Similarly, there is no reason for an audience to believe that Olivia has made meaningful discoveries about the nature of love. If she was headstrong and reckless in loving Cesario, it is hard to see her as docile and prudent in her relations with Sebastian. At the end of the play, as at the beginning, Olivia is doing precisely what she wants to do.

While Olivia and Orsino have not really learned anything about love during the play, we in the audience have. As I have suggested earlier, when external obstacles to the pursuit of love are removed, as they are in Illyria, it is the nature of passion itself that lovers must contend with. "Bright things come to confusion" readily enough in our world without the interference of blocking figures. Love, first of all, can be unrequited. It is, horribly enough, possible to love someone who—for no good reason—just does not return that love. Olivia makes it perfectly clear:

> I cannot love him,
> Yet I suppose him virtuous, know him
>   noble,
> Of great estate, of fresh and stainless youth;
> In voices well divulg'd, free, learn'd, and
>   valiant,
> And in dimension, and the shape of nature,
> A gracious person. But yet I cannot love
>   him.
>
>   (I.v.257-62)

Orsino responds, "I cannot be so answer'd," and continues to long for what he cannot have in a particularly elegant, "poetical" fashion. Olivia, faced with rejection by Cesario, takes a more active approach; her "headstrong potent fault" finds expression in direct, aggressive confrontation with Cesario. It is Viola whose response to loving without requital has become best known:

> She never told her love,
> But let concealement like a worm i' the bud
> Feed on her damask cheek; she pin'd in
>   thought,
> And with a green and yellow melancholy
> She sate like Patience on a monument,
> Smiling at grief.
>
>   (II.iv.110-15)

It has been argued that this is not really an accurate description of Viola; perhaps it is exaggerated, but certainly Viola's reaction to loving one who loves another is of this same kind; she waits for "Time" to resolve a painful situation made more painful by her concealed identity. It seems to me very peculiar to regard this as a norm or an ideal, as some critics suggest.

At last, of course, Viola has her reward; Orsino's love for Olivia, which could "give no place, bide no denay," suddenly turns to her. That love can so turn is another of its characteristics that *Twelfth Night* discovers to us; again, it is an old truth. Here, in a comic structure, love's capriciousness works toward a comic resolution of the plot. Orsino can, after all, love Viola; Olivia can just as well marry Sebastian as Cesario. Yet Dr. Johnson's objection [in *Johnson as a Critic,* 1973] to Olivia's marriage is, as one might expect, lucid and to the point. Only in myth and ritual are twins the same person, and while the stage world is, in part, a mythic realm, theater—and Shakespeare's theater in particular—is closely bound to the empirical, naturalistic world the audience inhabits. In that frame of reference, Olivia abandons her vow of chastity to pursue the first new man she meets, marries his (her) twin brother by mistake, and seems willing to transfer her affections to a man she does not know because he looks like the one she fell in love with.

The crucial point is this: at the end of the play we perceive that love really has little or nothing to do with personality. It is, as Kott has said of love in *As You Like It,* an electric current that passes through the bodies of men and women, boys and girls. Passion violates identity. That this is true in terms of the individual's consciousness is a truism. "Ourselves we do not owe," cries Olivia, succumbing to her feelings for Cesario. The action of *Twelfth Night* suggests that it is not only the personality of the lover that is disrupted by passion: it is personality itself, the whole concept of unique, distinct identity. Cesario, the beloved, is both Viola and Sebastian; it really doesn't matter. Olivia and Viola are ultimately as interchangeable as their names suggest. As in Spenser's Garden of Adonis, forms change, but Form remains; here, however, the "Form" is not a structure or a pattern, but energy, energy which propels individuals, sometimes against their will, toward others who may or may not be so moved.

Such, it seems to me, is love in *Twelfth Night.*

Shakespeare has made similar suggestions about the nature of love in *As You Like It* and *Midsummer Night's Dream,* plays which also deal with psychic liberation; yet these plays do not lead us to a dark vision of the psyche. Nor do they have the melancholy tone of *Twelfth Night;* the language of this comedy is unusual in being not bawdy but grim. There are remarkably few ribald puns in *Twelfth Night;* by my count, there are twenty-nine references to madness in the play, twenty-two references to disease, twenty-five to devilry, and thirty-seven to destruction and death. The play's somber language would seem to be at odds with its festive structure; in my view, the structure and language are particularly compatible given the nature of festivity in *Twelfth Night.*

One difference between Illyria and the Wood of Athens is that in the wood, powerful and ultimately benevolent beings exist to set things right, beings who are intimately allied with, indeed embodiments of, the natural world. Illyria is a city, not a forest. In *Twelfth Night,* unlike *As You Like It* and *Midsummer Night's Dream,* festivity is divorced from pastoral, and this is crucially important to our experience of the play, since it means that sexuality is not perceived in relation to nature.

The concept of nature which the Renaissance inherited from the Middle Ages made a distinction between material phenomena (natura naturata) and an organizing principle (natura naturans); the latter was conceived as a structuring energy which, under Divine Providence, brought the physical phenomena into existence and patterned their being. As a manifestation of natura naturans, sexuality may wreak havoc in individual lives, but pursues its own ends of fertility and generation. Thus, as in *Midsummer Night's Dream,* a loss of identity can result from being subsumed in forces greater than the conscious self; personality may be blurred or erased by these forces, but finally they are beneficent in that they drive towards the preservation of life. The multiple marriages at the end of *As You Like It* provoke even from Jacques the comment (the realization), "these couples are coming to the ark." But in *Twelfth Night,* the absence of pastoral distances festivity from fertility, just as the absence of bawdry distances sexuality from a simple, homely pleasure that all humans share with the beasts. Illyria is beautiful, aristocratic, and sterile.

Festivity in *Twelfth Night* is divorced not only from nature, but, as I have indicated, from occasion. It is not a temporary release from social restraints but a permanent condition. The Forest of Arden and the Wood of Athens are places into which people enter in the course of the play and from which they will return; there is, to paraphrase Ralph Berry, "no escape from Illyria." The marriages there do not seem to place erotic love in a community, or to anchor it in a social life where impulses are ordered—not necessarily repressed, but controlled and contained.

That ordering, in a healthy society, provides more, rather than less individual freedom; the ability to control drives and impulses means, for the individual, freedom from the tyranny of the unconscious, while societal restraints ultimately protect the individual from the tyranny of others. The real tragedy of Malvolio lies in the fact that in this play the principle of order has become too rigid and too perverse to accommodate pleasure. Of course we laugh at him, he is ridiculous, yet his expulsion from the comic world brings an end to "Shakespeare's Festive Comedy," since it means that sobriety and intoxication, parents and children, workday and holiday, restraint and release, cannot be reconciled. In this way, Malvolio's exit is as disturbing as Mercade's entrance in *Love's Labours Lost* with his message of death. We feel, in the audience, the necessity of somehow making peace with him, and he is gone. His last line must certainly include everyone in the theater.

The play itself has discovered to us the dangers of life without the principle of order that Malvolio stands for; Feste's final song serves as a vivid reminder. The Rabelaisian ideal of freedom (the Abbaye de Thélème) only is possible when human nature can be trusted; doing what we will can be a horror if the forces that drive us are dark. In *Twelfth Night* Shakespeare leads us to explore the possibility that our drives to pleasure are ultimately irreconcilable with social and moral norms of goodness; it is the antithesis of *As You Like It*, which works from the hypothesis that people are basically good at heart. In *As You Like It*, the characters and the audience arrive at a restoration of the world; in *Twelfth Night* what the characters and the audience come to are the limits of festival, and at that extremity are violence and indiscriminate passion.

The play does not so much tell us but show us that these are what we want. It is the audience who finally approve, with their laughter and applause, the actions of the characters. I do not mean to suggest that we should not laugh and applaud, or that we should become a community of Malvolios, hostile to pleasure. This is a very funny play, and nearly all the characters—certainly including Orsino and Olivia—are enormously appealing. That is just the point. What I am suggesting is this: to delight in the pranks of the revellers is to participate vicariously in a form of Dionysian frenzy; to assent to the ending, to confirm it as a "happy" one, is to embrace the possibility of erotic love as transpersonal and trans-sexual. But the play does not wholeheartedly confirm the value of Saturnalian pleasure; if it is not sentimentalized in production, if festivity is allowed to reach its limits,

then the play itself will create an awareness that "what we will" is potentially dark and dangerous.

ROLE PLAYING AND PROBLEMS OF IDENTITY

Many critics have identified the problem of identity as a major issue in *Twelfth Night* and correlate the self-deception and disguises which are prevalent in the play with this theme. Frank Kermode has explored the limits of "wonder and madness" as they relate to identity issues within the play. Critic S. Nagarajan argues that self-deception—demonstrated by the disguises adopted by many of the characters—clouds the reason of the characters involved.

While *Twelfth Night* is rich with characters who adopt disguises or play roles, many critics, including Karen Greif and **J. Dennis Huston,** both find Viola's gender-switching disguise to be the central focus of the play. In Greif's view, Viola is unlike the other characters in that she is keenly aware of her role-playing, and her admission of her true identity at the play's end is the event that makes it possible for Orsino and Olivia to drop their unfulfilling roles and find love. Grief also points out that Feste is aware of the untrustworthy nature of words and appearances. J. Dennis Huston places Viola's adoption of a disguise in psychoanalytical context: he sees her adoption of a masculine disguise as motivated by a reluctance to embrace her sexual identity.

J. Dennis Huston

SOURCE: "'When I Came to Man's Estate': *Twelfth Night* and Problems of Identity," in *Modern Language Quarterly*, Vol. 33, No. 3, September, 1972, pp. 274-88.

[*Huston outlines a number of "unanswered problems" in* Twelfth Night. *Among these are the juxtaposition of scenes which take place three months apart, Viola's puzzling reaction to the appearance of her brother, and the lack of any resolution to the matter of Antonio's imprisonment. The critic maintains that these questions arise from the sense of detachment the play creates in its audience by presenting Illyria as a kind of fairy-tale world. Huston goes on to offer a psychological analysis of Viola's masculine disguise, describing it in terms of an "identity crisis" brought about by her belief that her twin brother has died and by her arrival in a foreign land. According to Huston, Viola is reluctant to embrace her sexual identity in this new world and finds a sense of security and "masculine freedom" by adopting the identity of her lost brother.*]

One of the most perplexing difficulties confronting a reader of *Twelfth Night,* or any other Shakespearean play, is how to deal with what might be called its residual problems, those testy questions that critical analyses ignore or leave unanswered. Some such problems, indigenous to Shakespearean drama, are really unanswerable. And *Twelfth Night* has its share of these. Partly the condition of Shakespeare's text is to blame. We shall never know, for instance, whether the fourth stanza of Feste's final song is as it should be: there surely Shakespeare's, and Feste's, sense of context is hardly given just representation by the sentence fragment passed on in the text. But, just as surely, conjecture about this problem is essentially fruitless, since the content of the stanza is clear enough without textual emendation. The bed that should be the still, fixed center of a generatively fruitful marriage is instead fractured by the drunk's unproductive activity and, like him, spun out into the unstable perimeter of one-night stands, and falls, in the company of other tosspots.

Partly, too, insoluble problems are a necessary result of the way Shakespeare wrote—swiftly and commercially, so that accuracy of petty detail is sometimes sacrificed to more pressing immediate effects. The contradictory double time scheme in *Twelfth Night* is, as a consequence, neither very noticeable nor very important. It hardly matters that Sebastian and Viola collide spatially when they are temporally almost three months apart. Superficially, they meet at the same time, for Viola has served Orsino during the three months that Sebastian has accompanied Antonio with "not a minute's vacancy" (V.i.98) [quotations from the *Complete Works of Shakespeare,* ed. Hardin Craig (1951)]. Viola is, however, first sent as an emissary to Olivia only three days after her arrival in Orsino's court, and her return journey to that court is interrupted by the scene in which Sebastian takes leave of Antonio after a stay of three months, though the length of this stay is not revealed until we have forgotten its technical impossibility. Shakespeare is not so much anticipating the modern movie technique of the flash-forward as he is sacrificing consistency of detail to thematic effect, by assuring his audience that Sebastian lives, that Olivia's love can find a suitable object, and that all of the intricately interwoven complications of plot are under the guiding and beneficent control of a dramatist who means to bring them eventually to a harmonious conclusion. If in the process he can successfully employ one of his favorite dramatic sleights of hand, double time, that is only further proof of his suprahuman powers as creator.

Mostly, though, unanswered problems in *Twelfth Night* evolve out of the very nature of the dramatic form itself, with its carefully delimited boundaries of action and character. Such boundaries may appear almost unlimited, as the controversial complexity of a world like Hamlet's proves, but such complexity is the result of carefully controlled exclusion: we do not notice boundaries because we do not look for them. Fascinated by what we see and hear of Hamlet, we forget that what we see and hear of him is all there is. As a consequence, we often ignore problems that the dramatist ignores, although they could never pass unnoticed in real life. We may wonder briefly how Horatio could have remained a month at Elsinore without ever meeting Hamlet, and why everyone in Denmark has conveniently forgotten that Hamlet is the real heir to his father's throne, but we dismiss such queries as quibbles. Shakespeare does not worry about them, so why should we?

There are similar kinds of delitescent boundaries to the action of *Twelfth Night.* For example, Viola changes her plans for disguise between the time we first see her and the time she arrives at Orsino's court, where she appears as a page, not a eunuch. Her brother likewise alters his purpose after his initial appearance, for although he takes leave of Antonio specifically to go to Orsino's court, he next appears as a casual sight-seer who has apparently put aside all thoughts of count and court. Finally, Olivia could hardly marry Sebastian while confused about his identity, because the error would be exposed during the exchange of vows. Even in his euphoric state of wonder, Sebastian would have to recognize that he was not "Cesario."

But the reader fastidious enough to worry about problems like these must also wonder if he is not perhaps throwing in his lot with the likes of Pope's dunces and digging around in the fertile soil of Shakespeare's plays merely to turn up grubs and worms and bits of hair. Still, the plain fact about grubs and worms is that they often indicate where the soil is richest: trivial problems are not the only ones left unanswered in *Twelfth Night.* Others more substantial linger and tease us out of thought until, like Malvolio struggling to decode the cryptic content of Maria's note, we think we glimpse the figure of a grander, yet undisclosed, design. For instance, why is Viola, who is at least once called Sebastian and who has hoped from the first that her brother is not really drowned, so slow to realize that he is in Illyria? And why, when she finally sees him, does she initiate such an unnecessarily long and artificial recognition scene? What happens to Antonio, who is conspicuously ignored in the closing speeches of pardon? How are we to interpret Orsino's insistent desire to see Viola in feminine dress before accepting her as a woman? And finally, as a corollary to this question, we might wonder just how we are supposed to feel about the betrothal of this vain, self-serving Duke to such an energetic and interesting heroine.

These questions do overreach the boundaries of explicit

action in *Twelfth Night,* but the play itself encourages this kind of conjecturing by repeatedly calling forth the Renaissance equivalent of the *Verfremdungseffekt.* Almost never is the audience allowed to forget that it is watching a play whose world is manufactured out of the shaping imagination of the dramatist. That is why Sebastian first appears so early in the play, even at the cost of temporal consistency; that is why Malvolio, enthralled by Malaria's letter, does not notice his boisterous deceivers, who are near enough to hear *him* clearly as he reads; and that is why Fabian interrupts the gulling of Malvolio to exclaim, "If this were played upon a stage now, I could condemn it as an improbable fiction" (III.iv.140-41). In addition, there are other less obvious, but equally important, promptings to detachment. Riddles and puns are dominant figures of speech in the language of Feste and Viola, who use them in part to signal their detachment from the restrictive roles forced upon them in Illyria. And in the process their detachment is passed on to the audience, which is similarly encouraged to view the action critically from its own, even broader, perspective. Even the playwright's cursory suggestions about the geography of Illyria distance it from actual human experience by locating it somewhere in the middle distance between fairyland and reality.

At first the world of the play seems insulated like the setting of a fairy tale, which, even when its action is supposedly wide-ranging, presents us with a realm that is everywhere the same—ravaged by the same kind of giant, dragon, or wicked stepmother. Here the sea, through its mythical associations with tempest, leviathan, and chaos, laps at the edges of the land and people grounded there, threatening imminent dissolution. It already has robbed this world of considerable masculine force and left its women exposed and isolated. Sebastian has apparently drowned, and Viola is shipwrecked on a strange shore. Olivia's father and brother have died, and while her uncle drowns his days and nights in drink, she is undergoing a sea-change of her own by closing up her house and heart in order to "water once a day her chamber round / With eye-offending brine" (I.i.29-30). Even the ruling Duke is figuratively paralyzed by a love that, like the sea, swallows all that it encounters.

This world, too, seems characterized by the psychological simplicity of the bedtime story, where human motives are transparent and actions exaggerated. The Duke cares for nothing but his love of love; Olivia has resolved to honor her brother's memory by shutting herself off from the sun for seven years; and her uncle just as foolishly insulates himself against an outside world of time and responsibility by drunkenly obliterating all distinctions between late and betimes. Then there is Viola—orphaned, shipwrecked, and washed up on a strange shore—clearly an identifiable personage

from fairy tale: she is the quester, the young, untested hero of uncertain origins who has come to rejuvenate the wasteland and heal its languishing, impotent ruler. To emphasize her apparently mythical role, Shakespeare makes her introduction as simply direct as "once upon a time" and her motivation as transparent as fairyland love: "What country, friends, is this? . . . Who governs here? . . . Orsino! I have heard my father name him: / He was a bachelor then" (I.ii.1, 24, 28-29). Then, further identifying her with the questing hero, Shakespeare dresses her as a young man and sends her to court, in both senses of the word.

But as the action of the play moves inland from the sea, situation and motivation become much more complicated, and the sharp outlines of the fairy-tale world dissolve. In its place appear the vague perimeters of the realm on the other side of Illyria from the sea. There men do not open their arms and gates to shipwrecked strangers; they shut them tightly for fear of knaves and thieves. There revelers who drink through the night cannot forever playfully catch the sounds of morning by claiming to be up betimes; they must eventually confront the jarring dissonances of the morning after the night before. And there marriage is not the promise of joy lived happily ever afterwards; it is a perilous undertaking which all too often ends in misunderstanding and sorrow. This world on the other side of Illyria is less well known to the characters than to the audience, which, after all, inhabits it daily and has come to the play partly in flight from its wind and rain. But the play will not let the audience forget it altogether; Feste is there to remind it that such a world indelibly marks the souls of those who have been there, even if they can regularly return to the realm of imagination and play. Like the audience, Feste is thus a participant in two worlds. And, also like it, he enters and exits from the realm outside Illyria.

At his entrance the first thing we hear of him is that he has been away, and his habitual detachment from the action of the play suggests that the world he has been visiting still has him partly in its grasp. There he has learned that language shifts meaning according to context and that, as a result, boundaries are no longer distinct: "That that is is" (IV.ii.17) at one time, but at another "Nothing that is so is so" (IV.i.9). Like language, then, philosophy becomes for Feste a cheveril glove that can be turned at will to conceal wear and tear; from almost all that goes on around him he maintains a measure of detachment. Only once in the drama is he so completely drawn into an action that he does not manage to retain a degree of aloofness from it: he mistakes Sebastian for Viola-Cesario. And then his error may signal a confusion of identity that belongs as much to psychological complexity and the realm of the audience as to dramatic irony and the world of Illyria.

Feste's exit, though, is even more obviously out from Illyria into the world of the audience. In his closing lyric he sings of experience removed from, but relevant to, that of the play. Here also we are presented with fool's play, a closed house, revelry, and marriage, but what we are given is really the underside—or, in the spatial terms suggested by the play, the other side—of the human experience depicted in the drama. For Faste's talk of closed houses that remain locked up against outsiders, of revelry followed by collapse, and of marriage blighted by the failure of expectation can perhaps be taken as a comment upon the apparently harmonious resolution of the plot. At the very least, the song encourages speculation about a conclusion where closed houses are opened up and revelry is ceremonialized in multiple marriages, and where in the process so many troublesome questions are left unanswered.

Finally, a further complication to the original simplicity of story line and character is presented by the entrance of Sebastian, whose manner and dress resemble Viola's and whose situation is almost an exact parallel to hers: saved by a ship captain and lamenting the loss of his twin, he sets out to seek his fortune at Orsino's court. Now suddenly there are *two* questing heroes spawned by the same sea, appareled in the same clothes, and bound for the same court. And now too the problems facing the audience, as well as the Illyrians, are compounded almost fourfold, for with Sebastian's introduction come also the knotty questions of Viola's reluctance to admit him living to her consciousness, double time, Antonio's captivity, and Orsino's insistence on redressing his page before acknowledging her identity as woman. Sebastian's presence is no doubt dramatically necessary, since he is needed to satisfy Olivia, but for her a man like Antonio might have served just as well: all that is really necessary is someone radically different from the languishing Orsino. Why then bring on Sebastian? Shakespeare is not inalterably bound to use twins just because his source does. Once early in his dramatic career he added a set of twins to a plot borrowed from Plautus; here he might just as easily have taken one away and avoided some of the dramatic problems precipitated by Sebastian's appearance. But of course he never meant to avoid them, because what surely drew him to the story in the first place was the very presence of the twins; it is one of the few details in the source he does not alter.

Since the time of the Roman theater, separated twins have provided the dramatist with a wealth of ready-made possibilities for comedy nourished by misunderstanding and mistaken identity, and Shakespeare was hardly one to throw away a dramatic formula of proven worth. But the real reason he may have chosen to retain the twins from the source story has to do with mistaken—or uncertain—identity in a more complex way, for in this respect, as in so many things, he apparently anticipated some of the discoveries of modern psychology. Or if he did not actually anticipate them, he at least created a dramatic world expansive enough to hold them in suspension. For a moment let me, like Feste, enter the world of *Twelfth Night* from the side weathered by wind and rain.

One of the foremost concerns of modern psychoanalytic study—for theorists as radically different as R. D. Laing and Erik Erikson—is with problems of identity. "The patient of today," Erikson writes, [in *Childhood and Society* (1963)] "suffers most under the problem of what he should believe in and who he should—or, indeed, might—be or become. . . . The study of identity, then, becomes as strategic in our time as the study of sexuality was in Freud's time." Erikson suggests that modern man can expand his understanding of this problem by studying its manifestations in history, for in singular moments man's struggle with identity, if he is such a man as Luther or Gandhi, has unleashed forces of immeasurable creativity and reshaped his world. But Erikson does not draw his examples of identity crises from history alone. He finds them also in art, and particularly in Shakespeare's tragedies, which give us remarkably lifelike accounts of man's struggle to understand and fulfill his sense of identity. The most obvious example is Hamlet. For surely what Hamlet experiences as he struggles to integrate his remembrance of things past with a present time that seems out of joint is, in the language of contemporary psychology, an acute identity crisis. Repeatedly he reaches out for an identity that just as repeatedly dissolves before his self-lacerating violence:

> What a piece of work is a man! . . . And yet, to me, what is this quintessence of dust?
>
> (II.ii.314-22)

> O, what a rogue and peasant slave am I!
>
> (II.ii.576)

> To be, or not to be: that is the question. . . .
>
> (III.i.56)

> What should such fellows as I do crawling between earth and
> heaven?
>
> (III.i.130-32)

Shakespeare's interest in problems of identity is not restricted to his tragic drama, however. It is also recognizable as a concern in his comedies, where many of the problems that rack Hamlet are filtered through a different mode and mood. For instance, Shakespeare's comic heroines are often, like Hamlet, fatherless: Viola and Portia have lost their fathers to death, Rosalind has seen hers banished, and Beatrice and Helena are conspicuously fatherless in dramatic worlds where fathers play important roles. Sometimes, also like Hamlet, these heroines are called to answer the intransigent demands of their fathers' decrees: Hermia must wed Demetrius or choose between death and a nunnery, and Kate must marry if ever she is to escape endless unflattering comparisons with her sister. Portia's situation is most obviously like Hamlet's; the charge impressed by her father upon her comes from beyond the grave. Cut loose from a childhood identity secured by paternal protection, these heroines, also like the Danish Prince, soon discover the vulnerability of their newly exposed positions: Rosalind is banished under threat of death, Helena is abandoned in the enchanted wood, and Viola is stranded upon a strange shore.

In such a position Hamlet depends upon disguise to protect himself against violation of either the physical or psychological kind, and the heroines do the same thing. Most often they hide their sex, both literally and figuratively, behind the disguise of a page, with at least a twofold purpose. First, the disguise protects them from sexual attack; second, it secures for them a physical freedom that is the complementary corollary to their sudden vulnerability: without a father each is also without a circumscribed identity as a child and thus free to venture out into the broader world of adult responsibility and ultimately to choose a husband. Sometimes the disguise that these heroines wear is not consciously assumed, but even then it bespeaks a desire to enjoy the freedom associated with adulthood, particularly with the masculine role in the adult world. Kate and Beatrice do not actually dress themselves as young men; they just become masculinely independent and aggressive—by openly rebelling against the conventional feminine behavior expected of them.

No doubt there are other interesting similarities between the experiences of Hamlet and many of Shakespeare's heroines. Both undergo physical journeys that are related to psychological transportations; both are complemented by friends, often traveling companions, who speak for more socially conventional attitudes; and both experience setbacks in love which encourage doubt about the faithfulness, and ultimately about the very identity, of the loved one. To point out such similarities is not to argue that Shakespeare's comic heroines are really like Hamlet. Between them there is a world of difference: the difference between a comic and a tragic universe, between recreative psychic play and constrictive psychic paralysis, and, finally, between life and death. What *is* important about these similarities, from my point of view, is that they testify to Shakespeare's abiding concern with different forms of identity crisis. One such crisis is depicted in *Twelfth Night,* and it begins with Viola, stranded upon the shore.

Behind her is the sea of lost identity, which has washed away the foundations of her previous existence. Gone is her childhood tie to family, for her father is dead, her mother never to be heard of, and her brother apparently drowned. Gone too is Messaline, country of her birth, now so insulated by the perilous sea of experience that she cannot even think of returning there. Her world lies all before her, in thoughts of marriage and fulfilled sexual identity: "Orsino! I have heard my father name him: / He was a bachelor then" (I.ii.28-29). It is not by accident that she remembers her father as she thinks of Orsino, for she is in the process of turning from the security of parental protection to the uncertainty of sexual affection; but because the world of sexuality is also associated with pain and death—as Feste's first puns about hanging and Viola's later ones about dying emphasize—Viola is reluctant to commit herself completely to this new world. Her thoughts stray from Orsino to the softer figure of Olivia: "O that I served that lady / And might not be delivered to the world, / Till I had made mine own occasion mellow . . ." (I.ii.41-43). But occasion is not altogether under her control—Olivia will admit no kind of suit—and Viola is forced back to her original idea. She resolves to serve the Duke, though not yet with a clearly defined sexual identity. At first she thinks that she can obliterate all sexual considerations by appearing to Orsino as a eunuch; but once within his sphere of influence, she may sense that sexlessness is impossible and, still uncertain about the consequences of her female identity, adopts the disguise of a page to secure a measure of freedom and mobility. But what Viola is also doing by donning this disguise is providing herself with freedom in its manifestation as time.

In *Shakespeare's Festive Comedy* (1959), C. L. Barber made us aware of how important the concept of holiday is to Shakespearean comedy as a whole, where dramatic worlds often mirror the freedom of festival time when traditional rules are overturned and restrictions abandoned. But this kind of freedom is not limited to Shakespeare's dramatic universe in general; it may also find expression in the psyches of particular characters: an unloosening of bonds without may be matched by an equivalent unloosening of bonds within, and for similar reasons. In a time of revelry the state buys long-term obedience at the cost of short-term license; in the process of play the psyche often does the same thing, by temporarily putting away its usual restraints. The purpose of such a psychic holiday is obvious: it gives rein to impulses and energies in the psyche that might otherwise build to explosive proportions, and at the same time it allows for experimentation with, and maturation of, developing forms of identity.

In the development of the integrated human personality, modern psychoanalytic study suggests, the most important such psychic holiday occurs during adolescence. Erikson calls it a "psychosocial moratorium" and describes its crucial importance to adolescent girls:

> woman's life too contains . . . a sanctioned period of delay of adult functioning. The maturing girl . . . may venture into "outer space" with a bearing and a curiosity which often appears hermaphroditic if not outright "masculine." A special ambulatory dimension is thus added to the inventory of her spatial behavior . . . the young girl tries out a variety of possible identifications with the phallic-ambulatory male.

What is most interesting about this analysis, from my perspective, is its relevance to Viola. Here is an account of psychic development that includes newly acquired freedom, adventure into a realm formerly unknown, uncertain sexual identity with a tendency toward hermaphroditic and masculine behavior, and experimentation with a variety of identifications—all important components of Viola's experience in Illyria. Much of the action of *Twelfth Night* can thus be viewed as the depiction of an adolescent identity crisis in Viola, who is struggling with the problems of transition from childhood to adulthood. And, as if to focus attention on this crisis, Shakespeare has compounded it by putting Viola in an isolated position, where she cannot turn back to parental guidance for help. She is, in short, subjected to the tyranny of freedom; liberated from her past, she must play out different roles in order to discover what her mature identity is to be in the future: to discover who she is, she has to discover also who she is not.

First she attempts to put problems of sexuality aside by proclaiming herself a eunuch, but that plan is apparently rejected as soon as she gets close enough to discover that sexual impulses cannot be negated merely by proclamation. It is an idea that Shakespeare used twice before as the starting point for comedy—in *Love's Labour's Lost* and *The Taming of the Shrew*—and would use again with more serious overtones in *Measure for Measure*. Here, however, it is passed over quickly in Viola's experience because it is going to be given much more thorough treatment in the characterization of Olivia.

The next role that Viola assumes, and is least inclined to put away at the end, is the one obviously associated with her disguise. It is what Erikson, in talking about the adolescent female in general, calls her "identifications with the phallic-ambulatory male"—ambulatory because she tries out the freedom of movement that society generally denies young women, phallic because such freedom and mobility enable her to penetrate into realms of experience previously unknown. In her disguise as a young man Viola is free to move first from the seashore to the court and then back and forth between the court and Olivia's house. In addition, the increasingly phallic nature of her activity in this disguise is suggested by the progression from her penetration by stealth into Orsino's court, through her more obvious verbal and psychological assault of Olivia, to her blatant confrontation of Sir Andrew with the ultimately phallic weapon, the sword. Of course both Sir Andrew and Viola assume their roles as duelists with the greatest reluctance because they are, finally, not fitted to their usurped masculine attire. Though for obviously different reasons, each is inadequately equipped to deal with the manifold social, sexual, and psychological responsibilities of mature masculine identity. But each can discover his inadequacies only by playing out his assumed role to its inevitable conclusion.

Viola must do so because her initial freedom is accompanied by a concomitant confusion of sexual identity. Partly this is a result of conflicts attending her situation in general, for confusion of sexual identity is a common problem for a young woman trying to decide who and what she is, and will become. During such time, Erikson writes [in *Identity, Youth and Crisis*], "the young person does not feel himself clearly to be a member of one sex or the other," and she may as a consequence experiment with a variety of sexual identities. But mostly Viola's confusion of identity results from the fact that she is a twin. Since she and Sebastian, as twins, together constitute "A natural perspective, that is and not" (V.i.224)—an apparent singleness of identity within a doubleness of form—her sense of self must necessarily include a sense of other self that is her brother. Thus when he is apparently lost, she faces the psychic extinction of debilitating inaction. In almost her first speech Viola describes the feeling of paralysis that threatens to accompany the loss of her brother; without him she wonders if she can *do* anything: "And what should I do in Illyria? / My brother he is in Elysium" (I.ii.3-4). As a woman, then, she may imagine herself psychically incomplete, because her female identity does not take adequate account of her missing male counterpart. Perhaps to compensate for this feeling, Viola attempts to integrate Sebastian's masculineness into her own personality: she dons his clothes and moves with the freedom characteristic of a young man. She does not, however, like her forerunner in the source story, assume her brother's name, because she is not trying to obliterate her own feminine identity; she is not trying to *become* Sebastian. Instead, her intention is to secure for herself a temporary psychic holiday in order to try out various modes of behavior before settling on the finality of adult commitment. She does not understand the action in these terms, but the language of delay appears recurrently in her thoughts:

> O that I served that lady
> And might not be delivered to the world,

Till I had made mine own occasion mellow,
What my estate is!

                             (I.ii.41-44)

What else may hap to time I will commit;
Only shape thou thy silence to my wit.

                             (I.ii.60-61)

O time! thou must untangle this, not I;
It is too hard a knot for me to untie!

                             (II.ii.41-42)

In her choice of name Viola emphasizes the tenuousness of her position, because "Cesario" suggests, among other things, premature birth, delivery into a world before the attainment of full growth. Whether its sound also suggests Arion on the sea, and thereby Sebastian as he is described by Viola's nameless ship captain, is a matter of conjecture. Such a suggestion, though, would underscore the idea that Viola, in putting on her disguise as Cesario, is attempting to integrate aspects of Sebastian's personality into her own. It might also help to explain why Viola is later so reluctant to recognize Sebastian as an entity unto himself. Having lived so long with him as part of her personality, she may be unconsciously hesitant to admit him to the outside world again, partly because he will then no longer be under her psychic management and partly because his reappearance signals the end to her period of play: she must then put away her masculine usurped attire, and with it a mobility and masculine freedom that she will never know again.

It is no wonder that she may experience this kind of unconscious reaction to surrendering her masculine freedom, since the only clearly feminine role she tries on as Cesario is hardly more suited to her developing sexual identity than the role of eunuch. And, like her identity as eunuch, its expression is confined to language, not action. The role is that of the silent, passive, long-suffering female, and it significantly involves time, not as delay for the germination of action, but as permanent entrapment in inaction and grief:

My father had a daughter loved a man,

     . . . . .

       she pined in thought,
And with a green and yellow melancholy
She sat like patience on a monument,
Smiling at grief.

                           (II.iv.110-18)

Viola may be silent about her love for Orsino—though in moments like this one she no doubt hopes he will penetrate her disguise—but she hardly sits like patience on a monument. Instead, she counters her sorrow with the almost constant activity in "outer space" that goes with her disguise as a young man. In this respect she provides a marked contrast to other characters in the play who respond to love by various kinds of withdrawal.

For instance, Olivia first expresses her love for her dead brother by withdrawing into her house and closing out even the sun. Then later, when she has decided to put aside her mourning veil, she sends a servant after Cesario and bids him come to her, where they may confer in private. Even her courtship of Sebastian is essentially an act of withdrawal: what she really wants to do with her lover-husband is lock him up within her own private inner space—in her house, in her church, in her bedroom, and ultimately in her body. But during such withdrawal she at least admits another person, even if her union with him is constrictively possessive. Orsino and Malvolio cannot do even that, because their idea of love is really just a form of self-involvement. Their erotic fantasies leave no room for another person—only for a self-generated image of that person. As a result, each ultimately calls for the absolute privacy of autistic isolation. "I myself am best / When least in company" (I.iv.37-38), Orsino assures his servants, while Malvolio, as is his habit, is a good deal blunter: "let me enjoy my private" (III.iv.99). Shakespeare's pun here—it is surely his and not Malvolio's—is also instructive because it emphasizes the kind of adolescent constrictiveness that logically results from such a self-serving approach to love. Like Malvolio's other Freudian slip about winding his watch and "play [ing] with my—some rich jewel" (II.v.66), it directs us to the essentially masturbatory nature of his, and Orsino's, withdrawal. Locked in the love of vain, self-generated images, each experiences figuratively what it is Malvolio's misfortune to endure literally; imprisonment in darkness with only the self for company.

Malvolio's imprisonment, though, does more than draw attention to his and the Duke's limitations as lovers; it also gives explicit dramatic expression to a motif of implicit thematic importance throughout: entrapment. Few characters in *Twelfth Night* escape imprisonment of one kind or another. The most obvious victims besides Malvolio are Viola's rescuer and Antonio, who are locked forever in the limbo of indefinite incarceration. Before the ship captain can be released, Malvolio has to be relocated and pacified; before Antonio can be freed, he must be pardoned by Orsino. Neither captive is in an enviable position, for Malvolio's promise of revenge attests to an uncompromising bitterness hardly compatible with the reconciliations characteristic of comic resolutions, and Orsino's failure to grant Antonio pardon is almost as conspicuous as the silence of Duke Antonio in the last scene of *The Tempest*. Both may be versions in the comic mode of Iago's "From this time forth I never will speak word" (*Othello* V.ii.304), an intransigent refusal to communicate with those whose values one cannot accept. Whether the audience is supposed to be consciously aware of such problems is a debatable question, though surely some measure of awareness is generated by the Duke's order to pursue Malvolio and by Antonio's presence on the stage. What cannot be denied, however, is the fact that such problems focus attention on other examples of imprisonment, both voluntary and involuntary, in the play.

Olivia is for a time locked in her house, while Sebastian is confined first at Antonio's and then at Olivia's. Sir Andrew and Sir Toby, rebelling against the confinement of Olivia's exaggerated mourning plan, become imprisoned in another kind of excess as the monotonous circularity of their early-morning catch suggests. Orisino and Malvolio, each in his own special way, are trapped in self-generated, autistic love. Even Feste and Viola, who are the most mobile of Illyria's inhabitants, are ultimately constricted by their Illyrian dress. The Fool, continually forced to adjust his mood to the tastes of his superiors, faces as the price of possible failure the ultimate form of constriction: "my lady will hang thee for thy absence" (I.v.3-4). And Viola, who first dons the disguise of Cesario in order to secure a greater measure of freedom, finds that disguise ever more restricting until at last it threatens her with both confinement and self-annihilation: "Cesario, husband, stay" (V.i.146).

Such suggestions of entrapment qualify the happiness of the resolution. In a world so marked by constriction, marriage may also appear as another form of imprisonment, particularly when it is entered upon in such haste and for such foolish reasons. Olivia does not even know the name of her husband, Sir Toby has married Maria to repay her for gulling Malvolio, and Orsino is betrothed to Viola because he liked her when she was a boy. To the end his concerns are with surface judgments and self-generated images of the loved one: before recognizing Viola as a woman he must see her in feminine dress, and even then his intention is to make her his *fancy's* queen. Perhaps as testimony to the precariousness of this union, to the violence that can at any moment transform Orsino's totalitarian commitment from love to hate, is the figure of Antonio, whose faithful, vigorous love has not, like Viola's, been at last rewarded by Orsino's grace. Antonio's fate, we know, can become hers if the outlines of her character do not match the figures of Orsino's fancy: "Why should I not, had I the heart to do it, / Like to the Egyptian thief at point of death, / Kill what I love?" (V.i.120-22). Momentarily the energies of such potential violence threaten the apparent order of the resolution, but they are quickly pushed back down beneath the surface of things by the happy ending. In Viola's action, however, there is perhaps some evidence of uncertainty. She ignores Antonio, as if she were afraid

to recognize what his presence at her betrothal means. More noticeably, she seems to draw out the recognition scene with her brother interminably, as if, reluctant to discard her disguise, she were luxuriating for a few last, precious moments in the play world of masculine freedom. She talks about putting on her woman's weeds, but about this problem there is more than the necessary amount of talk, and less than the necessary amount of action. Then, at the end, she is strangely silent, as if she were fondly remembering all that is past. She might, though, for all we know, be joyfully anticipating the future and her role as Orsino's fancy's queen. If so, we wish her luck; but we cannot share her optimism, because we remember that Twelfth Night marks the conclusion of revelry and is always succeeded, as Feste reminds us, by a long season of wind and rain.

LANGUAGE AND COMMUNICATION

The use of language in *Twelfth Night* contributes to the sense of comedic festivity: much of the humor in the play centers on wordplay or choice of language. Feste and Viola both use words skillfully, revealing only as much as they choose to reveal. Some critics, such as Yumi Murakami, have examined the relationship between wordplay and characterization. Murakami argues that wordplay is used by Viola, Olivia, and Maria to engage their wit and intellect; by Feste to express humor and sarcasm; and by Orsino as a means of presenting his poetry. Other critics, including Terrence Eagleton, have anaylzed the destructive nature and power of language in *Twelfth Night*.

Critics take different views on whether the characters' speeches and messages communicate the truth or not. **Ralph Berry** contends that most of the acts of communications in *Twelfth Night* serve only to reinforce the characters' fantasies and convey no real truth. **Elizabeth Yearling**, however, argues that despite the disguises and deceptions of the characters, their speech conveys a true sense of their personalities. Both would agree, however, that the double meanings and jests of the play reinforce the thematic contrast of fantasy and reality.

Ralph Berry

SOURCE: "The Messages of *Twelfth Night*," in *Shakespeare's Comedies: Explorations in Form*, Princeton University Press, 1972, pp. 196-212.

[*Berry contends that the action in* Twelfth Night *centers on acts of communication—formal messages being sent and received. Most of these, in the critic's view, are not "true" communication: Olivia's message to Orsino in the first act, for example, is really an announcement to herself of her intention to continue mourning her brother. The letter that fools Malvolio is another instance of a message that fails to convey truth. In contrast, the critic describes Malvolio's message to Olivia from his confinement as the single act of true communication in the play.*]

The burden of the theme of fantasy and reality is entrusted to a particular device: the message. The action of *Twelfth Night* is in great part the business, literal and symbolic, of communication. Each Act sees one or more formal messages—I do not count informal and oral bringing of news. They constitute the archetypal action of the play.

The first scene contains an important message: Olivia to Orsino, a declaration of her absurd vow to mourn her brother for seven years. It is not a true communication, merely the publication of a fantasy; the "message" is a self-to-self statement. The same is true of Orsino's reply to Viola (I, 4); he, too, is announcing his own fantasy: "Surprise her with discourse of my dear faith; / It shall become thee well to act my woes." (1, 4, 24-25) The resonance of "act" is suggestive. Still, the nuncio's function is faithfully carried out by Viola:

> I will on with my speech in your praise and then
> show you the heart of my message. . . . Tell me
> your mind. I am a messenger. (I, 5, 181-2 . . . 194-5)

Viola has the understanding and intelligence for the discharge of her office. Even so, Olivia and Orsino cannot be said to communicate. The matter is repeated with greater emphasis and clarity in II, 4, when Orsino again sends his declaration of love. He is simply not interested in any answer but acceptance.

> *Viola:* But if she cannot love you, sir?
> *Duke:* I cannot be so answered.
>
> (II, 4, 86-87)

In other words, he will not accept the realities of the situation. It is a manifesto of noncommunication. Olivia's message to Viola (II, 2) is no more satisfactory. The messenger, Malvolio, has no idea of what is going on, but Viola immediately apprehends the situation: "She loves me sure." (II, 2, 21) The fault lies in the sender, prey to another species of illusion.

The play's main pseudo-message is the letter, supposedly from Olivia to Malvolio. His fantasy has been penetrated, and the "message" is no more than an inflation of his hopes. The scene in which Malvolio discovers the letter is, in addition to its other qualities, pure symbolist drama. The point is that Malvolio goes for a walk in the sun.

> *Maria:* He has been yonder i'the sun
> practicing behavior to his own shadow this
> half hour.
>
> (II, 5, 14-15)

And "sun," in the terms of this play, is the associate of folly. Feste makes the connection, to Viola: "Foolery, sir, does walk about the orb like the sun; it shines everywhere." (III, 1, 37-38) The connection is in any case confirmed by IV, 2 (the structural balance to II, 5, in the design of *Twelfth Night*), which presents the complementary paradox of reason in darkness. So Malvolio's journey into illusion takes the form of a walk in the sun.

Thus the comic business develops the serious concern of *Twelfth Night*, the fallibility of human communication. And the variations on this theme continue in Act III, through Sir Andrew's letter to Viola/Cesario. That letter is totally misconceived, a triumph of noncommunication. Sir Andrew has misjudged the situation, the identity of his addressee, his language—and to crown all, his message is not even delivered. His effort ranks with Malvolio's as the non-message of the play. Sir Toby (whose role now contrasts with Viola, the ideal messenger) delivers orally two lying messages, to Viola and Sir Andrew. Their purpose is merely deception. But Sir Toby's view of the essence of correspondence has already been made plain in his advice to Sir Andrew in III, 2: the key word is "lies." (III, 2, 40)

That is as far as *Twelfth Night* can go in its variations on failure of communication. The remainder of the play shows a struggling toward the light. Act IV, 2 is the critical scene. It reveals a Malvolio purged of fantasy, and striving only to make contact with the realities of the world. Matched with the sunfilled garden of II, 5, the cell completes the pairing of symbolist scenes. The darkness that figures ignorance—a form of illusion—closes about Malvolio, but his mind is clear:

> *Malvolio:* I am not mad, Sir Topas. I say to
> you this house is dark.
> *Clown:* Madman, thou errest. I say there is
> no darkness but ignorance, in which thou
> art more puzzled than the Egyptians in
> their fog.
> *Malvolio:* I say this house is as dark as
> ignorance, though ignorance were as dark
> as hell; and I say there was never man thus
> abused. I am no more mad than you are.
> Make the trial of it in any constant
> question.
>
> (IV, 2, 40-48)

Malvolio's attempts to penetrate the darkness are obstructed by the clown's feignings. But Malvolio has regained a human dignity, that of a man as disciplined guardian of his faculties. His language is controlled and just: "I think nobly of the soul and in no way approve his opinion." (IV, 2, 54-55) And he has, at last, a full grasp of the priorities of human needs. "Good fool, some ink, paper, and light; and convey what I will set down to my lady." (IV, 2, 106-108) The light of reason, a just message to compose, and the means of communication, he can command. The clown cannot refuse his cooperation.

And this message, from Malvolio to Olivia, is the apotheosis of the final Act. It is the message of a man in full possession of his senses and the situation; it is mediated, not by the clown (his tone, as he himself seems to feel, would be wrong) but by the nondescript and "neutral" Fabian; it finds an understanding audience, both the Duke ("This savors not much of distraction," V, 1, 304) and Olivia, "He hath been most notoriously abused." (V, 1, 368) Malvolio's letter has the distinction of being— of all the formal messages in *Twelfth Night*—the only true communication. It is the only occasion in the play when the human mind, unencumbered by fantasy, reaches out toward another human mind and finds its message fairly delivered, understandingly received, and answered. All the other messages are deceptions or self-illusions.

The principals, however, are not compelled to face reality in the same way as Malvolio. Orsino, the premier fantasist, merely switches faces in his image of the dream-woman. His first impulse on learning of Viola's sex is "let me see thee in thy woman's weeds" (V, 1, 265); and the unabashed auto-eroticism of his humor is underscored in his final words to Viola: "But when in other habits you are seen, / Orsino's mistress and his fancy's queen." (V, 1, 376-377) For "fancy," read "fantasy." His last line is a poised, ambiguous phrase. Will Viola control his fantasy, or embody it? One cannot prophesy. Olivia, too, is doubtless well off with the sensible Sebastian, but the "most extracting frenzy of mine own" (V, 1, 273) testifies to her susceptibility to the caprice of passion. As for the others, Sir Andrew's fantasy is ended. He had rather than forty pound he were at home; the phrase is a calculated multiplication of his earlier desire to exchange forty shillings for the trappings of folly. (II, 3, 18-19) His anagnorisis is to hear the truth from Sir Toby: "Will *you* help? An ass-head and a coxcomb and a knave, a thin-faced knave, a gull?" (V, 1, 198-199) We do not know his reactions; the audience will be able to savor his horrified face; but that truth, as with others in the play, must continue to fester. Sir Toby himself has married Maria "In recompense thereof . . ." (V, 1, 354), and in view of Maria's talents and shrewishness one is inclined to regard "recompense" as a pregnant word.

And there remains Malvolio. Here, I think, the critics have overcompensated. We have been told with considerable frequency of late years that one ought not to feel at all sorry for him, that he deserved all he got, that Elizabethan audiences would have laughed at his final disgrace, and that compassion is a nineteenth century invention anyway. No doubt all this is true. Elizabethan audiences, like modern ones, can never have been lacking in those who find only the most exquisite humor in the final "I'll be revenged on the whole pack of you." But I don't think it really matters whether one feels sorry for Malvolio, or not. The point, surely, is that he is *there*. Malvolio is an unassimilable element, a part of what is conceived to be the structure of comedy, that refuses to participate in the final dance. That dance is a gavotte of the realists coolly taking on the fantasists; it is scarcely the "communal integration" of the sentimentalists. The "golden time" that Orsino speaks of sounds hollowly.

The play as a whole is a masterly exposition of theme through device, that is to say of form. If we agree that the theme of *Twelfth Night* is reality and illusion, then this theme, obviously, is expressed through disguise, deception, and error. But the action of *Twelfth Night*, as I have shown, consists of a succession of pseudo-messages, products of the world of illusion. And it incorporates two scenes of startling theater, in which Malvolio receives, and sends, a message. At these points, the scenes of sunlight and of darkness, the symbolism of the drama becomes overt. Yet they are only the most compelling manifestation of an action that, in Shakespeare's way, is always reaching toward symbolism. The literal events generate their further meanings.

The form of *Twelfth Night,* as I maintain, should govern our interpretation. The open-ended invitation of the subtitle is no reason for disregarding the structure of the play. Its atmosphere one can in part ascribe to a particular production, and this will vary very greatly. Yet I think W. H. Auden [in *The Dyer's Hand,* 1962] is right to sense the "inverted commas around the 'fun.'" This stems from the nature of the action, and the questions left in the air concerning the principals. Exposure to reality has, in different ways, involved pain for the "comic" characters; Sir Toby, Sir Andrew, and Malvolio. But for Orsino and Olivia, the ending is illusion condoned. To speak of "unmasking" is surely misleading, for they have begun neither to understand nor confront their problems; nor need they. The cynicism of *Twelfth Night* lies in its acceptance of the truths that fantasy need not bring unhappiness, not exposure to reality happiness. The preoccupation with illusion and reality, madness and sanity, wisdom and folly, points unmistakably toward *King Lear.* The synthesis of theme and device could not be repeated within the genre of comedy.

Elizabeth M. Yearling

SOURCE: "Language, Theme, and Character in *Twelfth Night*," in *Shakespeare Survey: An Annual Survey of Shakspearean Study and Production*, Vol. 35, 1982, pp. 79-86.

[*Yearling contends that in* Twelfth Night, *language communicates truth, despite the play's deliberate deceptions and wordplay. Choice of language helps to convey a sense of character: Viola's ability to adapt to changing circumstances, for example, is reflected in her speech, which varies from courtly compliments to "rude jargon" depending on to whom she is speaking. Sir Toby mixes colloquial expressions with elaborate language, reflecting his "disorder" as a knight with questionable habits. Malvolio, even when he is alone, chooses pretentious words, reflecting his egotism. Yearling goes on to show how language supports a thematic contrast of the play: throughout* Twelfth Night, *characters abruptly switch from elaborate, indirect speech to short, direct, action-focused sentences, reflecting the contrast between the make-believe world of holiday festivities and the ordinary world of work and responsibility.*]

[By the late sixteenth century, if had become] fashionable to decry eloquence and to praise plain, unassuming style. But theory has to be tested in practice. The greatest practitioner of the period, Shakespeare, happend to be a playwright, and drama, where the author does not directly address readers or audience, has its special problems. The dramatist needs many styles, not just one plain style. He can allow his villains to exploit deceptive words, but he must also find words for his heroes and heroines, who usually need to speak more than Cordelia's 'nothing'. He cannot embark on a diction which expresses the essence of things. Spenser's technique is a matter for the study, often—as with his spelling—for eye rather than ear. Shakespeare has to find ways of communicating truth which are more complex than any theoretical straightforward relationship of word and subject-matter.

His problems are aired—semi-seriously—in *Twelfth Night*. Half-way through the play, Viola and Feste meet and jest about words and meaning (3.1.1-60). The significance of their exchange is uncertain. T. W. Craik writes [in the Preface to *Twelfth Night*, New Arden, (1975)] that the encounter sounds like 'a warming-up after a theatrical interval'. Yet this is the only meeting between Shakespeare's heroine and his fool. Their quibbling shows the two-facedness of words. Feste comments on how quickly 'the wrong side' of a sentence 'may be turned outward'. His own punning on Viola's description of words as 'wanton'—'equivocal'—turns to absurdity the idea that words equal things. He worries about his sister's name since 'her name's a word, and to dally with that word might make my sister wanton'. He

uses his theory that 'words are very rascals' to avoid justifying his opinion, for 'words are grown so false, I am loath to prove reason with them'. The debate itself embodies the slipperiness of words, and the confusion is compounded when Feste admits to being Olivia's 'corrupter of words'. His trade is to use words deceptively, and what he says cannot be trusted. Shakespeare makes it difficult to take the scene seriously.

Yet often in *Twelfth Night* he shows words to be frivolous, conventional, or false. Apart from Feste's comments there is Olivia's remark about the poetical being 'the more like to be feigned' (1.5.197) [quotations from New Arden Shakespeare (1975)]. Occasionally characters use words as mere decoration. The most blatant example is Sir Andrew, who stores useful vocabulary such as the 'odours', 'pregnant', and 'vouchsafed', of Viola's greeting to Olivia (3.1.92). Feste punctures words which he finds swollen. 'Vent thy folly somewhere else', Sebastian snaps incautiously, and is punished by some sarcastic variations on 'vent' which must cure him of the verb (4.1.10-17). Feste's mockery can conceal further jokes. To Viola he remarks, 'who you are and what you would are out of my welkin. I might say "element", but the word is overworn' (3.1.58-60). 'Welkin' too is an old-fashioned, poetic word. The overworn noun 'element' is used by several characters, from Viola to Malvolio. A time-bomb has been set for Malvolio's pompous 'I am not of your element' (3.4.125).

But tired or inflated vocabulary brings us to one of the play's complexities. A rich source of chiché was the language of compliment, the store of polite but often insincere coutesies which came naturally to the well-bred but had to be taught to the uncourtly in manuals which suggested the right phrases for wooing and suing. And it is the heroine who is the play's main speaker in this fossilized, conventional style. Olivia rejects Viola's address:

> *Viola.*
>   Cesario is your servant's name, fair
>   princess.
> *Olivia.*
>   My servant, sir? 'Twas never merry world
>   Since lowly feigning was call'd compliment:
>   Y'are servant to the Count Orsino, youth.

She could also have criticized the fashionable epithet, 'fair'. Viola justified her use of 'servant' by explaining the word literally:

> And he is yours, and his must needs be
>   yours:
> Your servant's servant is your servant,
>   madam.
>
>   (3.1.99-104)

The sentence Viola turns into a neat excuse was still paraded as a compliment half-way through the century, in Philomusus's *The Academy of Compliments* (1646): 'Sir, I am the servant of your servants' (p. 74). And Viola's 'vouchsafed', so admired by Sir Andrew, is something of an affectation. The verb 'vouchsafe' means 'grant in a condescending manner' and was appropriate between subject and monarch but less fitting in other relationships. Its use is mocked as over-deferential by many Elizabethan and Jacobean dramatists. Much of Viola's language, especially to Olivia, is affected, courtly, artificial, not the style we expect of a Shakespearian heroine. But Shakespeare exploits this conventional speech brilliantly. In act 1, scene 5, Viola's speeches in praise of Olivia are full of stock poetic phrases: 'red and white', 'cruell'st she alive', 'sighs of fire', 'call upon my soul', 'contemned love' (ll. 242-80). She borrows the standard phraseology of the sonnet-writers. But she also mocks herself. She worries about whether she is speaking to the right woman, and claims she is anxious to complete her penned speech. The scene turns on Viola's semiserious use of conventional vocabulary and images, her knowledge of what she is doing, and our share in that knowledge. Yet there is more. The stereotyped language conveys a considerable depth of feeling. ''Tis beauty truly blent' is a genuine appreciation of Olivia's beauty and of Viola's task as a rival. 'Make me a willow cabin . . .' is a powerful love speech. The strength and truth of feeling make it wrong to concentrate on the clichés and stock motifs, or on the speech's deception. Viola uses words devalued by overexposure; she speaks them as Cesario, whose existence is illusory, but their emotion convinces. We must add to Olivia's remark that the poetical is 'like to be feigned', Touchstone's ambiguous words in *As You Like It*: 'the truest poetry is the most feigning' (3.3.16).

Viola's poetry shows us Shakespeare's success in using falsehood to communicate truth. She deceives Olivia. Yet the audience, though undeceived, receives from the same language a sense of shared and genuine emotion. There is another way in which Viola's words communicate a truth. Her style expresses her nature. She is a linguistic chameleon who adapts her style to her companion. Her vocabulary ranges from courtly compliment to rude jargon (1.5.205). But her variousness is not just verbal: her nature is to deal confidently with sudden changes. And the assumed registers, coupled often with sincere feelings, capture the blend of truth and illusion which Viola represents. It is difficult not to see a convincing personality breaking through the polite fiction which is Cesario. This is most notable in Viola's discussion of love with Orsino in act 2, scene 4, but even the play's less spectacular passages can take us below Cesario's surface. After Antonio, in the belief that she is Sebastian, has interrupted her reluctant duelling, he asks for his money:

Viola.
What money, sir?
For the fair kindness you have show'd me
    here,
And part being prompted by your present
    trouble,
Out of my lean and low ability
I'll lend you something. My having is not
    much;
I'll make division of my present with you.
Hold, there's half my coffer.

                              (3.4.349-55)

The last line echoes, with an important difference, Antonio's 'Hold, sir, here's my purse' (3.3.38). Antonio's was a gift of unqualified generosity to a friend. Viola's is a carefully thought-out loan to a helpful but puzzling stranger. She moves slowly towards the offer. 'I'll lend' is preceded by a series of subordinate clauses and phrases outlining her reasons and stressing her poverty. 'My having is not much' repeats the content of the line before, and adds to our impression that Viola feels an uncomfortable need to justify herself. Her next speech contrasts in its vehemence. Antonio reminds Viola of his former 'kindnesses'.

Viola.   I know of none,
Nor know I you by voice or any feature.
I hate ingratitude more in a man
Than lying, vainness, babbling drunkenness,
Or any taint of vice whose strong corruption
Inhabits our frail blood.

                              (3.4.361-6)

There is no delay in reaching the point here. The verbs come first, several of them, forcefully stating an immediate reaction. We are persuaded that the speaker is not the illusory Cesario. No courteous surface falsifies these emotions.

Although *Twelfth Night* includes Feste's scepticism and many instances of verbal folly and deception, Shakespeare's practice encourages a positive belief in the power of words. Character and theme emerge from the nature of the words and the way they are combined. Here we are a little closer to the Platonic theory of names. Several characters in *Twelfth Night* have an individual vocabulary and syntax. Orsino's relatively short part in the play contains a high proportion of new and often slightly pompous words. In act 1, scene 4, he praises Viola's youthful appearance: 'Diana's lip / Is not more smooth and *rubious*'; 'And all is *semblative* a woman's part' (ll.31-4). In act 2, scene 4, he contributes 'cloyment' to the stodgy line, 'That suffers surfeit, cloyment, and revolt' (l.100). Act 5, scene 1 brings more new vocabulary—'baubling' and 'unprizable' describe Antonio's ship (ll. 52-3); Olivia, the 'marble-breasted' tyrant (l. 122), casts his faith to 'non-regardance' (l. 119). New words are common in

Orsino's vocabulary, especially words of several syllables ending in suffixes. His syntax is appropriate. Barbara Hardy notes his long sentences and sustained images, characteristics which are marked in the first scene. He uses little colloquial, easy speech.

Sir Toby is an interesting contrast. He also invents long words—'substractors' (1.3.34), 'consanguineous' (2.3.78), 'intercepter' (3.4.224). And his syntax is mannered. He teases Sir Andrew: 'Wherefore are these things hid? Wherefore have these gifts a curtain before 'em? Are they like to take dust, like Mistress Mall's picture? Why dost thou not go to church in a galliard, and come home in a coranto?' (1.3.122-6). The rhetorical questions and repeated 'wherefore' are part of a complete repetition of meaning in the first two questions, and there is syntactical balance in the last sentence. Sir Toby likes to put nouns in pairs, which sometimes alliterate: 'they are scoundrels and substractors' (1.3.34); 'he's a coward and a coistrel' (1.3.40). But Sir Toby's long words and patterned syntax are not enough to elevate his speech. His long words occur in prose, not verse, and their use undercuts their impressiveness: 'substractor' is a nonce-word meaning 'detractor' and it *sounds* like a drunken fumbling for words. Another good word to tumble over is 'consanguineous' which is accompanied by a gentle parody of the scholar's habit of pairing foreign imports with simpler words: 'Am not I consanguineous? Am I not of her blood?' M. M. Mahood notes that 'exquisite' (2.3.142) is 'a difficult word for the drunken knights to get their tongues round'. The same must be true of Sir Toby's compliment to Maria: 'Good night, Penthesilea' (2.3.177). The polysyllables are undermined by being spoken drunkenly, and also by the company they keep, since Sir Toby's speeches contain popular phrases and words of low origin. He is recorded as the first literary user of 'bum-baily' (3.4.178), the meanest kind of bailiff, a title which must have been current in the least reputable areas of London. His first words are 'What a plague' (1.3.1); he tells Malvolio to 'Sneck up!' (2.3.94); he uses the vulgar phrase 'call me cut' (2.3.187), and colloquial words such as 'coistrel' (1.3.40). He is also the play's most frequent user of the second person pronoun 'thou' instead of the more formal 'you'.

Sir Toby's speech mixes impressive vocabulary and mannered syntax with colloquial words. It reflects his disorder but at the same time a certain openness to experience. Malvolio's language indicates constraint. He introduces fewer new words than either Orsino or Sir Toby, but his mouth is full of pompous phrases and long words without the poetry of Orsino or the colloquialism of Sir Toby. He is at his worst in contemplation, in the letter scene (2.5.23-179). Inflated vocabulary is not simply a public front but is his very nature. 'A look round' becomes 'a demure travel of regard', 'what do these letters mean?' becomes

'what should that alphabetical position portend?'. Long abstract words abound: 'there is no consonancy in the sequel; that suffers under probation'. The homelier words of his tirade in act 2, scene 3 are there only to signify his disgust: 'Have you no wit, manners, nor honesty, but to gabble like tinkers at this time of night? Do ye make an ale-house of my lady's house, that ye squeak out your coziers' catches without any mitigation or remorse of voice?' (ll. 88-92). His style is noun-laden: nouns come in strings or separated by the preposition 'of'. The change when he woos Olivia (3.4.17-55) is interesting. He is still pompous and noun-obsessed—'this does make some obstruction in the blood'—but he throws in the fashionable word 'sweet' and quotes fragments of popular songs: 'Please one, and please all', 'Ay, sweetheart, and I'll come to thee'. Here he uses the familiar 'thou', unthinkable from a servant to his lady. The visible changes in appearance and behaviour are accompanied by more subtle changes in his language.

Other characters have personal styles. Sir Andrew, magpie-like, purloins impressive words, misuses long words (5.1.179-80), and tends to echo the speaker before him (1.3.62-3, 2.3.56). Feste parodies his superiors' polysyllables: 'I did impeticos thy gratillity' (2.3.27). He demands Olivia's attention to Malvolio's letter with the words 'perpend, my princess' (5.1.298), mocking—M. P. Tilley argues—the style of *Cambyses* [in 'Shakespeare and his Ridicule of "Cambyses"', *Modern Language Notes*, 24 (1909), 244-7, p. 244]. And he produces nonsense names, 'Pigrogromitus' (2.3.23), 'Quinapalus' (1.5.33). His verbal whimsy complicates the debate about words. His attacks on words and their falsehood tell us more about Feste than about words.

When we read or hear *Twelfth Night* we learn about the characters by attending to their vocabulary and syntax. Besides expressing character, the words and sentence structure can also clarify themes. One of the play's contrasts is between holiday and the work-a-day world. Although the title suggests festivity, recent criticism has qualified C. L. Barber's treatment of *Twelfth Night* as a festive comedy. Many modern critics dwell on the play's melancholy mood, but in more positive opposition to festivity are the characters' working lives. Sir Toby and Sir Andrew hope that life 'consists of eating and drinking' (2.3.11-12), but their fellows have more to do. Even Orsino, who has let his dukedom rule itself, at last resumes his function as ruler and magistrate. Viola is kept hard at work, Feste too—and when he is absent without leave he is threatened with dismissal. Malvolio and Maria have duties in Olivia's household, and Olivia has that household to organize (4.3.16-20).

The contrast between holiday and work results in an interesting structural device. There are repeated movements from musing or conversation back to some necessary task. These shifts are embodied in the dialogue, and centre on Viola. It is easy to note the difference between the first scene's languor and the second scene's sense of purpose, but even within scene 2 there is a distinct change of mood. Viola and the Captain discuss her brother's fate and she is encouraged to hope for his safety:

> Mine own escape unfoldeth to my hope,
> Whereto thy speech serves for authority,
> The like of him.
>
> (1.2.19-21)

The lines are in verse, the first has a formal old-fashioned -eth verb ending, and the object is delayed by a subordinate clause. Viola then switches to practical questions about her present situation: 'Know'st thou this country?'; 'Who governs here?'. The crisper -s ending for the third-person verb belongs with the simple questions and short prose lines which contrast with the Captain's verse replies. Viola's interest in what has or may have happened to her brother is superseded by a need to sort out her own affairs, and her style changes correspondingly. She installs herself in Orsino's service. As his attendant she has opportunities for leisurely talk, but she keeps remembering there are things to be done. In act 1, scene 5, she is Orsino's messenger to Olivia. At first she fences with Olivia but she suddenly returns to duty:

> Olivia. Are you a comedian?
> Viola. No, my profound heart: and yet, by
> the very fangs of malice I swear, I am not
> that I play. Are you the lady of the house?

Her ambiguity about herself is accompanied by an obscure oath. With her question, the conversation becomes more straightforward, only to hide in wordplay again.

> Olivia. If I do not usurp myself, I am.
> Viola. Most certain, if you are she, you do
> usurp yourself: for what is yours to bestow
> is not yours to reserve.

Viola's quibble is followed by an explanation both antithetical and cryptic. But then she changes to short statement—'But this is from my commission'—and a plain declaration of intent: 'I will on with my speech in your praise, and then show you the heart of my message' (1.5.183-92). Similarly her debate with Feste is interrupted by the direct question, 'Is thy lady within?'. Here too the preceding sentence is syntactically more elaborate and plays on words. Feste prays that Jove might send Cesario a beard and Viola replies: 'By my troth, I'll tell thee, I am almost sick for one, [Aside] though I would not have it grow on my chin' (3.1.45-9). In act 2, scene 4, the discussion of

love with Orsino, and the story of Cesario's 'sister', draw to a close with Viola's

> I am all the daughters of my father's house,
> And all the brothers too: and yet I know
> not.

The riddle is couched in repeated phrase-patterns—'all the daughters', 'all the brothers'—followed by a virtual aside. After this we are bound to read a meditative pause till Viola sharply changes the subject: 'Sir, shall I to this lady?' (2.4.121-3). On each of these occasions brief statements and questions replace more complex syntax, often punning or patterned. Viola delights in conversation and jesting debate but is aware of her present duty.

Other characters move similarly into action. Olivia's style in act 1, scene 5 also involves syntactical contrasts although her questions are misleadingly direct. She lingers over jokes such as the inventory of her beauty, but follows with a pertinent question. 'Were you sent hither to praise me?' (1.5.252-3). She continues with what seem to be the same sort of inquiries: 'How does he love me?'; 'Why, what would you?'; 'What is your parentage?' (ll. 258, 271, and 281). She is pursuing what has become important to her, but she has moved from the interview's business—Orsino—to Cesario-Viola, and she stops herself with crisp commands and statements which are more to the immediate purpose.

> Get you to your lord:
> I cannot love him: let him send no more,
> Unless, perchance, you come to me again,
> To tell me how he takes it. Fare you well:
> I thank you for your pains: spend this for
> me.
>
> (1.5.283-7)

The short clauses emphasize her business-like manner. The syntax is more flowing only in the lines where she provides for a return by Cesario, who distracts her from the task of rejecting Orsino, and she couches these lines in the conditional. The lingering 'unless' added to the brusque 'let him send no more' captures her feelings. During her second meeting with Viola, Olivia's ears recall her from distracting thoughts.

> O world, how apt the poor are to be proud!
> If one should be a prey, how much the
> better
> To fall before the lion than the Wolf! [Clock
> strikes.]
> The clock upbraids me with the waste of
> time.
> Be not afraid, good youth, I will not have
> you,

And yet when wit and youth is come to
  harvest,
Your wife is like to reap a proper man.
There lies your way, due west.

(3.1.129-36)

Again complex writing—subordination, apostrophe,
extended metaphor—accompanies the musing. Simple
statements interrupt it. We may compare with Olivia's 'waste of time' the First Officer's short, impatient
sentences when his prisoner Antonio procrastinates:
'What's that to us? The time goes by. Away!' (3.4.373).
These people do not have all the time in the world.
Tasks and duties press on them. Even Sebastian, who
has nothing in particular to do in Illyria, is not prepared just to stand talking to Antonio. Again the
transition is sudden; again questions replace condi-
tionals and balanced phrases.

But were my worth, as is my conscience,
  firm,
You should find better dealing. What's to
  do?
Shall we go see the relics of this town?

(3.3.17-19)

Note especially 'What's to *do*?'. He is later caught up
in Olivia's urge to action when she decides to marry
him. His meditative speech, 'This is the air, that is
the glorious sun' (4.3.1 ff.), is cut off by her arrival
with a request formed like a command: 'Blame not
this haste of mine' (4.3.22).

Orsino's resumption of office is the most elaborate
change in the speed of action. At last he comes to
woo Olivia himself. But before he can talk to her he
is brought some work. The officers enter with Antonio, and Orsino's questioning of that 'notable pirate' is interrupted by Olivia's arrival. For the audience this is their first meeting. The Duke's reaction
is oddly mechanical:

Here comes the Countess: now heaven walks
  on earth
But for thee, fellow—fellow, thy words are
  madness.

(5.1.95-6)

Orsino's 'but' sets the matter in hand against his
response to Olivia. Compare these words with the
equivalent passage in William Burnaby's eighteenth-
century revision of the play. There the Duke has
more to say about the woman he loves:

Now Heav'n walks on Earth, and Beauty
  round
Invades us all! Each glance devotes a Slave,
And every step, she treads upon a heart,
All of the Skies, but pitty you have brought.

Burnaby's addition is heavy-handed but shows he was
aware that Orsino's brief welcome in the original is
a little strange. It could be argued that since Orsino
seems more interested in his own moods than in
Olivia, he can offer only a commonplace compliment
when he actually meets her, and then directs his attention to the Antonio-Cesario conflict which fasci-
nates him. But this is not what happens. Olivia is
Orsino's business. When she appears he is needed as
a magistrate and after acknowledging her briskly he
returns to his case. Then, just as briskly, he quashes
Antonio's complaint and reserves judgement, so that
he can attend to his main concern:

But for thee, fellow—fellow, thy words are
  madness.
Three months this youth hath tended upon
  me;
But more of that anon. Take him aside.

(ll. 96-8)

Again simple, brusque statements announce Orsino's
despatching of business, and another 'but' emphasizes the transitions and oppositions of the passage.
Soon, Orsino resumes his polysyllables and complex sentences.

The words and syntax of *Twelfth Night* are interesting for what they say and for what they are. The
nature of the characters' vocabulary tells us something about them; the sentence structure also exposes
the characters and their moods, and points at thematic oppositions. Even if their surface meaning is deceptive, words can still communicate truthfully. Yet we
are also told that words deceive. And here we might
note a recurring syntactic pattern which embodies
the deceptions of *Twelfth Night*. Earlier I quoted 'I
am not that I play' from Viola's first encounter with
Olivia. This takes up her request to the Captain,
'Conceal me what I am' (1.2.53) and prefigures a
cryptic exchange with Olivia in act 3, scene 1:

Olivia.
  I prithee tell me what thou think'st of me.
Viola.
  That you do think you are not what you
    are.
Olivia.
  If I think so, I think the same of you.
Viola.
  Then think you right; I am not what I am.

(ll. 140-3)

The setting of negative against positive in conjunction with the verb 'to be' is repeated at the end of
the play when Orsino finds Sebastian and Viola
forming 'A natural perspective, that is, and is not!'
(5.1.215). And it is mocked in Feste's joking: '"That
that is, is": so, I, being Master Parson, am Master

511

Parson; for what is "that" but "that"? and "is" but "is"?' (4.2.15-17). In fact here, that that is, is not. Feste is more accurate, but without knowing it, when he tells Sebastian, whom he mistakes for Cesario, 'Nothing that is so, is so' (4.1.8-9). The repeated formula captures the confusion of actuality and fiction which these characters experience. Again the syntax tells us a truth while agreeing that words and events themselves can lie.

We cannot be certain about reality and falsehood when the genuine emotion of 'My father had a daughter loved a man' can move us so. Shakespeare's achievement with language in *Twelfth Night* is to encapsulate the conflict of truth and illusion, and to remind us that facts and truth are not necessarily the same, that the truest poetry often *is* the most feigning.

VIOLA AND OLIVIA

Although Viola and Olivia are closely linked as characters in *Twelfth Night*, critics often view Viola as the central character of the play. While critics H. N. Hudson and William H. Fleming identify Viola as a character who unifies the action, **Lydia Forbes** points out that Olivia serves the purpose of linking the plot elements as the woman who Orsino loves, Viola woos, and the head of the household that Malvolio, Feste, Sir Toby, and Maria all call home. Forbes also discusses the depth of Viola's self-knowledge, which allows her to adopt a disguise and to see with clarity beyond the self-deception of others in the play.

Critics have also focused on Viola as embodying Shakespeare's ideal of love in her patience and in her attitude of self-sacrifice. Critic Barbara Lewalski notes that Viola's behavior sets her apart from her fellow characters and represents "the Word made flesh," reflecting the spirit of Epiphany and Christmas. **Cynthia Lewis** chronicles Viola's moral growth and how it reflects the sacrificial nature of Antonio's love, Antonia being the Christ figure of *Twelfth Night*, according to Lewis. While Viola is generally regarded as the principle figure in the plot, Olivia's character parallels Viola on many levels. In his essay, **Douglas Parker** compares the women and outlines those qualities that lead him to describe them as non-genetic twins. For additional alayses of the characters of Viola and Olivia, see the essay by Harley Granville-Barker in the OVERVIEWS section, and the essay by **J. Dennis Huston** in the ROLE-PLAYING AND PROBLEMS OF IDENTITY section.

Lydia Forbes

SOURCE: "What You Will?" in *Shakespeare Quarter-ly*, Vol. XIII, No. 4, Autumn, 1962, pp. 475-85.

[Forbes illustrates Shakespeare's theme of disguise versus self-deception throughout the story of Viola. Viola is presented as a purposeful young woman who sets out to achieve her goal through any means. She recognizes the scope of her abilities and consents to disguise to buy herself time. Likewise, Olivia adopts the veil of mourning to keep Orsino at bay, who spends most of the play lost in self-delusion, and therefore is unsuitable for her. Viola judges Olivia by what she has heard of her and proceeds to romance Olivia in a way that cannot be successful for Orsino. Consequently, Viola's approach to Olivia wins her not to the Duke, but to Viola. The critic maintains that Olivia is a reasonable woman and perceives Viola to be a match for her in independence and wit, yet Olivia confuses Viola and Sebastian because of her deeper intuitive sense. Olivia perceives similar qualities of spirit in both Sebastian and Cesario: Sebastian matches Cesario in integrity, but is as impetuous as Viola is patient.]

. . . The story of the nobly born Viola, disguised as the page boy, "Cesario", is usually considered the principal plot of *Twelfth Night*. She sets her heart on the Duke Orsino of Illyria, and finally weds him. He is a good man and worthy of her, but temporarily so confused by a romantically far-fetched notion of love that he would not be able to appreciate her in her own feminine dress.

Beside this story we have a series of events engineered by a gentlewoman, Maria, attendant on the Countess Olivia. Maria's aim is to marry Olivia's uncle, Sir Toby Belch. By pretending to gratify Sir Toby's desire to be revenged on the officious steward, Malvolio, Maria succeeds in getting Sir Toby so far out of favor with his niece that he marries Maria in order to remain a member of the household.

Linking these two patterns, the Lady Olivia, as the unresponsive object of Orsino's attentions, moves briskly but with dignity, and an outstanding appreciation of honesty in respect to both the good and the bad.

In the opening scene of the play the audience is regaled with the full exuberance and verbal confusion that deception and self-delusion bring about. It is like a musical opening by Brahms, in which the themes are developed before they are stated. With the second scene, austere and isolated on the seacoast, the premises and the thesis of the play are demonstrated. The sea-captain, who rescues Viola from the shipwreck and brings her ashore in Illyria, describes the country and what he knows of its people. Viola gives us her own measure and his in her famous lines:

> There is a fair behavior in thee captain;
> And though that nature with a beauteous

wall
Doth oft close in pollution, yet of thee
I will believe thou hast a mind that suits
With this thy fair and outward character.

(I.ii.45)

While an ironic contrast exists between Viola's speech and her intention to disguise herself, her recognition of her own limitations and her own "fair behavior" after real peril clear the unreal atmosphere of the opening scene, and also put the following extravagances of Sir Toby and Sir Andrew in their place.

Viola's charm and wit and continual self-consciousness about her own disguise help us understand the people she is dealing with. She is so reasonable and patient that when she trusts someone we are persuaded that her faith is justified. Only the unreasonable in human nature forces her to disguise herself. As a woman of her position, and in such a situation, she could not be a free agent; so she dresses like her brother and calls herself "Cesario". She, like Olivia, needs time to get her bearings after a calamity in her family. She and Olivia dissemble in various ways to gain time.

Viola's first thought after being rescued is the hopeful one that her brother may also have survived. Her second thought is that she must now act on her own account. She has no family here. Since she has apparently heard of Orsino as a possible husband, she becomes a page in his household, to see for herself whether he might fill the bill. Though her deception serves her well, before the play is done Viola admits that disguise is, in fact, a "wickedness" wherein "the pregnant enemy [i.e. the Devil] does much."

The portrait of Viola shows that Shakespeare, in writing a stylized play, does not prevent his characters from coming alive. Their energy does not seem confined by any pattern, but occasionally the pattern becomes so clear that characterization takes second place. The two sea-captains who rescue Viola and Sebastian are a case in point. Shakespeare makes them both men of profound integrity. Antonio, who rescues Sebastian, scorns any disguise even though he knows his life is in danger here, and he is arrested by Orsino's men. Viola's nameless rescuer goes so far as to help her to disguise herself, and keeps her secret even when he is "in durance at Malvolio's suit". Both honest, both imprisoned in this odd land, these two men of the sea make a strong and arbitrary contrast to the prevailing distortions of life on shore in Illyria.

The first *sight* of Orsino, the Duke, should be as different from the first *sound*, as Viola's swaggering costume is from her very feminine nature. The reader of the play sees only the Duke's fantastic words, the actor will show the outward form of Orsino, who, in the last act, says to the sea-captain Antonio

That face of his I do remember well,
Yet, when I saw it last, it was besmear'd
As black as Vulcan in the smoke of war:
A bawbling vessel was the captain of,
For shallow draught and bulk unprizable;
With which most scathful grapple did he
    make
With the most noble bottom of our fleet,
That very envy and the tongue of loss
Cried fame and honor on him.

(V.i.55)

This Duke, who can recognize so well the quality of Antonio, is "noble in nature as in name". Yet for the greater part of the play he is baffled and deluded. Imagining that he is in love with Olivia, he feels both exalted and harassed by his "desires". He grants that he does not prize her riches, but he cannot see that he does not even prize her. Her beauty and her sex arouse in him a kind of emotion, conceit and mixed metaphor which he enjoys and thinks he needs so desperately that, at the end, he cries out for the heart to kill Olivia rather than lose her. So strong can the shape of fancy become!

By the fourth scene, Orsino has actually fallen in love with Viola. She wins him "liver and all" in the second act by talking to him in his own "fantastical" way. Her disguise lets him become devoted, without being confused by the erratic passions he associates with love of woman. That devotion is clear in one of the most comic moments in the last act, when his greeting to Olivia: "Now heaven walks on earth" is followed abruptly by a return to the puzzle of Antonio's identification of Cesario. The only sudden change in Orsino at the end of the play is his loss of the delusion that he loves Olivia.

Olivia's message to Orsino in the opening scene, refusing his suit, should seem like too much protestation, even without the benefit of hindsight. Here is a girl who is suddenly left all alone to manage the affairs of a great estate. She is saddled with her father's younger brother—a liability—and with an importunate neighbor who insists that she wed. She cannot accept him; so she publicly exaggerates out of all reason her natural grief at the death of her brother, so as to keep the unwelcome suitor at arm's length.

Viola, as Orsino's ambassador to Olivia, cannot help judging Olivia by what she has heard, and by the rebuffs encountered at the Countess's gate. To Viola, Olivia is like the subject of Shakespeare's 94th sonnet, one of those who "moving others, are themselves as stone", who take care to be "the lords and owners of their faces". Viola calls her "too proud" when Olivia's unveiling and itemizing of her face emphasize this attitude. There is certainly further deception, conscious or unconscious, by Viola in this first dialogue between these ladies. Viola carries out her master's orders to woo Olivia in a way that cannot succeed.

Viola's wit and aplomb, her independence and scorn for her own well-conned flowery speech are at once congenial to Olivia. When Viola, in exasperation, pulls out all the stops on her own natural poetry, Olivia dives into her bag of tricks to win "him". She tries to give "him" money, she sends "him" a ring, she wonders, when all her pleading seems to no avail: "How shall I feast him—what bestow of him—For youth is bought more oft than begged or borrowed."

Olivia is very young, then, and probably slight of figure to be suitably matched to "Cesario". Anyone as competent as she shows herself to be, as Sebastian notes that she is, and as a mistress would have to be to suit Malvolio, would not mismatch herself. She has been forced to grow up quickly in the last months, and her discovery of her own capabilities has gone to her head. But, since she is reasonable as well as practical, she can see that she is being swept off her feet and put suddenly into the position she has always objected to in Orsino (that of unrequited lover). This forces her to conceal her own nature from herself, to speak of "enchantment", and say in most un-Olivialike tones these lines, which are noticeably difficult to say naturally:

> Fate, show thy force: ourselves we do not
>   owe;
> What is decreed must be, and be this so.
>
> (I.v.331)

However this may comfort her, she does not actually leave to Fate anything which she can manage.

At her second visit as Cesario, careful to seem more courtly, formal and remote than the first time, Viola is met by the full storm of Olivia's recklessness. This is not only caused by passion, but by intuitive uneasiness:

> *Olivia.* Stay:
>   I prithee, tell me what thou think'st
> of me.
> *Viola.* That you do think you are not what
> you are.
> *Olivia.* If I think so, I think the same of
> you.
> *Viola.* Then think you right: I am not what I
> am.
> *Olivia.* I would you were as I would have
> you be.
>
> (III.i.151)

Sebastian, Viola's twin, is exactly what Olivia would have him be.

The most fundamental consideration in the relationship between "seems" and "is" arises with the confusion of Sebastian and Viola. When Olivia mistakes Sebastian for "Cesario", she is seeing the same spirit in both. Her eye is not stopped at the surface by any probable difference of height and voice. She did not fall in love with a physique. This is a difficult theatrical problem, certainly, but one to be tackled with bravado rather than coyness, because it is more than a casual assumption of the plot—it is a considered criticism of what we are accustomed to call "real", the façade. Olivia must be consistently shown as a person who is wary of letting her eye be "too great a flatterer for [her] mind". Her intuitive summing up of people is always made at a deeper level than this. As for the confusion of Antonio in mistaking Cesario for Sebastian, I believe that the only assumption the actor can make is that that honest stalwart could never entertain the suspicion of a disguise. He is far too much upset by the overwhelming sin of ingratitude to notice any surface changes in his erstwhile idol.

Sebastian has as much romantic venturesomeness, courage, charm and—all important to this play—integrity as Viola. But in his astonishing impetuosity he is a mirror image, rather than a copy, of his twin's equally astonishing patience. Their intentions are the same, their ways of carrying them out are very different.

Two such spirits as Viola and Sebastian are required as "fitting climax to the swelling act" which in the end unmasks all the characters of this play. They are needed by Olivia and Orsino as mates of the appropriate sex. They are used by Shakespeare to emphasize "what a piece of work is man". . . .

Cynthia Lewis

SOURCE: "Viola, Antonio, and Epiphany in *Twelfth Night*" in *Essays in Literature*, Vol. XIII, No. 2, Fall, 1986, pp. 187-99.

[*Lewis positions Antonio as a Christ figure against which Viola's moral growth, the central concern of the play, is measured throughout* Twelfth Night. *Viola demonstrates sacrificial qualities early in the play, but they only come to fruition through her service and ultimate sacrifice to Orsino. Her major obstacle is her fear of losing control, but her salvation, the critic asserts, is her clear-sightedness. This quality is demonstrated in Viola's interpretation of Olivia returning the ring she claimed Viola left behind as opposed to Malvolio's cloudy reasoning when attempting to decipher the letter he thinks is from Olivia. Antonio's example of sacrificing himself for Cesario, whom he believes to be Sebastian, is compared with Viola's sacrifice, when she offers to take the punishment Orsino who would like to deal to Olivia. The critic links the ideal sacrifice to the manifestation of the Messiah in the Epiphany and asserts that Christian love informs romantic love in the play.*]

Viola's characterization throughout *Twelfth Night* reveals that the play concerns itself fundamentally with her moral growth. Shakespeare continually plays Viola off the other characters to illustrate how far she has come and how much farther she has to go. Initially, she has all the makings of an Antonio. She generously rewards first the sea captain and then Feste (I.ii.18, III.i.43), and she lashes out at ingratitude when Antonio accuses her of it (III.iv.354-57). Her willingness to woo another woman for the man she loves also indicates her magnanimity.

Yet she often appears self-absorbed. Nowhere is this trait clearer than when she offers Antonio only half her coffer (III.iv.345-47). Next to the total altruism that Antonio showed Sebastian in the preceding scene (III.iii.38), Viola's reserve seems downright stingy. Granted, Viola is not rich; nor does she even know Antonio. Her giving anything at all under these circumstances could thus be admired. But the contrast between the two characters is evident: Viola is willing to go far for someone else, but only so far. Similarly, Viola has good reason in III.iv to be stunned by the sudden possibility that Sebastian may yet live and thus to ignore Antonio's arrest; but Antonio, having intervened to save her life, surely deserves more attention from Viola/Cesario than she gives. Even if Viola exits at the close of this scene in pursuit of Antonio and the officers, she apparently does so not to aid Antonio but to discover more about Sebastian's history.

This key episode in which Viola and Antonio are contrasted reveals the major obstacle that Viola must surmount before she can grow to love completely: fear of losing control. That she loves both her brother and her master is obvious to us, but a great deal of the potential and actual destructiveness in *Twelfth Night* arises from Viola's refusal to expose herself openly to others—to give herself away. She is consistently associated with walls—barriers to love—throughout the play. Her disguise becomes an emblem of her and others' fear: many such walls appear in the play and must be let down or broken through before genuine love can be enjoyed. Orsino uses clichéd love language to put a safe distance between himself and Olivia (e.g., I.i); Viola refers to the hypocrisy of most people, who hide their wickedness behind the "beauteous wall" of appearance (I.ii.48); Viola herself attempts to use language like Orsino's in wooing Olivia and in protecting herself, until she finds it will not shield her well (e.g., II.ii); Olivia hides in her house and behind her wit and her veil (II.ii, etc.). The spirit of Epiphany, represented by Antonio's willingness to manifest his true self for the sake of another, is stifled behind these barriers.

Viola's brilliant repartee with Feste demonstrates her capacity for folly, for letting go and enjoying another's company (III.i.1-59). Admiring his wit, she expresses appreciation for its wisdom and thus signals her own association with Christlike folly and her own understanding that folly comes in two forms: "For folly that he wisely shows is fit, / But wise men, folly-fall'n, quite taint their wit" (III.i.67-68). But when Feste cuts gently at Orsino's folly (ll. 39-41), Viola resists hearing more: "Nay, and thou pass upon me, I'll no more with thee" (ll. 42-43). Viola here seems reluctant to acknowledge the value of Feste's remarks. For a long time she appears unable either to admit that Orsino's attraction to Olivia is not genuine love or to deal directly with her feelings for Orsino. Her reaction to Feste's song in II.iv exemplifies the poor judgment that results from her infatuation. "Come away, come away, death" has got to be some of the most morbid verse ever set to music, as Feste kindly suggests to Orsino (II.iv.73-78), and the music that accompanies it would be anything but cheering. But Viola identifies with its gloom: "It gives a very echo to the seat / Where Love is thron'd" (II.iv.21-22). Viola's exaggerated sympathy for Orsino's pain mirrors his self-indulgence.

In its irrationality, Viola's love for Orsino resembles Antonio's love for Sebastian and Olivia's for Viola/Cesario. It is potentially good folly. But enclosed within her, it waxes overly melancholic. When she can express it in even veiled language, as she does in II.iv, it regains some of its health:

> **Vio.** My father had a daughter lov'd a man
> As it might be perhaps, were I a woman,
> I should your lordship.
> **Duke.**   And what's her history?
> **Vio.** A blank, my lord; she never told her love,
> But let concealment like a worm i' th' bud
> Feed on her damask cheek; she pin'd in thought,
> And with a green and yellow melancholy
> She sate like Patience on a monument,
> Smiling at grief. Was not this love indeed?
> (ll. 107-15)

Perhaps because this passage demands that Viola objectify her feelings, it is less self-pitying than her attraction to Feste's song. Furthermore, Viola's hidden love at least eventually permits her to instruct Orsino:

> **Vio.** But if she [Olivia] cannot love you, sir?
> **Duke.** I cannot be so answer'd.
> **Vio.**   Sooth, but you must.
> (II.iv.87-88)

Yet Viola herself realizes that secret longings fester

within, "like a worm i' th' bud." The self must be honestly exposed to survive; Viola must reveal her inner self to become fully human.

Another of Viola's potential virtues emerges as she is compared and contrasted with Malvolio. In much the same way that Malvolio seeks to unravel the letter he finds in II.v, Viola tries to read the significance of the allegedly returned ring in II.ii. The concept linking the two scenes is interpretation. On this score Viola obviously does much better than Malvolio. Her vision is not so dreamy-eyed as to obscure the true meaning of receiving the ring, whereas poor Malvolio's hopes absolutely blind him to the facts. Viola's visionary quality—composed of a clear-sightedness like Feste's and a power like Antonio's to perceive how others feel—will guide her through the snarls to come. Yet on this point too she fudges, when she thrusts all responsibility onto an external force: "O time, thou must untangle this, not I, / It is too hard a knot for me t' untie" (II.ii.40-41). Notwithstanding the partial truth of this statement, Viola will sooner or later have to participate in shaping her own life. Time can and does help, but it requires a cooperation from her, a total commitment of herself to love.

Whether or not Viola learns how to make such an investment directly from Antonio, the sea captain's dramatic purpose is to provide such an example, and Viola comes to reflect his behavior. The turning point for her, when all the potentially fine qualities we have seen in her come together, is also the heart of the play. It comes in her answer to Orsino's angry threat on her life:

> I'll sacrifice the lamb that I do love,
> To spite a raven's heart within a dove.
>
> (V.i.130-31)

The Christian implications of the "sacrificial lamb" ought to ring clear, and Viola's sudden "willingness" to give not just some, but all, endows her with new virtue:

> And I most jocund, apt, and willingly,
> To do you rest, a thousand deaths would die.
>
> (ll. 132-33)

Like Antonio, who has earlier offered to protect her with his life (III.iv.312-14), Viola now substitutes herself for Olivia, in order to give Orsino "rest." She gladly takes upon herself the punishment through which Orsino would "spite" another. Here lies the Epiphany in *Twelfth Night,* where the meaning of Christ's birth, His sacrifice for humanity, manifests itself in the actions of human beings. Viola's commitment of her life to love is the wisest folly she can pursue. To dismiss all barriers to love, to disregard even the welfare of one's physical being, is divine.

Viola's altruistic attitude toward love, which alludes to a Christian ideal, permits spiritual love and romantic love to be linked in *Twelfth Night.* Ultimately, we are not shown a world in which different types of love—say, physical and non-physical—are qualitatively different or are opposed. Rather, Christian love, as epitomized in Antonio, works itself into the worldliest of relationships through the four lovers, principally Viola, as well as through Feste. Thus, Christian love can *inform* romantic love, and the two comic traditions that shape the play—the romantic and the serious—are joined compatibly as Viola grows to become more like Antonio. Significantly, in this final scene Olivia also grows to accept Viola/Cesario as a "sister" and Orsino as her brother (ll. 326, 317). The good folly that is well on its way to triumphing over all is not limited to romantic love, but leads to general good will and fellowship.

Appropriately, after Viola's declaration of devotion to Orsino, the majority of the characters are in some respect set free. Viola's self-sacrifice is not the single twist in the plot that accounts for every subsequent revelation: many other actions, like Sebastian's entrance (l. 208), intervene before Viola's true identity is discovered. But Viola's new openness to love sets a tone early in the scene for the series of manifestations and apparent miracles to follow. The twins are reunited; the four lovers are rightly matched; the sea captain who has possession of Viola's clothes is "enlarged" (l. 278); and Malvolio is "deliver'd" (l. 315), though that does not guarantee his freedom, which only he can claim for himself. Even Fabian, caught up in the "wonder" of "this present hour," freely confesses the joke on Malvolio and tries to ease the tension between the revelers and the steward (ll. 355-68). "Golden time" is ripe for love like Antonio's.

But the play's problematic nature persists to the end, modifying and augmenting the harmonious resolution. For instance, what of Antonio? Are we to assume that Orsino will also set him free? It seems rather that the question of Antonio's future, like so many other questions at the closing, is left dangling for a reason. Interestingly, the other salient loose end here is that Viola has still not removed her disguise by the time *Twelfth Night* is finished. These two details do more than blur the play's resolution, as do questions about whether Malvolio will repair his ruined pride and whether Maria will help curb her new husband's former excesses. Most importantly, these unresolved elements involve the audience's sense of responsibility in determining their own future. Indeed, Act V would not challenge us morally if it clearly and simply showed that all ended well. *Twelfth Night* finally asks us whether *we* will make all well by divesting ourselves of the walls around *us* that shut out love like Antonio's and keep it imprisoned. Will we embrace the spirit of Epiphany, which shapes the play throughout, and thus free Christian love in our own world? By agreeing to, we will, in effect, liberate Antonio and change as radically as if we moved, along with Viola, from male to female. When *Twelfth Night* closes, it has already "pleased" us, as Feste promises (V.i.408). If it is also going to teach us when the "play is done" (l. 407), then we must respond to it by unveiling.

Douglas H. Parker

SOURCE: "Shakespeare's Female Twins in *Twelfth Night*: In Defense of Olivia" in *English Studies in Canada*, Vol. XIII, No. 1, March, 1987, pp. 23-34.

[*Parker outlines the parallels between Olivia and Viola in* Twelfth Night, *regarding them as non-genetic twins. He begins by describing the similarities between the characters: their loss of fathers and brothers, their respective disguises, and their pursuit of unrequited love. Viola relates to Olivia's inability to love Orsino because of her own inability to love Olivia. In her frustration with the situation, she communicates to them both the consequences of refusing to accept love. The critic demonstrates how Olivia and Viola are intellectual equals and that Olivia falls in love with Viola because of the qualities in herself that she sees Viola mirror back. The women also recognize that the are both intellectually bested by Feste, accept it with good humor, and are the only two in the play who can appreciate Feste's wit. Finally the critic considers the etymology of their names, explains why Olivia is not suffering from melancholy, and comments on the fitting conclusion that Viola and Olivia should become sisters-in-law.*]

. . . Shakespeare stresses the non-genetic twinning between Olivia and Viola at many points in the play in a number of ways: certain situations in which one character finds herself are mirrored in the other character's situations; particular scenes in which one character appears are repeated with slight variation for the other, or events in individual scenes in which both appear show remarkable similarities; and, finally, the outcome of the action of the play is essentially identical for both.

That Shakespeare wants us to regard Viola and Olivia's relationship as an important and close one is clear from the number of scenes in which the two appear in conversation together. No other pair of characters in the play has as many meetings stretching over as many lines as these two. Initially they meet in I.v. when Viola comes to Olivia's house to sue on Orsino's behalf; here the conversation lasts for about 150 lines; at the end of this scene we first recognize Olivia's developing love for Viola [quotations from Lothian and Craik's New Arden edition]. They meet again in III.i. and try to deal with Olivia's love for Orsino's

messenger; here the conversation runs to some 70 lines. And finally, their third and shortest meeting occurs in III.iv. where the matter of Olivia's love is again discussed for about 20 lines. These frequent encounters encourage us to feel that, if Sebastian had not appeared on the scene to satisfy Olivia's love, the two women might have gone on meeting indefinitely, for at the end of this final meeting Olivia encourages Viola to "come again to-morrow" (III.iv.218).

But the relationship between the two is far closer than a series of three meetings between them can suggest. In many of the play's situations, Viola and Olivia are identical characters: both have experienced the death of fathers; both think they have experienced the recent death of brothers. Both initially appear before the members of Illyrian society in disguise which serves a double function, even though the stress placed on each function differs for each woman. We learn early in the play from Valentine that out of respect for her recently dead brother, Olivia is "veiled" (I.i.28), and later we see this for ourselves in her first meeting with Viola. Olivia's veil serves as an obvious sign of her mourning; however, it also serves, secondarily, as a type of disguise, since it allows her to hide her face from Orsino's suitors thereby letting them know that their master is not for her. The fact that Olivia is prepared to lift her veil so quickly in Viola's presence indicates that her vow of seven years' mourning is as much an attempt to discourage Orsino's love pleas as it is an outward sign of grief. This is not to say that her sorrow for her brother's death is insincere; it is only to say that her grief is an interior sentiment which in these peculiar circumstances needs to be manifested in an outward fashion to encourage the Duke to credit it as valid. Hence Olivia's veil and the daily tearful watering of her chamber are not obvious indications, as many critics suggest, that Olivia is wallowing in melancholy as the Duke is in love; they are, rather, necessary props used to convince a love-struck Duke, who surrounds himself with his own props in the form of music and "sweet beds of flowers" (I.i.40) that her sorrow is sincere. In short, Olivia shows herself to be an admirable judge of Orsino's character by choosing his own methods of validating his experiences to convince him of the sincerity of her own. In this respect, Olivia, like Viola, has a sophisticated awareness of the importance of disguise in dealing with life's problems. And like Viola who, while sincerely mourning the death of her brother is, nevertheless, aware that she must deal with the new situation in which she finds herself after the shipwreck, since she is now a stranger in a strange land—and certainly unlike the inactive, prostrate figure of the love-struck Orsino—Olivia is also intent on imposing an order on her life, evident in her attempt early in the play to bring Sir Toby to heel (I.iii.) and to discover the whereabouts of the derelict Feste

(I.iv.). In short, while Orsino's love renders him "unstaid and skittish in all motions" (II.iv.18), Viola and Olivia's grief does not overwhelm them to the point that it becomes an obsession preventing them from carrying on with the necessary business of living one's life.

Viola, too, appears in disguise in the initial scenes of the play, and her male disguise, as purposeful as Olivia's veil, is used to protect her from the unknown dangers of a foreign country. But like Olivia's, Viola's disguise also serves as a sign of her mourning, if for no one but herself, since her physical resemblance to her brother coupled with her male attire must make her appear, to herself at least, very much like Sebastian. In fact, in III.iv. in soliloquy, she mentions that as Cesario she copies her brother, stating

> I my brother know
> Yet living in my glass; even such and so
> In favour was my brother, and he went
> Still in this fashion, colour, ornament,
> For him I imitate.
>
> (389-93)

For Viola, as much as for Olivia, these disguises initially both protect them from dangers of one sort or another, and also permit them to legitimately keep their brothers' memories "fresh / And lasting, in . . . [their] sad remembrance" (I.i.31-32).

The entire love situation in which Olivia and Viola find themselves entangled is also very similar. As is often the case in romantic comedy, both fall in love rapidly, Olivia after her first meeting with Viola, and Viola after only three days in Orsino's company. However, in this latter case, Shakespeare makes the three-day span seem as instantaneous as Olivia's more sudden love affliction by sacrificing chronological time to dramatic time. Although we hear from Valentine at the beginning of I.iv. that the Duke "hath known . . . [Viola] but three days" (3), their first actual stage encounter to which the audience is privy occurs in this same scene, and, as a result, Viola's love for the Duke seems as sudden as Olivia's for Viola. Both women must also endure unrequited love: despite the love tokens that each receives, Olivia cannot love Orsino any more than Viola can Olivia. And, further, just as Viola acts as the Duke's emissary, informing Olivia why she should love Orsino, Olivia herself, quite inadvertently no doubt, plays the same role as Viola as she informs her and us the audience about Orsino's inherent worthiness as a husband. Lest Orsino has left a bad taste in the audience's mouth after his first horribly self-indulgent appearance, and lest, as a result, we cannot understand the commonsensical Viola's passion for him, Olivia tells us that even though she cannot love him, she supposes him

> virtuous . . . noble,
> Of great estate, of fresh and stainless youth;
> In voices well divulg'd, free, learn'd, and
> valiant,
> And in dimension, and the shape of nature,
> A gracious person.
>
> (I.v.262-66)

Expecting to find Viola in I.v. suing on Orsino's behalf, the audience not only discovers this, but also the more unexpected, dramatically delightful event of Olivia serving as Orsino's spokesman and thereby mirroring Viola's role as go-between.

Viola's sense of the closeness of the two apparently hopeless love relationships is evident at a couple of points in the play. She is poignantly aware and understanding of Olivia's inability to love Orsino because she feels such an inability herself in her relationship with Olivia. Even though it is a sexual barrier that separates Olivia and Viola in contrast to an emotional one that separates Olivia and Orsino, the audience feels Viola mirroring her own frustration with Olivia's persistence when she says to the tenacious Orsino after he encourages her once again to return to Olivia to plead on his behalf: "But if she cannot love you, sir?" (II.iv.88). Also, in the same scene, perhaps reflecting on the apparent hopelessness of her own love for Orsino, she tells the Duke a story of a woman (actually Viola herself) who

> never told her love,
> But let concealment like a worm i' th' bud
> Feed on her damask cheek: she pin'd in
> thought,
> And with a green and yellow melancholy
> She sat like Patience on a monument,
> Smiling at grief.
>
> (II.iv.111-16)

This sad commentary on the loveless life, with its emphasis on death and decay, mirrors an earlier warning that Viola gave Olivia about her refusal to accept love—a warning which Shakespeare had given time and again in his sonnet sequence. Complimenting Olivia on her beauty, and, at the same time, encouraging her to capitalize on it while she can, she states:

> 'Tis beauty truly blent, whose red and white
> Nature's own sweet and cunning hand laid
> on.
> Lady, you are the cruell'st she alive
> If you will lead these graces to the grave
> And leave the world no copy.
>
> (I.v.241-46)

It is interesting to note the important similarities between these two speeches. The reference to the decay of female beauty is poignantly expressed in both;

Viola's "damask cheek" in the first passage finds its counterpart in the second in the reference to Olivia's "red and white" beauty. Both images clearly refer to the feminine complexion and both are interchangeable commonplaces in Renaissance love poetry. The image of the "worm i' th' bud" is less metaphorically expressed in the second passage through the reference to the "grave" as the final and inevitable resting place of all earthly beauty. And finally, there is an admonitory tone present in both passages even though it is more obliquely expressed in the first. In the first passage Viola, although addressing Orsino, seems to be telling herself that pining in thought, rather than acting by expressing her love to Orsino, could lead to a life of unfulfilled wishes ending in death, as the reference to "monument" suggests. In the second passage she more straightforwardly warns Olivia that the inevitable result of not acknowledging and accepting love is personal annihilation and "the grave."

In summary, in Olivia's and Viola's love situations, Shakespeare keeps the reader's mind fixed on the way in which each female reflects or mirrors the other's character, actions, or predicaments. The initial disguises of the two are clear mirrors of each other as each woman uses masking both to defend herself from unwanted advances or happenings and to serve as appropriate symbols of mourning reflecting a true inner grief. Further, each woman can be seen fulfilling the role of go-between for Orsino. As Viola confronts Olivia to sue on Orsino's behalf, so Olivia, through her complimentary comments on Orsino's character, assures Viola and the audience of his worthiness as a future husband. And finally, Viola herself, commenting in two different speeches on the nature of the two major female love patterns, sees a close relationship between her situation and Olivia's which Shakespeare stresses by using similar images, a similar admonitory tone, and by drawing similar conclusions.

Certain scenes in the play also emphasize the twin relationship that I see in Viola and Olivia. In the early part of the first meeting between the two women, Olivia shows anger at Viola's behaviour and asks why she began her conversation "rudely" (I.v.215). Viola's reply stresses the mirroring that runs through the play by making clear that she simply responded in kind to the reception she received at Olivia's hands; she states: "The rudeness that hath appeared in me have I learned from my entertainment" (217-18). Indeed, this entire first meeting between the two women is remarkable for the skill that each shows in conversing with the other, proving that each possesses a sharp wit. Initially the conversation begins with a display of verbal wit conducted in prose by both women. The ironically posturing Petrarchan love messenger, Viola, gets as good as she gives from the determined lady of the house, Olivia, whose true skill at repartee becomes evident when the messenger

introduces the imagery of the religion of love. Both instinctively seem to recognize when the witty prologue to this first meeting concludes, for after this initial period of feeling each other out, both immediately switch from prose to poetry, a switch which indicates a movement that Berry characterizes [in *Shakespeare's Comedies: Exploration in Form* (1972)] as one from "the language of fencing and social deception" to "the language of truth and intensely felt emotion." Unlike so many of the other scenes in this play where one character takes advantage of or capitalizes on the linguistic or personality weaknesses of another, there is no sense that there is a clear victor-victim relationship at the end of this scene. This is a conversation between intellectual equals with no clear winner emerging at its conclusion. And the fact that by the end of the scene Olivia has fallen in love with the messenger seems to prove the point that the two women are alike; after Viola exits, Olivia comments on Viola's character as revealed in this scene by stating that "Thy tongue, thy face, thy limbs, actions, and spirit / Do give thee five-fold blazon" (I.v.296-97). Earlier she had ironically catalogued her own beauty in a not entirely dissimilar way when she assured Viola that she would "give out divers schedules of my beauty" (247-48). That Shakespeare wants us to see that Olivia falls in love with Viola in this scene because she recognizes in her aspects of herself is evident in his uses of the word "blazon" to describe Viola's beauty and "schedules of beauty" to describe Olivia's. On the surface of it, there seems to be no apparent similarity between the two expressions, "blazon" being glossed in most editions as heraldic insignia, and "schedules" as written statements. But, in fact, the word "blazon" also has a more general meaning which the *OED* gives as "a description or record of any kind; *esp.* a record of virtues or excellencies," and adds the further meaning of "'publication.'" Taken in this more general sense, Viola's "fivefold blazon" can be seen as the beauty she publicly displays or "publishes" in Olivia's presence; in other words, Viola's qualities serve as an obvious record of her virtues just as Olivia's qualities are ones that she ironically intends to make public by giving out "divers schedules," that is, written statements or publications of them. That Olivia should talk about the public demonstration of her beauty and then go on to describe Viola's in essentially the same terms, makes the point clear: at the end of this scene, Olivia has come to love Viola because she sees herself mirrored in her, a mirroring which we, the audience, have also been made to see through the skilful and equal ironic verbal exchanges that have occurred in the scene. If it is, therefore, valid to claim that Olivia falls in love with Viola because the latter is, in fact, her alter ego—a view which Plato's Aristophanes would have no trouble accepting— then a new interpretation of Olivia's final words in this scene emerges. When, at the end of this scene, Olivia claims that "ourselves we do not owe" (314), she means, no doubt, as the traditional gloss of the lines states, that there are greater powers beyond us which seem to direct, shape and control us despite ourselves; but in the light of my interpretation of this scene, which sees Olivia's love for Viola emerging because of the similarities she comes to recognize between them, the line might also suggest Olivia's new awareness that her self is not something owned or possessed solely by her; it is, in fact, also part of her new love in whom she has just glimpsed characteristics of her own person.

In terms of the characters involved, methods of argumentation used and sentiments expressed by both Viola and Olivia, two other scenes in the play emphasize the character twinning with which this essay is concerned. Feste's catechizing of Olivia in I.v. in which he proves his mistress a "fool" for the undue grief she feels over the death of her brother, is mirrored in his extended verbal victory over Viola in III.i. which Viola recognizes as a type of instruction in the power and versatility of language. In the first exchange with Olivia, Feste's victory over his mistress is merely a verbal one; although by asking her the right questions he can demonstrate to her why she should not mourn her brother's death knowing his soul to be in heaven, he, nevertheless, cannot convince Olivia or the audience that her grief is unnecessary. The profound emotional effects of death go well beyond the logical conclusions derived from this form of verbal catechizing. One can find very little true consolation in Feste's argument, even as one admires its logic. The same phenomenon is evident in his exchange with Viola in III.i. Words once again appear to be infinitely capable of meaning what Feste wants them to as the skilful word crafter, or "corrupter of words" as he calls himself (37), attains victory over Viola by disabling her expectations—as he does Olivia's—and showing her his skill at turning language to his advantage. One example from this scene will suffice to make the point. When Feste tells Viola that he lives "by

Olivia, Maria, and Malvolio at Olivia's house (Act III, scene iv).

the church" and she asks him "Art thou a church-man?" his response undermines her line of thought. He answers:

> No such matter, sir. I do live by the church, for
> I do live at my house, and my house doth stand by
> the church. (5-7)

While we cannot help admiring Feste's skilful response here—as we admired his rational and verbal victory over Olivia—we must, at the same time, recognize that he is not really answering Viola's question—as earlier he was not truly convincing Olivia or us of her folly. In both cases he is merely using the symbols of thought—language itself—as tools for a clever but essentially specious game of verbal one-upmanship. What is interesting and important to notice is the women's almost identical responses to Feste's victory over them in each of these scenes. In Feste's exchange with Olivia, the dour steward of her household, Malvolio, is outraged at what he regards as Feste's impertinence. Obviously failing to see that Feste's victory is merely verbal and not substantial, he regards the clown's behaviour as insufferable. Olivia, clearly recognizing the true nature of Feste's "victory," takes his catechizing in the spirit in which it was intended and comments on Feste's effects:

> There is no slander in an allowed fool, though he
> do nothing but rail; nor no railing in a known
> discreet man, though he do nothing but reprove.
> (I.v.93-96)

In a similar vein, at the conclusion of her exchange with Feste, Viola fleshes out Olivia's comment by analyzing the skill of the "allowed fool," a skill which Olivia has shown that she understands implicitly in the lines just quoted. Viola states:

> This fellow is wise enough to play the fool,
> And to do that well, craves a kind of wit:
> He must observe their mood on whom he
>   jests,
> The quality of persons, and the time,
> And like the haggard, check at every feather
> That comes before his eye. This is a practice
> As full of labour as a wise man's art:
> For folly that he wisely shows is fit;
> But wise men, folly-fall'n, quite taint their
>   wit.
>
>   (III.i.61-69)

Of all the characters in the play, only these two women seem truly capable of appreciating Feste's verbal skill. Orsino, of course, is interested in Feste as well, but on a much more superficial and selfish level: he enjoys Feste's singing abilities because they help sustain his love mood. Viola and Olivia's good-spirited "defeats" at the clown's hands plus their comments

on the witty fool's talents following these defeats, indicate their shared view of his gifts, and, in Olivia's case, at least, give support to Feste's words about his mistress to Viola when he states that "the Lady Olivia has no folly" (III.i.33). This telling comment lets us know how the wise Feste regards Olivia, and also indicates how seriously he must have taken his attempt to prove her a fool.

The sentiments expressed by both women at the conclusion of two other scenes in the play also add to the mirroring pattern that I have been tracing. At the end of I.v. after Olivia has fallen in love with Viola, and, as a result, added another complication to her life, she is still level-headed enough to recognize how very much other forces are in control of an individual's situation. Hoping that her love might develop, and yet aware of her own impotence in making the outcome match her desires, she addresses fate:

> Fate, show thy force; ourselves we do not
>   owe.
> What is decreed, must be; and be this so.
>   (I.v.314-15)

Viola expresses a similar notion at the end of II.ii. Again, like Olivia earlier, Viola is contemplating her various love entanglements. And again, like Olivia, she is prudent enough to see how powerless she is to shape her own destiny in the face of these entanglements. As a result, she places her faith in time as Olivia has earlier placed hers in fate:

> O time, thou must untangle this, not I,
> It is too hard a knot for me t'untie.
>   (II.ii.39-40)

This faith in powers beyond themselves proves valid for both women at the end of the play where the final series of mirroring events occurs. It is not enough to state—as many others have—that the apparently hopeless love relationships work themselves out satisfactorily for Viola and Olivia. This is only the most obvious example of mirroring. What is also important to recognize is that Viola's happy recovery of her brother Sebastian is also found in Olivia's situation. Fate has indeed proven itself generous to Olivia as time has to Viola. For by steadfastly refusing to marry Orsino throughout the play, Olivia has managed by the play's end not only to marry the husband of her dreams, but also to recover a brother in the person of Orsino. That this recovery is at least as important as the marriage is evident in the way in which Shakespeare stresses the notion near the play's conclusion. Once the comic complications have been resolved, Olivia encourages Orsino "To think me as well a sister, as a wife" (V.i.316), and a few lines later Orsino complies by addressing his former beloved as "sweet sister" (383). These numerous similarities between Shakespeare's two principal female characters in *Twelfth Night* strike me as more than fortuitous; there are far too many of them and they are far too closely related to be attributed solely to chance. Besides, Shakespeare seems to be deliberately directing the reader's attention to this second pair of twins in his play not only through the various mirroring situations and scenes mentioned above, but also through their very names: both names etymologically derive from similar aspects of animate nature—Olivia's name originates with the olive plant and Viola's with the flower violet. Schleiner states [in "Orsino and Viola: Are the Names of Serious Character in *Twelfth Night* Meaningful?" *Shakespeare Studies,* 16 (1983)] that both of these flowers "possibly refer to purgatives" which might suggest the part that both characters play in purging the drama of its comic complications: Viola by constantly sounding the note of common sense and Olivia through her constant refusal to marry Orsino, which, of course, permits Viola to finally have him, thereby creating the play's happy ending. Is it, then, altogether surprising in light of these connections between the two women that each name—Viola and Olivia—should be essentially an anagram of the other?

In conclusion, Shakespeare's major female characters in *Twelfth Night,* despite their passports and their parentage, possess a dramatic kinship which makes each stand head and shoulders above the Illyrian folly in the play. If, as some credulous critics suggest, Olivia is "addicted to a melancholy" (II.v.202-03) because of the death of her brother, the spectators never see it. We only hear that she waters "once a day her chamber round / With eye-offending brine / All this to season / A brother's dead love" (I.i.29-31) from Valentine, Orsino's go-between, who has received the information from Olivia's handmaid. Further, melancholia in this period was generally regarded as a debilitating mental disease which left its victims free to do very little more than ponder their obsessive bitterness—witness, for instance, Hamlet and Jaques. As I have suggested earlier, Olivia is clearly concerned about the state of her household, the condition of Sir Toby and the whereabouts of Feste, concerns which would not enter the mind of a true melancholic. What we can truly speak of is Olivia's sadness which is clearly legitimate and understandable, and which, as I have suggested, mirrors Viola's. It is a sadness brought about by unrequited love just as Viola's is. Against the charges of self-deceit, one might counter that a self-deceived woman could scarcely hold out as long as Olivia does against Orsino's persistent wooing which, we sense, has been going on long before the play even opens. Further, the suggestion that Olivia will not marry Orsino because by doing so she would be marrying above her station, does not sound like the sentiment of a self-deceived person. As I have suggested above, she is no more self-deceived than Viola. Finally, it is through her refusal to marry Orsino that Olivia, as much as Viola or Sebastian,

helps bring the play to a happy conclusion by throwing Viola into Orsino's arms thereby fulfilling Viola's wishes. By contributing to the play's resolution, Olivia shows herself to be in the tradition of other enlightened Shakespearean female figures: the four ladies in *Love's Labour's Lost,* Rosalind in *As You Like It* and, of course, Viola in this play.

From the beginning of *Twelfth Night* we, as well as Viola, know that Olivia's love for Viola is doomed to failure because of the sex they share by nature. What we need to learn, however, is that this marriage of bodies which cannot be actualized, does not prevent Shakespeare from depicting a "marriage of true minds" between Olivia and Viola. It is, therefore, a fitting climax to this play that at its end each woman should become the other's sister-in-law since throughout both have been, as I hope I have shown, sisters in sentiment, intellect, and spirit.

MALVOLIO

Malvolio has intrigued critics more than any other character in *Twelfth Night.* In the seventeenth century, Charles I was so taken by Malvolio's mistreatment that he changed the name of the play in the Second Folio to "Malvolio."

Critics in the nineteenth century argued whether or not Malvolio was a Puritan, or represented the emerging bourgeoisie class, questions which are still being debated today. Twentieth-century critic Paul Siegel also identified Malvolio with Puritan self-discipline and predictability. **Melvin Seiden** identifies Malvolio with both the Puritans and the new bourgeoisie. However, he asserts that Shakespeare created those parallels only as a pretext for setting Malvolio up as the scapegoat, sacrificed to bring the Bard's comedy to life.

In a departure from the generally accepted interpretation, Seiden also argues that Malvolio's rigid adherence to order springs not from excessive self-love, but from a sense of inferiority. **David Wilbern** argues that Malvolio's gulling results from the emergence of his latent sexual desire for Olivia, and discusses the carnality at the core of the play. For further analysis of Malvolio's character, see the essay by **Thad Jenkins Logan** in the section on CELEBRATION AND FESTIVITY and the essay by **Ralph Berry** in the LANGUAGE AND COMMUNICATION section.

Melvin Seiden

SOURCE: "Malvolio Reconsidered," in *University of Kansas City Review,* Vol. XXVIII, No. 2, December, 1961, pp. 105-114.

[*Seiden examines Malvolio's role in the comic strategy of* Twelfth Night, *which is, the critic asserts, to divert the burden of comic scrutiny away from the festive lovers, and to lend a puritanical air which in contrast heightens the overriding sense of gaiety in the play. In the society of Illyria, Malvolio represents the new bourgeoisie, and is placed in conflict with the degenerate aristocracy of Sir Toby and Sir Andrew, and not with the patrician lovers, as other commentators have argued. On the contrary, Seiden explains that Malvolio strives to uphold the social standards of Olivia's household, by which he lives and earns his keep, and is threatened by any subversion of the system. In principle, he is opposed to frivolity and to endow Malvolio with a sense of humor, as some readers have mused, would serve to make him into a tragic figure, clearly not what Shakespeare had intended. Seiden claims that Malvolio plays the bad cop not out of an excessive sense of self-love, as other critics have suggested, but out of an underdeveloped sense of self. He enforces restraint because he lacks an independent spirit within himself, and suffers an inferiority complex as a result. In conclusion, Seiden compares the comic strategies of* Twelfth Night *to a typical catharsis in a Shakespearean tragedy and contrasts the fate of Malvolio to that of Falstaff in* Henry IV. *While the clown Falstaff was sacrificed as the world of comedy gave way to the reinstitution of normal life, Malvolio, who represents law and order in Illyria, was not heralded as the returning patron of seriousness and work, but at the finale remained unsatisfied and discredited, a scapegoat sacrificed to the gods of comedy.*]

. . . The miraculous, domesticated and made to serve the strategems of the dramatist, is one of the staples of comedy, especially that of Shakespeare. We recognize its power and beauty in the neatly-contrived and swiftly-executed denouement whereby the necessary "happy ending" is consummated. It is no less miraculous that the three lovers of *Twelfth Night* persistently escape involvement in the embarrassments and humiliations of the comic hurly-burly, and since this less obtrusive aspect of comic magic can lead us to a better understanding of what Shakespeare is up to in this play, we must examine its significance.

In the character of Falstaff and in the punitive comedy of Jonson one finds a curious phenomenon. Falstaff, Volpone, Subtle, and Face are comic impresarios; they cause others to appear ridiculous, thus ingratiating themselves without having to undergo as patients the comic action that, as agents, they have unleashed upon others. But the appetite for comedy that they have awakened in us is voracious and one not easily or quickly satisfied. Soon we want to see these impresarios sacrificed on altars of their own making. Jonson exploits this expectation, manipulating it to arouse suspense, and finally satisfying it by heaping on the heads of the comedy-makers comic punishments more extreme (and delightful to us) than anything that they, as agents, had been able to inflict

on their victims. One might expect, therefore, that the pristine status of the three lovers would in a similar fashion arouse comic expectations and desires that could be fulfilled only at *their* expense.

Shakespeare's grand strategy is to divert the current of our expectations into another channel, to provide us with another object for our promiscuous and destructive laughter in the figure of Malvolio. One can enumerate the various vices of Malvolio that make him a fair target, a worthy object of comic deflation. These will tell us what is ludicrous and laughable in Malvolio. But if we are concerned with the more interesting question of Malvolio's *raison d'être*, the answer must surely be that he exists so that Shakespeare's lovers may preserve their status free from the nothing-if-not-critical comic scrutiny which would otherwise expose their romantic pretensions to the withering winds of laughter. It is not Sir Andrew Aguecheek and Sir Toby Belch, patricians manqué, who are the true surrogates for the comic-"tragedies" that are never permitted to embroil the lovers, but the puritan Malvolio. He is the scapegoat; he is the man who undergoes a sacrificial comic death so that they may live unscathed; he is the man who, because of offensive seriousness (made to appear an antithetical ridiculousness) allows what is also ludicrous in the lovers to maintain its soberfaced pretense of impregnable seriousness.

Malvolio stands condemned of a mean, life-denying, but nevertheless principled utilitarianism. Shakespeare wants to excite our antipathy to Malvolio's anti-comic sobriety, his sour bourgeois version of Aristotle's ethical golden mean, and he provides us with many appropriate occasions for venting our antipathies. What Shakespeare does not want us to recognize, and what becomes clear once we are no longer involved emotionally in the play, is the fact that just as Malvolio is a creature of utility for his mistress Olivia, winning for his assiduous services only scorn and abuse, so for his creator Malvolio becomes an infinitely serviceable comic instrument. We recognize that without Malvolio the comedy of *Twelfth Night* would be impoverished; I would go farther and argue that without him the comedy, the play as a whole, would not *work*, and it is precisely this indebtedness to Malvolio's multifarious utilitarianism that Shakespeare cannot acknowledge, since we are not meant to see what the old magician has up his sleeve or in his hat.

The social issues involved in the struggle between Malvolio's code of calculating utility and the comic values suggested by the title of the play (the bacchanalia, before the holiday ends) are not as clear as some critics have made them out to be. Tallying Malvolio's traits, we have no trouble seeing what these stand for. He is efficient, music-hating, fun-denying, power-seeking, austere, pompous, officious, and melancholy—in short, he is a Puritan and, in the first decade of the seventeenth century, an ur-version of the man of the future, the petty bourgeois. Curiously, however, these values are not pitted against the lovers' aristocratic ones; the conflict is *not* between Malvolio's excessively rigid and stifling code of responsibility and that of love, leisure, music, sensibility, elegance, and the higher irresponsibility. Shakespeare is particularly careful to avoid representing a direct clash between Malvolio and his aristocratic betters. He is gulled, baited, and scourged by Maria and Feste, socially his inferiors, who are aided by Sir Toby and Sir Andrew, and the latter are grossly perverted specimens of nobility. We need not look any farther than Falstaff to see that for Shakespeare the fallen aristocrat can be morally worse than the erect man of lower degree. The idea of a social hierarchy necessitates such a judgment. The good man of the middle ranks is likely to have only middling virtues and vices, but he is at least in his proper place. The degenerate, of whatever rank, threatens the whole of the great chain of being.

The conflict in *Twelfth Night* is then between aristocracy at its worst (Toby and Aguecheek, aided by the roisterers)—perverted, and thus the antithesis of what is implied in the ideal of *noblesse oblige*—and a representative of the new bourgeoisie presented in its most perfect archetypal form, since Malvolio, whatever else he is not, is true to the principles he represents. He has a radical existential authenticity; he is the quintessential bourgeois.

Shakespeare's overt—but I think questionable—point is that in its purest manifestation such dour puritanism is worse even than the corrupt patrician irresponsibility of the Belches and Aguecheeks. The point that he is at some pains to conceal—or rather, what he wishes to avoid making a point of—is that he must avoid challenging the values of the patrician lovers with those of Malvolio.

Why? For one thing, the antithesis between Malvolio's grubby puritanism and the lovers' exquisite manners is not the unequivocal conflict between beauty and the beast that so many of our critics have made it out to be. We all recognize that Malvolio stands for work, order, duty, sobriety—everything, in short, that permits a society to function. Olivia clearly recognizes this. She understands that Malvolio's stewardship is necessary to the functioning of her household. As steward, then, Malvolio represents the police force: law and order. The love-making, the sweet melancholy of long leisure hours spent in contemplation, the delight in music, the poeticizing of life—all this is possible because of the mean prose of Malvolio's labors as a steward.

In the modern world, Marxist propaganda describes the police force as a contemptible tool of the capitalist system. More than that, the Marxist has tried to win over the police force to its revolutionary side by pointing up a social irony: the police, it is said, are themselves exploited by the very system which they uphold. One can imagine the Marxist pamphlet which says to the police of the capitalist states: "With every brutality you inflict upon the poor, the ignorant, the socially impotent, you brutalize yourselves; in suppressing the have-nots you only enslave those who would liberate you." One doubts whether such appeals have ever won many recruits to the revolutionary cause. Pride in work—no matter what the work may be—seems to be more deeprooted and compelling than any doubts or scruples the worker may feel about the utility or morality of his work. So it is with Malvolio. His arrogance is not the swollen amour-propre it seems to be. Clearly this is a man who believes in work and in particular in his own work. He is fanatically conscientious in trying to enforce law and order, not as the play so slyly makes us believe merely because he is temperamentally opposed to fun and play, but because he is also by principle antagonistic to whatever threatens to subvert the orderly social machinery of his mistress's household.

We in America have made a cult of that ambiguous virtue we call "a sense of humor." And so one hears it said, "If only Malvolio had a sense of humor, it would be possible to like him a little." What is being asked for here is that Malvolio be critical and detached, able to view his policeman's job skeptically and perhaps with the saving grace of an irony that would puncture the hypocrisies inherent in the job itself and his own seriousness. But this is impossible. Such a Malvolio would be a deeply divided man. Having the insight to see that in being Olivia's lackey he demeans himself and makes himself an object of contempt, Malvolio would indeed become what he comes perilously close to being in that extraordinary scene in which he suffers Feste's catechistic torments—a tragic figure. The so-called romantic critics assert that in this bitter, punitive scene, ending with the victim's impotent oath, "I'll be reveng'd on the whole pack of you!" Malvolio is in fact something like a tragic figure. But romantic critics and those who dismiss this view of Malvolio as sentimentality agree that it cannot have been Shakespeare's intention (or, seeking to avoid the dread intentional fallacy: that of the play) to endow Malvolio with tragic stature. Granting Malvolio the complex attitudes of a man with a sense of humor could all too easily engender tragic consequences.

There is in the American army the standard type of the supply or mess sergeant who is officious, bossy, and what is most damning, niggardly in dispensing food or clothing. "You'd think the stuff was his!" the indignant soldier cries out when his request for more (of whatever it is that he wants more of) has been turned down. The poor soldier sees only the irrationality of the sergeant's identifying his interest with Theirs (the army, the government, the taxpayers of America). From Their point of view, as expressed, say, by the officer who represents authority, it is precisely this identification between the underling, who has nothing to gain by being parsimonious, and constituted authority that makes a good supply sergeant or mess sergeant. The officer will soon want to get rid of the sergeant who recognizes that the stuff *isn't* his and acts accordingly.

Olivia, it can be assumed, would be the first to be displeased by a Malvolio who, winking broadly at Toby, had said, "Dost thou think because I must feign a steward's virtue I desire not the joys of cakes and ale?" Malvolio's frigid personality reflects his stern policies, and these are his mistress's. He is her surrogate, her cop; he is all superego in a libidinous society; and as we all come round to saying when we must justify whatever it is we do, Malvolio might have said, "That is what I'm paid to do." Malvolio, like the petty Nazi hireling defending himself at the Nuremberg trials, would have had to be a revolutionary to be different from what he was—not just a better man, but a radical critic of the society that created him, gave him employment, and provided sustenance.

Early in the play, in answer to Malvolio's contempt for the verbal tomfoolery with which Feste amuses his mistress, Olivia sums up Malvolio's chief vice neatly (and famously) in the line: "O, you are sick of self-love, Malvolio, and taste with a distemper'd appetite." The tag has stuck. Self-love seems to explain almost everything. But does it? Is Malvolio's behavior that of a man who, thinking well of himself, thinks poorly of others? One ought not answer Yes too quickly.

A common schematic analysis of the theme of love in *Twelfth Night* is the following: all of the major characters, with the exception of Viola, are seen to be motivated by some heretical or distorted version of love. Orsino is in love with love itself, Olivia is in love with grief, Malvolio is smitten with self-love, and only Viola expresses true—that is, a properly directed and controlled—love. In this account, Malvolio's narcissistic love disables him from loving others.

Now it is certainly true that more than anything else it is the passionless, calculating, mercenary fashion in which Malvolio responds to the imaginary love of his mistress that makes him so repugnant. Despite the social impropriety, we might forgive him were he to court his mistress with passion. If he were a man by love possessed, unable to control an imperious passion, he would be the type of the romantic sinner we have no difficulty forgiving. And, so far as the proprieties are concerned, it is no accident that the witty Maria, blessed because she is a wit, is fortunate enough

to marry above her station. Only a twentieth century reader of the play, his mind corrupted by democratic and psychological principles alien to the world of *Twelfth Night,* will question Maria's good luck. For the Elizabethan, it cannot have much mattered that Toby is an ass; even as ass, if affiliated with nobility, may be a good catch for one of the downstairs folk. The point then is that Shakespeare's social hierarchy can, for comic purposes, be flexible enough to permit one of those who has ingratiated herself to us by ingeniously performing her role as maker of comedy the good fortune of succeeding as a social climber.

Malvolio's social climbing is therefore not evil per se. In comedy, success is conferred only upon those who please us by aiding and abetting the flow of the comedy. Malvolio is the very embodiment of the anti-comic spirit and the failure of his social climbing is due not simply or primarily to the immorality and impiety of the aim itself, but to his not having as it were bribed us by affording us comic pleasure. If Malvolio had been an agent of joy and comic abandon, Shakespeare would have had little difficulty in winning the sympathy of his audience for a man who at play's end inherits rather than becomes, as he does become, dispossessed.

The critics agree that Malvolio is a loveless Snopes, and the orthodox view, based on Olivia's judgment, is that inflated self-love incapacitates him for loving others. I want to suggest that what seems to Olivia to be self-love in Malvolio is more likely to be a deficiency of self-esteem. Like all those whose work is primarily that of imposing discipline, coercing obedience, enforcing respect and orderly behavior, checking "the natural man" in whatever guise he may assume with the "civilizing" force of control, constraint, and censorship, Malvolio is well suited to this job precisely because he does not possess a well developed, assertive ego. Plato as well as Freud recognized that the natural man within us calls out Yes, Yes, to the heart's deepest desires, and, whether it be called Reason or the Superego, that which makes possible comity among men must depend heavily upon the negation of these disruptive, antisocial desires. In the dialectical tension between the impatient affirmations of freedom and the unfeeling restraints of society every man must work out his own never perfectly satisfactory compromise. Those whose social roles require, as does Malvolio's, that they be constantly saying no to others must first learn to be deaf to the alluring siren songs within themselves. Whoever does any of society's police work must either be able to silence the powerful voice of self within himself or be so constituted as to have few or weak urgings of the kind that lead to independence of character and freedom of behavior.

If Malvolio loved himself more one can imagine him

loving his policeman's work less. If this seeming self-love were genuine, Malvolio might have allowed himself to be caught up in the fun, the irresponsible high jinks, the holiday mood of the revelers. True self-love, witnessing the privileged hedonism of irresponsibility says, "Why should I be excluded? Why must I be the servant of fasting while others feast?" Malvolio earns the enmity of the other members of Olivia's household because his over-assertiveness seems to them to be an excess of self-love. To us, this aggressive and sullen wielding of authority and the peacock air of superiority are likely to seem the very opposite of what they pretend to be: not the firm conviction of integrity but a self-detructive sense of inferiority. Malvolio acts and talks like one whose show of strength is only a fantasy, the purpose of which is to abrogate a reality that is all weakness and self-contempt. It is no accident that in the first great scene of Malvolio's comic humiliation, where he is ensnared into ludicrous courtship of his mistress, it is precisely the fantasist in Malvolio that is played upon so outrageously and brilliantly by Maria and the other wits. And, if it be objected that the motives we impute to Malvolio are too serious, too sympathetic, the reply must be that we do not necessarily sympathize more with a self-deceived puritan than a simple moral bully, and, comedy or no comedy, Malvolio is a serious character; it is precisely his seriousness that we are asked to see as comic in the context of the others' horse-play. It seems perfectly legitimate and appropriate temporarily to remove that seriousness from its comic context and consider it seriously.

I have described the comic strategies of *Twelfth Night* as devious. It can also be said that they are curiously unShakespearean. In particular, I refer to the emotional and moral implications of the mechanism for resolving a comic action that is analogous to catharsis in tragedy.

It is a commonplace of the critical tradition to find in Shakespeare's Falstaff the embodiment of the comic spirit. Modern scholarship has tended to reinforce this tradition by showing that Falstaff derives from the character of Vice or Riot in the medieval morality plays. Because he is Riot, Falstaff represents the principle of the transvaluation of all normal values. The comedy of the *Henry IV* plays inheres precisely in the subverting of the normal, sane, responsible, ordered, workaday world. One can describe this opposition between the comic and the non-comic worlds in an almost endless series of antinomies—moral, social, political, psychological; but no matter how Falstaff's comic nature is described, one is inevitably led to the recognition that the fundamental differentiating trait is in his radical transvaluating of conventional values and attitudes.

Because more than being an impresario of comedy

Falstaff *is* comedy, it is inevitable that Falstaff be banished, purged, symbolically sacrificed after he has outlived his comic usefulness. The pattern of the *Henry IV* plays seems to be an archetypal one: the sane, sober, unmagical world of work and duty is turned topsy-turvy by comic anarchy; comic anarchy flourishes, evoking in us pleasure and wonder; the forces representing what most of us unphilosophically think of as "reality" reassert themselves, thus re-establishing a world that, whatever else it may be, is always a non-comic one.

This re-establishing of a non-comic world is, of course, equivalent to the return to a non-tragic world in tragic works. Indeed, the whole pattern is more than similar in comedy and tragedy: in both there is a radical overturning of that gray reality we all know best, followed by a return to equilibrium at every level at which the disharmony and disequilibrium had previously existed. What comedy and tragedy have in common is that in both a kind of insanity (one terrible, the other delightful) has been allowed to reign and is then purged.

Everything that has given us pleasure in *Henry IV* took place under the aegis of Falstaff. No wonder we are saddened and perhaps even indignant when we are forced to witness the humiliation of the fantastic creature that made all of this possible. The tensions of tragedy become increasingly intolerable and we demand that they be resolved. But we want the holidaying of comedy to go on and on—in our dreams, even forever. In both cases, however, we understand that life always provides a Fortinbras to insure that man and society will survive and that, for a similar but antithetical reason, King Henrys, judges, wives, babies, and empty cupboards contrive to bring the raptures of a comic holiday to an end.

There is no Falstaff in *Twelfth Night;* there are only those grossly inferior comedians, Feste, Maria, Toby, and Aguecheek and—quintessential antagonist to everything that Falstaff is and represents, that harsh and melancholy voice of the anti-comic spirit: Malvolio.

How clever of Shakespeare to get us to believe that puritanism is bad or ugly—so at least hundreds of college students of Shakespeare have unanimously believed—when in fact Malvolio's fundamental sin (I am tempted to say his only sin) is that in his very being he threatens the comic, holiday world that Maria, Feste and company are so gaily creating. It is irrelevant that Shakespeare the man may have loathed puritanism and everything it stood for. In this play, Malvolio's puritanism is a pretext, a convenient catch-all for traits and attitudes inimical to the lovely anarchy of comedy. He must be humiliated, gulled, baited, scourged, made to suffer the melancholy consequences of his melancholy personality, and, above all, rendered impotent so that the fever of comedy can range with full potency. If Malvolio is not the perfect mythic scapegoat, where in our literature does one find a figure who can be called a scapegoat? No, it simply will not do to say that one is sentimentalizing in describing Malvolio as a scapegoat sacrificed to the amoral, bacchanalian gods of comedy. To insist upon Malvolio's sacrificial status is not to excuse or justify his clearly repugnant personality. Least of all is it a covert plea for sympathy. Malvolio's function is to "die" a kind of comic death so that comedy may live. And so, throughout the play we see him "dying" in various ways. However, the immense—and in my opinion, unsatisfactorily resolved—problem arises when the comedy itself, as is always the case, must "die." What does—what can—the dramatist do with Malvolio at that point?

The logic that ought to impose itself upon Shakespeare would seem to be as follows: since the re-instituting of the non-comic world in *Henry IV* requires the literal and symbolic sacrificing of the patron of riot and comedy who is Falstaff, the same strategic necessities in *Twelfth Night* ought to allow Malvolio, by virtue of his antithetical role, to come into his own with the "dying" of the comedy. He is the patron of the non-comic and it would seem natural that he should preside over the re-establishment of the hegemony of the non-comic that ends the play. But Shakespeare has provided himself with no machinery and aroused in us no expectations that would permit Malvolio to receive the blessing of a magic (and thus appropriately comic) and symbolic rebirth. Lodged uncomfortably at the center of this genial, loving, musical comedy is the harsh, unpurged punitive fate of Malvolio. Olivia says, "He hath been most notoriously abus'd"; and that is the only soft chord in the dissonant Malvolio music.

Let us be perfectly clear about this point. If Shakespeare is "unfair" in his treatment of Malvolio it is not in the severity of the punishments meted out to him during the course of the play; it is in Shakespeare's trying to have it both ways. Denier of comedy and its claims that Malvolio is, by comedy's standards he "deserves" his fate, but, when the resolution of the action itself denies, negates, "kills" the comedy, one expects that with the return to the world that Malvolio has been immolated for upholding, Malvolio himself will have his day. But Malvolio has been totally discredited in serving this world. He is like the politician who lives to see his name become anathema while the principles that soiled his good name, having once been defeated, return triumphantly. But these principles, miraculously, are no longer associated with the man who gave them their name.

Malvolio is Shakespeare's comic Coriolanus, a man

beset by the wolves who are his enemies and the jackals who are or ought to be his friends. In America no one loves a cop—even when he's called a policeman. In Illyria the natives are apparently no different, and even light-hearted Illyrian comedy turns out to be a cannibalistic affair, at bottom.

David Willbern

SOURCE: "Malvolio's Fall," in *Shakespeare Quarterly*, Vol. 29, No. 1, Winter, 1978, pp. 85-90.

[*Wilbern discusses the carnal side of* Twelfth Night, *asserting that Malvolio's repressed desire is reciprocal to the lover's indulgence. The critic maintains that Malvolio's social aspirations are motivated by a desire to sleep with Olivia. However, as Malvolio fails to keep separate his covert desire from his overt behavior, he is undone by his desire, and becomes the butt of the merrymakers' fun. The critic considers Shakespeare's wordplay in the letter supposedly from Olivia, suggesting that it provides insight into the psychology of Malvolio the censor, and into Shakespeare's erotic play with language. Malvolio's actions after his gulling resemble someone who is possessed, which is explained by the critic as a parallel to the basic scheme of a medieval Morality Play. The critic also considers the tension created by Malvolio in the final act, pointing out that it is typical of Shakespearean comedies to leave elements of irresolution in the finale. Willbern speculates on the hidden meaning of the cryptogram Sir Andrew questions, explaining that it represents a secret carnality at the heart of the play. He points out that festivity and loss are presented as reciprocal, and erotic desire and symbolic death are intermixed, creating a tone of romantic melancholy. Finally he compares Feste and Malvolio as symbolic brothers.*]

Malvolio, that humorless steward, sick of merrymakers and self-love, seems almost a stranger to the festive world of Illyria. His very first words reveal his acrimonious opinion of Feste, the soul of festivity [quotations from *The Riverside Shakespeare*, 1974]:

> *Oli.* What think you of this fool, Malvolio? doth he not mend?
> *Mal.* Yes, and shall do till the pangs of death shake him. Infirmity, that decays the wise, doth ever make the better fool.
>
> (I. v. 73-77)

Everything about Malvolio's character sets him apart from frivolity.

Even his vocabulary isolates Malvolio. When he chastises a rowdy Sir Toby by demanding "Is there no respect of place, person, nor time in you?" Toby quips, "We did keep time, sir, in our catches" (II. iii. 91-94). For the solemn steward and the carousing knight, the word "time" has different meanings. Malvolio hears only a cacophonous violation of decorum; Toby hears only melody and lyrics. When, a few lines later, Toby and Feste "converse" with Malvolio in song, Malvolio simply does not understand (II. iii. 102 ff.).

But while Malvolio may have no use for festivity, festivity has considerable use for him. In the paragraphs that follow, I shall consider the steward's collision with the merrymakers, the nature of the damage he suffers, and its relevance to the general theme of festivity.

When Malvolio falls into Maria's cunning trap and makes his sole concession to frivolity by donning yellow cross-garters, the desires he has previously hidden beneath a staid composure suddenly emerge exultant. On the surface Malvolio's wish is to be a social climber, "to be Count Malvolio." Yet there is a deeper desire here, and even though cross-gartering "does make some obstruction in the blood," as he complains, it does not obstruct an unwitting expression of the steward's strongest yearning: to sleep with his lady Olivia. In the forged letter scene, he alludes to a daydream of "having come from a day-bed, where I have left Olivia sleeping" (II. v. 48-49). And he jumps eagerly at an imagined opportunity when Olivia, thinking that a man who dresses so oddly and smiles so incessantly must be deranged, suggests rest: "Wilt thou go to bed, Malvolio?" she asks. "To bed?" he exclaims. "Ay, sweet heart, and I'll come to thee" (III. iv. 29-31).

But Malvolio's latent sexual wishes are also evident in his reading of the forged letter. While his fantasy of leaving Olivia in their shared day-bed is romantic enough, his remark to Toby about fortune "having cast me on your niece" (II. v. 69-70) may be less so, and his spelling lesson betrays the crudest carnality. "By my life," he swears, "this is my lady's hand. These be her very c's, her u's, and her t's, and thus makes she her great P's." After thus spelling out the carnal focus of his fantasies, he sounds out the word it self, hidden within a term of disdain: "It is, in *contempt* of question, her hand" (II. v. 86-88). It must have been important to Shakespeare that the bawdy secret be heard, for Andrew immediately repeats, "Her c's, her u's, and her t's: Why that?"

Some fine and famous Shakespeareans have been unable or unwilling to hear the answer to this question. Arthur Innes reasoned in 1895 [in *A New Variorum Edition of Shakespeare: Twelfe Night, or, What you Will,* 1901] that "probably Shakespeare merely named letters that would sound well." [In *The Complete Works of Shakespeare,* 1971], G. L. Kittredge considered Andrew's question "impossible to answer." Once the bawdy note is sounded, of course, the question is embarrassingly easy to answer.

In one sense, the event illustrates Shakespeare's insight into the psychology of the bluenose censor, secretly fascinated by and desirous of the eroticism he contemns. But it may also demonstrate Shakespeare's playful insight into his own wordplay, so frequently erotic. As the body lies at the basis of metaphor, bawdiness is basic to much punning: playing around with language.

But Malvolio is not playing; he is being played, for a fool. His hidden desire emerges, but only cryptically. Later, Feste, with his characteristically well-disguised perspicacity, mockingly underscores Malvolio's latent wantonness. "Sir Topas, Sir Topas, good Sir Topas," cries Malvolio from his prison, "Go to my lady." To which the dissembling Feste replies, "Out, hyperbolical fiend! how vexest thou this man! Talkest thou nothing but of ladies?" (IV. ii. 23-26). Until his surrender to festivity, Malvolio's black suit and anti-comic bearing have concealed his "fiend"; now it is out in the open.

Up to the moment of his fall, Malvolio had been able to keep his overt behavior and his covert desires neatly separate, thereby maintaining the condition he had earlier demanded of Toby the reveler: "If you can separate yourself and your misdemeanors, you are welcome to the house" (II. iii. 98-99). But Malvolio's careful division between act and desire, reason and fantasy, collapses when he falls into Maria's trap, even though he himself is certain he has maintained it yet. "I do not now fool myself," he asserts, "to let imagination jade me, for every reason excites to this, that my lady loves me" (II. v. 164-65). From the inverted perspective in which reason "excites" rather than informs, Malvolio finds the way to shape the letter in terms of himself, and then to reform himself in terms of the letter: "M. O. A. I. . . . If I could make that resemble something in me!" (II. v. 109-20). It requires only a little "crush" to make the fit. Excited by false reasons, his reason fails him. His "madness" is thus his conviction that he is not mad, his illusion of maintaining control over circumstances when in fact he has lost control. "O peace!" Fabian cautions the impatient Andrew as they watch Malvolio drawing the net more tightly about himself: "Now he's deeply in. Look how imagination blows him" (II. v. 42-43). As he cleverly deciphers the forged letter, Malvolio believes that his supreme reason is shaping his destiny: "Thou art made," he reads, "if thou desir'st to be so" (II. v. 155). Instead of making him, however, his desire unmakes him. His efforts to reform his image lead to disgrace: a fall from grace which is not only personal and social, but has spiritual resonance as well.

Feste is not merely joking when he refers to Malvolio's "fiend." For indeed, the steward behaves, as Toby and Maria maliciously observe, as though he were "possessed." Maria claims that "Yond gull Malvolio is turn'd heathen, a very renegado; for there is no Christian that means to be sav'd by believing rightly can ever believe such impossible passages of grossness. He's in yellow stockings" (III. ii. 69-73). Malvolio's plight is comical, of course, but there is an undercurrent of seriousness throughout. Malvolio surely means to be saved by believing rightly, but erroneous beliefs and impure desires have placed his soul in precarious balance. A bit of Feste's seeming nonsense clarifies the situation. After paralleling himself and Malvolio (incarcerated) with the medieval figures of Vice and Devil, Feste departs with a song whose final line is "Adieu, goodman devil" (IV. ii. 120-31). A typical Festean riddle, the phrase makes appropriate sense. It is a syntactic representation of the basic Morality Play scheme: "man" is centered between "good" and "devil" and should turn in the right direction, "*à Dieu.*" This moment of mini-allegory prefigures Feste's later banter with Orsino, when the Duke tells the clown, "O, you give me ill counsel," and Feste continues: "Put your grace in your pocket, sir, for this once, and let your flesh and blood obey it" (V. i. 31-33). Feste's counsel here echoes the voice of the archdeceiver, perched on his victim's left shoulder: "let your flesh and blood run free," he advises, "just for this once. Don't worry about your soul, just hide it and the possibility of grace away temporarily, 'in your pocket, sir.'" Such brief transgressions, however, will not be forgotten. "Pleasure will be paid," Feste reminds us, "one time or another" (II. iv. 70-71).

The underlying seriousness of Malvolio's fall is further suggested by the nature of the punishment he suffers. On one level, he is imprisoned for the "madness" of being rigidly sane in a frivolous world. On another level, his humbling is a direct rebuke to his social-climbing aspirations. On a yet deeper level, he is punished for his hidden concupiscence, with the punishment combining various symbolic "deaths." Malvolio is not only mortified; metaphorically he is also mortally assaulted, killed, and buried. "I have dogg'd him," gloats Toby, "like his murtherer" (III. ii. 76). The steward who wanted to possess his lady is instead thrown into a small dark hole: having wished for a bed, he finds a grave. He complains to Feste, the singer of "Come away, come away, death, / And in sad cypress let me be laid" (II. iv. 51-52), saying that "they have laid me here in hideous darkness" (IV. ii. 29-30). Malvolio does symbolically "die," but not as he had hoped; his is not the sexual death of Feste's ambiguous song, but the comic scapegoat death of a victimized gull.

Even when released from his symbolic cell, however, the unrepentant steward refuses to participate in the lovers' celebrations. Faced again with merriment, he steadfastly clings to sobriety. His letter to Olivia from his cell—signed, accurately, "the madly-us'd Malvolio"—

is calm, reasonable, and correctly descriptive of his treatment (V. i. 302-11). His only request is "Tell me why."

> Why have you suffer'd me to be imprison'd,
> Kept in a dark house, visited by the priest,
> And made the most notorious geck and gull
> That e'er invention play'd on? Tell me why!
>
> (V. i. 341-44)

He receives no answer, and although Olivia promises him future justice, he is not appeased. The steward who earlier declared to Toby, Maria, and Fabian, "I am not of your element" (III. iv. 124), is thus alone at play's end. While Feste remains to sing his lovely and melancholy song, Malvolio exits, snarling promised revenge.

As Malvolio departs, he leaves behind an unresolved conclusion to the play, taking with him the key to any clear resolution. For all its conventional comic devices of repaired unions, the ending of *Twelfth Night* is indeterminate. We look for the settlement of disputes and the reunion of fragmented relationships, "confirm'd by mutual joinder of their hands," as the priest says of Olivia and Sebastian (V. i. 157). But though the final scene of *Twelfth Night* is in fact constructed so as to allow "mutual joinder," no such resolution occurs. The prolonged hesitation of Viola and Sebastian to identify each other which includes a careful scrutiny of all the evidence (names, sex, moles, age, clothing) finally results not in any embrace of recognition but in Viola's odd provision of postponement:

> Do not embrace me till each circumstance
> Of place, time, fortune, do cohere and jump
> That I am Viola.
>
> (V. i. 251-53)

One expects a coherence of circumstance place, time, and fortune at the conclusion of a successful comedy—and *Twelfth Night* has often been viewed as a paradigm of the form. But Shakespeare deliberately defers a denouement, and the play ends before we see one enacted. Viola maintains that the resumption of her true identity depends upon the old captain who brought her to Illyria, the captain who has kept her "maiden weeds." The captain, however, has been jailed by Malvolio, "upon some action" (V. i. 275-76). Malvolio is therefore essential to a final resolution of the plot; the ultimate coherence of time and circumstance depends upon the mistreated gull. When he stalks out, swearing revenge, he also disrupts the plot, refusing to fulfill his essential role in the final "mutual joinder." Orsino commands, "Pursue him and entreat him to a peace; he hath not told us of the captain yet" (V. i. 380-81). But we hear no more from Malvolio, nor from anyone else, for the play almost immediately concludes, with the loose ends of its unfinished plot knotted abruptly into Feste's final song.

Similar gestures of irresolution occur at the end of almost all of Shakespeare's comedies—as though he was habitually skeptical of the resolutions the genre typically provided. Whether through hints of failed marriage at the end of *As You Like It,* or the sudden mournful disruption at the end of *Love's Labor's Lost.* or the preposterous rapid-fire revelations at the end of *Cymbeline,* Shakespeare usually complicates the conventional comic ending, stressing the fragility of its artifice. As Feste's concluding song suggests in *Twelfth Night,* the momentary pleasures of plays and other toys are only transient episodes in a larger season of folly, thievery, drunkenness, and old age. To the extent that the tidy finales of conventional comedies deny such larger, extradramatic realities, Shakespeare seems to have been uneasy with them: the ending of *The Tempest* is his final manifestation of this uneasiness.

An aspect of Shakespeare's distrust of romantic conventions underlies Malvolio's spelling lesson, to return to that scene for a moment. I want to ask Andrew Aguecheek's question once more, and offer a speculative answer. "Her c's, her u's, and her t's: why that?" Why, indeed? Why does Shakespeare so carefully embed this grossest of verbal improprieties in a play which even Eric Partridge [in *Shakespeare's Bawdy,* (1968)] calls "the cleanest comedy except *A Midsummer Night's Dream*"?

One answer involves what Shakespeare evidently considered the natural and undeniable bases of human behavior. The romantic comedy of *Twelfth Night* transmutes our basic appetites, sublimating carnal hunger into romantic yearning: food becomes music, as Orsino's opening speech reveals (but melancholy music, with "a dying fall"). *Twelfth Night* enacts an elaborate dance around a central core of carnality, which Malvolio's unconscious cryptogram literally spells out. The idealized festivity of *Twelfth Night* is to its secret erotic core as the innocent Maypole dance is to the symbol around which it revolves—except that the joys and celebrations of Maygames are muted in Shakespeare's play by wintry, "dying" tones of mourning and loss. Erotic desire and symbolic death intermix throughout the play, creating a continuous undertone of romantic melancholy best personified in the figure of Feste. Festivity and loss are presented as reciprocal: carnival is a farewell to the carnal (*carne-vale*).

What makes *Twelfth Night* ultimately so melancholy, however, is not the sounding of these baser tones in the music of love, but the futile (albeit beautiful) effort spent trying to deny the facts of desire and death with the artificial toys of romantic wish-fulfillment. Finally it won't work. In retrospect, the festive fantasy of innocent indulgence looks like another version of the puritanical Malvolio's effort to deny

or repudiate base carnal desire. Illyria's romanticism is psychologically reciprocal to Malvolio's rigidity and restraint: both represent denials and sublimations. Feste's final song seems to admit the futility of both defenses against the real world.

For all their mutual antipathy, Malvolio and Feste are symbolic brothers: both estranged from yet integral to the festive yet melancholy world of Illyria. To achieve a comic world of reunion and restoration, it is necessary to omit or deny or banish their respective melancholies. But, since melancholy preceded and prompted the merriment, this is impossible. Malvolio therefore retreats to his threats of vengeance, Feste to his ambiguous lyric. Finally both characters withdraw from the comic world. But without them and the impulses of restraint and love they represent, that comic world has no motivation, no "reason" for being.

At Malvolio's fall we laughed all. Yet without the (scape) goat, there would have been no carnival to provide either the fall or the merriment attending it.

FESTE

Feste is considered by many critics to be the best of Shakespeare's fools. Some critics, such as Hermann Ulrici, consider Feste the central figure in *Twelfth Night.* Ulrici maintained that the meaning of the play was concentrated in the fool. Surabhi Bnerjee argues that Feste plays an integral role in the play in that he enhances the spirit of festivity. Similarly, Peter Hall argues that Feste is the central figure of the play, and describes him as bitter, insecure, and cynical.

Alan S. Downer points out that it is Feste who exposes the true motives behind the others' actions, and in so doing propels the theme that unifies the three subplots which make up the play, and lifts *Twelfth Night* above a conventional romantic comedy. While Downer asserts that Feste does not actually manipulate the plot, **Joan Hartwig** argues that the actions of Feste and Maria mimic the hand of Fate, driving Malvolio's destiny without the mercy that Fate actually bestows upon the others. For further analysis of Feste's character, see the essay by **Thad Jenkins Logan** in the CELEBRATION AND FESTIVITY section.

Alan S. Downer

SOURCE: "Feste's Night" in *College English,* Vol. 13, No. 5, February, 1952, pp. 258-65.

[*Downer examines Feste's role as the fool in* Twelfth Night, *which allows Feste to speak freely and peel away the pretenses of the other characters. He is a pivotal figure in the play, and his presence elevates the play above the level of a mere romantic farce. Feste operates in each of the three subplots to round off the action of the play: first, Orsino must understand the nature of true love so he may marry Viola; second, Malvolio's inflated sense of self must be punctured; and third, Sebastian must take Viola's place in Olivia's heart. By speaking the truth, he ensures that his lord and lady will not be fools, and he closes the play with a song.]*

. . . Feste is disguised both in costume and in behavior. His suit is motley, the uniform of the Fool, and he carries the tabor and perhaps the bauble as his badge of office. When, however, Olivia calls him a fool—and we must return to this scene again—he points out that "cucullus non facit monachum [the cowl doesn't make the monk]." And as the man inside the monk's robe may be anything but a monk in spirit, so he, Feste, wears not motley in his brain. His disguise, like Viola's, is a kind of protection; he is an allowed fool and may speak frankly what other men, in other disguises, must say only to themselves. . . .

Feste's whole art and function depend upon his talents as a "notable corrupter of words," and he has much wisdom to utter on what we should probably call the problem of semantics. He concludes one wit combat by declaring that "words are grown so false that I am loath to prove reason with them." In many ways he is the central figure of the play, the symbol of its meaning. The plot could get on without him, no doubt; his practical function as message-bearer could be taken over by Fabian, who has little enough to keep him busy. But he is no mere embellishment. Without Feste, *Twelfth Night* would not be the enduring comedy it is but another romantic farce like *The Comedy of Errors.* Twelfth Night is Feste's night.

The Fool is as conventional in Shakespearean comedy as the intriguing slave or parasite in Plautus or Molière. But, while Feste shares some of the characteristics of Tranio-Phormio-Sganarelle, he does not, like them, dazzle our eyes by juggling the elements of the plot into a complex pattern which only he can sort out for the necessary fortunate conclusion. Until the last act of the play, he does little but jest or sing. But for all his failure to take a positive part in the intrigue—emphasized perhaps when he drops out of the baiting of Malvolio—for all that he is not, that is to say, a protagonist, he nonetheless propounds the theme which gives *Twelfth Night* its unity and makes a single work of art out of what might have been a gorgeous patchwork.

A brief examination of the matter of the comedy will suggest the basis for such a conclusion. *Twelfth Night* is compounded of two, perhaps three, "plots," more or less independent actions, each of which must be rounded off before the play is concluded. In the first, Duke Orsino's eyes must be opened to the true nature of love that he may marry Viola; in the second, Malvolio must be reduced from the deluded superman to fallible humanity; in the third, which is closely tied with the first, Sebastian must be substituted for Viola in the affections of Olivia.

The structure is skilfully contrived not only to keep all three plots going and maintain a reasonable connection among them but to emphasize the similarity of their themes. Like most panoramic drama, the play may be divided into three organic movements rather than the meaningless editorial division into five acts. The first of these movements, from the introduction of Orsino to Viola's discovery that she has charmed Olivia (I, 1–II, 3), is concerned almost exclusively with establishing the triangular love affair. Toby, Andrew, and Maria are brought on to whet our appetites for their plot, and, just before the movement ends, Sebastian appears that we may be reassured all will come right before the play is over. However, we should note a speech of Feste's made to Maria during his first appearance (I, 5), in which he refers obliquely to the common subject of the separate actions: "If Sir Toby would leave drinking, thou wert as witty a piece of Eve's flesh as any in Illyria." If all were as it should be and according to the order of nature, Toby would wed Maria. But Toby drinks, and the Duke loves Olivia, and Olivia (as we shall see in a moment) loves Viola. All most *un*natural.

In the second movement (II, 3–IV, I) the love triangle remains unchanged, and the trapping of Malvolio occupies most of the action. We observe the offense for which he is to be punished, the plotting of revenge, and the success of the scheme. Sebastian has again made only a token appearance, but in the final scene of the movement (III, 4) all three actions are brought together with the greatest of ease as the deluded Malvolio is handed over to Toby, and Andrew and Viola are inveigled into a duel from which both are rescued by the intervention and arrest of Sebastian's friend, Antonio.

The final movement, the last two acts of the play, is in a sense Sebastian's. Mistaken for Viola, he brings about a fortunate unknotting of the love tangle, rescues his friend Antonio from the clutches of the Duke, and forces a confession of their machinations from Toby and company. The point to notice here is that Feste is the character who, innocently enough, drives Sebastian into Olivia's arms. It is Feste's only direct contribution to the action of the play; it is also the single decisive action which cuts the comic knot; and it is a visual dramatic symbol of his relationship to the whole play. It is the action of a man whose professional function is to perceive and declare the true state of affairs in the face of scorn, threats, and discouragement from the self-deluded. Shakespeare has in fact prepared us for this action at several important points earlier in the play.

On his first appearance, with Maria, Feste demonstrates not only that he is able to more than hold his own in a wit combat but that he is shrewd enough to see the true state of affairs in the household. A moment later, with the license of an allowed fool, he is demonstrating to Olivia the folly of her resolution to withdraw from the world for seven years in mourning for her brother.

> FESTE: Good madonna, why mournest thou?
> OLIVIA: Good fool, for my brother's death.
> FESTE: I think his soul is in hell, madonna.
> OLIVIA: I know his soul is in heaven, fool.
> FESTE: The more fool, madonna, to mourn
>   for your brother's soul, being in heaven.
>   Taken away the fool, gentlemen
>
> [I, 5, 72-78].

The little passage is in the most artificial of dialogue forms, stichomythia, and it is perhaps only a bit of logic-chopping, but it presents the common-sense view of a sentimental and un-Christian attitude.

The exposure of Olivia takes place in the first movement of the play. In the second movement Feste undertakes to tell the Duke a few plain truths, but, since the undeceiving of the mighty is ticklish business, he goes about it in an oblique manner.

Shakespeare has introduced the Duke in a most ambiguous way. To him falls an opening speech as rich in texture and sound as any love poetry in the language. To him also falls an attitude that cannot fail to win both our admiration and our exasperation. We admire his constancy, that is, but are somewhat impatient with his refusal to "take his answer." Further, if we accept him at his own evaluation as presented in his speeches, his sudden switch to Viola in the last scene becomes pure comic convention without reason or meaning, a botched-up happy ending.

But, if we have been beguiled by our own sentimentality into sympathy with the Duke, Feste will set us right, and most particularly in that romantic scene (II, 4) where he has been thrust in to sing the song which Viola seems not prepared to perform. It is as early in the morning as the love-smitten Duke would arise from bed. He enters, calling at once for music, and requests Cesario (that is, Viola) for that "old and antique song" they heard last night. While his servant Curio goes in search of Feste to sing it, Orsino proceeds to analyze it for us. The description is famous and explicit:

> It is old and plain,

> The spinsters and the knitters in the sun,
> And the free maids that weave their thread
>   with bones,
> Do use to chant it. It is silly sooth,
> And dallies with the innocence of love
> Like the old age
>
> [II, 4, 44-49].

That is, a simple song, presumably a folk song or ballad, fit accompaniment to a household task. It is a love song, but not impassioned, not from the point of view of fervent youth. It dallies with the harmless pleasure of love as if the experience were but the memory of the old, a memory recollected in tranquillity. Whereupon Feste sings:

> Come away, come away, death,
>   And in sad cypress let me be laid.
> Fly away, fly away, breath;
>   I'm slain by a fair cruel maid.
> My shroud of white, stuck all with yew,
>   O prepare it!
> My part of death, no one so true
>   Did share it.

In the second stanza the love imagery becomes more extravagant.

> Not a flower, not a flower sweet,
>   On my black coffin let there be strown;
> Not a friend, not a friend greet
>   My poor corpse, where my bones shall be
>   thrown.
> A thousand, thousand sighs to save,
>   Lay me, O where
> Sad, true lover ne'er find my grave,
>   To weep there.

Without the original music, which cannot be traced, it is impossible to say for certain, but, from the striking difference between the song as anticipated and the song as sung, Feste seems to have been mocking, indirectly, the Duke's passion. "Come away, death" is indeed a love song, but it can hardly be said to dally with the innocence of love. This would explain the Duke's abrupt, "There's for thy pains," and his immediate dismissal, not only of the singer, but of his entire court. Perhaps he is afraid that there may have been some sniggering behind his back as Feste sang. There is just a hint in the play that his household is a little wearied of his unavailing pursuit of Olivia.

And Feste, going off, dares a parting thrust. "Now the melancholy god protect thee," he says, and bids him put to sea to make a good voyage of nothing. In this scene, I suggest, Feste "exposes" the Duke as he has earlier exposed Olivia. By mocking them both, he points out that their loves are sentimental and foolish. And the Duke, unlike Olivia, is angry. He dismisses his attendants and sends Viola once more to "same sovereign cruelty," with a stubborn determination to act out the role he has cast himself in.

With this as a clue to his character, the actor of course has it in his power to make evident the Duke's melancholy, his fashionable love-sickness, from the start. In the first scene, even in his gorgeous opening set-piece, he is plainly worshiping love for its own sake and fostering his emotion for sentimental purposes. His first words demand that the music play on, that he may experience again his pleasurable mood of Thwarted Lover. For all the beauty of the verse, the attitude is distinctly unhealthy. He must have music for his love to feed on, even upon arising in the morning; or, for a substitute, a garden of sweet-scented flowers. And is he not, like Romeo in the throes of puppy love for the equally unresponsive Rosaline, "best when least in company"?

The parallel exposing of Malvolio, which is capped by Feste in the third movement, is the clearest statement of the theme in action, since it is unencumbered by romantic love, an element which can blind an audience to the true state of affairs as effectively as it can blind the romantic lovers. Malvolio, in this play, is plain text. As Olivia's steward he is sufficiently in charge of her affairs to bring suit against a sea captain for dereliction of duty; as her butler, he is ready with falsehoods to defend her privacy; as her would-be husband, he has prepared schemes for the proper and efficient conduct of their household. These are all admirable traits for his several capacities: the alert businessman, the devoted servant, the careful husband. But there is a fault in him, an obvious fault. There is something too much of the cold gaze from half-shut eyes down the prominent beak, something too much of the demure travel of regard. Malvolio would not only be virtuous, he would have others so, and he would define the term. It is a cause of delight to discover that the elegant creature with snow-broth in his veins, so superior to the drunken carousing of Toby, the witty trifling of Feste, the dalliance of Olivia—that this man of virtue is only human, like ourselves. And in this exposure, that the whirligig of time may bring his revenges, Feste is permitted to play the visually dominant part.

The action is so arranged that, of all the conspirators, only Feste has a scene alone with Malvolio, in which, for nobody's pleasure but his own, he teases and torments the benighted steward and reduces the proud man to a state of wretched groveling: "I tell thee," cries Malvolio at last, "I am as well in my wits as any man in Illyria," and Feste replies, "Well-a-day that you were, sir."

This does not seem to be idly spoken. Feste is saying that he wishes Malvolio were not sick of self-love but like a normal Illyrian. Like Toby, for example, who would go to church in a galliard and return in a coranto, and whose fair round belly symbolizes his philosophy, that there is a place for cakes and ale even in a world turning Puritan. The point is made simply and emphatically, with Feste *solus* on the stage, and Malvolio perhaps clamoring behind the Judas window of the stage door: the Elizabethan equivalent of a motion-picture close-up—on Feste.

Thus it is Feste's function in both parts of the action to make plain to the audience the artificial, foolish attitudes of the principal figures. Malvolio loves himself, Orsino loves love, and Olivia loves a ghost. This, says Feste, is unnatural, against common sense. In this similarity of situation and Feste's single-minded attitude in each case lies the unity of *Twelfth Night*, its theme.

Feste states it clearly. Since he is primarily a singing fool, he states it in song:

> What is love? 'Tis not hereafter;
> Present mirth hath present laughter. . . .
> Youth's a stuff will not endure.

Feste's philosophy is as old as the hills, as old as the comic attitude, the acceptance of the facts of life. His philosophy, however, goes somewhat deeper than a mere sentimental optimism.

> Journeys end in lovers' meeting
> Every wise man's son doth know.

As a wise man's son, or as an understanding fool, he sees to it that there shall be a meeting of true lovers at the end of the journey of Viola and Sebastian. In his scene with Malvolio he even discards his priestly disguise and appears in his own motley to restore the vision of the self-blinded man. And, by his introduction of Sebastian to Olivia, he makes possible the shedding of all disguises both physical and spiritual at the dénouement.

Critical opinion has been somewhat divided about Feste. There is general agreement about his remarkable clean-spokenness; he has been called the merriest of Shakespeare's fools, and the loneliest. He has been taken to be the symbol of misrule that governs the Twelfth Night activities. Yet, when the recognition scene is over, all the characters romantically paired off, Malvolio reduced to a very human bellow—"I'll be revenged on the whole pack of you!"—and Feste prepares to sing his foolish little epilogue, does he not seem to be something more than merry, or lonely, or the spirit of misrule?

Observe him, alone on the great stage which is the emptier for the departure of the grandly dressed ladies and gentlemen who have crowded it during the last scene, and the quieter after the vigorous excitement that attended the dé ouement: the twins united, the marriage and betrothal, the explosion of Malvolio, the brawling of Andrew and Toby. Feste is perhaps older than the other characters, "a fool that the Lady Olivia's father took much delight in." But he has been, for a fool, a rather quiet character; no loud, bawdy jokes and very little slapstick. His brain is not parti-colored: *cucullus non facit monachum.* As Viola observes:

> This fellow's wise enough to play the fool,
> And to do that well craves a kind of wit.
> He must observe their mood on whom he
>　　jests,
> The quality of persons and the time;
> Not, like the haggard, check at every feather
> That comes before his eye. This is a practice
> As full of labor as a wise man's art.

It is the function of this fool to speak the truth, however quizzically he must phrase it. It is his task to persuade his lord and lady *not* to be fools. It is the task of comedy, too.

And now he is alone. Now he sings his lonely, foolish song:

> When that I was and a little tiny boy
>　　With hey, ho, the wind and the rain, etc.

Perhaps it is not so foolish. There is one constant thing in this world, he says, the facts of nature, the wind and the rain that raineth every day. Thieves may be shut out and evil men by bars and locks but not the rain that raineth every day. Like a true jester, he makes a little joke out of his moral. When he took a wife, he planned to be master in his own house, but nature defeated him, for it is the order of nature that men shall be henpecked, and suffer from hangovers, as surely as the rain shall fall. He emphasizes the antiquity of his wisdom:

> A great while ago, the world began
>　　With hey, ho, the wind and the rain.

Then, with a quizzical smile, as if to say, "I have made my point, or the comedy has made it for me; no need to quote history—"he slips into the epilogue pattern we have been awaiting:

> But that's all one, our play is done,
>　　And we'll strive to please you every day.

It is, after all, as he reminds us, just a play. But it has its purpose for being, just as the great tragedies have. *Twelfth Night* is Feste's night, and we may look to be well edified when the Fool delivers the Madmen.

Joan Hartwig

SOURCE: "Feste's 'Whirligig of Time' and the Comic Providence of *Twelfth Night*," in *ELH*, Vol. 40, No. 4, Winter, 1973, pp. 501-13.

[*Hartwig analyzes the relationship between Malvolio and Feste, suggesting that while Feste claims Malvolio's humiliation is "the whirligig of time" bringing its revenge back on Malvolio, it is really the result of Feste and Maria manipulating Malvolio by human means to achieve their own revenge. While Malvolio praises divine intervention when he finds the letter, believing that what Fate has decreed must be, he fails to anticipate the intrusion of Feste and Maria. When Malvolio is faced with the discrepancy between what he wants, and what really is, he refuses to broaden his spectrum of reality and is confronted by the possibility of madness. In the same way that Feste manipulates Malvolio into an unpredictable position, so comic providence leads the audience to an unexpected finale.*]

Shakespeare's plays frequently counterpose the powers of human and of suprahuman will, and the antithesis usually generates a definition of natures, both human and suprahuman. These definitions vary, however, according to the play. For instance, Hamlet's "providence" does not seem the same as the darker, equivocating power that encourages Macbeth to pit his will against a larger order; and these controls differ from Diana and Apollo in the later plays, *Pericles* and *The Winter's Tale*. Furthermore, Hamlet's submission and Macbeth's submission to non-human controls (if indeed they do submit their individual wills) cannot be understood as the same action or even to imply the same kind of human vision.

Many of the conflicts of *Twelfth Night* seem to be concerned with the contest between human will and suprahuman control; yet, the latter manifests itself in various ways and is called different names by the characters themselves. As each contest between the human will and another designer works itself out, the involved characters recognize that their will is fulfilled, but not according to their planning. The individual's will is finally secondary to a design that benevolently, but unpredictably, accords with what he truly desires. For example, when Olivia, at the end of Act I, implores Fate to accord with her will in allowing her love for Cesario to flourish, she has no idea that her will must be circumvented for her own happiness. Yet the substitution of Sebastian for Cesario in her love fulfills her wishes more appropriately than her own design could have done. Inversely, when Duke Orsino says in the opening scene that he expects to replace Olivia's brother in her "debt of love," he doesn't realize that literally he will become her "brother" (I.i.34-40) [quotations from *William Shakespeare: The Complete Works*, ed.

Alfred Harbage (1969).] As the closing moments of the play bring Olivia and the Duke together on the stage for the only time, she says to him, "think me as well a sister as a wife" (V.i.307); and the Duke responds in kind: "Madam, I am most apt t' embrace your offer," and a bit later, "Meantime, sweet sister, / We will not part from hence" (V.i.310, 373-74). The Duke had not understood the literal force of his prediction, but his early statement of his hope plants a subtle suggestion for the audience. When the play's action accords with Duke Orsino's "will," the discrepancy between intention and fulfillment is a delightful irony which points again to the fact that "what you will" may be realized, but under conditions which the human will cannot manipulate. Orsino's desire to love and be loved, on the other hand, is fulfilled by his fancy's true queen, Viola, more appropriately than his design for Olivia would have allowed.

The one character whose true desires are not fulfilled in the play is Malvolio. His hope to gain Olivia in marriage results in public humiliation at the hands of Feste, who takes obvious satisfaction in being able to throw Malvolio's former haughty words back at him under their new context of Malvolio's demonstrated foolishness:

> Why, 'some are born great, some achieve greatness, and some have greatness thrown upon them.' I was one, sir, in this interlude, one Sir Topas, sir; but that's all one. 'By the Lord, fool, I am not mad!' But do you remember, 'Madam, why laugh you at such a barren rascal? An you smile not, he's gagged'? And thus the whirligig of time brings in his revenges. (V.i.360-66)

Feste's assertion that the "whirligig of time" has brought this revenge upon Malvolio neglects the fact that Maria has been the instigator and Feste the enforcer of the plot to harass Malvolio. Time's design, insofar as Malvolio is concerned, depends upon Maria's and Feste's will, which differs significantly from a central point that the main plot makes—that human will is not the controller of events. The characters in the main plot learn from the play's confusing action that human designs are frequently inadequate for securing "what you will," and that a design outside their control brings fulfillment in unexpected ways. Feste's fallacy, of course, makes the results of the subplot *seem* to be the same as the results of the main plot, but Time's revenges on Malvolio are primarily human revenges, and this particular measure for measure is thoroughly within human control. Feste's justice allows no mitigation for missing the mark in human action; and the incipient cruelty that his precise justice manifests is felt, apparently, by other characters in the play.

When Olivia and her company hear Malvolio's case,

she responds with compassion: "Alas, poor fool, how have they baffled thee! . . . He hath been most notoriously abused" (V.i.359, 368). Duke Orsino, upon hearing Malvolio's letter of explanation, comments, "This savors not much of distraction" (V.i.304). And even Sir Toby has become uneasy about the harsh treatment of Malvolio in the imprisonment scene: "I would we were well rid of this knavery. If he may be conveniently delivered, I would he were; for I am now so far in offense with my niece that I cannot pursue with any safety this sport to the upshot" (IV.ii.66-70). Actually, to place the responses into this sequence reverses the play's order; and we should consider the fact that Shakespeare builds *toward* a compassionate comment, with Olivia's statement climaxing an unwillingness to condone the actions of Feste and Maria in gulling Malvolio—at least in its last phase. Feste's exact form of justice without mercy has always characterized revenge, and even the word "revenge" is stressed by several of the characters in the subplot. When Maria voices her apparently spontaneous plot to gull Malvolio, she says:

> The devil a Puritan that he is . . . the best persuaded of himself; so crammed, as he thinks, with excellencies that it is his grounds of faith that all that look on him love him; and on that vice in him will my revenge find notable cause to work. (II.iii.134-40)

Maria's successful implementation of her "revenge" elicits Sir Toby's total admiration. At the end of II.v, he exclaims, "I could marry this wench for this device" (168), and when Maria appears soon thereafter, he asks, "Wilt thou set thy foot o' my neck?" (174). The battlefield image of the victor and the victim is mockheroic, of course; but in the final scene Fabian testifies to its literal fruition: "Maria writ / The letter, at Sir Toby's great importance, / In recompense whereof he hath married her" (V.i.352-54). Sir Toby's submission to Maria's will is a comic parallel for two actions: the pairing off of lovers, and the submission of the individual's will to a design other than his own. Yet the inclusion of a parodic version of marriage-harmony in the subplot does not fully ease discomfort of the subplot's conclusion. Fabian tries to smooth it away when he suggests that the "sportful malice" of gulling Malvolio "may rather pluck on laughter than revenge" (V.i.355-58). Neither Feste nor Malvolio seems to be convinced, however. Feste's "whirligig of time brings in his revenges," and Malvolio quits the stage with, "I'll be revenged on the whole pack of you!" (V.i.366-67). The forgiveness that should conclude the comic pattern is "notoriously" missing from the subplot and cannot be absorbed successfully by the Duke's line, "Pursue him and entreat him to a peace." Malvolio seems unlikely to return. The major differences between the subplot and the main plot is clearest at this dramatic moment: revenge is a human action that destroys; love, graced by the sanction of a higher providence, creates a "golden time."

Feste's "whirligig" seems to be a parody of Fortune's wheel in its inevitable turning, particularly with its suggestions of giddy swiftness and change. It provides a perfect image for the wild but symmetrical comic conclusion of the play's action. Feste's speech which includes it gives the appearance of completion to a mad cycle of events over which no human had much control. Only in Malvolio's case was human control of events evident. In her forged letter, Maria caters to Malvolio's "will" and, by encouraging him to accept his own interpretation of circumstances as his desire dictates, she leads him not only into foolishness, but also into a defense of his sanity. The discrepancy between Malvolio's assumption that fortune is leading him on his way and the fact that Maria is in charge of his fate manifests itself clearly in the juxtaposition of her directions to the revelers (as she leaves the stage) with Malvolio's lines as he enters:

> MARIA Get ye all three into the box tree. . . . Observe him, for the love of mockery; for I know this letter will make a contemplative idiot of him. Close, in the name of jesting. [*The others hide.*] Lie thou there [*throws down a letter*]; for here comes the trout that must be caught with tickling. *Exit.*

Enter Malvolio.

> MALVOLIO 'Tis but fortune; all is fortune. Maria once told me she [Olivia] did affect me. (II.v.13-22)

The gulling of Malvolio which follows is hilariously funny, partly because Malvolio brings it all on himself. Even before he finds the letter, his assumptions of rank and his plans for putting Sir Toby in his place elicit volatile responses from the box tree. And after he finds the forged letter, Malvolio's self-aggrandizing interpretations of the often cryptic statements evoke howls of glee mixed with the already disdainful laughter. The comedy of this scene is simple in its objective exploitation of Malvolio's self-love, and Malvolio becomes an appropriately comic butt. The audience's hilarity is probably more controlled than Sir Toby's and the box tree audience's excessive laughter; still, we are united in laughing at Malvolio's foolishness. And when Malvolio appears in his yellow stockings and cross-garters, the visual comedy encourages a total release in the fun of the game—Malvolio is gulled and we need not feel the least bit guilty, because he is marvelously unaware of his own foolishness. Oblivious to any reality but his own, Malvolio thinks he is irresistibly appealing with his repugnant dress and his continuous smiles—so contrary to his usual solemnity—and Olivia concludes that he has gone mad. "Why, this is very midsummer madness," she says, and, then, as she is leaving to receive Cesario, she commends Malvolio to Maria's care.

Good Maria, let this fellow be looked to. Where's my cousin Toby? Let some of my people have a special care of him. I would not have him miscarry for the half of my dowry. (III.iv.55-58)

Malvolio misconstrues Olivia's generous concern as amorous passion and he thanks Jove for contriving circumstances so appropriately:

> I have limed her; but it is Jove's doing, and Jove make me thankful. . . . Nothing that can be can come between me and the full prospect of my hopes. Well, Jove, not I, is the doer of this, and he is to be thanked. (III.iv.68-77)

Malvolio's scrupulous praise of a higher designer than himself is a parodic echo of Olivia's earlier submission to Fate after she has begun to love Cesario: "What is decreed must be—and be this so!" (I.v.297). The impulses underlying Malvolio's speech (and to some extent, Olivia's speech as well) exert opposite pulls: Malvolio wants to attribute control of circumstances to Jove at the same time he wants divine identity. He attempts to simulate foreknowledge through predictive assertion: "Nothing that can be can come between me and the full prospect of my hopes." As long as events are in the hands of a non-human control, man cannot destroy or divert the predetermined order. But Malvolio cannot foresee the vindictive wit of Maria (often pronounced "Moriah"), nor can Olivia foresee the necessary substitution of Sebastian for Viola-Cesario. Each must learn that he, like the characters he wishes to control, is subject to an unpredictable will not his own. Precisely at this moment—when the character is forced to see a discrepancy between what he "wills" and what "is"—the possibility that he is mad confronts him.

Feste seems to adopt the disguise of Sir Topas to convince Malvolio that he is mad, and the imprisonment scene evokes a different response than the letter that exploits Malvolio by encouraging him to wear yellow stockings and cross-garters. In the earlier phase of the gulling, Malvolio is a comic butt after the fashion of Sir Andrew Aguecheek, unaware of his foolishness; however, imprisoned, Malvolio is a helpless victim, fully aware that he is being abused. With Olivia, his extraordinary costume and perpetual smiles make him a visible clown, and, as a result, he even seems good-humored. But with Maria and Feste in the imprisonment scene, he is not visible; we only hear him and his protestations of abuse. These different visual presentations produce a notable difference in comic effect because visual comedy often changes a serious tone in the dialogue.

In the imprisonment scene, Sir Topas keeps insisting that things are not as Malvolio perceives them; but Malvolio refuses to admit a discrepancy between what he perceives and reality. Accordingly, Malvolio insists that he is not mad.

Malvolio within.

MALVOLIO Who calls there?

CLOWN Sir Topas the curate, who comes to visit Malvolio the lunatic. . . .

MALVOLIO Sir Topas, never was man thus wronged. Good Sir Topas, do not think I am mad. They have laid me here in hideous darkness.

CLOWN Fie, thou dishonest Satan. I call thee by the most modest terms, for I am one of those gentle ones that will use the devil himself with courtesy. Say'st thou that house is dark?

MALVOLIO As hell, Sir Topas.

CLOWN Why, it hath bay windows transparent as barricadoes, and the clerestories toward the south north are as lustrous as ebony; and yet complainest thou of obstruction?

MALVOLIO I am not mad, Sir Topas. I say to you this house is dark.

CLOWN Madman, thou errest. I say there is no darkness but ignorance, in which thou art more puzzled than the Egyptians in their fog.

MALVOLIO I say this house is as dark as ignorance, though ignorance were as dark as hell; and I say there was never man thus abused. I am no more mad than you are.

(IV.ii.20-48)

In the darkness of his prison, Malvolio literally is unable to see, and Feste makes the most of the symbolic implications of Malvolio's blindness. The audience perceives with Feste that the house is not dark (that hypothetical Globe audience would have been able to see the literal daylight in the playhouse), yet the audience also knows that Malvolio is being "abused" because he cannot see the light. The audience is therefore led to a double awareness of values in this scene: we are able to absorb the emblematic significance of Malvolio's separation from good-humored sanity and to know at the same time that Malvolio is not mad in the literal way that Feste, Maria, and Sir Toby insist. Although the literal action engenders the emblematic awareness, the literal action does not necessarily support the emblematic meaning. This pull in two opposite directions occurs simultaneously and places the audience in a slightly uncomfortable position. We prefer to move in one direction or in the other. Yet it seems that here Shakespeare asks us to

forgo the either-or alternatives and to hold contradictory impressions together. Malvolio cannot be dismissed as a simple comic butt when his trial in the dark has such severe implications.

The ambiguities of his situation are clear to everyone except Malvolio, but he rigidly maintains his single point of view. Because he refuses to allow more than his own narrowed focus, he is *emblematically* an appropriate butt for the harsh comic action that blots out his power to see as well as to act. He must ultimately depend upon the fool to bring him "ink, paper, and light" so that he may extricate himself from his prison, a situation which would have seemed to Malvolio earlier in the play "mad" indeed. Feste thus does force Malvolio to act against his will in submitting to the fool, but Malvolio fails to change his attitudes. Malvolio remains a literalist—Feste's visual disguise is for the audience so that we can see as well as hear the ambiguities of his performance, a point that Maria brings into focus when she says "Thou mightest have done this without thy beard and gown. He sees thee not" (IV.ii.63-64).

In the very next scene, Sebastian presents a contrast which delineates even more clearly the narrowness of Malvolio's response to an uncontrollable situation. Sebastian, too, confronts the possibility that he is mad: his situation in Illyria is anything but under his control.

> This is the air; that is the glorious sun;
> This pearl she gave me, I do feel't and see't;
> And *though* 'tis wonder that enwraps me thus,
> *Yet* 'tis not madness. . . .
> For *though* my soul disputes well with my sense
> That this may be some error, *but* no madness,
> *Yet* doth this accident and flood of fortune
> So far exceed all instance, all discourse,
> That I am ready to distrust mine eyes
> And wrangle with my reason that persuades me
> To any other trust *but* that I am mad,
> Or *else* the lady's mad.
>
> (IV.iii.1-16: my italics)

Sebastian's pile of contrasting conjunctions ("though," "yet," "but") underlines his hesitance to form a final judgment, unlike Malvolio, whose point of view never changes despite the onslaught of unmanageable circumstances. The contradictions of his sensory perceptions lead Sebastian to a state of "wonder" in which he is able to suspend reason and delay judgment, and this signifies a flexibility of perception which Malvolio cannot attain. Malvolio is not stirred by the discrepancies of experience to consider that appearances may not be reality; but Sebastian can appreciate the undefinable workings of a power beyond the evident. Sebastian's ability to sense the "wonder" in a world where cause and effect have been severed gives him a stature that Malvolio cannot achieve. Yet the difference between them is due to the source of their manipulation as well as to their response. Sebastian is manipulated by Fate or by Fortune; Malvolio, by Maria and Feste. Human manipulators parody suprahuman control and because they do, Maria and Feste define both levels of action.

Feste, Maria, and Sir Toby are all in a set and predictable world of sporting gullery, and the rules for their games are known. Feste's "whirligig" associates Time with a toy (perhaps even with an instrument of torture) and limits Time to human terms of punishment. On the other hand, the Time that Viola addresses does untie her problematic knot of disguise. Feste's attribution of revenge to this "whirligig of Time" points up the difference between the two controls. The whirligig becomes a parodic substitute for the larger providence that other characters talk about under other titles: Time, Jove, Fate, Fortune, or Chance. Significantly, Malvolio's humiliation is the only humanly designed action that fulfills itself as planned. The subplot performs its parody in many other ways, but in Feste's summary "whirligig" it displays the double vision that Shakespearean parody typically provides. The foibles of the romantics in Illyria are seen in their reduced terms through Sir Toby, Maria, and Sir Andrew, but the limitations of the parodic characters also heighten by contrast the expansive and expanding world of the play. Love, not revenge, is celebrated.

But even Feste's whirligig takes another spin and does not stop at revenge: in the play's final song the playwright extends an embrace to his audience. Feste's song creates an ambiguity of perspective which fuses the actual world with an ideal one: "the rain it raineth every day" is hardly the world described by the play. Romantic Illyria seems to have little to do with such realistic intrusions. Yet, the recognition of continuous rain is in itself an excess—it does not rain every day in the actual world, at least not in the same place. Thus, the pessimistic excess of the song balances the optimistic excesses of the romance world of Illyria; neither excess accurately reflects the actual world. Despite the apparent progress the song describes of a man's growing from infancy to maturity and to old age, it remains something of an enigma. The ambiguities of the first four stanzas build to a contrast of direct statements in the final stanza.

> A great while ago the world begun,
>   With hey, ho, the wind and the rain;
> But that's all one, our play is done,
>   And we'll strive to please you every day.

The first line of this stanza seems to imply that the world has its own, independent design; and it also suggests that man's actions must take their place and find meaning within this larger and older pattern. The specific meaning of that larger design, however, remains concealed within the previous ambiguities of Feste's song. His philosophic pretensions to explain that design are comically vague and he knows it. He tosses them aside to speak directly to the audience: "But that's all one, our play is done." This is the same phrase Feste uses with Malvolio in his summary speech in Act V: "I was one, sir, in this interlude, one Sir Topas, sir; but that's all one." In both cases, Feste avoids an explanation.

Turning to the audience and shattering the dramatic illusion is typical in epilogues, but Feste's inclusion of the audience into his consciousness of the play as a metaphor for actual experience has a special significance here. Throughout *Twelfth Night*, Feste has engaged various characters in dialogues of self-determination. In one game of wit, he points out that Olivia is a fool "to mourn for your brother's soul, being in heaven" (I.v.65-66). By his irrefutable logic, he wins Olivia's favor and her tacit agreement that her mourning has been overdone. The Duke also is subject to Feste's evaluation in two scenes. Following his performance, upon the Duke's request, of a sad song of unrequited love, Feste leaves a paradoxical benediction:

> Now the melancholy god protect thee, and the tailor make thy doublet of changeable taffeta, for thy mind is a very opal. I would have men of such constancy put to sea, that their business might be everything, and their intent everywhere; for that's it that always makes a good voyage of nothing. (II.iv.72-77)

And later, when the Duke is approaching Olivia's house, Feste encounters him with one of his typically unique and audaciously applied truisms:

DUKE I know thee well. How dost thou, my good fellow?

CLOWN Truly, sir, the better for my foes, and the worse for my friends.

DUKE Just the contrary: the better for thy friends.

CLOWN No, sir, the worse.

DUKE How can that be?

CLOWN Marry, sir, they praise me and make an ass of me. Now my foes tell me plainly I am an ass; so that by my foes, sir, I profit in the knowledge of myself, and by my friends I am abused; so that, conclusions to be as kisses, if your four negatives make your two affirmatives, why then, the worse for my friends, and the better for my foes.

(V.i.9-20)

The Duke has in fact lacked some knowledge of himself, and Feste's pointed remark makes it clear that he is using his role as fool to point up the true foolishness of others. In the prison scene with Malvolio, Feste provides a confusing game of switching identities from the Clown to Sir Topas. In each situation, Feste provides the other person with a different perspective for seeing himself. Thus, it is more than merely appropriate that at the end of the play Feste engages the audience in its own definition of self. By asking them to look at their participation in the dramatic illusion, Feste is requesting them to recognize their own desire for humanly willed happiness.

The playwright, like the comic providence in the play, has understood "what we will" and has led us to a pleasurable fulfillment of our desires, but in ways which we could not have foreseen or controlled. The substitution of the final line, "And we'll strive to please you every day," for the refrain, "For the rain it raineth every day," is a crucial change. Like the incremental repetition in the folk ballad, this pessimistic refrain has built a dynamic tension which is released in the recognition that the play is an actual experience in the lives of the audience, even though it is enacted in an imagined world. The players, and the playwright who arranges them, are engaged in an ongoing effort to please the audience. The providential design remains incomplete within the play's action and only promises a "golden time"; similarly, the playwright promises further delightful experiences for his audience. The subplot's action, on the other hand, is limited within the framework of revenge: the revenge of the subplot characters elicits Malvolio's cry for revenge.

Malvolio is the only one who refuses to see himself in a subservient position to a larger design. And possibly because that design is too small, we cannot feel that his abuse and final exclusion from the happy community of lovers and friends allows the golden time to be fulfilled within the play. Feste's manipulation of Malvolio resembles the playwright's manipulation of his audience's will, but in such a reduced way that we cannot avoid seeing the difference between merely human revenge and the larger benevolence that controls the play's design.

SOURCES FOR FURTHER STUDY

Literary Commentary

Barber, C. L. "Testing Courtesy and Humanity in *Twelfth Night*," in *Shakespeare's Festive Comedy*, Princeton University Press, 1959, pp. 240-61.

Provides an overview of the play by considering different themes, first centering the argument on the key word "madness." The critic also considers social and sexual roles, and how their temporary inversion serves to solidify what is considered normal.

Berry, Ralph. "The Season of *Twelfth Night*." *New York Literary Forum* 1 (Spring 1978): 139-149.

Compares late nineteenth-century productions of the play with modern ones, finding that the former emphasized comedic elements of the play at the expense of its darker themes.

———. "'Twelfth Night': The Experience of the Audience." *Shakespeare Survey* 34 (1981): 111-19.

Contends that the play would have had a disturbing effect on its original audiences, much like a joke that goes too far.

Charney, Maurice. "Comic Premises of *Twelfth Night*." *New York Literary Forum* 1 (Spring 1978): 151-65.

Examines Robert Herrick's 1648 poem "Twelfe night, or King and Queene" from Hesperides, and discusses the cultural context it provides for Twelfth Night festivities of that era.

Crane, Milton. "*Twelfth Night* and Shakespearean Comedy." *Shakespeare Quarterly* VI, No. 1 (Winter 1955): 1-8.

Places *Twelfth Night* in the context of Shakespeare's comedies, which Crane contends are based upon themes of classical comedy but depart from these conventions to an increasingly larger degree in the later plays.

Donno, Elizabeth Story. Introduction to *Twelfth Night or What You Will*, by William Shakespeare, edited by Elizabeth Story Donno, pp. 1-40. Cambridge: Cambridge University Press, 1985.

Provides an overview of issues relating to the play, including its sources, theatrical history, and critical commentary.

Eagleton, Terrence. "Language and Reality in 'Twelfth Night.'" *The Critical Quarterly* 9, No. 3 (Autumn 1967): 217-28.

Delves into the complex relationship between language, roles, and illusion in the play.

Fleming, William H. "*Twelfth Night*." *Shakespeare' Plots: A Study in Dramatic Construction*, pp. 68-76. London: Hutchinson & Co (Publishers) Ltd, 1949.

Praises the lyrical elements of *Twelfth Night* as a means of expressing the theme of love, and discusses the humor, farce, and satire within the play.

Fortin, René E. "*Twelfth Night*: Shakespeare's Drama of Initiation." *Papers on Language and Literature* VIII, No. 2 (Spring 1972): 135-46.

Provides a symbolic interpretation of the play as a

drama centering on Viola's search for her sexual identity.

Furnivall, F. J. *New Variorum Edition of Shakespeare: "Twelfe Night or, What You Will".* Written by William Shakespeare. Translated and edited by Horace Howard Furness. New York: J. B. Lippincott Company, 1901, pp. 385.

Argues that despite the happy spirit of the play, there is a "shadow of death and distress" in the play.

Gaskill, Gayle. "The Role of Fortune in *Twelfth Night.*" *Iowa English Bulletin* 30, No. 1 (Fall 1980): 20-23, 32.

Examines the workings of fortune in the play, and how each character's nature is revealed by their reaction to it.

Gerard, Albert. "Shipload of Fools: A Note on *Twelfth Night.*" *English Studies* 45, No. 2 (Autumn 1964): 109.

Sees in *Twelfth Night* intimations of the tragic themes of Shakespeare's later plays.

Greif, Karen. "Plays and Playing in *Twelfth Night.*" *Shakespeare Survey: An Annual Survey of Shakespearean Study and Production* 34 (1981): 121-30.

Greif examines the relationship between appearance and reality in Twelfth Night, exploring ways in which each character engages in self-deception or the deception of others.

Hotson, Leslie. *The First Night of "Twelfth Night."* London: Rupert Hart-Davis, 1954, 256 p.

Suggests that *Twelfth Night* was originally commisioned by Queen Elizabeth for a Twelfth Night performance given in 1600-01, in honor of Virginio Orsino, Duke of Bracciano. Provides evidence for the earliest performance of *Twelfth Night* and offers insights on the thematic importance of festivity.

Hudson, H. N. "Shakespeare's Characters: "Twelfth Night." *Shakespeare: His Life, Art, and Characters,* Vol. I, revised edition. Morristown, NJ: Ginn & Company, 1872, pp. 351-73.

Discusses Shakespeare's supposed aversion to the Puritans of his time and argues that Shakespeare wanted us to pity Malvolio.

Legatt, Alexander. "Twelfth Night" and "Conclusion: Beyond Twelfth Night." In his *Shakespeare's Comedy of Love,* pp. 221-66. London: Methuen, 1974.

Offers an extended analysis of the play, concluding that *Twelfth Night* is unique among Shakespeare's comedies in its depiction of the opposition between an ideal "golden world" of order and the seemingly disordered everyday world.

Lewalski, Barbara K. "Thematic Patterns in *Twelfth Night.*" *Shakespeare Studies: An Annual Gathering of Research, Criticism, and Reviews* I, (1965): 168-81.

Discusses the pagan celebration of Twelfth Night and examines the Christian concept of Epiphany in the play.

Montegut, E. *New Variorum Edition of Shakespeare: "Twelfe Night or, What You Will".* Written by William Shakespeare. Translated and edited by Horace Howard Furness. New York: J. B. Lippincott Company, 1901, pp. 382-84.

Presents the theory that *Twelfth Night* is a masquerade and carnival farce. Stresses the ambiguity in the play and discusses how the characters are "slaves" of their individual defects and perspectives.

Schwartz, Elias. "*Twelfth Night* and the Meaning of Shakespearean Comedy." *College English* 28, No. 7 (April 1967): 508-19.

Contends that *Twelfth Night* is not a satiric comedy but a profound vision of merriment and festivity.

Siegel, Paul N. "Malvolio: Comic Puritan Automaton." *New York Literary Forum* 6 (1980): 217-30.

Analyzes Malvolio as a representation of Puritan self-discipline and predictability.

Stane, Bob. "The Genealogy of Sir Andrew Aguecheek." *The Shakespeare Newsletter* XXXII, Nos. 5 and 6 (Winter 1982): 32.

Suggests that the role of Sir Andrew Aguecheek was inspired by a personality type readily recognizable to all levels of English society.

Swander, Homer. "*Twelfth Night*: Critics, Players, and a Script." *Educational Theatre Journal* XVI, No. 2 (May 1964): 114-21.

Surveys critical reactions to various New York productions of the play, arguing that to be successful a production must convey the underlying moral warning against self-love and folly.

Ulrici, Hermann. "Criticisms of Shakspeare's Dramas: "Twelfth Night." *Shakespeare's Dramatic Art: And His Relation to Calderon and Goethe.* Translated by A. J. W. Morrison. London: Chapman Brothers, 1846, pp. 246-53.

Argues that in *Twelfth Night* Shakespeare creates a world of contradiction, fantasy, and chaos, and that Feste is the central figure in *Twelfth Night*. Ulrici maintains that the meaning of the play was concentrated in the fool.

Warren, Roger. "Orsino and Sonnet 56." *Notes and Queries* 18, No. 4 (April 1971): 146-47.

Relates Orsino's opening speech to Shakespeare's Sonnet 56, suggesting that a deeper understanding of love underlies Orsino's idealism.

———. "'Smiling at Grief': Some Techniques of Comedy in 'Twelfth Night' and 'Così Fan Tutte.'" *Shakespeare Survey* 32 (1979): 79-84.

Compares the comic elements of the play to Mozart's

opera *Così Fan Tutte*, finding similarities in the artists' approaches and their willingness to explore the complexities of human emotions.

Williams, Porter, Jr. "Mistakes in *Twelfth Night* and Their Resolution: A Study in Some Relationships of Plot and Theme." *PMLA* LXXVI, No. 3 (June 1961): 193-99.

Shows how the mistakes made by characters in the play reveal themes of love and personal relationships common to all of Shakespeare's comedies.

Media Adaptations

Twelfth Night. Cedric Messina, Dr. Jonathan Miller, BBC, 1980.

Set in an aristocratic country house. Part of the "Shakespeare Plays" series. Distributed by Ambrose Video Publishing, Inc. 124 minutes.

Twelfth Night: An Introduction. BHE Education Ltd., Seabourn Enterprises Ltd., 1969.

Brief narrative bridges connect the performances of key scenes. Distributed by Phoenix/BFA Films. 23 minutes.

Glossary

Note to the reader: This glossary includes terms commonly encountered in the study of Shakespeare's work. It is not intended to be comprehensive.

Allegory: an extended metaphor or analogy in which characters in a drama or story and the characters' actions are equated with abstract ideas outside of the drama or story being told.

Aside: a dramatic device by which an actor directly addresses the audience but is not heard by the other actors on the stage. In Act I, scene iv of *Twelfth Night*, for example, Viola, in male disguise as Cesario, delivers an aside while in Duke Orsino's presence revealing that she has fallen in love with him.

Burlesque: a form of comedy characterized by mockery or exaggeration. Commentators have noted that throughout *Henry IV, Part One*, Falstaff's words and actions serve as a burlesque of the main action of the play.

Comedy: a form of drama in which the primary purpose is to amuse and which ends happily.

Denouement: the final explanation or outcome of the plot.

Dramatic irony: achieved when the audience understands the real significance of a character's words or actions but the character or those around him or her do not.

Early modern literature: in England, literature from the late sixteenth and early seventeenth centuries.

Farce: a humorous play marked by broad satirical comedy and an improbable plot.

Foil: in literature, a character who, through contrast with another character, highlights or enhances the second character's distinctive qualities. Shakespearean characters often appear in pairs that serve as foils to one another: the docile Bianca and the stubborn Katherina, for example, in *The Taming of the Shrew*, or the Puritan Malvolio and hedonistic Sir Toby Belch in *Twelfth Night*.

Folio: a piece of paper folded in half or a volume made up of folio sheets. In 1623, Shakespeare's plays were assembled into a folio edition. The term folio is also used to designate any early collection of Shakespeare's works.

Gender role: behavior that a society expects or accepts from a man or a woman because of his or her sex. Commentators often note that Bianca and Katherina from *The Taming of the Shrew* represent two extremes of gender roles available to women in Shakespeare's time: the seemingly compliant young woman who waits to be wooed, and the "shrewish" woman who uses her temper to intimidate men.

History play: a drama set in a time period earlier than that during which the play was written. Shakespeare treated both very recent and ancient Brithish history in his plays. *Henry IV, Henry V, and Richard III* are three of Shakespeare's history plays.

Induction: introductory scene or scenes that precede the main action of a play. The Christopher Sly episode that begins the action of *The Taming of the Shrew* is such an induction.

Machiavellianism: the theory, based on the work and beliefs of Italian political philosopher Niccolo Machiavelli (1469-1527), that the attainment of political power is justified by any means. Commentators often note that Shakespeare's Richard III is a Machiavellian character, as he is willing to use deception and murder to gain power.

Masque: in medieval England and Europe, a game or party in which participants wore masks. In *Much Ado About Nothing,* the masked Don Pedro, Prince of Aragon, woos Hero for Claudio at a masque, while Beatrice takes advantage of the disguises worn by partygoers to mock Benedick to his face, pretending she does not know who he is.

Morality play: a medieval drama in which abstract vices and virtues are presented in human form.

Mystery play: a medieval drama depicting a story from the Bible.

Parody: a composition or work which imitates another, usually serious, work.

Plot: the sequence of events in a drama or story.

Pun: a play on words. For example, the lovesick Duke Orsino puns on the homophones *hart* and *heart* in his opening speech in *Twelfth Night.*

Satire: a piece of literature that presents human vices or foolishness in a way that invites ridicule or scorn.

Soliloquy: a character's speech within in a play delivered while the character is alone. The speech is intended to inform the audience of the character's thoughts or feelings or to provide information about other characters in the play.

Stock character: a conventional character type which belongs to a particular form of literature. In Elizabethan and Jacobean-era drama, stock characters included the clownish rustic, whose attempts to mimic the speech and behavior of the upper classes result in humorous misuses of words and phrases (malapropisms). *Henry IV*'s Falstaff is said to resemble this figure (*see also* **Vice-figure**). The constable Dogberry from *Much Ado About Nothing* is another example of this stock figure. Another stock figure in the drama of this era, the Machiavellian plotter and evil-doer, is often depicted as an illegitimate half-brother of a morally upright character, such as the bastard Don John in *Much Ado About Nothing.*

Subplot: a plot that is secondary to the main plot of the drama. In *King Lear,* for example, the intrigue generated by Edmund's attempt to discredit his legitimate half-brother, Edgar, functions as one subplot, while the attempts of Regan and Goneril to win Edmund as a lover functions as another subplot.

Theme: a central idea in a work of literature or representational art.

Tragedy: a drama which recounts the significant events or actions in a protagonist's life, which, taken together, bring about catastrophe.

Unities: a term referring to the dramatic structures of action, time, and place. Each unity is defined by several characteristics. The unity of action requires that the action of the play have a beginning, a middle, and an end. The unity of time requires that the action of a play take place in one day. The unity of place limits the action of the play to one place. Many plays violate all three unities. In *The Tempest,* Shakespeare observes all three unities.

Vice or **Vice-figure**: a **stock character** in the **morality play**, who, as a tempter, possesses both evil and comic qualities. Many commentators maintain that the character of the drunken and disreputable knight Sir John Falstaff from the *Henry IV* plays, though based in part on a historical figure, also derives some of his characteristics from the standard Vice-figure from the Morality plays.

Cumulative Index to Major Themes and Characters

The Cumulative Index to Major Themes and Characters identifies the principal themes and characters discussed in the criticism of each play. The themes and characters are arranged alphabetically. Page references indicate the beginning page number of each essay containing substantial commentary on that theme or character. The number "1" appearing after a play name indicates that the play appeared in the first edition of *Shakespeare for Students*; the number "2" appearing after a play name indicates that the play appears in *Shakespeare for Students, Book II.*

Theme and Character Index